1 MONTH OF
FREE
READING

at

www.ForgottenBooks.com

By purchasing this book you are
eligible for one month membership to
ForgottenBooks.com, giving you
unlimited access to our entire
collection of over 1,000,000 titles via
our web site and mobile apps.

To claim your free month visit:

www.forgottenbooks.com/free931771

ISBN 978-0-260-16213-7
PIBN 10931771

Forgotten Books is a registered trademark of FB &c Ltd.
Copyright © 2018 FB &c Ltd.
FB &c Ltd, Dalton House, 60 Windsor Avenue, London, SW19 2RR.
Company number 08720141. Registered in England and Wales.

For support please visit www.forgottenbooks.com

A COMPILATION

OF THE

AGES AND PAPERS

OF THE

'RESIDENTS

1789-1897

ISHED BY AUTHORITY OF CONGRESS

BY

JAMES D. RICHARDSON

A REPRESENTATIVE FROM THE STATE OF TENNESSEE

VOLUME VIII

WASHINGTON

OFFICE

430043

Illustrations

	Page.
LIBRARY OF CONGRESS	Frontispiece.
JAMES A. GARFIELD	2
CHESTER A. ARTHUR	30
GROVER CLEVELAND	296

VII

Democrat who had been chosen by his party had held the office since the retirement of Buchanan, in 1861. President Cleveland's papers fill 558 pages of this volume, occupying more space than any other Chief Magistrate, Andrew Johnson being next with 457 pages. At an early date after Mr. Cleveland's inauguration he became involved in an important and rather acrimonious discussion with the Senate on the subject of suspensions from office. The Senate demanded of him and of the heads of some of the Executive Departments the reasons for the suspension of certain officials and the papers and correspondence incident thereto. In an exhaustive and interesting paper he declined to comply with the demand. His annual message of December, 1887, was devoted exclusively to a discussion of the tariff. It is conceded by all to be an able document, and is the only instance where a President in his annual message made reference to only one question. His vetoes are more numerous than those of any other Chief Executive, amounting within the four years to over three hundred, or more than twice the number in the aggregate of all his predecessors. These vetoes relate to almost all subjects of legislation, but mainly to pension cases and bills providing for the erection of public buildings throughout the country.

JAMES D. RICHARDSON.

JULY 4, 1898.

Contents of Volume VIII

	Page.
PREFATORY NOTE	III–IV

JAMES A. GARFIELD, MARCH 4, 1881, TO SEPTEMBER 19, 1881

PORTRAIT	2
BIOGRAPHICAL SKETCH	3–6
INAUGURAL ADDRESS	6–12
SPECIAL MESSAGES	12
EXECUTIVE ORDER	13
DEATH OF PRESIDENT GARFIELD	13–27

CHESTER A. ARTHUR, SEPTEMBER 19, 1881, TO MARCH 4, 1885

PORTRAIT	30
BIOGRAPHICAL SKETCH	31–33
INAUGURAL ADDRESS	33–34
PROCLAMATIONS	34–35
SPECIAL MESSAGES	35
PROCLAMATION	36
EXECUTIVE ORDER	37
FIRST ANNUAL MESSAGE	37–65
SPECIAL MESSAGES	66–112
VETO MESSAGES	112–122
PROCLAMATIONS	122–124
EXECUTIVE ORDERS	124–126
SECOND ANNUAL MESSAGE	126–148
SPECIAL MESSAGES	148–158
PROCLAMATIONS	159–160
EXECUTIVE ORDERS	160–169
THIRD ANNUAL MESSAGE	170–188
SPECIAL MESSAGES	188–221
VETO MESSAGE	221–223
PROCLAMATIONS	223–226
EXECUTIVE ORDERS	226–235
FOURTH ANNUAL MESSAGE	235–254
SPECIAL MESSAGES	254–280
PROCLAMATIONS	280–286
EXECUTIVE ORDERS	286–294

Illustrations

                                                              Page
LIBRARY OF CONGRESS... Frontispiece.
JAMES A. GARFIELD..   2
CHESTER A. ARTHUR   30
GROVER CLEVELAND   296

James A. Garfield

March 4, 1881, to September 19, 1881

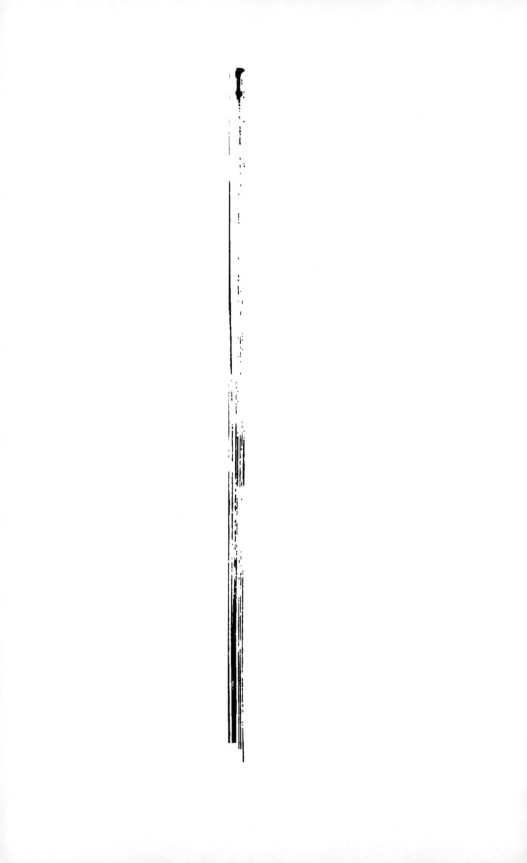

JAMES A. GARFIELD

James A. Garfield

JAMES ABRAM GARFIELD was born in Orange, Cuyahoga County, Ohio, November 19, 1831. His father, Abram Garfield, was a native of New York, but of Massachusetts ancestry; descended from Edward Garfield, an English Puritan, who in 1630 was one of the founders of Watertown. His mother, Eliza Ballou, was born in New Hampshire, of a Huguenot family that fled from France to New England after the revocation of the Edict of Nantes in 1685. Garfield, therefore, was from lineage well represented in the struggles for civil and religious liberty, both in the Old and in the New World. His father moved to Ohio in 1830 and settled in what was then known as the "Wilderness," now as the "Western Reserve," which was occupied by Connecticut people. He died at the age of 33, leaving a widow and four small children, of whom James was the youngest. Mrs. Garfield brought up her family unaided, and impressed upon them a high standard of moral and intellectual worth. James attended school in a log hut at the age of 3 years, learned to read, and began that habit of omnivorous reading which ended only with his life. At 10 years of age was accustomed to manual labor, helping out his mother's meager income by work at home or on the farms of the neighbors. Attended the district school in the winter months, made good progress, and was conspicuous for his assiduity. At the age of 14 had a fair knowledge of arithmetic and grammar, and was particularly apt in the facts of American history. His imagination was especially kindled by tales of the sea, and he so far yielded to his love of adventure that in 1848 he went to Cleveland and proposed to ship as a sailor on board a lake schooner. Seeing that this life was not the romance he had conceived, he turned promptly from the lake; but loath to return home without adventure and without money, he drove some months for a boat on the Ohio Canal, when he was promoted from the towpath to the boat. Attended the Geauga Seminary at Chester, Ohio, during the winter of 1849-50. In the vacations learned and practiced the trade of a carpenter, helped at harvest, taught—did anything and everything to earn money to pay for his schooling. After the first term he asked and needed no aid from home: he had reached the point where he could support himself. Was converted under the instructions of a Christian preacher, was baptized and received into that denomination. As soon as he finished his studies in Chester entered (1851) the Hiram Eclectic Institute (now Hiram College), at Hiram, Portage County, Ohio, the principal educational institution of his church. He was not very quick of acquisition, but his perseverance was indomitable and he soon had an excellent knowledge of Latin and a fair acquaintance with algebra, natural philosophy, and botany. His superiority was easily recognized in the prayer meetings and debating societies of the college, where he was assiduous and conspicuous. Living here was inexpensive, and he readily made his expenses by teaching in the English departments, and also gave instruction in the ancient languages. Entered Williams College in the autumn of 1854, and graduated with the highest honors in the class of 1856. Returned to Ohio and resumed his place as a teacher of Latin and Greek at Hiram Institute, and the next year, being then only 26 years of age, was made its president. The regulations and practices of his church, known as the Christian Church, or Church of the Disciples, permitted him to preach, and he used the permission. He also pursued the study of law, entering his name in 1858 as a student in a law office in Cleveland, but studying in Hiram. Cast his first vote in 1856 for John C. Frémont, the first Republican candidate for the Presidency. Married Lucretia Rudolph November 11, 1858. In 1859 was chosen to represent the counties of Summit and Portage in the Ohio senate. In August, 1861, Governor William Dennison commissioned him lieutenant-colonel in the Forty-second Regiment Ohio Volunteers. Was promoted to the command of this regiment. In December, 1861, reported to General Buell in Louisville, Ky. Was given a brigade and assigned the difficult task of driving the Confederate general Humphrey Marshall from eastern Kentucky. General Garfield triumphed over the Confederate forces at the battle of Middle Creek, January 10, 1862, and in recognition of his services was made a brigadier-general by President Lincoln. During the campaign of the Big Sandy, while Garfield was engaged in breaking up some scattered Confederate encampments, his supplies gave out and he was threatened with starvation. Going himself to the Ohio River, he seized a steamer, loaded it with provisions, and on the refusal of any pilot to undertake the perilous voyage, because of a freshet that had swelled the river, he stood at the helm for forty-eight hours and piloted the craft through the dangerous channel. In order to surprise Marshall, then intrenched in Cumberland Gap, Garfield marched his soldiers 100 miles in four days through a blinding snowstorm. Returning to Louisville, he found that General Buell was away; overtook him at Columbia, Tenn., and was assigned to the command of the Twentieth Brigade. Reached Shiloh in time to take part in the second day's fight. Was engaged in all the operations in front of Corinth, and in June, 1862, rebuilt the bridges on the Memphis and Charleston Railroad, and exhibited noticeable engineering skill in repairing the fortifications of

Huntsville. Was granted leave of absence July 30, 1862, on account of ill health, and returned to Hiram, Ohio, where he lay ill for two months. Went to Washington on September 25, 1862, and was ordered on court-martial duty. November 25 was assigned to the case of General Fitz John Porter. In February, 1863, returned to duty under General Rose-crans, then in command of the Army of the Cumberland. Rosecrans made him his chief of staff, with responsibilities beyond those usually given to this office. In this field Garfield's influence on the campaign in middle Tennessee was most important. One familiar incident shows and justifies the great influence he wielded in its counsels. Before the battle of Chickamauga, June 24, 1863, General Rosecrans asked the written opinion of seventeen of his generals on the advisability of an immediate advance. All others opposed, but Garfield advised it, and his arguments were so convincing that Rosecrans determined to seek an engagement. General Garfield wrote out all the orders of that fateful day, September 19, excepting one, and that one was the blunder that lost the day. Garfield volunteered to take the news of the defeat on the right to General George H. Thomas, who held the left of the line. It was a bold ride, under constant fire, but he reached Thomas and gave the information that saved the Army of the Cumberland. For this action he was made a major-general September 19, 1863—promoted for gallantry on a field that was lost. Yielded to Mr. Lincoln's urgent request and on December 5, 1863, resigned his commission and hastened to Washington to sit in Congress, to which he had been chosen fifteen months before. Was offered a division in the Army of the Cumberland by General Thomas, but yielded to the representations of the President and Secretary Stanton that he would be more useful in the House of Representatives. Was placed on the Committee on Military Affairs, then the most important in Congress. In the Thirty-ninth Congress (1865) was changed, at his own request, from the Committee on Military Affairs to the Committee on Ways and Means. In the Fortieth Congress (1867) was restored to the Committee on Military Affairs and made its chairman. In the Forty-first Congress the Committee on Banking and Currency was created and he was made its chairman. Served also on the Select Committee on the Census and on the Committee on Rules. Was chairman of the Committee on Appropriations in the Forty-second and Forty-third Congresses. In the Forty-fourth, Forty-fifth, and Forty-sixth Congresses (the House being Democratic) was assigned to the Committee on Ways and Means. In 1876, at President Grant's request, went to New Orleans in company with Senators Sherman and Matthews and other Republicans, to watch the counting of the Louisiana vote. He made a special study of the West Feliciana Parish case, and embodied his views in a brief but significant report. In January, 1877, made two notable speeches in the House on the duty of Congress in a Presidential election, and claimed that the Vice-President had a constitutional right to count the electoral vote. Opposed the Electoral Commission, yet when the commission was ordered was chosen by acclamation to fill one of the two seats allotted to Republican Representatives. Mr. Blaine left the House for the Senate in 1877, and this made Mr. Garfield the undisputed leader of his party in the House. At this time and subsequently was its candidate for Speaker. Was elected to the United States Senate January 13, 1880. Attended the Republican convention which met at Chicago in June, 1880, where he opposed the renomination of President Grant and supported Senator Sherman. On the thirty-sixth ballot the delegates broke their ranks, and, rushing to General Garfield, he was unanimously nominated for President on June 8, 1880. Was elected November 2, 1880, receiving 214 electoral votes to 144 that were cast for Winfield S. Hancock. Was shot July 2, 1881, by an assassin in the Baltimore and Potomac Railroad station, in Washington, and died from the effects of the wound September 19 at Elberon, N. J. He was buried at Cleveland, Ohio.

INAUGURAL ADDRESS.

FELLOW-CITIZENS: We stand to-day upon an eminence which overlooks a hundred years of national life—a century crowded with perils, but crowned with the triumphs of liberty and law. Before continuing the onward march let us pause on this height for a moment to strengthen our faith and renew our hope by a glance at the pathway along which our people have traveled.

It is now three days more than a hundred years since the adoption of the first written constitution of the United States—the Articles of Confederation and Perpetual Union. The new Republic was then beset with danger on every hand. It had not conquered a place in the family of nations. The decisive battle of the war for independence, whose centennial anniversary will soon be gratefully celebrated at Yorktown, had not yet been fought. The colonists were struggling not only against the armies of a great nation, but against the settled opinions of mankind; for the world did not then believe that the supreme authority of government could be safely intrusted to the guardianship of the people themselves.

We can not overestimate the fervent love of liberty, the intelligent courage, and the sum of common sense with which our fathers made the great experiment of self-government. When they found, after a short trial, that the confederacy of States was too weak to meet the necessities of a vigorous and expanding republic, they boldly set it aside, and in its
ead established a National Union, founded directly upon the will of the

people, endowed with full power of self-preservation and ample authority for the accomplishment of its great object.

Under this Constitution the boundaries of freedom have been enlarged, the foundations of order and peace have been strengthened, and the growth of our people in all the better elements of national life has indicated the wisdom of the founders and given new hope to their descendants. Under this Constitution our people long ago made themselves safe against danger from without and secured for their mariners and flag equality of rights on all the seas. Under this Constitution twenty-five States have been added to the Union, with constitutions and laws, framed and enforced by their own citizens, to secure the manifold blessings of local self-government.

The jurisdiction of this Constitution now covers an area fifty times greater than that of the original thirteen States and a population twenty times greater than that of 1780.

The supreme trial of the Constitution came at last under the tremendous pressure of civil war. We ourselves are witnesses that the Union emerged from the blood and fire of that conflict purified and made stronger for all the beneficent purposes of good government.

And now, at the close of this first century of growth, with the inspirations of its history in their hearts, our people have lately reviewed the condition of the nation, passed judgment upon the conduct and opinions of political parties, and have registered their will concerning the future administration of the Government. To interpret and to execute that will in accordance with the Constitution is the paramount duty of the Executive.

Even from this brief review it is manifest that the nation is resolutely facing to the front, resolved to employ its best energies in developing the great possibilities of the future. Sacredly preserving whatever has been gained to liberty and good government during the century, our people are determined to leave behind them all those bitter controversies concerning things which have been irrevocably settled, and the further discussion of which can only stir up strife and delay the onward march.

The supremacy of the nation and its laws should be no longer a subject of debate. That discussion, which for half a century threatened the existence of the Union, was closed at last in the high court of war by a decree from which there is no appeal—that the Constitution and the laws made in pursuance thereof are and shall continue to be the supreme law of the land, binding alike upon the States and the people. This decree does not disturb the autonomy of the States nor interfere with any of their necessary rights of local self-government, but it does fix and establish the permanent supremacy of the Union.

The will of the nation, speaking with the voice of battle and through the amended Constitution, has fulfilled the great promise of 1776 by proclaiming "liberty throughout the land to all the inhabitants thereof."

The elevation of the negro race from slavery to the full rights of citizenship is the most important political change we have known since the adoption of the Constitution of 1787. No thoughtful man can fail to appreciate its beneficent effect upon our institutions and people. It has freed us from the perpetual danger of war and dissolution. It has added immensely to the moral and industrial forces of our people. It has liberated the master as well as the slave from a relation which wronged and enfeebled both. It has surrendered to their own guardianship the manhood of more than 5,000,000 people, and has opened to each one of them a career of freedom and usefulness. It has given new inspiration to the power of self-help in both races by making labor more honorable to the one and more necessary to the other. The influence of this force will grow greater and bear richer fruit with the coming years.

No doubt this great change has caused serious disturbance to our Southern communities. This is to be deplored, though it was perhaps unavoidable. But those who resisted the change should remember that under our institutions there was no middle ground for the negro race between slavery and equal citizenship. There can be no permanent disfranchised peasantry in the United States. Freedom can never yield its fullness of blessings so long as the law or its administration places the smallest obstacle in the pathway of any virtuous citizen.

The emancipated race has already made remarkable progress. With unquestioning devotion to the Union, with a patience and gentleness not born of fear, they have ''followed the light as God gave them to see the light.'' They are rapidly laying the material foundations of self-support, widening their circle of intelligence, and beginning to enjoy the blessings that gather around the homes of the industrious poor. They deserve the generous encouragement of all good men. So far as my authority can lawfully extend, they shall enjoy the full and equal protection of the Constitution and the laws.

The free enjoyment of equal suffrage is still in question, and a frank statement of the issue may aid its solution. It is alleged that in many communities negro citizens are practically denied the freedom of the ballot. In so far as the truth of this allegation is admitted, it is answered that in many places honest local government is impossible if the mass of uneducated negroes are allowed to vote. These are grave allegations. So far as the latter is true, it is the only palliation that can be offered for opposing the freedom of the ballot. Bad local government is certainly a great evil, which ought to be prevented; but to violate the freedom and sanctities of the suffrage is more than an evil. It is a crime which, if persisted in, will destroy the Government itself. Suicide is not a remedy. If in other lands it be high treason to compass the death of the king, it shall be counted no less a crime here to strangle our sover-

power and stifle its voice.

as been said that unsettled questions have no pity for the repose of nations. It should be said with the utmost emphasis that this question of the suffrage will never give repose or safety to the States or to the nation until each, within its own jurisdiction, makes and keeps the ballot free and pure by the strong sanctions of the law.

But the danger which arises from ignorance in the voter can not be denied. It covers a field far wider than that of negro suffrage and the present condition of the race. It is a danger that lurks and hides in the sources and fountains of power in every state. We have no standard by which to measure the disaster that may be brought upon us by ignorance and vice in the citizens when joined to corruption and fraud in the suffrage.

The voters of the Union, who make and unmake constitutions, and upon whose will hang the destinies of our governments, can transmit their supreme authority to no successors save the coming generation of voters, who are the sole heirs of sovereign power. If that generation comes to its inheritance blinded by ignorance and corrupted by vice, the fall of the Republic will be certain and remediless.

The census has already sounded the alarm in the appalling figures which mark how dangerously high the tide of illiteracy has risen among our voters and their children.

To the South this question is of supreme importance. But the responsibility for the existence of slavery did not rest upon the South alone. The nation itself is responsible for the extension of the suffrage, and is under special obligations to aid in removing the illiteracy which it has added to the voting population. For the North and South alike there is but one remedy. All the constitutional power of the nation and of the States and all the volunteer forces of the people should be surrendered to meet this danger by the savory influence of universal education.

It is the high privilege and sacred duty of those now living to educate their successors and fit them, by intelligence and virtue, for the inheritance which awaits them.

In this beneficent work sections and races should be forgotten and partisanship should be unknown. Let our people find a new meaning in the divine oracle which declares that "a little child shall lead them," for our own little children will soon control the destinies of the Republic.

My countrymen, we do not now differ in our judgment concerning the controversies of past generations, and fifty years hence our children will not be divided in their opinions concerning our controversies. They will surely bless their fathers and their fathers' God that the Union was preserved, that slavery was overthrown, and that both races were made equal before the law. We may hasten or we may retard, but we can not prevent, the final reconciliation. Is it not possible for us now to make a truce with time by anticipating and accepting its inevitable verdict?

Enterprises of the highest importance to our moral and material well-being unite us and offer ample employment of our best powers. Let all our people, leaving behind them the battlefields of dead issues, move forward and in their strength of liberty and the restored Union win the grander victories of peace.

The prosperity which now prevails is without parallel in our history. Fruitful seasons have done much to secure it, but they have not done all. The preservation of the public credit and the resumption of specie payments, so successfully attained by the Administration of my predecessors, have enabled our people to secure the blessings which the seasons brought.

By the experience of commercial nations in all ages it has been found that gold and silver afford the only safe foundation for a monetary system. Confusion has recently been created by variations in the relative value of the two metals, but I confidently believe that arrangements can be made between the leading commercial nations which will secure the general use of both metals. Congress should provide that the compulsory coinage of silver now required by law may not disturb our monetary system by driving either metal out of circulation. If possible, such an adjustment should be made that the purchasing power of every coined dollar will be exactly equal to its debt-paying power in all the markets of the world.

The chief duty of the National Government in connection with the currency of the country is to coin money and declare its value. Grave doubts have been entertained whether Congress is authorized by the Constitution to make any form of paper money legal tender. The present issue of United States notes has been sustained by the necessities of war; but such paper should depend for its value and currency upon its convenience in use and its prompt redemption in coin at the will of the holder, and not upon its compulsory circulation. These notes are not money, but promises to pay money. If the holders demand it, the promise should be kept.

The refunding of the national debt at a lower rate of interest should be accomplished without compelling the withdrawal of the national-bank notes, and thus disturbing the business of the country.

I venture to refer to the position I have occupied on financial questions during a long service in Congress, and to say that time and experience have strengthened the opinions I have so often expressed on these subjects.

The finances of the Government shall suffer no detriment which it may be possible for my Administration to prevent.

The interests of agriculture deserve more attention from the Government than they have yet received. The farms of the United States afford homes and employment for more than one-half our people, and furnish much the largest part of all our exports. As the Government lights our coasts for the protection of mariners and the benefit of commerce, so it should give to the tillers of the soil the best lights of practical science
ience.

Our manufactures are rapidly making us industrially independent, and are opening to capital and labor new and profitable fields of employment. Their steady and healthy growth should still be matured. Our facilities for transportation should be promoted by the continued improvement of our harbors and great interior waterways and by the increase of our tonnage on the ocean.

The development of the world's commerce has led to an urgent demand for shortening the great sea voyage around Cape Horn by constructing ship canals or railways across the isthmus which unites the continents. Various plans to this end have been suggested and will need consideration, but none of them has been sufficiently matured to warrant the United States in extending pecuniary aid. The subject, however, is one which will immediately engage the attention of the Government with a view to a thorough protection to American interests. We will urge no narrow policy nor seek peculiar or exclusive privileges in any commercial route; but, in the language of my predecessor, I believe it to be the right "and duty of the United States to assert and maintain such supervision and authority over any interoceanic canal across the isthmus that connects North and South America as will protect our national interest."

The Constitution guarantees absolute religious freedom. Congress is prohibited from making any law respecting an establishment of religion or prohibiting the free exercise thereof. The Territories of the United States are subject to the direct legislative authority of Congress, and hence the General Government is responsible for any violation of the Constitution in any of them. It is therefore a reproach to the Government that in the most populous of the Territories the constitutional guaranty is not enjoyed by the people and the authority of Congress is set at naught. The Mormon Church not only offends the moral sense of manhood by sanctioning polygamy, but prevents the administration of justice through ordinary instrumentalities of law.

In my judgment it is the duty of Congress, while respecting to the uttermost the conscientious convictions and religious scruples of every citizen, to prohibit within its jurisdiction all criminal practices, especially of that class which destroy the family relations and endanger social order. Nor can any ecclesiastical organization be safely permitted to usurp in the smallest degree the functions and powers of the National Government.

The civil service can never be placed on a satisfactory basis until it is regulated by law. For the good of the service itself, for the protection of those who are intrusted with the appointing power against the waste of time and obstruction to the public business caused by the inordinate pressure for place, and for the protection of incumbents against intrigue and wrong, I shall, at the proper time ask Congress to fix the tenure of the minor offices of the several Executive Departments and prescribe the grounds upon which removals shall be made during the terms for which incumbents have been appointed.

Finally, acting always within the authority and limitations of the Constitution, invading neither the rights of the States nor the reserved rights of the people, it will be the purpose of my Administration to maintain the authority of the nation in all places within its jurisdiction; to enforce obedience to all the laws of the Union in the interests of the people; to demand rigid economy in all the expenditures of the Government, and to require the honest and faithful service of all executive officers, remembering that the offices were created, not for the benefit of incumbents or their supporters, but for the service of the Government.

And now, fellow-citizens, I am about to assume the great trust which you have committed to my hands. I appeal to you for that earnest and thoughtful support which makes this Government in fact, as it is in law, a government of the people.

I shall greatly rely upon the wisdom and patriotism of Congress and of those who may share with me the responsibilities and duties of administration, and, above all, upon our efforts to promote the welfare of this great people and their Government I reverently invoke the support and blessings of Almighty God.

MARCH 4, 1881.

SPECIAL MESSAGES.

EXECUTIVE MANSION,
Washington, April 6, 1881.

To the Senate of the United States:

I transmit herewith, in response to the resolution of the Senate of the 18th ultimo, a report of the Secretary of State, with accompanying papers, in relation to the capitulations of the Ottoman Empire.

JAMES A. GARFIELD.

EXECUTIVE MANSION,
Washington, May 20, 1881.

To the Senate of the United States:

I transmit herewith a report of the Secretary of State, with accompanying papers, submitted in response to the Senate resolution of the 12th ultimo, touching the case of Michael P. Boyton.*

JAMES A. GARFIELD.

*Arrested and imprisoned by authorities of Great Britain.

EXECUTIVE ORDER.

EXECUTIVE MANSION,
Washington, May 28, 1881.

DEAR SIR:* I am directed by the President to inform you that the several Departments of the Government will be closed on Monday, the 30th instant, to enable the employees to participate in the decoration of the graves of the soldiers who fell during the rebellion.

Very respectfully,

J. STANLEY BROWN, *Private Secretary.*

DEATH OF PRESIDENT GARFIELD.

ANNOUNCEMENT OF THE ASSASSINATION TO REPRESENTATIVES OF THE UNITED STATES ABROAD.

[From the Washington Post, July 3, 1881.]

DEPARTMENT OF STATE,
Washington, July 2, 1881.

JAMES RUSSELL LOWELL,
Minister, etc., London:

The President of the United States was shot this morning by an assassin named Charles Guiteau. The weapon was a large-sized revolver. The President had just reached the Baltimore and Potomac station, at about 9.20, intending, with a portion of his Cabinet, to leave on the limited express for New York. I rode in the carriage with him from the Executive Mansion and was walking by his side when he was shot. The assassin was immediately arrested, and the President was conveyed to a private room in the station building and surgical aid at once summoned. He has now, at 10.20, been removed to the Executive Mansion. The surgeons, on consultation, regard his wounds as very serious, though not necessarily fatal. His vigorous health gives strong hopes of his recovery. He has not lost consciousness for a moment. Inform our ministers in Europe.

JAMES G. BLAINE, *Secretary of State.*

PUBLIC ANNOUNCEMENT OF DEATH BY THE PHYSICIANS.

[From the New York Herald, September 20, 1881.]

ELBERON, N. J., *September 19—11.30 p. m.*

The President died at thirty-five minutes past 10 p. m. After the bulletin was issued at half past 5 this evening the President continued in much the same condition as during the afternoon, the pulse varying from 102 to 106, with rather increased force and volume. After taking

*Addressed to the heads of the Executive Departments, etc.

nourishment he fell into a quiet sleep about thirty-five minutes before his death, and while asleep his pulse ran to 120 and was somewhat more feeble. At ten minutes after 10 o'clock he awoke, complaining of severe pain over the region of the heart, and almost immediately became unconscious, and ceased to breathe at twenty-five minutes to 11.

D. W. BLISS.
FRANK H. HAMILTON.
D. HAYES AGNEW.

ANNOUNCEMENT TO THE VICE-PRESIDENT.

[From the New-York Times, September 20, 1881.]

[LONG BRANCH, N. J., *September 19, 1881.*]

Hon. CHESTER A. ARTHUR,
No. 123 Lexington Avenue, New York:

It becomes our painful duty to inform you of the death of President Garfield and to advise you to take the oath of office as President of the United States without delay. If it concur with your judgment, we will be very glad if you will come here on the earliest train to-morrow morning.

WILLIAM WINDOM,
Secretary of the Treasury.
WILLIAM H. HUNT,
Secretary of the Navy.
THOMAS L. JAMES,
Postmaster-General.
WAYNE MacVEAGH,
Attorney-General.
S. J. KIRKWOOD,
Secretary of the Interior.

[The Secretaries of State and of War were absent from Long Branch.]

REPLY OF THE VICE-PRESIDENT.

[From the Evening Star, Washington, September 20, 1881.]

NEW YORK, *September 20, 1881.**

I have your message announcing the death of President Garfield. Permit me to renew through you the expression of sorrow and sympathy which I have already telegraphed to Attorney-General MacVeagh. In accordance with your suggestion, I have taken the oath of office as President before the Hon. John R. Brady, justice of the supreme court of the State of New York. I will soon advise you further in regard to the other suggestion in your telegram.

C. A. ARTHUR.

*Addressed to the Cabinet.

RESENTATIVES **OF THE UNITED STATES**
    ABROAD.

m, New York, September 21, 881.]

G BRANCH, N. J., *September 20, 1881.*]

ent of the United States, died at Elberon,
es before 11 o'clock.   For nearly eighty days
during the entire period exhibited extraordi-
'hristian resignation.   The sorrow through-
universal.   Fifty millions of people stand as
y, at his residence in the city of New York,
sident, took the oath of office as President,
ue of the Constitution.   President Arthur
ge of his duties.   You will formally commu-
ish Government and transmit this dispatch
ministers on the Continent for like commu-
to which they are respectively accredited.
                                            BLAINE, *Secretary.*

SENTATIVES OF FOREIGN GOVERNMENTS
IE UNITED STATES.

al records, Department of State.]

      DEPARTMENT OF STATE,
          Washington, September 20, 1881.

o announce to you that the illness of the
s, which you have followed with an anxiety
npathy which you have repeatedly testified
he sorrowful period that has passed since he
he 2d of July, terminated last evening, when
utes past 10 o'clock.
etails of the funeral ceremonies are arranged
ereof.   ROBERT R. HITT,
                          Acting Secretary.

EMENT TO THE ARMY.

ial records, War Department.]

RAL ORDERS, No. 71.

HEADQUARTERS OF THE ARMY,
      ADJUTANT-GENERAL'S OFFICE,
          Washington, September 20, 1881.

the Secretary of War announces to the Army
ld, President of the United States:

WAR DEPARTMENT, *September 20, 1881.*

· Secretary of War announces to the Army
dent of the United States, died at Elberon,

N. J., at twenty-five minutes before 11 in the evening of September 19, 1881.

The great grief which is felt by the nation at the untimely death of the President will be especially felt by the Army, in whose service he bore so distinguished a part during the War of the Rebellion. In him the Army has lost a beloved Commander in Chief, friend, and former comrade.

Proper honors will be paid to the memory of the late Chief Magistrate of the nation at headquarters of each military department and division and at each military station.

The General of the Army will give the necessary instructions for carrying this order into effect.

ROBT. T. LINCOLN, Secretary of War.

II. On the day after the receipt of this order at the headquarters of military commands in the field, and at each military station, and at the Military Academy at West Point, the troops and cadets will be paraded at 10 o'clock a. m. and the order read to them, after which all labor for the day will cease.

At dawn of day thirteen guns will be fired at each military post, and afterwards at intervals of thirty minutes between the rising and setting sun a single gun, and at the close of the day a national salute of thirty-eight guns.

The national flag will be displayed at half-staff at the headquarters of the several military divisions and departments and at all military stations until the remains of the late Chief Magistrate are consigned to their final resting place at Cleveland, Ohio, at 2 p. m. on the 26th instant.

The officers of the Army of the United States will wear the badge of mourning on the left arm and on their swords and the colors of the regiments will be draped in mourning for the period of six months.

III. The following officers of the Army will, with a like number of officers of the Navy selected for the purpose, compose the guard of honor and accompany the remains of their late Commander in Chief from the national capital to Cleveland, Ohio, and continue with them until they are consigned to their final resting place: The General of the Army, Major-General Winfield S. Hancock, Quartermaster-General M. C. Meigs, Adjutant-General R. C. Drum, Inspector-General D. B. Sacket.

By command of General Sherman:

R. C. DRUM, Adjutant-General.

[From official records, War Department.]

GENERAL ORDERS, No. 72.

HEADQUARTERS OF THE ARMY,
ADJUTANT-GENERAL'S OFFICE,
Washington, September 20, 1881.

The following order has been received from the War Department:

The Secretary of War announces to the Army that upon the death of James A. Garfield, President of the United States, Chester A. Arthur,

Vice-President, on the 20th day of September, 1881, at his residence in the city of New York, took the oath of office as President of the United States, to which office he succeeded by virtue of the Constitution. President Arthur has entered upon the discharge of his official duties.

ROBT. T. LINCOLN,
Secretary of War.

By command of General Sherman:

R. C. DRUM, *Adjutant-General.*

ANNOUNCEMENT TO THE NAVY.

[From official records, Navy Department.]

GENERAL ORDER.

NAVY DEPARTMENT,
Washington, September 20, 1881.

The officers and men of the Navy and of the Marine Corps of the United States are hereby notified that President Garfield died at Long Branch on the 19th instant at 10 o'clock and 40 minutes p. m. Under the Constitution and laws of the Government Chester A. Arthur, then Vice-President, duly took the oath as President of the United States, and has entered upon the duties of that office. As President and Commander in Chief of the Navy of the United States he will be obeyed and respected by all persons connected with this Department. It is becoming that at a time when the heart of the nation is heavy with grief a proper expression should be given to the respect and affection so sincerely and universally entertained for the memory of the wise, patriotic, and noble Chief Magistrate who has departed this life under circumstances so distressing. To this end the officers of the Navy will see to it that all honors and ceremonies befitting the occasion are observed by their respective commands in accordance with the regulations of the service.

The offices of the Department will remain closed for all business during the time the remains of the President shall lie in state at the Capitol.

WILLIAM H. HUNT,
Secretary of the Navy.

[From official records, Navy Department.]

SPECIAL ORDER.

NAVY DEPARTMENT,
Washington, September 23, 1881.

Struck down by the hand of a cowardly assassin, in the day of his vigor and usefulness, on the eve of departure from the capital in search of much-needed rest from the toils and cares of office, our Chief Magistrate, President, and Commander in Chief, James A. Garfield, after bearing with heroic fortitude untold suffering, succumbed to the dread summons and yielded up his life at Elberon, N. J., on the evening of the 19th instant. The nation mourns its loss. The funeral services will take place at Cleveland, Ohio, on Monday, the 26th instant. It is eminently fit and proper that special honors should be paid to the memory of the late President on that day, and the Department therefore directs that at all naval stations and on board all vessels in commission the flags shall be at half-mast from sunrise to sunset and a gun fired every half hour during that period. The period of mourning by half-masted colors will cease at sunset. On foreign stations this order will be carried out on the day after its receipt. The navy-yards will be closed and all work suspended during the day. Officers of the Navy and Marine Corps will, as a further mark of respect, wear crape on the left arm and sword hilt for six months from the 20th instant.

ED. T. NICHOLS,
Acting Secretary of the Navy.

ACTION OF SENATORS AND OF REPRESENTATIVES ELECT IN WASHINGTON.

The members of the Senate and members elect of the House of Representatives in Washington held meetings on September 22 and selected the following gentlemen to accompany the remains of the late President to Cleveland, Ohio:

Senators Henry B. Anthony, of Rhode Island; John Sherman, of Ohio; Thomas F. Bayard, of Delaware; John J. Ingalls, of Kansas; James L. Pugh, of Alabama; Henry W. Blair, of New Hampshire; Johnson N. Camden, of West Virginia, and John T. Morgan, of Alabama.

Representatives elect John Randolph Tucker, of Virginia; John A. Kasson, of Iowa; Samuel J. Randall, of Pennsylvania; Frank Hiscock, of New York; Benjamin Wilson, of West Virginia; John R. Thomas, of Illinois; Amos Townsend, of Ohio, and Charles M. Shelley, of Alabama.

ORDERS OF THE HEADS OF THE EXECUTIVE DEPARTMENTS.

[From the National Republican, Washington, September 21, 1881.]

LONG BRANCH, *September 20.**

It has been agreed here by all the heads of Departments that the Departments shall remain closed from this time until the conclusion of President Garfield's funeral ceremonies in Washington, and it is understood that you will notify the acting heads of all Departments of this arrangement. * * *

ROBERT T. LINCOLN,
Secretary of War.

* Sent to the chief clerk of the War Department.

nds, Treasury Department.]

ORDER.

RY DEPARTMENT,

OFFICE OF THE SECRETARY,
shington, D. C., September 20, 1881.

:ct to the memory of President Garfield,
: closed during this day.

H. F. FRENCH,
Acting Secretary.

ds, Treasury Department.]

;OTICE.

RY DEPARTMENT,

OFFICE OF THE SECRETARY,
shington, D. C., September 21, 1881.

nemory of the late President, James A.
t will be closed to public business to-day
osed Thursday and Friday, the 22d and

H. F. FRENCH,
Acting Secretary.

ds, Treasury Department.]

)RDER.

RY DEPARTMENT,

OFFICE OF THE SECRETARY,
shington, D. C., September 24, 1881.

ation of the President* appointing Mon-
as a day of humiliation and mourning,
: late President, James A. Garfield, it is
:losed during that day.

H. F. FRENCH,
Acting Secretary.

la, Post-Office Department.]

POST-OFFICE DEPARTMENT,
shington, D. C., September 20, 1881.

ath of President James A. Garfield, this
ic business until after the funeral party
hio.

RICHD. A. ELMER,
Acting Postmaster-General.

See p. 34.

[From official records, Post-Office Department.]

POST-OFFICE DEPARTMENT,
Washington, D. C., September 24, 1881.

Ordered, That, in conformity with the action of other executive branches of the Government, this Department be closed on Monday next, the 26th instant, and that the day be fittingly observed by all persons connected therewith as the occasion of the consignment to their final resting place of the remains of the late beloved and honored Chief Magistrate of the United States, James A. Garfield.

RICHD. A. ELMER, *Acting Postmaster-General.*

[From official records, Interior Department.]

ORDER.

DEPARTMENT OF THE INTERIOR,
Washington, September 20, 1881.

As a token of respect to the memory of the late President, James A. Garfield, the Department of the Interior and the several bureaus and offices thereof will be closed to public business until Saturday, the 24th instant.

A. BELL, *Acting Secretary.*

[From official records, Interior Department.]

ORDER.

DEPARTMENT OF THE INTERIOR,
Washington, September 24, 1881.

In pursuance of the proclamation of the President of the United States* appointing Monday, the 26th instant, as a day of humiliation and mourning for the death of the late President, this Department and the several bureaus and offices thereof will be closed to business on that day.

A. BELL, *Acting Secretary.*

FUNERAL ANNOUNCEMENT TO THE PUBLIC.

[From the New-York Times, September 21, 1881.]

[ELBERON, N. J., *September 20, 1881.*]

The remains of the late President of the United States will be removed to Washington by special train on Wednesday, September 21, leaving Elberon at 10 a. m. and reaching Washington at 4 p. m. Detachments from the United States Army and from the marines of the Navy will be in attendance on arrival at Washington to perform escort duty. The remains will lie in state in the Rotunda of the Capitol on Thursday and

*See p. 34.

Friday, and will be guarded by deputations from the Executive Departments and by officers of the Senate and House of Representatives.

Religious ceremonies will be observed in the Rotunda at 3 o'clock on Friday afternoon. At 5 o'clock the remains will be transferred to the funeral car and be removed to Cleveland, Ohio, *via* the Pennsylvania Railroad, arriving there Saturday at 2 p. m. In Cleveland the remains will lie in state until Monday at 2 p. m., and be then interred in Lakeview Cemetery. No ceremonies are expected ·in the cities and towns along the route of the funeral train beyond the tolling of bells. Detailed arrangements for final sepulture are committed to the municipal authorities of Cleveland, under the direction of the executive of the State of Ohio.

JAMES G. BLAINE,
Secretary of State.

OFFICIAL ARRANGEMENTS FOR THE FUNERAL.

[From official records, War Department.]

ORDER OF ARRANGEMENT FOR THE FUNERAL AT WASHINGTON CITY OF JAMES A. GARFIELD, LATE PRESIDENT OF THE UNITED STATES.

The remains of the late President will lie in state in the Rotunda of the Capitol until 3 o'clock p. m. on Friday, the 23d instant, when they will be borne to the depot of the Baltimore and Potomac Railroad and thence conveyed to their final resting place at Cleveland, Ohio.

ORDER OF PROCESSION.

FUNERAL ESCORT.
(Under command of Brevet Major-General R. B. Ayres.)
Battalion of District of Columbia Volunteers.
Battalion of marines.
Battalion of foot artillery.
Battery of light artillery.

CIVIC PROCESSION.
(Under command of Chief Marshal Colonel Robert Boyd.)
Clergymen in attendance.
Physicians who attended the late President.
Guard of honor. Hearse. Guard of honor.
Bearers. Bearers.
(The officers of the Army, Navy, and Marine Corps in the city, and not on duty with the troops forming the escort, in full dress, will form, right in front, on either side of the hearse—the Army on the right and the Navy and Marine Corps on the left—and compose the guard of honor.)
Family of the late President.
Relatives of the late President.
Ex-Presidents of the United States.
The President.
The Cabinet ministers.
The Diplomatic Corps.

The Chief Justice and Associate Justices of the Supreme Court of the United States.
The Senators of the United States.
Members of the United States House of Representatives.
Governors of States and Territories and Commissioners of the District of Columbia.
The judges of the Court of Claims, the judiciary of the District of Columbia, and judges of the United States courts.
The Assistant Secretaries of State, Treasury, and Interior Departments.
The Assistant Postmasters-General.
The Solicitor-General and the Assistant Attorneys-General.
Organized societies.
Citizens and strangers.

The troops designated to form the escort will assemble on the east side of the Capitol and form line fronting the eastern portico of the Capitol precisely at 2 o'clock p. m. on Friday the 23d instant.

The procession will move on the conclusion of the religious services at the Capitol appointed to commence at 3 o'clock, when minute guns will be fired at the navy-yard by the vessels of war which may be in port, at Fort Myer and by the battery of artillery stationed near the Capitol for that purpose. At the same hour the bells of the several churches, fire-engine houses, and the schoolhouses will be tolled.

The civic procession will form in accordance with directions to be given by the chief marshal.

The officers of the Army and Navy selected to compose the guard of honor and accompany the remains to their final resting place will assemble at 4 p. m. at the Baltimore and Potomac Railroad depot, where they will receive the body of the late President and deposit it in the car prepared for the purpose.

ROBERT T. LINCOLN,
Secretary of War.

WILLIAM H. HUNT,
Secretary of the Navy.

J. DENT,
President Board of Commissioners District of Columbia.

[From the Washington Post, September 23, 1881.]

CIRCULAR.

HEADQUARTERS OF THE ARMY,
ADJUTANT-GENERAL'S OFFICE,
Washington, September 22, 1881.

The officers of the Army in this city not otherwise ordered for special duty on this occasion will assemble in full uniform at 3 p. m. on the 23d instant on the east front of the Capitol and form line, right in front, on the right of the hearse, to act as a guard of honor to the remains of the late President of the United States from the Capitol to the Baltimore and Potomac Railroad depot.

By command of General Sherman:

R. C. DRUM, *Adjutant-General.*

[From records in possession of Colonel Amos Webster.]

GENERAL ORDERS, No. 22.

ADJUTANT-GENERAL'S OFFICE,
DISTRICT OF COLUMBIA MILITIA,
September 21, 1881.

Pursuant to orders from the honorable Secretary of War, the troops comprising the militia of the District of Columbia will assemble in full-dress uniform at 3 p. m. on the 21st instant on Sixth street NW., the right resting on Pennsylvania avenue, the left extended south, to take part in and form a portion of the escort to the remains of the late President, and will also hold themselves in readiness to participate at the funeral ceremonies on Friday, the 23d instant. The formation will be as follows on both occasions:

Washington Light Infantry Corps, Captain W. G. Moore.
Union Veteran Corps, Captain S. E. Thomason.
National Rifles, Captain J. O. P. Burnside.
Washington Light Guards, Lieutenant F. S. Hodgson.
Butler Zouaves, Captain C. B. Fisher.
Capital City Guards, Captain W. S. Kelly.
Washington Cadets, Captain C. A. Dolan.

The officers of Light Battery A, District of Columbia Artillery, will report to adjutant-general District of Columbia Militia for duty as aids on both occasions.

A. WEBSTER,
Adjutant-General District of Columbia Militia.

[From records in possession of Colonel Amos Webster.]

GENERAL ORDER No. 23.

ADJUTANT-GENERAL'S OFFICE,
DISTRICT OF COLUMBIA MILITIA,
September 22, 1881.

Pursuant to orders from the honorable Secretary of War, and in compliance with general order No. 22 from these headquarters, all the organizations comprising the militia of the District of Columbia will assemble in full-dress uniform at 2 p. m. on the 23d instant on the ground east of the Capitol, right resting on B street N., the left extending south, facing west. The formation will be the same as designated in general order No. 22. Upon their arrival on the ground designated each commanding officer will report in person to the commanding officer of the District Volunteers.

By order of the Commissioners of the District of Columbia:

AMOS WEBSTER,
Adjutant-General District of Columbia Militia, Commanding.

[From the Washington Post, September 23, 1881.]

SPECIAL ORDER.

NAVY DEPARTMENT,
Washington, September 22, 1881.

The officers of the Navy and Marine Corps on duty and resident in Washington will assemble to-morrow, the 23d instant, at 3 o'clock p. m., at the east front of the Capitol, in full dress, to accompany the remains of the late President Garfield to the Baltimore and Potomac Railroad depot.

Commander H. L. Howison, United States Navy, is hereby appointed adjutant, and will direct the formation of the officers of the Navy and Marine Corps.

ED. T. NICHOLS,
Acting Secretary of the Navy.

[From the Medical Record, New York, 1881, vol. 20, p. 364.]

OFFICIAL BULLETIN OF THE AUTOPSY ON THE BODY OF PRESIDENT GARFIELD.

The following official bulletin was prepared by the surgeons who have been in attendance upon the late President:

By previous arrangement a *post-mortem* examination of the body of President Garfield was made this afternoon in the presence and with the assistance of Drs. Hamilton, Agnew, Bliss, Barnes, Woodward, Reyburn, Andrew H. Smith, of Elberon, and Acting Assistant Surgeon D. S. Lamb, of the Army Medical Museum, of Washington. The operation was performed by Dr. Lamb. It was found that the ball, after fracturing the right eleventh rib, had passed through the spinal column in front of the spinal cord, fracturing the body of the first lumbar vertebra, driving a number of small fragments of bone into the adjacent soft parts, and lodging below the pancreas, about $2\frac{1}{2}$ inches to the left of the spine and behind the peritoneum, where it had become completely encysted.

The immediate cause of death was secondary hemorrhage from one of the mesenteric arteries adjoining the track of the ball, the blood rupturing the peritoneum and nearly a pint escaping into the abdominal cavity. This hemorrhage is believed to have been the cause of the severe pain in the lower part of the chest complained of just before death. An abscess cavity 6 inches by 4 in dimensions was found in the vicinity of the gall bladder, between the liver and the transverse colon, which were strongly adherent. It did not involve the substance of the liver, and no communication was found between it and the wound.

A long suppurating channel extended from the external wound, between the loin muscles and the right kidney, almost to the right groin. This channel, now known to be due to the burrowing of pus from the l, was supposed during life to have been the track of the ball.

On an examination of the organs of the chest evidences of severe bronchitis were found on both sides, with broncho-pneumonia of the lower portions of the right lung, and, though to a much less extent, of the left. The lungs contained no abscesses and the heart no clots. The liver was enlarged and fatty, but not from abscesses. Nor were any found in any other organ except the left kidney, which contained near its surface a small abscess about one-third of an inch in diameter.

In reviewing the history of the case in connection with the autopsy it is quite evident that the different suppurating surfaces, and especially the fractured, spongy tissue of the vertebræ, furnish a sufficient explanation of the septic condition which existed.

> D. W. BLISS.
> J. K. BARNES.
> J. J. WOODWARD.
> ROBERT REYBURN.
> FRANK H. HAMILTON.
> D. HAYES AGNEW.
> ANDREW H. SMITH.
> D. S. LAMB.

[SEPTEMBER 20, 1881.]

FORMAL OATH OF OFFICE ADMINISTERED TO PRESIDENT ARTHUR.

President Chester A. Arthur took the formal oath of office as President of the United States in the room of the Vice-President, in the Capitol, Thursday, September 22, 1881, at 12.10 o'clock p. m. Chief Justice Morrison R. Waite administered the oath prescribed by the Constitution in the presence of the members of the Cabinet, the Justices of the Supreme Court, ex-Presidents Grant and Hayes, General W. T. Sherman, and a number of Senators and Representatives.

[For Inaugural Address of President Arthur see pp. 33–34.]

ACTION OF CONGRESS.

President Arthur, in his first annual message to the first session of the Forty-seventh Congress, thus announced the death of his predecessor:

An appalling calamity has befallen the American people since their chosen representatives last met in the halls where you are now assembled. We might else recall with unalloyed content the rare prosperity with which throughout the year the nation has been blessed. Its harvests have been plenteous; its varied industries have thriven; the health of its people has been preserved; it has maintained with foreign governments the undisturbed relations of amity and peace. For these manifestations of His favor we owe to Him who holds our destiny in His hands the tribute of our

To that mysterious exercise of His will which has taken from us the loved and illustrious citizen who was but lately the head of the nation we bow in sorrow and submission.

The memory of his exalted character, of his noble achievements, and of his patriotic life will be treasured forever as a sacred possession of the whole people.

The announcement of his death drew from foreign governments and peoples trib. utes of sympathy and sorrow which history will record as signal tokens of the kin. ship of nations and the federation of mankind.

The Senate on December 6, 1881, adopted the following resolution:

Resolved, That a committee of six Senators be appointed on the part of the Sen. ate to join such committee as may be appointed on the part of the House to consider and report by what token of respect and affection it may be proper for the Congress of the United States to express the deep sensibility of the nation to the event of the decease of the late President, James A. Garfield, and that so much of the message of the President as relates to that melancholy event be referred to said committee.

The committee on the part of the Senate, having been subsequently increased to eight, comprised the following-named gentlemen:

John Sherman, of Ohio; George H. Pendleton, of Ohio; Henry L. Dawes, of Massachusetts; Elbridge G. Lapham, of New York; Thomas F. Bayard, of Delaware; John T. Morgan, of Alabama; Omar D. Conger, of Michigan, and Joseph E. Brown, of Georgia.

The House of Representatives on December 6, 1881, passed the following resolution:

Resolved, That a committee of one member from each State represented in this House be appointed on the part of the House to join such committee as may be appointed on the part of the Senate to consider and report by what token of respect and affection it may be proper for the Congress of the United States to express the deep sensibility of the nation to the event of the decease of their late President, James Abram Garfield, and that so much of the message of the President as refers to that melancholy event be referred to said committee.

The committee on the part of the House of Representatives comprised the following-named gentlemen:

William M. Springer, of Ohio; Romualdo Pacheco, of California; ... . of Colorado, John T. Wait, of Connecticut; William .... Poindexter Dunn, of Arkansas; Edward L. .... Robert H. M. Davidson, of Florida; Alexander H. .... Joseph G. Cannon, of Illinois; Godlove S. Orth, John N. Kasson, of Iowa; John A. Anderson, of Kansas; .... of Kentucky; Randall L. Gibson, of Louisiana; Nel- .... of Maine; Robert M. McLane, of Maryland; Benjamin .... of Massachusetts; Roswell G. Horr, of Michigan; Mark H. .... of Minnesota; Charles E. Hooker, of Mississippi; Nicholas Ford, of Missouri; Edward K. Valentine, of Nebraska; George W. Cassidy, of Nevada; Joshua G. Hall, of New Hampshire; John Hill, of New Jersey; S. Cox, of New York; Robert B. Vance, of North Carolina; Mel- george, of Oregon; Charles O'Neill, of Pennsylvania; Jonathan

Chace, of Rhode Island; D. Wyatt Aiken, of South Carolina; Augustus H. Pettibone, of Tennessee; Roger Q. Mills, of Texas; Charles H. Joyce, of Vermont; J. Randolph Tucker, of Virginia; Benjamin Wilson, of West Virginia, and Charles G. Williams, of Wisconsin.

The following concurrent resolutions were adopted by both Houses of Congress on December 21, 1881:

Whereas the melancholy event of the violent and tragic death of James Abram Garfield, late President of the United States, having occurred during the recess of Congress, and the two Houses sharing in the general grief and desiring to manifest their sensibility upon the occasion of the public bereavement: Therefore

Be it resolved by the House of Representatives (the Senate concurring), That the two Houses of Congress will assemble in the Hall of the House of Representatives on a day and hour to be fixed and announced by the joint committee, and that in the presence of the two Houses there assembled an address upon the life and character of James Abram Garfield, late President of the United States, be pronounced by Hon. James G. Blaine, and that the President of the Senate *pro tempore* and the Speaker of the House of Representatives be requested to invite the President and ex-Presidents of the United States, the heads of the several Departments, the judges of the Supreme Court, the representatives of the foreign governments near this Government, the governors of the several States, the General of the Army, and the Admiral of the Navy, and such officers of the Army and Navy as have received the thanks of Congress who may then be at the seat of Government to be present on the occasion.

And be it further resolved, That the President of the United States be requested to transmit a copy of these resolutions to Mrs. Lucretia R. Garfield, and to assure her of the profound sympathy of the two Houses of Congress for her deep personal affliction and of their sincere condolence for the late national bereavement.

February 1, 1882, both Houses of Congress adopted the following resolution:

Resolved by the House of Representatives (the Senate concurring), That Monday, the 27th day of February, 1882, be set apart for the memorial services upon the late President, James A. Garfield.

[For proclamation of President Arthur appointing, in consequence of the death of James Abram Garfield, late President of the United States, a day of humiliation and mourning, see p. 34.]

Chester A. Arthur

September 19, 1881, to March 4, 1885

Chester A. Arthur

CHESTER ALAN ARTHUR was born in Fairfield, Franklin County, Vt., October 5, 1830. He was the eldest son of Rev. William Arthur and Malvina Stone. His father, a Baptist minister, was born in Ireland and emigrated to the United States. Chester prepared for college at Union Village in Greenwich and at Schenectady, N. Y., and in 1845 entered the sophomore class of Union College. While in his sophomore year taught school for a term at Schaghticoke, Rensselaer County, and a second term at the same place during his last year in college. Joined the Psi Upsilon Society, and was one of six in a class of one hundred who were elected members of the Phi Beta Kappa Society, the condition of admission being high scholarship. After his graduation in 1848, at the age of 18, attended a law school at Ballston Spa, N. Y.; returned to Lansingburg, N. Y., where his father then resided, and continued his legal studies. Was principal of an academy at North Pownal, Bennington County, Vt., in 1851. In 1853 entered the law office of Erastus D. Culver in New York City as a student; was admitted to the bar during the same year, and at once became a member of the firm of Culver, Parker & Arthur. Having formed from early associations sentiments of hostility to slavery, as a law student and after his admission to the bar became an earnest advocate for the slaves. Became a Henry Clay Whig, and cast his first vote in 1852 for Winfield Scott for President. Participated in the first Republican State convention, at Saratoga, and took an active part in the Frémont campaign of 1856. October 29, 1859, married Ellen Lewis Herndon, of Fredericksburg, Va. January 1, 1861, was appointed on Governor Edwin D. Morgan's staff as engineer in chief, with the rank of brigadier-general. Had previously taken part in the organization of the State militia, and had been judge-advocate of the Second Brigade. When the civil war began, in April, 1861, he became acting quartermaster-general, and as such began in New York City the work of preparing and forwarding the State's quota of troops. Was called to Albany in December for consultation concerning the defenses of New York Harbor. Summoned a board of engineers on December 24, of which he became a member, and on January 18, 1862, submitted an elaborate report on the condition of the national forts both on the seacoast and on the inland border of the State. Was appointed inspector-general February 10, 1862, with the rank of brigadier-general, and in May inspected the New York troops at Fredericksburg and on the Chickahominy. In June, 1862, Governor Morgan ordered his return from the Army of the Potomac, and he acted as secretary of the meeting of the governors of the loyal States which was held June 28 in New York City. At Governor Morgan's request, General Arthur resumed his former work, resigned as inspector-general, and on July 10 was appointed quartermaster-general. Retired from the office December 31, 1862, when Horatio Seymour succeeded Governor Morgan. Between 1862 and 1872 was engaged in continuous and active law practice—in partnership with Henry G. Gardner from 1862 till 1867, then for five years alone, and on January 1, 1872, formed the firm of Arthur, Phelps & Knevals. Was for a short time counsel for the department of assessments and taxes, but resigned the place. Continued during all this period to take an active part in politics. Was chairman in 1868 of the Central Grant Club of New York, and became chairman of the executive committee of the Republican State committee in 1879. Was appointed collector of the port of New York by President Grant on November 20, 1871; was reappointed on December 17, 1875, and confirmed by the Senate on the same day without reference to a committee, a courtesy never before extended to an appointee who had not been a Senator; retained the office until July 11, 1878, when he was suspended by President Hayes. On retiring from the office of collector resumed the practice of law with the firm of Arthur, Phelps, Knevals & Ransom. Advocated in 1880 the nomination of General Grant to succeed President Hayes. Was a delegate at large to the Chicago convention, which met June 2, 1880. After the nomination of General Garfield for the Presidency a general desire arose in the convention to nominate for Vice-President some advocate of General Grant and a resident of New York State. The New York delegation indicated their preference for General Arthur, and he was nominated on the first ballot. Was elected Vice-President November 2, 1880; took the oath of office March 4, 1881, and presided over the extraordinary session of the Senate that then began, which was very exciting. That body being equally divided, he was frequently called upon to exercise the right of casting the controlling vote. President Garfield was shot July 2, 1881, and died September 19. His Cabinet announced his death to the Vice-President, then in New York, and at their suggestion he took the oath as President on the 20th at his residence in New York City before Judge John R. Brady, of the New York supreme court. On the 22d the oath was formally administered again in the Vice-President's room in the Capitol at Washington by Chief Justice Waite. President Arthur's name was presented to the Republican Presidential convention which met at Chicago June 3, 1884. On the first ballot he received 278 votes against 540 for all others, 276 on the second, 274 on the third, and 207 on the fourth, which resulted in the nomination of James G. Blaine. In the canvass which ensued Mr. Arthur rendered all possible assistance to the Republican cause and candidates. Died suddenly at his residence in New York City November 18, 1886, and was buried in Rural Cemetery at Albany.

INAUGURAL ADDRESS.

For the fourth time in the history of the Republic its Chief Magistrate has been removed by death. All hearts are filled with grief and horror at the hideous crime which has darkened our land, and the memory of the murdered President, his protracted sufferings, his unyielding fortitude, the example and achievements of his life, and the pathos of his death will forever illumine the pages of our history.

For the fourth time the officer elected by the people and ordained by the Constitution to fill a vacancy so created is called to assume the Executive chair. The wisdom of our fathers, foreseeing even the most dire possibilities, made sure that the Government should never be imperiled because of the uncertainty of human life. Men may die, but the fabrics of our free institutions remain unshaken. No higher or more assuring proof could exist of the strength and permanence of popular government than the fact that though the chosen of the people be struck down his constitutional successor is peacefully installed without shock or strain except the sorrow which mourns the bereavement. All the noble aspirations of my lamented predecessor which found expression in his life, the measures devised and suggested during his brief Administration to correct abuses, to enforce economy, to advance prosperity, and to promote the general welfare, to insure domestic security and maintain friendly and honorable relations with the nations of the earth, will be garnered in the hearts of the people; and it will be my earnest endeavor to profit, and to see that the nation shall profit, by his example and experience.

Prosperity blesses our country. Our fiscal policy is fixed by law, is well grounded and generally approved. No threatening issue mars our foreign intercourse, and the wisdom, integrity, and thrift of our people may be trusted to continue undisturbed the present assured career of peace, tranquillity, and welfare. The gloom and anxiety which have enshrouded the country must make repose especially welcome now. No demand for speedy legislation has been heard; no adequate occasion is apparent for an unusual session of Congress. The Constitution defines the functions and powers of the executive as clearly as those of either of the other two departments of the Government, and he must answer for the just exercise of the discretion it permits and the performance of the duties it imposes. Summoned to these high duties and responsibilities and profoundly conscious of their magnitude and gravity, I assume the trust imposed by the Constitution, relying for aid on divine guidance and the virtue, patriotism, and intelligence of the American people.

SEPTEMBER 22, 1881.

PROCLAMATIONS.

BY THE PRESIDENT OF THE UNITED STATES OF AMERICA.

A PROCLAMATION.

Whereas in His inscrutable wisdom it has pleased God to remove from us the illustrious head of the nation, James A. Garfield, late President of the United States; and

Whereas it is fitting that the deep grief which fills all hearts should manifest itself with one accord toward the throne of infinite grace, and that we should bow before the Almighty and seek from Him that consolation in our affliction and that sanctification of our loss which He is able and willing to vouchsafe:

Now, therefore, in obedience to sacred duty and in accordance with the desire of the people, I, Chester A. Arthur, President of the United States of America, do hereby appoint Monday next, the 26th day of September—on which day the remains of our honored and beloved dead will be consigned to their last resting place on earth—to be observed throughout the United States as a day of humiliation and mourning; and I earnestly recommend all the people to assemble on that day in their respective places of divine worship, there to render alike their tribute of sorrowful submission to the will of Almighty God and of reverence and love for the memory and character of our late Chief Magistrate.

In witness whereof I have hereunto set my hand and caused the seal of the United States to be affixed.

[SEAL.] Done at the city of Washington, the 22d day of September, A. D. 1881, and of the Independence of the United States of America the one hundred and sixth.

CHESTER A. ARTHUR.

By the President:

JAMES G. BLAINE, *Secretary of State.*

BY THE PRESIDENT OF THE UNITED STATES OF AMERICA.

A PROCLAMATION.

Whereas objects of interest to the United States require that the Senate should be convened at an early day to receive and act upon such communications as may be made to it on the part of the Executive:

Now, therefore, I, Chester A. Arthur, President of the United States, have considered it to be my duty to issue this my proclamation, declaring that an extraordinary occasion requires the Senate of the United States to convene for the transaction of business at the Capitol, in the city of Washington, on Monday, the 10th day of October next, at 12 o'clock noon on that day, of which all who shall at that time be entitled to act as members of that body are hereby required to take notice.

Given under my hand and the seal of the United States, at Washington, the 23d day of September, A. D. 1881, and of the Independence of the United States the one hundred and sixth.

[SEAL.]

CHESTER A. ARTHUR.

By the President:

JAMES G. BLAINE,
Secretary of State.

SPECIAL MESSAGES.

WASHINGTON, *October 12, 1881.*

To the Senate of the United States:

I transmit herewith to the Senate a communication from the Secretary of State, submitting the text, in the English and French languages, of the proceedings of the International Sanitary Conference, provided for by the joint resolution of the Senate and House of Representatives of the United States of America, held at Washington in the early part of 1881.

CHESTER A. ARTHUR.

To the Senate:

I transmit herewith the report of the Secretary of State in answer to the resolution of the Senate of October 14, with accompanying document.*

CHESTER A. ARTHUR.

OCTOBER 24, 1881.

WASHINGTON, *October 26, 1881.*

To the Senate of the United States:

I transmit to the Senate, for its consideration with a view to ratification, a convention between the United States and His Majesty the King of Roumania, defining the rights, immunities, and privileges of consular officers, signed on the 17th day of June, 1881.

CHESTER A. ARTHUR.

* Letter of instruction to United States ministers in Europe relative to protecting the rights and interests of the United States in the projected interoceanic canal at Panama.

PROCLAMATION.

By the President of the United States of America.

A PROCLAMATION.

It has long been the pious custom of our people, with the closing of the year, to look back upon the blessings brought to them in the changing course of the seasons and to return solemn thanks to the all-giving source from whom they flow. And although at this period, when the falling leaf admonishes us that the time of our sacred duty is at hand, our nation still lies in the shadow of a great bereavement, and the mourning which has filled our hearts still finds its sorrowful expression toward the God before whom we but lately bowed in grief and supplication, yet the countless benefits which have showered upon us during the past twelvemonth call for our fervent gratitude and make it fitting that we should rejoice with thankfulness that the Lord in His infinite mercy has most signally favored our country and our people. Peace without and prosperity within have been vouchsafed to us, no pestilence has visited our shores, the abundant privileges of freedom which our fathers left us in their wisdom are still our increasing heritage; and if in parts of our vast domain sore affliction has visited our brethren in their forest homes, yet even this calamity has been tempered and in a manner sanctified by the generous compassion for the sufferers which has been called forth throughout our land. For all these things it is meet that the voice of the nation should go up to God in devout homage.

Wherefore I, Chester A. Arthur, President of the United States, do recommend that all the people observe Thursday, the 24th day of November instant, as a day of national thanksgiving and prayer, by ceasing, so far as may be, from their secular labors and meeting in their several places of worship, there to join in ascribing honor and praise to Almighty God, whose goodness has been so manifest in our history and in our lives, and offering earnest prayers that His bounties may continue to us and to our children.

In witness whereof I have hereunto set my hand and caused the seal of the United States to be affixed.

[SEAL.]   Done at the city of Washington, this 4th day of November, A. D. 1881, and of the Independence of the United States the one hundred and sixth.

CHESTER A. ARTHUR.

By the President:

JAMES G. BLAINE,
Secretary of State.

EXECUTIVE ORDER.*

YORKTOWN, VA., *October 19, 1881.*

In recognition of the friendly relations so long and so happily subsisting between Great Britain and the United States, in the trust and confidence of peace and good will between the two countries for all the centuries to come, and especially as a mark of the profound respect entertained by the American people for the illustrious sovereign and gracious lady who sits upon the British throne

It is hereby ordered, That at the close of the ceremonies commemorative of the valor and success of our forefathers in their patriotic struggle for independence the British flag shall be saluted by the forces of the Army and Navy of the United States now at Yorktown.

The Secretary of War and the Secretary of the Navy will give orders accordingly.

CHESTER A. ARTHUR.

By the President:
JAMES G. BLAINE,
Secretary of State.

FIRST ANNUAL MESSAGE.

WASHINGTON, *December 6, 1881.*

To the Senate and House of Representatives of the United States:

An appalling calamity has befallen the American people since their chosen representatives last met in the halls where you are now assembled. We might else recall with unalloyed content the rare prosperity with which throughout the year the nation has been blessed. Its harvests have been plenteous; its varied industries have thriven; the health of its people has been preserved; it has maintained with foreign governments the undisturbed relations of amity and peace. For these manifestations of His favor we owe to Him who holds our destiny in His hands the tribute of our grateful devotion. .

To that mysterious exercise of His will which has taken from us the loved and illustrious citizen who was but lately the head of the nation we bow in sorrow and submission.

The memory of his exalted character, of his noble achievements, and of his patriotic life will be treasured forever as a sacred possession of the whole people.

*Read by the Secretary of State before the people assembled to celebrate the Yorktown Centennial.

The announcement of his death drew from foreign governments and peoples tributes of sympathy and sorrow which history will record as signal tokens of the kinship of nations and the federation of mankind.

The feeling of good will between our own Government and that of Great Britain was never more marked than at present. In recognition of this pleasing fact I directed, on the occasion of the late centennial celebration at Yorktown, that a salute be given to the British flag.

Save for the correspondence to which I shall refer hereafter in relation to the proposed canal across the Isthmus of Panama, little has occurred worthy of mention in the diplomatic relations of the two countries.

Early in the year the Fortune Bay claims were satisfactorily settled by the British Government paying in full the sum of £15,000, most of which has been already distributed. As the terms of the settlement included compensation for injuries suffered by our fishermen at Aspee Bay, there has been retained from the gross award a sum which is deemed adequate for those claims.

The participation of Americans in the exhibitions at Melbourne and Sydney will be approvingly mentioned in the reports of the two exhibitions, soon to be presented to Congress. They will disclose the readiness of our countrymen to make successful competition in distant fields of enterprise.

Negotiations for an international copyright convention are in hopeful progress.

The surrender of Sitting Bull and his forces upon the Canadian frontier has allayed apprehension, although bodies of British Indians still cross the border in quest of sustenance. Upon this subject a correspondence has been opened which promises an adequate understanding. Our troops have orders to avoid meanwhile all collisions with alien Indians.

The presence at the Yorktown celebration of representatives of the French Republic and descendants of Lafayette and of his gallant compatriots who were our allies in the Revolution has served to strengthen the spirit of good will which has always existed between the two nations.

You will be furnished with the proceedings of the Bimetallic Conference held during the summer at the city of Paris. No accord was reached, but a valuable interchange of views was had, and the conference will next year be renewed.

At the Electrical Exhibition and Congress, also held at Paris, this country was creditably represented by eminent specialists, who, in the absence of an appropriation, generously lent their efficient aid at the instance of the State Department. While our exhibitors in this almost distinctively American field of achievement have won several valuable awards, I recommend that Congress provide for the repayment of the personal expenses incurred in the public interest by the honorary commissioners and delegates.

No new questions respecting the status of our naturalized citizens in

ırisen during the year, and the causes of complaint, espe-
and Lorraine, have practically ceased through the liberal
ımperial Government in accepting our often-expressed
ıbject. The application of the treaty of 1868 to the
Rhenish provinces has received very earnest attention,
ınd lasting agreement on this point is confidently ex-
ırticipation of the descendants of Baron von Steuben in
ıstivities, and their subsequent reception by their Amer-
ırikingly evinced the ties of good will which unite the
and our own.

ʿse with Spain has been friendly. An agreement con-
ary last fixes a term for the labors of the Spanish and
ns Commission. The Spanish Government has been
ıy the late awards of that Commission, and will, it is
to the request as promptly and courteously as on former

ıslation onerous fines have been imposed upon American
nish and colonial ports for slight irregularities in mani-
ı of hardship is specially worthy of attention. The bark
for Japan, entered Manila in distress, and is there sought
ı under Spanish revenue laws for an alleged shortage in
d cargo. Though efforts for her relief have thus far
ıg, it is expected that the whole matter will be adjusted
rit.

ısolutions of condolence on the assassination of the Czar
ere appropriately communicated to the Russian Govern-
turn has expressed its sympathy in our late national
It is desirable that our cordial relations with Russia
gthened by proper engagements assuring to peaceable
visit the Empire the consideration which is due to them
ʿriendly state. This is especially needful with respect to
ıtes, whose classification with the native Hebrews has
ı remonstrances from this Government.

ʿary consular agreement with Italy has been sanctioned
which puts at rest conflicts of jurisdiction in the case of
ıtd.

tant international conferences have been held in Italy
. At the Geographical Congress of Venice, the Benefi-
ıf Milan, and the Hygienic Congress of Turin this coun-
ıted by delegates from branches of the public service or
ns duly accredited in an honorary capacity. It is hoped
ʿill give such prominence to the results of their partici-
ıay seem to deserve.

of all discriminating duties against such colonial pro-
Dutch East Indies as are imported hither from Holl:

has been already considered by Congress. I trust that at the present session the matter may be favorably concluded.

The insecurity of life and property in many parts of Turkey has given rise to correspondence with the Porte looking particularly to the better protection of American missionaries in the Empire. The condemned murderer of the eminent missionary Dr. Justin W. Parsons has not yet been executed, although this Government has repeatedly demanded that exemplary justice be done.

The Swiss Government has again solicited the good offices of our diplomatic and consular agents for the protection of its citizens in countries where it is not itself represented. This request has, within proper limits, been granted.

Our agents in Switzerland have been instructed to protest against the conduct of the authorities of certain communes in permitting the emigration to this country of criminals and other objectionable persons. Several such persons, through the cooperation of the commissioners of emigration at New York, have been sent back by the steamers which brought them. A continuance of this course may prove a more effectual remedy than diplomatic remonstrance.

Treaties of commerce and navigation and for the regulation of consular privileges have been concluded with Roumania and Servia since their admission into the family of European States.

As is natural with contiguous states having like institutions and like aims of advancement and development, the friendship of the United States and Mexico has been constantly maintained. This Government has lost no occasion of encouraging the Mexican Government to a beneficial realization of the mutual advantages which will result from more intimate commercial intercourse and from the opening of the rich interior of Mexico to railway enterprise. I deem it important that means be provided to restrain the lawlessness unfortunately so common on the frontier and to suppress the forays of the reservation Indians on either side of the Rio Grande.

The neighboring States of Central America have preserved internal peace, and their outward relations toward us have been those of intimate friendship. There are encouraging signs of their growing disposition to subordinate their local interests to those which are common to them by reason of their geographical relations.

The boundary dispute between Guatemala and Mexico has afforded this Government an opportunity to exercise its good offices for preventing a rupture between those States and for procuring a peaceable solution of the question. I cherish strong hope that in view of our relations of amity with both countries our friendly counsels may prevail.

A special envoy of Guatemala has brought to me the condolences of his Government and people on the death of President Garfield.

The Costa Rican Government lately framed an engagement with

Colombia for settling by arbitration the boundary question between those countries, providing that the post of arbitrator should be offered successively to the King of the Belgians, the King of Spain, and the President of the Argentine Confederation. The King of the Belgians has declined to act, but I am not as yet advised of the action of the King of Spain. As we have certain interests in the disputed territory which are protected by our treaty engagements with one of the parties, it is important that the arbitration should not without our consent affect our rights, and this Government has accordingly thought proper to make its views known to the parties to the agreement, as well as to intimate them to the Belgian and Spanish Governments.

The questions growing out of the proposed interoceanic waterway across the Isthmus of Panama are of grave national importance. This Government has not been unmindful of the solemn obligations imposed upon it by its compact of 1846 with Colombia, as the independent and sovereign mistress of the territory crossed by the canal, and has sought to render them effective by fresh engagements with the Colombian Republic looking to their practical execution. The negotiations to this end, after they had reached what appeared to be a mutually satisfactory solution here, were met in Colombia by a disavowal of the powers which its envoy had assumed and by a proposal for renewed negotiation on a modified basis.

Meanwhile this Government learned that Colombia had proposed to the European powers to join in a guaranty of the neutrality of the proposed Panama canal—a guaranty which would be in direct contravention of our obligation as the sole guarantor of the integrity of Colombian territory and of the neutrality of the canal itself. My lamented predecessor felt it his duty to place before the European powers the reasons which make the prior guaranty of the United States indispensable, and for which the interjection of any foreign guaranty might be regarded as a superfluous and unfriendly act.

Foreseeing the probable reliance of the British Government on the provisions of the Clayton-Bulwer treaty of 1850 as affording room for a share in the guaranties which the United States covenanted with Colombia four years before, I have not hesitated to supplement the action of my predecessor by proposing to Her Majesty's Government the modification of that instrument and the abrogation of such clauses thereof as do not comport with the obligations of the United States toward Colombia or with the vital needs of the two friendly parties to the compact.

This Government sees with great concern the continuance of the hostile relations between Chile, Bolivia, and Peru. An early peace between these Republics is much to be desired, not only that they may themselves be spared further misery and bloodshed, but because their continued antagonism threatens consequences which are, in my judgment, dangerous to the interests of republican government on this continent and calculated to destroy the best elements of our free and peaceful civilization.

As in the present excited condition of popular feeling in these countries there has been serious misapprehension of the position of the United States, and as separate diplomatic intercourse with each through independent ministers is sometimes subject, owing to the want of prompt reciprocal communication, to temporary misunderstanding, I have deemed it judicious at the present time to send a special envoy accredited to all and each of them, and furnished with general instructions which will, I trust, enable him to bring these powers into friendly relations.

The Government of Venezuela maintains its attitude of warm friendship and continues with great regularity its payment of the monthly quota of the diplomatic debt. Without suggesting the direction in which Congress should act, I ask its attention to the pending questions affecting the distribution of the sums thus far received.

The relations between Venezuela and France growing out of the same debt have been for some time past in an unsatisfactory state, and this Government, as the neighbor and one of the largest creditors of Venezuela, has interposed its influence with the French Government with the view of producing a friendly and honorable adjustment.

I regret that the commercial interests between the United States and Brazil, from which great advantages were hoped a year ago, have suffered from the withdrawal of the American lines of communication between the Brazilian ports and our own.

Through the efforts of our minister resident at Buenos Ayres and the United States minister at Santiago, a treaty has been concluded between the Argentine Republic and Chile, disposing of the long-pending Patagonian boundary question. It is a matter of congratulation that our Government has been afforded the opportunity of successfully exerting its good influence for the prevention of disagreements between these Republics of the American continent.

I am glad to inform you that the treaties lately negotiated with China have been duly ratified on both sides and the exchange made at Peking. Legislation is necessary to carry their provisions into effect. The prompt and friendly spirit with which the Chinese Government, at the request of the United States, conceded the modification of existing treaties should secure careful regard for the interests and susceptibilities of that Government in the enactment of any laws relating to Chinese immigration.

Those clauses of the treaties which forbid the participation of citizens or vessels of the United States in the opium trade will doubtless receive your approval. They will attest the sincere interest which our people and Government feel in the commendable efforts of the Chinese Government to put a stop to this demoralizing and destructive traffic.

In relation both to China and Japan some changes are desirable in our present system of consular jurisdiction. I hope at some future time to lay before you a scheme for its improvement in the entire East.

The intimacy between our own country and Japan, the most advanced of the Eastern nations, continues to be cordial. I am advised that the Emperor contemplates the establishment of full constitutional government, and that he has already summoned a parliamentary congress for the purpose of effecting the change. Such a remarkable step toward complete assimilation with the Western system can not fail to bring Japan into closer and more beneficial relationship with ourselves as the chief Pacific power.

A question has arisen in relation to the exercise in that country of the judicial functions conferred upon our ministers and consuls. The indictment, trial, and conviction in the consular court at Yokohama of John Ross, a merchant seaman on board an American vessel, have made it necessary for the Government to institute a careful examination into the nature and methods of this jurisdiction.

It appeared that Ross was regularly shipped under the flag of the United States, but was by birth a British subject. My predecessor felt it his duty to maintain the position that during his service as a regularly shipped seaman on board an American merchant vessel Ross was subject to the laws of that service and to the jurisdiction of the United States consular authorities.

I renew the recommendation which has been heretofore urged by the Executive upon the attention of Congress, that after the deduction of such amount as may be found due to American citizens the balance of the indemnity funds heretofore obtained from China and Japan, and which are now in the hands of the State Department, be returned to the Governments of those countries.

The King of Hawaii, in the course of his homeward return after a journey around the world, has lately visited this country. While our relations with that Kingdom are friendly, this Government has viewed with concern the efforts to seek replenishment of the diminishing population of the islands from outward sources, to a degree which may impair the native sovereignty and independence, in which the United States was among the first to testify a lively interest.

Relations of unimpaired amity have been maintained throughout the year with the respective Governments of Austria-Hungary, Belgium, Denmark, Brazil, Paraguay and Uruguay, Portugal, and Sweden and Norway. This may also be said of Greece and Ecuador, although our relations with those States have for some years been severed by the withdrawal of appropriations for diplomatic representatives at Athens and Quito. It seems expedient to restore those missions, even on a reduced scale, and I decidedly recommend such a course with respect to Ecuador, which is likely within the near future to play an important part among the nations of the Southern Pacific.

At its last extra session the Senate called for the text of the Geneva convention for the relief of the wounded in war. I trust that this action foreshadows such interest in the subject as will result in the adhesion of the United States to that humane and commendable engagement.

I invite your attention to the propriety of adopting the new code of international rules for the prevention of collisions on the high seas and of conforming the domestic legislation of the United States thereto, so that no confusion may arise from the application of conflicting rules in the case of vessels of different nationalities meeting in tidal waters. These international rules differ but slightly from our own. They have been adopted by the Navy Department for the governance of the war ships of the United States on the high seas and in foreign waters, and, through the action of the State Department in disseminating the rules and in acquainting shipmasters with the option of conforming to them without the jurisdictional waters of the United States, they are now very generally known and obeyed.

The State Department still continues to publish to the country the trade and manufacturing reports received from its officers abroad. The success of this course warrants its continuance and such appropriation as may be required to meet the rapidly increasing demand for these publications. With special reference to the Atlanta Cotton Exposition, the October number of the reports was devoted to a valuable collection of papers on the cotton-goods trade of the world.

The International Sanitary Conference for which, in 1879, Congress made provision assembled in this city early in January last, and its sessions were prolonged until March. Although it reached no specific conclusions affecting the future action of the participant powers, the interchange of views proved to be most valuable. The full protocols of the sessions have been already presented to the Senate.

As pertinent to this general subject, I call your attention to the operations of the National Board of Health. Established by act of Congress approved March 3, 1879, its sphere of duty was enlarged by the act of June 2 in the same year. By the last-named act the board was required to institute such measures as might be deemed necessary for preventing the introduction of contagious or infectious diseases from foreign countries into the United States or from one State into another.

The execution of the rules and regulations prepared by the board and approved by my predecessor has done much to arrest the progress of epidemic disease, and has thus rendered substantial service to the nation.

The International Sanitary Conference, to which I have referred, adopted a form of a bill of health to be used by all vessels seeking to enter the ports of the countries whose representatives participated in its deliberations. This form has since been prescribed by the National Board of Health and incorporated with its rules and regulations, which have been approved by me in pursuance of law.

ople is of supreme importance. All measures
be against the spread of contagious diseases and
sanitary knowledge for such purposes deserve

etary of the Treasury presents in detail a highly
he state of the finances and the condition of the
public service administered by that Department.
s from all sources for the fiscal year ending June

```
..............................................  $198, 159, 676. 02
..............................................  135, 264, 385. 51
..............................................  2, 201, 863. 17
d deposits of national banks...............  8, 116, 115. 72
t by Pacific Railway companies...............  810, 833. 80
i6c Railway companies ......................  805, 180. 54
ssities, etc.  .. .  1, 225, 514. 86
i patent, and lands...............  2, 244, 983. 98
overnment property......  262, 174. 00
..............................................  3, 468, 485. 61
ict of Columbia......  ......  2, 016, 199. 23
s..............................................  6, 206, 880. 13
 is..............................................  360, 782, 292. 57
```

tures for the same period were:

```
..............................................  $17, 941, 177. 19
..............................................  1, 093, 954. 92
..............................................  6, 514, 161. 09
..............................................  50, 059, 779. 62
nent, including river and harbor improve-
..............................................  40, 466, 460. 55
t, including vessels, machinery, and improve-
..............................................  15, 686, 671. 66
ures, including public buildings, light-houses,
r..............................................  41, 837, 280. 57
it of the District of Columbia...............  3, 543, 912. 03
idit..............................................  82, 508, 741. 18
thousand..............................................  1, 061, 248. 78
                                               _____
shares..............................................  260, 712, 887. 59
```

nue of $100,069,404.98, which was applied as

```
and..............................................  $74, 371, 200. 00
the sinking fund............................  109, 001. 05
s be..............................................  7, 418, 000. 00
s..............................................  2, 016, 150. 00
..............................................  18, 300. 00
s.d.d..............................................  3, 400. 00
s..............................................  37, 300. 00
s..............................................  143, 150. 00
s..............................................  959, 150. 00
s..............................................  337, 400. 00
i..............................................  1, 000. 00
interest, and other notes ...............  18, 330. 00
ith in the Treasury...............  14, 637, 023. 93
                                               _____
                                               100, 069, 404. 98
```

the sinking fund for the year amounted to
um included a balance of $49,817,128.78.

provided for during the previous fiscal year. The sum of $74,480,201.05 was applied to this fund, which left a deficit of $16,305,873.47. The increase of the revenues for 1881 over those of the previous year was $29,352,901.10. It is estimated that the receipts during the present fiscal year will reach $400,000,000 and the expenditures $270,000,000, leaving a surplus of $130,000,000 applicable to the sinking fund and the redemption of the public debt.

I approve the recommendation of the Secretary of the Treasury that provision be made for the early retirement of silver certificates and that the act requiring their issue be repealed. They were issued in pursuance of the policy of the Government to maintain silver at or near the gold standard, and were accordingly made receivable for all customs, taxes, and public dues. About sixty-six millions of them are now outstanding. They form an unnecessary addition to the paper currency, a sufficient amount of which may be readily supplied by the national banks.

In accordance with the act of February 28, 1878, the Treasury Department has monthly caused at least two millions in value of silver bullion to be coined into standard silver dollars. One hundred and two millions of these dollars have been already coined, while only about thirty-four millions are in circulation.

For the reasons which he specifies, I concur in the Secretary's recommendation that the provision for coinage of a fixed amount each month be repealed, and that hereafter only so much be coined as shall be necessary to supply the demand.

The Secretary advises that the issue of gold certificates should not for the present be resumed, and suggests that the national banks may properly be forbidden by law to retire their currency except upon reasonable notice of their intention so to do. Such legislation would seem to be justified by the recent action of certain banks on the occasion referred to in the Secretary's report.

Of the fifteen millions of fractional currency still outstanding, only about eighty thousand has been redeemed the past year. The suggestion that this amount may properly be dropped from future statements of the public debt seems worthy of approval.

So also does the suggestion of the Secretary as to the advisability of relieving the calendar of the United States courts in the southern district of New York by the transfer to another tribunal of the numerous suits there pending against collectors.

The revenue from customs for the past fiscal year was $198,159,676.02, an increase of $11,637,611.42 over that of the year preceding. One hundred and thirty-eight million ninety-eight thousand five hundred and sixty-two dollars and thirty-nine cents of this amount was collected at the port of New York, leaving $50,251,113.63 as the amount collected at all the other ports of the country. Of this sum $47,977,137.63 was

collected on sugar, melado, and molasses; $27,285,624.78 on wool and
~~manufactures~~, ~~$64,534.34~~ on iron and steel and manufactures
~~thereof; $9,998,663.81~~ on manufactures of silk; $10,825,115.21 on man-
~~ufactures of cotton, and $6,469,643.04~~ on wines and spirits, making a
~~total revenue from these sources~~ of $133,058,720.81.

The expenses of collection for the past year were $6,419,345.20, an
increase over the preceding year of $387,410.04. Notwithstanding the
increase in the revenue from customs over the preceding year, the gross
value of the imports, including free goods, decreased over $25,000,000.
The most marked decrease was in the value of unmanufactured wool,
$14,023,682, and in that of scrap and pig iron, $12,810,671. The value
of imported sugar, on the other hand, showed an increase of $7,457,474;
of steel rails, $4,345,521; of barley, $2,154,204, and of steel in bars,
ingots, etc., $1,620,046.

Contrasted with the imports during the last fiscal year, the exports
were as follows:

Domestic merchandise	$883,925,947
Foreign merchandise	18,451,399
Total	902,377,346
Imports of merchandise	642,664,628
Excess of exports over imports of merchandise	259,712,718
Aggregate of exports and imports	1,545,041,974

Compared with the previous year, there was an increase of $66,738,688
in the value of exports of merchandise and a decrease of $25,290,118 in
the value of imports. The annual average of the excess of imports of
merchandise over exports thereof for ten years previous to June 30, 1873,
was $104,706,922, but for the last six years there has been an excess
of exports over imports of merchandise amounting to $1,180,668,105,
an annual average of $196,778,017. The specie value of the exports
of domestic merchandise was $376,616,473 in 1870 and $883,925,947
in 1881, an increase of $507,309,474, or 135 per cent. The value of im-
ports was ~~$435,958,408~~ in 1870 and $642,664,628 in 1881, an increase of
$206,706,220, or 47 per cent.

During each ~~year from~~ 1862 to 1879, inclusive, the exports of specie
exceeded the imports. The largest excess of such exports over imports
was reached during the year 1864, when it amounted to $92,280,929.
But during the year ended June 30, 1880, the imports of coin and bullion
exceeded the exports by $75,891,391, and during the last fiscal year the
excess of imports over exports was $91,168,650.

In the last annual report of the Secretary of the Treasury the attention of Congress was called to the fact that $469,651,050 in 5 per cent
bonds and $203,573,750 in 6 per cent bonds would become redeemable
during the year, and Congress was asked to authorize the refunding of
these bonds at a lower rate of interest. The bill for such refunding
having failed to become a law, the Secretary of the Treasury in April

last notified the holders of the $195,690,400 6 per cent bonds then outstanding that the bonds would be paid at par on the 1st day of July following, or that they might be "continued" at the pleasure of the Government, to bear interest at the rate of 3½ per cent per annum.

Under this notice $178,055,150 of the 6 per cent bonds were continued at the lower rate and $17,635,250 were redeemed.

In the month of May a like notice was given respecting the redemption or continuance of the $439,841,350 of 5 per cent bonds then outstanding, and of these $401,504,900 were continued at 3½ per cent per annum and $38,336,450 redeemed.

The 6 per cent bonds of the loan of February 8, 1861, and of the Oregon war debt, amounting together to $14,125,800, having matured during the year, the Secretary of the Treasury gave notice of his intention to redeem the same, and such as have been presented have been paid from the surplus revenues. There have also been redeemed at par $16,179,100 of the 3½ per cent "continued" bonds, making a total of bonds redeemed or which have ceased to bear interest during the year of $123,969,650.

The reduction of the annual interest on the public debt through these transactions is as follows:

By reduction of interest to 3½ per cent	$10,473,952.25
By redemption of bonds	6,352,340.00
Total	16,826,292.25

The 3½ per cent bonds, being payable at the pleasure of the Government, are available for the investment of surplus revenues without the payment of premiums.

Unless these bonds can be funded at a much lower rate of interest than they now bear, I agree with the Secretary of the Treasury that no legislation respecting them is desirable.

It is a matter for congratulation that the business of the country has been so prosperous during the past year as to yield by taxation a large surplus of income to the Government. If the revenue laws remain unchanged, this surplus must year by year increase, on account of the reduction of the public debt and its burden of interest and because of the rapid increase of our population. In 1860, just prior to the institution of our internal-revenue system, our population but slightly exceeded 30,000,000; by the census of 1880 it is now found to exceed 50,000,000. It is estimated that even if the annual receipts and expenditures should continue as at present the entire debt could be paid in ten years.

In view, however, of the heavy load of taxation which our people have already borne, we may well consider whether it is not the part of wisdom to reduce the revenues, even if we delay a little the payment of the debt.

It seems to me that the time has arrived when the people may justly demand some relief from their present onerous burden, and that by due economy in the various branches of the public service this may readily be afforded.

I therefore concur with the Secretary in recommending the abolition of all internal-revenue taxes except those upon tobacco in its various forms and upon distilled spirits and fermented liquors, and except also the special tax upon the manufacturers of and dealers in such articles. The retention of the latter tax is desirable as affording the officers of the Government a proper supervision of these articles for the prevention of fraud. I agree with the Secretary of the Treasury that the law imposing a stamp tax upon matches, proprietary articles, playing cards, checks, and drafts may with propriety be repealed, and the law also by which banks and bankers are assessed upon their capital and deposits. There seems to be a general sentiment in favor of this course.

In the present condition of our revenues the tax upon deposits is especially unjust. It was never imposed in this country until it was demanded by the necessities of war, and was never exacted, I believe, in any other country even in its greatest exigencies. Banks are required to secure their circulation by pledging with the Treasurer of the United States bonds of the General Government. The interest upon these bonds, which at the time when the tax was imposed was 6 per cent, is now in most instances 3½ per cent. Besides, the entire circulation was originally limited by law and no increase was allowable. When the existing banks had practically a monopoly of the business, there was force in the suggestion that for the franchise to the favored grantees the Government might very properly exact a tax on circulation; but for years the system has been free and the amount of circulation regulated by the public demand.

The retention of this tax has been suggested as a means of reimbursing the Government for the expense of printing and furnishing the circulating notes. If the tax should be repealed, it would certainly seem proper to require the national banks to pay the amount of such expense to the Comptroller of the Currency.

It is perhaps doubtful whether the immediate reduction of the rate of taxation upon liquors and tobacco is advisable, especially in view of the drain upon the Treasury which must attend the payment of arrears of pensions. A comparison, however, of the amount of taxes collected under the varying rates of taxation which have at different times prevailed suggests the intimation that some reduction may soon be made without material diminution of the revenue.

The tariff laws also need revision; but, that a due regard may be paid to the conflicting interests of our citizens, important changes should be made with caution. If a careful revision can not be made at this session, a simple measure such as was lately approved by the Senate and is now recommended by the Secretary of the Treasury would doubtless lighten the labors of Congress whenever this subject shall be brought to its consideration.

The accompanying report of the Secretary of War will make known to you the operations of that Department for the past year.

He suggests measures for promoting the efficiency of the Army without adding to the number of its officers, and recommends the legislation necessary to increase the number of enlisted men to 30,000, the maximum allowed by law.

This he deems necessary to maintain quietude on our ever-shifting frontier; to preserve peace and suppress disorder and marauding in new settlements; to protect settlers and their property against Indians, and Indians against the encroachments of intruders; and to enable peaceable immigrants to establish homes in the most remote parts of our country.

The Army is now necessarily scattered over such a vast extent of territory that whenever an outbreak occurs reenforcements must be hurried from many quarters, over great distances, and always at heavy cost for transportation of men, horses, wagons, and supplies.

I concur in the recommendations of the Secretary for increasing the Army to the strength of 30,000 enlisted men.

It appears by the Secretary's report that in the absence of disturbances on the frontier the troops have been actively employed in collecting the Indians hitherto hostile and locating them on their proper reservations; that Sitting Bull and his adherents are now prisoners at Fort Randall; that the Utes have been moved to their new reservation in Utah; that during the recent outbreak of the Apaches it was necessary to reenforce the garrisons in Arizona by troops withdrawn from New Mexico; and that some of the Apaches are now held prisoners for trial, while some have escaped, and the majority of the tribe are now on their reservation.

There is need of legislation to prevent intrusion upon the lands set apart for the Indians. A large military force, at great expense, is now required to patrol the boundary line between Kansas and the Indian Territory. The only punishment that can at present be inflicted is the forcible removal of the intruder and the imposition of a pecuniary fine, which in most cases it is impossible to collect. There should be a penalty by imprisonment in such cases.

The separate organization of the Signal Service is urged by the Secretary of War, and a full statement of the advantages of such permanent organization is presented in the report of the Chief Signal Officer. A detailed account of the useful work performed by the Signal Corps and the Weather Bureau is also given in that report.

I ask attention to the statements of the Secretary of War regarding the requisitions frequently made by the Indian Bureau upon the Subsistence Department of the Army for the casual support of bands and tribes of Indians whose appropriations are exhausted. The War Department should not be left, by reason of inadequate provision for the Indian Bureau, to contribute for the maintenance of Indians.

The report of the Chief of Engineers furnishes a detailed account of the operations for the improvement of rivers and harbors.

I commend to your attention the suggestions contained in this report in regard to the condition of our fortifications, especially our coast defenses, and recommend an increase of the strength of the Engineer Battalion, by which the efficiency of our torpedo system would be improved.

I also call your attention to the remarks upon the improvement of the South Pass of the Mississippi River, the proposed free bridge over the Potomac River at Georgetown, the importance of completing at an early day the north wing of the War Department building, and other recommendations of the Secretary of War which appear in his report.

The actual expenditures of that Department for the fiscal year ending June 30, 1881, were $42,122,201.39. The appropriations for the year 1882 were $44,889,725.42. The estimates for 1883 are $44,541,276.91.

The report of the Secretary of the Navy exhibits the condition of that branch of the service and presents valuable suggestions for its improvement. I call your especial attention also to the appended report of the Advisory Board which he convened to devise suitable measures for increasing the efficiency of the Navy, and particularly to report as to the character and number of vessels necessary to place it upon a footing commensurate with the necessities of the Government.

I can not too strongly urge upon you my conviction that every consideration of national safety, economy, and honor imperatively demands a thorough rehabilitation of our Navy.

With a full appreciation of the fact that compliance with the suggestions of the head of that Department and of the Advisory Board must involve a large expenditure of the public moneys, I earnestly recommend such appropriations as will accomplish an end which seems to me so desirable.

Nothing can be more inconsistent with true public economy than withholding the means necessary to accomplish the objects intrusted by the Constitution to the National Legislature. One of those objects, and one which is of paramount importance, is declared by our fundamental law to be the provision for the "common defense." Surely nothing is more essential to the defense of the United States and of all our people than the efficiency of our Navy.

We have for many years maintained with foreign governments the relations of honorable peace, and that such relations may be permanent is desired by every patriotic citizen of the Republic. But if we heed the teachings of history we shall not forget that in the life of every nation emergencies may arise when a resort to arms can alone save it from dishonor.

No danger from abroad now threatens this people, nor have we any cause to distrust the friendly professions of other governments. But for avoiding as well as for repelling dangers that may threaten us in the future we must be prepared to enforce any policy which we think wise to adopt.

We must be ready to defend our harbors against aggression; to protect, by the distribution of our ships of war over the highways of commerce, the varied interests of our foreign trade and the persons and property of our citizens abroad; to maintain everywhere the honor of our flag and the distinguished position which we may rightfully claim among the nations of the world.

The report of the Postmaster-General is a gratifying exhibit of the growth and efficiency of the postal service.

The receipts from postage and other ordinary sources during the past fiscal year were $36,489,816.58. The receipts from the money-order business were $295,581.39, making a total of $36,785,397.97. The expenditure for the fiscal year was $39,251,736.46. The deficit supplied out of the general Treasury was $2,481,129.35, or 6.3 per cent of the amount expended. The receipts were $3,469,918.63 in excess of those of the previous year, and $4,575,397.97 in excess of the estimate made two years ago, before the present period of business prosperity had fairly begun.

The whole number of letters mailed in this country in the last fiscal year exceeded 1,000,000,000.

The registry system is reported to be in excellent condition, having been remodeled during the past four years with good results. The amount of registration fees collected during the last fiscal year was $712,882.20, an increase over the fiscal year ending June 30, 1877, of $345,443.40.

The entire number of letters and packages registered during the year was 8,338,919, of which only 2,061 were lost or destroyed in transit.

The operations of the money-order system are multiplying yearly under the impulse of immigration, of the rapid development of the newer States and Territories, and the consequent demand for additional means of intercommunication and exchange.

During the past year 338 additional money-order offices have been established, making a total of 5,499 in operation at the date of this report.

During the year the domestic money orders aggregated in value $105,075,769.35.

A modification of the system is suggested, reducing the fees for money orders not exceeding $5 from 10 cents to 5 cents and making the maximum limit $100 in place of $50.

Legislation for the disposition of unclaimed money orders in the possession of the Post-Office Department is recommended, in view of the fact that their total value now exceeds $1,000,000.

The attention of Congress is again invited to the subject of establishing a system of savings depositories in connection with the Post-Office Department.

The statistics of mail transportation show that during the past year railroad routes have been increased in length 6,249 miles and in cost

$1,114,382, while steamboat routes have been decreased in length 2,182 miles and in cost $134,054. The so-called star routes have been decreased in length 3,949 miles and in cost $364,144.

Nearly all of the more expensive routes have been superseded by railroad service. The cost of the star service must therefore rapidly decrease in the Western States and Territories.

The Postmaster-General, however, calls attention to the constantly increasing cost of the railway mail service as a serious difficulty in the way of making the Department self-sustaining.

Our postal intercourse with foreign countries has kept pace with the growth of the domestic service. Within the past year several countries and colonies have declared their adhesion to the Postal Union. It now includes all those which have an organized postal service except Bolivia, Costa Rica, New Zealand, and the British colonies in Australia.

As has been already stated, great reductions have recently been made in the expense of the star-route service. The investigations of the Department of Justice and the Post-Office Department have resulted in the presentation of indictments against persons formerly connected with that service, accusing them of offenses against the United States. I have enjoined upon the officials who are charged with the conduct of the cases on the part of the Government, and upon the eminent counsel who before my accession to the Presidency were called to their assistance, the duty of prosecuting with the utmost vigor of the law all persons who may be found chargeable with frauds upon the postal service.

The Acting Attorney-General calls attention to the necessity of modifying the present system of the courts of the United States—a necessity due to the large increase of business, especially in the Supreme Court. Litigation in our Federal tribunals became greatly expanded after the close of the late war. So long as that expansion might be attributable to the abnormal condition in which the community found itself immediately after the return of peace, prudence required that no change be made in the constitution of our judicial tribunals. But it has now become apparent that an immense increase of litigation has directly resulted from the wonderful growth and development of the country. There is no ground for belief that the business of the United States courts will ever be less in volume than at present. Indeed, that it is likely to be much greater is generally recognized by the bench and bar.

In view of the fact that Congress has already given much consideration to this subject, I make no suggestion as to detail, but express the hope that your deliberations may result in such legislation as will give early relief to our overburdened courts.

The Acting Attorney-General also calls attention to the disturbance of the public tranquillity during the past year in the Territory of Arizona. A band of armed desperadoes known as "Cowboys," probably numbering from fifty to one hundred men, have been engaged for months in committing acts of lawlessness and brutality which the local authorities have been unable to repress. The depredations of these "Cowboys" have also extended into Mexico, which the marauders reach from the Arizona frontier. With every disposition to meet the exigencies of the case, I am embarrassed by lack of authority to deal with them effectually. The punishment of crimes committed within Arizona should ordinarily, of course, be left to the Territorial authorities; but it is worthy consideration whether acts which necessarily tend to embroil the United States with neighboring governments should not be declared crimes against the United States. Some of the incursions alluded to may perhaps be within the scope of the law (U. S. Revised Statutes, sec. 5286) forbidding "military expeditions or enterprises" against friendly states; but in view of the speedy assembling of your body I have preferred to await such legislation as in your wisdom the occasion may seem to demand.

It may perhaps be thought proper to provide that the setting on foot within our own territory of brigandage and armed marauding expeditions against friendly nations and their citizens shall be punishable as an offense against the United States.

I will add that in the event of a request from the Territorial government for protection by the United States against "domestic violence" this Government would be powerless to render assistance.

The act of 1795, chapter 36, passed at a time when Territorial governments received little attention from Congress, enforced this duty of the United States only as to the State governments. But the act of 1807, chapter 39, applied also to Territories. This law seems to have remained in force until the revision of the statutes, when the provision for the Territories was dropped. I am not advised whether this alteration was intentional or accidental; but as it seems to me that the Territories should be offered the protection which is accorded to the States by the Constitution, I suggest legislation to that end.

It seems to me, too, that whatever views may prevail as to the policy of recent legislation by which the Army has ceased to be a part of the *posse comitatus*, an exception might well be made for permitting the military to assist the civil Territorial authorities in enforcing the laws of the United States. This use of the Army would not seem to be within the alleged evil against which that legislation was aimed. From sparseness of population and other circumstances it is often quite impracticable to summon a civil posse in places where officers of justice require assistance and where a military force is within easy reach.

The report of the Secretary of the Interior, with accompanying documents, presents an elaborate account of the business of that Department. A summary of it would be too extended for this place. I ask your careful attention to the report itself.

Prominent among the matters which challenge the attention of Congress at its present session is the management of our Indian affairs.

While this question has been a cause of trouble and embarrassment from the infancy of the Government, it is but recently that any effort has been made for its solution at once serious, determined, consistent, and promising success.

It has been easier to resort to convenient makeshifts for tiding over temporary difficulties than to grapple with the great permanent problem, and accordingly the easier course has almost invariably been pursued.

It was natural, at a time when the national territory seemed almost illimitable and contained many millions of acres far outside the bounds of civilized settlements, that a policy should have been initiated which more than aught else has been the fruitful source of our Indian complications.

I refer, of course, to the policy of dealing with the various Indian tribes as separate nationalities, of relegating them by treaty stipulations to the occupancy of immense reservations in the West, and of encouraging them to live a savage life, undisturbed by any earnest and well-directed efforts to bring them under the influences of civilization.

The unsatisfactory results which have sprung from this policy are becoming apparent to all.

As the white settlements have crowded the borders of the reservations, the Indians, sometimes contentedly and sometimes against their will, have been transferred to other hunting grounds, from which they have again been dislodged whenever their new-found homes have been desired by the adventurous settlers.

These removals and the frontier collisions by which they have often been preceded have led to frequent and disastrous conflicts between the races.

It is profitless to discuss here which of them has been chiefly responsible for the disturbances whose recital occupies so large a space upon the pages of our history.

We have to deal with the appalling fact that though thousands of lives have been sacrificed and hundreds of millions of dollars expended in the attempt to solve the Indian problem, it has until within the past few years seemed scarcely nearer a solution than it was half a century ago. But the Government has of late been cautiously but steadily feeling its way to the adoption of a policy which has already produced gratifying results, and which, in my judgment, is likely, if Congress and the Executive accord in its support, to relieve us ere long from the difficulties which have hitherto beset us.

For the success of the efforts now making to introduce among the Indians the customs and pursuits of civilized life and gradually to absorb them into the mass of our citizens, sharing their rights and holden to their responsibilities, there is imperative need for legislative action.

My suggestions in that regard will be chiefly such as have been already called to the attention of Congress and have received to some extent its

First. I recommend the passage of an act making the laws of the various States and Territories applicable to the Indian reservations within their borders and extending the laws of the State of Arkansas to the portion of the Indian Territory not occupied by the Five Civilized Tribes.

The Indian should receive the protection of the law. He should be allowed to maintain in court his rights of person and property. He has repeatedly begged for this privilege. Its exercise would be very valuable to him in his progress toward civilization.

Second. Of even greater importance is a measure which has been frequently recommended by my predecessors in office, and in furtherance of which several bills have been from time to time introduced in both Houses of Congress. The enactment of a general law permitting the allotment in severalty, to such Indians, at least, as desire it, of a reasonable quantity of land secured to them by patent, and for their own protection made inalienable for twenty or twenty-five years, is demanded for their present welfare and their permanent advancement.

In return for such considerate action on the part of the Government, there is reason to believe that the Indians in large numbers would be persuaded to sever their tribal relations and to engage at once in agricultural pursuits. Many of them realize the fact that their hunting days are over and that it is now for their best interests to conform their manner of life to the new order of things. By no greater inducement than the assurance of permanent title to the soil can they be led to engage in the occupation of tilling it.

The well-attested reports of their increasing interest in husbandry justify the hope and belief that the enactment of such a statute as I recommend would be at once attended with gratifying results. A resort to the allotment system would have a direct and powerful influence in dissolving the tribal bond, which is so prominent a feature of savage life, and which tends so strongly to perpetuate it.

Third. I advise a liberal appropriation for the support of Indian schools, because of my confident belief that such a course is consistent with the wisest economy.

Even among the most uncultivated Indian tribes there is reported to be a general and urgent desire on the part of the chiefs and older members for the education of their children. It is unfortunate, in view of this fact, that during the past year the means which have been at the command of the Interior Department for the purpose of Indian instruction have proved to be utterly inadequate.

The success of the schools which are in operation at Hampton, Carlisle, and Forest Grove should not only encourage a more generous provision for the support of those institutions, but should prompt the establishment of others of a similar character.

They are doubtless much more potent for good than the day schools upon the reservation, as the pupils are altogether separated from the surroundings of savage life and brought into constant contact with civilization.

There are many other phases of this subject which are of great interest, but which can not be included within the becoming limits of this communication. They are discussed ably in the reports of the Secretary of the Interior and the Commissioner of Indian Affairs.

For many years the Executive, in his annual message to Congress, has urged the necessity of stringent legislation for the suppression of polygamy in the Territories, and especially in the Territory of Utah. The existing statute for the punishment of this odious crime, so revolting to the moral and religious sense of Christendom, has been persistently and contemptuously violated ever since its enactment. Indeed, in spite of commendable efforts on the part of the authorities who represent the United States in that Territory, the law has in very rare instances been enforced, and, for a cause to which reference will presently be made, is practically a dead letter.

The fact that adherents of the Mormon Church, which rests upon polygamy as its corner stone, have recently been peopling in large numbers Idaho, Arizona, and other of our Western Territories is well calculated to excite the liveliest interest and apprehension. It imposes upon Congress and the Executive the duty of arraying against this barbarous system all the power which under the Constitution and the law they can wield for its destruction.

Reference has been already made to the obstacles which the United States officers have encountered in their efforts to punish violations of law. Prominent among these obstacles is the difficulty of procuring legal evidence sufficient to warrant a conviction even in the case of the most notorious offenders.

Your attention is called to a recent opinion of the Supreme Court of the United States, explaining its judgment of reversal in the case of Miles, who had been convicted of bigamy in Utah. The court refers to the fact that the secrecy attending the celebration of marriages in that Territory makes the proof of polygamy very difficult, and the propriety is suggested of modifying the law of evidence which now makes a wife incompetent to testify against her husband.

This suggestion is approved. I recommend also the passage of an act providing that, in the Territories of the United States the fact that a woman has been married to a person charged with bigamy shall not disqualify her as a witness upon his trial for that offense. I further recommend legislation by which any person solemnizing a marriage in any of the Territories shall be required, under stringent penalties for neglect or refusal, to file a certificate of such marriage in the supreme court of the Territory.

Doubtless Congress may devise other practicable measures for obviating the difficulties which have hitherto attended the efforts to suppress this iniquity. I assure you of my determined purpose to cooperate with you in any lawful and discreet measures which may be proposed to that end.

Although our system of government does not contemplate that the nation should provide or support a system for the education of our people, no measures calculated to promote that general intelligence and virtue upon which the perpetuity of our institutions so greatly depends have ever been regarded with indifference by Congress or the Executive.

A large portion of the public domain has been from time to time devoted to the promotion of education.

There is now a special reason why, by setting apart the proceeds of its sales of public lands or by some other course, the Government should aid the work of education. Many who now exercise the right of suffrage are unable to read the ballot which they cast. Upon many who had just emerged from a condition of slavery were suddenly devolved the responsibilities of citizenship in that portion of the country most impoverished by war. I have been pleased to learn from the report of the Commissioner of Education that there has lately been a commendable increase of interest and effort for their instruction; but all that can be done by local legislation and private generosity should be supplemented by such aid as can be constitutionally afforded by the National Government.

I would suggest that if any fund be dedicated to this purpose it may be wisely distributed in the different States according to the ratio of illiteracy, as by this means those localities which are most in need of such assistance will reap its special benefits.

The report of the Commissioner of Agriculture exhibits the results of the experiments in which that Department has been engaged during the past year and makes important suggestions in reference to the agricultural development of the country.

The steady increase of our population and the consequent addition to the number of those engaging in the pursuit of husbandry are giving to this Department a growing dignity and importance. The Commissioner's suggestions touching its capacity for greater usefulness deserve attention, as it more and more commends itself to the interests which it was created to promote.

It appears from the report of the Commissioner of Pensions that since 1860 789,063 original pension claims have been filed; 450,949 of these have been allowed and inscribed on the pension roll; 72,539 have been rejected and abandoned, being 13+ per cent of the whole number of claims settled.

There are now pending for settlement 265,575 original pension claims, 227,040 of which were filed prior to July 1, 1880. These, when allowed, will involve the payment of arrears from the date of discharge in case of an invalid and from date of death or termination of a prior right in all other cases.

From all the data obtainable it is estimated that 15 per cent of the number of claims now pending will be rejected or abandoned. This would show the probable rejection of 34,050 cases and the probable admission of about 193,500 claims, all of which involve the payment of arrears of pension.

With the present force employed, the number of adjudications remaining the same and no new business intervening, this number of claims (193,000) could be acted upon in a period of six years; and taking January 1, 1884, as a near period from which to estimate in each case an average amount of arrears, it is found that every case allowed would require for the first payment upon it the sum of $1,350. Multiplying this amount by the whole number of probable admissions gives $250,-000,000 as the sum required for first payment. This represents the sum which must be paid upon claims which were filed before July 1, 1880, and are now pending and entitled to the benefits of the arrears act. From this amount ($250,000,000) may be deducted from ten to fifteen millions for cases where, the claimant dying, there is no person who under the law would be entitled to succeed to the pension, leaving $235,000,000 as the probable amount to be paid.

In these estimates no account has been taken of the 38,500 cases filed since June 30, 1880, and now pending, which must receive attention as current business, but which do not involve the payment of any arrears beyond the date of filing the claim. Of this number it is estimated that 85 per cent will be allowed.

As has been stated, with the present force of the Pension Bureau (675 clerks) it is estimated that it will take six years to dispose of the claims now pending.

It is stated by the Commissioner of Pensions that by an addition of 250 clerks (increasing the adjudicating force rather than the mechanical) double the amount of work could be accomplished, so that these cases could be acted upon within three years.

Aside from the considerations of justice which may be urged for a speedy settlement of the claims now on the files of the Pension Office, it is no less important on the score of economy, inasmuch as fully one-third of the clerical force of the office is now wholly occupied in giving attention to correspondence with the thousands of claimants whose cases have been on the files for the past eighteen years. The fact that a sum so enormous must be expended by the Government to meet demands for arrears of pensions is an admonition to Congress and the Executive to give cautious consideration to any similar project in the future. The great temptation to the presentation of fictitious claims afforded by the fact that the average sum obtained upon each application is $1,300 leads me to suggest the propriety of making some special appropriation for the prevention of fraud.

I advise appropriations for such internal improvements as the wisdom of Congress may deem to be of public importance. The necessity of improving the navigation of the Mississippi River justifies a special allusion to that subject. I suggest the adoption of some measure for the removal of obstructions which now impede the navigation of that great channel of commerce.

In my letter accepting the nomination for the Vice-Presidency I stated that in my judgment—

No man should be the incumbent of an office the duties of which he is for any cause unfit to perform; who is lacking in the ability, fidelity, or integrity which a proper administration of such office demands. This sentiment would doubtless meet with general acquiescence, but opinion has been widely divided upon the wisdom and practicability of the various reformatory schemes which have been suggested and of certain proposed regulations governing appointments to public office.

The efficiency of such regulations has been distrusted mainly because they have seemed to exalt mere educational and abstract tests above general business capacity and even special fitness for the particular work in hand. It seems to me that the rules which should be applied to the management of the public service may properly conform in the main to such as regulate the conduct of successful private business:

Original appointments should be based upon ascertained fitness.

The tenure of office should be stable.

Positions of responsibility should, so far as practicable, be filled by the promotion of worthy and efficient officers.

The investigation of all complaints and the punishment of all official misconduct should be prompt and thorough.

The views expressed in the foregoing letter are those which will govern my administration of the executive office. They are doubtless shared by all intelligent and patriotic citizens, however divergent in their opinions as to the best methods of putting them into practical operation.

For example, the assertion that "original appointments should be based upon ascertained fitness" is not open to dispute.

But the question how in practice such fitness can be most effectually ascertained is one which has for years excited interest and discussion. The measure which, with slight variations in its details, has lately been urged upon the attention of Congress and the Executive has as its principal feature the scheme of competitive examination. Save for certain exceptions, which need not here be specified, this plan would allow admission to the service only in its lowest grade, and would accordingly demand that all vacancies in higher positions should be filled by promotion alone. In these particulars it is in conformity with the existing civil-service system of Great Britain; and indeed the success which has attended that system in the country of its birth is the strongest argument which has been urged for its adoption here.

The fact should not, however, be overlooked that there are certain features of the English system which have not generally been received with favor in this country, even among the foremost advocates of civil-service reform.

Among them are:

1. A tenure of office which is substantially a life tenure.

2. A limitation of the maximum age at which an applicant can enter the service, whereby all men in middle life or older are, with some exceptions, rigidly excluded.

3. A retiring allowance upon going out of office.

These three elements are as important factors of the problem as any of the others. To eliminate them from the English system would effect a most radical change in its theory and practice.

The avowed purpose of that system is to induce the educated young men of the country to devote their lives to public employment by an assurance that having once entered upon it they need never leave it, and that after voluntary retirement they shall be the recipients of an annual pension. That this system as an entirety has proved very successful in Great Britain seems to be generally conceded even by those who once opposed its adoption.

To a statute which should incorporate all its essential features I should feel bound to give my approval; but whether it would be for the best interests of the public to fix upon an expedient for immediate and extensive application which embraces certain features of the English system, but excludes or ignores others of equal importance, may be seriously doubted, even by those who are impressed, as I am myself, with the grave importance of correcting the evils which inhere in the present methods of appointment.

If, for example, the English rule which shuts out persons above the age of 25 years from a large number of public employments is not to be made an essential part of our own system, it is questionable whether the attainment of the highest number of marks at a competitive examination should be the criterion by which all applications for appointment should be put to test. And under similar conditions it may also be questioned whether admission to the service should be strictly limited to its lowest ranks.

There are very many characteristics which go to make a model civil servant. Prominent among them are probity, industry, good sense, good habits, good temper, patience, order, courtesy, tact, self-reliance, manly deference to superior authority, and manly consideration for inferiors. The absence of these traits is not supplied by wide knowledge of books, or by promptitude in answering questions, or by any other quality likely to be brought to light by competitive examination.

To make success in such a contest, therefore, an indispensable condition of public employment would very likely result in the practical exclusion of the older applicants, even though they might possess qualifications far superior to their younger and more brilliant competitors.

These suggestions must not be regarded as evincing any spirit of opposition to the competitive plan, which has been to some extent successfully employed already, and which may hereafter vindicate the claim of its most earnest supporters; but it ought to be seriously considered whether the application of the same educational standard to persons of mature years and to young men fresh from school and college would not be likely to exalt mere intellectual proficiency above other qualities of equal or greater importance.

Another feature of the proposed system is the selection by promotion of all officers of the Government above the lowest grade, except such as would fairly be regarded as exponents of the policy of the Executive and the principles of the dominant party.

To afford encouragement to faithful public servants by exciting in their minds the hope of promotion if they are found to merit it is much to be desired.

But would it be wise to adopt a rule so rigid as to permit no other mode of supplying the intermediate walks of the service?

There are many persons who fill subordinate positions with great credit, but lack those qualities which are requisite for higher posts of duty; and, besides, the modes of thought and action of one whose service in a governmental bureau has been long continued are often so cramped by routine procedure as almost to disqualify him from instituting changes required by the public interests. An infusion of new blood from time to time into the middle ranks of the service might be very beneficial in its results.

The subject under discussion is one of grave importance. The evils which are complained of can not be eradicated at once; the work must be gradual.

The present English system is a growth of years, and was not created by a single stroke of executive or legislative action.

Its beginnings are found in an order in council promulgated in 1855, and it was after patient and cautious scrutiny of its workings that fifteen years later it took its present shape.

Five years after the issuance of the order in council, and at a time when resort had been had to competitive examinations as an experiment much more extensively than has yet been the case in this country, a select committee of the House of Commons made a report to that House which, declaring its approval of the competitive plan, deprecated, nevertheless, any precipitancy in its general adoption as likely to endanger its ultimate success.

During this tentative period the results of the two methods of pass examination and competitive examination were closely watched and compared. It may be that before we confine ourselves upon this important question within the stringent bounds of statutory enactment we may profitably await the result of further inquiry and experiment.

The submission of a portion of the nominations to a central board of examiners selected solely for testing the qualifications of applicants may

: to the competitive test, put an end to the mis-
ie present system of appointment, and it may be
a board a wide discretion to ascertain the charac-
s of candidates in those particulars which I have
being no less important than mere intellectual

em it advisable at the present session to establish
mission to the service, no doubts such as have been
ie from giving the measure my earnest support.
mend, should there be a failure to pass any other
hat an appropriation of $25,000 per year may be
nt of section 1753 of the Revised Statutes.
forded me I shall strive to execute the provisions
) its letter and spirit.
stice to the present civil servants of the Govern-
bject without declaring my dissent from the severe
ite censure with which they have been recently
e as a class indolent, inefficient, and corrupt is a
en often made and widely credited; but when the
r, and importance of their duties are considered
ie employees of the Government are, in my judg-
i commendation.
ne of the merchant marine of the United States
d. In view of the fact that we furnish so large
ghts of the commercial world and that our ship-
rapidly increasing, it is cause of surprise that not
interest diminishing, but it is less than when our
re not half so large as now, either in bulk or value.
culiar hindrance to the development of this inter-
id energy of American mechanics and capitalists
ountry at least abreast of our rivals in the friendly
macy.
ron for wood and of steam for sail have wrought
e carrying trade of the world; but these changes
wane to America if we had given to our naviga-
i of the aid and protection which have been so
our manufactures. I commend the whole sub-
Congress, with the suggestion that no question
e farther reaching importance can engage their

Court of the United States declared unconstitu-
rtain States which imposed upon shipowners or
.50 for each passenger arriving from a foreign
eof required a bond to indemnify the State and
t expense for the future relief or support of such

passenger. Since this decision the expense attending the care and super-vision of immigrants has fallen on the States at whose ports they have landed.   As a large majority of such immigrants, immediately upon their arrival, proceed to the inland States and the Territories to seek permanent homes, it is manifestly unjust to impose upon the State whose shores they first reach the burden which it now bears.   For this reason, and because of the national importance of the subject, I recommend legislation regarding the supervision and transitory care of immigrants at the ports of debarkation.

I regret to state that the people of Alaska have reason to complain that they are as yet unprovided with any form of government by which life or property can be protected.   While the extent of its population does not justify the application of the costly machinery of Territorial administration, there is immediate necessity for constituting such a form of government as will promote the education of the people and secure the administration of justice.

The Senate at its last session passed a bill providing for the construc-tion of a building for the Library of Congress, but it failed to become a law.   The provision of suitable protection for this great collection of books and for the copyright department connected with it has become a subject of national importance and should receive prompt attention.

The report of the Commissioners of the District of Columbia herewith transmitted will inform you fully of the condition of the affairs of the District.

They urge the vital importance of legislation for the reclamation and improvement of the marshes and for the establishment of the harbor lines along the Potomac River front.

It is represented that in their present condition these marshes seriously affect the health of the residents of the adjacent parts of the city, and that they greatly mar the general aspect of the park in which stands the Washington Monument.   This improvement would add to that park and to the park south of the Executive Mansion a large area of valuable land, and would transform what is now believed to be a dangerous nui-sance into an attractive landscape extending to the river front.

They recommend the removal of the steam railway lines from the sur-face of the streets of the city and the location of the necessary depots in such places as may be convenient for the public accommodation, and they call attention to the deficiency of the water supply, which seriously affects the material prosperity of the city and the health and comfort of its inhabitants.

I commend these subjects to your favorable consideration.

The importance of timely legislation with respect to the ascertainment and declaration of the vote for Presidential electors was sharply called to the attention of the people more than four years ago.

It is to be hoped that some well-defined measure may be devised before another national election which will render unnecessary a resort to any expedient of a temporary character for the determination of questions upon contested returns.

Questions which concern the very existence of the Government and the liberties of the people were suggested by the prolonged illness of the late President and his consequent incapacity to perform the functions of his office.

It is provided by the second article of the Constitution, in the fifth clause of its first section, that "in case of the removal of the President from office, or of his death, resignation, or inability to discharge the powers and duties of the said office, the same shall devolve on the Vice-President."

What is the intendment of the Constitution in its specification of "inability to discharge the powers and duties of the said office" as one of the contingencies which calls the Vice-President to the exercise of Presidential functions?

Is the inability limited in its nature to long-continued intellectual incapacity, or has it a broader import?

What must be its extent and duration?

How must its existence be established?

Has the President whose inability is the subject of inquiry any voice in determining whether or not it exists, or is the decision of that momentous and delicate question confided to the Vice-President, or is it contemplated by the Constitution that Congress should provide by law precisely what should constitute inability and how and by what tribunal or authority it should be ascertained?

If the inability proves to be temporary in its nature, and during its continuance the Vice-President lawfully exercises the functions of the Executive, by what tenure does he hold his office?

Does he continue as President for the remainder of the four years' term?

Or would the elected President, if his inability should cease in the interval, be empowered to resume his office?

And if, having such lawful authority, he should exercise it, would the Vice-President be thereupon empowered to resume his powers and duties as such?

I cannot doubt that these important questions will receive your early and thoughtful consideration.

Deeply impressed with the gravity of the responsibilities which have so unexpectedly devolved upon me, it will be my constant purpose to cooperate with you in such measures as will promote the glory of the country and the prosperity of its people.

CHESTER A. ARTHUR.

SPECIAL MESSAGES.

EXECUTIVE MANSION,
Washington, December 12, 1881.

To the Senate of the United States:

I transmit herewith, in response to the resolution of the Senate of the 17th of May last, a report of the Secretary of State, with accompanying papers, touching the Geneva convention for the relief of the wounded in war.

CHESTER A. ARTHUR.

EXECUTIVE MANSION, *December 15, 1881.*

To the Senate and House of Representatives:

I transmit herewith a communication from the Secretary of the Interior, with accompanying papers, in reference to the applications of the Chicago, Texas and Mexican Central and the St. Louis and San Francisco Railway companies for a right of way across the lands of the Choctaw Nation in the Indian Territory for the building of a proposed railroad and telegraph line.

The matter is commended to the careful attention of Congress.

CHESTER A. ARTHUR.

EXECUTIVE MANSION, *December 15, 1881.*

To the Senate of the United States:

I transmit herewith, in response to a resolution of the Senate of the 12th instant, a report from the Secretary of State, with an accompanying paper, touching the proposed modification of the Clayton-Bulwer treaty of April 19, 1850, between the United States and Great Britain.

CHESTER A. ARTHUR.

WASHINGTON, *December 15, 1881.*

To the Senate of the United States:

I transmit to the Senate, for its consideration with a view to ratification, a treaty of peace, friendship, and commerce between the United States of America and the Kingdom of Madagascar, signed on the 13th day of May, 1881, together with certain correspondence relating thereto.

CHESTER A. ARTHUR.

WASHINGTON, *December 19, 1881.*

To the Senate of the United States:

I transmit herewith to the Senate a report from the Secretary of State, in response to its resolution of the 13th of October last, calling for the transmission to the Senate of papers on file in the Department of State relating to the seizure of one Vicenzo Rebello, an Italian, in the city of New Orleans, in June, 1881, by one James Mooney, under a warrant of arrest issued by John A. Osborn, United States commissioner in and for the city of New York.

CHESTER A. ARTHUR.

WASHINGTON, *December 19, 1881.*

To the Senate of the United States:

I transmit herewith to the Senate a report of the Secretary of State, in relation to the necessity of modifying the present system of consular jurisdiction of the United States in the countries of the East. I regard this subject, to which I have adverted in my general message to Congress, as one deserving the earnest attention of the National Legislature.

CHESTER A. ARTHUR.

[A similar message was sent to the House of Representatives.]

WASHINGTON, *December 19, 1881.*

To the House of Representatives:

I transmit herewith to the House of Representatives, for the consideration of Congress, a communication from the Secretary of State, setting forth the expediency of organizing a class of supernumerary secretaries of legation to meet the needs of our diplomatic service abroad.

CHESTER A. ARTHUR.

WASHINGTON, *December 19, 1881.*

To the Senate of the United States:

I transmit herewith, in reply to the resolution of the Senate of the 19th of May last, a report from the Secretary of State, with an accompanying paper.*

CHESTER A. ARTHUR.

EXECUTIVE MANSION, *December 21, 1881.*

To the House of Representatives:

I transmit herewith, for the consideration of Congress, a communication from the Secretary of the Interior, with an accompanying paper, in which he recommends a further appropriation for the payment of the expenses of the Tenth Census; also an appropriation of $2,000 to recompense the disbursing clerk of the Department of the Interior for his services in disbursing the appropriations for the Tenth Census.

CHESTER A. ARTHUR.

* List of officers, clerks, etc., in the Department of State.

EXECUTIVE MANSION, *December 21, 1881.*

To the Senate of the United States:

I transmit herewith, in response to a resolution of the Senate of the 6th instant, a letter from the Secretary of the Treasury and its accompanying papers.*

CHESTER A. ARTHUR.

EXECUTIVE MANSION, *January 6, 1882.*

To the Senate and House of Representatives:

I transmit a communication† received this day from the late Postmaster-General, to which I invite your careful attention.

Though the period limited for the reception of bids under the existing advertisement expires on the 7th instant, several weeks must necessarily elapse before they can be classified and examined and the actual letting take place.

If, therefore, Congress shall be of the opinion that a change in the law is needed, it may, I presume, be made immediately applicable.

CHESTER A. ARTHUR.

EXECUTIVE MANSION, *January 9, 1882.*

To the Senate of the United States:

I transmit herewith a communication from the Secretary of the Interior, with accompanying papers, in reference to the bill of the Choctaw Council approved November 10, 1881, granting a right of way through the Choctaw Nation to the St. Louis and San Francisco Railway Company, a bill (S. No. 60) for the ratification of which is now understood to be pending before your honorable body.

CHESTER A. ARTHUR.

EXECUTIVE MANSION, *January 11, 1882.*

To the Senate and House of Representatives:

I transmit herewith a communication from the Secretary of the Interior, with draft of a bill and accompanying papers, in reference to an agreement by the Shoshone and Bannock Indians with the United States for the disposal of certain of their lands in the Fort Hall Indian Reservation, in Idaho, for the use of the Utah and Northern Railway.

The matter is commended to the careful consideration of Congress.

CHESTER A. ARTHUR.

---

* Instructions to, and reports of certain, examiners of national banks.
† Relating to fraudulent bonds accompanying certain bids and contracts for carrying United States mail.

EXECUTIVE MANSION, *January 18, 1882.*

To the Senate and House of Representatives:

I transmit herewith a communication from the Secretary of the Interior, with draft of a bill to appropriate money to meet a deficiency in the Indian service for the fiscal year ending June 30, 1882.

A copy of report of the Commissioner of Indian Affairs, dated 13th instant, in regard to the bill is also inclosed.

The subject is commended to the attention of Congress.

CHESTER A. ARTHUR.

EXECUTIVE MANSION, *January 18, 1882.*

To the Senate and House of Representatives:

I transmit herewith a communication from the Secretary of the Interior, with draft of a bill and accompanying papers, amendatory of the act of March 3, 1880, for the sale of the Otoe and Missouria Indian Reservation, in the States of Nebraska and Kansas.

The subject is presented to the consideration of Congress.

CHESTER A. ARTHUR.

EXECUTIVE MANSION,
Washington, January 18, 1882.

To the Senate and House of Representatives:

I transmit herewith a letter from the Secretary of the Interior, forwarding copy of a letter addressed to him by the Commissioner of Indian Affairs, inclosing draft of a bill to create the office of medical inspector for the United States Indian service.

CHESTER A. ARTHUR.

EXECUTIVE MANSION, *January 18, 1882.*

To the Senate and House of Representatives:

I transmit herewith a communication from the Secretary of the Interior, with draft of bill and accompanying papers, providing for the improvement of the condition of Indians occupying reservations, and for other purposes.

The matter is commended to the consideration of Congress.

CHESTER A. ARTHUR.

EXECUTIVE MANSION, *January 18, 1882.*

To the Senate and House of Representatives:

I transmit herewith a communication from the Secretary of the Interior, and accompanying letter from the Commissioner of Indian Affairs, recommending a renewal of the appropriation of $10,000 heretofore made for defraying the expenses of the Board of Indian Commissioners.

The subject is commended to the consideration of Congress.

CHESTER A. ARTHUR.

EXECUTIVE MANSION, *January 18, 1882.*

To the Senate and House of Representatives:

I transmit herewith a communication from the Secretary of the Interior, with draft of a bill and accompanying papers, in reference to the settlement of the estate of deceased Kickapoo Indians in the State of Kansas, and for other purposes.

The matter is commended to the attention of Congress.

CHESTER A. ARTHUR.

EXECUTIVE MANSION, *January 18, 1882.*

To the Senate and House of Representatives:

I transmit herewith a communication from the Secretary of the Interior, with a draft of a bill and accompanying papers, to accept and ratify an agreement with the Crow Indians for the sale of a portion of their reservation in the Territory of Montana, required for the Northern Pacific Railroad, and to make the necessary appropriation for carrying the same into effect.

The subject is presented for the consideration of Congress.

CHESTER A. ARTHUR.

EXECUTIVE MANSION, *January 19, 1882.*

To the Senate and House of Representatives:

I transmit herewith, for the consideration of Congress, a communication from the Secretary of War, with accompanying papers, recommending an appropriation for the purchase of a site and the erection of a fireproof building to contain the records, library, and museum of the Surgeon-General's Office.

CHESTER A. ARTHUR.

OFFICE OF THE PRESIDENT OF THE UNITED STATES,
Washington, January 19, 1882.

To the Senate and House of Representatives:

I transmit herewith, for the consideration of Congress, a letter from the Secretary of War, inclosing a copy of one from the Chief Signal Officer of the Army, dated the 11th instant, setting forth the necessity for additional room for the Signal Office and recommending that Congress provide that of the amount estimated ($350,000) for "observation and report transmission to the Senate of papers on file in the Department of State relating to the seizure of one Vicenzo Rebello, an Italian, in the city of New Orleans, in June, 1881, by one James Mooney, under a warrant of arrest issued by John A. Osborn, United States commissioner in and for the city of New York.

CHESTER A. ARTHUR.

WASHINGTON, *December 19, 1881.*

To the Senate of the United States:

I transmit herewith to the Senate a report of the Secretary of State, in relation to the necessity of modifying the present system of consular jurisdiction of the United States in the countries of the East. I regard this subject, to which I have adverted in my general message to Congress, as one deserving the earnest attention of the National Legislature.

CHESTER A. ARTHUR.

[A similar message was sent to the House of Representatives.]

WASHINGTON, *December 19, 1881.*

To the House of Representatives:

I transmit herewith to the House of Representatives, for the consideration of Congress, a communication from the Secretary of State, setting forth the expediency of organizing a class of supernumerary secretaries of legation to meet the needs of our diplomatic service abroad.

CHESTER A. ARTHUR.

WASHINGTON, *December 19, 1881.*

To the Senate of the United States:

I transmit herewith, in reply to the resolution of the Senate of the 19th of May last, a report from the Secretary of State, with an accompanying paper.*

CHESTER A. ARTHUR.

EXECUTIVE MANSION, *December 21, 1881.*

To the House of Representatives:

I transmit herewith, for the consideration of Congress, a communication from the Secretary of the Interior, with an accompanying paper, in which he recommends a further appropriation for the payment of the expenses of the Tenth Census; also an appropriation of $2,000 to recompense the disbursing clerk of the Department of the Interior for his services in disbursing the appropriations for the Tenth Census.

CHESTER A. ARTHUR.

* List of officers, clerks, etc., in the Department of State.

General Land Office and to create the offices of Assistant Commissioner of the General Land Office and inspectors of surveyors-general and district land officers.

The matter is commended to the attention of Congress.

CHESTER A. ARTHUR.

EXECUTIVE MANSION, *January 24, 1882.*

To the Senate and House of Representatives:

I transmit herewith a communication from the Secretary of the Interior, with draft of a bill for the per capita distribution of the sum of $2,000 to the band of Eastern Shawnee Indians at Quapaw Agency, Ind. T., with accompanying papers noted in said communication.

CHESTER A. ARTHUR.

EXECUTIVE MANSION, *January 24, 1882.*

To the Senate and House of Representatives:

I transmit herewith a communication from the Secretary of the Interior, with draft of a bill to increase the salary of the Commissioner of Indian Affairs and to create the office of Assistant Commissioner of Indian Affairs.

The matter is commended to the attention of Congress.

CHESTER A. ARTHUR.

EXECUTIVE MANSION, *January 24, 1882.*

To the Senate and House of Representatives:

I transmit herewith a communication from the Secretary of the Interior, with draft of a bill and accompanying papers, in reference to the proposition of the Creek Nation of Indians for the cession of certain of their lands in the Indian Territory occupied by the Seminole Indians.

The subject is commended to the consideration of Congress.

CHESTER A. ARTHUR.

EXECUTIVE MANSION, *January 24, 1882.*

To the Senate and House of Representatives:

I transmit herewith a communication from the Secretary of the Interior, with draft of a bill authorizing the sale of certain pine timber cut upon the Menomonee Reservation in Wisconsin, together with the accompanying papers noted in said communication.

CHESTER A. ARTHUR.

.tion of Congress.
CHESTER A. ARTHUR.

MANSION, *January 18, 1882.*

s:

from the Secretary of the Inte-
g papers, amendatory of the act
e and Missouria Indian Reser-
nsas.
ration of Congress.
CHESTER A. ARTHUR.

EXECUTIVE MANSION,
ashington, January 18, 1882.

s:

Secretary of the Interior, for-
by the Commissioner of Indian
the office of medical inspector

CHESTER A. ARTHUR.

MANSION, *January 18, 1882.*

s:

from the Secretary of the Inte-
papers, providing for the im-
ccupying reservations, and for

leration of Congress.
CHESTER A. ARTHUR.

MANSION, *January 18, 1882.*

s:

from the Secretary of the Inte-
Commissioner of Indian Affairs-

recommending a renewal of the appropriation of $10,000 heretofore made for defraying the expenses of the Board of Indian Commissioners.

The subject is commended to the consideration of Congress.

CHESTER A. ARTHUR.

EXECUTIVE MANSION, *January 18, 1882.*

To the Senate and House of Representatives:

I transmit herewith a communication from the Secretary of the Interior, with draft of a bill and accompanying papers, in reference to the settlement of the estate of deceased Kickapoo Indians in the State of Kansas, and for other purposes.

The matter is commended to the attention of Congress.

CHESTER A. ARTHUR.

EXECUTIVE MANSION, *January 18, 1882.*

To the Senate and House of Representatives:

I transmit herewith a communication from the Secretary of the Interior, with a draft of a bill and accompanying papers, to accept and ratify an agreement with the Crow Indians for the sale of a portion of their reservation in the Territory of Montana, required for the Northern Pacific Railroad, and to make the necessary appropriation for carrying the same into effect.

The subject is presented for the consideration of Congress.

CHESTER A. ARTHUR.

EXECUTIVE MANSION, *January 19, 1882.*

To the Senate and House of Representatives:

I transmit herewith, for the consideration of Congress, a communication from the Secretary of War, with accompanying papers, recommending an appropriation for the purchase of a site and the erection of a fireproof building to contain the records, library, and museum of the Surgeon-General's Office.

CHESTER A. ARTHUR.

OFFICE OF THE PRESIDENT OF THE UNITED STATES,
Washington, January 19, 1882.

To the Senate and House of Representatives:

I transmit herewith, for the consideration of Congress, a letter from the Secretary of War, inclosing a copy of one from the Chief Signal Officer of the Army, dated the 11th instant, setting forth the necessity for additional room for the Signal Office and recommending that Congress provide that of the amount estimated ($350,000) for "observation and report of storms, 1883,'' the sum of $10,000 may be expended for the hire of a safe and suitable building in Washington City for the office of the Chief Signal Officer.

CHESTER A. ARTHUR.

OFFICE OF THE PRESIDENT OF THE UNITED STATES,
January 19, 1882.

To the Senate and House of Representatives:

I transmit herewith, for the consideration of Congress, a communication from the Secretary of War, dated the 14th instant, and accompanying letter from the Chief Signal Officer of the Army, recommending the passage of a joint resolution, in accordance with the inclosed draft, authorizing the printing and binding of 10,000 additional copies of the latter's annual report for the year 1881.

CHESTER A. ARTHUR.

WASHINGTON, *January 23, 1882.*

To the Senate of the United States:

I transmit to the Senate, for its consideration with a view to ratification, a treaty of commerce and navigation between the United States of America and His Majesty the King of Roumania, signed on the 11th day of April last.

CHESTER A. ARTHUR.

WASHINGTON, *January 24, 1882.*

To the Senate of the United States:

I transmit to the Senate, for its consideration with a view to ratification, a treaty of commerce between the United States and the Prince of Serbia, signed on the 14th of October last.

    *   *   *   *   *   *

CHESTER A. ARTHUR.

WASHINGTON, *January 24, 1882.*

To the Senate of the United States:

I transmit to the Senate, for its consideration with a view to ratification, a convention defining the rights, immunities, and privileges of consular officers, between the United States and the Prince of Serbia, signed on the 14th of October last.

    *   *   *   *   *   *

CHESTER A. ARTHUR.

EXECUTIVE MANSION, *January 24, 1882.*

To the Senate and House of Representatives:

I transmit herewith a communication from the Secretary of the Interior, with draft of a bill to increase the salary of the Commissioner of the

Senate with the former dispatches, because at that time no advice had been received that its contents had been communicated to the British Government.

CHESTER A. ARTHUR.

EXECUTIVE MANSION, *February 1, 1882.*

To the House of Representatives:

I transmit herewith a communication from the Secretary of the Interior, inclosing a letter from the Commissioner of Pensions, giving, in compliance with the resolution of the House of Representatives passed on the 26th of January, 1882, estimates of the amounts which will be required annually to pay pensions for the next twenty-five years, based on the presumed conditions stated in the resolution.

CHESTER A. ARTHUR.

EXECUTIVE MANSION, *February 2, 1882.*

To the Senate and House of Representatives:

I transmit herewith a letter from the Secretary of the Interior, with accompanying papers, relative to lawlessness which prevails in parts of Arizona, and in connection therewith call attention to that portion of my message of the 6th of December last in which suggestions were made as to legislation which seems to be required to enable the General Government to assist the local authorities of the Territory in restoring and maintaining order.

CHESTER A. ARTHUR.

EXECUTIVE MANSION, *February 2, 1882.*

To the Senate and House of Representatives:

I transmit herewith a communication from the Secretary of the Interior, with a draft of a bill authorizing the disposal of dead and damaged timber upon Indian reservations under the direction of the Interior Department, and correspondence noted by the Secretary.

The subject is presented for the consideration of Congress.

CHESTER A. ARTHUR.

EXECUTIVE MANSION,
Washington, February 2, 1882.

To the Senate and House of Representatives:

I transmit herewith a letter from the Secretary of the Interior, inclosing copy of a letter addressed to him by the Commissioner of the General Land Office, asking, for reasons stated therein, that Congress may be requested to make a special appropriation for a temporary increase of the clerical force of the General Land Office.

A draft of a bill for that purpose is herewith inclosed, and the subject is commended to the consideration of Congress.

CHESTER A. ARTHUR.

EXECUTIVE MANSION,
Washington, February 2, 1882.

To the Senate of the United States:

I transmit herewith, in further response to the resolution of the Senate of the 18th of March, 1881, a report of the Secretary of State, with its accompaniment, touching the capitulations of the Ottoman Empire.

CHESTER A. ARTHUR.

EXECUTIVE MANSION, *February 2, 1882.*

To the Senate and House of Representatives:

I transmit herewith, for the consideration of Congress, a communication from the Secretary of War, dated the 27th of January, 1882, and accompanying estimates for new buildings for the general recruiting service at Davids Island, New York Harbor, and Columbus Barracks, Ohio.

CHESTER A. ARTHUR.

EXECUTIVE MANSION, *February 2, 1882.*

To the Senate and House of Representatives:

I transmit herewith a communication from the Secretary of the Interior, with the draft of a bill to authorize the settlement of certain accounts for advertising the sale of Kansas Indian lands, with accompanying papers referred to in said communication.

The subject is commended to the consideration of Congress.

CHESTER A. ARTHUR.

EXECUTIVE MANSION, *February 2, 1882.*

To the Senate and House of Representatives:

I transmit herewith a communication from the Secretary of the Interior, with a draft of a bill for the payment of certain settlers in the State of Nevada for improvements on lands in Duck Valley, in said State, taken for the use and occupancy of the Shoshone Indians.

CHESTER A. ARTHUR.

EXECUTIVE MANSION, *February 2, 1882.*

To the Senate and House of Representatives:

I transmit herewith, for the consideration of Congress, a communication from the Secretary of the Interior, dated January 31, 1882, upon the subject of additional legislation for the expenses of the Tenth Census, and inclose draft of an act supplemental to the act approved January 28, 1882.

CHESTER A. ARTHUR.

EXECUTIVE MANSION, *February 3, 1882.*
To the Senate and House of Representatives:

I transmit herewith, for the consideration of Congress, a communication of the Secretary of the Interior of the 27th ultimo, with accompanying papers, on the subject of the confirmation of the homestead entries of certain lands in Marquette district, Michigan, made by Hugh Foster and John Waishkey, jr.

CHESTER A. ARTHUR.

EXECUTIVE MANSION, *February 3, 1882.*
To the Senate and House of Representatives:

I transmit herewith a communication from the Secretary of the Interior, with a draft of a bill to prevent timber depredations on Indian reservations, and correspondence noted by the Secretary.

The subject is presented for the consideration of Congress.

CHESTER A. ARTHUR.

EXECUTIVE MANSION, *February 3, 1882.*
To the Senate of the United States:

I transmit herewith a report of the Secretary of State of this date, with accompanying papers, furnished in obedience to a resolution of the Senate of the 12th ultimo, calling for certain correspondence in the case of claim of Antonio Pelletier against the Government of Hayti.

CHESTER A. ARTHUR.

[A similar message was sent to the House of Representatives.]

EXECUTIVE MANSION, *February 8, 1882.*
To the Senate and House of Representatives:

I transmit herewith a communication of 1st instant from the Secretary of the Interior, covering information respecting the lands granted to the State of Oregon for the Willamette Valley and Cascade Mountain Wagon Road Company.

The subject is commended to the consideration of Congress.

CHESTER A. ARTHUR.

EXECUTIVE MANSION, *February 8, 1882.*
To the Senate and House of Representatives:

I transmit herewith, for the consideration of Congress, a communication from the Secretary of War, inclosing copies of papers relating to the site of Fort Bliss, at El Paso, Tex., with special reference to certain errors contained in the deeds conveying the land to the United States, and recommending the passage by Congress of an act, a draft of which is also inclosed, to rectify and establish the title of the United States to the site in question. CHESTER A. ARTHUR.

EXECUTIVE MANSION, *February 8, 1882.*
To the Senate and House of Representatives:

I transmit herewith, for the consideration of Congress, a letter from the Secretary of War of the 6th instant, together with plans and estimates for barracks and quarters in the Military Division of the Pacific and at Fort Monroe, Va., for the fiscal year ending June 30, 1883; also the correspondence accompanying the same. CHESTER A. ARTHUR.

EXECUTIVE MANSION, *February 15, 1882.*
To the Senate and House of Representatives:

I transmit herewith, for the consideration of Congress, a letter from the Secretary of War, dated the 11th instant, covering plans and estimates for completing the new barracks at Fort Leavenworth, Kans., and for the erection of additional quarters for officers thereat, in connection with the School of Cavalry and Infantry; also the correspondence accompanying the same. CHESTER A. ARTHUR.

EXECUTIVE MANSION, *February 15, 1882.*
To the Senate and House of Representatives:

I transmit herewith, for the information of Congress, the report of the Board of Indian Commissioners for the year 1881, accompanied by a letter from the Secretary of the Interior, dated the 9th instant, suggesting legislation regarding reports from said board. The report is sent with the message to the House of Representatives. CHESTER A. ARTHUR.

EXECUTIVE MANSION, *February 15, 1882.*
To the Senate and House of Representatives:

I transmit herewith a communication from the Secretary of the Navy, dated the 8th instant; and accompanying copies of letters from Rear-Admiral John Rodgers, Superintendent of the Naval Observatory, Professor J. E. Nourse, United States Navy, and Hon. John Eaton, Commissioner of Education, suggesting the publication of a second edition of the Second Arctic Expedition made by Captain C. F. Hall. CHESTER A. ARTHUR.

EXECUTIVE MANSION, *February 15, 1882.*

To the Senate and House of Representatives:

I transmit herewith, for the consideration of Congress, a letter from the Secretary of the Interior, inclosing a letter from the Commissioner of Education, in which the recommendation is made that an appropriation of $50,000 be made for the purpose of education in Alaska.

CHESTER A. ARTHUR.

EXECUTIVE MANSION, *February 15, 1882.*

To the House of Representatives:

I transmit herewith the response of the Secretary of State to your resolution of the 30th ultimo, calling for certain information relative to the amount of fees collected by consuls of the United States from American vessels.

CHESTER A. ARTHUR.

EXECUTIVE MANSION, *February 17, 1882.*

To the House of Representatives:

In answer to the resolution of the House of Representatives of the 6th instant, requesting a further compliance with its call for correspondence respecting the war on the Pacific, I transmit herewith a report of the Secretary of State and its accompanying papers.

CHESTER A. ARTHUR.

EXECUTIVE MANSION, *February 17, 1882.*

To the Senate of the United States:

In answer to the resolution of the Senate of the 12th of December, 1881, respecting the Clayton-Bulwer treaty, I transmit herewith a further report by the Secretary of State, accompanied by copies of papers on the subject.   CHESTER A. ARTHUR.

EXECUTIVE MANSION, *February 17, 1882.*

To the Senate of the United States:

In answer to the resolution of the Senate of the 31st of January last, calling for the correspondence touching the relations of the United States with Guatemala and Mexico and their relations with each other, I transmit a report of the Secretary of State, which is accompanied by a copy of the papers called for by the resolution.

CHESTER A. ARTHUR.

EXECUTIVE MANSION, *February 21, 1882.*

To the Senate and House of Representatives:

I submit herewith, for the consideration of Congress, a letter from the Secretary of the Interior, and accompanying papers, in which he recommends that authority be given for the payment of certain damages which unexpectedly occurred to the property of private persons on the Government reservation at Hot Springs, Ark., in consequence of work performed under the direction of the superintendent in the performance of his duty.   CHESTER A. ARTHUR.

EXECUTIVE MANSION, *February 21, 1882.*

To the Senate and House of Representatives:

I transmit herewith, for the consideration of Congress, a communication from the Secretary of the Interior, inclosing a copy of a communication from the Commissioner of Pensions, in which he recommends that more adequate provision be made for the payment of the expenses of obtaining evidence of the extent of the disability of those pensioners of the United States and applicants for pension who reside in foreign countries.   CHESTER A. ARTHUR.

EXECUTIVE MANSION, *February 21, 1882.*

To the Senate and House of Representatives:

I transmit herewith, for the consideration of Congress, a communication from the Secretary of the Navy, with accompanying papers, asking, for reasons stated by him, that Congress may be requested to make a special appropriation for the payment of the claim of Isaac A. Sylvester against the Navy Department.   CHESTER A. ARTHUR.

EXECUTIVE MANSION, *February 21, 1882.*

To the Senate and House of Representatives:

I transmit herewith a communication of the Secretary of the Interior, dated the 16th instant, relative to the necessity for a deficiency appropriation for the payment of salaries of clerks and laborers in the Patent Office during the present fiscal year.

The subject is commended to the consideration of Congress.

CHESTER A. ARTHUR.

EXECUTIVE MANSION, *February 28, 1882.*

To the Senate and House of Representatives:

I transmit herewith a communication from the Secretary of the Navy, with a copy of a letter from the Superintendent of the United States

Naval Observatory, accompanied by a draft of a bill, with estimates for an observation of the transit of Venus on the 6th of December, 1882.

The matter is commended to the consideration of Congress.

CHESTER A. ARTHUR.

EXECUTIVE MANSION, *February 28, 1882.*

To the Senate and House of Representatives:

I transmit herewith a letter from the Secretary of the Interior, inclosing a memorial and papers from the Seneca Nation of New York Indians embodying a resolution and remonstrance against the passage of Senate bill No. 19, "to provide for the allotment of lands in severalty to Indians on the various reservations," etc., together with a report thereon of the Commissioner of Indian Affairs, recommending an amendment to the seventh section thereof excluding the lands of said Indians.

The accompanying papers are transmitted with the message to the Senate.

CHESTER A. ARTHUR.

EXECUTIVE MANSION, *February 28, 1882.*

To the Senate and House of Representatives:

I submit herewith, for the consideration of Congress, a letter from the Secretary of the Interior, inclosing a petition of Mr. P. W. Norris for compensation for services rendered and expenses incurred by him as superintendent of the Yellowstone National Park from the 18th of April, 1877, to the 1st of July, 1878.

CHESTER A. ARTHUR.

EXECUTIVE MANSION, *February 28, 1882.*

To the Senate of the United States:

I transmit herewith a communication of the Secretary of the Interior of the 23d instant, with accompanying papers, furnished in obedience to a resolution of the Senate of the 30th ultimo, calling for certain information in relation to the Malheur Indian Reservation, in the State of Oregon.

CHESTER A. ARTHUR.

EXECUTIVE MANSION, *February 28, 1882.*

To the House of Representatives:

In reply to the resolution of the House of Representatives of the 24th ultimo, I transmit herewith copies of letters from the Secretary of the Treasury and the chairman of the Civil Service Commission, dated the 3d and 13th instant, respectively, from which it will be seen that the appropriation of $15,000 made at the last session of Congress for the promotion of efficiency in the different branches of the civil service is still unexpended, and that in order to execute the provisions of section 1753 of the Revised Statutes an annual appropriation of $25,000 would be necessary.

CHESTER A. ARTHUR.

WASHINGTON, March 1, 1882.

To the Senate of the United States:

I transmit herewith, in response to a resolution of the Senate of May 19, 1881, a communication, with accompanying papers, from the Secretary of State, respecting the collection by consular officers of certain official fees in connection with the authentication of invoices, and the compensation of such officers.

CHESTER A. ARTHUR.

EXECUTIVE MANSION, March 1, 1882.

To the Senate and House of Representatives:

I transmit herewith a communication, dated the 28th of February, 1882, from the Secretary of the Interior, with accompanying papers, in relation to the request of the Cherokee Indians of the Indian Territory for payment for lands belonging to them in said Territory ceded to the United States by the sixteenth article of their treaty of July 19, 1866, for the settlement of friendly Indians.

CHESTER A. ARTHUR.

EXECUTIVE MANSION, March 2, 1882.

To the Senate and House of Representatives:

I transmit herewith, for the consideration of Congress, a communication from the Secretary of War, dated the 18th ultimo, inclosing plans and estimates for the construction of the post of Fort Thornburg, in Utah Territory, and recommending an appropriation of $84,000 for that purpose and that the same be made available for immediate use.

CHESTER A. ARTHUR.

EXECUTIVE MANSION, March 3, 1882.

To the Senate and House of Representatives:

I transmit herewith, for the consideration of Congress, a communication from the Secretary of War, transmitting plans and estimates for the large military post proposed to be constructed at Fort Selden, N. Mex.

CHESTER A. ARTHUR.

WASHINGTON, March 3, 1882.

To the Senate of the United States:

I transmit to the Senate, for its action thereon, the accession of the United States to the convention concluded at Geneva on the 22d August,

1864, between various powers, for the amelioration of the wounded of armies in the field, and to the additional articles thereto, signed at Geneva on the 20th October, 1868.

CHESTER A. ARTHUR.

EXECUTIVE MANSION, *March 3, 1882.*

To the Senate and House of Representatives:

I transmit herewith a communication from the Secretary of the Interior, dated the 2d instant, with accompanying papers, submitting an estimate of appropriations for the payment of expenses of removal of certain Eastern Cherokee Indians to the Indian Territory.

The subject is presented for the consideration of Congress.

CHESTER A. ARTHUR.

EXECUTIVE MANSION, *March 7, 1882.*

To the Senate and House of Representatives:

I transmit a communication from the Secretary of the Navy, with a copy of a letter from the Chief of the Bureau of Equipment and Recruiting and a draft of a bill recommending an increase of 500 enlisted men for the naval service.

The matter is commended to the consideration of Congress.

CHESTER A. ARTHUR.

EXECUTIVE MANSION, *March 8, 1882.*

To the Senate and House of Representatives:

I transmit herewith a communication from the Secretary of the Interior, dated the 6th instant, with accompanying papers* from the Commissioner of Indian Affairs and draft of a bill to amend section 2135, Revised Statutes.

The subject is commended to the consideration of Congress.

CHESTER A. ARTHUR.

EXECUTIVE MANSION, *March 10, 1882.*

To the Senate and House of Representatives:

I transmit herewith, for the consideration of Congress, a communication from the Secretary of the Navy, with accompanying papers, asking, for reasons stated by him, that Congress may be requested to make a special appropriation for paving a portion of the roadway of Hanover street and curbing and paving the sidewalk of that street on the side next the Government property at the Naval Academy, Annapolis, Md.

CHESTER A. ARTHUR.

* Relating to the selling and trading of annuity goods by Lower Brulé Indians.

EXECUTIVE MANSION, *March 10, 1882.*

To the Senate and House of Representatives:

I transmit herewith a communication from the Secretary of the Interior of the 9th instant, submitting, with accompanying papers, an estimate of appropriation for the purpose of defraying the expenses of the Ute Commission, appointed under section 2 of the act of June 15, 1880.

The matter is commended to the early action of Congress.

CHESTER A. ARTHUR.

EXECUTIVE MANSION, *March 10, 1882.*

To the Senate and House of Representatives:

I transmit herewith, for the consideration of Congress, a communication from the Secretary of War of the 6th instant, and accompanying papers, recommending the passage of an act making certain debts incurred by soldiers a lien against their pay.

CHESTER A. ARTHUR.

EXECUTIVE MANSION, *March 10, 1882.*

To the House of Representatives:

I herewith transmit, in response to a resolution of the House of Representatives of the 7th ultimo, a report of the Secretary of State, touching the arrest and imprisonment in Mexico of Thomas Shields and two other American citizens to which that resolution relates.

CHESTER A. ARTHUR.

EXECUTIVE MANSION, *March 10, 1882.*

To the House of Representatives:

I transmit herewith, in answer to the resolution of the House of Representatives of the 30th of January last, a report from the Secretary of State, with accompanying paper.* CHESTER A. ARTHUR.

EXECUTIVE MANSION, *March 13, 1882.*

To the Senate and House of Representatives:

I transmit herewith a communication from the president of the National Board of Health, calling attention to the necessity for additional legislation to prevent the introduction of contagious and infectious diseases into the United States from foreign countries.

The subject is commended to the careful consideration of Congress.

CHESTER A. ARTHUR.

*List of promotions, removals, and appointments in the consular service since March 4, 1877.

EXECUTIVE MANSION, *March 14, 1882.*

To the House of Representatives:

I inclose herewith an amended estimate for an increase in the clerical force of the office of the Commissioner of Pensions, which I recommend to your consideration.

CHESTER A. ARTHUR.

[The same message was sent to the Senate.]

EXECUTIVE MANSION, *March 16, 1882.*

To the Senate of the United States:

I transmit herewith a report of the Secretary of State and an accompanying paper, in further response to the resolution of the Senate of the 13th of December last, calling for correspondence touching affairs in or between Peru and Chile.

CHESTER A. ARTHUR.

EXECUTIVE MANSION, *March 17, 1882.*

To the Senate and House of Representatives:

I transmit herewith a communication from the Secretary of the Interior, with accompanying papers, covering the action of the Osage Indians declining to accede to the terms of the act of March 3, 1881, reducing the price of their lands in Kansas.

CHESTER A. ARTHUR.

EXECUTIVE MANSION, *March 18, 1882.*

To the House of Representatives:

In response to the resolution of the House of Representatives adopted March 16, 1882, in which the President is requested, if not incompatible with the public interests, to furnish to the House all the facts before him at the time he authorized the sending or employment of troops or military forces of the United States in the State of Nebraska during the present month, together with his reasons therefor, I have the honor to state that the employment of military forces of the United States as to which it is understood that information is desired by the House of Representatives was authorized on the 10th instant, and that all the facts before me at that time are set forth in telegraphic communications, dated the 9th and 10th instant, from the governor of the State of Nebraska and Brigadier-General Crook, commanding the Department of the Platte, of which copies are herewith submitted.

For the further information of the House of Representatives, I transmit copies of telegraphic correspondence had on the 9th, 10th, and 11th instant between the Secretary of War and the governor of Nebraska and the Secretary of War and the Lieutenant-General of the Army, of which the instructions issued by my direction for the employment of the military forces upon the application of the governor of Nebraska are a part.

From these papers it will be seen that the authority to employ troops was given upon the application of the governor of Nebraska in order to protect the State against domestic violence. The instructions were given in compliance with the requirements of that part of section 4 of Article IV of the Constitution which provides that the United States shall, on application of the legislature, or of the executive (when the legislature can not be convened), protect each of the States against domestic violence.

CHESTER A. ARTHUR.

EXECUTIVE MANSION, *March 20, 1882,*

To the Senate of the United States:

In compliance with a resolution of the Senate of the 9th instant, instructing the Secretary of State to ascertain and report to the Senate the cause for the alleged imprisonment by the British Government of Daniel McSweeney, a citizen of the United States, I transmit herewith a report on the subject from the Secretary of State, with its accompanying papers.

CHESTER A. ARTHUR.

EXECUTIVE MANSION, *March 21, 1882.*

To the Senate and House of Representatives:

I transmit herewith, for the consideration of Congress, a communication from the Secretary of War, dated the 18th instant, inclosing plans and estimates for a brick building for the post of Fort Leavenworth, Kans., to contain quarters for two companies of troops, to replace the one destroyed by fire on the 1st February last, and recommending an appropriation of $18,745.77, in accordance with the estimates.

CHESTER A. ARTHUR.

EXECUTIVE MANSION, *March 21, 1882.*

To the Senate and House of Representatives:

I transmit herewith, for the consideration of Congress, a communication from the Secretary of the Interior, dated the 6th instant, with accompanying papers and draft of a bill "to authorize payment for Government transportation over certain railroads."

CHESTER A. ARTHUR.

EXECUTIVE MANSION, *March 21, 1882.*

To the Senate and House of Representatives:

transmit herewith a communication from the Secretary of the Navy, calling attention to the necessity of appropriating the sum of $12,000

EXECUTIVE MANSION, *April 4, 1882.*

To the Senate and House of Representatives:

I transmit herewith, for the consideration of Congress, a letter from the Secretary of War, dated March 31, 1882, and accompanying report from the Chief of Engineers, with its inclosures, relative to the construction of a bridge across the Potomac River at or near Georgetown, in the District of Columbia, under the provisions of the act approved February 23, 1881, in which he requests that an additional appropriation of $80,000 be made to give practical effect to the act referred to in accordance with the recommendations of the Chief of Engineers.

CHESTER A. ARTHUR.

EXECUTIVE MANSION, *April 5, 1882.*

To the Senate and House of Representatives:

I transmit herewith a communication from the Secretary of the Interior, setting forth the necessity for an increased number of law clerks in the office of the Assistant Attorney-General in the Department of the Interior, because of the growing amount of business in that office.

The matter is commended to the attention and favorable action of Congress.

CHESTER A. ARTHUR.

EXECUTIVE MANSION, *April 5, 1882.*

To the Senate and House of Representatives:

I transmit herewith a communication from the Secretary of the Interior of this date, with draft of bill for the relief of Pierre Garrieaux and correspondence in relation thereto.

CHESTER A. ARTHUR.

EXECUTIVE MANSION, *April 5, 1882.*

To the House of Representatives:

I transmit herewith, in reply to the resolution of the House of Representatives of the 31st of January last, a report from the Secretary of State, with accompanying papers.*

CHESTER A. ARTHUR.

To the Senate: WASHINGTON, *April 5, 1882.*

I transmit herewith, in reply to the resolution of the Senate of the 29th of March last, the report of the Secretary of State, with accompanying papers.*

CHESTER A. ARTHUR.

*Correspondence, etc., relative to American citizens imprisoned in Ireland.

EXECUTIVE MANSION, *March 27, 1882.*

To the Senate and House of Representatives:

I transmit herewith a communication from the Secretary of the Interior, dated the 24th instant, and the accompanying letter of the Commissioner of Patents, submitting a supplemental estimate for an appropriation of $52,500 for the employment of twenty-five assistant principal examiners of patents, at an annual salary of $2,100 each.

The matter is commended to the consideration of Congress.

CHESTER A. ARTHUR.

EXECUTIVE MANSION, *March 28, 1882.*

To the Senate and House of Representatives:

I transmit herewith a communication from the Secretary of the Navy, with accompanying papers, on the subject of purchasing from the American Wood Preserving Company the machinery which was erected by that company at the navy-yard, Boston, under contract with the Navy Department, for the purpose of fully testing the company's process of preserving timber for use in the Navy.

The attention of Congress is invited to the subject.

CHESTER A. ARTHUR.

EXECUTIVE MANSION, *March 28, 1882.*

To the House of Representatives:

I transmit herewith, in response to the resolution of the House of Representatives of yesterday, the 27th instant, a report of the Secretary of State, with accompanying papers, touching the negotiations for the restoration of peace in South America.

CHESTER A. ARTHUR.

WASHINGTON, *March 28, 1882.*

To the Senate of the United States:

I transmit to the Senate, for its consideration with a view to ratification, a convention for the protection of trade-marks, concluded between the United States and His Majesty the King of Roumania on the 7th of October, 1881.

CHESTER A. ARTHUR.

EXECUTIVE MANSION, *March 29, 1882.*

To the Senate and House of Representatives:

I transmit herewith a communication from the Secretary of the Interior, dated 24th instant, in relation to the urgent necessity for action on the part of Congress for the prevention of trespasses upon Indian lands, with copy of report from Commissioner of Indian Affairs upon the subject and draft of bill for the object indicated.

The subject is commended to the consideration of Congress.

CHESTER A. ARTHUR.

EXECUTIVE MANSION, *March 29, 1882.*
To the Senate and House of Representatives:

I transmit herewith, for the consideration of Congress, a communication from the Secretary of War, dated March 25, 1882, with accompanying correspondence, plans, and estimates, in which he recommends an appropriation of $40,000 for the completion of the new post at Fort Lewis, Colo.

CHESTER A. ARTHUR.

EXECUTIVE MANSION, *March 30, 1882.*
To the Senate and House of Representatives:

I transmit herewith a communication from the Secretary of the Interior, dated the 28th instant, and the accompanying letter of the Superintendent of the Government Hospital for the Insane, submitting an estimate for a deficiency appropriation of $20,792.51 for the support of that institution for the remaining portion of the present fiscal year.

CHESTER A. ARTHUR.

EXECUTIVE MANSION, *March 30, 1882.*
To the Senate and House of Representatives:

I transmit herewith a letter from the Secretary of the Interior, inclosing draft of a bill to amend section 2056 of the Revised Statutes of the United States, relating to the term of office of Indian inspectors and Indian agents.

The subject is commended to the consideration of Congress.

CHESTER A. ARTHUR.

EXECUTIVE MANSION, *March 30, 1882.*
To the Senate and House of Representatives:

I transmit herewith a communication from the Secretary of the Interior, dated the 29th of March, and the accompanying letter of the Commissioner of the General Land Office, submitting an estimate for the additions of $34,200 and $20,000, respectively, to the appropriations for salaries, fees, and commissions of registers and receivers, and for contingent expenses, land offices, for the next fiscal year.

CHESTER A. ARTHUR.

EXECUTIVE MANSION, *March 30, 1882.*

To the House of Representatives:

I transmit herewith a report of the Secretary of State and accompanying documents, in response to a resolution of the House of Representatives of February 13, 1882, touching the protection of American citizens in Persia and the establishment of diplomatic relations with that country. CHESTER A. ARTHUR.

EXECUTIVE MANSION, *April 3, 1882.*

To the Senate and House of Representatives:

I transmit herewith, for the consideration of Congress, a letter from the Secretary of the Interior, in which he sets forth the necessity which will exist for an appropriation for the payment of the commissioners to be appointed under the recent act of Congress entitled "An act to amend section 5352 of the Revised Statutes of the United States in reference to bigamy, and for other purposes," and also for the payment of the election officers to be appointed by said commissioners.

In this connection I submit to Congress that, in view of the important and responsible duties devolved upon the commissioners under this act, their compensation at $3,000 per annum, as provided therein, should be increased to a sum not less than $5,000 per annum.

Such increased compensation, in my judgment, would secure a higher order of ability in the persons to be selected and tend more effectually to carry out the objects of the act. CHESTER A. ARTHUR.

EXECUTIVE MANSION, *April 3, 1882.*

To the House of Representatives:

I forward herewith, in compliance with a resolution of the House of Representatives of the 6th of February ultimo, calling for information in reference to the arrest and imprisonment in Mexico of certain American citizens, a further report from the Secretary of State and its accompanying paper, concerning the cases of Thomas Shields and Charles Weber, to which that resolution refers. CHESTER A. ARTHUR.

EXECUTIVE MANSION, *April 4, 1882.*

To the House of Representatives:

In partial response to the resolution of the House of Representatives of the 31st of January last, on the subject of American citizens imprisoned in Ireland, I transmit herewith a report of the Secretary of State. CHESTER A. ARTHUR.

EXECUTIVE MANSION, *April 4, 1882.*

To the Senate and House of Representatives:

I transmit herewith, for the consideration of Congress, a letter from the Secretary of War, dated March 31, 1882, and accompanying report from the Chief of Engineers, with its inclosures, relative to the construction of a bridge across the Potomac River at or near Georgetown, in the District of Columbia, under the provisions of the act approved February 23, 1881, in which he requests that an additional appropriation of $80,000 be made to give practical effect to the act referred to in accordance with the recommendations of the Chief of Engineers.

CHESTER A. ARTHUR.

EXECUTIVE MANSION, *April 5, 1882.*

To the Senate and House of Representatives:

I transmit herewith a communication from the Secretary of the Interior, setting forth the necessity for an increased number of law clerks in the office of the Assistant Attorney-General in the Department of the Interior, because of the growing amount of business in that office.

The matter is commended to the attention and favorable action of Congress.

CHESTER A. ARTHUR.

EXECUTIVE MANSION, *April 5, 1882.*

To the Senate and House of Representatives:

I transmit herewith a communication from the Secretary of the Interior of this date, with draft of bill for the relief of Pierre Garrieaux and correspondence in relation thereto.

CHESTER A. ARTHUR.

EXECUTIVE MANSION, *April 5, 1882.*

To the House of Representatives:

I transmit herewith, in reply to the resolution of the House of Representatives of the 31st of January last, a report from the Secretary of State, with accompanying papers.*

CHESTER A. ARTHUR.

WASHINGTON, *April 5, 1882.*

To the Senate:

I transmit herewith, in reply to the resolution of the Senate of the 29th of March last, the report of the Secretary of State, with accompanying papers.*

CHESTER A. ARTHUR.

*Correspondence, etc., relative to American citizens imprisoned in Ireland.

EXECUTIVE MANSION, *April 6, 1882.*

To the Senate and House of Representatives:

I transmit herewith, for the consideration of Congress, a letter from the Secretary of War, dated the 4th instant, inclosing plans and estimates for the completion of the post of Fort McKinney, Wyoming Territory, and recommending an appropriation of $50,000 for the purpose in accordance with the estimates. CHESTER A. ARTHUR.

EXECUTIVE MANSION, *April 6, 1882.*

To the Senate and House of Representatives:

I transmit herewith, for the consideration of Congress, a communication from the Secretary of War, dated the 4th instant, inclosing estimates for deficiency in the appropriation for the transportation of the Army and its supplies for the fiscal year ending June 30, 1882, and recommending an appropriation in accordance therewith. CHESTER A. ARTHUR.

EXECUTIVE MANSION, *April 11, 1882.*

To the Senate and House of Representatives:

I transmit herewith, for the consideration of Congress, a letter from the Secretary of War, dated the 6th instant, in which he recommends a reappropriation of the unexpended balances of two appropriations of $50,000 each, made in 1880 and 1881, "for continuing the improvement of the water-power pool" at the Rock Island Arsenal, and that the additional sum of $30,000 be granted for the same purpose; also the additional sum of $70,000 "for deepening the canal and for opening six waterways in connection with the water power." CHESTER A. ARTHUR.

EXECUTIVE MANSION, *April 12, 1882.*

To the Senate and House of Representatives:

I transmit herewith a communication from the Secretary of the Interior, with the accompanying report from the Commissioner of Indian Affairs, dated 29th ultimo, recommending an increase of item for "transportation of Indian supplies for the fiscal year 1882" (deficiency), as designated in Senate Executive Document 57, Forty-seventh Congress, first session. CHESTER A. ARTHUR.

EXECUTIVE MANSION, *April 12, 1882.*

To the Senate and House of Representatives:

I transmit herewith a communication from the Secretary of the Interior, inclosing draft of bill prepared in the Office of Indian Affairs, submitted with Commissioner's report of 27th ultimo, confirming to the

Cheyenne and Arapahoe Indians the lands in the Indian Territory set apart for their occupancy by an Executive order dated August 10, 1869, which lands are in lieu of those set apart for their use and occupancy by the second article of the treaty with said Indians concluded October 28, 1867.

CHESTER A. ARTHUR.

EXECUTIVE MANSION, *April 12, 1882.*

To the Senate and House of Representatives:

I transmit herewith, for the consideration of Congress, a letter from the Secretary of War, dated the 6th instant, inclosing one from the acting chief clerk of the War Department on the subject, recommending an additional appropriation of $2,000 for contingent expenses of the War Department for 1882; also that appropriation provided for the purpose for the next fiscal year be increased $10,000.

CHESTER A. ARTHUR.

OFFICE OF THE PRESIDENT OF THE UNITED STATES,
Washington, April 14, 1882.

To the Senate of the United States:

I transmit herewith, for the consideration of Congress, the inclosed letter and accompanying statement from the Secretary of the Navy, in relation to the necessity of building a new boiler shop at the navy-yard, New York, and repairing the caisson gate of the dry dock at that station, in which it is requested that an appropriation of $147,243.04 be made for these objects.

CHESTER A. ARTHUR.

[The same message was sent to the House of Representatives.]

EXECUTIVE MANSION, *April 14, 1882.*

To the House of Representatives:

I transmit herewith, with commendation to the attention of Congress, a report of the Secretary of State and its accompanying papers, concerning the proposed establishment of an international bureau of exchanges.

CHESTER A. ARTHUR. ·

EXECUTIVE MANSION, *April 14, 1882.*

To the Senate and House of Representatives:

I transmit herewith a communication from the Secretary of the Interior, with correspondence, relative to right of way of the Republican Valley Railroad across the Otoe and Missouria Reservation in the State of Nebraska, and draft of an amendment to S. No. 930, "A bill to amend an act entitled 'An act to provide for the sale of the remainder of the reservation of 'the confederated Otoe and Missouria tribes of Indians in the States of Nebraska and Kansas, and for other purposes,' approved March 3, 1881.''

CHESTER A. ARTHUR.

EXECUTIVE MANSION, *April 17, 1882.*

To the Senate and House of Representatives:

I transmit herewith a letter, dated the 29th ultimo, from the Secretary of War, inclosing copy of a communication from the Mississippi River Commission, in which the commission recommends that an appropriation may be made of $1,010,000 for "closing existing gaps in levees," in addition to the like sum for which an estimate has already been submitted.

The subject is one of such importance that I deem it proper to recommend early and favorable consideration of the recommendations of the commission. Having possession of and jurisdiction over the river, Congress, with a view of improving its navigation and protecting the people of the valley from floods, has for years caused surveys of the river to be made for the purpose of acquiring knowledge of the laws that control it and of its phenomena. By act approved June 28, 1879, the Mississippi River Commission was created, composed of able engineers. Section 4 of the act provides that—

It shall be the duty of said commission to take into consideration and mature such plan or plans and estimates as will correct, permanently locate, and deepen the channel and protect the banks of the Mississippi River; improve and give safety and ease to the navigation thereof; prevent destructive floods; promote and facilitate commerce, trade, and the postal service.

The constitutionality of a law making appropriations in aid of these objects can not be questioned. While the report of the commission submitted and the plans proposed for the river's improvement seem justified as well on scientific principles as by experience and the approval of the people most interested, I desire to leave it to the judgment of Congress to decide upon the best plan for the permanent and complete improvement of the navigation of the river and for the protection of the valley.

The immense losses and widespread suffering of the people dwelling near the river induce me to urge upon Congress the propriety of not only making an appropriation to close the gaps in the levees occasioned by the recent floods, as recommended by the commission, but that Congress should inaugurate measures for the permanent improvement of the navigation of the river and security of the valley. It may be that such a system of improvement would as it progressed require the appropriation of twenty or thirty millions of dollars. Even such an expenditure, extending, as it must, over several years, can not be regarded as extravaga in view of the immense interest involved. The safe and convenient navigation of the Mississippi is a matter of concern to all sections of the country, but to the Northwest, with its immense harvests, needing cheap transportation to the sea, and to the inhabitants of the river valley, whose lives and property depend upon the proper construction of the safeguards which protect them from the floods, it is of vital importance that a well-matured and comprehensive plan for improvement should be put into operation with as little delay as possible. The cotton product of the region subject to the devastating floods is a source of wealth to the nation and of great importance to keeping the balances of trade in our favor.

It may not be inopportune to mention that this Government has imposed and collected some $ per cent by a tax on cotton, in the production of which the population of the Lower Mississippi is largely engaged, and it does not seem inequitable to return a portion of this tax to those who contributed it, particularly as such an action will also result in an important gain to the country at large, and especially so to the great and rich States of the Northwest and the Mississippi Valley.

CHESTER A. ARTHUR.

EXECUTIVE MANSION, *April 17, 1882.*

To the Senate and House of Representatives:

I transmit herewith a communication, dated the 14th instant, from the Secretary of the Interior, with draft of bill, and accompanying papers, for the establishment of an Indian training school on the site of the old Fort Ripley Military Reservation, in the State of Minnesota.

The subject is commended to the consideration of Congress.

CHESTER A. ARTHUR.

EXECUTIVE MANSION, *April 17, 1882.*

To the Senate and House of Representatives:

I transmit herewith a communication from the Secretary of the Interior of the 12th instant, with accompanying papers, in relation to coal lands upon the San Carlos Reservation, in the Territory of Arizona.

The subject is presented for the consideration of Congress.

CHESTER A. ARTHUR.

EXECUTIVE MANSION, *April 17, 1882.*

To the Senate:

I transmit herewith a report from the Secretary of State and its accompanying papers, concerning the international regulations for preventing collisions at sea, and I earnestly commend this important subject to the early and favorable consideration of Congress.

CHESTER A. ARTHUR.

[The same message was sent to the House of Representatives.]

EXECUTIVE MANSION, *April 18, 1882.*

To the Senate and House of Representatives:

I send herewith a copy of the circular invitation extended to all the independent countries of North and South America to participate in a general congress to be held in the city of Washington on the 22d of November next for the purpose of considering and discussing the methods of preventing war between the nations of America.

In giving this invitation I was not unaware that there existed differences between several of the Republics of South America which would militate against the happy results which might otherwise be expected from such an assemblage. The differences indicated are such as exist between Chile and Peru, between Mexico and Guatemala, and between the States of Central America.

It was hoped that these differences would disappear before the time fixed for the meeting of the congress. This hope has not been realized.

Having observed that the authority of the President to convene such a congress has been questioned, I beg leave to state that the Constitution confers upon the President the power, by and with the advice and consent of the Senate, to make treaties, and that this provision confers the power to take all requisite measures to initiate them, and to this end the President may freely confer with one or several commissioners or delegates from other nations. The congress contemplated by the invitation could only effect any valuable results by its conclusions eventually taking the form of a treaty of peace between the States represented; and, besides, the invitation to the States of North and South America is merely a preliminary act, of which constitutionality or the want of it can hardly be affirmed.

It has been suggested that while the international congress would have no power to affect the rights of nationalities there represented, still Congress might be unwilling to subject the existing treaty rights of the United States on the Isthmus and elsewhere on the continent to be clouded and rendered uncertain by the expression of the opinions of a congress composed largely of interested parties.

I am glad to have it in my power to refer to the Congress of the United States, as I now do, the propriety of convening the suggested international congress, that I may thus be informed of its views, which it will be my pleasure to carry out.

Inquiry having been made by some of the Republics invited whether it is intended that this international congress shall convene, it is important

that Congress should at as early a day as is convenient inform me
lution or otherwise of its opinion in the premises.   My action w
harmony with such expression.

CHESTER A. ARTE

DEPARTMENT OF STATE, *Washington, Novembr*

SIR:* The attitude of the United States with respect to the question
peace on the American continent is well known through its persistent
years past to avert the evils of warfare, or, these efforts failing, to bring posi
flicts to an end through pacific counsels or the advocacy of impartial arl
This attitude has been consistently maintained, and always with such fair
leave no room for imputing to our Government any motive except the hun
disinterested one of saving the kindred States of the American continent
burdens of war.   The position of the United States as the leading power of
World might well give to its Government a claim to authoritative utteranc
purpose of quieting discord among its neighbors, with all of whom the most
relations exist.   Nevertheless, the good offices of this Government are not
not at any time been tendered with a show of dictation or compulsion, bu
exhibiting the solicitous good will of a common friend.

For some years past a growing disposition has been manifested by certa
of Central and South America to refer disputes affecting grave questions ol
tional relationship and boundaries to arbitration rather than to the sword
been on several such occasions a source of profound satisfaction to the Go
of the United States to see that this country is in a large measure looked
the American powers as their friend and mediator.

The just and impartial counsel of the President in such cases has ne
withheld, and his efforts have been rewarded by the prevention of sanguin
or angry contentions between peoples whom we regard as brethren.

The existence of this growing tendency convinces the President that th
ripe for a proposal that shall enlist the good will and active cooperation o
States of the Western Hemisphere, both north and south, in the interest of t
and for the common weal of nations.

He conceives that none of the Governments of America can be less alive
own to the dangers and horrors of a state of war, and especially of war betw
men.   He is sure that none of the chiefs of Governments on the continent ca
sensitive than he is to the sacred duty of making every endeavor to do a
the chances of fratricidal strife.   And he looks with hopeful confidence
active assistance from them as will serve to show the broadness of our
humanity and the strength of the ties which bind us all together as a g
harmonious system of American Commonwealths.

Impressed by these views, the President extends to all the independent
of North and South America an earnest invitation to participate in a general
to be held in the city of Washington on the 24th day of November, 1882, for
pose of considering and discussing the methods of preventing war between th
of America.   He desires that the attention of the congress shall be strictly
to this one great object; that its sole aim shall be to seek a way of perm
averting the horrors of cruel and bloody combat between countries, oftene
blood and speech, or the even worse calamity of internal commotion and ci

cities, of paralyzed industries, of devastated fields, of ruthless conscription, of the slaughter of men, of the grief of the widow and the orphan, of imbittered resentments that long survive those who provoked them and heavily afflict the innocent generations that come after.

The President is especially desirous to have it understood that in putting forth this invitation the United States does not assume the position of counseling, or attempting through the voice of the congress to counsel, any determinate solution of existing questions which may now divide any of the countries of America. Such questions can not properly come before the congress. Its mission is higher. It is to provide for the interests of all in the future, not to settle the individual differences of the present. For this reason especially the President has indicated a day for the assembling of the congress so far in the future as to leave good ground for hope that by the time named the present situation on the South Pacific coast will be happily terminated, and that those engaged in the contest may take peaceable part in the discussion and solution of the general question affecting in an equal degree the well-being of all.

It seems also desirable to disclaim in advance any purpose on the part of the United States to prejudge the issues to be presented to the congress. It is far from the intent of this Government to appear before the congress as in any sense the protector of its neighbors or the predestined and necessary arbitrator of their disputes. The United States will enter into the deliberations of the congress on the same footing as the other powers represented, and with the loyal determination to approach any proposed solution not merely in its own interest or with a view to asserting its own power, but as a single member among many coordinate and coequal States. So far as the influence of this Government may be potential, it will be exerted in the direction of conciliating whatever conflicting interests of blood or government or historical tradition may necessarily come together in response to a call embracing such vast and diverse elements.

You will present these views to the minister of foreign relations of Mexico, enlarging, if need be, in such terms as will readily occur to you, upon the great mission which it is within the power of the proposed congress to accomplish in the interest of humanity, and upon the firm purpose of the United States to maintain a position of the most absolute and impartial friendship toward all. You will thereupon, in the name of the President of the United States, tender to His Excellency the President of the Mexican Republic a formal invitation to send two commissioners to the congress, provided with such powers and instructions on behalf of their Government as will enable them to consider the questions brought before that body within the limit of submission contemplated by this invitation.

The United States as well as the other powers will in like manner be represented by two commissioners, so that equality and impartiality will be amply secured in the proceedings of the congress.

In delivering this invitation through the minister of foreign affairs you will read this dispatch to him and leave with him a copy, intimating that an answer is desired by this Government as promptly as the just consideration of so important a proposition will permit.

I am, sir, your obedient servant,   JAMES G. BLAINE.

EXECUTIVE MANSION, *April 18, 1882.*

To the Senate and House of Representatives:

I transmit herewith, for the consideration of Congress, a note addressed by the minister plenipotentiary of Mexico to the Secretary of State, proposing the conclusion of a convention between the two countries for defining the boundary between the United States and Mexico from the Rio Grande westward to the Pacific Ocean by the erection of durable monuments. I lay before Congress a letter on the same subject, with its accompaniment from the Secretary of War, to whom the proposition was referred by the Secretary of State for the expression of his views thereon.

I deem it important that the boundary line between the two countries, as defined by existing treaties and already once surveyed, should be run anew and defined by suitable permanent monuments. By so doing uncertainty will be prevented as to jurisdiction in criminal and municipal affairs and questions be averted which may at any time in the near future arise with the growth of population on the border.

Moreover, I conceive that the willing and speedy assent of the Government of the United States to the proposal thus to determine the existing stipulated boundary with permanence and precision will be in some sense an assurance to Mexico that the unauthorized suspicion which of late years seems to have gained some credence in that Republic that the United States covets and seeks to annex neighboring territory is without foundation. That which the United States seeks and which the definite settlement of the boundary in the proposed manner will promote, is a confiding and friendly feeling between the two nations leading to advantageous commerce and closer commercial relations.

I have to suggest that in accepting this proposal suitable provision be made for an adequate military force on the frontier to protect the surveying parties from hostile Indians. The troops so employed will at the same time protect the settlers on the border and help to prevent marauding on both sides by the nomadic Indians.

CHESTER A. ARTHUR.

EXECUTIVE MANSION, *April 20, 1882.*

To the Senate and House of Representatives:

I transmit herewith, for the consideration of Congress, a letter from the Secretary of War of the 8th instant inclosing plans and estimates for the completion of the post of Fort Maginnis, Montana Territory, and recommending an appropriation to the amount of $95,000, as called for by the estimates.

CHESTER A. ARTHUR.

EXECUTIVE MANSION, *April 20, 1882.*

To the Senate and House of Representatives:

I transmit herewith a communication, dated the 15th instant, from the Secretary of the Interior, with draft of bill, and accompanying papers, touching the amendment of section 2142 of the Revised Statutes of the United States.

The subject is presented for the consideration of Congress.

CHESTER A. ARTHUR.

OFFICE OF THE PRESIDENT OF THE UNITED STATES,
Washington, April 21, 1882.

To the Senate of the United States:

I transmit herewith a communication addressed to me by the Secretary of the Navy, with accompanying papers, in which an appropriation is asked for the purpose of observing the transit of Venus in 1882.

The matter is commended to the favorable action of Congress.

CHESTER A. ARTHUR.

[The same message was sent to the House of Representatives.]

EXECUTIVE MANSION, *April 25, 1882.*

To the House of Representatives:

I transmit herewith a report of the Secretary of State, presented in compliance with the request of the House of Representatives in a resolution of the 10th instant, asking for information touching the existing restrictions on the importation of American neat cattle into Great Britain.

CHESTER A. ARTHUR.

EXECUTIVE MANSION, *April 25, 1882.*

To the House of Representatives:

I transmit herewith, for the consideration of the House of Representatives, a report from the Secretary of State, in relation to the International Fisheries Exhibition which is to be held at London in May, 1883. Fully approving of the suggestions contained in the report, I would earnestly recommend that favorable action be taken upon the subject at the present session of Congress, in order that there may be ample time for making the appropriations necessary to enable this country to participate in the exhibition.

CHESTER A. ARTHUR.

EXECUTIVE MANSION, *April 26, 1882.*

To the Senate and House of Representatives:

By recent information received from official and other sources I am advised that an alarming state of disorder continues to exist within the

...came, such head
... repress it
... the utmost, rejects
... Jones County and
... resistance to law
... that the people
... protection of the
... especial attention

... Jackson. Army, on
... that, in rears of
... that the civil
... the prisoners

... known
... within the
... carried into
... present
... suggested
... armed
... citizens be
... obey this

... Territory
... another
... nature
... the force
... referred
... it
... the civil
... same
... upon

...
...
...
...
...
...
...
...
...

EXECUTIVE MANSION,
Washington, May 2, 1882.

To the House of Representatives:

In answer to a resolution of the House of Representatives of the 30th of January last, calling for correspondence respecting the condition of Israelites in Russia, I transmit herewith a report from the Secretary of State and its accompanying papers.

CHESTER A. ARTHUR.

EXECUTIVE MANSION,
Washington, May 2, 1882.

To the Senate and House of Representatives:

I transmit herewith, for the consideration of Congress, a letter from the Secretary of the Interior, in which he requests that an appropriation of $108,000 be made for constructing a fireproof roof over the south and east wings of the building occupied by the Department of the Interior.

CHESTER A. ARTHUR.

EXECUTIVE MANSION,
Washington, May 2, 1882.

To the Senate of the United States:

I transmit herewith, in response to the resolution of the Senate of the 18th ultimo, a report of the Secretary of State, with copies of certain diplomatic correspondence* with Spain in 1876, called for by that resolution.

CHESTER A. ARTHUR.

EXECUTIVE MANSION, May 5, 1882.

To the Senate and House of Representatives:

I transmit herewith a communication from the Secretary of the Interior of the 3d instant, with accompanying papers, in relation to a proposed amendment of the act of the 15th December, 1880, providing for the disposal of the Fort Dodge Military Reservation, Kans.

The subject is commended to the consideration of Congress.

CHESTER A. ARTHUR.

EXECUTIVE MANSION, May 9, 1882.

To the Senate and House of Representatives:

I transmit herewith, for the consideration of Congress, a communication from the Secretary of the Interior, inclosing a letter from the Superintendent of Census, submitting an estimate for an appropriation of $80,000 to defray the expenses of the Census Office during the remainder of the present fiscal year.

CHESTER A. ARTHUR.

*Relating to United States citizens condemned to death in Cuba, etc.

EXECUTIVE MANSION, *May 9, 1882.*

To the Senate and House of Representatives:

I transmit herewith, for the consideration of Congress, a communication from the Secretary of the Interior, inclosing a letter from the Commissioner of the General Land Office, submitting an estimate for a special appropriation of $3,200 for completing an exhibit of all the private land claims in the State of Louisiana.   CHESTER A. ARTHUR.

EXECUTIVE MANSION, *May 11, 1882.*

To the Senate and House of Representatives:

I submit herewith, for the consideration of Congress, a letter from the Secretary of the Interior, inclosing a copy of a letter from the governor of Arizona, in which he requests that an appropriation of $2,000 be made for the contingent expenses of the Territory for the next fiscal year.

CHESTER A. ARTHUR.

EXECUTIVE MANSION, *May 15, 1882.*

To the Senate and House of Representatives:

I transmit herewith a communication from the Secretary of the Interior, submitting a copy of a letter from the Commissioner of Pensions inviting attention to the fact that the "deficiency" appropriation of $16,000,000 to meet the June payment of army pensions should be available as early as the 25th instant if practicable, in order to avoid any delay in payment.   CHESTER A. ARTHUR.

EXECUTIVE MANSION, *May 15, 1882.*

To the Senate and House of Representatives:

I transmit herewith a communication, dated the 11th instant, from the Secretary of the Interior, together with estimate of appropriation and accompanying papers, to provide, in accordance with treaty stipulations and existing laws, for the payment of certain interest due the Osage Indians.

The subject is presented for the consideration of Congress.

CHESTER A. ARTHUR.

EXECUTIVE MANSION, *May 15, 1882.*

To the Senate of the United States:

I transmit herewith a report of the Secretary of State, with accompanying papers, submitted in response to the Senate resolution of the 21st of March last, requesting a copy of instructions given to Mr. George F.

Seward, when minister to China, concerning Chinese immigration, etc., and Mr. Seward's dispatches on that subject.

CHESTER A. ARTHUR.

EXECUTIVE MANSION, *May 18, 1882.*

To the House of Representatives:

I transmit herewith a concluding report from the Secretary of State of the 17th instant, and its accompanying papers, relative to Thomas Shields and Charles Weber, who were imprisoned at Apan, Mexico, and whose cases formed the subject of the resolution of the House of Representatives of February 6, 1882.

CHESTER A. ARTHUR.

EXECUTIVE MANSION, Washington, *May 18, 1882.*

To the Senate of the United States:

I transmit herewith a letter from the Secretary of State, accompanied by a copy of the correspondence referred to in Senate resolution of the 26th ultimo, in relation to the Japanese indemnity.

CHESTER A. ARTHUR.

EXECUTIVE MANSION, *May 22, 1882.*

To the Senate and House of Representatives:

I transmit herewith a communication from the Secretary of the Interior, dated 18th instant, and accompanying report from the Commissioner of Indian Affairs, relative to the necessity for buildings at the Mescalero Agency, N. Mex., and for an appropriation for the support, civilization, etc., of the Apaches at the Mescalero and Jicarilla agencies, together with an estimate for the same, in the form of a proposed clause for insertion in the sundry civil bill now pending for consideration in committee.

The subject is presented for the consideration of Congress.

CHESTER A. ARTHUR.

EXECUTIVE MANSION, *May 22, 1882.*

To the Senate and House of Representatives:

I transmit herewith a communication from the Secretary of the Interior of the 18th instant, with accompanying papers, submitting the draft of a proposed clause for insertion in one of the pending appropriation bills, to provide for the payment for improvements made by certain settlers on the Round Valley Indian Reservation, in California, as appraised under the act approved March 3, 1873.

The subject is presented for the consideration of Congress.

CHESTER A. ARTHUR.

Territory of Arizona, and that lawlessness has already gained such head there as to require a resort to extraordinary means to repress it.

The governor of the Territory, under date of the 31st ultimo, reports that violence and anarchy prevail, particularly in Cochise County and along the Mexican border; that robbery, murder, and resistance to law have become so common as to cease causing surprise, and that the people are greatly intimidated and losing confidence in the protection of the law. I transmit his communication herewith and call especial attention thereto.

In a telegram from the General of the Army dated at Tucson, Ariz., on the 11th instant, herewith transmitted, that officer states that he hears of lawlessness and disorders which seem well attested, and that the civil officers have not sufficient force to make arrests and hold the prisoners for trial or punish them when convicted.

Much of this disorder is caused by armed bands of desperadoes known as "Cowboys," by whom depredations are not only committed within the Territory, but it is alleged predatory incursions are made therefrom into Mexico. In my message to Congress at the beginning of the present session I called attention to the existence of these bands and suggested that the setting on foot within our own territory of brigandage and armed marauding expeditions against friendly nations and their citizens be made punishable as an offense against the United States. I renew this suggestion.

To effectually repress the lawlessness prevailing within the Territory a prompt execution of the process of the courts and vigorous enforcement of the laws against offenders are needed. This the civil authorities there are unable to do without the aid of other means and forces than they can now avail themselves of. To meet the present exigencies the governor asks that provision be made by Congress to enable him to employ and maintain temporarily a volunteer militia force to aid the civil authorities, the members of which force to be invested with the same powers and authority as are conferred by the laws of the Territory upon peace officers thereof.

On the ground of economy as well as effectiveness, however, it appears to me to be more advisable to permit the cooperation with the civil authorities of a part of the Army as a *posse comitatus*. Believing that this, in addition to such use of the Army as may be made under the powers already conferred by section 5298, Revised Statutes, would be adequate to secure the accomplishment of the ends in view, I again call the attention of Congress to the expediency of so amending section 15 of the act of June 18, 1878, chapter 263, as to allow the military forces to be employed as a *posse comitatus* to assist the civil authorities within a Territory to execute the laws therein. This use of the Army, as I have in my former message observed, would not seem to be within the alleged evil against which that legislation was aimed.

CHESTER A. ARTHUR

EXECUTIVE MANSION,
Washington, May 2, 1882.

To the House of Representatives:

In answer to a resolution of the House of Representatives of the 30th of January last, calling for correspondence respecting the condition of Israelites in Russia, I transmit herewith a report from the Secretary of State and its accompanying papers.

CHESTER A. ARTHUR.

EXECUTIVE MANSION,
Washington, May 2, 1882.

To the Senate and House of Representatives:

I transmit herewith, for the consideration of Congress, a letter from the Secretary of the Interior, in which he requests that an appropriation of $108,000 be made for constructing a fireproof roof over the south and east wings of the building occupied by the Department of the Interior.

CHESTER A. ARTHUR.

EXECUTIVE MANSION,
Washington, May 2, 1882.

To the Senate of the United States:

I transmit herewith, in response to the resolution of the Senate of the 18th ultimo, a report of the Secretary of State, with copies of certain diplomatic correspondence* with Spain in 1876, called for by that resolution.

CHESTER A. ARTHUR.

EXECUTIVE MANSION, *May 5, 1882.*

To the Senate and House of Representatives:

I transmit herewith a communication from the Secretary of the Interior of the 3d instant, with accompanying papers, in relation to a proposed amendment of the act of the 15th December, 1880, providing for the disposal of the Fort Dodge Military Reservation, Kans.

The subject is commended to the consideration of Congress.

CHESTER A. ARTHUR.

EXECUTIVE MANSION, *May 9, 1882.*

To the Senate and House of Representatives:

I transmit herewith, for the consideration of Congress, a communication from the Secretary of the Interior, inclosing a letter from the Superintendent of Census, submitting an estimate for an appropriation of $80,000 to defray the expenses of the Census Office during the remainder of the present fiscal year.

CHESTER A. ARTHUR.

* Relating to United States citizens condemned to death in Cuba, etc.

EXECUTIVE MANSION, *May 9, 1882.*

To the Senate and House of Representatives:

I transmit herewith, for the consideration of Congress, a communication from the Secretary of the Interior, inclosing a letter from the Commissioner of the General Land Office, submitting an estimate for a special appropriation of $3,200 for completing an exhibit of all the private land claims in the State of Louisiana.

CHESTER A. ARTHUR.

EXECUTIVE MANSION, *May 11, 1882.*

To the Senate and House of Representatives:

I submit herewith, for the consideration of Congress, a letter from the Secretary of the Interior, inclosing a copy of a letter from the governor of Arizona, in which he requests that an appropriation of $2,000 be made for the contingent expenses of the Territory for the next fiscal year.

CHESTER A. ARTHUR.

EXECUTIVE MANSION, *May 15, 1882.*

To the Senate and House of Representatives:

I transmit herewith a communication from the Secretary of the Interior, submitting a copy of a letter from the Commissioner of Pensions inviting attention to the fact that the "deficiency" appropriation of $16,000,000 to meet the June payment of army pensions should be available as early as the 25th instant if practicable, in order to avoid any delay in payment.

CHESTER A. ARTHUR.

EXECUTIVE MANSION, *May 15, 1882.*

To the Senate and House of Representatives:

I transmit herewith a communication, dated the 11th instant, from the Secretary of the Interior, together with estimate of appropriation and accompanying papers, to provide, in accordance with treaty stipulations and existing laws, for the payment of certain interest due the Osage Indians.

The subject is presented for the consideration of Congress.

CHESTER A. ARTHUR.

EXECUTIVE MANSION, *May 15, 1882.*

To the Senate of the United States:

I transmit herewith a report of the Secretary of State, with accompanying papers, submitted in response to the Senate resolution of the 21st of March last, requesting a copy of instructions given to Mr. George F.

Seward, when minister to China, concerning Chinese immigration, etc., and Mr. Seward's dispatches on that subject.

CHESTER A. ARTHUR.

EXECUTIVE MANSION, *May 18, 1882.*

To the House of Representatives:

I transmit herewith a concluding report from the Secretary of State of the 17th instant, and its accompanying papers, relative to Thomas Shields and Charles Weber, who were imprisoned at Apan, Mexico, and whose cases formed the subject of the resolution of the House of Representatives of February 6, 1882.

CHESTER A. ARTHUR.

EXECUTIVE MANSION,
Washington, May 18, 1882.

To the Senate of the United States:

I transmit herewith a letter from the Secretary of State, accompanied by a copy of the correspondence referred to in Senate resolution of the 26th ultimo, in relation to the Japanese indemnity.

CHESTER A. ARTHUR.

EXECUTIVE MANSION, *May 22, 1882.*

To the Senate and House of Representatives:

I transmit herewith a communication from the Secretary of the Interior, dated 18th instant, and accompanying report from the Commissioner of Indian Affairs, relative to the necessity for buildings at the Mescalero Agency, N. Mex., and for an appropriation for the support, civilization, etc., of the Apaches at the Mescalero and Jicarilla agencies, together with an estimate for the same, in the form of a proposed clause for insertion in the sundry civil bill now pending for consideration in committee.

The subject is presented for the consideration of Congress.

CHESTER A. ARTHUR.

EXECUTIVE MANSION, *May 22, 1882.*

To the Senate and House of Representatives:

I transmit herewith a communication from the Secretary of the Interior of the 19th instant, with accompanying papers, submitting the draft of a proposed clause for insertion in one of the pending appropriation bills to provide for the payment for improvements made by certain settlers on the Round Valley Indian Reservation, in California, as appraised under the act approved March 3, 1873.

The subject is presented for the consideration of Congress.

CHESTER A. ARTHUR.

EXECUTIVE MANSION, *May 22, 1882.*

To the House of Representatives:

I transmit herewith a letter from the Secretary of State and accompanying documents, submitted in compliance with resolution of the House of Representatives of the 20th ultimo, calling for additional information respecting cases of American citizens under arrest in Ireland.

CHESTER A. ARTHUR.

EXECUTIVE MANSION, *May 22, 1882.*

To the Senate and House of Representatives:

I transmit herewith a letter from the Secretary of War, dated the 18th instant, and accompanying papers from the Acting Chief Signal Officer, representing the necessity of a special appropriation being made not later than the 1st of June proximo for the purpose of dispatching a vessel, with men and supplies, for the relief of the expedition which was last year sent to Lady Franklin Bay, Grinnell Land.

CHESTER A. ARTHUR.

EXECUTIVE MANSION, *May 24, 1882.*

To the Senate of the United States:

In compliance with a resolution of the Senate of the 1st of March last, I transmit a communication from the Secretary of the Navy, accompanied by the report (with the exception of such parts thereof as it is deemed incompatible with the public interests to furnish) of Commodore R. W. Shufeldt, United States Navy, of his cruise around the world in the United States steamer *Ticonderoga.*

CHESTER A. ARTHUR.

EXECUTIVE MANSION,
Washington, May 25, 1882.

To the Senate and House of Representatives:

I transmit herewith a letter from the Secretary of State, concerning the awards made against Venezuela by the mixed commission under the convention of April 25, 1866. I earnestly invite the attention of Congress to this communication and the accompanying inclosures. In case neither House takes action upon it during the present Congress I shall feel it my duty to direct that this prolonged discussion be definitely terminated by recognizing the absolute validity of all the awards.

CHESTER A. ARTHUR.

EXECUTIVE MANSION, *May 26, 1882.*

To the House of Representatives:

In answer to the resolution of the House of Representatives of the 10th of April ultimo, calling upon the Secretary of State for information in regard to the restrictions imposed by the French Government upon pork exported from the United States, I transmit herewith a report of that officer and its accompanying papers.

CHESTER A. ARTHUR.

EXECUTIVE MANSION, *June 5, 1882.*

To the Senate and House of Representatives:

I transmit herewith a communication from the Secretary of the Interior of the 24th ultimo, with accompanying papers, submitting the draft of a proposed clause for insertion in one of the pending appropriation bills, to provide for the payment of certain legal services rendered to the Cherokee Indians in North Carolina in 1881, amounting to $150.

The subject is presented for the consideration of Congress.

CHESTER A. ARTHUR.

EXECUTIVE MANSION,
Washington, June 5, 1882.

To the Senate of the United States:

In further answer to the Senate's resolution of the 12th of December last, I transmit herewith a report of the Secretary of State and its accompanying paper, in regard to the modification of the Clayton-Bulwer treaty.

CHESTER A. ARTHUR.

EXECUTIVE MANSION, *June 14, 1882.*

To the Senate and House of Representatives:

I transmit herewith a letter from the Secretary of the Interior, respecting the Louisiana private land claim of Antonio Vaca, deceased, to which, with the accompanying papers, I invite the attention of Congress.

CHESTER A. ARTHUR.

EXECUTIVE MANSION,
Washington, June 14, 1882.

To the Senate of the United States:

I transmit herewith, in response to the resolution of the Senate of the 5th instant, a report from the Secretary of State, submitting copies of the full correspondence between the Department of State and Hon. William Henry Trescot, special envoy extraordinary to the Republics of Peru, Chile, and Bolivia, and Walker Blaine, Third Assistant Secretary of State.

CHESTER A. ARTHUR.

EXECUTIVE MANSION, *June 16, 1882.*

To the Senate and House of Representatives:

I submit herewith, for the consideration of Congress, a communication from the Secretary of the Interior, in which he recommends that the sum of $245,000, the amount which the Superintendent estimates will be required to complete the work of the Tenth Census, be appropriated for the purpose.

CHESTER A. ARTHUR.

EXECUTIVE MANSION, *June 16, 1882.*

To the Senate and House of Representatives:

I transmit herewith, for the consideration of Congress, a letter from the Secretary of War, dated the 14th instant, covering plans and estimates for repairs, additions, and alterations to public buildings at the depot of the mounted recruiting service, Jefferson Barracks, Mo., and in which he recommends that the sum of $24,938.44 be appropriated for the purpose, in accordance with the estimates, during the present session of Congress.

CHESTER A. ARTHUR.

To the Senate: EXECUTIVE MANSION, *June 16, 1882.*

I transmit herewith a report from the Secretary of State and its accompanying papers, concerning the Smoke Abatement Exhibition which was held at South Kensington, London, last winter.

CHESTER A. ARTHUR.

WASHINGTON, *June 16, 1882.*

To the Senate of the United States:

I transmit herewith to the Senate, for its consideration with a view to ratification, a convention between the United States and His Majesty the King of the Belgians, touching the reciprocal surrender of fugitives from justice, signed on the 13th day of June, 1882, and intended to supersede the convention for extradition of criminals between both countries which was concluded on the 19th day of March, 1874.

CHESTER A. ARTHUR.

EXECUTIVE MANSION, *June 19, 1882.*

To the Senate and House of Representatives:

I transmit herewith a communication, dated the 16th instant, from the Secretary of the Interior, inclosing, with accompanying papers, a draft of a bill "to enlarge the Pawnee Indian Reservation in Indian Territory."

The subject is presented for the consideration of Congress.

CHESTER A. ARTHUR.

EXECUTIVE MANSION, *June 19, 1882.*

To the House of Representatives:

I transmit herewith a letter from the Secretary of State, referring a communication from the Mexican minister at this capital touching the arrest and imprisonment in Mexico of Thomas Shields and two other American citizens, to which the resolution of the House of Representatives of the 6th day of February last relates.

CHESTER A. ARTHUR.

WASHINGTON, *June 23, 1882.*

To the Senate of the United States:

I transmit herewith to the Senate, with a view to ratification, a convention between the United States and His Majesty the King of Spain, for securing reciprocal protection for the trade-marks and manufactured articles of their respective citizens and subjects within the dominions or territories of the other country, signed on the 19th day of June, 1882.

CHESTER A. ARTHUR.

EXECUTIVE MANSION, *June 26, 1882.*

To the Senate and House of Representatives:

I transmit herewith a communication from the Secretary of War, dated the 9th instant, and its accompanying copy of the telegram from the general commanding the Military Division of the Pacific and Department of California, relative to the construction of additional quarters, barracks, storehouses, etc., within the limits of the Military Department of Arizona.

The Secretary of War recommends that for the purpose of constructing the additional buildings referred to the sum of their estimated cost, $205,000, be appropriated during the present session of Congress.

CHESTER A. ARTHUR.

EXECUTIVE MANSION, *June 28, 1882.*

To the Senate and House of Representatives:

I transmit herewith a communication from the Secretary of the Interior of the 22d instant, with accompanying papers, submitting the draft of a proposed clause for insertion in one of the pending appropriation bills, to provide for the payment for improvements made by certain settlers on the Jicarilla Apache Indian Reservation, in New Mexico.

The subject is presented for the consideration of Congress.

CHESTER A. ARTHUR.

EXECUTIVE MANSION, *July 3, 1882.*

To the House of Representatives:

In answer to the resolution of the House of Representatives of the 25th of April last, calling for information in regard to the reassembling of the Paris Monetary Conference during the current year and other matters connected therewith, I transmit herewith a report on the subject and its accompanying papers.   CHESTER A. ARTHUR.

EXECUTIVE MANSION,
Washington, July 20, 1882.

To the Senate of the United States:

I transmit herewith a report of the Secretary of State and accompanying papers, furnished in response to the resolution of the Senate of December 21, 1881, calling for the correspondence with the Mexican Government in regard to the claims of Benjamin Weil and La Abra Silver Mining Company against Mexico.

CHESTER A. ARTHUR.

EXECUTIVE MANSION,
Washington, July 20, 1882.

To the Senate of the United States:

I transmit herewith to the Senate, for its consideration with a view to ratification, a convention between the United States and Mexico, providing for the reopening and retrying of the claims of Benjamin Weil and La Abra Silver Mining Company against Mexico, which was signed on the 13th instant.

A report of the Secretary of State, with its accompanying correspondence, transmitted to the Senate this day in response to the resolution of December 21, 1881, will show the antecedents of the negotiation which resulted in the accompanying convention. In view of the accumulation of testimony presented by Mexico relative to these two claims, I have deemed it proper to avail myself of the authority given to the Executive by the Constitution, and of which authority the act of Congress of June 18, 1878, is declarative, to effect a rehearing of these cases. I therefore empowered the Secretary of State to negotiate with the minister of Mexico a convention to that end.

The more important correspondence preliminary to the treaty is herewith transmitted.

It will be seen by the stipulations of the treaty that the rehearing will have no retroactive effect as to payments already distributed, that the *bona fide* interests of third parties are amply secured, and that the Government of the United States is fully guarded against any liability resulting from the rehearing.   CHESTER A. ARTHUR.

EXECUTIVE MANSION,
Washington, July 20, 1882.

To the Senate of the United States:

I transmit herewith to the Senate, for consideration with a view to ratification, a supplementary convention between the United States and the French Republic, signed at Washington on the 19th instant, extending the term of duration of the commission organized under the convention of January 15, 1880, between the two countries.

CHESTER A. ARTHUR.

EXECUTIVE MANSION,
Washington, July 29, 1882.

To the Senate of the United States:

I transmit herewith, in response to the Senate resolution of the 15th instant, a report of the Secretary of State and accompanying papers, relating to the Clayton-Bulwer treaty.

CHESTER A. ARTHUR.

EXECUTIVE MANSION,
Washington, July 29, 1882.

To the Senate of the United States:

I transmit herewith to the Senate, for consideration with a view to ratification, a treaty between the United States and the Kingdom of Korea, or Chosen, concluded on the 22d May last. For the information of the Senate the accompanying letter of the Secretary of State is also transmitted.

CHESTER A. ARTHUR.

EXECUTIVE MANSION,
Washington, August 1, 1882.

To the Senate of the United States:

I transmit herewith to the Senate, for consideration with a view to ratification, a convention concluded on the 29th of July, 1882, between the United States and Mexico, providing for an international boundary survey to relocate the existing frontier line between the two countries west of the Rio Grande.

CHESTER A. ARTHUR.

OFFICE OF THE PRESIDENT OF THE UNITED STATES,
Washington, August 4, 1882.

To the Senate of the United States:

In reply to a resolution of the Senate passed April 25, 1882, I transmit herewith a communication, with accompanying papers, from the Secretary of the Navy, in relation to the title by which the United States holds the land now occupied as a navy-yard at Boston, Mass.

CHESTER A. ARTHUR.

EXECUTIVE MANSION, *August 5, 1882.*

To the House of Representatives:

I transmit herewith a report of the Secretary of State, submitted in compliance with the resolution of the House of Representatives of the 28th of June, calling for additional information respecting the case of American citizens under arrest in Ireland.

CHESTER A. ARTHUR.

EXECUTIVE MANSION,
Washington, August 7, 1882.

To the Senate of the United States:

I transmit herewith to the Senate, with a view to ratification, a convention concluded this day between the United States of America and His Majesty the King of Spain, supplementary to the extradition convention concluded between said countries on the 5th day of January, 1877.

CHESTER A. ARTHUR.

VETO MESSAGES.

EXECUTIVE MANSION,
Washington, April 4, 1882.

To the Senate of the United States:

After careful consideration of Senate bill No. 71, entitled "An act to execute certain treaty stipulations relating to Chinese," I herewith return it to the Senate, in which it originated, with my objections to its passage.

A nation is justified in repudiating its treaty obligations only when they are in conflict with great paramount interests. Even then all possible reasonable means for modifying or changing those obligations by mutual agreement should be exhausted before resorting to the supreme right of refusal to comply with them.

These rules have governed the United States in their past intercourse with other powers as one of the family of nations. I am persuaded that if Congress can feel that this act violates the faith of the nation as pledged to China it will concur with me in rejecting this particular mode of regulating Chinese immigration, and will endeavor to find another which shall meet the expectations of the people of the United States without coming in conflict with the rights of China.

The present treaty relations between that power and the United States spring from an antagonism which arose between our paramount domestic interests and our previous relations.

The treaty commonly known as the Burlingame treaty conferred upon Chinese subjects the right of voluntary emigration to the United States for the purposes of curiosity or trade or as permanent residents, and was in all respects reciprocal as to citizens of the United States in China. It gave to the voluntary emigrant coming to the United States the right to travel there or to reside there, with all the privileges, immunities, or exemptions enjoyed by the citizens or subjects of the most favored nation.

Under the operation of this treaty it was found that the institutions of the United States and the character of its people and their means of obtaining a livelihood might be seriously affected by the unrestricted introduction of Chinese labor. Congress attempted to alleviate this condition by legislation, but the act which it passed proved to be in violation of our treaty obligations, and, being returned by the President with his objections, failed to become a law.

Diplomatic relief was then sought. A new treaty was concluded with China. Without abrogating the Burlingame treaty, it was agreed to modify it so far that the Government of the United States might regulate, limit, or suspend the coming of Chinese laborers to the United States or their residence therein, but that it should not absolutely prohibit them, and that the limitation or suspension should be reasonable and should apply only to Chinese who might go to the United States as laborers, other classes not being included in the limitations. This treaty is unilateral, not reciprocal. It is a concession from China to the United States in limitation of the rights which she was enjoying under the Burlingame treaty. It leaves us by our own act to determine when and how we will enforce those limitations. China may therefore fairly have a right to expect that in enforcing them we will take good care not to overstep the grant and take more than has been conceded to us.

It is but a year since this new treaty, under the operation of the Constitution, became part of the supreme law of the land, and the present act is the first attempt to exercise the more enlarged powers which it relinquishes to the United States.

In its first article the United States is empowered to decide whether the coming of Chinese laborers to the United States or their residence therein affects or threatens to affect our interests or to endanger good order, either within the whole country or in any part of it. The act recites that "in the opinion of the Government of the United States the coming of Chinese laborers to this country endangers the good order of certain localities thereof." But the act itself is much broader than the recital. It acts upon residence as well as immigration, and its provisions are effective throughout the United States. I think it may fairly be accepted as an expression of the opinion of Congress that the coming of such laborers to the United States or their residence here affects our interests and endangers good order throughout the country.   On this point I should feel it my duty to accept the views of Congress.

The first article further confers the power upon this Government to regulate, limit, or suspend, but not actually to prohibit, the coming of such laborers to or their residence in the United States.   The negotiators of the treaty have recorded with unusual fullness their understanding of the sense and meaning with which these words were used.

As to the class of persons to be affected by the treaty, the Americans inserted in their draft a provision that the words "Chinese laborers" signify all immigration other than that for "teaching, trade, travel, study, and curiosity."   The Chinese objected to this that it operated to include artisans in the class of laborers whose immigration might be forbidden. The Americans replied that they "could" not consent that artisans shall be excluded from the class of Chinese laborers, for it is this very competition of skilled labor in the cities where the Chinese labor immigration concentrates which has caused the embarrassment and popular discontent.   In the subsequent negotiations this definition dropped out, and does not appear in the treaty.   Article II of the treaty confers the rights, privileges, immunities, and exemptions which are accorded to citizens and subjects of the most favored nation upon Chinese subjects proceeding to the United States as teachers, students, merchants, or from curiosity.   The American commissioners report that the Chinese Government claimed that in this article they did by exclusion provide that nobody should be entitled to claim the benefit of the general provisions of the Burlingame treaty but those who might go to the United States in those capacities or for those purposes.   I accept this as the definition of the word "laborers" as used in the treaty.

As to the power of legislating respecting this class of persons, the new treaty provides that we "may not absolutely prohibit" their coming or their residence.   The Chinese commissioners gave notice in the outset that they would never agree to a prohibition of voluntary emigration.   Notwithstanding this the United States commissioners submitted a draft, in which it was provided that the United States might "regulate, limit, suspend, or prohibit" it.   The Chinese refused to accept this.   The Americans replied that they were "willing to consult the wishes of the Chinese Government in preserving the principle of free intercourse between the people of the two countries, as established by existing treaties, provided that the right of the United States Government to use its discretion in guarding against any possible evils of immigration of Chinese laborers is distinctly recognized.   Therefore if such concession removes all difficulty on the part of the Chinese commissioners (but only in that case) the United States commissioners will agree to remove the word 'prohibit' from their article and to use the words 'regulate, limit, or suspend.'"   The Chinese reply to this can only be inferred from the fact that in the place of an agreement, as proposed by our commissioners, that we might prohibit the coming or residence of Chinese laborers, there was inserted in the treaty an agreement that we might not do it.

The remaining words, "regulate, limit, and suspend," first appear in the American draft. When it was submitted to the Chinese, they said:

We infer that of the phrases regulate, limit, suspend, or prohibit, the first is a general expression referring to the others. * * * We are entirely ready to negotiate with your excellencies to the end that a limitation either in point of time or of numbers may be fixed upon the emigration of Chinese laborers to the United States.

At a subsequent interview they said that "by limitation in number they meant, for example, that the United States, having, as they supposed, a record of the number of immigrants in each year, as well as the total number of Chinese now there, that no more should be allowed to go in any one year in future than either the greatest number which had gone in any year in the past, or that the total number should never be allowed to exceed the number now there. As to limitation of time they meant, for example, that Chinese should be allowed to go in alternate years, or every third year, or, for example, that they should not be allowed to go for two, three, or five years."

At a subsequent conference the Americans said:

The Chinese commissioners have in their project explicitly recognized the right of the United States to use some discretion, and have proposed a limitation as to time and number. This *is* the right to regulate, limit, or suspend.

In one of the conferences the Chinese asked the Americans whether they could give them any idea of the laws which would be passed to carry the powers into execution. The Americans answered that this could hardly be done; that the United States Government might never deem it necessary to exercise this power. It would depend upon circumstances. If Chinese immigration concentrated in cities where it threatened public order, or if it confined itself to localities where it was an injury to the interests of the American people, the Government of the United States would undoubtedly take steps to prevent such accumulations of Chinese. If, on the contrary, there was no large immigration, or if there were sections of the country where such immigration was clearly beneficial, then the legislation of the United States under this power would be adapted to such circumstances. For example, there might be a demand for Chinese labor in the South and a surplus of such labor in California, and Congress might legislate in accordance with these facts. In general, the legislation would be in view of and depend upon the circumstances of the situation at the moment such legislation became necessary. The Chinese commissioners said this explanation was satisfactory; that they had not intended to ask for a draft of any special act, but for some general idea how the power would be exercised. What had just been said gave them the explanation which they wanted.

With this entire accord as to the meaning of the words they were

about to employ and the object of the legislation which might be had in
consequence, the parties signed the treaty, in Article I of which—

The Government of China agrees that the Government of the United States may
regulate, limit, or suspend such coming or residence, but may not absolutely prohibit it. The limitation or suspension shall be reasonable, and shall apply only
to Chinese who may go to the United States as laborers, other classes not being
included in the limitations. Legislation taken in regard to Chinese laborers will
be of such a character only as is necessary to enforce the regulation, limitation, or
suspension of immigration.

The first section of the act provides that—

From and after the expiration of sixty days next after the passage of this act, and
until the expiration of twenty years next after the passage of this act, the coming of
Chinese laborers be, and the same is hereby, suspended; and during such suspension
it shall not be lawful for any Chinese laborer to come, or, having so come after the
expiration of said sixty days, to remain within the United States.

The examination which I have made of the treaty and of the declarations which its negotiators have left on record of the meaning of its language leaves no doubt in my mind that neither contracting party in
concluding the treaty of 1880 contemplated the passage of an act prohibiting immigration for twenty years, which is nearly a generation, or
thought that such a period would be a reasonable suspension or limitation, or intended to change the provisions of the Burlingame treaty
to that extent. I regard this provision of the act as a breach of our
national faith, and being unable to bring myself in harmony with the
views of Congress on this vital point the honor of the country constrains
me to return the act with this objection to its passage.

Deeply convinced of the necessity of some legislation on this subject,
and concurring fully with Congress in many of the objects which are
sought to be accomplished, I avail myself of the opportunity to point
out some other features of the present act which, in my opinion, can
be modified to advantage.

The classes of Chinese who still enjoy the protection of the Burlingame treaty are entitled to the privileges, immunities, and exemptions
accorded to citizens and subjects of the most favored nation. We have
treaties with many powers which permit their citizens and subjects to
reside within the United States and carry on business under the same
laws and regulations which are enforced against citizens of the United
States. I think it may be doubted whether provisions requiring personal registration and the taking out of passports which are not imposed
upon natives can be required of Chinese. Without expressing an opinion on that point, I may invite the attention of Congress to the fact that
the system of personal registration and passports is undemocratic and
hostile to the spirit of our institutions. I doubt the wisdom of putting an
entering wedge of this kind into our laws. A nation like the United
States, jealous of the liberties of its citizens, may well hesitate before it
incorporates into its polity a system which is fast disappearing in Europe

before the progress of liberal institutions. A wide experience has shown how futile such precautions are, and how easily passports may be borrowed, exchanged, or even forged by persons interested to do so.

If it is, nevertheless, thought that a passport is the most convenient way for identifying the Chinese entitled to the protection of the Burlingame treaty, it may still be doubted whether they ought to be required to register. It is certainly our duty under the Burlingame treaty to make their stay in the United States, in the operation of general laws upon them, as nearly like that of our own citizens as we can consistently with our right to shut out the laborers. No good purpose is served in requiring them to register.

My attention has been called by the Chinese minister to the fact that the bill as it stands makes no provision for the transit across the United States of Chinese subjects now residing in foreign countries. I think that this point may well claim the attention of Congress in legislating on this subject.

I have said that good faith requires us to suspend the immigration of Chinese laborers for a less period than twenty years; I now add that good policy points in the same direction.

Our intercourse with China is of recent date. Our first treaty with that power is not yet forty years old. It is only since we acquired California and established a great seat of commerce on the Pacific that we may be said to have broken down the barriers which fenced in that ancient Monarchy. The Burlingame treaty naturally followed. Under the spirit which inspired it many thousand Chinese laborers came to the United States. No one can say that the country has not profited by their work. They were largely instrumental in constructing the railways which connect the Atlantic with the Pacific. The States of the Pacific Slope are full of evidences of their industry. Enterprises profitable alike to the capitalist and to the laborer of Caucasian origin would have lain dormant but for them. A time has now come when it is supposed that they are not needed, and when it is thought by Congress and by those most acquainted with the subject that it is best to try to get along without them. There may, however, be other sections of the country where this species of labor may be advantageously employed without interfering with the laborers of our own race. In making the proposed experiment it may be the part of wisdom as well as of good faith to fix the length of the experimental period with reference to this fact.

Experience has shown that the trade of the East is the key to national wealth and influence. The opening of China to the commerce of the whole world has benefited no section of it more than the States of our own Pacific Slope. The State of California, and its great maritime port especially, have reaped enormous advantages from this source. Blessed with an exceptional climate, enjoying an unrivaled harbor, with the riches of a great agricultural and mining State in its rear and the wealth of the whole Union pouring into it over its lines of railway, San Francisco has before it an incalculable future if our friendly and amicable relations with Asia remain undisturbed.   It needs no argument to show that the policy which we now propose to adopt must have a direct tendency to repel Oriental nations from us and to drive their trade and commerce into more friendly lands.   It may be that the great and paramount interest of protecting our labor from Asiatic competition may justify us in a permanent adoption of this policy; but it is wiser in the first place to make a shorter experiment, with a view hereafter of maintaining permanently only such features as time and experience may commend.

I transmit herewith copies of the papers relating to the recent treaty with China, which accompanied the confidential message of President Hayes to the Senate of the 10th January, 1881, and also a copy of a memorandum respecting the act herewith returned, which was handed to the Secretary of State by the Chinese minister in Washington.

CHESTER A. ARTHUR.

Executive Mansion, *July 1, 1882.*

To the House of Representatives of the United States:

Herewith I return House bill No. 2744, entitled "An act to regulate the carriage of passengers by sea," without my approval.   In doing this I regret that I am not able to give my assent to an act which has received the sanction of the majority of both Houses of Congress.

The object proposed to be secured by the act is meritorious and philanthropic.   Some correct and accurate legislation upon this subject is undoubtedly necessary.   Steamships that bring large bodies of emigrants must be subjected to strict legal enactments, so as to prevent the passengers from being exposed to hardship and suffering; and such legislation should be made as will give them abundance of space and air and light, protecting their health by affording all reasonable comforts and conveniences and by providing for the quantity and quality of the food to be furnished and all of the other essentials of roomy, safe, and healthful accommodations in their passage across the sea.

A statute providing for all this is absolutely needed, and in the spirit of humane legislation must be enacted.   The present act, by most of its provisions, will obtain and secure this protection for such passengers, and were it not for some serious errors contained in it it would be most willingly approved by me.

My objections are these: In the first section, in lines from 13 to 24, inclusive, it is provided "that the compartments or spaces," etc., "shall be of sufficient dimensions to allow for each and any passenger," etc., "100 cubic feet, if the compartment or space is located on the first deck next below the uppermost deck of the vessel," etc., "or 120 cubic feet for each passenger," etc., "if the compartment or space is located on the second deck below the uppermost deck of the vessel," etc. "It shall not be lawful to carry or bring passengers on any deck other than the two decks mentioned," etc.

Nearly all of the new and most of the improved ocean steamers have a spar deck, which is above the main deck. The main deck was in the old style of steamers the only uppermost deck. The spar deck is a comparatively new feature of the large and costly steamships, and is now practically the uppermost deck. Below this spar deck is the main deck. Because of the misuse of the words "uppermost deck" instead of the use of the words "main deck" by this act, the result will be to exclude nearly all of the large steamships from carrying passengers anywhere but on the main deck and on the deck below, which is the steerage deck, and to leave the orlop, or lower deck, heretofore used for passengers, useless and unoccupied by passengers. This objection, which is now presented in connection with others that will be presently explained, will, if this act is enforced as it is now phrased, render useless for passenger traffic and expose to heavy loss all of the great ocean steam lines; and it will also hinder emigration, as there will not be ships enough that could accept these conditions to carry all who may now wish to come.

The use of the new and the hitherto unknown term "uppermost deck" creates this difficulty, and I can not consent to have an abuse of terms like this to operate thus injuriously to these large fleets of ships. The passengers will not be benefited by such a statute, but emigration will be hindered, if not for a while almost prevented for many.

Again, the act in the first section, from line 31 to line 35, inclusive, provides: "And such passengers shall not be carried or brought in any between-decks, nor in any compartment," etc., "the clear height of which is less than 7 feet." Between the decks of all ships are the beams; they are about a foot in width. The legal method of ascertaining tonnage for the purpose of taxation is to measure between the beams from the floor to the ceiling. If this becomes a law the space required would be 8 feet from floor to ceiling, and this is impracticable, for in all ships the spaces between decks are adjusted in proportion to the dimensions of the ship; and if these spaces between decks are changed so as not to correspond in their proportions with the dimensions of the vessel, the ship will not work well in the sea, her sailing qualities will be injured, and she will be rendered unfit for service.

It is only in great ships of vast tonnage that the height between decks can be increased. All the ordinary-sized ships are necessarily constructed with 7 feet space in the interval between the beams from the floor to the ceiling. To adopt this act, with this provision, would be to drive out of the service of transporting passengers most all of the steamships now in such trade, and no practical good obtained by it, for really, with the exception of the narrow beam, the space between the decks is now 7 feet. The purpose of the space commanded by the act is to obtain sufficient air and ventilation, and that is actually now given to the passenger by the 7 feet that exists in all of these vessels between floor and ceiling.

There is also another objection that I must suggest. In section 12, from line 14 to line 24, it is provided: "Before such vessel shall be cleared or may lawfully depart," etc., "the master of said vessel shall furnish," etc. "a correct list of all passengers who have been or are intended to be taken on board the vessel, and shall specify," etc. This provision would prevent the clearing of the vessel. Steam vessels start at an appointed hour and with punctuality. Down almost to the very hour of their departure new passengers, other than those who have engaged their passage, constantly come on board. If this provision is to be the law, they must be rejected, for the ship can not, without incurring heavy penalties, take passengers whose names are not set forth on the list required before such vessel shall be cleared. They should be allowed to take such new passengers upon condition that they would furnish an additional list containing such persons' names. There are other points of objection of a minor character that might be presented for consideration if the bill could be reconsidered and amended, but the three that I have recited are conspicuous defects in a bill that ought to be a code for such a purpose, clear and explicit, free from all such objections. The practical result of this law would be to subject all of the competing lines of large ocean steamers to great losses. By restricting their carrying accommodations it would also stay the current of emigration that it is our policy to encourage as well as to protect. A good bill, correctly phrased, and expressing and naming in plain, well-known technical terms the proper and usual places and decks where passengers are and ought to be placed and carried, will receive my prompt and immediate assent as a public necessity and blessing

CHESTER A. ARTHUR.

EXECUTIVE MANSION, *August 1, 1882.*

To the House of Representatives:

Having watched with much interest the progress of House bill No. 6242, entitled "An act making appropriations for the construction, repair, and preservation of certain works on rivers and harbors, and for other purposes," and having since it was received carefully examined it, after mature consideration I am constrained to return it herewith to the House of Representatives, in which it originated, without my signature and with my objections to its passage.

Many of the appropriations in the bill are clearly for the general welfare and most beneficent in their character. Two of the objects for which provision is made were by me considered so important that I felt it my duty to direct to them the attention of Congress. In my annual message in December last I urged the vital importance of legislation for the reclamation of the marshes and for the establishment of the harbor lines along the Potomac front. In April last, by special message, I recommended an appropriation for the improvement of the Mississippi River. It is not necessary that I say that when my signature would make the bill appropriating for these and other valuable national objects a law it is with great reluctance and only under a sense of duty that I withhold it.

My principal objection to the bill is that it contains appropriations for purposes not for the common defense or general welfare, and which do not promote commerce among the States. These provisions, on the contrary, are entirely for the benefit of the particular localities in which it is proposed to make the improvements. I regard such appropriation of the public money as beyond the powers given by the Constitution to Congress and the President.

I feel the more bound to withhold my signature from the bill because of the peculiar evils which manifestly result from this infraction of the Constitution. Appropriations of this nature, to be devoted purely to local objects, tend to an increase in number and in amount. As the citizens of one State find that money, to raise which they in common with the whole country are taxed, is to be expended for local improvements in another State, they demand similar benefits for themselves, and it is not unnatural that they should seek to indemnify themselves for such use of the public funds by securing appropriations for similar improvements in their own neighborhood. Thus as the bill becomes more objectionable it secures more support. This result is invariable and necessarily follows a neglect to observe the constitutional limitations imposed upon the lawmaking power.

The appropriations for river and harbor improvements have, under the influences to which I have alluded, increased year by year out of proportion to the progress of the country, great as that has been. In 1870 the aggregate appropriation was $3,975,900; in 1875, $6,648,517.50; in 1880, $8,976,500; and in 1881, $11,451,000; while by the present act there is appropriated $18,743,875.

While feeling every disposition to leave to the Legislature the responsibility of determining what amount should be appropriated for the purposes of the bill, so long as the appropriations are confined to objects indicated by the grant of power, I can not escape the conclusion that, as a part of the lawmaking power of the Government, the duty devolves upon me to withhold my signature from a bill containing appropriations which in my opinion greatly exceed in amount the needs of the country for the present fiscal year. It being the usage to provide money for these purposes by annual appropriation bills, the President is in effect directed to expend so large an amount of money within so brief a period that the expenditure can not be made economically and advantageously.

The extravagant expenditure of public money is an evil not to be measured by the value of that money to the people who are taxed for it.

They sustain a greater injury in the demoralizing effect produced upon those who are intrusted with official duty through all the ramifications of government.

These objections could be removed and every constitutional purpose readily attained should Congress enact that one-half only of the aggregate amount provided for in the bill be appropriated for expenditure during the fiscal year, and that the sum so appropriated be expended only for such objects named in the bill as the Secretary of War, under the direction of the President, shall determine; provided that in no case shall the expenditure for any one purpose exceed the sum now designated by the bill for that purpose.

I feel authorized to make this suggestion because of the duty imposed upon the President by the Constitution "to recommend to the consideration of Congress such measures as he shall judge necessary and expedient," and because it is my earnest desire that the public works which are in progress shall suffer no injury. Congress will also convene again in four months, when this whole subject will be open for their consideration.

CHESTER A. ARTHUR.

PROCLAMATIONS.

By the President of the United States of America.

A PROCLAMATION.

Whereas it is provided in the laws of the United States that—

Whenever, by reason of unlawful obstructions, combinations, or assemblages of persons or rebellion against the authority of the Government of the United States, it shall become impracticable, in the judgment of the President, to enforce by the ordinary course of judicial proceedings the laws of the United States within any State or Territory, it shall be lawful for the President to call forth the militia of any or all the States and to employ such parts of the land and naval forces of the United States as he may deem necessary to enforce the faithful execution of the laws of the United States or to suppress such rebellion, in whatever State or Territory thereof the laws of the United States may be forcibly opposed or the execution thereof forcibly obstructed.

And whereas it has been made to appear satisfactorily to me, by information received from the governor of the Territory of Arizona and from the General of the Army of the United States and other reliable sources, that in consequence of unlawful combinations of evil-disposed persons who are banded together to oppose and obstruct the execution of the laws it has become impracticable to enforce by the ordinary course of judicial proceedings the laws of the United States within that Territory, and that the laws of the United States have been therein forcibly opposed and the execution thereof forcibly resisted; and

Whereas the laws of the United States require that whenever it may be necessary, in the judgment of the President, to use the military forces for the purpose of enforcing the faithful execution of the laws of the United States, he shall forthwith, by proclamation, command such insurgents to disperse and retire peaceably to their respective abodes within a limited time:

Now, therefore, I, Chester A. Arthur, President of the United States, do hereby admonish all good citizens of the United States, and especially of the Territory of Arizona, against aiding, countenancing, abetting, or taking part in any such unlawful proceedings; and I do hereby warn all persons engaged in or connected with said obstruction of the laws to disperse and retire peaceably to their respective abodes on or before noon of the 15th day of May.

In witness whereof I have hereunto set my hand and caused the seal of the United States to be affixed.

[SEAL.] Done at the city of Washington, this 3d day of May, A. D. 1882, and of the Independence of the United States the one hundred and sixth. CHESTER A. ARTHUR.

By the President:
FREDK. T. FRELINGHUYSEN,
Secretary of State.

BY THE PRESIDENT OF THE UNITED STATES OF AMERICA.

A PROCLAMATION.

In conformity with a custom the annual observance of which is justly held in honor by this people, I, Chester A. Arthur, President of the United States, do hereby set apart Thursday, the 30th day of November next, as a day of public thanksgiving.

The blessings demanding our gratitude are numerous and varied. For the peace and amity which subsist between this Republic and all the nations of the world; for the freedom from internal discord and violence; for the increasing friendship between the different sections of the land; for liberty, justice, and constitutional government; for the devotion of the people to our free institutions and their cheerful obedience to mild laws; for the constantly increasing strength of the Republic while extending its privileges to fellow-men who come to us; for the improved means of internal communication and the increased facilities of intercourse with other nations; for the general prevailing health of the year; for the prosperity of all our industries, the liberal return for the mechanic's toil affording a market for the abundant harvests of the husbandman;

for the preservation of the national faith and credit; for wise and generous provision to effect the intellectual and moral education of our youth; for the influence upon the conscience of a restraining and transforming religion, and for the joys of home—for these and for many other blessings we should give thanks.

Wherefore I do recommend that the day above designated be observed throughout the country as a day of national thanksgiving and prayer, and that the people, ceasing from their daily labors and meeting in accordance with their several forms of worship, draw near to the throne of Almighty God, offering to Him praise and gratitude for the manifold goodness which He has vouchsafed to us and praying that His blessings and His mercies may continue.

And I do further recommend that the day thus appointed be made a special occasion for deeds of kindness and charity to the suffering and the needy, so that all who dwell within the land may rejoice and be glad in this season of national thanksgiving.

In witness whereof I have hereunto set my hand and caused the seal of the United States to be affixed.

[SEAL.]   Done at the city of Washington, this 25th day of October, A. D. 1882, and of the Independence of the United States the one hundred and seventh.

CHESTER A. ARTHUR.

By the President:

EREDK. T. FRELINGHUYSEN, *Secretary of State.*

EXECUTIVE ORDERS.

To Collectors of Customs: TREASURY DEPARTMENT, *March 30, 1882.*

Under the provisions of section 1955, Revised Statutes, so much of Department instructions of July 3, 1875,[*] approved by the President, as prohibits the importation and use of breech-loading rifles and suitable ammunition therefor into and within the limits of the Territory of Alaska is hereby amended and modified so as to permit emigrants who intend to become actual *bona fide* settlers upon the mainland to ship to the care of the collector of customs at Sitka, for their own personal protection and for the hunting of game, not exceeding one such rifle and suitable ammunition therefor to each male adult; also to permit actual *bona fide* residents of the mainland of Alaska (not including Indians or traders), upon application to the collector and with his approval, to order and ship for personal use such arms and ammunition to his care, not exceeding one rifle for each such person, and proper ammunition.

The sale of such arms and ammunition is prohibited except by persons about to leave the Territory, and then only to *bona fide* residents (excluding Indians and traders) upon application to and with the approval of the collector.

H. F. FRENCH, *Acting Secretary.*

Approved:

CHESTER A. ARTHUR.

[*] See Vol. VII, p. 328.

CHESTER A. ARTHUR, PRESIDENT OF THE UNITED STATES OF
AMERICA.

To all to whom these presents shall come, greeting:

Whereas on the 10th day of January, 1863, Fitz John Porter, then
major-general of volunteers in the military service of the United States,
and also colonel of the Fifteenth Regiment of Infantry and brevet brigadier-general in the United States Army, was by a general court-martial,
for certain offenses of which he had been thereby convicted, sentenced
" to be cashiered and to be forever disqualified from holding any office of
trust or profit under the Government of the United States;" and

Whereas on the 21st day of January, 1863, that sentence was duly confirmed by the President of the United States, and by his order of the
same date carried into execution; and

Whereas so much of that sentence as forever disqualified the said Fitz
John Porter from holding office imposed upon him a continuing penalty and is still being executed; and

Whereas doubts have since arisen concerning the guilt of the said Fitz
John Porter of the offenses whereof he was convicted by the said court-
martial, founded upon the result of an investigation ordered on the 12th
day of April, 1878, by the President of the United States, which are
deemed by me to be of sufficient gravity to warrant the remission of that
part of said sentence which has not yet been completely executed:

Now, therefore, know ye that I, Chester A. Arthur, President of the
United States, by virtue of the power vested in me by the Constitution
of the United States and in consideration of the premises, do hereby
grant to the said Fitz John Porter full remission of the hereinbefore-
mentioned continuing penalty.

In witness whereof I have hereunto signed my name and caused the
seal of the United States to be affixed.

Done at the city of Washington, this 4th day of May, A. D. 1882, and
of the Independence of the United States the one hundred and
[SEAL.] sixth.

CHESTER A. ARTHUR.

By the President:
    FREDK. T. FRELINGHUYSEN, *Secretary of State.*

EXECUTIVE MANSION, *Washington, May 26, 1882.*

SIR:* I am directed by the President to inform you that the several
Departments of the Government will be closed on Tuesday, the 30th
instant, to enable the employees to participate in the decoration of the
graves of the soldiers who fell during the rebellion.

Very respectfully,
    FRED. J. PHILLIPS, *Private Secretary.*

*Addressed to the heads of the Executive Departments, etc.

WAR DEPARTMENT,
Washington, July 13, 1882.

I. By direction of the President, the Military Department of West Point will be discontinued September 1, 1882.

II. By direction of the President, sections 1 and 2 of Article I of the general regulations for the United States Military Academy are hereby amended to read as follows:

1. The General of the Army, under the War Department, shall have supervision and charge of the United States Military Academy. He will watch over its administration and discipline and the instruction of the Corps of Cadets, and will make reports thereof to the Secretary of War.

2. The Superintendent, and in his absence the next in rank, shall have the immediate government and military command of the Academy, and shall be commandant of the military post of West Point. The Superintendent will render, through the Adjutant-General, to the General of the Army, for submission to the Secretary of War, all required reports, returns, and estimates concerning the Academy.

ROBERT T. LINCOLN,
Secretary of War.

SECOND ANNUAL MESSAGE.

WASHINGTON, *December 4, 1882.*

To the Senate and House of Representatives of the United States:

It is provided by the Constitution that the President shall from time to time give to the Congress information of the state of the Union and recommend to their consideration such measures as he shall judge necessary and expedient.

In reviewing the events of the year which has elapsed since the commencement of your sessions. I first call your attention to the gratifying condition of our foreign affairs. Our intercourse with other powers has continued to be of the most friendly character.

Such slight differences as have arisen during the year have been already settled or are likely to reach an early adjustment. The arrest of citizens of the United States in Ireland under recent laws which owe their origin to the disturbed condition of that country has led to a somewhat extended correspondence with the Government of Great Britain. A disposition to respect our rights has been practically manifested by the release of the arrested parties.

The claim of this nation in regard to the supervision and control of any interoceanic canal across the American Isthmus has continued to be the subject of conference.

It is likely that time will be more powerful than discussion in removing the divergence between the two nations whose friendship is so closely

cemented by the intimacy of their relations and the community of their interests.

Our long-established friendliness with Russia has remained unshaken. It has prompted me to proffer the earnest counsels of this Government that measures be adopted for suppressing the proscription which the Hebrew race in that country has lately suffered. It has not transpired that any American citizen has been subjected to arrest or injury, but our courteous remonstrance has nevertheless been courteously received. There is reason to believe that the time is not far distant when Russia will be able to secure toleration to all faiths within her borders.

At an international convention held at Paris in 1880, and attended by representatives of the United States, an agreement was reached in respect to the protection of trade-marks, patented articles, and the rights of manufacturing firms and corporations. The formulating into treaties of the recommendations thus adopted is receiving the attention which it merits.

The protection of submarine cables is a subject now under consideration by an international conference at Paris. Believing that it is clearly the true policy of this Government to favor the neutralization of this means of intercourse, I requested our minister to France to attend the convention as a delegate. I also designated two of our eminent scientists to attend as our representatives at the meeting of an international committee at Paris for considering the adoption of a common unit to measure electric force.

In view of the frequent occurrence of conferences for the consideration of important matters of common interest to civilized nations, I respectfully suggest that the Executive be invested by Congress with discretionary powers to send delegates to such conventions, and that provision be made to defray the expenses incident thereto.

The difference between the United States and Spain as to the effect of a judgment and certificate of naturalization has not yet been adjusted, but it is hoped and believed that negotiations now in progress will result in the establishment of the position which seems to this Government so reasonable and just.

I have already called the attention of Congress to the fact that in the ports of Spain and its colonies onerous fines have lately been imposed upon vessels of the United States for trivial technical offenses against local regulations. Efforts for the abatement of these exactions have thus far proved unsuccessful.

I regret to inform you also that the fees demanded by Spanish consuls in American ports are in some cases so large, when compared with the value of the shipment, as to amount in effect to a considerable export duty, and that our remonstrances in this regard have not as yet received the attention which they seem to deserve.

The German Government has invited the United States to participate in an international exhibition of domestic cattle to be held at Hamburg

in July, 1883. If this country is to be represented, it is important that in the early days of this session Congress should make a suitable appropriation for that purpose.

The death of Mr. Marsh, our late minister to Italy, has evoked from that Government expressions of profound respect for his exalted character and for his honorable career in the diplomatic service of his country. The Italian Government has raised a question as to the propriety of recognizing in his dual capacity the representative of this country recently accredited both as secretary of legation and as consul-general at Rome. He has been received as secretary, but his exequatur as consul-general has thus far been withheld.

The extradition convention with Belgium, which has been in operation since 1874, has been lately supplanted by another. The Senate has signified its approval, and ratifications have been duly exchanged between the contracting countries. To the list of extraditable crimes has been added that of the assassination or attempted assassination of the chief of the State.

Negotiations have been opened with Switzerland looking to a settlement by treaty of the question whether its citizens can renounce their allegiance and become citizens of the United States without obtaining the consent of the Swiss Government.

I am glad to inform you that the immigration of paupers and criminals from certain of the Cantons of Switzerland has substantially ceased and is no longer sanctioned by the authorities.

The consideration of this subject prompts the suggestion that the act of August 3, 1882, which has for its object the return of foreign convicts to their own country, should be so modified as not to be open to the interpretation that it affects the extradition of criminals on preferred charges of crime.

The Ottoman Porte has not yet assented to the interpretation which this Government has put upon the treaty of 1830 relative to its jurisdictional rights in Turkey. It may well be, however, that this difference will be adjusted by a general revision of the system of jurisdiction of the United States in the countries of the East, a subject to which your attention has been already called by the Secretary of State.

In the interest of justice toward China and Japan, I trust that the question of the return of the indemnity fund to the Governments of those countries will reach at the present session the satisfactory solution which I have already recommended, and which has recently been foreshadowed by Congressional discussion.

The treaty lately concluded with Korea awaits the action of the Senate.

During the late disturbance in Egypt the timely presence of American vessels served as a protection to the persons and property of many of our own citizens and of citizens of other countries, whose governments have expressed their thanks for this assistance.

The recent legislation restricting immigration of laborers from China has given rise to the question whether Chinese proceeding to or from mother country may lawfully pass through our own.

Construing the act of May 6, 1882, in connection with the treaty of November 7, 1880, the restriction would seem to be limited to Chinese immigrants coming to the United States as laborers, and would not forbid a mere transit across our territory. I ask the attention of Congress to the subject, for such action, if any, as may be deemed advisable.

This Government has recently had occasion to manifest its interest in the Republic of Liberia by seeking to aid the amicable settlement of the boundary dispute now pending between that Republic and the British possession of Sierra Leone.

The reciprocity treaty with Hawaii will become terminable after September 9, 1883, on twelve months' notice by either party. While certain provisions of that compact may have proved onerous, its existence has fostered commercial relations which it is important to preserve. I suggest, therefore, that early consideration be given to such modifications of the treaty as seem to be demanded by the interests of our people.

In view of our increasing trade with both Hayti and Santo Domingo, I advise that provision be made for diplomatic intercourse with the latter by enlarging the scope of the mission at Port au Prince.

I regret that certain claims of American citizens against the Government of Hayti have thus far been urged unavailingly.

A recent agreement with Mexico provides for the crossing of the frontier by the armed forces of either country in pursuit of hostile Indians. In my message of last year I called attention to the prevalent lawlessness upon the borders and to the necessity of legislation for its suppression. I again invite the attention of Congress to the subject.

A partial relief from these mischiefs has been sought in a convention, which now awaits the approval of the Senate, as does also another touching the establishment of the international boundary between the United States and Mexico. If the latter is ratified, the action of Congress will be required for establishing suitable commissions of survey. The boundary dispute between Mexico and Guatemala, which led this Government to proffer its friendly counsels to both parties, has been amicably settled.

No change has occurred in our relations with Venezuela. I again invoke your action in the matter of the pending awards against that Republic, to which reference was made by a special message from the Executive at your last session.

An invitation has been received from the Government of Venezuela to send representatives in July, 1883, to Caracas for participating in the centennial celebration of the birth of Bolivar, the founder of South American independence. In connection with this event it is designed to commence the erection at Caracas of a statue of Washington and to conduct an industrial exhibition which will be open to American products. I recommend that the United States be represented and that suitable provision be made therefor.

The elevation of the grade of our mission in Central America to the plenipotentiary rank, which was authorized by Congress at its late session, has been since effected.

The war between Peru and Bolivia on the one side and Chile on the other began more than three years ago. On the occupation by Chile in 1880 of all the littoral territory of Bolivia, negotiations for peace were conducted under the direction of the United States. The allies refused to concede any territory, but Chile has since become master of the whole coast of both countries and of the capital of Peru. A year since, as you have already been advised by correspondence transmitted to you in January last, this Government sent a special mission to the belligerent powers to express the hope that Chile would be disposed to accept a money indemnity for the expenses of the war and to relinquish her demand for a portion of the territory of her antagonist.

This recommendation, which Chile declined to follow, this Government did not assume to enforce; nor can it be enforced without resort to measures which would be in keeping neither with the temper of our people nor with the spirit of our institutions.

The power of Peru no longer extends over its whole territory, and in the event of our interference to dictate peace would need to be supplemented by the armies and navies of the United States. Such interference would almost inevitably lead to the establishment of a protectorate— a result utterly at odds with our past policy, injurious to our present interests, and full of embarrassments for the future.

For effecting the termination of hostilities upon terms at once just to the victorious nation and generous to its adversaries, this Government has spared no efforts save such as might involve the complications which I have indicated.

It is greatly to be deplored that Chile seems resolved to exact such rigorous conditions of peace and indisposed to submit to arbitration the terms of an amicable settlement. No peace is likely to be lasting that is not sufficiently equitable and just to command the approval of other nations.

About a year since invitations were extended to the nations of this continent to send representatives to a peace congress to assemble at Washington in November, 1882. The time of meeting was fixed at a period then remote, in the hope, as the invitation itself declared, that in the meantime the disturbances between the South American Republics would be adjusted. As that expectation seemed unlikely to be realized, I asked in April last for an expression of opinion from the two Houses of Congress as to the advisability of holding the proposed convention at the time appointed. This action was prompted in part by doubts which mature reflection had suggested whether the diplomatic usage and traditions of the Government did not make it fitting that the Executive should consult the representatives of the people before pursuing a line of policy somewhat novel in its character and far reaching in its possible consequences. In view of the fact that no action was taken by Congress in the premises and that no provision had been made for necessary expenses, I subsequently decided to postpone the convocation, and so notified the several Governments which had been invited to attend.

I am unwilling to dismiss this subject without assuring you of my support of any measures the wisdom of Congress may devise for the promotion of peace on this continent and throughout the world, and I trust that the time is nigh when, with the universal assent of civilized peoples, all international differences shall be determined without resort to arms by the benignant processes of arbitration.

Changes have occurred in the diplomatic representation of several foreign powers during the past year. New ministers from the Argentine Republic, Austria-Hungary, Brazil, Chile, China, France, Japan, Mexico, the Netherlands, and Russia have presented their credentials. The missions of Denmark and Venezuela at this capital have been raised in grade. Switzerland has created a plenipotentiary mission to this Government, and an embassy from Madagascar and a minister from Siam will shortly arrive.

Our diplomatic intercourse has been enlarged by the establishment of relations with the new Kingdom of Servia, by the creation of a mission to Siam, and by the restoration of the mission to Greece. The Shah of Persia has expressed his gratification that a chargé d'affaires will shortly be sent to that country, where the rights of our citizens have been hitherto courteously guarded by the representatives of Great Britain.

I renew my recommendation of such legislation as will place the United States in harmony with other maritime powers with respect to the international rules for the prevention of collisions at sea.

In conformity with your joint resolution of the 3d of August last, I have directed the Secretary of State to address foreign governments in respect to a proposed conference for considering the subject of the universal adoption of a common prime meridian to be used in the reckoning of longitude and in the regulation of time throughout the civilized world. Their replies will in due time be laid before you.

An agreement was reached at Paris in 1875 between the principal powers for the interchange of official publications through the medium of their respective foreign departments.

The admirable system which has been built up by the enterprise of the Smithsonian Institution affords a practical basis for our cooperation in this scheme, and an arrangement has been effected by which that institution will perform the necessary labor, under the direction of the Department of State. A reasonable compensation therefor should be provided by law.

A clause in the act making appropriations for the diplomatic and consular service contemplates the reorganization of both branches of such service on a salaried basis, leaving fees to inure to the benefit of the Treasury. I cordially favor such a project, as likely to correct abuses in the present system. The Secretary of State will present to you at an early day a plan for such reorganization.

A full and interesting exhibit of the operations of the Treasury Department is afforded by the report of the Secretary.

It appears that the ordinary revenues from all sources for the fiscal year ended June 30, 1882, were as follows:

From customs	$220,410,730.25
From internal revenue	146,497,595.45
From sales of public lands	4,753,140.37
From tax on circulation and deposits of national banks	8,956,794.45
From repayment of interest by Pacific Railway companies	840,554.37
From sinking fund for Pacific Railway companies	796,271.42
From customs fees, fines, penalties, etc	1,343,348.00
From fees—consular, letters patent, and lands	2,638,990.97
From proceeds of sales of Government property	314,959.85
From profits on coinage, bullion deposits, and assays	4,116,693.73
From Indian trust funds	5,705,243.22
From deposits by individuals for surveying public lands	2,052,306.36
From revenues of the District of Columbia	1,715,176.41
From miscellaneous sources	3,383,445.43
Total ordinary receipts	403,525,250.28

The ordinary expenditures for the same period were—

For civil expenses	$18,042,386.42
For foreign intercourse	1,307,583.19
For Indians	9,736,747.40
For pensions	61,345,193.95
For the military establishment, including river and harbor improvements, and arsenals	43,570,494.19
For the naval establishment, including vessels, machinery, and improvements at navy-yards	15,032,046.26
For miscellaneous expenditures, including public buildings, light-houses, and collecting the revenue	34,539,237.50
For expenditures on account of the District of Columbia	3,330,543.87
For interest on the public debt	71,077,206.79
Total ordinary expenditures	257,981,439.57

Leaving a surplus revenue of $145,543,810.71, which, with an amount drawn from the cash balance in the Treasury of $20,737,694.84, making $166,281,505.55, was applied to the redemption—

Of bonds for the sinking fund	$60,079,150.00
Of fractional currency for the sinking fund	58,705.55
Of loan of July and August, 1861	62,572,050.00
Of loan of March, 1863	4,472,900.00
Of funded loan of 1881	37,194,450.00
Of loan of 1858	1,000.00
Of loan of February, 1861	303,000.00
Of five-twenties of 1862	2,100.00
Of five-twenties of 1864	7,400.00
Of five-twenties of 1865	6,500.00
Of ten-forties of 1864	254,550.00
Of consols of 1865	86,450.00
Of consols of 1867	408,250.00
Of consols of 1868	141,400.00
Of Oregon War debt	675,250.00
Of old demand, compound-interest, and other notes	18,350.00
	166,281,505.55

The foreign commerce of the United States during the last fiscal year, including imports and exports of merchandise and specie, was as follows:

```
Exports:
    Merchandise................................................... $750,542,257
    Specie ....................................................      49,417,479
        Total....................................................  799,959,736
Imports:
    Merchandise .................................................  724,639,574
    Specie ......................................................   42,472,390
        Total ...................................................  767,111,964
Excess of exports over imports of merchandise................      25,902,683
```

This excess is less than it has been before for any of the previous six years, as appears by the following table:

Year ended June 30—	Excess of exports over imports of merchandise.
1876	$79,643,481
1877	151,152,094
1878	257,814,234
1879	264,661,666
1880	167,683,912
1881	259,712,718
1882	25,902,683

During the year there have been organized 171 national banks, and of those institutions there are now in operation 2,269, a larger number than ever before. The value of their notes in active circulation on July 1, 1882, was $324,656,458.

I commend to your attention the Secretary's views in respect to the likelihood of a serious contraction of this circulation, and to the modes by which that result may, in his judgment, be averted.

In respect to the coinage of silver dollars and the retirement of silver certificates, I have seen nothing to alter but much to confirm the sentiments to which I gave expression last year.

A comparison between the respective amounts of silver-dollar circulation on November 1, 1881, and on November 1, 1882, shows a slight increase of a million and a half of dollars; but during the interval there had been in the whole number coined an increase of twenty-six millions. Of the one-hundred and twenty-eight millions thus far minted, little more than thirty-five millions are in circulation. The mass of accumulated coin has grown so great that the vault room at present available for storage is scarcely sufficient to contain it. It is not apparent why it is desirable to continue this coinage, now so enormously in excess of the

As to the silver certificates, in addition to the grounds which seemed last year to justify their retirement may be mentioned the effect which is likely to ensue from the supply of gold certificates for whose issuance Congress recently made provision, and which are now in active circulation.

You can not fail to note with interest the discussion by the Secretary as to the necessity of providing by legislation some mode of freeing the Treasury of an excess of assets in the event that Congress fails to reach an early agreement for the reduction of taxation.

I heartily approve the Secretary's recommendation of immediate and extensive reductions in the annual revenues of the Government.

It will be remembered that I urged upon the attention of Congress at its last session the importance of relieving the industry and enterprise of the country from the pressure of unnecessary taxation. It is one of the tritest maxims of political economy that all taxes are burdensome, however wisely and prudently imposed; and though there have always been among our people wide differences of sentiment as to the best methods of raising the national revenues, and, indeed, as to the principles upon which taxation should be based, there has been substantial accord in the doctrine that only such taxes ought to be levied as are necessary for a wise and economical administration of the Government. Of late the public revenues have far exceeded that limit, and unless checked by appropriate legislation such excess will continue to increase from year to year. For the fiscal year ended June 30, 1881, the surplus revenue amounted to $100,000,000; for the fiscal year ended on the 30th of June last the surplus was more than one hundred and forty-five millions.

The report of the Secretary shows what disposition has been made of these moneys. They have not only answered the requirements of the sinking fund, but have afforded a large balance applicable to other reductions of the public debt.

But I renew the expression of my conviction that such rapid extinguishment of the national indebtedness as is now taking place is by no means a cause for congratulation; it is a cause rather for serious apprehension.

If it continues, it must speedily be followed by one of the evil results so clearly set forth in the report of the Secretary.

Either the surplus must lie idle in the Treasury or the Government will be forced to buy at market rates its bonds not then redeemable, and which under such circumstances can not fail to command an enormous premium, or the swollen revenues will be devoted to extravagant expenditure, which, as experience has taught, is ever the bane of an overflowing treasury.

It was made apparent in the course of the animated discussions which this question aroused at the last session of Congress that the policy of diminishing the revenue by reducing taxation commanded the general approval of the members of both Houses.

I regret that because of conflicting views as to the best methods by which that policy should be made operative none of its benefits have as yet been reaped.

In fulfillment of what I deem my constitutional duty, but with little hope that I can make valuable contribution to this vexed question, I shall proceed to intimate briefly my own views in relation to it.

Upon the showing of our financial condition at the close of the last fiscal year, I felt justified in recommending to Congress the abolition of all internal revenue taxes except those upon tobacco in its various forms and upon distilled spirits and fermented liquors, and except also the special tax upon the manufacturers of and dealers in such articles.

I venture now to suggest that unless it shall be ascertained that the probable expenditures of the Government for the coming year have been underestimated all internal taxes save those which relate to distilled spirits can be prudently abrogated.

Such a course, if accompanied by a simplification of the machinery of collection, which would then be easy of accomplishment, might reasonably be expected to result in diminishing the cost of such collection by at least $2,500,000 and in the retirement from office of from 1,500 to 2,000 persons.

The system of excise duties has never commended itself to the favor of the American people, and has never been resorted to except for supplying deficiencies in the Treasury when, by reason of special exigencies, the duties on imports have proved inadequate for the needs of the Government. The sentiment of the country doubtless demands that the present excise tax shall be abolished as soon as such a course can be safely pursued.

It seems to me, however, that, for various reasons, so sweeping a measure as the total abolition of internal taxes would for the present be an unwise step.

Two of these reasons are deserving of special mention:

First. It is by no means clear that even if the existing system of duties on imports is continued without modification those duties alone will yield sufficient revenue for all the needs of the Government. It is estimated that $100,000,000 will be required for pensions during the coming year, and it may well be doubted whether the maximum annual demand for that object has yet been reached. Uncertainty upon this question would alone justify, in my judgment, the retention for the present of that portion of the system of internal revenue which is least objectionable to the people.

Second. A total abolition of excise taxes would almost inevitably prove a serious if not an insurmountable obstacle to a thorough revision of the tariff and to any considerable reduction in import duties.

The present tariff system is in many respects unjust. It makes unequal distributions both of its burdens and its benefits. This fact was practically recognized by a majority of each House of Congress in the passage of the act creating the Tariff Commission. The report of that commission will be placed before you at the beginning of this session, and will, I trust, afford you such information as to the condition and prospects of the various commercial, agricultural, manufacturing, mining, and other interests of the country and contain such suggestions for statutory revision as will practically aid your action upon this important subject.

The revenue from customs for the fiscal year ended June 30, 1879, amounted to $137,000,000.

It has in the three succeeding years reached, first, $186,000,000, then $198,000,000, and finally, as has been already stated, $220,000,000.

The income from this source for the fiscal year which will end on June 30, 1883, will doubtless be considerably in excess of the sum last mentioned.

If the tax on domestic spirits is to be retained, it is plain, therefore, that large reductions from the customs revenue are entirely feasible. While recommending this reduction, I am far from advising the abandonment of the policy of so discriminating in the adjustment of details as to afford aid and protection to domestic labor. But the present system should be so revised as to equalize the public burden among all classes and occupations and bring it into closer harmony with the present needs of industry.

Without entering into minute detail, which under present circumstances is quite unnecessary, I recommend an enlargement of the free list so as to include within it the numerous articles which yield inconsiderable revenue, a simplification of the complex and inconsistent schedule of duties upon certain manufactures, particularly those of cotton, iron, and steel, and a substantial reduction of the duties upon those articles and upon sugar, molasses, silk, wool, and woolen goods.

If a general revision of the tariff shall be found to be impracticable at this session, I express the hope that at least some of the more conspicuous inequalities of the present law may be corrected before your final adjournment. One of them is specially referred to by the Secretary. In view of a recent decision of the Supreme Court, the necessity of amending the law by which the Dutch standard of color is adopted as the test of the saccharine strength of sugars is too obvious to require comment.

From the report of the Secretary of War it appears that the only outbreaks of Indians during the past year occurred in Arizona and in the southwestern part of New Mexico. They were promptly quelled, and the quiet which has prevailed in all other parts of the country has permitted such an addition to be made to the military force in the region endangered by the Apaches that there is little reason to apprehend trouble in the future.

Those parts of the Secretary's report which relate to our seacoast defenses and their armament suggest the gravest reflections. Our existing fortifications are notoriously inadequate to the defense of the great harbors and cities for whose protection they were built.

The question of providing an armament suited to our present necessities has been the subject of consideration by a board, whose report was transmitted to Congress at the last session. Pending the consideration of that report, the War Department has taken no steps for the manufacture or conversion of any heavy cannon, but the Secretary expresses the hope that authority and means to begin that important work will be soon provided. I invite the attention of Congress to the propriety of making more adequate provision for arming and equipping the militia than is afforded by the act of 1808, which is still upon the statute book. The matter has already been the subject of discussion in the Senate, and a bill which seeks to supply the deficiencies of existing laws is now upon its calendar.

The Secretary of War calls attention to an embarrassment growing out of the recent act of Congress making the retirement of officers of the Army compulsory at the age of 64. The act of 1878 is still in force, which limits to 400 the number of those who can be retired for disability or upon their own application. The two acts, when construed together, seem to forbid the relieving, even for absolute incapacity, of officers who do not fall within the purview of the later statute, save at such times as there chance to be less than 400 names on the retired list. There are now 420. It is not likely that Congress intended this result, and I concur with the Secretary that the law ought to be amended.

The grounds that impelled me to withhold my signature from the bill entitled "An act making appropriations for the construction, repair, and preservation of certain works on rivers and harbors," which became a law near the close of your last session, prompt me to express the hope that no similar measure will be deemed necessary during the present session of Congress. Indeed, such a measure would now be open to a serious objection in addition to that which was lately urged upon your attention. I am informed by the Secretary of War that the greater portion of the sum appropriated for the various items specified in that act remains unexpended.

Of the new works which it authorized, expenses have been incurred upon two only, for which the total appropriation was $210,000. The present available balance is disclosed by the following table:

Amount of appropriation by act of August 2, 1882	$18,738,875
Amount of appropriation by act of June 19, 1882	10,000
Amount of appropriation for payments to J. B. Eads	304,000
Unexpended balance of former appropriations	4,738,263
	23,791,138
Less amount drawn from Treasury between July 1, 1882, and November 30, 1882	6,056,194
	17,734,944

It is apparent by this exhibit that so far as concerns most of the items to which the act of August 2, 1882, relates there can be no need of further appropriations until after the close of the present session. If, however, any action should seem to be necessary in respect to particular objects, it will be entirely feasible to provide for those objects by appropriate legislation. It is possible, for example, that a delay until the assembling of the next Congress to make additional provision for the Mississippi River improvements might be attended with serious consequences. If such should appear to be the case, a just bill relating to that subject would command my approval.

This leads me to offer a suggestion which I trust will commend itself to the wisdom of Congress. Is it not advisable that grants of considerable sums of money for diverse and independent schemes of internal improvement should be made the subjects of separate and distinct legislative enactments? It will scarcely be gainsaid, even by those who favor the most liberal expenditures for such purposes as are sought to be accomplished by what is commonly called the river and harbor bill, that the practice of grouping in such a bill appropriations for a great diversity of objects, widely separated either in their nature or in the locality with which they are concerned, or in both, is one which is much to be deprecated unless it is irremediable. It inevitably tends to secure the success of the bill as a whole, though many of the items, if separately considered, could scarcely fail of rejection. By the adoption of the course I have recommended every member of Congress, whenever opportunity should arise for giving his influence and vote for meritorious appropriations, would be enabled so to do without being called upon to sanction others undeserving his approval. So also would the Executive be afforded thereby full opportunity to exercise his constitutional prerogative of opposing whatever appropriations seemed to him objectionable without imperiling the success of others which commended themselves to his judgment.

It may be urged in opposition to these suggestions that the number of works of internal improvement which are justly entitled to governmental aid is so great as to render impracticable separate appropriation bills therefor, or even for such comparatively limited number as make disposition of large sums of money. This objection may be well founded, and, whether it be or not, the advantages which would be likely to ensue from the adoption of the course I have recommended may perhaps be more effectually attained by another, which I respectfully submit to Congress as an alternative proposition.

It is provided by the constitutions of fourteen of our States that the executive may disapprove any item or items of a bill appropriating money, whereupon the part of the bill approved shall be law and the part disapproved shall fail to become law unless repassed according to the provisions prescribed for the passage of bills over the veto of the executive. The States wherein some such provision as the foregoing is a, part of the fundamental law are Alabama, California, Colorado, Florida, Georgia, Louisiana, Minnesota, Missouri, Nebraska, New Jersey, New York, Pennsylvania, Texas, and West Virginia. I commend to your careful consideration the question whether an amendment of the Federal Constitution in the particular indicated would not afford the best remedy for what is often a grave embarrassment both to members of Congress and to the Executive, and is sometimes a serious public mischief.

The report of the Secretary of the Navy states the movements of the various squadrons during the year, in home and foreign waters, where our officers and seamen, with such ships as we possess, have continued to illustrate the high character and excellent discipline of the naval organization.

On the 21st of December, 1881, information was received that the exploring steamer *Jeannette* had been crushed and abandoned in the Arctic Ocean. The officers and crew, after a journey over the ice, embarked in three boats for the coast of Siberia. One of the parties, under the command of Chief Engineer George W. Melville, reached the land, and, falling in with the natives, was saved. Another, under Lieutenant-Commander De Long, landed in a barren region near the mouth of the Lena River. After six weeks had elapsed all but two of the number had died from fatigue and starvation. No tidings have been received from the party in the third boat, under the command of Lieutenant Chipp, but a long and fruitless investigation leaves little doubt that all its members perished at sea. As a slight tribute to their heroism I give in this communication the names of the gallant men who sacrificed their lives on this expedition: Lieutenant-Commander George W. De Long, Surgeon James M. Ambler, Jerome J. Collins, Hans Halmer Erichsen, Heinrich H. Kaacke, George W. Boyd, Walter Lee, Adolph Dressler, Carl A. Görtz, Nelse Iverson, the cook Ah Sam, and the Indian Alexy. The officers and men in the missing boat were Lieutenant Charles W. Chipp, commanding; William Dunbar, Alfred Sweetman, Walter Sharvell, Albert C. Kuehne, Edward Star, Henry D. Warren, and Peter E. Johnson.

Lieutenant Giles B. Harber and Master William H. Scheutze are now bringing home the remains of Lieutenant De Long and his comrades, in pursuance of the directions of Congress.

The *Rodgers*, fitted out for the relief of the *Jeannette* in accordance with the act of Congress of March 3, 1881, sailed from San Francisco June 16 under the command of Lieutenant Robert M. Berry. On November 30 she was accidentally destroyed by fire while in winter quarters in St. Lawrence Bay, but the officers and crew succeeded in escaping to the shore. Lieutenant Berry and one of his officers, after making a search for the *Jeannette* along the coast of Siberia, fell in with Chief Engineer Melville's party and returned home by way of Europe. The other officers and the crew of the *Rodgers* were brought from St. Lawrence Bay by the whaling steamer *North Star*. Master Charles F. Putnam, who had been placed in charge of a depot of supplies at Cape Serdze, returning to his post from St. Lawrence Bay across the ice in a blinding snow-storm, was carried out to sea and lost, notwithstanding all efforts to rescue him.

It appears by the Secretary's report that the available naval force of the United States consists of 37 cruisers, 14 single-turreted monitors, built during the rebellion, a large number of smoothbore guns and Parrott rifles, and 87 rifled cannon.

The cruising vessels should be gradually replaced by iron or steel ships, the monitors by modern armored vessels, and the armament by high-power rifled guns.   .

The reconstruction of our Navy, which was recommended in my last message, was begun by Congress authorizing, in its recent act, the construction of two large unarmored steel vessels of the character recommended by the late Naval Advisory Board, and subject to the final approval of a new advisory board to be organized as provided by that act. I call your attention to the recommendation of the Secretary and the board that authority be given to construct two more cruisers of smaller dimensions and one fleet dispatch vessel, and that appropriations be made for high-power rifled cannon for the torpedo service and for other harbor defenses.

Pending the consideration by Congress of the policy to be hereafter adopted in conducting the eight large navy-yards and their expensive establishments, the Secretary advocates the reduction of expenditures therefor to the lowest possible amounts.

For the purpose of affording the officers and seamen of the Navy opportunities for exercise and discipline in their profession, under appropriate control and direction, the Secretary advises that the Light-House Service and Coast Survey be transferred, as now organized, from the Treasury to the Navy Department; and he also suggests, for the reasons which he assigns, that a similar transfer may wisely be made of the cruising revenue vessels.

The Secretary forcibly depicts the intimate connection and interdependence of the Navy and the commercial marine, and invites attention to the continued decadence of the latter and the corresponding transfer of our growing commerce to foreign bottoms.

This subject is one of the utmost importance to the national welfare. Methods of reviving American shipbuilding and of restoring the United States flag in the ocean carrying trade should receive the immediate attention of Congress. We have mechanical skill and abundant material for the manufacture of modern iron steamships in fair competition with our commercial rivals. Our disadvantage in building ships is the greater cost of labor, and in sailing them, higher taxes, and greater interest on capital, while the ocean highways are already monopolized by our formidable competitors. These obstacles should in some way be overcome, and for our rapid communication with foreign lands we should not continue to depend wholly upon vessels built in the yards of other countries and sailing under foreign flags. With no United States steamers on the principal ocean lines or in any foreign ports, our facilities for extending our commerce are greatly restricted, while the nations which build and sail the ships and carry the mails and passengers obtain thereby conspicuous advantages in increasing their trade.

The report of the Postmaster-General gives evidence of the satisfactory condition of that Department and contains many valuable data and accompanying suggestions which can not fail to be of interest.

The information which it affords that the receipts for the fiscal year have exceeded the expenditures must be very gratifying to Congress and to the people of the country.

As matters which may fairly claim particular attention, I refer you to his observations in reference to the advisability of changing the present basis for fixing salaries and allowances, of extending the money-order system, and of enlarging the functions of the postal establishment so as to put under its control the telegraph system of the country, though from this last and most important recommendation I must withhold my concurrence.

At the last session of Congress several bills were introduced into the House of Representatives for the reduction of letter postage to the rate of 2 cents per half ounce.

I have given much study and reflection to this subject, and am thoroughly persuaded that such a reduction would be for the best interests of the public.

It has been the policy of the Government from its foundation to defray as far as possible the expenses of carrying the mails by a direct tax in the form of postage. It has never been claimed, however, that this service ought to be productive of a net revenue.

As has been stated already, the report of the Postmaster-General shows that there is now a very considerable surplus in his Department and that henceforth the receipts are likely to increase at a much greater ratio than the necessary expenditures. Unless some change is made in the existing laws, the profits of the postal service will in a very few years swell the revenues of the Government many millions of dollars. The time seems auspicious, therefore, for some reduction in the rates of postage. In what shall that reduction consist?

A review of the legislation which has been had upon this subject during the last thirty years discloses that domestic letters constitute the only class of mail matter which has never been favored by a substantial reduction of rates. I am convinced that the burden of maintaining the service falls most unequally upon that class, and that more than any other it is entitled to present relief.

That such relief may be extended without detriment to other public interests will be discovered upon reviewing the results of former reductions.

Immediately prior to the act of 1845 the postage upon a letter composed of a single sheet was as follows:

If conveyed—	Cents.
30 miles or less	6
Between 30 and 80 miles	10
Between 80 and 150 miles	12½
Between 150 and 400 miles	18¾
Over 400 miles	25

By the act of 1845 the postage upon a single letter conveyed for any distance under 300 miles was fixed at 5 cents and for any greater distance at 10 cents.

By the act of 1851 it was provided that a single letter, if prepaid, should be carried any distance not exceeding 3,000 miles for 3 cents and any greater distance for 6 cents.

It will be noticed that both of these reductions were of a radical character and relatively quite as important as that which is now proposed.

In each case there ensued a temporary loss of revenue, but a sudden and large influx of business, which substantially repaired that loss within three years.

Unless the experience of past legislation in this country and elsewhere goes for naught, it may be safely predicted that the stimulus of 33⅓ per cent reduction in the tax for carriage would at once increase the number of letters consigned to the mails.

The advantages of secrecy would lead to a very general substitution of sealed packets for postal cards and open circulars, and in divers other ways the volume of first-class matter would be enormously augmented. Such increase amounted in England, in the first year after the adoption of penny postage, to more than 125 per cent.

As a result of careful estimates, the details of which can not be here set out, I have become convinced that the deficiency for the first year after the proposed reduction would not exceed 7 per cent of the expenditures, or $3,000,000, while the deficiency after the reduction of 1845 was more than 14 per cent, and after that of 1851 was 27 per cent.

Another interesting comparison is afforded by statistics furnished me by the Post-Office Department.

The act of 1845 was passed in face of the fact that there existed a deficiency of more than $30,000. That of 1851 was encouraged by the slight surplus of $132,000. The excess of revenue in the next fiscal year is likely to be $3,500,000.

If Congress should approve these suggestions, it may be deemed desirable to supply to some extent the deficiency which must for a time result by increasing the charge for carrying merchandise, which is now only 16 cents per pound; but even without such an increase I am confident that the receipts under the diminished rates would equal the expenditures after the lapse of three or four years.

The report of the Department of Justice brings anew to your notice the necessity of enlarging the present system of Federal jurisprudence so as effectually to answer the requirements of the ever-increasing litigation with which it is called upon to deal.

The Attorney-General renews the suggestions of his predecessor that in the interests of justice better provision than the existing laws afford should be made in certain judicial districts for fixing the fees of witnesses and jurors.

In my message of December last I referred to pending criminal proceedings growing out of alleged frauds in what is known as the star-route service of the Post-Office Department, and advised you that I had enjoined upon the Attorney-General and associate counsel, to whom the interests of the Government were intrusted, the duty of prosecuting with the utmost vigor of the law all persons who might be found chargeable with those offenses. A trial of one of these cases has since occurred. It occupied for many weeks the attention of the supreme court of this District and was conducted with great zeal and ability. It resulted in a disagreement of the jury, but the cause has been again placed upon the calendar and will shortly be retried. If any guilty persons shall finally escape punishment for their offenses, it will not be for lack of diligent and earnest efforts on the part of the prosecution.

I trust that some agreement may be reached which will speedily enable Congress, with the concurrence of the Executive, to afford the commercial community the benefits of a national bankrupt law.

The report of the Secretary of the Interior, with its accompanying documents, presents a full statement of the varied operations of that Department. In respect to Indian affairs nothing has occurred which has changed or seriously modified the views to which I devoted much space in a former communication to Congress. I renew the recommendations therein contained as to extending to the Indian the protection of the law, allotting land in severalty to such as desire it, and making suitable provision for the education of youth. Such provision, as the Secretary forcibly maintains, will prove unavailing unless it is broad enough to include all those who are able and willing to make use of it, and should not solely relate to intellectual training, but also to instruction in such manual labor and simple industrial arts as can be made practically available.

Among other important subjects which are included within the Secretary's report, and which will doubtless furnish occasion for Congressional action, may be mentioned the neglect of the railroad companies to which large grants of land were made by the acts of 1862 and 1864 to take title thereto, and their consequent inequitable exemption from local taxation.

No survey of our material condition can fail to suggest inquiries as to the moral and intellectual progress of the people.

The census returns disclose an alarming state of illiteracy in certain portions of the country, where the provision for schools is grossly inadequate.

It is a momentous question for the decision of Congress whether immediate and substantial aid should not be extended by the General Government for supplementing the efforts of private beneficence and of State and Territorial legislation in behalf of education.

The regulation of interstate commerce has already been the subject of your deliberations. One of the incidents of the marvelous extension of the railway system of the country has been the adoption of such measures by the corporations which own or control the roads as have tended to impair the advantages of healthful competition and to make hurtful discriminations in the adjustment of freightage.

These inequalities have been corrected in several of the States by appropriate legislation, the effect of which is necessarily restricted to the limits of their own territory.

So far as such mischiefs affect commerce between the States or between any one of the States and a foreign country, they are subjects of national concern, and Congress alone can afford relief.

The results which have thus far attended the enforcement of the recent statute for the suppression of polygamy in the Territories are reported by the Secretary of the Interior. It is not probable that any additional legislation in this regard will be deemed desirable until the effect of existing laws shall be more closely observed and studied.

I congratulate you that the commissioners under whose supervision those laws have been put in operation are encouraged to believe that the evil at which they are aimed may be suppressed without resort to such radical measures as in some quarters have been thought indispensable for success.

The close relation of the General Government to the Territories preparing to be great States may well engage your special attention. It is there that the Indian disturbances mainly occur and that polygamy has found room for its growth. I can not doubt that a careful survey of Territorial legislation would be of the highest utility. Life and property would become more secure. The liability of outbreaks between Indians and whites would be lessened. The public domain would be more securely guarded and better progress be made in the instruction of the young.

Alaska is still without any form of civil government. If means were provided for the education of its people and for the protection of their lives and property, the immense resources of the region would invite permanent settlements and open new fields for industry and enterprise.

the extremes of climate, and in regulating and sustaining the flow of springs and streams is now well understood, and their importance in relation to the growth and prosperity of the country can not be safely disregarded. They are fast disappearing before destructive fires and the legitimate requirements of our increasing population, and their total extinction can not be long delayed unless better methods than now prevail shall be adopted for their protection and cultivation. The attention of Congress is invited to the necessity of additional legislation to secure the preservation of the valuable forests still remaining on the public domain, especially in the extreme Western States and Territories, where the necessity for their preservation is greater than in less mountainous regions, and where the prevailing dryness of the climate renders their restoration, if they are once destroyed, well-nigh impossible.

The communication which I made to Congress at its first session, in December last, contained a somewhat full statement of my sentiments in relation to the principles and rules which ought to govern appointments to public service.

Referring to the various plans which had theretofore been the subject of discussion in the National Legislature (plans which in the main were modeled upon the system which obtains in Great Britain, but which lacked certain of the prominent features whereby that system is distinguished), I felt bound to intimate my doubts whether they, or any of them, would afford adequate remedy for the evils which they aimed to correct.

I declared, nevertheless, that if the proposed measures should prove acceptable to Congress they would receive the unhesitating support of the Executive.

Since these suggestions were submitted for your consideration there has been no legislation upon the subject to which they relate, but there has meanwhile been an increase in the public interest in that subject, and the people of the country, apparently without distinction of party, have in various ways and upon frequent occasions given expression to their earnest wish for prompt and definite action. In my judgment such action should no longer be postponed.

I may add that my own sense of its pressing importance has been quickened by observation of a practical phase of the matter, to which attention has more than once been called by my predecessors.

The civil list now comprises about 100,000 persons, far the larger part of whom must, under the terms of the Constitution, be selected by the President either directly or through his own appointees.

In the early years of the administration of the Government the personal direction of appointments to the civil service may not have been an irksome task for the Executive, but now that the burden has increased fully a hundredfold it has become greater than he ought to bear, and it necessarily diverts his time and attention from the proper discharge of other duties no less delicate and responsible, and which in the very nature of things can not be delegated to other hands.

In the judgment of not a few who have given study and reflection to this matter, the nation has outgrown the provisions which the Constitution has established for filling the minor offices in the public service.

But whatever may be thought of the wisdom or expediency of changing the fundamental law in this regard, it is certain that much relief may be afforded, not only to the President and to the heads of the Departments, but to Senators and Representatives in Congress, by discreet legislation. They would be protected in a great measure by the bill now pending before the Senate, or by any other which should embody its important features, from the pressure of personal importunity and from the labor of examining conflicting claims and pretensions of candidates.

I trust that before the close of the present session some decisive action may be taken for the correction of the evils which inhere in the present methods of appointment, and I assure you of my hearty cooperation in any measures which are likely to conduce to that end.

As to the most appropriate term and tenure of the official life of the subordinate employees of the Government, it seems to be generally agreed that, whatever their extent or character, the one should be definite and the other stable, and that neither should be regulated by zeal in the service of party or fidelity to the fortunes of an individual.

It matters little to the people at large what competent person is at the head of this department or of that bureau if they feel assured that the removal of one and the accession of another will not involve the retirement of honest and faithful subordinates whose duties are purely administrative and have no legitimate connection with the triumph of any political principles or the success of any political party or faction. It is to this latter class of officers that the Senate bill, to which I have already referred, exclusively applies.

While neither that bill nor any other prominent scheme for improving the civil service concerns the higher grade of officials, who are appointed by the President and confirmed by the Senate, I feel bound to correct a prevalent misapprehension as to the frequency with which the present Executive has displaced the incumbent of an office and appointed another in his stead.

It has been repeatedly alleged that he has in this particular signally departed from the course which has been pursued under recent Administrations of the Government. The facts are as follows:

The whole number of Executive appointments during the four years immediately preceding Mr. Garfield's accession to the Presidency was 2,696. Of this number 244, or 9 per cent, involved the removal of previous incumbents.

The ratio of removals to the whole number of appointments was much the ～e during each of those four years.

In the first year, with 790 appointments, there were 74 removals, or 9.3 per cent; in the second, with 917 appointments, there were 85 removals, or 8.5 per cent; in the third, with 480 appointments, there were 48 removals, or 10 per cent; in the fourth, with 429 appointments, there were 37 removals, or 8.6 per cent. In the four months of President Garfield's Administration there were 390 appointments and 89 removals, or 22.7 per cent. Precisely the same number of removals (89) has taken place in the fourteen months which have since elapsed, but they constitute only 7.8 per cent of the whole number of appointments (1,118) within that period and less than 2.6 of the entire list of officials (3,459), exclusive of the Army and Navy, which is filled by Presidential appointment.

I declare my approval of such legislation as may be found necessary for supplementing the existing provisions of law in relation to political assessments.

In July last I authorized a public announcement that employees of the Government should regard themselves as at liberty to exercise their pleasure in making or refusing to make political contributions, and that their action in that regard would in no manner affect their official status.

In this announcement I acted upon the view, which I had always maintained and still maintain, that a public officer should be as absolutely free as any other citizen to give or to withhold a contribution for the aid of the political party of his choice. It has, however, been urged, and doubtless not without foundation in fact, that by solicitation of official superiors and by other modes such contributions have at times been obtained from persons whose only motive for giving has been the fear of what might befall them if they refused. It goes without saying that such contributions are not voluntary, and in my judgment their collection should be prohibited by law. A bill which will effectually suppress them will receive my cordial approval.

I hope that, however numerous and urgent may be the demands upon your attention, the interests of this District will not be forgotten.

The denial to its residents of the great right of suffrage in all its relations to national, State, and municipal action imposes upon Congress the duty of affording them the best administration which its wisdom can devise.

The report of the District Commissioners indicates certain measures whose adoption would seem to be very desirable. I instance in particular those which relate to arrears of taxes, to steam railroads, and to assessments of real property.

Among the questions which have been the topic of recent debate in the halls of Congress none are of greater gravity than those relating to the ascertainment of the vote for Presidential electors and the intendment of the Constitution in its provisions for devolving Executive functions upon the Vice-President when the President suffers from inability to discharge the powers and duties of his office.

I trust that no embarrassments may result from a failure to determine these questions before another national election.

The closing year has been replete with blessings, for which we owe to the Giver of All Good our reverent acknowledgment. For the uninterrupted harmony of our foreign relations, for the decay of sectional animosities, for the exuberance of our harvests and the triumphs of our mining and manufacturing industries, for the prevalence of health, the spread of intelligence, and the conservation of the public credit, for the growth of the country in all the elements of national greatness—for these and countless other blessings we should rejoice and be glad. I trust that under the inspiration of this great prosperity our counsels may be harmonious, and that the dictates of prudence, patriotism, justice, and economy may lead to the adoption of measures in which the Congress and the Executive may heartily unite.

CHESTER A. ARTHUR.

SPECIAL MESSAGES.

EXECUTIVE MANSION, *December 6, 1882.*

To the Senate and House of Representatives:

I transmit herewith a communication from the Secretary of War, dated the 4th instant, and its accompanying papers, in which it is recommended that section 1216, Revised Statutes, be so amended as to include in its provisions the enlisted men of the Army, and that section 1285, Revised Statutes, be modified so as to read:

A certificate of merit granted to an enlisted man for distinguished service shall entitle him thereafter to additional pay, at the rate of $2 per month, while he is in the military service, although such service may not be continuous.

CHESTER A. ARTHUR.

EXECUTIVE MANSION, *December 6, 1882.*

To the Senate and House of Representatives:

I transmit herewith a communication from the Secretary of War, dated the 4th instant, setting forth certain facts respecting the title to the peninsula of Presque Isle, at Erie, Pa., and recommending that the subject be presented to Congress with the view of legislation by that body modifying the act of May 27, 1882, entitled "An act to authorize the Secretary of War to accept the peninsula in Lake Erie opposite the harbor of Erie, in the State of Pennsylvania" (17 U. S. Statutes at Large, p. 162), so as to authorize the Secretary of War to accept title to the said peninsula, proffered by the marine hospital of Pennsylvania pursuant to an act of the legislature of that State approved by the governor May 11, 1871.

CHESTER A. ARTHUR

EXECUTIVE MANSION, *December 6, 1882.*

To the Senate and House of Representatives:

I transmit herewith, for the consideration of Congress, a communication from the Secretary of War, inclosing one from the commanding general Department of the Missouri, indorsed by the division commander, urging the advisability of prompt action in the matter of perfecting the title to the site of Fort Bliss, Tex.

Accompanying also is a copy of Senate Executive Document No. 96, Forty-seventh Congress, first session, which presents fully the facts in the case, as well as the character of the legislation necessary to secure to the United States proper title to the land in question.

The Secretary of War expresses his concurrence in the views of the military authorities as to the importance of this subject and urges that the requisite legislation be had by Congress at its present session.

CHESTER A. ARTHUR.

EXECUTIVE MANSION, *December 8, 1882.*

To the Senate and House of Representatives:

I transmit herewith a communication from the Secretary of the Interior, with a draft of a bill and accompanying papers, to accept and ratify an agreement made by the Pi-Ute Indians, and granting a right of way to the Carson and Colorado Railroad Company through the Walker River Reservation, in Nevada.

The subject is presented for the consideration of Congress.

CHESTER A. ARTHUR.

EXECUTIVE MANSION,
Washington, December 13, 1882.

To the House of Representatives:

In response to the resolution of the House of Representatives of the 30th of January, 1882, on the subject of the tariff of consular fees, I transmit herewith a report of the Secretary of State.

CHESTER A. ARTHUR.

EXECUTIVE MANSION, *December 15, 1882.*

To the Senate and House of Representatives:

I transmit herewith, for the consideration of Congress, a letter from the Secretary of the Interior, inclosing a copy of a letter from the acting governor of New Mexico, in which he sets forth reasons why authority should be given and provision made for holding a session of the Territorial legislature of New Mexico in January, 1883, or soon thereafter.

CHESTER A. ARTHUR.

EXECUTIVE MANSION, *December 19, 1882.*

To the Senate and House of Representatives:

I transmit herewith, for the consideration of Congress, a communication from the Secretary of War, upon the subject of abandoned military reservations, and renewing his former recommendation for such legislation as will provide for the disposal of military sites that are no longer needed for military purposes.

CHESTER A. ARTHUR.

EXECUTIVE MANSION, *December 21, 1882.*

To the Senate and House of Representatives:

I transmit herewith a communication from the Secretary of the Interior of the 18th instant, with accompanying papers, submitting a draft of a bill ''for the relief of the Nez Percé Indians in the Territory of Idaho and of the allied tribes residing upon the Grande Ronde Indian Reservation, in the State of Oregon.''

The subject is presented for the consideration of Congress.

CHESTER A. ARTHUR.

EXECUTIVE MANSION, *December 27, 1882.*

To the Senate and House of Representatives:

I submit herewith a letter from the Secretary of the Interior, inclosing a communication from the secretary of the Territory of New Mexico, who has custody of the public buildings at Santa Fe, in which are set forth reasons why an appropriation should be made for the completion of the capitol at Santa Fe, and commend the same to the consideration of Congress.

CHESTER A. ARTHUR.

EXECUTIVE MANSION, *January 5, 1883.*

To the Senate and House of Representatives:

I transmit herewith a communication from the Secretary of the Interior, together with a letter from the Superintendent of the Census, requesting an additional appropriation of $100,000 to complete the work of the Tenth Census, and recommend the same to Congress for its favorable consideration.

CHESTER A. ARTHUR.

EXECUTIVE MANSION, *January 5, 1883.*

To the Senate and House of Representatives:

I transmit herewith, for the consideration of Congress, a communication from the Secretary of War, dated the 2d instant, and inclosing one from Lieutenant Robert Craig, Fourth Artillery, indorsed by the Chief

Signal Officer of the Army, recommending that Congress authorize the printing and binding for the use of the Signal Office of 10,000 copies of the Annual Report of the Chief Signal Officer for the fiscal year 1882, and inclosing a draft of a joint resolution for the purpose.

CHESTER A. ARTHUR.

EXECUTIVE MANSION, *January 9, 1883.*
To the Senate and House of Representatives:

I transmit herewith a communication from the Secretary of the Interior, submitting a report, with accompanying papers, regarding the condition of the several libraries of said Department and the consolidation of the same.

CHESTER A. ARTHUR.

EXECUTIVE MANSION,
Washington, January 10, 1883.
To the Senate of the United States:

The Senate having by executive resolution of the 20th ultimo returned to me the supplemental convention of extradition signed August 7, 1882, in order that certain verbal changes therein might be made, as requested by the Spanish Government, as explained in the letter of the Secretary of State to the Committee on Foreign Relations of the Senate dated the 15th ultimo, I now lay the said convention so modified before the Senate, with a view to its ratification.

CHESTER A. ARTHUR.

EXECUTIVE MANSION, *January 11, 1883.*
To the Senate and House of Representatives:

I transmit herewith, for the consideration of Congress, a communication from the Secretary of War, dated the 10th instant, inclosing one from the Chief of Ordnance, together with one from Lieutenant-Colonel D. W. Flagler, commanding the Rock Island Arsenal, Ill., setting forth the insufficiency of the sum appropriated by the sundry civil appropriation act of August 7, 1882, for the deepening of the water-power tail-race canal at that arsenal, and recommending that a special appropriation of $20,000 be made for the completion of said work.

CHESTER A. ARTHUR.

EXECUTIVE MANSION, *January 12, 1883.*
To the House of Representatives:

I transmit herewith a report of the Secretary of State and accompanying papers, furnished in response to the resolution of the House of Representatives of July 15, 1882, calling for any information in the possession of the Department of State in reference to any change or modification of the stipulations which the French Cable Company made with the Government.

CHESTER A. ARTHUR.

EXECUTIVE MANSION, *January 19, 1883.*
To the Senate and House of Representatives:

I transmit herewith, for the consideration of Congress, a communication from the Secretary of War, dated the 17th instant, inclosing, with other papers on the subject, a petition of Thomas Mulvihill, of Pittsburg, Pa., praying for the repossession of certain shore lands at Pittsburg erroneously conveyed by him to the United States.

CHESTER A. ARTHUR.

EXECUTIVE MANSION, *January 19, 1883.*
To the Senate and House of Representatives:

I transmit herewith a communication, dated the 18th instant, from the Secretary of the Interior, with accompanying papers, in relation to the request of the Cherokee Indians in the Indian Territory for payment for lands in that Territory west of the ninety-sixth degree west longitude, the cession of which to the United States for the settlement of friendly Indians thereon is provided for in the sixteenth article of the treaty of July 19, 1866.

CHESTER A. ARTHUR.

EXECUTIVE MANSION, *January 19, 1883.*
To the Senate and House of Representatives:

I transmit herewith, for the consideration of Congress, a communication from the Secretary of War, dated the 17th instant, inclosing copies of letters respectively from the Chief of Engineers and Colonel A. F. Rockwell, in charge of public buildings and grounds in this city, urging the importance of an immediate appropriation of $1,000 for removing snow and ice from the walks and pavements in and around the various public reservations under his control during the remainder of the present fiscal year.

CHESTER A. ARTHUR.

EXECUTIVE MANSION, *January 19, 1883.*
To the Senate of the United States:

I have carefully considered the provisions of Senate bill No. 561, entitled "An act for the relief of Robert Stodart Wyld."

I am of the opinion that the general statute is sufficiently liberal to provide relief in all proper cases of destroyed United States bonds, and I believe that the act above referred to constitutes an evil precedent.

It is not, however, so objectionable as to call for my formal disapproval, and I have allowed it to become a law under the constitutional provision, contenting myself with communicating to the Senate, in which the bill originated, my disapproval of special legislation of this character.

CHESTER A. ARTHUR.

EXECUTIVE MANSION, *January 19, 1883.*
To the Senate and House of Representatives:

I transmit herewith, for the consideration of Congress, a communication from the Secretary of War, dated the 18th instant, inclosing an extract copy of a report of the Adjutant-General respecting the military reservation of Fort Cameron, Utah Territory, and recommending that authority be granted during the present session of Congress for the disposal of said reservation, it being no longer needed for military purposes.

CHESTER A. ARTHUR.

EXECUTIVE MANSION, *January 19, 1883.*
To the Senate and House of Representatives:

I transmit herewith a communication from the Secretary of the Interior, with a draft of a bill, and accompanying papers, to accept and ratify an agreement with the confederated tribes of Flathead, Kootenay, and Upper Pend d'Oreille Indians for the sale of a portion of their reservation in the Territory of Montana, required for the Northern Pacific Railroad, and to make the necessary appropriation for carrying the same into effect.

The subject is presented for the consideration of the Congress.

CHESTER A. ARTHUR.

EXECUTIVE MANSION,
Washington, January 23, 1883.
To the Senate of the United States:

In response to the resolution of the Senate of the United States dated January 5, 1883, requesting "that the Secretary of State be directed to transmit to the Senate copies of any letters on file in his Department from the consular service upon the subject of the shipment and discharge of seamen or payment of extra wages to seamen," I have to transmit a report of the Secretary of State on the subject.

CHESTER A. ARTHUR.

EXECUTIVE MANSION, *January 25, 1883.*
To the Senate and House of Representatives:

I transmit herewith a communication from the Secretary of State, concerning the character and condition of the library of the Department of

CHESTER A. ARTHUR.

EXECUTIVE MANSION, *January 26, 1883.*

To the House of Representatives:

It is hereby announced to the House of Congress in which it originated that the joint resolution (H. Res. 190) to refer certain claims to the
Court of Claims has been permitted to become a law under the constitutional provision. Its apparent purpose is to allow certain bankers to sue
in the Court of Claims for the amount of internal-revenue tax collected
from them without lawful authority, upon showing as matter of excuse
for not having brought their suits within the time limited by law that
they had entered into an agreement with the district attorney which was
in substance that they should be relieved of that necessity. I can not
concur in the policy of setting aside the bar of the statute in those cases
on such ground, but I have not deemed it necessary to return the joint
resolution with my objections for reconsideration.

CHESTER A. ARTHUR.

EXECUTIVE MANSION, *January 30, 1883.*

To the Senate of the United States:

I transmit herewith a copy of a communication to me from the Secretary of the Treasury.*

I have acted in conformity with the recommendations, oral and written,
which are therein set forth, concerning the action suggested to be that
which would best effectuate the purpose of section 1768 of the Revised
Statutes of the United States and be most considerate of the reputation
and interests of the public officer to be affected and most subservient to
the public interest.

CHESTER A. ARTHUR.

EXECUTIVE MANSION,
Washington, February 3, 1883.

To the Senate of the United States:

I transmit to the Senate, for consideration with a view to ratification,
the treaty of commerce which was signed in duplicate January 20, 1883,
by commissioners on the part of the United States and Mexico, with
accompanying papers.

The attention of the Senate is called to the statement in the third
protocol as to the insertion of the word "steel" in item No. (35) 66 of
the list appended to article 2 of the treaty. No further information as
to the possible correction therein referred to has yet reached me; but
as the session of the Senate will soon terminate, I deem it advisable to
transmit the treaty as signed, in the hope that its ratification may be
assented to.

While the treaty does not contain all the provisions desired by the

---

* Relating to the suspension of William H. Daniels, collector of customs for the district of Oswe-
gatchie, N. Y.

United States, the difficulties in the way of a full and complete settlement of matters of common interest to the two countries were such as to make me willing to approve it as an important step toward a desirable result, not doubting that, as time shall show the advantages of the system thus inaugurated, the Government will be able by supplementary agreements to insert the word "steel" and to perfect what is lacking in the instrument.

CHESTER A. ARTHUR.

EXECUTIVE MANSION, *February 3, 1883.*

To the Senate and House of Representatives:

I transmit herewith a communication from the Secretary of the Interior of the 1st instant, submitting a report made by the commission appointed under the provisions of the act of August 7, 1882, to treat with the Sioux Indians for a modification of their existing treaties, together with a copy of the agreement negotiated by that commission. The subject is presented for the favorable consideration of Congress.

CHESTER A. ARTHUR.

EXECUTIVE MANSION, *February 5, 1883.*

To the Senate and House of Representatives:

I transmit herewith, for the consideration of Congress, a communication from the Secretary of War, dated the 2d instant, in relation to the subject of invasion of the Indian Territory, and urging the importance of amending section 2148 of the Revised Statutes so as to impose a penalty of imprisonment for unlawful entry upon the Indian lands.

CHESTER A. ARTHUR.

EXECUTIVE MANSION,
Washington, February 5, 1883.

To the Senate of the United States:

Referring to my message to the Senate of the 3d instant, wherewith was transmitted, for consideration with a view to ratification, the treaty of commerce between Mexico and the United States which was signed at Washington on the 20th ultimo, I have now to inform the Senate that this Government is officially advised by that of Mexico, through its minister at this capital, that it assents to the insertion of the word "steel" in item No. (35) 86 of the list appended to article 2 of that treaty.

It is desired that the treaty be returned to me that the amendment may be made, after which it will be again sent to the Senate for final action.

CHESTER A. ARTHUR.

EXECUTIVE MANSION, *February 6, 1883.*

To the Senate of the United States:

I retransmit to the Senate the commercial treaty recently signed in this city by the commissioners of the United States and Mexico, as amended by the insertion of the word "steel" in item (35) 66 of the list appended to article 2 thereof.

CHESTER A. ARTHUR.

EXECUTIVE MANSION, *February 7, 1883.*

To the Senate and House of Representatives:

I transmit herewith a communication of the 3d instant, with accompanying papers, from the Secretary of the Interior, being a partial report upon the Cherokee Indian matters required under a clause in the sundry civil appropriation act of August 7, 1882.

CHESTER A. ARTHUR.

EXECUTIVE MANSION, *February 8, 1883.*

To the Senate and House of Representatives:

I transmit herewith a communication from the Secretary of the Interior of the 7th instant, with accompanying papers, setting forth the urgent necessity of stringent measures for the repression of the rapidly increasing evasions and violations of the laws relating to public lands, and of a special appropriation for the purpose both in the current and approaching fiscal years.

The subject is presented for the consideration of Congress.

CHESTER A. ARTHUR.

EXECUTIVE MANSION, *Washington, February 9, 1883.*

To the Senate of the United States:

I transmit herewith to the Senate, for its consideration with a view to ratification, a convention between the United States of America and the French Republic, for extending the term of the French and American claims convention, concluded at Washington on the 8th day of February, 1883.

CHESTER A. ARTHUR.

EXECUTIVE MANSION, *February 10, 1883.*

To the Senate and House of Representatives:

I transmit herewith, for the information of Congress, a copy of the report of the Board of Indian Commissioners for the year 1882. The report accompanies the message to the House of Representatives.

CHESTER A. ARTHUR.

EXECUTIVE MANSION, *February 10, 1883.*
To the House of Representatives:

I transmit herewith, in response to a resolution of the House of Representatives of the 25th ultimo, a report of the Secretary of State, in relation to export duties levied in foreign countries having commercial relations with the United States.

CHESTER A. ARTHUR.

EXECUTIVE MANSION, *February 12, 1883.*
To the Senate and House of Representatives:

I transmit herewith a communication of the 8th instant, with accompanying papers, from the Secretary of the Interior, comprising the further report in relation to matters of difference between the Eastern and Western bands of Cherokee Indians required by an item in the sundry civil act approved August 7, 1882 (pamphlet statutes, page 328).

CHESTER A. ARTHUR.

EXECUTIVE MANSION, *Washington, February 15, 1883.*
To the Senate of the United States:

I transmit herewith, in compliance with the resolution of the Senate of December 18, 1882, the report of Mr. George Earl Church upon Ecuador, which I have this day received from the Secretary of State.

CHESTER A. ARTHUR.

EXECUTIVE MANSION, *February 20, 1883.*
To the Senate and House of Representatives:

I transmit herewith, for the consideration of Congress, a letter from the Secretary of War, dated the 19th instant, inclosing a copy of one from Major George L. Gillespie, Corps of Engineers, dated the 15th instant, referring to the insufficiency of the sum ($39,000) appropriated by the sundry civil bill of August 7, 1882, for building the sea wall on Governors Island, New York Harbor, together with a copy of the indorsement of the Chief Engineer, showing the necessity for an additional appropriation of $15,000 for this purpose. The Secretary of War recommends that said additional sum of $15,000 be appropriated at the present session of Congress for the object stated.

CHESTER A. ARTHUR.

EXECUTIVE MANSION, *Washington, February 23, 1883.*
To the House of Representatives of the United States of America:

With reference to my message of the 12th ultimo on the same subject, I transmit herewith a further report of the Secretary of State, furnishing additional papers received since the date of his former report in response to a resolution of the House of Representatives of July 5, 1882, calling for any information in the possession of the Department of State in reference to any changes or modifications of the stipulations which the French Cable Company made with this Government.

CHESTER A. ARTHUR.

EXECUTIVE MANSION, *February 26, 1883.*

To the Senate and House of Representatives:

I transmit herewith, for the information of Congress, a copy of the annual report of the Government directors of the Union Pacific Railway Company, under date of the 19th instant.

The copy of the report referred to accompanies the message to the House of Representatives.

CHESTER A. ARTHUR.

EXECUTIVE MANSION, *February 27, 1883.*

To the Senate of the United States:

I transmit herewith a report of the Secretary of State, furnished in response to the resolution of the Senate of February 26, 1883, requesting information touching an alleged joint agreement between the ministers of the United States, of Great Britain, of France, and of Italy now serving in Peru.

CHESTER A. ARTHUR.

EXECUTIVE MANSION, *March 1, 1883.*

To the Senate of the United States:

Having approved the act recently passed by Congress "to regulate and improve the civil service of the United States," I deem it my duty to call your attention to the provision for the employment of a "chief examiner" contained in the third section of the act, which was the subject of consideration at the time of its approval.

I am advised by the Attorney-General that there is great doubt whether such examiner is not properly an officer of the United States because of the nature of his employment, its duration, emolument, and duties. If he be such, the provision for his employment (which involves an appointment by the Commission) is not in conformity with section 2, Article II of the Constitution. Assuming this to be the case, the result would be that the appointment of the chief examiner must be deemed to be vested in the President, by and with the advice and consent of the Senate, since in such case the appointment would not be otherwise provided for by law. Concurring in this opinion, I nominate Silas W. Burt, of New York, to be chief examiner of the Civil Service Commission.

CHESTER A. ARTHUR.

PROCLAMATIONS.

BY THE PRESIDENT OF THE UNITED STATES OF AMERICA.

A PROCLAMATION.

Whereas by the eighth section of an act entitled "An act to encourage the holding of a World's Industrial and Cotton Centennial Exposition in the year 1884," approved February 10, 1883, it was enacted as follows:

That whenever the President shall be informed by the said board of management that provision has been made for suitable buildings, or the erection of the same, for the purposes of said exposition, the President shall, through the Department of State, make proclamation of the same, setting forth the time at which the exhibition will open and the place at which it will be held; and such board of management shall communicate to the diplomatic representatives of all nations copies of the same and a copy of this act, together with such regulations as may be adopted by said board of management, for publication in their respective countries.

And whereas the duly constituted board of managers of the aforesaid World's Industrial and Cotton Centennial Exposition has informed me that provision has been made for the erection of suitable buildings for the purposes of said exposition:

Now, therefore, I, Chester A. Arthur, President of the United States of America, by authority of and in fulfillment of the requirements of said act approved February 10, 1883, do hereby declare and make known that the World's Industrial and Cotton Centennial Exposition will be opened on the first Monday in December, 1884, at the city of New Orleans, in the State of Louisiana, and will there be holden continuously until the 31st day of May, 1885.

In testimony whereof I have hereunto set my hand and caused the seal of the United States to be affixed.

[SEAL.] Done at the city of Washington, this 10th day of September, 1883, and of the Independence of the United States the one hundred and eighth.

CHESTER A. ARTHUR.

By the President:
FREDK. T. FRELINGHUYSEN,
Secretary of State.

BY THE PRESIDENT OF THE UNITED STATES OF AMERICA.

A PROCLAMATION.

In furtherance of the custom of this people at the closing of each year to engage, upon a day set apart for that purpose, in a special festival of praise to the Giver of All Good, I, Chester A. Arthur, President of the

United States, do hereby designate Thursday, the 29th day of November next, as a day of national thanksgiving.

The year which is drawing to an end has been replete with evidences of divine goodness.

The prevalence of health, the fullness of the harvests, the stability of peace and order, the growth of fraternal feeling, the spread of intelligence and learning, the continued enjoyment of civil and religious liberty—all these and countless other blessings are cause for reverent rejoicing.

I do therefore recommend that on the day above appointed the people rest from their accustomed labors and, meeting in their several places of worship, express their devout gratitude to God that He hath dealt so bountifully with this nation and pray that His grace and favor abide with it forever.

In witness whereof I have hereunto set my hand and caused the seal of the United States to be affixed.

[SEAL.]   Done at the city of Washington, this 26th day of October, A. D. 1883, and of the Independence of the United States the one hundred and eighth.

CHESTER A. ARTHUR.

By the President:
FREDK. T. FRELINGHUYSEN,
Secretary of State.

EXECUTIVE ORDERS.

DEPARTMENT OF STATE,
Washington, March 26, 1883.

SIR:* It is my melancholy duty to inform you that the Hon. Timothy O. Howe, Postmaster-General, and lately a Senator of the United States, died yesterday at Kenosha, Wis., at 2 o'clock in the afternoon. By reason of this afflicting event the President directs that the Executive Departments of the Government and the offices dependent thereon throughout the country will be careful to manifest by all customary and appropriate observances due honor to the memory of one so eminent in successive offices of public esteem and trust and so distinguished and respected as a citizen.

To this end the President directs that the Post-Office Department and its dependencies in this capital shall be draped in mourning for a period of thirty days; that the several Executive Departments shall be closed on Wednesday next, the day of the funeral of the deceased, and that on

---

* Addressed to the heads of the Executive Departments, etc.

all public buildings of the Government throughout the United States the national flag shall be draped in mourning and displayed at half-mast.

I have the honor to be, sir, your obedient servant,

FREDK. T. FRELINGHUYSEN.

EXECUTIVE MANSION,
Washington, April 2, 1883.

Under the provisions of section 1 of the "act making appropriations for the naval service for the fiscal year ending June 30, 1884, and for other purposes," approved March 3, 1883, the following-named officers of the Army and Navy will constitute a board for the purpose of examining and reporting to Congress which of the navy-yards or arsenals owned by the Government has the best location and is best adapted for the establishment of a Government foundry, or what other method, if any, should be adopted for the manufacture of heavy ordnance adapted to modern warfare, for the use of the Army and Navy of the United States, the cost of all buildings, tools, and implements necessary to be used in the manufacture thereof, including the cost of a steam hammer or apparatus of sufficient size for the manufacture of the heaviest guns:

Commodore Edward Simpson, United States Navy; Captain Edmund O. Matthews, United States Navy; Colonel Thomas G. Baylor, Ordnance Department, United States Army; Lieutenant-Colonel Henry L. Abbot, Engineer Corps, United States Army; Major Samuel S. Elder, Second Artillery, United States Army; Lieutenant William H. Jacques, United States Navy.

CHESTER A. ARTHUR.

EXECUTIVE MANSION, *May 7, 1883.*

In the exercise of the power vested in the President by the Constitution, and by virtue of the seventeen hundred and fifty-third section of the Revised Statutes and of the civil-service act approved January 16, 1883, the following rules for the regulation and improvement of the executive civil service are hereby promulgated:

RULE I.

No person in the public service shall use his official authority or influence either to coerce the political action of any person or body or to interfere with any election.

RULE II.

No person in the public service shall for that reason be under any obligations to contribute to any political fund or to render any political service, and he will not be removed or otherwise prejudiced for refusing to do so.

RULE III.

It shall be the duty of collectors, postmasters, assistant treasurers, naval officers, surveyors, appraisers, and custodians of public buildings at places where examinations are to be held to allow and arrange for the reasonable use of suitable rooms in the public buildings in their charge, and for heating, lighting, and furnishing the same for the purposes of such examinations; and all other executive officers shall in all legal and proper ways facilitate such examinations and the execution of these rules.

RULE IV.

1. All officials connected with any office where or for which any examination is to take place will give the Civil Service Commission and the chief examiner such information as may be reasonably required to enable the Commission to select competent and trustworthy examiners; and the examinations by those selected as examiners, and the work incident thereto, will be regarded as a part of the public business to be performed at such office.

2. It shall be the duty of every executive officer promptly to inform the Commission, in writing, of the removal or discharge from the public service of any examiner in his office or of the inability or refusal of any such examiner to act in that capacity.

RULE V.

There shall be three branches of the service classified under the civil-service act (not including laborers or workmen or officers required to be confirmed by the Senate), as follows:

1. Those classified in the Departments at Washington shall be designated "The classified departmental service."

2. Those classified under any collector, naval officer, surveyor, or appraiser in any customs district shall be designated "The classified customs service."

3. Those classified under any postmaster at any post-office, including that at Washington, shall be designated "The classified postal service."

4. The classified customs service shall embrace the several customs districts where the officials are as many as fifty, now the following: New York City, N. Y.; Boston, Mass.; Philadelphia, Pa.; San Francisco, Cal.; Baltimore, Md.; New Orleans, La.; Chicago, Ill.; Burlington, Vt.; Portland, Me.; Detroit, Mich.; Port Huron, Mich.

5. The classified postal service shall embrace the several post-offices where the officials are as many as fifty, now the following: Albany, N. Y.; Baltimore, Md.; Boston, Mass.; Brooklyn, N. Y.; Buffalo, N. Y.; Chicago, Ill.; Cincinnati, Ohio; Cleveland, Ohio; Detroit, Mich.; Indianapolis, Ind.; Kansas City, Mo.; Louisville, Ky.; Milwaukee, Wis.; Newark, N. J.; New Orleans, La.; New York City, N. Y.; Philadelphia, Pa.; Pittsburg, Pa.; Providence, R. I.; Rochester, N. Y.; St. Louis, Mo.; San Francisco, Cal.; Washington, D. C.

RULE VI.

1. There shall be open competitive examinations for testing the fitness of applicants for admission to the service. Such examinations shall be practical in their character and, so far as may be, shall relate to those matters which will fairly test the relative capacity and fitness of the persons examined to discharge the duties of the branch of the service which they seek to enter.

2. There shall also be competitive examinations of a suitable character to test the fitness of persons for promotion in the service.

RULE VII.

1. The general examinations under the first clause of Rule VI for admission to the service shall be limited to the following subjects: (1) Orthography, penmanship,

and copying; 2 arithmetic—fundamental rules, fractions and percentage; 3 interest, discount, and elements of bookkeeping and 4 four other 5 elements of the English language, letter writing, and the proper construction of sentences; 5 elements of the geography, history, and government of the United States.

2. Proficiency in each of these subjects shall be tested by grading the standing of the persons examined in proportion to the nature of the knowledge of such subjects in the branch or part of the service which the applicant seeks to enter.

3. No one shall be entitled to be certified for appointment who se standing upon a just grading in the general examination shall be less than 65 per cent of complete proficiency in the first three subjects mentioned in this rule, and that measure of proficiency shall be deemed adequate.

4. But for places in which a lower degree of education will suffice the Commission may limit the examination to first penmanship, copying and orthography, second, the fundamental rules of arithmetic. But no person shall be certified under this examination of a less grading than 65 per cent in each subject.

5. The Commission may also order examinations of a higher grade or upon additional or special subjects, to test the capacity and fitness which may be needed in any special place or branch of the service.

RULE VIII

No question in any examination or proceeding by or under the Commission or examiners shall call for the expression or disclosure of any political or religious opinion or affiliation; nor shall any discrimination be made by reason thereof if known; and the Commission and its examiners shall discountenance all disclosure before either of them of such opinion by or concerning any applicants for examination or by or concerning anyone whose name is on any register awaiting appointment.

All regular applications for the competitive examinations for admission to the classified service must be made on blanks to be furnished as approved by the Commission. All requests for such blanks and all applications for examination must be addressed as follows: 1 If for the classified departmental service to the United States Civil Service Commission, Washington, D. C.; 2 if for the classified postal service to the postmaster under whom service is sought; 3 if for the classified customs service to the head of either customs office in which service is sought. All officers receiving such applications will indorse thereon the date of the reception thereof and transmit the same to the proper examining board of the district or office where service is sought or, if in Washington, to the Civil Service Commission.

RULE X.

Every examining board shall keep such records and such papers on file and make such reports as the Commission shall require, and any such paper or record in the charge of any examining board or any officer shall at all times be open to examination as the Commission shall direct, and upon its request shall be forwarded to the Commission for inspection and revision.

RULE XI.

Every application, in order to entitle the applicant to appear for examination or to be examined, must state under oath the facts on the following subjects: 1 Full name, residence, and post-office address; 2 citizenship; 3 age; 4 place of birth; (5) health and physical capacity for the public service; 6 right of preference by reason of military or naval service; (7) previous employment in the public service; (8) business or employment and residence for the previous five years; (9) education. Such other information shall be furnished as the Commission may reasonably require touching the applicant's fitness for the public service. The applicant must also state the number of members of his family in the public service and where employed, and must also assert that he is not disqualified under section 3 of the civil-service act, which is as follows:

"That no person habitually using intoxicating beverages to excess shall be appointed to or retained in any office, appointment, or employment to which the provisions of this act are applicable."

RULE XII.

1. Every regular application must be supported by proper certificates of good moral character, health, and physical and mental capacity for doing the public work, the certificates to be in such form and number as the regulations of the Commission shall provide; but no certificate will be received which is inconsistent with the tenth section of the civil-service act.

2. No one shall be entitled to be examined for admission to the classified postal service if under 16 or over 35 years of age, or to the classified customs service or to the classified departmental service if under 18 or over 45 years of age; but no one shall be examined for appointment to any place in the classified customs service, except that of clerk or messenger, who is under 21 years of age; but these limitations of age shall not apply to honorably discharged soldiers and sailors of the last war who are otherwise duly qualified.

RULE XIII.

1. The date of the reception of all regular applications for the classified departmental service shall be entered of record by the Commission, and of all other regular applications by the proper examining boards of the district or office for which they are made; and applicants, when in excess of the number that can be examined at a single examination, shall be notified to appear in their order on the respective records. But any applicants in the several States and Territories for appointment in the classified departmental service may be notified to appear for examination at any place at which an examination is to be held, whether in any State or Territory or in Washington, which shall be deemed most convenient for them.

2. The Commission is authorized, in aid of the apportionment among the States and Territories, to hold examinations at places convenient for applicants from different States and Territories, or for those examination districts which it may designate and which the President shall approve.

RULE XIV.

Those examined shall be graded, and shall have their grade marked upon a register after those previously thereon, in the order of their excellence as shown by their examination papers, except that those from the same State or Territory may be entered upon the register together, in the order of relative excellence, to facilitate apportionment. Separate registers may be kept of those seeking to enter any part of the service in which special qualifications are required.

RULE XV.

The Commission may give a certificate to any person examined, stating the grade which such person attained and the proficiency in the several subjects, shown by the markings.

RULE XVI.

1. Whenever any officer having the power of appointment or employment shall so request, there shall be certified to him by the Commission or the proper examining board four names for the vacancy specified, to be taken from those graded highest on the proper register of those in his branch of the service and remaining eligible, regard being had to the apportionment of appointments to States and Territories; and from the said four a selection shall be made for the vacancy.

2. These certifications for the service at Washington shall be made in such order as to apportion, as nearly as may be practicable, the original appointments thereto among the States and Territories and the District of Columbia upon the basis of population as ascertained at the last preceding census.

3. In case the request for any such certification or any law or regulation shall call for those of either sex, the four highest of that sex shall be certified; otherwise sex shall be disregarded in such certification.

4. No person upon any register shall be certified more than three times to the same officer in the customs or postal service or more than twice to any department at Washington, unless upon request of the appointing officer; nor shall anyone remain eligible more than one year upon any register. And no person while remaining eligible on any register shall be admitted to a new examination of the same grade.

RULE XVII.

1. Every original appointment or employment in said classified service shall be for the probationary period of six months, at the end of which time, if the conduct and capacity of the person appointed have been found satisfactory, the probationer shall be absolutely appointed or employed, but otherwise be deemed out of the service.

2. Every officer under whom any probationer shall serve during any part of the probation provided for by these rules shall carefully observe the quality and value of the service rendered by such probationer, and shall report to the proper appointing officer, in writing, the facts observed by him, showing the character and qualifications of such probationer and of the service performed by him; and such reports shall be preserved on file.

3. Every false statement knowingly made by any person in his application for examination and every connivance by him at any false statement made in any certificate which may accompany his application shall be regarded as good cause for the removal or discharge of such person during his probation.

RULE XVIII.

Every head of a Department or office shall notify the Commission of the name of every person appointed to or employed in the classified service under him (giving the date of the appointment and the designation of the office or place) from those examined under the Commission, and shall also inform the Commission of the date of any rejection or final appointment or employment of any probationer and of the promotion, removal, discharge, resignation, transfer, or death of any such person after probation.

RULE XIX.

There are excepted from examination the following: (1) The confidential clerk or secretary of any head of a Department or office; (2) cashiers of collectors; (3) cashiers of postmasters; (4) superintendents of money-order divisions in post-offices; (5) the direct custodians of money for whose fidelity another officer is under official bond, but these exceptions shall not extend to any official below the grade of assistant cashier or teller; (6) persons employed exclusively in the secret service of the Government, or as translators or interpreters or stenographers; (7) persons whose employment is exclusively professional: 1 8 chief clerks, superintendents, and chiefs of divisions or bureaus. But no person so excepted shall be either transferred, appointed, or promoted, unless to some excepted place, without an examination under the Commission. Promotions may be made without examinations in offices where examinations for promotion are not now held until rules on the subject shall be promulgated.

RULE XX.

If the failure of competent persons to attend and be examined or the prevalence of contagious disease or other sufficient cause shall make it impracticable to supply in due season for any appointment the names of persons who have passed a competitve examination, the appointment may be made of a person who has passed a noncompetitive examination, which examination the Commission may provide for; but its next report shall give the reason for such resort to noncompetitive examination.

RULE XXI.

The Civil Service Commission will make appropriate regulations for carrying these rules into effect.

RULE XXII.

Every violation by any officer in the executive civil service of these rules or of the eleventh, twelfth, thirteenth, or fourteenth section of the civil-service act, relating to political assessments, shall be good cause for removal.

CHESTER A. ARTHUR.

EXECUTIVE MANSION, *May 21, 1883.*

Under the provisions of section 4 of the act approved March 3, 1883, it is hereby ordered that the several Executive Departments, the Department of Agriculture, and the Government Printing Office be closed on Wednesday, the 30th instant, to enable the employees to participate in the decoration of the graves of the soldiers who fell during the rebellion.

CHESTER A. ARTHUR.

WAR DEPARTMENT, *October 13, 1883.*

I. The President, having acceded to the request of General William T. Sherman to be relieved from the command of the Army on the 1st of November, 1883, preparatory to his retirement from active service, directs the following changes and assignments to command:

General William T. Sherman will be relieved from the command of the Army on the above-mentioned date and will repair to his home, St. Louis, Mo., to await his retirement. The General will be attended prior to his retirement by those of his aids-de-camp whom he may designate to the Adjutant-General.

Lieutenant-General Philip H. Sheridan will proceed to Washington, and on the above-mentioned date assume command of the Army.

Major-General John M. Schofield will proceed to Chicago, Ill., and will on the above-mentioned date assume command of the Military Division of the Missouri.

Major-General John Pope will proceed to the Presidio of San Francisco, Cal., and will on the above-mentioned date assume command of the Military Division of the Pacific and of the Department of California.

Brigadier-General Christopher C. Augur will proceed to Fort Leavenworth, and will on the above-mentioned date assume command of the Department of the Missouri.

Brigadier-General Ranald S. Mackenzie will proceed to San Antonio, Tex., and will on the above-mentioned date assume command of the Department of Texas.

II. The Department of the South will on the 1st day of November, 1883, be merged in the Department of the East, under the command of Major-General Hancock, commanding the Military Division of the Atlantic and the Department of the East.

ROBERT T. LINCOLN,
Secretary of War.

In the exercise of the power vested in the President by the Constitution, and by virtue of the seventeen hundred and fifty-third section of the Revised Statutes and of the civil-service act approved January 16, 1883, the following rules for the regulation and improvement of the executive civil service are hereby amended and promulgated, as follows:

RULE VI.

1. There shall be open competitive examinations for testing the fitness of applicants for admission to the service. Such examinations shall be practical in their character and, so far as may be, shall relate to those matters which will fairly test the relative capacity and fitness of the persons examined to discharge the duties of the branch of the service which they seek to enter.

2. There shall, so far as they may be deemed useful, be competitive examinations of a suitable character to test the fitness of persons for promotion in the service.

RULE VII.

1. The general examinations under the first clause of Rule VI for admission to the service shall be limited to the following subjects: (1) Orthography, penmanship, and copying; (2) arithmetic—fundamental rules, fractions, and percentage; (3) interest, discount, and elements of bookkeeping and of accounts; (4) elements of the English language, letter writing, and the proper construction of sentences; (5) elements of the geography, history, and government of the United States.

2. Proficiency in each of these subjects shall be credited in grading the standing of the persons examined in proportion to the value of a knowledge of such subjects in the branch or part of the service which the applicant seeks to enter.

3. No one shall be entitled to be certified for appointment whose standing upon a just grading in the general examination shall be less than 65 per cent of complete proficiency in the first three subjects mentioned in this rule, and that measure of proficiency shall be deemed adequate.

4. But for places in which a lower degree of education will suffice the Commission may limit the examinations to less than the five subjects above mentioned; but no

person shall be certified for appointment under this clause whose grading shall be less than an average of 65 per cent on such of the first three subjects or parts thereof as the examination may embrace.

5. The Commission may also order examinations upon other subjects, of a technical or special character, to test the capacity which may be needed in any part of the classified service which requires peculiar information or skill. Examinations hereunder may be competitive or noncompetitive, and the maximum limitations of age contained in the twelfth rule shall not apply to applicants for the same. The application for and notice of these special examinations, the records thereof, and the certification of those found competent shall be such as the Commission may provide for. After consulting the head of any Department or office the Commission may from time to time designate, subject to the approval of the President, the positions therein for which applicants may be required to pass this special examination.

RULE VIII.

No question in any examination or proceeding by or under the Commission or examiners shall call for the expression or disclosure of any political or religious opinion or affiliation, and if such opinion or affiliation be known no discrimination shall be made by reason thereof by the examiners, the Commission, or the appointing power. The Commission and its examiners shall discountenance all disclosure before either of them of such opinion by or concerning any applicant for examination or by or concerning anyone whose name is on any register awaiting appointment.

RULE XI.

Every application, in order to entitle the applicant to appear for examination or to be examined, must state under oath the facts on the following subjects: (1) Full name, residence, and post-office address; (2) citizenship; (3) age; (4) place of birth; (5) health and physical capacity for the public service; (6) right of preference by reason of military or naval service; (7) previous employment in the public service; (8) business or employment and residence for the previous five years; (9) education. Such other information shall be furnished as the Commission may reasonably require touching the applicant's fitness for the public service. The applicant must also state the number of members of his family in the public service and where employed, and must also assert that he is not disqualified under section 8 of the civil-service act, which is as follows:

"That no person habitually using intoxicating beverages to excess shall be appointed to or retained in any office, appointment, or employment to which the provisions of this act are applicable."

No person under enlistment in the Army or Navy of the United States shall be examined under these rules.

RULE XIII.

1. The date of the reception of all regular applications for the classified departmental service shall be entered of record by the Commission, and of all other regular applications by the proper examining boards of the district or office for which they are made; and applicants, when in excess of the number that can be examined at a single examination, shall, subject to the needs of apportionment, be notified to appear in their order on the respective records. But any applicants in the several States and Territories for appointment in the classified departmental service may be notified to appear for examination at any place at which an examination is to be held, whether in any State or Territory or in Washington, which shall be deemed most convenient for them.

2. The Commission is authorized, in aid of the apportionment among the States

and Territories, to hold examinations at places convenient for applicants from different States and Territories, or for those examination districts which it may designate and which the President shall approve.

RULE XVI.

1. Whenever any officer having the power of appointment or employment shall so request, there shall be certified to him by the Commission or the proper examining board four names for the vacancy specified, to be taken from those graded highest on the proper register of those in his branch of the service and remaining eligible, regard being had to the apportionment of appointments to States and Territories; and from the said four a selection shall be made for the vacancy.

2. These certifications for the service at Washington shall be made in such order as to apportion, as nearly as may be practicable, the original appointments thereto among the States and Territories and the District of Columbia upon the basis of population as ascertained at the last preceding census.

3. In case the request for any such certification or any law or regulation shall call for those of either sex, the four highest of that sex shall be certified; otherwise sex shall be disregarded in such certification.

4. No person upon any register shall be certified more than four times to the same officer in the customs or postal service or more than twice to any Department at Washington, unless upon request of the appointing officer; nor shall anyone remain eligible more than one year upon any register. No person while remaining eligible on any register shall be admitted to a new examination, and no person having failed upon any examination shall within six months thereafter be admitted to another examination without the consent of the Commission; but these restrictions shall not extend to examinations under clause 5 of Rule VII.

RULE XVIII.

Every head of a Department or office shall notify the Commission of the name of every person appointed to or employed in the classified service under him (giving the date of the appointment and the designation of the office or place) from those examined under the Commission, and shall also inform the Commission of the date of any rejection or final appointment or employment of any probationer, and of the promotion, removal, discharge, resignation, transfer, or death of any such person after probation. Every head of an office in the postal or customs service shall give such information on these subjects to the board of examiners for his office as the regulations of the Commission may provide for.

RULE XIX.

There are excepted from examination the following: (1) The confidential clerk or secretary of any head of Department or office; (2) cashiers of collectors; (3) cashiers of postmasters; (4) superintendents of money-order divisions in post-offices; (5) the direct custodians of money for whose fidelity another officer is under official bond, but these exceptions shall not extend to any official below the grade of assistant cashier or teller; (6) persons employed exclusively in the secret service of the Government, or as translators or interpreters or stenographers; (7) persons whose employment is exclusively professional; (8) chief clerks, deputy collectors, and superintendents or chiefs of divisions or bureaus. But no person so excepted shall be either transferred, appointed, or promoted, unless to some excepted place, without an examination under the Commission. Promotions may be made without examinations in offices where examinations for promotion are not now held until rules on the subject shall be promulgated.

Approved, November 7, 1883.   CHESTER A. ARTHUR.

THIRD ANNUAL MESSAGE.

WASHINGTON, *December 4, 1883.*

To the Congress of the United States:

At the threshold of your deliberations I congratulate you upon the favorable aspect of the domestic and foreign affairs of this Government.

Our relations with other countries continue to be upon a friendly footing. With the Argentine Republic, Austria, Belgium, Brazil, Denmark, Hayti, Italy, Santo Domingo, and Sweden and Norway no incident has occurred which calls for special comment. The recent opening of new lines of telegraphic communication with Central America and Brazil permitted the interchange of messages of friendship with the Governments of those countries.

During the year there have been perfected and proclaimed consular and commercial treaties with Servia and a consular treaty with Roumania, thus extending our intercourse with the Danubian countries, while our Eastern relations have been put upon a wider basis by treaties with Korea and Madagascar. The new boundary-survey treaty with Mexico, a trade-marks convention and a supplementary treaty of extradition with Spain, and conventions extending the duration of the Franco-American Claims Commission have also been proclaimed.

Notice of the termination of the fisheries articles of the treaty of Washington was duly given to the British Government, and the reciprocal privileges and exemptions of the treaty will accordingly cease on July 1, 1885. The fisheries industries, pursued by a numerous class of our citizens on the northern coasts, both of the Atlantic and Pacific oceans, are worthy of the fostering care of Congress. Whenever brought into competition with the like industries of other countries, our fishermen, as well as our manufacturers of fishing appliances and preparers of fish products, have maintained a foremost place. I suggest that Congress create a commission to consider the general question of our rights in the fisheries and the means of opening to our citizens, under just and enduring conditions, the richly stocked fishing waters and sealing grounds of British North America.

Question has arisen touching the deportation to the United States from the British Islands, by governmental or municipal aid, of persons unable there to gain a living and equally a burden on the community here. Such of these persons as fall under the pauper class as defined by law have been sent back in accordance with the provisions of our statutes. Her Majesty's Government has insisted that precautions have been taken before shipment to prevent these objectionable visitors from coming hither without guaranty of support by their relatives in this country. The action of the British authorities in applying measures for relief has, however, in so many cases proved ineffectual, and especially so in certain recent instances of needy emigrants reaching our territory through Canada, that a revision of our legislation upon this subject may be deemed advisable.

Correspondence relative to the Clayton-Bulwer treaty has been continued and will be laid before Congress.

The legislation of France against the importation of prepared swine products from the United States has been repealed. That result is due no less to the friendly representations of this Government than to a growing conviction in France that the restriction was not demanded by any real danger to health.

Germany still prohibits the introduction of all swine products from America. I extended to the Imperial Government a friendly invitation to send experts to the United States to inquire whether the use of those products was dangerous to health. This invitation was declined. I have believed it of such importance, however, that the exact facts should be ascertained and promulgated that I have appointed a competent commission to make a thorough investigation of the subject. Its members have shown their public spirit by accepting their trust without pledge of compensation, but I trust that Congress will see in the national and international bearings of the matter a sufficient motive for providing at least for reimbursement of such expenses as they may necessarily incur.

The coronation of the Czar at Moscow afforded to this Government an occasion for testifying its continued friendship by sending a special envoy and a representative of the Navy to attend the ceremony.

While there have arisen during the year no grave questions affecting the status in the Russian Empire of American citizens of other faith than that held by the national church, this Government remains firm in its conviction that the rights of its citizens abroad should be in no wise affected by their religious belief.

It is understood that measures for the removal of the restrictions which now burden our trade with Cuba and Puerto Rico are under consideration by the Spanish Government.

The proximity of Cuba to the United States and the peculiar methods of administration which there prevail necessitate constant discussion and appeal on our part from the proceedings of the insular authorities. I regret to say that the just protests of this Government have not as yet produced satisfactory results.

The commission appointed to decide certain claims of our citizens against the Spanish Government, after the recognition of a satisfactory rule as to the validity and force of naturalization in the United States, has finally adjourned. Some of its awards, though made more than two years ago, have not yet been paid. Their speedy payment is expected.

Claims to a large amount which were held by the late commission to be without its jurisdiction have been diplomatically presented to the

Spanish Government. As the action of the colonial authorities which has given rise to these claims was admittedly illegal, full reparation for the injury sustained by our citizens should be no longer delayed.

The case of the *Masonic* has not yet reached a settlement. The Manila court has found that the proceedings of which this Government has complained were unauthorized, and it is hoped that the Government of Spain will not withhold the speedy reparation which its sense of justice should impel it to offer for the unusual severity and unjust action of its subordinate colonial officers in the case of this vessel.

The Helvetian Confederation has proposed the inauguration of a class of international treaties for the referment to arbitration of grave questions between nations. This Government has assented to the proposed negotiation of such a treaty with Switzerland.

Under the treaty of Berlin liberty of conscience and civil rights are assured to all strangers in Bulgaria. As the United States have no distinct conventional relations with that country and are not a party to the treaty, they should, in my opinion, maintain diplomatic representation at Sofia for the improvement of intercourse and the proper protection of the many American citizens who resort to that country as missionaries and teachers. I suggest that I be given authority to establish an agency and consulate-general at the Bulgarian capital.

The United States are now participating in a revision of the tariffs of the Ottoman Empire. They have assented to the application of a license tax to foreigners doing business in Turkey, but have opposed the oppressive storage tax upon petroleum entering the ports of that country.

The Government of the Khedive has proposed that the authority of the mixed judicial tribunals in Egypt be extended so as to cover citizens of the United States accused of crime, who are now triable before consular courts. This Government is not indisposed to accept the change, but believes that its terms should be submitted for criticism to the commission appointed to revise the whole subject.

At no time in our national history has there been more manifest need of close and lasting relations with a neighboring state than now exists with respect to Mexico. The rapid influx of our capital and enterprise into that country shows, by what has already been accomplished, the vast reciprocal advantages which must attend the progress of its internal development. The treaty of commerce and navigation of 1848 has been terminated by the Mexican Government, and in the absence of conventional engagements the rights of our citizens in Mexico now depend upon the domestic statutes of that Republic. There have been instances of harsh enforcement of the laws against our vessels and citizens in Mexico and of denial of the diplomatic resort for their protection. The initial step toward a better understanding has been taken in the negotiation by the commission authorized by Congress of a treaty which is still before the Senate awaiting its approval.

The provisions for the reciprocal crossing of the frontier by the troops in pursuit of hostile Indians have been prolonged for another year. The operations of the forces of both Governments against these savages have been successful, and several of their most dangerous bands have been captured or dispersed by the skill and valor of United States and Mexican soldiers fighting in a common cause.

The convention for the resurvey of the boundary from the Rio Grande to the Pacific having been ratified and exchanged, the preliminary reconnoissance therein stipulated has been effected. It now rests with Congress to make provision for completing the survey and relocating the boundary monuments.

A convention was signed with Mexico on July 13, 1882, providing for the rehearing of the cases of Benjamin Weil and the Abra Silver Mining Company, in whose favor awards were made by the late American and Mexican Claims Commission. That convention still awaits the consent of the Senate. Meanwhile, because of those charges of fraudulent awards which have made a new commission necessary, the Executive has directed the suspension of payments of the distributive quota received from Mexico.

Our geographical proximity to Central America and our political and commercial relations with the States of that country justify, in my judgment, such a material increase of our consular corps as will place at each capital a consul-general.

The contest between Bolivia, Chile, and Peru has passed from the stage of strategic hostilities to that of negotiation, in which the counsels of this Government have been exercised. The demands of Chile for absolute cession of territory have been maintained and accepted by the party of General Iglesias to the extent of concluding a treaty of peace with the Government of Chile in general conformity with the terms of the protocol signed in May last between the Chilean commander and General Iglesias. As a result of the conclusion of this treaty General Iglesias has been formally recognized by Chile as President of Peru and his government installed at Lima, which has been evacuated by the Chileans. A call has been issued by General Iglesias for a representative assembly, to be elected on the 13th of January, and to meet at Lima on the 1st of March next. Meanwhile the provisional government of General Iglesias has applied for recognition to the principal powers of America and Europe. When the will of the Peruvian people shall be manifested, I shall not hesitate to recognize the government approved by them.

Diplomatic and naval representatives of this Government attended at Caracas the centennial celebration of the birth of the illustrious Bolivar. At the same time the inauguration of the statue of Washington in the Venezuelan capital testified to the veneration in which his memory is there held.

Congress at its last session authorized the Executive to propose to Venezuela a reopening of the awards of the mixed commission of Caracas. The departure from this country of the Venezuelan minister has delayed the opening of negotiations for reviving the commission. This Government holds that until the establishment of a treaty upon this subject the Venezuelan Government must continue to make the payments provided for in the convention of 1866.

There is ground for believing that the dispute growing out of the unpaid obligations due from Venezuela to France will be satisfactorily adjusted. The French cabinet has proposed a basis of settlement which meets my approval, but as it involves a recasting of the annual quotas of the foreign debt it has been deemed advisable to submit the proposal to the judgment of the cabinets of Berlin, Copenhagen, The Hague, London, and Madrid.

At the recent coronation of His Majesty King Kalakaua this Government was represented both diplomatically and by the formal visit of a vessel of war.

The question of terminating or modifying the existing reciprocity treaty with Hawaii is now before Congress. I am convinced that the charges of abuses and frauds under that treaty have been-exaggerated, and I renew the suggestion of last year's message that the treaty be modified wherever its provisions have proved onerous to legitimate trade between the two countries. I am not disposed to favor the entire cessation of the treaty relations which have fostered good will between the countries and contributed toward the equality of Hawaii in the family of nations.

In pursuance of the policy declared by this Government of extending our intercourse with the Eastern nations, legations have during the past year been established in Persia, Siam, and Korea. It is probable that permanent missions of those countries will ere long be maintained in the United States. A special embassy from Siam is now on its way hither.

Treaty relations with Korea were perfected by the exchange at Seoul, on the 19th of May last, of the ratifications of the lately concluded convention, and envoys from the King of Tah Chosen have visited this country and received a cordial welcome. Korea, as yet unacquainted with the methods of Western civilization, now invites the attention of those interested in the advancement of our foreign trade, as it needs the implements and products which the United States are ready to supply. We seek no monopoly of its commerce and no advantages over other nations, but as the Chosenese, in reaching for a higher civilization, have confided in this Republic, we can not regard with indifference any encroachment on their rights.

China, by the payment of a money indemnity, has settled certain of the long-pending claims of our citizens, and I have strong hopes that the remainder will soon be adjusted.

Questions have arisen touching the rights of American and other foreign manufacturers in China under the provisions of treaties which permit aliens to exercise their industries in that country. On this specific point our own treaty is silent, but under the operation of the most-favored-nation clause we have like privileges with those of other powers. While it is the duty of the Government to see that our citizens have the full enjoyment of every benefit secured by treaty, I doubt the expediency of leading in a movement to constrain China to admit an interpretation which we have only an indirect treaty right to exact. The transference to China of American capital for the employment there of Chinese labor would in effect inaugurate a competition for the control of markets now supplied by our home industries.

There is good reason to believe that the law restricting the immigration of Chinese has been violated, intentionally or otherwise, by the officials of China upon whom is devolved the duty of certifying that the immigrants belong to the excepted classes.

Measures have been taken to ascertain the facts incident to this supposed infraction, and it is believed that the Government of China will cooperate with the United States in securing the faithful observance of the law.

The same considerations which prompted Congress at its last session to return to Japan the Simonoseki indemnity seem to me to require at its hands like action in respect to the Canton indemnity fund, now amounting to $300,000.

The question of the general revision of the foreign treaties of Japan has been considered in an international conference held at Tokyo, but without definite result as yet. This Government is disposed to concede the requests of Japan to determine its own tariff duties, to provide such proper judicial tribunals as may commend themselves to the Western powers for the trial of causes to which foreigners are parties, and to assimilate the terms and duration of its treaties to those of other civilized states.

Through our ministers at London and at Monrovia this Government has endeavored to aid Liberia in its differences with Great Britain touching the northwestern boundary of that Republic. There is a prospect of adjustment of the dispute by the adoption of the Mannah River as the line. This arrangement is a compromise of the conflicting territorial claims and takes from Liberia no country over which it has maintained effective jurisdiction.

The rich and populous valley of the Kongo is being opened to commerce by a society called the International African Association, of which the King of the Belgians is the president and a citizen of the United States the chief executive officer. Large tracts of territory have been ceded to the association by native chiefs, roads have been opened, steamboats placed on the river, and the nuclei of states established at twenty-two stations under one flag which offers freedom to commerce and prohibits the slave trade.   The objects of the society are philanthropic.   It does not aim at permanent political control, but seeks the neutrality of the valley.   The United States can not be indifferent to this work nor to the interests of their citizens involved in it.   It may become advisable for us to cooperate with other commercial powers in promoting the rights of trade and residence in the Kongo Valley free from the interference or political control of any one nation.

In view of the frequency of invitations from foreign governments to participate in social and scientific congresses for the discussion of important matters of general concern, I repeat the suggestion of my last message that provision be made for the exercise of discretionary power by the Executive in appointing delegates to such convocations.   Able specialists are ready to serve the national interests in such capacity without personal profit or other compensation than the defrayment of expenses actually incurred, and this a comparatively small annual appropriation would suffice to meet.

I have alluded in my previous messages to the injurious and vexatious restrictions suffered by our trade in the Spanish West Indies. Brazil, whose natural outlet for its great national staple, coffee, is in and through the United States, imposes a heavy export duty upon that product.   Our petroleum exports are hampered in Turkey and in other Eastern ports by restrictions as to storage and by onerous taxation. For these mischiefs adequate relief is not always afforded by reciprocity treaties like that with Hawaii or that lately negotiated with Mexico and now awaiting the action of the Senate.   Is it not advisable to provide some measure of equitable retaliation in our relations with governments which discriminate against our own?   If, for example, the Executive were empowered to apply to Spanish vessels and cargoes from Cuba and Puerto Rico the same rules of treatment and scale of penalties for technical faults which are applied to our vessels and cargoes in the Antilles, a resort to that course might not be barren of good results.

The report of the Secretary of the Treasury gives a full and interesting exhibit of the financial condition of the country.

It shows that the ordinary revenues from all sources for the fiscal year ended June 30, 1883, amounted to $398,287,581.95, whereof there was received—

From customs	$214,706,496.93
From internal revenue	144,720,368.98
From sales of public lands	7,955,864.42
From tax on circulation and deposits of national banks	9,111,008.85
From profits on coinage, bullion deposits, and assays	4,460,205.17
From other sources	17,333,637.60
Total	398,287,581.95

For the same period the ordinary expenditures were:

For civil expenses	$22,343,285.76
For foreign intercourse	2,419,275.24
For Indians	7,362,590.34

For pensions.. $66,012,573.64
For the military establishment, including river and harbor improvements and arsenals... 48,911,382.93
For the naval establishment, including vessels, machinery, and improvements at navy-yards............... .... 15,283,437.17
For miscellaneous expenditures, including public buildings, light-houses, and collecting the revenue 40,098,432.73
For expenditures on account of the District of Columbia............... 3,817,028.48
For interest on the public debt 59,160,131.25

    Total... 265,408,137.54

Leaving a surplus revenue of $132,879,444.41, which, with an amount drawn from the cash balance in the Treasury of $1,299,312.55, making $134,178,756.96, was applied to the redemption—

Of bonds for the sinking fund... $44,850,700.00
Of fractional currency for the sinking fund.............................. 46,556.96
Of funded loan of 1881, continued at 3½ per cent 65,380,250.00
Of loan of July and August, 1861, continued at 3½ per cent..... ...... 20,594,600.00
Of funded loan of 1907.. 1,418,850.00
Of funded loan of 1881.. 719,150.00
Of loan of February, 1861 .... 18,000.00
Of loan of July and August, 1861.......... .... 266,600.00
Of loan of March, 1863......... .... 116,850.00
Of loan of July, 1882... 47,650.00
Of five-twenties of 1862... 10,300.00
Of five-twenties of 1864... 7,050.00
Of five-twenties of 1865... 9,600.00
Of ten-forties of 1864... 133,550.00
Of consols of 1865.. 40,800.00
Of consols of 1867.. 235,700.00
Of consols of 1868.. 154,650.00
Of Oregon War debt... 5,450.00
Of refunding certificates.. 109,150.00
Of old demand, compound-interest, and other notes.................... 13,300.00

    Total... 134,178,756.96

The revenue for the present fiscal year, actual and estimated, is as follows:

Source.	For the quarter ended September 30, 1883 (actual).	For the remaining three quarters of the year (estimated).
From customs........................ ...	$57,402,975.67	$137,597,024.33
From internal revenue.............	29,662,078.60	90,337,921.40
From sales of public lands	2,012,635.17	5,067,364.83
From tax on circulation and deposits of national banks	1,557,800.88	1,542,199.12
From repayment of interest and sinking fund, Pacific Railway companies...................	521,050.51	1,478,949.49
From customs fees, fines, penalties, etc	398,676.78	901,303.22
From fees—consular, letters patent, and lands .	863,380.80	2,436,700.20
From proceeds of sales of Government property	112,562.23	167,437.77
From profits on coinage, etc	950,229.46	3,146,770.54
From deposits for surveying public lands	172,461.31	327,558.60
From revenues of the District of Columbia	256,017.99	1,643,952.01
From miscellaneous sources	1,237,189.63	2,382,816.87
Total receipts..........................	95,946,917.03	247,033,082.07

The actual and estimated expenses for the same period are:

Object.	For the quarter ended September 30, 1883 (actual).	For the remaining three quarters of the year (estimated).
For civil and miscellaneous expenses, including public buildings, light-houses, and collecting the revenue.......................	$15,385,799.42	$51,114,200.58
For Indians..................................	2,623,390.54	4,126,609.46
For pensions....................................	16,285,261.98	53,714,738.02
For military establishment, including fortifications, river and harbor improvements, and arsenals......................................	13,512,204.33	26,487,795.67
For naval establishment, including vessels and machinery, and improvements at navy-yards..	4,199,299.69	12,300,700.31
For expenditures on account of the District of Columbia...........	1,138,836.41	2,611,163.59
For interest on the public debt..................	14,797,297.96	39,702,702.04
Total ordinary expenditures..............	67,942,090.33	190,057,909.67

Total receipts, actual and estimated $343,000,000.00
Total expenditures, actual and estimated........................... .... 258,000,000.00

85,000,000.00
Estimated amount due the sinking fund................................. 45,816,741.07

Leaving a balance of... .... 39,183,258.93

If the revenue for the fiscal year which will end on June 30, 1885, be estimated upon the basis of existing laws, the Secretary is of the opinion that for that year the receipts will exceed by $60,000,000 the ordinary expenditures including the amount devoted to the sinking fund.

Hitherto the surplus, as rapidly as it has accumulated, has been devoted to the reduction of the national debt.

As a result the only bonds now outstanding which are redeemable at the pleasure of the Government are the 3 percents, amounting to about $305,000,000.

The 4½ percents, amounting to $250,000,000, and the $737,000,000 4 percents are not payable until 1891 and 1907, respectively.

If the surplus shall hereafter be as large as the Treasury estimates now indicate, the 3 per cent bonds may all be redeemed at least four years before any of the 4½ percents can be called in. The latter at the same rate of accumulation of surplus can be paid at maturity, and the moneys requisite for the redemption of the 4 percents will be in the Treasury many years before those obligations become payable.

There are cogent reasons, however, why the national indebtedness should not be thus rapidly extinguished. Chief among them is the fact that only by excessive taxation is such rapidity attainable.

In a communication to the Congress at its last session I recommended that all excise taxes be abolished except those relating to distilled spirits and that substantial reductions be also made in the revenues from customs. A statute has since been enacted by which the annual tax and tariff receipts of the Government have been cut down to the extent of at least fifty or sixty millions of dollars.

While I have no doubt that still further reductions may be wisely made, I do not advise the adoption at this session of any measures for large diminution of the national revenues. The results of the legislation of the last session of the Congress have not as yet become sufficiently apparent to justify any radical revision or sweeping modifications of existing law.

In the interval which must elapse before the effects of the act of March 3, 1883, can be definitely ascertained a portion at least of the surplus revenues may be wisely applied to the long-neglected duty of rehabilitating our Navy and providing coast defenses for the protection of our harbors. This is a matter to which I shall again advert.

Immediately associated with the financial subject just discussed is the important question what legislation is needed regarding the national currency.

The aggregate amount of bonds now on deposit in the Treasury to support the national-bank circulation is about $350,000,000. Nearly $200,000,000 of this amount consists of 3 percents, which, as already stated, are payable at the pleasure of the Government and are likely to be called in within less than four years unless meantime the surplus revenues shall be diminished.

The probable effect of such an extensive retirement of the securities which are the basis of the national-bank circulation would be such a contraction of the volume of the currency as to produce grave commercial embarrassments.

How can this danger be obviated? The most effectual plan, and one whose adoption at the earliest practicable opportunity I shall heartily approve, has already been indicated.

If the revenues of the next four years shall be kept substantially commensurate with the expenses, the volume of circulation will not be likely to suffer any material disturbance; but if, on the other hand, there shall be great delay in reducing taxation, it will become necessary either to substitute some other form of currency in place of the national-bank notes or to make important changes in the laws by which their circulation is now controlled.

In my judgment the latter course is far preferable. I commend to your attention the very interesting and thoughtful suggestions upon this subject which appear in the Secretary's report.

The objections which he urges against the acceptance of any other securities than the obligations of the Government itself as a foundation for national-bank circulation seem to me insuperable.

For averting the threatened contraction two courses have been suggested, either of which is probably feasible. One is the issuance of new bonds, having many years to run, bearing a low rate of interest, and exchangeable upon specified terms for those now outstanding. The other course, which commends itself to my own judgment as the better, is the enactment of a law repealing the tax on circulation and permitting the banks to issue notes for an amount equal to 90 per cent of the market value instead of, as now, the face value of their deposited bonds. I agree with the Secretary in the belief that the adoption of this plan would afford the necessary relief.

The trade dollar was coined for the purpose of traffic in countries where silver passed at its value as ascertained by its weight and fineness. It never had a legal-tender quality. Large numbers of these coins entered, however, into the volume of our currency. By common consent their circulation in domestic trade has now ceased, and they have thus become a disturbing element. They should not be longer permitted to embarrass our currency system. I recommend that provision be made for their reception by the Treasury and the mints, as bullion, at a small percentage above the current market price of silver of like fineness.

The Secretary of the Treasury advises a consolidation of certain of the customs districts of the country, and suggests that the President be vested with such power in relation thereto as is now given him in respect to collectors of internal revenue by section 3141 of the Revised Statutes. The statistics upon this subject which are contained in his report furnish of themselves a strong argument in defense of his views.

At the adjournment of Congress the number of internal-revenue collection districts was 126. By Executive order dated June 25, 1883, I directed that certain of these districts be consolidated. The result has been a reduction of one-third their number, which at present is but 83.

From the report of the Secretary of War it will be seen that in only a single instance has there been any disturbance of the quiet condition of our Indian tribes. A raid from Mexico into Arizona was made in March last by a small party of Indians, which was pursued by General Crook into the mountain regions from which it had come. It is confidently hoped that serious outbreaks will not again occur and that the Indian tribes which have for so many years disturbed the West will hereafter remain in peaceable submission.

I again call your attention to the present condition of our extended seacoast, upon which are so many large cities whose wealth and importance to the country would in time of war invite attack from modern armored ships, against which our existing defensive works could give no adequate protection. Those works were built before the introduction of modern heavy rifled guns into maritime warfare, and if they are not put in an efficient condition we may easily be subjected to humiliation by a hostile power greatly inferior to ourselves. As germane to this subject, I call your attention to the importance of perfecting our submarine-torpedo defenses. The board authorized by the last Congress to report upon the method which should be adopted for the manufacture of heavy ordnance adapted to modern warfare has visited the principal iron and steel works in this country and in Europe. It is hoped that its report will soon be made, and that Congress will thereupon be disposed to provide suitable facilities and plant for the manufacture of such guns as are now imperatively needed.

On several occasions during the past year officers of the Army have at the request of the State authorities visited their militia encampments for inspection of the troops. From the reports of these officers I am induced to believe that the encouragement of the State militia organizations by the National Government would be followed by very gratifying results, and would afford it in sudden emergencies the aid of a large body of volunteers educated in the performance of military duties.

The Secretary of the Navy reports that under the authority of the acts of August 5, 1882, and March 3, 1883, the work of strengthening our Navy by the construction of modern vessels has been auspiciously begun. Three cruisers are in process of construction—the *Chicago*, of 4,500 tons displacement, and the *Boston* and *Atlanta*, each of 2,500 tons. They are to be built of steel, with the tensile strength and ductility prescribed by law, and in the combination of speed, endurance, and armament are expected to compare favorably with the best unarmored war vessels of other nations. A fourth vessel, the *Dolphin*, is to be constructed of similar material, and is intended to serve as a fleet dispatch boat.

The double-turreted monitors *Puritan*, *Amphitrite*, and *Terror* have been launched on the Delaware River and a contract has been made for the supply of their machinery. A similar monitor, the *Monadnock*, has been launched in California.

The Naval Advisory Board and the Secretary recommend the completion of the monitors, the construction of four gunboats, and also of three additional steel vessels like the *Chicago*, *Boston*, and *Dolphin*.

As an important measure of national defense, the Secretary urges also the immediate creation of an interior coast line of waterways across the peninsula of Florida, along the coast from Florida to Hampton Roads, between the Chesapeake Bay and the Delaware River, and through Cape Cod.

I feel bound to impress upon the attention of Congress the necessity of continued progress in the reconstruction of the Navy. The condition of the public Treasury, as I have already intimated, makes the present an auspicious time for putting this branch of the service in a state of efficiency.

It is no part of our policy to create and maintain a Navy able to cope with that of the other great powers of the world.

We have no wish for foreign conquest, and the peace which we have long enjoyed is in no seeming danger of interruption.

But that our naval strength should be made adequate for the defense of our harbors, the protection of our commercial interests, and the maintenance of our national honor is a proposition from which no patriotic citizen can withhold his assent.

The report of the Postmaster-General contains a gratifying exhibit of the condition and prospects of the interesting branch of the public service committed to his care.

It appears that on June 30, 1883, the whole number of post-offices was 47,863, of which 1,632 were established during the previous fiscal year. The number of offices operating under the system of free delivery was 154.

At these latter offices the postage on local matter amounted to $4,195,230.52, a sum exceeding by $1,021,894.01 the entire cost of the carrier service of the country.

The rate of postage on drop letters passing through these offices is now fixed by law at 2 cents per half ounce or fraction thereof. In offices where the carrier system has not been established the rate is only half as large.

It will be remembered that in 1863, when free delivery was first established by law, the uniform single-rate postage upon local letters was 1 cent, and so it remained until 1872, when in those cities where carrier service was established it was increased in order to defray the expense of such service.

It seems to me that the old rate may now with propriety be restored, and that, too, even at the risk of diminishing, for a time at least, the receipts from postage upon local letters.

I can see no reason why that particular class of mail matter should be held accountable for the entire cost of not only its own collection and delivery, but the collection and delivery of all other classes; and I am confident, after full consideration of the subject, that the reduction of rate would be followed by such a growing accession of business as to occasion but slight and temporary loss to the revenues of the Post-Office. The Postmaster-General devotes much of his report to the consideration in its various aspects of the relations of the Government to the telegraph. Such reflection as I have been able to give to this subject since my last annual message has not led me to change the views which I there expressed in dissenting from the recommendation of the then Postmaster-General that the Government assume the same control over the telegraph which it has always exercised over the mail.

Admitting that its authority in the premises is as ample as has ever been claimed for it, it would not, in my judgment, be a wise use of that authority to purchase or assume the control of existing telegraph lines, or to construct others with a view of entering into general competition with private enterprise.

The objections which may be justly urged against either of those projects, and indeed against any system which would require an enormous increase in the civil-service list, do not, however, apply to some of the plans which have lately provoked public comment and discussion. It has been claimed, for example, that Congress might wisely authorize the Postmaster-General to contract with some private persons or corporation for the transmission of messages, or of a certain class of messages, at specified rates and under Government supervision. Various such schemes, of the same general nature, but widely differing in their special characteristics, have been suggested in the public prints, and the arguments by which they have been supported and opposed have doubtless attracted your attention.

It is likely that the whole subject will be considered by you at the present session.

In the nature of things it involves so many questions of detail that your deliberations would probably be aided slightly, if at all, by any particular suggestions which I might now submit.

I avow my belief, however, that the Government should be authorized by law to exercise some sort of supervision over interstate telegraphic communication, and I express the hope that for attaining that end some measure may be devised which will receive your approbation.

The Attorney-General criticises in his report the provisions of existing law fixing the fees of jurors and witnesses in the Federal courts. These provisions are chiefly contained in the act of February 26, 1853, though some of them were introduced into that act from statutes which had been passed many years previous. It is manifest that such compensation as might when these laws were enacted have been just and reasonable would in many instances be justly regarded at the present day as inadequate. I concur with the Attorney-General in the belief that the statutes should be revised by which these fees are regulated.

So, too, should the laws which regulate the compensation of district attorneys and marshals. They should be paid wholly by salaries instead of in part by fees, as is now the case.

The change would prove to be a measure of economy and would discourage the institution of needless and oppressive legal proceedings, which it is to be feared have in some instances been conducted for the mere sake of personal gain.

Much interesting and varied information is contained in the report of the Secretary of the Interior.

I particularly call your attention to his presentation of certain phases of the Indian question, to his recommendations for the repeal of the preemption and timber-culture acts, and for more stringent legislation to prevent frauds under the pension laws. The statutes which prescribe the definitions and punishments of crimes relating to pensions could doubtless be made more effective by certain amendments and additions which are pointed out in the Secretary's report.

I have previously referred to the alarming state of illiteracy in certain portions of the country, and again submit for the consideration of Congress whether some Federal aid should not be extended to public primary education wherever adequate provision therefor has not already been made.

The Utah Commission has submitted to the Secretary of the Interior its second annual report. As a result of its labors in supervising the recent election in that Territory, pursuant to the act of March 22, 1882, it appears that persons by that act disqualified to the number of about 12,000, were excluded from the polls. This fact, however, affords little cause for congratulation, and I fear that it is far from indicating any real and substantial progress toward the extirpation of polygamy. All the members elect of the legislature are Mormons. There is grave reason to believe that they are in sympathy with the practices that this Government is seeking to suppress, and that its efforts in that regard will be more likely to encounter their opposition than to receive their encouragement and support. Even if this view should happily be erroneous, the law under which the commissioners have been acting should be made more effective by the incorporation of some such stringent amendments as they recommend, and as were included in bill No. 2238 on the Calendar of the Senate at its last session.

I am convinced, however, that polygamy has become so strongly intrenched in the Territory of Utah that it is profitless to attack it with any but the stoutest weapons which constitutional legislation can fashion. I favor, therefore, the repeal of the act upon which the existing government depends, the assumption by the National Legislature of the entire political control of the Territory, and the establishment of a commission with such powers and duties as shall be delegated to it by law.

The Department of Agriculture is accomplishing much in the direction of the agricultural development of the country, and the report of the Commissioner giving the results of his investigations and experiments will be found interesting and valuable.

At his instance a convention of those interested in the cattle industry of the country was lately held at Chicago. The prevalence of pleuropneumonia and other contagious diseases of animals was one of the chief topics of discussion. A committee of the convention will invite your cooperation in investigating the causes of these diseases and providing methods for their prevention and cure.

I trust that Congress will not fail at its present session to put Alaska under the protection of law. Its people have repeatedly remonstrated against our neglect to afford them the maintenance and protection expressly guaranteed by the terms of the treaty whereby that Territory was ceded to the United States. For sixteen years they have pleaded in vain for that which they should have received without the asking.

They have no law for the collection of debts, the support of education, the conveyance of property, the administration of estates, or the enforcement of contracts; none, indeed, for the punishment of criminals, except such as offend against certain customs, commerce, and navigation acts.

The resources of Alaska, especially in fur, mines, and lumber, are considerable in extent and capable of large development, while its geographical situation is one of political and commercial importance.

The promptings of interest, therefore, as well as considerations of honor and good faith, demand the immediate establishment of civil government in that Territory.

Complaints have lately been numerous and urgent that certain corporations, controlling in whole or in part the facilities for the interstate carriage of persons and merchandise over the great railroads of the country, have resorted in their dealings with the public to divers measures unjust and oppressive in their character.

In some instances the State governments have attacked and suppressed these evils, but in others they have been unable to afford adequate relief because of the jurisdictional limitations which are imposed upon them by the Federal Constitution.

The question how far the National Government may lawfully interfere in the premises, and what, if any, supervision or control it ought to exercise, is one which merits your careful consideration.

While we can not fail to recognize the importance of the vast railway systems of the country and their great and beneficent influences upon the development of our material wealth, we should, on the other hand, remember that no individual and no corporation ought to be invested with absolute power over the interest of any other citizen or class of citizens. The right of these railway corporations to a fair and profitable return upon their investments and to reasonable freedom in their regulations must be recognized; but it seems only just that, so far as its constitutional authority will permit, Congress should protect the people at large in their interstate traffic against acts of injustice which the State governments are powerless to prevent.

In my last annual message I called attention to the necessity of protecting by suitable legislation the forests situated upon the public domain. In many portions of the West the pursuit of general agriculture is only made practicable by resort to irrigation, while successful irrigation would itself be impossible without the aid afforded by forests in contributing to the regularity and constancy of the supply of water.

During the past year severe suffering and great loss of property have been occasioned by profuse floods followed by periods of unusually low water in many of the great rivers of the country.

These irregularities were in great measure caused by the removal from about the sources of the streams in question of the timber by which the water supply had been nourished and protected.

The preservation of such portions of the forests on the national domain as essentially contribute to the equable flow of important water courses is of the highest consequence.

Important tributaries of the Missouri, the Columbia, and the Saskatchewan rise in the mountain region of Montana, near the northern boundary of the United States, between the Blackfeet and Flathead Indian reservations. This region is unsuitable for settlement, but upon the rivers which flow from it depends the future agricultural development of a vast tract of country. The attention of Congress is called to the necessity of withdrawing from public sale this part of the public domain and establishing there a forest preserve.

The industrial exhibitions which have been held in the United States during the present year attracted attention in many foreign countries, where the announcement of those enterprises had been made public through the foreign agencies of this Government. The Industrial Exhibition at Boston and the Southern Exposition at Louisville were largely attended by the exhibitors of foreign countries, notwithstanding the absence of any professed national character in those undertakings.

The Centennial Exposition to be held next year at New Orleans in commemoration of the centenary of the first shipment of cotton from a port of the United States bids fair to meet with like gratifying success. Under the act of Congress of the 10th of February, 1883, declaring that exposition to be national and international in its character, all foreign governments with which the United States maintain relations have been invited to participate.

The promoters of this important undertaking have already received assurances of the lively interest which it has excited abroad.

The report of the Commissioners of the District of Columbia is herewith transmitted. I ask for it your careful attention, especially for those portions which relate to assessments, arrears of taxes, and increase of water supply.

The commissioners who were appointed under the act of January 16, 1883, entitled "An act to regulate and improve the civil service of the United States," entered promptly upon the discharge of their duties.

A series of rules, framed in accordance with the spirit of the statute, was approved and promulgated by the President.

In some particulars wherein they seemed defective those rules were subsequently amended. It will be perceived that they discountenance any political or religious tests for admission to those offices of the public service to which the statute relates.

The act is limited in its original application to the classified clerkships in the several Executive Departments at Washington (numbering about 5,600) and to similar positions in customs districts and post-offices where as many as fifty persons are employed. A classification of these positions analogous to that existing in the Washington offices was duly made before the law went into effect. Eleven customs districts and twenty-three post-offices were thus brought under the immediate operation of the statute.

The annual report of the Civil Service Commission which will soon be submitted to Congress will doubtless afford the means of a more definite judgment than I am now prepared to express as to the merits of the new system. I am persuaded that its effects have thus far proved beneficial. Its practical methods appear to be adequate for the ends proposed, and there has been no serious difficulty in carrying them into effect. Since the 16th of July last no person, so far as I am aware; has been appointed to the public service in the classified portions thereof at any of the Departments, or at any of the post-offices and customs districts above named, except those certified by the Commission to be the most competent on the basis of the examinations held in conformity to the rules.

At the time when the present Executive entered upon his office his death, removal, resignation, or inability to discharge his duties would have left the Government without a constitutional head.

It is possible, of course, that a similar contingency may again arise unless the wisdom of Congress shall provide against its recurrence.

The Senate at its last session, after full consideration, passed an act relating to this subject, which will now, I trust, commend itself to the approval of both Houses of Congress.

The clause of the Constitution upon which must depend any law regulating the Presidential succession presents also for solution other questions of paramount importance.

These questions relate to the proper interpretation of the phrase "inability to discharge the powers and duties of said office," our organic law providing that when the President shall suffer from such inability the Presidential office shall devolve upon the Vice-President, who must himself under like circumstances give place to such officer as Congress may by law appoint to act as President.

I need not here set forth the numerous and interesting inquiries which are suggested by these words of the Constitution. They were fully stated in my first communication to Congress and have since been the subject of frequent deliberations in that body.

It is greatly to be hoped that these momentous questions will find speedy solution, lest emergencies may arise when longer delay will be impossible and any determination, albeit the wisest, may furnish cause for anxiety and alarm.

For the reasons fully stated in my last annual message I repeat my recommendation that Congress propose an amendment to that provision of the Constitution which prescribes the formalities for the enactment of laws, whereby, in respect to bills for the appropriation of public moneys, the Executive may be enabled, while giving his approval to particular items, to interpose his veto as to such others as do not commend them-

The fourteenth amendment of the Constitution confers the rights of citizenship upon all persons born or naturalized in the United States and subject to the jurisdiction thereof.   It was the special purpose of this amendment to insure to members of the colored race the full enjoyment of civil and political rights.   Certain statutory provisions intended to secure the enforcement of those rights have been recently declared unconstitutional by the Supreme Court.

Any legislation whereby Congress may lawfully supplement the guaranties which the Constitution affords for the equal enjoyment by all the citizens of the United States of every right, privilege, and immunity of citizenship will receive my unhesitating approval.

                                        CHESTER A. ARTHUR.

SPECIAL MESSAGES.

EXECUTIVE MANSION, *December 10, 1883.*
To the Senate and House of Representatives:

I transmit herewith a communication from the Secretary of the Interior of the 3d instant, submitting, with accompanying papers, draft of a bill to accept and ratify certain agreements made with the Sioux Indians and to grant a right of way to the Dakota Central Railway Company through the Sioux Reservation in Dakota.

The matter is presented for the consideration of the Congress.

                                        CHESTER A. ARTHUR.

EXECUTIVE MANSION, *December 10, 1883.*
To the Senate and House of Representatives:

I transmit herewith a communication from the Secretary of the Interior of the 3d instant, with accompanying papers, submitting draft of a bill to prevent timber depredations on Indian reservations.

The subject is presented for the consideration of the Congress.

                                        CHESTER A. ARTHUR.

EXECUTIVE MANSION, *December 10, 1883.*
To the Senate and House of Representatives:

I transmit herewith a communication of the 3d instant from the Secretary of the Interior, in relation to the urgent necessity of action on the part of the Congress for the more adequate prevention of trespasses upon Indian lands, with copy of report from the Commissioner of Indian Affairs upon the subject, draft of bill for the object indicated, and copy of correspondence from the Secretary of War recommending action in the premises.

The matter is commended to the consideration of the Congress.

CHESTER A. ARTHUR.

EXECUTIVE MANSION, *December 10, 1883.*

To the Senate and House of Representatives:

I transmit herewith a communication of the 3d instant from the Secretary of the Interior, with the draft of a bill "to accept and ratify an agreement made by the Pi-Ute Indians, and granting a right of way to the Carson and Colorado Railroad Company through the Walker River Reservation, in Nevada," and accompanying papers in relation to the subject.

The matter is presented for the consideration of the Congress.

CHESTER A. ARTHUR.

EXECUTIVE MANSION, *December 10, 1883.*

To the Senate and House of Representatives:

I transmit herewith a communication from the Secretary of the Interior of the 3d instant, with accompanying papers, submitting a draft of a bill "providing for the allotment of lands in severalty to certain Chippewa Indians of Lake Superior residing in the State of Wisconsin, and granting patents therefor."

The subject is presented for the consideration of the Congress.

CHESTER A. ARTHUR.

EXECUTIVE MANSION, *December 10, 1883.*

To the Senate and House of Representatives:

I transmit herewith a communication from the Secretary of the Interior of the 3d instant, with draft of bill for the payment of certain settlers in the State of Nevada for improvements on lands in Duck Valley, in that State, taken for the use and occupancy of the Shoshone Indians, with accompanying papers.

The subject is presented for the consideration of the Congress.

CHESTER A. ARTHUR.

EXECUTIVE MANSION, *December 10, 1883.*

To the Senate and House of Representatives:

I transmit herewith a communication from the Secretary of the Interior of the 3d instant, submitting, with accompanying papers, draft of a bill "to provide for the settlement of the estates of deceased Kickapoo Indians in the State of Kansas, and for other purposes."

The matter is presented for the consideration of the Congress.

CHESTER A. ARTHUR.

EXECUTIVE MANSION, *December 11, 1883.*

To the Senate and House of Representatives:

I transmit herewith a letter from the Secretary of the Interior, inclosing a communication from the Commissioner of Indian Affairs setting forth the necessity of a deficiency appropriation of $60,000 for the immediate wants of his Bureau.

CHESTER A. ARTHUR.

EXECUTIVE MANSION, *December 13, 1883.*

To the Senate and House of Representatives:

I transmit herewith, for the consideration of Congress, a letter from the Secretary of War, inclosing copies of official reports, etc., by the military authorities touching the necessity for the acquisition of additional land for the military reservation of Fort Preble, Me., and expressing his concurrence in the recommendation of the Lieutenant-General of the Army that the sum of $8,000 be appropriated by Congress for the purchase of such additional land.

CHESTER A. ARTHUR.

EXECUTIVE MANSION, *December 13, 1883.*

To the Senate and House of Representatives:

I transmit herewith, for the consideration of Congress, a communication from the Secretary of War, touching the question of the reconstruction of a bridge over the Republican River at or near Fort Riley, in the State of Kansas, and recommending such legislation as will authorize the reconstruction of said bridge by the United States in accordance with the terms and provisions of a joint resolution of the legislature of the State of Kansas approved March 6, 1883, a copy of which is herewith inclosed.

CHESTER A. ARTHUR.

EXECUTIVE MANSION, *December 13, 1883.*

To the Senate and House of Representatives:

I transmit herewith, for the consideration of Congress, a communication from the Secretary of War, dated the 4th instant, inclosing and commending to favorable consideration a letter from the board of commissioners of the Soldiers' Home, dated Washington, D. C., November 27, 1883, recommending such legislation as will confer upon said board of commissioners authority to advance a sum not exceeding $40,000 annually from funds found to be due the Soldiers' Home on settlements to be made in the offices of the Second Comptroller and Second Auditor, to pay for the services of extra clerks to be employed under the direction of the Secretary of the Treasury in making such settlements.

CHESTER A. ARTHUR.

EXECUTIVE MANSION, *December 13, 1883.*
To the Senate and House of Representatives:

I transmit herewith, for the consideration of Congress, a copy of a communication from the Secretary of War, dated the 8th instant, inclosing one from Captain S. M. Mills, Fifth Artillery, indorsed by the Chief Signal Officer of the Army, recommending that Congress authorize the printing and binding, for the use of the Signal Office, of 5,000 copies of the Annual Report of the Chief Signal Officer for the fiscal year 1882, and inclosing a draft of a joint resolution for that purpose.

CHESTER A. ARTHUR.

EXECUTIVE MANSION, *December 13, 1883.*
To the Senate and House of Representatives:

I transmit herewith, for the consideration of Congress, a letter from the Secretary of War, dated the 8th instant, and its accompanying papers, relative to the reconveyance to Mr. Thomas Mulvihill, of Pittsburg, Pa., of certain land erroneously conveyed by him to the United States, the particular facts regarding which are fully set forth in the inclosed copy of Senate Executive Document No. 46, Forty-seventh Congress, second session.

It appearing that the land in question was through error alone transferred to the United States, and that to retransfer the same to Mr. Mulvihill would be a measure of simple justice, it is recommended that such legislation be had as may be necessary to restore to Mr. Mulvihill his rights in the premises.

CHESTER A. ARTHUR.

EXECUTIVE MANSION, *December 17, 1883.*
To the Senate and House of Representatives:

I transmit herewith a communication from the Secretary of the Interior of the 4th instant, with accompanying papers, submitting a draft of a bill "to confirm the title to certain land in the Indian Territory to the Cheyennes and Arapahoes and the Wichitas and affiliated bands, to provide for the issuance of patents therefor, and for other purposes."

The subject is presented for the consideration of the Congress.

CHESTER A. ARTHUR.

EXECUTIVE MANSION, *December 17, 1883.*

To the Senate and House of Representatives:

I transmit herewith a communication of the 11th instant from the Secretary of the Interior, submitting, with accompanying papers, draft of a bill "to provide for the issuance of patents for certain lands in the Indian Territory occupied by the Kickapoo, Iowa, and other Indians."

The matter is presented for the consideration of the Congress.

CHESTER A. ARTHUR.

EXECUTIVE MANSION, *December 17, 1883.*

To the Senate and House of Representatives:

I transmit herewith a communication of the 6th instant from the Secretary of the Interior, submitting, with accompanying papers, a draft of a bill "to accept and ratify an agreement with the confederated tribes of the Flathead, Kootenay, and Upper Pend d'Oreille Indians for the sale of a portion of their reservation in the Territory of Montana required for the use of the Northern Pacific Railroad, and for other purposes."

The subject is presented for the consideration of the Congress.

CHESTER A. ARTHUR.

EXECUTIVE MANSION, *December 17, 1883.*

To the Senate and House of Representatives:

I transmit herewith a communication from the Secretary of the Interior of the 4th instant, submitting, with accompanying papers, draft of a bill "to accept and ratify the agreement submitted by the Shoshones, Bannocks, and Sheepeaters of the Fort Hall and Lemhi reservations, in Idaho, May 14, 1880, for the sale of a portion of their land in said Territory and for other purposes, and to make the necessary appropriations for carrying out the same."

The matter is presented for the consideration of the Congress.

CHESTER A. ARTHUR.

EXECUTIVE MANSION, *December 17, 1883.*

To the Senate and House of Representatives:

I transmit herewith a communication from the Secretary of the Interior, submitting a draft of a bill "providing for allotment of lands in severalty to the Indians residing upon the Chehalis Reservation, in Washington Territory, and granting patents therefor," with accompanying report from the Commissioner of Indian Affairs upon the subject.

The matter is presented for the consideration of the Congress.

CHESTER A. ARTHUR.

EXECUTIVE MANSION, *December 17, 1883.*
To the Senate and House of Representatives:

I transmit herewith a communication from the Secretary of the Interior of the 3d instant, with accompanying papers, submitting a draft of a bill for the relief of the Nez Percé Indians in the Territory of Idaho and of the allied tribes residing on the Grande Ronde Indian Reservation, in the State of Oregon.

The subject is presented for the consideration of the Congress.

CHESTER A. ARTHUR.

EXECUTIVE MANSION, *December 17, 1883.*
To the Senate and House of Representatives:

I transmit herewith a communication from the Secretary of the Interior of the 4th instant, submitting, with accompanying papers, draft of a bill to accept and ratify certain agreements made with the Sioux Indians and to grant a right of way to the Chicago, Milwaukee, and St. Paul Railway Company through the Sioux Reservation in Dakota.

The matter is presented for the consideration of the Congress.

CHESTER A. ARTHUR.

EXECUTIVE MANSION, *December 17, 1883.*
To the Senate and House of Representatives:

I transmit herewith, for the consideration of Congress, a letter from the Secretary of War, dated December 13 instant, inclosing one from the Surgeon-General of the Army submitting a special estimate for funds in the sum of $200,000 for the erection in this city of a suitable fireproof building to contain the records, library, and museum of the Medical Department of the Army, together with preliminary plans for said building and copies of reports, etc., in relation to the subject.

CHESTER A. ARTHUR.

EXECUTIVE MANSION, *December 17, 1883.*
To the Senate and House of Representatives:

I transmit herewith, for the consideration of Congress, a communication from the Secretary of the Navy, dated the 10th instant, inclosing a letter from the Surgeon-General of the Navy respecting the advisability of providing for representation on the part of the United States in any international convention that may be organized for the purpose of establishing uniform standards of measure of color perception and acuteness of vision.

CHESTER A. ARTHUR.

EXECUTIVE MANSION, *December 17, 1883.*

To the Senate and House of Representatives:

I transmit herewith a communication of the 3d instant from the Secretary of the Interior, submitting, with accompanying papers, a draft of a bill for the payment of the value of certain improvements made by certain settlers on the Round Valley Indian Reservation, in the State of California, as appraised under the act approved March 3, 1873.

The subject is presented for the consideration of the Congress.

CHESTER A. ARTHUR.

EXECUTIVE MANSION, *December 17, 1883.*

To the Senate and House of Representatives:

I transmit herewith a communication of the 12th instant from the Secretary of the Interior, submitting a report of the Commissioner of Indian Affairs of December 8, 1883, and accompanying papers, on the subject of the "Old Settler" or "Western" Cherokees."

CHESTER A. ARTHUR.

EXECUTIVE MANSION, *December 17, 1883.*

To the Senate and House of Representatives:

I transmit herewith a communication of the 4th instant from the Secretary of the Interior, with draft of a bill to accept and ratify an agreement made with Chief Moses and other Indians for the relinquishment of certain lands in Washington Territory, and to make the necessary appropriations for carrying the same into effect, with accompanying papers.

The subject is presented for the consideration of the Congress.

CHESTER A. ARTHUR.

EXECUTIVE MANSION, *December 19, 1883.*

To the Senate and House of Representatives:

I transmit herewith, for the consideration of Congress, a letter from the Secretary of War, dated the 15th instant, inclosing one from the Quartermaster-General setting forth the necessity for the construction of a fireproof building in this city for the storage of the public records.

CHESTER A. ARTHUR.

EXECUTIVE MANSION, *December 19, 1883.*

To the Senate and House of Representatives:

I transmit herewith a letter from the Secretary of the Interior, inclosing a copy of a communication from the Commissioner of Indian Affairs setting forth the necessity of a deficiency appropriation of $78,110 for the purchase of supplies for the balance of the present fiscal year for the Crow Indians.

CHESTER A. ARTHUR.

EXECUTIVE MANSION,
Washington, December 19, 1883.

To the Senate of the United States:

I transmit herewith, in response to the Senate resolution of the 18th instant, a report of the Secretary of State and accompanying papers, relating to the treaty between the United States and Great Britain signed April 19, 1850.

CHESTER A. ARTHUR.

EXECUTIVE MANSION, *December 19, 1883.*

To the Senate and House of Representatives:

I transmit herewith, for the consideration of Congress, a communication from the Secretary of War, dated December 14, 1883, upon the subject of abandoned military reservations, and renewing his former recommendation for such legislation as will provide for the disposal of military sites that are no longer needed for military purposes.

CHESTER A. ARTHUR.

EXECUTIVE MANSION,
Washington, December 19, 1883.

To the Senate of the United States of America:

I transmit herewith to the Senate, for its consideration with a view to ratification, a treaty of extradition between the United States of America and the Grand Duchy of Luxemburg, concluded at Berlin on the 29th of October, A. D. 1883.

CHESTER A. ARTHUR.

EXECUTIVE MANSION,
Washington, December 24, 1883.

To the House of Representatives:

The House of Representatives having adopted on the 19th instant a resolution in the following words—

Resolved, That the Secretary of State be, and he is hereby, requested to furnish for the information of this House, without delay, if not incompatible with the public service, all communications, documents, and papers in his possession relating to the trial, conviction, and execution of the late Patrick O'Donnell by the British Government—

I transmit herewith a report made to me by the Secretary of State, with the papers enumerated in the subjoined list, as answering said resolution.

CHESTER A. ARTHUR.

EXECUTIVE MANSION, *January 7, 1884.*

To the Senate and House of Representatives:

I transmit herewith a communication from the Secretary of the Interior of the 19th ultimo, submitting, with accompanying papers, a draft of a bill providing for the allotment of lands in severalty to the Arickaree, Gros Ventre, and Mandan Indians on the Fort Berthold Indian Reservation, in Dakota, and the granting of patents therefor, and for other purposes.

The matter is presented for the action of the Congress.

CHESTER A. ARTHUR.

EXECUTIVE MANSION, *January 7, 1884.*

To the Senate and House of Representatives:

I transmit herewith a communication from the Secretary of the Interior of the 19th ultimo, submitting, with accompanying papers, a draft of a bill "to allow Indian homestead entries in certain cases without the payment of fees and commissions."

The matter is presented for the consideration and action of the Congress.

CHESTER A. ARTHUR.

EXECUTIVE MANSION, *January 7, 1884.*

To the Senate and House of Representatives:

I transmit herewith, for the consideration of Congress, a letter from the Secretary of War, dated the 2d instant, inclosing copies of official correspondence, reports, etc., in relation to the military post of Fort Sullivan, Me., and recommending such legislation as will authorize the sale of the site to the highest bidder after public advertisement, the same being no longer needed for military purposes.

CHESTER A. ARTHUR.

EXECUTIVE MANSION, *January 8, 1884.*

To the Senate and House of Representatives:

I submit a communication from the governor of the State of Illinois, with a copy of an act of the general assembly of that State tendering to the United States the cession of the Illinois and Michigan Canal upon condition that it shall be enlarged and maintained as a national waterway for commercial purposes.

The proposed cession is an element of the subject which Congress had under consideration in directing by the act of August 2, 1882, a survey for a canal from a point on the Illinois River at or near the town of Hennepin by the most practicable route to the Mississippi River at or above the city of Rock Island, the canal to be not less than 70 feet wide at the water line and not less than 7 feet in depth of water, and with capacity for vessels of at least 280 tons burden; and also a survey of the Illinois and Michigan Canal and an estimate of the cost of enlarging it to the dimensions of the proposed canal between Hennepin and the Mississippi River.

The surveys ordered in the above act have been completed and the report upon them is included in the last annual report of the Secretary of War, and a copy is herewith submitted. It is estimated in the report that by the enlargement of the Illinois and Michigan Canal and the construction of the proposed canal by the shortest route between Hennepin and the Mississippi River a direct and convenient thoroughfare for vessels of 280 tons burden may be opened from the Mississippi River to Lake Michigan at a cost of $8,110,286.65, and that the annual charge for maintenance would be $138,600.

It appears from these papers that the estimated yield of corn, wheat, and oats for 1882 in the States of Illinois, Wisconsin, Iowa, Minnesota, Kansas, and Nebraska was more than 1,000,000,000 bushels. It is claimed that if the cheap water transportation route which is now continuous from the Atlantic Ocean to Chicago is extended to the Upper Mississippi by such a canal a great benefit in the reduction of freight charges would result to the people of the Upper Mississippi Valley, whose productions I have only partly noted, not only upon their own shipments, but upon the articles of commerce used by them, which are now taken from the Eastern States by water only as far as Chicago.

As a matter of great interest, especially to the citizens of that part of the country, I commend the general subject to your consideration.

CHESTER A. ARTHUR.

EXECUTIVE MANSION,
Washington, January 8, 1884.

To the House of Representatives:

In answer to the resolution of the House of Representatives of the 7th instant, respecting the alleged distribution of circulars in some of the Departments asking contributions for political purposes, I hereby transmit the reply of the Secretary of State.

CHESTER A. ARTHUR.

EXECUTIVE MANSION, *January 8, 1884.*

To the Senate and House of Representatives:

I transmit herewith to the House of Representatives a communication from the Secretary of War, submitting the annual report of the Mississippi River Commission.

I take this occasion to invite the early attention of Congress to the continuation of the work on the Mississippi River which is being carried on under the plans of the commission. My sense of the importance of the improvement of this river, not only to the people of the Northwest, but especially to the inhabitants of the Lower Mississippi Valley, has already been expressed in a special communication to the last Congress. The harvests of grain and cotton produced in the region bordering upon the Mississippi are so vast as to be of national importance, and the project now being executed for their cheap transportation should be sufficiently provided for.

The commission report that the results due to the still uncompleted works have been remarkable, and give the highest encouragement for expecting the ultimate success of the improvement.

The act of August 2, 1882, appropriated $4,123,000 for the work on that part of the river below Cairo. The estimates of the commission already transmitted to Congress call for $3,000,000 for the continuation of the work below Cairo, and it appears from their report that all of the last appropriation available for active operations has been exhausted and that there is urgently needed an immediate appropriation of $1,000,-000 to continue the work without loss of time, in view of the approach of the flood season, with its attendant dangers.

I therefore recommend to Congress the early passage of a separate bill on this subject.

CHESTER A. ARTHUR.

EXECUTIVE MANSION, *January 9, 1884.*
To the Senate and House of Representatives:

I transmit herewith, for the consideration of Congress, a letter from the Secretary of War of the 7th instant, inclosing a copy of one from the Quartermaster-General of the Army submitting plans and estimates for the construction of walls, etc., at the Schuylkill Arsenal, Philadelphia, Pa., rendered necessary by the opening of Peltz street, and recommending that an appropriation be made of the amount estimated to be requisite for the work referred to.

CHESTER A. ARTHUR.

EXECUTIVE MANSION, *January 14, 1884.*
To the Senate and House of Representatives:

I transmit herewith a communication from the Secretary of the Interior, submitting, with accompanying papers, an estimate of appropriation in the sum of $25,000 for the settlement under existing treaties of certain freedmen and their descendants upon lands known as the Oklahoma district, within the Indian Territory.

The matter is presented for the consideration of the Congress.

CHESTER A. ARTHUR.

EXECUTIVE MANSION, *January 14, 1884.*

To the Senate and House of Representatives:

I transmit herewith a communication of the 11th instant from the Secretary of the Interior, submitting, with accompanying papers, an item of appropriation in the sum of $3,000 for the location and survey of boundary lines of certain lands purchased by the United States from the Creek Indians for the use of the Seminole Indians in the Indian Territory.

The matter is presented for the consideration of the Congress.

CHESTER A. ARTHUR.

EXECUTIVE MANSION, *January 14, 1884.*

To the Senate and House of Representatives:

I transmit herewith a communication from the Secretary of the Interior, submitting, with accompanying papers, a draft of a bill "for the relief of the Mission Indians in the State of California."

The subject is presented for the consideration of the Congress.

CHESTER A. ARTHUR.

EXECUTIVE MANSION,
Washington, January 15, 1884.

To the Senate of the United States:

In response to the resolution of the Senate of the 8th instant, calling for the correspondence on file upon the subject of discriminating duties upon commerce between the United States and Cuba and Puerto Rico, I transmit herewith a report made to me by the Secretary of State, with accompanying papers.

CHESTER A. ARTHUR.

EXECUTIVE MANSION, *January 16, 1884.*

To the Senate and House of Representatives:

I transmit herewith, for the consideration of Congress, a copy of a letter from the secretary of state of the State of Pennsylvania, dated November 26, 1883, inclosing a duly authenticated copy of an act of the legislature of that State entitled "An act to provide for the preservation, use, custody, and disposition of the marine hospital at Erie, and making an appropriation for the repair of the same," approved July 5, 1883, and tendering to the United States Government, on behalf of the governor, in pursuance of the provisions of the act, the said marine hospital for use as a soldiers' and sailors' home.

The papers having upon their receipt been referred by me to the Secretary of War, I inclose also a copy of his letter of the 12th instant returning the same, together with a copy of the report of Captain Edwar'

Maguire, Corps of Engineers, dated the 10th ultimo, giving a description of the property referred to and expressing his views as to its adaptability for a soldiers and sailors' home.

CHESTER A. ARTHUR.

EXECUTIVE MANSION, *January 16, 1884.*

To the Senate and House of Representatives:

I transmit herewith a letter from the Secretary of the Interior, dated the 11th instant, suggesting further action by Congress in the matter of granting leases of bath houses and bath-house sites at the Hot Springs Reservation, Ark.

The subject is presented for the consideration of the Congress.

CHESTER A. ARTHUR.

EXECUTIVE MANSION, *January 17, 1884.*

To the Senate and House of Representatives:

I transmit, for the consideration of Congress, a communication from the Secretary of War and the Secretary of the Navy, on the subject of an expedition for the relief of Lieutenant A. W. Greely and his party, composing what is known as the "Lady Franklin Bay Expedition," which was sent to the arctic regions in 1881 under the provisions of the acts of Congress approved May 1, 1880, and March 3, 1881.

In the plans for the relief of this party, as arranged with Lieutenant Greely, it was contemplated that an effort would be made to communicate with him and furnish him any needed assistance in 1882 and again in 1883.

Subsequently legislation was enacted which required the expedition of 1883 to bring the party home. It was a part of the arrangement that if communication should not be made with him on or before the 1st of September, 1883, he should, with his party, abandon his station at Lady Franklin Bay not later than the above-mentioned date and proceed southward, and would find a well-supplied relief station at the entrance to Smiths Sound, a point where it would not be difficult to reach him during a part of each year. The expeditions of 1882 and 1883 were sent, but neither one of them was able to communicate with Lieutenant Greely; and the last one failed to accomplish any part of its object beyond leaving a very small quantity of stores in the neighborhood of the entrance to Smiths Sound.

The situation of Lieutenant Greely and his party under these circumstances is one of great peril, and in presenting the preliminary views of the board appointed by me to take into consideration an expedition for their relief I urgently recommend prompt action by Congress to enable the recommendations of the Secretary of War and the Secretary of the Navy to be carried out without delay.

CHESTER A. ARTHUR.

EXECUTIVE MANSION, *January 22, 1884.*

To the House of Representatives:

I transmit herewith, in response to the resolution of the House dated January 11, 1883, a letter, dated the 21st instant, from the Secretary of War, together with a report submitted to him by the Chief of Engineers, embodying the information, so far as the same can be furnished from the records of his office, and a statement prepared in the Treasury Department, respecting the expenditures for rivers and harbors, called for by the said resolution.　　　CHESTER A. ARTHUR.

EXECUTIVE MANSION, *January 28, 1884.*

To the Senate and House of Representatives:

I transmit to Congress a communication from the Secretary of War, in relation to the necessity of an immediate appropriation of not less than $42,000 to enable the engineer in charge to make next autumn the explosion required for the removal of Flood Rock, in the East River, New York. The importance of the work is well known, and as it appears that without a speedy appropriation a delay of a year must follow, accompanied by large expenses to protect from injury the work already done, I commend the subject to the early and favorable consideration of Congress.　　　CHESTER A. ARTHUR.

EXECUTIVE MANSION,
Washington, January 30, 1884.

To the Senate of the United States:

In further response to the resolution of the Senate of the 8th instant, calling for the correspondence on file upon the subject of discriminating duties upon commerce between the United States and Cuba and Puerto Rico, I transmit certain papers additional to the papers which accompanied the report sent to you on the 15th instant.　　　CHESTER A. ARTHUR.

EXECUTIVE MANSION, *January 31, 1884.*

To the Senate and House of Representatives:

I transmit herewith a communication of the 29th instant from the Secretary of the Interior, submitting, with accompanying papers, a report of the Commissioner of Indian Affairs upon the subject of the right of way of the Chicago, Milwaukee and St. Paul Railway Company through the Lake Traverse Indian Reservation, in Dakota.

The subject is commended to the consideration of the Congress.

CHESTER A. ARTHUR.

EXECUTIVE MANSION, *January 31, 1884.*

To the House of Representatives of the United States:

I transmit herewith, in response to the resolutions of the House of Representatives, the following report of the Secretary of State, with accompanying papers, relative to the restrictions upon the importation of American hog products into Germany and France.

CHESTER A. ARTHUR.

EXECUTIVE MANSION, *February 6, 1884.*

To the Senate and House of Representatives: .

I transmit herewith, for the consideration of Congress, a communication, under date of the 2d instant, from the Secretary of the Interior, transmitting the last annual report of the Government directors of the Union Pacific Railway Company.

The report accompanying the Secretary's communication has been sent to the House of Representatives.

CHESTER A. ARTHUR.

EXECUTIVE MANSION,
Washington, February 7, 1884.

To the House of Representatives:

I transmit herewith a report of the Secretary of State, in response to the resolution of the House of Representatives of the 16th ultimo, respecting the arrest and imprisonment of John E. Wheelock in Venezuela in 1879.

CHESTER A. ARTHUR.

EXECUTIVE MANSION,
Washington, February 7, 1884.

To the House of Representatives:

I transmit herewith, in response to a resolution of the House of Representatives of the 15th instant [ultimo], a report of the Secretary of State, with accompanying papers, in relation to the reported arrest at Lodz, in Russian Poland, of Reinhardt Wagner, a citizen of the United States.

CHESTER A. ARTHUR.

WASHINGTON, *February 7, 1884.*

To the Senate of the United States:

I transmit herewith to the Senate, for its consideration with a view to its ratification, an agreement concerning trade-marks between the United States and Italy, signed June 1, 1882, provided the terms thereof commend themselves to the Senate.

CHESTER A. ARTHUR.

EXECUTIVE MANSION, *February 11, 1884.*

To the Senate and House of Representatives:

I transmit a communication, under date of the 8th instant, addressed to me by the Secretary of the Navy, covering a report of Professor Simon Newcomb, United States Navy, on the subject of recent improvements in astronomical observatories, instruments, and methods of observations, as noted during his visit to the principal observatories of Europe in the year 1883, made in pursuance of orders of the Navy Department.

The request of the Secretary is commended to the consideration of Congress.

CHESTER A. ARTHUR.

EXECUTIVE MANSION,
Washington, February 12, 1884.

To the Senate of the United States:

I transmit herewith, for the consideration of the Senate in connection with the commercial convention of January 20, 1883, between the United States and Mexico, now pending before the Senate, a protocol of an agreement, signed on the 11th instant by the Secretary of State and the representative of Mexico at this capital, explaining and correcting an error of translation found in the Spanish text of said convention.

CHESTER A. ARTHUR.

EXECUTIVE MANSION, *February 13, 1884.*

To the Senate and House of Representatives:

I transmit herewith a communication of the 8th ultimo from the Secretary of the Interior, and the accompanying papers, relating to the establishment of the boundary line between the United States and the State of Texas.

The matter is presented for the consideration of the Congress.

CHESTER A. ARTHUR.

EXECUTIVE MANSION, *February 13, 1884.*

To the Senate of the United States:

In compliance with the resolution of the Senate of February 6, 1884, directing "that the President be requested, if in his judgment not incompatible with the public interests, to communicate to the Senate the record of the proceedings, testimony, and findings of the court of inquiry in relation to the events connected with the loss of the steamer *Proteus* in the Arctic Ocean," I have the honor to transmit herewith a copy of the record called for in said resolution, together with the letter of the Secretary of War, dated the 12th instant, submitting the same to me.

CHESTER A. ARTHUR.

EXECUTIVE MANSION,
Washington, February 13, 1884.

To the Senate of the United States:

In reply to the resolution of the Senate of the 11th instant, I have the honor to inclose a communication* from the Secretary of State.

CHESTER A. ARTHUR.

EXECUTIVE MANSION, *February 18, 1884.*

To the Senate and House of Representatives:

I transmit herewith the report of a board of Army and Navy officers appointed by me in accordance with the act of Congress approved March 3, 1883, "for the purpose of examining and reporting to Congress which of the navy-yards or arsenals owned by the Government has the best location and is best adapted for the establishment of a Government foundry, or what other method, if any, should be adopted for the manufacture of heavy ordnance adapted to modern warfare, for the use of the Army and Navy of the United States, the cost of all buildings, tools, and implements necessary to be used in the manufacture thereof, including the cost of a steam hammer or apparatus of sufficient size for the manufacture of the heaviest guns."

CHESTER A. ARTHUR.

EXECUTIVE MANSION, *February 21, 1884.*

To the Senate and House of Representatives:

I transmit herewith a report of the Secretary of State of the 21st instant, whereby your honorable body, and through you the people of the United States, may become apprised of the generous contribution made by Her Britannic Majesty's Government toward the efforts for the relief of Lieutenant Greely's arctic exploring party by presenting to the United States the arctic steamship *Alert.*

CHESTER A. ARTHUR.

DEPARTMENT OF STATE,
Washington, February 21, 1884.

The PRESIDENT:

In the search for vessels suitable for the expedition now preparing to relieve Lieutenant Greely and his party, attention was early directed to the *Alert*, which is the property of the British Government, and was the advance ship of the expedition under Sir George Nares. It was desirable to secure this vessel, as she is peculiarly fitted for the intended service, and as the inspecting officers recommended her Mr. Lowell was therefore instructed to ask whether she could be spared for the service.

Information of the wish of this Government having previously and informally reached the British admiralty, a private intimation was conveyed to the United States minister to the effect that the British Government had not forgotten the very considerate conduct of this Government on the occasion of the recovery of the *Resolute*, and that should any suggestion be made that the vessel would be of use to the expedition she would be presented. The *Resolute*, a vessel, as the President remem-

* Relating to the demand of Mexico for the extradition of Alexander Trimble.

bers, formerly belonging to Her Majesty's navy, having been abandoned in the arctic region, was discovered and brought to the United States by American seamen, and thereupon was purchased by this Government of her sailors, repaired, and returned to Great Britain. On her arrival in England the vessel was received by the Queen in person, and the officers of the United States Navy who took the ship thither were treated with every official and personal courtesy.

The Government of Her Majesty has now given the *Alert* to the United States unconditionally, with her anchors, chains, and such of her equipment as can be utilized.

Recognizing this graceful and opportune act of courtesy on the part of Her Majesty's Government, the undersigned to-day instructed Mr. Lowell as follows, by telegraph:

"Her Majesty's Government having presented to the Government of the United States the ship *Alert* to aid in the relief of Lieutenant Greely and his party, you will inform the secretary of state for foreign affairs that the spirit which prompts this act of generosity, and this evidence of sympathy with the object in view, receives the highest appreciation of the President, as it will that of the people of the United States. The President sends his cordial thanks for the opportune gift of this vessel, which he accepts in the name of the United States, and which will be used in the humane enterprise for which it is so peculiarly adapted."

Respectfully submitted.

FREDK. T. FRELINGHUYSEN.

EXECUTIVE MANSION, *February 21, 1884.*

To the Senate and House of Representatives:

I transmit herewith, for the consideration of Congress, a letter from the Secretary of War, dated the 19th instant, submitting a letter from the Chief Signal Officer of the Army, dated the 2d instant, and its accompanying plan of a proposed meteorological observatory at Fort Myer, Va., together with an estimate of the cost of the same in the sum of $4,000 and a statement giving various reasons why the said observatory should be established.

CHESTER A. ARTHUR.

EXECUTIVE MANSION, *February 25, 1884.*

To the House of Representatives:

In answer to so much of the resolution of the House of Representatives of the 17th ultimo as calls for the correspondence with the Mexican Government respecting the payment of claims specified in the fifth section of the act of Congress approved June 17, 1878, I transmit herewith the report of the Secretary of State and its accompanying papers.

CHESTER A. ARTHUR.

EXECUTIVE MANSION, *February 29, 1884.*

To the Senate and House of Representatives:

In compliance with the act of Congress approved January 16, 1883, entitled "An act to regulate and improve the civil service of the United

States,'' the Civil Service Commission has made to the President its first annual report.

That report is herewith transmitted, together with communications from the heads of the several Executive Departments of the Government respecting the practical workings of the law under which the Commission has been acting.

Upon the good results which that law has already accomplished I congratulate Congress and the people, and I avow my conviction that it will henceforth prove to be of still more signal benefit to the public service.

I heartily commend the zeal and fidelity of the Commissioners and their suggestion for further legislation, and I advise the making of such an appropriation as shall be adequate for their needs.

CHESTER A. ARTHUR.

EXECUTIVE MANSION,
Washington, February 29, 1884.

To the Senate and House of Representatives:

I transmit herewith, for the consideration of Congress, a report of the Secretary of State, accompanying a report made by the commission lately designated by me to examine and report upon the asserted unhealthfulness of the swine products of this country. The views and conclusions of the commission deserve the most careful consideration of Congress, to the end that if any path be legitimately open for removing the prohibition which closes important foreign markets to those products it may be followed and appropriate legislation devised.

I earnestly recommend that Congress provide for reimbursing the expenses incurred by the commissioners in this praiseworthy service, and I should be glad also if some remunerative recognition of their public-spirited action in accepting the onerous and responsible duties imposed on them were to suggest itself to Congress. At all events, in view of the conflicting theories touching the origin and propagation of trichiniasis and the means of isolating and extirpating it among domestic swine, and considering the important bearing which precise knowledge on these points would have on the commercial aspects of the matter, I recommend provision for special research in this direction.

CHESTER A. ARTHUR.

EXECUTIVE MANSION,
Washington, March 5, 1884.

To the House of Representatives:

In further response to the resolution of the House of Representatives of the 15th January last, calling for copies of correspondence on file in the Department of State in relation to the reported arrest at Lodz, in Russia, of Reinhardt Wagner, a citizen of the United States, I transmit, in addition to the papers sent you on the 7th ultimo, a copy of a dispatch subsequently received.

CHESTER A. ARTHUR.

EXECUTIVE MANSION,
Washington, March 6, 1884.

To the House of Representatives of the United States:

I transmit herewith to the House of Representatives a report from the Secretary of State, in response to a resolution of that body of the 5th ultimo, calling for correspondence concerning the representations made to this Government in relation to the existing tariff discrimination against the works of foreign artists.

CHESTER A. ARTHUR.

EXECUTIVE MANSION,
Washington, March 10, 1884.

To the House of Representatives:

I transmit herewith the following documents, received from the Secretary of State, relative to the resolution of the House of Representatives upon the death of Mr. Edward Lasker.

CHESTER A. ARTHUR.

EXECUTIVE MANSION,
Washington, March 11, 1884.

To the Senate of the United States:

I submit herewith, for the consideration of the Senate with a view to obtaining its advice and consent thereto, a draft of a proclamation whereby the United States accede and adhere to an international convention for the protection of industrial property, signed at Paris March 20, 1883, and in explanation of the purport of that convention and the proposed mode of effecting the adhesion of the United States thereto I subjoin a report of the Secretary of State.

CHESTER A. ARTHUR.

EXECUTIVE MANSION, *March 14, 1884.*

To the Senate and House of Representatives:

I transmit herewith, for the consideration of Congress, a communication from the Secretary of War of the 12th instant, and accompanying papers, requesting an appropriation of $230,869.44 for the erection at the Presidio of San Francisco of additional buildings at headquarters Military Division of the Pacific, rendered necessary in consequence of the proposed increase of the garrison by removal of troops from points in San Francisco Harbor.

CHESTER A. ARTHUR.

EXECUTIVE MANSION, *March 18, 1884.*
To the Senate and House of Representatives:

I transmit herewith, for the consideration of Congress, a communication from the Secretaries of War and the Navy, concerning the expediency of offering rewards for the rescue of Lieutenant Greely and party by the independent efforts of private vessels, in addition to sending the three ships constituting the national relief expedition.

CHESTER A. ARTHUR.

EXECUTIVE MANSION,
Washington, March 18, 1884.
To the Senate of the United States:

In answer to the resolution of the Senate of the 15th of January last, respecting the discovery of phosphates upon the coast of Brazil by a citizen of the United States, I transmit herewith a report from the Secretary of State upon the subject, together with the accompanying papers.

CHESTER A. ARTHUR.

EXECUTIVE MANSION, *March 20, 1884.*
To the Senate and House of Representatives:

In accordance with the provisions of the act making appropriations for the diplomatic and consular service for the year ending June 30, 1883, I transmit herewith a communication from the Secretary of State in relation to the consular service.

CHESTER A. ARTHUR.

EXECUTIVE MANSION, *March 20, 1884.*
To the Senate and House of Representatives:

I transmit herewith a communication from the Secretary of War of the 18th instant, submitting a letter from Colonel A. F. Rockwell, United States Army, in charge of public buildings and grounds, embodying an estimate in the sum of $30,000 for a pedestal for the statue of General James A. Garfield, to be erected in the city of Washington by the Society of the Army of the Cumberland, together with a letter upon the subject from General Anson G. McCook, on behalf of the Society of the Army of the Cumberland, the object in view being the procurement of an appropriation by Congress of the amount of the accompanying estimate.

I commend the subject to the favorable consideration of Congress.

CHESTER A. ARTHUR.

EXECUTIVE MANSION, *March 26, 1884.*

e and House of Representatives:

ual message I impressed upon Congress the necessity of con-
ess in the reconstruction of the Navy. The recommendations
ion of the Secretary of the Navy and of the Naval Advisory
submitted by me unaccompanied by specific expressions of
now deem it my duty to advise that appropriations be made
tuptation toward designing and commencing the construction
of those additional steel cruisers and the four gunboats thus
i, the cost of which, including their armament, will not ex-
ooo, of which sum one-half should be appropriated for the
bur.

ro, *Boston*, *Atlanta*, and *Dolphin* have been designed and are
rith care and skill, and there is every reason to believe that
>ve creditable and serviceable modern cruisers. Technical
acerning the details of these or of additional vessels can not
tled except by experts, and the Naval Advisory Board, organ-
tion of Congress under the act of August 5, 1882, and con-
ree line officers, a naval constructor, and a naval engineer,
th reference only to character, experience, knowledge, and
. naval architect and a marine engineer from civil life ''of
eputation and standing as experts in naval or marine con-
s an appropriate authority to decide finally all such ques-
unwilling to see the gradual reconstruction of our naval
' happily begun in conformity with modern requirements,
full year for any unsubstantial reason.

conditions Congress may see fit to impose in order to
ous designs and honest and economical construction will be
> me, but to relinquish or postpone the policy already delib-
red will be, in my judgment, an act of national imprudence.
tions should also be made without delay for finishing the
:urreted monitors, the *Puritan*, *Amphitrite*, *Terror*, and *Mo-
> for procuring their armament and that of the *Miantono-*
hulls are built, and their machinery is under contract and
completion, except that of the *Monadnock*, on the Pacific
should also be built, and the armor and heavy guns of all
>cured at the earliest practicable moment.

amount appropriated up to this time for the four vessels is
1. A sum not exceeding $3,838,769.62, including $866,725
erful rifled cannon and for the remainder of the ordnance
>mplete and equip them for service. Of the sum required,
llions need be appropriated for the next fiscal year. It is
that one of the monitors will be a match for the heaviest
>nclads which certain other Governments have constructed
>ur or five millions each, but they will be armored vessels of

an approved and useful type. presenting limited surfaces for the shot of an enemy, and possessed of such seagoing capacity and offensive power as fully to answer our immediate necessities. Their completion having been determined upon in the recent legislation of Congress. no time should be lost in accomplishing the necessary object.

The Gun Foundry Board, appointed by direction of Congress. consisting of three army and three navy officers, has submitted its report. duly transmitted on the 20th day of February, 1884, recommending that the Government should promote the production at private steel works of the required material for heavy cannon, and that two Government factories, one for the Army and one for the Navy, should be established for the fabrication of guns from such material. An early consideration of the report is recommended, together with such action as will enable the Government to construct its ordnance upon its own territory and so to provide the armaments demanded by considerations which concern the national safety and honor.

CHESTER A. ARTHUR.

EXECUTIVE MANSION, *April 1, 1884.*

To the House of Representatives:

In response to a resolution of the House of Representatives of January 15, 1884, requesting the President to forward to the House information, including reports from consuls and others, concerning the undervaluation, false classification, and other irregular practices in the importation of foreign merchandise, and to recommend what legislation, if any, is needed to prevent such frauds on the revenue, I have the honor to transmit herewith a letter of the Secretary of the Treasury of the 28th ultimo, inclosing a draft of a bill on the subject, together with copies of reports taken from the files of the Treasury Department concerning the information desired.

CHESTER A. ARTHUR.

EXECUTIVE MANSION,
Washington, April 1, 1884.

To the House of Representatives:

I transmit herewith a report of the Secretary of State and accompanying papers, furnished in response to a resolution of the House of Representatives of January 16, 1884, calling for information as to the payments made by Spain in accordance with the terms of its treaty with the United States concluded February 17, 1834.

CHESTER A. ARTHUR.

EXECUTIVE MANSION, *April 2, 1884.*

To the Senate and House of Representatives:

I transmit to Congress a communication from the Secretary of War, embodying the views of the president of the Mississippi River Commis-

sion upon a report from Major Stickney, of the Engineer Corps, in relation to the protection of existing levees from destruction by the floods
in the lower part of the Mississippi River. It appears that there is an
urgent need of an appropriation of $100,000 to be used for this purpose, and that an enormous destruction of property may be thereby
averted. I recommend an immediate appropriation of the sum required
for the purpose, to be expended under the direction of the Mississippi
River Commission.

CHESTER A. ARTHUR.

EXECUTIVE MANSION, *April 2, 1884.*
To the House of Representatives:

In response to the resolution of the House of Representatives of 5th of
February last, respecting the arrest and imprisonment of certain American citizens by the authorities of Colombia, at Aspinwall, I transmit a
report of the Secretary of State.

CHESTER A. ARTHUR.

EXECUTIVE MANSION, *April 11, 1884.*
To the Senate and House of Representatives:

The condition of our seacoast defenses and their armament has been
brought to the attention of Congress in my annual messages, and I now
submit a special estimate of the Chief of Ordnance, United States Army,
transmitted by the Secretary of War, for a permanent annual appropriation of $1,500,000 to provide the necessary armament for our fortifications.

This estimate is founded upon the report of the Gun Foundry Board
recently transmitted, to which I have heretofore invited the early attention of Congress.

In presenting this estimate I do not think it necessary to enumerate
the considerations which make it of the highest importance that there
should be no unnecessary delay in entering upon the work, which must
be commensurate with the public interests to be guarded, and which
will take much time.

CHESTER A. ARTHUR.

EXECUTIVE MANSION, *April 14, 1884.*
To the Senate and House of Representatives:

I transmit herewith, for the consideration of Congress, a communication from the Secretary of War of the 5th instant, submitting copies of
certain papers, consisting of a letter, dated February 16 last, from Mr.
Haughwout Howe, of New York City, presenting a proposition for the
sale to the Government for the sum of $5,500 of certain hospital and
other records pertaining to an association founded in New York City in
April, 1862, for the purpose of extending relief to soldiers of the late

war; a report of an examination made of these records by a representative of the War Department, and a report of the Adjutant-General stating that the records would prove of great value to the Department in the settlement of claims of deserving soldiers, as well as in detecting fraudulent claims, as the books, etc., contain information not now of record in the War Department.

The Secretary of War, it will be observed, recommends that an appropriation be made by Congress of the necessary sum for the purchase of the records referred to.

CHESTER A. ARTHUR.

EXECUTIVE MANSION,
Washington, April 14, 1884.

To the Senate of the United States of America:

I transmit herewith to the Senate, for its consideration with a view to ratification, a convention concluded between the United States of America and France and the twenty-four other powers named in said convention for the protection of submarine cables, concluded at Paris on the 14th day of March, A. D. 1884. I also inclose, for the information of the Senate, a copy of Mr. Morton's dispatch No. 518, of the 18th ultimo, in relation to the subject.

CHESTER A. ARTHUR.

WASHINGTON, *April 14, 1884.*

To the Senate of the United States:

I transmit to the Senate, for its consideration with a view to ratification, a convention concerning trade-marks and trade-labels between the United States and Belgium, signed on the 7th instant.

CHESTER A. ARTHUR.

EXECUTIVE MANSION,
Washington, April 18, 1884.

To the Senate and House of Representatives:

I transmit herewith a communication from the Secretary of State of the 16th instant, relative to the approaching visit of a special embassy from Siam to the United States, and recommend that the appropriation asked by the Secretary of State to suitably defray the expenses of such embassy while in this country be made.

CHESTER A. ARTHUR.

EXECUTIVE MANSION,
Washington, April 18, 1884.

To the House of Representatives:

I transmit herewith a copy of a report of the Secretary of State of the 16th instant, in relation to the final award made by the late French and

American Claims Commission against the United States for the sum of $625,566.35, for the payment of the claims of French citizens against this Government. I recommend that an appropriation of the above sum be made to enable the Government to fulfill its obligations under the treaty of January 15, 1880, between this country and France.

CHESTER A. ARTHUR.

EXECUTIVE MANSION,
Washington, April 18, 1884.

To the Senate and House of Representatives:

I transmit herewith a communication from the Secretary of State, dated the 16th instant, respecting the approaching international conference at Washington, D. C., for the purpose of fixing upon a meridian proper to be employed as a common zero of longitude and standard of time reckoning throughout the globe, and recommend that the sum of $10,000 be appropriated to enable the Secretary of State to meet the expenses of the same.

CHESTER A. ARTHUR.

EXECUTIVE MANSION,
Washington, April 18, 1884.

To the Senate of the United States:

In response to the resolution of the Senate of the 5th of December last, respecting the execution by the United States of the ninth article of the treaty of 1819 with Spain, I transmit herewith a report of the Secretary of State and its accompanying papers.

CHESTER A. ARTHUR.

EXECUTIVE MANSION,
Washington, April 22, 1884.

To the Senate of the United States:

I transmit herewith a report of the Secretary of State, in response to a resolution of the Senate of February 29, 1884, requesting information concerning the respective average production, consumption, exportation, and importation of wheat, rye, corn, and cotton in foreign countries, together with statistics showing the production and surplus or deficiency in the crops of the past two years in each of such countries, an estimate of the probable requirements of such products from the United States to meet the wants of these countries before the crops of the coming crop year are ready for market, and other available information concerning the questions to which the resolution refers.

CHESTER A. ARTHUR.

EXECUTIVE MANSION,
Washington, April 24, 1884.

To the House of Representatives:

I transmit herewith, in answer to a resolution of the House of Representatives of the 21st instant, a report of the Secretary of State, with the accompanying papers, in relation to the threatened confiscation of the American college at Rome by the Italian Government.

CHESTER A. ARTHUR.

EXECUTIVE MANSION,
Washington, April 28, 1884.

To the House of Representatives:

I transmit herewith a report of the Secretary of State, in relation to the bill for the support of the diplomatic and consular services.

CHESTER A. ARTHUR.

EXECUTIVE MANSION,
Washington, May 3, 1884.

To the House of Representatives:

I transmit herewith, for your consideration, a communication from the Secretary of State, recommending the appropriation of the sum of $22,500, or so much thereof as may be necessary, to meet the proper obligations of the Government on account of the courteous services of the various umpires of the late American-Spanish Commission.

CHESTER A. ARTHUR.

EXECUTIVE MANSION,
Washington, May 6, 1884.

To the Senate of the United States:

In answer to the resolution of the Senate of March 12, 1884, requesting to be furnished with a copy of correspondence between this Government and that of China respecting the Ward claims and the claim of Charles E. Hill, I herewith submit a letter of the Secretary of State, together with its accompanying papers.

CHESTER A. ARTHUR.

EXECUTIVE MANSION,
Washington, May 6, 1884.

To the Senate and House of Representatives:

I transmit herewith, for the information of Congress, a communication from the Secretary of the Interior, submitting a copy of the report of the Utah Commission.

CHESTER A. ARTHUR.

EXECUTIVE MANSION,
Washington, May 6, 1884.

To the Senate and House of Representatives:

I transmit herewith, for the information of Congress, a copy of the preliminary report of the board of management of the World's Industrial and Cotton Centennial Exposition, showing their operations and containing observations upon other matters concerning the project deemed of importance.
CHESTER A. ARTHUR.

EXECUTIVE MANSION, *May 6, 1884.*

To the House of Representatives:

In answer to that part of the resolution of the House of Representatives of the 17th of January last respecting the question of boundaries between the Republics of Mexico and Guatemala, I transmit herewith the report of the Secretary of State and its accompanying papers.
CHESTER A. ARTHUR.

EXECUTIVE MANSION,
Washington, May 12, 1884.

To the House of Representatives:

I transmit herewith, in answer to the resolution of the House of Representatives of the 6th of February last, a communication from the Secretary of State, respecting the extradition of criminals under the treaty of 1842 with Great Britain.
CHESTER A. ARTHUR.

EXECUTIVE MANSION,
Washington, May 12, 1884.

To the House of Representatives:

I transmit herewith a communication from the Secretary of State, transmitting a draft of a resolution providing for the presentation of a testimonial to Mr. E. L. Oxenham, British consul at Chin-Kiang, in acknowledgment of services rendered the United States.
CHESTER A. ARTHUR.

EXECUTIVE MANSION,
Washington, May 14, 1884.

To the Senate and House of Representatives:

I transmit herewith a communication from the Secretary of State of the 14th instant, with accompanying papers, relative to the necessity of an appropriation by Congress to enable this Government to execute the provisions of the convention between the United States and Mexico of

July 29, 1882, for the relocation of the monuments marking the boundary line between the two countries, and recommend that the amount asked, $224,556.75, be immediately provided.

CHESTER A. ARTHUR.

EXECUTIVE MANSION,
Washington, May 15, 1884.

To the Senate:

I transmit herewith to the Senate, for consideration with a view to advising and consenting thereto, an agreement, signed May 14, 1884, between the Secretary of State and the minister plenipotentiary of Siam, for the regulation of the liquor traffic in Siam when citizens of the United States engage in the importation or sale of liquors there.

CHESTER A. ARTHUR.

EXECUTIVE MANSION, *May 19, 1884.*

To the House of Representatives:

I transmit herewith, for such action as is deemed proper, a communication from the Secretary of State, recommending an additional appropriation of $6,000 for the construction of a wharf and roadway as a means of approach to the monument to be erected at Wakefield, Westmoreland County, Va., to mark the birthplace of George Washington.

I commend the matter to your favorable attention.

CHESTER A. ARTHUR.

EXECUTIVE MANSION, *May 19, 1884.*

To the House of Representatives:

I transmit herewith a report from the Secretary of State, with accompanying copies of correspondence, in further response to the resolution of the House of Representatives of January 16, 1884, respecting the arrest and imprisonment of John E. Wheelock in Venezuela in 1879.

CHESTER A. ARTHUR.

EXECUTIVE MANSION, *May 29, 1884.*

To the House of Representatives:

I transmit herewith, for such action as is deemed proper, a communication from the Secretary of State, accompanied by several inclosures, in which he recommends an appropriation for rewarding the services of the Osette Indians in rescuing and caring for the crew of the American steamer *Umatilla*, which vessel was wrecked in February last near the Vancouvers Island.

CHESTER A. ARTHUR.

EXECUTIVE MANSION,
Washington, May 29, 1884.

░░░ ░░ *United States:*

it herewith, in response to the resolution of the Senate of
last, a report from the Secretary of State, with accompanying
regard to the claim of Edward H. Ladd against the Govern-
░░░░░░.

CHESTER A. ARTHUR.

EXECUTIVE MANSION,
Washington, June 9, 1884.

░░ ░░░ *House of Representatives:*

it herewith, for the consideration of Congress, a letter and
anying estimate, submitted by the board charged with pre-
epartmental exhibit for the World's Industrial and Cotton
Exposition to be held at New Orleans, beginning December
'his board was appointed by Executive order of May 13, 1884,*
posed of representatives of the several Executive Departments,
ment of Agriculture, and the Smithsonian Institution. It is
th the important and responsible duty of making arrangements
)lete and harmonious collection of the articles and materials
;irable to place on exhibition, in illustration of the resources of
y, its methods of governmental administration, and its means
ind defense.

rd submits an estimate calling for an appropriation of $588,000
ish the desired end. That amount is distributed among the
ts as shown in the table. The War, Navy, and Interior De-
call for the largest share, representing as they do the national
y land and sea, the progress of naval architecture and ord-
geological survey and mineral wealth of the Territories, the
of the Indians, and the education of the masses, all of which
iried and instructive exhibits. The Smithsonian Institution,
ier its general care the National Museum and the Fish Com-
prepared to make a display second in interest to none of
ys. The remaining Departments can present instructive and
exhibits, which will attract popular attention and convey an
ir extensively ramified duties and of the many points where
icially affect the life of the people as a nation and as indi-

iibit of the Government at the Centennial Exhibition held
lphia in 1876 was admitted to be one of the most attractive
that great national undertaking and a valuable addition to it.
of intelligence and scientific attainments, at home and abroad,
the highest encomiums, showing the interest it awakened

* See pp. 230-231.

among those whose lives are given to the improvement of the social and material condition of the people.

The reproduction of such a display now on a more extensive plan is rendered possible by the advancement of science and invention during the eight years that have passed since the Philadelphia exhibit was collected.

The importance, purposes, and benefits of the New Orleans Exhibition are continental in their scope. Standing at the threshold of the almost unopened markets of Spanish and Portuguese America, New Orleans is a natural gateway to their trade, and the exhibition offers to the people of Mexico and Central and South America an adequate knowledge of our farming implements, metal manufactures, cotton and woolen goods, and the like necessities of existence, in respect to which those countries are either deficient or supplied to a limited extent. The breaking down of the barriers which still separate us from the Republics of America whose productions so entirely complement our own will aid greatly in removing the disparity of commercial intercourse under which less than 10 per cent of our exports go to American countries.

I trust that Congress will realize the urgency of this recommendation and make its appropriation immediately available, so that the board may lose no time in undertaking the extensive preparations necessary to spread a more intimate knowledge of our Government institutions and national resources among the people of our country and of neighboring states in a way to command the respect due it in the family of nations.

CHESTER A. ARTHUR.

EXECUTIVE MANSION,
Washington, June 9, 1884.

To the Senate of the United States:

I transmit herewith, for consideration by the Senate and appropriate action thereon, a report of the Secretary of State, communicating the proposal of the King of Hawaii that the duration of the existing reciprocity treaty with the United States be extended for a further definite period of seven years.

The treaty having been heretofore under consideration by your honorable body, I deem it fitting to consult the Senate in the matter before directing the negotiations to proceed.

CHESTER A. ARTHUR.

EXECUTIVE MANSION,
Washington, June 11, 1884.

To the House of Representatives:

In compliance with the resolution of the House of Representatives of the 10th instant, I return House bill No. 2344, entitled "An act for the relief of Melissa G. Polar."

CHESTER A. ARTHUR.

EXECUTIVE MANSION,
To the House of Representatives: *Washington, June 11, 1884.*

I transmit herewith to the House of Representatives, in response to a resolution of that body of the 21st of April last, a copy of the material correspondence on file in the Department of State relative to the claim of W. J. Hale against the Argentine Republic, and a list of the papers.

CHESTER A. ARTHUR.

EXECUTIVE MANSION,
To the Senate of the United States: *Washington, June 12, 1884.*

I transmit herewith, in response to a resolution of the Senate dated May 2, 1884, the following report of the Secretary of State, with an accompanying paper, relative to the latest law of the Mexican Republic creating or modifying the *zona libre* in relation to importations of merchandise.

CHESTER A. ARTHUR.

EXECUTIVE MANSION,
To the Senate: *Washington, June 13, 1884.*

I transmit to the Senate, for its consideration with a view to ratification, a convention signed on the 11th instant, supplementary to the extradition convention concluded between the United States and Italy on the 23d of March, 1868.

CHESTER A. ARTHUR.

EXECUTIVE MANSION,
To the House of Representatives: *Washington, June 19, 1884.*

I transmit herewith, in answer to the resolution of the House of Representatives of the 31st of March last, a communication from the Secretary of State, with accompanying papers, concerning the rent of consular premises in China.

CHESTER A. ARTHUR.

EXECUTIVE MANSION, *June 21, 1884.*
To the Senate and House of Representatives:

I have permitted House bill No. 4689, entitled "An act for the relief of Eliza W. Patterson," to become a law by withholding action upon it for ten days after it was presented to me.

The affairs and interests of the District of Columbia are committed to Congress as its legislature. I do not question the constitutional right of Congress to pass a law relieving the family of an officer, in view of the services he had rendered his country, from the burdens of taxation, but I submit to Congress that this just gift of the nation to the family of such faithful officer should come from the National Treasury rather than from that of this District, and I therefore recommend that an appropriation be made to reimburse the District for the amount of taxes which would have been due to it had this act not become a law.

CHESTER A. ARTHUR.

EXECUTIVE MANSION,
To the House of Representatives: *Washington, June 24, 1884.*

In answer to a resolution of the House of Representatives of the 7th instant, making an inquiry regarding the expenditure of moneys appropriated by Congress to meet the expenses of the French and American Claims Commission, I transmit herewith a report of the Secretary of State upon the subject.   CHESTER A. ARTHUR.

EXECUTIVE MANSION, *June 28, 1884.*
To the Senate and House of Representatives:

I transmit herewith a communication from the Secretary of the Interior, calling attention to certain omissions, etc., in the act (H. R. 1340) entitled "An act to establish a Bureau of Labor Statistics," and invite the attention of the Congress to the same.

CHESTER A. ARTHUR.

EXECUTIVE MANSION,
To the House of Representatives: *Washington, June 30, 1884.*

I transmit herewith, in compliance with resolutions of the House of Representatives respectively dated March 22 and April 19, 1884, a report from the Secretary of State, communicating information in regard to moneys received from Venezuela under the treaty of April 25, 1866, and their distribution to holders of awards by the Department of State.

CHESTER A. ARTHUR.

EXECUTIVE MANSION,
To the Senate of the United States: *Washington, July 3, 1884.*

I transmit herewith, in response to a resolution of the Senate of the 11th of February last, a report of the Secretary of State, relative to the papers on file in the Department of State touching the unsettled claims of citizens of the United States against France for spoliations prior to July 31, 1801.   CHESTER A. ARTHUR.

EXECUTIVE MANSION, *July 7, 1884.*
To the House of Representatives:

In compliance with the concurrent resolution of the Senate and House nresentatives of the 5th instant, I return herewith House bill 6770, entitled "An act making appropriations for the consular and diplomatic service of the Government for the fiscal year ending June 30, 1885, and for other purposes."

CHESTER A. ARTHUR.

VETO MESSAGE.

EXECUTIVE MANSION, *July 2, 1884.*

To the House of Representatives:

After careful consideration of the bill entitled "An act for the relief of Fitz John Porter," I herewith return it with my objections to that House of Congress in which it originated. Its enacting clause is in terms following:

That the President be, and he is hereby, authorized to nominate and, by and with the advice and consent of the Senate, to appoint Fitz John Porter, late a major-general of the United States Volunteers and a brevet brigadier-general and colonel of the Army, to the position of colonel in the Army of the United States, of the same grade and rank held by him at the time of his dismissal from the Army by sentence of court-martial promulgated January 27, 1863. * * *

It is apparent that should this bill become a law it will create a new office which can be filled by the appointment of the particular individual whom it specifies, and can not be filled otherwise; or it may be said with perhaps greater precision of statement that it will create a new office upon condition that the particular person designated shall be chosen to fill it. Such an act, as it seems to me, is either unnecessary and ineffective or it involves an encroachment by the legislative branch of the Government upon the authority of the Executive. As the Congress has no power under the Constitution to nominate or appoint an officer and can not lawfully impose upon the President the duty of nominating or appointing to office any particular individual of its own selection, this bill, if it can fairly be construed as requiring the President to make the nomination and, by and with the advice and consent of the Senate, the appointment which it authorizes, is in manifest violation of the Constitution. If such be not its just interpretation, it must be regarded as a mere enactment of advice and counsel, which lacks in the very nature of things the force of positive law and can serve no useful purpose upon the statute books.

There are other causes that deter me from giving this bill the sanction of my approval. The judgment of the court-martial by which more than twenty years since General Fitz John Porter was tried and convicted was pronounced by a tribunal composed of nine general officers of distinguished character and ability. Its investigation of the charges of which it found the accused guilty was thorough and conscientious, and its find-·ings and sentence were in due course of law approved by Abraham

Lincoln, then President of the United States. Its legal competency, its jurisdiction of the accused and of the subject of the accusation, and the substantial regularity of all of its proceedings are matters which have never been brought into question. Its judgment, therefore, is final and conclusive in its character.

The Supreme Court of the United States has recently declared that a court-martial such as this was is the organism provided by law and clothed with the duty of administering justice in this class of cases. Its judgments, when approved, rest on the same basis and are surrounded by the same considerations which give conclusiveness to the judgments of other legal tribunals, including as well the lowest as the highest. It follows, accordingly, that when a lawfully constituted court-martial has duly declared its findings and its sentence and the same have been duly approved neither the President nor the Congress has any power to set them aside. The existence of such power is not openly asserted, nor perhaps is it necessarily implied, in the provisions of the bill which is before me, but when its enacting clauses are read in the light of the recitations of its preamble it will be seen that it seeks in effect the practical annulment of the findings and the sentence of a competent court-martial.

A conclusion at variance with these findings has been reached after investigation by a board consisting of three officers of the Army. This board was not created in pursuance of any statutory authority and was powerless to compel the attendance of witnesses or to pronounce a judgment which could have been lawfully enforced. The officers who constituted it, in their report to the Secretary of War, dated March 19, 1879, state that in their opinion—

Justice requires * * * such action as may be necessary to annul and set aside the findings and sentence of the court-martial in the case of Major-General Fitz John Porter and to restore him to the positions of which that sentence deprived him, such restoration to take effect from the date of his dismissal from the service.

The provisions of the bill now under consideration are avowedly based on the assumption that the findings of the court-martial have been discovered to be erroneous; but it will be borne in mind that the investigation which is claimed to have resulted in this discovery was made many years after the events to which that evidence related and under circumstances that made it impossible to reproduce the evidence on which they were based.

It seems to me that the proposed legislation would establish a dangerous precedent, calculated to imperil in no small measure the binding force and effect of the judgments of the various tribunals established under our Constitution and laws.

I have already, in the exercise of the pardoning power with which the President is vested by the Constitution, remitted the continuing penalty which had made it impossible for Fitz John Porter to hold any office of trust or profit under the Government of the United States; but I am unwilling to give my sanction to any legislation which shall practically annul and set at naught the solemn and deliberate conclusions of the tribunal by which he was convicted and of the President by whom its findings were examined and approved.

CHESTER A. ARTHUR.

PROCLAMATIONS.

BY THE PRESIDENT OF THE UNITED STATES OF AMERICA.

A PROCLAMATION.

Whereas both Houses of Congress did on the 20th instant request the commemoration, on the 23d instant, of the one hundredth anniversary of the surrender by George Washington, at Annapolis, of his commission as Commander in Chief of the patriot forces of America; and

Whereas it is fitting that this memorable act, which not only signalized the termination of the heroic struggle of seven years for independence, but also manifested Washington's devotion to the great principle that ours is a civic government of and by the people, should be generally observed throughout the United States:

Now, therefore, I, Chester A. Arthur, President of the United States, do hereby recommend that either by appropriate exercises in connection with the religious services of the 23d instant or by such public observances as may be deemed proper on Monday, the 24th instant, this signal event in the history of American liberty be commemorated; and further, I hereby direct that at 12 o'clock noon on Monday next the national salute be fired from all the forts throughout the country.

In witness whereof I have hereunto set my hand and caused the seal of the United States to be affixed.

[SEAL.]   Done this 21st day of December, A. D. 1883, and of the Independence of the United States the one hundred and eighth.

CHESTER A. ARTHUR.

By the President:
FREDK. T. FRELINGHUYSEN,
Secretary of State.

BY THE PRESIDENT OF THE UNITED STATES OF AMERICA.

A PROCLAMATION.

Whereas by a memorandum of an agreement executed at Madrid on the 13th day of February, A. D. 1884, by and between the duly authorized agents and representatives of the Government of the United States of America and of the Government of His Majesty the King of Spain, satisfactory evidence has been given to me that the Government of that country has abolished the discriminating customs duty heretofore imposed upon the products of and articles proceeding from the United States of America imported into the islands of Cuba and Puerto Rico, said abolition to take effect on and after the 1st day of March next:

Now, therefore, I, Chester A. Arthur, President of the United States of America, by virtue of the authority vested in me by section 4228 of the Revised Statutes, do hereby declare and proclaim that on and after the said 1st day of March next, so long as the products of and articles proceeding from the United States imported into the islands of Cuba and Puerto Rico shall be exempt from discriminating customs duties, any such duties on the products of and articles proceeding from Cuba and Puerto Rico under the Spanish flag shall be suspended and discontinued.

In witness whereof I have hereunto set my hand and caused the seal of the United States to be affixed.

[SEAL.]   Done at the city of Washington, this 14th day of February, A. D. 1884, and of the Independence of the United States the one hundred and eighth.

CHESTER A. ARTHUR.

By the President:

FREDK. T. FRELINGHUYSEN, *Secretary of State.*

BY THE PRESIDENT OF THE UNITED STATES OF AMERICA.

A PROCLAMATION.

Whereas it is alleged that certain persons have within the territory and jurisdiction of the United States begun and set on foot preparations for an organized and forcible possession of and settlement upon the lands of what is known as the Oklahoma lands, in the Indian Territory, which Territory is designated, recognized, and described by the treaties and laws of the United States and by the executive authorities as Indian country, and as such is subject to occupation by Indian tribes only; and

Whereas the laws of the United States provide for the removal of all persons residing or being found in said Indian Territory without express permission of the Interior Department:

Now, therefore, for the purpose of properly protecting the interests of the Indian nations and tribes in said Territory, and that settlers may not be induced to go into a country, at great expense to themselves, where they can not be allowed to remain, I, Chester A. Arthur, President of the United States, do admonish and warn all such persons so intending or preparing to remove upon said lands or into said Territory against any attempt to so remove or settle upon any of the lands of said Territory; and I do further warn and notify any and all such persons who do so offend that they will be speedily and immediately removed therefrom by the proper officers of the Interior Department, and, if necessary, the aid and assistance of the military forces of the United States will be invoked to remove all such intruders from the said Indian Territory.

In testimony whereof I have hereunto set my hand and caused the seal of the United States to be affixed.

[SEAL.]   Done at the city of Washington, this 1st day of July, A. D. 1884, and of the Independence of the United States the one hundred and eighth.

CHESTER A. ARTHUR.

By the President:

FREDK. T. FRELINGHUYSEN, *Secretary of State.*

BY THE PRESIDENT OF THE UNITED STATES OF AMERICA.

A PROCLAMATION.

While quarantine regulations are committed to the several States, the General Government has reposed certain powers in the President, to be used at his discretion in preventing a threatened epidemic.

Feeling it my duty, I hereby call upon all persons who under existing systems in the several States are intrusted with the execution of quarantine regulations to be diligent and on the alert in order to prevent the introduction of the pestilence which we all regret to learn has made its appearance in some of the countries of Europe between which and the ports of the United States intercourse is direct and frequent.

I further advise that the cities and towns of the United States, whether on the coast or on the lines of interior communication, by sound sanitary regulations and the promotion of cleanliness, be prepared to resist the power of the disease and to mitigate its severity.

And I further direct the consuls of the United States in the ports where the pestilence has made or may make its appearance to exercise vigilance in carrying out the instructions heretofore given and in communicating to the Government of the United States any information of value relating to the progress or treatment of the disease.

Given under my hand and the seal of the United States, at the city of Washington, this 19th day of July, A. D. 1884, and of the Independence of the United States the one hundred and ninth.

[SEAL.]

CHESTER A. ARTHUR.

By the President:

FREDK T. FRELINGHUYSEN, *Secretary of State.*

BY THE PRESIDENT OF THE UNITED STATES OF AMERICA.

A PROCLAMATION.

The season is nigh when it is the yearly wont of this people to observe day appointed for that purpose by the President as an especial occasion for thanksgiving unto God.

Now, therefore, in recognition of this hallowed custom, I, Chester A. Arthur, President of the United States, do hereby designate as such day of general thanksgiving Thursday, the 27th day of this present November.

And I do recommend that throughout the land the people, ceasing from their accustomed occupations, do then keep holiday at their several homes and their several places of worship, and with heart and voice pay reverent acknowledgment to the Giver of All Good for the countless blessings wherewith He hath visited this nation.

In witness whereof I have hereunto set my hand and caused the seal of the United States to be affixed.

[SEAL.] Done at the city of Washington, this 7th day of November, A. D. 1884, and of the Independence of the United States the one hundred and ninth. CHESTER A. ARTHUR.

By the President:
FREDK. T. FRELINGHUYSEN,
Secretary of State.

EXECUTIVE ORDERS.

In the exercise of the power vested in the President by the Constitution, and by virtue of the seventeen hundred and fifty-third section of the Revised Statutes and of the civil-service act approved January 16, 1883, the following rule for the regulation and improvement of the executive civil service is hereby amended and promulgated, as follows:

RULE XII.

1. Every regular application must be supported by proper certificates of good moral character, health, and physical and mental capacity for doing the public work, the certificates to be in such form and number as the regulations of the Commission shall provide; but no certificate will be received which is inconsistent with the tenth section of the civil-service act.

2. No one shall be entitled to be examined for admission to the classified postal service if under 16 or over 35 years of age, or to the classified customs service or to the classified departmental service if under 18 or over 45 years of age; but no one shall be examined for appointment to any place in the classified customs service, except that of clerk or messenger, who is under 21 years of age; but these limitations of age shall not apply to persons honorably discharged from the military or naval service of the country who are otherwise duly qualified.

Approved, December 5, 1883. CHESTER A. ARTHUR.

EXECUTIVE MANSION, *December 17, 1883.*

The following-named officers of the Army and Navy will constitute a board to consider an expedition to be sent for the relief of Lieutenant Greely and his party, composing what is known as the "Lady Franklin Bay Expedition," and to recommend to the Secretaries of War and the

Navy, jointly, the steps the board may consider necessary to be taken for the equipment and transportation of the relief expedition, and to suggest such plan for its control and conduct and for the organization of its personnel as may seem to them best adapted to accomplish its purpose:

Brigadier-General William B. Hazen, Chief Signal Officer, United States Army; Captain James A. Greer, United States Navy; Lieutenant-Commander B. H. McCalla, United States Navy; Captain George W. Davis, Fourteenth Infantry, United States Army.

The board will meet in Washington, D. C., on the 20th instant.

CHESTER A. ARTHUR.

In the exercise of the power vested in the President by the Constitution, and by virtue of the seventeen hundred and fifty-third section of the Revised Statutes and of the civil-service act approved January 16, 1883, the following rule and the amendment to Rule XVI for the regulation and improvement of the executive civil service are hereby promulgated:

RULE XXI.

1. No person shall be promoted, without examination under these rules, from any position for which an examination is not required to any position for which an examination is required under the rules; nor shall any person who has passed only a limited examination under clause 4 of Rule VII for the lower classes or grades in the departmental or customs service be promoted within two years after appointment to any position giving a salary of $1,000 or upward without first passing an examination under clause 1 of said rule, and such examination shall not be allowed within the first year after appointment.

2. But a person who has passed the examination under said clause 1 and has accepted a position giving a salary of $900 or less shall have the same right of promotion as if originally appointed to a position giving a salary of $1,000 or more.

3. The Commission may at any time certify for a $900 or any lower place in the classified service any person upon the register who has passed the examination under clause 1 of Rule VII if such person does not object before such certification is made.

II. The following words are added as a fifth clause at the end of Rule XVI, viz:

5. Any person appointed to or employed in any part of the classified service, after due certification for the same under these rules, who shall be dismissed or separated therefrom without fault or delinquency on his part may be reappointed or reemployed in the same part or grade of such service at the same office, within eight months next following such dismissal or separation, without further examination.

III. It is further ordered that the rule heretofore designated XXI be hereafter designated XXII, and XXII as Rule XXIII.

Approved, January 18, 1884.

CHESTER A. ARTHUR.

EXECUTIVE MANSION, *February 8, 1884.*

General William T. Sherman, General of the Army, having this day reached the age of 64 years, is, in accordance with law, placed upon the retired list of the Army without reduction in his current pay and allow-

The announcement of the severance from the command of the Army of one who has been for so many years its distinguished chief can but awaken in the minds, not only of the Army, but of the people of the United States, mingled emotions of regret and gratitude—regret at the withdrawal from active military service of an officer whose lofty sense of duty has been a model for all soldiers since he first entered the Army in July, 1840, and gratitude, freshly awakened, for the services, of incalculable value, rendered by him in the war for the Union, which his great military genius and daring did so much to end.

The President deems this a fitting occasion to give expression in this manner to the gratitude felt toward General Sherman by his fellow-citizens, and to the hope that Providence may grant him many years of health and happiness in the relief from the active duties of his profession.

CHESTER A. ARTHUR.

DEPARTMENT OF JUSTICE,
Washington, March 12, 1884.

To the District Attorneys and Marshals of the United States:

By direction of the President, I have to inform you it is reported that certain persons are aiding in the prosecution of heinous crimes by shipping to foreign ports explosives dangerous in the highest degree to life and property. No proof has been adduced that this rumor is founded upon fact, and the President can not believe its truth. The honor of this nation, however, requires that it should not be open to the imputation, unfounded though it be, of the slightest appearance of tolerating such crimes, whether to be committed against our people or those of other countries.

Your attention is therefore called to sections 5353, 5354, 5355, 4278, and 4279 of the Revised Statutes of the United States, which regulate the shipment of explosives and the punishment of those who infringe their provisions; and you are instructed to be diligent in your efforts to prevent the offenses described and to detect and prosecute those who have or may commit them.

Very respectfully,

BENJAMIN HARRIS BREWSTER,
Attorney-General.

BY THE PRESIDENT OF THE UNITED STATES.

EXECUTIVE ORDER.

Whereas it has been brought to the notice of the President of the United States that in the World's Industrial and Cotton Centennial Exhibition of Arts, Manufactures, and Products of the Soil and Mines, to be held in the city of New Orleans, commencing December 1, 1884, for the purpose of celebrating the one hundredth anniversary of the production, manufacture, and commerce of cotton, it is desirable that from the Executive Departments of the Government of the United States in which there may be articles suitable for the purpose intended there should appear such articles and materials as will, when presented in a collective exhibition, illustrate the functions and administrative faculties of the Government in time of peace and its resources as a war power, and thereby serve to demonstrate the nature of our institutions and their adaptation to the wants of the people:

Now, for the purpose of securing a complete and harmonious arrangement of the articles and materials designed to be exhibited from the Executive Departments of the Government, it is ordered that a board, to be composed of one person to be named by the head of each of the Executive Departments which may have articles and materials to be exhibited, and also of one person to be named in behalf of the Smithsonian Institution, and one to be named in behalf of the Department of Agriculture, and one to be named in behalf of the Bureau of Education, be charged with the preparation, arrangement, and safe-keeping of such articles and materials as the heads of the several Departments and the Commissioner of Agriculture, the Director of the Smithsonian Institution, and the Commissioner of Education may respectively decide shall be embraced in the collection; that one of the persons thus named, to be designated by the President, shall be chairman of such board, and that the board appoint from their number such other officers as they may think necessary; and that the said board, when organized, shall be authorized, under the direction of the President, to confer with the executive officers of the World's Industrial Cotton Centennial Exhibition in relation to such matters connected with the subject as may pertain to the respective Departments having articles and materials on exhibition, and that the names of the persons thus selected by the heads of the several Departments, the Commissioner of Agriculture, the Director of the Smithsonian Institution, and the Commissioner of Education shall be submitted to the President for designation.

Done at the city of Washington, this 9th day of April, 1884, and of the Independence of the United States the one hundred and eighth.

CHESTER A. ARTHUR.

By the President:
  FREDK. T. FRELINGHUYSEN,
    Secretary of State.

In the exercise of the power vested in the President by the Constitution and by virtue of the seventeen hundred and fifty-third section of the Revised Statutes and of the civil-service act approved January 16, 1883, the following rules for the regulation and improvement of the executive civil service are amended as stated below, and are hereby promulgated:

1. Rule XI is amended by adding thereto a second clause, as follows:

2. The Commission may by regulations, subject to change at any time by the President, declare the kind and measure of ill health, physical incapacity, misrepresentation, and bad faith which may properly exclude any person from the right of examination, grading, or certification under these rules. It may also provide for medical certificates of physical capacity in the proper cases, and for the appropriate certification of persons so defective in sight, speech, hearing, or otherwise as to be apparently disqualified for some of the duties of the part of the service which they seek to enter.

2. The second clause of Rule XII is amended by substituting for the first line and the second line thereof down to the word "age" therein (as printed in the annual report of the Commission) the following words:

No one shall be entitled to be examined for admission to the classified postal service if under 16 or over 35 years of age, excepting messengers, stampers, and other junior assistants, who must not be under 14 years of age.

3. Rule XXI, as printed in said report, is amended by substituting for the first two lines and the third line down to the word "rules" therein the following words:

No person, unless excepted under Rule XIX, shall be admitted into the classified civil service from any place not within said service without an examination and certification under the rules.

Approved, April 23, 1884.

CHESTER A. ARTHUR.

In the exercise of the power vested in the President by the Constitution, and by virtue of the seventeen hundred and fifty-third section of the Revised Statutes and of the civil-service act approved January 16, 1883, the following rule for the regulation and improvement of the executive civil service is amended as stated below, and is hereby promulgated:

Rule XI is amended by striking out the last sentence of said rule as printed in the annual report of the Commission and inserting in place thereof the following, namely:

No person under enlistment in the Army or Navy of the United States shall be examined under these rules except for some place in the Department under which he is enlisted requiring special qualifications, and with the consent in writing of the head of such Department.

Approved, April 23, 1884.

CHESTER A. ARTHUR.

BY THE PRESIDENT OF THE UNITED STATES.

EXECUTIVE ORDER.

In conformity with the Executive order directing the organization of a board, to be composed of one person to be named by the head of each of the Executive Departments which may have articles and materials to be exhibited at the World's Industrial and Cotton Centennial Exhibition, I hereby direct the persons who have been so designated, viz, Major and Brevet Lieutenant-Colonel Stephen C. Lyford, United States Army, of the War Department, president of the board; Charles S. Hill, of the Department of State; Lieutenant B. H. Buckingham, United States Navy, of the Navy Department; William F. McLennan, of the Treasury Department; Abraham D. Hazen, Assistant Postmaster-General; Benjamin Butterworth, of the Interior Department; Cecil Clay, of the Department of Justice; William Saunders, of the Agricultural Department; G. Brown Goode, of the Smithsonian Institution; Lyndon A. Smith, of the Bureau of Education, Interior Department, to assemble at the Department of State, in the city of Washington, at noon on the 17th day of May, 1884, and then and there to organize said board; and said board when so organized shall immediately proceed to the discharge of its duties.

I also designate W. A. De Caindry as the secretary of said board.

Done at the city of Washington, this 13th day of May, 1884, and of the Independence of the United States the one hundred and eighth.

CHESTER A. ARTHUR.

By the President:

FREDK. T. FRELINGHUYSEN,
Secretary of State.

EXECUTIVE MANSION,
Washington, May 26, 1884.

Under the provisions of section 4 of the act approved March 3, 1883, it is hereby ordered that the several Executive Departments, the Department of Agriculture, and the Government Printing Office be closed on Friday, the 30th instant, to enable the employees to participate in the decoration of the graves of the soldiers who fell during the rebellion.

CHESTER A. ARTHUR.

In the exercise of the power vested in the President by the Constitution, and by virtue of the seventeen hundred and fifty-third section of the Revised Statutes and of the civil-service act approved January 16, 1883, the following special rule for the regulation and improvement of the executive civil service is hereby promulgated:

SPECIAL RULE.

Any person who was employed on or before the 16th day of January, 1883, in any Executive Department at Washington in a position not included in the classified service in said Department, but who was at that date exclusively engaged in the duties of a clerk or copyist, and who has since been continuously so engaged, may, in the discretion of the head of the Department, be treated as within the classified service for the Department in a grade corresponding to such duties, provided such person has either already passed an examination under the civil-service rules or shall pass an appropriate competitive or noncompetitive examination thereunder at a grade of 65 per cent or upward.

Approved, June 12, 1884.

CHESTER A. ARTHUR.

EXECUTIVE MANSION, *July 8, 1884.*

In order to carry out the provisions of that portion of the act entitled "An act making appropriations for sundry civil expenses of the Government for the fiscal year ending June 30, 1885, and for other purposes," approved July 7, 1884, which contemplates the participation of the several Executive Departments, the Department of Agriculture, and the Smithsonian Institution in the World's Industrial and Cotton Centennial Exposition of 1884-85, the board heretofore appointed by Executive order to take charge of the articles and materials to be exhibited by these Departments, the Department of Agriculture, and the Smithsonian Institution is hereby continued under the following regulations and distribution of duties, viz:

The funds appropriated for such participation will be drawn from the Treasury upon the requisition of the president of the board, and will be disbursed and accounted for as are other public moneys under the existing laws and regulations relating to disbursing officers.

An officer of the Army will be detailed by the Secretary of War and an officer of the Navy will be detailed by the Secretary of the Navy to report to the president of the board for duty as disbursing officers of the board.

The representatives of the several Executive Departments, the representative of the Department of Agriculture, and the representative of the Smithsonian Institution will have charge of the matter pertaining to their respective Departments, subject to the general advisement of the board, and all bills will be paid by the disbursing officers upon vouchers certified by such representatives and countersigned by the president of the board.

The disbursing officers will render, through the president of the board, monthly accounts current of all advances and disbursements by them to the First Auditor of the Treasury for audit and settlement in the same manner as are other accounts of disbursing officers of the Government.

Each representative will be held responsible to the head of his respective Department for all public property of the United States furnished by the head of such Department or otherwise coming to his hands for the purposes of the exposition, and will render proper accounts of the same to such head of Department until the property is returned.

CHESTER A. ARTHUR.

EXECUTIVE MANSION, *July 10, 1884.*

The participation of the several Executive Departments, the Department of Agriculture, and the Smithsonian Institution in the Cincinnati

Industrial Exposition at Cincinnati, Ohio, and the Southern Exposition at Louisville, Ky., as contemplated by the ''act making appropriations for sundry civil expenses of the Government for the fiscal year ending June 30, 1885, and for other purposes,'' is hereby placed under the management of the board referred to in Executive order of July 8, 1884, relating to the participation of said Departments and Institution in the World's Industrial and Cotton Centennial Exposition of 1884–85, the provisions of which order being hereby extended to embrace said Cincinnati and Louisville expositions.

CHESTER A. ARTHUR.

EXECUTIVE MANSION, *July 16, 1884.*

No appropriation having been specifically made for the participation of the Bureau of Education, Interior Department, in the World's Industrial and Cotton Centennial Exposition at New Orleans, La., the Industrial Exposition, Cincinnati, Ohio, or the Southern Exposition, Louisville, Ky., the representative on behalf of that Bureau in the board appointed by Executive order of May 13, 1884,* is relieved from further duty as a member of the board, and the display of that Bureau will be made as a part of the exhibit of the Interior Department out of the moneys appropriated for the participation of that Department in said expositions.

CHESTER A. ARTHUR.

In the exercise of the power vested in the President by the Constitution, and by virtue of the seventeen hundred and fifty-third section of the Revised Statutes and of the civil-service act approved January 16, 1883, the following special rule for the regulation and improvement of the executive civil service is hereby promulgated:

SPECIAL RULE.

The names of all persons who shall have successfully passed their examination under the civil-service rules previous to July 16, 1884, may remain on the register of persons eligible for appointment two years from the date of their respective registrations, unless sooner appointed.

Approved, July 18, 1884.

CHESTER A. ARTHUR.

In the exercise of the power vested in the President by the Constitution, and by virtue of the seventeen hundred and fifty-third section of the Revised Statutes and of the civil-service act approved January 16, 1883, the following special rule for the regulation and improvement of the executive civil service is hereby promulgated:

SPECIAL RULE NO. 3.

Appointments to the 150 places in the Pension Office provided to be filled by the act of July 7, 1884, except so far as they may be filled by promotions, must be

* See pp. 230–231.

separately apportioned by the appointing power in as near conformity to the second section of the act of January 16, 1883, as the need of filling them promptly and the residence and qualifications of the applicants will permit.

Approved, July 22, 1884.

CHESTER A. ARTHUR.

DEPARTMENT OF STATE,
Washington, September 5, 1884.

SIR:* With deep regret I announce to you that the Hon. Charles J. Folger, Secretary of the Treasury of the United States, yesterday died at his home in Geneva, State of New York.

Thus has closed the life of a distinguished and respected citizen, who by his services as an executive officer of the United States and as a legislator and judge of his own State won the esteem and regard of his fellow-countrymen.

The President directs that all Departments of the executive branch of the Government and the offices subordinate to them shall manifest due honor for the memory of this eminent citizen, in a manner consonant with the dignity of the office thus made vacant and with the upright character of him who held it.

To this end the President directs that the Treasury Department and its dependencies in this capital shall be draped in mourning for a period of thirty days, the several Executive Departments shall be closed on the day of the funeral of the deceased, and that on all public buildings of the Government throughout the United States the national flag shall be draped in mourning and displayed at half-mast.

I have the honor to be, sir, your obedient servant,

FREDK. T. FRELINGHUYSEN.

In the exercise of the power vested in the President by the Constitution, and by virtue of the seventeen hundred and fifty-third section of the Revised Statutes and of the civil-service act approved January 16, 1883, the following rule for the regulation and improvement of the executive civil service is hereby amended and promulgated:

RULE XIX.

There are excepted from examination the following: (1) The confidential clerk or secretary of any head of Department or office; (2) cashiers of collectors; (3) cashiers of postmasters; (4) superintendents of money-order divisions in post-offices; (5) the direct custodians of money for whose fidelity another officer is under official bond and disbursing officers having the custody of money who give bonds, but these exceptions shall not extend to any official below the grade of assistant cashier or teller; (6) persons employed exclusively in the secret service of the Government, or as translators or interpreters or stenographers; (7) persons whose employment is exclusively professional; (8) chief clerks, deputy collectors, and superintendents, or chiefs

* Addressed to the heads of the Executive Departments, etc.

of divisions and bureaus. But no person so excepted shall be either transferred, appointed, or promoted, unless to some excepted place, without an examination under the Commission. Promotions may be made without examination in offices where examinations for promotion are not now held until rules on this subject shall be promulgated.

Approved, November 10, 1884.   CHESTER A. ARTHUR.

FOURTH ANNUAL MESSAGE.

WASHINGTON, *December 1, 1884.*

To the Congress of the United States:

Since the close of your last session the American people, in the exercise of their highest right of suffrage, have chosen their Chief Magistrate for the four years ensuing.

When it is remembered that at no period in the country's history has the long political contest which customarily precedes the day of the national election been waged with greater fervor and intensity, it is a subject of general congratulation that after the controversy at the polls was over, and while the slight preponderance by which the issue had been determined was as yet unascertained, the public peace suffered no disturbance, but the people everywhere patiently and quietly awaited the result.

Nothing could more strikingly illustrate the temper of the American citizen, his love of order, and his loyalty to law. Nothing could more signally demonstrate the strength and wisdom of our political institutions.

Eight years have passed since a controversy concerning the result of a national election sharply called the attention of the Congress to the necessity of providing more precise and definite regulations for counting the electoral vote.

It is of the gravest importance that this question be solved before conflicting claims to the Presidency shall again distract the country, and I am persuaded that by the people at large any of the measures of relief thus far proposed would be preferred to continued inaction.

Our relations with all foreign powers continue to be amicable.

With Belgium a convention has been signed whereby the scope of present treaties has been so enlarged as to secure to citizens of either country within the jurisdiction of the other equal rights and privileges in the acquisition and alienation of property. A trade-marks treaty has also been concluded.

The war between Chile and Peru is at an end. For the arbitration of the claims of American citizens who during its continuance suffered through the acts of the Chilean authorities a convention will soon be

The state of hostilities between France and China continues to be an embarrassing feature of our Eastern relations. The Chinese Government has promptly adjusted and paid the claims of American citizens whose property was destroyed in the recent riots at Canton. I renew the recommendation of my last annual message, that the Canton indemnity fund be returned to China.

The true interpretation of the recent treaty with that country permitting the restriction of Chinese immigration is likely to be again the subject of your deliberations. It may be seriously questioned whether the statute passed at the last session does not violate the treaty rights of certain Chinese who left this country with return certificates valid under the old law, and who now seem to be debarred from relanding for lack of the certificates required by the new.

The recent purchase by citizens of the United States of a large trading fleet heretofore under the Chinese flag has considerably enhanced our commercial importance in the East. In view of the large number of vessels built or purchased by American citizens in other countries and exclusively employed in legitimate traffic between foreign ports under the recognized protection of our flag, it might be well to provide a uniform rule for their registration and documentation, so that the *bona fide* property rights of our citizens therein shall be duly evidenced and properly guarded.

· Pursuant to the advice of the Senate at the last session, I recognized the flag of the International Association of the Kongo as that of a friendly government, avoiding in so doing any prejudgment of conflicting territorial claims in that region. Subsequently, in execution of the expressed wish of the Congress, I appointed a commercial agent for the Kongo basin.

The importance of the rich prospective trade of the Kongo Valley has led to the general conviction that it should be open to all nations upon equal terms. At an international conference for the consideration of this subject called by the Emperor of Germany, and now in session at Berlin, delegates are in attendance on behalf of the United States. Of the results of the conference you will be duly advised.

The Government of Korea has generously aided the efforts of the United States minister to secure suitable premises for the use of the legation. As the conditions of diplomatic intercourse with Eastern nations demand that the legation premises be owned by the represented power, I advise that an appropriation be made for the acquisition of this property by the Government. The United States already possess valuable premises at Tangier as a gift from the Sultan of Morocco. As is stated hereafter, they have lately received a similar gift from the Siamese Government. The Government of Japan stands ready to present to us extensive grounds at Tokyo whereon to erect a suitable building for the legation, court-house, and jail, and similar privileges can probably be secured in China and Persia. The owning of such premises would not only effect a large saving of the present rentals, but would permit of the due assertion of extraterritorial rights in those countries, and would the better serve to maintain the dignity of the United States.

The failure of Congress to make appropriation for our representation at the autonomous court of the Khedive has proved a serious embarrassment in our intercourse with Egypt; and in view of the necessary intimacy of diplomatic relationship due to the participation of this Government as one of the treaty powers in all matters of administration there affecting the rights of foreigners, I advise the restoration of the agency and consulate-general at Cairo on its former basis. I do not conceive it to be the wish of Congress that the United States should withdraw altogether from the honorable position they have hitherto held with respect to the Khedive, or that citizens of this Republic residing or sojourning in Egypt should hereafter be without the aid and protection of a competent representative.

With France the traditional cordial relationship continues. The colossal statue of Liberty Enlightening the World, the generous gift of the people of France, is expected to reach New York in May next. I suggest that Congressional action be taken in recognition of the spirit which has prompted this gift and in aid of the timely completion of the pedestal upon which it is to be placed.

Our relations with Germany, a country which contributes to our own some of the best elements of citizenship, continue to be cordial. The United States have extradition treaties with several of the German States, but by reason of the confederation of those States under the imperial rule the application of such treaties is not as uniform and comprehensive as the interests of the two countries require. I propose, therefore, to open negotiations for a single convention of extradition to embrace all the territory of the Empire.

It affords me pleasure to say that our intercourse with Great Britain continues to be of a most friendly character.

The Government of Hawaii has indicated its willingness to continue for seven years the provisions of the existing reciprocity treaty. Such continuance, in view of the relations of that country to the American system of States, should, in my judgment, be favored.

The revolution in Hayti against the established Government has terminated. While it was in progress it became necessary to enforce our neutrality laws by instituting proceedings against individuals and vessels charged with their infringement. These prosecutions were in all cases successful.

Much anxiety has lately been displayed by various European Governments, and especially by the Government of Italy, for the abolition of our import duties upon works of art. It is well to consider whether the present discrimination in favor of the productions of American artists abroad is not likely to result, as they themselves seem very generally to believe it may, in the practical exclusion of our painters and sculptors from the rich fields for observation, study, and labor which they have hitherto enjoyed.

There is prospect that the long-pending revision of the foreign treaties of Japan may be concluded at a new conference to be held at Tokyo. While this Government fully recognizes the equal and independent station of Japan in the community of nations, it would not oppose the general adoption of such terms of compromise as Japan may be disposed to offer in furtherance of a uniform policy of intercourse with Western nations.

During the past year the increasing good will between our own Government and that of Mexico has been variously manifested. The treaty of commercial reciprocity concluded January 20, 1883, has been ratified and awaits the necessary tariff legislation of Congress to become effective. This legislation will, I doubt not, be among the first measures to claim your attention.

A full treaty of commerce, navigation, and consular rights is much to be desired, and such a treaty I have reason to believe that the Mexican Government stands ready to conclude.

Some embarrassment has been occasioned by the failure of Congress at its last session to provide means for the due execution of the treaty of July 29, 1882, for the resurvey of the Mexican boundary and the relocation of boundary monuments.

With the Republic of Nicaragua a treaty has been concluded which authorizes the construction by the United States of a canal, railway, and telegraph line across the Nicaraguan territory.

By the terms of this treaty 60 miles of the river San Juan, as well as Lake Nicaragua, an inland sea 40 miles in width, are to constitute a part of the projected enterprise.

This leaves for actual canal construction 17 miles on the Pacific side and 36 miles on the Atlantic. To the United States, whose rich territory on the Pacific is for the ordinary purposes of commerce practically cut off from communication by water with the Atlantic ports, the political and commercial advantages of such a project can scarcely be overestimated.

It is believed that when the treaty is laid before you the justice and liberality of its provisions will command universal approval at home and abroad.

The death of our representative at Russia while at his post at St. Petersburg afforded to the Imperial Government a renewed opportunity to testify its sympathy in a manner befitting the intimate friendliness which has ever marked the intercourse of the two countries.

The course of this Government in raising its representation at Bangkok to the diplomatic rank has evoked from Siam evidences of warm friendship and augurs well for our enlarged intercourse. The Siamese Government has presented to the United States a commodious mansion and grounds for the occupancy of the legation, and I suggest that by joint resolution Congress attest its appreciation of this generous gift.

This Government has more than once been called upon of late to take action in fulfillment of its international obligations toward Spain. Agitation in the island of Cuba hostile to the Spanish Crown having been fomented by persons abusing the sacred rights of hospitality which our territory affords, the officers of this Government have been instructed to exercise vigilance to prevent infractions of our neutrality laws at Key West and at other points near the Cuban coast. I am happy to say that in the only instance where these precautionary measures were successfully eluded the offenders, when found in our territory, were subsequently tried and convicted.

The growing need of close relationship of intercourse and traffic between the Spanish Antilles and their natural market in the United States led to the adoption in January last of a commercial agreement looking to that end. This agreement has since been superseded by a more carefully framed and comprehensive convention, which I shall submit to the Senate for approval. It has been the aim of this negotiation to open such a favored reciprocal exchange of productions carried under the flag of either country as to make the intercourse between Cuba and Puerto Rico and ourselves scarcely less intimate than the commercial movement between our domestic ports, and to insure a removal of the burdens on shipping in the Spanish Indies, of which in the past our shipowners and shipmasters have so often had cause to complain.

The negotiation of this convention has for a time postponed the prosecution of certain claims of our citizens which were declared to be without the jurisdiction of the late Spanish-American Claims Commission, and which are therefore remitted to diplomatic channels for adjustment. The speedy settlement of these claims will now be urged by this Government.

Negotiations for a treaty of commercial reciprocity with the Dominican Republic have been successfully concluded, and the result will shortly be laid before the Senate.

Certain questions between the United States and the Ottoman Empire still remain unsolved. Complaints on behalf of our citizens are not satisfactorily adjusted. The Porte has sought to withhold from our commerce the right of favored treatment to which we are entitled by existing conventional stipulations, and the revision of the tariffs is unaccomplished.

The final disposition of pending questions with Venezuela has not as yet been reached, but I have good reason to expect an early settlement which will provide the means of reexamining the Caracas awards in conformity with the expressed desire of Congress, and which will recognize the justice of certain claims preferred against Venezuela.

The Central and South American Commission appointed by authority of the act of July 7, 1884, will soon proceed to Mexico. It has been furnished with instructions which will be laid before you. They contain a statement of the general policy of the Government for enlarging its commercial intercourse with American States. The commissioners have been actively preparing for their responsible task by holding conferences in the principal cities with merchants and others interested in Central and South American trade.

The International Meridian Conference lately convened in Washington upon the invitation of the Government of the United States was composed of representatives from twenty-five nations. The conference concluded its labors on the 1st of November, having with substantial unanimity agreed upon the meridian of Greenwich as the starting point whence longitude is to be computed through 180 degrees eastward and westward, and upon the adoption, for all purposes for which it may be found convenient, of a universal day which shall begin at midnight on the initial meridian and whose hours shall be counted from zero up to twenty-four.

The formal report of the transactions of this conference will be hereafter transmitted to the Congress.

This Government is in frequent receipt of invitations from foreign states to participate in international exhibitions, often of great interest and importance. Occupying, as we do, an advanced position in the world's production, and aiming to secure a profitable share for our industries in the general competitive markets, it is a matter of serious concern that the want of means for participation in these exhibitions should so often exclude our producers from advantages enjoyed by those of other countries. During the past year the attention of Congress was drawn to the formal invitations in this regard tendered by the Governments of England, Holland, Belgium, Germany, and Austria. The Executive has in some instances appointed honorary commissioners. This is, however, a most unsatisfactory expedient, for without some provision to meet the necessary working expenses of a commission it can effect little or nothing in behalf of exhibitors. An International Inventions Exhibition is to be held in London next May. This will cover a field of special importance, in which our country holds a foremost rank; but the Executive is at present powerless to organize a proper representation of our vast national interests in this direction.

I have in several previous messages referred to this subject. ˙ It seems to me that a statute giving to the Executive general discretionary authority to accept such invitations and to appoint honorary commissioners, without salary, and placing at the disposal of the Secretary of State a small fund for defraying their reasonable expenses, would be of great public utility.

This Government has received official notice that the revised international regulations for preventing collisions at sea have been adopted by all the leading maritime powers except the United States, and came into force on the 1st of September last. For the due protection of our shipping interests the provisions of our statutes should at once be brought into conformity with these regulations.

The question of securing to authors, composers, and artists copyright privileges in this country in return for reciprocal rights abroad is one that may justly challenge your attention. It is true that conventions will be necessary for fully accomplishing this result; but until Congress shall by statute fix the extent to which foreign holders of copyright shall be here privileged it has been deemed inadvisable to negotiate such conventions. For this reason the United States were not represented at the recent conference at Berne.

I recommend that the scope of the neutrality laws of the United States be so enlarged as to cover all patent acts of hostility committed in our territory and aimed against the peace of a friendly nation. Existing statutes prohibit the fitting out of armed expeditions and restrict the shipment of explosives, though the enactments in the latter respect were not framed with regard to international obligations, but simply for the protection of passenger travel. All these statutes were intended to meet special emergencies that had already arisen. Other emergencies have arisen since, and modern ingenuity supplies means for the organization of hostilities without open resort to armed vessels or to filibustering parties.

I see no reason why overt preparations in this country for the commission of criminal acts such as are here under consideration should not be alike punishable whether such acts are intended to be committed in our own country or in a foreign country with which we are at peace.

The prompt and thorough treatment of this question is one which intimately concerns the national honor.

Our existing naturalization laws also need revision. Those sections relating to persons residing within the limits of the United States in 1795 and 1798 have now only a historical interest. Section 2172, recognizing the citizenship of the children of naturalized parents, is ambiguous in its terms and partly obsolete. There are special provisions of law favoring the naturalization of those who serve in the Army or in merchant vessels, while no similar privileges are granted those who serve in the Navy or the Marine Corps.

"An uniform rule of naturalization" such as the Constitution contemplates should, among other things, clearly define the status of persons born within the United States subject to a foreign power (section 1992) and of minor children of fathers who have declared their intention to become citizens but have failed to perfect their naturalization. It might be wise to provide for a central bureau of registry, wherein should be filed authenticated transcripts of every record of naturalization in the several Federal and State courts, and to make provision also for the vacation or cancellation of such record in cases where fraud had been practised upon the court by the applicant himself or where he had renounced or forfeited his acquired citizenship. A just and uniform law in this respect would strengthen the hands of the Government in protecting its citizens abroad and would pave the way for the conclusion of treaties of naturalization with foreign countries.

The legislation of the last session effected in the diplomatic and consular service certain changes and reductions which have been productive of embarrassment. The population and commercial activity of our country are steadily on the increase, and are giving rise to new, varying, and often delicate relationships with other countries. Our foreign establishment now embraces nearly double the area of operations that it occupied twenty years ago. The confinement of such a service within the limits of expenditure then established is not, it seems to me, in accordance with true economy. A community of 60,000,000 people should be adequately represented in its intercourse with foreign nations.

A project for the reorganization of the consular service and for recasting the scheme of extraterritorial jurisdiction is now before you. If the limits of a short session will not allow of its full consideration, I trust that you will not fail to make suitable provision for the present needs of the service.

It has been customary to define in the appropriation acts the rank of each diplomatic office to which a salary is attached. I suggest that this course be abandoned and that it be left to the President, with the advice and consent of the Senate, to fix from time to time the diplomatic grade of the representatives of this Government abroad as may seem advisable, provision being definitely made, however, as now, for the amount of salary attached to the respective stations.

The condition of our finances and the operations of the various branches of the public service which are connected with the Treasury Department are very fully discussed in the report of the Secretary.

It appears that the ordinary revenues for the fiscal year ended June 30, 1884, were:

From customs	$195,067,489.76
From internal revenue	121,586,072.51
From all other sources	31,866,307.65
Total ordinary revenues	348,519,869.92

The public expenditures during the same period were:

For civil expenses	$22,312,907.71
For foreign intercourse	1,260,766.37
For Indians	6,475,999.29
For pensions	55,429,228.06
For the military establishment, including river and harbor improvements and arsenals	39,429,603.36
For the naval establishment, including vessels, machinery, and improvements at navy-yards	17,292,601.44
For miscellaneous expenditures, including public buildings, light-houses, and collecting the revenue	43,939,710.00
For expenditures on account of the District of Columbia	3,407,049.62
For interest on the public debt	54,578,378.48
For the sinking fund	46,790,229.50
Total ordinary expenditures	290,916,473.83
Leaving a surplus of	57,603,396.09

As compared with the preceding fiscal year, there was a net decrease of over $21,000,000 in the amount of expenditures. The aggregate receipts were less than those of the year previous by about $54,000,000. The falling off in revenue from customs made up nearly $20,000,000 of this deficiency, and about $23,000,000 of the remainder was due to the diminished receipts from internal taxation.

The Secretary estimates the total receipts for the fiscal year which will end June 30, 1885, at $330,000,000 and the total expenditures at $290,620,201.16, in which sum are included the interest on the debt and the amount payable to the sinking fund. This would leave a surplus for the entire year of about $39,000,000.

The value of exports from the United States to foreign countries during the year ending June 30, 1884, was as follows:

Domestic merchandise	$724,964,852
Foreign merchandise	15,548,757
Total merchandise	740,513,609
Specie	67,133,383
Total exports of merchandise and specie	807,646,992

The cotton and cotton manufactures included in this statement were valued at $208,900,415; the breadstuffs at $162,544,715; the provisions at $114,416,547, and the mineral oils at $47,103,248.

During the same period the imports were as follows:

Merchandise	$667,697,693
Gold and silver	37,426,262
Total	705,123,955

More than 63 per cent of the entire value of imported merchandise consisted of the following articles:

Sugar and molasses	$103,884,274
Wool and woolen manufactures	53,542,392
Silk and its manufactures	49,949,128
Coffee	49,666,705
Iron and steel and manufactures thereof	41,464,599
Chemicals	38,464,965
Flax, hemp, jute, and like substances, and manufactures thereof	33,463,398
Cotton and manufactures of cotton	30,454,476
Hides and skins other than fur skins	22,350,906

I concur with the Secretary of the Treasury in recommending the immediate suspension of the coinage of silver dollars and of the issuance of silver certificates. This is a matter to which in former communications I have more than once invoked the attention of the National Legislature.

It appears that annually for the past six years there have been coined, in compliance with the requirements of the act of February 28, 1878, more than 27,000,000 silver dollars.

The number now outstanding is reported by the Secretary to be nearly 185,000,000, whereof but little more than 40,000,000, or less than 22 per cent, are in actual circulation. The mere existence of this fact seems to me to furnish of itself a cogent argument for the repeal of the statute which has made such fact possible.

But there are other and graver considerations that tend in the same direction.

The Secretary avows his conviction that unless this coinage and the issuance of silver certificates be suspended silver is likely at no distant day to become our sole metallic standard. The commercial disturbance and the impairment of national credit that would be thus occasioned can scarcely be overestimated.

I hope that the Secretary's suggestions respecting the withdrawal from circulation of the $1 and $2 notes will receive your approval. It is likely that a considerable portion of the silver now encumbering the vaults of the Treasury might thus find its way into the currency.

While trade dollars have ceased, for the present at least, to be an element of active disturbance in our currency system, some provision should be made for their surrender to the Government. In view of the circumstances under which they were coined and of the fact that they have never had a legal-tender quality, there should be offered for them only a slight advance over their bullion value.

The Secretary in the course of his report considers the propriety of beautifying the designs of our subsidiary silver coins and of so increasing their weight that they may bear their due ratio of value to the standard dollar. His conclusions in this regard are cordially approved.

In my annual message of 1882 I recommended the abolition of all excise taxes except those relating to distilled spirits. This recommendation is now renewed. In case these taxes shall be abolished the revenues that will still remain to the Government will, in my opinion, not only suffice to meet its reasonable expenditures, but will afford a surplus large enough to permit such tariff reduction as may seem to be advisable when the results of recent revenue laws and commercial treaties shall have shown in what quarters those reductions can be most judiciously effected.

One of the gravest of the problems which appeal to the wisdom of Congress for solution is the ascertainment of the most effective means for increasing our foreign trade and thus relieving the depression under which our industries are now languishing. The Secretary of the Treasury advises that the duty of investigating this subject be intrusted in the first instance to a competent commission. While fully recognizing the considerations that may be urged against this course, I am nevertheless of the opinion that upon the whole no other would be likely to effect speedier or better results.

That portion of the Secretary's report which concerns the condition of our shipping interests can not fail to command your attention. He emphatically recommends that as an incentive to the investment of American capital in American steamships the Government shall, by liberal payments for mail transportation or otherwise, lend its active assistance to individual enterprise, and declares his belief that unless that course be pursued our foreign carrying trade must remain, as it is to-day, almost exclusively in the hands of foreigners.

One phase of this subject is now especially prominent in view of the repeal by the act of June 26, 1884, of all statutory provisions arbitrarily compelling American vessels to carry the mails to and from the United States. As it is necessary to make provision to compensate the owners of such vessels for performing that service after April, 1885, it is hoped that the whole subject will receive early consideration that will lead to the enactment of such measures for the revival of our merchant marine as the wisdom of Congress may devise.

The 3 per cent bonds of the Government to the amount of more than $100,000,000 have since my last annual message been redeemed by the Treasury. The bonds of that issue still outstanding amount to little over $200,000,000, about one-fourth of which will be retired through the operations of the sinking fund during the coming year. As these bonds still constitute the chief basis for the circulation of the national banks, the question how to avert the contraction of the currency caused by their retirement is one of constantly increasing importance.

It seems to be generally conceded that the law governing this matter exacts from the banks excessive security, and that upon their present bond deposits a larger circulation than is now allowed may be granted with safety. I hope that the bill which passed the Senate at the last session, permitting the issue of notes equal to the face value of the deposited bonds, will commend itself to the approval of the House of Representatives.

In the expenses of the War Department the Secretary reports a decrease of more than $9,000,000. Of this reduction $5,600,000 was effected in the expenditures for rivers and harbors and $2,700,000 in expenditures for the Quartermaster's Department.

Outside of that Department the annual expenses of all the Army bureaus proper (except possibly the Ordnance Bureau) are substantially fixed charges, which can not be materially diminished without a change in the numerical strength of the Army. The expenditures in the Quartermaster's Department can readily be subjected to administrative discretion, and it is reported by the Secretary of War that as a result of exercising such discretion in reducing the number of draft and pack animals in the Army the annual cost of supplying and caring for such animals is now $1,108,085.90 less than it was in 1881.

The reports of military commanders show that the last year has been notable for its entire freedom from Indian outbreaks.

In defiance of the President's proclamation of July 1, 1884,* certain intruders sought to make settlements in the Indian Territory. They were promptly removed by a detachment of troops.

* See pp. 224-225.

During the last session of Congress a bill to provide a suitable fire-proof building for the Army Medical Museum and the library of the Surgeon-General's Office received the approval of the Senate. A similar bill reported favorably in the House of Representatives by one of its committees is still pending before that body. It is hoped that during the coming session the measure may become a law and that thereafter immediate steps may be taken to secure a place of safe deposit for these valuable collections now in a state of insecurity.

The funds with which the works for the improvement of rivers and harbors were prosecuted during the past year were derived from the appropriations of the act of August 2, 1882, together with such few balances as were on hand from previous appropriations. The balance in the Treasury subject to requisition July 1, 1883, was $........... The amount appropriated during the fiscal year 1884 was $........... and the amount drawn from the Treasury during the fiscal year was $........... leaving a balance of $........... in the Treasury subject to requisition July 1, 1884.

The Secretary of War submits the report of the Chief of Engineers as to the practicability of protecting our important cities on the seaboard by fortifications and other defenses able to repel modern methods of attack. The time has now come when such defenses can be prepared with confidence that they will not prove abortive, and when the possible result of delay in making such preparation is seriously considered delay seems inexcusable. For the most important cities—those whose destruction or capture would be a national humiliation—adequate defenses, inclusive of guns, may be made by the gradual expenditure of $60,000,000—a sum much less than a victorious enemy could levy as a contribution. An appropriation of about one-tenth of that amount is asked to begin the work, and I concur with the Secretary of War in urging that it be granted.

The War Department is proceeding with the conversion of 10-inch smoothbore guns into 8-inch rifles by lining the former with tubes of forged steel or of coil wrought iron. Fifty guns will be thus converted within the year. This, however, does not obviate the necessity of providing means for the construction of guns of the highest power both for the purposes of coast defense and for the armament of war vessels.

The report of the Gun Foundry Board, appointed April 2, 1883, in pursuance of the act of March 3, 1883, was transmitted to Congress in a special message of February 18, 1884.* In my message of March 26, 1884,† I called attention to the recommendation of the board that the Government should encourage the production at private steel works of the required material for heavy cannon, and that two Government factories, one for the Army and one for the Navy, should be established for the fabrication of guns from such material. No action having been taken, the board was subsequently reconvened to determine more fully the plans and estimates necessary for carrying out its recommendation. It has received information which indicates that there are responsible steel manufacturers in this country who, although not provided at present with the necessary plant, are willing to construct the same and to make bids for contracts with the Government for the supply of the requisite material for the heaviest guns adapted to modern warfare if a guaranteed order of sufficient magnitude, accompanied by a positive appropriation extending over a series of years, shall be made by Congress. All doubts as to the feasibility of the plan being thus removed, I renew my recommendation that such action be taken by Congress as will enable the Government to construct its own ordnance upon its own territory, and so to provide the armaments demanded by considerations of national safety and honor.

The report of the Secretary of the Navy exhibits the progress which has been made on the new steel cruisers authorized by the acts of August 5, 1882, and March 3, 1883. Of the four vessels under contract, one, the *Chicago*, of 4,500 tons, is more than half finished; the *Atlanta*, of 3,000 tons, has been successfully launched, and her machinery is now fitting; the *Boston*, also of 3,000 tons, is ready for launching, and the *Dolphin*, a dispatch steamer of 1,500 tons, is ready for delivery.

Certain adverse criticisms upon the designs of these cruisers are discussed by the Secretary, who insists that the correctness of the conclusions reached by the Advisory Board and by the Department has been demonstrated by recent developments in shipbuilding abroad.

The machinery of the double-turreted monitors *Puritan*, *Terror*, and *Amphitrite*, contracted for under the act of March 3, 1883, is in process of construction. No work has been done during the past year on their armor for lack of the necessary appropriations. A fourth monitor, the *Monadnock*, still remains unfinished at the navy-yard in California. It is recommended that early steps be taken to complete these vessels and to provide also an armament for the monitor *Miantonomoh*.

The recommendations of the Naval Advisory Board, approved by the Department, comprise the construction of one steel cruiser of 4,500 tons, one cruiser of 3,000 tons, two heavily armed gunboats, one light cruising gunboat, one dispatch vessel armed with Hotchkiss cannon, one armored ram, and three torpedo boats. The general designs, all of which are calculated to meet the existing wants of the service, are now well advanced, and the construction of the vessels can be undertaken as soon as you shall grant the necessary authority.

The act of Congress approved August 7, 1882, authorized the removal to the United States of the bodies of Lieutenant-Commander George W. De Long and his companions of the *Jeannette* expedition. This removal has been successfully accomplished by Lieutenants Harber and Schuetze. The remains were taken from their grave in the Lena Delta in March,

1883, and were retained at Yakutsk until the following winter, the season being too far advanced to admit of their immediate transportation. They arrived at New York February 20, 1884, where they were received with suitable honors.

In pursuance of the joint resolution of Congress approved February 13, 1884, a naval expedition was fitted out for the relief of Lieutenant A. W. Greely, United States Army, and of the party who had been engaged under his command in scientific observations at Lady Franklin Bay. The fleet consisted of the steam sealer *Thetis*, purchased in England; the *Bear*, purchased at St. Johns, Newfoundland, and the *Alert*, which was generously provided by the British Government. Preparations for the expedition were promptly made by the Secretary of the Navy, with the active cooperation of the Secretary of War. Commander George W. Coffin was placed in command of the *Alert* and Lieutenant William H. Emory in command of the *Bear*. The *Thetis* was intrusted to Commander Winfield S. Schley, to whom also was assigned the superintendence of the entire expedition.

Immediately upon its arrival at Upernavik the fleet began the dangerous navigation of Melville Bay, and in spite of every obstacle reached Littleton Island on June 22, a fortnight earlier than any vessel had before attained that point. On the same day it crossed over to Cape Sabine, where Lieutenant Greely and the other survivors of his party were discovered. After taking on board the living and the bodies of the dead, the relief ships sailed for St. Johns, where they arrived on July 17. They were appropriately received at Portsmouth, N. H., on August 1 and at New York on August 8. One of the bodies was landed at the former place. The others were put on shore at Governors Island, and, with the exception of one, which was interred in the national cemetery, were forwarded thence to the destinations indicated by friends. The organization and conduct of this relief expedition reflects great credit upon all who contributed to its success.

In this the last of the stated messages that I shall have the honor to transmit to the Congress of the United States I can not too strongly urge upon its attention the duty of restoring our Navy as rapidly as possible to the high state of efficiency which formerly characterized it. As the long peace that has lulled us into a sense of fancied security may at any time be disturbed, it is plain that the policy of strengthening this arm of the service is dictated by considerations of wise economy, of just regard for our future tranquillity, and of true appreciation of the dignity and honor of the Republic.

The report of the Postmaster-General acquaints you with the present condition and needs of the postal service.

It discloses the gratifying fact that the loss of revenue from the reduction in the rate of letter postage recommended in my message of December 4, 1882, and effected by the act of March 3, 1883, has been much less than was generally anticipated. My recommendation of this reduction was based upon the belief that the actual falling off in receipts from letter postages for the year immediately succeeding the change of rate would be $3,000,000. It has proved to be only $2,275,000.

This is a trustworthy indication that the revenue will soon be restored to its former volume by the natural increase of sealed correspondence.

I confidently repeat, therefore, the recommendation of my last annual message that the single-rate postage upon drop letters be reduced to 1 cent wherever the payment of 2 cents is now required by law. The double rate is only exacted at offices where the carrier system is in operation, and it appears that at those offices the increase in the tax upon local letters defrays the cost not only of its own collection and delivery, but of the collection and delivery of all other mail matter. This is an inequality that ought no longer to exist.

I approve the recommendation of the Postmaster-General that the unit of weight in the rating of first-class matter should be 1 ounce instead of one-half ounce, as it now is. In view of the statistics furnished by the Department, it may well be doubted whether the change would result in any loss of revenue. That it would greatly promote the convenience of the public is beyond dispute.

The free-delivery system has been lately applied to five cities, and the total number of offices in which it is now in operation is 159. Experience shows that its adoption, under proper conditions, is equally an accommodation to the public and an advantage to the postal service. It is more than self-sustaining, and for the reasons urged by the Postmaster-General may properly be extended.

In the opinion of that officer it is important to provide means whereby exceptional dispatch in dealing with letters in free-delivery offices may be secured by payment of extraordinary postage. This scheme might be made effective by employment of a special stamp whose cost should be commensurate with the expense of the extra service.

In some of the large cities private express companies have undertaken to outstrip the Government mail carriers by affording for the prompt transmission of letters better facilities than have hitherto been at the command of the Post-Office.

It has always been the policy of the Government to discourage such enterprises, and in no better mode can that policy be maintained than in supplying the public with the most efficient mail service that, with due regard to its own best interests, can be furnished for its accommodation.

The Attorney-General renews the recommendation contained in his report of last year touching the fees of witnesses and jurors.

He favors radical changes in the fee bill, the adoption of a system by which attorneys and marshals of the United States shall be compensated solely by salaries, and the erection by the Government of a penitentiary for the confinement of offenders against its laws.

Of the varied governmental concerns in charge of the Interior Department the report of its Secretary presents an interesting summary. Among the topics deserving particular attention I refer you to his observations respecting our Indian affairs, the preemption and timber-culture acts, the failure of railroad companies to take title to lands granted by the Government, and the operations of the Pension Office, the Patent Office, the Census Bureau, and the Bureau of Education.

Allusion has been made already to the circumstance that, both as between the different Indian tribes and as between the Indians and the whites, the past year has been one of unbroken peace.

In this circumstance the President is glad to find justification for the policy of the Government in its dealing with the Indian question and confirmation of the views which were fully expressed in his first communication to the Forty-seventh Congress.

The Secretary urges anew the enactment of a statute for the punishment of crimes committed on the Indian reservations, and recommends the passage of the bill now pending in the House of Representatives for the purchase of a tract of 18,000 square miles from the Sioux Reservation. Both these measures are worthy of approval.

I concur with him also in advising the repeal of the preemption law, the enactment of statutes resolving the present legal complications touching lapsed grants to railroad companies, and the funding of the debt of the several Pacific railroads under such guaranty as shall effectually secure its ultimate payment.

The report of the Utah Commission will be read with interest.

It discloses the results of recent legislation looking to the prevention and punishment of polygamy in that Territory. I still believe that if that abominable practice can be suppressed by law it can only be by the most radical legislation consistent with the restraints of the Constitution.

I again recommend, therefore, that Congress assume absolute political control of the Territory of Utah and provide for the appointment of commissioners with such governmental powers as in its judgment may justly and wisely be put into their hands.

In the course of this communication reference has more than once been made to the policy of this Government as regards the extension of our foreign trade. It seems proper to declare the general principles that should, in my opinion, underlie our national efforts in this direction.

The main conditions of the problem may be thus stated:

We are a people apt in mechanical pursuits and fertile in invention. We cover a vast extent of territory rich in agricultural products and in nearly all the raw materials necessary for successful manufacture. We have a system of productive establishments more than sufficient to supply our own demands. The wages of labor are nowhere else so great. The scale of living of our artisan classes is such as tends to secure their personal comfort and the development of those higher moral and intellectual

qualities that go to the making of good citizens. Our system of tax and tariff legislation is yielding a revenue which is in excess of the present needs of the Government.

These are the elements from which it is sought to devise a scheme by which, without unfavorably changing the condition of the workingman, our merchant marine shall be raised from its enfeebled condition and new markets provided for the sale beyond our borders of the manifold fruits of our industrial enterprises.

The problem is complex and can be solved by no single measure of innovation or reform.

The countries of the American continent and the adjacent islands are for the United States the natural marts of supply and demand. It is from them that we should obtain what we do not produce or do not produce in sufficiency, and it is to them that the surplus productions of our fields, our mills, and our workshops should flow, under conditions that will equalize or favor them in comparison with foreign competition.

Four paths of policy seem to point to this end:

First. A series of reciprocal commercial treaties with the countries of America which shall foster between us and them an unhampered movement of trade. The conditions of these treaties should be the free admission of such merchandise as this country does not produce, in return for the admission free or under a favored scheme of duties of our own products, the benefits of such exchange to apply only to goods carried under the flag of the parties to the contract; the removal on both sides from the vessels so privileged of all tonnage dues and national imposts, so that those vessels may ply unhindered between our ports and those of the other contracting parties, though without infringing on the reserved home coasting trade; the removal or reduction of burdens on the exported products of those countries coming within the benefits of the treaties, and the avoidance of the technical restrictions and penalties by which our intercourse with those countries is at present hampered.

Secondly. The establishment of the consular service of the United States on a salaried footing, thus permitting the relinquishment of consular fees not only as respects vessels under the national flag, but also as respects vessels of the treaty nations carrying goods entitled to the benefits of the treaties.

Thirdly. The enactment of measures to favor the construction and maintenance of a steam carrying marine under the flag of the United States.

Fourthly. The establishment of an uniform currency basis for the countries of America, so that the coined products of our mines may circulate on equal terms throughout the whole system of commonwealths. This would require a monetary union of America, whereby the output of the bullion-producing countries and the circulation of those which yield neither gold nor silver could be adjusted in conformity with the

population, wealth, and commercial needs of each. As many of the countries furnish no bullion to the common stock, the surplus production of our mines and mints might thus be utilized and a step taken toward the general remonetization of silver.

To the accomplishment of these ends, so far as they can be attained by separate treaties, the negotiations already concluded and now in progress have been directed; and the favor which this enlarged policy has thus far received warrants the belief that its operations will ere long embrace all, or nearly all, the countries of this hemisphere.

It is by no means desirable, however, that the policy under consideration should be applied to these countries alone. The healthful enlargement of our trade with Europe, Asia, and Africa should be sought by reducing tariff burdens on such of their wares as neither we nor the other American States are fitted to produce, and thus enabling ourselves to obtain in return a better market for our supplies of food, of raw materials, and of the manufactures in which we excel.

It seems to me that many of the embarrassing elements in the great national conflict between protection and free trade may thus be turned to good account; that the revenue may be reduced so as no longer to overtax the people; that protective duties may be retained without becoming burdensome; that our shipping interests may be judiciously encouraged, the currency fixed on firm bases, and, above all, such an unity of interests established among the States of the American system as will be of great and ever-increasing advantage to them all.

All treaties in the line of this policy which have been negotiated or are in process of negotiation contain a provision deemed to be requisite under the clause of the Constitution limiting to the House of Representatives the authority to originate bills for raising revenue.

On the 29th of February last * I transmitted to the Congress the first annual report of the Civil Service Commission, together with communications from the heads of the several Executive Departments of the Government respecting the practical workings of the law under which the Commission had been acting. The good results therein foreshadowed have been more than realized.

The system has fully answered the expectations of its friends in securing competent and faithful public servants and in protecting the appointing officers of the Government from the pressure of personal importunity and from the labor of examining the claims and pretensions of rival candidates for public employment.

The law has had the unqualified support of the President and of the heads of the several Departments, and the members of the Commission have performed their duties with zeal and fidelity. Their report will shortly be submitted, and will be accompanied by such recommendations for enlarging the scope of the existing statute as shall commend them-

* See pp. 205-206.

selves to the Executive and the Commissioners charged with its administration.

In view of the general and persistent demand throughout the commercial community for a national bankrupt law, I hope that the differences of sentiment which have hitherto prevented its enactment may not outlast the present session.

The pestilence which for the past two years has been raging in the countries of the East recently made its appearance in European ports with which we are in constant communication.

The then Secretary of the Treasury, in pursuance of a proclamation of the President,* issued certain regulations restricting and for a time prohibiting the importation of rags and the admission of baggage of immigrants and of travelers arriving from infected quarters. Lest this course may have been without strict warrant of law, I approve the recommendation of the present Secretary that the Congress take action in the premises, and I also recommend the immediate adoption of such measures as will be likely to ward off the dreaded epidemic and to mitigate its severity in case it shall unhappily extend to our shores.

The annual report of the Commissioners of the District of Columbia reviews the operations of the several departments of its municipal government. I ask your careful consideration of its suggestions in respect to legislation, especially commending such as relate to a revision of the civil and criminal code, the performance of labor by persons sentenced to imprisonment in the jail, the construction and occupation of wharves along the river front, and the erection of a suitable building for District offices.

I recommend that in recognition of the eminent services of Ulysses S. Grant, late General of the armies of the United States and twice President of this nation, the Congress confer upon him a suitable pension.

Certain of the measures that seem to me necessary and expedient I have now, in obedience to the Constitution, recommended for your adoption.

As respects others of no less importance I shall content myself with renewing the recommendations already made to the Congress, without restating the grounds upon which such recommendations were based.

The preservation of forests on the public domain, the granting of Government aid for popular education, the amendment of the Federal Constitution so as to make effective the disapproval by the President of particular items in appropriation bills, the enactment of statutes in regard to the filling of vacancies in the Presidential office, and the determining of vexed questions respecting Presidential inability are measures which may justly receive your serious consideration.

As the time draws nigh when I am to retire from the public service, I can not refrain from expressing to the members of the National Legislature with whom I have been brought into personal and official intercourse my sincere appreciation of their unfailing courtesy and of their

*See p. 225.

harmonious cooperation with the Executive in so many measures calculated to promote the best interests of the nation.

And to my fellow-citizens generally I acknowledge a deep sense of obligation for the support which they have accorded me in my administration of the executive department of this Government.

CHESTER A. ARTHUR.

SPECIAL MESSAGES.

EXECUTIVE MANSION,
Washington, December 3, 1884.

To the Senate of the United States:

I transmit to the Senate, for its consideration with a view to ratification, a convention for regulating the right of succession to and acquisition of property, etc., concluded between the United States and Belgium on the 4th ultimo.

CHESTER A. ARTHUR.

EXECUTIVE MANSION,
Washington, December 3, 1884.

To the Senate of the United States:

I herewith transmit, for the consideration of the Senate with a view to its ratification, a convention between the United States of America and the United States of Mexico, touching the boundary line between the two countries where it follows the bed of the Rio Grande and the Rio Gila, concluded November 12, 1884, and add that the convention is in accordance with an opinion of the Hon. Caleb Cushing, Attorney-General, dated November 11, 1856. (See Opinions of Attorneys-General, Vol. XIII, p. 175, "Arcifinious boundaries.")

CHESTER A. ARTHUR.

EXECUTIVE MANSION,
Washington, December 4, 1884.

To the Senate and House of Representatives:

I transmit herewith a communication from the Secretary of State, submitting the text, in the English and French languages, of the proceedings of the International Meridian Conference, provided for by the act of Congress approved August 3, 1882, held at Washington during the mouth of October, 1884.

CHESTER A. ARTHUR.

EXECUTIVE MANSION,
Washington, December 9, 1884.
To the Senate of the United States:

I herewith transmit, for the consideration of the Senate with a view to its ratification, a supplementary convention to limit the duration of the convention respecting commercial reciprocity between the United States of America and the Hawaiian Kingdom, concluded January 30, 1875.

CHESTER A. ARTHUR.

EXECUTIVE MANSION,
Washington, December 9, 1884.
To the Senate of the United States:

I transmit herewith, for the consideration of the Senate with a view to obtaining its advice thereon and consent thereto, a convention for commercial reciprocity between the United States and the Dominican Republic, which was signed in this capital on the 4th instant.

This convention aims to carry out the principles which, as explained in my last annual message to the Congress, should, it is conceived, control all commercial arrangements entered into with our neighbors of the American system with whom trade must be conducted by sea. Santo Domingo is the first of the independent Republics of the Western Hemisphere with which an engagement of this character has been concluded, and the precedent now set will command your fullest attention as affecting like future negotiations.

CHESTER A. ARTHUR.

EXECUTIVE MANSION,
Washington, December 10, 1884.
To the Senate of the United States:

I transmit herewith, for consideration by the Senate with a view to advising and consenting to its ratification, a convention for commercial reciprocity between the United States and Spain, providing for an intimate and favored exchange of products with the islands of Cuba and Puerto Rico, which convention was signed at Madrid on the 18th ultimo.

The negotiations for this convention have been in progress since April last, in pursuance of the understanding reached by the two Governments on the 2d of January, 1884, for the improvement of commercial relations between the United States and the Spanish Antilles, by the eighth article of which both Governments engaged "to begin at once negotiations for a complete treaty of commerce and navigation between the United States of America and the said Provinces of Cuba and Puerto Rico." Although this clause was by common consent omitted from the substitutionary agreement of February 13, 1884 (now in force until replaced by this convention being carried into effect), the obligation to enter upon such negotiation was deemed to continue. With the best desire manif both sides to reach a common accord, the negotiation has been necessarily protracted, owing to the complexity of the details to be incorporated in order that the convention might respond to the national policy of intercourse with the neighboring communities of the American system, which is outlined in my late annual message to the Congress in the following words:

The conditions of these treaties should be the free admission of such merchandise as this country does not produce, in return for the admission free, or under a favored scheme of duties, of our own products, the benefits of such exchange to apply only to goods carried under the flag of the parties to the contract; the removal on both sides from the vessels so privileged of all tonnage dues and national imposts, so that those vessels may ply unhindered between our ports and those of the other contracting parties, though without infringing on the reserved home coasting trade; the removal or reduction of burdens on the exported products of those countries coming within the benefits of the treaties, and the avoidance of the technical restrictions and penalties by which our intercourse with those countries is at present hampered.

A perusal of the convention now submitted will suffice to show how fully it carries out the policy of intercourse thus announced. I commend it to you in the confident expectation that it will receive your sanction.

It does not seem necessary to my present purpose to enter into detailed consideration of the many immediate and prospective advantages which will flow from this convention to our productions and our shipping interests.

CHESTER A. ARTHUR.

EXECUTIVE MANSION,
Washington, December 10, 1884.

To the Senate of the United States:

I transmit herewith to the Senate, for consideration with a view to ratification, a treaty signed on the 1st of December with the Republic of Nicaragua, providing for the construction of an interoceanic canal across the territory of that State.

The negotiation of this treaty was entered upon under a conviction that it was imperatively demanded by the present and future political and material interests of the United States.

The establishment of water communication between the Atlantic and Pacific coasts of the Union is a necessity, the accomplishment of which, however, within the territory of the United States is a physical impossibility. While the enterprise of our citizens has responded to the duty of creating means of speedy transit by rail between the two oceans, these great achievements are inadequate to supply a most important requisite of national union and prosperity.

For all maritime purposes the States upon the Pacific are more distant from those upon the Atlantic than if separated by either ocean alone. Europe and Africa are nearer to New York, and Asia nearer to California, than are these two great States to each other by sea. Weeks

qualities that go to the making of good citizens. Our system of tax and tariff legislation is yielding a revenue which is in excess of the present needs of the Government.

These are the elements from which it is sought to devise a scheme by which, without unfavorably changing the condition of the workingman, our merchant marine shall be raised from its enfeebled condition and new markets provided for the sale beyond our borders of the manifold fruits of our industrial enterprises.

The problem is complex and can be solved by no single measure of innovation or reform.

The countries of the American continent and the adjacent islands are for the United States the natural marts of supply and demand. It is from them that we should obtain what we do not produce or do not produce in sufficiency, and it is to them that the surplus productions of our fields, our mills, and our workshops should flow, under conditions that will equalize or favor them in comparison with foreign competition.

Four paths of policy seem to point to this end:

First. A series of reciprocal commercial treaties with the countries of America which shall foster between us and them an unhampered movement of trade. The conditions of these treaties should be the free admission of such merchandise as this country does not produce, in return for the admission free or under a favored scheme of duties of our own products, the benefits of such exchange to apply only to goods carried under the flag of the parties to the contract; the removal on both sides from the vessels so privileged of all tonnage dues and national imposts, so that those vessels may ply unhindered between our ports and those of the other contracting parties, though without infringing on the reserved home coasting trade; the removal or reduction of burdens on the exported products of those countries coming within the benefits of the treaties, and the avoidance of the technical restrictions and penalties by which our intercourse with those countries is at present hampered.

Secondly. The establishment of the consular service of the United States on a salaried footing, thus permitting the relinquishment of consular fees not only as respects vessels under the national flag, but also as respects vessels of the treaty nations carrying goods entitled to the benefits of the treaties.

Thirdly. The enactment of measures to favor the construction and maintenance of a steam carrying marine under the flag of the United States.

Fourthly. The establishment of an uniform currency basis for the countries of America, so that the coined products of our mines may circulate on equal terms throughout the whole system of commonwealths. This would require a monetary union of America, whereby the output of the bullion-producing countries and the circulation of those which yield neither gold nor silver could be adjusted in conformity with the

Of the varied governmental concerns in charge of the Interior Department the report of its Secretary presents an interesting summary. Among the topics deserving particular attention I refer you to his observations respecting our Indian affairs, the preemption and timber-culture acts, the failure of railroad companies to take title to lands granted by the Government, and the operations of the Pension Office, the Patent Office, the Census Bureau, and the Bureau of Education.

Allusion has been made already to the circumstance that, both as between the different Indian tribes and as between the Indians and the whites, the past year has been one of unbroken peace.

In this circumstance the President is glad to find justification for the policy of the Government in its dealing with the Indian question and confirmation of the views which were fully expressed in his first communication to the Forty-seventh Congress.

The Secretary urges anew the enactment of a statute for the punishment of crimes committed on the Indian reservations, and recommends the passage of the bill now pending in the House of Representatives for the purchase of a tract of 18,000 square miles from the Sioux Reservation. Both these measures are worthy of approval.

I concur with him also in advising the repeal of the preemption law, the enactment of statutes resolving the present legal complications touching lapsed grants to railroad companies, and the funding of the debt of the several Pacific railroads under such guaranty as shall effectually secure its ultimate payment.

The report of the Utah Commission will be read with interest.

It discloses the results of recent legislation looking to the prevention and punishment of polygamy in that Territory. I still believe that if that abominable practice can be suppressed by law it can only be by the most radical legislation consistent with the restraints of the Constitution.

I again recommend, therefore, that Congress assume absolute political control of the Territory of Utah and provide for the appointment of commissioners with such governmental powers as in its judgment may justly and wisely be put into their hands.

In the course of this communication reference has more than once been made to the policy of this Government as regards the extension of our foreign trade. It seems proper to declare the general principles that should, in my opinion, underlie our national efforts in this direction.

The main conditions of the problem may be thus stated:

We are a people apt in mechanical pursuits and fertile in invention. We cover a vast extent of territory rich in agricultural products and in nearly all the raw materials necessary for successful manufacture. We have a system of productive establishments more than sufficient to supply our own demands. The wages of labor are nowhere else so great. The scale of living of our artisan classes is such as tends to secure their personal comfort and the development of those higher moral and intellectual

qualities that go to the making of good citizens. Our system of tax and tariff legislation is yielding a revenue which is in excess of the present needs of the Government.

These are the elements from which it is sought to devise a scheme by which, without unfavorably changing the condition of the workingman, our merchant marine shall be raised from its enfeebled condition and new markets provided for the sale beyond our borders of the manifold fruits of our industrial enterprises.

The problem is complex and can be solved by no single measure of innovation or reform.

The countries of the American continent and the adjacent islands are for the United States the natural marts of supply and demand. It is from them that we should obtain what we do not produce or do not produce in sufficiency, and it is to them that the surplus productions of our fields, our mills, and our workshops should flow, under conditions that will equalize or favor them in comparison with foreign competition.

Four paths of policy seem to point to this end:

First. A series of reciprocal commercial treaties with the countries of America which shall foster between us and them an unhampered movement of trade. The conditions of these treaties should be the free admission of such merchandise as this country does not produce, in return for the admission free or under a favored scheme of duties of our own products, the benefits of such exchange to apply only to goods carried under the flag of the parties to the contract; the removal on both sides from the vessels so privileged of all tonnage dues and national imposts, so that those vessels may ply unhindered between our ports and those of the other contracting parties, though without infringing on the reserved home coasting trade; the removal or reduction of burdens on the exported products of those countries coming within the benefits of the treaties, and the avoidance of the technical restrictions and penalties by which our intercourse with those countries is at present hampered.

Secondly. The establishment of the consular service of the United States on a salaried footing, thus permitting the relinquishment of consular fees not only as respects vessels under the national flag, but also as respects vessels of the treaty nations carrying goods entitled to the benefits of the treaties.

Thirdly. The enactment of measures to favor the construction and maintenance of a steam carrying marine under the flag of the United States.

Fourthly. The establishment of an uniform currency basis for the countries of America, so that the coined products of our mines may circulate on equal terms throughout the whole system of commonwealths. This would require a monetary union of America, whereby the output of the bullion-producing countries and the circulation of those which yield neither gold nor silver could be adjusted in conformity with the

in the confident expectation that it will receive approval, and that by appropriate legislation means may be provided for inaugurating the work without delay after the treaty shall have been ratified.

In conclusion I urge the justice of recognizing the aid which has recently been rendered in this matter by some of our citizens. The efforts of certain gentlemen connected with the American company which received the concession from Nicaragua (now terminated and replaced by this international compact) accomplished much of the preliminary labors leading to the conclusion of the treaty.

You may have occasion to examine the matter of their services, when such further information as you may desire will be furnished you.

I may add that the canal can be constructed by the able Engineer Corps of our Army, under their thorough system, cheaper and better than any work of such magnitude can in any other way be built.

CHESTER A. ARTHUR.

EXECUTIVE MANSION,
Washington, December 10, 1884.

To the Senate of the United States:

I transmit herewith, for consideration by the Senate with a view to advising and consenting to its ratification, a convention for commercial reciprocity between the United States and Spain, providing for an intimate and favored exchange of products with the islands of Cuba and Puerto Rico, which convention was signed at Madrid on the 18th ultimo.

The negotiations for this convention have been in progress since April last, in pursuance of the understanding reached by the two Governments on the 2d of January, 1884, for the improvement of commercial relations between the United States and the Spanish Antilles, by the eighth article of which both Governments engaged "to begin at once negotiations for a complete treaty of commerce and navigation between the United States of America and the said Provinces of Cuba and Puerto Rico." Although this clause was by common consent omitted from the substitutionary agreement of February 13, 1884 (now in force until replaced by this convention being carried into effect), the obligation to enter upon such a negotiation was deemed to continue. With the best desire manifest on both sides to reach a common accord, the negotiation has been necessarily protracted, owing to the complexity of the details to be incorporated in order that the convention might respond to the national policy of intercourse with the neighboring communities of the American system, which is outlined in my late annual message to the Congress in the following words:

The conditions of these treaties should be the free admission of such merchandise as this country does not produce, in return for the admission free or under a favored scheme of duties of our own products, the benefits of such exchange to apply only to goods carried under the flag of the parties to the contract; the removal on both sides from the vessels so privileged of all tonnage dues and national imposts, so that those vessels may ply unhindered between our ports and those of the other contracting parties, though without infringing on the reserved home coasting trade; the removal or reduction of burdens on the exported products of those countries coming within the benefits of the treaties, and the avoidance of the technical restrictions and penalties by which our intercourse with those countries is at present hampered.

A perusal of the convention now submitted will suffice to show how fully it carries out the policy of intercourse thus announced. I commend it to you in the confident expectation that it will receive your sanction.

It does not seem necessary to my present purpose to enter into detailed consideration of the many immediate and prospective advantages which will flow from this convention to our productions and our shipping interests.

CHESTER A. ARTHUR.

EXECUTIVE MANSION,
Washington, December 10, 1884.

To the Senate and House of Representatives:

With reference to the recommendations on the subject in my recent annual message, I transmit herewith a report of the Secretary of State of the 9th instant, showing the necessity for immediate legislation for the purpose of bringing the statutes of the United States into conformity with the international regulations for preventing collisions at sea, which have now been adopted by all the leading maritime powers of the world except this country.

CHESTER A. ARTHUR.

EXECUTIVE MANSION, *December 11, 1884.*

To the Senate of the United States:

I transmit herewith to the Senate a communication of this date from the Secretary of State, in relation to the reciprocity treaty recently signed between the United States and Spain.

CHESTER A. ARTHUR.

EXECUTIVE MANSION, *December 16, 1884.*

The SPEAKER OF THE HOUSE OF REPRESENTATIVES:

In compliance with the following resolution, adopted by the House on the 10th instant—

Resolved, That the President be requested to furnish this House, as early as convenient, with the necessary information showing the authority of law for which certain commodores of the Navy have been given the rank of acting rear-admirals when, as is alleged, no vacancy existed to justify such action—

I transmit herewith a communication from the Secretary of the Navy, containing the information called for by the resolution.

CHESTER A. ARTHUR.

EXECUTIVE MANSION,
Washington, December 17, 1884.

To the Senate of the United States:

I transmit to the Senate, for its consideration with a view to ratification, an agreement signed by Mr. N. D. Comanos, on the part of the United States of America, and Nubar Pasha, on behalf of the Government of the Khedive of Egypt, relative to a commercial and customs-house convention. The agreement is dated November 16, 1884.

CHESTER A. ARTHUR.

EXECUTIVE MANSION, *December 22, 1884.*

To the Senate and House of Representatives:

I transmit herewith the supplementary report, dated December 20, 1884, made in pursuance of orders of the Secretary of War and the Secretary of the Navy by the Gun Foundry Board, appointed by me in accordance with the act of Congress approved March 3, 1883.

CHESTER A. ARTHUR.

EXECUTIVE MANSION, *January 5, 1885.*

To the House of Representatives:

In accordance with the provisions of the act making appropriations for the diplomatic and consular service for the year ending June 30, 1883, I transmit herewith a further communication from the Secretary of State in relation to the consular service.

CHESTER A. ARTHUR.

EXECUTIVE MANSION, *January 5, 1885.*

To the House of Representatives:

I transmit herewith, with a recommendation for its favorable consideration, a communication from the Secretary of State, in which he urges the adoption of measures to secure the consul at Buenos Ayres against loss through the dropping of his salary at the last session of Congress.

CHESTER A. ARTHUR.

EXECUTIVE MANSION, *January 5, 1885.*

To the Senate and House of Representatives:

I transmit herewith a communication of the 2d instant from the Secretary of the Interior, inclosing certain papers in relation to the present condition of the Cheyenne and Arapahoe Indians in the Indian Territory, and recommending that some provision of law be enacted for disarming those and other Indians when such action may be found necessary for their advancement in civilized pursuits, and that means be provided for compensating the Indians for the weapons so taken from or surrendered by them.

The subject is commended to the favorable consideration and action of the Congress.

CHESTER A. ARTHUR.

EXECUTIVE MANSION, *January 12, 1885.*

To the Senate and House of Representatives:

I transmit herewith, for the consideration of Congress, the annual report of Government directors of the Union Pacific Railway Company for the year 1884.

The report accompanies the message to the House of Representatives.

CHESTER A. ARTHUR.

EXECUTIVE MANSION, *January 13, 1885.*

To the Senate:

I transmit herewith a communication from the Secretary of State, respecting the compensation for special electoral messengers to be appointed under the provisions of existing law.

I earnestly invite the attention of Congress to this communication and recommend that an appropriation be made without delay, to be immediately available, for the purposes indicated.

CHESTER A. ARTHUR.

EXECUTIVE MANSION, *January 13, 1885.*

To the Senate and House of Representatives:

I transmit herewith a communication from the Secretary of War, dated January 9, 1885, inclosing a copy of one dated January 5, 1885, from Lieutenant-Colonel William P. Craighill, Corps of Engineers, who was charged with the building of the monument at Yorktown, reporting the completion of the monument and recommending that the balance of the appropriation for building the same be used in paying the wages of a watchman and erecting a suitable keeper's dwelling on the site.

The matter is commended to the consideration of Congress.

CHESTER A. ARTHUR.

EXECUTIVE MANSION, *January 16, 1885.*

To the United States Senate:

I transmit herewith a copy of a letter addressed to the Secretary of War by General W. T. Sherman, under date of January 6, 1885, as called for by resolution of the Senate of January 13, 1885, as follows:

That the President of the United States be, and he is hereby, requested, if in his opinion it be not incompatible with the public interest, to communicate to the Senate a historical statement concerning the public policy of the executive department of the Confederate States during the late War of the Rebellion, reported to have been lately filed in the War Department by General William T. Sherman.

CHESTER A. ARTHUR.

EXECUTIVE MANSION, *January 20, 1885.*

To the Senate:

In response to the resolution of the Senate passed December 16, 1884, I transmit herewith a letter of the Secretary of State of the 19th instant, submitting a report containing certain information in the Department of State in relation to the foreign trade of Mexico, Central and South America, the Spanish West Indies, Hayti, and Santo Domingo, and also in relation to the share of the United States to the trade in question.

CHESTER A. ARTHUR.

EXECUTIVE MANSION, *January 23, 1885.*

To the Senate of the United States:

I transmit herewith, in answer to a resolution of the Senate dated January 5, 1885, a report of the Secretary of State and accompanying copies of such treaties and conventions between the United States and foreign powers as are requested by the resolution.

CHESTER A. ARTHUR.

EXECUTIVE MANSION, *January 23, 1885.*

To the Senate and House of Representatives:

I transmit herewith a communication of the 20th instant from the Secretary of the Interior, presenting, with accompanying papers, a draft of proposed legislation providing for the settlement of certain claims of Omaha Indians in Nebraska against the Winnebago Indians on account of horses stolen by members of the latter tribe from the Omahas.

The subject is commended to the favorable consideration and action of the Congress.

CHESTER A. ARTHUR.

EXECUTIVE MANSION, *January 23, 1885.*

To the Senate and House of Representatives:

I transmit herewith a report of the Secretary of State of the 22d instant, respecting an estimate of an appropriation to enable the Department of State to cause a preliminary search to be made of the records of the French prize courts from 1792 to 1801, inclusive, to ascertain whether any evidence or documents relating to the claims in question still exist, and, if so, the nature and character thereof; said preliminary search being intended to aid the Department of State to carry out the requirements of section 5 of the act approved January 20, 1885, to provide for the ascertainment of the claims of American citizens for spoliations committed by the French prior to the 31st of July, 1801.

CHESTER A. ARTHUR.

EXECUTIVE MANSION, *January 27, 1885.*
To the House of Representatives:

I transmit herewith, as desired by the House resolution of the 9th instant, a report, with accompanying papers, from the Secretary of State, in relation to the arrest and the imprisonment of Thomas R. Monahan by the authorities of Mexico.

CHESTER A. ARTHUR.

EXECUTIVE MANSION, *January 27, 1885.*
To the House of Representatives:

I transmit herewith a preliminary report of the Secretary of State of the 26th instant, in response to a resolution of the House of Representatives passed on the 9th day of January, 1885, calling for copies of accounts and vouchers of the disbursing officers of the French and American Claims Commission and certain other information in relation to the transactions of said commission.

CHESTER A. ARTHUR.

EXECUTIVE MANSION, *January 27, 1885.*
To the Senate of the United States:

I have carefully considered the provisions of Senate bill No. 862, entitled "An act for the relief of Uriel Crocker."

The general statute provides for relief in case of the destruction of coupon bonds.

In my opinion this provision of law is sufficiently liberal to meet all cases of missing coupon bonds worthy of favorable action, and I do not deem it advisable to encourage this class of legislation.

The bill is not, however, so flagrantly inexpedient as to call for my formal disapproval, and I have allowed it to become a law under the constitutional provision, contenting myself with communicating to the Senate, in which the bill originated, my disapproval of special legislation of this character.

CHESTER A. ARTHUR.

EXECUTIVE MANSION,
Washington, January 27, 1885.
To the Senate of the United States:

I transmit to the Senate, for its consideration with a view to ratification, an additional article, signed on the 23d of June last, to the treaty of friendship, commerce, and navigation which was concluded between the United States and the Argentine Confederation July 27, 1853.

CHESTER A. ARTHUR.

EXECUTIVE MANSION, *January 27, 1885.*
To the Senate and House of Representatives:

I transmit herewith a letter from the Secretary of State, concerning the awards made against Venezuela by the mixed commission under the convention of April 25, 1866.

I earnestly invite the attention of Congress to this communication and the accompanying documents.

CHESTER A. ARTHUR.

EXECUTIVE MANSION, *January 27, 1885.*
To the Senate of the United States:

I transmit herewith a report of the Secretary of State and accompanying papers, furnished in response to a resolution of the Senate of May 2, 1884, calling for information relative to the landing of foreign telegraphic cables upon the shores of the United States.

CHESTER A. ARTHUR.

EXECUTIVE MANSION, *January 27, 1885.*
To the Senate and House of Representatives:

I have the honor to transmit communications from the Secretary of the Navy, recommending certain action by the Government in recognition of the services, official and personal, extended in Russia to the survivors of the arctic exploring steamer *Jeannette* and to the search parties subsequently sent to Siberia.

The authority of Congress is requested for extending the specific rewards mentioned in the paper accompanying one of the communications of the Secretary. The suggestion concerning the thanks of Congress is also submitted for consideration.

CHESTER A. ARTHUR.

EXECUTIVE MANSION, *January 27, 1885.*
To the Senate of the United States:

In response to the resolution of the Senate of the 22d instant, setting forth that—

Whereas the United States, in 1866, acquired from the Creek and Seminole Indians by treaty certain lands situate in the Indian Territory, a portion of which have remained unoccupied until the present time; and

Whereas a widely extended belief exists that such unoccupied lands are public lands of the United States, and as such subject to homestead and preemption settle-
    and pursuant to such belief a large number of citizens of the United States

have gone upon them claiming the right to settle and acquire title thereto under the general land laws of the United States; and

Whereas it is understood that the President of the United States does not regard said lands as open to settlement and believes it to be his duty to remove all persons who go upon the same claiming the right to settle thereon, and for that purpose has directed the expulsion of the persons now on said lands by the use of military force, and there seems to be a probability of a conflict growing out of the attempt to expel said persons so claiming right and attempting to settle: Therefore,

Resolved, That the President be requested to advise the Senate as to the status of the lands in question as viewed by the Executive, the action taken, if any, to expel persons seeking to settle thereon, and the reasons for the same, together with any other information in his possession bearing upon the existing controversy—

I have the honor to state that the matter was referred to the Secretaries of War and the Interior and to transmit herewith their respective reports thereon, dated the 26th instant.

The report of the Commissioner of Indian Affairs accompanying that of the Secretary of the Interior recites fully the provisions of the treaties made with the Indian tribes ceding the lands in question to the United States, showing the condition and purposes expressed in said treaties regarding said lands, as well as the action taken with reference thereto, from which it will be seen that they are not open to settlement under any laws of the United States.

The report of the Secretary of War shows the action of the military authorities at the request of the Interior Department under section 2147 of the Revised Statutes.

The status of these lands was considered by my predecessor, President Hayes, who on the 26th day of April, 1879, issued a proclamation* warning all persons intending to go upon said lands without proper permission of the Interior Department that they would be speedily and immediately removed therefrom according to the laws made and provided, and that if necessary the aid and assistance of the military forces of the United States would be invoked to carry into proper execution the laws of the United States referring thereto. A similar proclamation† was issued by President Hayes on the 12th day of February, 1880. On the 1st day of July, 1884, I considered it to be my duty to issue a proclamation‡ of like import.

These several proclamations were at the request of the Secretary of the Interior.

As will be seen by the report of the Secretary of War, the military forces of the United States have been repeatedly employed to remove intruders from the lands in question, and that notwithstanding such removals and in disregard of law and the Executive proclamations a large body of intruders is now within the territory in question, and that an adequate force of troops has been ordered to remove the intruders and is now being concentrated for that purpose.

*See Vol. VII, pp. 547-548.   †See Vol. VII, pp. 598-599.   ‡See pp. 224-225.

None of the land or general laws of the United States have been extended over these lands except as to the punishment for crimes and other provisions contained in the intercourse act which relate to trade and the introduction of spirituous liquors and arms among Indians, and do not sanction settlement. It is clear that no authorized settlement can be made by any person in the territory in question.

Until the existing status of these lands shall have been changed by agreement with the Indians interested, or in some other manner as may be determined by Congress, the treaties heretofore made with the Indians should be maintained and the power of the Government to the extent necessary should be exercised to keep off intruders and all unauthorized persons.

CHESTER A. ARTHUR.

EXECUTIVE MANSION, *January 29, 1885.*

To the House of Representatives:

In response to the resolution of the House of Representatives of the 5th of January, 1885, calling for information as to the Kongo conference at Berlin, I transmit herewith a report of the Secretary of State of the 28th instant, in relation to the subject.

CHESTER A. ARTHUR.

EXECUTIVE MANSION, *January 29, 1885.*

To the Senate and House of Representatives:

I transmit herewith a communication of 27th instant, with inclosures, from the Secretary of the Interior, in relation to objections on the part of the Creek Nation of Indians to pending legislation providing for the opening up to homestead settlement of certain lands in the Indian Territory.

The matter is presented to the consideration of the Congress.

CHESTER A. ARTHUR.

EXECUTIVE MANSION, *January 29, 1885.*

To the House of Representatives:

In compliance with a resolution of the House of Representatives (which was concurred in by the Senate) of January 28, 1885, I return herewith the bill (H. R. 1017) relative to the Inspector-General's Department of the Army.

CHESTER A. ARTHUR.

EXECUTIVE MANSION, *January 30, 1885.*

To the Senate and House of Representatives:

When the expedition for the relief of Lieutenant Greely and his party was being prepared, in the early part of the year 1884, and a search for suitable vessels was being made, the *Alert*, then the property of Great Britain, and which had been the advance ship of the expedition under Sir George Nares, was found to be peculiarly fitted for the intended service, and this Government immediately offered to purchase that vessel, upon which Her Majesty's Government generously presented her to the United States, refusing to accept any pay whatever for the vessel. The *Alert* rendered important and timely service in the expedition for the relief of Lieutenant Greely and party, which in its results proved so satisfactory to the Government and people of this country.

I am of the opinion that the *Alert* should now be returned to Her Majesty's Government, with suitable acknowledgments for its generous and graceful acts of courtesy in so promptly putting the vessel at the service of the United States, and I therefore recommend that authority be given me by Congress to carry out this purpose.

CHESTER A. ARTHUR.

EXECUTIVE MANSION, *January 30, 1885.*
To the House of Representatives:

I transmit herewith, in response to a resolution of the House of Representatives of the 28th of January, 1885, a report by the Secretary of State, in relation to the case of Julio R. Santos, an American citizen imprisoned in Ecuador.

CHESTER A. ARTHUR.

EXECUTIVE MANSION, *January 30, 1885.*
To the Senate and House of Representatives of the United States:

I herewith transmit a communication from the Secretary of State, in regard to the desire of the Government of Korea to obtain the services of one or more officers of the United States as military instructors in that country, and recommend the adoption of a joint resolution authorizing such officers as may be conveniently spared, and who may be selected for that duty, to proceed to Korea for the purpose indicated.

CHESTER A. ARTHUR.

EXECUTIVE MANSION, *February 2, 1885.*
To the Senate and House of Representatives of the United States:

I transmit herewith to the Senate a communication from the Secretary of State, submitting, at the request of a delegate from the United States to the Third International Conference of the Red Cross, held in September, 1884, a copy of the preliminary report of that conference.

CHESTER A. ARTHUR.

EXECUTIVE MANSION, *February 2, 1885.*

To the Senate and House of Representatives:

I transmit herewith, for the consideration of Congress, the report of the National Board of Health for the year 1884.

CHESTER A. ARTHUR.

EXECUTIVE MANSION,
Washington, February 2, 1885.

To the Senate of the United States of America:

With reference to the resolution of the Senate of the 12th of June, 1884, declining to advise and consent to the ratification of an accession of the United States to an international convention for the protection of industrial property, signed at Paris March 20, 1883, I now return the proposed instrument of accession to the Senate for reconsideration in connection with the views and recommendations contained in the accompanying report of the Secretary of State, dated January 29, 1885.

CHESTER A. ARTHUR.

EXECUTIVE MANSION, *February 2, 1885.*

To the House of Representatives:

In response to the resolution of the House of Representatives of January 28, 1885, "that the President be respectfully requested to transmit to this House a copy of the recent appeal of Fitz John Porter, together with the accompanying papers," I transmit herewith a copy of a communication from Fitz John Porter, addressed to the President from Morristown, N. J., under date of October 14, 1884, together with copies of the accompanying papers.

CHESTER A. ARTHUR.

EXECUTIVE MANSION, *February 3, 1885.*

To the Senate and House of Representatives:

I take especial pleasure in laying before Congress the generous offer made by Mrs. Grant to give to the Government, in perpetual trust, the swords and military (and civil) testimonials lately belonging to General Grant. A copy of the deed of trust and of a letter addressed to me by Mr. William H. Vanderbilt, which I transmit herewith, will explain the nature and motives of this offer.

Appreciation of General Grant's achievements and recognition of his just fame have in part taken the shape of numerous mementoes and gifts which, while dear to him, possess for the nation an exceptional interest.

These relics, of great historical value, have passed into the hands of another, whose considerate action has restored the collection to Mrs. Grant as a life trust, on the condition that at the death of General Grant, or sooner, at Mrs. Grant's option, it should become the property of the Government, as set forth in the accompanying papers. In the exercise of the option thus given her Mrs. Grant elects that the trust shall forthwith determine, and asks that the Government designate a suitable place of deposit and a responsible custodian for the collection

The nature of this gift and the value of the relics which the generosity of a private citizen, joined to the high sense of public regard which animates Mrs. Grant, have thus placed at the disposal of the Government, demand full and signal recognition on behalf of the nation at the hands of its representatives. I therefore ask Congress to take suitable action to accept the trust and to provide for its secure custody, at the same time recording the appreciative gratitude of the people of the United States to the donors.

In this connection I may pertinently advert to the pending legislation of the Senate and House of Representatives looking to a national recognition of General Grant's eminent services by providing the means for his restoration to the Army on the retired list. That Congress, by taking such action, will give expression to the almost universal desire of the people of this nation is evident, and I earnestly urge the passage of an act similar to Senate bill No. 2530, which, while not interfering with the constitutional prerogative of appointment, will enable the President in his discretion to nominate General Grant as general upon the retired list.

CHESTER A. ARTHUR.

DEED OF TRUST.

Whereas I, William H. Vanderbilt, of the city of New York, by virtue of a sale made under a judgment in a suit to foreclose a chattel mortgage in the supreme court of this State, in which I was plaintiff and Ulysses S. Grant defendant, which judgment was entered on the 6th day of December, 1884, and under an execution in another suit in said court between the same parties upon a judgment entered December 9, 1884, have become the owner of the property and the articles described in the schedule hereto annexed, formerly the property of Ulysses S. Grant:

Now, therefore, to carry out a purpose formed by me, and in consideration of $1 to me paid, I do hereby transfer and convey each and every one of the articles mentioned and itemized in the said schedule to Julia Dent Grant, to have and to hold the same to her, her executors and administrators, upon the trust and agreement, nevertheless, hereby accepted and made by her, that on the death of the said Ulysses S. Grant, or previously thereto, at her or their option, the same shall become and be the property of the nation and shall be taken to Washington and transferred and conveyed by her and them to the United States of America.

In witness whereof the said William H. Vanderbilt and Julia Dent Grant have executed these presents, this 10th day of January, A. D. 1885.

Sealed and delivered in presence of—

W. H. VANDERBILT.
JULIA DENT GRANT.

Schedule of swords and medals, paintings, bronzes, portraits, commissions and addresses, and objects of value and art presented by various governments in the world to General Ulysses S. Grant.

Mexican onyx cabinet, presented to General Grant by the people of Puebla, Mexico.

Aerolite, part of which passed over Mexico in 1871.

Bronze vases, presented to General Grant by the Japanese citizens of Yokohama, Japan.

Marble bust and pedestal, presented by workingmen of Philadelphia.

General Grant and family, painted by Coggswell.

Large elephant tusks, presented by the King of Siam.

Small elephant tusks, from the Maharajah of Johore.

Picture of General Scott, by Page, presented by gentlemen of New York.

Crackleware bowls (very old), presented by Prince Koon, of China.

Cloisonné jars (old), presented by Li Hung Chang.

Chinese porcelain jars (old), presented by Prince Koon, of China.

Arabian Bible.

Coptic Bible, presented by Lord Napier, who captured it with King Theodore, of Abyssinia.

Sporting rifle.

Sword of Donelson, presented to General Grant after the fall of Fort Donelson, by officers of the Army, and used by him until the end of the war.

New York sword, voted to General Grant by the citizens of New York at the fair held in New York.

Sword of Chattanooga, presented to General Grant by the citizens of Jo Daviess County, Ill. (Galena), after the battle of Chattanooga.

Roman mug and pitcher.

Silver menu and card, farewell dinner of San Francisco, Cal.

Silver menu of Paris dinner.

Horn and silver snuff box.

Silver match box, used by General Grant.

Gold table, modeled after the table in Mr. McLean's house on which General R. E. Lee signed the articles of surrender. This was presented to General Grant by ex-Confederate soldiers.

Gold cigar case (enameled), presented by the Celestial King of Siam.

Gold cigar case (plain), presented by the Second King of Siam.

Gold-handled knife, presented by miners of Idaho Territory.

Nine pieces of jade stone, presented by Prince Koon, of China.

Silver trowel, used by General Grant in laying the corner stone of the American Museum of Natural History, New York.

Knife, made at Sheffield for General Grant.

Gold pen, General Grant's.

Embroidered picture (cock and hen), presented to General Grant by citizens of Japan.

Field glasses, used by General Grant during the war.

Iron-headed cane, made from the rebel ram *Merrimac.*

Silver-headed cane, made from wood used in the defense of Fort Sumter.

Gold-headed cane, made out of wood from old Fort Du Quesne, Pa.

Gold-headed cane, presented to General Grant as a tribute of regard for his humane treatment of the soldiers and kind consideration of those who ministered to the sick and wounded during the war.

Gold-headed cane, used by General Lafayette, and presented to General Grant by the ladies of Baltimore, Md.

Carved wood cane, from the estate of Sir Walter Scott.

Uniform as general of the United States Army.

Fifteen buttons, cut from the coats during the war by Mrs. Grant after the different battles.

Hat ornament, used at Belmont.

Hat ornament, used at Fort Donelson.

Shoulder straps (brigadier-general), worn by General Grant at Belmont, Fort Donelson, and Shiloh.

Shoulder straps (lieutenant-general), cut from the coat used by General Grant in the campaigns against Richmond and Petersburg and Lee's army.

Shoulder straps (lieutenant-general), cut from General Grant's coat.

Pair of shoulder straps (general), cut from a coat General Grant used after the war.

Medal from the American Congress (gold) for opening the Mississippi.

Gold medal, from Philadelphia.

Twenty-one medals (gold, silver, and bronze), badges of armies and corps.

Ten medals (silver and bronze), sent to General Grant at different times.

Fourteen medals (bronze), in memory of events.

Silk paper (Louisville Commercial), printed for General Grant.

Silk paper (Daily Chronicle), printed for General Grant.

Silk paper (Burlington Hawkeye), printed for General Grant.

Collection of coin (Japanese). This is the only complete set, except one which is in the Japanese treasury. Seven of these pieces cost $5,000. This set was presented by the Government of Japan.

Warrant as cadet at West Point.

Commission, brevet second lieutenant (missing).

Commission, second lieutenant (missing).

Commission, brevet first lieutenant (missing).

Commission as first lieutenant, United States Army.

Commission as brevet captain, United States Army.

Commission as captain, United States Army.

Commission as colonel of volunteers.

Commission as brigadier-general.

Commission as major-general.

Commission as major-general, United States Army.

Commission as lieutenant-general, United States Army.

Commission as general, United States Army.

Commission as honorary member of M. L. A., San Francisco.

Commission as member of Sacramento Society of Pioneers.

Commission as honorary member Royal Historical Society.

Commission as Military Order of Loyal Legion.

Commission as member of the Aztec Club.

Certificate of election President of the United States.

Certificate of reelection President of the United States.

Certificate of honorary membership Territorial Pioneers of California.

Certificate of honorary membership St. Andrew's Society.

Certificate of election LL. D., Harvard College.

Certificate of election honorary membership of the Sacramento Society.

Certificate of Pioneers of California.

Certificate of election honorary member Mercantile Library, San Francisco.

Freedom of the city of Dublin, Ireland.

Freedom of the city of Stratford-on-Avon.

Freedom of the city of London, England.

Freedom of the city of Glasgow, Scotland.

Freedom of the city of Edinburgh, Scotland.

Freedom of the city of Ayr, Scotland.

Freedom of the burgh of Inverness, Scotland.

Freedom of the city of Oakland, America.

Freedom of the city of San Francisco, America.

Freedom of the city of Londonderry, Ireland.

The freedom of many other cities.

Address to General Grant from the Chamber of Commerce, Newcastle-upon-Tyne, 1877.

Address to General Grant from the mayor, aldermen, and citizens of the city of Manchester, England, May 13, 1877.

Address to General Grant by the workingmen of Birmingham, England, October 16, 1877.

Address to General Grant from the Chamber of Commerce and Board of Trade, San Francisco, Cal., September, 1879.

Address to General Grant by mayor, aldermen, and burgesses of the borough of Gateshead, England.

Address to General Grant by the mayor, aldermen, magistrates, aldermen, and councilors of the borough of Leicester, England.

Address to General Grant by the Americans of Shanghai, China, May 19, 1879.

Address to General Grant by the Calumet Club, of Chicago, Ill.

Address to General Grant from the Society of Friends in Great Britain.

Address to General Grant from Chamber of Commerce of Penang.

Address to General Grant by the mayor, aldermen, and burgesses of the borough of Southampton, England.

Address to General Grant by the provost, magistrates, and town council of the royal borough of Stirling.

Address to General Grant by the mayor, aldermen, and burgesses of Tynemouth, England.

Address to General Grant by the mayor and town council of Sunderland.

Address to General Grant by the trade and friendly societies of Sunderland.

Address to General Grant by the public schools of Louisville, Ky.

Address to General Grant by the colored men of Louisville, Ky.

Address to General Grant by ex-Confederate soldiers.

Address to General Grant by the State of Louisiana.

Address to General Grant by the Chamber of Commerce and Board of Trade of San Francisco, Cal.

Address to General Grant by the British workmen of London, England.

Address to General Grant by the North Shields Shipowners' Society, England.

Address to General Grant by the Chamber of Commerce, Sheffield, England.

Address to General Grant from mayor, aldermen, and burgesses of borough of Royal Leamington Spa, England.

Address to General Grant by the mayor, aldermen, and burgesses of Sheffield, England.

Address to General Grant by wardens, etc., and commonalty of the town of Sheffield, England.

Address to General Grant from the provost, magistrates, and town council of the city and royal burgh of Elgin, Scotland.

Address to General Grant from the mayor, aldermen, and burgesses of the borough of Folkestone, England.

Address to General Grant by the mayor, aldermen, and burgesses of the borough of Jarrow, England.

Address to General Grant by the mayor, aldermen, and burgesses of Gateshead, England.

dress to General Grant from the Carpenters' Company.

Address to General Grant from the citizens of Cincinnati, congratulating him on his second election as President of the United States.

Address to General Grant from the citizens of Nagasaki, Japan.

Resolutions of the Territorial Pioneers, admitting General Grant to membership.

Resolution of the Caledonian Club, of San Francisco, enrolling General Grant as an honorary member.

Resolutions of the citizens of Jo Daviess County, presenting a sword to General Grant (sword of Chattanooga).

Resolutions of the Washington Camp, of Brooklyn, Long Island.

First resolutions of thanks of the Congress of the United States.

First resolutions inviting General Grant to visit the house of representatives of the Commonwealth of Pennsylvania.

Second resolutions of thanks from the Congress of the United States.

Letter from citizens of Jersey City thanking General Grant for his Des Moines, Iowa, speech on the question of public schools.

Presentation of a silver medal by the Union League Club, of Philadelphia, for gallantry and distinguished services.

Vote of thanks by Congress to General U. S. Grant, etc.

Other resolutions, addresses, votes of thanks, and freedom of cities.

640 FIFTH AVENUE, *January 20, 1885.*

His Excellency CHESTER A. ARTHUR,
President of the United States.

DEAR SIR: I purchased the articles of historical interest belonging to General Grant and gave them to Mrs. Grant in trust to hold during the lifetime of the General, and at his death, or sooner, at her option, they to become the property of the Government. They consist of his swords, memorials of his victories from the United States, States, and cities, and tributes to his fame and achievements from governments all over the world. In their proper place at Washington they will always be secure and will afford pleasure and instruction to succeeding generations. This trust has been accepted by Mrs. Grant, and the disposition of the articles is in conformity to the wishes of the General. I transmit to you herewith the deed of trust. Mrs. Grant informs me that she prefers to close the trust at once and send the memorials to Washington. May I ask, therefore, that you will designate some official, representing the proper Department, to receive them, and direct him to notify Mrs. Grant of the arrangements necessary to perfect the transfer and deposit in such of the Government buildings as may be most suitable?

Yours, respectfully,

W. H. VANDERBILT.

EXECUTIVE MANSION, *February 5, 1885.*

To the Senate and House of Representatives of the United States:

I herewith transmit a communication from the Secretary of State, relative to the Japanese Government's offer to donate a valuable piece of land to the United States in fee simple for legation purposes, and earnestly recommend that the Executive may be immediately authorized to accept the gift in the name of the United States and to tender to his Imperial Japanese Majesty's Government a suitable expression of this Government's thanks for the generosity which prompted the presentation of so desirable a site of ground.

I deem it unnecessary to enlarge upon the statement of the Secretary of State. I feel certain, however, that a perusal of his communication will at once commend itself to the favorable attention of Congress, and doubt not that the necessary authorization of Congress will be immediately given for the acceptance of the gift, as well as insure early action looking to the erection on the premises of suitable public buildings for the use of the legation of the United States at Tokyo. This step can not but be favorable to the United States in every honorable way, while the disinterested motives of a friendly foreign government deserve from us a proper and just recognition.   CHESTER A. ARTHUR.

EXECUTIVE MANSION, *February 11, 1885.*

To the Senate and House of Representatives:

In compliance with the act of Congress approved January 16, 1883, entitled "An act to regulate and improve the civil service of the United States," the Civil Service Commission has made to the President its second annual report.

That report is herewith transmitted.

The Commission is in the second year of its existence. The President congratulates the country upon the success of its labors, commends the subject to the favorable consideration of Congress, and asks for an appropriation to continue the work.   CHESTER A. ARTHUR.

EXECUTIVE MANSION, *February 12, 1885.*

To the Senate and House of Representatives:

I transmit herewith a copy of the report of the board of management of the World's Industrial and Cotton Centennial Exposition, dated February 2, 1885, requesting an additional appropriation to extinguish a deficit in its accounts, and asking authority to reopen the exhibition during the winter of 1885–86.

A failure on the part of the management to carry out the original intent in regard to the exposition might reflect upon the honor of the United States Government, since twenty-one foreign nations and forty-six States and Territories have joined in the enterprise through faith in the sanction of the Government. In view of this fact and in consideration of the value of the exposition to the cause of material progress and general education, I respectfully submit the report mentioned for the favorable consideration of Congress.   CHESTER A. ARTHUR.

EXECUTIVE MANSION, *February 13, 1885.*

To the Senate and House of Representatives:

I herewith transmit, as desired by the act of Congress approved July 7, 1884, a letter from the Secretary of State, with accompanying report from the Central and South American commissioners.

                    CHESTER A. ARTHUR.

EXECUTIVE MANSION, *February 17, 1885.*

To the House of Representatives:

In response to the resolution of the House of Representatives of the 9th of January, 1885, calling for certain correspondence concerning the transactions of the late French and American Commission, I transmit herewith a report of the Secretary of State of the 16th instant, in relation to the subject.

CHESTER A. ARTHUR.

WASHINGTON, *February 17, 1885.*

To the Senate of the United States:

Referring your honorable body to the message of December 1, 1884, by which I transmitted to the Senate, with a view to ratification, a treaty negotiated with Belgium touching the succession to and acquirement of real property, etc., by the citizens or subjects of the one Government in the domain of the other, I now address you in order to recall the treaty thus transmitted for reexamination.

CHESTER A. ARTHUR.

EXECUTIVE MANSION, *February 17, 1885.*

To the Senate of the United States:

Referring to my message of the 13th instant, concerning the report of the Central and South American commissioners, I have the honor to inform the Senate that the report therein stated as accompanying the message was transmitted with a like message to the House of Representatives.

A note of explanation to this effect was inadvertently omitted from the former message.

CHESTER A. ARTHUR.

EXECUTIVE MANSION, *February 19, 1885.*

To the Senate and House of Representatives:

I transmit herewith a report of the Secretary of State of the 19th instant, recommending the enactment of a law for the protection of submarine cables in pursuance of our treaty obligations under the international convention in relation to the subject signed at Paris on the 14th day of March, 1884.

I commend the matter to the favorable consideration of Congress.

CHESTER A. ARTHUR.

EXECUTIVE MANSION, *February 19, 1885.*

To the Senate and House of Representatives:

I transmit herewith a communication of the 16th instant from the Secretary of the Interior, submitting, with accompanying papers, a draft of a bill "to accept and ratify an agreement with the confederated tribes and bands of Indians occupying the Yakima Reservation in the Territory of Washington for the extinguishment of their title to so much of said reservation as is required for the use of the Northern Pacific Railroad, and to make the necessary appropriation for carrying out the same."

The matter is presented for the consideration and action of the Congress.

CHESTER A. ARTHUR.

EXECUTIVE MANSION, *February 19, 1885.*

To the House of Representatives:

I transmit herewith, in response to a resolution of the House of Representatives of the 5th instant, requesting copies of all the communications which have been received respecting the Kongo conference, and especially copies of the text of the commissions or powers sent by this Government to each of the three American plenipotentiaries or agents, a report of the Secretary of State.

CHESTER A. ARTHUR.

EXECUTIVE MANSION, *February 19, 1885.*

To the House of Representatives:

With reference to my communication of the 27th ultimo, transmitting to the House of Representatives a preliminary report of the Secretary of State, dated the 26th of January, 1885, in response to the resolution of the House of the 9th of January, 1885, calling for copies of the accounts and vouchers of the disbursing officers of the French-American Claims Commission and containing other information in relation to the transactions of said commission, I now transmit herewith a further report on the subject by the Secretary of State, dated the 17th instant, which is accompanied by the desired copies of the accounts and vouchers in question.

CHESTER A. ARTHUR.

EXECUTIVE MANSION, *February 25, 1885.*

To the House of Representatives:

In answer to the resolution of the House of Representatives of the 13th instant, requesting me to inform that body, if not incompatible with the public interest, what were the reasons which moved me to appoint commissioners to examine and report upon the California and Oregon Railroad from Reading northwardly, I transmit herewith a communication on that subject addressed to me on the 24th instant by the Secretary of the Interior, setting forth the practice under which my action was taken.

CHESTER A. ARTHUR.

Executive Mansion, *February 26, 1885.*

To the Senate of the United States:

I transmit to the Senate, for its consideration with a view to ratification, a provisional article of agreement modifying the latter clause of Article XXVI of the pending commercial treaty between the United States and Spain, concluded November 18, 1884, so as to extend the time for the approval of the laws necessary to carry the said treaty into operation if ratified.

CHESTER A. ARTHUR.

Executive Mansion,
Washington, D. C., February 26, 1885.

To the Senate of the United States:

I herewith transmit, for the consideration of the Senate with a view to ratification, an additional article, signed by the Secretary of State and the minister of Mexico here, on behalf of their respective Governments, the 25th instant, providing for the extension of the time for the approval of the necessary legislation in order to carry into effect the commercial reciprocity treaty between the United States and Mexico of January 20, 1883.

CHESTER A. ARTHUR.

Executive Mansion,
Washington, February 28, 1885.

To the Senate of the United States:

Referring to my message to the Senate of the 25th instant, by which I transmitted, with a view to ratification, an additional article to the commercial treaty with Spain concluded November 18, 1884, I now have the honor to request the return of that instrument.

CHESTER A. ARTHUR.

Executive Mansion,
Washington, March 2, 1885.

To the Senate of the United States:

I herewith transmit to the Senate, with a view to examination and sanction by that body, a treaty signed in this city to-day by the Secretary of State and the Spanish minister, consisting of four supplementary articles amendatory of the commercial treaty of November 18, 1884, between the United States and Spain, which is now pending in the Senate. The accompanying report of the Secretary of State recites the particulars of the modifications which have been made in deference to the representations made on behalf of important commercial interests of the United States, whereby it is believed all well-founded objections on their part to the ratification of that treaty are obviated.

CHESTER A. ARTHUR.

EXECUTIVE MANSION, *March 2, 1885.*

To the Senate of the United States:

I transmit herewith, for the consideration of the Senate with a view to its ratification, a convention concluded February 20, 1885, between the United States of America and the United States of Mexico, for the extradition of criminals. A report of the Secretary of State, touching the negotiation of the convention, is also transmitted.

CHESTER A. ARTHUR.

EXECUTIVE MANSION, *March 3, 1885.*

To the Senate of the United States:

I nominate Ulysses S. Grant, formerly commanding the armies of the United States, to be general on the retired list of the Army, with the full pay of such rank.

CHESTER A. ARTHUR.

PROCLAMATIONS.

BY THE PRESIDENT OF THE UNITED STATES OF AMERICA.

A PROCLAMATION.

Whereas the treaty concluded between the United States of America and Her Majesty the Queen of Great Britain and Ireland, concluded at Washington on the 8th day of May, 1871, contains among other articles the following, viz:

ARTICLE XVIII.

It is agreed by the high contracting parties that, in addition to the liberty secured to the United States fishermen by the convention between the United States and Great Britain signed at London on the 20th day of October, 1818, of taking, curing, and drying fish on certain coasts of the British North American colonies therein defined, the inhabitants of the United States shall have, in common with the subjects of Her Britannic Majesty, the liberty, for the term of years mentioned in Article XXXIII of this treaty, to take fish of every kind, except shellfish, on the seacoasts and shores and in the bays, harbors, and creeks of the Provinces of Quebec, Nova Scotia, and New Brunswick, and the colony of Prince Edwards Island, and of the several islands thereunto adjacent, without being restricted to any distance from the shore, with permission to land upon the said coasts and shores and islands, and also upon the Magdalen Islands, for the purpose of drying their nets and curing their fish; provided that in so doing they do not interfere with the rights of private property or with British fishermen in the peaceable use of any part of the said coasts in their occupancy for the same purpose.

It is understood that the above-mentioned liberty applies solely to the sea fishery, and that the salmon and shad fisheries, and all other fisheries in rivers and the mouths of rivers, are hereby reserved exclusively for British fishermen.

ARTICLE XIX.

It is agreed by the high contracting parties that British subjects shall have, in common with the citizens of the United States, the liberty, for the term of years mentioned in Article XXXIII of this treaty, to take fish of every kind, except shell-fish, on the eastern seacoasts and shores of the United States north of the thirty-ninth parallel of north latitude, and on the shores of the several islands thereunto adjacent, and in the bays, harbors, and creeks of the said seacoasts and shores of the United States and of the said islands, without being restricted to any distance from the shore, with permission to land upon the said coasts of the United States and of the islands aforesaid, for the purpose of drying their nets and curing their fish; provided that in so doing they do not interfere with the rights of private property or with the fishermen of the United States in the peaceable use of any part of the said coasts in their occupancy for the same purpose.

It is understood that the above-mentioned liberty applies solely to the sea fishery; and that salmon and shad fisheries, and all other fisheries in rivers and mouths of rivers, are hereby reserved exclusively for fishermen of the United States.

ARTICLE XX.

It is agreed that the places designated by the commissioners appointed under the first article of the treaty between the United States and Great Britain concluded at Washington on the 5th of June, 1854, upon the coasts of Her Britannic Majesty's dominions and the United States, as places reserved from the common right of fishing under that treaty, shall be regarded as in like manner reserved from the common right of fishing under the preceding articles. In case any question should arise between the Governments of the United States and of Her Britannic Majesty as to the common right of fishing in places not thus designated as reserved, it is agreed that a commission shall be appointed to designate such places, and shall be constituted in the same manner and have the same powers, duties, and authority as the commission appointed under the said first article of the treaty of the 5th of June, 1854.

ARTICLE XXI.

It is agreed that for the term of years mentioned in Article XXXIII of this treaty fish oil and fish of all kinds (except fish of the inland lakes and of the rivers falling into them, and except fish preserved in oil), being the produce of the fisheries of the United States, or of the Dominion of Canada, or of Prince Edwards Island, shall be admitted into each country, respectively, free of duty.

ARTICLE XXII.

Inasmuch as it is asserted by the Government of Her Britannic Majesty that the privileges accorded to the citizens of the United States under Article XVIII of this treaty are of greater value than those accorded by Articles XIX and XXI of this treaty to the subjects of Her Britannic Majesty, and this assertion is not admitted by the Government of the United States, it is further agreed that commissioners shall be appointed to determine, having regard to the privileges accorded by the United States to the subjects of Her Britannic Majesty, as stated in Articles XIX and XXI of this treaty, the amount of any compensation which in their opinion ought to be paid by the Government of the United States to the Government of Her Britannic Majesty in return for the privileges accorded to the citizens of the United States under Article XVIII of this treaty; and that any sum of money which the said commissioners may so award shall be paid by the United States Government, in a gross sum, within twelve months after such award shall have been given.

ARTICLE XXIII.

The commissioners referred to in the preceding article shall be appointed in the following manner; that is to say: One commissioner shall be named by the President of the United States, one by Her Britannic Majesty, and a third by the President of the United States and Her Britannic Majesty conjointly; and in case the third commissioner shall not have been so named within a period of three months from the date when this article shall take effect, then the third commissioner shall be named by the representative at London of His Majesty the Emperor of Austria and King of Hungary. In case of the death, absence, or incapacity of any commissioner, or in the event of any commissioner omitting or ceasing to act, the vacancy shall be filled in the manner hereinbefore provided for making the original appointment, the period of three months in case of such substitution being calculated from the date of the happening of the vacancy.

The commissioners so named shall meet in the city of Halifax, in the Province of Nova Scotia, at the earliest convenient period after they have been respectively named, and shall before proceeding to any business make and subscribe a solemn declaration that they will impartially and carefully examine and decide the matters referred to them to the best of their judgment and according to justice and equity; and such declaration shall be entered on the record of their proceedings.

Each of the high contracting parties shall also name one person to attend the commission as its agent, to represent it generally in all matters connected with the commission.

ARTICLE XXIV.

The proceedings shall be conducted in such order as the commissioners appointed under Articles XXII and XXIII of this treaty shall determine. They shall be bound to receive such oral or written testimony as either Government may present. If either party shall offer oral testimony, the other party shall have the right of cross-examination, under such rules as the commissioners shall prescribe.

If in the case submitted to the commissioners either party shall have specified or alluded to any report or document in its own exclusive possession, without annexing a copy, such party shall be bound, if the other party thinks proper to apply for it, to furnish that party with a copy thereof; and either party may call upon the other, through the commissioners, to produce the originals or certified copies of any papers adduced as evidence, giving in each instance such reasonable notice as the commissioners may require.

The case on either side shall be closed within a period of six months from the date of the organization of the commission, and the commissioners shall be requested to give their award as soon as possible thereafter. The aforesaid period of six months may be extended for three months in case of a vacancy occurring among the commissioners under the circumstances contemplated in Article XXIII of this treaty.

ARTICLE XXV.

The commissioners shall keep an accurate record and correct minutes or notes of all their proceedings, with the dates thereof, and may appoint and employ a secretary and any other necessary officer or officers to assist them in the transaction of the business which may come before them.

Each of the high contracting parties shall pay its own commissioner and agent or counsel; all other expenses shall be defrayed by the two Governments in equal moieties.

ARTICLE XXX.

It is agreed that for the term of years mentioned in Article XXXIII of this treaty subjects of Her Britannic Majesty may carry in British vessels, without payment of duty, goods, wares, or merchandise from one port or place within the territory of the United States upon the St. Lawrence, the Great Lakes, and the rivers connecting the same, to another port or place within the territory of the United States as aforesaid: *Provided*, That a portion of such transportation is made through the Dominion of Canada by land carriage and in bond, under such rules and regulations as may be agreed upon between the Government of Her Britannic Majesty and the Government of the United States.

Citizens of the United States may for the like period carry in United States vessels, without payment of duty, goods, wares, or merchandise from one port or place within the possessions of Her Britannic Majesty in North America to another port or place within the said possessions: *Provided*, That a portion of such transportation is made through the territory of the United States by land carriage and in bond, under such rules and regulations as may be agreed upon between the Government of the United States and the Government of Her Britannic Majesty.

The Government of the United States further engages not to impose any export duties on goods, wares, or merchandise carried under this article through the territory of the United States; and Her Majesty's Government engages to urge the parliament of the Dominion of Canada and the legislatures of the other colonies not to impose any export duties on goods, wares, or merchandise carried under this article; and the Government of the United States may, in case such export duties are imposed by the Dominion of Canada, suspend during the period that such duties are imposed the right of carrying granted under this article in favor of the subjects of Her Britannic Majesty.

The Government of the United States may suspend the right of carrying granted in favor of the subjects of Her Britannic Majesty under this article in case the Dominion of Canada should at any time deprive the citizens of the United States of the use of the canals in the said Dominion on terms of equality with the inhabitants of the Dominion, as provided in Article XXVII.

ARTICLE XXXII.

It is further agreed that the provisions and stipulations of Articles XVIII to XXV of this treaty, inclusive, shall extend to the colony of Newfoundland, so far as they are applicable. But if the Imperial Parliament, the legislature of Newfoundland, or the Congress of the United States shall not embrace the colony of Newfoundland in their laws enacted for carrying the foregoing articles into effect, then this article shall be of no effect; but the omission to make provision by law to give it effect by either of the legislative bodies aforesaid shall not in any way impair any other articles of this treaty.

And whereas, pursuant to the provisions of Article XXXIII of said treaty, due notice has been given to the Government of Her Britannic Majesty of the intention of the Government of the United States of America to terminate the above-recited articles of the treaty in question on the 1st day of July, 1885; and

Whereas, pursuant to the terms of said treaty and of the notice given thereunder by the Government of the United States of America to that of Her Britannic Majesty, the above-recited articles of the treaty of Washington, concluded May 8, 1871, will expire and terminate on the 1st day of July, 1885:

Now, therefore, I, Chester A. Arthur, President of the United States of America, do hereby give public notice that Articles XVIII, XIX, XX, XXI, XXII, XXIII, XXIV, XXV, XXX, and XXXII of the treaty of Washington, concluded May 8, 1871, will expire and terminate on the 1st day of July, 1885,'and all citizens of the United States are hereby warned that none of the privileges secured by the above-recited articles of the treaty in question will exist after the 1st day of July next. All American fishermen should govern themselves accordingly.

Done at the city of Washington, this 31st day of January, A. D. 1885, [SEAL.] and of the Independence of the United States of America the one hundred and ninth.

CHESTER A. ARTHUR.

By the President:

FREDK. T. FRELINGHUYSEN,
Secretary of State.

BY THE PRESIDENT OF THE UNITED STATES OF AMERICA.

A PROCLAMATION.

Whereas satisfactory evidence has been received by me that upon vessels of the United States arriving in ports of the Province of Ontario, in the Dominion of Canada, or arriving at any port in the island of Monserrat, in the West Indies, or at Panama or Aspinwall, United States of Colombia, or at the ports of San Juan and Mayaguez, in the island of Puerto Rico, no duty is imposed by the ton as tonnage tax or as light money, and that no other equivalent tax on vessels of the United States is imposed at said ports by the governments to which said ports are immediately subject; and

Whereas by the provisions of section 14 of an act approved June 26, 1884, "to remove certain burdens on the American merchant marine and encourage the American foreign carrying trade, and for other purposes," the President of the United States is authorized to suspend the collection in ports of the United States from vessels arriving from any port in the Dominion of Canada, Newfoundland, the Bahama Islands, the Bermuda Islands, the West India Islands, Mexico, and Central America down to and including Aspinwall and Panama of so much of the duty at the rate of 3 cents per ton as may be in excess of the tonnage and light-house dues, or other equivalent tax or taxes, imposed on American vessels by the government of the foreign country in which such port is situated:

Now, therefore, I, Chester A. Arthur, President of the United States of America, by virtue of the authority vested in me by the act and section hereinbefore mentioned, do hereby declare and proclaim that on and after the first Tuesday in February, 1885, the collection of said tonnage duty of 3 cents per ton shall be suspended as regards all vessels arriving in any port of the United States from any port in the Province of Ontario, in the Dominion of Canada, or from a port in the island of Monserrat, in the West Indies, or from the ports of Panama and Aspinwall, or the ports of San Juan and Mayaguez, in the island of Puerto Rico.

In testimony whereof I have hereunto set my hand and caused the seal of the United States to be affixed.

[SEAL.] Done at the city of Washington, this 31st day of January, 1885, and of the Independence of the United States of America the one hundred and ninth.

CHESTER A. ARTHUR.

By the President:

FREDK. T. FRELINGHUYSEN,
Secretary of State.

BY THE PRESIDENT OF THE UNITED STATES OF AMERICA.

A PROCLAMATION.

Whereas satisfactory evidence has been received by me that upon vessels of the United States arriving at the port of San Juan del Norte (Greytown), Nicaragua, no duty is imposed by the ton as tonnage tax or as light money, and that no other equivalent tax on vessels of the United States is imposed at said port by the Government of Nicaragua; and

Whereas, by the provisions of section 14 of an act approved June 26, 1884, "to remove certain burdens on the American merchant marine and encourage the American foreign carrying trade, and for other purposes," the President of the United States is authorized to suspend the collection in ports of the United States from vessels arriving from any port in the Dominion of Canada, Newfoundland, the Bahama Islands, the Bermuda Islands, the West India Islands, Mexico, and Central America down to and including Aspinwall and Panama of so much of the duty at the rate of 3 cents per ton as may be in excess of the tonnage and light-house dues, or other equivalent tax or taxes, imposed on American vessels by the government of the foreign country in which such port is situated:

Now, therefore, I, Chester A. Arthur, President of the United States of America, by virtue of the authority vested in me by the act and section hereinbefore mentioned, do hereby declare and proclaim that on and after the first Tuesday in March, 1885, the collection of said tonnage duty of 3 cents per ton shall be suspended as regards all vessels arriving in any port of the United States from the port of San Juan del Norte (Greytown), Nicaragua.

In testimony whereof I have hereunto set my hand and caused the seal of the United States to be affixed.

[SEAL.] Done at the city of Washington, this 26th day of February, 1885, and of the Independence of the United States of America the one hundred and ninth.

CHESTER A. ARTHUR.

By the President:

FREDK. T. FRELINGHUYSEN,
Secretary of State.

BY THE PRESIDENT OF THE UNITED STATES OF AMERICA.

A PROCLAMATION.

Whereas objects of interest to the United States require that the Senate should be convened at 12 o'clock on the 4th day of March next to receive and act upon such communications as may be made to it on the part of the Executive:

Now, therefore, I, Chester A. Arthur, President of the United States, have considered it to be my duty to issue this my proclamation, declaring that an extraordinary occasion requires the Senate of the United States to convene for the transaction of business at the Capitol, in the city of Washington, on the 4th day of March next, at 12 o'clock at noon on that day, of which all who shall at that time be entitled to act as members of that body are hereby required to take notice.

Given under my hand and the seal of the United States, at Washington, the 27th day of February, A. D. 1885, and of the Independence of the United States of America the one hundred and ninth.

[SEAL.]

CHESTER A. ARTHUR.

By the President:

FREDK. T. FRELINGHUYSEN, *Secretary of State.*

EXECUTIVE ORDERS.

In the exercise of the power vested in the President by the Constitution, and by virtue of the seventeen hundred and fifty-third section of the Revised Statutes and of the civil-service act approved January 16, 1883, the following rules for the regulation and improvement of the executive civil service are hereby amended and promulgated, as follows:

RULE V.

There shall be three branches of the service classified under the civil-service act (not including laborers or workmen or officers required to be confirmed by the Senate), as follows:

1. Those classified in the Departments at Washington shall be designated "The classified departmental service."

2. Those classified under any collector, naval officer, surveyor, or appraiser in any customs district shall be designated "The classified customs service."

3. Those classified under any postmaster at any post-office, including that at Washington, shall be designated "The classified postal service."

4. The classified customs service shall embrace the several customs districts where the officials are as many as fifty, now the following: New York City, N. Y.; Boston, Mass.; Philadelphia, Pa.; San Francisco, Cal.; Baltimore, Md.; New Orleans, La.; Chicago, Ill.; Burlington, Vt.; Portland, Me.; Detroit, Mich.; Port Huron, Mich.

5. The classified postal service shall embrace the several post-offices where the officials are as many as fifty, now the following: Albany, N. Y.; Baltimore, Md.; Boston, Mass.; Brooklyn, N. Y.; Buffalo, N. Y.; Chicago, Ill.; Cincinnati, Ohio; Cleveland,

Ohio; Detroit, Mich.; Indianapolis, Ind.; Jersey City, N. J.; Kansas City, Mo.; Louisville, Ky.; Milwaukee, Wis.; Minneapolis, Minn.; Newark, N. J.; New Orleans, La.; New York City, N. Y.; Philadelphia, Pa.; Pittsburg, Pa.; Providence, R. I.; Rochester, N. Y.; St. Louis, Mo.; St. Paul, Minn.; San Francisco, Cal.; Washington, D. C.

RULE VII.

1. The general examinations under the first clause of Rule VI for admission to the service shall be limited to the following subjects: (1) Orthography, penmanship, and copying; (2) arithmetic—fundamental rules, fractions, and percentage; (3) interest, discount, and elements of bookkeeping and of accounts; (4) elements of the English language, letter writing, and the proper construction of sentences; (5) elements of the geography, history, and government of the United States.

2. Proficiency in any subject upon which an examination shall be held shall be credited in grading the standing of the persons examined in proportion to the value of a knowledge of such subject in the branch or part of the service which the applicant seeks to enter.

3. No one shall be entitled to be certified for appointment whose standing upon a just grading in the general examination shall be less than 65 per cent of complete proficiency in the first three subjects mentioned in this rule, and that measure of proficiency shall be deemed adequate.

4. For places in which a lower degree of education will suffice the Commission may limit the examinations to less than the five subjects above mentioned; but no person shall be certified for appointment under this clause whose grading shall be less than an average of 65 per cent on such of the first three subjects or parts thereof as the examination may embrace.

5. The Commission may also order examinations upon other subjects of a technical or special character to test the capacity which may be needed in any part of the classified service which requires peculiar information or skill. Examinations hereunder may be competitive or noncompetitive, and the maximum limitations of age contained in the twelfth rule shall not apply to applicants for the same. The application for and notice of these special examinations, the records thereof, and the certification of those found competent shall be such as the Commission may provide for. After consulting the head of any Department or office the Commission may from time to time designate, subject to the approval of the President, the positions therein for which applicants may be required to pass the special examination. .

RULE XI.

1. Every application, in order to entitle the applicant to appear for examination or to be examined, must state under oath the facts on the following subjects: (1) Full name, residence, and post-office address; (2) citizenship; (3) age; (4) place of birth; (5) health and physical capacity for the public service; (6) right of preference by reason of military or naval service; (7) previous employment in the public service; (8) business or employment and residence for the previous five years; (9) education. Such other information shall be furnished as the Commission may reasonably require touching the applicant's fitness for the public service. The applicant must also state the number of members of his family in the public service and where employed, and must also assert that he is not disqualified under section 8 of the civil-service act, which is as follows:

"That no person habitually using intoxicating beverages to excess shall be appointed to or retained in any office, appointment, or employment to which the provisions of this act are applicable."

No person dismissed from the public service for misconduct shall be admitted to examination within two years thereafter.

2. No person under enlistment in the Army or Navy of the United States shall be

as to apportion, as nearly as may be practicable, the original appointments thereto among the States and Territories and the District of Columbia upon the basis of population as ascertained at the last preceding census.

3. In case the request for any such certification or any law or regulation shall call for those of either sex, persons of that sex shall be certified; otherwise sex shall be disregarded in such certification.

4. No person upon any register shall be certified more than four times to the same officer in the customs or postal service or more than three times to any Department at Washington, unless upon request of the appointing officer; nor shall anyone remain eligible more than one year upon any register; but these restrictions shall not extend to examinations under clause 5 of Rule VII. No person while remaining eligible on any register shall be admitted to a new examination, and no person having failed upon any examination shall within six months thereafter be admitted to another examination without the consent of the Commission.

5. Any person appointed to or employed in any part of the classified service, after due certification for the same under these rules, who shall be dismissed or separated therefrom without fault or delinquency on his part, may be reappointed or reemployed in the same part or grade of such service in the same Department or office within one year next following such dismissal or separation, without further examination, on such certification as the Commission may provide.

Approved, January 24, 1885.   **CHESTER A. ARTHUR.**

In the exercise of the power vested in the President by the Constitution, and by virtue of the seventeen hundred and fifty-third section of the Revised Statutes and of the civil-service act approved January 16, 1883, the following rule for the regulation and improvement of the executive civil service is hereby amended and promulgated, as follows:

RULE XVI.

1. Whenever any officer having the power of appointment or employment shall so request, there shall be certified to him by the Commission or the proper examining board four names for the vacancy specified, to be taken from those graded highest on the proper register of those in his branch of the service and remaining eligible, regard being had to any right of preference and to the apportionment of appointments to States and Territories; and from the said four a selection shall be made for the vacancy. But if a person is on both a general and a special register he need be certified from the former only, at the discretion of the Commission, until he has remained two months upon the latter.

2. These certifications for the service at Washington shall be made in such order as to apportion, as nearly as may be practicable, the original appointments thereto among the States and Territories and the District of Columbia upon the basis of population as ascertained at the last preceding census.

3. In case the request for any such certification or any law or regulation shall call for those of either sex, persons of that sex shall be certified; otherwise sex shall be disregarded in such certification.

4. No person upon any register shall be certified more than four times to the same officer in the customs or postal service or more than three times to any Department at Washington, unless upon request of the appointing officer; nor shall anyone remain eligible more than one year upon any register; but these restrictions shall not extend to examinations under clause 5 of Rule VII. No person while remaining eligible on any register shall be admitted to a new examination, and no person having failed

upon any examination shall within six months thereafter be admitted to another examination without the consent of the Commission.

5. Any person appointed to or employed in any part of the classified service, after due certification for the same under these rules, who shall be dismissed or separated therefrom without fault or delinquency on his part, may be reappointed or reemployed in the same part or grade of such service in the same Department or office within one year next following such dismissal or separation, without further examination, on such certification as the Commission may provide.

Approved, February 11, 1885.   CHESTER A. ARTHUR.

EXECUTIVE MANSION, *February 17, 1885.*

Under the provisions of section 4 of the act of Congress approved March 3, 1883, it is hereby ordered that the several Executive Departments, the Department of Agriculture, and the Government Printing Office be closed on Saturday, the 21st instant, to enable the employees to participate in the ceremonies attending the dedication of the Washington Monument.

CHESTER A. ARTHUR.

TREASURY DEPARTMENT,
OFFICE OF THE SECRETARY,
Washington, D. C., February 26, 1885.

Attention is called to the following section of the act of May 17, 1884, entitled "An act providing a civil government for Alaska:"

"SEC. 14. That the provisions of chapter 3, Title XXIII, of the Revised Statutes of the United States, relating to the unorganized Territory of Alaska, shall remain in full force except as herein specially otherwise provided; and the importation, manufacture, and sale of intoxicating liquors in said district, except for medicinal, mechanical, and scientific purposes, is hereby prohibited under the penalties which are provided in section 1955 of the Revised Statutes for the wrongful importation of distilled spirits; and the President of the United States shall make such regulations as are necessary to carry out the provisions of this section."

To enforce this section of law the following regulations are prescribed:

No intoxicating liquors shall be landed at any port or place in said Territory without a permit from the chief officer of the customs at such port or place, to be issued upon evidence satisfactory to such officer that the liquors are imported and are to be used solely for medicinal, mechanical, and scientific purposes.

No person shall manufacture or sell intoxicating liquors within the Territory of Alaska without first having obtained a license from the governor of said Territory, to be issued upon evidence satisfactory to that officer that the making and sale of such liquor will be conducted strictly in accordance with the requirements of the statute.

Any intoxicating liquors imported, manufactured, or sold within the limits of said Territory in violation of these regulations, and the persons engaged in such violation, will be dealt with in the manner prescribed in section 1955 of the Revised Statutes; and the governor of Alaska and the officers of the customs at any port or place in the United States from which intoxicating liquors may be shipped to that Territory, as well as officers of the United States within that Territory, are hereby authorized respectively to exact, in their discretion, a bond of the character mentioned in section 1955, Revised Statutes, from the master or mate of any vessel and from the persons in such Territory to whom the liquors may be sent.

The penalty prescribed by section 1955, Revised Statutes, for violation of the law is a fine not exceeding $500, or imprisonment not more than six months, and the forfeiture of the vessel bringing the merchandise and her cargo, together with her tackle, apparel, and furniture, where the value of the merchandise exceeds $400. Where the value does not exceed $400, the penalty is forfeiture of the merchandise.

The proper officers within the Territory are charged with the execution of the law and these regulations. Intoxicating liquors forfeited under the provisions of this act will be subject to sale under the same provisions of law as govern the sale of other goods that may have become liable to forfeiture, but will only be delivered for removal beyond the limits of the Territory.

H. McCULLOCH, *Secretary.*

Approved:

CHESTER A. ARTHUR.

In the exercise of the power vested in the President by the Constitution, and by virtue of the seventeen hundred and fifty-third section of the Revised Statutes and of the civil-service act approved January 16, 1883, the following rule for the regulation and improvement of the executive civil service is hereby amended and promulgated, as follows:

RULE XVI.

1. Whenever any officer having the power of appointment or employment shall so request, there shall be certified to him by the Commission or the proper examining board four names for the vacancy specified, to be taken from those graded highest on the proper register of those in his branch of the service and remaining eligible, regard being had to any right of preference and to the apportionment of appointments to States and Territories; and from the said four a selection shall be made for the vacancy. But if a person is on both a general and a special register he need be certified from the former only, at the discretion of the Commission, until he has remained two months upon the latter.

2. These certifications for the service at Washington shall be made in such order as to apportion, as nearly as may be practicable, the original appointments thereto among the States and Territories and the District of Columbia upon the basis of population as ascertained at the last preceding census.

3. In case the request for any such certification or any law or regulation shall call for those of either sex, persons of that sex shall be certified; otherwise sex shall be disregarded in such certification.

4. No person upon any register shall be certified more than four times to the same officer in the customs or postal service or more than three times to any Department at Washington, unless upon request of the appointing officer; nor shall anyone remain eligible more than one year upon any register, except as may be provided by regulation; but these restrictions shall not extend to examinations under clause 5 of Rule VII. No person while remaining eligible on any register shall be admitted to a new examination, and no person having failed upon any examination shall within six months thereafter be admitted to another examination without the consent of the Commission.

5. Any person appointed to or employed in any part of the classified service who shall be dismissed or separated therefrom without fault or delinquency on his part may be reappointed or reemployed in the same part or grade of such service in the same Department or office within one year next following such dismissal or separation, without further examination, on such certification as the Commission may provide.

Approved, February 27, 1885.

CHESTER A. ARTHUR.

EXECUTIVE MANSION, *March 3, 1885.*

Under the provisions of section 4 of the act of Congress approved March 3, 1883, it is hereby ordered that the several Executive Departments, the Department of Agriculture, and the Government Printing Office be closed on Wednesday, the 4th instant, to enable the employees to witness the ceremonies incident to the inauguration on that day.

CHESTER A. ARTHUR.

Grover Cleveland

March 4, 1885, to March 4, 1889

Grover Cleveland

GROVER CLEVELAND was born in Caldwell, Essex County, N. J., March 18, 1837. On the paternal side he is of English origin. Moses Cleveland emigrated from Ipswich, County of Suffolk, England, in 1635, and settled at Woburn, Mass., where he died in 1701. His descendant William Cleveland was a silversmith and watchmaker at Norwich, Conn. Richard Falley Cleveland, son of the latter named, was graduated at Yale in 1824, was ordained to the Presbyterian ministry in 1829, and in the same year married Ann Neal, daughter of a Baltimore merchant of Irish birth. These two were the parents of Grover Cleveland. The Presbyterian parsonage at Caldwell, where he was born, was first occupied by the Rev. Stephen Grover, in whose honor he was named; but the first name was early dropped, and he has been since known as Grover Cleveland. When he was 4 years old his father accepted a call to Fayetteville, near Syracuse, N. Y., where the son had common and academic schooling, and afterwards was a clerk in a country store. The removal of the family to Clinton, Oneida County, gave him additional educational advantages in the academy there. In his seventeenth year he became a clerk and an assistant teacher in the New York Institution for the Blind, in New York City, in which his elder brother, William, a Presbyterian clergyman, was then a teacher. In 1855 he left Holland Patent, in Oneida County, where his mother at that time resided, to go to the West in search of employment. On his way he stopped at Black Rock, now a part of Buffalo, and called on his uncle, Lewis F. Allen, who induced him to remain and aid him in the compilation of a volume of the American Herd Book, receiving for six weeks' service $60. He afterwards, and while studying law, assisted in the preparation of several other volumes of this work, and the preface to the fifth volume (1861) acknowledges his services. In August, 1855, he secured a place as clerk and copyist for the law firm of Rogers, Bowen & Rogers, in Buffalo, began to read Blackstone, and in the autumn of that year was receiving $4 per week for his work. He was admitted to the bar in 1859, but for three years longer remained with the firm that first employed him, acting as managing clerk at a salary of $600, a part of which he devoted to the support of his widowed mother, who died in 1882. Was appointed assistant district attorney of Erie County January 1, 1863, and held the office for three years. At this time the Civil War was raging. Two of his brothers were in the Army, and his mother and sisters were largely dependent upon him for support. Unable himself to enlist, he borrowed money and sent a substitute to the war, and it was not till long after the war that he was able to repay the loan. In 1865, at the age of 28, he was the Democratic candidate for district attorney, but was defeated by the Republican candidate, his intimate friend, Lyman K. Bass. He then became the law partner of Isaac V. Vanderpool, and in 1869 became a member of the firm of Lanning, Cleveland & Folsom. He continued a successful practice till 1870, when he was elected sheriff of Erie County. At the expiration of his three years' term he formed a law partnership with his personal friend and political antagonist, Lyman K. Bass, the firm being Bass, Cleveland & Bissell, and, after the forced retirement, from failing health, of Mr. Bass, Cleveland & Bissell. In 1881 he was nominated the Democratic candidate for mayor of Buffalo, and was elected by a majority of 3,530, the largest ever given to a candidate in that city. In the same election the Republican State ticket was carried in Buffalo by an average majority of over 1,600. He entered upon the office January 1, 1882, and soon became known as the "Veto Mayor," using that prerogative fearlessly in checking unwise, illegal, and extravagant expenditures. By his vetoes he saved the city nearly $1,000,000 in the first half year of his administration. He opposed giving $500 of the taxpayers' money to the Firemen's Benevolent Society on the ground that such appropriation was not permissible under the terms of the State constitution and the charter of the city. He vetoed a resolution diverting $500 from the Fourth of July appropriations to the observance of Decoration Day for the same reason, and immediately subscribed one-tenth of the sum wanted for the purpose. His administration of the office won tributes to his integrity and ability from the press and the people irrespective of party. On the second day of the Democratic State convention at Syracuse, September 22, 1882, on the third ballot, was nominated for governor in opposition to the Republican candidate, Charles J. Folger, then Secretary of the United States Treasury. He had the united support of his own party, while the Republicans were not united on his opponent, and at the election in November he received a plurality over Mr. Folger of 192,854. His State administration was only an expansion of the fundamental principles that controlled his official action while mayor of Buffalo. In a letter written to his brother on the day of his election he announced a policy he intended to adopt, and afterwards carried out, "that is, to make the matter a business engagement between the people of the State and myself, in which the obligation on my side is to perform the duties assigned me with an eye single to the interest of my employers." The

Democratic national convention met at Chicago July 8, 1884. On July 11 he was nominated as their candidate for President. The Republicans made James G. Blaine their candidate, while Benjamin F. Butler, of Massachusetts, was the Labor and Greenback candidate, and John P. St. John, of Kansas, was the Prohibition candidate. At the election, November 4, Mr. Cleveland received 219 and Mr. Blaine 182 electoral votes. He was unanimously renominated for the Presidency by the national Democratic convention in St. Louis on June 6, 1888. At the election in November he received 168 electoral votes, while 233 were cast for Benjamin Harrison, the Republican candidate. Of the popular vote, however, he received 5,540,329, and Mr. Harrison received 5,439,853. At the close of his Administration, March 4, 1889, he retired to New York City, where he reentered upon the practice of his profession. It soon became evident, however, that he would be prominently urged as a candidate for renomination in 1892. At the national Democratic convention which met in Chicago June 21, 1892, he received more than two-thirds of the votes on the first ballot. At the election in November he received 277 of the electoral votes, while Mr. Harrison received 145 and Mr. James B. Weaver, the candidate of the People's Party, 22. Of the popular vote Mr. Cleveland received 5,553,142, Mr. Harrison 5,186,931, and Mr. Weaver 1,030,128. He retired from office March 4, 1897, and removed to Princeton, N. J., where he has since resided. He is the first of our Presidents who served a second term without being elected as his own successor. President Cleveland was married in the White House on June 2, 1886, to Miss Frances Folsom, daughter of his deceased friend and partner, Oscar Folsom, of the Buffalo bar. Mrs. Cleveland was the youngest (except the wife of Mr. Madison) of the many mistresses of the White House, having been born in Buffalo, N. Y., in 1864. She is the first wife of a President married in the White House, and the first to give birth to a child there, their second daughter (Esther) having been born in the Executive Mansion in 1893.

INAUGURAL ADDRESS.

FELLOW-CITIZENS: In the presence of this vast assemblage of my countrymen I am about to supplement and seal by the oath which I shall take the manifestation of the will of a great and free people. In the exercise of their power and right of self-government they have committed to one of their fellow-citizens a supreme and sacred trust, and he here consecrates himself to their service.

This impressive ceremony adds little to the solemn sense of responsibility with which I contemplate the duty I owe to all the people of the land. Nothing can relieve me from anxiety lest by any act of mine their interests may suffer, and nothing is needed to strengthen my resolution to engage every faculty and effort in the promotion of their welfare.

Amid the din of party strife the people's choice was made, but its attendant circumstances have demonstrated anew the strength and safety of a government by the people. In each succeeding year it more clearly appears that our democratic principle needs no apology, and that in its fearless and faithful application is to be found the surest guaranty of good government.

But the best results in the operation of a government wherein every citizen has a share largely depend upon a proper limitation of purely partisan zeal and effort and a correct appreciation of the time when the heat of the partisan should be merged in the patriotism of the citizen.

To-day the executive branch of the Government is transferred to new keeping. But this is still the Government of all the people, and it should be none the less an object of their affectionate solicitude. At this hour the animosities of political strife, the bitterness of partisan defeat, and the exultation of partisan triumph should be supplanted by an ungrudging acquiescence in the popular will and a sober, conscientious concern for the general weal. Moreover, if from this hour we cheerfully and honestly abandon all sectional prejudice and distrust, and determine, with manly confidence in one another, to work out harmoniously the achievements of our national destiny, we shall deserve to realize all the benefits which our happy form of government can bestow.

On this auspicious occasion we may well renew the pledge of our devotion to the Constitution, which, launched by the founders of the Republic and consecrated by their prayers and patriotic devotion, has for almost a century borne the hopes and the aspirations of a great people through prosperity and peace and through the shock of foreign conflicts and the perils of domestic strife and vicissitudes.

By the Father of his Country our Constitution was commended for adoption as "the result of a spirit of amity and mutual concession." In that same spirit it should be administered, in order to promote the lasting welfare of the country and to secure the full measure of its priceless benefits to us and to those who will succeed to the blessings of our national life. The large variety of diverse and competing interests subject to Federal control, persistently seeking the recognition of their claims, need give us no fear that "the greatest good to the greatest number" will fail to be accomplished if in the halls of national legislation that spirit of amity and mutual concession shall prevail in which the Constitution had its birth. If this involves the surrender or postponement of private interests and the abandonment of local advantages, compensation will be found in the assurance that the common interest is subserved and the general welfare advanced.

In the discharge of my official duty I shall endeavor to be guided by a just and unstrained construction of the Constitution, a careful observance of the distinction between the powers granted to the Federal Government and those reserved to the States or to the people, and by a cautious appreciation of those functions which by the Constitution and laws have been especially assigned to the executive branch of the Government.

But he who takes the oath to-day to preserve, protect, and defend the Constitution of the United States only assumes the solemn obligation which every patriotic citizen—on the farm, in the workshop, in the busy marts of trade, and everywhere—should share with him. The Constitution which prescribes his oath, my countrymen, is yours; the Government you have chosen him to administer for a time is yours; the suffrage which executes the will of freemen is yours; the laws and the entire scheme of our civil rule, from the town meeting to the State capitals and the national capital, is yours. Your every voter, as surely as your Chief Magistrate, under the same high sanction, though in a different sphere, exercises a public trust. Nor is this all. Every citizen owes to the country a vigilant watch and close scrutiny of its public servants and a fair and reasonable estimate of their fidelity and usefulness. Thus is the people's will impressed upon the whole framework of our civil polity—municipal, State, and Federal; and this is the price of our liberty and the inspiration of our faith in the Republic.

It is the duty of those serving the people in public place to closely limit public expenditures to the actual needs of the Government economically administered, because this bounds the right of the Government to exact tribute from the earnings of labor or the property of the citizen, and because public extravagance begets extravagance among the people. We should never be ashamed of the simplicity and prudential economies which are best suited to the operation of a republican form of government and most compatible with the mission of the American people. Those who are selected for a limited time to manage public affairs are still of the people, and may do much by their example to encourage, consistently with the dignity of their official functions, that plain way of life which among their fellow-citizens aids integrity and promotes thrift and prosperity.

The genius of our institutions, the needs of our people in their home life, and the attention which is demanded for the settlement and development of the resources of our vast territory dictate the scrupulous avoidance of any departure from that foreign policy commended by the history, the traditions, and the prosperity of our Republic. It is the policy of independence, favored by our position and defended by our known love of justice and by our power. It is the policy of peace suitable to our interests. It is the policy of neutrality, rejecting any share in foreign broils and ambitions upon other continents and repelling their intrusion here. It is the policy of Monroe and of Washington and Jefferson—" Peace, commerce, and honest friendship with all nations; entangling alliance with none."

A due regard for the interests and prosperity of all the people demands that our finances shall be established upon such a sound and sensible basis as shall secure the safety and confidence of business interests and make the wage of labor sure and steady, and that our system of revenue shall be so adjusted as to relieve the people of unnecessary taxation, having a due regard to the interests of capital invested and workingmen employed in American industries, and preventing the accumulation of a surplus in the Treasury to tempt extravagance and waste.

Care for the property of the nation and for the needs of future settlers requires that the public domain should be protected from purloining schemes and unlawful occupation.

The conscience of the people demands that the Indians within our boundaries shall be fairly and honestly treated as wards of the Government and their education and civilization promoted with a view to their ultimate citizenship, and that polygamy in the Territories, destructive of the family relation and offensive to the moral sense of the civilized world, shall be repressed.

The laws should be rigidly enforced which prohibit the immigration of a servile class to compete with American labor, with no intention of acquiring citizenship, and bringing with them and retaining habits and customs repugnant to our civilization.

The people demand reform in the administration of the Government and the application of business principles to public affairs. As a means to this end, civil-service reform should be in good faith enforced. Our citizens have the right to protection from the incompetency of public employees who hold their places solely as the reward of partisan service, and from the corrupting influence of those who promise and the vicious methods of those who expect such rewards; and those who worthily seek public employment have the right to insist that merit and competency shall be recognized instead of party subserviency or the surrender of honest political belief.

In the administration of a government pledged to do equal and exact justice to all men there should be no pretext for anxiety touching the protection of the freedmen in their rights or their security in the enjoyment of their privileges under the Constitution and its amendments. All discussion as to their fitness for the place accorded to them as American citizens is idle and unprofitable except as it suggests the necessity for their improvement. The fact that they are citizens entitles them to all the rights due to that relation and charges them with all its duties, obligations, and responsibilities.

These topics and the constant and ever-varying wants of an active and enterprising population may well receive the attention and the patriotic endeavor of all who make and execute the Federal law. Our duties are practical and call for industrious application, an intelligent perception of the claims of public office, and, above all, a firm determination, by united action, to secure to all the people of the land the full benefits of the best form of government ever vouchsafed to man. And let us not trust to human effort alone, but humbly acknowledging the power and goodness of Almighty God, who presides over the destiny of nations, and who has at all times been revealed in our country's history, let us invoke His aid and His blessing upon our labors.

MARCH 4, 1885.

SPECIAL MESSAGES.

EXECUTIVE MANSION, *March 13, 1885.*

To the Senate of the United States:

For the purpose of their reexamination I withdraw certain treaties and conventions now pending in the Senate which were communicated to that body by my predecessor in office, and I therefore request the return to me of the commercial convention between the United States and the Dominican Republic which was transmitted to the Senate December 9, 1884; of the commercial treaty between the United States and Spain which was transmitted to the Senate December 10, 1884, together with the supplementary articles thereto of March 2, 1885; and of the treaty between the United States and Nicaragua for the construction of an interoceanic canal which was transmitted to the Senate December 10, 1884.

GROVER CLEVELAND.

EXECUTIVE MANSION,
Washington, April 2, 1885.

To the Senate of the United States:

For the purpose of its reconsideration I withdraw the additional article, now pending in the Senate, signed on the 23d of June last, to the treaty of friendship, commerce, and navigation which was concluded between the United States and the Argentine Confederation July 27, 1853, and communicated to the Senate by my predecessor in office 27th of January, 1885.

GROVER CLEVELAND.

PROCLAMATIONS.

BY THE PRESIDENT OF THE UNITED STATES OF AMERICA.

A PROCLAMATION.

Whereas it is alleged that certain individuals, associations of persons, and corporations are in the unauthorized possession of portions of the territory known as the Oklahoma lands, within the Indian Territory, which are designated, described, and recognized by the treaties and laws of the United States and by the executive authority thereof as Indian lands; and

Whereas it is further alleged that certain other persons or associations within the territory and jurisdiction of the United States have begun and set on foot preparations for an organized and forcible entry and settlement upon the aforesaid lands and are now threatening such entry and occupation; and

Whereas the laws of the United States provide for the removal of all persons residing or being found upon such Indian lands and territory without permission expressly and legally obtained of the Interior Department:

Now, therefore, for the purpose of protecting the public interests, as well as the interests of the Indian nations and tribes, and to the end that no person or persons may be induced to enter upon said territory, where they will not be allowed to remain without the permission of the authority aforesaid, I, Grover Cleveland, President of the United States, do hereby warn and admonish all and every person or persons now in the occupation of such lands, and all such person or persons as are intending, preparing, or threatening to enter and settle upon the same, that they will neither be permitted to enter upon said territory nor, if already there, to remain thereon, and that in case a due regard for and voluntary obedience to the laws and treaties of the United States and if this admonition and warning be not sufficient to effect the purposes and intentions of the Government as herein declared, the military power of the United States will be invoked to abate all such unauthorized possession, to prevent such threatened entry and occupation, and to remove all such intruders from the said Indian lands.

In testimony whereof I have hereunto set my hand and caused the seal of the United States to be affixed.

[SEAL.]   Done at the city of Washington, this 13th day of March, 1885, and of the Independence of the United States of America the one hundred and ninth.   GROVER CLEVELAND.

By the President:

T. F. BAYARD, *Secretary of State.*

BY THE PRESIDENT OF THE UNITED STATES OF AMERICA.

A PROCLAMATION.

Whereas satisfactory evidence has been received by me that upon vessels of the United States arriving at the island of Trinidad, British West Indies, no duty is imposed by the ton as tonnage tax or as light money, and that no other equivalent tax on vessels of the United States is imposed at said island by the British Government; and

Whereas by the provisions of section 14 of an act approved June 26,

1884, "to remove certain burdens on the American merchant marine and encourage the American foreign carrying trade, and for other purposes," the President of the United States is authorized to suspend the collection in ports of the United States from vessels arriving from any port in the island of Trinidad of so much of the duty at the rate of 3 cents per ton as may be in excess of the tonnage and light-house dues, or other equivalent of tax or taxes, imposed on American vessels by the government of the foreign country in which such port is situated:

Now, therefore, I, Grover Cleveland, President of the United States of America, by virtue of the authority vested in me by the act and section hereinbefore mentioned, do hereby declare and proclaim that on and after this 7th day of April, 1885, the collection of said tonnage duty of 3 cents per ton shall be suspended as regards all vessels arriving in any port of the United States from a port in the island of Trinidad, British West Indies.

In testimony whereof I have hereunto set my hand and caused the seal of the United States to be affixed.

[SEAL.]   Done at the city of Washington, this 7th day of April, 1885, and of the Independence of the United States of America the one hundred and ninth.   GROVER CLEVELAND.

By the President:

T. F. BAYARD, *Secretary of State.*

BY THE PRESIDENT OF THE UNITED STATES OF AMERICA.

A PROCLAMATION.

Whereas, by an Executive order bearing date the 27th day of February, 1885, it was ordered that "all that tract of country in the Territory of Dakota known as the Old Winnebago Reservation and the Sioux or Crow Creek Reservation, and lying on the east bank of the Missouri River, set apart and reserved by Executive order dated January 11, 1875, and which is not covered by the Executive order dated August 9, 1879, restoring certain of the lands reserved by the order of January 11, 1875, except the following-described tracts: Townships No. 108 north, range 71 west; 108 north, range 72 west; fractional township 108 north, range 73 west; the west half of section 4, sections 5, 6, 7, 8, 9, 16, 17, 18, 19, 20, 21, 28, 29, 30, 31, 32, and 33 of township 107 north, range 70 west; fractional townships 107 north, range 71 west; 107 north, range 72 west; 107 north, range 73 west; the west half of township 106 north, range 70 west; and fractional township 106 north, range 71 west; and except also all tracts within the limits of the aforesaid Old Winnebago Reservation and the Sioux or Crow Creek Reservation which are outside of the limits of the above-described tracts, and which may have heretofore been allotted to the Indians residing upon said reservation, or which may have heretofore been selected or occupied by the said Indians under and in accordance with the provisions of article 6 of the treaty with the Sioux Indians of April 29, 1868, be, and the same is hereby, restored to the public domain;'' and

Whereas upon the claim being made that said order is illegal and in violation of the plighted faith and obligations of the United States contained in sundry treaties heretofore entered into with the Indian tribes or bands occupants of said reservation, and that the further execution of said order will not only occasion much distress and suffering to peaceable Indians, but retard the work of their civilization and engender amongst them a distrust of the National Government, I have determined, after a careful examination of the several treaties, acts of Congress, and other official data bearing on the subject, aided and assisted therein by the advice and opinion of the Attorney-General of the United States duly rendered in that behalf, that the lands so proposed to be restored to the public domain by said Executive order of February 27, 1885, are included as existing Indian reservations on the east bank of the Missouri River by the terms of the second article of the treaty with the Sioux Indians concluded April 29, 1868, and that consequently, being treaty reservations, the Executive was without lawful power to restore them to the public domain by said Executive order, which is therefore deemed and considered to be wholly inoperative and void; and

Whereas the laws of the United States provide for the removal of all persons residing or being found upon Indian lands and territory without permission expressly and legally obtained of the Interior Department:

Now, therefore, in order to maintain inviolate the solemn pledges and plighted faith of the Government as given in the treaties in question, and for the purpose of properly protecting the interests of the Indian tribes as well as of the United States in the premises, and to the end that no person or persons may be induced to enter upon said lands, where they will not be allowed to remain without the permission of the authority aforesaid, I, Grover Cleveland, President of the United States, do hereby declare and proclaim the said Executive order of February 27, 1885, to be in contravention of the treaty obligations of the United States with the Sioux tribe of Indians, and therefore to be inoperative and of no effect; and I further declare that the lands intended to be embraced therein are existing Indian reservations, and as such available for Indian purposes alone and subject to the Indian-intercourse acts of the United States. I do further warn and admonish all and every person or persons now in the occupation of said lands under color of said Executive order, and all such person or persons as are intending or preparing to enter and settle upon the same thereunder, that they will neither be permitted to remain or enter upon said lands, and such persons as are already there are hereby required to vacate and remove therefrom with their effects within sixty days from the date hereof; and in case a due regard for and voluntary obedience to the laws and treaties of the United States and this admonition and warning be not sufficient to effect the purpose and intentions as herein declared, all the power of the Government will be employed to carry into proper execution the treaties and laws of the United States herein referred to.

In testimony thereof I hereunto set my hand and cause the seal of the United States to be affixed.

[SEAL.]   Done at the city of Washington, this 17th day of April, 1885, and of the Independence of the United States of America the one hundred and ninth.   **GROVER CLEVELAND.**

By the President:

T. F. BAYARD, *Secretary of State.*

BY THE PRESIDENT OF THE UNITED STATES OF AMERICA:

A PROCLAMATION.

Whereas certain portions of the Cheyenne and Arapahoe, Indian Reservation, in the Indian Territory, are occupied by persons other than Indians, who claim the right to keep and graze cattle thereon by agreement made with the Indians for whose special possession and occupancy the said lands have been reserved by the Government of the United States, or under other pretexts and licenses; and

Whereas all such agreements and licenses are deemed void and of no effect, and the persons so occupying said lands with cattle are considered unlawfully upon the domain of the United States so reserved as aforesaid; and

Whereas the claims of such persons under said leases and licenses and their unauthorized presence upon such reservation have caused complaint and discontent on the part of the Indians located thereon, and are likely to cause serious outbreaks and disturbances:

Now, therefore, I, Grover Cleveland, President of the United States, do hereby order and direct that all persons other than Indians who are now upon any part of said reservation for the purpose of grazing cattle thereon, and their servants and agents, and all other unauthorized persons now upon said reservation, do, within forty days from the date of this proclamation, depart and entirely remove therefrom with their cattle, horses, and other property.

In witness whereof I have hereunto set my hand and caused the seal of the United States to be affixed.

[SEAL.]   Done at the city of Washington on this 23d day of July, 1885, and the year of the Independence of the United States the one hundred and tenth.

          GROVER CLEVELAND.

By the President:

T. F. BAYARD, *Secretary of State.*

BY THE PRESIDENT OF THE UNITED STATES OF AMERICA.

A PROCLAMATION.

The President of the United States has just received the sad tidings of the death of that illustrious citizen and ex-President of the United States, General Ulysses S. Grant, at Mount McGregor, in the State of New York, to which place he had lately been removed in the endeavor to prolong his life.

In making this announcement to the people of the United States the President is impressed with the magnitude of the public loss of a great military leader, who was in the hour of victory magnanimous, amid disaster serene and self-sustained; who in every station, whether as a soldier or as a Chief Magistrate, twice called to power by his fellow-countrymen, trod unswervingly the pathway of duty, undeterred by doubts, single-minded and straightforward.

The entire country has witnessed with deep emotion his prolonged and patient struggle with painful disease, and has watched by his couch of suffering with tearful sympathy.

The destined end has come at last, and his spirit has returned to the Creator who sent it forth.

The great heart of the nation that followed him when living with love and pride bows now in sorrow above him dead, tenderly mindful of his virtues, his great patriotic services, and of the loss occasioned by his death.

In testimony of respect to the memory of General Grant, it is ordered that the Executive Mansion and the several Departments at Washington be draped in mourning for a period of thirty days and that all public business shall on the day of the funeral be suspended; and the Secretaries of War and of the Navy will cause orders to be issued for appropriate military and naval honors to be rendered on that day.

In witness whereof I have hereunto set my hand and caused the seal of the United States to be affixed.

[SEAL.]   Done at the city of Washington, this 23d day of July, 1885, and of the Independence of the United States the one hundred and tenth.

                                    GROVER CLEVELAND.

By the President:
     T. F. BAYARD, *Secretary of State.*

BY THE PRESIDENT OF THE UNITED STATES OF AMERICA.

A PROCLAMATION.

Whereas public policy demands that the public domain shall be reserved for the occupancy of actual settlers in good faith, and that our people who seek homes upon such domain shall in no wise be prevented by any wrongful interference from the safe and free entry thereon to which they may be entitled; and

Whereas, to secure and maintain this beneficent policy, a statute was passed by the Congress of the United States on the 25th day of February, in the year 1885, which declared to be unlawful all inclosures of any public lands in any State or Territory to any of which land included within said inclosure the person, party, association, or corporation making or controlling such inclosure had no claim or color of title made or acquired in good faith, or an asserted right thereto by or under claim made in good faith with a view to entry thereof at the proper land office; and which statute also prohibited any person, by force, threats, intimidation, or by any fencing or inclosure or other unlawful means, from preventing or obstructing any person from peaceably entering upon or establishing a settlement or residence on any tract of public land subject to settlement or entry under the public-land laws of the United States, and from preventing or obstructing free passage and transit over or through the public lands; and

Whereas it is by the fifth section of said act provided as follows:

That the President is hereby authorized to take such means as shall be necessary to remove and destroy any unlawful inclosure of any of said lands, and to employ civil or military force as may be necessary for that purpose.

And whereas it has been brought to my knowledge that unlawful inclosures, and such as are prohibited by the terms of the aforesaid statute, exist upon the public domain, and that actual legal settlement thereon is prevented and obstructed by such inclosures and by force, threats, and intimidation:

Now, therefore, I, Grover Cleveland, President of the United States, do hereby order and direct that any and every unlawful inclosure of the public lands maintained by any person, association, or corporation be immediately removed; and I do hereby forbid any person, association, or corporation from preventing or obstructing by means of such inclosures, or by force, threats, or intimidation, any person entitled thereto from peaceably entering upon and establishing a settlement or residence on any part of such public land which is subject to entry and settlement under the laws of the United States.

And I command and require each and every officer of the United States upon whom the duty is legally devolved to cause this order to be obeyed and all the provisions of the act of Congress herein mentioned to be faithfully enforced.

In testimony whereof I have hereunto set my hand and caused the seal of the United States to be affixed.

[SEAL.] Done at the city of Washington, this 7th day of August, 1885, and of the Independence of the United States of America the one hundred and tenth.

GROVER CLEVELAND.

By the President:
T. F. BAYARD,
Secretary of State.

BY THE PRESIDENT OF THE UNITED STATES OF AMERICA.

A PROCLAMATION.

Whereas satisfactory evidence has been received by me that upon vessels of the United States arriving at the port of Boca del Toro, United States of Colombia, no duty is imposed by the ton as tonnage tax or as light money, and that no other equivalent tax on vessels of the United States is imposed at said port by the Colombian Government; and

Whereas by the provisions of section 14 of an act approved June 26, 1884, "to remove certain burdens on the American merchant marine and encourage the American foreign carrying trade, and for other purposes," the President of the United States is authorized to suspend the collection in ports of the United States from vessels arriving from any port in "Central America down to and including Aspinwall and Panama" of so much of the duty at the rate of 3 cents per ton as may be in excess of the tonnage and light-house dues, or other equivalent tax or taxes, imposed on American vessels by the government of the foreign country in which such port is situated:

Now, therefore, I, Grover Cleveland, President of the United States of America, by virtue of the authority vested in me by the act and section hereinbefore mentioned, do hereby declare and proclaim that on and after this 9th day of September, 1885, the collection of said tonnage duty of 3 cents per ton shall be suspended as regards all vessels arriving in any port of the United States from the port of Boca del Toro, United States of Colombia.

In testimony whereof I have hereunto set my hand and caused the seal of the United States to be affixed.

[SEAL.]   Done at the city of Washington, this 9th day of September, 1885, and of the Independence of the United States of America the one hundred and tenth.

GROVER CLEVELAND.

By the President:

T. F. BAYARD, *Secretary of State.*

BY THE PRESIDENT OF THE UNITED STATES OF AMERICA.

A PROCLAMATION.

The American people have always abundant cause to be thankful to Almighty God, whose watchful care and guiding hand have been manifested in every stage of their national life, guarding and protecting them in time of peril and safely leading them in the hour of darkness and of danger.

It is fitting and proper that a nation thus favored should on one day in every year, for that purpose especially appointed, publicly acknowledge the goodness of God and return thanks to Him for all His gracious gifts.

Therefore, I, Grover Cleveland, President of the United States of America, do hereby designate and set apart Thursday, the 26th day of November instant, as a day of public thanksgiving and prayer, and do invoke the observance of the same by all the people of the land.

On that day let all secular business be suspended, and let the people assemble in their usual places of worship and with prayer and songs of praise devoutly testify their gratitude to the Giver of Every Good and Perfect Gift for all that He has done for us in the year that has passed; for our preservation as a united nation and for our deliverance from the shock and danger of political convulsion; for the blessings of peace and for our safety and quiet while wars and rumors of wars have agitated and afflicted other nations of the earth; for our security against the scourge of pestilence, which in other lands has claimed its dead by thousands and filled the streets with mourners; for plenteous crops which reward the labor of the husbandman and increase our nation's wealth, and for the contentment throughout our borders which follows in the train of prosperity and abundance.

And let there also be on the day thus set apart a reunion of families, sanctified and chastened by tender memories and associations; and let the social intercourse of friends, with pleasant reminiscence, renew the ties of affection and strengthen the bonds of kindly feeling.

And let us by no means forget while we give thanks and enjoy the comforts which have crowned our lives that truly grateful hearts are inclined to deeds of charity, and that a kind and thoughtful remembrance of the poor will double the pleasures of our condition and render our praise and thanksgiving more acceptable in the sight of the Lord.

Done at the city of Washington, this 2d day of November, 1885, and
[SEAL.]　of the Independence of the United States the one hundred and tenth.

GROVER CLEVELAND.

By the President:

T. F. BAYARD,
Secretary of State.

BY THE PRESIDENT OF THE UNITED STATES OF AMERICA.

A PROCLAMATION.

Whereas it is represented to me by the governor of the Territory of Washington that domestic violence exists within the said Territory, and that by reason of unlawful obstructions and combinations and the assemblage of evil-disposed persons it has become impracticable to enforce by the ordinary course of judicial proceedings the laws of the United States at Seattle and at other points and places within said Territory, whereby life and property are there threatened and endangered; and

Whereas the legislature of said Territory can not be convened, and in the judgment of the President an emergency has arisen and a case is now presented which justifies and requires, under the Constitution and laws of the United States, the employment of military force to suppress domestic violence and enforce the faithful execution of the laws of the United States if the command and warning of this proclamation be disobeyed or disregarded:

Now, therefore, I, Grover Cleveland, President of the United States of America, do hereby command and warn all insurgents and all persons who have assembled at any point within the said Territory of Washington for the unlawful purposes aforesaid to desist therefrom and to disperse and retire peaceably to their respective abodes on or before 12 o'clock meridian on the 8th day of November instant.

And I do admonish all good citizens of the United States and all persons within the limits and jurisdiction thereof against aiding, abetting, countenancing, or taking any part in such unlawful acts or assemblages.

In witness whereof I have set my hand and caused the seal of the United States to be hereunto affixed.

[SEAL.]   Done at the city of Washington, this 7th day of November, A. D. 1885, and of the Independence of the United States the one hundred and tenth.

GROVER CLEVELAND.

By the President:

T. F. BAYARD,
Secretary of State.

EXECUTIVE ORDERS.

In the exercise of the power vested in the President by the Constitution, and by virtue of the seventeen hundred and fifty-third section of the Revised Statutes and of the civil-service act approved January 16, 1883, the following rule for the regulation and improvement of the executive civil service is hereby amended and promulgated, as follows:

RULE XXII.

Any person who has been in the classified departmental service for one year or more immediately previous may, when the needs of the service require it, be transferred or appointed to any other place therein upon producing a certificate from the Civil Service Commission that such person has passed at the required grade one or more examinations which are together equal to that necessary for original entrance to the place which would be secured by the transfer or appointment; and any person who has for three years last preceding served as a clerk in the office of the President of the United States may be transferred or appointed to any place in the classified service without examination.

Approved, March 18, 1885.

GROVER CLEVELAND.

BY THE PRESIDENT OF THE UNITED STATES.

EXECUTIVE ORDER.

Whereas the Government of His Majesty the King of Italy has extended to the Government of the United States an invitation to participate in a sanitary conference to be held, at Rome on the 15th day of May, 1885, for the purpose of devising efficient measures to prevent the invasion of cholera and to mitigate its disastrous consequences; and

Whereas, by a provision of the act of Congress entitled "An act making appropriations for sundry civil expenses of the Government for the fiscal year ending June 30, 1886, and for other purposes," approved March 3, 1885, for the suppression of epidemic diseases, the President of the United States is authorized, in case of threatened or actual epidemic of cholera or yellow fever, to use certain appropriated sums, made immediately available, "in aid of State and local boards or otherwise, in his discretion, in preventing and suppressing the spread of the same and for maintaining quarantine and maritime inspections at points of danger;" and

Whereas there is imminent danger of a recurrence of a cholera epidemic in Europe, which may be brought to our shores unless adequate measures of international or local quarantine and maritime inspection are taken in season, which measures of preventive inspection are proper to be considered by the aforesaid conference, to the end that their efficiency in divers countries may be secured:

Now, therefore, in virtue of the discretionary authority conferred upon me by the aforesaid act of Congress, I hereby designate and appoint Major George M. Sternberg, surgeon in the United States Army, to attend said conference at Rome as the delegate thereto on the part of the Government of the United States, under the directions and instructions of the Secretary of State; and I hereby direct the Secretary of War to detail the said George M. Sternberg to perform the special service to which he is thus assigned, with full pay and allowances as on active service; and I further direct that the reasonable and necessary expenses of travel and sojourn of the said George M. Sternberg in proceeding from Washington to Rome, and during his attendance there upon the sessions of the said conference, and in returning, upon the conclusion thereof, from Rome to Washington, be adjusted and paid from the appropriation available under the aforesaid act of March 3, 1885, upon his statement of account approved by the Secretary of State.

Done at the city of Washington, this 25th day of April, A. D. 1885, and of the Independence of the United States the one hundred and ninth.

GROVER CLEVELAND.

By the President:

T. F. BAYARD, *Secretary of State.*

EXECUTIVE MANSION,
Washington, May 12, 1885.

Under a provision of an act of Congress entitled "An act making appropriations for fortifications and other works of defense, and for the armament thereof, for the fiscal year ending June 30, 1886, and for other purposes," approved March 3, 1885, a board, to consist of the officers and civilians hereinafter named, is appointed to "examine and report at what ports fortifications or other defenses are most urgently required, the character and kind of defenses best adapted for each, with reference to armament," and "the utilization of torpedoes, mines, or other defensive appliances:" Hon. William C. Endicott, Secretary of War, president of the board; Brigadier-General Stephen V. Benét, Chief of Ordnance; Brigadier-General John Newton, Chief of Engineers; Lieutenant-Colonel Henry L. Abbot, Corps of Engineers; Captain Charles S. Smith, Ordnance Department; Commander W. T. Sampson, United States Navy; Commander Caspar F. Goodrich, United States Navy; Mr. Joseph Morgan, jr., of Pennsylvania; Mr. Erastus Corning, of New York.

GROVER CLEVELAND.

EXECUTIVE MANSION, *May 26, 1885.*

Under the provisions of section 4 of the act approved March 3, 1883, it is hereby ordered that the several Executive Departments, the Department of Agriculture, and the Government Printing Office be closed on Saturday, the 30th instant, to enable the employees to participate in the decoration of the graves of the soldiers who fell during the rebellion.

GROVER CLEVELAND.

In the exercise of the power vested in the President by the Constitution, and by virtue of the seventeen hundred and fifty-third section of the Revised Statutes and of the civil-service act approved January 16, 1883, the following rule for the regulation and improvement of the executive civil service is hereby amended and promulgated, as follows:

RULE XI.

1. Every application, in order to entitle the applicant to appear for examination or to be examined, must state under oath the facts on the following subjects: (1) Full name, residence, and post-office address; (2) citizenship; (3) age; (4) place of birth; (5) health and physical capacity for the public service; (6) right of preference by reason of military or naval service; (7) previous employment in the public service; (8) business or employment and residence for the previous five years; (9) education. Such other information shall be furnished as the Commission may reasonably require touching the applicant's fitness for the public service. The applicant must also state the number of members of his family in the public service and where employed, and must also assert that he is not disqualified under section 8 of the civil-service act, which is as follows:

"That no person habitually using intoxicating beverages to excess shall be appointed to or retained in any office, appointment, or employment to which the provisions of this act are applicable."

No person dismissed from the public service for misconduct and no person who has not been absolutely appointed or employed after probation shall be admitted to examination within two years thereafter.

2. No person under enlistment in the Army or Navy of the United States shall be examined under these rules, except for some place in the Department under which he is enlisted requiring special qualifications, and with the consent in writing of the head of such Department.

3. The Commission may by regulations, subject to change at any time by the President, declare the kind and measure of ill health, physical incapacity, misrepresentation, and bad faith which may properly exclude any person from the right of examination, grading, or certification under these rules. It may also provide for medical certificates of physical capacity in the proper cases, and for the appropriate certification of persons so defective in sight, speech, hearing, or otherwise as to be apparently disqualified for some of the duties of the part of the service which they seek to enter.

Approved, June 2, 1885.   GROVER CLEVELAND.

In the exercise of the power vested in the President by the Constitution, and by virtue of the seventeen hundred and fifty-third section of the Revised Statutes and of the civil-service act approved January 16, 1883, the eighth clause of Rule XIX for the regulation and improvement of the executive civil service is hereby amended so as to read as follows:

8. Chief clerks, deputy collectors, deputy naval officers, deputy surveyors of customs, and superintendents or chiefs of divisions or bureaus.

And the same is hereby promulgated.

Approved, June 15, 1885.   GROVER CLEVELAND.

In the exercise of the power vested in the President by the Constitution, and by virtue of the seventeen hundred and fifty-third section of the Revised Statutes and of the civil-service act approved January 16, 1883, the following special rule for the regulation and improvement of the executive civil service is hereby promulgated:

SPECIAL RULE NO. 4.

Appointments to the 150 places in the Pension Office provided to be filled by the act of March 3, 1885, except so far as they may be filled by promotions or transfers, must be separately apportioned by the appointing power in as near conformity to the second section of the act of January 16, 1883, as the need of filling them promptly and the residence and qualifications of the applicants will permit.

Approved, July 16, 1885.   GROVER CLEVELAND.

EXECUTIVE MANSION, *July 23, 1885.*

Heads of all Government Departments:

Ex-President Ulysses S. Grant died this morning at 8 o'clock.

In respect to his memory it is ordered that all of the offices of the Executive Departments in the city of Washington be closed to-day at 1 o'clock.   GROVER CLEVELAND.

GENERAL ORDERS, No. 81.

HEADQUARTERS OF THE ARMY,
ADJUTANT-GENERAL'S OFFICE,
Washington, July 23, 1885.

I. The following proclamation has been received from the President

[For proclamation see p. 308.]

II. In compliance with the instructions of the President, on the day of the funeral, at each military post, the troops and cadets will be paraded and this order read to them, after which all labors for the day will cease.

The national flag will be displayed at half-staff.

At dawn of day thirteen guns will be fired, and afterwards at intervals of thirty minutes between the rising and setting of the sun a single gun, and at the close of the day a national salute of thirty-eight guns.

The officers of the Army will wear crape on the left arm and on their swords, and the colors of the Battalion of Engineers, of the several regiments, and of the United States Corps of Cadets will be put in mourning for the period of six months.

The date and hour of the funeral will be communicated to department commanders by telegraph, and by them to their subordinate commanders.

By command of Lieutenant-General Sheridan:

R. C. DRUM, *Adjutant-General.*

SPECIAL ORDER.

NAVY DEPARTMENT,
Washington, July 23, 1885.

The President of the United States announces the death of ex-President Ulysses S. Grant in the following proclamation:

[For proclamation see p. 308.]

In pursuance of the President's instructions, it is hereby directed that the ensign at each naval station and of each vessel of the United States Navy in commission be hoisted at half-mast, and that a gun be fired at intervals of every half hour from sunrise to sunset at each naval station and on board of flagships and of vessels acting singly on the day of the funeral, where this order may be received in time, otherwise on the day after its receipt.

The officers of the Navy and Marine Corps will wear the usual badge of mourning attached to the sword hilt and on the left arm for a period of thirty days.

WILLIAM C. WHITNEY,
Secretary of the Navy.

In the exercise of the power vested in the President by the Constitution, and by virtue of the seventeen hundred and fifty-third section of the Revised Statutes and of the civil-service act approved January 16, 1883, the seventh clause of Rule XIX for the regulation and improvement of the executive civil service is hereby amended so as to read as follows:

7. Persons whose employment is exclusively professional; but medical examiners are not included among such persons.

And the same is hereby promulgated.

Approved, August 5, 1885.

GROVER CLEVELAND.

By the President of the United States.

EXECUTIVE ORDER.

EXECUTIVE MANSION, *August 6, 1885.*

To Head of each Executive Department:

It is hereby ordered, That the several Executive Departments, the Department of Agriculture, and the Government Printing Office be closed to-morrow, Friday, August 7, at 3 o'clock p. m., to enable such employees as may desire to attend the funeral of the late ex-President, General Grant, in New York.

GROVER CLEVELAND.

EXECUTIVE MANSION,
Washington, September 23, 1885.

Under a provision of an act of Congress entitled ''An act to authorize the appointment of a commission by the President of the United States to run and mark the boundary lines between a portion of the Indian Territory and the State of Texas, in connection with a similar commis-sion to be appointed by the State of Texas,'' the following officers of the Army are detailed, in obedience to the provisions of said act of Congress, to act in conjunction with such persons as have been appointed by the State of Texas to ascertain and mark the point where the one hundredth meridian of longitude crosses the Red River: Major W. R. Livermore, Corps of Engineers; First Lieutenant Thomas L. Casey, jr., Corps of Engineers; First Lieutenant Lansing H. Beach, Corps of Engineers.

GROVER CLEVELAND.

By the President of the United States.

EXECUTIVE ORDER.

Whereas, by a provision of the act of Congress entitled ''An act making appropriations for sundry civil expenses of the Government for the fiscal year ending June 30, 1886, and for other purposes,'' approved March 3, 1885, for the suppression of epidemic diseases, the President of the United States is authorized, in case of threatened or actual epidemic of cholera or yellow fever, to use certain appropriated sums, made immediately available, ''in aid of State and local boards or otherwise, in his discretion, in preventing and suppressing the spread of the same and for maintaining quarantine and maritime inspections at points of danger;'' and

Whereas there is imminent danger of a recurrence of a cholera epidemic in Europe, which may be brought to our shores unless adequate measures of international or local quarantine inspections are taken in season, which measures of preventive inspection are proper subjects to be considered, to the end that their efficiency in divers countries may be secured:

Now, therefore, in virtue of the discretionary authority conferred upon me by the aforesaid act of Congress, I hereby designate and appoint Dr. E. O. Shakespeare, M. D., of Pennsylvania, as a representative of the Government of the United States, to proceed, under the directions of the Secretary of State, to Spain and such other countries in Europe where the cholera exists, and make investigation of the causes, progress, and proper prevention and cure of the said diseases, in order that a full report may be made of them to Congress during the next ensuing session; and I direct that the reasonable and necessary expenses of travel and sojourn of the said E. O. Shakespeare in proceeding from Washington to Spain and elsewhere in Europe as he may find it absolutely necessary to go in pursuit of the desired information, and in returning to Washington at the conclusion of his labors, be adjusted and paid from the appropriation available under the aforesaid act of March 3, 1885, upon his statement of account approved by the Secretary of State.

Done at the city of Washington, this 1st day of October, 1885, and of the Independence of the United States the one hundred and tenth.

GROVER CLEVELAND.

By the President:

T. F. BAYARD, *Secretary of State.*

In the exercise of the power vested in the President by the Constitution, and by virtue of the seventeen hundred and fifty-third section of the Revised Statutes and of the civil-service act approved January 16, 1883, the following special rule for the regulation and improvement of the executive civil service is hereby made and promulgated:

SPECIAL RULE NO. 5.

Special Rule No. 2, approved July 18, 1884, is hereby revoked. All applicants on any register for the postal or customs service who on the 1st day of November next shall have been thereon one year or more shall, in conformity with Rule XVI, be no longer eligible for appointment from such register.

Approved, October 1, 1885.

GROVER CLEVELAND.

EXECUTIVE MANSION, ·
Washington, October 24, 1885.

Under a provision of an act of Congress entitled "An act to authorize the appointment of a commission by the President of the United States to run and mark the boundary lines between a portion of the Indian Territory and the State of Texas, in connection with a similar commission to be appointed by the State of Texas," Major S. M. Mansfield, Corps of Engineers, is detailed, in addition to those officers named in Executive order dated September 23, 1885, in obedience to the provisions of said act of Congress, to act in conjunction with such persons as have been appointed by the State of Texas to ascertain and mark the point where the one hundredth meridian of longitude crosses the Red River.

GROVER CLEVELAND.

EXECUTIVE MANSION, *October 29, 1885.**

The death of George B. McClellan, at one time the Major-General Commanding the Army of the United States, took place at an early hour this morning. As a mark of public respect to the memory of this distinguished soldier and citizen, whose military ability and civic virtues have shed luster upon the history of his country, it is ordered by the President that the national flag be displayed at half-mast upon all the buildings of the Executive Departments in the city until after his funeral shall have taken place.

DANIEL S. LAMONT,
Private Secretary.

WAR DEPARTMENT,
ADJUTANT-GENERAL'S OFFICE,
Washington, November 25, 1885.

I. The following proclamation [order] of the President of the United States is published for the information and guidance of all concerned:

EXECUTIVE MANSION,
Washington, November 25, 1885.

To the People of the United States:

Thomas A. Hendricks, Vice-President of the United States, died to-day at 5 o'clock p. m. at Indianapolis, and it becomes my mournful duty to announce the distressing fact to his fellow-countrymen.

In respect to the memory and the eminent and varied services of this high official and patriotic public servant, whose long career was so full of usefulness and honor to his State and to the United States, it is ordered that the national flag be displayed at half-mast upon all the public buildings of the United States; that the Executive Mansion and

---

* Sent to the heads of the Executive Departments, etc.

the several Executive Departments in the city of Washington be closed on the day of the funeral and be draped in mourning for the period of thirty days; that the usual and appropriate military and naval honors be rendered, and that on all the legations and consulates of the United States in foreign countries the national flag shall be displayed at half-mast on the reception of this order, and the usual emblems of mourning be adopted for thirty days.   GROVER CLEVELAND.

By the President:
>   T. F. BAYARD,
>   *Secretary of State.*

II. On the day next succeeding the receipt of this order at each military post the troops will be paraded at 10 o'clock a. m. and this order read to them.

The national flag will be displayed at half-mast. At dawn of day thirteen guns will be fired. Commencing at 12 o'clock m., nineteen minute guns will be fired, and at the close of the day the national salute of thirty-eight guns.

The usual badge of mourning will be worn by officers of the Army, and the colors of the several regiments, of the United States Corps of Cadets, and of the Battalion of Engineers will be put in mourning for the period of thirty days.

By order of the Secretary of War:
>   R. C. DRUM,
>   *Adjutant-General.*

SPECIAL ORDER.

NAVY DEPARTMENT,
Washington, November 25, 1885.

The President of the United States announces the death of Vice-President Thomas A. Hendricks in the following order:

[For order see preceding page.]

In pursuance of the foregoing order, it is hereby directed that upon the day following the receipt of this the ensign at each United States naval station and of each United States naval vessel in commission be hoisted at half-mast from sunrise to sunset, and that thirteen guns be fired at sunrise, nineteen minute guns at meridian, and a national salute at sunset at each United States naval station and on board flagships and vessels acting singly, at home or abroad.

The officers of the Navy and Marine Corps will wear the usual badge of mourning for three months.

>   WILLIAM C. WHITNEY,
>   *Secretary of the Navy.*

In the exercise of the power vested in the President by the Constitution, and by virtue of the seventeen hundred and fifty-third section of the Revised Statutes and of the civil-service act approved January 16, 1883, the following rules for the regulation and improvement of the executive civil service are hereby amended and promulgated so as to read as follows:

RULE IV.

1. All officials connected with any office where or for which any examination is to take place will give the Civil Service Commission and the chief examiner such information as may be reasonably required to enable the Commission to select competent and trustworthy examiners; and the examinations by those selected as examiners, and the work incident thereto, will be regarded as a part of the public business to be performed at such office, and with due regard to other parts of the public business said examiners shall be allowed time during office hours to perform the duties required of them.

2. It shall be the duty of every executive officer promptly to inform the Commission, in writing, of the removal or discharge from the public service of any examiner in his office, or of the inability or refusal of any such examiner to act in that capacity; and, on the request of the Commission, such officer shall thereupon name not less than two persons serving under him whom he regards as most competent for a place on an examining board, stating generally their qualifications; and from all those who may be named for any such place the Commission shall select a person to fill the same.

RULE XI.

1. Every application, in order to entitle the applicant to appear for examination or to be examined, must state under oath the facts on the following subjects: (1) Full name, residence, and post-office address; (2) citizenship; (3) age; (4) place of birth; (5) health and physical capacity for the public service; (6) right of preference by reason of military or naval service; (7) previous employment in the public service; (8) business or employment and residence for the previous five years; (9) education. Such other information shall be furnished as the Commission may reasonably require touching the applicant's fitness for the public service. The applicant must also state the number of members of his family in the public service and where employed, and must also assert that he is not disqualified under section 8 of the civil-service act, which is as follows:

"That no person habitually using intoxicating beverages to excess shall be appointed to or retained in any office, appointment, or employment to which the provisions of this act are applicable."

No person dismissed from the public service for misconduct shall be admitted to examination within two years thereafter, and no person not absolutely appointed or employed after probation shall be admitted to an examination within one year thereafter.

2. No person under enlistment in the Army or Navy of the United States shall be examined under these rules, except for some place requiring special qualifications, and with the consent in writing of the head of the Department under which he is enlisted.

3. The Commission may, by regulations subject to change at any time by the President, declare the kind and measure of ill health, physical incapacity, misrepresentation, and bad faith which may properly exclude any person from the right of examination, grading, or certification under these rules. It may also provide for medical certificates of physical capacity in the proper cases, and for the appropriate

certification of persons so defective in sight, speech, hearing, or otherwise as to be apparently disqualified for some of the duties of the part of the service which they seek to enter.

RULE XII.

1. Every regular application must be supported by proper certificates of good moral character, health, and physical and mental capacity for doing the public work, the certificates to be in such form and number as the regulations of the Commission shall provide; but no certificate will be received which is inconsistent with the tenth section of the civil-service act.

2. No one shall be examined for admission to the classified postal service if under 16 or over 35 years of age, excepting messengers, stampers, and other junior assistants, who must not be under 14 years of age, or to the classified customs service or to the classified departmental service if under 18 or over 45 years of age; but no one shall be examined for appointment to any place in the classified customs service, except that of clerk or messenger, who is under 21 years of age; but these limitations of age shall not apply to persons honorably discharged from the military or naval service of the country who are otherwise duly qualified.

RULE XVI.

1. Whenever any officer having the power of appointment or employment shall so request, there shall be certified to him by the Commission or the proper examining board four names for the vacancy specified, to be taken from those graded highest on the proper register of those in his branch of the service and remaining eligible, regard being had for any right of preference and to the apportionments to States and Territories; and from the said four a selection shall be made for the vacancy. But if a person is on both a general and a special register he need not be certified for the former, except at the discretion of the Commission, until he has remained two months upon the latter.

2. These certifications for the service at Washington shall be made in such order as to apportion, as nearly as may be practicable, the original appointments thereto among the States and Territories and the District of Columbia upon the basis of population as ascertained at the last preceding census.

3. In case the request for any such certification or any law or regulation shall call for those of either sex, persons of that sex shall be certified; otherwise sex shall be disregarded in such certification.

4. Subject to the other provisions of this rule, persons eligible on any register shall be entitled to three certifications only to the same officer, but with his request in writing there may be a fourth certification of such persons to him when reached in order. No one shall remain eligible for more than one year upon any register, except as may be provided by regulation; but these restrictions shall not extend to examinations under clause 5 of Rule VII. No person while remaining eligible on any register shall be admitted to a new examination, and no person having failed upon any examination shall within six months be admitted to another examination without the consent of the Commission.

5. Any person appointed to or employed in any place in the classified service who shall be dismissed or separated therefrom without fault or delinquency on his part may be reappointed or reemployed in the same Department or office, at a grade for which no higher examination is required than that for the position he last held, within one year next following such dismissal or separation, without further examination, on such certification as the Commission may provide.

RULE XVII.

1. Every original appointment or employment in said classified service shall be for the probationary period of six months, at the end of which time, if the conduct and

capacity of the person appointed have been found satisfactory to the officer having the duty of selection, the probationer shall be absolutely appointed or employed, but otherwise be deemed out of the service.

2. Every officer under whom any probationer shall serve during any part of the probation provided for by these rules shall carefully observe the quality and value of the service rendered by such probationer, and shall report to the proper appointing officer in writing the facts observed by him, showing the character and qualifications of such probationer and of the service performed by him; and such reports shall be preserved on file.

3. Every false statement knowingly made by any person in his application for examination, and every connivance by him at any false statement made in any certificate which may accompany his application, and every deception or fraud practiced by him or by any person in his behalf and with his knowledge to influence his examination, certification, or appointment, shall be regarded as good cause for refusing to certify such person or for the removal or discharge of such person during his probation or thereafter.

RULE XIX.

There are excepted from examination the following: (1) The confidential clerk or secretary of any head of a Department or office; (2) cashiers of collectors; (3) cashiers of postmasters; (4) superintendents of money-order divisions in post-offices; (5) the direct custodians of money for whose fidelity another officer is under official bond, and disbursing officers having the custody of money who give bond; but these exceptions shall not extend to any official below the grade of assistant cashier or teller; (6) persons employed exclusively in the secret service of the Government, or as translators, or interpreters, or stenographers; (7) persons whose employment is exclusively professional, but medical examiners are not included among such persons; (8) chief clerks, deputy collectors, deputy naval officers, deputy surveyors of customs, and superintendents or chiefs of divisions or bureaus. But no person so excepted shall be either transferred, appointed, or promoted, unless to some excepted place, without an examination under the Commission, which examination shall not take place within six months after entering the service. Promotions may be made without examination in offices where examinations are not now held until rules on the subject shall be promulgated.

RULE XXI.

1. No person, unless excepted under Rule XIX, shall be admitted into the classified civil service from any place not within said service without an examination and certification under the rules; with this exception, that any person who shall have been an officer for one year or more last preceding in any Department or office, in a grade above the classified service thereof, may be transferred or appointed to any place in the service of the same without examination.

2. No person who has passed only a limited examination under clause 4 of Rule VII for the lower classes or grades in the departmental or customs service shall be appointed, or be promoted within two years after appointment, to any position giving a salary of $1,000 or upward, without first passing an examination under clause 1 of said rule; and such examination shall not be allowed within the first year after appointment.

3. But a person who has passed the examination under said clause 1, and has accepted a position giving a salary of $900 or less, shall have the same right of promotion as if originally appointed to a position giving a salary of $1,000 or more.

4. The Commission may at any time certify for a $900 or any lower place in the classified service any person upon the register who has passed the examination under clause 1 of Rule VII if such person does not object before such certification is made.

RULE XXII.

Any person who has been in the classified departmental service for six months or more immediately previous may, when the needs of the service require it, be transferred or appointed to any other place therein upon producing a certificate from the Civil Service Commission that such person has passed at the required grade one or more examinations which are together equal to that necessary for original entrance to the place which would be secured by the transfer or appointment; and any person who has for three years last preceding served as a clerk in the office of the President of the United States may be transferred or appointed to any place in the classified service without examination.

Approved, November 27, 1885.   GROVER CLEVELAND.

By the President of the United States.

EXECUTIVE ORDER.

EXECUTIVE MANSION,
Washington, November 28, 1885.

It is hereby ordered, That the Department of Agriculture, the Government Printing Office, and all other Government offices in the District of Columbia be closed on Tuesday, December 1, 1885, the day of the funeral of the late Thomas A. Hendricks, Vice-President of the United States.

GROVER CLEVELAND.

FIRST ANNUAL MESSAGE.

WASHINGTON, *December 8, 1885.*
To the Congress of the United States:

Your assembling is clouded by a sense of public bereavement, caused by the recent and sudden death of Thomas A. Hendricks, Vice-President of the United States. His distinguished public services, his complete integrity and devotion to every duty, and his personal virtues will find honorable record in his country's history.

Ample and repeated proofs of the esteem and confidence in which he was held by his fellow-countrymen were manifested by his election to offices of the most important trust and highest dignity; and at length, full of years and honors, he has been laid at rest amid universal sorrow and benediction.

The Constitution, which requires those chosen to legislate for the people to annually meet in the discharge of their solemn trust, also requires the President to give to Congress information of the state of the Union and recommend to their consideration such measures as he shall deem necessary and expedient. At the threshold of a compliance with these constitutional directions it is well for us to bear in mind that our usefulness to the people's interests will be promoted by a constant appreciation of the scope and character of our respective duties as they relate to Federal legislation. While the Executive may recommend such measures as he shall deem expedient, the responsibility for legislative action must and should rest upon those selected by the people to make their laws.

Contemplation of the grave and responsible functions assigned to the respective branches of the Government under the Constitution will disclose the partitions of power between our respective departments and their necessary independence, and also the need for the exercise of all the power intrusted to each in that spirit of comity and cooperation which is essential to the proper fulfillment of the patriotic obligations which rest upon us as faithful servants of the people.

The jealous watchfulness of our constituencies, great and small, supplements their suffrages, and before the tribunal they establish every public servant should be judged.

It is gratifying to announce that the relations of the United States with all foreign powers continue to be friendly. Our position after nearly a century of successful constitutional government, maintenance of good faith in all our engagements, the avoidance of complications with other nations, and our consistent and amicable attitude toward the strong and weak alike furnish proof of a political disposition which renders professions of good will unnecessary. There are no questions of difficulty pending with any foreign government.

The Argentine Government has revived the long dormant question of the Falkland Islands by claiming from the United States indemnity for their loss, attributed to the action of the commander of the sloop of war *Lexington* in breaking up a piratical colony on those islands in 1831, and their subsequent occupation by Great Britain. In view of the ample justification for the act of the *Lexington* and the derelict condition of the islands before and after their alleged occupation by Argentine colonists, this Government considers the claim as wholly groundless.

Question has arisen with the Government of Austria-Hungary touching the representation of the United States at Vienna. Having under my constitutional prerogative appointed an estimable citizen of unimpeached probity and competence as minister at that court, the Government of Austria-Hungary invited this Government to take cognizance of certain exceptions, based upon allegations against the personal acceptability of Mr. Keiley, the appointed envoy, asking that in view thereof the appointment should be withdrawn. The reasons advanced were such as could not be acquiesced in without violation of my oath of office and the precepts of the Constitution, since they necessarily involved a limitation in favor of a foreign government upon the right of selection by the Executive and required such an application of a religious test as a qualification for office under the United States as would have resulted in the practical disfranchisement of a large class of our citizens and the abandonment of a vital principle in our Government. The Austro-Hungarian Government finally decided not to receive Mr. Keiley as the envoy of the United States, and that gentleman has since resigned his commission, leaving the post vacant. I have made no new nomination, and the interests of this Government at Vienna are now in the care of the secretary of legation, acting as chargé d'affaires *ad interim.*

Early in March last war broke out in Central America, caused by the attempt of Guatemala to consolidate the several States into a single government. In these contests between our neighboring States the United States forebore to interfere actively, but lent the aid of their friendly offices in deprecation of war and to promote peace and concord among the belligerents, and by such counsel contributed importantly to the restoration of tranquillity in that locality.

Emergencies growing out of civil war in the United States of Colombia demanded of the Government at the beginning of this Administration the employment of armed forces to fulfill its guaranties under the thirty-fifth article of the treaty of 1846, in order to keep the transit open across the Isthmus of Panama. Desirous of exercising only the powers expressly reserved to us by the. treaty, and mindful of the rights of Colombia, the forces sent to the Isthmus were instructed to confine their action to "positively and efficaciously" preventing the transit and its accessories from being "interrupted or embarrassed."

. The execution of this delicate and responsible task necessarily involved police control where the local authority was temporarily powerless, but always in aid of the sovereignty of Colombia.

The prompt and successful fulfillment of its duty by this Government was highly appreciated by the Government of Colombia, and has been followed by expressions of its satisfaction.

High praise is due to the officers and men engaged in this service.

The restoration of peace on the Isthmus by the reestablishment of the constituted Government there being thus accomplished, the forces of the United States were withdrawn.

Pending these occurrences a question of much importance was presented by decrees of the Colombian Government proclaiming the closure of certain ports then in the hands of insurgents and declaring vessels held by the revolutionists to be piratical and liable to capture by any power. To neither of these propositions could the United States assent. An effective closure of ports not in the possession of the Government, but held by hostile partisans, could not be recognized; neither could the vessels of insurgents against the legitimate sovereignty be deemed *hostes humani generis* within the precepts of international law, whatever might be the definition and penalty of their acts under the municipal law of the State against whose authority they were in revolt. The denial by this Government of the Colombian propositions did not, however, imply the admission of a belligerent status on the part of the insurgents.

The Colombian Government has expressed its willingness to negotiate conventions for the adjustment by arbitration of claims by foreign citizens arising out of the destruction of the city of Aspinwall by the insurrectionary forces.

The interest of the United States in a practicable transit for ships across the strip of land separating the Atlantic from the Pacific has been repeatedly manifested during the last half century.

My immediate predecessor caused to be negotiated with Nicaragua a treaty for the construction, by and at the sole cost of the United States, of a canal through Nicaraguan territory, and laid it before the Senate. Pending the action of that body thereon, I withdrew the treaty for reexamination. Attentive consideration of its provisions leads me to withhold it from resubmission to the Senate.

Maintaining, as I do, the tenets of a line of precedents from Washington's day, which proscribe entangling alliances with foreign states, I do not favor a policy of acquisition of new and distant territory or the incorporation of remote interests with our own.

The laws of progress are vital and organic, and we must be conscious of that irresistible tide of commercial expansion which, as the concomitant of our active civilization, day by day is being urged onward by those increasing facilities of production, transportation, and communication to which steam and electricity have given birth; but our duty in the present instructs us to address ourselves mainly to the development of the vast resources of the great area committed to our charge and to the cultivation of the arts of peace within our own borders, though jealously alert in preventing the American hemisphere from being involved in the political problems and complications of distant governments. Therefore I am unable to recommend propositions involving paramount privileges of ownership or right outside of our own territory, when coupled with absolute and unlimited engagements to defend the territorial integrity of the state where such interests lie. While the general project of connecting the two oceans by means of a canal is to be encouraged, I am of opinion that any scheme to that end to be considered with favor should be free from the features alluded to.

The Tehuantepec route is declared by engineers of the highest repute and by competent scientists to afford an entirely practicable transit for vessels and cargoes, by means of a ship railway, from the Atlantic to the Pacific. The obvious advantages of such a route, if feasible, over others more remote from the axial lines of traffic between Europe and the Pacific, and particularly between the Valley of the Mississippi and the western coast of North and South America, are deserving of consideration.

Whatever highway may be constructed across the barrier dividing the two greatest maritime areas of the world must be for the world's benefit—a trust for mankind, to be removed from the chance of domination by any single power, nor become a point of invitation for hostilities or a prize for warlike ambition. An engagement combining the construction, ownership, and operation of such a work by this Government, with an offensive and defensive alliance for its protection, with the foreign state whose responsibilities and rights we would share is, in my judgment, inconsistent with such dedication to universal and neutral use, and would, moreover, entail measures for its realization beyond the scope of our national polity or present means.

The lapse of years has abundantly confirmed the wisdom and foresight of those earlier Administrations which, long before the conditions of maritime intercourse were changed and enlarged by the progress of the age, proclaimed the vital need of interoceanic transit across the American Isthmus and consecrated it in advance to the common use of mankind by their positive declarations and through the formal obligation of treaties. Toward such realization the efforts of my Administration will be applied, ever bearing in mind the principles on which it must rest, and which were declared in no uncertain tones by Mr. Cass, who, while Secretary of State, in 1858, announced that "what the United States want in Central America, next to the happiness of its people, is the security and neutrality of the interoceanic routes which lead through it."

The construction of three transcontinental lines of railway, all in successful operation, wholly within our territory, and uniting the Atlantic and the Pacific oceans, has been accompanied by results of a most interesting and impressive nature, and has created new conditions, not in the routes of commerce only, but in political geography, which powerfully affect our relations toward and necessarily increase our interests in any transisthmian route which may be opened and employed for the ends of peace and traffic, or, in other contingencies, for uses inimical to both.

Transportation is a factor in the cost of commodities scarcely second to that of their production, and weighs as heavily upon the consumer.

Our experience already has proven the great importance of having the competition between land carriage and water carriage fully developed, each acting as a protection to the public against the tendencies to monopoly which are inherent in the consolidation of wealth and power in the hands of vast corporations.

These suggestions may serve to emphasize what I have already said on the score of the necessity of a neutralization of any interoceanic transit; and this can only be accomplished by making the uses of the route open to all nations and subject to the ambitions and warlike necessities of none.

The drawings and report of a recent survey of the Nicaragua Canal route, made by Chief Engineer Menocal, will be communicated for your information.

The claims of citizens of the United States for losses by reason of the late military operations of Chile in Peru and Bolivia are the subject of negotiation for a claims convention with Chile, providing for their submission to arbitration.

The harmony of our relations with China is fully sustained.

In the application of the acts lately passed to execute the treaty of 1880, restrictive of the immigration of Chinese laborers into the United States, individual cases of hardship have occurred beyond the power of the Executive to remedy, and calling for judicial determination.

The condition of the Chinese question in the Western States and Territories is, despite this restrictive legislation, far from being satisfactory. The recent outbreak in Wyoming Territory, where numbers of unoffending Chinamen, indisputably within the protection of the treaties and the law, were murdered by a mob, and the still more recent threatened outbreak of the same character in Washington Territory, are fresh in the minds of all, and there is apprehension lest the bitterness of feeling against the Mongolian race on the Pacific Slope may find vent in similar lawless demonstrations. All the power of this Government should be exerted to maintain the amplest good faith toward China in the treatment of these men, and the inflexible sternness of the law in bringing the wrongdoers to justice should be insisted upon.

Every effort has been made by this Government to prevent these violent outbreaks and to aid the representatives of China in their investigation of these outrages; and it is but just to say that they are traceable to the lawlessness of men not citizens of the United States engaged in competition with Chinese laborers.

Race prejudice is the chief factor in originating these disturbances, and it exists in a large part of our domain, jeopardizing our domestic peace and the good relationship we strive to maintain with China.

The admitted right of a government to prevent the influx of elements hostile to its internal peace and security may not be questioned, even where there is no treaty stipulation on the subject. That the exclusion of Chinese labor is demanded in other countries where like conditions prevail is strongly evidenced in the Dominion of Canada, where Chinese immigration is now regulated by laws more exclusive than our own. If existing laws are inadequate to compass the end in view, I shall be prepared to give earnest consideration to any further remedial measures, within the treaty limits, which the wisdom of Congress may devise.

The independent State of the Kongo has been organized as a government under the sovereignty of His Majesty the King of the Belgians, who assumes its chief magistracy in his personal character only, without making the new State a dependency of Belgium. It is fortunate that a benighted region, owing all it has of quickening civilization to the beneficence and philanthropic spirit of this monarch, should have the advantage and security of his benevolent supervision.

The action taken by this Government last year in being the first to recognize the flag of the International Association of the Kongo has been followed by formal recognition of the new nationality which succeeds to its sovereign powers.

A conference of delegates of the principal commercial nations was held at Berlin last winter to discuss methods whereby the Kongo basin might be kept open to the world's trade. Delegates attended on behalf of the United States on the understanding that their part should be merely deliberative, without imparting to the results any binding character so far as the United States were concerned. This reserve was due to the indisposition of this Government to share in any disposal by an international congress of jurisdictional questions in remote foreign territories. The results of the conference were embodied in a formal act of the nature of an international convention, which laid down certain obligations purporting to be binding on the signatories, subject to ratification within one year. Notwithstanding the reservation under which the delegates of the United States attended, their signatures were attached to the general act in the same manner as those of the plenipotentiaries of other governments, thus making the United States appear, without reserve or qualification, as signatories to a joint international engagement imposing on the signers the conservation of the territorial integrity of distant regions where we have no established interests or control.

This Government does not, however, regard its reservation of liberty of action in the premises as at all impaired; and holding that an engagement to share in the obligation of enforcing neutrality in the remote valley of the Kongo would be an alliance whose responsibilities we are not in a position to assume, I abstain from asking the sanction of the Senate to that general act.

The correspondence will be laid before you, and the instructive and interesting report of the agent sent by this Government to the Kongo country and his recommendations for the establishment of commercial agencies on the African coast are also submitted for your consideration.

The commission appointed by my predecessor last winter to visit the Central and South American countries and report on the methods of enlarging the commercial relations of the United States therewith has submitted reports, which will be laid before you.

No opportunity has been omitted to testify the friendliness of this Government toward Korea, whose entrance into the family of treaty powers the United States were the first to recognize. I regard with favor the application made by the Korean Government to be allowed to employ American officers as military instructors, to which the assent of Congress becomes necessary, and I am happy to say this request has the concurrent sanction of China and Japan.

The arrest and imprisonment of Julio R. Santos, a citizen of the United States, by the authorities of Ecuador gave rise to a contention with that Government, in which his right to be released or to have a speedy and impartial trial on announced charges and with all guaranties of defense stipulated by treaty was insisted upon by us. After an elaborate correspondence and repeated and earnest representations on our part Mr.

Santos was, after an alleged trial and conviction, eventually included in a general decree of amnesty and pardoned by the Ecuadorian Executive and released, leaving the question of his American citizenship denied by the Ecuadorian Government, but insisted upon by our own.

The amount adjudged by the late French and American Claims Commission to be due from the United States to French claimants on account of injuries suffered by them during the War of Secession, having been appropriated by the last Congress, has been duly paid to the French Government.

The act of February 25, 1885, provided for a preliminary search of the records of French prize courts for evidence bearing on the claims of American citizens against France for spoliations committed prior to 1801. The duty has been performed, and the report of the agent will be laid before you.

I regret to say that the restrictions upon the importation of our pork into France continue, notwithstanding the abundant demonstration of the absence of sanitary danger in its use; but I entertain strong hopes that with a better understanding of the matter this vexatious prohibition will be removed. It would be pleasing to be able to say as much with respect to Germany, Austria, and other countries, where such food products are absolutely excluded, without present prospect of reasonable change.

The interpretation of our existing treaties of naturalization by Germany during the past year has attracted attention by reason of an apparent tendency on the part of the Imperial Government to extend the scope of the residential restrictions to which returning naturalized citizens of German origin are asserted to be liable under the laws of the Empire. The temperate and just attitude taken by this Government with regard to this class of questions will doubtless lead to a satisfactory understanding.

The dispute of Germany and Spain relative to the domination of the Caroline Islands has attracted the attention of this Government by reason of extensive interests of American citizens having grown up in those parts during the past thirty years, and because the question of ownership involves jurisdiction of matters affecting the status of our citizens under civil and criminal law. While standing wholly aloof from the proprietary issues raised between powers to both of which the United States are friendly, this Government expects that nothing in the present contention shall unfavorably affect our citizens carrying on a peaceful commerce or there domiciled, and has so informed the Governments of Spain and Germany.

The marked good will between the United States and Great Britain has been maintained during the past year.

The termination of the fishing clauses of the treaty of Washington, in pursuance of the joint resolution of March 3, 1883, must have resulted in the abrupt cessation on the 1st of July of this year, in the midst of their ventures, of the operations of citizens of the United States engaged in fishing in British American waters but for a diplomatic understanding reached with Her Majesty's Government in June last, whereby assurance was obtained that no interruption of those operations should take place during the current fishing season.

In the interest of good neighborhood and of the commercial intercourse of adjacent communities, the question of the North American fisheries is one of much importance. Following out the intimation given by me when the extensory arrangement above described was negotiated, I recommend that the Congress provide for the appointment of a commission in which the Governments of the United States and Great Britain shall be respectively represented, charged with the consideration and settlement, upon a just, equitable, and honorable basis, of the entire question of the fishing rights of the two Governments and their respective citizens on the coasts of the United States and British North America. The fishing interests being intimately related to other general questions dependent upon contiguity and intercourse, consideration thereof in all their equities might also properly come within the purview of such a commission, and the fullest latitude of expression on both sides should be permitted.

The correspondence in relation to the fishing rights will be submitted.

The arctic exploring steamer *Alert*, which was generously given by Her Majesty's Government to aid in the relief of the Greely expedition, was, after the successful attainment of that humane purpose, returned to Great Britain, in pursuance of the authority conferred by the act of March 3, 1885.

The inadequacy of the existing engagements for extradition between the United States and Great Britain has been long apparent. The tenth article of the treaty of 1842, one of the earliest compacts in this regard entered into by us, stipulated for surrender in respect of a limited number of offenses. Other crimes no less inimical to the social welfare should be embraced and the procedure of extradition brought in harmony with present international practice. Negotiations with Her Majesty's Government for an enlarged treaty of extradition have been pending since 1870, and I entertain strong hopes that a satisfactory result may be soon attained.

The frontier line between Alaska and British Columbia, as defined by the treaty of cession with Russia, follows the demarcation assigned in a prior treaty between Great Britain and Russia. Modern exploration discloses that this ancient boundary is impracticable as a geographical fact. In the unsettled condition of that region the question has lacked importance, but the discovery of mineral wealth in the territory the line is supposed to traverse admonishes that the time has come when an accurate ·dge of the boundary is needful to avert jurisdictional complications.

I recommend, therefore, that provision be made for a preliminary reconnoissance by officers of the United States, to the end of acquiring more precise information on the subject. I have invited Her Majesty's Government to consider with us the adoption of a more convenient line, to be established by meridian observations or by known geographical features without the necessity of an expensive survey of the whole.

The late insurrectionary movements in Hayti having been quelled, the Government of that Republic has made prompt provision for adjudicating the losses suffered by foreigners because of hostilities there, and the claims of certain citizens of the United States will be in this manner determined.

The long-pending claims of two citizens of the United States, Pelletier and Lazare, have been disposed of by arbitration, and an award in favor of each claimant has been made, which by the terms of the engagement is final. It remains for Congress to provide for the payment of the stipulated moiety of the expenses.

A question arose with Hayti during the past year by reason of the exceptional treatment of an American citizen, Mr. Van Bokkelen, a resident of Port-au-Prince, who, on suit by creditors residing in the United States, was sentenced to imprisonment, and, under the operation of a Haytian statute, was denied relief secured to a native Haytian. This Government asserted his treaty right to equal treatment with natives of Hayti in all suits at law. Our contention was denied by the Haytian Government, which, however, while still professing to maintain the ground taken against Mr. Van Bokkelen's right, terminated the controversy by setting him at liberty without explanation.

An international conference to consider the means of arresting the spread of cholera and other epidemic diseases was held at Rome in May last, and adjourned to meet again on further notice. An expert delegate on behalf of the United States has attended its sessions and will submit a report.

Our relations with Mexico continue to be most cordial, as befits those of neighbors between whom the strongest ties of friendship and commercial intimacy exist, as the natural and growing consequence of our similarity of institutions and geographical propinquity.

The relocation of the boundary line between the United States and Mexico westward of the Rio Grande, under the convention of July 29, 1882, has been unavoidably delayed, but I apprehend no difficulty in securing a prolongation of the period for its accomplishment.

The lately concluded commercial treaty with Mexico still awaits the stipulated legislation to carry its provisions into effect, for which one year's additional time has been secured by a supplementary article signed in February last and since ratified on both sides.

As this convention, so important to the commercial welfare of the two adjoining countries, has been constitutionally confirmed by the treaty-making branch, I express the hope that legislation needed to make it effective may not be long delayed.

The large influx of capital and enterprise to Mexico from the United States continues to aid in the development of the resources and in augmenting the material well-being of our sister Republic. Lines of railway, penetrating to the heart and capital of the country, bring the two peoples into mutually beneficial intercourse, and enlarged facilities of transit add to profitable commerce, create new markets, and furnish avenues to otherwise isolated communities.

I have already adverted to the suggested construction of a ship railway across the narrow formation of the territory of Mexico at Tehuantepec.

With the gradual recovery of Peru from the effects of her late disastrous conflict with Chile, and with the restoration of civil authority in that distracted country, it is hoped that pending war claims of our citizens will be adjusted.

In conformity with notification given by the Government of Peru, the existing treaties of commerce and extradition between the United States and that country will terminate March 31, 1886.

Our good relationship with Russia continues.

An officer of the Navy, detailed for the purpose, is now on his way to Siberia bearing the testimonials voted by Congress to those who generously succored the survivors of the unfortunate *Jeannette* expedition.

It is gratifying to advert to the cordiality of our intercourse with Spain.

The long-pending claim of the owners of the ship *Masonic* for loss suffered through the admitted dereliction of the Spanish authorities in the Philippine Islands has been adjusted by arbitration and an indemnity awarded. The principle of arbitration in such cases, to which the United States have long and consistently adhered, thus receives a fresh and gratifying confirmation.

Other questions with Spain have been disposed of or are under diplomatic consideration with a view to just and honorable settlement.

The operation of the commercial agreement with Spain of January 2–February 13, 1884, has been found inadequate to the commercial needs of the United States and the Spanish Antilles, and the terms of the agreement are subjected to conflicting interpretations in those islands.

Negotiations have been instituted at Madrid for a full treaty not open to these objections and in the line of the general policy touching the neighborly intercourse of proximate communities, to which I elsewhere advert, and aiming, moreover, at the removal of existing burdens and annoying restrictions; and although a satisfactory termination is promised, I am compelled to delay its announcement.

An international copyright conference was held at Berne in September, on the invitation of the Swiss Government. The envoy of the United States attended as a delegate, but refrained from committing this

Government to the results, even by signing the recommendatory protocol adopted. The interesting and important subject of international copyright has been before you for several years. Action is certainly desirable to effect the object in view; and while there may be question as to the relative advantage of treating it by legislation or by specific treaty, the matured views of the Berne conference can not fail to aid your consideration of the subject.

The termination of the commercial treaty of 1862 between the United States and Turkey has been sought by that Government. While there is question as to the sufficiency of the notice of termination given, yet as the commercial rights of our citizens in Turkey come under the favored-nation guaranties of the prior treaty of 1830, and as equal treatment is admitted by the Porte, no inconvenience can result from the assent of this Government to the revision of the Ottoman tariffs, in which the treaty powers have been invited to join.

Questions concerning our citizens in Turkey may be affected by the Porte's nonacquiescence in the right of expatriation and by the imposition of religious tests as a condition of residence, in which this Government can not concur. The United States must hold in their intercourse with every power that the status of their citizens is to be respected and equal civil privileges accorded to them without regard to creed, and affected by no considerations save those growing out of domiciliary return to the land of original allegiance or of unfulfilled personal obligations which may survive, under municipal laws, after such voluntary return.

The negotiation with Venezuela relative to the rehearing of the awards of the mixed commission constituted under the treaty of 1866 was resumed in view of the recent acquiescence of the Venezuelan envoy in the principal point advanced by this Government, that the effects of the old treaty could only be set aside by the operation of a new convention. A result in substantial accord with the advisory suggestions contained in the joint resolution of March 3, 1883, has been agreed upon and will shortly be submitted to the Senate for ratification.

Under section 3659 of the Revised Statutes all funds held in trust by the United States and the annual interest accruing thereon, when not otherwise required by treaty, are to be invested in stocks of the United States bearing a rate of interest not less than 5 per cent per annum. There being now no procurable stocks paying so high a rate of interest, the letter of the statute is at present inapplicable, but its spirit is subserved by continuing to make investments of this nature in current stocks bearing the highest interest now paid. The statute, however, makes no provision for the disposal of such accretions. It being contrary to the general rule of this Government to allow interest on claims, I recommend the repeal of the provision in question and the disposition, under a u' form rule, of the present accumulations from investment of trust funds

The inadequacy of existing legislation touching citizenship and naturalization demands your consideration.

While recognizing the right of expatriation, no statutory provision exists providing means for renouncing citizenship by an American citizen, native born or naturalized, nor for terminating and vacating an improper acquisition of citizenship. Even a fraudulent decree of naturalization can not now be canceled. The privilege and franchise of American citizenship should be granted with care, and extended to those only who intend in good faith to assume its duties and responsibilities when attaining its privileges and benefits. It should be withheld from those who merely go through the forms of naturalization with the intent of escaping the duties of their original allegiance without taking upon themselves those of their new status, or who may acquire the rights of American citizenship for no other than a hostile purpose toward their original governments. These evils have had many flagrant illustrations.

I regard with favor the suggestion put forth by one of my predecessors that provision be made for a central bureau of record of the decrees of naturalization granted by the various courts throughout the United States now invested with that power.

The rights which spring from domicile in the United States, especially when coupled with a declaration of intention to become a citizen, are worthy of definition by statute. The stranger coming hither with intent to remain, establishing his residence in our midst, contributing to the general welfare, and by his voluntary act declaring his purpose to assume the responsibilities of citizenship, thereby gains an inchoate status which legislation may properly define. The laws of certain States and Territories admit a domiciled alien to the local franchise, conferring on him the rights of citizenship to a degree which places him in the anomalous position of being a citizen of a State and yet not of the United States within the purview of Federal and international law.

It is important within the scope of national legislation to define this right of alien domicile as distinguished from Federal naturalization.

The commercial relations of the United States with their immediate neighbors and with important areas of traffic near our shores suggest especially liberal intercourse between them and us.

Following the treaty of 1883 with Mexico, which rested on the basis of a reciprocal exemption from customs duties, other similar treaties were initiated by my predecessor.

Recognizing the need of less obstructed traffic with Cuba and Puerto Rico, and met by the desire of Spain to succor languishing interests in the Antilles, steps were taken to attain those ends by a treaty of commerce. A similar treaty was afterwards signed by the Dominican Republic. Subsequently overtures were made by Her Britannic Majesty's Government for a like mutual extension of commercial intercourse with the British West Indian and South American dependencies, but without result.

On taking office I withdrew for reexamination the treaties signed with Spain and Santo Domingo, then pending before the Senate. The result has been to satisfy me of the inexpediency of entering into engagements of this character not covering the entire traffic.

These treaties contemplated the surrender by the United States of large revenues for inadequate considerations. Upon sugar alone duties were surrendered to an amount far exceeding all the advantages offered in exchange. Even were it intended to relieve our consumers, it was evident that so long as the exemption but partially covered our importation such relief would be illusory. To relinquish a revenue so essential seemed highly improvident at a time when new and large drains upon the Treasury were contemplated. Moreover, embarrassing questions would have arisen under the favored-nation clauses of treaties with other nations.

As a further objection, it is evident that tariff regulation by treaty diminishes that independent control over its own revenues which is essential for the safety and welfare of any government. Emergency calling for an increase of taxation may at any time arise, and no engagement with a foreign power should exist to hamper the action of the Government.

By the fourteenth section of the shipping act approved June 26, 1884, certain reductions and contingent exemptions from tonnage dues were made as to vessels entering ports of the United States from any foreign port in North and Central America, the West India Islands, the Bahamas and Bermudas, Mexico, and the Isthmus as far as Aspinwall and Panama. The Governments of Belgium, Denmark, Germany, Portugal, and Sweden and Norway have asserted, under the favored-nation clause in their treaties with the United States, a claim to like treatment in respect of vessels coming to the United States from their home ports. This Government, however, holds that the privileges granted by the act are purely geographical, inuring to any vessel of any foreign power that may choose to engage in traffic between this country and any port within the defined zone, and no warrant exists under the most-favored-nation clause for the extension of the privileges in question to vessels sailing to this country from ports outside the limitation of the act.

Undoubtedly the relations of commerce with our near neighbors, whose territories form so long a frontier line difficult to be guarded, and who find in our country, and equally offer to us, natural markets, demand special and considerate treatment. It rests with Congress to consider what legislative action may increase facilities of intercourse which contiguity makes natural and desirable.

I earnestly urge that Congress recast the appropriations for the maintenance of the diplomatic and consular service on a footing commensurate with the importance of our national interests. At every post where a representative is necessary the salary should be so graded as to permit him to live with comfort. With the assignment of adequate salaries the so-called notarial extraofficial fees, which our officers abroad are now permitted to treat as personal perquisites, should be done away with. Every act requiring the certification and seal of the officer should be taxable at schedule rates and the fee therefor returned to the Treasury. By restoring these revenues to the public use the consular service would be self-supporting, even with a liberal increase of the present low salaries.

In further prevention of abuses a system of consular inspection should be instituted.

The appointment of a limited number of secretaries of legation at large, to be assigned to duty wherever necessary, and in particular for temporary service at missions which for any cause may be without a head, should also be authorized.

I favor also authorization for the detail of officers of the regular service as military or naval attachés at legations.

Some foreign governments do not recognize the union of consular with diplomatic functions. Italy and Venezuela will only receive the appointee in one of his two capacities, but this does not prevent the requirement of a bond and submission to the responsibilities of an office whose duties he can not discharge. The superadded title of consul-general should be abandoned at all missions.

I deem it expedient that a well-devised measure for the reorganization of the extraterritorial courts in Oriental countries should replace the present system, which labors under the disadvantage of combining judicial and executive functions in the same office.

In several Oriental countries generous offers have been made of premises for housing the legations of the United States. A grant of land for that purpose was made some years since by Japan, and has been referred to in the annual messages of my predecessor. The Siamese Government has made a gift to the United States of commodious quarters in Bangkok. In Korea the late minister was permitted to purchase a building from the Government for legation use. In China the premises rented for the legation are favored as to local charges. At Tangier the house occupied by our representative has been for many years the property of this Government, having been given for that purpose in 1822 by the Sultan of Morocco. I approve the suggestion heretofore made, that, in view of the conditions of life and administration in the Eastern countries, the legation buildings in China, Japan, Korea, Siam, and perhaps Persia, should be owned and furnished by the Government with a view to permanency and security. To this end I recommend that authority be given to accept the gifts adverted to in Japan and Siam, and to purchase in the other countries named, with provision for furniture and repairs. A considerable saving in rentals would result.

The World's Industrial Exposition, held at New Orleans last winter, with the assistance of the Federal Government, attracted a large number of foreign exhibits, and proved of great value in spreading among the concourse of visitors from Mexico and Central and South America a wider knowledge of the varied manufactures and productions of this country and their availability in exchange for the productions of those regions.

Past Congresses have had under consideration the advisability of abolishing the discrimination made by the tariff laws in favor of the works of American artists. The odium of the policy which subjects to a high rate of duty the paintings of foreign artists and exempts the productions of American artists residing abroad, and who receive gratuitously advantages and instruction, is visited upon our citizens engaged in art culture in Europe, and has caused them with practical unanimity to favor the abolition of such an ungracious distinction; and in their interest, and for other obvious reasons, I strongly recommend it.

The report of the Secretary of the Treasury fully exhibits the condition of the public finances and of the several branches of the Government connected with his Department. The suggestions of the Secretary relating to the practical operations of this important Department, and his recommendations in the direction of simplification and economy, particularly in the work of collecting customs duties, are especially urged upon the attention of Congress.

The ordinary receipts from all sources for the fiscal year ended June 30, 1885, were $322,690,706.38. Of this sum $181,471,939.34 was received from customs and $112,498,725.54 from internal revenue. The total receipts, as given above, were $24,829,163.54 less than those for the year ended June 30, 1884. This diminution embraces a falling off of $13,595,550.42 in the receipts from customs and $9,687,346.97 in the receipts from internal revenue.

The total ordinary expenditures of the Government for the fiscal year were $260,226,935.50, leaving a surplus in the Treasury at the close of the year of $63,463,771.27. This is $40,929,854.32 less than the surplus reported at the close of the previous year.

The expenditures are classified as follows:

For civil expenses	$23,826,942.11
For foreign intercourse	5,439,609.11
For Indians	6,552,494.63
For pensions	56,102,267.49
For the military, including river and harbor improvements and arsenals	42,670,578.47
For the Navy, including vessels, machinery, and improvements of navy-yards	16,021,079.69
For interest on the public debt	51,386,256.47
For the District of Columbia	3,499,650.95
For miscellaneous expenditures, including public buildings, light-houses, and collecting the revenue	54,728,056.21

The amount paid on the public debt during the fiscal year ended June 30, 1885, was $45,993,235.43, and there has been paid since that date and up to November 1, 1885, the sum of $369,828, leaving the amount of the debt at the last-named date $1,514,475,860.47. There was, however, at that time in the Treasury, applicable to the general purposes of the Government, the sum of $66,818,292.38.

The total receipts for the current fiscal year ending June 30, 1886, ascertained to October 1, 1885, and estimated for the remainder of the year, are $315,000,000. The expenditures ascertained and estimated for the same time are $245,000,000, leaving a surplus at the close of the year estimated at $70,000,000.

The value of the exports from the United States to foreign countries during the last fiscal year was as follows:

Domestic merchandise	$726,682,946.00
Foreign merchandise	15,506,809.00
	742,189,755.00
Gold	8,477,892.00
Silver	33,753,633.00
	784,421,280.00

Some of the principal exports, with their values and the percentage they respectively bear to the total exportation, are given as follows:

Articles.	Value.	Percentage.
Cotton and cotton manufactures	$213,799,049	29.42
Breadstuffs	160,370,821	22.07
Provisions	107,332,456	14.77
Oils—mineral, vegetable, and animal	54,326,202	7.48
Tobacco and its manufactures	24,767,305	3.41
Wood and its manufactures	21,464,322	2.95

Our imports during the year were as follows:

Merchandise	$579,580,053.80
Gold	26,691,696.00
Silver	16,550,627.00
	622,822,376.80

The following are given as prominent articles of import during the year, with their values and the percentage they bear to the total importation:

Articles.	Value.	Percentage.
Sugar and molasses	$76,738,713	13.29
Coffee	46,723,318	8.09
Wool and its manufactures	44,656,482	7.73
Silk and its manufactures	40,393,002	6.99
Chemicals, dyes, drugs, and medicines	35,070,816	6.07
Iron and steel and their manufactures	34,563,689	5.98
Flax, hemp, jute, and their manufactures	32,854,874	5.69
Cotton and its manufactures	28,152,001	4.88
Hides and skins other than fur skins	20,586,443	3.56

Of the entire amount of duties collected 70 per cent was collected from the following articles of import:

	Percentage.
Sugar and molasses	29
Wool and its manufactures	15
Silk and its manufactures	8
Iron and steel and their manufactures	7
Cotton manufactures	6
Flax, hemp, and jute, and their manufactures	5

The fact that our revenues are in excess of the actual needs of an economical administration of the Government justifies a reduction in the amount exacted from the people for its support. Our Government is but the means established by the will of a free people by which certain principles are applied which they have adopted for their benefit and protection; and it is never better administered and its true spirit is never better observed than when the people's taxation for its support is scrupulously limited to the actual necessity of expenditure and distributed according to a just and equitable plan.

The proposition with which we have to deal is the reduction of the revenue received by the Government, and indirectly paid by the people, from customs duties. The question of free trade is not involved, nor is there now any occasion for the general discussion of the wisdom or expediency of a protective system.

Justice and fairness dictate that in any modification of our present laws relating to revenue the industries and interests which have been encouraged by such laws, and in which our citizens have large investments, should not be ruthlessly injured or destroyed. We should also deal with the subject in such manner as to protect the interests of American labor, which is the capital of our workingmen. Its stability and proper remuneration furnish the most justifiable pretext for a protective policy.

Within these limitations a certain reduction should be made in our customs revenue. The amount of such reduction having been determined, the inquiry follows, Where can it best be remitted and what articles can best be released from duty in the interest of our citizens?

I think the reduction should be made in the revenue derived from a tax upon the imported necessaries of life. We thus directly lessen the cost of living in every family of the land and release to the people in every humble home a larger measure of the rewards of frugal industry.

During the year ended November 1, 1885, 145 national banks were organized, with an aggregate capital of $16,938,000, and circulating notes have been issued to them amounting to $4,274,910. The whole number of these banks in existence on the day above mentioned was 2,727.

The very limited amount of circulating notes issued by our national banks, compared with the amount the law permits them to issue upon a deposit of bonds for their redemption, indicates that the volume of our circulating medium may be largely increased through this instrumentality.

Nothing more important than the present condition of our currency and coinage can claim your attention.

Since February, 1878, the Government has, under the compulsory provisions of law, purchased silver bullion and coined the same at the rate of more than $2,000,000 every month. By this process up to the present date 215,759,431 silver dollars have been coined.

A reasonable appreciation of a delegation of power to the General Government would limit its exercise, without express restrictive words, to the people's needs and the requirements of the public welfare.

Upon this theory the authority to "coin money" given to Congress by the Constitution, if it permits the purchase by the Government of bullion for coinage in any event, does not justify such purchase and coinage to an extent beyond the amount needed for a sufficient circulating medium.

The desire to utilize the silver product of the country should not lead to a misuse or the perversion of this power.

The necessity for such an addition to the silver currency of the nation as is compelled by the silver-coinage act is negatived by the fact that up to the present time only about 50,000,000 of the silver dollars so coined have actually found their way into circulation, leaving more than 165,000,000 in the possession of the Government, the custody of which has entailed a considerable expense for the construction of vaults for its deposit. Against this latter amount there are outstanding silver certificates amounting to about $93,000,000.

Every month two millions of gold in the public Treasury are paid out for two millions or more of silver dollars, to be added to the idle mass already accumulated.

If continued long enough, this operation will result in the substitution of silver for all the gold the Government owns applicable to its general purposes. It will not do to rely upon the customs receipts of the Government to make good this drain of gold, because the silver thus coined having been made legal tender for all debts and dues, public and private, at times during the last six months 58 per cent of the receipts for duties has been in silver or silver certificates, while the average within that period has been 20 per cent. The proportion of silver and its certificates received by the Government will probably increase as time goes on, for the reason that the nearer the period approaches when it will be obliged to offer silver in payment of its obligations the greater inducement there will be to hoard gold against depreciation in the value of silver or for the purpose of speculating.

This hoarding of gold has already begun.

When the time comes that gold has been withdrawn from circulation, then will be apparent the difference between the real value of the silver dollar and a dollar in gold, and the two coins will part company. Gold, still the standard of value and necessary in our dealings with other countries, will be at a premium over silver; banks which have substituted gold for the deposits of their customers may pay them with silver bought with such gold, thus making a handsome profit; rich speculators will sell their hoarded gold to their neighbors who need it to liquidate their foreign debts, at a ruinous premium over silver, and the laboring men and women of the land, most defenseless of all, will find that the dollar received for the wage of their toil has sadly shrunk in its purchasing power. It may be said that the latter result will be but temporary, and that ultimately the price of labor will be adjusted to the change; but even if this takes place the wage-worker can not possibly gain, but must inevitably lose, since the price he is compelled to pay for his living will not only be measured in a coin heavily depreciated and fluctuating and uncertain in its value, but this uncertainty in the value of the purchasing medium will be made the pretext for an advance in prices beyond that justified by actual depreciation.

The words uttered in 1834 by Daniel Webster in the Senate of the United States are true to-day:

> The very man of all others who has the deepest interest in a sound currency, and who suffers most by mischievous legislation in money matters, is the man who earns his daily bread by his daily toil.

The most distinguished advocate of bimetallism, discussing our silver coinage, has lately written:

> No American citizen's hand has yet felt the sensation of cheapness, either in receiving or expending the silver-act dollars.

And those who live by labor or legitimate trade never will feel that sensation of cheapness. However plenty silver dollars may become, they will not be distributed as gifts among the people; and if the laboring man should receive four depreciated dollars where he now receives but two, he will pay in the depreciated coin more than double the price he now pays for all the necessaries and comforts of life.

Those who do not fear any disastrous consequences arising from the continued compulsory coinage of silver as now directed by law, and who suppose that the addition to the currency of the country intended as its result will be a public benefit, are reminded that history demonstrates that the point is easily reached in the attempt to float at the same time two sorts of money of different excellence when the better will cease to be in general circulation. The hoarding of gold which has already taken place indicates that we shall not escape the usual experience in such cases. So if this silver coinage be continued we may reasonably expect that gold and its equivalent will abandon the field of circulation to silver alone. This of course must produce a severe contraction of our circulating medium, instead of adding to it.

It will not be disputed that any attempt on the part of the Government to cause the circulation of silver dollars worth 80 cents side by side with gold dollars worth 100 cents, even within the limit that legislation does not run counter to the laws of trade, to be successful must be seconded by the confidence of the people that both coins will retain the same purchasing power and be interchangeable at will.   A special effort has been made by the Secretary of the Treasury to increase the amount of our silver coin in circulation; but the fact that a large share of the limited amount thus put out has soon returned to the public Treasury in payment of duties leads to the belief that the people do not now desire to keep it in hand, and this, with the evident disposition to hoard gold, gives rise to the suspicion that there already exists a lack of confidence among the people touching our financial processes.   There is certainly not enough silver now in circulation to cause uneasiness, and the whole amount coined and now on hand might after a time be absorbed by the people without apprehension; but it is the ceaseless stream that threatens to overflow the land which causes fear and uncertainty.

What has been thus far submitted upon this subject relates almost entirely to considerations of a home nature, unconnected with the bearing which the policies of other nations have upon the question.   But it is perfectly apparent that a line of action in regard to our currency can not wisely be settled upon or persisted in without considering the attitude on the subject of other countries with whom we maintain intercourse through commerce, trade, and travel.   An acknowledgment of this fact is found in the act by virtue of which our silver is compulsorily coined.   It provides that—

The President shall invite the governments of the countries composing the Latin Union, so called, and of such other European nations as he may deem advisable, to join the United States in a conference to adopt a common ratio between gold and silver for the purpose of establishing internationally the use of bimetallic money and securing fixity of relative value between those metals.

This conference absolutely failed, and a similar fate has awaited all subsequent efforts in the same direction.   And still we continue our coinage of silver at a ratio different from that of any other nation.   The most vital part of the silver-coinage act remains inoperative and unexecuted, and without an ally or friend we battle upon the silver field in an illogical and losing contest.

To give full effect to the design of Congress on this subject I have made careful and earnest endeavor since the adjournment of the last Congress.

To this end I delegated a gentleman well instructed in fiscal science to proceed to the financial centers of Europe and, in conjunction with our ministers to England, France, and Germany, to obtain a full knowledge of the attitude and intent of those governments in respect of the establishment of such an international ratio as would procure free coinage of both metals at the mints of those countries and our own.   By my direction our consul-general at Paris has given close attention to the proceedings of the congress of the Latin Union, in order to indicate our interest in its objects and report its action.

It may be said in brief, as the result of these efforts, that the attitude of the leading powers remains substantially unchanged since the monetary conference of 1881, nor is it to be questioned that the views of these governments are in each instance supported by the weight of public opinion.

The steps thus taken have therefore only more fully demonstrated the uselessness of further attempts at present to arrive at any agreement on the subject with other nations.

In the meantime we are accumulating silver coin, based upon our own peculiar ratio, to such an extent, and assuming so heavy a burden to be provided for in any international negotiations, as will render us an undesirable party to any future monetary conference of nations.

It is a significant fact that four of the five countries composing the Latin Union mentioned in our coinage act, embarrassed with their silver currency, have just completed an agreement among themselves that no more silver shall be coined by their respective Governments and that such as has been already coined and in circulation shall be redeemed in gold by the country of its coinage. The resort to this expedient by these countries may well arrest the attention of those who suppose that we can succeed without shock or injury in the attempt to circulate upon its merits all the silver we may coin under the provisions of our silver-coinage act.

The condition in which our Treasury may be placed by a persistence in our present course is a matter of concern to every patriotic citizen who does not desire his Government to pay in silver such of its obligations as should be paid in gold. Nor should our condition be such as to oblige us, in a prudent management of our affairs, to discontinue the calling in and payment of interest-bearing obligations which we have the right now to discharge, and thus avoid the payment of further interest thereon.

The so-called debtor class, for whose benefit the continued compulsory coinage of silver is insisted upon, are not dishonest because they are in debt, and they should not be suspected of a desire to jeopardize the financial safety of the country in order that they may cancel their present debts by paying the same in depreciated dollars. Nor should it be forgotten that it is not the rich nor the money lender alone that must submit to such a readjustment, enforced by the Government and their debtors. The pittance of the widow and the orphan and the incomes of helpless beneficiaries of all kinds would be disastrously reduced. The depositors in savings banks and in other institutions which hold in trust the savings of the poor, when their little accumulations are scaled down to meet the new order of things, would in their distress painfully realize the delusion of the promise made to them that plentiful money would improve their condition.

We have now on hand all the silver dollars necessary to supply the present needs of the people and to satisfy those who from sentiment wish to see them in circulation, and if their coinage is suspended they can be readily obtained by all who desire them.   If the need of more is at any time apparent, their coinage may be renewed.

That disaster has not already overtaken us furnishes no proof that danger does not wait upon a continuation of the present silver coinage. We have been saved by the most careful management and unusual expedients, by a combination of fortunate conditions, and by a confident expectation that the course of the Government in regard to silver coinage would be speedily changed by the action of Congress.

Prosperity hesitates upon our threshold because of the dangers and uncertainties surrounding this question.   Capital timidly shrinks from trade, and investors are unwilling to take the chance of the questionable shape in which their money will be returned to them, while enterprise halts at a risk against which care and sagacious management do not protect.

As a necessary consequence, labor lacks employment and suffering and distress are visited upon a portion of our fellow-citizens especially entitled to the careful consideration of those charged with the duties of legislation.   No interest appeals to us so strongly for a safe and stable currency as the vast army of the unemployed.

I recommend the suspension of the compulsory coinage of silver dollars, directed by the law passed in February, 1878.

The Steamboat-Inspection Service on the 30th day of June, 1885, was composed of 140 persons, including officers, clerks, and messengers.   The expenses of the service over the receipts were $138,822.22 during the fiscal year.   The special inspection of foreign steam vessels, organized under a law passed in 1882, was maintained during the year at an expense of $36,641.63.   Since the close of the fiscal year reductions have been made in the force employed which will result in a saving during the current year of $17,000 without affecting the efficiency of the service.

The Supervising Surgeon-General reports that during the fiscal year 41,714 patients have received relief through the Marine-Hospital Service, of whom 12,803 were treated in hospitals and 28,911 at the dispensaries.

Active and effective efforts have been made through the medium of this service to protect the country against an invasion of cholera, which has prevailed in Spain and France, and the smallpox, which recently broke out in Canada.

The most gratifying results have attended the operations of the Life-Saving Service during the last fiscal year.   The observance of the provision of law requiring the appointment of the force employed in this service to be made "solely with reference to their fitness, and without reference to their political or party affiliation," has secured the result which may confidently be expected in any branch of public employment where such a rule is applied. As a consequence, this service is composed of men well qualified for the performance of their dangerous and exceptionally important duties.

The number of stations in commission at the close of the year was 203. The number of disasters to vessels and craft of all kinds within their field of action was 371. The number of persons endangered in such disasters was 2,439, of whom 2,428 were saved and only 11 lost. Other lives which were imperiled, though not by disasters to shipping, were also rescued, and a large amount of property was saved through the aid of this service. The cost of its maintenance during the year was $828,474.43.

The work of the Coast and Geodetic Survey was during the last fiscal year carried on within the boundaries and off the coasts of thirty-two States, two Territories, and the District of Columbia. In July last certain irregularities were found to exist in the management of this Bureau, which led to a prompt investigation of its methods. The abuses which were brought to light by this examination and the reckless disregard of duty and the interests of the Government developed on the part of some of those connected with the service made a change of superintendency and a few of its other officers necessary. Since the Bureau has been in new hands an introduction of economies and the application of business methods have produced an important saving to the Government and a promise of more useful results.

This service has never been regulated by anything but the most indefinite legal enactments and the most unsatisfactory rules. It was many years ago sanctioned apparently for a purpose regarded as temporary and related to a survey of our coast. Having gained a place in the appropriations made by Congress, it has gradually taken to itself powers and objects not contemplated in its creation and extended its operations until it sadly needs legislative attention.

So far as a further survey of our coast is concerned, there seems to be a propriety in transferring that work to the Navy Department. The other duties now in charge of this establishment, if they can not be profitably attached to some existing Department or other bureau, should be prosecuted under a law exactly defining their scope and purpose, and with a careful discrimination between the scientific inquiries which may properly be assumed by the Government and those which should be undertaken by State authority or by individual enterprise.

It is hoped that the report of the Congressional committee heretofore appointed to investigate this and other like matters will aid in the accomplishment of proper legislation on this subject.

The report of the Secretary of War is herewith submitted. The attention of Congress is invited to the detailed account which it contains of the administration of his Department, and his recommendations and suggestions for the improvement of the service.

The Army consisted, at the date of the last consolidated returns, of 2,154 officers and 24,705 enlisted men.

The expenses of the Departments for the fiscal year ended June 30, 1885, including $13,164,394.60 for public works and river and harbor improvements, were $45,850,999.54.

Besides the troops which were dispatched in pursuit of the small band of Indians who left their reservation in Arizona and committed murders and outrages, two regiments of cavalry and one of infantry were sent last July to the Indian Territory to prevent an outbreak which seemed imminent. They remained to aid, if necessary, in the expulsion of intruders upon the reservation, who seemed to have caused the discontent among the Indians, but the Executive proclamation* warning them to remove was complied with without their interference.

Troops were also sent to Rock Springs, in Wyoming Territory, after the massacre of Chinese there, to prevent further disturbance, and afterwards to Seattle, in Washington Territory, to avert a threatened attack upon Chinese laborers and domestic violence there. In both cases the mere presence of the troops had the desired effect.

It appears that the number of desertions has diminished, but that during the last fiscal year they numbered 2,927; and one instance is given by the Lieutenant-General of six desertions by the same recruit. I am convinced that this number of desertions can be much diminished by better discipline and treatment; but the punishment should be increased for repeated offenses.

These desertions might also be reduced by lessening the term of first enlistments, thus allowing a discontented recruit to contemplate a nearer discharge and the Army a profitable riddance. After one term of service a reenlistment would be quite apt to secure a contented recruit and a good soldier.

The Acting Judge-Advocate-General reports that the number of trials by general courts-martial during the year was 2,328, and that 11,851 trials took place before garrison and regimental courts-martial. The suggestion that probably more than half the Army have been tried for offenses, great and small, in one year may well arrest attention. Of course many of these trials before garrison and regimental courts-martial were for offenses almost frivolous, and there should, I think, be a way devised to dispose of these in a more summary and less inconvenient manner than by court-martial.

If some of the proceedings of courts-martial which I have had occasion to examine present the ideas of justice which generally prevail in these tribunals, I am satisfied that they should be much reformed if the honor and the honesty of the Army and Navy are by their instrumentality to be vindicated and protected.

The Board on Fortifications or other defenses, appointed in pursuance

*See pp. 303-304.

of the provisions of the act of Congress approved March 3, 1885, will in a short time present their report, and it is hoped that this may greatly aid the legislation so necessary to remedy the present defenseless condition of our seacoasts.

The work of the Signal Service has been prosecuted during the last year with results of increasing benefit to the country. The field of instruction has been enlarged with a view of adding to its usefulness. The number of stations in operation June 30, 1885, was 489. Telegraphic reports are received daily from 160 stations. Reports are also received from 25 Canadian stations, 375 volunteer observers, 52 army surgeons at military posts, and 333 foreign stations. The expense of the service during the fiscal year, after deducting receipts from military telegraph lines, was $792,592.97. In view of the fact referred to by the Secretary of War, that the work of this service ordinarily is of a scientific nature, and the further fact that it is assuming larger proportions constantly and becoming more and more unsuited to the fixed rules which must govern the Army, I am inclined to agree with him in the opinion that it should be separately established. If this is done, the scope and extent of its operations should, as nearly as possible, be definitely prescribed by law and always capable of exact ascertainment.

The Military Academy at West Point is reported as being in a high state of efficiency and well equipped for the satisfactory accomplishment of the purposes of its maintenance.

The fact that the class which graduates next year is an unusually large one has constrained me to decline to make appointments to second lieutenancies in the Army from civil life, so that such vacancies as exist in these places may be reserved for such graduates; and yet it is not probable that there will be enough vacancies to provide positions for them all when they leave the military school. Under the prevailing law and usage those not thus assigned to duty never actively enter the military service. It is suggested that the law on this subject be changed so that such of these young men as are not at once assigned to duty after graduation may be retained as second lieutenants in the Army if they desire it, subject to assignment when opportunity occurs, and under proper rules as to priority of selection.

The expenditures on account of the Military Academy for the last fiscal year, exclusive of the sum taken for its purposes from appropriations for the support of the Army, were $290,712.07.

The act approved March 3, 1885, designed to compensate officers and enlisted men for loss of private property while in the service of the United States, is so indefinite in its terms and apparently admits so many claims the adjustment of which could not have been contemplated that if it is to remain upon the statute book it needs amendment.

There should be a general law of Congress prohibiting the construction of bridges over navigable waters in such manner as to obstruct navigation, with provisions for preventing the same. It seems that under existing statutes the Government can not intervene to prevent such a construction when entered upon without its consent, though when such consent is asked and granted upon condition the authority to insist upon such condition is clear. Thus it is represented that while the officers of the Government are with great care guarding against the obstruction of navigation by a bridge across the Mississippi River at St. Paul a large pier for a bridge has been built just below this place directly in the navigable channel of the river. If such things are to be permitted, a strong argument is presented against the appropriation of large sums of money to improve the navigation of this and other important highways of commerce.

The report of the Secretary of the Navy gives a history of the operations of his Department and the present condition of the work committed to his charge.

He details in full the course pursued by him to protect the rights of the Government in respect of certain vessels unfinished at the time of his accession to office, and also concerning the dispatch boat *Dolphin*, claimed to be completed and awaiting the acceptance of the Department. No one can fail to see from recitals contained in this report that only the application of business principles has been insisted upon in the treatment of these subjects, and that whatever controversy has arisen was caused by the exaction on the part of the Department of contract obligations as they were legally construed. In the case of the *Dolphin*, with entire justice to the contractor, an agreement has been entered into providing for the ascertainment by a judicial inquiry of the complete or partial compliance with the contract in her construction, and further providing for the assessment of any damages to which the Government may be entitled on account of a partial failure to perform such contract, or the payment of the sum still remaining unpaid upon her price in case a full performance is adjudged.

The contractor, by reason of his failure in business, being unable to complete the other three vessels, they were taken possession of by the Government in their unfinished state under a clause in the contract permitting such a course, and are now in process of completion in the yard of the contractor, but under the supervision of the Navy Department.

Congress at its last session authorized the construction of two additional new cruisers and two gunboats, at a cost not exceeding in the aggregate $2,995,000. The appropriation for this purpose having become available on the 1st day of July last, steps were at once taken for the procurement of such plans for the construction of these vessels as would be likely to insure their usefulness when completed. These are of the utmost importance, considering the constant advance in the art of building vessels of this character, and the time is not lost which is spent *in* their careful consideration and selection.

All must admit the importance of an effective navy to a nation like ours, having such an extended seacoast to protect; and yet we have not a single vessel of war that could keep the seas against a first-class vessel of any important power. Such a condition ought not longer to continue. The nation that can not resist aggression is constantly exposed to it. Its foreign policy is of necessity weak and its negotiations are conducted with disadvantage because it is not in condition to enforce the terms dictated by its sense of right and justice.

Inspired, as I am, by the hope, shared by all patriotic citizens, that the day is not very far distant when our Navy will be such as befits our standing among the nations of the earth, and rejoiced at every step that leads in the direction of such a consummation, I deem it my duty to especially direct the attention of Congress to the close of the report of the Secretary of the Navy, in which the humiliating weakness of the present organization of his Department is exhibited and the startling abuses and waste of its present methods are exposed. The conviction is forced upon us with the certainty of mathematical demonstration that before we proceed further in the restoration of a Navy we need a thoroughly reorganized Navy Department. The fact that within seventeen years more than $75,000,000 have been spent in the construction, repair, equipment, and armament of vessels, and the further fact that instead of an effective and creditable fleet we have only the discontent and apprehension of a nation undefended by war vessels, added to the disclosures now made, do not permit us to doubt that every attempt to revive our Navy has thus far for the most part been misdirected, and all our efforts in that direction have been little better than blind gropings and expensive, aimless follies.

Unquestionably if we are content with the maintenance of a Navy Department simply as a shabby ornament to the Government, a constant watchfulness may prevent some of the scandal and abuse which have found their way into our present organization, and its incurable waste may be reduced to the minimum. But if we desire to build ships for present usefulness instead of naval reminders of the days that are past, we must have a Department organized for the work, supplied with all the talent and ingenuity our country affords, prepared to take advantage of the experience of other nations, systematized so that all effort shall unite and lead in one direction, and fully imbued with the conviction that war vessels, though new, are useless unless they combine all that the ingenuity of man has up to this day brought forth relating to their construction.

I earnestly commend the portion of the Secretary's report devoted to this subject to the attention of Congress, in the hope that his suggestions touching the reorganization of his Department may be adopted as the first step toward the reconstruction of our Navy.

The affairs of the postal service are exhibited by the report of the Postmaster-General, which will be laid before you.

The postal revenue, whose ratio of gain upon the rising prosperity of 1882 and 1883 outstripped the increasing expenses of our growing service, was checked by the reduction in the rate of letter postage which took effect with the beginning of October in the latter year, and it diminished during the two past fiscal years $2,790,000, in about the proportion of $2,270,000 in 1884 to $520,000 in 1885. Natural growth and development have meantime increased expenditure, resulting in a deficiency in the revenue to meet the expenses of the Department of five and a quarter million dollars for the year 1884 and eight and a third million in the last fiscal year. The anticipated and natural revival of the revenue has been oppressed and retarded by the unfavorable business condition of the country, of which the postal service is a faithful indicator. The gratifying fact is shown, however, by the report that our returning prosperity is marked by a gain of $380,000 in the revenue of the latter half of the last year over the corresponding period of the preceding year.

The change in the weight of first-class matter which may be carried for a single rate of postage from a half ounce to an ounce, and the reduction by one-half of the rate of newspaper postage, which, under recent legislation, began with the current year, will operate to restrain the augmentation of receipts which otherwise might have been expected to such a degree that the scale of expense may gain upon the revenue and cause an increased deficiency to be shown at its close. Yet, after no long period of reawakened prosperity, by proper economy it is confidently anticipated that even the present low rates, now as favorable as any country affords, will be adequate to sustain the cost of the service.

The operation of the Post-Office Department is for the convenience and benefit of the people, and the method by which they pay the charges of this useful arm of their public service, so that it be just and impartial, is of less importance to them than the economical expenditure of the means they provide for its maintenance and the due improvement of its agencies, so that they may enjoy its highest usefulness.

A proper attention has been directed to the prevention of waste or extravagance, and good results appear from the report to have already been accomplished.

I approve the recommendation of the Postmaster-General to reduce the charges on domestic money orders of $5 and less from 8 to 5 cents. This change will materially aid those of our people who most of all avail themselves of this instrumentality, but to whom the element of cheapness is of the greatest importance. With this reduction the system would still remain self-supporting.

The free-delivery system has been extended to 19 additional cities during the year, and 178 now enjoy its conveniences. Experience has commended it to those who enjoy its benefits, and further enlargement of its facilities is due to other communities to which it is adapted. In the cities where it has been established, taken together, the local postage exceeds its maintenance by nearly $1,300,000. The limit to which this system is now confined by law has been nearly reached, and the reasons given justify its extension, which is proposed.

It was decided, with my approbation, after a sufficient examination, to be inexpedient for the Post-Office Department to contract for carrying our foreign mails under the additional authority given by the last Congress. The amount limited was inadequate to pay all within the purview of the law the full rate of 50 cents per mile, and it would have been unjust and unwise to have given it to some and denied it to others. Nor could contracts have been let under the law to all at a rate to have brought the aggregate within the appropriation without such practical prearrangement of terms as would have violated it.

The rate of sea and inland postage which was proffered under another statute clearly appears to be a fair compensation for the desired service, being three times the price necessary to secure transportation by other vessels upon any route, and much beyond the charges made to private persons for services not less burdensome.

Some of the steamship companies, upon the refusal of the Postmaster-General to attempt, by the means provided, the distribution of the sum appropriated as an extra compensation, withdrew the services of their vessels and thereby occasioned slight inconvenience, though no considerable injury, the mails having been dispatched by other means.

Whatever may be thought of the policy of subsidizing any line of public conveyance or travel, I am satisfied that it should not be done under cover of an expenditure incident to the administration of a Department, nor should there be any uncertainty as to the recipients of the subsidy or any discretion left to an executive officer as to its distribution. If such gifts of the public money are to be made for the purpose of aiding any enterprise in the supposed interest of the public, I can not but think that the amount to be paid and the beneficiary might better be determined by Congress than in any other way.

The international congress of delegates from the Postal Union countries convened at Lisbon, in Portugal, in February last, and after a session of some weeks the delegates signed a convention amendatory of the present postal-union convention in some particulars designed to advance its purposes. This additional act has had my approval and will be laid before you with the departmental report.

I approve the recommendation of the Postmaster-General that another assistant be provided for his Department. I invite your consideration to the several other recommendations contained in his report.

The report of the Attorney-General contains a history of the conduct of the Department of Justice during the last year and a number of valuable suggestions as to needed legislation, and I invite your careful attention to the same.

The condition of business in the courts of the United States is such that there seems to be an imperative necessity for remedial legislation on the subject. Some of these courts are so overburdened with pending causes that the delays in determining litigation amount often to a denial of justice. Among the plans suggested for relief is one submitted by the Attorney-General. Its main features are: The transfer of all the original jurisdiction of the circuit courts to the district courts and an increase of judges for the latter where necessary; an addition of judges to the circuit courts, and constituting them exclusively courts of appeal, and reasonably limiting appeals thereto; further restrictions of the right to remove causes from the State to Federal courts: permitting appeals to the Supreme Court from the courts of the District of Columbia and the Territories only in the same cases as they are allowed from State courts, and guarding against an unnecessary number of appeals from the circuit courts.

I approve the plan thus outlined, and recommend the legislation necessary for its application to our judicial system.

The present mode of compensating United States marshals and district attorneys should, in my opinion, be changed. They are allowed to charge against the Government certain fees for services, their income being measured by the amount of such fees within a fixed limit as to their annual aggregate. This is a direct inducement for them to make their fees in criminal cases as large as possible in an effort to reach the maximum sum permitted. As an entirely natural consequence, unscrupulous marshals are found encouraging frivolous prosecutions, arresting people on petty charges of crime and transporting them to distant places for examination and trial, for the purpose of earning mileage and other fees; and district attorneys uselessly attend criminal examinations far from their places of residence for the express purpose of swelling their accounts against the Government. The actual expenses incurred in these transactions are also charged against the Government.

Thus the rights and freedom of our citizens are outraged and public expenditures increased for the purpose of furnishing public officers pretexts for increasing the measure of their compensation.

I think marshals and district attorneys should be paid salaries, adjusted by a rule which will make them commensurate with services fairly rendered.

In connection with this subject I desire to suggest the advisability, if it be found not obnoxious to constitutional objection, of investing United States commissioners with the power to try and determine certain violations of law within the grade of misdemeanors. Such trials might be made to depend upon the option of the accused. The multiplication of small and technical offenses, especially under the provisions of our internal-revenue law, render some change in our present system very desirable in the interests of humanity as well as economy. The district courts are now crowded with petty prosecutions, involving a punishment, in case of conviction, of only a slight fine, while the parties accused are harassed by an enforced attendance upon courts held hundreds of miles from their homes. If poor and friendless, they are obliged to remain in jail during months, perhaps, that elapse before a session of the court is held, and are finally brought to trial surrounded by strangers and with but little real opportunity for defense. In the meantime frequently the marshal has charged against the Government his fees for an arrest, the transportation of the accused and the expense of the same, and for summoning witnesses before a commissioner, a grand jury, and a court; the witnesses have been paid from the public funds large fees and traveling expenses, and the commissioner and district attorney have also made their charges against the Government.

This abuse in the administration of our criminal law should be remedied; and if the plan above suggested is not practicable, some other should be devised.

The report of the Secretary of the Interior, containing an account of the operations of this important Department and much interesting information, will be submitted for your consideration.

The most intricate and difficult subject in charge of this Department is the treatment and management of the Indians. I am satisfied that some progress may be noted in their condition as a result of a prudent administration of the present laws and regulations for their control.

But it is submitted that there is lack of a fixed purpose or policy on this subject, which should be supplied. It is useless to dilate upon the wrongs of the Indians, and as useless to indulge in the heartless belief that because their wrongs are revenged in their own atrocious manner, therefore they should be exterminated.

They are within the care of our Government, and their rights are, or should be, protected from invasion by the most solemn obligations. They are properly enough called the wards of the Government; and it should be borne in mind that this guardianship involves on our part efforts for the improvement of their condition and the enforcement of their rights. There seems to be general concurrence in the proposition that the ultimate object of their treatment should be their civilization and citizenship. Fitted by these to keep pace in the march of progress with the advanced civilization about them, they will readily assimilate with the mass of our population, assuming the responsibilities and receiving the protection incident to this condition.

The difficulty appears to be in the selection of the means to be at present employed toward the attainment of this result.

Our Indian population, exclusive of those in Alaska, is reported as numbering 260,000, nearly all being located on lands set apart for their use and occupation, aggregating over 134,000,000 acres. These lands are included in the boundaries of 171 reservations of different dimensions, scattered in 21 States and Territories, presenting great variations in climate and in the kind and quality of their soils.   Among the Indians upon these several reservations there exist the most marked differences in natural traits and disposition and in their progress toward civilization. While some are lazy, vicious, and stupid, others are industrious, peaceful, and intelligent; while a portion of them are self-supporting and independent, and have so far advanced in civilization that they make their own laws, administered through officers of their own choice, and educate their children in schools of their own establishment and maintenance, others still retain, in squalor and dependence, almost the savagery of their natural state.

In dealing with this question the desires manifested by the Indians should not be ignored.   Here again we find a great diversity.   With some the tribal relation is cherished with the utmost tenacity, while its hold upon others is considerably relaxed; the love of home is strong with all, and yet there are those whose attachment to a particular locality is by no means unyielding; the ownership of their lands in severalty is much desired by some, while by others, and sometimes among the most civilized, such a distribution would be bitterly opposed.

The variation of their wants, growing out of and connected with the character of their several locations, should be regarded.   Some are upon reservations most fit for grazing, but without flocks or herds; and some, on arable land, have no agricultural implements.   While some of the reservations are double the size necessary to maintain the number of Indians now upon them, in a few cases, perhaps, they should be enlarged.

Add to all this the difference in the administration of the agencies. While the same duties are devolved upon all, the disposition of the agents and the manner of their contact with the Indians have much to do with their condition and welfare.   The agent who perfunctorily performs his duty and slothfully neglects all opportunity to advance their moral and physical improvement and fails to inspire them with a desire for better things will accomplish nothing in the direction of their civilization, while he who feels the burden of an important trust and has an interest in his work will, by consistent example, firm yet considerate treatment, and well-directed aid and encouragement, constantly lead those under his charge toward the light of their enfranchisement.

The history of all the progress which has been made in the civilization of the Indian I think will disclose the fact that the beginning has been religious teaching, followed by or accompanying secular education. While the self-sacrificing and pious men and women who have aided in this good work by their independent endeavor have for their reward the beneficent results of their labor and the consciousness of Christian duty well performed, their valuable services should be fully acknowledged by all who under the law are charged with the control and management of our Indian wards.

What has been said indicates that in the present condition of the

Indians no attempt should be made to apply a fixed and unyielding plan of action to their varied and varying needs and circumstances.

The Indian Bureau, burdened as it is with their general oversight and with the details of the establishment, can hardly possess itself of the minute phases of the particular cases needing treatment; and thus the propriety of creating an instrumentality auxiliary to those already established for the care of the Indians suggests itself.

I recommend the passage of a law authorizing the appointment of six commissioners, three of whom shall be detailed from the Army, to be charged with the duty of a careful inspection from time to time of all the Indians upon our reservations or subject to the care and control of the Government, with a view of discovering their exact condition and needs and determining what steps shall be taken on behalf of the Government to improve their situation in the direction of their self-support and complete civilization; that they ascertain from such inspection what, if any, of the reservations may be reduced in area, and in such cases what part not needed for Indian occupation may be purchased by the Government from the Indians and disposed of for their benefit; what, if any, Indians may, with their consent, be removed to other reservations, with a view of their concentration and the sale on their behalf of their abandoned reservations; what Indian lands now held in common should be allotted in severalty; in what manner and to what extent the Indians upon the reservations can be placed under the protection of our laws and subjected to their penalties, and which, if any, Indians should be invested with the right of citizenship. The powers and functions of the commissioners in regard to these subjects should be clearly defined, though they should, in conjunction with the Secretary of the Interior, be given all the authority to deal definitely with the questions presented deemed safe and consistent.

They should be also charged with the duty of ascertaining the Indians who might properly be furnished with implements of agriculture, and of what kind; in what cases the support of the Government should be withdrawn; where the present plan of distributing Indian supplies should be changed; where schools may be established and where discontinned; the conduct, methods, and fitness of agents in charge of reservations; the extent to which such reservations are occupied or intruded upon by unauthorized persons, and generally all matters related to the welfare and improvement of the Indian.

They should advise with the Secretary of the Interior concerning these matters of detail in management, and he should be given power to deal with them fully, if he is not now invested with such power.

This plan contemplates the selection of persons for commissioners who are interested in the Indian question and who have practical ideas upon the subject of their treatment.

The expense of the Indian Bureau during the last fiscal year was more than six and a half million dollars. I believe much of this expenditure might be saved under the plan proposed; that its economical effects would be increased with its continuance; that the safety of our frontier settlers would be subserved under its operation, and that the nation would be saved through its results from the imputation of inhumanity, injustice, and mismanagement.

In order to carry out the policy of allotment of Indian lands in severalty, when deemed expedient, it will be necessary to have surveys completed of the reservations, and I hope that provision will be made for the prosecution of this work.

In May of the present year a small portion of the Chiricahua Apaches on the White Mountain Reservation, in Arizona, left the reservation and committed a number of murders and depredations upon settlers in that neighborhood. Though prompt and energetic action was taken by the military, the renegades eluded capture and escaped into Mexico. The formation of the country through which these Indians passed, their thorough acquaintance with the same, the speed of their escape, and the manner in which they scattered and concealed themselves among the mountains near the scene of their outrages put our soldiers at a great disadvantage in their efforts to capture them, though the expectation is still entertained that they will be ultimately taken and punished for their crimes.

The threatening and disorderly conduct of the Cheyennes in the Indian Territory early last summer caused considerable alarm and uneasiness. Investigation proved that their threatening attitude was due in a great measure to the occupation of the land of their reservation by immense herds of cattle, which their owners claimed were rightfully there under certain leases made by the Indians. Such occupation appearing upon examination to be unlawful notwithstanding these leases, the intruders were ordered to remove with their cattle from the lands of the Indians by Executive proclamation.* The enforcement of this proclamation had the effect of restoring peace and order among the Indians, and they are now quiet and well behaved.

By an Executive order issued on February 27, 1885, by my predecessor, a portion of the tract of country in the territory known as the Old Winnebago and Crow Creek reservations was directed to be restored to the public domain and opened to settlement under the land laws of the United States, and a large number of persons entered upon those lands. This action alarmed the Sioux Indians, who claimed the territory as belonging to their reservation under the treaty of 1868. This claim was determined, after careful investigation, to be well founded, and consequently the Executive order referred to was by proclamation of April 17, 1885,† declared to be inoperative and of no effect, and all persons upon the land were warned to leave. This warning has been substantially complied with.

*See pp. 224-225. †See pp. 305-307.

The public domain had its origin in cessions of land by the States to the General Government. The first cession was made by the State of New York, and the largest, which in area exceeded all the others, by the State of Virginia. The territory the proprietorship of which became thus vested in the General Government extended from the western line of Pennsylvania to the Mississippi River. These patriotic donations of the States were encumbered with no condition except that they should be held and used "for the common benefit of the United States." By purchase with the common fund of all the people additions were made to this domain until it extended to the northern line of Mexico, the Pacific Ocean, and the Polar Sea. The original trust, "for the common benefit of the United States," attached to all. In the execution of that trust the policy of many homes, rather than large estates, was adopted by the Government. That these might be easily obtained, and be the abode of security and contentment, the laws for their acquisition were few, easily understood, and general in their character. But the pressure of local interests, combined with a speculative spirit, have in many instances procured the passage of laws which marred the harmony of the general plan and encumbered the system with a multitude of general and special enactments which render the land laws complicated, subject the titles to uncertainty, and the purchasers often to oppression and wrong. Laws which were intended for the "common benefit" have been perverted so that large quantities of land are vesting in single ownerships. From the multitude and character of the laws, this consequence seems incapable of correction by mere administration.

It is not for the "common benefit of the United States" that a large area of the public lands should be acquired, directly or through fraud, in the hands of a single individual. The nation's strength is in the people. The nation's prosperity is in their prosperity. The nation's glory is in the equality of her justice. The nation's perpetuity is in the patriotism of all her people. Hence, as far as practicable, the plan adopted in the disposal of the public lands should have in view the original policy, which encouraged many purchasers of these lands for homes and discouraged the massing of large areas. Exclusive of Alaska, about three-fifths of the national domain has been sold or subjected to contract or grant. Of the remaining two-fifths a considerable portion is either mountain or desert. A rapidly increasing population creates a growing demand for homes, and the accumulation of wealth inspires an eager competition to obtain the public land for speculative purposes. In the future this collision of interests will be more marked than in the past, and the execution of the nation's trust in behalf of our settlers will be more difficult. I therefore commend to your attention the recommendations contained in the report of the Secretary of the Interior with reference to the repeal and modification of certain of our land laws.

The nation has made princely grants and subsidies to a system of railroads projected as great national highways to connect the Pacific States with the East.   It has been charged that these donations from the people have been diverted to private gain and corrupt uses, and thus public indignation has been aroused and suspicion engendered.   Our great nation does not begrudge its generosity, but it abhors peculation and fraud; and the favorable regard of our people for the great corporations to which these grants were made can only be revived by a restoration of confidence, to be secured by their constant, unequivocal, and clearly manifested integrity.   A faithful application of the undiminished proceeds of the grants to the construction and perfecting of their roads, an honest discharge of their obligations, and entire justice to all the people in the enjoyment of their rights on these highways of travel are all the public asks, and it will be content with no less.   To secure these things should be the common purpose of the officers of the Government, as well as of the corporations.   With this accomplishment prosperity would be permanently secured to the roads, and national pride would take the place of national complaint.

It appears from the report of the Commissioner of Pensions that there were on the 1st day of July, 1885, 345,125 persons borne upon the pension rolls, who were classified as follows: Army invalids, 241,456; widows, minor children, and dependent relatives of deceased soldiers, 78,841; navy invalids, 2,745; navy widows, minor children, and dependents, 1,926; survivors of the War of 1812, 2,945; and widows of those who served in that war, 17,212.   About one man in ten of all those who enlisted in the late war are reported as receiving pensions, exclusive of the dependents of deceased soldiers.   On the 1st of July, 1875, the number of pensioners was 234,821, and the increase within the ten years next thereafter was 110,304.

While there is no expenditure of the public funds which the people more cheerfully approve than that made in recognition of the services of our soldiers living and dead, the sentiment underlying the subject should not be vitiated by the introduction of any fraudulent practices.   Therefore it is fully as important that the rolls should be cleansed of all those who by fraud have secured a place thereon as that meritorious claims should be speedily examined and adjusted.   The reforms in the methods of doing the business of this Bureau which have lately been inaugurated promise better results in both these directions.

The operations of the Patent Office demonstrate the activity of the inventive genius of the country.   For the year ended June 30, 1885, the applications for patents, including reissues, and for the registration of trade-marks and labels, numbered 35,688.   During the same period there were 22,928 patents granted and reissued and 1,429 trade-marks and labels registered.   The number of patents issued in the year 1875 was 14,387.   The receipts during the last fiscal year were $1,074,974.35, and the total expenditures, not including contingent expenses, $934,123.11.

There were 9,788 applications for patents pending on the 1st day of July, 1884, and 5,786 on the same date in the year 1885. There has been considerable improvement made in the prompt determination of applications and a consequent relief to expectant inventors.

A number of suggestions and recommendations are contained in the report of the Commissioner of Patents which are well entitled to the consideration of Congress.

In the Territory of Utah the law of the United States passed for the suppression of polygamy has been energetically and faithfully executed during the past year, with measurably good results. A number of convictions have been secured for unlawful cohabitation, and in some cases pleas of guilty have been entered and a slight punishment imposed, upon a promise by the accused that they would not again offend against the law, nor advise, counsel, aid, or abet in any way its violation by others.

The Utah commissioners express the opinion, based upon such information as they are able to obtain, that but few polygamous marriages have taken place in the Territory during the last year. They further report that while there can not be found upon the registration lists of voters the name of a man actually guilty of polygamy, and while none of that class are holding office, yet at the last election in the Territory all the officers elected, except in one county, were men who, though not actually living in the practice of polygamy, subscribe to the doctrine of polygamous marriages as a divine revelation and a law unto all higher and more binding upon the conscience than any human law, local or national. Thus is the strange spectacle presented of a community protected by a republican form of government, to which they owe allegiance, sustaining by their suffrages a principle and a belief which set at naught that obligation of absolute obedience to the law of the land which lies at the foundation of republican institutions.

The strength, the perpetuity, and the destiny of the nation rest upon our homes, established by the law of God, guarded by parental care, regulated by parental authority, and sanctified by parental love.

These are not the homes of polygamy.

The mothers of our land, who rule the nation as they mold the characters and guide the actions of their sons, live according to God's holy ordinances, and each, secure and happy in the exclusive love of the father of her children, sheds the warm light of true womanhood, unperverted and unpolluted, upon all within her pure and wholesome family circle.

These are not the cheerless, crushed, and unwomanly mothers of polygamy.

The fathers of our families are the best citizens of the Republic. Wife and children are the sources of patriotism, and conjugal and parental affection beget devotion to the country. The man who, undefiled with plural marriage, is surrounded in his single home with his wife and children has a stake in the country which inspires him with respect for its laws and courage for its defense.

These are not the fathers of polygamous families.

There is no feature of this practice or the system which sanctions it which is not opposed to all that is of value in our institutions.

There should be no relaxation in the firm but just execution of the law now in operation, and I should be glad to approve such further discreet legislation as will rid the country of this blot upon its fair fame.

Since the people upholding polygamy in our Territories are reenforced by immigration from other lands, I recommend that a law be passed to prevent the importation of Mormons into the country.

The agricultural interest of the country demands just recognition and liberal encouragement. It sustains with certainty and unfailing strength our nation's prosperity by the products of its steady toil, and bears its full share of the burden of taxation without complaint. Our agriculturists have but slight personal representation in the councils of the nation, and are generally content with the humbler duties of citizenship and willing to trust to the bounty of nature for a reward of their labor. But the magnitude and value of this industry are appreciated when the statement is made that of our total annual exports more than three-fourths are the products of agriculture, and of our total population nearly one-half are exclusively engaged in that occupation.

The Department of Agriculture was created for the purpose of acquiring and diffusing among the people useful information respecting the subjects it has in charge, and aiding in the cause of intelligent and progressive farming, by the collection of statistics, by testing the value and usefulness of new seeds and plants, and distributing such as are found desirable among agriculturists. This and other powers and duties with which this Department is invested are of the utmost importance, and if wisely exercised must be of great benefit to the country. The aim of our beneficent Government is the improvement of the people in every station and the amelioration of their condition. Surely our agriculturists should not be neglected. The instrumentality established in aid of the farmers of the land should not only be well equipped for the accomplishment of its purpose, but those for whose benefit it has been adopted should be encouraged to avail themselves fully of its advantages.

The prohibition of the importation into several countries of certain of our animals and their products, based upon the suspicion that health is endangered in their use and consumption, suggests the importance of such precautions for the protection of our stock of all kinds against disease as will disarm suspicion of danger and cause the removal of such an injurious prohibition.

If the laws now in operation are insufficient to accomplish this protection, I recommend their amendment to meet the necessities of the situation; and I commend to the consideration of Congress the suggestions contained in the report of the Commissioner of Agriculture calculated to increase the value and efficiency of this Department.

The report of the Civil Service Commission, which will be submitted, contains an account of the manner in which the civil-service law has been executed during the last year and much valuable information on this important subject.

I am inclined to think that there is no sentiment more general in the minds of the people of our country than a conviction of the correctness of the principle upon which the law enforcing civil-service reform is based. In its present condition the law regulates only a part of the subordinate public positions throughout the country. It applies the test of fitness to applicants for these places by means of a competitive examination, and gives large discretion to the Commissioners as to the character of the examination and many other matters connected with its execution. Thus the rules and regulations adopted by the Commission have much to do with the practical usefulness of the statute and with the results of its application.

The people may well trust the Commission to execute the law with perfect fairness and with as little irritation as is possible. But of course no relaxation of the principle which underlies it and no weakening of the safeguards which surround it can be expected. Experience in its administration will probably suggest amendment of the methods of its execution, but I venture to hope that we shall never again be remitted to the system which distributes public positions purely as rewards for partisan service. Doubts may well be entertained whether our Government could survive the strain of a continuance of this system, which upon every change of Administration inspires an immense army of claimants for office to lay siege to the patronage of Government, engrossing the time of public officers with their importunities, spreading abroad the contagion of their disappointment, and filling the air with the tumult of their discontent.

The allurements of an immense number of offices and places exhibited to the voters of the land, and the promise of their bestowal in recognition of partisan activity, debauch the suffrage and rob political action of its thoughtful and deliberative character. The evil would increase with the multiplication of offices consequent upon our extension, and the mania for office holding, growing from its indulgence, would pervade our population so generally that patriotic purpose, the support of principle, the desire for the public good, and solicitude for the nation's welfare would be nearly banished from the activity of our party contests and cause them to degenerate into ignoble, selfish, and disgraceful struggles for the possession of office and public place.

Civil-service reform enforced by law came none too soon to check the progress of demoralization.

One of its effects, not enough regarded, is the freedom it brings to the

political action of those conservative and sober men who, in fear of the confusion and risk attending an arbitrary and sudden change in all the public
offices with a change of party rule, cast their ballots against such a chance.

Parties seem to be necessary, and will long continue to exist; nor can
it be now denied that there are legitimate advantages, not disconnected
with office holding, which follow party supremacy. While partisanship
continues bitter and pronounced and supplies so much of motive to
sentiment and action, it is not fair to hold public officials in charge
of important trusts responsible for the best results in the performance of
their duties, and yet insist that they shall rely in confidential and important places upon the work of those not only opposed to them in political
affiliation, but so steeped in partisan prejudice and rancor that they have
no loyalty to their chiefs and no desire for their success. Civil-service
reform does not exact this, nor does it require that those in subordinate
positions who fail in yielding their best service or who are incompetent
should be retained simply because they are in place. The whining of a
clerk discharged for indolence or incompetency, who, though he gained
his place by the worst possible operation of the spoils system, suddenly
discovers that he is entitled to protection under the sanction of civil-
service reform, represents an idea no less absurd than the clamor of the
applicant who claims the vacant position as his compensation for the most
questionable party work.

The civil-service law does not prevent the discharge of the indolent or
incompetent clerk, but it does prevent supplying his place with the unfit
party worker. Thus in both these phases is seen benefit to the public
service. And the people who desire good government, having secured
this statute, will not relinquish its benefits without protest. Nor are
they unmindful of the fact that its full advantages can only be gained
through the complete good faith of those having its execution in charge.
And this they will insist upon.

I recommend that the salaries of the Civil Service Commissioners be
increased to a sum more nearly commensurate to their important duties.

It is a source of considerable and not unnatural discontent that no
adequate provision has yet been made for accommodating the principal
library of the Government. Of the vast collection of books and pam-
phlets gathered at the Capitol, numbering some 700,000, exclusive of
manuscripts, maps, and the products of the graphic arts, also of great
volume and value, only about 300,000 volumes, or less than half the
collection, are provided with shelf room. The others, which are increasing at the rate of from twenty-five to thirty thousand volumes a year, are
not only inaccessible to the public, but are subject to serious damage and
deterioration from other causes in their present situation.

A consideration of the facts that the library of the Capitol has twice
been destroyed or damaged by fire, its daily increasing value, and its
importance as a place of deposit of books under the law relating to copy-

right makes manifest the necessity of prompt action to insure its proper accommodation and protection.

My attention has been called to a controversy which has arisen from the condition of the law relating to railroad facilities in the city of Washington, which has involved the Commissioners of the District in much annoyance and trouble. I hope this difficulty will be promptly settled by appropriate legislation.

The Commissioners represent that enough of the revenues of the District are now on deposit in the Treasury of the United States to repay the sum advanced by the Government for sewer improvements under the act of June 30, 1884. They desire now an advance of the share which ultimately should be borne by the District of the cost of extensive improvements to the streets of the city. The total expense of these contemplated improvements is estimated at $1,000,000, and they are of the opinion that a considerable sum could be saved if they had all the money in hand, so that contracts for the whole work could be made at the same time. They express confidence that if the advance asked for should be made the Government would be reimbursed the same within a reasonable time. I have no doubt that these improvements could be made much cheaper if undertaken together and prosecuted according to a general plan.

The license law now in force within the District is deficient and uncertain in some of its provisions and ought to be amended. The Commissioners urge, with good reason, the necessity of providing a building for the use of the District government which shall better secure the safety and preservation of its valuable books and records.

The present condition of the law relating to the succession to the Presidency in the event of the death, disability, or removal of both the President and Vice-President is such as to require immediate amendment. This subject has repeatedly been considered by Congress, but no result has been reached. The recent lamentable death of the Vice-President, and vacancies at the same time in all other offices the incumbents of which might immediately exercise the functions of the Presidential office, has caused public anxiety and a just demand that a recurrence of such a condition of affairs should not be permitted.

In conclusion I commend to the wise care and thoughtful attention of Congress the needs, the welfare, and the aspirations of an intelligent and generous nation. To subordinate these to the narrow advantages of partisanship or the accomplishment of selfish aims is to violate the people's trust and betray the people's interests; but an individual sense of responsibility on the part of each of us and a stern determination to perform our duty well must give us place among those who have added in their day and generation to the glory and prosperity of our beloved land.

GROVER CLEVELAND.

SPECIAL MESSAGES.

EXECUTIVE MANSION,
Washington, December 14, 1885.

To the Senate of the United States:

In response to the resolution of the Senate of the 9th instant, calling for the correspondence on file in relation to the appointment of Mr. A. M. Keiley as envoy extraordinary and minister plenipotentiary, first to the Government of Italy and then to that of Austria-Hungary, I transmit herewith a report from the Secretary of State, with accompanying papers.

GROVER CLEVELAND.

EXECUTIVE MANSION, *December 14, 1885.*

To the Senate and House of Representatives:

I transmit herewith a communication of 10th instant from the Secretary of the Interior, inclosing a report from the Commissioner of Indian Affairs upon the subject of the condition of the Northern Cheyenne Indians upon the Rosebud and Tongue rivers, in Montana, the inadequacy of the appropriation made for their support during the current fiscal year, and requesting legislative authority for the use of certain funds indicated for their relief.

The proposed legislation does not involve any additional appropriation, and the necessity for the authority requested is urgent. I therefore recommend the matter to the early and favorable consideration and action of Congress.

GROVER CLEVELAND.

EXECUTIVE MANSION,
Washington, December 14, 1885.

To the Senate of the United States:

I transmit to the Senate, for its consideration with a view to ratification, a convention between the United States and Venezuela for the reopening of the claims of citizens of the United States against that Government under the treaty of April 25, 1866, signed on the 5th instant

GROVER CLEVELAND.

EXECUTIVE MANSION,
Washington, December 14, 1885.

To the Senate:

I transmit, for the consideration of the Senate with a view to ratification, an additional article, signed the 5th instant, extending for a period of eighteen months from the date of the exchange of ratifications of the same the provisions of Article VIII of the convention of July 29, 1882, between the United States and Mexico, in regard to the resurvey of the boundary line, a copy of which convention is herewith inclosed.

GROVER CLEVELAND.

EXECUTIVE MANSION,
Washington, December 21, 1885.
To the Senate of the United States:

I nominate James P. Kimball, of Pennsylvania, to be Director of the Mint, in place of Horatio C. Burchard, removed; and the reasons for such removal are herewith communicated to the Senate, pursuant to the statute in such case made and provided. GROVER CLEVELAND.

EXECUTIVE MANSION, *December 21, 1885.*
To the Senate of the United States:

In the matter of the removal of Horatio C. ⎱
   Burchard as Director of the Mint. ⎰

In conformity to section 343 of the Revised Statutes of the United States, the following is respectfully communicated to the Senate as reasons of the removal above referred to:

The Director of the Mint is the head of one of the most important of the bureaus of the Treasury Department, to which are attached duties of a highly technical and varied nature.

By the express terms of the law creating the office the incumbent is "under the direction of the Secretary of the Treasury."

This last-named officer, under whose direction M.. Burchard was thus placed, reported to me that his mode of conducting the business of the office was unsatisfactory and inefficient and that the public interest required a change.

And therefore I removed Mr. Burchard and appointed Mr. Kimball in his place, believing him to possess especial qualifications for the proper administration of the important duties involved.

GROVER CLEVELAND.

EXECUTIVE MANSION, *December 21, 1885.*
To the Senate and House of Representatives:

I transmit herewith a communication of the 17th instant from the Secretary of the Interior, submitting, with accompanying papers, a draft of a bill granting a right of way to the Jamestown and Northern Railroad Company through the Devils Lake Indian Reservation, in the Territory of Dakota.

The matter is presented for the consideration and action of Congress.

GROVER CLEVELAND.

EXECUTIVE MANSION, *December 21, 1885.*

To the Senate and House of Representatives:

I transmit herewith a communication of the 15th instant from the Secretary of the Interior, submitting, with accompanying papers upon the subject, a draft of a bill to amend section 2148 of the Revised Statutes of the United States, relating to trespasses upon Indian lands.

The subject is one of great importance, and is commended to the early and favorable action of Congress.   GROVER CLEVELAND.

EXECUTIVE MANSION, *December 21, 1885.*

To the Senate and House of Representatives:

I transmit herewith a report, together with accompanying documents, made to me by the board of management of the World's Industrial and Cotton Centennial Exposition, held at New Orleans from December 16, 1884, to May 31, 1885.   GROVER CLEVELAND.

EXECUTIVE MANSION, *December 21, 1885.*

To the Senate and House of Representatives:

I transmit herewith a communication of the 17th instant from the Secretary of the Interior, submitting, with accompanying papers, a draft of a bill to accept and ratify an agreement made by the Pi-Ute Indians, and granting a right of way to the Carson and Colorado Railroad Company through the Walker River Reservation, in Nevada.

The matter is presented for the consideration and action of Congress.

GROVER CLEVELAND.

EXECUTIVE MANSION, *December 21, 1885.*

To the Senate and House of Representatives:

I transmit herewith a communication of the 17th instant from the Secretary of the Interior, submitting, with accompanying papers, a report of the Commissioner of Indian Affairs concerning the failure of the Utah and Northern Railroad Company to compensate the Indians upon the Fort Hall Reservation, in Idaho, for lands taken and used in construction of their line of road crossing the reservation from north to south.

The subject is recommended to the early attention and action of Congress.   GROVER CLEVELAND.

EXECUTIVE MANSION, *December 21, 1885.*

Senate and House of Representatives:

ısmit herewith a communication of the 15th instant from the Secof the Interior, submitting, with accompanying papers upon the subject, a draft of a bill "to provide for the settlement of the estates of deceased Kickapoo Indians in the State of Kansas, and for other purposes."

The matter is presented for the favorable consideration of Congress.

GROVER CLEVELAND.

EXECUTIVE MANSION, *December 21, 1885.*

To the Senate and House of Representatives:

I transmit herewith a communication of the 15th instant from the Secretary of the Interior, submitting, with accompanying papers upon the subject, a draft of a bill for the relief of the Mission Indians in California.

The subject is presented for the action of Congress.

GROVER CLEVELAND.

EXECUTIVE MANSION, *December 21, 1885.*

To the Senate and House of Representatives:

I transmit herewith a communication of the 17th instant from the Secretary of the Interior, submitting, with accompanying papers, a draft of a bill to accept and ratify an agreement made by the Sisseton and Wahpeton Indians, and to grant a right of way for the Chicago, Milwaukee and St. Paul Railway through the Lake Traverse Reservation, in Dakota.

The subject is presented for the consideration and action of Congress.

GROVER CLEVELAND.

EXECUTIVE MANSION, *December 21, 1885.*

To the Senate and House of Representatives:

I transmit herewith a communication of the 15th instant from the Secretary of the Interior, submitting, with accompanying papers on the subject, a draft of a bill to amend section 5388 of the Revised Statutes of the United States, relating to timber depredations upon lands reserved or purchased for military, Indian, or other purposes, etc.

This is an important subject, and is commended to the early attention of Congress.

GROVER CLEVELAND.

EXECUTIVE MANSION, *December 21, 1885.*

To the Senate and House of Representatives:

I transmit herewith a communication of the 15th instant from the Secretary of the Interior, submitting, with accompanying papers, a draft of a bill to accept and ratify an agreement made with the confederated tribes and bands of Indians occupying the Yakima Reservation, in Washington

Territory, for the right of way of the Northern Pacific Railroad across said reservation, etc.

The matter is presented for the consideration and action of Congress.

GROVER CLEVELAND.

EXECUTIVE MANSION, *January 5, 1886.*
To the Senate and House of Representatives:

I transmit herewith a communication of the 19th ultimo from the Secretary of the Interior, submitting, with accompanying papers in relation thereto, a draft of a bill "to provide for allotments of lands in severalty to the Indians residing upon the Round Valley Reservation, in the State of California, and granting patents therefor, and for other purposes."

The matter is presented for the early consideration and action of Congress.

GROVER CLEVELAND.

To the Senate: EXECUTIVE MANSION, *January 7, 1886.*

I transmit herewith, in response to a resolution of the Senate of the 9th ultimo, a report of the Secretary of State, in answer to the request for any documents or information received from our consul-general at Paris or from the special agent sent to the financial centers of Europe in respect to the establishment of an international ratio of gold and silver coinage as would procure the free coinage of both metals at the mints of those countries and our own.

GROVER CLEVELAND.

EXECUTIVE MANSION, *January 12, 1886.*
To the Senate and House of Representatives:

In continuation of the message of my predecessor of the 13th of February last, I now transmit herewith a letter from the Secretary of State, which is accompanied by the final report of the commissioners appointed under the act of July 7, 1884, to visit the States of Central and South America.

GROVER CLEVELAND.

EXECUTIVE MANSION, *January 12, 1886.*
To the Senate and House of Representatives:

I transmit herewith a communication of the 2d instant from the Secretary of the Interior, submitting, with accompanying papers, a draft of a bill to amend section 9 of the act of March 3, 1885, relating to the trial and punishment of Indians committing certain specified crimes.

The subject is presented for the consideration and action of Congress.

GROVER CLEVELAND.

To the Senate: EXECUTIVE MANSION, *January 12, 1886.*

I transmit herewith a report of the Secretary of State, in response to a resolution of the Senate of the 14th ultimo, requesting a copy of "any report of an actual instrumental survey of a line for a ship railroad across the Isthmus of Tehuantepec and any map of the same that has been made to or placed on file in any of the Executive Departments, and of any canal or canals designed to connect such ship railway with the Gulf of Mexico or the Pacific Ocean."

GROVER CLEVELAND.

EXECUTIVE MANSION, *January 12, 1886.*

To the Senate of the United States:

I transmit herewith a communication from the Secretary of State, accompanied by a report of Hon. James O. Broadhead and Somerville P. Tuck, appointed to carry out certain of the provisions of section 5 of an act entitled "An act to provide for the ascertainment of claims of American citizens for spoliations committed by the French prior to the 31st day of July, 1801," approved January 20, 1885.

GROVER CLEVELAND.

To the Senate: EXECUTIVE MANSION, *January 12, 1886.*

I transmit herewith, in response to a resolution of the Senate of the 5th instant, a report of the Secretary of State, containing all the correspondence and information in the custody of his Department relative to the extension of certain fishing rights and privileges under the treaty of Washington from July 1, 1885, to January 1, 1886.

GROVER CLEVELAND.

EXECUTIVE MANSION, *January 25, 1886.*

To the Senate and House of Representatives:

I transmit herewith a letter from the Secretary of State, which is accompanied by the report of the United States Electrical Commission of the proceedings of the National Conference of Electricians held at the city of Philadelphia in the month of September, 1884.

GROVER CLEVELAND.

EXECUTIVE MANSION, *January 25, 1886.*

To the Senate and House of Representatives:

I transmit herewith a communication of the 16th instant from the Secretary of the Interior, submitting, with accompanying papers, a draft of proposed legislation providing for negotiations with the various tribes and bands of Chippewa Indians in the State of Minnesota, with a view to the improvement of their present condition.

It is requested that the matter may have early attention, consideration, and action by Congress.

GROVER CLEVELAND.

EXECUTIVE MANSION, *January 28, 1886.*
To the Senate:

In continuing accord with the Senate resolution of December 9, 1885, I transmit herewith a letter from the Secretary of State, accompanied by information received from the United States minister to Belgium in relation to the action of the Belgian Government in concluding its adhesion to the monetary convention of the States comprising the "Latin Union."

GROVER CLEVELAND.

EXECUTIVE MANSION, *January 28, 1886.*
To the Senate and House of Representatives:

I transmit herewith a communication of 25th instant from the Secretary of the Interior, submitting, with accompanying papers, the draft of a proposed amendment to the first section of the act ratifying an agreement with the Crow Indians in Montana, approved April 11, 1882, requested by said Indians, for the purpose of increasing the amount of the annual payments under said agreement and reducing the number thereof, in order that sufficient means may be provided for establishing them on their individual allotments.

The matter is presented for the consideration and action of Congress.

GROVER CLEVELAND.

EXECUTIVE MANSION,
Washington, February 4, 1886.
To the Senate:

By its resolution in executive session of March 18, 1885, the Senate advised and consented to the ratification of the convention concluded November 12, 1884, between the United States of America and the United States of Mexico, touching the boundary line between the two countries where it follows the bed of the Rio Grande and the Rio Gila.

The ratifications could not, however, be exchanged between the two contracting parties and the convention proclaimed until after it had received the constitutional sanction of the Government of Mexico, whose Congress but recently convened.

In a note to the Secretary of State of December 26, 1885, Mr. Matias Romero, the minister of Mexico here, advises him of a decree issued by the Mexican Senate in its session of December 11 last, approving, with certain modifications, the convention in question:

"The modifications made in the said treaty by the Mexican Senate are not essential," says Mr. Romero, "since they consist mainly in the rectification of the mistake made when the Gila River was mentioned as a part of the boundary line, the Colorado River being omitted, and in the correction of an error in the Spanish translation."

That the Senate may have the matter fully before it, I herewith transmit a copy of Mr. Romero's note of December 26, 1885, with its inclosure, and return the convention in the original for such further consideration and direction as the Senate in its constitutional prerogative may deem necessary and proper.   GROVER CLEVELAND.

EXECUTIVE MANSION, *February 4, 1886.*

The PRESIDENT OF THE SENATE PRO TEMPORE.

SIR: In response to the Senate resolution dated January 5, 1886—

That the Secretary of the Interior be, and hereby is, directed to communicate to the Senate a copy of each report made by the Government directors of the Union Pacific Railroad Company from date of first appointment of such directors to the present time—

I transmit herewith a communication from the Secretary of the Interior, dated the 2d instant, with the copies required.

GROVER CLEVELAND.

EXECUTIVE MANSION, *February 4, 1886.*

The SPEAKER OF THE HOUSE OF REPRESENTATIVES.   •

SIR: In response to House resolution of January 27, 1886—

That the Secretary of the Interior be, and is hereby, requested to furnish this House with copies of any and all contracts or leases which are to be found on file in said Department between the Southern Pacific Company and any and every railroad or railroads to which land grants were made, or which received any subsidies from the United States; also a copy of the charter of incorporation of the Southern Pacific Company; also all and every contract or contracts on file between the Pacific Steamship Company and any and every land grant or subsidized railroad company or companies—

I transmit herewith a communication from the Secretary of the Interior, dated the 2d instant, inclosing the copies required.

GROVER CLEVELAND.

EXECUTIVE MANSION, *February 4, 1886.*

To the Senate and House of Representatives:

I transmit herewith a communication of 3d instant from the Secretary of the Interior, submitting, with accompanying papers, a draft of a bill authorizing the use of certain funds belonging to the Miami Indians in

Indian Territory, proceeds of sales of their lands, for the purpose of relieving their present pressing necessities.

The matter is presented for the consideration and action of Congress.

GROVER CLEVELAND.

EXECUTIVE MANSION, *February 8, 1886.*

To the Senate and House of Representatives:

I transmit herewith a letter from the Secretary of the Interior, dated 5th instant, inclosing the recommendation of the Commissioner of Indian Affairs for the insertion in the act making appropriations for the current and contingent expenses of the Indian Department for the year ending June 30, 1887, of an item providing for an agent for the Winnebago Indians in Wisconsin, at a salary of $1,500 per annum.

The matter is respectfully submitted for the consideration and action of Congress.

GROVER CLEVELAND.

EXECUTIVE MANSION, *February 8, 1886.*

The PRESIDENT OF THE SENATE PRO TEMPORE.

SIR: In response to Senate resolution of January 7, 1886—

That the Secretary of the Interior be, and hereby is, directed to communicate to the Senate whether any surveys of the public lands have been made within the last two years in the State of Nebraska; whether there are any unsurveyed public lands within said State; also what recommendations have been made within the last three years by the surveyors-general of said district as to the discontinuance of said office, and whether it is advisable that the office of surveyor-general of said district should cease and be discontinued under the provisions of section 2218 of the Revised Statutes of the United States—

I transmit herewith a communication from the Secretary of the Interior, dated the 3d instant, inclosing the information desired.

GROVER CLEVELAND.

EXECUTIVE MANSION, *February 15, 1886.*

To the Senate and House of Representatives:

I transmit herewith, for the consideration of Congress, a communication, under date of the 9th instant, from the Secretary of the Interior, and the accompanying last annual report of the Government directors of the Union Pacific Railway Company.

GROVER CLEVELAND.

EXECUTIVE MANSION, *February 15, 1886.*

To the Senate and House of Representatives:

I transmit herewith a communication of the 12th instant from the Secretary of the Interior, submitting, with accompanying papers, the draft of a bill prepared by the Commissioner of Indian Affairs to amend the third section of the act of March 3, 1885, "to provide for the sale of the Sac and Fox and Iowa Indian reservations in the States of Nebraska and Kansas, and for other purposes."

The matter is presented for the consideration and action of Congress.

GROVER CLEVELAND.

EXECUTIVE MANSION, *February 16, 1886.*

To the Senate of the United States:

I transmit herewith, in response to a resolution of the Senate of the 9th instant, a statement showing the payments of awards of the commissioners appointed under the conventions between the United States and France concluded April 30, 1803, and July 4, 1831, and between the United States and Spain concluded February 22, 1819, prepared from the books in the Department of the Treasury, under the direction of the Secretary of the Treasury, at the request of the Secretary of State.

Also, for the further information of the Senate, a report prepared by direction of the Secretary of State, from the original records in his custody, of the awards made by the said commissioners in claims allowed by them.

GROVER CLEVELAND.

EXECUTIVE MANSION,
Washington, D. C., March 1, 1886.

To the Senate of the United States:

Ever since the beginning of the present session of the Senate the different heads of the Departments attached to the executive branch of the Government have been plied with various requests and demands from committees of the Senate, from members of such committees, and at last from the Senate itself, requiring the transmission of reasons for the suspension of certain officials during the recess of that body, or for the papers touching the conduct of such officials, or for all papers and documents relating to such suspensions, or for all documents and papers filed in such Departments in relation to the management and conduct of the offices held by such suspended officials.

The different terms from time to time adopted in making these requests and demands, the order in which they succeeded each other, and the fact that when made by the Senate the resolution for that purpose was passed in executive session have led to the presumption, the correctness of which will, I suppose, be candidly admitted, that from first to last the information thus sought and the papers thus demanded were desired for use by the Senate and its committees in considering the propriety of the suspensions referred to.

Though these suspensions are my executive acts, based upon considerations addressed to me alone and for which I am wholly responsible, I have had no invitation from the Senate to state the position which I have felt constrained to assume in relation to the same or to interpret for myself my acts and motives in the premises.

In this condition of affairs I have forborne addressing the Senate upon the subject, lest I might be accused of thrusting myself unbidden upon the attention of that body.

But the report of the Committee on the Judiciary of the Senate lately presented and published, which censures the Attorney-General of the United States for his refusal to transmit certain papers relating to a suspension from office, and which also, if I correctly interpret it, evinces a misapprehension of the position of the Executive upon the question of such suspensions, will, I hope, justify this communication.

This report is predicated upon a resolution of the Senate directed to the Attorney-General and his reply to the same. This resolution was adopted in executive session devoted entirely to business connected with the consideration of nominations for office. It required the Attorney-General ''to transmit to the Senate copies of all documents and papers that have been filed in the Department of Justice since the 1st day of January, 1885, in relation to the management and conduct of the office of district attorney of the United States for the southern district of Alabama.''

The incumbent of this office on the 1st day of January, 1885, and until the 17th day of July ensuing, was George M. Duskin, who on the day last mentioned was suspended by an Executive order, and John D. Burnett designated to perform the duties of said office. At the time of the passage of the resolution above referred to the nomination of Burnett for said office was pending before the Senate, and all the papers relating to said nomination were before that body for its inspection and information.

In reply to this resolution the Attorney-General, after referring to the fact that the papers relating to the nomination of Burnett had already been sent to the Senate, stated that he was directed by the President to say that—

The papers and documents which are mentioned in said resolution and still remaining in the custody of this Department, having exclusive reference to the suspension by the President of George M. Duskin, the late incumbent of the office of district attorney for the southern district of Alabama, it is not considered that the public interests will be promoted by a compliance with said resolution and the transmission of the papers and documents therein mentioned to the Senate in executive session.

Upon this resolution and the answer thereto the issue is thus stated by the Committee on the Judiciary at the outset of the report:

The important question, then, is whether it is within the constitutional competence of either House of Congress to have access to the official papers and documents in the various public offices of the United States created by laws enacted by themselves.

I do not suppose that "the public offices of the United States" are regulated or controlled in their relations to either House of Congress by the fact that they were "created by laws enacted by themselves." It must be that these instrumentalities were created for the benefit of the people and to answer the general purposes of government under the Constitution and the laws, and that they are unencumbered by any lien in favor of either branch of Congress growing out of their construction, and unembarrassed by any obligation to the Senate as the price of their creation.

The complaint of the committee that access to official papers in the public offices is denied the Senate is met by the statement that at no time has it been the disposition or the intention of the President or any Department of the executive branch of the Government to withhold from the Senate official documents or papers filed in any of the public offices. While it is by no means conceded that the Senate has the right in any case to review the act of the Executive in removing or suspending a public officer, upon official documents or otherwise, it is considered that documents and papers of that nature should, because they are official, be freely transmitted to the Senate upon its demand, trusting the use of the same for proper and legitimate purposes to the good faith of that body; and though no such paper or document has been specifically demanded in any of the numerous requests and demands made upon the Departments, yet as often as they were found in the public offices they have been furnished in answer to such applications.

· The letter of the Attorney-General in response to the resolution of the Senate in the particular case mentioned in the committee's report was written at my suggestion and by my direction. There had been no official papers or documents filed in his Department relating to the case within the period specified in the resolution. The letter was intended, by its description of the papers and documents remaining in the custody of the Department, to convey the idea that they were not official; and it was assumed that the resolution called for information, papers, and documents of the same character as were required by the requests and demands which preceded it.

Everything that had been written or done on behalf of the Senate from the beginning pointed to all letters and papers of a private and unofficial nature as the objects of search, if they were to be found in the Departments, and provided they had been presented to the Executive with a view to their consideration upon the question of suspension from office.

Against the transmission of such papers and documents I have interposed my advice and direction. This has not been done, as is suggested in the committee's report, upon the assumption on my part that the Attorney-General or any other head of a Department "is the servant of the President, and is to give or withhold copies of documents in his office according to the will of the Executive and not otherwise," but because I regard the papers and documents withheld and addressed to me or intended for my use and action purely unofficial and private, not infrequently confidential, and having reference to the performance of a duty exclusively mine. I consider them in no proper sense as upon the files of the Department, but as deposited there for my convenience, remaining still completely under my control. I suppose if I desired to take them into my custody I might do so with entire propriety, and if I saw fit to destroy them no one could complain.

Even the committee in its report appears to concede that there may be with the President or in the Departments papers and documents which, on account of their unofficial character, are not subject to the inspection of the Congress. A reference in the report to instances where the House of Representatives ought not to succeed in a call for the production of papers is immediately followed by this statement:

The committee feels authorized to state, after a somewhat careful research, that within the foregoing limits there is scarcely in the history of this Government, until now, any instance of a refusal by a head of a Department, or even of the President himself, to communicate official facts and information, as distinguished from private and unofficial papers, motions, views, reasons, and opinions, to either House of Congress when unconditionally demanded.

To which of the classes thus recognized do the papers and documents belong that are now the objects of the Senate's quest?

They consist of letters and representations addressed to the Executive or intended for his inspection; they are voluntarily written and presented by private citizens who are not in the least instigated thereto by any official invitation or at all subject to official control. While some of them are entitled to Executive consideration, many of them are so irrelevant, or in the light of other facts so worthless, that they have not been given the least weight in determining the question to which they are supposed to relate.

Are all these, simply because they are preserved, to be considered official documents and subject to the inspection of the Senate? If not, who is to determine which belong to this class? Are the motives and purposes of the Senate, as they are day by day developed, such as would be satisfied with my selection? Am I to submit to theirs at the risk of being charged with making a suspension from office upon evidence which was not even considered?

Are these papers to be regarded official because they have not only been presented but preserved in the public offices?

Their nature and character remain the same whether they are kept in the Executive Mansion or deposited in the Departments. There is no mysterious power of transmutation in departmental custody, nor is there magic in the undefined and sacred solemnity of Department files. If the presence of these papers in the public offices is a stumbling block in the way of the performance of Senatorial duty, it can be easily removed.

The papers and documents which have been described derive no official character from any constitutional, statutory, or other requirement making them necessary to the performance of the official duty of the Executive.

It will not be denied, I suppose, that the President may suspend a public officer in the entire absence of any papers or documents to aid his official judgment and discretion; and I am quite prepared to avow that the cases are not few in which suspensions from office have depended more upon oral representations made to me by citizens of known good repute and by members of the House of Representatives and Senators of the United States than upon any letters and documents presented for my examination. I have not felt justified in suspecting the veracity, integrity, and patriotism of Senators, or ignoring their representations, because they were not in party affiliation with the majority of their associates; and I recall a few suspensions which bear the approval of individual members identified politically with the majority in the Senate.

While, therefore, I am constrained to deny the right of the Senate to the papers and documents described, so far as the right to the same is based upon the claim that they are in any view of the subject official, I am also led unequivocally to dispute the right of the Senate by the aid of any documents whatever, or in any way save through the judicial process of trial on impeachment, to review or reverse the acts of the Executive in the suspension, during the recess of the Senate, of Federal officials.

I believe the power to remove or suspend such officials is vested in the President alone by the Constitution, which in express terms provides that "the executive power shall be vested in a President of the United States of America," and that "he shall take care that the laws be faithfully executed."

The Senate belongs to the legislative branch of the Government. When the Constitution by express provision superadded to its legislative duties the right to advise and consent to appointments to office and to sit as a court of impeachment, it conferred upon that body all the control and regulation of Executive action supposed to be necessary for the safety of the people; and this express and special grant of such extraordinary powers, not in any way related to or growing out of general Senatorial duty, and in itself a departure from the general plan of our Government, should be held, under a familiar maxim of construction, to exclude every other right of interference with Executive functions.

In the first Congress which assembled after the adoption of the Constitution, comprising many who aided in its preparation, a legislative construction was given to that instrument in which the independence of the Executive in the matter of removals from office was fully sustained.

I think it will be found that in the subsequent discussions of this question there was generally, if not at all times, a proposition pending to in some way curtail this power of the President by legislation, which furnishes evidence that to limit such power it was supposed to be necessary to supplement the Constitution by such legislation.

The first enactment of this description was passed under a stress of partisanship and political bitterness which culminated in the President's impeachment.

This law provided that the Federal officers to which it applied could only be suspended during the recess of the Senate when shown by evidence satisfactory to the President to be guilty of misconduct in office, or crime, or when incapable or disqualified to perform their duties, and that within twenty days after the next meeting of the Senate it should be the duty of the President "to report to the Senate such suspension, with the evidence and reasons for his action in the case."

This statute, passed in 1867, when Congress was overwhelmingly and bitterly opposed politically to the President, may be regarded as an indication that even then it was thought necessary by a Congress determined upon the subjugation of the Executive to legislative will to furnish itself a law for that purpose, instead of attempting to reach the object intended by an invocation of any pretended constitutional right.

The law which thus found its way to our statute book was plain in its terms, and its intent needed no avowal. If valid and now in operation, it would justify the present course of the Senate and command the obedience of the Executive to its demands. It may, however, be remarked in passing that under this law the President had the privilege of presenting to the body which assumed to review his executive acts his reasons therefor, instead of being excluded from explanation or judged by papers found in the Departments.

Two years after the law of 1867 was passed, and within less than five weeks after the inauguration of a President in political accord with both branches of Congress, the sections of the act regulating suspensions from office during the recess of the Senate were entirely repealed, and in their place were substituted provisions which, instead of limiting the causes of suspension to misconduct, crime, disability, or disqualification, expressly permitted such suspension by the President "in his discretion," and completely abandoned the requirement obliging him to report to the Senate "the evidence and reasons" for his action.

With these modifications and with all branches of the Government in political harmony, and in the absence of partisan incentive to captions obstruction, the law as it was left by the amendment of 1869 was much less destructive of Executive discretion. And yet the great general and patriotic citizen who on the 4th day of March, 1869, assumed the duties of Chief Executive, and for whose freer administration of his high office the most hateful restraints of the law of 1867 were, on the 5th day of April, 1869, removed, mindful of his obligation to defend and protect every prerogative of his great trust, and apprehensive of the injury threatened the public service in the continued operation of these statutes

even in their modified form, in his first message to Congress advised
their repeal and set forth their unconstitutional character and hurtful
tendency in the following language:

It may be well to mention here the embarrassment possible to arise from leaving
on the statute books the so-called "tenure-of-office acts," and to earnestly recommend their total repeal. It could not have been the intention of the framers of
the Constitution, when providing that appointments made by the President should
receive the consent of the Senate, that the latter should have the power to retain in
office persons placed there by Federal appointment against the will of the President.
The law is inconsistent with a faithful and efficient administration of the Government. What faith can an Executive put in officials forced upon him, and those, too,
whom he has suspended for reason? How will such officials be likely to serve an
Administration which they know does not trust them?

I am unable to state whether or not this recommendation for a repeal
of these laws has been since repeated. If it has not, the reason can probably be found in the experience which demonstrated the fact that the
necessities of the political situation but rarely developed their vicious
character.

And so it happens that after an existence of nearly twenty years of
almost innocuous desuetude these laws are brought forth—apparently
the repealed as well as the unrepealed—and put in the way of an Executive who is willing, if permitted, to attempt an improvement in the
methods of administration.

The constitutionality of these laws is by no means admitted. But why
should the provisions of the repealed law, which required specific cause
for suspension and a report to the Senate of "evidence and reasons," be
now in effect applied to the present Executive, instead of the law, afterwards passed and unrepealed, which distinctly permits suspensions by the
President "in his discretion" and carefully omits the requirement that
"evidence and reasons for his action in the case" shall be reported to the
Senate.

The requests and demands which by the score have for nearly three
months been presented to the different Departments of the Government,
whatever may be their form, have but one complexion. They assume
the right of the Senate to sit in judgment upon the exercise of my exclusive discretion and Executive function, for which I am solely responsible
to the people from whom I have so lately received the sacred trust of
office. My oath to support and defend the Constitution, my duty to the
people who have chosen me to execute the powers of their great office
and not to relinquish them, and my duty to the Chief Magistracy, which
I must preserve unimpaired in all its dignity and vigor, compel me to
refuse compliance with these demands.

To the end that the service may be improved, the Senate is invited to
the fullest scrutiny of the persons submitted to them for public office, in
recognition of the constitutional power of that body to advise and consent to their appointment. I shall continue, as I have thus far done, to
furnish, at the request of the confirming body, all the information I possess

touching the fitness of the nominees placed before them for their action, both when they are proposed to fill vacancies and to take the place of suspended officials. Upon a refusal to confirm I shall not assume the right to ask the reasons for the action of the Senate nor question its determination. I can not think that anything more is required to secure worthy incumbents in public office than a careful and independent discharge of our respective duties within their well-defined limits.

Though the propriety of suspensions might be better assured if the action of the President was subject to review by the Senate, yet if the Constitution and the laws have placed this responsibility upon the executive branch of the Government it should not be divided nor the discretion which it involves relinquished.

It has been claimed that the present Executive having pledged himself not to remove officials except for cause, the fact of their suspension implies such misconduct on the part of a suspended official as injures his character and reputation, and therefore the Senate should review the case for his vindication.

I have said that certain officials should not, in my opinion, be removed during the continuance of the term for which they were appointed solely for the purpose of putting in their place those in political affiliation with the appointing power, and this declaration was immediately followed by a description of official partisanship which ought not to entitle those in whom it was exhibited to consideration. It is not apparent how an adherence to the course thus announced carries with it the consequences described. If in any degree the suggestion is worthy of consideration, it is to be hoped that there may be a defense against unjust suspension in the justice of the Executive.

Every pledge which I have made by which I have placed a limitation upon my exercise of executive power has been faithfully redeemed. Of course the pretense is not put forth that no mistakes have been committed; but not a suspension has been made except it appeared to my satisfaction that the public welfare would be improved thereby. Many applications for suspension have been denied, and the adherence to the rule laid down to govern my action as to such suspensions has caused much irritation and impatience on the part of those who have insisted upon more changes in the offices.

The pledges I have made were made to the people, and to them I am responsible for the manner in which they have been redeemed. I am not responsible to the Senate, and I am unwilling to submit my actions and official conduct to them for judgment.

There are no grounds for an allegation that the fear of being found false to my professions influences me in declining to submit to the demands of the Senate. I have not constantly refused to suspend officials, and thus incurred the displeasure of political friends, and yet willfully broken faith with the people for the sake of being false to them.

Neither the discontent of party friends, nor the allurements constantly offered of confirmations of appointees conditioned upon the avowal that suspensions have been made on party grounds alone, nor the threat proposed in the resolutions now before the Senate that no confirmations will be made unless the demands of that body be complied with, are sufficient to discourage or deter me from following in the way which I am convinced leads to better government for the people.

GROVER CLEVELAND.

EXECUTIVE MANSION, *March 1, 1886.*

To the Senate and House of Representatives:

It is made the constitutional duty of the President to recommend to the consideration of Congress from time to time such measures as he shall judge necessary and expedient. In no matters can the necessity of this be more evident than when the good faith of the United States under the solemn obligation of treaties with foreign powers is concerned.

The question of the treatment of the subjects of China sojourning within the jurisdiction of the United States presents such a matter for the urgent and earnest consideration of the Executive and the Congress.

In my first annual message, upon the assembling of the present Congress, I adverted to this question in the following words:

The harmony of our relations with China is fully sustained.

In the application of the acts lately passed to execute the treaty of 1880, restrictive of the immigration of Chinese laborers into the United States, individual cases of hardship have occurred beyond the power of the Executive to remedy, and calling for judicial determination.

The condition of the Chinese question in the Western States and Territories is, despite this restrictive legislation, far from being satisfactory. The recent outbreak in Wyoming Territory, where numbers of unoffending Chinamen, indisputably within the protection of the treaties and the law, were murdered by a mob, and the still more recent threatened outbreak of the same character in Washington Territory, are fresh in the minds of all, and there is apprehension lest the bitterness of feeling against the Mongolian race on the Pacific Slope may find vent in similar lawless demonstrations. All the power of this Government should be exerted to maintain the amplest good faith toward China in the treatment of these men, and the inflexible sternness of the law in bringing the wrongdoers to justice should be insisted upon.

Every effort has been made by this Government to prevent these violent outbreaks and to aid the representatives of China in their investigation of these outrages; and it is but just to say that they are traceable to the lawlessness of men not citizens of the United States engaged in competition with Chinese laborers.

Race prejudice is the chief factor in originating these disturbances, and it exists in a large part of our domain, jeopardizing our domestic peace and the good relationship we strive to maintain with China.

The admitted right of a government to prevent the influx of elements hostile to its internal peace and security may not be questioned, even where there is no treaty stipulation on the subject. That the exclusion of Chinese labor is demanded in other countries where like conditions prevail is strongly evidenced in the Dominion of Canada, where Chinese immigration is now regulated by laws more exclusive than our own. If existing laws are inadequate to compass the end in view, I shall be prepared to give earnest consideration to any further remedial measures, within the treaty limits, which the wisdom of Congress may devise.

At the time I wrote this the shocking occurrences at Rock Springs, in Wyoming Territory, were fresh in the minds of all, and had been recently presented anew to the attention of this Government by the Chinese minister in a note which, while not unnaturally exhibiting some misconception of our Federal system of administration in the Territories while they as yet are not in the exercise of the full measure of that sovereign self-government pertaining to the States of the Union, presents in truthful terms the main features of the cruel outrage there perpetrated upon inoffensive subjects of China. In the investigation of the Rock Springs outbreak and the ascertainment of the facts on which the Chinese minister's statements rest the Chinese representatives were aided by the agents of the United States, and the reports submitted, having been thus framed and recounting the facts within the knowledge of witnesses on both sides, possess an impartial truthfulness which could not fail to give them great impressiveness.

The facts, which so far are not controverted or affected by any exculpatory or mitigating testimony, show the murder of a number of Chinese subjects in September last at Rock Springs, the wounding of many others, and the spoliation of the property of all when the unhappy survivors had been driven from their habitations. There is no allegation that the victims by any lawless or disorderly act on their part contributed to bring about a collision; on the contrary, it appears that the law-abiding disposition of these people, who were sojourners in our midst under the sanction of hospitality and express treaty obligations, was made the pretext for an attack upon them. This outrage upon law and treaty engagements was committed by a lawless mob. None of the aggressors—happily for the national good fame—appear by the reports to have been citizens of the United States. They were aliens engaged in that remote district as mining laborers, who became excited against the Chinese laborers, as it would seem, because of their refusal to join them in a strike to secure higher wages. The oppression of Chinese subjects by their rivals in the competition for labor does not differ in violence and illegality from that applied to other classes of native or alien labor. All are equally under the protection of law and equally entitled to enjoy the benefits of assured public order.

Were there no treaty in existence referring to the rights of Chinese subjects; did they come hither as all other strangers who voluntarily resort to this land of freedom, of self-government, and of laws, here peaceably to win their bread and to live their lives, there can be no question that they would be entitled still to the same measure of protection from violence and the same free forum for the redress of their grievances as any other aliens.

So far as the treaties between the United States and China stipulate for the treatment of the Chinese subjects actually in the United States as the citizens or subjects of "the most favored nation" are treated, they create no new status for them; they simply recognize and confirm a general and existing rule, applicable to all aliens alike, for none are favored above others by domestic law, and none by foreign treaties unless it be the Chinese themselves in some respects. For by the third article of the treaty of November 17, 1880, between the United States and China it is provided that—

ART. III. If Chinese laborers, or Chinese of any other class, now either permanently or temporarily residing in the territory of the United States, meet with ill treatment at the hands of any other persons, the Government of the United States will exert all its power to devise measures for their protection and to secure to them the same rights, privileges, immunities, and exemptions as may be enjoyed by the citizens or subjects of the most favored nation, and to which they are entitled by treaty.

This article may be held to constitute a special privilege for Chinese subjects in the United States, as compared with other aliens; not that it creates any peculiar rights which others do not share, but because, in case of ill treatment of the Chinese in the United States, this Government is bound to "exert all its power to devise measures for their protection," by securing to them the rights to which equally with any and all other foreigners they are entitled.

Whether it is now incumbent upon the United States to amend their general laws or devise new measures in this regard I do not consider in the present communication, but confine myself to the particular point raised by the outrage and massacre at Rock Springs.

The note of the Chinese minister and the documents which accompany it give, as I believe, an unexaggerated statement of the lamentable incident, and present impressively the regrettable circumstance that the proceedings, in the name of justice, for the ascertainment of the crime and fixing the responsibility therefor were a ghastly mockery of justice. So long as the Chinese minister, under his instructions, makes this the basis of an appeal to the principles and convictions of mankind, no exception can be taken; but when he goes further, and, taking as his precedent the action of the Chinese Government in past instances where the lives of American citizens and their property in China have been endangered, argues a reciprocal obligation on the part of the United States to indemnify the Chinese subjects who suffered at Rock Springs, it became necessary to meet his argument and to deny most emphatically the conclusions he seeks to draw as to the existence of such a liability and the right of the Chinese Government to insist upon it.

I draw the attention of the Congress to the latter part of the note of the Secretary of State of February 18, 1886, in reply to the Chinese minister's representations, and invite especial consideration of the cogent reasons by which he reaches the conclusion that whilst the United States

Government is under no obligation, whether by the express terms of its treaties with China or the principles of international law, to indemnify these Chinese subjects for losses caused by such means and under the admitted circumstances; yet that in view of the palpable and discreditable failure of the authorities of Wyoming Territory to bring to justice the guilty parties or to assure to the sufferers an impartial forum in which to seek and obtain compensation for the losses which those subjects have incurred by lack of police protection, and considering further the entire absence of provocation or contribution on the part of the victims, the Executive may be induced to bring the matter to the benevolent consideration of the Congress, in order that that body in its high discretion may direct the bounty of the Government in aid of innocent and peaceful strangers whose maltreatment has brought discredit upon the country, with the distinct understanding that such action is in no wise to be held as a precedent, is wholly gratuitous, and is resorted to in a spirit of pure generosity toward those who are otherwise helpless.

The correspondence exchanged is herewith submitted for the information of the Congress, and accompanies a like message to the House of Representatives.

GROVER CLEVELAND.

EXECUTIVE MANSION, *June 2, 1886.*

To the Senate and House of Representatives:

I transmit herewith a communication of the 29th ultimo from the Secretary of the Interior, submitting, with accompanying papers, a draft of a bill, prepared in the Office of Indian Affairs for the purpose of securing to the Cherokees and others, citizens of the Cherokee Nation, by allotment and incorporation, a sum equal to their proportion of the $300,000 proceeds of lands west of 96° in the Indian Territory appropriated by the act of March 3, 1883.

The matter is presented for the consideration of Congress.

GROVER CLEVELAND.

EXECUTIVE MANSION, *June 2, 1886.*

To the Senate and House of Representatives:

I transmit herewith a communication of the 29th ultimo from the Secretary of the Interior, submitting, with accompanying papers, a draft of a bill recommended by the Commissioner of Indian Affairs for the payment of moneys claimed under alleged existing treaty stipulations and laws by such Eastern Cherokee Indians as have removed or shall hereafter remove themselves to the Indian Territory.

The matter is presented for the consideration of Congress.

GROVER CLEVELAND.

EXECUTIVE MANSION, *March 2, 1886.*

To the Senate and House of Representatives:

I transmit herewith a communication of 26th ultimo from the Secretary of the Interior, with inclosures, requesting legislation to provide for the reappraisement and sale of a small tract of land in the State of Nebraska belonging to the Sac and Fox Indian Reservation.

The matter is presented for the action of Congress.

GROVER CLEVELAND.

EXECUTIVE MANSION, *March 3, 1886.*

To the Senate and House of Representatives:

I transmit herewith, for the information of Congress, the seventeenth annual report of the Board of Indian Commissioners, for the year 1885, submitted to the Secretary of the Interior in pursuance of the act of May 17, 1882.

The report accompanies the message to the House of Representatives.

GROVER CLEVELAND.

EXECUTIVE MANSION, *March 10, 1886.*

To the Senate and House of Representatives:

I transmit herewith a communication of the 5th instant from the Secretary of the Interior, submitting, with accompanying papers, a draft of a bill, prepared in the Office of Indian Affairs, "for the relief of the Omaha tribe of Indians in the State of Nebraska."

The matter is presented for the consideration of Congress.

GROVER CLEVELAND.

EXECUTIVE MANSION, *March 10, 1886.*

To the Senate and House of Representatives:

I transmit herewith, for the consideration of Congress, the report of the National Board of Health for the year 1885.

GROVER CLEVELAND.

EXECUTIVE MANSION, *March 17, 1886.*

To the Senate of the United States:

I transmit herewith a communication from the Secretary of State, being a revised list of papers on file in the Department of State touching the unpaid claims of citizens of the United States against France for spoliation prior to July 31, 1881.

GROVER CLEVELAND.

EXECUTIVE MANSION, *March 17, 1886.*

To the Senate of the United States:

In response to the resolution of the Senate of the 17th of February, requesting to be furnished with a copy of the report made by the consul-general of the United States at Berlin upon the shipping interest of Germany, I transmit a report of the Secretary of State upon the subject.

GROVER CLEVELAND.

EXECUTIVE MANSION,
Washington, March 17, 1886.

To the Senate of the United States:

In compliance with the resolution of the Senate in executive session of the 27th of January, I transmit herewith the report of the Secretary of State and the papers accompanying it, relating to the emigration of Chinese to the United States.

GROVER CLEVELAND.

EXECUTIVE MANSION, *March 18, 1886.*

To the Senate and House of Representatives:

I transmit herewith a communication of 16th instant from the Secretary of the Interior, submitting, with accompanying papers, a draft of a bill, prepared by the Commissioner of Indian Affairs, providing for the use of certain funds, proceeds of Indian reservations, covered into the Treasury under the provisions of the act of March 3, 1883, for the benefit of the Indians on whose account the same is covered in.

The subject is recommended to the favorable consideration and action of Congress.

GROVER CLEVELAND.

EXECUTIVE MANSION, *March 18, 1886.*

To the Senate and House of Representatives:

I transmit herewith a communication of the 16th instant from the Secretary of the Interior, submitting, with accompanying papers, a draft of a bill, prepared by the Commissioner of Indian Affairs, ''to authorize the purchase of a tract of land near Salem, Oreg., for the use of the Indian training school.''

The subject is presented for the consideration and action of Congress.

GROVER CLEVELAND.

EXECUTIVE MANSION, *March 18, 1886.*

To the Senate:

In compliance with a resolution of the Senate of February 9, 1886, I herewith transmit a report from the Secretary of State, with its accom--

panying documents, relative to the commerce between the United States and certain foreign countries in cereals, and the cotton product during the years 1884 and 1885.

GROVER CLEVELAND.

EXECUTIVE MANSION, *March 22, 1886.*

To the House of Representatives:

In answer to the resolution of the House of Representatives of the 15th of February last, calling upon the Secretary of State for copies of all the correspondence relating to the claims of certain governments to be accorded the reductions and exemptions of tonnage dues accorded to vessels entering ports of the United States from certain ports named in the shipping act of June 26, 1884, I transmit the report of that officer, together with the correspondence.

GROVER CLEVELAND.

EXECUTIVE MANSION, *March 25, 1886.*

To the Senate and House of Representatives:

I transmit herewith the report of the Civil Service Commission for the year ended on the 16th day of January last.

The exhibit thus made of the operations of the Commission and the account thus presented of the results following the execution of the civil-service law can not fail to demonstrate its usefulness and strengthen the conviction that this scheme for a reform in the methods of administering the Government is no longer an experiment.

Wherever this reform has gained a foothold it has steadily advanced in the esteem of those charged with public administrative duties, while the people who desire good government have constantly been confirmed in their high estimate of its value and efficiency.

With the benefits it has already secured to the public service plainly apparent, and with its promise of increased usefulness easily appreciated, this cause is commended to the liberal care and jealous protection of the Congress.

GROVER CLEVELAND.

EXECUTIVE MANSION, *March 30, 1886.*

To the House of Representatives:

In further answer to the resolution of the House of Representatives of the 15th of February last, calling upon the Secretary of State for copies of all correspondence relating to the claims of governments to be accorded the reductions and exemptions of tonnage dues accorded to vessels entering the ports of the United States from certain ports named in the shipping act of June 26, 1884, I transmit herewith a copy of the reply of the Attorney-General to the letter of the Secretary of State of December 15,

1885, as found on pages 35 and 36 of Executive Document No. 132, House of Representatives, Forty-ninth Congress, first session, communicated on the 22d instant.

GROVER CLEVELAND.

EXECUTIVE MANSION, *April 1, 1886.*
To the House of Representatives:

In response to a resolution of the House of Representatives of the 24th of March, relative to the employment of substitutes in the Department of State, I transmit herewith a report of the Secretary of State on the subject.

GROVER CLEVELAND.

EXECUTIVE MANSION, *April 1, 1886.*
To the Senate and House of Representatives:

I transmit herewith a letter from the Secretary of the Interior and the accompanying report, submitted by the governor of Alaska in compliance with section 5 of the act of May 17, 1884, entitled "An act providing a civil government for Alaska."

GROVER CLEVELAND.

EXECUTIVE MANSION, *April 1, 1886.*
To the Senate and House of Representatives:

I transmit herewith a report of the Secretary of State, in relation to the claim of the representatives of the late Hon. James Crooks, a British subject, against this Government for the seizure of the schooner *Lord Nelson* in 1812.

The matter is commended to the favorable consideration of Congress.

GROVER CLEVELAND.

EXECUTIVE MANSION, *April 6, 1886.*
To the Senate and House of Representatives of the United States:

I transmit herewith, for the consideration of Congress with a view to appropriate legislation in the premises, a report of the Secretary of State, with certain correspondence touching the treaty right of Chinese subjects other than laborers "to go and come of their own free will and accord."

In my annual message of the 8th of December last I said:

In the application of the acts lately passed to execute the treaty of 1880, restrictive of the immigration of Chinese laborers into the United States, individual cases of hardship have occurred beyond the power of the Executive to remedy, and calling for judicial determination.

These cases of individual hardship are due to the ambiguous and defective provisions of the acts of Congress approved respectively on the

6th May, 1882, and 5th July, 1884. The hardship has in some cases been remedied by the action of the courts. In other cases, however, where the phraseology of the statutes has appeared to be conclusive against any discretion on the part of the officers charged with the execution of the law, Chinese persons expressly entitled to free admission under the treaty have been refused a landing and sent back to the country whence they came without being afforded any opportunity to show in the courts or otherwise their right to the privilege of free ingress and egress which it was the purpose of the treaty to secure.

In the language of one of the judicial determinations of the Supreme Court of the United States to which I have referred—

> The supposition should not be indulged that Congress, while professing to faithfully execute the treaty stipulations and recognizing the fact that they secure to a certain class the right to go from and come to the United States, intended to make its protection depend upon the performance of conditions which it was physically impossible to perform. (112 U. S. Reports, p. 554, Chew Heong *vs.* United States.)

The act of July 5, 1884, imposes such an impossible condition in not providing for the admission, under proper certificate, of Chinese travelers of the exempted classes in the cases most likely to arise in ordinary commercial intercourse.

The treaty provisions governing the case are as follows:

> ART. I. * * * The limitation or suspension shall be reasonable, and shall apply only to Chinese who may go to the United States as laborers, other classes not being included in the limitations. * * *
>
> ART. II. Chinese subjects, whether proceeding to the United States as teachers, students, merchants, or from curiosity, together with their body and household servants, * * * shall be allowed to go and come of their own free will and accord, and shall be accorded all the rights, privileges, immunities, and exemptions which are accorded to the citizens and subjects of the most favored nation.

Section 6 of the amended Chinese immigration act of 1884 purports to secure this treaty right to the exempted classes named by means of prescribed certificates of their status, which certificates shall be the *prima facie* and the sole permissible evidence to establish a right of entry into the United States. But it provides in terms for the issuance of certificates in two cases only:

(*a*) Chinese subjects departing from a port of China; and

(*b*) Chinese persons (*i. e.*, of the Chinese race) who may at the time be subjects of some foreign government other than China, and who may depart for the United States from the ports of such other foreign government.

A statute is certainly most unusual which, purporting to execute the provisions of a treaty with China in respect of Chinese subjects, enacts strict formalities as regards the subjects of other governments than that of China.

It is sufficient that I should call the earnest attention of Congress to the circumstance that the statute makes no provision whatever for the somewhat numerous class of Chinese persons who, retaining their Chinese subjection in some countries other than China, desire to come from such countries to the United States.

Chinese merchants have trading operations of magnitude throughout the world. They do not become citizens or subjects of the country where they may temporarily reside and trade; they continue to be subjects of China, and to them the explicit exemption of the treaty applies. Yet if such a Chinese subject, the head of a mercantile house at Hongkong or Yokohama or Honolulu or Havana or Colon, desires to come from any of these places to the United States, he is met with the requirement that he must produce a certificate, in prescribed form and in the English tongue, issued by the Chinese Government. If there be at the foreign place of his residence no representative of the Chinese Government competent to issue a certificate in the prescribed form, he can obtain none, and is under the provisions of the present law unjustly debarred from entry into the United States. His usual Chinese passport will not suffice, for it is not in the form which the act prescribes shall be the sole permissible evidence of his right to land. And he can obtain no such certificate from the Government of his place of residence, because he is not a subject or citizen thereof ''at the time,'' or at any time.

There being, therefore, no statutory provision prescribing the terms upon which Chinese persons resident in foreign countries but not subjects or citizens of such countries may prove their status and rights as members of the exempted classes in the absence of a Chinese representative in such country, the Secretary of the Treasury, in whom the execution of the act of July 5, 1884, was vested, undertook to remedy the omission by directing the revenue officers to recognize as lawful certificates those issued in favor of Chinese subjects by the Chinese consular and diplomatic officers at the foreign port of departure, when viséed by the United States representative thereat. This appears to be a just application of the spirit of the law, although enlarging its letter, and in adopting this rule he was controlled by the authority of high judicial decision as to what evidence is necessary to establish the fact that an individual Chinaman belongs to the exempted class.

He, however, went beyond the spirit of the act and the judicial decisions, by providing, in a circular dated January 14, 1885, for the original issuance of such a certificate by the United States consular officer at the port of departure, in the absence of a Chinese diplomatic or consular representative thereat; for it is clear that the act of Congress contemplated the intervention of the United States consul only in a supervisory capacity, his function being to check the proceeding and see that no abuse of the privilege followed. The power or duty of original certification is wholly distinct from that supervisory function. It either dispenses with .
reign certificate altogether, leaving the consular visé to stand alone .

and sufficient, or else it combines in one official act the distinct functions of certification and verification of the fact certified.

The official character attaching to the consular certification contemplated by the unamended circular of January 14, 1885, is to be borne in mind. It is not merely *prima facie* evidence of the status of the bearer, such as the courts may admit in their discretion; it was prescribed as an official attestation, on the strength of which the customs officers at the port of entry were to admit the bearer without further adjudication of his status unless question should arise as to the truth of the certificate itself.

It became, therefore, necessary to amend the circular of January 14, 1885, and this was done on the 13th of June following, by striking out the clause prescribing original certification of status by the United States consuls. The effect of this amendment is to deprive any certificate the United States consuls may issue of the value it purported to possess as sole permissible evidence under the statute when its issuance was prescribed by Treasury regulations. There is, however, nothing to prevent consuls giving certificates of facts within their knowledge to be received as evidence in the absence of statutory authentication.

The complaint of the Chinese minister in his note of March 24, 1886, is that the Chinese merchant Lay Sang, of the house of King Lee & Co., of San Francisco, having arrived at San Francisco from Hongkong and exhibited a certificate of the United States consul at Hongkong as to his status as a merchant, and consequently exempt under the treaty, was refused permission to land and was sent back to Hongkong by the steamer which brought him. While the certificate he bore was doubtless insufficient under the present law, it is to be remembered that there is at Hongkong no representative of the Government of China competent or authorized to issue the certificate required by the statute. The intent of Congress to legislate in execution of the treaty is thus defeated by a prohibition directly contrary to the treaty, and conditions are exacted which, in the words of the Supreme Court hereinbefore quoted, ''it was physically impossible to perform.''

This anomalous feature of the act should be reformed as speedily as possible, in order that the occurrence of such cases may be avoided and the imputation removed which would otherwise rest upon the good faith of the United States in the execution of their solemn treaty engagements.

GROVER CLEVELAND.

EXECUTIVE MANSION, *April 9, 1886.*

To the House of Representatives:

I transmit herewith a report of the Secretary of State, in relation to the mercantile marines of France, Germany, Great Britain, and Italy.

GROVER CLEVELAND.

EXECUTIVE MANSION, *April 14, 1886.*

To the House of Representatives:

In response to a resolution of the House of Representatives of the 17th ultimo, requesting the Secretary of State " to communicate to the House of Representatives, if not incompatible with the public interest, copies of the recent correspondence and dispatches between the Secretary of State and the minister of the United States at The Hague touching the subject of taxation of petroleum in Holland and in the Dutch colonies, and that of the export therefrom of leaf tobacco to the United States," I transmit herewith the report of the Secretary of State on the subject.

GROVER CLEVELAND.

EXECUTIVE MANSION, *April 14, 1886.*

To the House of Representatives:

In response to a resolution of the House of Representatives of the 6th instant, requesting the Secretary of State " to transmit, if not incompatible with the public interest, copies of all correspondence between his Department and the representatives of France, Germany, Austria, and any other European country which has partially or entirely restricted the importation of American pork," I transmit herewith the report of the Secretary of State on the subject.

GROVER CLEVELAND.

EXECUTIVE MANSION, *April 20, 1886.*

To the House of Representatives:

I transmit herewith a report of the Secretary of State on the manufacture of milk sugar in Switzerland.

GROVER CLEVELAND.

EXECUTIVE MANSION, *April 22, 1886.*

To the Senate and House of Representatives:

The Constitution imposes upon the President the duty of recommending to the consideration of Congress from time to time such measures as he shall judge necessary and expedient.

I am so deeply impressed with the importance of immediately and thoughtfully meeting the problem which recent events and a present condition have thrust upon us, involving the settlement of disputes arising between our laboring men and their employers, that I am constrained to recommend to Congress legislation upon this serious and pressing subject.

Under our form of government the value of labor as an element of l prosperity should be distinctly recognized, and the welfare of the laboring man should be regarded as especially entitled to legislative care. In a country which offers to all its citizens the highest attainment of social and political distinction its workingmen can not justly or safely be considered as irrevocably consigned to the limits of a class and entitled to no attention and allowed no protest against neglect.

The laboring man, bearing in his hand an indispensable contribution to our growth and progress, may well insist, with manly courage and as a right, upon the same recognition from those who make our laws as is accorded to any other citizen having a valuable interest in charge; and his reasonable demands should be met in such a spirit of appreciation and fairness as to induce a contented and patriotic cooperation in the achievement of a grand national destiny.

While the real interests of labor are not promoted by a resort to threats and violent manifestations, and while those who, under the pretext of an advocacy of the claims of labor, wantonly attack the rights of capital and for selfish purposes or the love of disorder sow seeds of violence and discontent should neither be encouraged nor conciliated, all legislation on the subject should be calmly and deliberately undertaken, with no purpose of satisfying unreasonable demands or gaining partisan advantage.

The present condition of the relations between labor and capital is far from satisfactory. The discontent of the employed is due in a large degree to the grasping and heedless exactions of employers and the alleged discrimination in favor of capital as an object of governmental attention. It must also be conceded that the laboring men are not always careful to avoid causeless and unjustifiable disturbance.

Though the importance of a better accord between these interests is apparent, it must be borne in mind that any effort in that direction by the Federal Government must be greatly limited by constitutional restrictions. There are many grievances which legislation by Congress can not redress, and many conditions which can not by such means be reformed.

I am satisfied, however, that something may be done under Federal authority to prevent the disturbances which so often arise from disputes between employers and the employed, and which at times seriously threaten the business interests of the country; and, in my opinion, the proper theory upon which to proceed is that of voluntary arbitration as the means of settling these difficulties.

But I suggest that instead of arbitrators chosen in the heat of conflicting claims, and after each dispute shall arise, for the purpose of determining the same, there be created a commission of labor, consisting of three members, who shall be regular officers of the Government, charged among other duties with the consideration and settlement, when possible, of all controversies between labor and capital.

A commission thus organized would have the advantage of being a stable body, and its members, as they gained experience, would constantly improve in their ability to deal intelligently and usefully with the questions which might be submitted to them.   If arbitrators are chosen for temporary service as each case of dispute arises, experience and familiarity with much that is involved in the question will be lacking, extreme partisanship and bias will be the qualifications sought on either side, and frequent complaints of unfairness and partiality will be inevitable.   The imposition upon a Federal court of a duty so foreign to the judicial function as the selection of an arbitrator in such cases is at least of doubtful propriety.

The establishment by Federal authority of such a bureau would be a just and sensible recognition of the value of labor and of its right to be represented in the departments of the Government.   So far as its conciliatory offices shall have relation to disturbances which interfere with transit and commerce between the States, its existence would be justified under the provision of the Constitution which gives to Congress the power ''to regulate commerce with foreign nations and among the several States;'' and in the frequent disputes between the laboring men and their employers, of less extent, and the consequences of which are confined within State limits and threaten domestic violence, the interposition of such a commission might be tendered, upon the application of the legislature or executive of a State, under the constitutional provision which requires the General Government to ''protect'' each of the States ''against domestic violence.''

If such a commission were fairly organized, the risk of a loss of popular support and sympathy resulting from a refusal to submit to so peaceful an instrumentality would constrain both parties to such disputes to invoke its interference and abide by its decisions.   There would also be good reason to hope that the very existence of such an agency would invite application to it for advice and counsel, frequently resulting in the avoidance of contention and misunderstanding.

If the usefulness of such a commission is doubted because it might lack power to enforce its decisions, much encouragement is derived from the conceded good that has been accomplished by the railroad commissions which have been organized in many of the States, which, having little more than advisory power, have exerted a most salutary influence in the settlement of disputes between conflicting interests.

In July, 1884, by a law of Congress, a Bureau of Labor was established and placed in charge of a Commissioner of Labor, who is required to ''collect information upon the subject of labor, its relations to capital, the hours of labor and the earnings of laboring men and women, and the means of promoting their material, social, intellectual, and moral prosperity.''

The commission which I suggest could easily be ingrafted upon the bureau thus already organized by the addition of two more commissioners supplementing the duties now imposed upon it by such other powers and functions as would permit the commissioners to act as arbitrators when necessary between labor and capital, under such limitations and upon such occasions as should be deemed proper and useful.

Power should also be distinctly conferred upon this bureau to investigate the causes of all disputes as they occur, whether submitted for arbitration or not, so that information may always be at hand to aid legislation on the subject when necessary and desirable.

GROVER CLEVELAND.

EXECUTIVE MANSION, *April 26, 1886.*
To the House of Representatives:

I transmit herewith a communication from the Secretary of State, accompanied by a report of Mr. Somerville P. Tuck, appointed to carry out certain provisions of section 5 of an act entitled "An act to provide for the ascertainment of claims of American citizens for spoliations committed by the French prior to the 31st day of July, 1801," approved January 20, 1885.

GROVER CLEVELAND.

[The same message was sent to the Senate.]

EXECUTIVE MANSION, *May 5, 1886.*
To the Senate and House of Representatives:

I transmit herewith a communication of 1st instant from the Secretary of the Interior, submitting a draft of a bill recommended by the Commissioner of Indian Affairs, providing for the payment of improvements made by settlers on the lands of the Mescalero Indian Reservation in the Territory of New Mexico.

The subject is presented for the consideration and action of Congress.

GROVER CLEVELAND.

EXECUTIVE MANSION, *May 11, 1886.*
To the Senate and House of Representatives:

I herewith transmit a report from the Secretary of State, dated the 6th instant, touching the claims of Benjamin Weil and La Abra Silver Mining Company against the Government of Mexico.

GROVER CLEVELAND.

EXECUTIVE MANSION, *May 11, 1886.*
To the Senate and House of Representatives:

By a joint resolution of Congress approved March 3. 1877, the President was authorized and directed to accept the colossal statue of "Liberty Enlightening the World" when presented by the citizens of the French Republic, and to designate and set apart for the erection thereof a suitable site upon either Governors or Bedloes Island, in the harbor of New York, and upon the completion thereof to cause the statue ''to be inaugurated with such ceremonies as will serve to testify the gratitude of our people for this expressive and felicitous memorial of the sympathy of the citizens of our sister Republic.''

The President was further thereby ''authorized to cause suitable regulations to be made for its future maintenance as a beacon and for the permanent care and preservation thereof as a monument of art and the continued good will of the great nation which aided us in our struggle for freedom.''

Under the authority of this resolution, on the 4th day of July, 1884, the minister of the United States to the French Republic, by direction of the President of the United States, accepted the statue and received a deed of presentation from the Franco-American Union, which is now preserved in the archives of the Department of State.

I now transmit to Congress a letter to the Secretary of State from Joseph W. Drexel, esq., chairman of the executive committee of ''the American committee on the pedestal of the great statue of 'Liberty Enlightening the World,''' dated the 27th of April, 1886, suggesting the propriety of the further execution by the President of the joint resolution referred to by prescribing the ceremonies of inauguration to be observed upon the complete erection of the statue upon its site on Bedloes Island, in the harbor of New York.

Thursday, the 3d of September, being the anniversary of the signing of the treaty of peace at Paris by which the independence of these United States was recognized and secured, has been suggested by this committee under whose auspices and agency the pedestal for the statue has been constructed as an appropriate day for the ceremonies of inauguration.

The international character which has been imprinted upon this work by the joint resolution of 1877 makes it incumbent upon Congress to provide means to carry their resolution into effect.

Therefore I recommend the appropriation of such sum of money as in the judgment of Congress shall be deemed adequate and proper to defray the cost of the inauguration of this statue.

I have been informed by the committee that certain expenses have been incurred in the care and custody of the statue since it was deposited on Bedloes Island, and the phraseology of the joint resolution providing for ''the permanent care and preservation thereof as a monument of art'' would seem to include the payment by the United States of the expense so incurred since the reception of the statue in this country.

The action of the French Government and people in relation to the presentation of this statue to the United States will, I hope, meet with hearty and responsive action upon the part of Congress, in which the Executive will be most happy to cooperate.

GROVER CLEVELAND.

EXECUTIVE MANSION, *May 11, 1886.*

To the Senate and House of Representatives:

The last general appropriation bill passed by the legislature of Utah was vetoed by the then governor of that Territory. It made an appropriation of money for the support of the district courts of the Territory, including the pay of reporters, jurors, and witnesses, and for the completion and maintenance of the Deseret University and the education of the deaf mutes therein. It also appropriated for the support of the Territorial insane asylum, as well as the salaries of Territorial officers, including that of the superintendent of the district schools, the auditor, the librarian, and the treasurer of the Territory. It also provided for internal improvements, such as roads and bridges.

The appropriation for the district courts, for the payment of witnesses and jurors in criminal cases, was $40,000; that for the Deseret University and the deaf mutes was $66,000, and for the insane asylum $25,000.

The board of regents of the Deseret University have borrowed money for the completion of the university buildings which were authorized by legislative action, and which is now due and no provision made for the payment. The act appropriating for the benefit of the Territorial insane asylum passed by the legislature was also vetoed. This included the sum of $13,000, which had been borrowed by the board of directors of the asylum for its completion and furnishing, and which now remains due and unpaid. It also included the sum of $3,548.85 for the care and maintenance of the indigent insane.

The legislature of the Territory, under existing law, will not again convene for nearly two years, there being no authority for a special session. In the meantime, under present conditions, the good order of society will be jeopardized, educational and charitable institutions will be paralyzed, and internal improvements stopped until the legislature meets and makes provision for their support.

A determination on the part of the General Government to suppress certain unlawful practices in this Territory demands neither the refusal of the means to support the local government nor the sacrifice of the interests of the community.

I therefore recommend the immediate enactment of such legislation as will authorize the assembling of the legislature of that Territory in special session at an early day, so that provision can be made to meet the difficulties herein suggested. GROVER CLEVELAND.

EXECUTIVE MANSION,
Washington, May 17, 1886.

To the Senate:

I transmit to the Senate, for its consideration with a view to ratification, a supplementary article, signed the 14th instant by the Secretary of State and the minister of Mexico here, extending until May 20, 1887, the time specified in Article VIII of the commercial reciprocity treaty of January 20, 1883, between the United States and Mexico, for the approval of the laws necessary to carry the said treaty into effect.

GROVER CLEVELAND.

EXECUTIVE MANSION,
Washington, May 17, 1886.

To the Senate:

In response to a resolution of the Senate of the 5th instant, inquiring as to the necessity for the continuance of the present charge for passports for American citizens desiring to visit foreign countries, I transmit herewith the report of the Secretary of State on the subject.

GROVER CLEVELAND.

EXECUTIVE MANSION,
Washington, May 17, 1886.

To the Senate and House of Representatives:

With reference to the paragraph in my annual message to Congress in which I called attention to the uncertainty that exists as to the location of the frontier line between Alaska and British Columbia as defined by the treaty of cession with Russia of March 30, 1867, I now transmit herewith, for the information and consideration of Congress, a report of the Secretary of State upon the subject, with accompanying papers.

In view of the importance of the subject, I recommend that provision be made by law for a preliminary survey of the boundary line in question by officers of the United States, in order that the information necessary for the basis of a treaty between this country and Great Britain for the establishment of a definite boundary line may be obtained; and I also recommend that the sum of $100,000, or so much thereof as may be necessary, be appropriated for the expenses of making such survey.

GROVER CLEVELAND.

EXECUTIVE MANSION,
Washington, May 21, 1886.

To the Senate of the United States:

I transmit herewith, for your consideration with a view to their ratification, the "convention concerning the international exchanges for official documents and literary publications" and the "convention for assuring the immediate exchange of the official journal as well as of the parliamentary annals and documents."

The first was signed at Brussels on the 15th of March, 1886, by the plenipotentiaries of the United States, Belgium, Brazil, Spain, Italy, Portugal, Servia, and Switzerland.

The second was signed at the same place and on the same date by the plenipotentiaries of the above-named powers, with the exception of Switzerland.

GROVER CLEVELAND.

EXECUTIVE MANSION, *May 21, 1886.*

To the Senate and House of Representatives:

I herewith transmit a report from the Secretary of State, dated the 19th instant, touching the necessity of legislation to carry into effect the provisions of Article II of the treaty between the United States and China of November 17, 1880, for the repression of the opium traffic, and recommend that appropriate legislation to fulfill that treaty promise of this Government be provided without further delay.

GROVER CLEVELAND.

EXECUTIVE MANSION, *May 28, 1886.*

To the House of Representatives:

I transmit herewith a report of the Secretary of State, accompanying the report of consuls of the United States on the trade and commerce of foreign countries.

GROVER CLEVELAND.

EXECUTIVE MANSION, *June 1, 1886.*

To the House of Representatives:

In response to a resolution of the House of Representatives of the 17th of March last, requesting the Secretary of State "to communicate to the House of Representatives, if not incompatible with the public interest, copies of recent correspondence and dispatches between the Secretary of State and the minister of the United States at The Hague touching the subject of taxation on petroleum in Holland and in the Dutch colonies, and that of the export therefrom of leaf tobacco to the United States," with reference to my message to the House of Representatives of the 14th ultimo [April], I now transmit a further report of the Secretary of State on the subject.

GROVER CLEVELAND.

EXECUTIVE MANSION, *June 2, 1886.*

To the House of Representatives:

In compliance with the request of the House of Representatives of this date, I return herewith House bill No. 6391, entitled "An act to authorize the Kansas City, Fort Scott and Gulf Railway Company to construct and operate a railway through the Indian Territory, and for other purposes."

GROVER CLEVELAND.

EXECUTIVE MANSION, *June 1, 1886.*

To the Senate and House of Representatives:

I herewith transmit a letter from the Secretary of State. with an accompanying paper. in relation to the distribution of the fund appropriated by the act of April 20. 1882. for the relief of the captain. owners. officers. and crew of the brig *General Armstrong*.

GROVER CLEVELAND.

EXECUTIVE MANSION.
Washington, June 2, 1886.

To the Senate of the United States:

I transmit herewith. for your consideration with a view to its ratification. a convention for the extradition of criminals. signed at Tokyo on the 29th day of April. 1886. by the plenipotentiaries of the United States and the Empire of Japan.

The negotiation which led to the conclusion of this convention was caused immediately by the case of a forger in San Francisco. who. having fled to Japan. was delivered up to the authorities of the State of California. It was not possible for this Government to ask his surrender. but the Japanese Government of its own motion caused his delivery as a friendly act. It then suggested the conclusion of an extradition convention between the two countries. The suggestion was favorably entertained by this Government. not only on account of the importance of such a treaty to the execution of the criminal laws of the United States. but also because of the support which its conclusion would give to Japan in her efforts toward judicial autonomy and complete sovereignty.

GROVER CLEVELAND

EXECUTIVE MANSION. *June 15. 1886.*

To the House of Representatives:

I transmit herewith a report from the Secretary of State. concerning the claim of Benjamin Weil and La Abra Mining Company. of Mexico. agreeably to the resolution of the House of Representatives dated May 13. 1886.

GROVER CLEVELAND.

EXECUTIVE MANSION. *June 10. 1886.*

To the House of Representatives:

Upon an examination of a bill originating in the House of Representatives. No. 4838. entitled "An act to abolish certain fees for official services to American vessels. and to amend the laws relating to shipping commissioners. seamen, and owners of vessels, and for other purposes." I find that there is such a failure to adjust existing laws to the new de-
    ure proposed by the bill as to greatly endanger the public service if

this bill should not be amended or at once supplemented by additional legislation.

The fees which are at present collected from vessels for services performed by the Bureau of Inspection, and which made up the fund from which certain expenses appurtenant to that Bureau were paid, are by the proposed bill abolished, but no provision has been substituted directing that such expenses shall be paid from the public Treasury or any other source.

The objects of the bill are in the main so useful and important that I have concluded to approve the same upon the assurance of those actively promoting its passage that another bill shall at once be introduced to cover the defect above referred to.

The necessity of such supplemental legislation is so obvious that I hope it will receive the immediate action of the Congress.

GROVER CLEVELAND.

EXECUTIVE MANSION, *June 28, 1886.*
To the Senate and House of Representatives:

I herewith inclose a report from the Secretary of State, with its accompanying copies of papers, relative to the case of the American schooner *Ounalaska,* which was duly condemned by the Government of Salvador for having been employed in aid of an insurrection against that Republic, and was subsequently presented to the United States. It seems that an act of Congress accepting the gift on the part of this Government is necessary to complete the transfer, and I recommend that legislation in this sense be adopted. It further appears that one Isidore Gutte, of San Francisco, has sought to obtain possession of the condemned vessel, and I therefore suggest that a second provision to the law accepting her be made giving authority to the Court of Claims to hear and determine the question of title.

GROVER CLEVELAND.

EXECUTIVE MANSION, *June 28, 1886.*
To the Senate and House of Representatives:

I transmit herewith a communication, with an accompanying paper, from the Secretary of State, in relation to the distribution of the award of the late Mexican Claims Commission in the case of S. A. Belden & Co. against the Republic of Mexico.

GROVER CLEVELAND.

To the Senate:　　　　　　　EXECUTIVE MANSION, *June 30, 1886.*

In response to the resolution of the Senate of the 28th of April last, I transmit herewith a report of the Secretary of State in relation to the affairs of the independent State of the Kongo.

GROVER CLEVELAND.

EXECUTIVE MANSION, *July 6, 1886.*

To the House of Representatives:

In compliance with a concurrent resolution of this date, I return herewith House bill No. 3501, entitled "An act granting a pension to Daniel J. Bingham."

GROVER CLEVELAND.

EXECUTIVE MANSION,
Washington, July 8, 1886.

To the Senate of the United States:

I transmit herewith, for your consideration with a view to its ratification, a convention signed at London June 25, 1886, between the United States of America and Great Britain, concerning the extradition of persons charged with crime.

I also inclose a report from the Secretary of State and a copy of a dispatch from the United States minister at London dated June 26, 1886, in reference thereto.

The question of extradition has been discussed between the two countries by Secretaries Fish, Evarts, and Frelinghuysen, as well as by the present Secretary of State, and the method adopted by the inclosed convention, namely, that of amending and extending the provisions of the tenth article of the treaty of 1842, has seemed the most convenient and expeditious.

In view of the continued pendency of the question and its great importance owing to the contiguity of Her Majesty's territories with those of the United States, I respectfully urge the consideration of the convention by the Senate during the present session.

GROVER CLEVELAND.

EXECUTIVE MANSION, *July 9, 1886.*

To the Senate and House of Representatives:

I transmit herewith, for your information, a report from the Secretary of State, inclosing the correspondence which has been exchanged between the Department of State and the Governments of Switzerland and Italy on the subject of international copyright.

GROVER CLEVELAND.

EXECUTIVE MANSION, *July 12, 1886.*

To the Senate and House of Representatives:

I transmit herewith a communication of 3d instant, with inclosures, from the Secretary of the Interior, recommending legislative authority for the use of funds from appropriation, Sioux, etc., 1887, for the subsistance of certain Northern Cheyenne Indians who have gone or who may go from the Sioux Reservation in Dakota to the Tongue River Indian Agency or vicinity, in Montana.

The matter is presented for the favorable consideration of Congress.

GROVER CLEVELAND.

EXECUTIVE MANSION, *July 24, 1886.*
To the Senate of the United States:

In response to the resolutions of the Senate dated respectively May 10 and July 10, 1886, touching alleged seizures and detentions of vessels of the United States in British North American waters, I transmit herewith a report of the Secretary of State, with accompanying papers.

GROVER CLEVELAND.

EXECUTIVE MANSION, *July 27, 1886.*
To the House of Representatives:

I transmit herewith, in response to the House resolution of the 10th instant, a report from the Secretary of State, and accompanying papers, relating to the imprisonment in Ecuador and subsequent release of Julio R. Santos.

GROVER CLEVELAND.

EXECUTIVE MANSION, *July 29, 1886.*
To the House of Representatives:

I transmit herewith a report of the Secretary of State, in reply to the resolution of the House of Representatives of the 27th of May last, in relation to trust funds.

GROVER CLEVELAND.

EXECUTIVE MANSION, *July 29, 1886.*
To the Senate of the United States:

I transmit herewith reports from the heads of the several Executive Departments of the Government, in answer to a resolution of the Senate of June 18, 1886, which requested certain information regarding appointments in such Departments, and having relation to the civil-service law.

GROVER CLEVELAND.

EXECUTIVE MANSION, *July 30, 1886.*
To the Senate of the United States:

· In further response to the Senate resolutions of the 10th of May and 10th of July, 1886, touching the seizure and detention of American vessels in Canadian waters, I transmit herewith a letter from the Secretary of State dated the 29th instant, accompanied by a report from the consul-general at Halifax relative to the subject.

GROVER CLEVELAND.

EXECUTIVE MANSION, *July 31, 1886.*

To the House of Representatives:

I have approved House bill No. 4335, entitled "An act making an appropriation to continue the construction of a public building at Clarksburg, W. Va., and changing the limit of cost thereof."

A law passed by the last Congress authorized the construction of this building and appropriated $50,000 for that purpose, which was declared to be the limit of its cost. A site has been purchased for said building, and, as is too often the case, it is now discovered that the sum appropriated is insufficient to meet the expense of such a building as is really needed.

The object of the bill which I have approved is to extend the limit of the cost to $80,000 and to make the additional appropriation to reach that sum. The first section fixes the limit above mentioned, but the second section appropriates $35,000, and thus, with the appropriation of $50,000 heretofore made, the aggregate appropriations exceed the sum to which the cost of the building is limited by $5,000.

Inasmuch as this latter sum can not properly be applied to the construction of the building, attention is called to the existence of this excess of appropriation and the suggestion made that it be returned to the Treasury.

                                        GROVER CLEVELAND.

EXECUTIVE MANSION, *August 2, 1886.*

To the Senate of the United States:

In response to the resolution of your honorable body of the 26th ultimo, I transmit a report of the Secretary of State, with accompanying papers, communicating the information possessed by the Department of State "concerning the alleged illegal detention of A. K. Cutting, an American citizen, by the Mexican authorities at El Paso del Norte;" and as to the further inquiry contained in said resolution, "whether any additional United States troops have been recently ordered to Fort Bliss," I answer in the negative.

                                        GROVER CLEVELAND.

EXECUTIVE MANSION, *August 2, 1886.*

To the House of Representatives:

In performance of the duty imposed upon me by the Constitution, I herewith transmit for your information (the same having heretofore been communicated to the Senate in response to a resolution of inquiry adopted by that body July 26, 1886) certain correspondence and accompanying documents in relation to the arrest and imprisonment at Paso del Norte by Mexican authority of A. K. Cutting, a citizen of the United States.

                                        GROVER CLEVELAND.

To the House of Representatives:

I have this day approved a bill originating in the House of Representatives entitled "An act defining butter, also imposing a tax upon and regulating the manufacture, sale, importation, and exportation of oleomargarine."

This legislation has awakened much interest among the people of the country, and earnest argument has been addressed to the Executive for the purpose of influencing his action thereupon. Many in opposition have urged its dangerous character as tending to break down the boundaries between the proper exercise of legislative power by Federal and State authority; many in favor of the enactment have represented that it promised great advantages to a large portion of our population who sadly need relief; and those on both sides of the question whose advocacy or opposition is based upon no broader foundation than local or personal interest have outnumbered all the others.

This upon its face and in its main features is a revenue bill, and was first introduced in the House of Representatives, wherein the Constitution declares that all bills for raising revenue shall originate.

The Constitution has invested Congress with a very wide legislative discretion both as to the necessity of taxation and the selection of the objects of its burdens; and though if the question was presented to me as an original proposition I might doubt the present need of increased taxation, I deem it my duty in this instance to defer to the judgment of the legislative branch of the Government, which has been so emphatically announced in both Houses of Congress upon the passage of this bill.

Moreover, those who desire to see removed the weight of taxation now pressing upon the people from other directions may well be justified in the hope and expectation that the selection of an additional subject of internal taxation so well able to bear it will in consistency be followed by legislation relieving our citizens from other revenue burdens, rendered by the passage of this bill even more than heretofore unnecessary and needlessly oppressive.

It has been urged as an objection to this measure that while purporting to be legislation for revenue its real purpose is to destroy, by the use of the taxing power, one industry of our people for the protection and benefit of another.

If entitled to indulge in such a suspicion as a basis of official action in this case, and if entirely satisfied that the consequences indicated would ensue, I should doubtless feel constrained to interpose Executive dissent.

But I do not feel called upon to interpret the motives of Congress otherwise than by the apparent character of the bill which has been presented to me, and I am convinced that the taxes which it creates can not possibly destroy the open and legitimate manufacture and sale of the thing upon which it is levied. If this article has the merit which its friends claim for it, and if the people of the land, with full knowledge of its real character, desire to purchase and use it, the taxes exacted by this bill will permit a fair profit to both manufacturer and dealer. If the existence of the commodity taxed and the profits of its manufacture and sale depend upon disposing of it to the people for something else which it deceitfully imitates, the entire enterprise is a fraud and not an industry; and if it can not endure the exhibition of its real character which will be effected by the inspection, supervision, and stamping which this bill directs, the sooner it is destroyed the better in the interest of fair dealing.

Such a result would not furnish the first instance in the history of legislation in which a revenue bill produced a benefit which was merely incidental to its main purpose.

There is certainly no industry better entitled to the incidental advantages which may follow this legislation than our farming and dairy interests, and to none of our people should they be less begrudged than our farmers and dairymen. The present depression of their occupations, the hard, steady, and often unremunerative toil which such occupations exact, and the burdens of taxation which our agriculturists necessarily bear entitle them to every legitimate consideration.

Nor should there be opposition to the incidental effect of this legislation on the part of those who profess to be engaged honestly and fairly in the manufacture and sale of a wholesome and valuable article of food which by its provisions may be subject to taxation. As long as their business is carried on under cover and by false pretenses such men have bad companions in those whose manufactures, however vile and harmful, take their place without challenge with the better sort in a common crusade of deceit against the public. But if this occupation and its methods are forced into the light and all these manufactures must thus either stand upon their merits or fall, the good and bad must soon part company and the fittest only will survive.

Not the least important incident related to this legislation is the defense afforded to the consumer against the fraudulent substitution and sale of an imitation for a genuine article of food of very general household use. Notwithstanding the immense quantity of the article described in this bill which is sold to the people for their consumption as food, and notwithstanding the claim made that its manufacture supplies a cheap substitute for butter, I venture to say that hardly a pound ever entered a poor man's house under its real name and in its true character.

While in its relation to an article of this description there should be no governmental regulation of what the citizen shall eat, it is certainly not a cause of regret if by legislation of this character he is afforded a means by which he may better protect himself against imposition in meeting the needs and wants of his daily life.

Having entered upon this legislation, it is manifestly a duty to render it as effective as possible in the accomplishment of all the good which should legitimately follow in its train.

This leads to the suggestion that the article proposed to be taxed and the circumstances which subject it thereto should be clearly and with great distinctness defined in the statute. It seems to me that this object has not been completely attained in the phraseology of the second section of the bill, and that question may well arise as to the precise condition the article to be taxed must assume in order to be regarded as "made in imitation or semblance of butter, or, when so made, calculated or intended to be sold as butter or for butter."

The fourteenth and fifteenth sections of the bill, in my opinion, are in danger of being construed as an interference with the police powers of the States. Not being entirely satisfied of the unconstitutionality of these provisions, and regarding them as not being so connected and interwoven with the other sections as, if found invalid, to vitiate the entire measure, I have determined to commend them to the attention of the House with a view to an immediate amendment of the bill if it should be deemed necessary and if it is practicable at this late day in the session of Congress.

The fact, too, that the bill does not take effect by its terms until ninety days have elapsed after its approval, thus leaving it but one month in operation before the next session of Congress, when, if time does not now permit, the safety and efficiency of the measure may be abundantly protected by remedial legislative action, and the desire to see realized the beneficial results which it is expected will immediately follow the inauguration of this legislation, have had their influence in determining my official action.

The considerations which have been referred to will, I hope, justify this communication and the suggestions which it contains.

GROVER CLEVELAND.

EXECUTIVE MANSION, *August 4, 1886.*
To the House of Representatives:

In compliance with a resolution of the House of Representatives of the 3d instant (the Senate concurring), I return herewith Senate bill No. 2056, entitled "An act to amend the pension laws by increasing the pensions of soldiers and sailors who have lost an arm or leg in the service."

GROVER CLEVELAND.

VETO MESSAGES.

EXECUTIVE MANSION, *March 10, 1886.*
To the Senate of the United States:

I have carefully considered Senate bill No. 193, entitled "An act for the relief of John Hollins McBlair," and hereby return the same without approval to the Senate, where it originated, with my objections to the same.

The object of this bill is to suspend the provisions of law regulating appointments in the Army by promotion so far as they affect John Hollins McBlair, and to authorize the President to nominate and, by and with the advice and consent of the Senate, appoint said McBlair a first lieutenant in the Army and to place him upon the retired list as of the date of April 8, 1864, with the pay of his rank from April 30, 1884.

The beneficiary named in this bill was appointed a first lieutenant in the Army, from civil life, in June, 1861, with rank from May 14, 1861.

It appears from his own testimony, afterwards taken before a retiring board, that at the time he was commissioned he was but 17 years of age.

In October, 1861, he was in the field for five days with his regiment, within which time he participated in no battle, skirmish, or engagement of any kind.

After five days spent in marching and camping he was taken sick, and after remaining in camp six or seven weeks, his illness still continuing, he was granted sick leave and came to Washington.

In June, 1862, he was put on duty in the Commissary Department at Washington and remained there until August, 1863, when he was summoned before a retiring board convened for the purpose of retiring disabled officers.

From testimony before this board it appears that the illness which caused him to leave his regiment was one not uncommon in the Army, and yielded to treatment, so that in April or May, 1862, he was completely cured.

About this time, however, he was attacked with convulsions, which were pronounced by the physicians examined before the board to be a form of epilepsy, and for this cause he was found to be incapacitated for active service.

The medical testimony, while it suggested various causes for this epileptic condition, negatives entirely any claim that these attacks were at all related to the illness which obliged this officer to abandon service with his regiment. He testified himself that he had been told he had one or two convulsions in childhood, but there is no direct testimony that he was subject to epileptic attacks before he entered the Army.

The retiring board determined upon the proof that this incapacity did not result from any incident of military service, and therefore Lieutenant McBlair was in October, 1863, retired wholly from the service with one year's pay and allowances, which is the usual action in such cases, and which was approved by the President.

But in April, 1864, the President, in a review of the case, made an order that instead of this officer being wholly retired he should be placed upon the retired list as of the date when the action of the retiring board was originally approved.

For about twenty years, and up to April 30, 1884, he remained upon the retired list and received the pay to which this position entitled him.

Quite recently, in consequence of a claim of additional pay which he made upon the Government, his status was examined by the Court of Claims, which decided that the action of the President in April, 1864, by which he sought to change the original disposition of the case upon the findings of the retiring board, was nugatory, and that ever since October, 1863, this officer had not been connected with the Army and had been receiving from the Government money to which he was not entitled.

If the bill herewith returned becomes a law, it makes valid all payments made, and if its purpose is carried out causes such payments to be resumed.

The finding of the retiring board seems so satisfactory and the merits of this case so slight in the light of the large sum already paid to the applicant, while the claims of thousands of wounded and disabled soldiers wait for justice at the hands of the Government, that I am constrained to interpose an objection to a measure which proposes to suspend general and wholesome laws for the purpose of granting what appears to me to be an undeserved gratuity.

GROVER CLEVELAND.

EXECUTIVE MANSION, *March 11, 1886.*

To the Senate of the United States:

I return herewith without approval, and with a statement of my objections thereto, Senate bill No. 150, entitled "An act to quiet title of settlers on the Des Moines River lands in the State of Iowa, and for other purposes."

This proposed legislation grows out of a grant of land made to the Territory of Iowa in the year 1846 to aid in the improvement of the navigation of the Des Moines River.

The language of this grant was such that it gave rise to conflicting decisions on the part of the Government Departments as to its extent, and it was not until 1860 that this question was authoritatively and finally settled by the Supreme Court of the United States. Its decision diminished the extent of the grant to a quantity much less than had been insisted on by certain interested parties and rendered invalid the titles of parties who held, under the Territory or State of Iowa, lands beyond the limit of the grant fixed by the decision of the court.

For the purpose of validating such titles and to settle all disputes so far as the General Government was concerned, the Congress, in the year 1861, by a joint resolution, transferred to the State of Iowa all the title then retained by the United States to the lands within the larger limits which had been claimed, and then held by *bona fide* purchasers from the State; and in 1862 an act of Congress was passed for the same general purpose.

Without detailing the exact language of this resolution and statute, it certainly seems to be such a transfer and relinquishment of all interests in the land mentioned on the part of the United States as to relieve the Government from any further concern therein.

The questions unfortunately growing out of this grant and the legislation relating thereto have been passed upon by the United States Supreme Court in numerous cases, and as late as 1883 that court, referring to its many previous decisions, adjudged that "the act of 1862 (12 U. S. Statutes at Large, ch. 161, p. 543) transferred the title from the United States and vested it in the State of Iowa for the use of its grantees under the river grant."

Bills similar to this have been before Congress for a number of years and have failed of passage; and at least on one occasion the Committee on the Judiciary of the Senate reported adversely upon a measure covering the same ground.

I have carefully examined the legislation upon the subject of this grant, and studied the decisions of the court upon the numerous and complicated questions which have arisen from such legislation, and the positions of the parties claiming an interest in the land covered by said grant, and I can not but think that every possible question that can be raised, or at least that ought to be raised, in any suit relating to these lands has been determined by the highest judicial authority in the land; and if any substantial point remains yet unsettled, I believe there is no difficulty in presenting it to the proper tribunal.

This bill declares that certain lands which nearly twenty-four years ago the United States entirely relinquished are still public lands, and directs the Attorney-General to begin suits to assert and protect the title of the United States in such lands.

If it be true that these are public lands, the declaration that they are so by enactment is entirely unnecessary; and if they are wrongfully withheld from the Government, the duty and authority of the Attorney-General are not aided by the proposed legislation. If they are not public lands because the United States have conveyed them to others, the bill is subject to grave objections as an attempt to destroy vested rights and disturb interests which have long since become fixed.

If a law of Congress could, in the manner contemplated by the bill, change, under the Constitution, the existing rights of any of the parties claiming interests in these lands, it hardly seems that any new questions could be presented to the courts which would do more than raise false hopes and renew useless and bitter strife and litigation.

It seems to me that all controversies which can hereafter arise between those claiming these lands have been fairly remitted to the State of Iowa, and that there they can be properly and safely left; and the Government, through its Attorney-General, should not be called upon to litigate the rights of private parties.

It is not pleasant to contemplate loss threatened to any party acting in good faith, caused by uncertainty in the language of laws or their conflicting interpretation; and if there are persons occupying these lands who labor under such disabilities as prevent them from appealing to the courts for a redress of their wrongs, a plain statute, directed simply to a remedy for such disabilities, would not be objectionable.

Should there be meritorious cases of hardship and loss, caused by an invitation on the part of the Government to settle upon lands apparently public, but to which no right or lawful possession can be secured, it would be better, rather than to attempt a disturbance of titles already settled, to ascertain such losses and do equity by compensating the proper parties through an appropriation for that purpose.

A law to accomplish this very object was passed by Congress in the year 1873.

Valuable proof is thus furnished, by the only law ever passed upon the subject, of the manner in which it was thought proper by the Congress at that time to meet the difficulties suggested by the bill now under consideration.

Notwithstanding the fact that there may be parties in the occupancy of these lands who suffer hardship by the application of strict legal principles to their claims, safety lies in noninterference by Congress with matters which should be left to judicial cognizance; and I am unwilling to concur in legislation which, if not an encroachment upon judicial power, trenches so closely thereon as to be of doubtful expediency, and which at the same time increases the elements of litigation that have heretofore existed and endangers vested rights.

GROVER CLEVELAND.

EXECUTIVE MANSION, *April 26, 1886.*

To the Senate of the United States:

I herewith return Senate bill No. 349, entitled "An act for the promotion of anatomical science and to prevent the desecration of graves," without my approval.

The purpose of this bill is to permit the delivery of certain dead bodies to the medical colleges located in the District of Columbia for dissection.

Such disposition of the bodies of unknown and pauper dead is only excused by the necessity of acquiring by this means proper and useful anatomical knowledge, and the laws by which it is permitted should, in deference to a decent and universal sentiment, carefully guard against abuse and needless offense.

The measure under consideration does not with sufficient care specify and limit the officers and the parties who it is proposed to invest with discretion in the disposition of dead bodies remaining in the institutions and places mentioned in the bill. The second section indicates an intention to prevent the use of said bodies for any other purpose than the promotion of anatomical and surgical knowledge within the District of Columbia, and to secure after such use the decent burial of the remains.   It declares that a bond shall be given providing for the performance of these conditions.   But instead of exacting the bond from the medical colleges, to which alone, by the terms of the first section, the bodies are to be delivered, such bond is required of "every physician or surgeon before receiving such dead body."

The bill also provides that a relative by blood or marriage, or a friend, may, within forty-eight hours after death, demand that any body be buried, upon satisfying "the authorities" of the relationship claimed to the deceased.

The "authorities" to be thus satisfied should be clearly defined, and the determination of a question so important should be left with those only who will perform this duty with proper care and consideration.

GROVER CLEVELAND.

EXECUTIVE MANSION,
Washington, April 30, 1886.

To the Senate of the United States:

I herewith return without my approval Senate bill No. 141, entitled "An act to extend the provisions of the act of June 10, 1880, entitled 'An act to amend the statutes in relation to immediate transportation of dutiable goods, and for other purposes,' to the port of Omaha, in the State of Nebraska."

The statute, which was passed June 10, 1880, referred to in the title of this bill permitted certain merchandise imported at specified ports, but which was consigned to certain other ports which were mentioned by name in the seventh section of said act, to be shipped immediately after entry at the port of arrival to such destination.

The seventh section of said act contained the names of more than seventy ports or places to which imported merchandise might be thus immediately shipped.   One of the places thus named is "Omaha, in Nebraska."

But it was declared in a proviso which was made a part of this section that the privilege of immediate transportation contemplated by the act should "not extend to any place at which there are not the necessary officers for the appraisement of merchandise and the collection of duties."

Because there were no such officers at Omaha the privilege mentioned was withheld from that place by the Treasury Department.

The bill submitted to me for approval provides that these privileges conferred by the act of June 10, 1880, be "extended to the port of Omaha, in the State of Nebraska, as provided for as to the ports mentioned in section 7 of said act."

I can not see that anything is gained by this legislation.

If the circumstances should warrant such a course, the authority which withholds such privileges from any of the places mentioned in the law of 1880 can confer the same without the aid of a new statute. This position is sustained by an opinion of the Attorney-General, dated in February, 1885.

If the legislation now proposed should become operative, the privileges extended to the city of Omaha would still be subject to the proviso attached to the seventh section of the law of 1880, and such newly granted privileges would be liable to immediate withdrawal by the Secretary of the Treasury.

Thus, if the design of this bill is to restore to the city named the privileges permitted by the law of 1880, it seems to be entirely unnecessary, since the power of such restoration is now fully vested in the Treasury Department. If the object sought is to bestow such privileges entirely free from the operation of the proviso above recited, the language of the bill does not accomplish that result.

I understand that the Government has not now at Omaha "the necessary officers for the appraisement of merchandise and the collection of duties," which by such proviso are necessary in order to secure to any place the advantages of immediate transportation. In the absence of such officers the proposed legislation would be nugatory and inoperative.

GROVER CLEVELAND.

EXECUTIVE MANSION, *May 8, 1886.*

To the House of Representatives:

I herewith return without approval a bill numbered 3019, entitled "An act to increase the pension of Abigail Smith," which bill originated in the House of Representatives.

This proposed legislation does injustice to a very worthy pensioner who was on the pension roll at the time of the passage of the law which took effect on the 19th day of March last, and by virtue of which all pensions of her class were increased from $8 to $12 per-month. Under this law she became entitled to her increased pension from the date of its passage. The bill now returned allows her the same amount, but if it became a law I suppose it would supersede her claim under the previous statute and postpone the receipt by her of the increase to the date of the passage of the new law.

She would thus lose for nearly two months the increase of pension already secured to her.

GROVER CLEVELAND.

EXECUTIVE MANSION, *May 8, 1886.*

To the House of Representatives:

I return without my approval House bill No. 1471, entitled "An act increasing the pension of Andrew J. Hill."

This bill doubles the pension which the person named therein has been receiving for a number of years. It appears from the report of the committee to which the bill was referred that a claim made by him for increased pension has been lately rejected by the Pension Bureau "on the ground that the claimant is now receiving a pension commensurate with the degree of disability found to exist."

The policy of frequently reversing by special enactment the decisions of the Bureau invested by law with the examination of pension claims, fully equipped for such examination, and which ought not to be suspected of any lack of liberality to our veteran soldiers, is exceedingly questionable. It may well be doubted if a committee of Congress has a better opportunity than such an agency to judge of the merits of these claims. If, however, there is any lack of power in the Pension Bureau for a full investigation, it should be supplied; if the system adopted is inadequate to do full justice to claimants, it should be corrected, and if there is a want of sympathy and consideration for the defenders of our Government the Bureau should be reorganized.

The disposition to concede the most generous treatment to the disabled, aged, and needy among our veterans ought not to be restrained; and it must be admitted that in some cases justice and equity can not be done nor the charitable tendencies of the Government in favor of worthy objects of its care indulged under fixed rules. These conditions sometimes justify a resort to special legislation, but I am convinced that the interposition by special enactment in the granting of pensions should be rare and exceptional. In the nature of things if this is lightly done and upon slight occasion, an invitation is offered for the presentation of claims to Congress which upon their merits could not survive the test of an examination by the Pension Bureau, and whose only hope of success depends upon sympathy, often misdirected, instead of right and justice. The instrumentality organized by law for the determination of pension claims is thus often overruled and discredited, and there is danger that in the end popular prejudice will be created against those who are worthily entitled to the bounty of the Government.

There has lately been presented to me, on the same day, for approval, nearly 240 special bills granting and increasing pensions and restoring to the pension list the names of parties which for cause have been dropped. To aid Executive duty they were referred to the Pension Bureau for examination and report. After a delay absolutely necessary they have been returned to me within a few hours of the limit constitutionally permitted for Executive action. Two hundred and thirty-two of these bills are thus classified:

Eighty-one cover cases in which favorable action by the Pension Bureau was denied by reason of the insufficiency of the testimony filed to prove the facts alleged.

These bills I have approved on the assumption that the claims were meritorious and that by the passage of the bills the Government has waived full proof of the facts.

Twenty-six of the bills cover claims rejected by the Pension Bureau because the evidence produced tended to prove that the alleged disability existed before the claimant's enlistment; 21 cover claims which have been denied by such Bureau because the evidence tended to show that the disability, though contracted in the service, was not incurred in the line of duty; 33 cover claims which have been denied because the evidence tended to establish that the disability originated after the soldier's discharge from the Army; 47 cover claims which have been denied because the general pension laws contain no provisions under which they could be allowed, and 24 of the claims have never been presented to the Pension Bureau.

I estimate the expenditure involved in these bills at more than $35,000 annually.

Though my conception of public duty leads me to the conclusion, upon the slight examination which I have been able to give such of these bills as are not comprised in the first class above mentioned, that many of them should be disapproved, I am utterly unable to submit within the time allowed me for that purpose my objections to the same.

They will therefore become operative without my approval.

A sufficient reason for the return of the particular bill now under consideration is found in the fact that it provides that the name of Andrew J. Hill be placed upon the pension roll, while the records of the Pension Bureau, as well as a medical certificate made a part of the committee's report, disclose that the correct name of the intended beneficiary is Alfred J. Hill.

GROVER CLEVELAND.

EXECUTIVE MANSION, *May 17, 1886.*

To the Senate of the United States:

I return without approval Senate bill No. 1397, entitled "An act to establish a port of delivery at Springfield, in the State of Massachusetts."

It appears that the best reasons urged for the passage of this bill are that Springfield has a population of about 40,000, that the imports to the section of country where the city is located for the last year amounted in value to nearly $3,000,000, and that the importers at this point labored under a disadvantage in being obliged to go to New York and Boston to clear their goods, which are frequently greatly delayed.

The Government is now subjected to great loss of revenue through the intricacies of the present system relating to the collection of customs dues, and through the frauds and evasions which that system permits and invites. It is also the cause of much of the delay and vexation to which the honest importer is subjected.

I am of the opinion that the reforms of present methods which have been lately earnestly pressed upon Congress should be inaugurated, instead of increasing the number of ports where present evils may be further extended.

The bill now under consideration provides that a surveyor of customs shall be appointed to reside at said port, who shall receive a salary not to exceed $1,000 per annum.

It is quite obvious that an experienced force of employees at the ports where goods for Springfield are entered would be much better qualified to adjust the duties upon the same than the person thus proposed to be added to the vast army of Federal officials.

There are many cities in the different States having larger populations than Springfield, and fully as much entitled, upon every ground presented, to the advantages sought by this bill; and yet it is clear that the following of the precedent which the proposed legislation would establish could not fail to produce confusion and uncertainty in the adjustment of customs dues, leading to irritating discriminations and probable loss to the Government.

GROVER CLEVELAND.

EXECUTIVE MANSION, *May 24, 1886.*

To the Senate of the United States:

I herewith return without approval Senate bill No. 2186, entitled "An act granting a pension to Louis Melcher."

This claimant enlisted on the 25th day of May, 1861, and was discharged for disability on the 16th day of August, 1861, having been in the service less than three months.

The certificate of the surgeon of his regiment, made at the time of his discharge, stated his disability to be "lameness, caused by previous repeated and extensive ulcerations of his legs, extending deeply among the muscles and impairing their powers and action by cicatrices, all existing before enlistment and not mentioned to the mustering officers at the time."

Upon this certificate, given at the time of the claimant's discharge and while he was actually under the surgeon's observation, an application for a pension was rejected by the Pension Bureau.

In the absence of anything impeaching the ability and integrity of the surgeon of the regiment, his certificate should, in my opinion, be regarded as a true statement of the condition of the claimant at the time of his discharge, though the committee's report suggests that the surgeon's skill may have been at fault when he declared that the ulcers existed before enlistment. The cicatrices showing beyond a doubt the previous existence of this difficulty would be plainly apparent upon an examination by a surgeon, and their origin could hardly be mistaken. The term of the claimant's service was not sufficiently long to have developed and healed, even imperfectly, in a location previously healthy, ulcers of the kind mentioned in the claimant's application.

My approval of this bill is therefore withheld upon the ground that I find nothing in my examination of the facts connected with the case which impeaches the value of the surgeon's certificate upon which the adverse action of the Pension Bureau was predicated.

GROVER CLEVELAND.

EXECUTIVE MANSION, *May 24, 1886.*

To the Senate of the United States:

A bill which originated in the Senate, entitled "An act granting a pension to Edward Ayers," and numbered 363, is herewith returned without approval.

The person named in this bill enlisted October 3, 1861, in an Indiana regiment and was mustered out of the service December 13, 1865. He represents that he was injured in the hip at the battle of Days Gap, April 30, 1863, and for this a pension is provided for him by the bill under consideration. His application for pension has been rejected by the Pension Bureau on the ground that it was proved on a special examination of the case that the claimant was injured by a fall when a boy, and that the injury complained of existed prior to his enlistment.

There is not a particle of proof or a fact stated either in the committee's report or the records in the Pension Bureau, so far as they are brought to my notice, tending to show that the claimant was in hospital or under medical care a single day during the whole term of his enlistment.

The report of the committee contains the following statement:

The record evidence proves that he was in this engagement, but there is no proof from this source that he was wounded. By numerous comrades who were present it is proven that he was hurt by the explosion of a shell as claimed. It is also shown that he has been disabled ever since; and the examining surgeon specifically describes the wound, and twice verifies that he is permanently disabled. From the fact that a man was exceedingly liable to injury under the circumstances in which he was placed, and from the evidence of eyewitnesses, the committee are of opinion that he was wounded as alleged.

A wound from a shell causing the person injured to be "disabled ever since" usually results in hospital or medical treatment. Not only is there no such claim made in this case, but, on the contrary, it appears that the claimant served in his regiment two years and nearly eight months after the alleged injury, and until he was mustered out.

It is represented to me by a report from the Pension Bureau that after his alleged wound, and in May or June, 1863, the claimant deserted, and in July of that year was arrested in the State of Indiana and returned to duty without trial. If this report is correct, the party now seeking a pension at the hands of the Government for disability incurred in the service seems to have been capable of considerable physical exertion, though not very creditable, within a few weeks after he claims to have received the injury upon which his application is based.

GROVER CLEVELAND.

EXECUTIVE MANSION, *May 24, 1886.*

To the Senate of the United States:

I return without approval Senate bill No. 1630, entitled "An act granting a pension to James C. Chandler."

It appears from the report of the committee to whom this bill was referred and from an examination of the official records that the proposed beneficiary first enlisted on the 27th day of August, 1861, and about nine months thereafter, on the 1st day of June, 1862, was discharged on account of disability arising from chronic bronchitis.

Notwithstanding the chronic character of his alleged disability, he enlisted again on the 3d day of January, 1864, seventeen months after such discharge.

No statement is presented of the bounty received by him upon either enlistment.

He was finally mustered out on the 19th day of September, 1865.

He first applied for a pension under the general law in May, 1869, alleging that in April, 1862, he was run over by a wagon and injured in his ankle. This accident occurred during his first enlistment; but instead of the injury having been then regarded a disability, he was discharged from such enlistment less than two months thereafter on account of chronic bronchitis.

It appears from the committee's report that his application was rejected and that another was afterwards made, alleging that the claimant had been afflicted with typhoid fever contracted in May, 1862, resulting in "rheumatism and disease of the back in region of kidneys."

This application was also rejected, on the ground that any disability that might have arisen from the cause alleged "had not existed in a pensionable degree since the date of filing the claim therefor," which was February 10, 1885.

There still remained an appeal to Congress, and probably there were not wanting those who found their interests in advising such an appeal and who had at hand Congressional precedents which promised a favorable result. That the parties interested did not miscalculate the chances of success is demonstrated by the bill now before me, which, in direct opposition to the action of the Pension Bureau, grants a pension to a man who, though discharged from enlistment for a certain alleged disability, made two applications for a pension based upon two distinct causes, both claimed to exist within two months prior to such discharge, and both different from the one upon which he accepted the same, and notwithstanding the fact that the proposed beneficiary, after all these disabilities had occurred, passed an examination as to his physical fitness for reenlistment, actually did reenlist, and served till finally mustered out at the close of the war.

If any money is to be given this man from the public Treasury, it should not be done under the guise of a pension.

GROVER CLEVELAND.

EXECUTIVE MANSION, *May 24, 1886.*

To the Senate of the United States:

I hereby return without approval Senate bill No. 857, entitled "An act granting a pension to Dudley B. Branch."

This claim is based upon the allegation, as appears by the committee's report, that the person named in the bill has a hernia, and that on the 9th day of June, 1862, while in the military service and in the line of duty, "in getting over a fence he fell heavily, striking a stone or hard substance, and received the hernia in his left side."

In December, 1875, thirteen and a half years thereafter, he filed an application for a pension, which was rejected by the Pension Bureau on the ground that there was no record of the alleged hernia, and the claimant was unable to furnish satisfactory evidence of its origin in the service.

The fact is stated in the committee's report that late in the year 1863 this soldier was transferred to the Invalid Corps, and the records show that he was thus transferred for a disability entirely different from that upon which he now bases his claim. He was mustered out in September, 1864, at the end of his term of service.

I am convinced that the rejection of this claim by the Pension Bureau was correct, and think its action should not be reversed.

I suppose an injury of the description claimed, if caused by violence directly applied, is quite palpable, its effect usually immediate, and its existence easily proved. The long time which elapsed between the injury and the claimant's application for a pension may be fairly considered as bearing upon the merits of such application, while the fact that the claimant was transferred to the Invalid Corps more than a year after he alleges the injury occurred, for an entirely different disability, can not be overlooked. In the committee's report the statement is found that the beneficiary named in the bill was in two different hospitals during the year 1863, and yet it is not claimed that the history of his hospital treatment furnishes any proof of the injury upon which his claim is now based.

GROVER CLEVELAND.

EXECUTIVE MANSION, *May 25, 1886.*

To the Senate of the United States:

I return without approval Senate bill No. 1998, entitled "An act for the relief of John D. Ham," which grants a pension to the party named.

The claimant alleges that he enrolled in the Army in January, 1862, and was "sworn in at his own home;" that the next day he started on horseback to go to the regiment he was to join, and that on the way his horse fell upon his left ankle, whereby he sustained an injury which entitles him to a pension.

His name is not borne upon any of the rolls of the regiment he alleges he was on his way to join.

He filed his application for pension in the Pension Bureau October 17, 1879 (seventeen years after his alleged injury), which was rejected apparently on the ground that he was not in the military service when the disability claimed was incurred.

He was drafted in 1863 and served until he was mustered out in 1865.

It is entirely clear that this claimant was not in the military service at the time he claims to have been injured; and his conduct in remaining at home until he was drafted, nearly two years afterwards, furnishes proof that he did not regard himself as in the meantime owing any military duty. These considerations, and the further facts that upon being drafted he was accepted as physically qualified for service, that he actually thereafter served a year and eight months, and that he waited seventeen years before claiming pension for his injury, in my mind present a case upon which the claimant is entitled to no relief even if charity instead of just liberality is invoked.

GROVER CLEVELAND.

EXECUTIVE MANSION, *May 25, 1886.*
To the Senate of the United States:

I herewith return without approval Senate bill No. 1290, entitled "An act granting a pension to David W. Hamilton."

A claim for pension filed by him in November, 1879, was rejected by the Pension Bureau on the ground that his alleged disability existed prior to his enlistment.

An examination of the records in the Adjutant-General's Office and a statement from the Pension Bureau derived from the claimant's application there for pension, with a reference to the report of the committee to whom this bill was referred, disclose the following facts:

The claimant was mustered in the service as first lieutenant in September, 1861, and as captain June 12, 1862. He is reported as present with his company until the 30th of that month. For the six months immediately following the latter date he is reported as "absent sick," and for the ten months next succeeding, and until October 27, 1863, as "absent on detached service." On the day last mentioned he tendered his resignation at Camp Morton, in the State of Indiana, to enable him to accept an appointment as captain in the Invalid Corps. He was thereupon so appointed upon account of "chronic enlargement of the spermatic cord of several years' standing, consequent upon hydrocele." He remained in the Invalid Corps until July 12, 1864, when, upon the tender of his resignation, he was discharged.

Less than four months afterwards, and on the 6th day of November, 1864, he was mustered in the service as a captain in another regiment of volunteers, and on the 17th day of November, 1865, again tendered his resignation, and was finally discharged.

Upon his application for pension under the general law, fourteen years thereafter, he admitted that he suffered from hydrocele as early as 1856, but claimed that an operation then performed for the same had given him permanent relief.

It will be seen that the claimant's term of service was liberally interspersed with sick leave, detached service, resignations, and membership in the Invalid Corps. He admits having the trouble which would naturally result in his alleged disability long before he entered the service. The surgeon upon whose certificate he was appointed to the Invalid Corps must have stated to him the character of his difficulty and that it was chronic. No application for pension was made until fourteen years after his discharge and just prior to the expiration of the time within which large arrearages might have been claimed. There is no hint of any medical testimony at all contradicting the certificate of the army surgeon made in 1863, but it is stated in the report of the committee that he can not procure medical testimony as to his soundness before entering the service because his family physician is dead. If he had filed his application earlier, it would have appeared in better faith, and it may be that he could have secured the evidence of his family physician if it was of the character he desired.

After the Pension Bureau has been in operation for a score of years since the late civil war, equipped with thousands of employees charged with no other duty except the ascertainment and adjustment of the claims of our discharged soldiers and their surviving relatives, it seems to me that a stronger case than this should be presented to justify the passage of a special act, twenty-three years after an alleged disability, granting a pension which has been refused by the Bureau especially organized for the purpose of allowing the same under just and liberal laws.

I am by no means insensible to that influence which leads the judgment toward the allowance of every claim alleged to be founded upon patriotic service in the nation's cause; and yet I neither believe it to be a duty nor a kindness to the worthy citizens for whose benefit our scheme of pensions was provided to permit the diversion of the nation's bounty to objects not within its scope and purpose.

GROVER CLEVELAND.

EXECUTIVE MANSION, *May 28, 1886.*

To the Senate:

I hereby return without approval Senate bill No. 1850, entitled "An act granting a pension to Mrs. Annie C. Owen."

The husband of the claimant was mustered into the service as second lieutenant December 14, 1861, and discharged October 16, 1862. It appears that he died in 1876 from neuralgia of the heart. In 1883 the present claimant filed her application for pension, alleging that her husband received two shell wounds, one in the calf of his left leg and one in his left side, on the 1st day of July, 1862, and claiming that they were in some way connected with the cause of his death.

On the records of his command there is no mention made of either wound, but it does appear that on the 8th day of July, seven days after the date of the alleged wounds, he was granted a leave of absence for thirty days on account, as stated in a medical certificate, of "remittent fever and diarrhea." A medical certificate dated August 5, 1862, while absent on leave, represents him to be at that time suffering from "chronic bronchitis and acute dysentery."

The application made for pension by the widow was rejected by the Pension Bureau February 1, 1886.

There is nothing before me showing that the husband of the claimant ever filed an application for pension, though he lived nearly fourteen years after his discharge; and his widow's claim was not made until twenty-one years after the alleged wounds and seven years after her husband's death.

If the information furnished concerning this soldier's service is correct, this claim for pension must be based upon a mistake. It is hardly possible that wounds such as are alleged should be received in battle by a second lieutenant and no record made of them; that he should seven days thereafter receive a leave of absence for other sickness, with no mention of these wounds, and that a medical certificate should be made (probably with a view of prolonging his leave) stating still other ailments, but silent as to wounds. The further facts that he made no claim for pension and that the claim of his widow was long delayed are worthy of consideration. And if the wounds were received as described there is certainly no necessary connection between them and death fourteen years afterwards from neuralgia of the heart.   GROVER CLEVELAND.

EXECUTIVE MANSION, *May 28, 1886.*
To the House of Representatives:

I return without approval a bill originating in the House of Representatives, numbered 2145, and entitled "An act for the relief of Rebecca Eldridge."

This bill provides for the payment of a pension to the claimant as the widow of Wilber H. Eldridge, who was mustered into the service on the 24th day of July, 1862, and discharged June 21, 1865. He was pensioned at the rate of $2 per month for a slight wound in the calf of the left leg, received on the 25th day of March, 1865. There is no pretense that this wound was at all serious, and a surgeon who examined it in 1880 reported that in his opinion the wounded man "was not incapacitated from obtaining his subsistence by manual labor;'' that the ball passed "rather superficially through the muscles," and that the party examined said there was no lameness "unless after long standing or walking a good deal." .

On the 28th of January, 1881, while working about a building, he fell backward from a ladder and fractured his skull, from which he died the same day.

Without a particle of proof and with no fact established which connects the fatal accident in the remotest degree with the wound referred to, it is proposed to grant a pension to the widow of $12 per month.

It is not a pleasant thing to interfere in such a case; but we are dealing with pensions, and not with gratuities.

GROVER CLEVELAND.

EXECUTIVE MANSION, *May 28, 1886.*

To the Senate:

I hereby return without approval Senate bill No. 1253, entitled "An act granting a pension to J. D. Haworth."

It is proposed by this bill to grant a pension to the claimant for the alleged loss of sight in one eye and the impairment of the vision of the other.

From the information furnished me I am convinced that the difficulty alleged by this applicant had its origin in causes existing prior to his enlistment, and that his present condition of disability is not the result of his service in the Army.

GROVER CLEVELAND.

EXECUTIVE MANSION, *May 28, 1886.*

To the House of Representatives:

I hereby return without approval a bill which originated in the House of Representatives, numbered 1582, and entitled "An act for the relief of Eleanor C. Bangham."

The claimant in this case is the widow of John S. Bangham, who was mustered into the service of the United States as a private on the 26th day of March, 1864, and was discharged by general order June 23, 1865.

It appears that during his fifteen months of service he was sick a considerable part of the time, and the records in two of the hospitals to which he was admitted show that his sickness was epilepsy. There are no records showing the character of his illness in other hospitals.

His widow, the present claimant, filed an application for pension March 12, 1878, alleging that her husband committed suicide September 10, 1873, from the effects of chronic diarrhea and general debility contracted in the service. Upon the evidence then produced her claim was allowed at the rate of $8 a month. She remained upon the rolls until July, 1885, when a special examination of the case was made, upon which it was developed and admitted by the pensioner that the deceased service seems to have been capable of considerable physical exertion, though not very creditable, within a few weeks after he claims to have received the injury upon which his application is based.

GROVER CLEVELAND.

EXECUTIVE MANSION, *May 24, 1886.*

To the Senate of the United States:

I return without approval Senate bill No. 1630, entitled "An act granting a pension to James C. Chandler."

It appears from the report of the committee to whom this bill was referred and from an examination of the official records that the proposed beneficiary first enlisted on the 27th day of August, 1861, and about nine months thereafter, on the 1st day of June, 1862, was discharged on account of disability arising from chronic bronchitis.

Notwithstanding the chronic character of his alleged disability, he enlisted again on the 3d day of January, 1864, seventeen months after such discharge.

No statement is presented of the bounty received by him upon either enlistment.

He was finally mustered out on the 19th day of September, 1865.

He first applied for a pension under the general law in May, 1869, alleging that in April, 1862, he was run over by a wagon and injured in his ankle. This accident occurred during his first enlistment; but instead of the injury having been then regarded a disability, he was discharged from such enlistment less than two months thereafter on account of chronic bronchitis.

It appears from the committee's report that his application was rejected and that another was afterwards made, alleging that the claimant had been afflicted with typhoid fever contracted in May, 1862, resulting in "rheumatism and disease of the back in region of kidneys."

This application was also rejected, on the ground that any disability that might have arisen from the cause alleged "had not existed in a pensionable degree since the date of filing the claim therefor," which was February 10, 1885.

There still remained an appeal to Congress, and probably there were not wanting those who found their interests in advising such an appeal and who had at hand Congressional precedents which promised a favorable result. That the parties interested did not miscalculate the chances of success is demonstrated by the bill now before me, which, in direct opposition to the action of the Pension Bureau, grants a pension to a man who, though discharged from enlistment for a certain alleged disability, made two applications for a pension based upon two distinct causes, both claimed to exist within two months prior to such discharge, and both different from the one upon which he accepted the same, and notwithstanding the fact that the proposed beneficiary, after all these disabilities had occurred, passed an examination as to his physical fitness for reenlistment, actually did reenlist, and served till finally mustered out at the close of the war.

If any money is to be given this man from the public Treasury, it should not be done under the guise of a pension.

GROVER CLEVELAND.

EXECUTIVE MANSION, *May 24, 1886.*

To the Senate of the United States:

I hereby return without approval Senate bill No. 857, entitled "An act granting a pension to Dudley B. Branch."

This claim is based upon the allegation, as appears by the committee's report, that the person named in the bill has a hernia, and that on the 9th day of June, 1862, while in the military service and in the line of duty, "in getting over a fence he fell heavily, striking a stone or hard substance, and received the hernia in his left side."

In December, 1875, thirteen and a half years thereafter, he filed an application for a pension, which was rejected by the Pension Bureau on the ground that there was no record of the alleged hernia, and the claimant was unable to furnish satisfactory evidence of its origin in the service.

The fact is stated in the committee's report that late in the year 1863 this soldier was transferred to the Invalid Corps, and the records show that he was thus transferred for a disability entirely different from that upon which he now bases his claim. He was mustered out in September, 1864, at the end of his term of service.

I am convinced that the rejection of this claim by the Pension Bureau was correct, and think its action should not be reversed.

I suppose an injury of the description claimed, if caused by violence directly applied, is quite palpable, its effect usually immediate, and its existence easily proved. The long time which elapsed between the injury and the claimant's application for a pension may be fairly considered as bearing upon the merits of such application, while the fact that the claimant was transferred to the Invalid Corps more than a year after he alleges the injury occurred, for an entirely different disability, can not be overlooked. In the committee's report the statement is found that the beneficiary named in the bill was in two different hospitals during the year 1863, and yet it is not claimed that the history of his hospital treatment furnishes any proof of the injury upon which his claim is now based.

GROVER CLEVELAND.

EXECUTIVE MANSION, *May 25, 1886.*

To the Senate of the United States:

I return without approval Senate bill No. 1998, entitled "An act for the relief of John D. Ham," which grants a pension to the party named.

From the report of the committee to whom this bill was referred I learn that the claimant enlisted in April, 1861, and was discharged in October, 1864.

He filed a claim in the Pension Bureau alleging that he received a saber wound in the head March 7, 1862, and a gunshot wound in the left leg in the autumn of the same year.

It appears upon examination of his military record that there is no mention of either disability, and that he served two years after the time he claims to have received these injuries. So far from being disabled, it is reported as an incident of his army life that in the year 1864 this soldier was found guilty of desertion and sentenced to forfeit all pay and allowances for the time he was absent.

The report of the committee, in apparent explanation of the lack of any official mention of the injuries alleged, declares that "the fact that the records of the War Department are often imperfect works great hardship to men who apply for pensions;" and his conviction of desertion and the lack of proof to sustain his allegations as to his injuries are disposed of as follows in the committee's report:

The Adjutant-General's report shows that the man was under discipline for some irregularities, but notwithstanding this and the lack of the required proof that he was wounded in the line of duty the committee are of the opinion that, situated as he was, he was very liable to and very probably did receive the wound from which he has suffered and is still suffering.

I am convinced that there exists serious difficulty on the part of the claimant instead of in the record of the War Department; that the kind of irregularity for which he was under discipline is calculated to produce a lack of confidence in his merits as a pensioner, and that the fact of his situation being such as to render him liable to receive a wound is hardly sufficient to establish his right to a soldier's pension, which is only justified by injuries actually received and affirmatively proven.

GROVER CLEVELAND.

To the Senate: EXECUTIVE MANSION, *June 2, 1886.*

I return herewith without approval Senate bill No. 1726, entitled "An act granting a pension to Augustus Field Stevens."

It appears that this claimant enlisted August 21, 1861, and was discharged on the 3d day of October, 1861, after a service of less than two months, upon a medical certificate of disability which represented him as "incapable of performing the duties of a soldier because of general debility, advanced age, unfit for service before entering."

His claim is not based upon any wound or injury, but he alleges that he contracted chronic diarrhea or dysentery while in the service. The committee to whom the bill was referred by the Senate admit that "there is a quantity of contradictory testimony, biased in about equal proportion for and against the claimant."

His claim was rejected by the Pension Bureau in 1882 and again in 1885, after a special examination concerning the facts, on the ground that the claimant had failed to show any pensionable disability contracted while he was in the service.

The medical certificate upon which he was discharged makes no mention of the disorders of which the applicant for pension now complains, but contains other statements which demonstrate that no allowance should be made to him by way of pension, unless such pension is to be openly and confessedly regarded as a mere charity, or unless the medical certificate made at the time of discharge, with the patient under observation, is to be, without any allegation to that effect, impeached.

I am not prepared either to gratuitously set at naught two determinations of the Pension Bureau, one very lately made after a special examination, and especially when the evidence produced before the committee to reverse the Bureau's action is admitted to be "contradictory" and "biased in about equal proportion for and against the claimant."

GROVER CLEVELAND.

To the Senate: EXECUTIVE MANSION, *June 19, 1886.*

I return herewith Senate bill No. 226, entitled "An act granting a pension to Margaret D. Marchand," without approval.

The beneficiary named in this bill is the widow of John B. Marchand, who entered the United States Navy in 1828, who was promoted to the rank of commodore in 1866, and who was placed upon the retired list in 1870. He died in August, 1875, of heart disease.

His widow filed an application for pension in 1883, claiming that his fatal disease was caused by exposure and exertion in the service during the War of the Rebellion. The application was rejected because of the inability to furnish evidence to prove that the death had any relation to the naval service of the deceased.

I am unable to see how any other conclusion could have been reached. The information furnished by the report of the committee to whom this bill was referred and derived from other data before me absolutely fails to connect the death of Commodore Marchand with any incident of his naval service.

This officer was undoubtedly brave and efficient, rendering his country valuable service; but it does not appear to have been of so distinguished a character, nor are the circumstances of his widow alleged to be such, as to render a gratuity justifiable. GROVER CLEVELAND.

To the Senate: EXECUTIVE MANSION, *June 19, 1886.*

I hereby return without my approval Senate bill No. 183, entitled "An act for the relief of Thomas S. Hopkins, late of Company C, Sixteenth Maine Volunteers."

This soldier was enrolled in the Army June 2, 1862, and discharged June 30, 1865. He was sent to the Government hospital September 20, 1863, and thereupon transferred to the Invalid Corps.

He filed his declaration for a pension in November, 1880, alleging that while in the service he contracted malarial fever and chronic diarrhea, and was seized with convulsions, suffering from great general debility.

A pension of $50 a month was granted to him in June, 1881, dating from the time of filing his application, which sum he has been receiving up to the present time.

This bill proposes to remove the limitation fixed by the law of 1879 prescribing the date prior to which an application for pension must be filed in order to entitle the claimant to draw the pension allowed from the time of his discharge from the service.

If this bill should become a law, it would entitle the claimant to about $9,000 of back pension. This is claimed upon the ground that the soldier was so sick from the time of the passage of the act creating the limitation up to the date allowed him to avail himself of the privileges of the act that he could not file his claim.

I think the limitation thus fixed a very wise one, and that it should not, in fairness to other claimants, be relaxed for causes not mentioned in the statute; nor should the door be opened to applications of this kind.

The beneficiary named in this bill had fifteen years after the accruing of his claim, and before it is alleged that he was incapacitated, within which he might have filed his application and entitled himself to the back pension now applied for.

The facts here presented come so far short of furnishing a satisfactory excuse for his delay that, in my judgment, the discrimination asked in his favor should not be granted.

GROVER CLEVELAND.

To the Senate: EXECUTIVE MANSION, *June 19, 1886.*

I return without approval Senate bill No. 763, entitled "An act for the erection of a public building at Sioux City, Iowa."

The report of the committee of the House of Representatives to whom this bill was referred states that by the census of 1880 the population of Sioux City was nearly 8,000, and that by other enumerations since made its population would seem to exceed 23,000. It is further stated in the report that for the accommodation of this population the city contains 393 brick and 2,984 frame buildings.

It seems to me that in the consideration of the merits of this bill the necessities of the Government should control the question, and that it should be decided as a business proposition, depending upon the needs of a Government building at the point proposed in order to do the Government work.

This greatly reduces the value of statistics showing population, extent of business, prospective growth, and matters of that kind, which, though exceedingly interesting, do not always demonstrate the necessity of the expenditure of a large sum of money for a public building.

I find upon examination that United States courts are sometimes held at Sioux City, but that they have been thus far held in the county court-house without serious inconvenience and without any expense to the Government. There are actually no other Federal officers there for whom the Government in any view should provide accommodations except the postmaster. The post-office is now located in a building rented by the Government until the 1st day of January, 1889, at the rate of $2,200 per annum.

By the last report of the Supervising Architect it appears that on October 1, 1885, there were 80 new public buildings in course of con-struction, and that the amount expended thereon during the preceding year was nearly $2,500,000, while large appropriations are asked to be expended on these buildings during the current year.

In my judgment the number of public buildings should not at this time be increased unless a greater public necessity exists therefor than is apparent in this case. GROVER CLEVELAND.

To the Senate: EXECUTIVE MANSION, *June 19, 1886.*

I return without approval Senate bill No. 206, entitled "An act to provide for the erection of a public building in the city of Zanesville, Ohio."

No Federal courts are held at Zanesville, and there are no Govern-ment officers located there who should be provided for at the public expense except the postmaster.

So far as I am informed the patrons of the post-office are fairly well accommodated in a building which is rented by the Government at the rate of $800 per annum; and though the postmaster naturally certifies that he and his fourteen employees require much more spacious sur-roundings, I have no doubt he and they can be induced to continue to serve the Government in its present quarters.

The public buildings now in process of construction, numbering 80, involving constant supervision, are all the building projects which the Government ought to have on hand at one time, unless a very palpable necessity exists for an increase in the number. The multiplication of these structures involves not only the appropriations made for their com-pletion, but great expense in their care and preservation thereafter.

While a fine Government building is a desirable ornament to any town or city, and while the securing of an appropriation therefor is often considered as an illustration of zeal and activity in the interest of a con-stituency, I am of the opinion that the expenditure of public money for such a purpose should depend upon the necessity of such a building for public uses.

In the case under consideration I have no doubt the Government can be well accommodated for some time to come in all its business relations with the people of Zanesville by renting quarters, at less expense than the annual cost of maintaining the proposed new building after its completion.

GROVER ·CLEVELAND.

EXECUTIVE MANSION, *June 19, 1886.*
To the House of Representatives:

I hereby return without approval House bill No. 1990, entitled "An act granting a pension to John Hunter."

The claimant was enrolled July 20, 1864, and was discharged by expiration of his term of service July 13, 1865.

During four months of the twelve while he remained in the service he is reported as "absent sick." His hospital record shows that he was treated for intermittent fever and rheumatism. In 1879, fourteen years after his discharge, he filed his claim for a pension, alleging that in May, 1864, he received a gunshot wound in the right leg while in a skirmish. The month of May, 1864, is included in the time during which, by the record, he appears to have been absent sick and undergoing treatment for fever and rheumatism. His claim was rejected in December, 1884, on the ground that there was no record of the alleged wound and the claimant was unable, though aided by the Bureau, to prove that the injury claimed was due to the service.

The evidence recited in the report of the Congressional committee to whom this bill was referred, though it tends to show, if reliable, that when the soldier returned from his service his leg was affected, fails to show a continuous disability from that cause. It is stated that about five years ago, while the claimant was gathering dandelions, in stepping across a ditch his leg broke. The doctor who attended him states that the leg was about four weeks longer in uniting than is usual, but he is not represented as giving an opinion that the fracture had anything to do with his patient's military service.

I find no reference to his condition since his recovery from the fracture of his leg, and there seems to be no allegation of present disability either from army service or the injury sustained while gathering dandelions.

GROVER CLEVELAND.

EXECUTIVE MANSION, *June 19, 1886.*
To the House of Representatives:

I return without my approval House bill No. 4002, entitled "An act granting a pension to Carter W. Tiller."

The records of the War Department show that George W. Tiller, the son of the claimant, enlisted in a Kentucky regiment on the 8th day of October, 1861, and that he deserted on the 20th day of September, 1863; that he was captured by the Confederates afterwards, but the time and circumstances are not given. On the 21st day of July, 1864, he was admitted to the Andersonville hospital, and died the same day of scorbutus.

The father filed his claim for a pension in 1877, alleging his dependence upon the deceased soldier. It is probably true that the son while in the Army sent money to the claimant, though he appears to have been employed as a policeman in the city of Louisville ever since his son's death, at a fair salary.

The claim thus made was rejected by the Pension Bureau on the ground that the claimant was not dependent upon his son.

I am entirely satisfied of the correctness of this determination, and if the records presented to me are reliable I think the fact which appears therefrom, that the death of the soldier occurred ten months after desertion and had no apparent relation to any service in the Union Army, is conclusive against the claim now made.

GROVER CLEVELAND.

EXECUTIVE MANSION, *June 19, 1886.*

To the House of Representatives:

I return without approval House bill No. 3826, entitled "An act for the relief of John Taylor."

By this bill it is proposed to increase the pension of the beneficiary named to $16 a month. He has been receiving a pension under the general law, dating from his discharge in 1865. His pension has been twice already increased, once by the Pension Bureau and once by a special act passed in 1882. His wound is not such as to cause his disability to become aggravated by time. The increase allowed by this bill, when applied for at the Pension Bureau in 1885, was denied on the ground that "the rate he was receiving was commensurate with the degree of his disability, a board of surgeons having reported that he was receiving a liberal rating."

I can discover no just ground for reversing this determination and making a further discrimination in favor of this pensioner.

GROVER CLEVELAND.

EXECUTIVE MANSION, *June 19, 1886.*

To the House of Representatives:

I return without approval House bill No. 5997, entitled "An act granting a pension to Elizabeth Luce."

The claimant named in this bill is the widow of John W. Luce, who entered the Army in August, 1861, and who was discharged in January,

1864, for a disability declared at the time in the surgeon's certificate to arise from "organic stricture of the urethra," which, from his statement, existed at the time of his enlistment.

Notwithstanding the admission which thus appears to have been made by him at the time of his discharge, he soon afterwards made an application for a pension, alleging that his difficulty arose from his being thrown forward on the pommel of his saddle when in the service.

Upon an examination of this claim by a special examiner, it is stated that no one could be found who had any knowledge of such an injury, and the claim was rejected.

In 1883, twenty years after the soldier alleged he was injured in the manner stated, he died, and the cause of his death was declared to be "chronic gastritis, complicated with kidney difficulty."

It is alleged that the examinations made by the Pension Bureau developed the fact that the deceased soldier was a man of quite intemperate habits.

The theory upon which this widow should be pensioned can only be that the death of her husband resulted from a disability or injury contracted or received in the military service. It seems to me that however satisfactorily the injury which he described may be established, and though every suspicion as to his habits be dismissed, there can hardly possibly be any connection between such an injury and the causes to which his death is attributed.

GROVER CLEVELAND.

EXECUTIVE MANSION, *June 19, 1886.*

To the House of Representatives:

I return without approval House bill No. 4058, entitled "An act for the relief of Joel D. Monroe."

The claimant mentioned in this bill enlisted in August, 1864, and was discharged with his regiment June 4, 1865.

The record of his short military service exhibits no mention of any injury or disability; but in June, 1880, fifteen years after his discharge, he filed in the Pension Bureau a claim for a pension based upon the allegation that in December, 1864, he was injured by the falling of a tree, which struck him on his head, affecting both of his eyes. He added to this allegation the further complaint that he contracted rheumatism while in the service.

The application for a pension was rejected by the Pension Bureau because there was no record of the disabilities claimed, nor was satisfactory proof furnished that any such disabilities originated in the service.

I am so entirely satisfied with this determination of the Pension Bureau that I am constrained to withhold my approval of this bill.

GROVER CLEVELAND.

EXECUTIVE MANSION, *June 21, 1886.*

To the House of Representatives:

I return without approval House bill No. 3624, entitled "An act granting a pension to Fred. J. Leese."

This claimant enlisted September 7, 1864, and was discharged June 4, 1865. During his short term of service there does not appear on the records any evidence of disability.

But in November, 1883, eighteen years after his discharge, he filed his application for a pension, alleging that in November, 1864, he contracted chronic diarrhea from exposure and severe work.

His claim has not yet been fully passed upon by the Pension Bureau, which, in my opinion, is sufficient reason why this bill should not become a law. I am also thoroughly convinced, from examination of the case, that the claimant should not be pensioned.

GROVER CLEVELAND.

EXECUTIVE MANSION, *June 21, 1886.*

To the House of Representatives:

I herewith return without approval House bill No. 6897, entitled "An act granting a pension to Henry Hipple, jr."

This claimant entered the Army as a drummer August 6, 1862, and was discharged May 29, 1863.

In 1879, sixteen years after his discharge, he appears to have discovered that during his short term of military service in the inhospitable climate of Port Tobacco, within the State of Maryland, he contracted rheumatism to such an extent as to entitle him to pension, for which he then applied.

It is conceded that he received no medical treatment while in the Army for this complaint, nor does he seem to have been attended by a physician since his discharge.

Without commenting further upon the features of this case which tend to discredit it, I deem myself obliged to disapprove this bill on the ground that there is an almost complete failure to state any facts that should entitle the claimant to a pension.

GROVER CLEVELAND.

EXECUTIVE MANSION, *June 21, 1886.*

To the House of Representatives:

I hereby return without approval a bill originating in the House of Representatives, entitled "An act granting an increase of pension to John W. Farris," which bill is numbered 6136.

The claimant mentioned in this bill enlisted in the month of October, 1861, and was mustered out of the service in August, 1865.

In 1881, sixteen years after his discharge, he filed an application for a pension, alleging that he was afflicted with chronic diarrhea contracted in the Army, and in 1885 his claim was allowed, and he was granted a pension for that cause.

In September of the same year, and after this pension was granted, he filed an application for an increase of his rate, alleging that in 1884 his eyes became affected in consequence of his previous ailments and the debility consequent thereupon.

The ingenuity developed in the constant and persistent attacks upon the public Treasury by those claiming pensions, and the increase of those already granted, is exhibited in bold relief by this attempt to include sore eyes among the results of diarrhea.

I am entirely satisfied with the opinion of the medical referee, who, after examining this case in October, 1885, reported that "the disease of the eyes can not be admitted to be a result of chronic diarrhea."

On all grounds it seems to me that this claimant should be contented with the pension which has been already allowed him.

GROVER CLEVELAND.

EXECUTIVE MANSION, *June 21, 1886.*

To the House of Representatives:

I hereby return without approval House bill No. 1707, entitled "An act granting a pension to Elijah P. Hensley."

The records of the War Department show that this claimant was mustered into the Third North Carolina Regiment, but on the muster-out roll of his company he is reported to have deserted April 3, 1865, and there is no record of any discharge or disability.

In September, 1866, an order was issued from his department headquarters removing the charge of desertion against him. Thirteen days afterwards, and on the 25th day of September, 1866, he filed an application for pension, which in 1868 was granted. He drew such pension dating from 1865 until 1877, when, upon evidence that the injury for which he was pensioned was not received in the line of duty, his name was dropped from the rolls.

The pensioner appealed from this determination of the Pension Bureau to the Secretary of the Interior, who, as lately as May, 1885, rendered a decision sustaining the action of the Bureau.

I find nothing in the facts presented to me which, in my opinion, justifies the reversal of the judgment of the Bureau and the Secretary of the Interior.

GROVER CLEVELAND.

EXECUTIVE MANSION, *June 21, 1886.*

To the Senate:

I return without approval Senate bill No. 2223, entitled "An act granting a pension to Elizabeth S. De Krafft."

My objection to this bill is that it is of no possible advantage to the beneficiary therein mentioned. It directs that her name be placed upon the pension roll, subject to the provisions and limitations of the pension laws. The effect of such legislation would be to permit Mrs. De Krafft to draw a pension at the rate of $30 each month from the date of the approval of the bill.

On the 26th day of February, 1886, under the provisions of the general pension law, she was allowed a pension of this exact sum, but the payments were to date from November 10, 1885.

I am so thoroughly tired of disapproving gifts of public money to individuals who in my view have no right or claim to the same, notwithstanding apparent Congressional sanction, that I interpose with a feeling of relief a veto in a case where I find it unnecessary to determine the merits of the application. In speaking of the promiscuous and ill-advised grants of pensions which have lately been presented to me for approval, I have spoken of their "apparent Congressional sanction" in recognition of the fact that a large proportion of these bills have never been submitted to a majority of either branch of Congress, but are the result of nominal sessions held for the express purpose of their consideration and attended by a small minority of the members of the respective Houses of the legislative branch of Government.

Thus in considering these bills I have not felt that I was aided by the deliberate judgment of the Congress; and when I have deemed it my duty to disapprove many of the bills presented, I have hardly regarded my action as a dissent from the conclusions of the people's representatives.

I have not been insensible to the suggestions which should influence every citizen, either in private station or official place, to exhibit not only a just but a generous appreciation of the services of our country's defenders. In reviewing the pension legislation presented to me many bills have been approved upon the theory that every doubt should be resolved in favor of the proposed beneficiary. I have not, however, been able to entirely divest myself of the idea that the public money appropriated for pensions is the soldiers' fund, which should be devoted to the indemnification of those who in the defense of the Union and in the nation's service have worthily suffered, and who in the day of their dependence resulting from such suffering are entitled to the benefactions of their Government. This reflection lends to the bestowal of pensions a kind of sacredness which invites the adoption of such principles and regulations as will exclude perversion as well as insure a liberal and generous application of grateful and benevolent designs. Heedlessness and a disregard of the principle which underlies the granting of pensions is unfair to the wounded, crippled soldier who is honored in the just recognition of his Government. Such a man should never find himself side by side on the pension roll with those who have been tempted to attribute the natural ills to which humanity is heir to service in the Army. Every relaxation of principle in the granting of pensions invites applications without merit and encourages those who for gain urge honest men to become dishonest. Thus is the demoralizing lesson taught the people that as against the public Treasury the most questionable expedients are allowable.

During the present session of Congress 493 special pension bills have been submitted to me, and I am advised that 111 more have received the favorable action of both Houses of Congress and will be presented within a day or two, making over 600 of these bills which have been passed up to this time during the present session, nearly three times the number passed at any entire session since the year 1861. With the Pension Bureau, fully equipped and regulated by the most liberal rules, in active operation, supplemented in its work by constant special legislation, it certainly is not unreasonable to suppose that in all the years that have elapsed since the close of the war a majority of the meritorious claims for pensions have been presented and determined.

I have now more than 130 of these bills before me awaiting Executive action. It will be impossible to bestow upon them the examination they deserve, and many will probably become operative which should be rejected.

In the meantime I venture to suggest the significance of the startling increase in this kind of legislation and the consequences involved in its continuance.

GROVER CLEVELAND.

To the Senate:
EXECUTIVE MANSION, *June 21, 1886.*

I hereby return without approval Senate bill No. 1584, entitled "An act for the relief of Cornelia R. Schenck."

It is proposed by this bill to grant a pension to Mrs. Schenck as the widow of Daniel F. Schenck, who entered the military service of the United States in August, 1861, and was mustered out October 21, 1864.

The record of his service contains no mention of any disability. He died in December, 1875, of a disease called gastroenteritis, which, being interpreted, seems to denote "inflammation of the stomach and small intestines." So far as the facts are made to appear, the soldier, neither during the term of his service nor during the eleven years he lived after his discharge, made any claim of any disability.

The claim of his widow was filed in the Pension Bureau in 1885, ten years after her husband's death, and is still undetermined.

The fact that her application is still pending in that Bureau is sufficient reason why this bill should not become a law.

A better reason is based upon the entire lack of any facts shown to exist which entitle the beneficiary named to a pension.

GROVER CLEVELAND.

To the Senate:

I return herewith without approval Senate bill No. 1192, entitled "An act granting a pension to Alfred Denny."

It appears that the claimant entered the United States military service as captain and assistant quartermaster of volunteers on the 12th day of June, 1863. After remaining in such position for less than a year he resigned to accept a civil position.

The short record of his military service discloses no mention of any accident or disability. But twenty years after his resignation, and on the 12th day of March, 1884, he reappears as an applicant for a pension, and alleges in his declaration filed in the Pension Bureau that in August, 1863, while in the line of duty, he was, by a sudden movement of the horse he was riding, thrown forward upon the horn of his saddle and thereby received a rupture in his right side, which at some time and in a manner wholly unexplained subsequently caused a rupture in his left side also.

The number of instances in which those of our soldiers who rode horses during the war were injured by being thrown forward upon their saddles indicate that those saddles were very dangerous contrivances.

I am satisfied there is not a particle of merit in this claim, and no facts are presented to me which entitle it to charitable consideration.

GROVER CLEVELAND.

To the Senate:

I hereby return without approval Senate bill No. 1400, entitled "An act granting a pension to William H. Beck."

This claimant enlisted in 1861. He reenlisted as a veteran volunteer January 1, 1864, and was finally mustered out April 20, 1866. In all this time of service his record shows no medical treatment or claim of disability. Indeed, an abstract of his reenlistment January 1, 1864, shows a medical examination and perfect soundness.

Notwithstanding all this, he filed his declaration on the 4th day of April, 1879, nearly thirteen years after his discharge, alleging that in June, 1863, he incurred epilepsy, to which he has been subject since, and that his fits have been from one to ten days apart. To connect this in some way with his military service he stated that the doctor at a hospital said his epilepsy was caused "by jar to the head from heavy firing." .

Six months after this alleged "jar" and his consequent epilepsy he reenlisted upon a medical certificate of perfect soundness and served more than two years thereafter.

Every conceded fact in the case negatives the allegations of his declaration, and the rejection of his claim necessarily followed.

If this disease can be caused in the manner here detailed, its manifestations are such as to leave no doubt of its existence, and it seems to me simply impossible under the circumstances detailed that there should be any lack of evidence to support the claim upon which this bill is predicated.

GROVER CLEVELAND.

EXECUTIVE MANSION, *June 22, 1886.*

To the Senate:

I hereby return without approval Senate bill No. 2005, entitled "An act granting a pension to Mary J. Nottage."

The beneficiary named in this bill is the widow of Thomas Nottage, who enlisted in August, 1861, and was discharged for disability September 17, 1862. The assistant surgeon of his regiment, upon his discharge, certified the cause to be "disease of the urinary organs," which had troubled him several years.

He died of consumption January 8, 1879, nearly seventeen years after his discharge, without ever having made any application for a pension.

In 1880 his widow made an application for pension, alleging that he contracted in the service "malarial poisoning, causing remittent fever, piles, general debility, consumption, and death," and that he left two children, both born after his discharge, one in 1866 and the other in 1874.

The only medical testimony which has been brought to my attention touching his condition since his discharge is that of a single physician to the effect that he attended him from the year 1873 to the time of his death in 1879. He states that the patient had during that time "repeated attacks of remittent fever and irritability of the bladder, with organic deposits;" that "in the spring of 1878 he had sore throat and cough, which resulted in consumption, of which he died."

The claim of the widow was rejected in July, 1885, on the ground that "the soldier's death was not the result of his service."

I am satisfied that this conclusion of the Pension Bureau was correct.

GROVER CLEVELAND.

EXECUTIVE MANSION, *June 22, 1886.*

To the Senate:

I return herewith without approval Senate bill No. 342, entitled "An act granting a pension to Marrilla Parsons, of Detroit, Mich."

No claim has ever been made for a pension in this case to the Pension Bureau, probably for the reason that there is no pretext that the beneficiary named is entitled to a pension under any general law.

Daniel P. Parsons was her stepson, who enlisted in 1861 and died of consumption on the 13th day of August, 1864.

There are no special circumstances to distinguish this case from many others whose claims might be made by stepparents, and there are no facts stated in support of the conclusion embodied in the committee's report that the soldier was taken sick from exposure incident to the service.

To depart from all rules regulating the granting of pensions by such an enactment as is proposed would establish a precedent which could not fail to cause embarrassment and perplexity.

GROVER CLEVELAND.

To the Senate:　　　　　　　EXECUTIVE MANSION, *June 22, 1886.*

I return without approval Senate bill No. 1383, entitled "An act granting a pension to Harriet Welch."

The beneficiary named in this bill asks for a pension as the widow of Syreannous Welch, who was wounded in 1864 while in the service, and was pensioned therefor in 1867. In 1876 his rate of pension was increased. In 1877 he appears to have applied to have his pension again increased. It is alleged that upon such application he was directed to appear before an examining board or a surgeon at Green Bay, Wis., for examination, and in returning to his home from that place on the 7th day of September, 1877, he fell from the cars and was killed, his remains having been found on the track the next morning.

No one appears to have seen the accident, but it is claimed that he could not depend upon his wounded leg, and that it "gave way many times and caused him to fall." From this statement the inference seems to have been indulged that his death was attributable to the wound he had received thirteen years before.

The widow's claim based upon this state of facts was rejected by the Pension Bureau on the ground that the accident resulting in death was not the result of his military service, and on an appeal taken to the Secretary of the Interior from that determination the same was sustained.

Though this widow admits that prior to her marriage with the deceased soldier she had married another man whom she could only say she believed to be dead, I believe her case to be a pitiable one and wish that I could join in her relief; but, unfortunately, official duty can not always be well done when directed solely by sympathy and charity.

GROVER CLEVELAND.

To the Senate:　　　　　　　EXECUTIVE MANSION, *June 22, 1886.*

I return without approval Senate bill No. 1288, entitled "An act granting a pension to Robert Holsey."

This claimant enlisted in 1862, and though he appears to have been sick on two occasions during his term of service, he remained with his company until it was mustered out in 1865.

This soldier was really sick during the time he remained in the Army, and in this respect his claim for a pension has a better origin than many that are presented. But the fact must be recognized, I suppose, that every army ailment does not necessarily result in death or disability.

In 1882, seventeen years after his discharge, this soldier filed his declaration for a pension, alleging that in 1863 he contracted intermittent fever, affecting his lungs, kidneys, and stomach.

A board of surgeons, upon an examination made in 1882, find disease of kidneys, but no indication of lung and stomach trouble; and a medical referee reported in 1885 that there had been no disease of the stomach and lungs since the filing of the claim, and that the difficulty affecting the kidneys had no relation to the sickness for which the claimant had been treated while in the Army.

I am of the opinion that a correct conclusion was reached when the application for pension in this case was denied by the Pension Bureau.

GROVER CLEVELAND.

EXECUTIVE MANSION, *June 22, 1886.*

To the House of Representatives:

I return herewith without approval House bill No. 7979, entitled "An act granting a pension to Jackson Steward."

This claimant's application for pension is now pending in the Pension Bureau, and has been sent to a special examiner for the purpose of taking additional proof.

This I deem sufficient reason why the proposed bill should not now become a law.

GROVER CLEVELAND.

EXECUTIVE MANSION, *June 22, 1886.*

To the Senate:

I hereby return without approval Senate bill No. 2025, entitled "An act granting a pension to James Butler."

This claimant was enrolled as a private in a New Hampshire regiment August 23, 1864, but on the organization of his company, on the 12th day of September, 1864, he was discharged on account of a fracture of his leg, which happened on the 11th day of September, 1864.

It appears that before the organization of the company to which he was attached, and on the 10th day of September, he obtained permission to leave the place of rendezvous for the purpose of visiting his family, and was to return the next day. At a very early hour in the morning, either while preparing to return or actually on his way, he fell into a new cellar and broke his leg. It is said that the leg fractured is now shorter than the other.

His claim for pension was rejected in December, 1864, by the Pension Bureau, and its action was affirmed in 1871 upon the ground that the injury was received while the claimant was on an individual furlough, and therefore not in the line of duty.

Considering the fact that neither his regiment nor his company had at the time of his accident been organized, and that he was in no sense in the military service of the United States, and that his injury was received while on a visit, and not in the performance of duty, I can see no pretext for allowing a pension in this case.

GROVER CLEVELAND.

EXECUTIVE MANSION, *June 23, 1886.*

To the House of Representatives:

I hereby return without approval House bill No. 6688, entitled "An act for the relief of William Bishop."

This claimant was enrolled as a substitute on the 25th day of March, 1865. He was admitted to a post hospital at Indianapolis on the 3d day of April, 1865, with the measles; was removed to the City General Hospital, in Indianapolis, on the 5th day of May, 1865; was returned to duty May 8, 1865, and was mustered out with a detachment of unassigned men on the 11th day of May, 1865.

This is the military record of this soldier, who remained in the Army one month and seventeen days, having entered it as a substitute at a time when high bounties were paid.

Fifteen years after this brilliant service and this terrific encounter with the measles, and on the 28th day of June, 1880, the claimant discovered that his attack of the measles had some relation to his army enrollment and that this disease had "settled in his eyes, also affecting his spinal column."

This claim was rejected by the Pension Bureau, and I have no doubt of the correctness of its determination.

GROVER CLEVELAND.

EXECUTIVE MANSION, *June 23, 1886.*

To the House of Representatives:

I herewith return without approval House bill No. 6266, entitled "An act granting a pension to Philip Arner."

It is conceded in the application for a pension made by this claimant that he was perfectly well prior to his enlistment, during his service, and for a year thereafter. He was discharged in July, 1864, and the proof is that he was taken seriously ill in the fall of 1865, since which time he has been troubled with lung difficulty.

He filed his application for pension in 1883. This was rejected on the ground that the sickness which produced his disability having occurred more than a year after his discharge from the Army, it can not be accepted as a result of his military service.

There is absolutely no allegation of any incident of his service which it is claimed is at all related to his sickness and disability.

GROVER CLEVELAND.

EXECUTIVE MANSION, *June 23, 1886.*

To the House of Representatives:

I herewith return without approval House bill No. 6170, entitled "An act granting a pension to Mary A. Van Etten."

In her declaration for a pension, filed July 28, 1885, this claimant alleges that her husband was drowned upon attempting to cross Braddocks Bay, near his residence, in the State of New York, on the 16th day of July, 1875.

It is claimed that in an effort to drive across that bay in a buggy with his young son the buggy was overturned and both were drowned. The application for pension was based upon the theory that during his military service the deceased soldier contracted rheumatism, which so interfered with his ability to save himself by swimming that his death may be fairly traced to a disability incurred in the service.

He does not appear to have been treated while in the Army for rheumatism, though some evidence is presented of his complaining of rheumatic symptoms.

He was mustered out in 1863, and though he lived twelve years thereafter it does not appear that he ever applied for a pension; and though he was drowned in 1875, his widow apparently did not connect his military service with his death until ten years thereafter.

It seems to me that there is such an entire absence of direct and tangible evidence that the death of this soldier resulted from any incident of his service that the granting of a pension upon such a theory is not justified.

GROVER CLEVELAND.

EXECUTIVE MANSION, *June 23, 1886.*

To the House of Representatives:

I return herewith without approval House bill No. 6117, entitled "An act granting a pension to James D. Cotton."

The claim for a pension in this case is on behalf of the father of Thomas Cotton, who was killed at Pittsburg Landing April 6, 1862.

The application of this claimant still remains in the Pension Bureau undetermined. The doubt in the case appears to relate to the dependence of the father upon his son at the time of his death.

This is a question which the Bureau is so well fitted to investigate and justly determine that it is, in my opinion, best to permit the same to be there fully examined.

GROVER CLEVELAND.

EXECUTIVE MANSION, *June 23, 1886.*

To the House of Representatives:

I return herewith without approval House bill No. 6753, entitled "An act granting a pension to Mrs. Alice E. Travers."

The husband of the beneficiary, John T. Travers, enlisted August 25, 1864, and was discharged June 11, 1866.

He died January 6, 1881, from the effects of an overdose of morphine which he administered himself. He was a druggist, and when suffering severely was in the habit of taking opiates for relief and sleep.

The disease from which it is said he suffered was lung difficulty, claimed to have been caused by a severe cold contracted in the service.

It does not appear that he ever applied for a pension, and the widow's claim seems to have been properly rejected by the Pension Bureau on the ground that the soldier's death was not due to his military service.

GROVER CLEVELAND.

EXECUTIVE MANSION, *June 23, 1886.*

To the House of Representatives:

I return herewith without approval House bill No. 1816, entitled "An act granting a pension to Mary Ann Miller."

Hamilton Miller, the husband of the claimant, enlisted April 22, 1861, and was sent with his regiment to Camp Dennison, in the suburbs of Cincinnati.

While thus in camp, apparently before he had ever been to the front, and on the 3d of June, 1861, he obtained permission to go to the city of Cincinnati, and was there killed by a blow received from some person who appears to be unknown; but undoubtedly the injury occurred in a fight or as the result of an altercation.

It is very clear to me that the Pension Bureau properly rejected the widow's claim for pension, for the reason that the soldier was not in the line of duty at the date of his death. It is also impossible to connect the death with any incident of the soldier's military service.

GROVER CLEVELAND.

EXECUTIVE MANSION, *June 23, 1886.*

To the House of Representatives:

I return herewith without approval House bill No. 7436, entitled "An act to grant a pension to Mary Anderson."

This claimant is the widow of Richard Anderson, who at the time of his death was receiving a pension on account of chronic diarrhea contracted in the service.

On the 7th day of February, 1882, the deceased pensioner went to Sparta, in the State of Wisconsin, to be examined for an increase of his pension. He called on the surgeon and was examined, and the next morning was found beheaded on the railroad track under such circumstances as indicated suicide.

The claim of the widow was rejected by the Pension Bureau on the ground that the cause of the death of her husband was in no way connected with his military service.

His wife and family present pitiable objects for sympathy, but I am unable to see how they have any claim to a pension.

GROVER CLEVELAND.

EXECUTIVE MANSION, *June 23, 1886.*

To the House of Representatives:

I hereby return without approval House bill 576, entitled "An act for the relief of Louisa C. Beezeley."

By this bill it is proposed to grant a pension to the beneficiary named, as the widow of Nathaniel Beezeley, who was enrolled in an Indiana regiment as a farrier in September, 1861. He was discharged July 17, 1862, after having been in the hospital considerable of the short time he was connected with the Army. The surgeon's certificate on his discharge stated that it was granted by reason of "old age," he then being 60 years old.

He never made any claim for pension, but in 1877 his widow filed her declaration, stating that her husband died in 1875 from disease contracted in the service.

I am convinced that the Pension Bureau acted upon entirely satisfactory evidence when this claim was rejected upon the ground that the cause of death originated subsequent to the soldier's discharge.

GROVER CLEVELAND.

EXECUTIVE MANSION, *June 23, 1886.*

To the House of Representatives:

I return herewith without approval House bill No. 6895, entitled "An act granting a pension to Sarah Harbaugh."

The husband of this claimant enlisted August 1, 1861, and was discharged September 7, 1864. He received a gunshot wound in the left ankle in May, 1863, and died suddenly of disease of the heart October 4, 1881. He was insane before his death, but in my opinion any connection between his injury and his service in the Army is next to impossible.

GROVER CLEVELAND.

EXECUTIVE MANSION, *June 23, 1886.*

To the House of Representatives:

I hereby return without approval House bill No. 7167, entitled "An act for the relief of Mrs. Maria Hunter."

The beneficiary named in this bill, to whom it is therein proposed to grant a pension at the rate of $50 a month, on the 23d day of March, 1886, filed her application for a pension in the Pension Bureau, where it is still pending undetermined.

Although the deceased soldier held a high rank, I have no doubt his widow will receive ample justice through the instrumentality organized for the purpose of dispensing the nation's grateful acknowledgment of military service in its defense.   GROVER CLEVELAND.

EXECUTIVE MANSION, *June 23, 1886.*

To the House of Representatives:

I return herewith without approval House bill No. 3205, entitled "An act granting a pension to George W. Guyse."

The claimant filed his declaration for a pension in 1878, alleging that about the 25th day of December, 1863, he received a gunshot wound in his left knee while engaged in a skirmish.

There has been much testimony taken in this case, and a great deal of it is exceedingly contradictory.   Three of the claimant's comrades, who originally testified to the receipt of the injury by him, afterwards denied that he was wounded in the service, and a portion of the evidence taken by the Bureau tends to establish the fact that the claimant cut his left knee with a knife shortly after his discharge.

An examining surgeon in November, 1884, reports that he finds "no indication of a gunshot wound, there being no physical or rational signs to sustain claimant in his application for pension."

He further reports that there "seems to be an imperfect scar near the knee, so imperfect as to render its origin uncertain, but in no respect resembling a gunshot wound."

I think upon all the facts presented the Pension Bureau properly rejected this claim, because there was no record of the injury and no satisfactory evidence produced showing that it was incurred in service and in line of duty, "all sources of information having been exhausted."

GROVER CLEVELAND.

EXECUTIVE MANSION, *June 23, 1886.*

To the House of Representatives:

I return without approval House bill No. 7401, entitled "An act granting a pension to Samuel Miller."

This man was discharged from one enlistment June 16, 1864, and enlisted again in August of that year.   He was finally discharged July 1, 1865.

In 1880 he filed an application for a pension, alleging that in May, 1862, he contracted in the service "kidney disease and weakness of the back."

A board of surgeons in 1881 reported that they failed to "discover any evidence of disease of kidneys."

It will be observed that since the date when it is claimed his disabilities visited him Mr. Miller not only served out his first term of enlistment, but reenlisted, and necessarily must have passed a medical examination.

I am entirely satisfied with the rejection of this claim by the Pension Bureau.
GROVER CLEVELAND.

EXECUTIVE MANSION, *June 23, 1886.*

To the House of Representatives:

I return herewith without approval House bill No. 424, entitled "An act to pension Giles C. Hawley."

This claimant enlisted August 5, 1861, and was discharged November 14, 1861, upon a surgeon's certificate, in which he stated: "I deem him unfit to stay in the service on account of deafness. He can not hear an ordinary command."

Seventeen years after his discharge from a military service of a little more than three months' duration, and in the year 1878, the claimant filed an application for pension, in which he alleged that "from exposure and excessive duty in the service his hearing was seriously affected."

There is no doubt that his disability existed to quite an extent at least before his enlistment, and there was plenty of opportunity for its increase between the time of discharge and of his application for pension.

I am entirely satisfied that it should not be altogether charged to the three months he spent in the service.
GROVER CLEVELAND.

EXECUTIVE MANSION, *June 23, 1886.*

To the House of Representatives:

I return herewith without approval House bill No. 7222, entitled "An act granting a pension to Callie West."

I base my action upon the opinion, derived from an examination of the circumstances attending the death of the claimant's husband, that his fatal disease did not have its origin in his military service and was entirely disconnected therewith.
GROVER CLEVELAND.

EXECUTIVE MANSION, *June 23, 1886.*

To the House of Representatives:

I return without approval House bill No. 6257, entitled "An act for the relief of Julia Connelly."

It is proposed by this bill to grant a pension to the beneficiary named as the widow of Thomas Connelly.

This man was mustered into the service October 26, 1861. He never did a day's service so far as his name appears, and the muster-out roll of his company reports him as having deserted at Camp Cameron, Pa., November 14, 1861.

He visited his family about the 1st day of December, 1861, and was found December 30, 1861, drowned in a canal about 6 miles from his home.

Those who prosecute claims for pensions have grown very bold when cases of this description are presented for consideration.

GROVER CLEVELAND.

EXECUTIVE MANSION, *June 23, 1886.*

To the House of Representatives:

I herewith return without approval House bill No. 6774, entitled "An act granting a pension to Bruno Schultz."

The application of this claimant for a pension, which was filed a number of years ago, though at one time rejected, has been since opened for reexamination, and is now awaiting additional evidence.

In this condition of this case I think this bill should not be approved.

GROVER CLEVELAND.

EXECUTIVE MANSION, *June 23, 1886.*

To the House of Representatives:

I hereby return without approval House bill No. 7298, entitled "An act for the relief of Charles Schuler."

It is proposed by this bill to grant a pension to the person above named, who was discharged from the military service in December, 1864. He filed a declaration for a pension in the Pension Bureau in January, 1883. This application is still pending. Without referring to the merits of the case, I am of the opinion that the matter should be determined by the Bureau to which it has properly been presented before special legislation should be invoked.

GROVER CLEVELAND.

EXECUTIVE MANSION, *June 23, 1886.*

To the House of Representatives:

I return herewith without approval House bill No. 7073, entitled "An act granting a pension to Mary S. Woodson."

Henry Woodson, the husband of the beneficiary named, enlisted in September, 1861, and was discharged in October, 1863, on account of valvular disease of the heart.

The application for pension on behalf of his widow was filed August 5, 1881.

M P—VOL VIII—29

She concedes that she is unable to furnish any evidence of the date or the cause of her husband's death.

It appears that he left home in March, 1874, for the purpose of finding work, and neither she nor her friends have ever heard from him since. His death may naturally be presumed, and the condition of his family is such that it would be a positive gratification to aid them in the manner proposed; but the entire and conceded absence of any presumption, however weak, that he died from any cause connected with his military service seems to render it improper to place the widow's name upon the pension rolls.

GROVER CLEVELAND.

Executive Mansion, *June 23, 1886.*

To the House of Representatives:

I return without approval House bill No. 7108, entitled "An act granting a pension to Andrew J. Wilson."

It appears that this man was drafted and entered the service in February, 1865, and was discharged in September of the same year on account of "chronic nephritis and deafness."

In 1882 he filed his application for a pension, alleging that in June, 1865, from exposure, he contracted rheumatism. Afterwards he described his trouble as inflammation of the muscles of the back, with pain in the kidneys. In another statement, filed in December, 1884, he alleges that while in the service he contracted diarrhea and was injured in one of his testicles, producing a rupture.

Whatever else may be said of this claimant's achievements during his short military career, it must be conceded that he accumulated a great deal of disability.

There is no doubt in my mind that whatever ailments he may honestly lay claim to, his title to the same was complete before he entered the Army.

GROVER CLEVELAND.

Executive Mansion, *June 23, 1886.*

To the House of Representatives:

I return herewith without approval House bill No. 7703, entitled "An act granting a pension to Anna A. Probert."

The husband of this beneficiary was pensioned in 1864. He was a druggist and apothecary at Norwalk, in the State of Ohio. Shortly before his death, in 1878, he went to Memphis for the purpose of giving his professional assistance to those suffering from yellow fever at that place. He was himself attacked by that disease, and died on the 28th day of October, 1878.

His widow has never herself applied for a pension, but a power of attorney has been filed, authorizing the prosecution of her claim by another.

That she has employed an ingenious attorney or agent is demonstrated by the fact that the bill now before me seems to be based upon the theory that Mr. Probert might have recovered from his attack of yellow fever if he had been free from the ailments for which he had been pensioned fourteen years before.

If such speculations and presumptions as this are to be indulged, we shall find ourselves surrounded and hedged in by the rule that all men entering an army were free from disease or the liability to disease before their enlistment, and every infirmity which is visited upon them thereafter is the consequence of army service.

GROVER CLEVELAND.

EXECUTIVE MANSION, *June 23, 1886.*

To the House of Representatives:

I return without approval House bill No. 7162, entitled "An act granting a pension to Martha McIlwain."

R. J. McIlwain, the husband of the claimant, enlisted in 1861, and was discharged in 1862 because of the loss of his right leg by a gunshot wound. He was pensioned for this disability. He died May 15, 1883, from an overdose of morphia. It is claimed by the widow that her husband was in the habit of taking morphia to alleviate the pain he endured from his stump, and that he accidentally took too much.

The case was investigated by a special examiner upon the widow's application for pension, and his report shows that the deceased had been in the habit of taking morphia and knew how to use it; that he had been in the habit of buying 6 grains at a time, and that his death was caused by his taking one entire purchase of 6 grains while under the influence of liquor.

In any event it is quite clear that the taking of morphia in any quantity was not the natural result of military service or injury received therein.

I concur in the judgment of the Pension Bureau, which rejected the widow's claim for pension on the ground that "the death of the soldier was not due to his military service."

GROVER CLEVELAND.

EXECUTIVE MANSION, *June 23, 1886.*

To the House of Representatives:

I hereby return without approval House bill No. 7931, entitled "An act increasing the pension of Clark Boon."

This claimant filed his declaration for pension February 3, 1874, in which he states that he lost his health while a prisoner at Tyler, Tex.

On the 19th day of October, 1874, he filed an affidavit claiming that he contracted diseases of the heart and head while in the service. In a further application, filed January 16, 1878, he abandoned his allegations as to disease, and asks for a pension on account of a gunshot wound in the left ankle. Medical testimony was produced on his behalf tending to show not only a gunshot wound, but a disease of the eyes.

A small pension was at last granted him upon the theory advanced by a board of surgeons in 1880 that it was "possible that applicant was entitled to a small rating for weakness of ankle."

A declaration was filed June 4, 1885, by which this claimant insists upon an increase of pension on account of the wound and also for disease of eyes and rheumatism.

I am entirely satisfied that all has been done in this case that the most liberal treatment demands.

GROVER CLEVELAND.

EXECUTIVE MANSION, *June 23, 1886.*

To the House of Representatives:

I hereby return without approval House bill No. 7257, entitled "An act granting a pension to James H. Darling."

This man enlisted in November, 1861, and was reported as having deserted March 5, 1862. The charge of desertion was, however, removed, and it is stated that he went to his home in Ohio at the date stated, by proper authority, where he remained sick till December, 1862, when he was discharged for disability caused "by a disease of the kidneys known as Bright's disease," from which, the physician making the certificate thought, "there was no reasonable prospect of his recovery."

The claimant filed his application for pension, alleging that in January, 1862, he contracted rheumatism.

The claim was investigated by a special examiner and rejected on the ground that the evidence produced failed to show the alleged disability was contracted in the service and in the line of duty.

A medical examination made in 1877 showed that the claimant was "a well-nourished man, 65 years old; height, 5 feet 8 inches; weight, 165 pounds." No disability was discovered, "but a general stiffness of joints, especially of legs, which he says is much aggravated in stormy, cold weather."

Another examination in 1882 found this victim of war disability with "the appearance of a hale, hearty old man—no disease that was discoverable by examination (without chemical test), except some lameness from rheumatism." His weight upon this examination is stated to be 186 pounds.

It is evident to me that this man ought not to be pensioned.

GROVER CLEVELAND.

EXECUTIVE MANSION, *June 23, 1886.*

To the House of Representatives:

I return herewith without my approval House bill No. 6372, entitled "An act to pension Charles A. Chase."

This claimant was enrolled September 6, 1864, and mustered out with his detachment June 1, 1865. His brief service contains no record of disability.

But in 1880 he filed a declaration for pension, in which he claims that by reason of exposure suffered in the service about the 20th of October, 1864, he contracted disease of the liver and kidneys.

The application for pension was denied January 9, 1884, because there was no record of the alleged diseases, and no satisfactory proof of their contraction in the Army was produced, and because of the meager and unconvincing evidence of disability found by the surgeon on an actual examination of the claimant.

I adopt these as the reasons for my action in withholding my approval of this bill.

GROVER CLEVELAND.

EXECUTIVE MANSION, *June 23, 1886.*

To the House of Representatives:

I return herewith without approval House bill No. 6192, entitled "An act granting a pension to Mary Norman."

The husband of this claimant was enrolled May 22, 1863, and was mustered out of the service June 1, 1866.

He was wounded in the head February 20, 1864; was treated for the same, and returned to duty September 3, 1864.

In her declaration for pension, filed in February, 1880, the claimant claims a pension because of his wound and deafness consequent therefrom, and that he died after he left the service.

In a letter, however, dated October 13, 1880, she states that her husband was drowned while trying to cross Roanoke River in December, 1868.

Her claim was rejected in 1881 on the ground that the cause of the soldier's death was accidental drowning, and was not due to his military service.

In an attempt to meet this objection it was claimed as lately as 1885, on behalf of the widow, that her husband's wound caused deafness to such an extent that at the time he was drowned he was unable to hear the ferryman, with whom he was crossing the river, call out that the boat was sinking.

How he could have saved his life if he had heard the warning is not stated.

It seems very clear to me that this is not a proper case for the granting of a pension.

GROVER CLEVELAND.

EXECUTIVE MANSION, *June 23, 1886.*

To the House of Representatives:

I return herewith without my approval House bill No. 7614, entitled "An act granting an increase of pension to Hezekiah Tillman."

This claimant, in his declaration for pension, filed in 1866, alleges that he received a gunshot wound in his right leg November 25, 1862. He was mustered out with his company September 22, 1864.

He was pensioned for the wound which he claimed to have received as his only injury.

In another declaration, filed in 1872, he alleged that in December, 1862, he was struck in his left eye by some hard substance, which destroyed the vision of that organ.

In a subsequent declaration, filed in 1878, he claimed that he received a shell wound in his left knee in November, 1863.

This latter claim has not been finally acted upon by the Pension Bureau, and I am of the opinion that with the diverse claims for injuries which have been there presented on behalf of the beneficiary named justice will be done in the case.

GROVER CLEVELAND.

EXECUTIVE MANSION, *June 23, 1886.*

To the House of Representatives:

I return without approval House bill No. 6718, entitled "An act granting a pension to William H. Starr."

An application made by this claimant to the Pension Bureau is still pending there, and additional evidence has been called for, which the claim is awaiting before final decision.

I am of the opinion that the investigation there should be fully completed before special legislation is resorted to.

GROVER CLEVELAND.

EXECUTIVE MANSION, *June 23, 1886.*

To the House of Representatives:

I return without approval House bill No. 7109, entitled "An act granting a pension to Joseph Tuttle."

This man claims a pension as the dependent father of Charles Tuttle, who enlisted in 1861 and was killed in action May 31, 1862.

The claimant, being, as he says, poor, took his son Charles, at the age of 9 years, and placed him in charge of an uncle living in Ohio. An arrangement was afterwards made by which the boy should live with a stranger named Betts. Upon the death of this gentleman the lad was transferred to one Captain Hill, with whom he remained until his enlistment in 1861.

It is stated that during the time he remained with Mr. Hill he sent his father $5; but the fatherly care and interest of the claimant in his son is exhibited by his statement that though the son was killed in 1862 his father was not aware of it until the year 1864.

After the exhibition of heartlessness and abandonment on the part of a father which is a prominent feature in this case, I should be sorry to be a party to a scheme permitting him to profit by the death of his patriotic son. The claimant relinquished the care of his son, and should be held to have relinquished all claim to his assistance and the benefits so indecently claimed as the result of his death.

GROVER CLEVELAND.

EXECUTIVE MANSION, *June 23, 1886.*

To the House of Representatives:

I return herewith without approval House bill No. 5995, entitled "An act granting a pension to David T. Elderkin."

This claimant enlisted August 5, 1862. From his record it appears that he was dishonorably discharged the service, to date from June 11, 1863, with a loss of all pay, bounty, and allowances.

He filed a declaration for a pension in 1882, claiming that he was wounded in the head by a shell January 1, 1863, which cut his cheek close to his right ear, causing almost total deafness.

There is conflicting evidence as to the claimant's freedom from deafness prior to enlistment, and on a special examination it was shown that he was slightly hard of hearing before enlistment. Indeed the claimant himself stated to the special examiner and also to the board of surgeons that he had been somewhat deaf from childhood.

In 1882 an examining surgeon reports that he finds no scar or evidence of wound, but his hearing is very much impaired.

The claim was rejected in 1885 on the ground that deafness existed prior to enlistment, and also because of no ratable disability by reason of alleged wound in the cheek.

I think, considering the manner of the soldier's discharge and the facts developed, that the claimant should not be pensioned.

GROVER CLEVELAND.

EXECUTIVE MANSION, *June 29, 1886.*

To the Senate:

I hereby return Senate bill No. 1797, entitled "An act granting a pension to John S. Kirkpatrick."

This claimant appears to have enlisted December 10, 1861, and to have been discharged December 20, 1864. He is borne upon the rolls of his company as present up to June, 1862; in July and August, 1862, as on detached service as hospital attendant, and so reported February 28, 1863. In March and April, 1863, he is reported as present, and in May and June, 1863, as on detached service.   There is nowhere in his service any record of disability.

He filed his application for a pension in 1880, in which he alleged that from hardship and exposure on a long march in New Mexico in the month of December, 1862, he contracted varicose veins in his legs.

As I understand the record given above, this claimant was on detached service from July, 1862, to February, 1863.

It will be observed that his claim is that he contracted his disability within that time, and in December, 1862.   He appears also to have served for two years after the date of his alleged injury, and that he did not file his application for pension till about sixteen years afterwards.

His claim is still pending, undetermined, in the Pension Bureau, and if there is merit in it there is no doubt that he will be able to make it apparent.

GROVER CLEVELAND.

EXECUTIVE MANSION, *June 29, 1886.*

To the Senate:

I hereby return without approval Senate bill No. 1077, entitled "An act granting a pension to Newcomb Parker."

This claimant filed an application for a pension in the year 1880.

Before the passage of the bill herewith returned the Commissioner of Pensions, in ignorance of the action of Congress, allowed his claim under the general law.   As this decision of the Pension Bureau entitles the beneficiary named to draw a pension from the date of filing his application, which, under the provisions of the special bill in his favor, would only accrue from the time of its passage, I am unwilling that one found worthy to be placed upon the pension rolls by the Bureau, to which he properly applied, should be an actual loser by reason of a special interposition of Congress in his behalf.

GROVER CLEVELAND.

EXECUTIVE MANSION, *July 2, 1886.*

To the House of Representatives:

I return without approval House bill No. 473, entitled "An act granting a pension to William Boone."

There is not the slightest room for doubt as to the facts involved in this case.

No application for pension was ever made to the Pension Bureau by the beneficiary named in this bill.   He enlisted in August, 1862; was in action November, 1862, and taken prisoner and at once paroled.   During his parole, and at Aurora, in the State of Illinois, he took part in the celebration of the 4th day of July, 1863, and while so engaged was terribly injured by the discharge of a cannon.   He is poor, and has a wife and a number of children.

These facts are derived from the report of the committee in Congress to whom the bill was referred, and from a letter written by the soldier since favorable action was had upon said bill by both Houses of Congress, which letter is now before me. In this letter he says: ''I never thought of trying getting a pension until my old comrades urged me to do so.''

This declaration does not in the least, I think, militate against the present application for pension, but it tends to show the ideas that have become quite prevalent concerning the facts necessary to be established in order to procure a pension by special act of Congress.

Let it be conceded that during the three months which elapsed between the soldier's enlistment and his capture and parole he was constantly in the field and bravely did his duty. The case presented is that of a brave soldier, not injured in any engagement with the enemy, but honorably captured, and by his parole placed in a condition which prevented for the time being his further active military service. He proceeded to his home or to his friends and took his place among noncombatants. Eight months afterwards he joined the citizens of the place of his sojourn and the citizens of every town and hamlet in the loyal States in the usual and creditable celebration of our national holiday. Among the casualties which unfortunately always result from such celebrations there occurred a premature discharge of a cannon, which the present claimant for pension was assisting other citizens to discharge and manage.

Whether any of those thus engaged with him were injured is not disclosed, but it is certain that the paroled soldier was very badly hurt.

I am utterly unable to discover any relation between this accident and the military service, or any reason why, if a pension is granted as proposed by this bill, there should not also be a pension granted to any of the companions of the claimant who chanced to be injured at the same time.

A disabled man and a wife and family in need are objects which appeal to the sympathy and charitable feelings of any decent man; but it seems to me that it by no means follows that those intrusted with the people's business and the expenditure of the people's money are justified in so executing the pension laws as that they shall furnish a means of relief in every case of distress or hardship.　　GROVER CLEVELAND.

To the Senate:　　EXECUTIVE MANSION, *July 3, 1886.*

I hereby return without approval Senate bill No. 365, entitled ''An act for the relief of Martin L. Bundy.''

By this bill it is proposed to allow in the settlement by the United States with Mr. Bundy, who was lately a paymaster in the Army, the sum of $719.47 for the forage of two horses to which he claims he was entitled while in the service, and which has never been drawn by him. The time during which it is alleged this forage was due is stated to be between July 17, 1862, and April 15, 1866.

This claimant was mustered out as paymaster on the last-mentioned

EXECUTIVE MANSION, *July 5, 1886.*

To the House of Representatives:

I herewith return without approval House bill No. 1818, entitled "An act granting a pension to H. L. Kyler."

A pension was granted to the person named in this bill, dating from September, 1864, for neuralgia and disease of the eyes.

He was mustered into the service, to serve one hundred days, May 14, 1864, and mustered out September 8, 1864.

In 1880 information reached the Pension Bureau that the pensioner was treated for neuralgia and disease of the eyes at various times between the years 1859 and 1864, and this fact appearing to the satisfaction of the Bureau upon the examination which followed, the pensioner's name was dropped from the roll.

Afterwards another thorough examination of the case was made, when the pensioner was permitted to confront the witnesses against him and produce evidence in his own behalf.

It is claimed that a Dr. Saunders, who testified to treating the pensioner before his enlistment, was exceedingly unfriendly; but he was corroborated by his son and by entries on his books. Another physician, apparently disinterested, also testified to his treatment of the pensioner in 1860 for difficulties with his eyes and ears. The pensioner himself admitted that he had trouble with one of his eyes in 1860, but that he entirely recovered. Six other witnesses testified to the existence of disease of the pensioner's eyes before enlistment.

Though twelve neighbors of the pensioner testified that he was free from neuralgia and disease of the eyes before enlistment, I am of the opinion that the evidence against the pension was quite satisfactory, and that it should not be restored, as the bill before me proposes.

GROVER CLEVELAND.

EXECUTIVE MANSION, *July 5, 1886.*

To the House of Representatives:

I return herewith without approval House bill No. 3640, entitled "An act granting a pension to James T. Irwin."

This claimant enlisted in February, 1864, and was mustered out June 10, 1865. He is reported as absent sick from August 20, 1864, until mustered out. He seems to have been treated for remittent fever, chronic diarrhea, general debility, and palpitation of the heart.

In 1876 he filed a declaration for pension, alleging that at Petersburg, July 1, 1864, he contracted fever and inflammation of the eyes.

He filed an affidavit in January, 1877, in which he states that his diseased eyes resulted from diseased nerves, caused by a wound received June 18, 1864, at Petersburg, and from a consequent abscess on the back of the neck.

In an affidavit filed in July, 1878, he states that in June, 1864, in front of Petersburg, he had his gun smashed in front of his face and his eyes injured, and afterwards he had an abscess on the back of his neck, typhoid fever, and disease of the left lung.

His claim founded upon these various allegations of injury was rejected in February, 1879.

In September, 1884, a declaration was filed for a pension, alleging disease of the heart contracted at Petersburg June 16, 1864.

The claimant was examined once in 1882 and twice in 1884 by United States examining surgeons and boards, and it is stated that these examinations failed to reveal any disease or disability except disease of the eyes and an irritable heart, the result of indigestion.

An oculist who made an examination in 1884 reported that the unnatural condition of claimant's eyes was congenital and in no manner the result of injury or disease.

Upon a consideration of the very short time that the claimant was in actual service, the different claims he has made touching his alleged disability, and the positive results of medical examinations, I am satisfied this pension should not be allowed.

GROVER CLEVELAND.

EXECUTIVE MANSION, *July 5, 1886.*

To the House of Representatives:

` I return herewith without my approval House bill No. 5306, entitled "An act granting a pension to Roxana V. Rowley."

The beneficiary named in this bill is the widow of Franklin Rowley, who enlisted February 8, 1865, was promoted to first lieutenant March 13, 1865, and was discharged May 22, 1865, having tendered his resignation, as it is stated, on account of incompetency. His tender of resignation was indorsed by the commanding officer of his regiment as follows: "This man is wholly unfit for an officer."

It will be seen that he was in the service a little more than three months.

In 1880, fifteen years after his discharge, he applied for a pension, alleging that he contracted disease of the liver while in the service.

Upon an examination of the claim his attending physician before enlistment stated that as early as 1854 the claimant was afflicted with dyspepsia and functional disease of the liver; that he regarded him as incurable, so far as being restored to sound health was concerned, and that if he had been at home at the time when he enlisted he would have advised against it.

The testimony of this physician as to the claimant's condition after his discharge is referred to in the report of the Committee of the House to whom this bill was referred, and I do not understand that he is at all impeached. He certainly is better informed than any other person regarding the condition of the man who was his patient.

The soldier died in 1881, sixteen years after his discharge, and his widow filed her claim for pension in 1882, alleging that the death of her husband was caused by a disease of the liver contracted in the service.

Her claim was rejected in 1883 upon the ground that the disease of which her husband died existed prior to his enlistment.

I can not avoid the conclusion, upon all the facts presented, that his death was not chargeable to any incident of his brief military service.

GROVER CLEVELAND.

EXECUTIVE MANSION, *July 5, 1886.*

To the House of Representatives:

I herewith return without approval House bill No. 5021, entitled "An act granting a pension to Mrs. Margaret A. Jacoby."

A pension has been allowed on account of the disability of the claimant's husband, dating from his discharge in 1864.

The beneficiary named in this bill applied for pension in 1885, alleging that she married the soldier in 1864; that he incurred deafness and chronic diarrhea while in the service, from the combined effect of which he partially lost his mind; that on the 7th day of September, 1875, he disappeared, and that after diligent search and inquiry she is unable to learn anything of him since that time.

His disability from army service should be conceded and his death at some time and in some manner may well be presumed; but the fact that he died from any cause related to his disability or his service in the Army has no presumption and not a single particle of proof to rest upon.

With proper diligence something should be discovered to throw a little light upon this subject. GROVER CLEVELAND.

EXECUTIVE MANSION, *July 5, 1886.*

To the House of Representatives:

I return without approval House bill No. 3304, entitled "An act to restore the name of Abner Morehead to the pension roll."

The person mentioned in this bill was pensioned in November, 1867, upon the claim made by him that in 1863, from hardship and exposure incident to camp life and field duty, he contracted a fever which settled in his eyes, almost wholly destroying his sight. Afterwards his pension was increased to $15 a month, dating from December, 1867, and arrears at the rate of $8 a month from February, 1864. In 1876 the case was put in the hands of a special agent of the Pension Bureau for examination, and upon his report, showing that the claimant's disease of the eyes existed prior to enlistment, his name was dropped from the rolls.

An application for restoration was made in 1879, and a thorough examination was made by a special examiner in 1885, who reported that the testimony taken conclusively established the fact that the claimant had disease of the eyes prior to the time of enlistment, the result of a disorder which he specifically mentions, and that he was treated for the same more than a year subsequently to 1860.   He adds:

There is no merit whatever in this case, and it is evident that he obtained a large sum as pension to which he must have known he was not entitled.

The results of these examinations, instituted for the express purpose of developing the facts, and with nothing apparent to impeach them, should, I think, control as against the statements of neighbors and comrades based upon mere general observation, and not necessarily covering the period which is important to the controversy.

GROVER CLEVELAND.

EXECUTIVE MANSION, *July 5, 1886.*

To the House of Representatives:

I herewith return without approval House bill No. 4782, entitled "An act granting a pension to Elizabeth McKay."

The beneficiary named is the widow of Rowley S. McKay, who in 1862 seems to have been employed as pilot on the ram *Switzerland*.   He seems to have been upon the rolls of two other vessels of the United States, the *Covington* and *General Price*, but was discharged by Admiral Porter in June, 1864, with loss of all pay and emoluments.

He filed an application for pension in 1870, alleging that while on duty as pilot and in action with the rebel ram *Arkansas* his hearing became affected by heavy firing.   He also claimed that in February, 1863, while on the vessel *Queen of the West*, she grounded, and to escape capture he got off and floated down the river on a cotton bale, and, being in the water about three hours, the exposure caused a disease of the urinary organs; and that a few days after, while coming up the river on a transport, the boat was fired into and several balls passed through his left thigh.   It seems that this claim was not definitely passed upon, but it is stated that the records failed to show that McKay was in the service of the United States at the time he alleged the contraction of disease of the urinary organs and was wounded in the thigh.

The beneficiary named in this bill never made application for pension to the Pension Bureau, but it appears that she bases her claims to consideration by Congress upon the allegation that in 1862, while her husband was acting as pilot of the ram or gunboat *Switzerland*, he contracted chronic diarrhea, from which he never recovered, and that he died from the effects of said disease in May, 1874.

It will be observed that among the various causes which the soldier or sailor himself alleged as the grounds of his application for pension chronic diarrhea is not mentioned.

There does not appear to be any medical testimony to support the claim thus made by the widow, and the cause of death is not definitely stated.

Taking all together, it has the appearance of a case, by no means rare, where chronic diarrhea or rheumatism are appealed to as a basis for a pension claim in the absence of something more substantial and definite.

The fact that the claim of the beneficiary has never been presented to the Pension Bureau influences in some degree my action in withholding my approval of this bill.   GROVER CLEVELAND.

EXECUTIVE MANSION, *July 5, 1886.*

To the House of Representatives:

I return herewith without approval House bill No. 3623, entitled "An act granting a pension to William H. Nevil."

This bill directs that the name of the claimant be placed upon the pension roll "subject to the provisions and limitations of the pension laws."

This very thing was done on the 22d day of June, 1865, and the claimant is in the receipt at the present time of the full amount of pension allowed by our pension laws as administered by the Pension Bureau.

I suppose the intention of the bill was to increase this pension, but it is not framed in such a way as to accomplish that object or to benefit the claimant in any way whatever.   GROVER CLEVELAND.

EXECUTIVE MANSION, *July 5, 1886.*

To the House of Representatives:

I herewith return without approval House bill No. 1505, entitled "An act granting a pension to William Dermody."

By the records of the War Department which have been furnished me it appears that this claimant enlisted August 19, 1861; that he deserted August 29, 1862; in November and December, 1862, he is reported as present in confinement in regimental guardhouse, to forfeit one month's pay by sentence of regimental court-martial; he is reported as having deserted again in December, 1863, but as present for duty in January and February, 1864; he reenlisted in the latter month, and was mustered out July 17, 1865, and with his company was paid up to and including July 21, 1865.

He filed a declaration for pension in 1879, alleging that he received a gunshot wound in the thigh at Trenton, N. J., July 21, 1865, and that the wound was inflicted by a member of the Invalid Corps, who was whipping a drummer boy, and the claimant interfered in behalf of the boy.

It is quite certain that the transaction took place July 23.

An examining board, in 1880, found pistol shot in thigh, but refused to give the claimant a rating, because, as they report, "from the evidence before the board there is reason to suppose that he was deserting from the barracks at Trenton July 23, 1865, and was shot by the guard."

This may not be a just suspicion or finding, but he surely was not in the service nor in the performance of any military duty at the time of the injury, nor was he engaged in such manner as to entitle him to indemnification at the hands of the Government.

GROVER CLEVELAND.

EXECUTIVE MANSION, *July 5, 1886.*

To the House of Representatives:

I herewith return without approval House bill No. 1059, entitled "An act to grant a pension to Joseph Romiser."

The Pension Bureau reports that the records of the office fail to show that an application has been filed in favor of this claimant, though it is stated in the report of the House committee that such a claim was made and rejected on the ground that the claimant was not at the time of injury in the service of the United States.

It certainly appears from the report of the committee that the beneficiary named in this bill was not in the service of the Government at such a time, and also that he had not been mustered into the service of any State military organization. It is stated that he belonged to Captain Frank Mason's company of volunteers, of Frostburg, in the State of Maryland.

Whether this company was organized for the purpose of cooperating at any time with the Union or State forces is not alleged, and it may well have been existing merely for the purpose of neighborhood protection.

Such as it was, the company was ordered in June, 1861, to proceed to Cumberland to repel a threatened attack of Confederate forces. Upon arriving at that place the men were ordered to uncap their muskets. In doing this, and through the negligence of another member of the company, whose musket was discharged, the claimant was wounded.

It does not seem to me that the facts in this case, so far as they have been developed, justify the passage of this act.

GROVER CLEVELAND.

EXECUTIVE MANSION, *July 5, 1886.*

To the House of Representatives:

I herewith return without approval House bill No. 4226, entitled "An act granting a pension to Fannie E. Evans."

The beneficiary named in this bill is the widow of George S. Evans. He was a soldier in the Mexican War, and entered the Union Army in the War of the Rebellion, on the 16th day of October, 1861, as major of a California regiment. He became a colonel in February, 1863, and re-
d in April of that year, to take effect on the 31st of May ensuing.

His resignation seems to have been tendered on account of private matters, and no mention was then made of any disability. It is stated in the committee's report to the House that in 1864 he accepted the office of adjutant-general of the State of California, which he held for nearly four years.

He died in 1883 from cerebral apoplexy.

In March, 1884, his widow filed an application for pension, based upon the allegation that from active and severe service in a battle with the Indians at Spanish Fort in 1863 her husband incurred a hernia, which incapacitated him for active service.

There appears to be evidence to justify this statement, notwithstanding the fact that the deceased during the twenty years that followed before his death made no claim for such disability.

But it seems to me that the effort to attribute his death by apoplexy to the existence of hernia ought not to be successful.

GROVER CLEVELAND.

EXECUTIVE MANSION, *July 5, 1886.*
To the House of Representatives:

I herewith return without approval House bill No. 2971, entitled "An act granting a pension to Francis Deming."

This claimant entered the service in August, 1861, and was discharged September 15, 1865.

His hospital record shows that during his service he was treated for various temporary ailments, among which rheumatism is not included.

He filed an application for pension in September, 1884, alleging that in August, 1864, he contracted rheumatism, which had resulted in blindness.

On an examination of his case in November, 1884, he stated that his eyesight began to fail in 1882.

There seems to be no testimony showing his condition from the time of his discharge to 1880, a period of fifteen years.

The claim that his present condition of blindness is the result of his army service is not insisted upon as a reason for granting him relief as strongly as his sad and helpless condition. The committee of the House to which this bill was referred, after detailing his situation, close their report with these words: "He served well his country in its dire need; his necessities now appeal for relief."

We have here presented the case of a soldier who did his duty during his army service, and who was discharged in 1865 without any record of having suffered with rheumatism and without any claim of disability arising from the same. He returned to his place as a citizen, and in peaceful pursuits, with chances certainly not impaired by the circumstance that he had served his country, he appears to have held his place in the race of life for fifteen years or more. Then, like many another, he was subjected to loss of sight, one of the saddest afflictions known to human life.

Thereupon, and after nineteen years had elapsed since his discharge from the Army, a pension is claimed for him upon a very shadowy allegation of the incurrence of rheumatism while in the service, coupled with the startling proposition that this rheumatism resulted, just previous to his application, in blindness. Upon medical examination it appeared that his blindness was caused by amaurosis, which is generally accepted as an affection of the optic nerve.

I am satisfied that a fair examination of the facts in this case justifies the statement that the bill under consideration can rest only upon the grounds that aid should be furnished to this ex-soldier because he served in the Army and because he a long time thereafter became blind, disabled, and dependent.

The question is whether we are prepared to adopt this principle and establish this precedent.

None of us are entitled to credit for extreme tenderness and consideration toward those who fought their country's battles. These are sentiments common to all good citizens. They lead to the most benevolent care on the part of the Government and deeds of charity and mercy in private life. The blatant and noisy self-assertion of those who, from motives that may well be suspected, declare themselves above all others friends of the soldier can not discredit nor belittle the calm, steady, and affectionate regard of a grateful nation.

An appropriation has just been passed setting apart $76,000,000 of the public money for distribution as pensions, under laws liberally constructed, with a view of meeting every meritorious case. More than $1,000,000 was added to maintain the Pension Bureau, which is charged with the duty of a fair, just, and liberal apportionment of this fund.

Legislation has been at the present session of Congress perfected considerably increasing the rate of pension in certain cases. Appropriations have also been made of large sums for the support of national homes where sick, disabled, or needy soldiers are cared for, and within a few days a liberal sum has been appropriated for the enlargement and increased accommodation and convenience of these institutions.

All this is no more than should be done.

But with all this, and with the hundreds of special acts which have been passed granting pensions in cases where, for my part, I am willing to confess that sympathy rather than judgment has often led to the discovery of a relation between injury or death and military service, I am constrained by a sense of public duty to interpose against establishing a principle and setting a precedent which must result in unregulated, partial, and unjust gifts of public money under the pretext of indemnifying those who suffered in their means of support as an incident of military service.

GROVER CLEVELAND.

EXECUTIVE MANSION, *July 6, 1886.*

To the House of Representatives:

I herewith return without approval House bill No. 4642, entitled "An act granting a pension to James Carroll."

The claimant alleges that he was wounded while in the service as a member of Company B, Third Regiment North Carolina Mounted Volunteers, while securing recruits for the regiment at Watauga, N. C., January 25, 1865.

The records of the War Department develop the fact that the name of this man is not borne upon any roll of the company to which he claims to belong.

He stated in his application that he was sworn in by one George W. Perkins, who, it appears, was a private in said company, and that Perkins was with him at the time he was shot.

This is undoubtedly true, and that the claimant was injured by a gunshot is also probably true. He was not, however, at the time regularly in the United States service, but this objection might in some circumstances be regarded as technical. The difficulty is that the fact that he was creditably employed in a service of benefit to the country is not satisfactorily shown. He gives two accounts of the business in which he was engaged, and Mr. Perkins's explanation of the manner in which the two were occupied is somewhat different still.

Carroll's claim, presented to the Pension Bureau, was rejected upon the ground that there was no record of his service on file; but in his testimony he stated that Perkins was wounded on the same occasion as himself, and that he (Perkins) was then a pensioner on account thereof.

The records of the Pension Bureau show that Perkins was pensioned in 1873 on account of three wounds received at the time and place of Carroll's injury.

It also appears that his name was dropped from the rolls in 1877 on the ground that his wounds were not received in the line of duty.

After an investigation made at that time by a special examiner, he reported that Perkins and Carroll had collected a number of men together, who made their headquarters at the home of Carroll's mother and were engaged in plundering the neighborhood, and that on account of their depredations they were hunted down by home guards and shot at the time they stated.

If this report is accepted as reliable, it should of course lead to the rejection of the claim for pension on the part of Mr. Carroll.

GROVER CLEVELAND.

EXECUTIVE MANSION, *July 6, 1886.*

To the House of Representatives:

I herewith return without approval House bill No. 3043, entitled "An act granting a pension to Lewis W. Scanland."

The claimant filed his declaration for a pension in 1884, alleging that he contracted chronic diarrhea while serving in a company of mounted Illinois volunteers in the Black Hawk War.

The records show that he served from April 18, 1832, to May 28, in the same year.

He was examined by a board of surgeons in 1884, when he was said to be 75 years old. In his examination he did not claim to have diarrhea for a good many years. On the contrary, he claimed to be affected with constipation, and said he had never had diarrhea of late years, except at times when he had taken medicine for constipation.

I am inclined to think it would have been a fortunate thing if in this case it could have been demonstrated that a man could thrive so well with the chronic diarrhea for fifty-two years as its éxistence in the case of this good old gentleman would prove. We should then, perhaps, have less of it in claims for pensions.

The fact is, in this case there is no disability which can be traced to the forty days' military service of fifty-four years ago, and I think little, if any, more infirmity than is usually found in men of the age of the claimant.

Entertaining this belief, I am constrained to withhold my signature from this bill.

GROVER CLEVELAND.

EXECUTIVE MANSION, *July 6, 1886.*
To the House of Representatives:

I return herewith without approval House bill No. 5414, entitled "An act granting a pension to Maria Cunningham."

The husband of the beneficiary named in this bill enlisted January 29, 1862, and was discharged January 20, 1865.

He applied for a pension in 1876, alleging a shell wound in the head. His claim was rejected on the ground that there appeared to be no disability from that cause. No other injury or disability was ever claimed by him, but at the time of his examination in 1876 he was found to be sickly, feeble, and emaciated, and suffering from an advanced stage of saccharine diabetes.

His widow filed an application for a pension in 1879, alleging that her husband died in December, 1877, of spinal disease and diabetes, contracted in the service.

Her claim was rejected because evidence was not furnished that the cause of the soldier's death had its origin in the military service.

There seems to be an entire absence of proof of this important fact.

GROVER CLEVELAND.

EXECUTIVE MANSION, *July 6, 1886.*
To the House of Representatives:

I herewith return without approval House bill No. 4797, entitled "An act granting a pension to Robert H. Stapleton."

This claimant filed an application for pension in the Pension Bureau in 1883, alleging that while acting as lieutenant-colonel of a New Mexico regiment, on February 21, 1862, the tongue of a caisson struck him, injuring his left side. A medical examination made in 1882 showed a fracture of the ninth, tenth, and eleventh ribs of the left side.

If these fractures were the result of the injury alleged, they were immediately apparent, and the delay of twenty-one years in presenting the claim for pension certainly needs explanation.

Claims of this description, by a wise provision of law, must, to be valid, be prosecuted to a successful issue prior to the 4th day of July, 1874.

The rank which this claimant held presupposes such intelligence as admits of no excuse on the ground of ignorance of the law for his failure to present his application within the time fixed by law.

The evidence of disability from the cause alleged is weak, to say the most of it, and I can not think that such a wholesome provision of law as that above referred to, which limits the time for the adjustment of such claims, should be modified upon the facts presented in this case.

GROVER CLEVELAND.

EXECUTIVE MANSION, *July 6, 1886.*
To the House of Representatives:

I herewith return without approval House bill No. 5550, entitled "An act to provide for the erection of a public building at Duluth, Minn."

After quite a careful examination of the public needs at the point mentioned I am entirely satisfied that the public building provided for in this bill is not immediately necessary.

Not a little legislation has lately been perfected, and very likely more will be necessary, to increase miscalculated appropriations for and correct blunders in the construction of many of the public buildings now in process of erection.

While this does not furnish a good reason for disapproving the erection of other buildings where actually necessary, it induces close scrutiny and gives rise to the earnest wish that new projects for public buildings shall for the present be limited to such as are required by the most pressing necessities of the Government's business.

GROVER CLEVELAND.

EXECUTIVE MANSION, *July 6, 1886.*
To the House of Representatives:

I return herewith without approval House bill No. 2043, entitled "An act to place Mary Karstetter on the pension roll."

The husband of this beneficiary, Jacob Karstetter, was enrolled June 30, 1864, as a substitute in a Pennsylvania regiment, and was discharged for disability June 20, 1865, caused by a gunshot wound in the left hand.

A declaration for pension was filed by him in 1865, based upon this wound, and the same was granted, dating from June in that year, which he drew till the time of his death, August 21, 1874.

In 1882 his widow filed her application for pension, alleging that he died of wounds received in battle. The claim was made that he was injured while in the Army by a horse running over him.

There is little or no evidence of such an injury having been received; and if this was presented there would be no necessary connection between that and the cause of the soldier's death, which was certified by the attending physician to be gastritis and congestion of the kidneys.

I can hardly see how the Pension Bureau could arrive at any conclusion except that the death of the soldier was not due to his military service, and the acceptance of this finding, after an examination of the facts, leads me to disapprove this bill.

GROVER CLEVELAND.

EXECUTIVE MANSION, *July 6, 1886.*

To the House of Representatives:

I herewith return without approval House bill No. 5394, entitled "An act granting a pension to Sallie Ann Bradley."

The husband of this proposed beneficiary was discharged from the military service in 1865, after a long service, and was afterwards pensioned for gunshot wound.

He died in 1882. The widow appears to have never filed a claim for pension in her own right.

No cause is given of the soldier's death, but it is not claimed that it resulted from his military service, her pension being asked for entirely because of her needs and the faithful service of her husband and her sons.

This presents the question whether a gift in such a case is a proper disposition of money appropriated for the purpose of paying pensions.

The passage of this law would, in my opinion, establish a precedent so far-reaching and open the door to such a vast multitude of claims not on principle within our present pension laws that I am constrained to disapprove the bill under consideration.

GROVER CLEVELAND.

EXECUTIVE MANSION, *July 6, 1886.*

To the House of Representatives:

I return herewith without approval House bill No. 5603, entitled "An act granting a pension to Mrs. Catherine McCarty."

The beneficiary is the widow of John McCarty, of the First Missouri Regiment of State Militia Volunteers, who died at Clinton, Mo., April 8, 64.

The widow filed her claim in 1866, alleging that her husband died while in the service from an overdose of colchicum.

The evidence shows without dispute that on the day previous to the death of the soldier a comrade procured some medicine from the regimental surgeon and asked McCarty to smell and taste it; that he did so, and shortly afterwards became very sick and died the next morning.

It is quite evident that the deceased soldier did more than taste this medicine.

Although it would be pleasant to aid the widow in this case, it is hardly fair to ask the Government to grant a pension for the freak or gross heedlessness and recklessness of this soldier.

GROVER CLEVELAND.

EXECUTIVE MANSION, *July 6, 1886.*

To the House of Representatives:

I herewith return without my approval House bill No. 6648, entitled "An act for the relief of Edward M. Harrington."

It appears that this claimant was enrolled as a recruit December 31, 1863, and mustered in at Dunkirk, N. Y. He remained at the barracks there until March, 1864, when he was received at the Elmira rendezvous. From there he was sent to his regiment on the 7th day of April, 1864.

He was discharged June 15, 1864, upon a surgeon's certificate of disability, declaring the cause of discharge to be epilepsy, produced by blows of violence over the hypochondrial region while in the service, producing a deformity of sternum.

The claimant filed an application for pension in June, 1879, and in that and subsequent affidavits he alleged that while in barracks at Dunkirk, N. Y., and about the 9th day of January, 1864, and in the line of duty, he was attacked by one Patrick Burnes, who struck him upon the head and stamped upon and kicked him, breaking his collar bone and a number of ribs, causing internal injury and fits, the latter recurring every two weeks.

It is hardly worth while considering the character of these alleged injuries or their connection with the fits with which the claimant is afflicted.

I am entirely unable to see how the injuries are related to the claimant's army service.

The Government ought not to be called upon to insure against the quarrelsome propensities of its individual soldiers, nor to compensate one who is worsted in a fight, or even in an unprovoked attack, when the cause of injury is in no way connected with or related to any requirement or incident of military service.

GROVER CLEVELAND.

EXECUTIVE MANSION, *July 7, 1886.*

To the Senate of the United States:

I return without approval Senate bill No. 2281, entitled "An act granting to railroads the right of way through the Indian reservation in northern Montana."

The reservation referred to stretches across the extreme northern part of Montana Territory, with British America for its northern boundary. It contains an area of over 30,000 square miles. It is dedicated to Indian occupancy by treaty of October 17, 1855, and act of Congress of April 15, 1874. No railroads are within immediate approach to its boundaries, and only one, as shown on recent maps, is under construction in the neighborhood leading in its direction. The surrounding country is sparsely settled, and I have been unable to ascertain that the necessities of commerce or any public exigencies demand this legislation, which would affect so seriously the rights and interests of the Indians occupying the reservation.

The bill is in the nature of a general right of way for railroads through this Indian reservation. The Indian occupants have not given their consent to it, neither have they been consulted regarding it, nor is there any provision in it for securing their consent or agreement to the location or construction of railroads upon their lands. No routes are described, and no general directions on which the line of any railroad will be constructed are given.

No particular organized railway company engaged in constructing a railroad toward the reservation and ready or desirous to build its road through the Indian lands to meet the needs and requirements of trade and commerce is named. The bill gives the right to any railroad in the country, duly organized under the laws of any Territory, of any State, or of the United States, except those of the District of Columbia, to enter this Indian country, prospect for routes of travel, survey them, and construct routes of travel wherever it may please, with no check save possible disapproval by the Secretary of the Interior of its maps of location, and no limitation upon its acts except such rules and regulations as he may prescribe.

This power vested in the Secretary of the Interior might itself be improvidently exercised and subject to abuse.

No limit of time is fixed within which the construction of railroads should begin or be completed. Without such limitations speculating corporations would be enabled to seek out and secure the right of way over the natural and most feasible routes, with no present intention of constructing railroads along such lines, but with the view of holding their advantageous easements for disposal at some future time to some other corporation for a valuable consideration. In this way the construction of needed railroad facilities in that country could be hereafter greatly obstructed and retarded.

If the United States must exercise its right of eminent domain over the Indian Territories for the general welfare of the whole country, it should be done cautiously, with due regard for the interests of the Indians, and to no greater extent than the exigencies of the public service require.

Bills tending somewhat in the direction of this general character of legislation, affecting the rights of the Indians reserved to them by treaty stipulations, have been presented to me during the present session of Congress. They have received my reluctant approval, though I am by no means certain that a mistake has not been made in passing such laws without providing for the consent to such grants by the Indian occupants and otherwise more closely guarding their rights and interests; and I hoped that each of those bills as it received my approval would be the last of the kind presented. They, however, designated particular railroad companies, laid down general routes over which the respective roads should be constructed through the Indian lands, and specified their direction and termini, so that I was enabled to reasonably satisfy myself that the exigencies of the public service and the interests of commerce probably demanded the construction of the roads, and that by their construction and operation the Indians would not be too seriously affected.

The bill now before me is much more general in its terms than those which have preceded it. It is a new and wide departure from the general tenor of legislation affecting Indian reservations. It ignores the right of the Indians to be consulted as to the disposition of their lands, opens wide the door to any railroad corporation to do what, under the treaty covering the greater portion of the reservation, is reserved to the United States alone; it gives the right to enter upon Indian lands to a class of corporations carrying with them many individuals not known for any scrupulous regard for the interest or welfare of the Indians; it invites a general invasion of the Indian country, and brings into contact and intercourse with the Indians a class of whites and others who are independent of the orders, regulations, and control of the resident agents.

Corporations operating railroads through Indian lands are strongly tempted to infringe at will upon the reserved rights and the property of Indians, and thus are apt to become so arbitrary in their dealings and domineering in their conduct toward them that the Indians become disquieted, often threatening outbreaks and periling the lives of frontier settlers and others.

I am impressed with the belief that the bill under consideration does not sufficiently guard against an invasion of the rights and a disturbance of the peace and quiet of the Indians on the reservation mentioned; nor am I satisfied that the legislation proposed is demanded by any exigency of the public welfare.

GROVER CLEVELAND.

EXECUTIVE MANSION, *July 9, 1886.*

To the House of Representatives:

I return herewith without approval House bill No. 524, entitled ''An act granting a pension to Daniel H. Ross.''

An application for pension was filed in the Pension Bureau by the beneficiary named in this bill, and considerable testimony was filed in support of the same. I do not understand that the claim has been finally rejected. But however that may be, the claimant died, as I am advised, on the 1st day of February last. This, of course, renders the proposed legislation entirely inoperative, if it would not actually prejudice the claim of his surviving widow. She has already been advised of the evidence necessary to complete the claim of her husband, and it is not at all improbable that she will be able to prosecute the same to a successful issue for her benefit.

At any rate, her rights should not be in the least jeopardized by the completion of the legislation proposed in this bill.

GROVER CLEVELAND.

EXECUTIVE MANSION, *July 9, 1886.*

To the Senate:

I herewith return without approval Senate bill No. 856, entitled ''An act to provide for the erection of a public building in the city of Dayton, Ohio.''

It is not claimed that the Government has any public department or business which it should quarter at Dayton except its post-office and internal-revenue office. The former is represented as employing ten clerks, sixteen regular and two substitute letter carriers, and two special-delivery employees, who, I suppose, are boys, only occasionally in actual service. I do not understand that the present post-office quarters are either insufficient or inconvenient. By a statement prepared by the present postmaster it appears that they are rented by the Government for a period of ten years from the 15th day of October, 1883, at an annual rent of $2,950, which includes the cost of heating the same.

The office of the internal-revenue collector is claimed to be inadequate, but I am led to believe that this officer is fairly accommodated at an annual rental of $900. It is not impossible that a suggestion to change the area of this revenue district may be adopted, which would relieve any complaint of inadequacy of office room.

With only these two offices to provide for, I am not satisfied that the expenditure of $150,000 for their accommodation, as proposed by this bill, is in accordance with sound business principles or consistent with that economy in public affairs which has been promised to the people.

GROVER CLEVELAND.

EXECUTIVE MANSION, *July 10, 1886.*

To the House of Representatives:

I herewith return without approval House bill No. 5546, entitled "An act for the erection of a public building at Asheville, N. C."

If the needs of the Government are alone considered, the proposed building is only necessary for the accommodation of two terms of the United States court in each year and to provide an office for the clerk of that court and more commodious quarters for the post-office.

The terms of the court are now held in the county court room at Asheville at an expense to the Government of $50 for each term; the clerk of the court occupies a room for which an annual rent of $150 is paid, and the rent paid for the rooms occupied by the post-office is $180 each year.

The postmaster reports that four employees are regularly engaged in his office, which is now rated as third class.

I have no doubt that the court could be much more conveniently provided for in a new building if one should be erected; but it is represented to me that the regular terms held at Asheville last only two or three weeks each, though special terms are ordered at times to clear the docket. It is difficult to see from any facts presented in support of this bill why the United States court does not find accommodations which fairly answer its needs in the rooms now occupied by it. The floor space furnished for the terms of the Federal court is stated to be 75 by 100 feet, which, it must be admitted, provides a very respectable court room.

It is submitted that the necessity to the Government of a proper place to hold its courts is the only consideration which should have any weight in determining upon the propriety of expending the money which will be necessary to erect the proposed new building.

The limit of its cost is fixed in the bill under consideration at the sum of $80,000, but the history of such projects justifies the expectation that this limit will certainly be exceeded.

I am satisfied that the present necessity for this building is not urgent, and that something may be gained by a delay which will demonstrate more fully the public needs, and thus better suggest the style and size of the building to be erected.   GROVER CLEVELAND.

EXECUTIVE MANSION, *July 30, 1886.*

To the Senate:

I return without approval Senate bill No. 63, entitled "An act to authorize the construction of a highway bridge across that part of the waters of Lake Champlain lying between the towns of North Hero and Alburg, in the State of Vermont."

On the 20th day of June, 1884, a bill was approved and became a law having the same title and containing precisely the same provisions and in the exact words of the bill herewith returned.

The records of the War Department indicate that nothing has been done toward building the bridge permitted by such prior act. It is hardly possible that the bill now before me is intended to authorize an additional bridge between the two towns named, and I have been unable to discover any excuse or necessity for new legislation on the subject.

I conclude, therefore, that Congress in passing this bill acted in ignorance of the fact that a law providing for its objects and purposes was already on the statute book.

My approval of the bill is withheld for this reason and in order to prevent an unnecessary and confusing multiplicity of laws.

GROVER CLEVELAND.

EXECUTIVE MANSION, *July 30, 1886.*
To the House of Representatives:

I hereby return without my approval House bill No. 1391, entitled "An act to provide for the erection of a public building at Springfield, Mo."

It appears from the report of the committee of the House of Representatives to which this bill was referred that the city of Springfield is in a thriving condition, with stores, banks, and manufactories, and having, with North Springfield, which is an adjoining town, about 20,000 inhabitants.

No Federal courts are held at this place, and apparently the only quarters which the Government should provide are such as are necessary for the accommodation of the post-office and the land-office located there.

The postmaster reports that six employees are engaged in his office.

The rooms used as a post-office are now furnished the Government free of expense, and the rent paid for the quarters occupied as a land-office amounts to $300 annually.

Upon the facts presented I am satisfied that the business of the Government at this point can be well transacted for the present without the construction of the proposed building.

GROVER CLEVELAND.

To the Senate: EXECUTIVE MANSION, *July 31, 1886.*

I return without approval Senate bill No. 2160, entitled "A bill granting a pension to Mary J. Hagerman."

The husband of this proposed beneficiary enlisted in 1861 and was wounded by a gunshot, which seriously injured his left forearm. In 1864 he was discharged; was afterwards pensioned for his wound, and died in August, 1884.

᠁ ᠁ageman, who attended the deceased in his last illness, testifies that he was called to attend him in August, 1884; that he was sick with typhomalarial fever, and that upon inquiry he (the physician) found that it was caused by hard work or overexertion and exposure. He was ill for about ten days.

The application of his widow for pension was rejected in 1885 on the ground that the fatal disease was not due to military service.

I am unable to discover how any different determination could have been reached.

To grant a pension in this case would clearly contravene the present policy of the Government, and either establish a precedent which, if followed, would allow a pension to the widow of every soldier wounded or disabled in the war, without regard to the cause of death, or would unjustly discriminate in favor of the few thus receiving the bounty of the Government against many whose cases were equally meritorious.

GROVER CLEVELAND.

To the Senate: EXECUTIVE MANSION, *July 31, 1886.*

I herewith return without my approval Senate bill No. 1421, entitled "An act granting a pension to William H. Weaver."

The claimant named in this bill enlisted August 12, 1862, and was mustered out of service June 12, 1865. During his service he was treated in hospital for diarrhea and lumbago, and in the reports for May and June, as well as July and August, 1864, he is reported as absent sick.

He filed his application for pension in November, 1877, alleging that in March, 1863, he contracted measles, and in May, 1864, remittent fever, and that as a result of the two attacks he was afflicted with weakness in the limbs and eyes. He made statements afterwards in support of his application that he was also troubled in the service with rheumatism and diarrhea.

The case was examined by several special examiners, from which, as reported to me, it appeared from the claimant's admission that he had sore eyes previous to his enlistment, though he claimed they were sound when he entered the Army.

A surgeon who made an examination in March, 1881, reported that he could not find any evidence whatever of disease of the eyes, and nothing to corroborate the claimant's assertion that he was suffering from rheumatism, piles, or diarrhea.

Another surgeon, who examined the claimant in 1879, reported that he found the eyelids slightly granulated, producing some irritation of the eyeball and rendering the eyes a little weak, and that he found no other disability.

In 1882 a surgeon who made an examination reported that he discovered indications that the claimant had suffered at some time with chronic ophthalmia, but that in his opinion his eyes did not disable him in the least, and that the claimant was well nourished and in good health.

The report of the committee to whom this bill was referred in the Senate states that six special examinations have been made in the case and that two of them were favorable to the claim.

The trouble and expense incurred by the Pension Bureau to ascertain the truth and to deal fairly by this claimant, and the entire absence of any suspicion of bias against the claim in that Bureau, ought to give weight to its determination.

The claim was rejected by the Pension Bureau in July, 1885, upon the ground that disease of the eyes existed prior to enlistment and that the evidence failed to show that there had existed a pensionable degree of disability, since discharge, from diarrhea or rheumatism.

It will be observed that this is not a case where there was a lack of the technical proof required by the Pension Bureau, but that its judgment was based upon the merits of the application and affected the very foundation of the claim.

I think it should be sustained; and its correctness is somewhat strengthened by the fact that the claimant continued in active service for more than a year after his alleged sickness, that after filing his claim he added thereto allegations of additional disabilities, and that he made no application for pension until more than twelve years after his discharge.

GROVER CLEVELAND.

EXECUTIVE MANSION, *July 31, 1886.*

To the House of Representatives:

I herewith return without approval House bill No. 3363, entitled "An act granting a pension to Jennette Dow."

The husband of the claimant enlisted August 7, 1862; received a gunshot wound in his left knee in September, 1863, and was mustered out with his company June 10, 1865. He was pensioned for his wound in 1878 at the rate of $4 per month, dating from the time of his discharge, which amount was increased to $8 per month from June 4, 1880. The pensioned soldier died December 17, 1882, and in 1883 his widow, the claimant, filed an application for pension, alleging that her husband's death resulted from his wound. Her claim was rejected in 1885 upon the ground that death was not caused by the wound.

The physician who was present at the time of the death certifies that the same resulted from apoplexy in twelve hours after the deceased was attacked.

It also appears from the statement of this physician that the deceased was employed for years after his discharge from the Army as a railroad conductor, and that at the time of his death he had with difficulty reached his home. He then describes as following the attack the usual manifestations of apoplexy, and adds that he regards the case as one of "hemiplegia, the outgrowth primarily of nerve injury, aggravated by the life's calling, and eventuating in apoplexy as stated."

Evidence is filed in the Pension Bureau showing that after his discharge he was more or less troubled with his wound, though one witness testifies that he railroaded with him for fifteen years after his injury. I find no medical testimony referred to which with any distinctness charges death to the wound, and it would be hardly credible if such evidence was found.

I am sure that in no case except in an application for pension would an attempt be made in the circumstances here developed to attribute death from apoplexy to a wound in the knee received nineteen years before the apoplectic attack.

GROVER CLEVELAND.

EXECUTIVE MANSION, *July 31, 1886.*

To the House of Representatives:

I return without approval House bill No. 9106, entitled "An act granting a pension to Rachel Barnes."

William Barnes, the husband of the beneficiary named in this bill, enlisted in the United States infantry in February, 1838, and was discharged February 24, 1841.

In 1880 he applied for a pension, alleging that while serving in Florida in 1840 and 1841 he contracted disease of the eyes. He procured considerable evidence in support of his claim, but in 1882, and while still endeavoring to furnish further proof, he committed suicide by hanging.

The inference that his death thus occasioned was the result of despondency and despair brought on by his failure to procure a pension, while it adds a sad feature to the case, does not aid in connecting his death with his military service.

That this was the view of the committee of the House to whom the bill was referred is evidenced by the conclusion of their report in these words:

And while your committee do not feel justified under the law as at present existing in recommending that the name of the widow be placed upon the pension roll for the purpose of a pension in her own right as widow of the deceased soldier and by reason of the soldier's death, they do think that she should be allowed such pension as, had her husband's claim been favorably determined on the day of his decease, he would have received.

And yet the bill under consideration directs the Secretary of the Interior to place this widow's name on the pension roll and to "pay her a pension as such widow from and after the passage of this act, subject to the provisions and limitations of the pension laws."

GROVER CLEVELAND.

EXECUTIVE MANSION, *July 31, 1886.*

To the House of Representatives:

I return herewith without approval House bill No. 8336, entitled "An act granting an increase of pension to Duncan Forbes."

The beneficiary named in this bill enlisted, under the name of Alexander Sheret, January 7, 1862, in the Regular Army, and was discharged January 8, 1865.

He applied for a pension in 1879, alleging that he was wounded in his right breast December 31, 1862, and in his right ankle September 20, 1863. He was pensioned in 1883, dating from January 9, 1865, for the ankle wound, but that part of his claim based upon the wound in his breast was rejected upon the ground that there was no record of the same and the testimony failed to show that such a wound had its origin in the service.

Though the lack of such a record is sufficiently accounted for, I am convinced that, conceding both the wounds alleged were received, this pensioner has been fairly and justly treated.

It appears from the allegations of his application to the Pension Bureau that after the wound in his breast, in December, 1862, he continued his service till September, 1863, when he was wounded again in the ankle, and that with both wounds he served until his discharge in January, 1865. It also appears from the records that after his discharge from the Army, and on the 3d day of February, 1865, he enlisted as landsman in the United States Navy, and served in that branch of the service for three years.

A medical examination in May, 1885, disclosed the appearance of a gunshot wound in the right breast, which is thus described:

The missile struck the seventh rib of right side and glanced off, leaving a horizontal scar 2¼ inches long and one-half inch wide, deeply depressed and firmly adherent.

I credit this claimant with being a good soldier, and I am willing to believe that his insistence upon a greater pension than that already allowed by the Pension Bureau, under liberal general laws, enacted for the benefit of himself and all his comrades, is the result of the demoralization produced by ill-advised special legislation on the subject.

GROVER CLEVELAND.

EXECUTIVE MANSION, *August 4, 1886.*

To the House of Representatives:

I return without approval House bill No. 5389, entitled "An act granting a pension to Ann Kinney."

This beneficiary applied for a pension in 1877 as the widow of Edward Kinney, alleging that he died September 5, 1875, from the effects of a wound received in the Army. He enlisted November 4, 1861, and was discharged July 28. 1862. on account of a gunshot wound in his left elbow. for which wound he was pensioned in the year 1865.

A physician testifies that the pensioned soldier's death was. in his opinion. brought on indirectly by the intemperate use of intoxicating liquors. and that he died from congestion of the brain.

The marshal of the city where he resided states that on the day of the soldier's death he was called to remove him from a house in which he was making a disturbance. and that finding him intoxicated he arrested him and took him to the lockup and placed him in a cell. In a short time, not exceeding an hour. thereafter he was found dead. He further states that he was addicted to periodical sprees.

Another statement is made that the soldier was an intemperate man. and died very suddenly in the city lockup. where he had been taken by an officer while on a drunken spree.

This is not a pleasant recital. and as against the widow I should be glad to avoid its effect. But the most favorable phase of the case does not aid her, since her claim rests upon the allegation that her husband was subject to epileptic fits and died from congestion of the brain while in one of these fits. Even upon this showing the connection between the fits and the wound in the elbow is not made apparent.

GROVER CLEVELAND.

EXECUTIVE MANSION. *August 4. 1886.*

To the House of Representatives:

I herewith return without approval House bill No. 8556, entitled "An act granting a pension to Abraham Points."

This soldier enlisted August 11. 1864. and was mustered out June 28, 1865.

He was treated during his short term of service for "catarrhal," "constipation," "diarrhea." "jaundice," and "colic."

He filed an application for pension in 1878. alleging that some of his comrades in a joke twisted his arm in such a manner that the elbow joint became stiffened and anchylosed. and that his eyes became sore and have continued to grow worse ever since. There is no record of either of these disabilities.

The application was denied upon the ground. as stated in the report from the Pension Bureau. that the claim "was specially examined, and it was shown conclusively. from the evidence of neighbors and acquaintances of good repute and standing. that the alleged disabilities existed at and prior to claimant's enlistment."

I am satisfied from an examination of the facts submitted to me that this determination was correct.

GROVER CLEVELAND.

EXECUTIVE MANSION, *August 4, 1886.*

To the House of Representatives:

I herewith return without approval House bill No. 3551, entitled "An act granting a pension to George W. Cutler, late a private in Company B, Ninth New Hampshire Volunteers."

This claimant enlisted July 12, 1862, and was discharged June 22, 1863, for disability resulting from "scrofulous ulceration of the tibia and fibula of right leg; loss of sight of left eye."

He made a claim for pension in 1865, alleging an injury while loading commissary stores, resulting in spitting of blood, injury to lungs, and heart disease.

This claim was rejected August 31, 1865.

In 1867 he again enlisted in the United States infantry, and was discharged from that enlistment March 29, 1869, for disability, the certificate stating that—

He is unfit for military service by reason of being subject to bleeding of the lungs. He was wounded, while in the line of his duty in the United States Army, at Fredericksburg, Va., December 13, 1862. Said wound is not the cause of his disability.

Afterwards, and in the year 1879, he filed affidavits claiming that he was wounded by a minie ball at the battle of Fredericksburg, December 13, 1862, and was injured by falling down an embankment.

In 1883 he filed an affidavit in which he stated that the disability for which he claims a pension arose from injuries received in falling down a bank at Fredericksburg and being tramped on by troops, causing a complication of diseases resulting in general debility.

The statement in the certificate of discharge from his second enlistment as to the wound he received by a minie ball at Fredericksburg was of course derived from his own statement, as it was related to a prior term of service.

The records of the Adjutant-General's Office furnish no evidence of wounds or injury at Fredericksburg.

The injury alleged at first as a consequence of loading commissary stores seems to have been abandoned by the claimant for the adoption of a wound at Fredericksburg, which in its turn seems to have been abandoned and a fall down a bank and trampling upon by troops substituted.

Whatever injuries he may have suffered during his first enlistment, and to whatever cause he chooses at last to attribute them, they did not prevent his reenlistment and passing the physical examination necessary before acceptance.

The surgeon of the Ninth New Hampshire Volunteers, in which he first enlisted, states that he remembers the claimant well; that he was mustered and accepted as a recruit in spite of his (the surgeon's) protest; that he was physically unfit for duty; that he had the appearance of impaired health, and that his face and neck were marked by one or more deep scars, the result, as the claimant himself alleged, of scrofulous abscesses in early youth. He expresses the opinion that he is attempting to palm off these old scars as evidence of wounds received, and that if he had been wounded as he claimed he (the surgeon) would have known it and remembered it.

It is true that whenever in this case a wound is described it is located in the jaw, while some of the medical testimony negatives the existence of any wound.

The contrariety of the claimant's statements and the testimony and circumstances tend so strongly to impeach his claim that I do not think the decision of the Pension Bureau should be reversed and the claimant pensioned.

GROVER CLEVELAND.

EXECUTIVE MANSION, *August 4, 1886.*

To the House of Representatives:

I herewith return without my approval House bill No. 7234, entitled "An act granting a pension to Susan Hawes."

The beneficiary named in this bill is the mother of Jeremiah Hawes, who enlisted in February, 1861, in the United States artillery, and was discharged in February, 1864. He filed a claim for pension in 1881, alleging that in 1862, by the premature discharge of a cannon, he sustained paralysis of his right arm and side. In 1883, while his claim was still pending, he died.

He does not appear to have made his home with his mother altogether, if at all. For some years prior to his death and at the time of its occurrence he was an inmate, or had been an inmate, of a soldiers' home in Ohio.

But whatever may be said of the character of any injuries he may have received in the service or of his relations to his mother, the cause of his death, it seems to me, can not possibly upon any reasonable theory be attributable to any incident of his military service.

It appears that in July, 1883, while the deceased was on his way from Buffalo, where he had been in a hospital, to the soldiers' home in Ohio, he attempted to step on a slowly moving freight train, and making a misstep a wheel of the car passed over his foot, injuring it so badly that it was deemed necessary by two physicians who were called to amputate the foot. An anæsthetic was administered preparatory to the operation, but before it was entered upon the injured man died, having survived the accident but two hours.

The physicians who were present stated that in their opinion death was due to heart disease.

The above account of the death of the soldier is derived from a report furnished by the Pension Bureau, and differs somewhat from the statement contained in the report of the House Committee on Invalid Pensions as related to the intention of the physicians to amputate the injured

foot and their administration of an anæsthetic.   But the accident and
the death two hours thereafter under the treatment of the physicians are
conceded facts.

GROVER CLEVELAND.

EXECUTIVE MANSION, *August 4, 1886.*

To the House of Representatives:

I herewith return without approval House bill No. 1584, entitled "An
act for the relief of Mrs. Aurelia C. Richardson."

Albert H. Fillmore, the son of the beneficiary mentioned in this bill,
enlisted in August, 1862, and died in the service, of smallpox, May 20,
1865.

His father having died some time prior to the soldier's enlistment, his
mother in 1858 married Lorenzo D. Richardson.   It is stated in the
report upon this case from the Pension Bureau that the deceased did not
live with his mother after her marriage to Richardson, and that there
is no competent evidence that he contributed to her support after that
event.

At the time of the soldier's death his stepfather was a blacksmith,
earning at about that time, as it is represented, not less than $70 a month,
and owning considerable property, a part of which still remains to him.

While in ordinary cases of this kind I am by no means inclined to distinguish very closely between dependence at the date of the soldier's
death and the date of proposed aid to a needy mother, I think the circumstances here presented, especially the fact of nonresidence by the
son with his mother since her second marriage, do not call for a departure from the law governing claims based upon dependence.

GROVER CLEVELAND.

POCKET VETOES.

EXECUTIVE MANSION,
Washington, August 17, 1886.

Hon. THOS. F. BAYARD,
       Secretary of State.

DEAR SIR: The President directs me to transmit to you the accompanying bills and joint resolutions, which failed to become laws at the close
of the late session of Congress, being unsigned and not having been presented to him ten days prior to adjournment.

I may add that the printed copy of memorandum (without signature)
is by the President, and is attached to each bill and resolution by his
direction.

Very respectfully,

O. L. PRUDEN,
Assistant Secretary.

["An act for the relief of Francis W. Haldeman."—Received July 28, 1886.]

This bill appropriates $200 to the party named therein "as compensation for services performed and money expended for the benefit of the United States Army." It appears from a report of the House Committee on War Claims that in the fall of 1863 Haldeman, a lad 12 years of age, purchased a uniform and armed himself and attached himself to various Ohio regiments, and, as is said, performed various duties connected with the army service until the end of the year 1864, and for this it is proposed to give him $200.

Of course he never enlisted and never was regularly attached to any regiment. What kind of arms this boy 12 years of age armed himself with is not stated, and it is quite evident that his military service could not have amounted to much more than the indulgence of a boyish freak and his being made a pet of the soldiers with whom he was associated. There is a pleasant sentiment connected with this display of patriotism and childish military ardor, and it is not a matter of surprise that he should, as stated by the committee, have "received honorable mention by name in the history of his regiment;" but when it is proposed twenty-two years after his one year's experience with troops to pay him a sum nearly if not quite equal to the pay of a soldier who fought and suffered all the dangers and privations of a soldier's life, I am constrained to dissent.

["An act for the relief of R. D. Beckley and Leon Howard."—Received July 28, 1886.]

These two men were employed by the Doorkeeper of the Forty-eighth Congress as laborers at the rate of $720 per annum.

They claim that in both sessions of that Congress they not only performed the duties appertaining to their positions as laborers, but also performed the full duties of messengers. Having received their pay as laborers, this bill proposes to appropriate for them the difference between their compensation as laborers and $1,200, the pay allowed messengers.

Congress, in appropriation bills covering the period in which these men claim to have performed these dual duties, provided for a certain specified number of messengers and a fixed number of laborers. They both accepted the latter position. If they actually performed the duties of both places, their ability to do so is evidence that the labor of either place was very light. In any case they owed their time and services to the Government, and while they were performing the duties of messengers they were not engaged in the harder tasks which might have been required of them as laborers. They ought not to complain if they have received the amount for which they agreed to work, and which was allowed for as the wages of a place which they were glad enough to secure. If they really did the work of both places, I don't see why they should not be paid both compensations. This proposition of course would not be entertained for a moment.

I am of the opinion that claims for extra compensation such as these should be firmly discountenanced, and I am sure no injustice will be done by my declining to approve this bill.

["An act for the relief of Thomas P. Morgan, jr."—Received July 31, 1886.—Memorandum.]

Thomas P. Morgan, jr., in the year 1881 entered into a contract with the Government to do certain excavating in the harbor of Norfolk.

He performed considerable of the work, but though the time limited by the contract for the completion was extended by the Government, he failed to complete the work, which necessitated other arrangements, to the damage of the Government in quite a large sum. His contract was forfeited by the Government because the progress he made was so slow and unsatisfactory. It seems that a certain percentage of the money earned by him in the progress of the work was, under the terms of the contract, retained by the Government to insure its completion, and when work was terminated the sum thus retained amounted to $4,898.04, which sum was justly forfeited to the Government.

The object of this bill is to waive this forfeiture and pay this sum to the derelict contractor.

Inasmuch as I am unable to see any equities in this case that should overcome the fact that the amount of loss to the Government through the contract is greater than the sum thus sought to be released to him, I am not willing to agree to his release from the consequence of his failure to perform his contract.

["An act for the relief of Charles F. Bowers."—Received August 2, 1886.]

It appears that Charles F. Bowers, while acting as regimental quartermaster in 1862, received of John Weeks, assistant quartermaster of volunteers, the sum of $230, for which he gave a receipt. On the settlement of his accounts he was unable to account for said sum, for the reason, as he alleges, that certain of his papers were lost and destroyed. Thus in the statement of his account he is represented as a debtor of the Government in that amount.

This bill directs that a credit be allowed to him of the said sum of $230. But since his account was adjusted as above stated, showing him in debt to the Government in the amount last stated, he has paid the sum of $75 and been allowed a credit of $125 for the value of a horse; so that whatever may be said of the merits of his claim that he should not be charged with the sum of $230, if he should now be credited with that sum the Government would owe him upon its books the sum of $30.

The bill is therefore not approved.

["An act to provide for the erection of a public building in the city of Annapolis, Md."—Received August 3, 1886.—Memorandum.]

The post-office at Annapolis is now accommodated in quarters for which the Government pays rent at the rate of $500 per annum, and the office occupied by the collector of customs is rented for $75 per annum.

The Government has no other use for a public building at Annapolis than is above indicated, and the chief argument urged why a building should be constructed there is based upon the fact that this city is the capital of the State of Maryland and should have a Government building because most if not all the other capitals of the States have such edifices.

There seems to be so little necessity for the building proposed for the transaction of Government business, and if there is anything in the argument last referred to it seems so well answered by the maintenance of the Naval Academy at Annapolis, this bill is allowed to remain inoperative.

["An act for the relief of J. A. Henry and others."—Received August 3, 1886.—Memorandum.]

This bill appropriates various sums to the parties named therein, being claims of rent of quarters occupied during the war by the Quartermaster's Department of the Army.

Among the appropriations there proposed to be made is one of the sum of $51 to L. F. Green. This account has been once paid, a special act directing such payment having been approved February 12, 1885. The fact of this payment and important information bearing upon the validity of some of the other claims mentioned in the bill could have been easily obtained by application to the Third Auditor.

["An act for the relief of William H. Wheeler."—Received August 3, 1886.]

This bill directs the payment of the sum of $633.50 to William H. Wheeler for quartermaster's stores furnished the Army in the year 1862.

From the data furnished me by the Quartermaster-General I am quite certain that this claim has been once paid. The circumstances presented to prove this are so strong that they should be explained before the relief provided by this bill is afforded the claimant.

["An act granting a pension to Margaret D. Marchand."—Received August 5, 1886.—Memorandum.]

A bill presented to me for approval, granting a pension of $50 per month to the beneficiary named, was disapproved upon the ground that the death of her husband did not appear to be in any way related to any incident of his military service.

This bill differs from the prior one simply in granting a pension subject to the provisions and limitations of the pension laws instead of fixing the rate of pension at a specified sum. I am still unable to see how the objection to the first bill has been obviated.

["Joint resolution providing for the distribution of the Official Register of the United States."—Received August 5, 1886.—Memorandum.]

This resolution reached me five minutes after the adjournment of the two Houses of Congress, and is the only enactment of the session which came to me too late for official action.

I do not understand this resolution nor the purposes sought to be accomplished by its passage, and while in that frame of mind should have been constrained to withhold my approval from the same even if it had reached me in time for consideration.

["Joint resolution directing payment of the surplus in the Treasury on the public debt."—Received August 5, 1886.—Memorandum.]

This resolution involves so much and is of such serious import that I do not deem it best to discuss it at this time. It is not approved because I believe it to be unnecessary and because I am by no means convinced that its mere passage and approval at this time may not endanger and embarrass the successful and useful operations of the Treasury Department and impair the confidence which the people should have in the management of the finances of the Government.

PROCLAMATIONS.

By the President of the United States of America.

A PROCLAMATION.

Whereas it is represented to me by the governor of the Territory of Washington that domestic violence exists within the said Territory, and that by reason of unlawful obstructions and combinations and the assemblage of evil-disposed persons it has become impracticable to enforce by the ordinary course of judicial proceedings the laws of the United States at Seattle and at other points and places within said Territory, whereby life and property are there threatened and endangered; and

Whereas, in the judgment of the President, an emergency has arisen and a case is now presented which justifies and requires, under the Constitution and laws of the United States, the employment of military force to suppress domestic violence and enforce the faithful execution of the laws of the United States if the command and warning of this proclamation be disobeyed and disregarded:

Now, therefore, I, Grover Cleveland, President of the United States of America, do hereby command and warn all insurgents and all persons who have assembled at any point within the said Territory of Washington for the unlawful purposes aforesaid to desist therefrom and to disperse and retire peaceably to their respective abodes on or before 6 o'clock in the afternoon of the 10th day of February instant.

And I do admonish all good citizens of the United States and all persons within the limits and jurisdiction thereof against aiding, abetting, countenancing, or taking any part in such unlawful acts or assemblages.

In witness whereof I have set my hand and caused the seal of the United States to be hereunto affixed.

[SEAL.]   Done at the city of Washington, this 9th day of February, A. D. 1886, and of the Independence of the United States the one hundred and tenth.

GROVER CLEVELAND.

By the President:

T. F. BAYARD, *Secretary of State.*

BY THE PRESIDENT OF THE UNITED STATES OF AMERICA.

A PROCLAMATION.

Whereas by a proclamation of the President of the United States dated the 14th day of February, in the year 1884,* upon evidence then appearing satisfactory to him that the Government of Spain had abolished the discriminating customs duty theretofore imposed upon the products of and articles proceeding from the United States of America imported into the islands of Cuba and Puerto Rico, such abolition to take effect on and after the 1st day of March of said year 1884, and, by virtue of the authority vested in him by section 4228 of the Revised Statutes of the United States, the President did thereby declare and proclaim that on and after the said 1st day of March, 1884, so long as the products of and articles proceeding from the United States imported into the islands of Cuba and Puerto Rico should be exempt from discriminating customs duties, any such duties on the products of and articles proceeding from Cuba and Puerto Rico under the Spanish flag should be suspended and discontinued; and

Whereas by Article I of the commercial agreement signed at Madrid the 13th day of February, 1884, it was stipulated and provided that "the duties of the third column of the customs tariffs of Cuba and Puerto Rico, which implies the suppression of the differential flag duty," should at once be applied to the products of and articles proceeding from the United States of America; and

Whereas the complete suppression of the differential flag duty in respect of all vessels of the United States and their cargoes entering the ports of Cuba and Puerto Rico is by the terms of the said agreement expressly made the consideration for the exercise of the authority conferred upon the President in respect of the suspension of the collection of foreign discriminating duties of tonnage and imposts upon merchandise brought within the United States from Cuba and Puerto Rico in Spanish vessels by said section 4228 of the Revised Statutes, which section reads as follows:

SEC. 4228. Upon satisfactory proof being given to the President by the government of any foreign nation that no discriminating duties of tonnage or imposts are imposed or levied in the ports of such nation upon vessels wholly belonging to citizens of the United States, or upon the produce, manufactures, or merchandise imported in the same from the United States or from any foreign country, the President may issue his proclamation declaring that the foreign discriminating duties of tonnage and impost within the United States are suspended and discontinued so far as respects the vessels of such foreign nation, and the produce, manufactures, or merchandise imported into the United States from such foreign nation or from any other foreign country; the suspension to take effect from the time of such notification being given to the President, and to continue so long as the reciprocal exemption of vessels belonging to citizens of the United States, and their cargoes, shall be continued, and no longer.

*See pp. 223-224.

And whereas proof is given to me that such complete suppression of the differential flag duty in respect of vessels of the United States and their cargoes entering the ports of Cuba and Puerto Rico has not in fact been secured, but that, notwithstanding the said agreement dated at Madrid, February 13, 1884, and in contravention thereof, as well as of the provisions of the said section 4228 of the Revised Statutes, higher and discriminating duties continue to be imposed and levied in said ports upon certain produce, manufactures, or merchandise imported into said ports from the United States or from any foreign country in vessels of the United States than is imposed and levied on the like produce, manufactures, or merchandise carried to said ports in Spanish vessels:

Now, therefore, I, Grover Cleveland, President of the United States of America, in execution of the aforesaid section 4228 of the Revised Statutes, do hereby revoke the suspension of the discriminating customs imposed and levied in the ports of the United States on the products of and articles proceeding under the Spanish flag from Cuba and Puerto Rico, which is set forth and contained in the aforesaid proclamation dated the 14th day of February, 1884; this revocation of said proclamation to take effect on and after the 25th day of October instant.

In witness whereof I have hereunto set my hand and caused the seal of the United States to be affixed.

[SEAL.]   Done at the city of Washington, this 13th day of October, A. D. 1886, and of the Independence of the United States the one hundred and eleventh.

GROVER CLEVELAND.

By the President:

T. F. BAYARD,
Secretary of State.

BY THE PRESIDENT OF THE UNITED STATES OF AMERICA.

A PROCLAMATION.

Whereas satisfactory proof has been given to me by the Government of Spain that no discriminating duties of tonnage or imposts are imposed or levied in the islands of Cuba and Puerto Rico upon vessels wholly belonging to citizens of the United States, or upon the produce, manufactures, or merchandise imported in the same from the United States or from any foreign country; and

Whereas notification of such abolition of discriminating duties of tonnage and imposts as aforesaid has been given to me by a memorandum of agreement signed this day in the city of Washington between the Secretary of State of the United States and the envoy extraordinary and minister plenipotentiary of Her Majesty the Queen Regent of Spain accredited to the Government of the United States of America:

Now, therefore, I, Grover Cleveland, President of the United States of

America, by virtue of the authority vested in me by section 4228 of the Revised Statutes of the United States, do hereby declare and proclaim that from and after the date of this my proclamation, being also the date of the notification received as aforesaid, the foreign discriminating duties of tonnage and impost within the United States are suspended and discontinued so far as respects the vessels of Spain and the produce, manufactures, or merchandise imported in said vessels into the United States from the islands of Cuba and Puerto Rico or from any other foreign country; such suspension to continue so long as the reciprocal exemption of vessels belonging to citizens of the United States, and their cargoes, shall be continued in the said islands of Cuba and Puerto Rico, and no longer.

In witness whereof I have hereunto set my hand and caused the seal of the United States to be affixed.

[SEAL.]   Done at the city of Washington, this 27th day of October, A. D. 1886, and of the Independence of the United States the one hundred and eleventh.

GROVER CLEVELAND.

By the President:

T. F. BAYARD,
Secretary of State.

A PROCLAMATION

BY THE PRESIDENT OF THE UNITED STATES.

It has long been the custom of the people of the United States, on a day in each year especially set apart for that purpose by their Chief Executive, to acknowledge the goodness and mercy of God and to invoke His continued care and protection.

In observance of such custom I, Grover Cleveland, President of the United States, do hereby designate and set apart Thursday, the 25th day of November instant, to be observed and kept as a day of thanksgiving and prayer.

On that day let all our people forego their accustomed employments and assemble in their usual places of worship to give thanks to the Ruler of the Universe for our continued enjoyment of the blessings of a free government, for a renewal of business prosperity throughout our land, for the return which has rewarded the labor of those who till the soil, and for our progress as a people in all that makes a nation great.

And while we contemplate the infinite power of God in earthquake, flood, and storm let the grateful hearts of those who have been shielded from harm through His mercy be turned in sympathy and kindness toward those who have suffered through His visitations.

Let us also in the midst of our thanksgiving remember the poor and needy with cheerful gifts and alms so that our service may by deeds of charity be made acceptable in the sight of the Lord.

In witness whereof I have hereunto set my hand and caused the seal of the United States to be affixed.

[SEAL.]   Done at the city of Washington, this 1st day of November, A. D. 1886, and of the Independence of the United States of America the one hundred and eleventh.

GROVER CLEVELAND.

By the President:

T. F. BAYARD, *Secretary of State.*

EXECUTIVE ORDERS.

Whereas in an Executive order dated the 21st day of July, 1875, directing the distribution of the fund of 400,000 pesetas received from the Spanish Government in satisfaction of the reclamation of the United States arising from the capture of the *Virginius*, it was provided "that should any further order or direction be required the same will hereafter be made in addition hereto;" and

Whereas a further order or direction is deemed necessary.

Now, therefore, I, Grover Cleveland, President of the United States, do hereby direct that all persons entitled to the benefit of any of the aforesaid fund of 400,000 pesetas who have not yet presented their claims thereto shall formulate and present their claims to the Secretary of State of the United States within six months from the date of this order, or be held as forever barred from the benefits of said fund.

And I hereby further direct that the balance of the fund which shall remain unclaimed at the expiration of the aforesaid period of six months shall be distributed *pro rata* among the beneficiaries under the original distribution provided they or their heirs or representatives shall within the six months next succeeding the said former period present to the Secretary of State of the United States petitions for their shares of said balance.

And to these ends the Secretary of State is requested to cause public notice to be given of the above direction.

In witness whereof I have hereunto set my hand at the city of Washington, this 10th day of December, A. D. 1885, and of the Independence of the United States of America the one hundred and tenth.

GROVER CLEVELAND.

EXECUTIVE MANSION,

Washington, February — —

Tidings of the death of Winfield Scott Hancock, the senior major-general of the Army of the United States, have just been received.

A patriotic and valiant defender of his country, an able and heroic soldier, a spotless and accomplished gentleman, crowned alike with the laurels of military renown and the highest tribute of his fellow-countrymen to his worth as a citizen, he has gone to his reward.

It is fitting that every mark of public respect should be paid to his memory.

Therefore it is now ordered by the President that the national flag be displayed at half-mast upon all the buildings of the Executive Departments in this city until after his funeral shall have taken place.

By direction of the President:

DANIEL S. LAMONT,
Private Secretary.

In the exercise of the power vested in the President by the Constitution, and by virtue of the seventeen hundred and fifty-third section of the Revised Statutes and of the civil-service act approved January 16, 1883, the following rule for the regulation and improvement of the executive civil service is hereby amended and promulgated, as follows:

RULE XXII.

Any person in the classified departmental service may be transferred and appointed to any other place therein upon the following conditions:

1. That he is not debarred by clause 2 of Rule XXI.

2. That the head of a Department has, in a written statement to be filed with the Commission, requested such transfer to a place in said Department, to be designated in the statement.

3. That said person is shown in the statement or by other evidence satisfactory to the Commission to have been during six consecutive months in such service since January 16, 1883.

4. That such person has passed at the required grade one or more examinations under the Commission which are together equal to that required for the place to which the transfer is to be made.

But any person who has for three years last preceding served as a clerk in the office of the President of the United States may be transferred or appointed to any place in the classified service without examination.

Approved, April 12, 1886.

GROVER CLEVELAND.

EXECUTIVE MANSION, *May 20, 1886.*

Under the provisions of section 4 of the act approved March 3, 1883, it is hereby ordered that the several Executive Departments, the Department of Agriculture, and the Government Printing Office be closed on Monday, the 31st instant, to enable the employees to participate in the decoration of the graves of the soldiers who fell during the rebellion.

GROVER CLEVELAND.

EXECUTIVE MANSION, *July 3, 1886.*

To Heads of the Government Departments:

Inasmuch as the 4th of July of the present year falls upon Sunday and the celebration of Independence Day is to be generally observed upon Monday, July 5, it is hereby ordered that the several Executive Departments, the Department of Agriculture, and the Government Printing Office be closed on Monday, the 5th instant.

GROVER CLEVELAND.

EXECUTIVE MANSION,
Washington, July 14, 1886.

To the Heads of Departments in the Service of the General Government:

I deem this a proper time to especially warn all subordinates in the several Departments and all officeholders under the General Government against the use of their official positions in attempts to control political movements in their localities.

Officeholders are the agents of the people, not their masters.   Not only is their time and labor due to the Government, but they should scrupulously avoid in their political action, as well as in the discharge of their official duty, offending by a display of obtrusive partisanship their neighbors·who have relations with them as public officials.

They should also constantly remember that their party friends from whom they have received preferment have not invested them with the power of arbitrarily managing their political affairs.   They have no right as officeholders to dictate the political action of their party associates or to throttle freedom of action within party lines by methods and practices which pervert every useful and justifiable purpose of party organization.

The influence of Federal officeholders should not be felt in the manipulation of political primary meetings and nominating conventions.   The use by these officials of their positions to compass their selection as delegates to political conventions is indecent and unfair; and proper regard for the proprieties and requirements of official place will also prevent their assuming the active conduct of political campaigns.

Individual interest and activity in political affairs are by no means condemned.   Officeholders are neither disfranchised nor forbidden the exercise of political privileges, but their privileges are not enlarged nor is their duty to party increased to pernicious activity by officeholding.

A just discrimination in this regard between the things a citizen may properly do and the purposes for which a public office should not be used is easy in the light of a correct appreciation of the relation between the people and those intrusted with official place and a consideration of the necessity under our form of government of political action free from official coercion.

You are requested to communicate the substance of these views to those for whose guidance they are intended.

GROVER CLEVELAND.

In the exercise of the power vested in the President by the Constitution, and by virtue of the seventeen hundred and fifty-third section of the Revised Statutes and of the civil-service act approved January 16, 1883, the following rule for the regulation and improvement of the executive civil service is hereby amended and promulgated, as follows:

RULE IX.

All applications for regular competitive examinations for admission to the classified civil service must be made on blank forms to be prescribed by the Commission.

Requests for blank forms of application for competitive examination for admission to the classified civil service and all regular applications for such examination shall be made—

1. If for the classified departmental service, to the United States Civil Service Commission at Washington, D. C.

2. If for the classified customs service, to the civil-service board of examiners for the customs district in which the person desiring to be examined wishes to enter the customs service.

3. If for the classified postal service, to the civil-service board of examiners for the post-office at which the person desiring to be examined wishes to enter the postal service.

Requests for blank forms of application to customs and postal boards of examiners must be made in writing by the persons desiring examination, and such blank forms shall not be furnished to any other persons.

Approved, August 13, 1886.

GROVER CLEVELAND.

EXECUTIVE MANSION,
Washington, November 16, 1886.

Hon. DANIEL MANNING,
Secretary of the Treasury.

DEAR SIR: In pursuance of a joint resolution of the Congress approved March 3. 1877, authorizing the President to cause suitable regulations to be made for the maintenance of the statue of "Liberty Enlightening the World," now located on Bedloes Island, in the harbor of New York, as a beacon, I hereby direct that said statue be at once placed under the care and superintendence of the Light-House Board, and that it be from henceforth maintained by said board as a beacon, and that it be so maintained, lighted, and tended in accordance with such rules and regulations as now exist applicable thereto, or such other and different rules and regulations as said board may deem necessary to carry out the design of said joint resolution and this order.

GROVER CLEVELAND.

GENERAL ORDERS, No. 84.

HEADQUARTERS OF THE ARMY,
ADJUTANT-GENERAL'S OFFICE,
Washington, November 18, 1886.

I. The following proclamation [order] has been received from the President:

EXECUTIVE MANSION,
Washington, D. C., November 18, 1886.

To the People of the United States:

It is my painful duty to announce the death of Chester Alan Arthur, lately the President of the United States, which occurred, after an illness of long duration, at an early hour this morning at his residence in the city of New York.

Mr. Arthur was called to the chair of the Chief Magistracy of the nation by a tragedy which cast its shadow over the entire Government.

His assumption of the grave duties was marked by an evident and conscientious sense of his responsibilities and an earnest desire to meet them in a patriotic and benevolent spirit.

With dignity and ability he sustained the important duties of his station, and the reputation of his personal worth, conspicuous graciousness, and patriotic fidelity will long be cherished by his fellow-countrymen.

In token of respect to the memory of the deceased it is ordered that the Executive Mansion and the several departmental buildings be draped in mourning for a period of thirty days and that on the day of the funeral all public business in the departments be suspended.

The Secretaries of War and of the Navy will cause orders to be issued for appropriate military and naval honors to be rendered on that day.

Done at the city of Washington this 18th day of November, A. D. 1886, and of the Independence of the United States of America the [SEAL.] one hundred and eleventh.

GROVER CLEVELAND.

By the President:

THOMAS F. BAYARD,
Secretary of State.

II. In compliance with the instructions of the President, on the day of the funeral, at each military post, the troops and cadets will be paraded and this order read to them, after which all labors for the day will cease.

The national flag will be displayed at half-staff.

At dawn of day thirteen guns will be fired, and afterwards at intervals of thirty minutes between the rising and setting of the sun a single gun, and at the close of the day a national salute of thirty-eight guns.

The officers of the Army will wear crape on the left arm and on their swords and the colors of the Battalion of Engineers, of the several regiments, and of the United States Corps of Cadets will be put in mourning for the period of six months.

The date and hour of the funeral will be communicated to department commanders by telegraph, and by them to their subordinate commanders. By command of Lieutenant-General Sheridan:

R. C. DRUM, *Adjutant-General.*

SPECIAL ORDER.

NAVY DEPARTMENT,
Washington, November 18, 1886.

The President of the United States announces the death of ex-President Chester Alan Arthur in the following proclamation [order]:

[For order see preceding page.]

It is hereby directed, in pursuance of the instructions of the President, that on the day of the funeral, where this order may be received in time, otherwise on the day after its receipt, the ensign at each naval station and of each of the vessels of the United States Navy in commission be hoisted at half-mast from sunrise to sunset, and that also, at each naval station and on board of flagships and vessels acting singly, a gun be fired at intervals of every half hour from sunrise to sunset.

The officers of the Navy and Marine Corps will wear the usual badge of mourning attached to the sword hilt and on the left arm for a period of thirty days.

WILLIAM C. WHITNEY,
Secretary of the Navy.

EXECUTIVE MANSION,
Washington, November 20, 1886.

It is hereby ordered, That the Department of Agriculture, the Government Printing Office, and all other Government offices in the District of Columbia be closed on Monday, the 22d instant, the day of the funeral of the late Chester Alan Arthur, ex-President of the United States.

GROVER CLEVELAND.

SECOND ANNUAL MESSAGE.

WASHINGTON, *December 6, 1886.*

To the Congress of the United States:

In discharge of a constitutional duty, and following a well-established precedent in the Executive office, I herewith transmit to the Congress at its reassembling certain information concerning the state of the Union, together with such recommendations for legislative consideration as appear necessary and expedient.

Our Government has consistently maintained its relations of friendship toward all other powers and of neighborly interest toward those whose possessions are contiguous to our own.   Few questions have arisen during the past year with other governments, and none of those are beyond the reach of settlement in friendly counsel.

We are as yet without provision for the settlement of claims of citizens of the United States against Chile for injustice during the late war with Peru and Bolivia.   The mixed commissions organized under claims conventions concluded by the Chilean Government with certain European States have developed an amount of friction which we trust can be avoided in the convention which our representative at Santiago is authorized to negotiate.

The cruel treatment of inoffensive Chinese has, I regret to say, been repeated in some of the far Western States and Territories, and acts of violence against those people, beyond the power of the local constituted authorities to prevent and difficult to punish, are reported even in distant Alaska.   Much of this violence can be traced to race prejudice and competition of labor, which can not, however, justify the oppression of strangers whose safety is guaranteed by our treaty with China equally with the most favored nations.

In opening our vast domain to alien elements the purpose of our lawgivers was to invite assimilation, and not to provide an arena for endless antagonism.   The paramount duty of maintaining public order and defending the interests of our own people may require the adoption of measures of restriction, but they should not tolerate the oppression of individuals of a special race.   I am not without assurance that the Government of China, whose friendly disposition toward us I am most happy to recognize, will meet us halfway in devising a comprehensive remedy by which an effective limitation of Chinese emigration, joined to protection of those Chinese subjects who remain in this country, may be secured.

Legislation is needed to execute the provisions of our Chinese convention of 1880 touching the opium traffic.

While the good will of the Colombian Government toward our country is manifest, the situation of American interests on the Isthmus of Panama has at times excited concern and invited friendly action looking to the performance of the engagements of the two nations concerning the territory embraced in the interoceanic transit.   With the subsidence of the Isthmian disturbances and the erection of the State of Panama into a federal district under the direct government of the constitutional administration at Bogota, a new order of things has been inaugurated, which, although as yet somewhat experimental and affording scope for arbitrary exercise of power by the delegates of the national authority, promises much improvement.

The sympathy between the people of the United States and France, born during our colonial struggle for independence and continuing to-day, has received a fresh impulse in the successful completion and dedication of the colossal statue of "Liberty Enlightening the World" in New York Harbor—the gift of Frenchmen to Americans.

A convention between the United States and certain other powers for the protection of submarine cables was signed at Paris on March 14, 1884, and has been duly ratified and proclaimed by this Government. By agreement between the high contracting parties this convention is to go into effect on the 1st of January next, but the legislation required for its execution in the United States has not yet been adopted. I earnestly recommend its enactment.

Cases have continued to occur in Germany giving rise to much correspondence in relation to the privilege of sojourn of our naturalized citizens of German origin revisiting the land of their birth, yet I am happy to state that our relations with that country have lost none of their accustomed cordiality.

The claims for interest upon the amount of tonnage dues illegally exacted from certain German steamship lines were favorably reported in both Houses of Congress at the last session, and I trust will receive final and favorable action at an early day.

The recommendations contained in my last annual message in relation to a mode of settlement of the fishery rights in the waters of British North America, so long a subject of anxious difference between the United States and Great Britain, was met by an adverse vote of the Senate on April 13 last, and thereupon negotiations were instituted to obtain an agreement with Her Britannic Majesty's Government for the promulgation of such joint interpretation and definition of the article of the convention of 1818 relating to the territorial waters and inshore fisheries of the British Provinces as should secure the Canadian rights from encroachment by the United States fishermen and at the same time insure the enjoyment by the latter of the privileges guaranteed to them by such convention.

The questions involved are of long standing, of grave consequence, and from time to time for nearly three-quarters of a century have given rise to earnest international discussions, not unaccompanied by irritation.

Temporary arrangements by treaties have served to allay friction, which, however, has revived as each treaty was terminated. The last arrangement, under the treaty of 1871, was abrogated after due notice by the United States on June 30, 1885, but I was enabled to obtain for our fishermen for the remainder of that season enjoyment of the full privileges accorded by the terminated treaty.

The joint high commission by whom the treaty had been negotiated, although invested with plenary power to make a permanent settlement, were content with a temporary arrangement, after the termination of which the question was relegated to the stipulations of the treaty of 1818, as to the first article of which no construction satisfactory to both countries has ever been agreed upon.

The progress of civilization and growth of population in the British Provinces to which the fisheries in question are contiguous and the expansion of commercial intercourse between them and the United States present to-day a condition of affairs scarcely realizable at the date of the negotiations of 1818.

New and vast interests have been brought into existence; modes of intercourse between the respective countries have been invented and multiplied; the methods of conducting the fisheries have been wholly changed; and all this is necessarily entitled to candid and careful consideration in the adjustment of the terms and conditions of intercourse and commerce between the United States and their neighbors along a frontier of over 3,500 miles.

This propinquity, community of language and occupation, and similarity of political and social institutions indicate the practicability and obvious wisdom of maintaining mutually beneficial and friendly relations.

Whilst I am unfeignedly desirous that such relations should exist between us and the inhabitants of Canada, yet the action of their officials during the past season toward our fishermen has been such as to seriously threaten their continuance.

Although disappointed in my efforts to secure a satisfactory settlement of the fishery question, negotiations are still pending, with reasonable hope that before the close of the present session of Congress announcement may be made that an acceptable conclusion has been reached.

As at an early day there may be laid before Congress the correspondence of the Department of State in relation to this important subject, so that the history of the past fishing season may be fully disclosed and the action and the attitude of the Administration clearly comprehended, a more extended reference is not deemed necessary in this communication.

The recommendation submitted last year that provision be made for a preliminary reconnoissance of the conventional boundary line between Alaska and British Columbia is renewed.

I express my unhesitating conviction that the intimacy of our relations with Hawaii should be emphasized. As a result of the reciprocity treaty of 1875, those islands, on the highway of Oriental and Australasian traffic, are virtually an outpost of American commerce and a stepping-stone to the growing trade of the Pacific. The Polynesian Island groups have been so absorbed by other and more powerful governments that the Hawaiian Islands are left almost alone in the enjoyment of their autonomy, which it is important for us should be preserved. Our treaty is now terminable on one year's notice, but propositions to abrogate it would be, in my judgment, most ill advised. The paramount influence we have there acquired, once relinquished, could only with difficulty be regained, and a valuable ground of vantage for ourselves might be con-
' into a stronghold for our commercial competitors. I earnestly
pd that the existing treaty stipulations be extended for a further

term of seven years.   A recently signed treaty to this end is now before
the Senate.

The importance of telegraphic communication between those islands
and the United States should not be overlooked.

The question of a general revision of the treaties of Japan is again
under discussion at Tokyo.   As the first to open relations with that Empire, and as the nation in most direct commercial relations with Japan,
the United States have lost no opportunity to testify their consistent
friendship by supporting the just claims of Japan to autonomy and independence among nations.

A treaty of extradition between the United States and Japan, the first
concluded by that Empire, has been lately proclaimed.

The weakness of Liberia and the difficulty of maintaining effective
sovereignty over its outlying districts have exposed that Republic to
encroachment.   It can not be forgotten that this distant community is
an offshoot of our own system, owing its origin to the associated benevolence of American citizens, whose praiseworthy efforts to create a nu-
cleus of civilization in the Dark Continent have commanded respect and
sympathy everywhere, especially in this country.   Although a formal
protectorate over Liberia is contrary to our traditional policy, the moral
right and duty of the United States to assist in all proper ways in the
maintenance of its integrity is obvious, and has been consistently announced during nearly half a century.   I recommend that in the reorganization of our Navy a small vessel, no longer found adequate to our
needs, be presented to Liberia, to be employed by it in the protection of
its coastwise revenues.

The encouraging development of beneficial and intimate relations between the United States and Mexico, which has been so marked within
the past few years, is at once the occasion of congratulation and of
friendly solicitude.   I urgently renew my former representation of the
need of speedy legislation by Congress to carry into effect the reciprocity
commercial convention of January 20, 1883.

Our commercial treaty of 1831 with Mexico was terminated, according to its provisions, in 1881, upon notification given by Mexico in pursuance of her announced policy of recasting all her commercial treaties.
Mexico has since concluded with several foreign governments new treaties of commerce and navigation, defining alien rights of trade, property,
and residence, treatment of shipping, consular privileges, and the like.
Our yet unexecuted reciprocity convention of 1883 covers none of these
points, the settlement of which is so necessary to good relationship.   I
propose to initiate with ,Mexico negotiations for a new and enlarged
treaty of commerce and navigation.

In compliance with a resolution of the Senate, I communicated to that
body on August 2 last, and also to the House of Representatives,* the

* See p. 406.

correspondence in the case of A. K. Cutting, an American citizen, then imprisoned in Mexico, charged with the commission of a penal offense in Texas, of which a Mexican citizen was the object.

After demand had been made for his release the charge against him was amended so as to include a violation of Mexican law within Mexican territory.

This joinder of alleged offenses, one within and the other exterior to Mexico, induced me to order a special investigation of the case, pending which Mr. Cutting was released.

The incident has, however, disclosed a claim of jurisdiction by Mexico novel in our history, whereby any offense committed anywhere by a foreigner, penal in the place of its commission, and of which a Mexican is the object, may, if the offender be found in Mexico, be there tried and punished in conformity with Mexican laws.

This jurisdiction was sustained by the courts of Mexico in the Cutting case, and approved by the executive branch of that Government, upon the authority of a Mexican statute. The appellate court in releasing Mr. Cutting decided that the abandonment of the complaint by the Mexican citizen aggrieved by the alleged crime (a libelous publication) removed the basis of further prosecution, and also declared justice to have been satisfied by the enforcement of a small part of the original sentence.

The admission of such a pretension would be attended with serious results, invasive of the jurisdiction of this Government and highly dangerous to our citizens in foreign lands. Therefore I have denied it and protested against its attempted exercise as unwarranted by the principles of law and international usages.

A sovereign has jurisdiction of offenses which take effect within his territory, although concocted or commenced outside of it; but the right is denied of any foreign sovereign to punish a citizen of the United States for an offense consummated on our soil in violation of our laws, even though the offense be against a subject or citizen of such sovereign. The Mexican statute in question makes the claim broadly, and the principle, if conceded, would create a dual responsibility in the citizen and lead to inextricable confusion, destructive of that certainty in the law which is an essential of liberty.

When citizens of the United States voluntarily go into a foreign country, they must abide by the laws there in force, and will not be protected by their own Government from the consequences of an offense against those laws committed in such foreign country; but watchful care and interest of this Government over its citizens are not relinquished because they have gone abroad, and if charged with crime committed in the foreign land a fair and open trial, conducted with decent regard for justice and humanity, will be demanded for them. With less than that this Government will not be content when the life or liberty of its citizens is at stake.

Whatever the degree to which extraterritorial criminal jurisdiction may have been formerly allowed by consent and reciprocal agreement among certain of the European States, no such doctrine or practice was ever known to the laws of this country or of that from which our institutions have mainly been derived.

In the case of Mexico there are reasons especially strong for perfect harmony in the mutual exercise of jurisdiction. Nature has made us irrevocably neighbors, and wisdom and kind feeling should make us friends.

The overflow of capital and enterprise from the United States is a potent factor in assisting the development of the resources of Mexico and in building up the prosperity of both countries.

To assist this good work all grounds of apprehension for the security of person and property should be removed; and I trust that in the interests of good neighborhood the statute referred to will be so modified as to eliminate the present possibilities of danger to the peace of the two countries.

The Government of the Netherlands has exhibited concern in relation to certain features of our tariff laws, which are supposed by them to be aimed at a class of tobacco produced in the Dutch East Indies. Comment would seem unnecessary upon the unwisdom of legislation appearing to have a special national discrimination for its object, which, although unintentional, may give rise to injurious retaliation.

The establishment, less than four years ago, of a legation at Teheran is bearing fruit in the interest exhibited by the Shah's Government in the industrial activity of the United States and the opportunities of beneficial interchanges.

Stable government is now happily restored in Peru by the election of a constitutional President, and a period of rehabilitation is entered upon; but the recovery is necessarily slow from the exhaustion caused by the late war and civil disturbances. A convention to adjust by arbitration claims of our citizens has been proposed and is under consideration.

The naval officer who bore to Siberia the testimonials bestowed by Congress in recognition of the aid given to the *Jeannette* survivors has successfully accomplished his mission. His interesting report will be submitted. It is pleasant to know that this mark of appreciation has been welcomed by the Russian Government and people as befits the traditional friendship of the two countries.

Civil perturbations in the Samoan Islands have during the past few years been a source of considerable embarrassment to the three Governments—Germany, Great Britain, and the United States—whose relations and extraterritorial rights in that important group are guaranteed by treaties. The weakness of the native administration and the conflict of opposing interests in the islands have led King Malietoa to seek alliance or protection in some one quarter, regardless of the distinct engagements whereby no one of the three treaty powers may acquire any paramount or exclusive interest. In May last Malietoa offered to place Samoa under the protection of the United States, and the late consul, without authority, assumed to grant it. The proceeding was promptly disavowed and the overzealous official recalled. Special agents of the three Governments have been deputed to examine the situation in the islands. With a change in the representation of all three powers and a harmonious understanding between them, the peace, prosperity, autonomous administration, and neutrality of Samoa can hardly fail to be secured.

It appearing that the Government of Spain did not extend to the flag of the United States in the Antilles the full measure of reciprocity requisite under our statute for the continuance of the suspension of discriminations against the Spanish flag in our ports, I was constrained in October last* to rescind my predecessor's proclamation of February 14, 1884,† permitting such suspension. An arrangement was, however, speedily reached, and upon notification from the Government of Spain that all differential treatment of our vessels and their cargoes, from the United States or from any foreign country, had been completely and absolutely relinquished, I availed myself of the discretion conferred by law and issued on the 27th of October my proclamation‡ declaring reciprocal suspension in the United States. It is most gratifying to bear testimony to the earnest spirit in which the Government of the Queen Regent has met our efforts to avert the initiation of commercial discriminations and reprisals, which are ever disastrous to the material interests and the political good will of the countries they may affect.

The profitable development of the large commercial exchanges between the United States and the Spanish Antilles is naturally an object of solicitude. Lying close at our doors, and finding here their main markets of supply and demand, the welfare of Cuba and Puerto Rico and their production and trade are scarcely less important to us than to Spain. Their commercial and financial movements are so naturally a part of our system that no obstacle to fuller and freer intercourse should be permitted to exist. The standing instructions of our representatives at Madrid and Havana have for years been to leave no effort unessayed to further these ends, and at no time has the equal good desire of Spain been more hopefully manifested than now.

The Government of Spain, by removing the consular tonnage fees on cargoes shipped to the Antilles and by reducing passport fees, has shown its recognition of the needs of less trammeled intercourse.

An effort has been made during the past year to remove the hindrances to the proclamation of the treaty of naturalization with the Sublime Porte, signed in 1874, which has remained inoperative owing to a disagreement of interpretation of the clauses relative to the effects of the return to and sojourn of a naturalized citizen in the land of origin. I trust soon to

*See pp. 497-498.   † See pp. 171-174.   ‡ See pp. 490-491.

be able to announce a favorable settlement of the differences as to this interpretation.

It has been highly satisfactory to note the improved treatment of American missionaries in Turkey, as has been attested by their acknowledgments to our late minister to that Government of his successful exertions in their behalf.

The exchange of ratifications of the convention of December 5, 1885, with Venezuela, for the reopening of the awards of the Caracas Commission under the claims convention of 1866, has not yet been effected, owing to the delay of the Executive of that Republic in ratifying the measure. I trust that this postponement will be brief; but should it much longer continue, the delay may well be regarded as a rescission of the compact and a failure on the part of Venezuela to complete an arrangement so persistently sought by her during many years and assented to by this Government in a spirit of international fairness, although to the detriment of holders of *bona fide* awards of the impugned commission.

I renew the recommendation of my last annual message that existing legislation concerning citizenship and naturalization be revised. We have treaties with many states providing for the renunciation of citizenship by naturalized aliens, but no statute is found to give effect to such engagements, nor any which provides a needed central bureau for the registration of naturalized citizens.

Experience suggests that our statutes regulating extradition might be advantageously amended by a provision for the transit across our territory, now a convenient thoroughfare of travel from one foreign country to another, of fugitives surrendered by a foreign government to a third state. Such provisions are not unusual in the legislation of other countries, and tend to prevent the miscarriage of justice. It is also desirable, in order to remove present uncertainties, that authority should be conferred on the Secretary of State to issue a certificate, in case of an arrest for the purpose of extradition, to the officer before whom the proceeding is pending, showing that a requisition for the surrender of the person charged has been duly made. Such a certificate, if required to be received before the prisoner's examination, would prevent a long and expensive judicial inquiry into a charge which the foreign government might not desire to press. I also recommend that express provision be made for the immediate discharge from custody of persons committed for extradition where the President is of opinion that surrender should not be made.

The drift of sentiment in civilized communities toward full recognition of the rights of property in the creations of the human intellect has brought about the adoption by many important nations of an international copyright convention, which was signed at Berne on the 18th of September, 1885.

Inasmuch as the Constitution gives to the Congress the power "to promote the progress of science and useful arts by securing for limited times to authors and inventors the exclusive right to their respective writings and discoveries," this Government did not feel warranted in becoming a signatory pending the action of Congress upon measures of international copyright now before it; but the right of adhesion to the Berne convention hereafter has been reserved. I trust the subject will receive at your hands the attention it deserves, and that the just claims of authors, so urgently pressed, will be duly heeded.

Representations continue to be made to me of the injurious effect upon American artists studying abroad and having free access to the art collections of foreign countries of maintaining a discriminating duty against the introduction of the works of their brother artists of other countries, and I am induced to repeat my recommendation for the abolition of that tax.

Pursuant to a provision of the diplomatic and consular appropriation act approved July 1, 1886, the estimates submitted by the Secretary of State for the maintenance of the consular service have been recast on the basis of salaries for all officers to whom such allowance is deemed advisable. Advantage has been taken of this to redistribute the salaries of the offices now appropriated for, in accordance with the work performed, the importance of the representative duties of the incumbent, and the cost of living at each post. The last consideration has been too often lost sight of in the allowances heretofore made. The compensation which may suffice for the decent maintenance of a worthy and capable officer in a position of onerous and representative trust at a post readily accessible, and where the necessaries of life are abundant and cheap, may prove an inadequate pittance in distant lands, where the better part of a year's pay is consumed in reaching the post of duty, and where the comforts of ordinary civilized existence can only be obtained with difficulty and at exorbitant cost. I trust that in considering the submitted schedules no mistaken theory of economy will perpetuate a system which in the past has virtually closed to deserving talent many offices where capacity and attainments of a high order are indispensable, and in not a few instances has brought discredit on our national character and entailed embarrassment and even suffering on those deputed to uphold our dignity and interests abroad.

In connection with this subject I earnestly reiterate the practical necessity of supplying some mode of trustworthy inspection and report of the manner in which the consulates are conducted. In the absence of such reliable information efficiency can scarcely be rewarded or its opposite corrected.

Increasing competition in trade has directed attention to the value of the consular reports printed by the Department of State, and the efforts of the Government to extend the practical usefulness of these reports have created a wider demand for them at home and a spirit of emulation abroad. Constituting a record of the changes occurring in trade and of the progress of the arts and invention in foreign countries, they are much sought for by all interested in the subjects which they embrace.

The report of the Secretary of the Treasury exhibits in detail the condition of the public finances and of the several branches of the Government related to his Department. I especially direct the attention of the Congress to the recommendations contained in this and the last preceding report of the Secretary touching the simplification and amendment of the laws relating to the collection of our revenues, and in the interest of economy and justice to the Government I hope they may be adopted by appropriate legislation.

The ordinary receipts of the Government for the fiscal year ended June 30, 1886, were $336,439,727.06. Of this amount $192,905,023.41 was received from customs and $116,805,936.48 from internal revenue. The total receipts, as here stated, were $13,749,020.68 greater than for the previous year, but the increase from customs was $11,434,084.10 and from internal revenue $4,407,210.94, making a gain in these items for the last year of $15,841,295.04, a falling off in other resources reducing the total increase to the smaller amount mentioned.

The expense at the different custom-houses of collecting this increased customs revenue was less than the expense attending the collection of such revenue for the preceding year by $490,608, and the increased receipts of internal revenue were collected at a cost to the Internal-Revenue Bureau $155,944.99 less than the expense of such collection for the previous year.

The total ordinary expenses of the Government for the fiscal year ended June 30, 1886, were $242,483,138.50, being less by $17,788,797 than such expenditures for the year preceding, and leaving a surplus in the Treasury at the close of the last fiscal year of $93,956,588.56, as against $63,463,771.27 at the close of the previous year, being an increase in such surplus of $30,492,817.29.

The expenditures are compared with those of the preceding fiscal year and classified as follows:

	Year ending June 30, 1886.	Year ending June 30, 1885.
For civil expenses................................	$21,955,604.04	$23,826,942.11
For foreign intercourse.........................	1,332,320.88	5,439,609.11
For Indians	6,099,158.17	6,552,494.63
For pensions	63,404,864.03	56,102,267.49
For the military, including river and harbor improvements and arsenals...	34,324,152.74	42,670,578.47
For the Navy, including vessels, machinery, and improvement of navy-yards...........................	13,907,887.74	16,021,079.69
For interest on public debt	50,580,145.97	51,386,256.47
For the District of Columbia.....................	2,892,321.89	3,499,650.95
Miscellaneous expenditures, including public buildings, light-houses, and collecting the revenue.......	47,986,683.04	54,728,056.21

For the current year to end June 30, 1887, the ascertained receipts up to October 1, 1886, with such receipts estimated for the remainder of the year, amount to $356,000,000.

The expenditures ascertained and estimated for the same period are $266,000,000, indicating an anticipated surplus at the close of the year of $90,000,000.

The total value of the exports from the United States to foreign countries during the fiscal year is stated and compared with the preceding year as follows:

	For the year ending June 30, 1886.	For the year ending June 30, 1885.
Domestic merchandise	$665,964,529	$726,682,946
Foreign merchandise	13,560,301	15,506,809
Gold	42,952,191	8,477,892
Silver	29,511,219	33,753,633

The value of some of our leading exports during the last fiscal year, as compared with the value of the same for the year immediately preceding, is here given, and furnishes information both interesting and suggestive:

	For the year ending June 30, 1886.	For the year ending June 30, 1885.
Cotton and cotton manufactures	$219,045,576	$213,799,049
Tobacco and its manufactures	30,424,908	24,767,305
Breadstuffs	125,846,558	160,370,821
Provisions	90,625,216	107,332,456

Our imports during the last fiscal year, as compared with the previous year, were as follows:

	1886.	1885.
Merchandise	$635,436,136.00	$579,580,053.80
Gold	20,743,349.00	26,691,696.00
Silver	17,850,307.00	16,550,627.00

In my last annual message to the Congress attention was directed to the fact that the revenues of the Government exceeded its actual needs, and it was suggested that legislative action should be taken to relieve the people from the unnecessary burden of taxation thus made apparent.

In view of the pressing importance of the subject I deem it my duty to again urge its consideration.

The income of the Government, by its increased volume and through economies in its collection, is now more than ever in excess of public necessities. The application of the surplus to the payment of such portion of the public debt as is now at our option subject to extinguishment, if continued at the rate which has lately prevailed, would retire that class of indebtedness within less than one year from this date. Thus a continuation of our present revenue system would soon result in the receipt of an annual income much greater than necessary to meet Government expenses, with no indebtedness upon which it could be applied. We should then be confronted with a vast quantity of money, the circulating medium of the people, hoarded in the Treasury when it should be in their hands, or we should be drawn into wasteful public extravagance, with all the corrupting national demoralization which follows in its train.

But it is not the simple existence of this surplus and its threatened attendant evils which furnish the strongest argument against our present scale of Federal taxation. Its worst phase is the exaction of such a surplus through a perversion of the relations between the people and their Government and a dangerous departure from the rules which limit the right of Federal taxation.

Good government, and especially the government of which every American citizen boasts, has for its objects the protection of every person within its care in the greatest liberty consistent with the good order of society and his perfect security in the enjoyment of his earnings with the least possible diminution for public needs. When more of the people's substance is exacted through the form of taxation than is necessary to meet the just obligations of the Government and the expense of its economical administration, such exaction becomes ruthless extortion and a violation of the fundamental principles of a free government.

The indirect manner in which these exactions are made has a tendency to conceal their true character and their extent. But we have arrived at a stage of superfluous revenue which has aroused the people to a realization of the fact that the amount raised professedly for the support of the Government is paid by them as absolutely if added to the price of the things which supply their daily wants as if it was paid at fixed periods into the hand of the taxgatherer.

Those who toil for daily wages are beginning to understand that capital, though sometimes vaunting its importance and clamoring for the protection and favor of the Government, is dull and sluggish till, touched by the magical hand of labor, it springs into activity, furnishing an occasion for Federal taxation and gaining the value which enables it to bear its burden. And the laboring man is thoughtfully inquiring whether in these circumstances, and considering the tribute he constantly pays into the public Treasury as he supplies his daily wants, he receives his fair share of advantages.

There is also a suspicion abroad that the surplus of our revenues indicates abnormal and exceptional business profits, which, under the system which produces such surplus, increase without corresponding benefit to the people at large the vast accumulations of a few among our citizens, whose fortunes, rivaling the wealth of the most favored in antidemo- cratic nations, are not the natural growth of a steady, plain, and indus- trious republic.

Our farmers, too, and those engaged directly and indirectly in supply- ing the products of agriculture, see that day by day, and as often as the daily wants of their households recur, they are forced to pay excessive and needless taxation, while their products struggle in foreign markets with the competition of nations, which, by allowing a freer exchange of productions than we permit, enable their people to sell for prices which distress the American farmer.

As every patriotic citizen rejoices in the constantly increasing pride of our people in American citizenship and in the glory of our national achievements and progress, a sentiment prevails that the leading strings useful to a nation in its infancy may well be to a great extent discarded in the present stage of American ingenuity, courage, and fearless self- reliance; and for the privilege of indulging this sentiment with true American enthusias. our citizens are quite willing to forego an idle sur- plus in the public Treasury.

And all the people know that the average rate of Federal taxation upon imports is to-day, in time of peace, but little less, while upon some articles of necessary consumption it is actually more, than was imposed by the grievous burden willingly borne at a time when the Government needed millions to maintain by war the safety and integrity of the Union.

It has been the policy of the Government to collect the principal part of its revenues by a tax upon imports, and no change in this policy is desirable. But the present condition of affairs constrains our people to demand that by a revision of our revenue laws the receipts of the Gov- ernment shall be reduced to the necessary expense of its economical administration; and this demand should be recognized and obeyed by the people's representatives in the legislative branch of the Government.

In readjusting the burdens of Federal taxation a sound public policy requires that such of our citizens as have built up large and important industries under present conditions should not be suddenly and to their injury deprived of advantages to which they have adapted their busi- ness; but if the public good requires it they should be content with such consideration as shall deal fairly and cautiously with their interests, while the just demand of the people for relief from needless taxation is honestly answered.

A reasonable and timely submission to such a demand should certainly be possible without disastrous shock to any interest; and a cheerful concession sometimes averts abrupt and heedless action, often the out- growth of impatience and delayed justice.

Due regard should be also accorded in any proposed readjustment to the interests of American labor so far as they are involved. We congratulate ourselves that there is among us no laboring class fixed within unyielding bounds and doomed under all conditions to the inexorable fate of daily toil. We recognize in labor a chief factor in the wealth of the Republic, and we treat those who have it in their keeping as citizens entitled to the most careful regard and thoughtful attention. This regard and attention should be awarded them, not only because labor is the capital of our workingmen, justly entitled to its share of Government favor, but for the further and not less important reason that the laboring man, surrounded by his family in his humble home, as a consumer is vitally interested in all that cheapens the cost of living and enables him to bring within his domestic circle additional comforts and advantages.

This relation of the workingman to the revenue laws of the country and the manner in which it palpably influences the question of wages should not be forgotten in the justifiable prominence given to the proper maintenance of the supply and protection of well-paid labor. And these considerations suggest such an arrangement of Government revenues as shall reduce the expense of living, while it does not curtail the opportunity for work nor reduce the compensation of American labor and injuriously affect its condition and the dignified place it holds in the estimation of our people.

But our farmers and agriculturists—those who from the soil produce the things consumed by all—are perhaps more directly and plainly concerned than any other of our citizens in a just and careful system of Federal taxation. Those actually engaged in and more remotely connected with this kind of work number nearly one-half of our population. None labor harder or more continuously than they. No enactments limit their hours of toil and no interposition of the Government enhances to any great extent the value of their products. And yet for many of the necessaries and comforts of life, which the most scrupulous economy enables them to bring into their homes, and for their implements of husbandry, they are obliged to pay a price largely increased by an unnatural profit, which by the action of the Government is given to the more favored manufacturer.

I recommend that, keeping in view all these considerations, the increasing and unnecessary surplus of national income annually accumulating be released to the people by an amendment to our revenue laws which shall cheapen the price of the necessaries of life and give freer entrance to such imported materials as by American labor may be manufactured into marketable commodities.

Nothing can be accomplished, however, in the direction of this much-needed reform unless the subject is approached in a patriotic spirit of devotion to the interests of the entire country and with a willingness to yield something for the public good.

The sum paid upon the public debt during the fiscal year ended June 30, 1886, was $44,551,043.36.

During the twelve months ended October 31, 1886, 3 per cent bonds were called for redemption amounting to $127,283,100, of which $80,643,200 was so called to answer the requirements of the law relating to the sinking fund and $46,639,900 for the purpose of reducing the public debt by application of a part of the surplus in the Treasury to that object. Of the bonds thus called $102,269,450 became subject under such calls to redemption prior to November 1, 1886. The remainder, amounting to $25,013,650, matured under the calls after that date.

In addition to the amount subject to payment and cancellation prior to November 1, there were also paid before that day certain of these bonds, with the interest thereon, amounting to $5,072,350, which were anticipated as to their maturity, of which $2,664,850 had not been called. Thus $107,341,800 had been actually applied prior to the 1st of November, 1886, to the extinguishment of our bonded and interest-bearing debt, leaving on that day still outstanding the sum of $1,153,443,112. Of this amount $86,848,700 were still represented by 3 per cent bonds. They, however, have been since November 1, or will at once be, further reduced by $22,606,150, being bonds which have been called, as already stated, but not redeemed and canceled before the latter date.

During the fiscal year ended June 30, 1886, there were coined, under the compulsory silver-coinage act of 1878, 29,838,905 silver dollars, and the cost of the silver used in such coinage was $23,448,960.01. There had been coined up to the close of the previous fiscal year under the provisions of the law 203,882,554 silver dollars, and on the 1st day of December, 1886, the total amount of such coinage was $247,131,549.

The Director of the Mint reports that at the time of the passage of the law of 1878 directing this coinage the intrinsic value of the dollars thus coined was 94¼ cents each, and that on the 31st day of July, 1886, the price of silver reached the lowest stage ever known, so that the intrinsic or bullion price of our standard silver dollar at that date was less than 72 cents. The price of silver on the 30th day of November last was such as to make these dollars intrinsically worth 78 cents each.

These differences in value of the coins represent the fluctuations in the price of silver, and they certainly do not indicate that compulsory coinage by the Government enhances the price of that commodity or secures uniformity in its value.

Every fair and legal effort has been made by the Treasury Department to distribute this currency among the people. The withdrawal of United States Treasury notes of small denominations and the issuing of small silver certificates have been resorted to in the endeavor to accomplish this result, in obedience to the will and sentiments of the representatives of the people in the Congress. On the 27th day of November, 1886, the people held of these coins, or certificates representing them, the nominal sum of $166,873,041, and we still had $79,464,345 in the Treasury, as against about $142,894,055 so in the hands of the people and $72,865,376 remaining in the Treasury one year ago. The Director of the Mint again urges the necessity of more vault room for the purpose of storing these silver dollars which are not needed for circulation by the people.

I have seen no reason to change the views expressed in my last annual message on the subject of this compulsory coinage, and I again urge its suspension on all the grounds contained in my former recommendation, reenforced by the significant increase of our gold exportations during the last year, as appears by the comparative statement herewith presented, and for the further reasons that the more this currency is distributed among the people the greater becomes our duty to protect it from disaster, that we now have abundance for all our needs, and that there seems but little propriety in building vaults to store such currency when the only pretense for its coinage is the necessity of its use by the people as a circulating medium.

The great number of suits now pending in the United States courts for the southern district of New York growing out of the collection of customs revenue at the port of New York and the number of such suits that are almost daily instituted are certainly worthy the attention of the Congress. These legal controversies, based upon conflicting views by importers and the collector as to the interpretation of our present complex and indefinite revenue laws, might be largely obviated by an amendment of those laws.

But pending such amendment the present condition of this litigation should be relieved. There are now pending about 2,500 of these suits. More than 1,100 have been commenced within the past eighteen months, and many of the others have been at issue for more than twenty-five years. These delays subject the Government to loss of evidence and prevent the preparation necessary to defeat unjust and fictitious claims, while constantly accruing interest threatens to double the demands involved.

In the present condition of the dockets of the courts, well filled with private suits, and of the force allowed the district attorney, no greater than is necessary for the ordinary and current business of his office, these revenue litigations can not be considered.

In default of the adoption by the Congress of a plan for the general reorganization of the Federal courts, as has been heretofore recommended, I urge the propriety of passing a law permitting the appointment of an additional Federal judge in the district where these Government suits have accumulated, so that by continuous sessions of the courts devoted to the trial of these cases they may be determined.

It is entirely plain that a great saving to the Government would be accomplished by such a remedy, and the suitors who have honest claims would not be denied justice through delay.

The report of the Secretary of War gives a detailed account of the administration of his Department and contains sundry recommendations for the improvement of the service, which I fully approve.

The Army consisted at the date of the last consolidated return of 2,103 officers and 24,946 enlisted men.

The expenses of the Department for the last fiscal year were $36,990,-903.38, including $6,294,305.43 for public works and river and harbor improvements.

I especially direct the attention of the Congress to the recommendation that officers be required to submit to an examination as a preliminary to their promotion. I see no objection, but many advantages, in adopting this feature, which has operated so beneficially in our Navy Department, as well as in some branches of the Army.

The subject of coast defenses and fortifications has been fully and carefully treated by the Board on Fortifications, whose report was submitted at the last session of Congress; but no construction work of the kind recommended by the board has been possible during the last year from the lack of appropriations for such purpose.

The defenseless condition of our seacoast and lake frontier is perfectly palpable. The examinations made must convince us all that certain of our cities named in the report of the board should be fortified and that work on the most important of these fortifications should be commenced at once. The work has been thoroughly considered and laid out, the Secretary of War reports, but all is delayed in default of Congressional action.

The absolute necessity, judged by all standards of prudence and foresight, of our preparation for an effectual resistance against the armored ships and steel guns and mortars of modern construction which may threaten the cities on our coasts is so apparent that I hope effective steps will be taken in that direction immediately.

The valuable and suggestive treatment of this question by the Secretary of War is earnestly commended to the consideration of the Congress.

In September and October last the hostile Apaches who, under the leadership of Geronimo, had for eighteen months been on the war path, and during that time had committed many murders and been the cause of constant terror to the settlers of Arizona, surrendered to General Miles, the military commander who succeeded General Crook in the management and direction of their pursuit.

Under the terms of their surrender as then reported, and in view of the understanding which these murderous savages seemed to entertain of the assurances given them, it was considered best to imprison them in such manner as to prevent their ever engaging in such outrages again, instead of trying them for murder. Fort Pickens having been selected as a safe place of confinement, all the adult males were sent thither and will be closely guarded as prisoners. In the meantime the residue of the band, who, though still remaining upon the reservation, were regarded as unsafe and suspected of furnishing aid to those on the war path, had been removed to Fort Marion. The women and larger children of the hostiles were also taken there, and arrangements have been made for putting the children of proper age in Indian schools.

The report of the Secretary of the Navy contains a detailed exhibit of the condition of his Department, with such a statement of the action needed to improve the same as should challenge the earnest attention of the Congress.

The present Navy of the United States, aside from the ships in course of construction, consists of—

First. Fourteen single-turreted monitors, none of which are in commission nor at the present time serviceable. The batteries of these ships are obsolete, and they can only be relied upon as auxiliary ships in harbor defense, and then after such an expenditure upon them as might not be deemed justifiable.

Second. Five fourth-rate vessels of small tonnage, only one of which was designed as a war vessel, and all of which are auxiliary merely.

Third. Twenty-seven cruising ships, three of which are built of iron, of small tonnage, and twenty-four of wood. Of these wooden vessels it is estimated by the Chief Constructor of the Navy that only three will be serviceable beyond a period of six years, at which time it may be said that of the present naval force nothing worthy the name will remain.

All the vessels heretofore authorized are under contract or in course of construction except the armored ships, the torpedo and dynamite boats, and one cruiser. As to the last of these, the bids were in excess of the limit fixed by Congress. The production in the United States of armor and gun steel is a question which it seems necessary to settle at an early day if the armored war vessels are to be completed with those materials of home manufacture. This has been the subject of investigation by two boards and by two special committees of Congress within the last three years. The report of the Gun Foundry Board in 1884, of the Board on Fortifications made in January last, and the reports of the select committees of the two Houses made at the last session of Congress have entirely exhausted the subject, so far as preliminary investigation is involved, and in their recommendations they are substantially agreed.

In the event that the present invitation of the Department for bids to furnish such of this material as is now authorized shall fail to induce domestic manufacturers to undertake the large expenditures required to prepare for this new manufacture, and no other steps are taken by Congress at its coming session, the Secretary contemplates with dissatisfaction the necessity of obtaining abroad the armor and the gun steel for the authorized ships. It would seem desirable that the wants of the Army and the Navy in this regard should be reasonably met, and that by uniting their contracts such inducement might be offered as would result in securing the domestication of these important interests.

The affairs of the postal service show marked and gratifying improvement during the past year. A particular account of its transactions and condition is given in the report of the Postmaster-General, which will be laid before you.

The reduction of the rate of letter postage in 1883, rendering the postal revenues inadequate to sustain the expenditures, and business depression also contributing, resulted in an excess of cost for the fiscal year ended June 30, 1885, of eight and one-third millions of dollars. An additional check upon receipts by doubling the measure of weight in rating sealed correspondence and diminishing one-half the charge for newspaper carriage was imposed by legislation which took effect with the beginning of the past fiscal year, while the constant demand of our territorial development and growing population for the extension and increase of mail facilities and machinery necessitates steady annual advance in outlay, and the careful estimate of a year ago upon the rates of expenditure then existing contemplated the unavoidable augmentation of the deficiency in the last fiscal year by nearly $2,000,000. The anticipated revenue for the last year failed of realization by about $64,000, but proper measures of economy have so satisfactorily limited the growth of expenditure that the total deficiency in fact fell below that of 1885, and at this time the increase of revenue is in a gaining ratio over the increase of cost, demonstrating the sufficiency of the present rates of postage ultimately to sustain the service. This is the more pleasing because our people enjoy now both cheaper postage proportionably to distances and a vaster and more costly service than any other upon the globe.

Retrenchment has been effected in the cost of supplies, some expenditures unwarranted by law have ceased, and the outlays for mail carriage have been subjected to beneficial scrutiny. At the close of the last fiscal year the expense of transportation on star routes stood at an annual rate of cost less by over $560,000 than at the close of the previous year and steamboat and mail-messenger service at nearly $200,000 less.

The service has been in the meantime enlarged and extended by the establishment of new offices, increase of routes of carriage, expansion of carrier-delivery conveniences, and additions to the railway mail facilities, in accordance with the growing exigencies of the country and the long-established policy of the Government.

The Postmaster-General calls attention to the existing law for compensating railroads and expresses the opinion that a method may be devised which will prove more just to the carriers and beneficial to the Government; and the subject appears worthy of your early consideration.

The differences which arose during the year with certain of the ocean steamship companies have terminated by the acquiescence of all in the policy of the Government approved by the Congress in the postal appropriation at its last session, and the Department now enjoys the utmost service afforded by all vessels which sail from our ports upon either ocean—a service generally adequate to the needs of our intercourse. Petitions have, however, been presented to the Department by numerous merchants and manufacturers for the establishment of a direct service to the Argentine Republic and for semimonthly dispatches to the Empire of Brazil, and the subject is commended to your consideration. It is an obvious duty to provide the means of postal communication which our commerce requires, and with prudent forecast of results the wise extension of it may lead to stimulating intercourse and become the harbinger of a profitable traffic which will open new avenues for the disposition of the products of our industry. The circumstances of the countries at the far south of our continent are such as to invite our enterprise and afford the promise of sufficient advantages to justify an unusual effort to bring about the closer relations which greater freedom of communication would tend to establish.

I suggest that, as distinguished from a grant or subsidy for the mere benefit of any line of trade or travel, whatever outlay may be required to secure additional postal service, necessary and proper and not otherwise attainable, should be regarded as within the limit of legitimate compensation for such service.

The extension of the free-delivery service as suggested by the Postmaster-General has heretofore received my sanction, and it is to be hoped a suitable enactment may soon be agreed upon.

The request for an appropriation sufficient to enable the general inspection of fourth-class offices has my approbation.

I renew my approval of the recommendation of the Postmaster-General that another assistant be provided for the Post-Office Department, and I invite your attention to the several other recommendations in his report.

The conduct of the Department of Justice for the last fiscal year is fully detailed in the report of the Attorney-General, and I invite the earnest attention of the Congress to the same and due consideration of the recommendations therein contained.

In the report submitted by this officer to the last session of the Congress he strongly recommended the erection of a penitentiary for the confinement of prisoners convicted and sentenced in the United States courts, and he repeats the recommendation in his report for the last year.

This is a matter of very great importance and should at once receive Congressional action. United States prisoners are now confined in more than thirty different State prisons and penitentiaries scattered in every part of the country. They are subjected to nearly as many different modes of treatment and discipline and are far too much removed from the control and regulation of the Government. So far as they are entitled to humane treatment and an opportunity for improvement and reformation, the Government is responsible to them and society that these things are forthcoming. But this duty can scarcely be discharged without more absolute control and direction than is possible under the present system.

Many of our good citizens have interested themselves, with the most beneficial results, in the question of prison reform. The General Government should be in a situation, since there must be United States prisoners, to furnish important aid in this movement, and should be able to illustrate what may be practically done in the direction of this reform and to present an example in the treatment and improvement of its prisoners worthy of imitation.

With prisons under its own control the Government could deal with the somewhat vexed question of convict labor, so far as its convicts were concerned, according to a plan of its own adoption, and with due regard to the rights and interests of our laboring citizens, instead of sometimes aiding in the operation of a system which causes among them irritation and discontent.

Upon consideration of this subject it might be thought wise to erect more than one of these institutions, located in such places as would best subserve the purposes of convenience and economy in transportation. The considerable cost of maintaining these convicts as at present, in State institutions, would be saved by the adoption of the plan proposed, and by employing them in the manufacture of such articles as were needed for use by the Government quite a large pecuniary benefit would be realized in partial return for our outlay.

I again urge a change in the Federal judicial system to meet the wants of the people and obviate the delays necessarily attending the present condition of affairs in our courts. All are agreed that something should be done, and much favor is shown by those well able to advise to the plan suggested by the Attorney-General at the last session of the Congress and recommended in my last annual message. This recommendation is here renewed, together with another made at the same time, touching a change in the manner of compensating district attorneys and marshals; and the latter subject is commended to the Congress for its action in the interest of economy to the Government, and humanity, fairness, and justice to our people.

The report of the Secretary of the Interior presents a comprehensive summary of the work of the various branches of the public service connected with his Department, and the suggestions and recommendations which it contains for the improvement of the service should receive your careful consideration.

The exhibit made of the condition of our Indian population and the progress of the work for their enlightenment, notwithstanding the many embarrassments which hinder the better administration of this important branch of the service, is a gratifying and hopeful one.

The funds appropriated for the Indian service for the fiscal year just passed, with the available income from Indian land and trust moneys, amounting in all to $7,850,775.12, were ample for the service under the conditions and restrictions of laws regulating their expenditure. There remained a balance on hand on June 30, 1886, of $1,660,023.30, of which $1,337,768.21 are permanent funds for fulfillment of treaties and other like purposes, and the remainder, $322,255.09, is subject to be carried to the surplus fund as required by law.

The estimates presented for appropriations for the ensuing fiscal year amount to $5,608,873.64, or $442,386.20 less than those laid before the Congress last year.

The present system of agencies, while absolutely necessary and well adapted for the management of our Indian affairs and for the ends in view when it was adopted, is in the present stage of Indian management inadequate, standing alone, for the accomplishment of an object which has become pressing in its importance—the more rapid transition from tribal organizations to citizenship of such portions of the Indians as are capable of civilized life.

When the existing system was adopted, the Indian race was outside of the limits of organized States and Territories and beyond the immediate reach and operation of civilization, and all efforts were mainly directed to the maintenance of friendly relations and the preservation of peace and quiet on the frontier. All this is now changed. There is no such thing as the Indian frontier. Civilization, with the busy hum of industry and the influences of Christianity, surrounds these people at every point. None of the tribes are outside of the bounds of organized government and society, except that the Territorial system has not been extended over that portion of the country known as the Indian Territory. As a race the Indians are no longer hostile, but may be considered as submissive to the control of the Government. Few of them only are troublesome. Except the fragments of several bands, all are now gathered upon reservations.

It is no longer possible for them to subsist by the chase and the spontaneous productions of the earth.

With an abundance of land, if furnished with the means and implements for profitable husbandry, their life of entire dependence upon Government rations from day to day is no longer defensible. Their inclination, long fostered by a defective system of control, is to cling to the habits and customs of their ancestors and struggle with persistence against the change of life which their altered circumstances press upon them. But barbarism and civilization can not live together. It is impossible that such incongruous conditions should coexist on the same soil.

They are a portion of our people, are under the authority of our Government, and have a peculiar claim upon and are entitled to the fostering care and protection of the nation. The Government can not relieve itself of this responsibility until they are so far trained and civilized as to be able wholly to manage and care for themselves. The paths in which they should walk must be clearly marked out for them, and they must be led or guided until they are familiar with the way and competent to assume the duties and responsibilities of our citizenship.

Progress in this great work will continue only at the present slow pace and at great expense unless the system and methods of management are improved to meet the changed conditions and urgent demands of the service.

The agents, having general charge and supervision in many cases of more than 5,000 Indians, scattered over large reservations, and burdened with the details of accountability for funds and supplies, have time to look after the industrial training and improvement of a few Indians only. The many are neglected and remain idle and dependent, conditions not favorable for progress and civilization.

The compensation allowed these agents and the conditions of the service are not calculated to secure for the work men who are fitted by ability and skill to properly plan and intelligently direct the methods best adapted to produce the most speedy results and permanent benefits.

Hence the necessity for a supplemental agency or system directed to the end of promoting the general and more rapid transition of the tribes from habits and customs of barbarism to the ways of civilization.

With an anxious desire to devise some plan of operation by which to secure the welfare of the Indians and to relieve the Treasury as far as possible from the support of an idle and dependent population, I recommended in my previous annual message the passage of a law authorizing the appointment of a commission as an instrumentality auxiliary to those already established for the care of the Indians. It was designed that this commission should be composed of six intelligent and capable persons—three to be detailed from the Army—having practical ideas upon the subject of the treatment of Indians and interested in their welfare, and that it should be charged, under the direction of the Secretary of the Interior, with the management of such matters of detail as can not with the present organization be properly and successfully conducted, and which present different phases, as the Indians themselves differ in their progress, needs, disposition, and capacity for improvement or immediate self-support.

By the aid of such a commission much unwise and useless expenditure of money, waste of materials, and unavailing efforts might be avoided; and it is hoped that this or some measure which the wisdom of Congress may better devise to supply the deficiency of the present system may receive your consideration and the appropriate legislation be provided.

The time is ripe for the work of such an agency.

There is less opposition to the education and training of the Indian youth, as shown by the increased attendance upon the schools, and there is a yielding tendency for the individual holding of lands. Development and advancement in these directions are essential, and should have every encouragement. As the rising generation are taught the language of civilization and trained in habits of industry they should assume the duties, privileges, and responsibilities of citizenship.

No obstacle should hinder the location and settlement of any Indian willing to take land in severalty; on the contrary, the inclination to do so should be stimulated at all times when proper and expedient. But there is no authority of law for making allotments on some of the reservations, and on others the allotments provided for are so small that the Indians, though ready and desiring to settle down, are not willing to accept such small areas when their reservations contain ample lands to afford them homesteads of sufficient size to meet their present and future needs.

These inequalities of existing special laws and treaties should be corrected and some general legislation on the subject should be provided, so that the more progressive members of the different tribes may be settled upon homesteads, and by their example lead others to follow, breaking away from tribal customs and substituting therefor the love of home, the interest of the family, and the rule of the state.

The Indian character and nature are such that they are not easily led while brooding over unadjusted wrongs. This is especially so regarding their lands. Matters arising from the construction and operation of railroads across some of the reservations, and claims of title and right of occupancy set up by white persons to some of the best land within other reservations require legislation for their final adjustment.

The settlement of these matters will remove many embarrassments to progress in the work of leading the Indians to the adoption of our institutions and bringing them under the operation, the influence, and the protection of the universal laws of our country.

The recommendations of the Secretary of the Interior and the Commissioner of the General Land Office looking to the better protection of public lands and of the public surveys, the preservation of national forests, the adjudication of grants to States and corporations and of private land claims, and the increased efficiency of the public-land service are commended to the attention of Congress. To secure the widest distribution of public lands in limited quantities among settlers for residence and cultivation, and thus make the greatest number of individual homes, was the primary object of the public-land legislation in the early days of the Republic. This system was a simple one. It commenced with an admirable scheme of public surveys, by which the humblest citizen could identify the tract upon which he wished to establish his home. The price of lands was placed within the reach of all the enterprising, industrious, and honest pioneer citizens of the country. It was soon, however, found that the object of the laws was perverted, under the system of cash sales, from a distribution of land among the people to an accumulation of land capital by wealthy and speculative persons. To check this tendency a preference right of purchase was given to settlers on the land, a plan which culminated in the general preemption act of 1841. The foundation of this system was actual residence and cultivation. Twenty years later the homestead law was devised to more surely place actual homes in the possession of actual cultivators of the soil. The land was given without price, the sole conditions being residence, improvement, and cultivation. Other laws have followed, each designed to encourage the acquirement and use of land in limited individual quantities. But in later years these laws, through vicious administrative methods and under changed conditions of communication and transportation, have been so evaded and violated that their beneficent purpose is threatened with entire defeat. The methods of such evasions and violations are set forth in detail in the reports of the Secretary of the Interior and Commissioner of the General Land Office. The rapid appropriation of our public lands without *bona fide* settlements or cultivation, and not only without intention of residence, but for the purpose of their aggregation in large holdings, in many cases in the hands of foreigners, invites the serious and immediate attention of the Congress.

The energies of the Land Department have been devoted during the present Administration to remedy defects and correct abuses in the public-land service. The results of these efforts are so largely in the nature of reforms in the processes and methods of our land system as to prevent adequate estimate; but it appears by a compilation from the reports of the Commissioner of the General Land Office that the immediate effect in leading cases which have come to a final termination has been the restoration to the mass of public lands of 2,750,000 acres; that 2,370,000 acres are embraced in investigations now pending before the Department or the courts, and that the action of Congress has been asked to effect the restoration of 2,790,000 acres additional; besides which 4,000,000 acres have been withheld from reservation and the rights of entry thereon maintained.

I recommend the repeal of the preemption and timber-culture acts, and that the homestead laws be so amended as to better secure compliance with their requirements of residence, improvement, and cultivation for the period of five years from date of entry, without commutation or provision for speculative relinquishment. I also recommend the repeal of the desert-land laws unless it shall be the pleasure of the Congress to so amend these laws as to render them less liable to abuses. As the chief motive for an evasion of the laws and the principal cause of their result in land accumulation instead of land distribution is the facility with which transfers are made of the right intended to be secured to settlers, it may be deemed advisable to provide by legislation some guards and checks upon the alienation of homestead rights and lands covered thereby until patents issue.

Last year an Executive proclamation* was issued directing the re-moval of fences which inclosed the public domain. Many of these have

* See pp. 308-309.

been removed in obedience to such order, but much of the public land still remains within the lines of these unlawful fences. The ingenious methods resorted to in order to continue these trespasses and the hardihood of the pretenses by which in some cases such inclosures are justified are fully detailed in the report of the Secretary of the Interior.

The removal of the fences still remaining which inclose public lands will be enforced with all the authority and means with which the executive branch of the Government is or shall be invested by the Congress for that purpose.

The report of the Commissioner of Pensions contains a detailed and most satisfactory exhibit of the operations of the Pension Bureau during the last fiscal year. The amount of work done was the largest in any year since the organization of the Bureau, and it has been done at less cost than during the previous year in every division.

On the 30th day of June, 1886, there were 365,783 pensioners on the rolls of the Bureau.

Since 1861 there have been 1,018,735 applications for pensions filed, of which 78,834 were based upon service in the War of 1812. There were 621,754 of these applications allowed, including 60,178 to the soldiers of 1812 and their widows.

The total amount paid for pensions since 1861 is $808,624,811.57.

The number of new pensions allowed during the year ended June 30, 1886, is 40,857, a larger number than has been allowed in any year save one since 1861. The names of 2,229 pensioners which had been previously dropped from the rolls were restored during the year, and after deducting those dropped within the same time for various causes a net increase remains for the year of 20,658 names.

From January 1, 1861, to December 1, 1885, 1,967 private pension acts had been passed. Since the last-mentioned date, and during the last session of the Congress, 644 such acts became laws.

It seems to me that no one can examine our pension establishment and its operations without being convinced that through its instrumentality justice can be very nearly done to all who are entitled under present laws to the pension bounty of the Government.

But it is undeniable that cases exist, well entitled to relief, in which the Pension Bureau is powerless to aid. The really worthy cases of this class are such as only lack by misfortune the kind or quantity of proof which the law and regulations of the Bureau require, or which, though their merit is apparent, for some other reason can not be justly dealt with through general laws. These conditions fully justify application to the Congress and special enactments. But resort to the Congress for a special pension act to overrule the deliberate and careful determination of the Pension Bureau on the merits or to secure favorable action when it could not be expected under the most liberal execution of general laws, it must be admitted opens the door to the allowance of questionable claims and presents to the legislative and executive branches of the Government applications concededly not within the law and plainly devoid of merit, but so surrounded by sentiment and patriotic feeling that they are hard to resist. I suppose it will not be denied that many claims for pension are made without merit and that many have been allowed upon fraudulent representations. This has been declared from the Pension Bureau, not only in this but in prior Administrations.

The usefulness and the justice of any system for the distribution of pensions depend upon the equality and uniformity of its operation.

It will be seen from the report of the Commissioner that there are now paid by the Government 131 different rates of pension.

He estimates from the best information he can obtain that 9,000 of those who have served in the Army and Navy of the United States are now supported, in whole or in part, from public funds or by organized charities, exclusive of those in soldiers' homes under the direction and control of the Government. Only 13 per cent of these are pensioners, while of the entire number of men furnished for the late war something like 20 per cent, including their widows and relatives, have been or now are in receipt of pensions.

The American people, with a patriotic and grateful regard for our ex soldiers, too broad and too sacred to be monopolized by any special advocates, are not only willing but anxious that equal and exact justice should be done to all honest claimants for pensions. In their sight the friendless and destitute soldier, dependent on public charity, if otherwise entitled, has precisely the same right to share in the provision made for those who fought their country's battles as those better able, through friends and influence, to push their claims. Every pension that is granted under our present plan upon any other grounds than actual service and injury or disease incurred in such service, and every instance of the many in which pensions are increased on other grounds than the merits of the claim, work an injustice to the brave and crippled, but poor and friendless, soldier, who is entirely neglected or who must be content with the smallest sum allowed under general laws.

There are far too many neighborhoods in which are found glaring cases of inequality of treatment in the matter of pensions, and they are largely due to a yielding in the Pension Bureau to importunity on the part of those, other than the pensioner, who are especially interested, or they arise from special acts passed for the benefit of individuals.

The men who fought side by side should stand side by side when they participate in a grateful nation's kind remembrance.

Every consideration of fairness and justice to our ex-soldiers and the protection of the patriotic instinct of our citizens from perversion and violation point to the adoption of a pension system broad and comprehensive enough to cover every contingency, and which shall make nunecessary an objectionable volume of special legislation.

As long as we adhere to the principle of granting pensions for service, and disability as the result of the service, the allowance of pensions should be restricted to cases presenting these features.

Every patriotic heart responds to a tender consideration for those who, having served their country long and well, are reduced to destitution and dependence, not as an incident of their service, but with advancing age or through sickness or misfortune. We are all tempted by the contemplation of such a condition to supply relief, and are often impatient of the limitations of public duty. Yielding to no one in the desire to indulge this feeling of consideration, I can not rid myself of the conviction that if these ex-soldiers are to be relieved they and their cause are entitled to the benefit of an enactment under which relief may be claimed as a right, and that such relief should be granted under the sanction of law, not in evasion of it; nor should such worthy objects of care, all equally entitled, be remitted to the unequal operation of sympathy or the tender mercies of social and political influence, with their unjust discriminations.

The discharged soldiers and sailors of the country are our fellow-citizens, and interested with us in the passage and faithful execution of wholesome laws. They can not be swerved from their duty of citizenship by artful appeals to their spirit of brotherhood born of common peril and suffering, nor will they exact as a test of devotion to their welfare a willingness to neglect public duty in their behalf.

On the 4th of March, 1885, the current business of the Patent Office was, on an average, five and a half months in arrears, and in several divisions more than twelve months behind. At the close of the last fiscal year such current work was but three months in arrears, and it is asserted and believed that in the next few months the delay in obtaining an examination of an application for a patent will be but nominal.

The number of applications for patents during the last fiscal year, including reissues, designs, trade-marks, and labels, equals 40,678, which is considerably in excess of the number received during any preceding year.

The receipts of the Patent Office during the year aggregate $1,205,-167.80, enabling the office to turn into the Treasury a surplus revenue, over and above all expenditures, of about $163,710.30.

The number of patents granted during the last fiscal year, including reissues, trade-marks, designs, and labels, was 25,619, a number also quite largely in excess of that of any preceding year.

The report of the Commissioner shows the office to be in a prosperous condition and constantly increasing in its business. No increase of force is asked for.

The amount estimated for the fiscal year ending June 30, 1886, was $890,760. The amount estimated for the year ending June 30, 1887, was $853,960. The amount estimated for the fiscal year ending June 30, 1888, is $778,770.

The Secretary of the Interior suggests a change in the plan for the payment of the indebtedness of the Pacific subsidized roads to the Government. His suggestion has the unanimous indorsement of the persons selected by the Government to act as directors of these roads and protect the interests of the United States in the board of direction. In considering the plan proposed the sole matters which should be taken into account, in my opinion, are the situation of the Government as a creditor and the surest way to secure the payment of the principal and interest of its debt.

By a recent decision of the Supreme Court of the United States it has been adjudged that the laws of the several States are inoperative to regulate rates of transportation upon railroads if such regulation interferes with the rate of carriage from one State into another. This important field of control and regulation having been thus left entirely unoccupied, the expediency of Federal action upon the subject is worthy of consideration.

The relations of labor to capital and of laboring men to their employers are of the utmost concern to every patriotic citizen. When these are strained and distorted, unjustifiable claims are apt to be insisted upon by both interests, and in the controversy which results the welfare of all and the prosperity of the country are jeopardized. Any intervention of the General Government, within the limits of its constitutional authority, to avert such a condition should be willingly accorded.

In a special message* transmitted to the Congress at its last session I suggested the enlargement of our present Labor Bureau and adding to its present functions the power of arbitration in cases where differences arise between employer and employed. When these differences reach such a stage as to result in the interruption of commerce between the States, the application of this remedy by the General Government might be regarded as entirely within its constitutional powers. And I think we might reasonably hope that such arbitrators, if carefully selected and if entitled to the confidence of the parties to be affected, would be voluntarily called to the settlement of controversies of less extent and not necessarily within the domain of Federal regulation.

I am of the opinion that this suggestion is worthy the attention of the Congress.

But after all has been done by the passage of laws, either Federal or State, to relieve a situation full of solicitude, much more remains to be accomplished by the reinstatement and cultivation of a true American sentiment which recognizes the equality of American citizenship. This, in the light of our traditions and in loyalty to the spirit of our institutions, would teach that a hearty cooperation on the part of all interests is the surest path to national greatness and the happiness of all our people; that capital should, in recognition of the brotherhood of our citizenship and in a spirit of American fairness, generously accord to labor its just compensation and consideration, and that contented labor is capital's

* See pp. 394-397.

best protection and faithful ally. It would teach, too, that the diverse situations of our people are inseparable from our civilization; that every citizen should in his sphere be a contributor to the general good; that capital does not necessarily tend to the oppression of labor, and that violent disturbances and disorders alienate from their promoters true American sympathy and kindly feeling.

The Department of Agriculture, representing the oldest and largest of our national industries, is subserving well the purposes of its organization. By the introduction of new subjects of farming enterprise and by opening new sources of agricultural wealth and the dissemination of early information concerning production and prices it has contributed largely to the country's prosperity. Through this agency advanced thought and investigation touching the subjects it has in charge should, among other things, be practically applied to the home production at a low cost of articles of food which are now imported from abroad. Such an innovation will necessarily, of course, in the beginning be within the domain of intelligent experiment, and the subject in every stage should receive all possible encouragement from the Government.

The interests of millions of our citizens engaged in agriculture are involved in an enlargement and improvement of the results of their labor, and a zealous regard for their welfare should be a willing tribute to those whose productive returns are a main source of our progress and power.

The existence of pleuro-pneumonia among the cattle of various States has led to burdensome and in some cases disastrous restrictions in an important branch of our commerce, threatening to affect the quantity and quality of our food supply. This is a matter of such importance and of such far-reaching consequences that I hope it will engage the serious attention of the Congress, to the end that such a remedy may be applied as the limits of a constitutional delegation of power to the General Government will permit.

I commend to the consideration of the Congress the report of the Commissioner and his suggestions concerning the interest intrusted to his care.

The continued operation of the law relating to our civil service has added the most convincing proofs of its necessity and usefulness. It is a fact worthy of note that every public officer who has a just idea of his duty to the people testifies to the value of this reform. Its staunchest friends are found among those who understand it best, and its warmest supporters are those who are restrained and protected by its requirements.

The meaning of such restraint and protection is not appreciated by those who want places under the Government regardless of merit and efficiency, nor by those who insist that the selection of such places should rest upon a proper credential showing active partisan work. They mean to public officers, if not their lives, the only opportunity afforded them to attend to public business, and they mean to the good people of the country the better performance of the work of their Government.

It is exceedingly strange that the scope and nature of this reform are so little understood and that so many things not included within its plan are called by its name. When cavil yields more fully to examination, the system will have large additions to the number of its friends.

Our civil-service reform may be imperfect in some of its details; it may be misunderstood and opposed; it may not always be faithfully applied; its designs may sometimes miscarry through mistake or willful intent;. it may sometimes tremble under the assaults of its enemies or languish under the misguided zeal of impracticable friends; but if the people of this country ever submit to the banishment of its underlying principle from the operation of their Government they will abandon the surest guaranty of the safety and success of American institutions.

I invoke for this reform the cheerful and ungrudging support of the Congress. I renew my recommendation made last year that the salaries of the Commissioners be made equal to other officers of the Government having like duties and responsibilities, and I hope that such reasonable appropriations may be made as will enable them to increase the usefulness of the cause they have in charge.

I desire to call the attention of the Congress to a plain duty which the Government owes to the depositors in the Freedman's Savings and Trust Company.

This company was chartered by the Congress for the benefit of the most illiterate and humble of our people, and with the intention of encouraging in them industry and thrift. Most of its branches were presided over by officers holding the commissions and clothed in the uniform of the United States. These and other circumstances reasonably, I think, led these simple people to suppose that the invitation to deposit their hard-earned savings in this institution implied an undertaking on the part of their Government that their money should be safely kept for them.

When this company failed, it was liable in the sum of $2,939,925.22 to 61,131 depositors. Dividends amounting in the aggregate to 62 per cent have been declared, and the sum called for and paid of such dividends seems to be $1,648,181.72. This sum deducted from the entire amount of deposits leaves $1,291,744.50 still unpaid. Past experience has shown that quite a large part of this sum will not be called for. There are assets still on hand amounting to the estimated sum of $16,000.

I think the remaining 38 per cent of such of these deposits as have claimants should be paid by the Government, upon principles of equity and fairness.

The report of the commissioner, soon to be laid before Congress, will give more satisfactory details on this subject.

The control of the affairs of the District of Columbia having been placed in the hands of purely executive officers, while the Congress still retains all legislative authority relating to its government, it becomes my duty to make known the most pressing needs of the District and recommend their consideration.

The laws of the District appear to be in an uncertain and unsatisfactory condition, and their codification or revision is much needed.

During the past year one of the bridges leading from the District to the State of Virginia became unfit for use, and travel upon it was forbidden. This leads me to suggest that the improvement of all the bridges crossing the Potomac and its branches from the city of Washington is worthy the attention of Congress.

The Commissioners of the District represent that the laws regulating the sale of liquor and granting licenses therefor should be at once amended, and that legislation is needed to consolidate, define, and enlarge the scope and powers of charitable and penal institutions within the District.

I suggest that the Commissioners be clothed with the power to make, within fixed limitations, police regulations. I believe this power granted and carefully guarded would tend to subserve the good order of the municipality.

It seems that trouble still exists growing out of the occupation of the streets and avenues by certain railroads having their termini in the city. It is very important that such laws should be enacted upon this subject as will secure to the railroads all the facilities they require for the transaction of their business and at the same time protect citizens from injury to their persons or property.

The Commissioners again complain that the accommodations afforded them for the necessary offices for District business and for the safe-keeping of valuable books and papers are entirely insufficient. I recommend that this condition of affairs be remedied by the Congress, and that suitable quarters be furnished for the needs of the District government.

In conclusion I earnestly invoke such wise action on the part of the people's legislators as will subserve the public good and demonstrate during the remaining days of the Congress as at present organized its ability and inclination to so meet the people's needs that it shall be gratefully remembered by an expectant constituency.

GROVER CLEVELAND.

SPECIAL MESSAGES.

EXECUTIVE MANSION, *December 8, 1886.*

To the Senate and House of Representatives of the United States:

I transmit herewith a letter from the Secretary of State, which is accompanied by the correspondence in relation to the rights of American fishermen in the British North American waters, and commend to your favorable consideration the suggestion that a commission be authorized by law to take perpetuating proofs of the losses sustained during the past year by American fishermen owing to their unfriendly and unwarranted treatment by the local authorities of the maritime provinces of the Dominion of Canada.

I may have occasion hereafter to make further recommendations during the present session for such remedial legislation as may become necessary for the protection of the rights of our citizens engaged in the open-sea fisheries in the North Atlantic waters.

GROVER CLEVELAND.

EXECUTIVE MANSION, *December 13, 1886.*

To the Senate and House of Representatives:

I transmit herewith a communication of the 8th instant from the Secretary of the Interior, submitting, with accompanying papers, an estimate of appropriation in the sum of $22,000, prepared in the Office of Indian Affairs, to provide for the payment to the Eel River band of Miami Indians of a principal sum in lieu of all annuities now received by them under existing treaty stipulations.

The matter is presented for the consideration of Congress.

GROVER CLEVELAND.

EXECUTIVE MANSION,
Washington, December 13, 1886.

To the Senate of the United States:

I transmit herewith, with a view to their ratification, an additional article, signed June 23, 1884, to the treaty of friendship, commerce, and navigation of July 27, 1853, between the United States and the Argentine Confederation; also an additional clause to the said additional article, signed June 25, 1885.

The report of the Secretary of State of even date and the papers inclosed therewith set forth the reasons which have, in my opinion, rendered it advisable to again transmit for ratification the additional article above mentioned, which was withdrawn from the Senate at my request on April 2, 1885.

GROVER CLEVELAND.

EXECUTIVE MANSION, *December 15, 1886.*

To the Senate and House of Representatives:

I transmit herewith, for your information, a report from the Secretary of State, inclosing the correspondence which has passed between the Department of State and the Governments of Switzerland and France on the subject of international copyright since the date of my message of July 9, 1886, on this question.

GROVER CLEVELAND.

To the Senate and House of Representatives:

I transmit herewith a report from the Secretary of State, in relation to the invitation from Her Britannic Majesty to this Government to participate in an international exhibition which is to be held at Adelaide, South Australia, in 1887.　　　　GROVER CLEVELAND.

EXECUTIVE MANSION, *December 21, 1886.*

To the Senate of the United States:

I nominate James C. Matthews, of New York, to be recorder of deeds in the District of Columbia, in the place of Frederick Douglass, resigned.

This nomination was submitted to the Senate at its last session, upon the retirement of the previous incumbent, who for a number of years had held the office to which it refers. In the last days of the session the Senate declined to confirm the nomination.

Opposition to the appointment of Mr. Matthews to the office for which he was named was developed among the citizens of the District of Columbia, ostensibly upon the ground that the nominee was not a resident of the District; and it is supposed that such opposition, to some extent at least, influenced the determination of the question of his confirmation.

Mr. Matthews has now been in occupancy of the office to which he was nominated for more than four months, and he has in the performance of the duties thereof won the approval of all those having business to transact with such office, and has rendered important service in rescuing the records of the District from loss and illegibility.

I am informed that his management of this office has removed much of the opposition to his appointment which heretofore existed.

I have ventured, therefore, in view of the demonstrated fitness of this nominee, and with the understanding that the objections heretofore urged against his selection have to a great extent subsided, and confessing a desire to cooperate in tendering to our colored fellow-citizens just recognition and the utmost good faith, to again submit this nomination to the Senate for confirmation, at the same time disclaiming any intention to question its previous action in the premises.

　　　　GROVER CLEVELAND.

EXECUTIVE MANSION, *January 5, 1887.*

To the Senate and House of Representatives:

Referring to my message of the 12th of January last,* transmitting the final report of the commissioners appointed under the act of July 7, 1884, to visit the States of Central and South America, I have now to submit

* See p. 370.

a special report by Commissioner Thomas C. Reynolds on the condition and commerce of Nicaragua, Honduras, and Salvador.

GROVER CLEVELAND.

EXECUTIVE MANSION, *January 5, 1887.*
To the House of Representatives:

I transmit herewith a letter from the Secretary of State, inclosing statement of customs duties levied by foreign nations upon the produce and manufactures of the United States.

GROVER CLEVELAND.

EXECUTIVE MANSION, *January 10, 1887.*
To the Senate and House of Representatives:

I transmit herewith a communication of 22d ultimo from the Secretary of the Interior, submitting, with accompanying papers, a draft of proposed legislation, prepared in the Office of Indian Affairs, providing for the per capita payment to the Delaware Indians resident in the Cherokee Nation, in Indian Territory, of the amount of their trust fund, principal and interest, held by the Government of the United States by virtue of the several treaties with the said Delaware Indians.

The matter is presented for the consideration and action of Congress.

GROVER CLEVELAND.

EXECUTIVE MANSION, *January 11, 1887.*
To the Senate and House of Representatives of the United States:

I transmit herewith a report from the Secretary of State, in relation to an invitation which has been extended to this Government to appoint a delegate or delegates to the Fourth International Prison Congress, to meet at St. Petersburg in the year 1890, and commend its suggestions to the favorable attention of Congress.

GROVER CLEVELAND.

EXECUTIVE MANSION,
Washington, January 13, 1887.
To the Senate of the United States:

I transmit to the Senate, for its consideration with a view to ratification, a declaration of the late international conference at Paris, explanatory of the convention of March 14, 1884, for the protection of submarine cables, made between the United States of America and Germany, Argentine Confederation, Austria-Hungary, Belgium, Brazil, Costa Rica, Denmark, Dominican Republic, Spain, United States of Colombia, France, Great Britain, Guatemala, Greece, Italy, Turkey, Netherlands, Persia,

Portugal, Roumania, Russia, Salvador, Servia, Sweden and Norway, and Uruguay.

The declaration has been generally accepted by the signatory powers, and Mr. McLane, the representative of the United States at the conference, has been instructed to sign it, subject to the approval of the Senate.

GROVER CLEVELAND.

EXECUTIVE MANSION, *January 17, 1887.*
To the Senate and House of Representatives:

I transmit herewith a communication of the 11th instant from the Secretary of the Interior, submitting, with accompanying papers, a copy of an agreement duly made under the provisions of the act of May 15, 1886 (24 U. S. Statutes at Large, p. 44), with the Indians residing upon the Fort Berthold Reservation, in Dakota, for the cession of a portion of their reservation in said Territory, and for other purposes.

The agreement, together with the recommendations of the Department, is presented for the action of Congress.

GROVER CLEVELAND.

EXECUTIVE MANSION,
Washington, January 18, 1887.
To the Senate of the United States:

Referring to the message of the President of the United States dated February 2, 1885,* I transmit herewith, for your consideration, a report from the Secretary of State, inclosing a translation of the convention for the protection of industrial property, of the *protocole de clôture* of said convention, and of a protocol proposed by the conference of 1886 for ratification by the Governments which have adhered to the convention.

GROVER CLEVELAND.

EXECUTIVE MANSION, *January 18, 1887.*
To the Senate and House of Representatives:

As a matter of national interest, and one solely within the discretion and control of Congress, I transmit the accompanying memorial of the executive committee of the subconstitutional centennial commission, proposing to celebrate on the 17th of September, in the city of Philadelphia, as the day upon which and the place where the convention that framed the Federal Constitution concluded their labors and submitted the results for ratification to the thirteen States then composing the United States.

The epoch was one of the deepest interest and the events well worthy of commemoration.

*See p. 270

I am aware that as each State acted independently in giving its adhesion to the new Constitution the dates and anniversaries of their several ratifications are not coincident. Some action looking to a national expression in relation to the celebration of the close of the first century of popular government under a written constitution has already been suggested, and whilst stating the great interest I share in the renewed examination by the American people of the historical foundations of their Government, I do not feel warranted in discriminating in favor or against the propositions to select one day or place in preference to all others, and therefore content myself with conveying to Congress these expressions of popular feeling and interest upon the subject, hoping that in a spirit of patriotic cooperation, rather than of local competition, fitting measures may be enacted by Congress which will give the amplest opportunity all over these United States for the manifestation of the affection and confidence of a free and mighty nation in the institutions of a Government of which they are the fortunate inheritors and under which unexampled prosperity has been enjoyed by all classes and conditions in our social system.

GROVER CLEVELAND.

EXECUTIVE MANSION, *January 18, 1887.*
To the Senate and House of Representatives:

I transmit herewith a communication of the 7th ultimo from the Secretary of the Interior, submitting, with accompanying papers, a draft of a bill "for the relief of Hiatt & Co., late traders for the Osage tribe of Indians, and for other purposes."

The matter is presented for the consideration of Congress.

GROVER CLEVELAND.

EXECUTIVE MANSION,
Washington, January 20, 1887.
To the Senate of the United States:

I transmit herewith, with a view to its ratification, a draft of declaration explanatory of Articles II and IV of the convention for the protection of submarine cables, which has been proposed by the conference of 1886 for ratification by the Governments adhering to the said convention.

GROVER CLEVELAND.

EXECUTIVE MANSION, *January 20, 1887.*
To the Senate and House of Representatives:

I herewith transmit a communication addressed to me by Mr. Samuel C. Reid, who offers to the United States the battle sword (now in my custody) of his father, Captain Samuel Chester Reid, who commanded the

United States private armed brig *General Armstrong* at the battle of Fayal, in September, 1814.

I respectfully recommend that appropriate action be taken by Congress for the acceptance of this gift.   GROVER CLEVELAND.

EXECUTIVE MANSION, *January 20, 1887.*
To the Senate of the United States:

I have the honor to transmit to the Senate herewith a report of the Secretary of State, in answer to the resolution of the Senate of the 11th instant, requesting "estimates for the contingent fund of each bureau" in the Department of State.   GROVER CLEVELAND.

To the Senate: EXECUTIVE MANSION, *January 20, 1887.*

I transmit herewith a report of the Secretary of State, in answer to the resolution of the Senate of December 8, 1886, relative to the claims of Antonio Pelletier and A. H. Lazare against the Republic of Hayti.

GROVER CLEVELAND.

EXECUTIVE MANSION, *January 25, 1887.*
To the Senate of the United States:

In response to the resolution of the Senate of the 21st ultimo, calling for certain correspondence touching the construction of a ship canal through Nicaragua, I transmit herewith a report from the Secretary of State on the subject, with accompanying papers.

GROVER CLEVELAND.

EXECUTIVE MANSION, *February 1, 1887.*
To the Senate and House of Representatives:

I transmit herewith a letter from the Secretary of State, together with a copy of the report, which it incloses, of Lieutenant William H. Schuetze, United States Navy, who was designated by the Secretary of the Navy, in pursuance of the act of Congress of March 3, 1885, making appropriations for the sundry civil expenses of the Government for the year ending June 30, 1886, to distribute the testimonials of the Government to subjects of Russia who extended aid to the survivors of the *Jeannette* exploring expedition and to the parties dispatched by this Government to aid the said survivors.

The report is interesting alike to the people of the United States and to the subjects of Russia, and will be gratifying to all who appreciate the generous and humane action of Congress in providing for the testimonials.   GROVER CLEVELAND.

EXECUTIVE MANSION, *February 1, 1887.*

To the House of Representatives of the United States:

In response to the resolution of the House of Representatives adopted on the 22d ultimo, calling upon me for a "copy of the treaty or convention proposed to the Senate and ratified by that body between the United States and the Government of the Hawaiian Islands," I transmit herewith a report of the Secretary of State, with accompanying papers.

It is proper to remark in this relation that no convention whatever has been "agreed to and ratified" by "the President and Senate," as is recited in the preamble to the said resolution of the House of Representatives, but that the documents referred to, exhibiting the action of the Executive and the Senate, respectively, are communicated in compliance with the request of the resolution.

GROVER CLEVELAND.

EXECUTIVE MANSION, *February 8, 1887.*

To the House of Representatives of the United States:

I transmit herewith, in response to a resolution of the House of the 24th ultimo, a report of the Secretary of State, with accompanying copies of correspondence between the Governments of the United States and Great Britain concerning the rights of American fishermen in the waters of British North America, supplemental to the correspondence already communicated to Congress with my message of December 8, 1886.*

GROVER CLEVELAND.

EXECUTIVE MANSION, *February 10, 1887.*

To the Senate and House of Representatives:

I transmit herewith a letter from the Secretary of State, accompanying reports by consular officers of the United States on the extent and character of the emigration from and immigration into their respective districts.

GROVER CLEVELAND.

EXECUTIVE MANSION,
Washington, February 14, 1887.

To the Senate of the United States:

I transmit herewith, with a view to its ratification, a treaty of amity, commerce, and navigation, concluded October 2, 1886, in the harbor of Nukualofa, Tongatabu, between the United States of America and the King of Tonga.

I also transmit, for your information, a report from the Secretary of State, inclosing copies of the treaties of friendship concluded between the Kingdom of Tonga and Germany and Great Britain.

GROVER CLEVELAND.

* See pp. 529-530.

EXECUTIVE MANSION, *February 14, 1887.*

To the Senate of the United States:

I transmit herewith a report furnished by the Secretary of State in response to a resolution of the Senate of January 31 ultimo, calling for particulars of the investment and distribution of the indemnity received in 1875 from Spain, and known as the "*Virginius* fund."

GROVER CLEVELAND.

EXECUTIVE MANSION, *February 15, 1887.*

To the House of Representatives:

In compliance with the resolution of the Senate of the 12th instant (the House of Representatives concurring), I return herewith the bill (H. R. 5652) for the relief of James W. Goodrich.

GROVER CLEVELAND.

EXECUTIVE MANSION, *February 16, 1887.*

To the Senate and House of Representatives:

I transmit herewith a letter from the Secretary of State, accompanying the annual reports of the consuls of the United States on the trade and industries of foreign countries.　　GROVER CLEVELAND.

EXECUTIVE MANSION, *February 19, 1887.*

To the House of Representatives of the United States:

I transmit herewith to the House of Representatives a report from the Secretary of State, in response to a resolution of that body of the 16th instant, inquiring as to the action of this Department to protect the interests of American citizens whose property was destroyed by fire caused by insurgents at Aspinwall in 1885.　　GROVER CLEVELAND.

To the Senate:　　EXECUTIVE MANSION, *February 23, 1887.*

In answer to the resolution of the Senate of the 14th instant, relating to the arrest, trial, and discharge of A. K. Cutting, a citizen of the United States, by the authorities of Mexico, I transmit herewith a letter from the Secretary of State of this date, with its accompaniment.

GROVER CLEVELAND.

EXECUTIVE MANSION, *February 25, 1887.*

To the House of Representatives:

In compliance with the resolution of the House of Representatives (the Senate concurring), I return herewith the bill (H. R. 367) to amend section 536 of the Revised Statutes of the United States, relating to the division of the State of Illinois into judicial districts, and to provide for holding terms of court of the northern district at the city of Peoria.

GROVER CLEVELAND.

EXECUTIVE MANSION,
Washington, February 25, 1887.

To the Senate of the United States:

I transmit herewith, with a view to its ratification, an additional article to the treaty of extradition concluded October 11, 1870, between the United States of America and the Republic of Guatemala.

GROVER CLEVELAND.

EXECUTIVE MANSION, *February 26, 1887.*

To the Senate:

I transmit herewith, in reply to a resolution of the Senate of the 21st ultimo, a report from the Secretary of State, relative to the seizure and sale of the American schooner *Rebecca* at Tampico and the resignation of Henry R. Jackson, esq., as minister of the United States to Mexico. It is not thought compatible with the public interests to publish the correspondence in either case at the present time.

GROVER CLEVELAND.

EXECUTIVE MANSION. *February 28, 1887.*

To the Senate and House of Representatives:

I transmit herewith a communication of 17th instant from the Secretary of the Interior, submitting, with accompanying papers, two agreements made with Chippewa Indians in the State of Minnesota under the provisions of the act of May 15, 1886 (24 U. S. Statutes at Large, p. 44).

The papers are presented for the consideration and action of Congress.

GROVER CLEVELAND.

EXECUTIVE MANSION,
Washington, March 1, 1887.

To the Senate of the United States:

In answer to the resolution of the Senate of the 22d ultimo, requesting copies of certain letters, dated June 8, 1886, and September 20, 1886, addressed by the counsel of A. H. Lazare to the Secretary of State, in regard to the award against the Republic of Hayti in favor of A. H. Lazare under the protocol signed by the Secretary of State and the minister of Hayti on May 24, 1884, I transmit a report from the Secretary of State upon the subject.

GROVER CLEVELAND.

EXECUTIVE MANSION,
Washington, March 1, 1887.

To the House of Representatives:

In compliance with the resolution of the House of Representatives of the 28th ultimo (the Senate concurring), I return herewith the bill of the House (H. R. 7310) granting a pension to Mrs. Arlanta T. Taylor.

GROVER CLEVELAND.

EXECUTIVE MANSION, *March 2, 1887.*

To the Senate of the United States:

In response to the resolution of the Senate of the 14th ultimo, requesting information concerning the service rendered by Count Casimir Pulaski, a brigadier-general of the Army of the United States in the years 1777, 1778, and 1779, and also respecting his pay and compensation, I transmit herewith reports upon the subject from the Secretary of State, the Secretary of the Treasury, and the Secretary of War.

GROVER CLEVELAND.

EXECUTIVE MANSION,
Washington, March 2, 1887.

To the Senate of the United States:

I transmit herewith a report of the Secretary of State, with accompanying papers, furnished in response to the resolution of the Senate of the 26th ultimo, calling for information touching the conditions under which certain transatlantic telegraph companies have been permitted to land their cables in the United States, and touching contracts of such companies with each other or with other cable or telegraph companies.

GROVER CLEVELAND.

VETO MESSAGES.

To the Senate:

EXECUTIVE MANSION, *January 19, 1887.*

I return without approval Senate bill No. 2269, entitled "An act granting a pension to William Dickens."

The beneficiary named in this bill filed his application for pension in the Pension Bureau in 1880, and in December, 1886, the same was granted, taking effect from the 15th day of October, 1864.

If the bill herewith returned should become a law, it would permit the payment of a pension only from the date of its approval. Thus, if it did not result in loss to the claimant by superseding the action of the Pension Bureau, it is plain that it would be a useless enactment.

GROVER CLEVELAND.

EXECUTIVE MANSION, *January 27, 1887.*

To the Senate:

I hereby return without approval Senate bill No. 2173, entitled "An act granting a pension to Benjamin Obekiah."

This bill directs that the beneficiary named therein be placed upon the pension roll, "subject to the provisions and limitations of the pension laws."

In July, 1886, the person named in this bill was placed upon the pension roll at a rate determined upon by the Pension Bureau, pursuant to the provisions and limitations of the pension laws; and it is entirely certain that the special act now presented to me would give the claimant no new rights or additional benefits.

GROVER CLEVELAND.

EXECUTIVE MANSION, *January 27, 1887.*

To the Senate:

I herewith return without approval Senate bill No. 127, entitled "An act for the relief of H. K. Belding."

This bill directs the sum of $1,566 to be paid to the said H. K. Belding "for carrying the mails of the United States between the years 1858 and 1862."

In April, 1858, a contract was awarded to the said Belding for carrying the mails from Brownsville, Minn., to Carimona, in the same State, a distance of 63 miles, and return, three times a week, for the sum of $1,800 per annum, said service to begin on the 1st day of July, 1858, and to terminate on the 30th day of June, 1862. This contract contained a provision that the Post-Office Department might discontinue the service in whole or in part, allowing to the contractor one month's extra pay therefor.

On May 9, 1859, in consequence of a failure on the part of the Congress to make the necessary appropriation, a general reduction of mail service was ordered, and the service under the contract with the claimant was reduced to two trips per week from May 10, 1859, instead of three, as stipulated in the contract, and a deduction of one-third of the annual sum to be paid by the contract was made for such reduced service; and thereupon one month's extra pay was allowed and paid the contractor on account of said reduction.

It is conceded that payment was made in full according to the terms of the contract up to the 10th day of May, 1859, but it is claimed that notwithstanding the reduction of the service to two trips per week and the receipt by the contractor of one month's extra pay by reason thereof, he continued to perform the full service of three trips per week from the 10th day of May, 1859, to the 30th day of September, 1860, being seventeen months.

Of the sum directed to be paid to him in the bill under consideration, $850 is allowed him on account of this service, he having been paid for the period stated at the rate of $1,200 per annum. The contractor claims that this full service was performed after the reduction by the Post-Office Department because he had received an intimation from the Postmaster-General that if the full service was continued after such reduction there was no doubt that the Congress would at its next session make provision for the payment of the sum deducted.

Of course no legal claim in favor of the contractor can be predicated upon the facts which he alleges; and if he did continue full service under the circumstances stated, it must be conceded that his conduct was hardly in accordance with the rules which regulate transactions of this kind.

But a thorough search of the correspondence and records in the Post-Office Department fails to disclose any letter, document, or record giving the least support to the allegation that any such intimation or assurance as is claimed was given; nor is there the least evidence in the Department that the full service was actually performed. There is, however, on the files of the Department a letter from the claimant, dated August 25, 1860, containing the following statement:

When I received official information of the curtailing service, the reasons why, I wrote to the Department that I would, if allowed, continue service three times a week and take certificates, if I could be allowed to connect with La Crosse at *pro rata* rates. That letter was never answered, and I continued service three times a week till 3d of September following, then run twice a week.

Thus it appears that this contractor, who in August, 1860, claimed that he continued full service upon the invitation of his own unanswered letter for less than four months, insists twenty-seven years after the date of the alleged service that he performed such service for seventeen months, and up to October, 1860. Not only has he himself in this manner almost conclusively shown that the claim now made and allowed is exorbitant, but the evidence gives rise to a strong presumption that it is entirely fictitious.

The remainder of the amount allowed to the claimant in this bill is based upon an alleged performance by the contractor of the same mail service which has been referred to from October 1, 1860, to February 14, 1861, a period of four months and fourteen days.

Prior to October 1, 1860, the claimant's contract was annulled and a new or more extended route established, entirely covering that upon which he had carried the mails. Thereupon a month's extra pay was allowed to him, and new contractors undertook the service and were paid therefor by the Government for the period covered by the claimant's alleged service. From the 14th day of February, 1861, Mr. Belding's contract with the Government was reinstated; but if he performed the service alleged during the period of four months and fourteen days immediately prior to that date, it is quite clear that he did so under an arrangement with the new contractors, and not under circumstances creating any legal or equitable claim against the Government.

GROVER CLEVELAND.

EXECUTIVE MANSION, *January 31, 1887.*

To the Senate:

I hereby return without approval Senate bill No. 2167, entitled "An act granting a pension to Mrs. Margaret Dunlap."

By this bill it is proposed to grant a pension to the beneficiary therein named as the mother of James F. Dunlap, who enlisted in the Seventh Missouri State Militia Cavalry in 1862 and died in July, 1864, of wounds received at the hand of a comrade.

The favorable action of the Senate upon this bill appears to be based, so far as the cause of death is concerned, upon an affidavit contained in the report of the committee to which the bill was referred, made by one G. Will Houts, second lieutenant in the company to which the deceased soldier belonged, in which the affiant deposes that some of the comrades of the deceased being engaged in an affray he attempted to separate the combatants, whereupon one of them, without cause or provocation, stabbed the deceased in the breast, from which, in a few days thereafter, he died; to which affidavit is added the finding of a court-martial that the party inflicting the wound was found guilty of manslaughter and sentenced to five years' imprisonment.

Upon this showing it might be difficult to spell out the facts that the injury to the soldier was received in the line of duty or that any theory of granting pensions covered the case.

But the weak features of this application are not alluded to in the committee's report.

The record of the soldier's death states that he was "killed by one of his comrades in a difficulty."

The same Lieutenant Houts who in 1872 made oath that the soldier was wounded while attempting to separate comrades who were fighting testified in 1864 before the court-martial upon the trial of the man who did the wounding, and whose name was Capehart, that Dunlap, the deceased, stated to him "that he was more to blame than Capehart, and that they had been scuffling, at first good-naturedly, and then both got angry; that he was rougher with Capehart than he ought to have been."

Another witness testified that the affray took place between Dunlap and Capehart; that Dunlap handled Capehart very roughly, kicking him, etc., and that finally Capehart stabbed Dunlap, upon which the latter attempted to get his gun, but was prevented from doing so by the witness.

Of course there can be no pretense of any kind of claim against the Government arising from these facts.

It is quite evident that the affidavit presented to the Senate committee was contrived to deceive, and it is to be feared that it is but a sample of many that are made in support of claims for pensions.

GROVER CLEVELAND.

To the House of Representatives:

I return without approval House bill No. 6443, entitled "An act granting a pension to Alexander Falconer."

This claimant filed his application for pension in 1879, alleging that in 1837, being then an enlisted man in the United States Army, he received a gunshot wound in his right leg below the knee at the battle of Okeechobee Lake, Florida.

The records disclose the fact that this soldier enlisted in 1834, and was almost continuously in the service and attached to the same company until 1846.

It further appears that he is reported sick during the month in which the battle was fought. The list of casualties does not contain his name among the wounded.

He reenlisted in 1846 and again in 1847, and was finally discharged in 1848. These latter enlistments were for service in the Mexican War.

His claim for pension was denied in 1885 on the ground that no disability existed in a pensionable degree from the alleged gunshot wound in his leg.

It is perfectly clear that the only pretexts for giving this claimant a pension are military service, old age, and poverty.

Inasmuch as he was a soldier in the Mexican War, his case is undoubtedly provided for by a general law approved within the last few days.

Under this bill the amount to be paid him is fixed, while if the bill herewith returned were approved the sum to be paid him would depend upon the determination of the Pension Bureau as to the extent of his disability as the result of his wound. As that Bureau has quite lately determined that there was no disability, it is evident that this old soldier can better rely upon the general law referred to.

GROVER CLEVELAND.

EXECUTIVE MANSION, *February 3, 1887.*
To the House of Representatives:

I herewith return without approval House bill No. 6132, entitled "An act granting a pension to William Lynch."

The claimant mentioned in this bill enlisted in the Fifth Regiment United States Infantry in 1849, and was discharged, after a reenlistment, September 8, 1859.

He filed a claim for pension more than twenty-four years afterwards, in April, 1884, claiming that he contracted rheumatism of the right hip and leg in the winter of 1857–58, while serving in Utah. He admitted that he was not under treatment while in the service and that he never consulted a physician in regard to his disability until he commenced proceedings for a pension.

The evidence disclosed to me falls far short of establishing this claim for pension upon its merits.

The application made to the Pension Bureau is still pending and awaiting answer to inquiries made by the Bureau in January, 1886.

I do not understand that the Congress intends to pass special acts in cases thus situated.

GROVER CLEVELAND.

EXECUTIVE MANSION, *February 4, 1887.*

To the House of Representatives:

I hereby return without approval House bill No. 7698, entitled "An act granting a pension to Robert K. Bennett."

The beneficiary named in this bill enlisted in September, 1862, and it appears that very soon after that he was detailed to the cook shop. This seems to be the only military service he rendered, and on February 7, 1863, five months after enlistment, he was received into the marine hospital at New Orleans for varicocele. He was discharged from the service February 22, 1863, and the cause of discharge is stated to be "varicocele, to which he was subject four years before enlistment."

Seventeen years thereafter, and in June, 1880, this claimant filed an application for pension in the Pension Bureau, alleging that about the 10th day of February, 1863, in unloading a barrel it fell upon him, producing a hernia, shortly after which he was affected by piles.

It will be seen that he fixes this injury as occurring three days after his admission to the hospital, but he might well be honestly mistaken as to this date. If the injury, however, was such as he stated, it is difficult to see why no mention was made of it in the hospital records.

He persisted at all times, as I understand the case, until the rejection of his claim in 1883, that his disability arose from hernia and piles. The reason of this rejection is stated to be that varicocele existed prior to enlistment and that there was no evidence of the existence of piles in the service or at discharge. From a medical examination made in December, 1882, it appears that there was "no evidence or symptoms of disability resulting from piles or hernia.

Subsequent to the rejection of this claim some proof was filed tending to show that the disability was in the right leg, but it is of such a nature, in the light of the claimant's own previous allegations, that I think the Pension Bureau did entirely right in informing his attorney that the additional evidence did not change the status of the case.

GROVER CLEVELAND.

EXECUTIVE MANSION, *February 4, 1887.*

To the House of Representatives:

I hereby return without approval House bill No. 7540, entitled "An act to increase the pension of Franklin Sweet."

This soldier was pensioned in 1863 as sergeant, though before that time he had been acting as captain, and was in command of his company when he was wounded. He is entitled in equity, and, I think, upon the theory of an act very recently approved, in law, to be treated in regard to his pension as a captain; and the Pension Bureau has within the last few days ordered a certificate for pension to issue to him as captain as of the date of his discharge.

I fully approve this action of the Bureau, and as this is much more favorable to a deserving soldier than his remedy under this bill, I am not willing that the action so lately and so justly taken in his behalf under the general law should be superseded by the approval of this act.

GROVER CLEVELAND.

EXECUTIVE MANSION, *February 4, 1887.*

To the House of Representatives:

I herewith return without approval House bill No. 8834, entitled "An act granting a pension to Abraham P. Griggs."

The claimant mentioned in this bill enlisted in a New Jersey regiment August 14, 1861, and was discharged for disability November 17, 1863.

He entered hospital January 2, 1863, and was transferred to general hospital at Newark, N. J., March 28, 1863, with "debility."

He was discharged from that hospital and from the service in November, 1863, as above stated, and the following statement from his certificate of discharge, if trustworthy, sheds some light upon the kind of debility with which he was afflicted:

This man has been in this hospital for the past eight months. We do not believe him sick, or that he has been sick, but completely worthless. He is obese and a malingerer to such an extent that he is almost an imbecile—worthlessness, obesity, and imbecility and laziness. He is totally unfit for the Invalid Corps or for any other military duty.

I do not regard it at all strange that this claimant, encouraged by the ease with which special acts are passed, seeks relief through such means, after his application, filed in the Pension Bureau nearly twenty years after his discharge, had been rejected.

Of the four comrades who make affidavit in support of his claim, two of them are recorded as deserters.

His claim is predicated upon rheumatism. He alleges that after his discharge from his enlistment he was drafted and served in the Third New York Cavalry, but the Adjutant-General reports that his name does not appear on the rolls of the company to which he says he was attached.

The board of United States examining surgeons at Trenton, N. J., report as the result of an examination as late as May 27, 1885, that they found "no disease of heart or lungs, no thickening or wasting of any of the joints of the body, no evidence of any rheumatic diathesis, no rupture or hemorrhoids, no disease of his spleen or kidney; hands are hard and indicate an ability to work."

I can not think that the official statements referred to, and which militate so strongly against the merits of the claimant, should be impeached or set aside by any of the other testimony which has been brought to my attention.

GROVER CLEVELAND.

EXECUTIVE MANSION, *February 4, 1887.*

To the House of Representatives:

I hereby return without approval House bill No. 927, entitled "An act granting a pension to Cudbert Stone."

The report of the committee of the House of Representatives to whom this bill was referred states that the claimant enlisted October 3, 1861, in Company H, Fourteenth Kentucky Volunteers, and was honorably discharged on the 31st day of January, 1865; that he filed his claim for pension July 20, 1881, more than sixteen years thereafter, alleging that he contracted piles while in the service, from exposure while in the line of duty, and that his claim was rejected in October, 1884, on the ground that the allegation of the claimant shows that his disability originated while undergoing the sentence of a court-martial, and therefore not in the line of duty.

The report of the committee closes with the statement that—

In view of the long and faithful service and high character of the claimant and the well-established facts that claimant was a stout and able-bodied man, free from any and all disease when he enlisted, and that by reason of his faithful service to his country and the great suffering and hardship through which he passed while in said service his health was permanently destroyed, the committee earnestly recommend the passage of the bill.

The records of the War Department show that the claimant enlisted October 25, 1861, and that on the muster-in roll of his company dated December 10, 1861, he is reported as present; that on the roll dated December 31, 1861, he is reported as absent without leave; that on the roll for January and February, 1862, he is reported as deserted; that he is not borne on subsequent rolls until that for November, 1864, when he is reported as gained from desertion; he was mustered out with his company January 31, 1865, and the records offered no evidence of disability; that in his claim for pension, filed in 1881, he alleges that he contracted piles in the winter of 1863.

In a subsequent statement he alleges that this date is erroneous, and that his disability was contracted in October, 1864, and that he believes it was the result of his having diarrhea for about twelve months prior to that date, contracted while he was being carried from place to place as a prisoner, he having been tried by a court-martial in May, 1862, for desertion and sentenced to imprisonment until the expiration of his term of enlistment.

Thus it quite plainly appears that this claimant spent the most of his term of enlistment in desertion or in imprisonment as a punishment of that offense; and thus is exhibited the "long and faithful service and the high character of the claimant" mentioned as entitling him to consideration by the committee who reported favorably upon this bill.

I withhold my assent from this bill because, if the facts before me, derived from the army records and the statements of the claimant are true, the allowance of this claim would, in my opinion, be a travesty upon our whole scheme of pensions and an insult to every decent veteran soldier.

GROVER CLEVELAND.

EXECUTIVE MANSION, *February 4, 1887.*

To the House of Representatives:

I return herewith without approval House bill No. 8150, entitled "An act granting a pension to Jesse Campbell."

The claim for a pension made by the beneficiary named in this bill to the Pension Bureau, and rejected in 1881, was reopened upon further proof in January, 1887, and the claimant was ordered before a board of examining surgeons, upon which a report has not yet been made.

Inasmuch as the only ground for the rejection of his claim was the nonexistence of pensionable disability from the cause he alleged, and in view of the fact that he now alleges a different disability, which the new evidence seems to support, there is no doubt that justice will be done the claimant under the general law.

This bill if passed would only place the name of the beneficiary upon the pension roll, "subject to the restrictions and limitations of the pension laws." Whether any sum was allowed him or not would still depend upon the existence of a disability; and if this is found upon the examination lately ordered, he will undoubtedly be put upon the pension roll, under existing law, in accordance with his supplementary claim.

GROVER CLEVELAND.

EXECUTIVE MANSION, *February 4, 1887.*

To the House of Representatives:

I hereby return without approval House bill No. 6832, entitled "An act granting a pension to Mrs. Catharine Sattler."

The beneficiary named in this bill claims a pension as the surviving widow of Julius Sattler, who enlisted in Company A, Seventh New York

Volunteers, and was in the service from March 10, 1864, to March 22, 1865, when be was discharged because of the amputation of his left forearm in consequence of a wound received in the battle of Deep Bottom, Virginia, on the 14th day of August, 1864.   He was pensioned in 1865 at the rate of $8 per month, which was afterwards increased to $15 per month, dating from June 6, 1866.

In October, 1867, he was employed as a watchman in the United States bonded warehouse in the city of New York, and on the 31st day of that month he received his monthly pay of $50.   He disappeared on that day, and on the 13th day of November, 1867, his body was found in the North River, at the foot of West Thirteenth street, in the city of New York, without his hat, coat, watch, or money.

These facts, with the further statement that he was a strong and healthy man at the time of his death, constitute the case on the part of the widow, who filed her application for a pension July 8, 1884, nearly seventeen years after her husband's death, alleging that she was married to the deceased in 1865, after the amputation of his arm.

Her claim was rejected in November, 1884, upon the ground that the soldier's death was not due to his military service.

This rejection was clearly right, unless the Government is to be held as an insurer against every fatal casualty incurred by those who have served in the Army, without regard to the manner of its occurrence.

GROVER CLEVELAND.

EXECUTIVE MANSION, *February 4, 1887.*

To the House of Representatives:

I herewith return without approval House bill No. 6825, entitled ''An act granting a pension to James R. Baylor.''

The claim of the beneficiary named in this bill is based upon an injury to his left ankle in 1862.

A medical examination in 1877 showed no appearance of there ever having been a fracture of the left ankle, as alleged by the claimant, and it was determined that there was no disability.   A later examination in the same year was had with the same result.   Still another medical examination was had in June, 1884, which, although nearly agreeing with the previous ones, and giving rise to some suspicion that the claimant was inclined to exaggerate and prevent a free and fair examination, still does not absolutely exclude a very slight disability.

Upon the report of this last examination the case has been reopened for further proof of disability since discharge, which if found will entitle the claimant to a pension under general laws.   On the question to be determined he would have no advantage under a special act, inasmuch as there must be a ratable disability to entitle him to any payment in pursuance of its provisions.

GROVER CLEVELAND.

EXECUTIVE MANSION, *February 11, 1887.*

To the House of Representatives:

I herewith return without my approval House bill No. 10457, entitled "An act for the relief of dependent parents and honorably discharged soldiers and sailors who are now disabled and dependent upon their own labor for support."

This is the first general bill that has been sanctioned by the Congress since the close of the late civil war permitting a pension to the soldiers and sailors who served in that war upon the ground of service and present disability alone, and in the entire absence of any injuries received by the casualties or incidents of such service.

While by almost constant legislation since the close of this war there has been compensation awarded for every possible injury received as a result of military service in the Union Army, and while a great number of laws passed for that purpose have been administered with great liberality and have been supplemented by numerous private acts to reach special cases, there has not until now been an avowed departure from the principle thus far adhered to respecting Union soldiers, that the bounty of the Government in the way of pensions is generously bestowed when granted to those who, in this military service and in the line of military duty, have to a greater or less extent been disabled.

But it is a mistake to suppose that service pensions, such as are permitted by the second section of the bill under consideration, are new to our legislation. In 1818, thirty-five years after the close of the Revolutionary War, they were granted to the soldiers engaged in that struggle, conditional upon service until the end of the war or for a term not less than nine months, and requiring every beneficiary under the act to be one " who is, or hereafter by reason of his reduced circumstances in life shall be, in need of assistance from his country for support." Another law of a like character was passed in 1828, requiring service until the close of the Revolutionary War; and still another, passed in 1832, provided for those persons not included in the previous statute, but who served two years at some time during the war, and giving a proportionate sum to those who had served not less than six months.

A service-pension law was passed for the benefit of the soldiers of 1812 in the year 1871, fifty-six years after the close of that war, which required only sixty days' service; and another was passed in 1878, sixty-three years after the war, requiring only fourteen days' service.

The service-pension bill passed at this session of Congress, thirty-nine years after the close of the Mexican War, for the benefit of the soldiers of that war, requires either some degree of disability or dependency or that the claimant under its provisions should be 62 years of age, and in either case that he should have served sixty days or been actually engaged in a battle.

It will be seen that the bill of 1818 and the Mexican pension bill, being thus passed nearer the close of the wars in which its beneficiaries were engaged than the others—one thirty-five years and the other thirty-nine years after the termination of such wars—embraced persons who were quite advanced in age, assumed to be comparatively few in number, and whose circumstances, dependence, and disabilities were clearly defined and could be quite easily fixed.

The other laws referred to appear to have been passed at a time so remote from the military service of the persons which they embraced that their extreme age alone was deemed to supply a presumption of dependency and need.

The number of enlistments in the Revolutionary War is stated to be 309,791, and in the War of 1812 576,622; but it is estimated that on account of repeated reenlistments the number of individuals engaged in these wars did not exceed one-half of the number represented by these figures. In the war with Mexico the number of enlistments is reported to be 112,230, which represents a greater proportion of individuals engaged than the reported enlistments in the two previous wars.

The number of pensions granted under all laws to soldiers of the Revolution is given at 62,069; to soldiers of the War of 1812 and their widows, 60,178; and to soldiers of the Mexican War and their widows, up to June 30, 1885, 7,619. The latter pensions were granted to the soldiers of a war involving much hardship for disabilities incurred as a result of such service; and it was not till within the last month that the few remaining survivors were awarded a service pension.

The War of the Rebellion terminated nearly twenty-two years ago; the number of men furnished for its prosecution is stated to be 2,772,408. No corresponding number of statutes have ever been passed to cover every kind of injury or disability incurred in the military service of any war. Under these statutes 561,576 pensions have been granted from the year 1861 to June 30, 1886, and more than 2,600 pensioners have been added to the rolls by private acts passed to meet cases, many of them of questionable merit, which the general laws did not cover.

On the 1st day of July, 1886, 365,763 pensioners of all classes were upon the pension rolls, of whom 305,605 were survivors of the War of the Rebellion and their widows and dependents. For the year ending June 30, 1887, $75,000,000 have been appropriated for the payment of pensions, and the amount expended for that purpose from 1861 to July 1, 1886, is $808,624,811.51.

While annually paying out such a vast sum for pensions already granted, it is now proposed by the bill under consideration to award a service pension to the soldiers of all wars in which the United States has been engaged, including of course the War of the Rebellion, and to pay those entitled to the benefits of the act the sum of $12 per month.

So far as it relates to the soldiers of the late civil war, the bounty it "ords them is given thirteen years earlier than it has been furnished the soldiers of any other war, and before a large majority of its beneficiaries have advanced in age beyond the strength and vigor of the prime of life.

It exacts only a military or naval service of three months, without any requirement of actual engagement with an enemy in battle, and without a subjection to any of the actual dangers of war.

The pension it awards is allowed to enlisted men who have not suffered the least injury, disability, loss, or damage of any kind, incurred in or in any degree referable to their military service, including those who never reached the front at all and those discharged from rendezvous at the close of the war, if discharged three months after enlistment. Under the last call of the President for troops, in December, 1864, 11,303 men were furnished who were thus discharged.

The section allowing this pension does, however, require, besides a service of three months and an honorable discharge, that those seeking the benefit of the act shall be such as "are now or may hereafter be suffering from mental or physical disability, not the result of their own vicious habits or gross carelessness, which incapacitates them for the performance of labor in such a degree as to render them unable to earn a support, and who are dependent upon their daily labor for support."

It provides further that such persons shall, upon making proof of the fact, "be placed on the list of invalid pensioners of the United States, and be entitled to receive for such total inability to procure their subsistence by daily labor $12 per month; and such pension shall commence from the date of the filing of the application in the Pension Office, upon proof that the disability then existed, and continue during the existence of the same in the degree herein provided: *Provided*, That persons who are now receiving pensions under existing laws, or whose claims are pending in the Pension Office, may, by application to the Commissioner of Pensions, in such form as he may prescribe, receive the benefit of this act."

It is manifestly of the utmost importance that statutes which, like pension laws, should be liberally administered as measures of benevolence in behalf of worthy beneficiaries should admit of no uncertainty as to their general objects and consequences.

Upon a careful consideration of the language of the section of this bill above given it seems to me to be so uncertain and liable to such conflicting constructions and to be subject to such unjust and mischievous application as to alone furnish sufficient ground for disapproving the proposed legislation.

Persons seeking to obtain the pension provided by this section must be now or hereafter—

1. "Suffering from mental or physical disability."

2. Such disability must not be "the result of their own vicious habits or gross carelessness."

3. Such disability must be such as "incapacitates them for the performance of labor in such a degree as to render them unable to earn a support."

4. They must be "dependent upon their daily labor for support."

5. Upon proof of these conditions they shall "be placed on the lists of invalid pensioners of the United States, and be entitled to receive for such total inability to procure their subsistence by daily labor $12 per month."

It is not probable that the words last quoted, "such total inability to procure their subsistence by daily labor," at all qualify the conditions prescribed in the preceding language of the section. The "total inability" spoken of must be "such" inability—that is, the inability already described and constituted by the conditions already detailed in the previous parts of the section.

It thus becomes important to consider the meaning and the scope of these last-mentioned conditions.

The mental and physical disability spoken of has a distinct meaning in the practice of the Pension Bureau and includes every impairment of bodily or mental strength and vigor. For such disabilities there are now paid 131 different rates of pension, ranging from $1 to $100 per month.

This disability must not be the result of the applicant's "vicious habits or gross carelessness." Practically this provision is not important. The attempt of the Government to escape the payment of a pension on such a plea would of course in a very large majority of instances, and regardless of the merits of the case, prove a failure. There would be that strange but nearly universal willingness to help the individual as between him and the public Treasury which goes very far to insure a state of proof in favor of the claimant.

The disability of applicants must be such as to "incapacitate them for the performance of labor in such a degree as to render them unable to earn a support."

It will be observed that there is no limitation or definition of the incapacitating injury or ailment itself. It need only be such a degree of disability from any cause as renders the claimant unable to earn a support by labor. It seems to me that the "support" here mentioned as one which can not be earned is a complete and entire support, with no diminution on account of the least impairment of physical or mental condition. If it had been intended to embrace only those who by disease or injury were totally unable to labor, it would have been very easy to express that idea, instead of recognizing, as is done, a "degree" of such inability.

What is a support? Who is to determine whether a man earns it, or has it, or has it not? Is the Government to enter the homes of claimants for pension and after an examination of their surroundings and circumstances settle those questions? Shall the Government say to one man that his manner of subsistence by his earnings is a support and to another that the things his earnings furnish are not a support? Any attempt, however honest, to administer this law in such a manner would

necessarily produce more unfairness and unjust discrimination and give
more scope for partisan partiality, and would result in more perversion
of the Government's benevolent intentions, than the execution of any
statute ought to permit.

If in the effort to carry out the proposed law the degree of disability as
related to earnings be considered for the purpose of discovering if in any
way it curtails the support which the applicant, if entirely sound, would
earn, and to which he is entitled, we enter the broad field long occupied
by the Pension Bureau, and we recognize as the only difference between
the proposed legislation and previous laws passed for the benefit of the
surviving soldiers of the Civil War the incurrence in one case of disabilities in military service and in the other disabilities existing, but in no
way connected with or resulting from such service.

It must be borne in mind that in no case is there any grading of this
proposed pension. Under the operation of the rule first suggested, if
there is a lack in any degree, great or small, of the ability to earn such
a support as the Government determines the claimant should have, and,
by the application of the rule secondly suggested, if there is a reduction
in any degree of the support which he might earn if sound, he is entitled
to a pension of $12.

In the latter case, and under the proviso of the proposed bill permitting persons now receiving pensions to be admitted to the benefits of the
act, I do not see how those now on the pension roll for disabilities incurred in the service, and which diminish their earning capacity, can be
denied the pension provided in this bill.

Of course none will apply who are now receiving $12 or more per
month. But on the 30th day of June, 1886, there were on the pension
rolls 202,621 persons who were receiving fifty-eight different rates of
pension from $1 to $11.75 per month. Of these, 28,142 were receiving
$2 per month; 63,116, $4 per month; 37,254, $6 per month, and 50,274,
whose disabilities were rated as total, $8 per month.

As to the meaning of the section of the bill under consideration there
appears to have been quite a difference of opinion among its advocates
in the Congress. The chairman of the Committee on Pensions in the
House of Representatives, who reported the bill, declared that there was
in it no provision for pensioning anyone who has a less disability than a
total inability to labor, and that it was a charity measure. The chairman of the Committee on Pensions in the Senate, having charge of the
bill in that body, dissented from the construction of the bill announced
in the House of Representatives, and declared that it not only embraced
all soldiers totally disabled, but, in his judgment, all who are disabled
to any considerable extent; and such a construction was substantially
given to the bill by another distinguished Senator, who, as a former Secretary of the Interior, had imposed upon him the duty of executing pension laws and determining their intent and meaning.

Another condition required of claimants under this act is that they shall be "dependent upon their daily labor for support."

This language, which may be said to assume that there exists within the reach of the persons mentioned "labor," or the ability in some degree to work, is more aptly used in a statute describing those not wholly deprived of this ability than in one which deals with those utterly unable to work.

I am of the opinion that it may fairly be contended that under the provisions of this section any soldier whose faculties of mind or body have become impaired by accident, disease, or age, irrespective of his service in the Army as a cause, and who by his labor only is left incapable of gaining the fair support he might with unimpaired powers have provided for himself, and who is not so well endowed with this world's goods as to live without work, may claim to participate in its bounty; that it is not required that he should be without property, but only that labor should be necessary to his support in some degree; nor is it required that he should be now receiving support from others.

Believing this to be the proper interpretation of the bill, I can not but remember that the soldiers of our Civil War in their pay and bounty received such compensation for military service as has never been received by soldiers before since mankind first went to war; that never before on behalf of any soldiery have so many and such generous laws been passed to relieve against the incidents of war; that statutes have been passed giving them a preference in all public employments; that the really needy and homeless Union soldiers of the rebellion have been to a large extent provided for at soldiers' homes, instituted and supported by the Government, where they are maintained together, free from the sense of degradation which attaches to the usual support of charity; and that never before in the history of the country has it been proposed to render Government aid toward the support of any of its soldiers based alone upon a military service so recent, and where age and circumstances appeared so little to demand such aid.

Hitherto such relief has been granted to surviving soldiers few in number, venerable in age, after a long lapse of time since their military service, and as a parting benefaction tendered by a grateful people.

I can not believe that the vast peaceful army of Union soldiers, who, having contentedly resumed their places in the ordinary avocations of life, cherish as sacred the memory of patriotic service, or who, having been disabled by the casualties of war, justly regard the present pension roll on which appear their names as a roll of honor, desire at this time and in the present exigency to be confounded with those who through such a bill as this are willing to be objects of simple charity and to gain a place upon the pension roll through alleged dependence.

Recent personal observation and experience constrain me to refer to another result which will inevitably follow the passage of this bill. It is

sad, but nevertheless true, that already in the matter of procuring pensions there exists a widespread disregard of truth and good faith, stimulated by those who as agents undertake to establish claims for pensions
heedlessly entered upon by the expectant beneficiary, and encouraged, or
at least not condemned, by those unwilling to obstruct a neighbor's plans.

In the execution of this proposed law under any interpretation a wide
field of inquiry would be opened for the establishment of facts largely
within the knowledge of the claimants alone, and there can be no doubt
that the race after the pensions offered by this bill would not only stimulate weakness and pretended incapacity for labor, but put a further premium on dishonesty and mendacity.

The effect of new invitations to apply for pensions or of new advantages added to causes for pensions already existing is sometimes startling.

Thus in March, 1879, large arrearages of pensions were allowed to be
added to all claims filed prior to July 1, 1880. For the year from July 1,
1879, to July 1, 1880, there were filed 110,673 claims, though in the year
immediately previous there were but 36,832 filed, and in the year following but 18,455.

While cost should not be set against a patriotic duty or the recognition
of a right, still when a measure proposed is based upon generosity or
motives of charity it is not amiss to meditate somewhat upon the expense
which it involves. Experience has demonstrated, I believe, that all estimates concerning the probable future cost of a pension list are uncertain
and unreliable and always fall far below actual realization.

The chairman of the House Committee on Pensions calculates that the
number of pensioners under this bill would be 33,105 and the increased
cost $4,767,120. This is upon the theory that only those who are entirely
unable to work would be its beneficiaries. Such was the principle of the
Revolutionary pension law of 1818, much more clearly stated, it seems to
me, than in this bill. When the law of 1818 was upon its passage in Congress, the number of pensioners to be benefited thereby was thought to
be 374; but the number of applicants under the act was 22,297, and the
number of pensions actually allowed 20,485, costing, it is reported, for
the first year, $1,847,900, instead of $40,000, the estimated expense for
that period.

A law was passed in 1853 for the benefit of the surviving widows of
Revolutionary soldiers who were married after January 1, 1800. It was
estimated that they numbered 300 at the time of the passage of the act;
but the number of pensions allowed was 3,742, and the amount paid
for such pensions during the first year of the operation of the act was
$180,000, instead of $24,000, as had been estimated.

I have made no search for other illustrations, and the above, being at
hand, are given as tending to show that estimates can not be relied upon
in such cases.

If none should be pensioned under this bill except those utterly unable to work, I am satisfied that the cost stated in the estimate referred to would be many times multiplied, and with a constant increase from year to year; and if those partially unable to earn their support should be admitted to the privileges of this bill, the probable increase of expense would be almost appalling.

I think it may be said that at the close of the War of the Rebellion every Northern State and a great majority of Northern counties and cities were burdened with taxation on account of the large bounties paid our soldiers; and the bonded debt thereby created still constitutes a large item in the account of the taxgatherer against the people. Federal taxation, no less borne by the people than that directly levied upon their property, is still maintained at the rate made necessary by the exigencies of war. If this bill should become a law, with its tremendous addition to our pension obligation, I am thoroughly convinced that further efforts to reduce the Federal revenue and restore some part of it to our people will, and perhaps should, be seriously questioned.

It has constantly been a cause of pride and congratulation to the American citizen that his country is not put to the charge of maintaining a large standing army in time of peace. Yet we are now living under a war tax which has been tolerated in peaceful times to meet the obligations incurred in war. But for years past, in all parts of the country, the demand for the reduction of the burdens of taxation upon our labor and production has increased in volume and urgency.

I am not willing to approve a measure presenting the objections to which this bill is subject, and which, moreover, will have the effect of disappointing the expectation of the people and their desire and hope for relief from war taxation in time of peace.

In my last annual message the following language was used:

Every patriotic heart responds to a tender consideration for those who, having served their country long and well, are reduced to destitution and dependence, not as an incident of their service, but with advancing age or through sickness or misfortune. We are all tempted by the contemplation of such a condition to supply relief, and are often impatient of the limitations of public duty. Yielding to no one in the desire to indulge this feeling of consideration, I can not rid myself of the conviction that if these ex-soldiers are to be relieved they and their cause are entitled to the benefit of an enactment under which relief may be claimed as a right, and that such relief should be granted under the sanction of law, not in evasion of it; nor should such worthy objects of care, all equally entitled, be remitted to the unequal operation of sympathy or the tender mercies of social and political influence, with their unjust discriminations.

I do not think that the objects, the conditions, and the limitations thus suggested are contained in the bill under consideration.

I adhere to the sentiments thus heretofore expressed. But the evil threatened by this bill is, in my opinion, such that, charged with a great responsibility in behalf of the people, I can not do otherwise than to bring to the consideration of this measure my best efforts of thought and judgment and perform my constitutional duty in relation thereto, regardless of all consequences except such as appear to me to be related to the best and highest interests of the country.

GROVER CLEVELAND.

EXECUTIVE MANSION, *February 16, 1887.*

To the House of Representatives:

I return without my approval House bill No. 10203, entitled "An act to enable the Commissioner of Agriculture to make a special distribution of seeds in the drought-stricken counties of Texas, and making an appropriation therefor."

It is represented that a long-continued and extensive drought has existed in certain portions of the State of Texas, resulting in a failure of crops and consequent distress and destitution.

Though there has been some difference in statements concerning the extent of the people's needs in the localities thus affected, there seems to be no doubt that there has existed a condition calling for relief; and I am willing to believe that, notwithstanding the aid already furnished, a donation of seed grain to the farmers located in this region, to enable them to put in new crops, would serve to avert a continuance or return of an unfortunate blight.

And yet I feel obliged to withhold my approval of the plan, as proposed by this bill, to indulge a benevolent and charitable sentiment through the appropriation of public funds for that purpose.

I can find no warrant for such an appropriation in the Constitution, and I do not believe that the power and duty of the General Government ought to be extended to the relief of individual suffering which is in no manner properly related to the public service or benefit. A prevalent tendency to disregard the limited mission of this power and duty should, I think, be steadfastly resisted, to the end that the lesson should be constantly enforced that though the people support the Government the Government should not support the people.

The friendliness and charity of our countrymen can always be relied upon to relieve their fellow-citizens in misfortune. This has been repeatedly and quite lately demonstrated. Federal aid in such cases encourages the expectation of paternal care on the part of the Government and weakens the sturdiness of our national character, while it prevents the indulgence among our people of that kindly sentiment and conduct which strengthens the bonds of a common brotherhood.

It is within my personal knowledge that individual aid has to some extent already been extended to the sufferers mentioned in this bill. The failure of the proposed appropriation of $10,000 additional to meet their remaining wants will not necessarily result in continued distress if the emergency is fully made known to the people of the country.

It is here suggested that the Commissioner of Agriculture is annually directed to expend a large sum of money for the purchase, propagation, and distribution of seeds and other things of this description, two-thirds of which are, upon the request of Senators, Representatives, and Delegates in Congress, supplied to them for distribution among their constituents.

The appropriation of the current year for this purpose is $100,000, and it will probably be no less in the appropriation for the ensuing year. I understand that a large quantity of grain is furnished for such distribution, and it is supposed that this free apportionment among their neighbors is a privilege which may be waived by our Senators and Representatives.

If sufficient of them should request the Commissioner of Agriculture to send their shares of the grain thus allowed them to the suffering farmers of Texas, they might be enabled to sow their crops, the constituents for whom in theory this grain is intended could well bear the temporary deprivation, and the donors would experience the satisfaction attending deeds of charity.

GROVER CLEVELAND.

To the Senate: EXECUTIVE MANSION, *February 19, 1887.*

I herewith return without approval Senate bill No. 859, entitled "An act granting a pension to Charlotte O'Neal."

This bill proposes to grant a pension to the beneficiary therein named as the widow of Richard O'Neal, late colonel of the Twenty-sixth Regiment Indiana Volunteers.

In the report of the committee in the Senate to whom this bill was referred it is stated that the deceased soldier was the first colonel of the regiment named; that he resigned from the Army, and was by order of the governor of Indiana put in charge of the United States camps at Indianapolis. A military order is made part of the report, announcing that the funeral of Lieutenant-Colonel Richard O'Neal will take place January 6, 1863, and reciting the fact that the deceased had charge of the camps near Indianapolis for the preceding four months.

It is distinctly alleged in the report that the beneficiary did not apply to the Pension Bureau for relief because the disease of which her husband died was incurred after his resignation.

The records of the War Department fail to show that there was a colonel of the Twenty-sixth Indiana Regiment named Richard O'Neal, but it does appear that Richard Neal was lieutenant-colonel of said regiment; that he was mustered in August 31, 1861, and resigned June 30, 1862.

If this is the officer whose widow is named in the bill, the proposition is to pension a widow of a soldier who, after ten months' service, resigned, and who seven months after his resignation died of disease which was in no manner related to his military service.

There is besides such a discrepancy between the name given in the bill and the name of the officer who served as lieutenant-colonel in the regiment mentioned that if the merits were with the widow the bill would need further Congressional consideration.

GROVER CLEVELAND.

To the Senate: EXECUTIVE MANSION, *February 19, 1887.*

I herewith return without approval Senate bill No. 1626, entitled "An act granting a pension to John Reed, sr."

The report of the Senate Committee on Pensions merely states that the mother of John Reed was granted a pension, commencing the 5th day of December, 1862; that she has since died, and that the proposed bill is to secure a pension to John Reed, sr., the aged and dependent father of the deceased soldier.

The records show that the beneficiary named in this bill filed an application for a pension in 1877, alleging that he was the father of John Reed, who died in the service, and that his wife, the mother of the deceased soldier, died May 10, 1872, and that he, the father, was mainly dependent upon his son for support. He filed evidence of the mother's death, and one witness alleged that he was present at her death and attended her funeral.

In 1864 Martha Reed, the mother of the soldier, filed her application for pension, in which she at first claimed to be the widow of John Reed. She afterwards, however, alleged that her husband, John Reed, abandoned his family in 1859 and had not thereafter contributed to their support, and that the soldier was her main support after such abandonment. She was allowed a pension as dependent mother, which commenced in 1862, the date of her son's death, and seems to have terminated July 22, 1884, when she died.

The claim of the father was rejected in 1883 for the reason that the mother, who had a prior right, was still living, and when his claim was again pressed in 1886 he was informed that his abandonment of his family in 1859 precluded the idea that he was entitled to a pension as being dependent upon the soldier for support.

Of course these decisions were correct in law, in equity, and in morals.

This case demonstrates the means employed in attempts to cheat the Government in applications for pensions—too often successful.

The allegation in 1877 of the man who now poses as the aged and dependent father of a dead soldier that the mother died in 1872, when at that time her claim was pending for pension largely based upon his abandonment; the affidavit of the man who testified that he saw her die in 1872; the effrontery of this unworthy father renewing his claim after the detection of his fraud and the actual death of the mother, and the allegation of the mother that she was a widow when in fact she was an abandoned wife, show the processes which enter into these claims for pensions and the boldness with which plans are sometimes concocted to rob the Government by actually trafficking in death and imposing upon the sacred sentiments of patriotism and national gratitude.

GROVER CLEVELAND.

To the Senate: EXECUTIVE MANSION, *February 21, 1887.*

I herewith return without approval Senate bill No. 2452, entitled "An act granting a pension to Rachel Ann Pierpont."

At the time this bill was introduced and passed an application for pension on behalf of the beneficiary named was pending in the Pension Bureau. This application was filed in December, 1879. Within the last few days, and on the 17th day of February, 1887, a pension was granted upon said application and a certificate issued at precisely the same rate which the bill herewith returned authorizes.

But the pension under the general laws dates from the time of filing the application in 1879, while under a special act it would date only from the time of its passage.

In the interest of the beneficiary and for her advantage the special bill is therefore disapproved.

GROVER CLEVELAND.

EXECUTIVE MANSION,
To the Senate: *Washington, February 21, 1887.*

I return herewith without approval Senate bill No. 2111, entitled "An act granting a pension to Jacob Smith."

The beneficiary named in this bill filed his claim for a pension November 11, 1882. He seems upon the facts presented to be justly entitled to it, and since this bill has been in my hands the Commissioner of Pensions has reported to me that a certificate therefor would at once be issued.

Under such a certificate this disabled soldier's pension will commence November 11, 1882. Under this bill, if approved, it would date only from the time of its approval. I suppose his certificate has already been issued, and I am unwilling to jeopardize the advantages he has gained thereunder, as might be done if the bill herewith returned became a law.

GROVER CLEVELAND.

To the Senate: EXECUTIVE MANSION, *February 21, 1887.*

I herewith return without approval Senate bill No. 1768, entitled "An act granting a pension to John D. Fincher."

The beneficiary named in this bill enlisted August 6, 1862, and was discharged for disability February 24, 1863.

The surgeon's certificate of disability given at the time of the soldier's discharge recites "general debility, which will disable him from performing the duties of a soldier for a good period of time. The disease was contracted by exposure and fatigue while performing the duties of a soldier."

The claimant filed his application for pension in September, 1882, nearly twenty years after his discharge, alleging that in November, 1862, he was attacked with bilious fever, followed by chronic diarrhea and lung trouble.

In support of his application an affidavit of a comrade was filed, setting forth the fact that the claimant was taken sick, as he alleged, in the fall of 1862, and that he was sent to the hospital on that account. The affidavit further expresses the belief that the claimant still suffers from the effects of his sickness and exposure.

So far as I am informed, and so far as the committee's report discloses, this is the only proof furnished of any continuance of disability at the time of filing the application for pension, and this proof, if it may be so regarded, is the mere expression of an opinion or belief, not necessarily based upon any personal knowledge, and which might have been honestly expressed if derived from representations of the claimant himself.

In this condition of the case the claimant was examined by a surgeon in 1882, whose report seems to negative all ailments except as one may be found in the fact alleged therein that he had pneumonia in 1868, and that there might be some pleuritic adhesions, plainly inferring that if such adhesions existed they were the result of the sickness to which he refers.

In February, 1885, the claimant was again examined by a board of surgeons. This examination seems to have been very carefully and thoroughly made, and as a result of the same the board reported that there was no disability. On this ground the claim was rejected.

There is no doubt as to the sickness of the claimant during his service and his disability at the time of his discharge, but unless the report of the board of surgeons is to be impeached without apparent reason there is as little doubt of the claimant's complete recovery.

No case has been presented to me in which the evidence afforded of a continuance of disability seems so inconclusive. In these circumstances the report of the board of surgeons appears to be upon the evidence before me almost uncontradicted.

GROVER CLEVELAND.

EXECUTIVE MANSION, *February 23, 1887.*

To the House of Representatives:

I herewith return without approval House bill No. 7327, entitled "An act granting a pension to Anthony McRobertson."

The beneficiary named in this bill was badly wounded in a battle which occurred about the 17th day of November, 1863.

He applied for pension in 1874, and the same was granted in November, 1886, to date from the time of his disability, November 17, 1863.

He is now receiving the highest rate allowed under the general law for cases such as his, and he would be entitled to no more under the special act.

It could not, therefore, by any possibility be of the least benefit to him, but, on the other hand, might jeopardize his advantages already gained.

GROVER CLEVELAND.

EXECUTIVE MANSION, *February 23, 1887.*

To the House of Representatives:

I herewith return without approval House bill No. 8002, entitled "An act to increase the pension of Loren Burritt."

The beneficiary named in this bill enlisted in October, 1863, and in December of that year was mustered in as major of the Eighth Regiment United States Colored Troops; was promoted to lieutenant-colonel and very badly wounded in February, 1864, and was mustered out with his regiment November 10, 1865.

His condition at the present time is most pitiable, and his helplessness is such that he needs the constant care and assistance of others. He was obliged to give up business about the year 1873.

In 1866 he was pensioned for his wound, which was in the right leg; and such pension has been increased from time to time until he is now in the receipt of $72 per month, the highest pension allowed under general laws. This rate was awarded him under a law passed in 1880, increasing from $50 to $72 per month the pensions of those who were rendered permanently and totally helpless, so that they required the regular and personal attendance of another.

On the 30th day of June, 1886, there were 1,009 persons on the rolls receiving this rate of pension.

This bill was reported upon adversely by the House Committee on Pensions, and they, while fully acknowledging the distressing circumstances surrounding the case, felt constrained to adverse action on the ground, as stated in the language of their report, that "there are many cases just as helpless and requiring as much attention as this one, and were the relief asked for granted in this instance it might reasonably be looked for in all."

No man can check, if he would, the feeling of sympathy and pity aroused by the contemplation of utter helplessness as the result of patriotic and faithful military service; but in the midst of all this I can not put out of mind the soldiers in this condition who were privates in the ranks, who sustained the utmost hardships of war, but who, because they were privates and in the humble walks of life, are not so apt to share in special favors of Congressional action. I find no reason why this beneficiary should be singled out from his class, except it be that he was a lieutenant-colonel instead of a private.

I am aware of a precedent for the legislation proposed, which is furnished by an enactment of the last session of Congress, to which I assented, as I think improvidently; but I am certain that exact equality and fairness in the treatment of our veterans is, after all, more just, beneficent, and useful than unfair discrimination in favor of officers or the special benefit born of sympathy in individual cases.

I am constrained, therefore, to agree with the House Committee on Pensions in their views of this bill.

GROVER CLEVELAND.

EXECUTIVE MANSION, *February 23, 1887.*

To the House of Representatives:

I herewith return without approval House bill No. 10082, entitled "An act to increase the pension of Margaret R. Jones."

The beneficiary mentioned in this bill is now receiving the highest rate of pension allowed in cases such as hers under the general law.

All the information which is available to me fails to furnish any reason why this pension should be specially increased, except the general statement in the claimant's petition that she is in necessitous circumstances and that the rate now allowed her is insufficient for her support.

The further statement in the petition that her husband's death "was caused prematurely by his endeavor to comply with unusual, disrespectful, and indefinite orders" to go to League Island Navy-Yard certainly does not in all its bearings furnish conclusive proof that his widow's pension should be increased beyond that furnished others in her situation.

GROVER CLEVELAND.

EXECUTIVE MANSION, *February 23, 1887.*

To the House of Representatives:

I return without approval House bill No. 5877, entitled "An act for the relief of William H. Morhiser."

This beneficiary, though apparently not regularly enlisted in the military service of the country during the time covered by this bill for his relief, performed military duty, was captured and imprisoned. No technicality should be interposed in considering this bill to prevent the receipt by him of the same pay and allowances awarded under like circumstances to soldiers regularly enlisted.

But this bill proposes to appropriate for the benefit of this claimant such sum as pay and allowances as would be allowed a private of cavalry from November 30, 1863, to January 1, 1865. It appears from the records of the War Department that he has already been paid for at least two months of that time.

The bill also provides that there shall also be allowed to the claimant such additional pay and allowances, as commutation of rations and so forth, as were allowed prisoners of war, from July 30, 1864, to January 1, 1865. The records disclose the fact that he has been allowed commutation of rations from July 30, 1864, to December 11, 1864.

As the purpose of this bill, as gathered from the report of the committee to whom it was referred, appears to be to secure for the claimant therein named compensation "at the rate at which other soldiers in the same situation were paid," and as he seems already to have received a considerable part of the compensation provided for in the bill, I am led to suppose that a mistake has been made in framing the same.

GROVER CLEVELAND.

EXECUTIVE MANSION, *February 24, 1887.*

To the House of Representatives:

I herewith return without approval House bill No. 7648, entitled "An act for the relief of the estate of the late John How, Indian agent, and his sureties."

John How was appointed Indian agent in July, 1878, and upon such appointment gave a bond to the Government in the penal sum of $10,000 conditioned for the faithful performance of his duties as such agent and to protect the Government from loss by mismanagement or malfeasance in his official conduct. The parties named in the bill were his sureties on said bond.

On the 23d day of December, 1881, upon a report of inspectors connected with the Indian Bureau suggesting frauds and mismanagement in the conduct of this agency, Mr. How was suspended from his office, which suspension was approved by the President in January, 1882.

After such suspension the accounts of the agent were examined and various explanations offered by him in relation thereto. It is stated, however, in a report from the Indian Office now before me, that such explanations were deemed by that office sufficient to remove only a small part of the items in the accounts which were questioned. The matter was thereupon referred to the Treasury Department for further examination and adjustment.

The Second Comptroller reports that the final settlement of this agent's accounts was pending before the accounting officers for upward of eighteen months, affording ample opportunity for any explanation which might be deemed necessary and proper, and that on the 21st day of July, 1885, a final adjustment was made of the said accounts, by which a sum very much in excess of the penalty of his bond was found due from said agent to the Government.

A suit was afterwards instituted against the agent and his sureties to recover the amount thus found due, so far as the bond covered the same.

This suit is still pending.

The object of the bill now under consideration is to wholly release and discharge these sureties from any liability upon said bond.

It seems to be the opinion of all the officers of the Government who have examined the matter at all that a debt exists in favor of the Government upon this bond. It is reported that a large amount of evidence has been taken, and that in the opinion of these officers the amount due the Government can not be reduced to a less amount than the penalty of the bond.

The Second Comptroller states, as results of examinations made in his office and by the Second Auditor, that it appears that many of the vouchers presented by the agent were fictitious, the persons in whose names they were given testifying that services and supplies therein mentioned were never rendered or furnished; that in other cases parties denied the genuineness of vouchers purporting to be made by them; that a large voucher apparently given for cattle was actually given for money loaned, and that supplies bought with Government funds were appropriated for the agent's personal benefit.

I do not suppose that it was intended by the Congress to entirely relieve these sureties if a condition exists such as is above set out, which results in an indebtedness to the Government. The proposed legislation, judging from the report of the House Committee on Claims, seems rather to proceed upon the theory that no sum is due the Government in the premises.

I think it will hardly be claimed that the patient investigation of the accounting officers should be lightly discredited in this case; and it seems to me that justness to the Government and fairness to the sureties seeking relief will presumably be secured by the further prosecution of the suit already instituted, in which the truth of all matters involved can be thoroughly tested.

GROVER CLEVELAND.

To the Senate: EXECUTIVE MANSION, *February 25, 1887.*

I herewith return without approval Senate bill No. 1162, entitled "An act for the erection of a post-office building at Lynn, Mass."

The title of this bill sufficiently indicates its purpose.

Congressional action in its favor appears to be based, as usual in such cases, upon representations concerning the population of the town in which it is proposed to erect the building, and the increase in such population, the number of railroad trains arriving and departing daily, and various other items calculated to demonstrate the importance of the city selected for Federal decoration.

These statements are supplemented by a report from the postmaster, setting forth that his postal receipts are increasing, giving the number of square feet now occupied by his office, the amount of rent paid, and the number of his employees.

This bill, unlike others of its class which seek to provide a place for a number of Federal offices, simply authorizes the construction of a building for the accommodation of the post-office alone.

The report of the postmaster differs also in this case from those which are usually furnished, inasmuch as it is therein distinctly stated that the space now furnished for his office is sufficient for its present operations. He adds, however, that from present indications there will be a large increase in the business of the office during the next ten years.

It is quite apparent that there is no necessity for the expenditure of $100,000, the amount limited in this bill, or any other sum, for the construction of the proposed building to meet the wants of the Government, and for this reason I am constrained to disapprove the proposed legislation.

GROVER CLEVELAND.

To the Senate: EXECUTIVE MANSION, *February 26, 1887.*

I herewith return without approval Senate bill No. 2045, entitled "An act granting a pension to Mrs. Sarah Hamilton."

Thomas Hamilton, the husband of the beneficiary named in this bill, enlisted September 2, 1862. Upon the records he is reported present to April 30, 1863; deserted May 27, 1863. His name is dropped from subsequent rolls to February 29, 1864, when he is reported as a deserter in arrest. He is not borne upon the rolls for March and April, 1864; for May and June, 1864, he is reported absent in arrest; for July and August, present under arrest; and for September and October, present for duty. He was mustered out with his company May 24, 1865.

He applied for a pension in 1872, alleging that he received an injury to his left leg about February 15, 1863, at St. Louis, by falling from a ladder, causing varicose veins and stiffening of the leg.

He was granted a pension January 29, 1881, to commence May 25, 1865.

He subsequently applied for an increase of pension, claiming that his eyes had become affected as a result of his varicose veins. This application was rejected upon the ground that the disability for which he was pensioned had not increased and that the disease of his eyes was not a result of such disability.

The pensioner died April 22, 1883, twenty years after his alleged injury, of cerebral apoplexy; and a physician states it as his judgment that the varicosed condition of the venous system was primarily the cause of his disabilities and death.

widow filed an application for pension October 31, 1883, which was rejected upon the ground that the soldier's death was not the result of his military service.

Notwithstanding the record of the deceased soldier, stained as it is with the charge of desertion, and the entire absence of any record proof of sickness and injury, I should consider myself, in favor of his widow, bound by the act of the Pension Bureau in allowing him a pension, and should cheerfully aid her attempt to procure a pension for herself in her needy condition, if I was not thoroughly convinced that her husband's death had no relation to his military service or any injury for which he was pensioned.

To the ordinary mind it seems impossible that apoplexy could result from such a varicosed condition as is described in this case. I do not understand that the physician who gives a contrary opinion bases his judgment upon actual observation at the time the soldier died. The last medical examination by the Pension Bureau before the soldier's death was in October, 1882, and resulted in the following report of the examining surgeon:

Weight, 180 pounds; age, 69 years; has varicose veins of left leg, but not to such an extent as to increase the size of the leg or result in marked disability; he is entirely blind in both eyes from glaucoma, which does not in any degree, in my opinion, depend upon the pensioned disability—varicose veins.

It appears that the benefit proposed by this bill can neither be properly regarded as a gratuity, based upon the honorable service and record of the soldier, nor predicated on his death resulting from a disability incurred in such service.

GROVER CLEVELAND.

To the Senate: EXECUTIVE MANSION, *February 26, 1887.*

I herewith return without approval Senate bill No. 2210, entitled "An act granting a pension to Anna Wright."

The beneficiary named in this bill was granted a pension on the 17th day of November, 1886, dating from May 25, 1863, and is now under the general law receiving precisely the pension which she would receive under the bill herewith returned if the same should be approved.

GROVER CLEVELAND.

EXECUTIVE MANSION,
Washington, February 26, 1887.

To the House of Representatives:

I herewith return without approval House bill No. 6976, entitled "An act to erect a public building at Portsmouth, Ohio."

It is represented in support of this bill that Portsmouth by its last census had a population of 11,321, and that it contains at present not less than 15,000 inhabitants; that it is a place of considerable manufacturing and commercial importance, and that there is no public building for the transaction of the business of the General Government nearer than Columbus or Cincinnati, both about 100 miles distant.

It is further stated in a communication from the promoter of this bill that—

> There is not a Federal public building in the State of Ohio east of the line drawn on the accompanying map from Cleveland through Columbus to Cincinnati; and when wealth and population and the needs of the public service are considered, the distribution of public buildings in the State is an unfair one.

Here is disclosed a theory of expenditure for public buildings which I can hardly think should be adopted. If an application for the erection of such a building is to be determined by the distance between its proposed location and another public building, or upon the allegation that a certain division of a State is without a Government building, or that the distribution of these buildings in a particular State is unfair, we shall rapidly be led to an entire disregard of the considerations of necessity and public need which it seems to me should alone justify the expenditure of public funds for such a purpose.

The care and protection which the Government owes to the people do not embrace the grant of public buildings to decorate thriving and prosperous cities and villages, nor should such buildings be erected upon any principle of fair distribution among localities.

The Government is not an almoner of gifts among the people, but an instrumentality by which the people's affairs should be conducted upon business principles, regulated by the public needs.

Applying these principles to the case embraced in the bill under consideration, we find that at Portsmouth there is a post-office and an internal-revenue collector's office for which the Government should provide.

It is represented that the quarters now furnished for these offices are inadequate and that more spacious rooms are desirable. In the post-office there are six employees, and the collector of internal revenue has five assistants. The annual rent paid for both these offices is $600.

Upon these facts the proposition is to expend $60,000 for a building to accommodate these offices, entailing after its completion quite a large sum annually for its care and superintendence.

Though the sum of $60,000 is the limit fixed for the cost of this building, if it should be completed for this sum it would be an exception to the rule in such cases; and if it is absolutely impossible to do the public business in the quarters now occupied by these offices, which does not appear to be claimed, there can be no difficulty in securing in this enterprising city adequate accommodations at a rent not largely in excess of that at present paid.

Upon the whole it does not appear, as a business proposition, that the building proposed should be undertaken.

GROVER CLEVELAND.

EXECUTIVE MANSION,
Washington, February 28, 1887.

To the Senate:

I herewith return without approval Senate bill No. 531, entitled "An act to provide for the erection of a public building at Lafayette, Ind."

This bill appropriates $50,000 for the purpose indicated in its title.

It is represented that a deputy internal-revenue collector is located at Lafayette, but no information is furnished that he has an office there which is or ought to be furnished by the Government. It is not claimed that the Federal business at this point requires other accommodation except for the post-office located there.

As usual in such cases, the postmaster reports, in reply to inquiries, that his present quarters are inadequate, and, as usual, it appears that the postal business is increasing. The rent paid for the rooms or building in which the post-office is kept is $1,100 per annum.

I have been informed since this bill has been in my hands that last spring a building was erected at Lafayette with special reference to its use for the post-office, and that a part of it was leased by the Government for that purpose for the term of five years. Upon the faith of such lease the premises thus rented were fitted up and furnished by the owner of the building in a manner especially adapted to postal uses, and an account of such fitting up and furnishing is before me, showing the expense of the same to have been more than $2,500.

In view of such new and recent arrangements made by the Government for the transaction of its postal business at this place, it seems that the proposed expenditure for the erection of a building for that purpose is hardly necessary or justifiable.

GROVER CLEVELAND.

PROCLAMATIONS.

BY THE PRESIDENT OF THE UNITED STATES OF AMERICA.

A PROCLAMATION.

Whereas satisfactory proof has been given to me by the Government of the Netherlands that no light-house and light dues, tonnage dues, or beacon and buoy dues are imposed in the ports of the Kingdom of the Netherlands; that no other equivalent tax of any kind is imposed upon vessels in said ports, under whatever flag they may sail; that vessels belonging to the United States of America and their cargoes are not required in the Netherlands to pay any fee or due of any kind or nature, or any import due higher or other than is payable by vessels of the Netherlands or their cargoes; that no export duties are imposed in the Netherlands; and that in the free ports of the Dutch East Indies, to wit, Riouw (in the island of Riouw), Pabeau, Saugrit, Loloan, and

Tamboekoes (in the island of Bali), Koepang (in the island of Timor), Makassar, Menado, Kema, and Gorontalo (in the island of Celebes), Amboina, Saparoa, Banda, Ternate, and Kajeli (in the Moluccas), Olehleh and Bengkalis (in the island of Sumatra), vessels are subjected to no fiscal tax, and no import or export duties are there levied:

Now, therefore, I, Grover Cleveland, President of the United States of America, by virtue of the authority vested in me by section 11 of the act of Congress entitled "An act to abolish certain fees for official services to American vessels, and to amend the laws relating to shipping commissioners, seamen, and owners of vessels, and for other purposes," approved June 19, 1886, do hereby declare and proclaim that from and after the date of this my proclamation shall be suspended the collection of the whole of the duty of 6 cents per ton, not to exceed 30 cents per ton per annum (which is imposed by said section of said act), upon vessels entered in the ports of the United States from any of the ports of the Kingdom of the Netherlands in Europe, or from any of the above-named free ports of the Dutch East Indies.

Provided, That there shall be excluded from the benefits of the suspension hereby declared and proclaimed the vessels of any foreign country in whose ports the fees or dues of any kind or nature imposed on vessels of the United States, or the import or export duties on their cargoes, are in excess of the fees, dues, or duties imposed on the vessels of such foreign country or their cargoes, or of the fees, dues, or duties imposed on the vessels of the country in which are the ports mentioned in this proclamation, or the cargoes of such vessels.

And the suspension hereby declared and proclaimed shall continue so long as the reciprocal exemption of vessels belonging to citizens of the United States and their cargoes shall be continued in the said ports of the Kingdom of the Netherlands in Europe and the said free ports of the Dutch East Indies, and no longer.

In witness whereof I have hereunto set my hand and caused the seal of the United States to be affixed.

[SEAL.]   Done at the city of Washington, this 22d day of April, A. D. 1887, and of the Independence of the United States the one hundred and eleventh.   GROVER CLEVELAND.

By the President:
T. F. BAYARD, *Secretary of State.*

BY THE PRESIDENT OF THE UNITED STATES OF AMERICA.

A PROCLAMATION.

Whereas satisfactory proof has been given to me by the Government of Spain that no discriminating duties of tonnage or imposts are imposed or levied in the islands of Cuba, Puerto Rico, and the Philippines, and all ~ies belonging to the Crown of Spain, upon vessels wholly belonging to citizens of the United States, or upon the produce, manufactures, or merchandise imported in the same from the United States or from any foreign country; and

Whereas notification of such abolition of discriminating duties of tonnage and imposts as aforesaid has been given to me by a memorandum of agreement signed this day at the city of Washington between the Secretary of State of the United States and the envoy extraordinary and minister plenipotentiary of Her Majesty the Queen Regent of Spain accredited to the Government of the United States of America:

Now, therefore, I, Grover Cleveland, President of the United States of America, by virtue of the authority vested in me by section 4228 of the Revised Statutes of the United States, do hereby declare and proclaim that from and after the date of this my proclamation, being also the date of the notification received as aforesaid, the foreign discriminating duties of tonnage and imposts within the United States are suspended and discontinued so far as respects the vessels of Spain and the produce, manufactures, or merchandise imported in said vessels into the United States from the islands of Cuba and Puerto Rico, the Philippines, and all other countries belonging to the Crown of Spain, or from any other foreign country; such suspension to continue so long as the reciprocal exemption of vessels belonging to citizens of the United States and their cargoes shall be continued in the said islands of Cuba and Puerto Rico, and the Philippines, and all other Spanish possessions, and no longer.

In witness whereof I have hereunto set my hand and caused the seal of the United States to be affixed.

[SEAL.]   Done at the city of Washington this 21st day of September, A. D. 1887, and of the Independence of the United States the one hundred and twelfth.

GROVER CLEVELAND.

By the President:

T. F. BAYARD, *Secretary of State.*

A PROCLAMATION

BY THE PRESIDENT OF THE UNITED STATES.

The goodness and the mercy of God, which have followed the American people during all the days of the past year, claim their grateful recognition and humble acknowledgment. By His omnipotent power He has protected us from war and pestilence and from every national calamity; by His gracious favor the earth has yielded a generous return to the labor of the husbandman, and every path of honest toil has led to comfort and contentment; by His loving kindness the hearts of our people have been replenished with fraternal sentiment and patriotic endeavor, and by His unerring guidance we have been directed in the way of national prosperity.

To the end that we may with one accord testify our gratitude for all these blessings, I, Grover Cleveland, President of the United States, do hereby designate and set apart Thursday, the 24th day of November next, as a day of thanksgiving and prayer, to be observed by all the people of the land.

On that day let all secular work and employment be suspended, and let our people assemble in their accustomed places of worship and with prayer and songs of praise give thanks to our Heavenly Father for all that He has done for us, while we humbly implore the forgiveness of our sins and a continuance of His mercy.

Let families and kindred be reunited on that day, and let their hearts, filled with kindly cheer and affectionate reminiscence, be turned in thankfulness to the source of all their pleasures and the giver of all that makes the day glad and joyous.

And in the midst of our worship and our happiness let us remember the poor, the needy, and the unfortunate, and by our gifts of charity and ready benevolence let us increase the number of those who with grateful hearts shall join in our thanksgiving.

In witness whereof I have set my hand and caused the seal of the United States to be hereunto affixed.

[SEAL.]   Done at the city of Washington, this 25th day of October, A. D. 1887, and of the Independence of the United States the one hundred and twelfth.

By the President: GROVER CLEVELAND.

T. F. BAYARD, *Secretary of State.*

EXECUTIVE ORDERS.

JANUARY 4, 1887.

In the exercise of the power vested in the President by the Constitution, and by virtue of the seventeen hundred and fifty-third section of the Revised Statutes and of the civil-service act approved January 16, 1883, the following regulations governing promotions in the customs service at the city of New York are hereby approved and promulgated:

REGULATION I.

The board of examiners at the New York customs district may at any time, with the approval of the Civil Service Commission, order an examination for promotion, and at least five days before the examination is to take place shall cause a notice to be posted conspicuously in the office for which such examination is to be held, and shall state in said notice the class or classes to test fitness for promotion to which the examination is to be held and the time and place of examination. Promotions shall be from class to class, and the examination of persons in one class shall be to test their fitness for promotion to the next higher class: *Provided, however,* That if in any examination for promotion the competitors in the next lower class shall not exceed three in number, the board may, at its discretion, open the competition to one or more of the classes below the class in which there are not more than three competitors. All persons in the class immediately below the class for which promotions are to be made, and who have been in said class at least six months, must be examined for promotion.

REGULATION 2.

The examination must be held upon such subjects as in the opinion of the board of examiners, with the approval of the Commission, the general nature of the business of the office and the special nature of the positions to be filled may require. In grading the competitors due weight must be given to the efficiency with which the several competitors shall have performed their duties in the office; but none who shall fail to attain a minimum standard of 75 per cent in the written examination shall be certified for promotion.

REGULATION 3.

The whole list of eligibles from which the promotion is to be made shall be certified to the nominating officer.

REGULATION 4.

Any person employed in any of the offices to which these regulations apply may be transferred without examination, after service of six months consecutively since January 16, 1883, from one office to a class no higher in another office, upon certification by the board of examiners that he has passed an examination for the class in which he is doing duty, and with the consent of the heads of the respective offices and the approval of the Secretary of the Treasury.

REGULATION 5.

The Civil Service Commission may at any time amend these regulations or substitute other regulations therefor.

The foregoing regulations are adopted and approved.

GROVER CLEVELAND.

In the exercise of the power vested in the President by the Constitution, and by virtue of the seventeen hundred and fifty-third section of the Revised Statutes and of the civil-service act approved January 16, 1883, the following rule for the regulation and improvement of the executive civil service is hereby amended and promulgated, as follows:

RULE IV.

1. The Civil Service Commission shall have authority to appoint the following-named boards of civil-service examiners:

The central board.—This board shall be composed of seven members, who shall be detailed from the Departments in which they may be serving at the time of appointment for continuous service at the office of the Civil Service Commission. Under the supervision of the Commission, the central board shall examine and mark the papers of all examinations for entrance to the departmental service, and also such of the papers of examinations for entrance to either the customs or the postal service as shall be submitted to it by the Commission. The Commission shall have authority to require any customs or postal board to send the papers of any examination conducted by said board to be examined and marked by the central board. The persons composing this board shall be in the departmental service.

Special boards.—These boards shall mark the papers of special examinations for the classified departmental service, and shall be composed of persons in the public service.

Supplementary boards.—These boards shall mark the papers of supplementary examinations for the classified departmental service, and shall be composed of persons in the public service.

Local departmental boards.—These boards shall be organized at one or more places in each State and Territory where examinations for the departmental service are to be held, and shall each be composed of persons in the public service residing in the State or Territory in which the board is to act.

Customs boards.—One for each classified customs district, to be composed of persons in the customs service in the district for which the board is to act. These boards shall conduct examinations for entrance to and promotion in the classified customs service.

Postal boards.—One for each classified post-office, to be composed of persons in the postal service at the post-office for which said board is to act. These boards shall conduct examinations for entrance to and promotions in the postal service.

2. No person shall be appointed a member of any board of examiners named herein until after consultation by the Civil Service Commission with the head of the Department or office in which the person whom it desires to appoint is serving.

3. It shall be the duty of the head of any classified customs office or classified post-office to promptly inform the Civil Service Commission, in writing, of the removal or resignation from the public service, or of the death, of any member of a board of examiners appointed from his office; and upon request of the Commission such officer shall state to the Commission which of the persons employed in his office he regards as most competent to fill the vacancy thus occasioned, or any vacancy which may otherwise occur; and in making this statement the officer shall mention generally the qualifications of each of the persons named therein by him.

4. The duties of a member of a special, supplementary, local, departmental, customs, or postal board of examiners shall be regarded as a part of the public duties of such examiner, and each examiner shall be allowed time during office hours to perform the duties required of him.

5. The Civil Service Commission shall have authority to adopt regulations which shall (1) prescribe the manner of organizing the several boards of civil-service examiners herein named, (2) more particularly state the powers of each of said boards, and (3) specifically define the duties of the members thereof.

6. The Civil Service Commission shall have authority to change at any time the membership of any of the above-named boards of civil-service examiners.

Approved, January 15, 1887.　　　　　GROVER CLEVELAND.

REGULATIONS FOR THE DISTRIBUTION OF ARMS, ORDNANCE STORES, QUARTERMASTER'S STORES, AND CAMP EQUIPAGE TO THE TERRITORIES AND THE DISTRICT OF COLUMBIA, PRESCRIBED BY THE PRESIDENT OF THE UNITED STATES IN CONFORMITY WITH THE SECOND SECTION OF THE ACT ENTITLED "AN ACT TO AMEND SECTION 1661, REVISED STATUTES, MAKING AN ANNUAL APPROPRIATION TO PROVIDE ARMS AND EQUIPMENTS FOR THE MILITIA."

EXECUTIVE MANSION, *April 22, 1887.*

1. Each Territory shall, if included within the provisions of said act, annually receive arms, ordnance stores, quartermaster's stores, and camp equipage equivalent to the quota of a State having the least representation in Congress, and the District of Columbia shall annually receive

arms, ordnance stores, quartermaster's stores, and camp equipage not exceeding double the quota of a State having the least representation in Congress.

2. Arms, ordnance stores, quartermaster's stores, and camp equipage shall be issued to the Territories on requisitions of the governors thereof and to the District of Columbia on requisitions approved by the senior general of the District Militia present for duty. Returns shall be made annually by the senior general of the District Militia in the manner as required by sections 3 and 4 of the act above referred to in the case of States and Territories.

3. It is forbidden to make issues to States and Territories in excess of the amount to their credit under the provisions of section 1161, Revised Statutes, as amended by the above act.

4. The regulations established by President Pierce April 30, 1855, under the act approved March 30, 1855, are hereby revoked.

GROVER CLEVELAND.

In the exercise of the power vested in the President by the Constitution, and by virtue of the seventeen hundred and fifty-third section of the Revised Statutes and of the civil-service act approved January 16, 1883, Rules IV, VI, XIX, XXI of the rules for the regulation and improvement of the executive civil service are hereby amended and promulgated as follows:

RULE IV.

1. The Commission may appoint boards of examiners as follows:

The central board.—A board composed of seven members, who shall be detailed from the Departments in which they are serving when appointed for continuous service at the office of the Commission. This board shall mark such papers of examinations for admission to the departmental, customs, and postal services as the Commission may direct.

Departmental special boards.—These boards shall mark such papers of special examinations for the departmental service as the Commission may direct, and shall be composed of persons in the public service.

Departmental supplementary boards.—These boards shall mark the papers of such supplementary examinations for the departmental service as the Commission may direct, and shall be composed of persons in the public service.

Departmental promotion boards.—One for each of the Executive Departments, of three members, and one auxiliary member for each bureau of the Department for which the board is to act.

Departmental local boards.—These boards shall be organized at one or more places in each State and Territory where examinations for the departmental service are to be held, and shall each be composed of persons in the public service residing in the State or Territory in which the board is to act.

Customs boards.—One for each classified customs district, to be composed of persons in the customs service in the district for which said board is to act. These boards shall conduct examinations for entrance to and promotions in the classified customs service, and shall mark such of the examination papers for that service as the Commission shall direct. They shall also conduct such departmental examinations as the Commission may direct.

Postal boards.—One for each classified post-office, to be composed of persons in the postal service at the post-office in which said board is to act. These boards shall conduct examinations for entrance to and promotions in the postal service, and shall mark such of the examination papers for that service as the Commission may direct. They shall also conduct such departmental examinations as the Commission may direct.

2. No person shall be appointed an examiner until after consultation by the Commission with the head of the Department or office in which the person whom it desires to appoint is serving.

3. It shall be the duty of the head of any classified customs office or post-office to promptly give written information to the Commission of the removal or resignation from the public service, or of the inability or refusal to act, of any examiner in his office; and on request of the Commission such officer shall state which of the persons in his office he regards as most competent to fill the vacancy, and shall mention generally the qualifications of each person named by him.

4. The duties of an examiner shall be regarded as a part of his public duties, and each examiner shall be allowed time during office hours to perform the duties required of him.

5. The Commission may adopt regulations which shall prescribe (1) the manner of organizing the boards of examiners, (2) the powers of each board, and (3) the duties of the members thereof.

6. The Commission may create additional boards of examiners and may change the membership of any board; and boards of examiners shall perform such other appropriate duties as the Commission may impose upon them.

RULE VI.

1. There shall be open competitive examinations for testing the fitness of applicants for admission to the service. Such examinations shall be practical in their character, and so far as may be shall relate to those matters which will fairly test the relative capacity and fitness of the persons examined to discharge the duties of the branch of the service which they seek to enter.

2. And for the purpose of establishing in the classified service the principle of compulsory competitive examination for promotion there shall be, so far as practicable and useful, such examinations of a suitable character to test the fitness of persons for promotion in the service, and the Commission may make regulations applying them to any classified Department, customs office, or post-office, under which regulations examinations for promotion shall be conducted and all promotions made; but until regulations made by the Commission in accordance herewith have been applied to a classified Department, customs office, or post-office, promotions therein may be made upon any test of fitness determined upon by the promoting officer. And in any classified Department, customs office, or post-office in which promotions are made under examinations as herein provided the Commission may, in special session, if the exigencies of the service require such action, provide noncompetitive examinations for promotion.

RULE XIX.

There are excepted from examination the following: (1) The confidential clerk or secretary of any head of a Department or office; (2) cashiers of collectors; (3) cashiers of postmasters; (4) superintendents of money-order divisions in post-offices; (5) the direct custodians of money for whose fidelity another officer is under official bond, and disbursing officers having the custody of money, who give bonds; but these exceptions shall not extend to any official below the grade of assistant cashier or teller; (6) persons employed exclusively in the secret service of the Government, or as translators or interpreters or stenographers; (7) persons whose employment is exclusively professional, but medical examiners are not included among such persons; (8) chief clerks, deputy collectors, deputy naval officers, deputy surveyors of customs, and superintendents or chiefs of divisions or bureaus. But no person so excepted shall be either transferred, appointed, or promoted, unless to some excepted place, without an examination under the Commission, which examination shall not take place within six months after entering the service.

RULE XXI.

1. No person, unless excepted under Rule XIX, shall be admitted into the classified civil service from any place not within said service without an examination and certification under the rules, with this exception, that any person who shall have been an officer for one year or more last preceding in any Department or office in a grade above the classified service thereof may be transferred or appointed to any place in the service of the same without examination.

2. No person who has passed only a limited examination under clause 4 of Rule VII for the lower classes or grades in the departmental or customs service shall be appointed or be promoted within two years after appointment to any position giving a salary of $1,000 or upward without first passing an examination under clause 1 of said rule; and such examination shall not be allowed within the first year after appointment.

3. But a person who has passed the examination under said clause 1 and has accepted a position giving a salary of $900 or less shall have the same right of promotion as if originally appointed to a position giving a salary of $1,000 or more.

4. The Commission may at any time certify for a $900 or any lower place in the classified service any person upon the register who has passed the examination under clause 1 of Rule VII, if such person does not object before such certification is made.

5. The provisions of this rule relating to promotions shall cease to be operative in any classified Department, customs office, or post-office when regulations for promotions have been applied thereto by the Commission under the authority conferred by clause 2 of Rule VI.

Approved, May 5, 1887.

GROVER CLEVELAND.

EXECUTIVE MANSION,
Washington, May 9, 1887.

The executive offices and Departments at the seat of Government, including the public printing establishment, will be closed at noon on Thursday, the 12th instant, to enable persons employed therein to attend the exercises at the unveiling of the statue of the late President Garfield.

And employees in such offices and Departments who desire to accompany any organization to which they belong in the parade or other exercises preceding on that day the unveiling ceremonies may, by permission of the heads of their respective offices or Departments, also be granted such leave of absence as may be necessary for that purpose.

Members of the Society of the Army of the Cumberland desiring to attend any meeting of such society on Wednesday, the 11th instant, may, by special permission of the respective heads of Departments and offices, be excused from duty during the hours on that day as said meetings may be held.

GROVER CLEVELAND.

WAR DEPARTMENT, ADJUTANT-GENERAL'S OFFICE,
Washington, April 30, 1887.

Hon. WILLIAM C. ENDICOTT,
    Secretary of War.

SIR: I have the honor to state that there are now in this office, stored in one of the attic rooms of the building, a number of Union flags captured in action, but recovered on the fall of the Confederacy and forwarded to the War Department for safe-keeping, together with a number of Confederate flags which the fortunes of war placed in our hands during the late Civil War.

While in the past favorable action has been taken on applications properly supported for the return of Union flags to organizations representing survivors of the military regiments in the service of the Government, I beg to submit that it would be a graceful act to anticipate future requests of this nature, and venture to suggest the propriety of returning all the flags (Union and Confederate) to the authorities of the respective States in which the regiments which bore these colors were organized, for such final disposition as they may determine.

While in all the civilized nations of the world trophies taken in war against foreign enemies have been carefully preserved and exhibited as proud mementos of the nation's military glories, wise and obvious reasons have always excepted from the rule evidences of past internecine troubles which by appeals to the arbitrament of the sword have disturbed the peaceful march of a people to its destiny.

Over twenty years have elapsed since the termination of the late Civil War. Many of the prominent leaders, civil and military, of the late Confederate States are now honored representatives of the people in the national councils, or in other eminent positions lend the aid of their talents to the wise administration of affairs of the whole country; and the people of the several States composing the Union are now united, treading the broader road to a glorious future.

Impressed with these views, I have the honor to submit the suggestion made in this letter for the careful consideration it will receive at your hands.

    Very truly, yours,

R. C. DRUM,
Adjutant-General.

[Indorsement.]

WAR DEPARTMENT, *May 26, 1887.*

The within recommendation approved by the President, and the Adjutant-General will prepare letters to governors of those States whose troops carried the colors and flags now in this Department, with the offer to return them as herein proposed. The history of each flag and the circumstances of its capture or recapture should be given.

WILLIAM C. ENDICOTT,
Secretary of War.

WAR DEPARTMENT, ADJUTANT-GENERAL'S OFFICE,
Washington, June 7, 1887.

Honorable GOVERNOR OF ———.

SIR: The President of the United States having approved the recommendation that all the flags in the custody of the War Department be returned to the authorities of the respective States in which the regiments which bore them were organized, for such final disposition as they may determine, I am instructed by the honorable Secretary of War to make you, in the name of the War Department, a tender of the flags now in this office belonging to the late volunteer organizations of the State of ———.

In discharging this pleasant duty I beg you will please advise me of your wishes in this matter. It is the intention in returning each flag to give its history as far as it is possible to do so, stating the circumstances of its capture and recovery.

I have the honor to be, very respectfully, your obedient servant,

R. C. DRUM, *Adjutant-General.*

The Secretary of War:

EXECUTIVE MANSION,
Washington, June 16, 1887.

I have to-day considered with more care than when the subject was orally presented me the action of your Department directing letters to be addressed to the governors of all the States offering to return, if desired, to the loyal States the Union flags captured in the War of the Rebellion by the Confederate forces and afterwards recovered by Government troops, and to the Confederate States the flags captured by the Union forces, all of which for many years have been packed in boxes and stored in the cellar and attic of the War Department.

I am of the opinion that the return of these flags in the manner thus contemplated is not authorized by existing law nor justified as an executive act.

I request, therefore, that no further steps be taken in the matter except to examine and inventory these flags and adopt proper measures for their preservation. Any direction as to the final disposition of them should originate with Congress.

Yours, truly,

GROVER CLEVELAND.

WAR DEPARTMENT, ADJUTANT-GENERAL'S OFFICE,
Hon. ——— ———,   *Washington, June —, 1887.*
     Governor of ———.

SIR: Referring to the letter from this office dated June —, 1887, on the subject of the return to the respective States of the flags now in the custody of the War Department, I am instructed by the Secretary of War to inform you of the withdrawal of the offer made therein, as on a more careful consideration of the legal points involved in the proposed action the President of the United States is of the opinion that the return of these flags is not authorized by existing law nor justified as an executive act, and that any direction as to their final disposition should originate with Congress.

I have the honor to be, very respectfully, your obedient servant,

——— ———, *Adjutant-General.*

EXECUTIVE MANSION,
Washington, August 25, 1887.

It appearing to me that the promoters of the International Military Encampment to be held in Chicago in October proximo, in commemoration of the fiftieth anniversary of the settlement of that city, have extended to the militia organizations of foreign countries, in behalf of the citizen soldiers of the State of Illinois, an invitation to take part in said encampment as the guests of the city of Chicago, and that representatives of the soldiery of certain foreign countries have accepted such invitation and are about to arrive in the United States:

I hereby direct the Secretary of the Treasury to instruct the collectors of customs at the several ports of entry that upon being satisfied that such visitors come as guests, in pursuance of the aforesaid invitation, they shall permit the entrance of such foreign soldiers into the United States, with their personal baggage, uniforms, arms, and equipments, without payment of customs duties thereon, and without other formality than such as may be necessary to insure the reexportation of said uniforms, baggage, arms, and equipments.

GROVER CLEVELAND.

DEPARTMENT OF STATE,
Washington, October 24, 1887.

By direction of the President the undersigned is charged with the sad duty of announcing the death, on the 22d instant, at 4 o'clock p. m., at his residence, Chicago, Ill., of Elihu B. Washburne, an illustrious citizen, formerly Secretary of State of the United States.

Mr. Washburne rendered great service to the people of the United States in many and important capacities. As a Representative from the State of Illinois in the National Legislature, and subsequently as envoy extraordinary and minister plenipotentiary of the United States to France, his career was marked by eminent usefulness, in which abilities of a high order were applied with unsparing devotion and fidelity in the performance of the trusts of public power.

His private life was unstained, his public service unquestionably great, and his memory will be cherished with affection and respect by his grateful countrymen.

On the day of his funeral this Department will be closed for all public business, and be draped in mourning for ten days thereafter.

The diplomatic and consular officers of the United States in foreign countries will be directed to make proper expression of the public sorrow experienced by the death of Mr. Washburne.

T. F. BAYARD, *Secretary of State.*

THIRD ANNUAL MESSAGE.

WASHINGTON, *December 6, 1887.*

To the Congress of the United States:

You are confronted at the threshold of your legislative duties with a condition of the national finances which imperatively demands immediate and careful consideration.

The amount of money annually exacted, through the operation of present laws, from the industries and necessities of the people largely exceeds the sum necessary to meet the expenses of the Government.

When we consider that the theory of our institutions guarantees to every citizen the full enjoyment of all the fruits of his industry and enterprise, with only such deduction as may be his share toward the careful and economical maintenance of the Government which protects him, it is plain that the exaction of more than this is indefensible extortion and a culpable betrayal of American fairness and justice. This wrong inflicted upon those who bear the burden of national taxation, like other wrongs, multiplies a brood of evil consequences. The public Treasury, which should only exist as a conduit conveying the people's tribute to its legitimate objects of expenditure, becomes a hoarding place for money needlessly withdrawn from trade and the people's use, thus crippling our national energies, suspending our country's development, preventing investment in productive enterprise, threatening financial disturbance, and inviting schemes of public plunder.

This condition of our Treasury is not altogether new, and it has more than once of late been submitted to the people's representatives in the Congress, who alone can apply a remedy. And yet the situation still continues, with aggravated incidents, more than ever presaging financial convulsion and widespread disaster.

It will not do to neglect this situation because its dangers are not now palpably imminent and apparent. They exist none the less certainly, and await the unforeseen and unexpected occasion when suddenly they will be precipitated upon us.

On the 30th day of June, 1885, the excess of revenues over public expenditures, after complying with the annual requirement of the sinking-fund act, was $17,859,735.84; during the year ended June 30, 1886, such excess amounted to $49,405,545.20, and during the year ended June 30, 1887, it reached the sum of $55,567,849.54.

The annual contributions to the sinking fund during the three years above specified, amounting in the aggregate to $138,058,320.94, and deducted from the surplus as stated, were made by calling in for that purpose outstanding 3 per cent bonds of the Government. During the six months prior to June 30, 1887, the surplus revenue had grown so large by repeated accumulations, and it was feared the withdrawal of this great sum of money needed by the people would so affect the business of the country, that the sum of $79,864,100 of such surplus was applied to the payment of the principal and interest of the 3 per cent bonds still outstanding, and which were then payable at the option of the Government. The precarious condition of financial affairs among the people still needing relief, immediately after the 30th day of June, 1887, the remainder of the 3 per cent bonds then outstanding, amounting with principal and interest to the sum of $18,877,500, were called in and applied to the sinking-fund contribution for the current fiscal year. Notwithstanding the operations of the Treasury Department, representations of distress in business circles not only continued, but increased, and absolute peril seemed at hand. In these circumstances the contribution to the sinking fund for the current fiscal year was at once completed by the expenditure of $27,684,283.55 in the purchase of Government bonds not yet due bearing 4 and 4½ per cent interest, the premium paid thereon averaging about 24 per cent for the former and 8 per cent for the latter. In addition to this, the interest accruing during the current year upon the outstanding bonded indebtedness of the Government was to some extent anticipated, and banks selected as depositories of public money were permitted to somewhat increase their deposits.

While the expedients thus employed to release to the people the money lying idle in the Treasury served to avert immediate danger, our surplus revenues have continued to accumulate, the excess for the present year amounting on the 1st day of December to $55,258,701.19, and estimated to reach the sum of $113,000,000 on the 30th of June next, at which date it is expected that this sum, added to prior accumulations, will swell the surplus in the Treasury to $140,000,000.

There seems to be no assurance that, with such a withdrawal from use of the people's circulating medium, our business community may not in the near future be subjected to the same distress which was quite lately produced from the same cause. And while the functions of our National Treasury should be few and simple, and while its best condition would be reached, I believe, by its entire disconnection with private business interests, yet when, by a perversion of its purposes, it idly holds money uselessly subtracted from the channels of trade, there seems to be reason for the claim that some legitimate means should be devised by the Government to restore in an emergency, without waste or extravagance, such money to its place among the people.

If such an emergency arises, there now exists no clear and undoubted executive power of relief. Heretofore the redemption of 3 per cent bonds, which were payable at the option of the Government, has afforded a means for the disbursement of the excess of our revenues; but these bonds have all been retired, and there are no bonds outstanding the payment of which we have a right to insist upon. The contribution to the sinking fund which furnishes the occasion for expenditure in the purchase of bonds has been already made for the current year, so that there is no outlet in that direction.

In the present state of legislation the only pretense of any existing executive power to restore at this time any part of our surplus revenues to the people by its expenditure consists in the supposition that the Secretary of the Treasury may enter the market and purchase the bonds of the Government not yet due, at a rate of premium to be agreed upon. The only provision of law from which such a power could be derived *is* found in an appropriation bill passed a number of years ago, and it is subject to the suspicion that it was intended as temporary and limited in its application, instead of conferring a continuing discretion and authority. No condition ought to exist which would justify the grant of power to a single official, upon his judgment of its necessity, to withhold from or release to the business of the people, in an unusual manner, money held in the Treasury, and thus affect at his will the financial situation of the country; and if it is deemed wise to lodge in the Secretary of the Treasury the authority in the present juncture to purchase bonds, it should be plainly vested, and provided, as far as possible, with such checks and limitations as will define this official's right and discretion and at the same time relieve him from undue responsibility.

In considering the question of purchasing bonds as a means of restoring to circulation the surplus money accumulating in the Treasury, it should be borne in mind that premiums must of course be paid upon such purchase, that there may be a large part of these bonds held as investments which can not be purchased at any price, and that combinations among holders who are willing to sell may unreasonably enhance the cost of such bonds to the Government.

It has been suggested that the present bonded debt might be refunded at a less rate of interest and the difference between the old and new security paid in cash, thus finding use for the surplus in the Treasury. The success of this plan, it is apparent, must depend upon the volition of the holders of the present bonds; and it is not entirely certain that the inducement which must be offered them would result in more financial benefit to the Government than the purchase of bonds, while the latter proposition would reduce the principal of the debt by actual payment instead of extending it.

The proposition to deposit the money held by the Government in banks throughout the country for use by the people is, it seems to me, exceedingly objectionable in principle, as establishing too close a relationship between the operations of the Government Treasury and the business of the country and too extensive a commingling of their money, thus fostering an unnatural reliance in private business upon public funds. If this scheme should be adopted, it should only be done as a temporary expedient to meet an urgent necessity. Legislative and executive effort should generally be in the opposite direction, and should have a tendency to divorce, as much and as fast as can be safely done, the Treasury Department from private enterprise.

Of course it is not expected that unnecessary and extravagant appropriations will be made for the purpose of avoiding the accumulation of an excess of revenue. Such expenditure, besides the demoralization of all just conceptions of public duty which it entails, stimulates a habit of reckless improvidence not in the least consistent with the mission of our people or the high and beneficent purposes of our Government.

·I have deemed it my duty to thus bring to the knowledge

countrymen, as well as to the attention of their representatives charged with the responsibility of legislative relief, the gravity of our financial situation.   The failure of the Congress heretofore to provide against the dangers which it was quite evident the very nature of the difficulty must necessarily produce caused a condition of financial distress and apprehension since your last adjournment which taxed to the utmost all the authority and expedients within executive control; and these appear now to be exhausted.   If disaster results from the continued inaction of Congress, the responsibility must rest where it belongs.

Though the situation thus far considered is fraught with danger which should be fully realized, and though it presents features of wrong to the people as well as peril to the country, it is but a result growing out of a perfectly palpable and apparent cause, constantly reproducing the same alarming circumstances—a congested National Treasury and a depleted monetary condition in the business of the country.   It need hardly be stated that while the present situation demands a remedy, we can only be saved from a like predicament in the future by the removal of its cause.

Our scheme of taxation, by means of which this needless surplus is taken from the people and put into the public Treasury, consists of a tariff or duty levied upon importations from abroad and internal-revenue taxes levied upon the consumption of tobacco and spirituous and malt liquors.   It must be conceded that none of the things subjected to internal-revenue taxation are, strictly speaking, necessaries.   There appears to be no just complaint of this taxation by the consumers of these articles, and there seems to be nothing so well able to bear the burden without hardship to any portion of the people.

But our present tariff laws, the vicious, inequitable, and illogical source of unnecessary taxation, ought to be at once revised and amended.   These laws, as their primary and plain effect, raise the price to consumers of all articles imported and subject to duty by precisely the sum paid for such duties.   Thus the amount of the duty measures the tax paid by those who purchase for use these imported articles.   Many of these things, however, are raised or manufactured in our own country, and the duties now levied upon foreign goods and products are called protection to these home manufactures, because they render it possible for those of our people who are manufacturers to make these taxed articles and sell them for a price equal to that demanded for the imported goods that have paid customs duty.   So it happens that while comparatively a few use the imported articles, millions of our people, who never used and never saw any of the foreign products, purchase and use things of the same kind made in this country, and pay therefor nearly or quite the same enhanced price which the duty adds to the imported articles.   Those who buy imports pay the duty charged thereon into the public Treasury, but the great majority of our citizens, who buy domestic articles of the same class, pay a sum at least approximately equal to this duty to the home manufacturer. This reference to the operation of our tariff laws is not made by way of instruction, but in order that we may be constantly reminded of the manner in which they impose a burden upon those who consume domestic products as well as those who consume imported articles, and thus create a tax upon all our people.

It is not proposed to entirely relieve the country of this taxation. It must be extensively continued as the source of the Government's income; and in a readjustment of our tariff the interests of American labor engaged in manufacture should be carefully considered, as well as the preservation of our manufacturers. It may be called protection or by any other name, but relief from the hardships and dangers of our present tariff laws should be devised with especial precaution against imperiling the existence of our manufacturing interests. But this existence should not mean a condition which, without regard to the public welfare or a national exigency, must always insure the realization of immense profits instead of moderately profitable returns. As the volume and diversity of our national activities increase, new recruits are added to those who desire a continuation of the advantages which they conceive the present system of tariff taxation directly affords them. So stubbornly have all efforts to reform the present condition been resisted by those of our fellow-citizens thus engaged that they can hardly complain of the suspicion, entertained to a certain extent, that there exists an organized combination all along the line to maintain their advantage.

We are in the midst of centennial celebrations, and with becoming pride we rejoice in American skill and ingenuity, in American energy and enterprise, and in the wonderful natural advantages and resources developed by a century's national growth. Yet when an attempt is made to justify a scheme which permits a tax to be laid upon every consumer in the land for the benefit of our manufacturers, quite beyond a reasonable demand for governmental regard, it suits the purposes of advocacy to call our manufactures infant industries still needing the highest and greatest degree of favor and fostering care that can be wrung from Federal legislation.

It is also said that the increase in the price of domestic manufactures resulting from the present tariff is necessary in order that higher wages may be paid to our workingmen employed in manufactories than are paid for what is called the pauper labor of Europe. All will acknowledge the force of an argument which involves the welfare and liberal compensation of our laboring people. Our labor is honorable in the eyes of every American citizen; and as it lies at the foundation of our development and progress, it is entitled, without affectation or hypocrisy, to the utmost regard. The standard of our laborers' life should not be measured by that of any other country less favored, and they are entitled to their full share of all our advantages.

By the last census it is made to appear that of the 17,392,099 of our population engaged in all kinds of industries 7,670,493 are employed in agriculture, 4,074,238 in professional and personal service (2,934,876 of whom are domestic servants and laborers), while 1,810,256 are employed in trade and transportation and 3,837,112 are classed as employed in manufacturing and mining.

For present purposes, however, the last number given should be considerably reduced. Without attempting to enumerate all, it will be conceded that there should be deducted from those which it includes 375,143 carpenters and joiners, 285,401 milliners, dressmakers, and seamstresses, 172,726 blacksmiths, 133,756 tailors and tailoresses, 102,473 masons, 76,241 butchers, 41,309 bakers, 22,083 plasterers, and 4,891 engaged in manufacturing agricultural implements, amounting in the aggregate to 1,214,023, leaving 2,623,089 persons employed in such manufacturing industries as are claimed to be benefited by a high tariff.

To these the appeal is made to save their employment and maintain their wages by resisting a change. There should be no disposition to answer such suggestions by the allegation that they are in a minority among those who labor, and therefore should forego an advantage in the interest of low prices for the majority. Their compensation, as it may be affected by the operation of tariff laws, should at all times be scrupulously kept in view; and yet with slight reflection they will not overlook the fact that they are consumers with the rest; that they too have their own wants and those of their families to supply from their earnings, and that the price of the necessaries of life, as well as the amount of their wages, will regulate the measure of their welfare and comfort.

But the reduction of taxation demanded should be so measured as not to necessitate or justify either the loss of employment by the workingman or the lessening of his wages; and the profits still remaining to the manufacturer after a necessary readjustment should furnish no excuse for the sacrifice of the interests of his employees, either in their opportunity to work or in the diminution of their compensation. Nor can the worker in manufactures fail to understand that while a high tariff is claimed to be necessary to allow the payment of remunerative wages, it certainly results in a very large increase in the price of nearly all sorts of manufactures, which, in almost countless forms, he needs for the use of himself and his family. He receives at the desk of his employer his wages, and perhaps before he reaches his home is obliged, in a purchase for family use of an article which embraces his own labor, to return in the payment of the increase in price which the tariff permits the hard-earned compensation of many days of toil.

The farmer and the agriculturist, who manufacture nothing, but who pay the increased price which the tariff imposes upon every agricultural implement, upon all he wears, and upon all he uses and owns, except the increase of his flocks and herds and such things as his husbandry produces from the soil, is invited to aid in maintaining the present situation; and he is told that a high duty on imported wool is necessary for the benefit of those who have sheep to shear, in order that the price of their wool may be increased. They, of course, are not reminded that the farmer who has no sheep is by this scheme obliged, in his purchases of clothing and woolen goods, to pay a tribute to his fellow-farmer as well as to the manufacturer and merchant; nor is any mention made of the fact that the sheep owners themselves and their households must wear clothing and use other articles manufactured from the wool they sell at tariff prices, and thus as consumers must return their share of this increased price to the tradesman.

I think it may be fairly assumed that a large proportion of the sheep owned by the farmers throughout the country are found in small flocks, numbering from twenty-five to fifty. The duty on the grade of imported wool which these sheep yield is 10 cents each pound if of the value of 30 cents or less and 12 cents if of the value of more than 30 cents. If the liberal estimate of 6 pounds be allowed for each fleece, the duty thereon would be 60 or 72 cents; and this may be taken as the utmost enhancement of its price to the farmer by reason of this duty. Eighteen dollars would thus represent the increased price of the wool from twenty-five sheep and $36 that from the wool of fifty sheep; and at present values this addition would amount to about one-third of its price. If upon its sale the farmer receives this or a less tariff profit, the wool leaves his hands charged with precisely that sum, which in all its changes will adhere to it until it reaches the consumer. When manufactured into cloth and other goods and material for use, its cost is not only increased to the extent of the farmer's tariff profit, but a further sum has been added for the benefit of the manufacturer under the operation of other tariff laws. In the meantime the day arrives when the farmer finds it necessary to purchase woolen goods and material to clothe himself and family for the winter. When he faces the tradesman for that purpose, he discovers that he is obliged not only to return in the way of increased prices his tariff profit on the wool he sold, and which then perhaps lies before him in manufactured form, but that he must add a considerable sum thereto to meet a further increase in cost caused by a tariff duty on the manufacture. Thus in the end he is aroused to the fact that he has paid upon a moderate purchase, as a result of the tariff scheme, which when he sold his wool seemed so profitable, an increase in price more than sufficient to sweep away all the tariff profit he received upon the wool he produced and sold.

When the number of farmers engaged in wool raising is compared with all the farmers in the country and the small proportion they bear to our population is considered; when it is made apparent that in the case of a large part of those who own sheep the benefit of tariff on wool is illusory; and, above all, when it must be conceded that the increase of the cost of living caused by such tariff becomes a burden upon those with moderate means and the poor, the employed and unemployed, the sick and well, and the young and old, and that it constitutes a tax which with relentless grasp is fastened upon the clothing of every man, woman, and child in the land, reasons are suggested why the removal or reduction of this duty should be included in a revision of our tariff laws.

In speaking of the increased cost to the consumer of our home manufactures resulting from a duty laid upon imported articles of the same description, the fact is not overlooked that competition among our domestic producers sometimes has the effect of keeping the price of their products below the highest limit allowed by such duty. But it is notorious that this competition is too often strangled by combinations quite prevalent at this time, and frequently called trusts, which have for their object the regulation of the supply and price of commodities made and sold by members of the combination. The people can hardly hope for any consideration in the operation of these selfish schemes.

If, however, in the absence of such combination, a healthy and free competition reduces the price of any particular dutiable article of home production below the limit which it might otherwise reach under our tariff laws, and if with such reduced price its manufacture continues to thrive, it is entirely evident that one thing has been discovered which should be carefully scrutinized in an effort to reduce taxation.

The necessity of combination to maintain the price of any commodity to the tariff point furnishes proof that someone is willing to accept lower prices for such commodity and that such prices are remunerative; and lower prices produced by competition prove the same thing. Thus where either of these conditions exists a case would seem to be presented for an easy reduction of taxation.

The considerations which have been presented touching our tariff laws are intended only to enforce an earnest recommendation that the surplus revenues of the Government be prevented by the reduction of our customs duties, and at the same time to emphasize a suggestion that in accomplishing this purpose we may discharge a double duty to our people by granting to them a measure of relief from tariff taxation in quarters where it is most needed and from sources where it can be most fairly and justly accorded.

Nor can the presentation made of such considerations be with any degree of fairness regarded as evidence of unfriendliness toward our manufacturing interests or of any lack of appreciation of their value and importance.

These interests constitute a leading and most substantial element of our national greatness and furnish the proud proof of our country's progress. But if in the emergency that presses upon us our manufacturers are asked to surrender something for the public good and to avert disaster, their patriotism, as well as a grateful recognition of advantages already afforded, should lead them to willing cooperation. No demand is made that they shall forego all the benefits of governmental regard; but they can not fail to be admonished of their duty, as well as their enlightened self-interest and safety, when they are reminded of the fact that financial panic and collapse, to which the present condition tends, afford no greater shelter or protection to our manufactures than to other important enterprises. Opportunity for safe, careful, and deliberate reform is now offered; and none of us should be unmindful of a time when an abused and irritated people, heedless of those who have resisted timely and reasonable relief, may insist upon a radical and sweeping rectification of their wrongs.

The difficulty attending a wise and fair revision of our tariff laws is not underestimated. It will require on the part of the Congress great labor and care, and especially a broad and national contemplation of the subject and a patriotic disregard of such local and selfish claims as are unreasonable and reckless of the welfare of the entire country.

Under our present laws more than 4,000 articles are subject to duty. Many of these do not in any way compete with our own manufactures, and many are hardly worth attention as subjects of revenue. A considerable reduction can be made in the aggregate by adding them to the free list. The taxation of luxuries presents no features of hardship; but the necessaries of life used and consumed by all the people, the duty upon which adds to the cost of living in every home, should be greatly cheapened.

The radical reduction of the duties imposed upon raw material used in manufactures, or its free importation, is of course an important factor in any effort to reduce the price of these necessaries. It would not only relieve them from the increased cost caused by the tariff on such material, but the manufactured product being thus cheapened that part of the tariff now laid upon such product, as a compensation to our manufacturers for the present price of raw material, could be accordingly modified. Such reduction or free importation would serve besides to largely reduce the revenue. It is not apparent how such a change can have any injurious effect upon our manufacturers. On the contrary, it would appear to give them a better chance in foreign markets with the manufacturers of other countries, who cheapen their wares by free material. Thus ot people might have the opportunity of extending their sales beyond tl limits of home consumption, saving them from the depression, inte ruption in business, and loss caused by a glutted domestic market anc affording their employees more certain and steady labor, with its resulting quiet and contentment.

The question thus imperatively presented for solution should be approached in a spirit higher than partisanship and considered in the light of that regard for patriotic duty which should characterize t those intrusted with the weal of a confiding people.   But the obligation to declared party policy and principle is not wanting to urge prompt and effective action.   Both of the great political parties now represented in the Government have by repeated and authoritative declarations condemned the condition of our laws which permit the collection from the people of unnecessary revenue, and have in the most solemn manner promised its correction; and neither as citizens nor partisans are our countrymen in a mood to condone the deliberate violation of these pledges.

Our progress toward a wise conclusion will not be improved by dwelling upon the theories of protection and free trade.   This savors too much of bandying epithets.   It is a *condition* which confronts us, not a theory. Relief from this condition may involve a slight reduction of the advantages which we award our home productions, but the entire withdrawal of such advantages should not be contemplated.   The question of free trade is absolutely irrelevant, and the persistent claim made in certain quarters that all the efforts to relieve the people from unjust and unnecessary taxation are schemes of so-called free traders is mischievous and far removed from any consideration for the public good.

The simple and plain duty which we owe the people is to reduce taxation to the necessary expenses of an economical operation of the Government and to restore to the business of the country the money which we hold in the Treasury through the perversion of governmental powers. These things can and should be done with safety to all our industries, without danger to the opportunity for remunerative labor which our workingmen need, and with benefit to them and all our people by cheapeuing their means of subsistence and increasing the measure of their comforts.

The Constitution provides that the President "shall from time to time give to the Congress information of the state of the Union."   It has been the custom of the Executive, in compliance with this provision, to annually exhibit to the Congress, at the opening of its session, the general condition of the country, and to detail with some particularity the operations of the different Executive Departments.   It would be especially agreeable to follow this course at the present time and to call attention to the valuable accomplishments of these Departments during the last fiscal year; but I am so much impressed with the paramount importance of the subject to which this communication has thus far been devoted that I shall forego the addition of any other topic, and only urge upon your immediate consideration the "state of the Union" as shown in the present condition of our Treasury and our general fiscal situation, upon which every element of our safety and prosperity depends.

The reports of the heads of Departments, which will be submitted, contain full and explicit information touching the transaction of the business intrusted to them and such recommendations relating to legislation in the public interest as they deem advisable.   I ask for these reports and recommendations the deliberate examination and action of the legislative branch of the Government.

There are other subjects not embraced in the departmental reports demanding legislative consideration, and which I should be glad to submit. Some of them, however, have been earnestly presented in previous messages, and as to them I beg leave to repeat prior recommendations.

As the law makes no provision for any report from the Department of State, a brief history of the transactions of that important Department, together with other matters which it may hereafter be deemed essential to commend to the attention of the Congress, may furnish the occasion for a future communication.

GROVER CLEVELAND.

SPECIAL MESSAGES.

EXECUTIVE MANSION,
Washington, December 14, 1887.

To the Senate of the United States:

I transmit herewith, with a view to its ratification, a final protocol, signed at Paris on the 7th day of July, 1887, by the plenipotentiaries of the United States and of the other powers parties to the convention of March 14, 1884, for the protection of submarine cables, fixing the 1st day of May, 1888, as the date on which the said convention of March 14, 1884, shall take effect, provided that those of the contracting Governments that have not adopted the measures provided for by article 12 of the said convention shall have conformed to that stipulation.

GROVER CLEVELAND.

EXECUTIVE MANSION,
Washington, December 14, 1887.

To the Senate of the United States:

I transmit herewith, with a view to its ratification, a convention between the United States and the Kingdom of the Netherlands for the extradition of criminals, signed at Washington on the 2d day of June, 1887.

GROVER CLEVELAND.

EXECUTIVE MANSION, *December 19, 1887.*

To the Senate and House of Representatives:

I transmit herewith a report from the Secretary of State, in relation to the invitation from Her Britannic Majesty to this Government to participate in the international exhibition which is to be held at Melbourne in 1888 to celebrate the centenary of the founding of New South Wales, the first Australian colony.

GROVER CLEVELAND.

EXECUTIVE MANSION, *December 19, 1887.*

To the Senate and House of Representatives:

I transmit herewith a report from the Secretary of State, in relation to an invitation which has been extended to this Government to appoint a delegate or delegates to the International Exposition of Labor to be held in April, 1888, at Barcelona, Spain, and commend its suggestions to the favorable attention of Congress.

GROVER CLEVELAND.

EXECUTIVE MANSION,
Washington, December 20, 1887.

To the Senate and House of Representatives:

I transmit herewith a communication from the Secretary of State, accompanied by the report of Mr. Edward Atkinson, of Massachusetts, who was specially designated by me, under the provisions of successive acts of Congress in that behalf, to visit the financial centers of Europe in order to ascertain the feasibility of establishing by international arrangement a fixity of rates between the two precious metals in free coinage of both.

GROVER CLEVELAND.

EXECUTIVE MANSION, *January 4, 1888.*

To the Senate and House of Representatives:

I transmit herewith a communication of 23d ultimo from the Secretary of the Interior, submitting, with accompanying papers, a draft of a bill to amend section 2148 of the Revised Statutes of the United States, relating to trespasses upon Indian lands.

GROVER CLEVELAND.

EXECUTIVE MANSION, *January 4, 1888.*

To the Senate and House of Representatives:

I transmit herewith a communication of 23d ultimo from the Secretary of the Interior, submitting, with accompanying papers, a draft of a bill granting a right of way to the Jamestown and Northern Railroad Company through the Devils Lake Indian Reservation, in the Territory of Dakota.

GROVER CLEVELAND.

EXECUTIVE MANSION, *January 4, 1888.*

To the Senate and House of Representatives:

I transmit herewith a communication of the 22d ultimo from the Secretary of the Interior, submitting, with accompanying papers, a draft of a bill to amend section 5388 of the Revised Statutes of the United States, relating to timber trespasses upon the public lands, so as to include Indian lands.

GROVER CLEVELAND.

EXECUTIVE MANSION, *January 4, 1888.*

To the Senate and House of Representatives:

I transmit herewith a communication of 27th December, 1887, from the Secretary of the Interior, submitting, with accompanying papers, draft of a bill "to authorize the Secretary of the Interior to fix the amount of compensation to be paid for the right of way for railroads through Indian reservations in certain contingencies."

The matter is commended to the consideration of Congress.

GROVER CLEVELAND.

EXECUTIVE MANSION, *January 4, 1888.*

To the Senate and House of Representatives:

I transmit herewith a communication of 22d ultimo from the Secretary of the Interior, submitting, with accompanying papers, a draft of a bill to accept and ratify an agreement made with the Indians of the Yakima Reservation, in Washington Territory, for the right of way of the Northern Pacific Railroad across said reservation, etc.

The matter is presented for the consideration and action of Congress.

GROVER CLEVELAND.

EXECUTIVE MANSION, *January 4, 1888.*

To the Senate and House of Representatives:

I transmit herewith a communication of 24th ultimo from the Secretary of the Interior, submitting, with accompanying papers, a draft of a bill to accept and ratify an agreement made by the Pi-Ute Indians, and granting a right of way to the Carson and Colorado Railroad Company through the Walker River Reservation, in Nevada.

GROVER CLEVELAND.

EXECUTIVE MANSION, *January 4, 1888.*

To the Senate and House of Representatives:

I transmit herewith a communication of the 24th ultimo from the Secretary of the Interior, submitting, with accompanying papers, a draft of a bill to accept and ratify an agreement made with the Sisseton and Wahpeton Indians, and to grant a right of way for the Chicago, Milwaukee and St. Paul Railway through the Lake Traverse Indian Reservation, in Dakota.

The matter is presented for the consideration and action of Congress.

GROVER CLEVELAND.

EXECUTIVE MANSION, *January 5, 1888.*

To the Senate and House of Representatives:

I transmit herewith a communication of the 23d ultimo from the Secretary of the Interior, submitting a draft of a bill "to provide for the reduction of the Round Valley Indian Reservation, in the State of California, and for other purposes," with accompanying papers relating thereto. The documents thus submitted exhibit extensive and entirely unjustifiable encroachments upon lands set apart for Indian occupancy and disclose a disregard of Indian rights so long continued that the Government can not further temporize without positive dishonor. Efforts to dislodge trespassers upon these lands have in some cases been resisted upon the ground that certain moneys due from the Government for improvements have not been paid. So far as this claim is well founded the sum necessary to extinguish the same should be at once appropriated and paid. In other cases the position of these intruders is one of simple and barefaced wrongdoing, plainly questioning the inclination of the Government to protect its dependent Indian wards and its ability to maintain itself in the guaranty of such protection.

These intruders should forthwith feel the weight of the Government's power. I earnestly commend the situation and the wrongs of the Indians occupying the reservation named to the early attention of the Congress, and ask for the bill herewith transmitted careful and prompt attention.

GROVER CLEVELAND.

To the Senate:　　　　 EXECUTIVE MANSION, *January 5, 1888.*

In answer to the resolution of the Senate of the 28th of February last, requesting the President of the United States to obtain certain information from the Government of Great Britain relative to the proceedings of the authorities of New Zealand concerning the titles to lands in that colony claimed by American citizens, I transmit a report of the Secretary of State, together with the accompanying documents.

GROVER CLEVELAND.

EXECUTIVE MANSION,
Washington, January 5, 1888.

To the Senate of the United States:

I transmit herewith, with a view to its ratification, a treaty of friendship, commerce, and navigation between the United States and the Republic of Peru, signed at Lima on the 31st day of August, 1887.

GROVER CLEVELAND.

EXECUTIVE MANSION,
Washington, January 5, 1888.

To the Senate of the United States:

I transmit, with a view to its ratification, an additional article, signed October 22, 1887, to the treaty for the extradition of criminals concluded October 11, 1870, between the United States and the Republic of Guatemala, and, for the reasons suggested by the Secretary of State in his report, request the return of the additional article to the above-mentioned treaty signed February 4, 1887, and transmitted to the Senate on February 24 [25] of the same year.* GROVER CLEVELAND.

EXECUTIVE MANSION, *January 9, 1888.*
To the Senate and House of Representatives:

I transmit herewith a communication of 30th of December, 1887, from the Secretary of the Interior, submitting, with accompanying papers, two additional reports from the commission appointed to conduct negotiations with certain tribes and bands of Indians for reduction of reservations, etc., under the provisions of the act of May 15, 1886 (24 U. S. Statutes at Large, p. 44), providing therefor. GROVER CLEVELAND.

EXECUTIVE MANSION, *January 9, 1888.*
To the Senate and House of Representatives:

I transmit herewith a communication from the Secretary of State, relative to the requests which have been received from various maritime associations and chambers of commerce of this country asking that measures be taken to convoke an international conference at Washington of representatives of all maritime nations to devise measures for the greater security of life and property at sea.

I commend this important subject to the favorable consideration of Congress. GROVER CLEVELAND.

EXECUTIVE MANSION, *January 9, 1888.*
To the Senate and House of Representatives:

I transmit herewith a report from the Secretary of State, recommending that this Government take action to approve the resolutions of the Washington International Meridian Conference, held in October, 1884, in favor of fixing a prime meridian and a universal day, and to invite the powers with whom this country has diplomatic relations to accede to the same.

GROVER CLEVELAND.

EXECUTIVE MANSION, *January 9, 1888.*
To the Senate and House of Representatives:

I transmit herewith a report of the Secretary of State, relative to the legislation required to carry into effect the international convention of March 14, 1884, for the protection of submarine cables, to which this country is a party. GROVER CLEVELAND.

* See p. 538.

EXECUTIVE MANSION, *January 12, 1888.*

To the Senate and House of Representatives:

I transmit herewith a report from the Secretary of State, in relation to the invitation from the Government of France to this Government to participate in the international exhibition which is to be held at Paris in 1889.

GROVER CLEVELAND.

EXECUTIVE MANSION,
Washington, January 16, 1888.

To the Senate of the United States:

I transmit herewith, in response to a resolution of the Senate of the 21st ultimo, a report of the Secretary of State touching correspondence of this Government with that of Hawaii, or of any foreign country, concerning any change or proposed change in the Government of the Hawaiian Islands.

GROVER CLEVELAND.

EXECUTIVE MANSION, *January 17, 1888.*

To the Senate and House of Representatives:

On the 3d day of March last an act was passed authorizing the appointment of three commissioners who should investigate the affairs of such railroads as have received aid from the United States Government. Among other things, the contemplated investigation included a history of the construction of these roads, their relations and indebtedness to the Government, and the question whether in the interest of the United States any extension of the time for the performance of the obligations of said roads to the Government should be granted; and if so, the said commissioners were directed to submit a scheme for such extension.

The commissioners were further directed by said act to report in full to the President upon all the matters submitted to them, and he was by said act required to forward said report to Congress with such recommendations or comments as he should see fit to make in the premises.

The commissioners immediately after their selection entered upon the discharge of their duties, and have prosecuted their inquiries with commendable industry, intelligence, and thoroughness. A large amount of testimony has been taken, and all the facts have been developed which appear to be necessary for the consideration of the questions arising from the condition of these aided railroads and their relations to the Government.

The commissioners have, however, been unable to agree upon the manner in which these railroads should be treated respecting their indebtedness to the United States, or to unite upon the plan best calculated to secure the payment of such indebtedness.

This disagreement has resulted in the preparation of two reports, both of which are herewith submitted to the Congress.

These reports exhibit such transactions and schemes connected with the construction of the aided roads and their management, and suggest the invention of such devices on the part of those having them in charge. for the apparent purpose of defeating any chance for the Government's reimbursement, that any adjustment or plan of settlement should be predicated upon the substantial interests of the Government rather than any forbearance or generosity deserved by the companies.

The wide publication which has already been given to the substance of the commissioners' reports obviates the necessity of detailing in this communication the facts found upon the investigation.

The majority report, while condemning the methods adopted by those who formerly had charge of the Union Pacific Railroad, declares that since its present management was inaugurated, in 1884, its affairs have been fairly and prudently conducted, and that the present administration "has devoted itself honestly and intelligently to the herculean task of rescuing the Union Pacific Railway from the insolvency which seriously threatened it at the inception of its work;" that it "has devoted itself, by rigid economy, by intelligent management, and by an application of every dollar of the earning capacity of the system to its improvement and betterment, to place that company on a sound and enduring financial foundation."

The condition of the present management of the Union Pacific Company has an important bearing upon its ability to comply with the terms of any settlement of its indebtedness which may be offered by the Government.

The majority of the commission are in favor of an extension of the time for the payment of the Government indebtedness of these companies, upon certain conditions; but the chairman of the commission, presenting the minority report, recommends, both upon principle and policy, the institution of proceedings for the forfeiture of the charters of the corporations and the winding up of their affairs.

I have been furnished with a statement or argument in defense of the transactions connected with the construction of the Central Pacific road and its branch lines, from which it may not be amiss to quote for the purpose of showing how some of the operations of the directors of such road, strongly condemned by the commissioners, are defended by the directors themselves. After speaking of a contract for the construction of one of these branch lines by a corporation called the Contract and Finance Company. owned by certain directors of the Central Pacific Railroad, this language is used:

It may be said of this contract, as of many others that were let to the different construction companies in which the directors of the Central Pacific have been stockholders, that they built the road with the moneys furnished by themselves and had the road for their outlay. In other words, they paid to the construction company the bonds and stock of the railroad so constructed, and waited until such time as they could develop sufficient business on the road built to induce the public to buy the

bonds or the stock. If the country through which the railroad ran developed sufficient business, then the project was a success; if it did not, then the operation was a
loss. These gentlemen took all the responsibility; any loss occurring was necessarily
theirs, and of right the profit belonged to them.

But it is said that they violated a well-known rule of equity in dealing with themselves; that they were trustees, and that they were representing both sides of the
contract.

The answer is that they did not find anybody else to deal with. They could not
find anyone who would take the chances of building a road through what was then
an almost uninhabited country and accept the bonds and stock of the road in payment. And when it is said that they were trustees, if they did occupy such relation
it was merely technical, for they represented only their own interests on both sides,
there being no one else concerned in the transaction. They became the incorporators
of the company that was to build the road, subscribed for its stock, and were the only
subscribers; therefore it is difficult to see how anyone was wronged by their action.
The rule of equity invoked, which has its origin in the injunction "No man can
serve two masters," certainly did not apply to them, because they were acting in
their own interests and were not charged with the duty of caring for others' rights,
there being no other persons interested in the subject-matter.

In view of this statement and the facts developed in the commissioners' reports, it seems proper to recall the grants and benefits derived from
the General Government by both the Union and Central Pacific companies for the purpose of aiding the construction of their roads.

By an act passed in 1862 it was provided that there should be advanced to said companies by the United States, to aid in such construction, the bonds of the Government amounting to $16,000 for every mile
constructed, as often as a section of 40 miles of said roads should be built;
that there should also be granted to said companies, upon the completion
of every said section of 40 miles of road, five entire sections of public land
for each mile so built; that the entire charges earned by said roads on
account of transportation and service for the Government should be
applied to the reimbursement of the bonds advanced by the United States
and the interest thereon, and that to secure the repayment of the bonds
so advanced, and interest, the issue and delivery to said companies of
said bonds should constitute a first mortgage on the whole line of their
roads and on their rolling stock, fixtures, and property of every kind and
description.

The liberal donations, advances, and privileges provided for in this
law were granted by the General Government for the purpose of securing the construction of these roads, which would complete the connection
between our eastern and western coasts; and they were based upon a
consideration of the public benefits which would accrue to the entire
country from such consideration.

But the projectors of these roads were not content, and the sentiment
which then seemed to pervade the Congress had not reached the limit
of its generosity. Two years after the passage of this law it was supplemented and amended in various important particulars in favor of these
companies by an act which provided, among other things, that the bonds,

at the rate already specified, should be delivered upon the completion of sections of 20 miles in length instead of 40; that the lands to be conveyed to said companies on the completion of each section of said road should be ten sections per mile instead of five; that only half of the charges for transportation and service due from time to time from the United States should be retained and applied to the advances made to said companies by the Government, thus obliging immediate payment to its debtor of the other half of said charges, and that the lien of the United States to secure the reimbursement of the amount advanced to said companies in bonds, which lien was declared by the law of 1862 to constitute a first mortgage upon all the property of said companies, should become a junior lien and be subordinated to a mortgage which the companies were by the amendatory act authorized to execute to secure bonds which they might from time to time issue in sums not exceeding the amount of the United States bonds which should be advanced to them.

The immense advantages to the companies of this amendatory act are apparent; and in these days we may well wonder that even the anticipated public importance of the construction of these roads induced what must now appear to be a rather reckless and unguarded appropriation of the public funds and the public domain.

Under the operation of these laws the principal of the bonds which have been advanced is $64,023,512, as given in the reports of the commissioners; the interest to November 1, 1887, is calculated to be $76,-024,206.58, making an aggregate at the date named of $140,047,718.58. The interest calculated to the maturity of the bonds added to the principal produces an aggregate of $178,884,759.50. Against these amounts there has been repaid by the companies the sum of $30,955,039.61.

It is almost needless to state that the companies have availed themselves to the utmost extent of the permission given them to issue their bonds and to mortgage their property to secure the payment of the same, by an incumbrance having preference to the Government's lien and precisely equal to it in amount.

It will be seen that there was available for the building of each mile of these roads $16,000 of United States bonds, due in thirty years, with 6 per cent interest; $16,000 in bonds of the companies, secured by a first mortgage on all their property, and ten sections of Government land, to say nothing of the stock of the companies.

When the relations created between the Government and these companies by the legislation referred to is considered, it is astonishing that the claim should be made that the directors of these roads owed no duty except to themselves in their construction; that they need regard no interests but their own, and that they were justified in contracting with themselves and making such bargains as resulted in conveying to their pockets all the assets of the companies. As a lienor the Government was vitally interested in the amount of the mortgage to which its security had been subordinated, and it had the right to insist that none of the bonds secured by this prior mortgage should be issued fraudulently or for the purpose of division among these stockholders without consideration.

The doctrine of complete independence on the part of the directors of these companies and their freedom from any obligation to care for other interests than their own in the construction of these roads seems to have developed the natural consequences of its application, portrayed as follows in the majority report of the commissioners:

The result is that those who have controlled and directed the construction and development of these companies have become possessed of their surplus assets through issues of bonds, stocks, and payment of dividends voted by themselves, while the great creditor, the United States, finds itself substantially without adequate security for the repayment of its loans.

The laws enacted in aid of these roads, while they illustrated a profuse liberality and a generous surrender of the Government's advantages, which it is hoped experience has corrected, were nevertheless passed upon the theory that the roads should be constructed according to the common rules of business, fairness, and duty, and that their value and their ability to pay their debts should not be impaired by unfair manipulations; and when the Government subordinated its lien to another it was in the expectation that the prior lien would represent in its amount only such bonds as should be necessarily issued by the companies for the construction of their roads at fair prices, agreed upon in an honest way between real and substantial parties. For the purpose of saving or improving the security afforded by its junior lien the Government should have the right now to purge this paramount lien of all that is fraudulent, fictitious, or unconscionable. If the transfer to innocent hands of bonds of this character secured by such first mortgage prevents their cancellation, it might be well to seek a remedy against those who issued and transferred them. If legislation is needed to secure such a remedy, the Congress can readily supply it.

I desire to call attention also to the fact that if all that was to be done on the part of the Government to fully vest in these companies the grants and advantages contemplated by the acts passed in their interest has not yet been perfected, and if the failure of such companies to perform in good faith their part of the contract justifies such a course, the power rests with the Congress to withhold further performance on the part of the Government. If donated lands are not yet granted to these companies, and if their violation of contract and of duty are such as in justice and morals forfeit their rights to such lands, Congressional action should intervene to prevent further consummation. Executive power must be exercised according to existing laws, and Executive discretion is probably not broad enough to reach such difficulties.

The California and Oregon Railroad is now a part of the Central Pacific system, and is a land-grant road. Its construction has been carried on with the same features and incidents which have characterized *the* other constructions of this system, as is made apparent on pages 78,

79, and 80 of the report of the majority of the commissioners. I have in my hands for approval the report of the commissioners appointed to examine two completed sections of this road. Upon such approval the company or the Central Pacific Company will be entitled to patents for a large quantity of public lands. I especially commend to the attention of Congress this condition of affairs, in order that it may determine whether or not it should intervene to save these lands for settlers, if such a course is justifiable.

It is quite time that the troublesome complications surrounding this entire subject, which has been transmitted to us as a legacy from former days, should be adjusted and settled.

No one, I think, expects that these railroad companies will be able to pay their immense indebtedness to the Government at its maturity.

Any proceeding or arrangement that would result now, or at any other time, in putting these roads, or any portion of them, in the possession and control of the Government is, in my opinion, to be rejected, certainly as long as there is the least chance for indemnification through any other means.

I suppose we are hardly justified in indulging the irritation and indignation naturally arising from a contemplation of malfeasance to such an extent as to lead to the useless destruction of these roads or loss of the advances made by the Government. I believe that our efforts should be in a more practical direction, and should tend, with no condonation of wrongdoing, to the collection by the Government, on behalf of the people, of the public money now in jeopardy.

While the plan presented by a majority of the commission appears to be well devised and gives at least partial promise of the results sought, the fact will not escape attention that its success depends upon its acceptance by the companies and their ability to perform its conditions after acceptance. It is exceedingly important that any adjustment now made should be final and effective. These considerations suggest the possibility that the remedy proposed in the majority report might well be applied to a part only of these aided railroad companies.

The settlement and determination of the questions involved are peculiarly within the province of the Congress. The subject has been made quite a familiar one by Congressional discussion. This is now supplemented in a valuable manner by the facts presented in the reports herewith submitted.

The public interest urges prompt and efficient action.

GROVER CLEVELAND.

EXECUTIVE MANSION, *January 23, 1888.*

To the Senate and House of Representatives:

I transmit herewith the first report of the board of control created by the act of Congress approved August 4, 1886 (24 U. S. Statutes at Large, p. 252), for the management of an industrial home in the Territory of

Utah, containing a statement of the action of the board in establishing the home and an account of expenditures from the appropriation made for that purpose in the act above mentioned.

GROVER CLEVELAND.

EXECUTIVE MANSION,
Washington, January 30, 1888.

To the Senate:

I transmit herewith, in response to the resolution of the Senate of the 21st of December last, a report from the Secretary of State, in relation to Midway Island.

GROVER CLEVELAND.

EXECUTIVE MANSION,
Washington, February 7, 1888.

To the Senate of the United States:

I transmit, with a view to its ratification, a declaration, signed December 1, 1886, and March 23, 1887, for Germany, by the delegates of the powers signatories of the convention of March 14, 1884, for the protection of submarine cables, defining the sense of articles 2 and 4 of the said convention.

GROVER CLEVELAND.

EXECUTIVE MANSION, *February 7, 1888.*

To the Senate and House of Representatives:

I transmit herewith a communication of 4th instant from the Secretary of the Interior, submitting, with other papers, a draft of a bill to accept and ratify an agreement made with the Shoshone and Bannock Indians for the surrender and relinquishment to the United States of a portion of the Fort Hall Reservation, in the Territory of Idaho, for the purposes of a town site, and for the grant of a right of way through said reservation to the Utah and Northern Railway Company, and for other purposes.

The matter is presented for the consideration of the Congress.

GROVER CLEVELAND.

EXECUTIVE MANSION, *February 20, 1888.*

To the Senate of the United States:

I transmit herewith a report furnished by the Secretary of State in response to a resolution of the Senate of the 2d instant, making inquiry respecting the present condition of the *Virginius* indemnity fund.

GROVER CLEVELAND.

EXECUTIVE MANSION, *February 20, 1888.*

To the Senate and House of Representatives:

I transmit herewith and commend to your favorable consideration a report from the Secretary of State, in relation to an invitation which this

Government has received from the Belgian Government to participate in an international exhibition of sciences and industry which will open at Brussels in the month of May next.

GROVER CLEVELAND.

EXECUTIVE MANSION, *February 20, 1888.*
To the Senate of the United States:

In my annual message transmitted to the Congress in December, 1886, it was stated that negotiations were then pending for the settlement of the questions growing out of the rights claimed by American fishermen in British North American waters.

As a result of such negotiations a treaty has been agreed upon between Her Britannic Majesty and the United States, concluded and signed in this capital, under my direction and authority, on the 15th of February instant, and which I now have the honor to submit to the Senate with the recommendation that it shall receive the consent of that body, as provided in the Constitution, in order that the ratifications thereof may be duly exchanged and the treaty be carried into effect.

Shortly after Congress had adjourned in March last, and in continuation of my efforts to arrive at such an agreement between the Governments of Great Britain and the United States as would secure to the citizens of the respective countries the unmolested enjoyment of their just rights under existing treaties and international comity in the territorial waters of Canada and of Newfoundland, I availed myself of opportune occurrences indicative of a desire to make without delay an amicable and final settlement of a long-standing controversy, productive of much irritation and misunderstanding between the two nations, to send through our minister in London proposals that a conference should take place on the subject at this capital.

The experience of the past two years had demonstrated the dilatory and unsatisfactory consequences of our indirect transaction of business through the foreign office in London, in which the views and wishes of the government of the Dominion of Canada were practically predominant, but were only to find expression at second hand.

To obviate this inconvenience and obstruction to prompt and well-defined settlement, it was considered advisable that the negotiations should be conducted in this city and that the interests of Canada and Newfoundland should be directly represented therein.

The terms of reference having been duly agreed upon between the two Governments and the conference arranged to be held here, by virtue of the power in me vested by the Constitution I duly authorized Thomas F. Bayard, the Secretary of State of the United States, William L. Putnam, a citizen of the State of Maine, and James B. Angell, a citizen of the State of Michigan, for and in the name of the United States, to meet and conf with the plenipotentiaries representing the Government of Her Britai

Majesty, for the purpose of considering and adjusting in a friendly spirit all or any questions relating to rights of fishery in the seas adjacent to British North America and Newfoundland which were in dispute between the Government of the United States and that of Her Britannic Majesty, and jointly and severally to conclude and sign any treaty or treaties touching the premises; and I herewith transmit for your information full copies of the power so given by me.

In execution of the powers so conveyed the said Thomas F. Bayard, William L. Putnam, and James B. Angell, in the month of November last, met in this city the plenipotentiaries of Her Britannic Majesty and proceeded in the negotiation of a treaty as above authorized. After many conferences and protracted efforts an agreement has at length been arrived at, which is embodied in the treaty which I now lay before you.

The treaty meets my approval, because I believe that it supplies a satisfactory, practical, and final adjustment, upon a basis honorable and just to both parties, of the difficult and vexed question to which it relates.

A review of the history of this question will show that all former attempts to arrive at a common interpretation, satisfactory to both parties, of the first article of the treaty of October 20, 1818, have been unsuccessful, and with the lapse of time the difficulty and obscurity have only increased.

The negotiations in 1854 and again in 1871 ended in both cases in temporary reciprocal arrangements of the tariffs of Canada and Newfoundland and of the United States, and the payment of a money award by the United States, under which the real questions in difference remained unsettled, in abeyance, and ready to present themselves anew just so soon as the conventional arrangements were abrogated.

The situation, therefore, remained unimproved by the results of the treaty of 1871, and a grave condition of affairs, presenting almost identically the same features and causes of complaint by the United States against Canadian action and British default in its correction, confronted us in May, 1886, and has continued until the present time.

The greater part of the correspondence which has taken place between the two Governments has heretofore been communicated to Congress, and at as early a day as possible I shall transmit the remaining portion to this date, accompanying it with the joint protocols of the conferences which resulted in the conclusion of the treaty now submitted to you.

You will thus be fully possessed of the record and history of the case since the termination on June 30, 1885, of the fishery articles of the treaty of Washington of 1871, whereby we were relegated to the provisions of the treaty of October 20, 1818.

As the documents and papers referred to will supply full information of the positions taken under my Administration by the representatives of the United States, as well as those occupied by the representatives of the ˹ ˙˙˙ment of Great Britain, it is not considered necessary or expedient to repeat them in this message. But I believe the treaty will be found to contain a just, honorable, and therefore satisfactory solution of the difficulties which have clouded our relations with our neighbors on our northern border.

Especially satisfactory do I believe the proposed arrangement will be found by those of our citizens who are engaged in the open-sea fisheries adjacent to the Canadian coast, and resorting to those ports and harbors under treaty provisions and rules of international law.

The proposed delimitation of the lines of the exclusive fisheries from the common fisheries will give certainty and security as to the area of their legitimate field. The headland theory of imaginary lines is abandoned by Great Britain, and the specification in the treaty of certain named bays especially provided for gives satisfaction to the inhabitants of the shores, without subtracting materially from the value or convenience of the fishery rights of Americans.

The uninterrupted navigation of the Strait of Canso is expressly and for the first time affirmed, and the four purposes for which our fishermen under the treaty of 1818 were allowed to enter the bays and harbors of Canada and Newfoundland within the belt of 3 marine miles are placed under a fair and liberal construction, and their enjoyment secured without such conditions and restrictions as in the past have embarrassed and obstructed them so seriously.

The enforcement of penalties for unlawfully fishing or preparing to fish within the inshore and exclusive waters of Canada and Newfoundland is to be accomplished under safeguards against oppressive or arbitrary action, thus protecting the defendant fishermen from punishment in advance of trial, delays, and inconvenience and unnecessary expense.

The history of events in the last two years shows that no feature of Canadian administration was more harassing and injurious than the compulsion upon our fishing vessels to make formal entry and clearance on every occasion of temporarily seeking shelter in Canadian ports and harbors.

Such inconvenience is provided against in the proposed treaty, and this most frequent and just cause of complaint is removed.

The articles permitting our fishermen to obtain provisions and the ordinary supplies of trading vessels on their homeward voyages, and under which they are accorded the further and even more important privilege on all occasions of purchasing such casual or needful provisions and supplies as are ordinarily granted to trading vessels, are of great importance and value.

The licenses, which are to be granted without charge and on application, in order to enable our fishermen to enjoy these privileges, are reasonable and proper checks in the hands of the local authorities to id$\prime$ the recipients and prevent abuse, and can form no impediment to who intend to use them fairly.

The hospitality secured for our vessels in all cases of actual distress, with liberty to unload and sell and transship their cargoes, is full and liberal.

These provisions will secure the substantial enjoyment of the treaty rights for our fishermen under the treaty of 1818, for which contention has been steadily made in the correspondence of the Department of State and our minister at London and by the American negotiators of the present treaty.

The right of our fishermen under the treaty of 1818 did not extend to the procurement of distinctive fishery supplies in Canadian ports and harbors, and one item supposed to be essential—to wit, bait—was plainly denied them by the explicit and definite words of the treaty of 1818, emphasized by the course of the negotiation and express decisions which preceded the conclusion of that treaty.

The treaty now submitted contains no provision affecting tariff duties, and, independently of the position assumed upon the part of the United States that no alteration in our tariff or other domestic legislation could be made as the price or consideration of obtaining the rights of our citizens secured by treaty, it was considered more expedient to allow any change in the revenue laws of the United States to be made by the ordinary exercise of legislative will and in the promotion of the public interests. Therefore the addition to the free list of fish, fish oil, whale and seal oil, etc., recited in the last article of the treaty, is wholly left to the action of Congress; and in connection therewith the Canadian and Newfoundland right to regulate sales of bait and other fishing supplies within their own jurisdiction is recognized, and the right of our fishermen to freely purchase these things is made contingent by this treaty upon the action of Congress in the modification of our tariff laws.

Our social and commercial intercourse with those populations who have been placed upon our borders and made forever our neighbors is made apparent by a list of United States common carriers, marine and inland, connecting their lines with Canada, which was returned by the Secretary of the Treasury to the Senate on the 7th day of February, 1888, in answer to a resolution of that body; and this is instructive as to the great volume of mutually profitable interchanges which has come into existence during the last half century.

This intercourse is still but partially developed, and if the amicable enterprise and wholesome rivalry between the two populations be not obstructed the promise of the future is full of the fruits of an unbounded prosperity on both sides of the border.

The treaty now submitted to you has been framed in a spirit of liberal equity and reciprocal benefits, in the conviction that mutual advantage and convenience are the only permanent foundation of peace and friendship between States, and that with the adoption of the agreement now placed before the Senate a beneficial and satisfactory intercourse between the two countries will be established so as to secure perpetual peace and harmony. .

In connection with the treaty herewith submitted I deem it also my duty to transmit to the Senate a written offer or arrangement, in the nature of a *modus vivendi*, tendered after the conclusion of the treaty on the part of the British plenipotentiaries, to secure kindly and peaceful relations during the period that may be required for the consideration of the treaty by the respective Governments and for the enactment of the necessary legislation to carry its provisions into effect if approved.

This paper, freely and on their own motion signed by the British conferees, not only extends advantages to our fishermen pending the ratification of the treaty, but appears to have been dictated by a friendly and amicable spirit.

I am given to understand that the other Governments concerned in this treaty will within a few days, in accordance with their methods of conducting public business, submit said treaty to their respective legislatures, when it will be at once published to the world. In view of such action it appears to be advisable that by publication here early and full knowledge of all that has been done in the premises should be afforded to our people.

It would also seem to be useful to inform the popular mind concerning the history of the long-continued disputes growing out of the subject embraced in the treaty and to satisfy the public interests touching the same, as well as to acquaint our people with the present status of the questions involved, and to give them the exact terms of the proposed adjustment, in place of the exaggerated and imaginative statements which will otherwise reach them.

I therefore beg leave respectfully to suggest that said treaty and all such correspondence, messages, and documents relating to the same as may be deemed important to accomplish those purposes be at once made public by the order of your honorable body.

GROVER CLEVELAND.

EXECUTIVE MANSION, *February 20, 1888.*

To the Senate and House of Representatives:

I transmit herewith a report from the Secretary of State, relative to an invitation from the Imperial German Government to the Government of the United States to become a party to the International Geodetic Association.

GROVER CLEVELAND.

EXECUTIVE MANSION, *February 27, 1888.*

To the Senate of the United States:

I transmit herewith a report furnished by the Secretary of State in response to a resolution of the Senate of January 12, 1888, making various inquiries respecting the awards of the late Spanish and American

Claims Commission and the disposition of moneys received in satisfaction thereof.   GROVER CLEVELAND.

EXECUTIVE MANSION, *March 5, 1888.*
To the Senate and House of Representatives of the United States of America:

I transmit herewith, for the information and consideration of Congress, a report of the Secretary of State, with accompanying correspondence, touching the action of the Government of Venezuela in conveying to that country for interment the remains of the distinguished Venezuelan soldier and statesman, General José Antonio Paez, and take pleasure in expressing my concurrence in the suggestion therein referred to, that the employment of a national vessel of war for the transportation of General Paez's remains from New York to La Guayra be authorized and provided for by Congress.   GROVER CLEVELAND.

EXECUTIVE MANSION, *March 5, 1888.*
To the Senate and House of Representatives:

I transmit herewith a report from the Secretary of State, relative to an invitation which the Royal Bavarian Government has extended to this Government to participate in the Third International Exhibition of the Fine Arts, which is to be held at Munich, Bavaria, during the present year.   GROVER CLEVELAND.

EXECUTIVE MANSION, *March 5, 1888.*
To the Senate and House of Representatives:

I herewith transmit a letter from the Secretary of State, accompanied by documents and correspondence, in relation to the recent negotiations with Great Britain concerning American fishing interests in British North American waters.   GROVER CLEVELAND.

To the Senate: EXECUTIVE MANSION, *March 5, 1888.*

I transmit herewith a report from the Secretary of State, with its inclosures, in response to the resolution of the Senate of the 21st of December, 1887, and the 16th of January, 1888, touching the awards of the late Mexican Claims Commission, and especially those in favor of Benjamin Weil and La Abra Silver Mining Company.

It will be seen that the report concludes with a suggestion that these claims be referred to the Court of Claims, or such other court as may be deemed proper, in order that the charges of fraud made in relation to said claims may be fully investigated.

If for any reason this proceeding be considered inadvisable, I respectfully ask that some final and definite action be taken directing the executive department of the Government what course to pursue in the premises.

In view of the long delay that has already occurred in these cases, it would seem but just to all parties concerned that the Congress should speedily signify its final judgment upon the awards referred to and make the direction contemplated by the act of 1878, in default of which the money now on hand applicable to such awards now remains undistributed.

GROVER CLEVELAND.

To the Senate: EXECUTIVE MANSION, *March 7, 1888.*

In compliance with the resolution of the Senate of the 24th of February, 1888, calling for information as to whether the Government of France has prohibited the importation into the country of any American products, and, if so, what products of the United States are affected thereby, and also as to whether any correspondence upon said subject has passed between the Governments of the United States and France, I transmit herewith a report from the Secretary of State on the subject, with the accompanying correspondence.

GROVER CLEVELAND.

To the Senate: EXECUTIVE MANSION, *March 8, 1888.*

A copy of the following resolution, passed by the Senate on the 1st day of the present month, was delivered to me on the 3d instant:

Resolved, That in view of the difficulties and embarrassments that have attended the regulation of the immigration of Chinese laborers to the United States under the limitations of our treaties with China, the President of the United States be requested to negotiate a treaty with the Emperor of China containing a provision that no Chinese laborer shall enter the United States.

The importance of the subject referred to in this resolution has by no means been overlooked by the executive branch of the Government, charged under the Constitution with the formulation of treaties with foreign countries.

Negotiation with the Emperor of China for a treaty such as is mentioned in said resolution was commenced many months ago and has been since continued. The progress of the negotiation thus inaugurated has heretofore been freely communicated to such members of the Senate and of its Committee on Foreign Relations as sought information concerning the same. It is, however, with much gratification that I deem myself now justified in expressing to the Senate, in response to its resolution, the hope and expectation that a treaty will soon be concluded concerning the immigration of Chinese laborers which will meet the wants of our people and the approbation of the body to which it will be submitted for confirmation.   GROVER CLEVELAND.

EXECUTIVE MANSION,
Washington, March 12, 1888.

To the Senate of the United States:

I transmit herewith, with a view to its ratification, a treaty between the United States of America and Zanzibar, concluded July 3, 1886, enlarging and defining the stipulations of the treaty of September 21, 1833, between the United States of America and His Majesty Seyed Syed bin Sultan of Muscat and Sovereign of Zanzibar, which treaty has continued in force as to Zanzibar and its dependencies after the separation of Zanzibar from Muscat, and has been accepted, ratified, and confirmed by the Sultan of Zanzibar on October 20, 1879.

GROVER CLEVELAND.

EXECUTIVE MANSION,
Washington, March 16, 1888.

To the Senate:

I have the honor to transmit herewith and recommend for your constitutional approval a convention signed and concluded in this city on the 12th instant, under my direction, between the United States and China, for the exclusion hereafter of Chinese laborers from coming into this country.

This treaty is accompanied by a letter from the Secretary of State in recital of its provisions and explanatory of the reasons for its negotiation, and with it are transmitted sundry documents giving the history of events connected with the presence and treatment of Chinese subjects in the United States.

In view of the public interest which has for a long time been manifested in relation to the question of Chinese immigration, it would seem advisable that the full text of this treaty should be made public, and I respectfully recommend that an order to that effect be made by your honorable body.

GROVER CLEVELAND.

EXECUTIVE MANSION, *March 16, 1888.*

To the Senate of the United States:

I herewith transmit, in compliance with the resolution of the Senate of the 16th ultimo, a report from the Secretary of State, accompanied by certain correspondence in regard to the Mexican *zona libre*.

GROVER CLEVELAND.

EXECUTIVE MANSION, *March 20, 1888.*

To the Senate and House of Representatives:

I transmit herewith a communication of the 13th instant from the Secretary of the Interior, with accompanying papers, and submitting the draft of a proposed bill to forfeit lands granted to the State of Oregon for the construction of certain wagon roads, and for other purposes.

The presentation of facts by the Secretary of the Interior herewith transmitted is the result of an examination made under his direction, which has developed, as it seems to me, the most unblushing frauds upon the Government, which, if remaining unchallenged, will divert several hundred thousand acres of land from the public domain and from the reach of honest settlers to those who have attempted to prevent and prostitute the beneficent designs of the Government. The Government sought by the promise of generous donations of land to promote the building of wagon roads for public convenience and for the purpose of encouraging settlement upon the public lands. The roads have not been built, and yet an attempt is made to claim the lands under a title which depends for its validity entirely upon the construction of these roads.

The evidence which has been collected by the Secretary of the Interior, plainly establishing this attempt to defraud the Government and exclude the settlers who are willing to avail themselves of the liberal policy adopted for the settlement of the public lands, is herewith submitted to the Congress, with the recommendation that the bill which has been prepared, and which is herewith transmitted, may become a law, and with the earnest hope that the opportunity thus presented to demonstrate a sincere desire to preserve the public domain for settlers and to frustrate unlawful attempts to appropriate the same may not be neglected.

GROVER CLEVELAND.

EXECUTIVE MANSION,
Washington, March 22, 1888.

To the Senate:

I transmit herewith, for your advice and consent to the ratification thereof, a convention between the United States and Venezuela, signed the 15th instant, supplementary to the convention between the same powers for the settlement of claims signed December 5, 1885.

I transmit also a report of the Secretary of State thereon and copies of correspondence had with the diplomatic representative of Venezuela at this capital in relation thereto.

GROVER CLEVELAND.

EXECUTIVE MANSION, *March 22, 1888.*

To the Senate:

In response to the resolution adopted by your honorable body on the 16th instant, as follows—

Resolved, That the President of the United States be requested, if in his judgment not incompatible with the public interest, to transmit to the Senate copies of the minutes and daily protocols of the meetings of the commissioners who negotiated the treaty with Great Britain submitted by the President to the Senate on the 20th of February, 1888—

I submit herewith a report of the Secretary of State, which I hope will satisfactorily meet the request for information embraced in said resolution.

GROVER CLEVELAN̄

EXECUTIVE MANSION, *March 27, 1888.*

To the Senate and House of Representatives:

I transmit herewith a report from Hon. George H. Pendleton, our minister to Germany, dated January 30, 1888, from which it appears that trichinosis prevails to a considerable extent in certain parts of Germany and that a number of persons have already died from the effects of eating the meat of diseased hogs which were grown in that country.

I also transmit a report from our consul at Marseilles, dated February 4, 1888, representing that for a number of months a highly contagious and fatal disease has prevailed among the swine of a large section of France, which disease is thought to be very similar to hog cholera by the Commissioner of Agriculture, whose statement is herewith submitted.

It is extremely doubtful if the law passed April 29, 1878, entitled "An act to prevent the introduction of contagious or infectious diseases into the United States," meets cases of this description.

In view of the danger to the health and lives of our people and the contagion that may be spread to the live stock of the country by the importation of swine or hog products from either of the countries named, I recommend the passage of a law prohibiting such importation, with proper regulations as to the continuance of such prohibition, and permitting such further prohibitions in other future cases of a like character as safety and prudence may require.

GROVER CLEVELAND.

EXECUTIVE MANSION,
Washington, April 2, 1888.

To the House of Representatives:

I transmit herewith a report from the Secretary of State, with its inclosures, in response to the resolution of the House of Representatives of the 8th ultimo, in relation to affairs in Samoa.

GROVER CLEVELAND.

[A similar message was sent to the Senate in answer to a resolution of that body of December 21, 1887.]

EXECUTIVE MANSION, *April 5, 1888.*

To the Senate and House of Representatives:

I transmit herewith a communication of the 3d instant from the Secretary of the Interior, submitting, with accompanying papers, a draft of a bill to provide for the revocation of the withdrawal of lands made for the benefit of certain railroads, and for other purposes.

GROVER CLEVELAND.

EXECUTIVE MANSION, *April 9, 1888.*

To the Senate and House of Representatives:

I transmit herewith a communication of the 6th instant from the Secretary of the Interior, submitting, with accompanying papers, a draft of proposed legislation, prepared in the Office of Indian Affairs, to authorize the use of certain funds therein specified in the purchase of lands in the State of Florida upon which to locate the Seminole Indians in that State. The matter is presented for the favorable consideration of Congress.

GROVER CLEVELAND.

EXECUTIVE MANSION, *April 12, 1888.*
To the Senate and House of Representatives:

I transmit herewith and commend to your favorable consideration a letter from the Secretary of State, outlining a plan for publishing the important collections of historical manuscripts now deposited in the Department of State.

GROVER CLEVELAND.

EXECUTIVE MANSION, *April 12, 1888.*
To the Senate of the United States:

In response to the resolution of the Senate dated March 8, calling for the correspondence respecting the seizure of the American steamships *Hero, San Fernando,* and *Nutrias,* the property of the Venezuela Steam Transportation Company of New York, and the imprisonment of their officers by the authorities in Venezuela, I transmit herewith the report of the Secretary of State on the subject, together with the accompanying documents.

GROVER CLEVELAND.

EXECUTIVE MANSION, *April 18, 1888.*
To the Senate of the United States:

In answer to the resolution of the Senate of the 5th of March last, calling upon the Secretary of State for copies of the correspondence relating to the claim of William H. Frear against the Government of France for money due him for provisions furnished in March, 1871, for revictualing Paris, I transmit a report from that officer, together with the correspondence called for by the resolution.

GROVER CLEVELAND.

EXECUTIVE MANSION,
Washington, April 23, 1888.
To the Senate:

I transmit herewith a report from the Secretary of State and accompanying papers, in response to the resolution of the Senate of the 25th of January last, requesting correspondence and other information in relation to the claims convention of December 5, 1885, between the United States and Venezuela.

This resolution was adopted in open session; but in view of the of circumstances since its adoption, by the signature on the 15th of the convention which I transmitted to the Senate with my message of the 22d ultimo,* and which is now under consideration there in executive session, I transmit the accompanying report as a confidential document also.

GROVER CLEVELAND.

EXECUTIVE MANSION,
Washington, *May 8, 1888.*

To the Senate of the United States:

I retransmit herewith a convention for the surrender of criminals between the United States and the Republic of Guatemala, concluded October 11, 1870, and ratified by the President of the United States, as amended by the Senate, on April 11, 1871, calling attention to the accompanying report of the Secretary of State as explanatory of my action.

GROVER CLEVELAND.

EXECUTIVE MANSION, *May 8, 1888.*

To the Senate of the United States:

In answer to the resolution of the Senate of April 12, directing the Secretary of State to transmit to the Senate a copy of the correspondence in his Department in regard to the case of John Fruchier, an American citizen who has been impressed into the military service of France, I transmit herewith a report in relation thereto from the Secretary of State, together with the accompanying papers, not considering their communication to be incompatible with the public interests.

GROVER CLEVELAND.

EXECUTIVE MANSION,
Washington, *May 14, 1888.*

To the Senate and House of Representatives:

I transmit herewith a report from the Secretary of State, relative to the claim of Mr. Rudolph Lobsiger, a Swiss citizen, against the United States, and recommend that provision be made by law for referring the matter to the Court of Claims for examination on its merits.

GROVER CLEVELAND.

EXECUTIVE MANSION,
Washington, *May 14, 1888.*

To the Senate and House of Representatives:

I transmit herewith a communication from the Secretary of State, accompanied by a report of Mr. Somerville P. Tuck, appointed to carry out

* See p. 611.

certain provisions of section 5 of an act entitled "An act to provide for the ascertainment of claims of American citizens for spoliations committed by the French prior to the 31st day of July, 1801," approved January 20, 1885.
GROVER CLEVELAND.

EXECUTIVE MANSION, *May 15, 1888.*
To the House of Representatives:

In compliance with a resolution originating in the House of Representatives and concurred in by the Senate, I return herewith the bill (H. R. 2699) entitled "An act for the relief of the heirs of the late Solomon Spitzer."
GROVER CLEVELAND.

EXECUTIVE MANSION,
Washington, June 14, 1888.
To the Senate of the United States:

I transmit herewith, in response to a resolution of the Senate of the 11th instant, a report of the Secretary of State, to whom said resolution was addressed, together with a copy of the letter addressed by William H. Seward, Secretary of State, to the governors of certain States of the Union, under date of October 14, 1861, as described in said resolution.
.GROVER CLEVELAND.

EXECUTIVE MANSION, *June 26, 1888.*
To the Senate and House of Representatives:

I transmit herewith a report from the Secretary of State, accompanied with selected correspondence relating to foreign affairs for the year 1887.
GROVER CLEVELAND.

EXECUTIVE MANSION,
Washington, July 5, 1888.
To the Senate:

I transmit herewith, with a view to its ratification, a convention for the extradition of criminals between the United States of America and the Republic of Colombia, signed at Bogota on the 7th of May, 1888, and I at the same time call attention to the accompanying report of the Secretary of State, suggesting certain amendments to the convention.
GROVER CLEVELAND.

EXECUTIVE MANSION,
Washington, July 18, 1888.
To the Senate:

I transmit, with a view to its ratification, a convention between the United States and Mexico, signed July 11, 1888, regulating the crossin and recrossing of the frontier between the two countries by pasturing estray or stolen cattle, and I at the same time call attention to the report of the Secretary of State and accompanying papers, relating to the convention in question.

GROVER CLEVELAND.

EXECUTIVE MANSION, *July 18, 1888.*

To the Senate and House of Representatives:

I transmit herewith a communication from the Secretary of State, submitting a series of reports on taxation, prepared by the consular officers of the United States.

GROVER CLEVELAND.

EXECUTIVE MANSION, *July 18, 1888.*

To the Senate and House of Representatives:

I transmit herewith a letter from the Secretary of State, accompanying the annual reports of the consuls of the United States on the trade and industries of foreign countries.

GROVER CLEVELAND.

EXECUTIVE MANSION, *July 18, 1888.*

To the Senate and House of Representatives:

I transmit herewith a letter from the Acting Secretary of State and accompanying documents, being reports from the consuls of the United States on the production of and trade in coffee among the Central and South American States.

GROVER CLEVELAND.

EXECUTIVE MANSION, *July 23, 1888.*

To the Congress of the United States:

Pursuant to the second section of chapter 27 of the laws of 1883, entitled "An act to regulate and improve the civil service of the United States," I herewith transmit the fourth report of the United States Civil Service Commission, covering the period between the 16th day of January, 1886, and the 1st day of July, 1887.

While this report has especial reference to the operations of the Commission during the period above mentioned, it contains, with its accompanying appendixes, much valuable information concerning the inception of civil-service reform and its growth and progress which can not fail to be interesting and instructive to all who desire improvement in administrative methods.

During the time covered by the report 15,852 persons were examined for admission in the classified civil service of the Government in all its branches, of whom 10,746 passed the examination and 5,106 failed. Of those who passed the examination 2,977 were applicants for admission to the departmental service at Washington, 2,547 were examined for admission to the customs service, and 5,222 for admission to the postal service. During the same period 547 appointments were made from the eligible lists to the departmental service, 641 to the customs service, and 3,254 to the postal service.

Concerning separations from the classified service, the report only informs us of such as have occurred among employees in the public service who had been appointed from eligible lists under civil-service rules. When these rules took effect, they did not apply to the persons then in the service, comprising a full complement of employees, who obtained their positions independently of the new law. The Commission has no record of the separations in this numerous class. And the discrepancy apparent in the report between the number of appointments made in the respective branches of the service from the lists of the Commission and the small number of separations mentioned is to a great extent accounted for by vacancies, of which no report was made to the Commission, occurring among those who held their places without examination and certification, which vacancies were filled by appointment from the eligible lists.

In the departmental service there occurred between the 16th day of January, 1886, and the 30th day of June, 1887, among the employees appointed from the eligible lists under civil-service rules, 17 removals, 36 resignations, and 5 deaths. This does not include 14 separations in the grade of special pension examiners—4 by removal, 5 by resignation, and 5 by death.

In the classified customs and postal services the number of separations among those who received absolute appointments under civil-service rules is given for the period between the 1st day of January, 1886, and the 30th day of June, 1887. It appears that such separations in the customs service for the time mentioned embraced 21 removals, 5 deaths, and 18 resignations, and in the postal service 256 removals, 23 deaths, and 469 resignations.

More than a year has passed since the expiration of the period covered by the report of the Commission. Within the time which has thus elapsed many important changes have taken place in furtherance of a reform in our civil service. The rules and regulations governing the execution of the law upon the subject have been completely remodeled in such manner as to render the enforcement of the statute more effective and greatly increase its usefulness.

Among other things, the scope of the examinations prescribed for those who seek to enter the classified service has been better defined and made more practical, the number of names to be certified from the eligible lists to the appointing officers from which a selection is made has been reduced from four to three, the maximum limitation of the age of persons seeking entrance to the classified service to 45 years has been changed, and reasonable provision has been made for the transfer of employees from one Department to another in proper cases. A plan has also been devised providing for the examination of applicants for promotion in the service, which, when in full operation, will eliminate all chance of favoritism in the advancement of employees, by making promotion a reward of merit and faithful discharge of duty.

Until within a few weeks there was no uniform classification of employees in the different Executive Departments of the Government. As a result of this condition, in some of the Departments positions could be obtained without civil-service examination, because they were not within the classification of such Department, while in other Departments an examination and certification were necessary to obtain positions of the same grade, because such positions were embraced in the classifications applicable to those Departments.

The exception of laborers, watchmen, and messengers from examination and classification gave opportunity, in the absence of any rule guarding against it, for the employment, free from civil-service restrictions, of persons under these designations, who were immediately detailed to do clerical work.

All this has been obviated by the application to all the Departments of an extended and uniform classification embracing grades of employees not theretofore included, and by the adoption of a rule prohibiting the detail of laborers, watchmen, or messengers to clerical duty.

The path of civil-service reform has not at all times been pleasant nor easy. The scope and purpose of the reform have been much misapprehended; and this has not only given rise to strong opposition, but has led to its invocation by its friends to compass objects not in the least related to it. Thus partisans of the patronage system have naturally condemned it. Those who do not understand its meaning either mistrust it or, when disappointed because in its present stage it is not applied to every real or imaginary ill, accuse those charged with its enforcement with faithlessness to civil-service reform. Its importance has frequently been underestimated, and the support of good men has thus been lost by their lack of interest in its success. Besides all these difficulties, those responsible for the administration of the Government in its executive branches have been and still are often annoyed and irritated by the disloyalty to the service and the insolence of employees who remain in place as the beneficiaries and the relics and reminders of the vicious system of appointment which civil-service reform was intended to displace.

And yet these are but the incidents of an advance movement which is radical and far-reaching. The people are, notwithstanding, to be congratulated upon the progress which has been made and upon the firm, practical, and sensible foundation upon which this reform now rests.

With a continuation of the intelligent fidelity which has hitherto characterized the work of the Commission; with a continuation and increase of the favor and liberality which have lately been evinced by the Congress in the proper equipment of the Commission for its work; with a firm but conservative and reasonable support of the reform by all its friends, and with the disappearance of opposition which must inevitably follow its better understanding, the execution of the civil-service law can not fail to ultimately answer the hopes in which it had its origin.

GROVER CLEVELAND.

EXECUTIVE MANSION, *July 26, 1888.*

To the Senate of the United States:

I transmit herewith, in response to a resolution of the Senate of 11th April last, a report of the Secretary of State, with accompanying correspondence, relating to the pending dispute between the Government of Venezuela and the Government of Great Britain concerning the boundaries between British Guiana and Venezuela.

GROVER CLEVELAND.

EXECUTIVE MANSION, *August 6, 1888.*

To the Senate and House of Representatives:

It becomes my painful duty to announce to the Congress and to the people of the United States the death of Philip H. Sheridan, General of the Army, which occurred at a late hour last night at his summer home in the State of Massachusetts.

The death of this valiant soldier and patriotic son of the Republic, though his long illness has been regarded with anxiety, has nevertheless shocked the country and caused universal grief.

He had established for himself a stronghold in the hearts of his fellow-countrymen, who soon caught the true meaning and purpose of his soldierly devotion and heroic temper.

His intrepid courage, his steadfast patriotism, and the generosity of his nature inspired with peculiar warmth the admiration of all the people.

Above his grave affection for the man and pride in his achievements will struggle for mastery, and too much honor can not be accorded to one who was so richly endowed with all the qualities which make his death a national loss.

GROVER CLEVELAND.

EXECUTIVE MANSION, *August 7, 1888.*

To the Senate:

In compliance with a resolution of the Senate of the 3d instant (the House of Representatives concurring), I return herewith the enrolled bill (S. 3303) amendatory of "An act relating to postal crimes and amendatory of the statutes therein mentioned," approved June 18, 1888.

GROVER CLEVELAND.

EXECUTIVE MANSION, *August 10, 1888.*

To the Senate and House of Representatives:

I transmit herewith a communication from the Secretary of State, accompanied by a report of the delegate on the part of the United States to the Fourth International Conference of the Red Cross Association, held at Carlsruhe, in the Grand Duchy of Baden, in September last.

GROVER CLEVELAND.

EXECUTIVE MANSION, *August 23, 1888.*

To the Congress:

The rejection by the Senate of the treaty lately negotiated for the settlement and adjustment of the differences existing between the United States and Great Britain concerning the rights and privileges of American fishermen in the ports and waters of British North America seems to justify a survey of the condition to which the pending question is thus remitted.

The treaty upon this subject concluded in 1818, through disagreements as to the meaning of its terms, has been a fruitful source of irritation and trouble. Our citizens engaged in fishing enterprises in waters adjacent to Canada have been subjected to numerous vexatious interferences and annoyances; their vessels have been seized upon pretexts which appeared to be entirely inadmissible, and they have been otherwise treated by the Canadian authorities and officials in a manner inexcusably harsh and oppressive.

This conduct has been justified by Great Britain and Canada by the claim that the treaty of 1818 permitted it and upon the ground that it was necessary to the proper protection of Canadian interests. We deny that treaty agreements justify these acts, and we further maintain that aside from any treaty restraints of disputed interpretation the relative positions of the United States and Canada as near neighbors, the growth of our joint commerce, the development and prosperity of both countries, which amicable relations surely guarantee, and, above all, the liberality always extended by the United States to the people of Canada furnished motives for kindness and consideration higher and better than treaty covenants.

While keenly sensitive to all that was exasperating in the condition and by no means indisposed to support the just complaints of our injured citizens, I still deemed it my duty, for the preservation of important American interests which were directly involved, and in view of all the details of the situation, to attempt by negotiation to remedy existing wrongs and to finally terminate by a fair and just treaty these ever-recurring causes of difficulty.

I fully believe that the treaty just rejected by the Senate was well 'o the exigency, and that its provisions were adequate for our security in the future from vexatious incidents and for the promotion of friendly neighborhood and intimacy, without sacrificing in the least our national pride or dignity.

I am quite conscious that neither my opinion of the value of the rejected treaty nor the motives which prompted its negotiation are of importance in the light of the judgment of the Senate thereupon. But it is of importance to note that this treaty has been rejected without any apparent disposition on the part of the Senate to alter or amend its provisions, and with the evident intention, not wanting expression, that no negotiation should at present be concluded touching the matter at issue.

The cooperation necessary for the adjustment of the long-standing national differences with which we have to deal by methods of conference and agreement having thus been declined, I am by no means disposed to abandon the interests and the rights of our people in the premises or to neglect their grievances; and I therefore turn to the contemplation of a plan of retaliation as a mode which still remains of treating the situation.

I am not unmindful of the gravity of the responsibility assumed in adopting this line of conduct, nor do I fail in the least to appreciate its serious consequences. It will be impossible to injure our Canadian neighbors by retaliatory measures without inflicting some damage upon our own citizens. This results from our proximity, our community of interests, and the inevitable commingling of the business enterprises which have been developed by mutual activity.

Plainly stated, the policy of national retaliation manifestly embraces the infliction of the greatest harm upon those who have injured us, with the least possible damage to ourselves. There is also an evident propriety, as well as an invitation to moral support, found in visiting upon the offending party the same measure or kind of treatment of which we complain, and as far as possible within the same lines. And above all things, the plan of retaliation, if entered upon, should be thorough and vigorous.

These considerations lead me at this time to invoke the aid and counsel of the Congress and its support in such a further grant of power as seems to me necessary and desirable to render effective the policy I have indicated.

The Congress has already passed a law, which received Executive assent on the 3d day of March, 1887, providing that in case American fishing vessels, being or visiting in the waters or at any of the ports of the British dominions of North America, should be or lately had been deprived of the rights to which they were entitled by treaty or law, or if they were denied certain other privileges therein specified or vexed and harassed in the enjoyment of the same, the President might deny to vessels and their masters and crews of the British dominions of North America any entrance into the waters, ports, or harbors of the United States, and also deny entry into any port or place of the United States of any product of said dominions or other goods coming from said dominions to the United States.

While I shall not hesitate upon proper occasion to enforce this act, it would seem to be unnecessary to suggest that if such enforcement is limited in such a manner as shall result in the least possible injury to our own people the effect would probably be entirely inadequate to the accomplishment of the purpose desired.

I deem it my duty, therefore, to call the attention of the Congress to certain particulars in the action of the authorities of the Dominion of Canada, in addition to the general allegations already made, which appear to be in such marked contrast to the liberal and friendly disposition of our country as in my opinion to call for such legislation as will, upon the principles already stated, properly supplement the power to inaugurate retaliation already vested in the Executive.

Actuated by the generous and neighborly spirit which has characterized our legislation, our tariff laws have since 1866 been so far waived in favor of Canada as to allow free of duty the transit across the territory of the United States of property arriving at our ports and destined to Canada, or exported from Canada to other foreign countries.

When the treaty of Washington was negotiated, in 1871, between the United States and Great Britain, having for its object very largely the modification of the treaty of 1818, the privileges above referred to were made reciprocal and given in return by Canada to the United States in the following language, contained in the twenty-ninth article of said treaty:

It is agreed that for the term of years mentioned in Article XXXIII of this treaty goods, wares, or merchandise arriving at the ports of New York, Boston, and Portland, and any other ports in the United States which have been or may from time to time be specially designated by the President of the United States, and destined for Her Britannic Majesty's possessions in North America, may be entered at the proper custom-house and conveyed in transit, without the payment of duties, through the territory of the United States, under such rules, regulations, and conditions for the protection of the revenue as the Government of the United States may from time to time prescribe; and, under like rules, regulations, and conditions, goods, wares, or merchandise may be conveyed in transit, without the payment of duties, from such possessions through the territory of the United States, for export from the said ports of the United States.

It is further agreed that for the like period goods, wares, or merchandise arriving at any of the ports of Her Britannic Majesty's possessions in North America, and destined for the United States, may be entered at the proper custom-house and conveyed in transit, without the payment of duties, through the said possessions, under such rules and regulations and conditions for the protection of the revenue as the governments of the said possessions may from time to time prescribe; and, under like rules, regulations, and conditions, goods, wares, or merchandise may be conveyed in transit, without payment of duties, from the United States through the said possessions to other places in the United States, or for export from ports in the said possessions.

In the year 1886 notice was received by the representatives of our

Government that our fishermen would no longer be allowed to ship their fish in bond and free of duty through Canadian territory to this country, and ever since that time such shipment has been denied.

The privilege of such shipment, which had been extended to our fishermen, was a most important one, allowing them to spend the time upon the fishing grounds which would otherwise be devoted to a voyage home with their catch, and doubling their opportunities for profitably prosecuting their vocation.

In forbidding the transit of the catch of our fishermen over their territory in bond and free of duty the Canadian authorities deprived us of the only facility dependent upon their concession and for which we could supply no substitute.

The value to the Dominion of Canada of the privilege of transit for their exports and imports across our territory and to and from our ports, though great in every aspect, will be better appreciated when it is remembered that for a considerable portion of each year the St. Lawrence River, which constitutes the direct avenue of foreign commerce leading to Canada, is closed by ice.

During the last six years the imports and exports of British Canadian Provinces carried across our territory under the privileges granted by our laws amounted in value to about $270,000,000, nearly all of which were goods dutiable under our tariff laws, by far the larger part of this traffic consisting of exchanges of goods between Great Britain and her American Provinces brought to and carried from our ports in their own vessels.

The treaty stipulation entered into by our Government was in harmony with laws which were then on our statute book and are still in force.

I recommend immediate legislative action conferring upon the Executive the power to suspend by proclamation the operation of all laws and regulations permitting the transit of goods, wares, and merchandise in bond across or over the territory of the United States to or from Canada.

There need be no hesitation in suspending these laws arising from the supposition that their continuation is secured by treaty obligations, for it seems quite plain that Article XXIX of the treaty of 1871, which was the only article incorporating such laws, terminated the 1st day of July, 1885.

The article itself declares that its provisions shall be in force "for the term of years mentioned in Article XXXIII of this treaty." Turning to Article XXXIII, we find no mention of the twenty-ninth article, but only a provision that Articles XVIII to XXV, inclusive, and Article XXX shall take effect as soon as the laws required to carry them into operation shall be passed by the legislative bodies of the different countries concerned, and that "they shall remain in force for the period of ten years from the date at which they may come into operation, and, further, until the expiration of two years after either of the high contracting parties shall have given notice to the other of its wish to terminate the same."

I am of the opinion that the "term of years mentioned in Article XXXIII," referred to in Article XXIX as the limit of its duration, means the period during which Articles XVIII to XXV, inclusive, and Article XXX, commonly called the "fishery articles," should continue in force under the language of said Article XXXIII.

That the joint high commissioners who negotiated the treaty so understood and intended the phrase is certain, for in a statement containing an account of their negotiations, prepared under their supervision and approved by them, we find the following entry on the subject:

The transit question was discussed, and it was agreed that any settlement that might be made should include a reciprocal arrangement in that respect for the period for which the fishery articles should be in force.

In addition to this very satisfactory evidence supporting this construction of the language of Article XXIX, it will be found that the law passed by Congress to carry the treaty into effect furnishes conclusive proof of the correctness of such construction.

This law was passed March 1, 1873, and is entitled "An act to carry into effect the provisions of the treaty between the United States and Great Britain signed in the city of Washington the 8th day of May, 1871, relating to the fisheries." After providing in its first and second sections for putting in operation Articles XVIII to XXV, inclusive, and Article XXX of the treaty, the third section is devoted to Article XXIX, as follows:

Sec. 3. That from the date of the President's proclamation authorized by the first section of this act, and so long as the articles eighteenth to twenty-fifth, inclusive, and article thirtieth of said treaty shall remain in force according to the terms and conditions of article thirty-third of said treaty, all goods, wares, and merchandise, arriving—

etc., etc., following in the remainder of the section the precise words of the stipulation on the part of the United States as contained in Article XXIX, which I have already fully quoted.

Here, then, is a distinct enactment of the Congress limiting the duration of this article of the treaty to the time that Articles XVIII to XXV, inclusive, and Article XXX should continue in force. That in fixing such limitation it but gave the meaning of the treaty itself is indicated by the fact that its purpose is declared to be to carry into effect the provisions of the treaty, and by the further fact that this law appears to have been submitted before the promulgation of the treaty to certain members of the joint high commission representing both countries, and met with no objection or dissent.

There appearing to be no conflict or inconsistency between the treaty and the act of the Congress last cited, it is not necessary to invoke the well-settled principle that in case of such conflict the statute governs the question.

In any event, and whether the law of 1873 construes the treaty or governs it, section 29 of such treaty, I have no doubt, terminated with the proceedings taken by our Government to terminate Articles XVIII to XXV, inclusive, and Article XXX of the treaty. These proceedings had their inception in a joint resolution of Congress passed May 3, 1883, declaring that in the judgment of Congress these articles ought to be terminated, and directing the President to give the notice to the Government of Great Britain provided for in Article XXXIII of the treaty. Such notice having been given two years prior to the 1st day of July, 1885, the articles mentioned were absolutely terminated on the last-named day, and with them Article XXIX was also terminated.

If by any language used in the joint resolution it was intended to relieve section 3 of the act of 1873, embodying Article XXIX of the treaty, from its own limitations, or to save the article itself, I am entirely satisfied that the intention miscarried.

But statutes granting to the people of Canada the valuable privileges of transit for their goods from our ports and over our soil, which had been passed prior to the making of the treaty of 1871 and independently of it, remained in force; and ever since the abrogation of the treaty, and notwithstanding the refusal of Canada to permit our fishermen to send their fish to their home market through her territory in bond, the people of that Dominion have enjoyed without diminution the advantages of our liberal and generous laws.

Without basing our complaint upon a violation of treaty obligations, it is nevertheless true that such refusal of transit and the other injurious acts which have been recited constitute a provoking insistence upon rights neither mitigated by the amenities of national intercourse nor modified by the recognition of our liberality and generous considerations.

The history of events connected with this subject makes it manifest that the Canadian government can, if so disposed administer its laws and protect the interests of its people without manifestation of unfriendliness and without the unneighborly treatment of our fishing vessels of which we have justly complained, and whatever is done on our part should be done in the hope that the disposition of the Canadian government may remove the occasion of a resort to the additional executive power now sought through legislative action.

I am satisfied that upon the principles which should govern retaliation our intercourse and relations with the Dominion of Canada furnish no better opportunity for its application than is suggested by the conditions herein presented, and that it could not be more effectively inaugurated than under the power of suspension recommended.

While I have expressed my clear conviction upon the question of the continuance of section 29 of the treaty of 1871, I of course fully concede the power and the duty of the Congress, in contemplating legislative action, to construe the terms of any treaty stipulation which might upon any possible consideration of good faith limit such action, and likewise the peculiar propriety in the case here presented of its interpretation of its own language, as contained in the laws of 1873 putting in operation said treaty and of 1883 directing the termination thereof; and if in the deliberate judgment of Congress any restraint to the proposed legislation exists, it is to be hoped that the expediency of its early removal will be recognized.

I desire also to call the attention of the Congress to another subject involving such wrongs and unfair treatment to our citizens as, in my opinion, require prompt action.

The navigation of the Great Lakes and the immense business and carrying trade growing out of the same have been treated broadly and liberally by the United States Government and made free to all mankind, while Canadian railroads and navigation companies share in our country's transportation upon terms as favorable as are accorded to our own citizens.

The canals and other public works built and maintained by the Government along the line of the lakes are made free to all.

In contrast to this condition, and evincing a narrow and ungenerous commercial spirit, every lock and canal which is a public work of the Dominion of Canada is subject to tolls and charges.

By Article XXVII of the treaty of 1871 provision was made to secure to the citizens of the United States the use of the Welland, St. Lawrence, and other canals in the Dominion of Canada on terms of equality with the inhabitants of the Dominion, and to also secure to the subjects of Great Britain the use of the St. Clair Flats Canal on terms of equality with the inhabitants of the United States.

The equality with the inhabitants of the Dominion which we were promised in the use of the canals of Canada did not secure to us freedom from tolls in their navigation, but we had a right to expect that we, being Americans and interested in American commerce, would be no more burdened in regard to the same than Canadians engaged in their own trade; and the whole spirit of the concession made was, or should have been, that merchandise and property transported to an American market through these canals should not be enhanced in its cost by tolls many times higher than such as were carried to an adjoining Canadian market. All our citizens, producers and consumers as well as vessel owners, were to enjoy the equality promised.

And yet evidence has for some time been before the Congress, furnished by the Secretary of the Treasury, showing that while the tolls charged in the first instance are the same to all, such vessels and cargoes as are destined to certain Canadian ports are allowed a refund of nearly the entire tolls, while those bound for American ports are not allowed any such advantage.

To promise equality, and then in practice make it conditional upon our vessels doing Canadian business instead of their own, is to fulfill a promise with the shadow of performance.

I recommend that such legislative action be taken as will give Canadian vessels navigating our canals, and their cargoes, precisely the advantages granted to our vessels and cargoes upon Canadian canals, and that the same be measured by exactly the same rule of discrimination.

The course which I have outlined and the recommendations made relate to the honor and dignity of our country and the protection and preservation of the rights and interests of all our people. A government does but half its duty when it protects its citizens at home and permits them to be imposed upon and humiliated by the unfair and overreaching disposition of other nations. If we invite our people to rely upon arrangements made for their benefit abroad, we should see to it that they are not deceived; and if we are generous and liberal to a neighboring country, our people should reap the advantage of it by a return of liberality and generosity.

These are subjects which partisanship should not disturb or confuse. Let us survey the ground calmly and moderately; and having put aside other means of settlement, if we enter upon the policy of retaliation let us pursue it firmly, with a determination only to subserve the interests of our people and maintain the high standard and the becoming pride of American citizenship.

GROVER CLEVELAND.

Executive Mansion, *August 27, 1888.*

To the House of Representatives:

In compliance with a resolution of the House of Representatives of the 27th instant (the Senate concurring), I return herewith House bill No. 10060, entitled "An act prescribing the times for sales and for notice of sales of property in the District of Columbia for overdue taxes."

GROVER CLEVELAND.

Executive Mansion, *September 7, 1888.*

To the Senate of the United States:

In reply to the resolution of the Senate in the words following—

In the Senate of the United States,
September 5, 1888.

Resolved, That the President is requested, if not incompatible with the public interests, to inform the Senate whether the recent treaty with China and the amendments adopted by the Senate have been ratified by the Emperor of China—

I have to communicate the annexed copies of dispatches from our minister to China, giving the only official information at hand in relation to the matter to which reference is had.

GROVER CLEVELAND.

To the Senate:

Responding to the inquiries contained in the subjoined resolution of the Senate of the 28th ultimo, I have the honor to state in reply to the subject first therein mentioned, calling upon the Executive for "copies of all communications, if any, addressed by his direction to the Government of Great Britain, remonstrating with that Government against the wrongs and unfair treatment to our citizens by the action of the Canadian Government in refunding to vessels and cargoes which pass through the Welland and other Canadian canals nearly the entire tolls if they are destined to Canadian ports, while those bound for American ports are not allowed any such advantage, and the breach of the engagement contained in the treaty of 1871 whereby Great Britain promised to the United States equality in the matter of such canal transportation; also copies of any demand made by his direction upon Great Britain for the redress of such wrongs, and the replies of Great Britain to such communication and demand," that I herewith transmit copies of all communications between the Department of State and the United States consul at Ottawa, which are accompanied by copies of the orders of the Canadian officials in relation to the subject inquired of; also correspondence between the Department of State and the British minister at this capital, with copies of the documents therein referred to.

I also inclose, as connected therewith, a copy of Executive Document No. 406, House of Representatives, Fiftieth Congress, first session, containing the answer of the Acting Secretary of the Treasury, dated July 23, 1888, in reply to a resolution of the House of Representatives relating to the navigation of the Welland Canal, and the documents thus transmitted comprise the entire correspondence in relation to the subjects referred to in that portion of the resolution of inquiry which is above quoted.

The second branch of inquiry is in the words following:

And also that there be communicated to the Senate copies of all papers, correspondence, and information touching the matter of the refusal of the British Government, or that of any of her North American dominions, to allow the entry at Dominion seaports of American fish or other cargoes for transportation in bond to the United States since the 1st day of July, 1885.

It will be remembered that though the fishing articles of the treaty of 1871 expired on the said 1st day of July, 1885, a temporary arrangement was made whereby the privileges accorded to our fishermen under said articles were continued during the remainder of that year's fishing season.

No instance of refusal by the Canadian authorities since July 1, 1885, up to the present time to allow the entry at Dominion seaports of American cargoes other than fish for transportation in bond across the territory of Canada to the United States has been made known to the Department of State.

The case of the fishing steamer *Novelty*, involving, among other things, a refusal, on July 1, 1886, of the right to permit the transshipment of fish in bond at the port of Pictou, Nova Scotia, was duly communicated to Congress in my message of December 8, 1886, a copy of which I herewith transmit. (Ex. Doc. No. 19, Forty-ninth Congress, second session, p. 1.)

On page 16 of this document will be found a copy of a communication addressed by the Secretary of State to the British minister, dated June 14, 1886, on the subject of the refusal of transshipment of fish in bond. At page 24 of the same publication will be found the protest of the Secretary of State in the case of the *Novelty*, and at pages 49–50 are the response of the British minister and report of the Canadian privy council.

On the 26th of January, 1887, a revised list of cases of alleged ill treatment of our fishing vessels in Canadian waters was furnished by the Secretary of State to the Committee on Foreign Relations of the Senate, in which the above case is included, a copy of which, being Senate Executive Document No. 55 of the second session Forty-ninth Congress, is herewith inclosed; and in the report by Mr. Edmunds, from the Committee on Foreign Relations (No. 1683 of the same session), the case referred to was again published. And, as relating to the subject of the resolution now before me, the following pertinent passage, taken from the said report, may be of interest:

As regards commercial and other friendly business intercourse between ports and places in the Dominion and the United States, it is, of course, of much importance that regulations affecting the same should be mutually reasonable and fairly administered. If an American vessel should happen to have caught a cargo of fish at sea 100 miles distant from some Canadian port, from which there is railway communication to the United States, and should be denied the privilege of landing and shipping its cargo therefrom to the United States, as the Canadians do, it would be, of course, a serious disadvantage; and there is, it is thought, nothing in the treaty of 1818 which would warrant such an exclusion. But the Dominion laws may make such a distinction, and it is understood that in fact the privilege of so shipping fish from American vessels has been refused during the last year.

I also respectfully refer to Senate Miscellaneous Document No. 54, Forty-ninth Congress, second session, being a communication from the Commissioner of Fish and Fisheries to Hon. George F. Edmunds, chairman of the Committee on Foreign Relations, dated February 5, 1887, which is accompanied by a partial list of vessels injuriously treated by the Canadian authorities, based upon information furnished to the United States Commissioner of Fish and Fisheries.

This list is stated to be supplementary to the revised list which had been transmitted to the committee by the Secretary of State January 26, 1887.

Of the sixty-eight vessels comprised in this list it is stated that six, to wit, the *Nellie M. Snow, Andrew Burnham, Harry G. French, Col. J. H. French, W. H. Wellington*, and *Ralph Hodgdon*, were refused permission to transship fish. None of these cases, however, were ever reported to the Department of State by the parties interested, or were accompanied by affidavit; nor does it appear the facts ever were investigated in any of the cases by the parties making the reports, which were obtained by circulars issued by order of the Commissioner of Fish and Fisheries.

The concluding inquiry is as follows:

And also that he communicate to the Senate what instances have occurred since the 3d of March, 1887, of wrongs to American fishing vessels or other American vessels in the ports or waters of British North America, and what steps, if any, have been taken in respect thereto.

Soon after the passage of the act of March 3, 1887, the negotiation which had been proceeding for several months previously progressed actively, and the proposed conference and the presence at this capital of the plenipotentiaries of the two Governments, out of which the since rejected treaty of February 7, 1888, eventuated, had their natural influence in repressing causes of complaint in relation to the fisheries. Therefore since March 3, 1887, no case has been reported to the Department of State wherein complaint was made of unfriendly or unlawful treatment of American fishing vessels on the part of the Canadian authorities in which reparation was not promptly and satisfactorily obtained by the United States consul-general at Halifax.

A single case of alleged unjust treatment of an American merchant vessel, not engaged in fishing, has been reported since March 3, 1887. This was the ship *Bridgewater*, which was first brought to the attention of the Department of State by the claimant by petition filed June 1, 1888.

On June 18, 1888, legal counsel, who appeared and desired to be heard, filed their formal authority and the claim was at once duly investigated, and on June 22, 1888, a communication was addressed by the Secretary of State to the British minister, which sets forth the history of the claim, and a copy of which is herewith transmitted; and of this formal acknowledgment was made, but no further reply has been received.

GROVER CLEVELAND.

To the Senate: EXECUTIVE MANSION, *September 18, 1888*.

I herewith transmit, in reply to the resolution of the Senate of the 11th instant, a copy of a report from the Secretary of State, with accompanying documents, relative to the pending treaty with China.

GROVER CLEVELAND.

To the Congress: EXECUTIVE MANSION, *October 1, 1888*.

I have this day approved House bill No. 11336, supplementary to an act entitled "An act to execute certain treaty stipulations relating to Chinese," approved the 6th day of May, 1882.

It seems to me that some suggestions and recommendations may properly accompany my approval of this bill.

Its object is to more effectually accomplish by legislation the exclusion from this country of Chinese laborers.

The experiment of blending the social habits and mutual race idio-syncrasies of the Chinese laboring classes with those of the great body of the people of the United States has been proved by the experience of twenty years, and ever since the Burlingame treaty of 1868, to be in every sense unwise, impolitic, and injurious to both nations. With the lapse of time the necessity for its abandonment has grown in force, until those having in charge the Government of the respective countries have resolved to modify and sufficiently abrogate all those features of prior conventional arrangements which permitted the coming of Chinese labor-ers to the United States.

In modification of prior conventions the treaty of November 17, 1880, was concluded, whereby, in the first article thereof, it was agreed that the United States should at will regulate, limit, or suspend the coming of Chinese laborers to the United States, but not absolutely prohibit it; and under this article an act of Congress, approved on May 6, 1882 (see 22 U. S. Statutes at Large, p. 58), and amended July 5, 1884 (23 U. S. Statutes at Large, p. 115), suspended for ten years the coming of Chinese laborers to the United States, and regulated the going and coming of such Chinese laborers as were at that time in the United States.

It was, however, soon made evident that the mercenary greed of the parties who were trading in the labor of this class of the Chinese popula-tion was proving too strong for the just execution of the law, and that the virtual defeat of the object and intent of both law and treaty was being fraudulently accomplished by false pretense and perjury, contrary to the expressed will of both Governments.

To such an extent has the successful violation of the treaty and the laws enacted for its execution progressed that the courts in the Pacific States have been for some time past overwhelmed by the examination of cases of Chinese laborers who are charged with having entered our ports under fraudulent certificates of return or seek to establish by perjury the claim of prior residence.

Such demonstration of the inoperative and inefficient condition of the treaty and law has produced deep-seated and increasing discontent among the people of the United States, and especially with those resident on the Pacific Coast. This has induced me to omit no effort to find an effectual remedy for the evils complained of and to answer the earnest popular demand for the absolute exclusion of Chinese laborers having objects and purposes unlike our own and wholly disconnected with American citizenship.

Aided by the presence in this country of able and intelligent diplo-matic and consular officers of the Chinese Government, and the repre-scutations made from time to time by our minister in China under the instructions of the Department of State, the actual condition of public sentiment and the status of affairs in the United States have been fully made known to the Government of China.

The necessity for remedy has been fully appreciated by that Government, and in August, 1886, our minister at Peking received from the Chinese foreign office a communication announcing that China, of her own accord, proposed to establish a system of strict and absolute prohibition of her laborers, under heavy penalties, from coming to the United States, and likewise to prohibit the return to the United States of any Chinese laborer who had at any time gone back to China, "in order" (in the words of the communication) "that the Chinese laborers may gradually be reduced in number and causes of danger averted and lives preserved."

This view of the Chinese Government, so completely in harmony with that of the United States, was by my direction speedily formulated in a treaty draft between the two nations, embodying the propositions so presented by the Chinese foreign office.

The deliberations, frequent oral discussions, and correspondence on the general questions that ensued have been fully communicated by me to the Senate at the present session, and, as contained in Senate Executive Document O, parts 1 and 2, and in Senate Executive Document No. 272, may be properly referred to as containing a complete history of the transaction.

It is thus easy to learn how the joint desires and unequivocal mutual understanding of the two Governments were brought into articulated form in the treaty, which, after a mutual exhibition of plenary powers from the respective Governments, was signed and concluded by the plenipotentiaries of the United States and China at this capital on March 12 last.

Being submitted for the advice and consent of the Senate, its confirmation, on the 7th day of May last, was accompanied by two amendments which that body ingrafted upon it.

On the 12th day of the same month the Chinese minister, who was the plenipotentiary of his Government in the negotiation and the conclusion of the treaty, in a note to the Secretary of State gave his approval to these amendments, "as they did not alter the terms of the treaty," and the amendments were at once telegraphed to China, whither the original treaty had previously been sent immediately after its signature on March 12.

On the 13th day of last month I approved Senate bill No. 3304, "to prohibit the coming of Chinese laborers to the United States." This bill was intended to supplement the treaty, and was approved in the confident anticipation of an early exchange of ratifications of the treaty and its amendments and the proclamation of the same, upon which event the legislation so approved was by its terms to take effect.

No information of any definite action upon the treaty by the Chinese Government was received until the 21st ultimo—the day the bill which I have just approved was presented to me—when a telegram from our minister at Peking to the Secretary of State announced the refusal of the Chinese Government to exchange ratifications of the treaty unless further discussion should be had with a view to shorten the period stipulated in the treaty for the exclusion of Chinese laborers and to change the conditions agreed on, which should entitle any Chinese laborer who might go back to China to return again to the United States.

By a note from the chargé d'affaires *ad interim* of China to the Secretary of State, received on the evening of the 25th ultimo (a copy of which is herewith transmitted, together with the reply thereto), a third amendment is proposed, whereby the certificate under which any departing Chinese laborer alleging the possession of property in the United States would be enabled to return to this country should be granted by the Chinese consul instead of the United States collector, as had been provided in the treaty.

The obvious and necessary effect of this last proposition would be practically to place the execution of the treaty beyond the control of the United States.

Article I of the treaty proposed to be so materially altered had in the course of the negotiations been settled in acquiescence with the request of the Chinese plenipotentiary and to his expressed satisfaction.

In 1886, as appears in the documents heretofore referred to, the Chinese foreign office had formally proposed to our minister strict exclusion of Chinese laborers from the United States without limitation, and had otherwise and more definitely stated that no term whatever for exclusion was necessary, for the reason that China would of itself take steps to prevent its laborers from coming to the United States.

In the course of the negotiations that followed suggestions from the same quarter led to the insertion in behalf of the United States of a term of "thirty years," and this term, upon the representations of the Chinese plenipotentiary, was reduced to "twenty years," and finally so agreed upon.

Article II was wholly of Chinese origination, and to that alone owes its presence in the treaty.

And it is here pertinent to remark that everywhere in the United States laws for the collection of debts are equally available to all creditors without respect to race, sex, nationality, or place of residence, and equally with the citizens or subjects of the most favored nations and with the citizens of the United States recovery can be had in any court of justice in the United States by a subject of China, whether of the laboring or any other class.

No disability accrues from nonresidence of a plaintiff, whose claim can be enforced in the usual way by him or his assignee or attorney in our courts of justice.

In this respect it can not be alleged that there exists the slightest discrimination against Chinese subjects, and it is a notable fact that large trading firms and companies and individual merchants and traders of that nation are profitably established at numerous points throughout the Union, in whose hands every claim transmitted by an absent Chinaman of a just and lawful nature could be completely enforced.

The admitted and paramount right and duty of every government to exclude from its borders all elements of foreign population which for any reason retard its prosperity or are detrimental to the moral and physical health of its people must be regarded as a recognized canon of international law and intercourse. China herself has not dissented from this doctrine, but has, by the expressions to which I have referred, led us confidently to rely upon such action on her part in cooperation with us as would enforce the exclusion of Chinese laborers from our country.

This cooperation has not, however, been accorded us. Thus from the unexpected and disappointing refusal of the Chinese Government to confirm the acts of its authorized agent and to carry into effect an international agreement, the main feature of which was voluntarily presented by that Government for our acceptance, and which had been the subject of long and careful deliberation, an emergency has arisen, in which the Government of the United States is called upon to act in self-defense by the exercise of its legislative power. I can not but regard the expressed demand on the part of China for a reexamination and renewed discussion of the topics so completely covered by mutual treaty stipulations as an indefinite postponement and practical abandonment of the objects we have in view, to which the Government of China may justly be considered as pledged.

The facts and circumstances which I have narrated lead me, in the performance of what seems to me to be my official duty, to join the Congress in dealing legislatively with the question of the exclusion of Chinese laborers, in lieu of further attempts to adjust it by international agreement.

But while thus exercising our undoubted right in the interest of our people and for the general welfare of our country, justice and fairness seem to require that some provision should be made by act or joint resolution under which such Chinese laborers as shall actually have embarked on their return to the United States before the passage of the law this day approved, and are now on their way, may be permitted to land, provided they have duly and lawfully obtained and shall present certificates heretofore issued permitting them to return in accordance with the provisions of existing law.

Nor should our recourse to legislative measures of exclusion cause us to retire from the offer we have made to indemnify such Chinese subjects as have suffered damage through violence in the remote and comparatively unsettled portions of our country at the hands of lawless men. Therefore I recommend that, without acknowledging legal liability therefor, but because it was stipulated in the treaty which has failed to take effect, and in a spirit of humanity befitting our nation, there be appropriated the sum of $276,619.75, payable to the Chinese.minister at this capital on behalf of his Government, as full indemnity for all losses and injuries sustained by Chinese subjects in the manner and under the circumstances mentioned.   GROVER CLEVELAND.

EXECUTIVE MANSION,
Washington, October 12, 1888.
To the Senate:

I transmit, with a view to its ratification, a convention between the United States of America and Venezuela to further extend the period for the exchange of ratifications of the claims convention of December 5, 1885, between the said contracting parties and to extend the period for the exchange of ratifications of the convention of March 15, 1888, between the same contracting parties, also relating to claims.

I invite attention to the accompanying report of the Secretary of State and the papers inclosed therein.   GROVER CLEVELAND.

VETO MESSAGES.

EXECUTIVE MANSION,
Washington, April 4, 1888.
To the House of Representatives:

I return herewith without approval House bill 2477, entitled "An act for the relief of Nathaniel McKay and the executors of Donald McKay."

It is proposed by this bill to allow the beneficiaries named therein to present to the Court of Claims for determination certain demands made by them against the Government on account of the construction of two ironclad monitors called the *Squando* and the *Nauset* and a side-wheel steamer called the *Ashuelot.*

The contracts for building these vessels were made early in 1863. It was agreed that they should be completed within six or eight months. It was also provided in these contracts that the Government "should have the privilege of making alterations and additions to the plans and specifications at any time during the progress of the work, as it may deem necessary and proper," and that if said alterations and additions should cause extra expense to the contractors the Government would "pay for the same at fair and reasonable rates."

It thus appears that the time allowed for the completion of these vessels was with the assent of the contractors made exceedingly short; that notwithstanding this fact they consented to permit such alterations of plans as must almost necessarily prolong the time, fixing no limit to such extension, and that in the same breath they fix their measure of compensation for such alterations and an extended time consequent thereon at "á fair and reasonable rate" for the extra expense caused thereby.

Almost immediately upon the beginning of their work alterations and changes were made in the original plans for these vessels, and they were repeated and continued to such a degree that the completion of the vessels was delayed many months.

In the latter part of the year 1864 and early in the year 1865 payments in excess of the contract price were made by the Navy Department to the contractors under the provisions of the contract above recited. The contract price for the *Squando* was $395,000. The contractors claimed extra compensation amounting to $337,329.46, and there was allowed $194,-525.70. The contract price of the *Nauset* was $386,000, the extra compensation claimed was $314,768.93, and the amount allowed $192,110.98. The contract price of the side-wheel steamer *Ashuelot* was $275,000, the extra compensation claimed was $81,447.50, and the amount allowed was $22,415.92. The different sums as thus adjusted were received by the contractors in settlement of their claims for extra expense, and receipts in full were given by them to the Government.

A number of other contractors had done like work for the Government and claimed to have demands growing out of the same for extra compensation.

Evidently with the view of investigating and settling these claims, on the 9th day of March, 1865, the Senate passed the following resolution:

Resolved, That the Secretary of the Navy be requested to organize a board of not less than three persons, whose duty it shall be to inquire into and determine how much the vessels of war and steam machinery contracted for by the Department in the years 1862 and 1863 cost the contractors over and above the contract price and allowance for extra work, and report the same to the Senate at its next session; none but those that have given satisfaction to the Department to be considered.

This board was appointed by the Secretary of the Navy on the 25th day of May, 1865, and consisted of a commodore, a chief engineer, and a paymaster in the Navy. Its powers were broad and liberal, and comprehended an inquiry touching all things that made up "the cost to the contractors" of their work in excess of the contract price and allowances for extra work.

The board convened on the 6th day of June, 1865, and sat continuously until the 23d day of December following, and made numerous awards to contractors. The parties mentioned in the bill now under consideration were notified on the 9th and 15th days of June, 1865, to prepare and submit testimony to the board in support of their claims, and they repeatedly signified their intention to do so.

Donald McKay was the contractor for the construction of the monitor *Nauset* and the steamer *Ashuelot*. The proceedings of the board show that on the 14th day of August, 1865, he notified the board that the only claim he made for loss was on the hull, boiler, and machinery of the *Ashuelot*, which he would be prepared to present in about six weeks.

Neither of these parties presented any statement to the board, and no claim of theirs was passed upon.

On the 2d day of March, 1867, an act was passed directing the Secretary of the Navy to investigate the claims of all contractors for building vessels of war and steam machinery for the same under contracts made after May 1, 1861, and before January 1, 1864. He was by said act required "to ascertain the additional cost which was necessarily incurred by each contractor in the completion of his work by reason of any changes or alterations in the plans and specifications required and delays in the prosecution of the work occasioned by the Government which were not provided for in the original contract." It was further provided that there should be reported to Congress a tabular statement of each case, which should contain "the name of the contractor, a description of the work, the contract price, the whole increased cost of the work over the contract price, and the amount of such increased cost caused by the delay and action of the Government as aforesaid, and the amount already paid the contractor over and above the contract price."

Under this act Commodore J. A. Marchand, Chief Engineer J. W. King, and Paymaster Edward Foster, of the Navy, were designated by the Secretary of the Navy to make the investigation required. These officers on the 26th day of November, 1867, made a report of their proceedings, which was submitted to the Senate with a tabulated statement of all the claims examined by them and their findings thereon

It appears by this report that the claims of the beneficiaries mentioned in the bill herewith returned were examined by the board, and that nothing was found due thereon under the terms of the law directing their examination.

These claims have frequently been before Congress since that time. They have been favorably reported and acted upon a number of times, and have also been more than once strongly condemned by committees to whom they were referred.

A resolution was passed in 1871 by the Congress referring these and other claims of a like character to the Court of Claims for adjudication, but it was vetoed by the President for reasons not necessarily affecting the merits of the claims.

The case of Chouteau *vs.* The United States, reported in Fifth Otto, page 61, which arose out of the contract to build a vessel called the *Etlah*, appears to present the same features that belong to the claims here considered. It is stated in the report of the House committee on this bill that "the *Squando* and *Nausct* were identical in the original plans and the changes and alterations thereon with the *Etlah* and *Shiloh*, built in St. Louis;" and yet the Supreme Court of the United States distinctly decided in the *Etlah* case that the only pretext for further compensation should be sought for in the contract, where the contractor had evidently been content to provide for all the remedy he desired.

It seems, then, that the contractors mentioned in this bill, after entering into contracts plainly indicating that changes of plans and consequent delay in their work were in their contemplation, availed themselves of the remedy which they themselves had provided, and thereupon received about 50 per cent in the case of two of these vessels of the contract price for extra work, giving the Government a receipt in full. When soon thereafter opportunity was offered them to make further claim of as broad a nature as they could desire, they failed to do so, and one of them disclaimed any right to recover on account of one of the vessels, though all are now included in the present bill. In 1867 the claims were fully examined under a law of Congress and rejected, and the Supreme Court in an exactly similar case finds neither law nor equity supporting them.

If it be claimed that no compensation has been yet allowed solely for the increase in the price of labor and material caused by delay in construction, it is no hardship to say that as the contractors made provision for change of plans and delay they must be held to have taken the risk of such rise in price and be satisfied with the provision they have made against it. Besides, much of the increase in the price of labor and material is included in the extra cost which has already been reimbursed to them.

But the bill does not provide that these contractors shall be limited in the Court of Claims to a recovery solely for loss occasioned by increase of the cost of labor and material during the delay caused by the Government. By the terms of the proposed act the court is directed to ascertain the additional cost necessarily incurred in building the vessels by reason of any changes or alterations in the plans and specifications and delays in the prosecution of the work. This, it seems to me, would enable these contractors to open the whole question of compensation for extra work.

It hardly seems fair to the Government to permit these claims to be presented after a lapse of twenty-three years since a settlement in full was made and receipts given, after the opportunity which has been offered for establishing further claims if they existed, and when, as a consequence of the contractor's neglect, the Government would labor under great disadvantages in its defense.

I am of the opinion, in view of the history of these claims and the suspicion naturally excited as to their merit, that no injustice will be done if they are laid at rest instead of being given new life and vigor in the Court of Claims.

                                                GROVER CLEVELAND.

EXECUTIVE MANSION, *April 16, 1888.*

To the House of Representatives:

I return herewith without approval House bill No. 445, entitled "An act granting a pension to Laura A. Wright."

The beneficiary named in this bill is the widow of Charles H. Wright, who was pensioned for a gunshot wound received in the military service of the United States on the 19th day of September, 1864. He continued in the receipt of such pension until June 25, 1884, when he committed suicide by hanging.

It is alleged on behalf of his widow that the pain caused by his wound was so great that it caused temporary insanity, under the influence of which he destroyed himself.

There is not a particle of proof that I can discover tending to show an unsound mind, unless it be the fact of his suicide. He suffered much pain at intervals. He was a farmer in comfortable circumstances, and according to the testimony of one of the physicians, filed in support of the widow's claim, his health was good up to the time of his death, except for the wound and its results. The day before his death he was engaged in work connected with his farming occupation, though he complained of pain from his wound. Early the next morning, still complaining, as it is alleged, of his wound, he went out, declaring he was going out to milk, and not returning in due time, upon search his body was found and his self-destruction discovered. This was nearly twenty years after the deceased received his wound, and there is not a suggestion of any act or word of his in all that time indicating insanity. It seems to me it can hardly be assumed in such circumstances that the insanity and death of the soldier resulted from pain arising from his wound, merely because no other explanation can be given. In numerous cases of suicide no cause or motive for self-destruction is discovered.

We have within our borders thousands of widows living in poverty, and some of them in need, whose dead husbands fought bravely and well in defense of the Government, but whose deaths were not occasioned by any incident of military service. In these cases the wife's long vigil at the bed of wasting disease, the poverty that came before the death, and the distressing doubt and uncertainty which darkened the future have not secured to such widows the aid of our pension laws.

With these in sight the bounty of the Government may without injustice be withheld from one whose soldier husband received a pension for nearly twenty years, though all that time able to labor, and who, having reached a stage of comfortable living, made his wife a widow by destroying his own life.

GROVER CLEVELAND.

To the Senate: EXECUTIVE MANSION, *April 16, 1888.*

I return herewith without approval Senate bill No. 809, entitled "An act granting a pension to Betsey Mannsfield."

It is proposed to grant a pension to the beneficiary named in this bill as the mother of Franklin J. Mannsfield, who enlisted as a private Apr¨

27, 1861, and died in camp of disease on the 14th day of November, in the same year. His mother filed an application for pension in June, 1882.

The testimony filed in the Pension Bureau discloses the following facts:

At the time of the death of the soldier the family, besides himself, consisted of three persons—his father and mother and an unmarried sister. They owned and resided upon a homestead in Wisconsin comprising 293 acres, 20 of which were cleared, the balance being in timber, all unencumbered. The assessed valuation was $1,170, the real value being considerably more. The father was a farmer and blacksmith, healthy and able-bodied, and furnishing a comfortable support, but shortly after the soldier's death he began to drink and his health began to fail. Upon the marriage of the daughter he deeded her 50 acres of the land. He became indebted, and from time to time sold portions of his homestead to pay debts; but in 1882, at the time the mother's application for pension was filed, there still remained 110 acres of land, valued at about $3,300, 40 acres of which was mortgaged in 1880 for $600. Since 1879 the farm had been rented, except 8 or 10 acres reserved for a residence for the family. They owned two cows, and the rent averaged about $125 a year.

This was the condition of affairs as late as 1886, when the claim of the mother for a pension was, after investigation, rejected by the Pension Bureau, and it is supposed to be substantially the same now.

It also appears that a son, born since the soldier's death, and upward of 18 years of age, resides with his parents and furnishes them some assistance.

The claimant certainly was not dependent in the least degree upon the soldier at the time of his death, and she did not file her claim for pension until nearly twenty-one years thereafter.

Though the lack of dependence at the date of the soldier's death is sufficient to defeat a parent's claim for pension under our laws, I believe that in proper cases a relaxation of rules and a charitable liberality should be shown to parents old and in absolute need through default of the help which, it may be presumed, a son would have furnished if his life had not been sacrificed in his country's service.

But it seems to me the case presented here can not be reached by any theory of pensions which has yet been suggested.

GROVER CLEVELAND.

EXECUTIVE MANSION, *April 16, 1888.*

To the Senate:

I return herewith without approval Senate bill No. 549, entitled "An act granting a pension to Hannah R. Langdon."

The husband of the beneficiary named in this bill entered the military service of the United States as assistant surgeon in a Vermont regiment on the 7th day of October, 1862, and less than six months thereafter tendered his resignation, based upon a surgeon's certificate of disability on account of chronic hepatitis (inflammation of the liver) and diarrhea.

On the 12th day of June, 1880, more than seventeen years after his discharge, he filed a claim for pension, alleging chronic diarrhea and resulting piles. He was allowed a pension in January, 1881, and died of consumption on the 24th day of September, in the same year.

Prior to the allowance of his claim for pension he wrote to the Bureau of Pensions a full history of his disability as resulting from chronic diarrhea and piles, and in that letter he made the following statement:

I have had no other disease, except last September (1880) I had pleurisy and congestion of my left lung.

From other sources the Bureau derived the information that the deceased had suffered an attack of pleuro-pneumonia on his left side, and that his recovery had been partial.

In December, 1880, he was examined by two members of the board of surgeons at Burlington, Vt., of which board he was also a member, and the following facts were certified:

For the past fifteen years claimant has practiced his profession in this city, and has up to within a year or a year and a half of this date shown a vigor and power of endurance quite equal to the labor imposed upon him by the popular demand for his services. About a year ago he evinced symptoms of breaking down, cough, emaciation, and debility.

These results—"breaking down, cough, emaciation, and debility"— are the natural effects of such an attack as the deceased himself reported, though not made by him any ground of a claim for pension, and it seems quite clear that his death in September, 1881, must be chargeable to the same cause.

His widow, the beneficiary named in this bill, filed her claim for pension December 5, 1881, based upon the ground that her husband's death from consumption was due to the chronic diarrhea for which he was pensioned. Upon such application the testimony of Dr. H. H. Atwater was filed, to the effect that about 1879 he began to treat the deceased regularly for pleuro-pneumonia, followed by abscesses and degeneration of lung tissue, which finally resulted in death, and that these diseased conditions were complicated with digestive affections, such as diarrhea, dyspepsia, and indigestion. Another affidavit of Dr. Atwater, made in 1886, will be found in the report upon this bill made by the House Committee on Invalid Pensions.

The claimant's application for a pension was rejected by the Pension Bureau on the ground that the cause of her husband's death was not shown to have been connected in any degree with the disease on account of which he was pensioned or with his military service.

I am entirely satisfied that this determination was correct.

I am constrained to disapprove the bill under consideration, because it is thus far our settled and avowed policy to grant pensions only to widows whose husbands have died from causes related to military service, and because the proposed legislation would, in my opinion, result in a discrimination in favor of this claimant unfair and unjust toward thousands of poor widows who are equally entitled to our sympathy and benevolence.

GROVER CLEVELAND.

EXECUTIVE MANSION, *April 18, 1888.*

To the Senate:

I return without approval Senate bill No. 258, entitled "An act for the relief of Major Daniel N. Bash, paymaster, United States Army."

The object of this bill is to release Paymaster Bash from all liability to the Government for the loss by theft of $7,350.93, which was intrusted to him for the payment of United States troops at various posts, one of which was Fort McKinney, in Wyoming Territory.

He started from Cheyenne Depot, accompanied by his clerk, D. F. Bash. Before starting he attempted to procure an iron safe in which he could deposit the money which he should have in his possession during his absence, but was unable to do so. It is alleged that it is customary for paymasters in such cases to be furnished with safes by the Government.

On the 17th day of March, 1887, Major Bash arrived at Douglas, Wyoming Territory, having in his possession $350.93, which was a balance left in his hands after making previous payments on the way. At Douglas he received by express $7,000, $250 of which were in silver. He was met here by an escort consisting of a sergeant and private soldier, who had been sent from Fort McKinney, and who were under orders to report to the paymaster at Douglas and to act as guard from that place to Fort McKinney.

Another unsuccessful attempt having been made at Douglas to obtain a safe or treasure box in which to carry the money, the same was put in a leather valise as the best thing that could be done in the circumstances. The money was first handed by the paymaster to his clerk, and by the clerk put in the valise and handed to the sergeant of the escort. There is evidence that the sergeant was told not to permit it to be out of his sight. Immediately after supper at Douglas the entire party entered the stage and proceeded upon their journey, the sergeant carrying the valise. Major Bash asserts that he said to the sergeant, "You must take good care of the valise; it contains the money."

The next morning, on the 18th day of March, the party arrived at Dry Cheyenne. When the paymaster went in to breakfast at that place, he found all the party at the breakfast table. After breakfast he walked out to the stage, the sergeant going at the same time. He asked him what he had done with the valise, and received the reply that it was in the stage. He then said to the sergeant, "You ought to have brought it in with you; you should take better care of that valise." The valise was then examined and the money was found untouched.

Pursuing their journey, the party arrived at Antelope Springs, Wyoming Territory, at half past 10 o'clock the same morning. The paymaster alleges that he asked the sergeant if he should take dinner there, and that, being answered in the negative, he remarked to him that he might then stay at the stage; that he then went to the stage station, leaving the two soldiers and the clerk at the stage; that he remained at the station warming himself a short time, finding there three citizens, one of whom he afterwards learned was Parker, the thief; that he left the room in which he had been warming himself and went to the dining room, passing along the front of the house, and as he did so noticed the stage standing there with no one near it except a stock tender; that on reaching the dining room he found his entire party at the table; that he looked "pretty sharp" at the sergeant, as he was surprised to see him there, but as he was just eating his pie he (the paymaster) said nothing to him; that not more than a minute after that the sergeant and driver got up and went out; that three or four minutes after they went out they rushed back and said that the valise had been taken.

It was found that the valise and money had been taken by Parker, who had mounted a horse and ridden away. He was pursued so closely that revolver shots were exchanged between the sergeant, who was badly mounted, and the thief. The sergeant alleged that he could have shot Parker if he had been provided with a gun instead of a revolver.

The facts in relation to this subject were developed upon a court of inquiry called for that purpose; and much of the above recited is derived from the evidence of Major Bash himself, taken upon such inquiry.

The following is the finding of the court concerning the conduct of the paymaster in the premises:

That Major Daniel N. Bash, paymaster, United States Army, did not give such direct and detailed orders to the members of the escort as to the manner in which they should guard the public money in his (Bash's) possession while en route to Fort McKinney as the importance of the matter required, and that he did not take the proper and necessary pains to see that any orders which he had given on this subject were duly obeyed.

This finding defines a case of negligence which renders the paymaster liable for the loss of these funds. But a number of army officers, including the members of the court of inquiry, suggest that the paymaster thus found at fault should be relieved from responsibility. This is much the fashion in these days.

It is said that a safe should have been provided; that the paymaster had the right to rely upon the fidelity and efficiency of the escort, and that the two men furnished him as an escort were unintelligent and negligent; that they should have been armed with guns instead of pistols, and that the instructions given to the escort by the paymaster were sufficient to acquit him of culpable neglect.

It seems to me that the omissions of care on the part of this officer are of such a nature as to render much that is urged in his favor irrelevant. He had the charge of this money. It was his care, vigilance, and intelligence which were the safeguards of its protection. If he had as full an appreciation as he indicates of the importance of having a safe, he must have known that in its absence additional care and watchfulness on his part were necessary, whatever his escort or his clerk might do.

But notwithstanding all this he seemed quite content to leave this large sum of money in the hands of those sent to him, not to have the custody of his funds, but to guard him from violence and robbery. On the very morning of the day the theft was committed he had found fault with the sergeant for leaving the money in the stage while he took breakfast, and had said to him that he (the sergeant) ought to have brought it in with him. He here furnishes his own definition of the kind of care which should have been taken of the money—the sergeant "ought to have brought it in with him;" and this suggests the idea that it would have been quite consistent with his duty, and perhaps not much beneath his dignity, if he had taken it in himself. (Chief Paymaster Terrell, in a letter favoring leniency, states that the coin could not have weighed less than 15 pounds.)

It must certainly be conceded that what then took place plainly warned him that to insure the safety of this money he must either take personal charge of it or he must at least be sure that those to whom he surrendered it were watchful and vigilant. And yet when, a few hours later, on the same day, upon arriving at Antelope Springs, he was informed by the sergeant that he did not propose to take dinner there, the paymaster almost casually said to him, "Then you stay at the stage," and he himself went to a room at the station to warm himself. When, as he went from there to the dining room, he passed the stage and saw no one near it except a stock tender, a very conservative idea of duty and care would have induced him to stop at the stage and ascertain the condition of affairs. If he had done so, he probably would have found the money there, and could have taken it in with him or watched it until some of his party came out from dinner. Instead of doing this, he himself went to the dining room, and indicated his surprise at seeing the sergeant there by looking at him sharply. However, as he was just eating his pie, nothing was said.

It is not improbable that the thief waited for the clerk and escort, and lastly the paymaster himself, to enter the dining room before venturing to take, entirely unmolested, the valise containing the money. When it is considered that after finishing his pie the sergeant came out to the stage so nearly the exact moment of the theft that, though badly mounted, he was able to approach near enough in pursuit of the fleeing thief to exchange revolver shots with him, it is quite apparent that the loss might have been prevented if the paymaster had remained a short time by the stage when he saw it unprotected, or had taken the valise in with him, or promptly diverted the attention of the sergeant from his pie to the money which all had abandoned.

When, therefore, it is said that this loss can be charged in any degree to the neglect or default of the Government, it is answered that the direct and immediate cause of the loss was the omission on the part of this paymaster of the Government, in whose custody these funds were placed, of the plainest and simplest acts of prudence and care.

The temptation is very strong to yield assent to the proposition for the relief of a citizen from liability to the Government arising from conduct not absolutely criminal; but the bonds and the security wisely exacted by the Government from its officers to insure proper discharge of public duty will be of very limited value if everything is to be excused except actual dishonesty.

I am thoroughly convinced that the interests of the public would be better protected if fewer private bills were passed relieving officials, upon slight and sentimental grounds, from their pecuniary responsibilities; and the readiness with which army officers join in applications for the condonation of negligence on the part of their army comrades does not tend, in my opinion, to maintain that regard for discipline and that scrupulous observance of duty which should characterize those belonging to their honorable profession.

I can not satisfy myself that the negligence made apparent in this case should be overlooked. GROVER CLEVELAND.

EXECUTIVE MANSION, *April 21, 1888.*

To the House of Representatives:

I return without approval House bill No. 823, entitled "An act granting a pension to Hannah C. De Witt."

An act the precise duplicate of this was passed at the present session of the Congress, and received Executive approval on the 10th day of March, 1888. Pursuant to said act the name of the beneficiary mentioned in the bill herewith returned has been placed upon the pension rolls. The second enactment is of course entirely useless, and was evidently passed by mistake. GROVER CLEVELAND.

EXECUTIVE MANSION, *April 21, 1888.*

To the House of Representatives:

I return without approval House bill No. 418, entitled "An act granting a pension to William H. Brokenshaw."

The history of the military service of the beneficiary mentioned in this bill, as derived from the records of the War Department, shows that he was received at draft rendezvous at Jackson, Mich., on the 25th day of March, 1865; that he was sent to the Twenty-fourth Regiment of Michigan Volunteers on the 29th day of the same month, and that he was present with his command, without any record of disability, from that date until the 30th day of June, 1865, when he was mustered out with his company. It will thus be seen that he was in the service a few days more than three months, just at the close of the war. It is not alleged that he did any actual fighting.

In 1883 he filed an application for pension, alleging that on the evening of the 25th of March, 1865, being the day he was received at rendezvous, he was injured in his ribs while getting into his bunk by three other recruits, who were scuffling in the room and who jumped upon him or crushed him against the side of his bunk.

An examination upon such application made in 1884 tended to show an injury to his ribs, but the claim was rejected upon the ground that no injury was incurred in the line of duty. It must be conceded that upon the claimant's own showing he was not injured as an incident to military service.

Aside from this objection, it is hardly possible that an injury of this kind, producing the consequences which it is alleged followed its infliction, could have been sustained by this soldier and not in the least interrupted the performance of his military service, though such service was very short and probably not severe. When with this it is considered that eighteen years elapsed between the date of the alleged injury and the soldier's application for pension, I am satisfied that no injustice will be done if the disposition made of this case by the Pension Bureau is allowed to stand.

GROVER CLEVELAND.

EXECUTIVE MANSION, *April 21, 1888.*

To the House of Representatives:

I return without approval House bill No. 4633, entitled ''An act granting a pension to Morris T. Mantor.''

The records in this case show that the beneficiary named in this bill enlisted on the 25th day of February, 1864, and that he was mustered out July 18, 1865.

It is also shown that though he was reported sick a considerable part of his period of service there is no mention of any trouble with his eyes.

In the year 1880 he filed an application for pension, alleging dropsy and disease of his eyes, caused by an explosion of ammunition.

The case was examined in 1882 and 1883, and was again specially examined very thoroughly and critically in 1885.

The evidence thus secured seemed to establish the fact that the claimant's eyes were sore for many years before enlistment, and that their condition before that date, during his service, and after his discharge did not materially differ. It also appeared that no pensionable disability from dropsy had existed since the filing of his application.

On these grounds the application was rejected, and I am convinced such action was entirely justified.

The reported conduct of the claimant on the last examination and his attempts to influence witnesses in their testimony add weight to the proposition, quite well established by the proof, that his claim to a pension lacks merit.

GROVER CLEVELAND.

EXECUTIVE MANSION, *April 24, 1888.*

To the House of Representatives:

I return without approval House bill No. 5247, entitled "An act granting a pension to William H. Brimmer."

The beneficiary named in this bill enlisted September 5, 1864, as a wagon master, and was discharged on the 30th day of May, 1865. There is no record of any disability during his short service.

In February, 1888, nearly twenty-three years after his discharge, he filed an application for a pension, alleging that in the fall of 1864 he was made to carry sacks of corn, which produced a weakness of the walls of the abdomen, resulting in rupture. In an affidavit filed upon said application the claimant testifies that he said nothing about his injury or disability to anyone while in the service and can furnish no evidence except his own statement.

The first and only medical evidence presented touching this claim is that of Dr. Reynolds, who examined him in 1880 or 1881, who then came to the conclusion that the claimant was suffering from an incomplete hernia, which a few months thereafter developed in the right groin. From this examination and testimony no hint is furnished that the injury was due to military service, nor any intimation that it might be.

In February, 1888, a medical examination was made under direction of the Pension Bureau, when it was found that the claimant had the general appearance of being healthy and well nourished, but that he had a small uncomplicated inguinal hernia on the right side, which was easily retained.

I can not believe upon the facts presented that an injury of the character alleged could have been sustained in the service and still permitted the performance of all the duties of wagon master for months thereafter, remaining undeveloped for so many years, and that there should now be such a lack of testimony connecting it with any incident of military service.

I believe the rejection of this claim was right and just upon its merits.

GROVER CLEVELAND.

EXECUTIVE MANSION, *April 24, 1888.*

To the House of Representatives:

I return without approval House bill 6908, entitled "An act granting a pension to William P. Witt."

The beneficiary named in the bill was enrolled for one hundred days' service on the 13th day of July, 1864, and was mustered out on the 16th day of November, in the same year. The record shows that he was reported present on all rolls until he was mustered out.

He filed a claim for pension in 1884, alleging that he incurred chronic diarrhea, liver disease, rheumatism, and a disease of the head affecting his hearing during his military service. Two comrades testify to his being sick and being in the hospital to such an extent as to wholly discredit his presence with his company. A physician testifies that he prescribed for him some time in the month of November, 1864, for liver disease and jaundice, to which rheumatism supervened, confining him six weeks or more.

There seems to be a complete hiatus of any medical or other evidence concerning his physical condition from that time until nearly twenty years thereafter, in July, 1884, when he was examined, and it was found that he had impaired hearing in both ears, but no symptoms of rheumatism, and that his liver was normal.

Without further detailing particulars, the entire complexion of this case satisfies me that the claimant contracted no pensionable disability during his one hundred days of service.

GROVER CLEVELAND.

EXECUTIVE MANSION, *April 24, 1888.*

To the House of Representatives:

I return without approval House bill No. 4550, entitled "An act granting a pension to Chloe Quiggle, widow of Phillip Quiggle."

The husband of the beneficiary named enlisted February 11, 1865, and was discharged September 27, 1865. The records show that he was reported August 31, 1865, as "absent, confined in post prison at Chattanooga since August 18, 1865."

He filed a claim for pension June 25, 1880, alleging that after a march from Chattanooga to a point 1½ miles distant and back he upon his return drank some water, which produced diarrhea, since which time he had been troubled also with disease of kidneys and rheumatism.

He died in September, 1882, and the claim then pending on his behalf was completed by his widow. After a special examination the claim for diarrhea was, on the 21st day of April, 1887, allowed from September 28, 1865, to January 1, 1870, when it was shown that any disability from this cause ceased. The claim for disease of kidneys and rheumatism was rejected upon the ground that no such disabilities were shown to be due to military service.

The widow filed a claim on her own behalf August 27, 1883, alleging the death of the soldier from the results of prostration by heat while marching near Nashville, Tenn., and also from disease of kidneys, rheumatism, and chronic diarrhea.

It is reported to me that the evidence taken during a special examination of this case established that before and after enlistment the soldier was addicted to the excessive use of intoxicating liquors.

One physician stated to the examiner that shortly after the soldier's discharge he found him suffering from disease of kidneys and from rheumatism and diarrhea, but that he concluded the disease of the kidneys had been coming on for a year; that it could not have been caused by a sunstroke a few weeks previously, and that the diseases were of longer standing than that.

Another physician who attended the soldier during his last illness testified that he did not know that he suffered from any disease until the summer of 1882; that he found him suffering from retention of urine, and that the difficulty rapidly developed into an acute attack of Bright's disease; that no indications of rheumatism were found, but that the disease progressed steadily and was a well-marked case of Bright's disease of the kidneys. He also testified that the origin of the disease was no doubt recent, though possibly it might have existed in a low form for some years.

A medical examination in May, 1882, developed no disease of the kidneys.

It seems to me that all the reliable testimony in the case tends to show beyond a doubt that the soldier's death was not due to any incident of his military service. I do not find that the medical testimony given by his neighbors makes a suggestion that it was, and upon all the facts I am of the opinion that the pension which has been already allowed was a liberal disposition of the case.

The beneficiary named in this bill is aged, and it would certainly be a gratification to grant her relief; but the question is whether we do well to establish a precedent for the allowance of claims of this character in the distribution of pension funds.   GROVER CLEVELAND.

To the Senate: EXECUTIVE MANSION, *April 30, 1888.*

I return without approval Senate bill No. 465, entitled "An act granting a pension to William Sackman, sr."

The beneficiary named in this bill served from December 24, 1861, to February 29, 1864, in the Fifth Regiment of the Missouri Militia Cavalry.

He was discharged on the day last named for disability. His certificate of discharge states his disability as follows:

Palpitation of the heart and defective lungs, the disability caused by falling off his horse near Fredericktown, Mo., while intoxicated, on detached service, in the month of September, 1862. Not having done any duty since, a discharge would benefit the Government and himself.

It appears that a claim for pension was filed in the year 1881, in which the claimant alleged that—

At Fredericktown, Mo., about the 10th or 12th of April, 1863, he had three ribs broken by falling from his horse while surrounded by guerrillas.

It will be seen that while the certificate of discharge mentions a fall in September, 1862, no allusion is made to any fracture of ribs, while the claimant alleges such an injury occurred in April, 1863.

In 1885 the surgeon who made the medical certificate attached to the discharge, in answer to an inquiry made by the Commissioner of Pensions, says:

I have to state that I remember the case very distinctly. I made the examination in person, and was thoroughly acquainted with the case. I read the statement on which the application for discharge was based to the man, and he consented to have the papers forwarded as they read. The application for pension is fraudulent and should not be allowed.

I have omitted references made to the habits of the soldier by this medical officer.

Of course much reliance should be placed upon these statements made by an officer whose business it was to know the exact facts, and who made his certificate at a time when such facts were fresh in his mind. There is no intimation that the surgeon who made the statement referred to was inimical to the soldier or influenced by any unjust motive.

The attempt to impeach the record thus made is based upon affidavits made by a number of the soldier's comrades, who testify to his character and habits, and only three of whom speak of an injury to the soldier caused by falling from his horse. Two of these affiants allege that they were with the claimant on detached duty when his horse took fright and ran away with him, injuring him so that he could not rise and get on his horse without assistance. So far as these affidavits are before me, no date of this occurrence is given, nothing is said as to the character of the injuries, and no reference is made to the condition of the soldier at the time. The third affiant, who speaks of an injury, says that it occurred while on duty on the march from Pilot Knob to Cape Girardeau, in the year 1862 or 1863, and that it was caused by the soldier's being thrown from his horse. He says further that the soldier was not intoxicated at that time.

No mention is made that I can discover of any fracture of the ribs except in the claimant's application for pension made in 1881, seventeen years after his discharge, and in a report of an examining surgeon made in 1882.

With no denial of the soldier's condition, as stated by the surgeon, on the part of the only parties who claim to have been present at the time of the injury, I can not satisfy myself, in view of the other circumstances surrounding this case, that the allegations contained in the claimant's discharge are discredited.　　GROVER CLEVELAND.

To the Senate:

I return without approval Senate bill No. 838, entitled "An act granting a pension to Mary Sullivan."

On the 1st day of July, 1886, an act was approved which is an exact copy of the one herewith returned. In pursuance of that act the beneficiary's name was placed upon the pension rolls.

A second law for the same purpose is of course unnecessary.

GROVER CLEVELAND.

To the House of Representatives:

I return without approval House bill No. 19, entitled "An act for the relief of H. B. Wilson, administrator of the estate of William Tinder, deceased."

The purpose of this bill is to refund to the estate of William Tinder the sum of $5,000, which was paid to the Government by his administrator in June, 1880, upon the following facts:

In 1876 two indictments were found against one Evans, charging him with passing counterfeit money. In May, 1878, he was tried upon one of said indictments and the jury failed to agree. Thereupon the prisoner entered into two recognizances in the sum of $5,000 each, with W. R. Evans and William Tinder as sureties, conditioned for the appearance of the prisoner Evans at the next term of the court, in November, 1878, for trial upon said indictment. Before that date, however, the prisoner fled the country and failed to appear according to the condition of his bond. In the meantime William Tinder died and H. B. Wilson was appointed his administrator.

Suits were brought upon the two bail bonds, and, the liability of the sureties not being admitted, the suits were tried in March, 1880, resulting in two judgments in favor of the United States and against the surety Evans and the estate of Tinder for $5,000 each and the costs.

Soon thereafter an application was made by the administrator of the estate of William Tinder for relief, and an offer was made by him to pay $5,000 and the costs in compromise and settlement of the liability of said estate upon said two judgments.

These judgments were a preferred claim against the estate, which was represented to be worth sixteen or eighteen thousand dollars. The other surety, Evans, was alleged to be worthless, and it was claimed that neither the administrator of the Tinder estate nor his attorneys had known the whereabouts of the indicted party since his flight, and that some time would elapse before certain litigation in which the estate was involved could be settled and the claims against it paid.

It was considered best by the officers of the Government to accept the proposition of the administrator, which was done in June, 1880. The sum of $5,099.06, the amount of one of said judgments, with interest and costs, was paid into the United States Treasury, and the estate of Tinder was in consideration thereof released and discharged from all liability upon both of said judgments.

Thus was the transaction closed, in exact accordance with the wishes and the prayer of the representative of this estate and by the favor and indulgence of the Government upon his application. There was, so far as I can learn, no condition attached, and no understanding or agreement that any future occurrence would affect the finality of the compromise by which the Government had accepted one-half of its claim in full settlement.

It appears that in 1881 the party indicted was arrested and brought to trial, which resulted in his conviction; and apparently for this reason alone it is proposed by the bill under consideration to open the settlement made at the request of the administrator and refund to him the sum which he paid on such settlement pursuant to his own offer.

I can see no fairness or justice to the Government in such a proposition. I do not find any statement that the administrator delivered the prisoner to the United States authorities for trial. On the contrary, it appears from an examination made in the First Comptroller's Office that he was arrested by the marshal on the 25th day of May, 1881, who charged and was paid his fees therefor. And if the administrator had surrendered the prisoner to justice it would not entitle him to the repayment of the money he has paid to compromise the two judgments against him.

The temptation to relieve from contracts with the Government upon plausible application is, in my opinion, not sufficiently resisted; but to refund money paid into the public Treasury upon such a liberal compromise as is exhibited in this case seems like a departure from all business principles and an unsafe concession that the interests of the Government are to be easily surrendered.

GROVER CLEVELAND.

EXECUTIVE MANSION, *May 3, 1888.*

To the House of Representatives:

I return without approval House bill No. 4534, entitled "An act for the relief of Emily G. Mills."

The object of this bill is to provide a pension for the beneficiary named therein as the widow of Oscar B. Mills, late a second assistant engineer, retired, in the United States Navy. The deceased was appointed an acting third assistant engineer in October, 1862, and in 1864 he was promoted to the place of second assistant engineer.

It is supposed that while in active service he did his full duty, though I am not informed of any distinguished acts of bravery or heroism. In February, 1871, he was before a naval retiring board, which found that he was incapacitated for active service on account of malarious fever, contracted in 1868, and recommended that he be allowed six months' leave of absence to recover his health.

In December, 1871, he was again examined for retirement, and the board found that he was not in any way incapacitated from performing the duties of his office. The next year, in 1872, another retiring board, upon an examination of his case, found that he was "laboring under general debility, the effect of intermittent fever acting upon an originally delicate constitution," and he was thereupon placed upon the retired list of the Navy.

On the 10th day of August, 1873, he was accidentally shot and killed by a neighbor, who was attempting to shoot an owl.

As long as there is the least pretense of limiting the bestowal of pensions to disability or death in some way related to the incidents of military and naval service, claims of this description can not consistently be allowed.

GROVER CLEVELAND.

EXECUTIVE MANSION, *May 7, 1888.*

To the House of Representatives:

I return without approval House bill No. 1406, entitled "An act to provide for the sale of certain New York Indian lands in Kansas."

Prior to the year 1838 a number of bands and tribes of New York Indians had obtained 500,000 acres of land in the State of Wisconsin, upon which they proposed to reside. In the year above named a treaty was entered into between the United States and these Indians whereby they relinquished to the Government these Wisconsin lands. In consideration thereof, and, as the treaty declares, "in order to manifest the deep interest of the United States in the future peace and prosperity of the New York Indians," it was agreed there should be set apart as a permanent home for all the New York Indians then residing in the State of New York, or in Wisconsin, or elsewhere in the United States, who had no permanent home, a tract of land amounting to 1,824,000 acres, directly west of the State of Missouri, and now included in the State of Kansas—being 320 acres for each Indian, as their number was then computed—"to have and to hold the same in fee simple to the said tribes or nations of Indians by patent from the President of the United States."

Full power and authority was also given to said Indians "to divide said lands among the different tribes, nations, or bands in severalty," with the right to sell and convey to and from each other under such rules and regulations as should be adopted by said Indians in their respective tribes or in general council.

The treaty further provided that such of the tribes of these Indians as did not accept said treaty and agree to remove to the country set apart for their new homes within five years or such other time as the President might from time to time appoint should forfeit all interest in the land so set apart to the United States; and the Government guaranteed to protect and defend them in the peaceable possession and enjoyment of their new homes.

I have no positive information that any considerable number of these Indians removed to the lands provided for them within the five years limited by the treaty. Their omission to do so may have been owing to the failure of the Government to appropriate the money to pay the expense of such removal, as it agreed to do in the treaty.

It is, however, stated in a letter of the Secretary of the Interior dated April 6, 1878, contained in the report of the Senate committee to whom the bill under consideration was referred, that in the year 1842 some of these Indians settled upon the lands described in the treaty; and it is further alleged in said report that in 1846 about two hundred more of them were removed to said lands.

The letter of the Secretary of the Interior above referred to contains the following statement concerning these Indian occupants:

From death and the hostility of the settlers, who were drawn in that direction by the fertility of the soil and other advantages, all of the Indians gradually relinquished their selections, until of the Indians who had removed thither from the State of New York only thirty-two remained in 1860.

And the following further statement is made:

The files of the Indian Office show abundant proof that they did not voluntarily relinquish their occupation.

The proof thus referred to is indeed abundant, and is found in official reports and affidavits made as late as the year 1859. By these it appears that during that year, in repeated instances, Indian men and widows of deceased Indians were driven from their homes by the threats of armed men; that in one case at least the habitation of an Indian woman was burned, and that the kind of outrages were resorted to which too often follow the cupidity of whites and the possession of fertile lands by defenseless and unprotected Indians.

An agent, in an official letter dated August 9, 1859, after detailing the cruel treatment of these occupants of the lands which the Government had given them, writes:

Since these Indians have been placed under my charge, which was, I think, in 1855, I have endeavored to protect them; but complaint after complaint has reached me, and I have reported their situation again and again; and I hope that it will not be long when the Indians who are entitled to land under the decision of the Indian Office shall have it set apart to them.

The same agent, under date of January 18, 1860, referring to these Indians, declares:

These Indians have been driven off their land and claims upon the New York tract by the whites, and they are now very much scattered and many of them are very destitute.

It was found in 1860 that of all the Indians who had prior to that date selected and occupied part of these lands but thirty-two remained, and it seems to have been deemed but justice to them to confirm their selections by some kind of governmental grant or declaration, though it does not appear that any of them had been able to maintain actual possession of all their selected lands against white intrusion. Thus certain special commissioners appointed to examine this subject, under date of May 29, 1860, make the following statement:

In this connection it may be proper to remark that many of the tracts so selected were claimed by lawless men who had compelled the Indians to abandon them under threats of violence; but we are confident that no serious injury will be done to anyone, as the improvements are of but little value.

On the 14th day of September, 1860, certificates were issued to the thirty-two Indians who had made selections of lands and who still survived, with a view of securing to them such selections and at the same time granting to them the number of acres which it was provided they should have by the treaty of 1838. These certificates were made by the Commissioner of Indian Affairs, and declared that in conformity with the provisions of the treaty of 1838 there had been assigned and allotted to the person named therein 320 acres of the land designated in said treaty, which land was particularly described in said certificates, which concluded as follows:

And the selection of said tract for the exclusive use and benefit of said reserve, having been approved by the Secretary of the Interior, is not subject to be alienated in fee, leased, or otherwise disposed of except to the United States.

In a letter dated September 13, 1860, from the Indian Commissioner to the agent in the neighborhood of these lands reference is made to the conduct of white intruders upon the same, and the following instructions were given to said agent:

In view of these representations and the fact that these white persons who are in possession of the land are intruders, I have to direct that you will visit the New York Reserve in Kansas at your earliest convenience, accompanied by those Indians living among the Osages to whom said lands have been allotted, with a view to place them in possession of the lands to which they are entitled; and if you should meet with any forcible resistance from white settlers you will report their names to this office, in order that appropriate action may be taken in the premises, and you will inform them that if they do not immediately abandon said lands they will be removed by force. When you shall have given the thirty-two Indians peaceable possession of their lands, or attempted to do so and have been prevented by forcible resistance, you will make a report of your action to this Bureau.

The records of the Indian Bureau do not disclose that any report was ever made by the agent to whom these instructions were given.

In 1861 and 1862 mention was made by the agents of the destitute condition of these Indians and of their being deprived of their lands, and in these years petitions were presented in their behalf asking that justice be done them on account of the failure of the Government to provide them with homes.

In the meantime, and in December, 1860, the remainder of the reserve not allotted to the thirty-two survivors was thrown open to settlement by Executive proclamation. Of course this was followed by increased conflict between the settlers and the Indians. It is presumed that it became dangerous for those to whom lands had been allotted to attempt to gain possession of them. On the 4th day of December, 1865, Agent Snow returned twenty-seven of the certificates of allotment which had not been delivered, and wrote as follows to the Indian Bureau:

A few of these Indians were at one time put in possession of their lands. They were driven off by the whites; one Indian was killed, others wounded, and their houses burned. White men at this time have possession of these lands, and have valuable improvements on them. The Indians are deterred even asking for possession. I would earnestly ask, as agent for these wronged and destitute people, that some measure be adopted by the Government to give these Indians their rights.

An official report made to the Secretary of the Interior dated February 16, 1871, gives the history of these lands, and concludes as follows:

These lands are now all or nearly all occupied by white persons who have driven the Indians from their homes—in some instances with violence. There is great necessity that some relief should be afforded to them by legislation of Congress, authorizing the issue of patents to the allottees or giving them power to sell and convey.

In this way they will be enabled to realize something from the land, and the occupants can secure titles for their homes.

Apparently in the line of this recommendation, and in an attempt to remedy the condition of affairs then existing, an act was passed on the 19th day of February, 1873, permitting heads of families and single persons over 21 years of age who had made settlements and improvements upon and were *bona fide* claimants and occupants of the lands for which the thirty-two certificates of allotments were issued to enter and purchase at the proper land office such lands so occupied by them, not exceeding 160 acres, upon paying therefor the appraised value of said tracts respectively, to be ascertained by three disinterested and competent appraisers, to be appointed by the Secretary of the Interior, who should report the value of such lands, exclusive of improvements, but that no sale should be made under said act for less than $3.75 per acre.

It was further provided that the entries allowed should be made within twelve months after the promulgation by the Secretary of the Interior of regulations to carry said act into effect, and that the money arising upon such sales should be paid into the Treasury of the United States in trust for and to be paid to the Indians respectively to whom such certificates of allotment had been issued, or to their heirs, upon satisfactory proof of their identity, at any time within five years from the passage of the act, and that in default of such proof the money should become a part of the public moneys of the United States.

It was also further provided that any Indian to whom any certificate of allotment had been issued, and who was then occupying the land allotted thereby, should be entitled to receive a patent therefor.

Pursuant to this statute these lands were appraised. The lowest value per acre fixed by the appraisers was $3.75, and the highest was $10, making the average for the whole $4.90 per acre.

It is reported that only eight pieces, containing 879.76 acres of land taken from six of these Indian allotments, were sold under this statute to the settlers thereon, producing the sum of $4,058.06, and that the price paid in no case was less than $4.50 per acre.

It is proposed by the bill under consideration to sell the remainder of this allotted land to those who failed to avail themselves of the law of 1873 for the sum of $2.50 per acre.

Whatever may be said of the effect of the action of the Indian Bureau in issuing certificates of allotment to individual Indians as it relates to the title of the lands described therein, it was the only way that the Government could perform its treaty obligation to furnish homes for any number of Indians less than a tribe or band; and if these allotments did not vest a title in these individual Indians they secured to them such rights to the lands as the Government was bound to protect and which it could not refuse to confirm if it became necessary by the issuance of patents therefor.

These rights are fully recognized by the statute of 1873, as well as by the bill under consideration.

The right and power of the Government to divest these allottees of their interests under their certificates is so questionable that perhaps it could only be done under the plan proposed, through an estoppel arising from the acceptance of the price for which their allotted lands were sold.

But whatever the effect of a compliance with the provisions of this bill would be upon the title of the settlers to these lands, I can see no fairness or justice in permitting them to enter and purchase such lands at a sum much less than their appraised value in 1873 and for hardly one-half the price paid by their neighbors under the law passed in that year.

The occupancy upon these lands of the settlers seeking relief, and of their grantors, is based upon wrong, violence, and oppression. A continuation of the wrongful exclusion of these Indians from their lands should not inure to the benefit of the wrongdoers. The opportunities afforded by the law of 1873 were neglected, perhaps, in the hope and belief that death would remove the Indians who by their appeals for justice annoyed those who had driven them from their homes, and perhaps in the expectation that the heedlessness of the Government concerning its obligations to the Indians would supply easier terms.   The idea is too prevalent that, as against those who by emigration and settlement upon our frontier extend our civilization and prosperity, the rights of the Indians are of but little consequence.   But it must be absolutely true that no development is genuine or valuable based upon the violence and cruelty of individuals or the faithlessness of a government.

While it might not result in exact justice or precisely rectify the wrong committed, it may well be that in existing circumstances the interests of the allottees or their heirs demand an adjustment of the kind now proposed.   But their lands certainly are worth much more than they were in 1873, and the settlers, if they are not subjected to a reappraisement, should at least pay the price at which the lands were appraised in that year.

If the holders of the interests of the allottees have such a title as will give them a standing in the courts of Kansas, I do not think they need fear defeat by being charged with improvements under the occupying claimants' act, for it has been decided in a case to be found in the twentieth volume of Kansas Reports, at page 374, that—

Neither the title nor possession of the Indian owner, secured by treaty with the United States Government, can be disturbed by State legislation; and the occupying claimants' act has no application in this case.

And yet the delay, uncertainty, and expense of legal contests should be considered.

I suggest that any bill which is passed to adjust the rights of these Indians by such a general plan as is embodied in the bill herewith returned should provide for the payment by the settlers within a reasonable time of an appraised value, and that in case the same is not paid by the respective occupants that the lands be sold at public auction for a price not less than the appraisement.

GROVER CLEVELAND.

EXECUTIVE MANSION, *May 9, 1888.*

To the House of Representatives:

I return without approval House bill No. 4357, entitled "An act to erect a public building at Allentown, Pa."

The accommodation of the postal business is the only public purpose for which the Government can be called on to provide, which is suggested as a pretext for the erection of this building.   It is proposed to expend $100,000 for a structure to be used as a post-office.   It is said that a deputy collector of internal revenue and a board of pension examiners are located at Allentown, but I do not understand that the Government is obliged to provide quarters for these officers.

The usual statement is made in support of this bill setting forth the growth of the city where it is proposed to locate the building and the amount and variety of the business which is there transacted; and the postmaster in stereotyped phrase represents the desirability of increased accommodation for the transaction of the business under his charge.

But I am thoroughly convinced that there is no present necessity for the expenditure of $100,000 for any purpose connected with the public business at this place.

The annual rent now paid for the post-office is $1,300.

The interest, at 3 per cent, upon the amount now asked for this new building is $3,000. As soon as it is undertaken the pay of a superintendent of its construction will begin, and after its completion the compensation of janitors and other expenses of its maintenance will follow.

The plan now pursued for the erection of public buildings is, in my opinion, very objectionable. They are often built where they are not needed, of dimensions and at a cost entirely disproportionate to any public use to which they can be applied, and as a consequence they frequently serve more to demonstrate the activity and pertinacity of those who represent localities desiring this kind of decoration at public expense than to meet any necessity of the Government.

GROVER CLEVELAND.

EXECUTIVE MANSION, *May 10, 1888.*

To the House of Representatives:

I return without approval House bill No. 7715, entitled "An act for the relief of Georgia A. Stricklett."

By the terms of this bill a pension is allowed to the beneficiary above named, whose husband died on the 21st day of July, 1873. It appears from the records that he was mustered into the service to date from October 10, 1863, to serve for one year. It is alleged in the report of the committee of the House who reported this bill that he was wounded with buckshot in the face and head by bushwhackers, when on recruiting service, on the 23d day of July, 1863. If these dates are correct, he was wounded before he entered the service; but this fact is not made the basis of the disapproval of the widow's application for relief. There seems, however, to be no mention of any such injury during his term of service, though he is reported sick much of the time when present with his regiment, and is reported as once in hospital for a disease which, to say the least of it, can not be recognized as related to the service.

The soldier himself made no application for pension.

A physician testifies that he was present on the 21st day of July, 1873, when the soldier died; that he examined the body after death, and to the best of his knowledge such death was caused partially by epilepsy, and that the epilepsy was the result of "wounds about the face and head received during his service during the war."

Another physician testifies that the soldier applied to him for treatment in 1868, and that his disability was the development of confirmed epilepsy, and he expresses the opinion that this was due to a wound from a buckshot. This physician, while not giving epilepsy as the cause of death, says that "had he lived to die a natural death he certainly would have died an insane epileptic."

The report speaks of his death by "an accidental shot."

The truth appears to be that he was killed by a pistol shot in an altercation with another man.

Unless it shall be assumed that the epilepsy was caused by the buckshot wound spoken of, and unless a pension should be allowed because, if the soldier had not been killed in an altercation, he might have soon died from such epilepsy, this bill is entirely devoid of merit.

Surely no one will seriously propose that a claim for pension should rest upon a conjecture as to what would have caused death if it had not occurred in an entirely different way.

The testimony of the physician who testified in this case that death was caused partially by epilepsy suggests the extreme recklessness which may characterize medical testimony in applications for pension.

GROVER CLEVELAND.

EXECUTIVE MANSION, *May 18, 1888.*

To the House of Representatives:

I return without approval House bill No. 2282, entitled "An act to pension Mrs. Theodora M. Piatt."

The deceased husband of the beneficiary named in this bill served faithfully and well in the volunteer service, and after his discharge as major entered the Regular Army and was on the retired list at the time of his death, which occurred on the 17th day of April, 1885. At that time he seems to have been engaged in the practice of the law at Covington, Ky.

He does not appear to have contracted any distinct and definite disability in his army service, though his health and strength were doubtless somewhat impaired by hardship and exposure.

It is conceded that he committed suicide by shooting himself with a pistol.

A coroner's inquest was held and the following verdict was returned:

Benjamin M. Piatt came to his death from a pistol bullet through the brain, fired from a pistol in his own hand, with suicidal intent, while laboring under a fit of temporary insanity, caused by morbid sensitiveness of wasted opportunities and constantly brooding over imaginary troubles and financial difficulties.

It is said in support of his widow's claim for pension that, being lame as a result, in part at least, of his military service, he, by reason of such lameness, fell from a staircase a few months before his death, the injury from which affected his mind, causing insanity, which in its turn resulted in his suicide.

Much interest is manifested in this case, based upon former friendship and intimacy with the deceased and kind feeling and sympathy for his widow. I should be glad to respond to these sentiments to the extent of approving this bill, but it is one of the misfortunes of public life and official responsibility that a sense of duty frequently stands between a conception of right and a sympathetic inclination.

The verdict returned upon the coroner's inquest, founded upon a friendly examination of all the facts surrounding the melancholy death of this soldier, made at the time of death and in the midst of his neighbors and friends, both by what it contains and by what is omitted, together with the other facts developed, leads me to the conclusion that if a pension is granted in this case no soldier's widow's application based upon suicide can be consistently rejected.

GROVER CLEVELAND.

EXECUTIVE MANSION, *May 18, 1888.*
To the House of Representatives:

I return without approval House bill No. 5545, entitled ''An act granting a pension to Nancy F. Jennings.''

William Jennings, the husband of the beneficiary named in this bill, enlisted in October, 1861, and was discharged June 24, 1862, upon a surgeon's certificate of disability, the cause of disability being therein stated as ''hemorrhoids.''

He never applied for a pension, and died in 1877 of apoplexy.

In the report of the committee which reported this bill the allegation is made that the deceased came home from the Army with chronic diarrhea and suffered from the same to the date of his death.

The widow filed a claim for pension in 1878, which was rejected on the ground that the fatal disease (apoplexy) was not due to military service nor the result of either of the complaints mentioned.

If we are to adhere to the rule that in order to entitle the widow of a soldier to a pension the death of her husband must be in some way related to his military service, there can be no doubt that upon its merits this case was properly disposed of by the Pension Bureau.

GROVER CLEVELAND.

EXECUTIVE MANSION, *May 18, 1888.*
To the House of Representatives:

I return without approval a joint resolution, which originated in the House of Representatives, ''authorizing the use and improvement of Castle Island, in Boston Harbor.''

This island is separated from the mainland of the city of Boston by a channel over one-half mile wide. Fort Independence is located on the island, and it is regarded by our military authorities as quite important to the defense of the city.

The proposition contained in the joint resolution is to permit the city of Boston, through its park commissioners, to improve and beautify this island in connection with a public park to be laid out in the city, with the intention of joining the mainland and the island by the construction of a viaduct or causeway across the water now separating the same.

It is quite plain that the occupancy of this island as a place of pleasure and recreation, as contemplated under this resolution, would be entirely inconsistent with military or defensive uses. I do not regard the control reserved in the resolution to the Secretary of War over such excavations, fillings, and structures upon the island as may be proposed as of much importance. When a park is established there, the island is no longer a defense in time of need.

This scheme, or one of the same character, was broached more than four years ago, and met the disapproval of the Secretary of War and the Engineer Department.

I am now advised by the Secretary of War, the Chief of Engineers, and the Lieutenant-General of the Army, in quite positive terms, that the resolution under consideration should not, for reasons fully stated by them, become operative.

I deem the opinions of these officers abundant justification for my disapproval of the resolution without further statement of objections.

GROVER CLEVELAND.

EXECUTIVE MANSION, *May 18, 1888.*

To the Senate:

I return without approval Senate bill No. 1064, entitled "An act for the relief of L. J. Worden."

This bill directs the Postmaster-General to allow to L. J. Worden, recently the postmaster at Lawrence, Kans., the sum of $625 paid out by him as such postmaster for clerk hire during the period from July 1, 1882, to June 30, 1883.

The allowances to these officers for clerk hire and other like expenses are fixed in each case by the Post-Office Department and are paid out of an appropriation made in gross to cover them all. The excess of receipts for box rents and commissions over and above the salary of the postmaster is adopted by law as the maximum amount of such allowances in each case, and within that limit the amount appropriated is apportioned by the Post-Office Department to the different offices according to their needs.

The allowances to the Lawrence post-office for the year ending June

30, 1883, was $3,100. This was fully its proportion of the appropriation made by Congress for that year, and as much as was in most cases given to other offices of the same grade. In September, 1882, during the first quarter of the year in question, the postmaster made application for an increase of his allowances, which was declined, and a similar application in December of the same year was also declined. The reason given for noncompliance with this request in both cases was a lack of funds. It is the rule to make only such allowances in any year as can be paid from the appropriation made for that period.

No further application for increase of allowances was made by Mr. Worden until March, 1884, when the same were increased $300 for the year, to date from the 1st day of January preceding.

It was found at that time, after a full and fair investigation by the Department, which had in hand abundant funds for an increase of these allowances, that notwithstanding the increase of business at this post-office, $300 added to the allowances for the year from July 1, 1882, to June 30, 1883, was sufficient; and yet more than twice that sum is added by the bill under consideration to the allowances for the year last named.

Forty-four postmasters have submitted vouchers, amounting to nearly $9,000, for clerk hire during that year in excess of allowances; but they were all rejected, and I understand have not been insisted upon.

I assume that the Post-Office Department in 1884 dealt justly and fairly by the postmaster at Lawrence, and upon this theory, if he should be reimbursed any expenditure for a previous year, the demand he now makes is excessive.

But the cases should be exceedingly rare in which postmasters are awarded any more than the allowances made by the Department officers. They have the very best means of ascertaining the amount necessary to meet the demands of the service in any particular case, and it certainly may be assumed that they desire to properly accommodate the public in the matter of postal facilities. When the appropriation is sufficient, the decision of the Department should be final; and when the money in hand does not admit of adequate allowances, postmasters should only be reimbursed money voluntarily expended by them when recommended by the Postmaster-General.

Any other course leads to the expenditure of money by postmasters for work which they should do themselves and to the employment of clerks which are unnecessary. The least encouragement that they may be repaid such expenditure by a special appropriation would dangerously tend to the substitution of their judgment for that of the Department and to the relaxation of wholesome discipline.

I think, when the application of Mr. Worden for an increase in his allowances was twice declined for any cause during the year covering his present demand, that if he made personal expenditures for clerk hire, and especially if he did so without the encouragement of the Department, they were made at his own risk.   It appears, too, that the amount of his claim is larger than can be justified in any event.

GROVER CLEVELAND.

The time allowed the Executive by the Constitution for the examination of bills presented to him by Congress for his action expired in the case of the bill herewith returned on Saturday, May 19.   The Senate adjourned or took a recess on Thursday afternoon, May 17, until to-day, the 21st of May.

On the day of said recess or adjournment the above message, disapproving said bill and accompanying its return to the Senate, where it originated, was drawn, and on May 18 was engrossed and signed.   On Saturday, the 19th of May, the Senate not being in session, the message and the bill were tendered to the Secretary of the Senate, who declined to receive them, and thereupon they were on the same day tendered to the President of the Senate, who also declined to receive the same, both of these officials claiming that the return of said bill and the delivery of said message could only properly be made to the Senate when in actual session.

They are therefore transmitted as soon as the Senate reconvenes after its recess, with this explanation.

GROVER CLEVELAND.

[May 22 the Senate proceeded, as the Constitution prescribes, to reconsider the said bill returned by the President of the United States with his objections, pending which it was ordered that the said bill and message be referred to the Committee on Privileges and Elections.   No action was taken.]

EXECUTIVE MANSION, *May 19, 1888.*

To the House of Representatives:

I return without approval House bill No. 88, entitled "An act granting a pension to Sally A. Randall."

Antipas Taber enlisted in the War of 1812 and was discharged in the year 1814.   There is no claim made that he received any injury in the Army or that his death, which happened long after his discharge, was in the slightest degree related to his military service.   It does not appear that he ever made any application for a pension or was ever upon the pension rolls.   He died at Trinidad, in the island of Cuba, April 11, 1831, leaving as his widow the beneficiary mentioned in this bill.   About twenty-two years after his death, and in February, 1853, she married Albert Randall, and twenty years thereafter, in October, 1873, Randall died, leaving her again a widow.

It is alleged in the report of the committee in the House to which this bill was referred that Mrs. Randall is a worthy woman, 75 years of age, needy circumstances, with health much impaired, and that the petition for her relief was signed by prominent citizens of Norwich, Conn., where she now resides.

All this certainly commends her case to the kindness and benevolence of the citizens mentioned, and the State of Connecticut ought not to allow her to be in needy circumstances.

It seems to me, however, that it would establish a bad precedent to provide for her from the Federal Treasury. From the statement of her present age she must have been born during the time of her first husband's enlistment. She knew nothing of his military service except as the same may have been detailed to her. Her first widowhood had no connection with any incident or condition of health traceable to such service, and her second husband, with whom she lived for twenty years, never entered the military service of the Government.

I do not see how the relief proposed can be granted in this case without an unjustifiable departure from the rules under which applications for pension should be determined.

GROVER CLEVELAND.

EXECUTIVE MANSION, *May 19, 1888.*
To the House of Representatives:

I return without approval House bill No. 879, entitled "An act granting a pension to Royal J. Hiar."

The beneficiary named in this bill enlisted November 11, 1861, in the First Regiment of Michigan Engineers and Mechanics. He is reported as absent without proper authority from May 24, 1862, to January 15, 1863, when he was discharged by reason of varicose veins of the left leg and thigh, claimed to have existed before enlistment.

He filed a claim for pension August 30, 1876, alleging disease of the right side and hip, due to typhoid pneumonia, contracted while repairing a hospital tent in March, 1862.

There is no record of this disease. The proof he furnishes of the same is extremely slight, though he was furnished ample opportunity. The disability of which he complains has no natural relation to the sickness he claims to have had during his service, but is quite a natural result of "an injury while logging," to which some of the witnesses examined in a special examination of the case attribute it.

GROVER CLEVELAND.

EXECUTIVE MANSION, *May 19, 1888.*
To the House of Representatives:

I return without approval House bill No. 5234, entitled "An act granting a pension to Cyrenius G. Stryker."

The beneficiary named in this bill enlisted for nine months in September, 1862, and was discharged June 27, 1863.

His enlistment was in Company A, Thirtieth New Jersey Regiment. The bill proposes to pension him as "a private in Company A, Thirtieth Regiment New York Volunteers."

He alleges that he was pushed or fell from the platform of a car in which he was transported to Washington after enlistment and injured his spine. On the claim which he presented to the Pension Bureau in June, 1879, repeated medical examinations failed to reveal any disability from the cause alleged, and after a special examination his claim was rejected because, with the assistance of such special examination, the claimant did not prove the origin of alleged injury in service and the line of duty or a pensionable degree of disability therefrom since discharge.

The evidence now offered in support of this claim appears to have reference to a time long anterior to its rejection by the Pension Bureau in 1886, and does not impeach the finding of the Bureau that at the latter date there existed no pensionable disability.

GROVER CLEVELAND.

EXECUTIVE MANSION, *May 19, 1888*.

To the House of Representatives:

I return without approval House bill No. 3579, entitled "An act granting a pension to Ellen Shea."

This beneficiary is an old lady and a widow. Her son, Michael Shea, enlisted in January, 1862. The records show that he was sick on one or two occasions during his service. He is also reported as a deserter and absent without leave and in arrest and confinement fully as often as he was sick. He was discharged January 20, 1865.

No application for a pension has been made on his behalf. The mother filed a claim for pension in July, 1884, alleging that her son contracted a fever in the service which resulted in insanity, which was the cause of his death on the 10th day of March, 1884.

He was killed by a snow slide in the State of Colorado. The only hint that his death was in any way connected with the service is the suggestion that not having the proper use of his mind he wandered away and was killed.

His mother now lives in Chicago and, I suppose, lived there at the time of her son's death. There is very little evidence offered of any unsoundness of mind, and his death occurring at Woodstock, Colo., it is hardly to be supposed that he wandered that far. And as tending to show that unsoundness of mind had nothing to do with his death it may be mentioned that an attorney having the mother's application for pension in charge withdrew from the case in October, 1884, for the reason that, having made inquiries at the place where the soldier was killed, he found that his death was caused by a snow slide, and that he was informed that a number of other persons lost their lives at the same time.

GROVER CLEVELAND.

EXECUTIVE MANSION, *May 19, 1888.*

To the House of Representatives:

I return without approval House bill No. 8164, entitled "An act granting a pension to William H. Hester."

It is claimed that the beneficiary named in this bill was injured by sand blowing in his eyes during a sand storm while in the service in the year 1869, resulting in nearly if not quite total blindness.

It is conceded in the report of the committee to which this bill was referred in the House that the claim for pension made by this man to the Pension Bureau was largely supported by perjury and forgery; but the criminality of these methods is made to rest upon three rogues and scoundrels who undertook to obtain a pension for the soldier, and it is stated by the committee as their opinion that the claimant himself was innocent of any complicity in the crimes committed and attempted.

I have quite a full report of the papers filed and proceedings taken in relation to the claim presented to the Pension Bureau, and I am sorry that I can not agree with the committee of the House as to the merits of the application now made or the good faith and honesty of the beneficiary named in the bill herewith returned.

Among the facts presented I shall refer to but one or two touching the conduct of the claimant himself.

Upon his examination, under oath, by a special examiner, he stated that he was brought to Washington to further his claim by a man named Miller, one of the rascally attorneys spoken of in the committee's report; that Miller was to pay his expenses while in Washington, and was to receive one-third of the money paid upon the claim.

This is not the conduct of a man claiming in good faith a pension from the Government.

He further stated under oath that his eyes became affected about January 15, 1869, by reason of a sand storm; that the sand blew into them and cut them all to pieces; that he was thereafter hardly able to see or get around and wait on himself, and that Edward N. Baldwin took care of him in his tent.

This Mr. Baldwin was found by the special examiner and testified that he knew the claimant and served in same regiment and bunked with him; that he never knew of the sand storm spoken of by Hester; that he never knew that he had sore eyes in the service; that he (Baldwin) did not take care of him when he was suffering with sore eyes, and that he never knew of Hester being sick but once, and that was when he had eaten too much. He was shown an affidavit purporting to be made by him and declared the entire thing to be false and a forgery.

I believe this claim for pension to be a fraud from beginning to end, and the effrontery with which it has been pushed shows the necessity of a careful examination of these cases.

GROVER CLEVELAND.

EXECUTIVE MANSION, *May 19, 1888.*

To the House of Representatives:

I return without approval House bill No. 6609, entitled "An act for the relief of Sarah E. McCaleb."

The husband of the beneficiary named in this bill was wounded in the head at the battle of Fort Donelson on the 15th day of February, 1862. He served thereafter and was promoted, and was discharged June 30, 1865.

He died by suicide in 1878.

He never applied for a pension.

The suggestion is made that the wound in his head predisposed him to mental unsoundness, but it does not appear to be claimed that he was insane.

I can not believe that his suicide had any connection with his army service.

GROVER CLEVELAND.

EXECUTIVE MANSION, *May 19, 1888.*

To the House of Representatives:

I return without approval House bill No. 4580, entitled "An act granting a pension to Farnaren Ball."

In the report of the committee to which this bill was referred the name of this beneficiary is given as "Farnasen Ball," and in a report from the Pension Bureau it is insisted that the correct name is "Tamezen Ball."

Her son, Augustus F. Coldecott, was pensioned for disease of the lungs up to the time of his death, which occurred June 2, 1872.

The cause of his death was an overdose of laudanum, and whether it was taken by mistake or design is uncertain.

The mother is not entirely destitute, deriving an income, though small, from the interest upon a mortgage given to her upon a sale of some real estate.

The proofs with which I have been furnished fail to satisfy me that the Government should grant a pension on account of death produced by a self-administered narcotic in the circumstances which surround this case.

As a general proposition I see nothing unjust or unfair in holding that if a pensioner is sick and through ignorance or design takes laudanum without the direction or regulation of a physician the Government should not be held responsible for the consequences.

GROVER CLEVELAND.

EXECUTIVE MANSION, *May 26, 1888.*

To the House of Representatives:

I return without approval House bill No. 339, entitled "An act for the relief of J. E. Pilcher."

This bill authorizes the Secretary of the Treasury to pay to the party named therein the sum of $905, being the amount of one bond of $100 and $805 in paper money of the Republic of Texas.

It is directed, however, that this money be paid out of the Texas indemnity fund.

This fund was created under a law passed on the 28th day of February, 1855, appropriating the sum of $7,750,000 to pay certain claims against the Republic of Texas. By the terms of said law a certain time was fixed within which such claims were to be presented to the Treasury Department.

Between the passage of said act and the year 1870 the sum of $7,648,-786.73 was paid upon said claims, leaving of the money appropriated an unexpended balance of $101,213.27.

This balance was on the 30th day of June, 1877, carried to the surplus fund and covered into the Treasury, pursuant to section 5 of chapter 328 of the laws of 1874.

Thus since that date it seems there has been no Texas indemnity fund, nor is there any such fund now from which the money mentioned in the bill herewith returned can be paid.

In this condition of affairs the proposed law could not be executed and would be of no possible use.

If the claims mentioned are such as should be paid by the United States, there appears to be no difficulty in making an appropriation for their payment from the general funds of the Government. I notice an item to meet a similar claim was inserted in a deficiency bill passed on the 7th day of July, 1884.   GROVER CLEVELAND.

To the Senate: EXECUTIVE MANSION, *May 28, 1888.*

I return without approval Senate bill No. 347, entitled "An act to provide for the erection of a public building in the city of Youngstown, Ohio."

By the census of 1880 the population of Youngstown appears to be 15,435. It is claimed by those urging the erection of a public building there that its population has nearly doubled since that date. The amount appropriated in the bill herewith returned is $75,000. There does not seem to be any governmental purpose to which such a building could be properly devoted except the accommodation of the post-office.

I have listened to an unusual amount of personal representation in favor of this bill from parties whose desires I should be glad to meet on this or any other question; but none of them have insisted that there is any present governmental need of the proposed new building even for postal purposes. On the contrary, I am informed that the post-office is at present well accommodated in quarters held under a lease which does not expire, I believe, until 1892. A letter addressed to the postmaster at Youngstown containing certain questions bearing upon the necessity of a new building failed to elicit a reply. This fact is very unusual and extraordinary, for the postmaster can almost always be relied upon to make an exhibit of the great necessity of larger quarters when a new public building is in prospect.

The fact was communicated to me early in the present session of the Congress that the aggregate sum of the appropriations contained in bills for the erection and extension of public buildings which had up to that time been referred to the House Committee on 'Public Buildings and Grounds was about $37,000,000.

Of course this fact would have no particular relevancy if all the buildings asked for were necessary for the transaction of public business, as long as we have the money to pay for them; but inasmuch as a large number of the buildings proposed are unnecessary and their erection would be wasteful and extravagant, besides furnishing precedents for further and more extended reckless expenditures of a like character, it seems to me that applications for new and expensive public buildings should be carefully scrutinized.

I am satisfied that the appropriation of $75,000 for a building at Youngstown is at present not justified.

GROVER CLEVELAND.

To the Senate: EXECUTIVE MANSION, *May 28, 1888.*

I return without approval Senate bill No. 1237, entitled "An act granting a pension to Anna Mertz."

The beneficiary named in this bill is the widow of Charles A. Mertz, who served in the Army as captain from April, 1862, to June, 1863, when he resigned on account of impaired health. It is stated in the committee's report that after his return from the Army he worked occasionally at his trade, though subject to attacks of very severe diarrhea, accompanied with acute catarrhal pains in the head and face, which he constantly attributed to his army service.

It is alleged that he had several times taken morphine, under medical advice, to allay pain caused by these attacks.

He did not apply for a pension.

On the 1st day of December, 1884, more than twenty-one years' after his discharge from the Army, he died from an overdose of morphine self-administered, for the purpose, it is claimed, of alleviating his suffering.

I do not think that in this case the death of the soldier was so related to his military service as to entitle his widow to a pension.

GROVER CLEVELAND.

To the Senate: EXECUTIVE MANSION, *May 28, 1888.*

I return without approval Senate bill No. 820, entitled "An act granting a pension to David A. Servis."

The beneficiary named in this bill enlisted August 14, 1862, and was discharged June 8, 1865.

It is alleged that about the month of January, 1863, a comrade, by way of a joke, put powder into a pipe which the beneficiary was accustomed to smoke and covered it with tobacco, so that when he lighted it the powder exploded and injured his eyes. The report of the Senate committee states that it does not appear that "any notice was taken of this wanton act of his tent mate."

There is no mention of any disability or injury in the record of the soldier's service. He seems to have served nearly two years and a half after the injury. He filed an application for a pension in May, 1885, more than twenty-two years thereafter.

Whatever may be the extent of the injury sustained, in regard to which the evidence is apparently quite meager, I can not see that it was such a result of military service as to entitle the applicant to a pension.

The utmost liberality to those who were in our Army hardly justifies a compensation by way of pension for injuries incurred in sport or pastime or as the result of a practical joke.

GROVER CLEVELAND.

To the Senate: EXECUTIVE MANSION, *May 28, 1888.*

I return without approval Senate bill No. 835, entitled "An act for the relief of Elisha Griswold."

The beneficiary named in this bill, which awards him a pension, enlisted in January, 1864, and was discharged February 12, 1866.

His claim for pension, as developed in the report of the Senate Committee on Pensions, is based upon the allegation that in January, 1866, he fell from a swing which had been put up in the building occupied as a barrack and struck on his head and shoulder.

The committee report in favor of the bill upon the grounds that the soldier was injured "while engaged in recreation" and that "such recreation is a necessary part of a soldier's life."

The beneficiary filed an application in January, 1880, and in support of such application he filed on the 16th day of July, 1886, an affidavit in which he testifies that at the time of the injury he was in prison at San Antonio, Tex., upon charges the character of which he could not ascertain, and that the swing from which he fell was erected by himself and others for pastime and exercise.

It will be seen that the injury complained of is alleged to have been sustained less than a month before his discharge. There is, however, no record of any disability.

His claim based upon this injury was, in my opinion, properly rejected as having no connection with his military service, and I think the facts in his case as herein detailed do not justify the award of a pension to him by special enactment.

On the 23d day of March, 1888, after the introduction of the bill herewith returned, the beneficiary, apparently having abandoned the claim
upon which the bill is predicated, filed another application for a pension
in the Pension Bureau, alleging that he contracted diarrhea and malarial
poisoning in the service. This application is still pending.

GROVER CLEVELAND.

EXECUTIVE MANSION, *May 29, 1888.*

To the House of Representatives:

I return without approval House bill No. 1275, entitled "An act for
the erection of a public building at Columbus, Ga., and appropriating
money therefor."

The city of Columbus, Ga., is undoubtedly a thriving, growing city.
The only present necessity for a public building there is for the accommodation of its post-office. It is stated in the report of the House committee that the gross revenues of the office for the year ending June 30,
1887, were $16,700. The postmaster, in a letter upon the subject, makes
the following statement:

> I estimate the gross receipts at $17,500 for the fiscal year ending March 31, which
> will be an increase of nearly 7 per cent over last year's receipts.

There are nine persons employed in the post-office at present, including the postmaster. The present quarters are leased by the Government
at an annual rent of $900. The postmaster represents that his accom-
modations are not adequate or convenient, and that instead of a space of
1,900 square feet, which he now has, he should be provided with 2,500
square feet.

The population of the city in 1880 was 10,123. It is claimed that it
is now about 20,000.

In my opinion the facts presented do not exhibit the necessity of the
expenditure of $100,000 to afford the increased room for the post-office
which may be desirable. I believe a private person would erect a building abundantly sufficient for all our postal needs in that city for many
years to come for one-third of that sum.

Business prudence and good judgment seem to dictate that the erection of the proposed building should be delayed until its necessity is
more manifest, and so that it can be better determined what expenditure
for such a purpose will be justified by the continued growth of the city
and the needs of the Government.

GROVER CLEVELAND.

EXECUTIVE MANSION, *June 5, 1888.*

To the House of Representatives:

I return herewith without approval House bill No. 4467, entitled "An
act for the erection of a public building at Bar Harbor, in Maine."

The entire town within which Bar Harbor is situated contained in 1880 1,639 inhabitants, as appears by the census of that year.

There is no pretense that there is any need of a public building there except to accommodate the post-office.

This is a third-class office, and the Government does not pay the rent for offices of that class. The gross receipts of the office for the year ended June 30, 1887, are reported by the Postmaster-General at $5,337. The postmaster reports that he employs five clerks in the summer and three in the winter. The fact that Bar Harbor is a place of very extensive summer resort makes its population exceedingly variable, and during a part of the year it is quite likely that the influx of pleasure seekers may make a more commodious post-office desirable, though there does not seem to be much complaint of present inconvenience.

The postmaster pays a rent of $500 per annum for his present quarters.

The amount appropriated by the bill is quite moderate, being only $25,000, but the postmaster expresses the opinion that a proper site alone would cost from twenty to thirty thousand dollars.

I am decidedly of the opinion that if a public building is to be erected at this place, of which at present there appears to be no necessity, it should be done under a system which will not give the post-office and the postmaster there an advantage over others of their class.

GROVER CLEVELAND.

EXECUTIVE MANSION, *June 5, 1888.*

To the House of Representatives:

I return without approval House bill No. 1394, entitled "An act authorizing the Secretary of the Treasury to purchase additional ground for the accommodation of Government offices in Council Bluffs, Iowa."

A new public building at Council Bluffs will be completed in a short time. The ground upon which it is located has a frontage of 192 feet and a depth of 106 feet and 10 inches. The proposition is to add 30 feet to its depth. The act under which this building has been thus far constructed provides that the ground purchased therefor shall be of such dimensions as to leave the building unexposed to fire by an open space of at least 40 feet, including streets and alleys. The building is located on land now belonging to the Government sufficient in size to comply with this provision, and in point of fact more than the open space required is left on all sides of the same. There is no pretense that any enlargement of the building is necessary or contemplated.

The report of the committee to which this bill was referred in the House simply states that "the grounds on which said building is situated are inadequate for its proper accommodation and safety."

If this is so, I can see no reason why additional ground should not be purchased for "the proper accommodation and safety" of a large proportion of the public buildings completed and in process of erection, since the provision that there shall exist 40 feet of open space on all sides is, I think, contained in all the bills authorizing their construction. In this view the proposed legislation would establish a very bad precedent.

It is provided in the bill that the additional 30 feet mentioned shall be purchased for a sum not to exceed $10,000. The adjoining 106 feet and 10 inches, located on the corner of two streets, were purchased in the year 1882 by the Government for $15,000. The permission to purchase this addition at a price per foot greatly in excess of that already owned by the Government seems so unnecessary, except to benefit the owner, that I am of the opinion it should not be granted.

GROVER CLEVELAND.

EXECUTIVE MANSION, *June 5, 1888.*

To the Senate:

I return without approval Senate bill No. 739, entitled "An act granting a pension to Johanna Loewinger."

The husband of the beneficiary named in this bill enlisted June 28, 1861, and was discharged May 8, 1862, upon a surgeon's certificate of disability. He was pensioned for chronic diarrhea. He died July 17, 1876. A coroner's inquest was held, who found by their verdict that the deceased came to his death "from suicide by cutting his throat with a razor, caused by long-continued illness."

This inquest was held immediately after the soldier's death, and it appears that the case was fully investigated, with full opportunities to discover the truth. Upon the verdict found, in the absence of insanity caused by any disability, it can hardly be claimed that his death was caused by his military service. The attempts afterwards to impeach this verdict and introduce another cause of death do not seem to be successful.

GROVER CLEVELAND.

EXECUTIVE MANSION, *June 12, 1888.*

To the Senate:

I return without approval Senate bill No. 1772, entitled "An act for the relief of John H. Marion."

It is proposed by this bill to relieve the party named therein from an indebtedness to the Government amounting to $1,042.45, arising from the nonfulfillment of a contract made by him in 1884 with the Government, by which he agreed to furnish for the use of the Quartermaster's Department a quantity of grama hay.

The contractor wholly failed to furnish the hay as agreed, and thereupon the Government, pursuant to the terms of the contract, obtained the hay in other quarters, paying therefor a larger sum by $1,042.45 than it would have been obliged to pay the contractor if he had fulfilled his agreement. This amount was charged against the contractor.

It is alleged that the crop of the particular kind of hay which was to be furnished under the contract failed the season in which it was to be supplied on account of drought, and that thus performance became impossible on the part of the contractor.

Between individuals no injustice could be claimed if the contractor in such circumstances should be held to have taken the chances of the crop; and if an equitable adjustment should be suggested in such a case as is here presented it would hardly be asked that the party suffering from the default or failure of the other should sustain all the loss.

It seems that the contractor was the proprietor of a newspaper in Arizona, and that he did some printing for the Government besides agreeing to furnish hay to the Quartermaster's Department. After the ascertainment of the loss to the Government arising out of the hay transactions, certain accounts for printing presented by the contractor were credited against the amount of such loss charged against him. In this way his debt to the Government has been reduced more than $700. The proposed legislation would cause to be paid to the contractor the sums so retained for printing and to relieve him from the remainder of the Government's claims.

Inquiry at the Quartermaster-General's Office fails to substantiate the allegation that there is any understanding when such contracts are made that their performance is to be at all relaxed by the failure of the crop.

There really seems to be no good reason why the contractor should not make good the entire loss consequent upon his default. If, however, strict rights are to be relinquished and the liberality of the Government invoked, it should not be taxed beyond the limit of sharing the loss with the delinquent. This result would be accomplished by discharging the remainder of the contractor's debt after crediting the bills for printing above referred to.

The Government is obliged in the transaction of its business to make numerous contracts with private parties, and if these contracts are to be of any use or protection they should not be lightly set aside on behalf of citizens who are disappointed as to their profitable nature or their ability to perform them.

GROVER CLEVELAND.

To the Senate: EXECUTIVE MANSION, *June 12, 1888.*

I return without approval Senate bill No. 1017, entitled "An act granting a pension to Stephen Schiedel."

The beneficiary named in this bill served in the First Regiment Missouri Light Artillery from October 24, 1861, to October, 1864. There is no record of any injury or disability while in the service.

In March, 1880, sixteen years after his discharge, he filed an application for a pension, alleging that about June, 1862, while carrying logs to aid in building quarters, a log slipped and fell upon a lever, which flew up and struck him, injuring his back and shoulder.

He furnished the testimony of two witnesses tending to support his statement of the manner in which he was injured, but upon investigation this evidence was found to be unreliable.

Medical examinations failed to disclose any disability from the cause alleged, but do tend to show that he was disabled since his discharge by an injury to his right hand and arm and some rheumatic trouble.

It is not claimed that he incurred any disability from rheumatism while in the Army. It appears distinctly that he was wounded in the right wrist and arm while firing a cannon at the village of Hamburg, Erie County, N. Y., on the 4th day of July, 1866. The doctor who testifies to this injury and who dressed the wound negatives any other illness before the accident.

Even if he has, since his discharge, suffered from rheumatism, he does not claim that this was incurred in the Army. He bases his right to a pension entirely upon an injury which he particularly describes, and which the medical examination does not sustain. It will be observed, too, that he continued his military service for two years and four months after the date of his alleged injury. It seems hardly possible that he could have done this if he had been injured in the manner he alleges.

GROVER CLEVELAND.

EXECUTIVE MANSION, *June 18, 1888.*
To the House of Representatives:

I return without approval House bill No. 3959, entitled "An act granting a pension to Dolly Blazer."

The husband of the beneficiary named in this bill was apparently a good soldier and was confined for a time in a Confederate prison. He was mustered out of the service in June, 1865, and never applied for a pension.

He died in 1878, leaving as survivors his widow and several children, two of whom are alleged to be still under 16 years of age.

The cause of the soldier's death was yellow fever. There is in my mind no doubt of this fact, and the attempt to establish any other cause of death, if successful, would go far toward fixing a precedent for the rejection of all evidence which stood in the way of a claim for pension.

The bill herewith returned is disapproved for the reason that the death of the soldier had no relation to his military service, and I do not think there should be a discrimination in favor of this applicant and against many thousands of widows fully as well entitled.

GROVER CLEVELAND.

EXECUTIVE MANSION, *June 18, 1888.*

To the House of Representatives:

I return without approval House bill No. 5522, entitled "An act for the relief of Elijah Martin."

By this bill it is proposed to increase the pension now paid to the beneficiary therein named, who was a soldier in the War of 1812, from $8 to $20 per month.

Prior to May 22, 1888, an application was made for reimbursement of the expenses attending the last sickness and burial of this pensioner, and on the day mentioned such application was transmitted to the proper auditing officer for adjustment.

I have no other information of the death of this soldier, but as his age is stated in the report of the House committee to be 87 years, and as there can hardly be a mistake as to the identity of the person named in the application mentioned, I am satisfied that the beneficiary has died since the introduction of the bill for his relief.

GROVER CLEVELAND.

EXECUTIVE MANSION, *June 19, 1888.*

To the House of Representatives:

I return without approval House bill No. 488, entitled "An act granting a pension to Elizabeth Burr."

It is proposed by this bill to grant a pension to the beneficiary therein named as the widow of William Burr, who enlisted for one hundred days in 1864 and was discharged on the 3d day of September in that year.

He is reported as present on all roll calls during his service. He died April 7, 1867, of dropsy, never having made any application for a pension.

His widow filed an application for pension in 1880, thirteen years after the soldier's death, alleging that the disease of which he died, claimed to be dropsy, was contracted in the service.

The claim was rejected by the Pension Bureau on the ground that the dropsy causing his death was not due to his military service, but that he was subject to the same before his enlistment.

I am perfectly satisfied that the rejection upon the ground claimed was correct.

GROVER CLEVELAND.

To the Senate: EXECUTIVE MANSION, *June 19, 1888.*

I return without approval Senate bill No. 1957, entitled "An act granting a pension to Virtue Smith."

The beneficiary named in this bill is the widow of David M. Smith (incorrectly named David W. Smith in the bill), who served as a bug[1] in a Minnesota regiment from August 22, 1862, to September 28, 1862, in a campaign against the Sioux Indians.

He received a gunshot wound in the right elbow, for which in 1867 he was granted a pension of $6 a month, which was very soon thereafter increased to $8, and in August, 1875, said pension was further increased to $10 a month, which he received to the date of his death.

He died in the city of Washington on the 22d day of January, 1880.

He obtained a position in the Second Auditor's Office of the Treasury Department in 1864, and worked steadily there until about six months before his death.

Medical examinations had from time to time up to 1877 seem to have found him in excellent physical condition except the wound in his right elbow, which caused stiffness, and an injury to his left forearm not received in the Army.

In 1879 he was examined by a physician of this city who stands among the best in the profession, and found in the last stages of consumption, and this physician declares he died from that cause. A female physician certified that the cause of death was "wounds in the Army."

The pensioner was 64 years old at the time of his death.

I am perfectly satisfied from the medical testimony and from other facts connected with this case that the death of the husband of the beneficiary was in no manner related to his military service.

GROVER CLEVELAND.

EXECUTIVE MANSION, *June 22, 1888.*
To the House of Representatives:

I return without approval House bill No. 3016, entitled "An act granting a pension to Mary F. Harkins."

The husband of this beneficiary was discharged from the military service in 1865, and was pensioned for a gunshot wound in the right foot at the rate of $6 per month.

He died in 1882, seventeen years after his discharge, "from rupture of the heart, caused by the bursting and parting of the fibers of the right ventricle."

The claim is now made that the death was the result of the wound in the foot.

An application to the Pension Bureau was rejected on the ground that the death cause was not the result of the wound.

I am satisfied that this was a just conclusion.

GROVER CLEVELAND.

EXECUTIVE MANSION, *June 22, 1888.*
To the House of Representatives:

I return without approval House bill No. 600, entitled "An act increasing the pension of Mary Minor Hoxey."

The husband of the beneficiary named in this bill was, while on military duty, wounded in the left hand and afterwards in the thigh. He was pensioned in 1871 on account of these wounds, and in 1879 was allowed arrearages from time of his discharge. He died in December, 1881, of consumption, being at that time in the receipt of a pension at the rate of $17 per month.

In 1884 his widow was allowed a pension at the same rate, with $2 a month each for two minor children. The children have now attained the age of 16 years, but the widow still receives the pension awarded to her, which is the same as that allowed to all widows of her class.

I discover no reason of any substance why this pension should be increased, and if it should be done it would only be a manifestation of unjust favoritism.

I can not forget the thousands of poor widows with claims superior to this beneficiary, but with no interested friends to push their claims for increase of pension, who would be discriminated against if this proposed bill becomes a law.

It seems to me that there is a chance to do injustice by unfair caprice in fixing the rates of pension, as well as by refusing them altogether when they should be granted.

GROVER CLEVELAND.

EXECUTIVE MANSION, *June 22, 1888.*

To the House of Representatives:

I return without approval House bill No. 8281, entitled "An act for the relief of Lieutenant James G. W. Hardy."

It is proposed by this bill to award a pension to the beneficiary above named.

In the month of January, 1864, he was on recruiting service in the State of Indiana. On the 15th day of that month he was traveling between Indianapolis and Lafayette in a railroad car, and he alleges that he raised a window of the car to obtain air, and placed his arm on the window sill, when it was struck by something from the outside and one of the bones of his arm broken.

In February, 1865, he resigned on account of disability caused by the accident above mentioned, the medical certificate then stating that he had a fracture of the right humerus of ten months' standing which had not been properly adjusted.

He made an application for a pension to the Pension Bureau, which was rejected.

Although it is stated in a general way that he was traveling on business connected with his recruiting service at the time of his injury, he has given no information as to the precise purpose of his journey; and it is conceded that he was guilty of such negligence that he had no right of action against the railroad company.

It also appears by the medical certificate upon which his resignation was permitted that the fracture, not necessarily serious, was never properly treated. It seems, too, that he remained in the service ten months after the injury.

I am unable to discover why a pension should be granted in this case, unless the Government is to be held as an insurer of the safety of every person in the military service in all circumstances and at all times and places.

GROVER CLEVELAND.

EXECUTIVE MANSION, *June 22, 1888.*

To the House of Representatives:

I return without approval House bill No. 8174, entitled "An act granting a pension to Ellen Sexton."

The husband of the beneficiary served in the Union Volunteer Army from October, 1862, to June, 1864, having been during the last seven months of his service in the Veteran Reserve Corps. He was discharged for a disability which, to say the least of it, certainly had no relation to his military service, unless the Government is to be held responsible for injury arising from vicious indulgence.

He died in the city of Cork, Ireland, May 29, 1875, of consumption, certified by the health authorities there to have been of seven years' duration.

GROVER CLEVELAND.

EXECUTIVE MANSION, *June 22, 1888.*

To the House of Representatives:

I return without approval House bill No. 2215, entitled "An act granting a pension to Charles Glamann."

This beneficiary served in an Illinois regiment from September, 1864, to July, 1865, and his record shows no injury or sickness except an attack of remittent fever.

He filed a claim for pension in 1880, alleging that he was struck accidentally with a half brick by a comrade and injured in his left arm.

There is no doubt that whatever disability he thus incurred was the result of a personal altercation between himself and the man who threw the brick.

The extent to which the power to grant pensions by special act has been made to cover all sorts of claims is illustrated by the fact that, in the light of many pensions that have been allowed, this case, though presenting an absurd claim, does not appear to be much out of the way. The effect of precedent as an inducement to increase and expand claims and causes for pensions is also shown by the allegation in the report of the House committee, as follows:

Your committee and Congress have, however, frequently relaxed the rule, and granted pension for injuries and disabilities incurred in such circumstances.

I believe that if the veterans of the war knew all that was going on in the way of granting pensions by private bills they would be more disgusted than any class of our citizens.

GROVER CLEVELAND.

To the Senate: EXECUTIVE MANSION, *June 26, 1888.*

I return without approval Senate bill No. 845, entitled "An act granting a pension to the widow of John A. Turley."

The husband of this beneficiary belonged to a Kentucky regiment of volunteers, and in 1863, having been in camp and on leave of absence, he and others of the regiment embarked on a steamboat, in charge of a lieutenant, to be taken to Louisville, whither they had been ordered.

While on the steamboat an altercation arose between two of the soldiers, and the deceased interfered to prevent, as is alleged, an affray. By so doing he was pushed or struck by one of the parties quarreling and fell upon the deck of the boat, striking his head against a plank, thus receiving a fatal injury.

It is quite clear to me that the death of this soldier was not the result of his military service. His presence on the boat was in the line of duty, but he had no charge of the rest of the men and was in no degree responsible for them, and whether he should be in any way implicated in the dispute which occurred was a matter entirely within his own control and determined by his own volition. If he had refrained from interference, he would have saved himself and performed to the utmost his military duty.

GROVER CLEVELAND.

To the Senate: EXECUTIVE MANSION, *July 5, 1888.*

I return without approval Senate bill No. 432, entitled "An act for the relief of Joel B. Morton."

Calvin Morton, the son of the beneficiary named in this bill, enlisted in the volunteer infantry in 1861, and after his discharge again enlisted in the United States cavalry, from which he was discharged in 1867.

It is alleged by his father that he was killed in the battle with the Indians at Little Big Horn, called the "Custer massacre," June 25, 1876.

His name does not appear in any record of the soldiers engaged in that battle. The casualty records of the affair are reported as very complete, but they contain no mention of any soldier of that name.

His father claims in his application before the Pension Bureau to have had a letter from his son in the fall of 1875, dated at some place in the Black Hills, stating that he was a lieutenant in the army under General Custer, but that the letter was lost. He also alleges that he read an account of the massacre in a newspaper, the name of which he has forgotten, and that his son was there mentioned as among the slain.

The report of the House committee states that the only evidence of the death of this soldier is found in a letter of Anderson G. Shaw, who writes that he was present on the field of the battle mentioned when the killed were buried, and that one of the burial party called a corpse found there Morton's. It is further claimed that the description of this body agreed with that given by the father of his son.

Considering the complete list of the casualties attending this battle now in the War Department, it must be conceded that the death of the son of the beneficiary is far from being satisfactorily established.

The claim of the father is still pending in the Pension Bureau, and perhaps with further effort more information on the subject can be obtained.

GROVER CLEVELAND.

EXECUTIVE MANSION, *July 5, 1888.*

To the Senate:

I return without approval Senate bill No. 43, entitled "An act granting a pension to Polly H. Smith."

John H. Smith, the husband of the beneficiary named in this bill, enlisted in the Regular Army in 1854 and served until the year 1870.

In 1868 a fistula developed, which was probably the result of quite continuous riding in the saddle. In 1870 he was placed upon the retired list as first lieutenant on account of the incapacity arising from such fistula.

In September, 1885, fifteen years after his retirement, he died suddenly at Portland, Oreg., of heart disease, while attempting to raise a trunk to his shoulder.

I can not see how the cause of death can be connected with his service or with the incapacity for which he was placed upon the retired list.

The application made by the widow for a pension is still pending before the Pension Bureau, and I understand that she or her friends prefer taking the chance of favorable consideration there to the approval of this bill.

GROVER CLEVELAND.

EXECUTIVE MANSION, *July 5, 1888.*

To the Senate:

I return without approval Senate bill No. 1547, entitled "An act granting a pension to Mary Ann Dougherty."

A large share of the report of the Senate committee to which this bill was referred, and which report is adopted by the committee of the House, as is usual in such cases, consists of a petition signed by Mary Ann Dougherty, addressed to the Congress, in which she states that she resides in Washington, having removed here with her husband in 1863 from New Jersey; that shortly after their arrival in this city her husband, Daniel Dougherty, returned to New Jersey and enlisted in the Thirty-fourth Regiment New Jersey Volunteers; that she obtained employment in the United States arsenal making cartridges, and that while so engaged she was injured by an explosion.

She also states that she had a young son killed by machinery in the navy-yard, and that at the grand review of the Army after the close of the war another son, 6 years old, was stolen by an officer of the Army and has not been heard of since. She further says that her husband left his home in 1865 and has not been heard of since, and that she believes he deserted her on account of her infirmities.

It is alleged in the report that she received a pension as the widow of Daniel Dougherty until it was discovered that he was alive, when her name was dropped from the rolls.

The petition of this woman is indorsed by the Admiral and several other officers of the Navy and a distinguished clergyman of Washington, certifying that they know Mrs. Dougherty and believe the facts stated to be true.

There is no pretense made now that this beneficiary is a widow, though she at one time claimed to be, and was allowed a pension on that allegation. Her present claim rests entirely upon injuries received by her when she was concededly not employed in the military service. If the pension now proposed is allowed her, it will be a mere act of charity.

Her husband, Daniel Dougherty, is now living in Philadelphia, and is a pensioner in his own right for disability alleged to have been incurred while serving in the Thirty-fourth New Jersey Volunteers. Of this fact this beneficiary has been repeatedly informed; and yet she states in her petition that her husband deserted her in 1865 and has not been heard of since.

It is alleged in the Pension Bureau that in 1878 she succeeded in securing a pension as the widow of Daniel Dougherty through fraudulent testimony and much false swearing on her part.

The police records of the precinct in which she has lived for years show that she is a woman of very bad character, and that she has been under arrest nine times for drunkenness, larceny, creating disturbance, and misdemeanors of that sort.

It happens that this claimant, by reason of her residence here, has been easily traced and her character and untruthfulness discovered. But there is much reason to fear that this case will find its parallel in many that have reached a successful conclusion.

I can not spell out any principle upon which the bounty of the Government is bestowed through the instrumentality of the flood of private pension bills that reach me. The theory seems to have been adopted that no man who served in the Army can be the subject of death or impaired health except they are chargeable to his service. Medical theories are set at naught and the most startling relation is claimed between alleged incidents of military service and disability or death. Fatal apoplexy is admitted as the result of quite insignificant wounds, heart disease is attributed to chronic diarrhea, consumption to hernia, and suicide is traced to army service in a wonderfully devious and curious way.

Adjudications of the Pension Bureau are overruled in the most peremptory fashion by these special acts of Congress, since nearly all the beneficiaries named in these bills have unsuccessfully applied to that Bureau for relief.

This course of special legislation operates very unfairly.

Those with certain influence or friends to push their claims procure pensions, and those who have neither friends nor influence must be content with their fate under general laws. It operates unfairly by increasing in numerous instances the pensions of those already on the rolls, while many other more deserving cases, from the lack of fortunate advocacy, are obliged to be content with the sum provided by general laws.

The apprehension may well be entertained that the freedom with which these private pension bills are passed furnishes an inducement to fraud and imposition, while it certainly teaches the vicious lesson to our people that the Treasury of the National Government invites the approach of private need.

None of us should be in the least wanting in regard for the veteran soldier, and I will yield to no man in a desire to see those who defended the Government when it needed defenders liberally treated. Unfriendliness to our veterans is a charge easily and sometimes dishonestly made.

I insist that the true soldier is a good citizen, and that he will be satisfied with generous, fair, and equal consideration for those who are worthily entitled to help.

I have considered the pension list of the Republic a roll of honor, bearing names inscribed by national gratitude, and not by improvident and indiscriminate almsgiving.

I have conceived the prevention of the complete discredit which must ensue from the unreasonable, unfair, and reckless granting of pensions by special acts to be the best service I can render our veterans.

In the discharge of what has seemed to me my duty as related to legislation, and in the interest of all the veterans of the Union Army, I have attempted to stem the tide of improvident pension enactments, though I confess to a full share of responsibility for some of these laws that should not have been passed.

I am far from denying that there are cases of merit which can not be reached except by special enactment, but I do not believe there is a member of either House of Congress who will not admit that this kind of legislation has been carried too far.

I have now before me more than 100 special pension bills, which can hardly be examined within the time allowed for that purpose.

My aim has been at all times, in dealing with bills of this character, to give the applicant for a pension the benefit of any doubt that might arise, and which balanced the propriety of granting a pension if there seemed any just foundation for the application; but when it seemed entirely outside of every rule in its nature or the proof supporting it, I have supposed I only did my duty in interposing an objection.

It seems to me that it would be well if our general pension laws should be revised with a view of meeting every meritorious case that can arise. Our experience and knowledge of any existing deficiencies ought to make the enactment of a complete pension code possible.

In the absence of such a revision, and if pensions are to be granted upon equitable grounds and without regard to general laws, the present methods would be greatly improved by the establishment of some tribunal to examine the facts in every case and determine upon the merits of the application.   GROVER CLEVELAND.

EXECUTIVE MANSION, *July 5, 1888.*
To the House of Representatives:

I return without approval House bill No. 8291, entitled "An act granting a pension to Julia Welch."

The husband of the beneficiary named in this bill served in the Army from December, 1863, to May, 1866.

He never filed an application for pension, and died February 24, 1880, of inflammation of the lungs.

The claim filed by his widow for pension alleged that her husband suffered from chronic diarrhea and disease of the heart and lungs as results of his army service.

The claim was rejected by the Pension Bureau on the ground that the soldier died from an acute disease which bore no relation to any complaint contracted in the Army.

I think the action of the Bureau was correct.

GROVER CLEVELAND.

EXECUTIVE MANSION, *July 5, 1888.*
To the House of Representatives:

I return without approval House bill No. 7907, entitled "An act granting a pension to Mary Ann Lang."

The husband of this beneficiary was wounded in the nose on the 1st day of June, 1864, and was mustered out of the service July 8, 1865. He was pensioned on account of this wound and died February 21, 1881. Prior to his death he had executed a declaration claiming pension also for rheumatism, but the application was not filed before he died.

The cause of his death was dropsy. The widow filed her claim for pension in 1884, which was rejected on the ground that the soldier's fatal disease was not the result of his military service.

A physician of good repute, who appears to have attended him more than any other physician for a number of years prior to his death, gives an account of rheumatic ailments and other troubles, and states that about a year and a half before he died he had a liver trouble which resulted in dropsy, which caused his death.   He adds that the soldier was a man who drank beer, and at times to excess, and that he drank harder toward the last of his life.   He further states that he is unable to connect the liver trouble with his rheumatism, and could not give any other reason for it except his long use of beer and liquor, and if that was not the cause it greatly aggravated it; that he had cautioned him about drinking, and at times he heeded the advice.

An appeal was taken from the action rejecting the claim and the case was submitted to the medical referee of the Pension Bureau, who decided upon all the testimony that the soldier's fatal disease (dropsy) was due to disease of the liver, which was not a sequence of rheumatism and was the result of excessive use of alcoholic stimulants.

It will be observed that no claim is made that death in any way resulted from the wound for which a pension had been allowed, and that even if rheumatism was connected with the death its incurrence in the Army had never been established.

I am satisfied that this case was properly disposed of by the Pension Bureau.

GROVER CLEVELAND.

EXECUTIVE MANSION, *July 6, 1888.*
To the House of Representatives:

I return without approval House bill No. 9184, entitled "An act granting a pension to William M. Campbell, jr."

This beneficiary was not enrolled in the service of the United States until August 5, 1862.   Previous to that time he had been a member of the same regiment in which he was so enrolled, and was in the service of the State of Kentucky.

He alleges that in the month of February, 1862, he was vaccinated with impure virus and in the same month contracted mumps.   He claims that as a result of these troubles he has been afflicted with ulcers and other serious consequences.

It is perfectly clear that at the time these disabilities were incurred, if they were incurred, the claimant was not in the military service of the United States.

The records show that he deserted September 16, 1862, a little more than a month after he was mustered into the United States service; that he was arrested April 25, 1864, one year and seven months after his desertion; that he was restored to duty by general court-martial with loss of pay and allowances during absence (the time lost by desertion to be made good), and that he was mustered out July 16, 1865.

This enactment seems neither to have law nor meritorious equity to support it.

GROVER CLEVELAND.

EXECUTIVE MANSION, *July 6, 1888.*

To the House of Representatives:

I return without approval House bill No. 8807, entitled "An act granting a pension to Harriet E. Cooper."

The husband of this beneficiary served as a major in an Illinois regiment from September 3, 1862, to April 1, 1863, when his resignation was accepted, it having been tendered on account of business affairs.

He was pensioned for rheumatism from April, 1863, and died October 3, 1883.

It is admitted on all hands that Major Cooper drank a good deal, but the committee allege that they can not arrive at the conclusion that death was attributable to that cause.

There is some medical testimony tending to show that death was caused from rheumatism, but one physician gives it as his opinion that death resulted from rheumatism and chronic alcoholism.

The physician who last attended the soldier testifies that the cause of death was chronic alcoholism. This should be the most reliable of all the medical testimony, and taken in connection with the conceded intemperate habits of the deceased and the fact that the brain was involved, it satisfies me that the rejection of the widow's claim by the Pension Bureau on the ground that the cause of death was mainly intemperance was correct.

GROVER CLEVELAND.

EXECUTIVE MANSION, *July 6, 1888.*

To the House of Representatives:

I return without approval House bill No. 6431, entitled "An act for the relief of Van Buren Brown."

The beneficiary named in this bill was discharged from the Army September 11, 1865.

He filed an application for pension in the Pension Bureau May 19, 1883, alleging chronic diarrhea, rheumatism, spinal disease the result of an injury, and deafness.

His claim was very thoroughly examined and reopened and examined again after rejection, and rejected a second time.

The case is full of uncertainty and contradiction. Without discussing these features, I am entirely satisfied that a pension should not be allowed, for the reason, among others, that three careful medical examinations made in 1883, 1884, and 1886 failed to disclose any pensionable disability.

GROVER CLEVELAND.

EXECUTIVE MANSION, *July 6, 1888.*

To the House of Representatives:

I return without approval House bill No. 367, entitled "An act granting a pension to Nathaniel D. Chase."

This beneficiary enlisted September 3, 1863. The records show that he was admitted to a hospital March 3, 1864, with a disease of a discreditable nature and by no means connected with the military service, and that he was discharged from the Army May 20, 1864, upon a certificate of paralysis of left arm, which came on suddenly February 20, 1864, and that the cause was unknown, but believed not to be incident to the service.

He filed an application for a pension in June, 1864, alleging paralysis of the left arm from causes unknown to him.

This claim was not prosecuted at that time, and the claimant reenlisted in January, 1865, and served until September 5, 1865, without any evidence of disability appearing upon the records.

He renewed his claim in 1870, stating that he was first taken with a pain in his left arm about March 1, 1864, and that it became partially paralyzed.

It will be observed that thus far in his application he gives no explanation of the incurrence of his disability which leads to the belief that it was related to his service.

In a letter dated May 31, 1864, his captain states that he can but think that the disability of the claimant was the result of his folly and indiscretion, and that he feels it his duty to decline giving him a certificate.

In 1880 the claimant stated the cause of his disability was an injury to his arm while expelling a soldier from a railroad train at Augusta, Me., he acting as provost guard at the time. Upon this allegation the case was reopened at the Pension Bureau.

In reply to a letter from the Bureau the captain of claimant's company stated that he had no knowledge of such an injury. The same officer, in a letter dated February 25, 1887, expresses the belief that the disability of the applicant, if any existed, was caused by the injudicious use of mercurial medicine self-administered for venereal disease contracted at Augusta, Me., in January, 1864, and that such was the rumor among his comrades when he was sent to the hospital.

I can not believe that an injury was sustained such as was specified by the applicant in 1880 and that nothing was said of it either in the claim made in 1864 or in 1870. In the absence of this or some other definite cause consistent with an honest claim we are left in the face of some contrary evidence to guess that his arm was injured in the service.

The application of this beneficiary is still pending in the Pension Bureau awaiting further information.

GROVER CLEVELAND.

EXECUTIVE MANSION, *July 16, 1888.*
To the House of Representatives:

I return without approval House bill No. 9520, entitled "An act for the relief of Mary Fitzmorris."

It is proposed by this bill to pension the beneficiary named therein, as the widow of Edmund Fitzmorris, under the provisions and limitations of the general pension laws. The name of the beneficiary is already upon the pension roll, and she is now entitled to receive precisely the sum as a pensioner which is allowed her under this bill.

As her application to the Pension Bureau was quite lately favorably acted upon, it is supposed this special bill for her relief was passed by the Congress in ignorance of that fact.

GROVER CLEVELAND.

To the Senate: EXECUTIVE MANSION, *July 16, 1888.*

I return without approval Senate bill No. 121, entitled "An act granting a pension to Tobias Baney."

This soldier was enrolled on the 28th day of February, 1865, and was discharged on the 31st day of January, 1866.

He filed an application for a pension in 1878, which was supplemented by statements from time to time, not always in exact agreement, but alleging uniformly that during his service, fixing the date at one time as in January, 1866, and at another time as in November, 1865, he was attacked in the city of Washington by palpitation of the heart, which increased after his discharge and resulted in disability. After a careful special examination by the Pension Bureau the claim was rejected upon the ground that origin of disability in the service and line of duty had not been shown, nor that the same existed for some time after discharge.

The beneficiary named in this bill enlisted shortly before the surrender of the Confederate forces, and it appears did little, if anything, more than garrison duty. He does not seem to have suffered any of the exposures usually incident to a soldier's service, and, as I understand his claim, does not himself give any instance of exposure or exertion from which his difficulty arose.

There is no record of any sickness or disability during the time he was in the Army nor any satisfactory proof that he was suffering with any ailment at the time of his discharge. His own statement, which some of the proof taken tends to show is not entirely reliable, goes no further than to claim that during his term of service his difficulty began.

On appeal from the rejection of the beneficiary's claim the case was thoroughly examined at the Interior Department and the rejection affirmed.

I am entirely satisfied that the case was properly determined.

GROVER CLEVELAND.

To the Senate: EXECUTIVE MANSION, *July 16, 1888.*

I return without approval Senate bill No. 470, entitled "An act granting a pension to Amanda F. Deck."

The husband of this beneficiary was pensioned for a gunshot wound in his right shoulder which he received in 1864 in a battle with Indians.

The report of the committee to which the bill was referred states nothing concerning the death of the soldier and gives no information as to the date or cause of the same, and the recommendation that a pension should be given the widow is based upon the service and injury of the soldier and the circumstances of the beneficiary.

No claim was filed in the Pension Bureau on behalf of the widow. This perhaps is accounted for by the fact that information is lodged in that Bureau to the effect that the deceased soldier died on the 21st day of September, 1883, "from a pistol ball fired by Luther Cultor."

If he was killed in a personal encounter, as the report of his death would seem to indicate, I am unable to see how his death can be in any way attributed to his military service or his widow be justly pensioned therefor.

GROVER CLEVELAND.

EXECUTIVE MANSION, *July 17, 1888.*

To the Senate:

I return without approval Senate bill No. 1613, entitled "An act granting an increase of pension to John F. Ballier."

This pensioner is now receiving the full amount of pension allowed for total disability to ex-soldiers of his rank.

Inasmuch as the bill herewith returned limits any increase to the rate fixed by law for cases of total disability, it appears to accomplish nothing of benefit to the beneficiary therein named.

GROVER CLEVELAND.

EXECUTIVE MANSION, *July 17, 1888.*

To the House of Representatives:

I return without approval House bill No. 5913, entitled "An act granting a pension to Thomas Shannon."

This beneficiary enlisted on the 31st day of May, 1870, in the Tenth Regiment of United States Infantry.

On the 4th day of July, 1872, he was upon leave at the city of Rio Grande, in the State of Texas. Some of the citizens were celebrating the day, and one of them had a can of powder in his hand which, according to the report of the accident, "was about to explode." The soldier endeavored to knock the can from the hand of the person who held it, when the powder exploded, severely injuring the soldier and necessitating the amputation of his right forearm.

Though this was a most unfortunate accident, it is quite plain that it had no connection with the military service.

To grant a pension in such a case would establish a precedent in the appropriation of money from the public Treasury which I can hardly think we should be justified in following.

GROVER CLEVELAND.

EXECUTIVE MANSION, *July 17, 1888.*
To the House of Representatives:

I return without approval House bill No. 9174, entitled "An act granting a pension to Woodford M. Houchin."

The beneficiary named in this bill was enrolled September 18, 1861, and discharged December 17, 1864.

He filed a claim for pension in the Pension Bureau December 22, 1876, alleging that he had a sore or ulcer on his left leg "which existed in a small way prior to enlistment," but was aggravated and enlarged by the exposures of the service.

This claim was rejected in 1877 on the ground that the disability existed prior to enlistment.

In September, 1879, he filed another application for pension, alleging a disability arising from an affection of his right eye caused by an attack of measles in September, 1861, and also again alleging ulcerated varicose veins of his left leg.

In October, 1886, the rejection of the claim for ulcerated varicose veins was adhered to and the added claim for disease of the eyes was rejected on the ground that it was not incurred in the service and line of duty.

On appeal from the action of the Pension Bureau to the Secretary of the Interior the rejection of the claim was sustained.

The claimant stated in support of his application that about three months before he enlisted a little yellow blister appeared on his left leg, which made a small sore, which existed when he enlisted; that while he was in Central America with General Walker he received a wound in the temple from a musket ball, and that he had also before enlistment been sick with the dropsy.

The case was very thoroughly examined by officers of the Pension Bureau, and a great mass of testimony was taken from numerous witnesses. Three brothers of the claimant testified to the existence of all the disabilities before his enlistment, and two of them stated facts which go far toward accounting for such disabilities in a way very discreditable to the claimant. Many other witnesses, with good opportunities of knowledge on the subject, testified to the same effect.

While testimony of a different character was also given, tending to establish the theory that the disabilities alleged were at least to some extent attributable to military service, the overwhelming weight of proof seems to establish that whatever disabilities exist are the result of disease contracted by vicious habits, and that such disabilities had their origin prior to enlistment.

GROVER CLEVELAND.

EXECUTIVE MANSION, *July 17, 1888.*

To the House of Representatives:

I return without approval House bill No. 8078, entitled "An act granting a pension to Theresa Herbst, widow of John Herbst, late private Company G, One hundred and fortieth Regiment of New York Volunteers."

John Herbst, the husband of the beneficiary named in this bill, enlisted August 26, 1862. He was wounded in the head at the battle of Gettysburg, July 2, 1863. He recovered from this wound, and on the 19th day of August, 1864, was captured by the enemy.

After his capture he joined the Confederate forces, and in 1865 was captured by General Stoneman while in arms against the United States Government. He was imprisoned and voluntarily made known the fact that he formerly belonged to the Union Army. Upon taking the oath of allegiance and explaining that he deserted to the enemy to escape the hardship and starvation of prison life, he was released and mustered out of the service on the 11th day of October, 1865.

He was regularly borne on the Confederate muster rolls for probably nine or ten months. No record is furnished of the number of battles in which he fought against the soldiers of the Union, and we shall never know the death and the wounds which he inflicted upon his former comrades in arms.

He never applied for a pension, though it is claimed now that at the time of his discharge he was suffering from rheumatism and dropsy, and that he died in 1868 of heart disease. If such disabilities were incurred in military service, they were quite likely the result of exposure in the Confederate army; but it is not improbable that this soldier never asked a pension because he considered that the generosity of his Government had been sufficiently taxed when the full forfeit of his desertion was not exacted.

The greatest possible sympathy and consideration are due to those who bravely fought, and being captured as bravely languished in rebel prisons.

But I will take no part in putting a name upon our pension roll which represents a Union soldier found fighting against the cause he swore he would uphold, nor should it be for a moment admitted that such desertion and treachery are excused when it avoids the rigors of honorable capture and confinement.

It would have been a sad condition of affairs if every captured Union soldier had deemed himself justified in fighting against his Government rather than to undergo the privations of capture.

GROVER CLEVELAND.

To the Senate: EXECUTIVE MANSION, *July 26, 1888.*

I return without approval Senate bill No. 1447, entitled "An act granting a pension to Bridget Foley."

Joseph F. Foley, the husband of the beneficiary named in this bill, enlisted on the 22d day of August, 1862, and was discharged February 13, 1863, for disability which was certified to arise from chronic rheumatism contracted prior to enlistment.

He appears to have been sick with rheumatism a large part of the time he was in the service, and because of that fact never reached a point nearer the front than the city of Washington.

He died May 13, 1873, of consumption.

His widow filed in 1884 a declaration executed by the deceased shortly before his death, in which he alleged that he was first attacked with rheumatism at Capitol Hill, in the District of Columbia, in October, 1862. The soldier never applied for a pension.

It is strenuously disputed that he had this complaint before enlistment. However this may be, it is certain that he died of consumption, and I can find no proof that this disease was contracted in the service or had any relation thereto.

GROVER CLEVELAND.

To the Senate:　　　　　　　EXECUTIVE MANSION, *July 26, 1888.*

I return without approval Senate bill No. 2644, entitled "An act granting the right of way to the Fort Smith, Paris and Dardanelle Railway Company to construct and operate a railroad, telegraph, and telephone line from Fort Smith, Ark., through the Indian Territory, to or near Baxter Springs, in the State of Kansas."

This bill grants a right of way 100 feet in width, with the use of adjoining lands for stations and other purposes, through the eastern part of that portion of the Indian Territory occupied by the Cherokee Indians under a treaty with the United States.

By the terms of the treaty concluded between the Government and the Cherokee Nation in 1866 these Indians expressly granted a right of way through their lands "to any company or corporation which shall be duly authorized by Congress to construct a railroad from any point north to any point south, and from any point east to any point west of, and which may pass through, the Cherokee Nation."

There are excellent reasons why this clause in the treaty should be construed as limiting the railroads which should run through these lands, at least without further permission of the Indians, to only one from north to south and one other from east to west.

It is evident, however, that the Congress has either not so interpreted this provision of the treaty or has determined that it should be disregarded, for there have been six or seven railroads constructed or authorized through these lands by the permission of the Government.

It has become very much the custom to grant these rights of way through Indian lands and reservations merely for the asking.

have been duplicated to such an extent that rival roads are found struggling for the advantage of a prior Congressional grant or for the possession of a contested route through these reservations.

I believe these indiscriminate grants to railroads permitting them to cross the lands occupied by the Indians, if not in absolute violation of their treaty rights, are dangerous to the success of our Indian management.

While maintaining their tribal condition they should not be easily subjected to the disturbance and the irritation of such encroachments. When they have advanced sufficiently for the allotment of their lands in severalty, they should be permitted, as a general rule, to enjoy and cultivate all the land set apart to them, and not discouraged by the forced surrender of a part of it for railroad purposes. In the solution of the problem of their civilization by allotments of land they need the land itself, and not compensation for its appropriation by others. They can not be expected to understand this process in any other way than an indication that their tenure is uncertain and the assurance that they shall hold their allotted land for cultivation a delusion.

It is not necessary in the treatment of this subject to insist that in no case should a railroad be permitted to cross Indian reservations. There may be valid public reasons why in some cases this should be allowed. Important lines of through travel should not be always obstructed or defeated by a refusal of such permission. But I think there should be shown in every case a justification in the public interest or in furtherance of general growth and progress, or at least in a plain local necessity or convenience, before such grants are made.

It seems to me also that the consent of the Indians for the passage of railroads through their land should, as a general rule, be required; that the means of determining the compensation to be made for land taken should be just and definite and easy of application; that the route of the proposed road should be as particularly described as is possible; that a reasonable time should be fixed for the construction of the road, and in default of such construction that the grant should be declared null and void without legislation or judicial action, and that in all cases the rights and interests of the Indians should be carefully considered.

The bill under consideration grants to the railroad company therein named the right to construct its road over substantially the same route described in a law already passed permitting the Kansas City, Fort Scott and Gulf Railway Company to build its road through this reservation. No necessity or good reason is apparent why these two roads should be built upon the same line.

The bill makes no provision for gaining the consent of the Indians occupying these lands. The Cherokee Nation of Indians have their head men and legislation, and are quite competent to pass upon this question. They have heretofore shown their interest in such subjects, I am informed, by

protesting against some of the grants which have been made for the construction of railroads through their lands.

The bill provides for the taking of lands held by individual occupants
and the manner of fixing the compensation therefor; but it is declared
that when any portion of the land taken by the company shall cease to be
used for the purposes for which it is taken the same shall revert to the
nation or tribe from which the same shall have been taken. There is no
provision that in any case land taken from individual occupants shall
revert to them.

In the fifth section of the bill it is provided that the railroad company
shall pay to the Secretary of the Interior, for the benefit of the particular
nation or tribe through whose lands its line may be located, in addition
to other compensation, the sum of $50.

It was, of course, intended to declare that this sum should be paid for
every mile of road built through Indian lands, but it is not so expressed.
I am by no means certain that the context will aid this omission, which
is quite palpable, when that part of the bill is compared with others of the
same character. In any event, this is a provision which should be free
from all doubt.

There is no time limited in the bill within which the proposed road
through the reservation shall be completed, and consequently no forfeiture fixed for noncompletion. The nearest approach to it is found in a
clause providing that the company shall build at least 50 miles of its road
in the Indian Territory within three years from the passage of the act, or
the rights granted shall be forfeited as to that portion not built. The
length of the proposed route through the Cherokee lands appears to be
considerably over 100 miles, and it is plain that there is no sufficient
guaranty in the bill that the entire road will be built within any particular time. There is no forfeiture and no limitation for the completion
of the road if 50 miles is built within three years, and there may be some
doubt how far the forfeiture would extend in case of a failure to finish
the 50 miles within the time specified.

I believe these grants to railroads should be sparingly made; that when
made they should present better reasons for their necessity and usefulness than are apparent in this case, and that they should be guarded and
limited by provisions which are not found in the bill herewith returned.

GROVER CLEVELAND.

EXECUTIVE MANSION, *August 3, 1888.*

To the House of Representatives:

I return without approval House bill No. 3008, entitled "An act for
the relief of P. A. Leatherbury."

This bill provides that the Secretary of the Treasury shall pay to the
person above named the sum of $601.27, being the amount paid by

to Lucy Roberts on two pension checks which were afterwards recalled and canceled.

The committee of the House to whom this bill was referred report that—

> The Department discovered, after the issuing of the checks, that the claim for pension was fraudulent, but not until after the purchase, in the ordinary course of business, by Mr. Leatherbury paying $601.27 therefor and giving his duebill for the balance, which balance he refused to pay after ascertaining that the check was repudiated by the Government.

Lucy Roberts, a colored woman, filed a claim for pension in 1868, alleging that she was the widow of Nelson Roberts, who died in the military service in 1865.

Her claim was allowed in 1876, and two checks, numbered 6863 and 6864, aggregating $1,301.27, were issued on account of said pension. Before payment of the checks information was received which caused an investigation by the Pension Bureau as to the honesty of the claim for pension. This investigation established its utterly fraudulent character, and thereupon the checks were canceled and the woman's name was dropped from the pension rolls.

Certain important facts are reported to me from the Pension Bureau as having been developed upon the investigation.

It appears that one Thomas had undertaken to act for the claimant in procuring her pension under an agreement that he should have $300 if successful. Mr. Leatherbury was a notary, postmaster, and claim agent, and acted as notary and general assistant to Thomas and the claimant, who was employed at Leatherbury's house. In the month of July, 1876, the same month the claim for pension was allowed, the woman Roberts was indicted for larceny, the complaining witness being Mr. Leatherbury. Shortly after the issue of the checks the woman disappeared, and it is reported that certain indications suggested that both Leatherbury and Thomas were not entirely ignorant of her whereabouts nor completely disconnected with her disappearance. The checks were obtained from Thomas by Leatherbury, he paying, as he alleges, to Thomas the fee of $300 which had been agreed upon. The checks remained in Leatherbury's possession until they were delivered by him to the special agent of the Pension Bureau upon the investigation. He claimed in his deposition that he considered that what money he had let the woman have and the goods she had obtained at his store while she worked for him, and the $300 which he had advanced to Thomas, her agent, justified him in holding her indebted to him in the sum of $600, and that he held the checks as security for the same, admitting that there was still $700 in her favor, written acknowledgment of which he had placed in the hands of his wife. He further stated that rather than gain notoriety in the matter he would return the checks to the special agent, but he trusted that the Government would pay him the $600 which he had sunk in the transaction.

The woman testified that she did take some goods from Leatherbury at his store at his suggestion, after the arrival of the checks and before she left, about August 16, 1876, which purchases amounted to no more than $100, and that he also advanced her $100; that he made no further payment and wrote to her that he had to give up the checks, and that she never indorsed the checks nor authorized anyone to do so.

Both Leatherbury and Thomas disclaimed any knowledge of the fraudulent character of the claim; but the fraudulent claimant lived in the house of one of them and he was assisting in procuring her claim to be allowed, while the other made an unlawful agreement for a liberal compensation for his services if the claim succeeded. The woman was indicted at the instance of Leatherbury at about the time of the issuance of the checks and fled, but if she is to be believed Leatherbury wrote to her during her absence. After her disappearance he ventures to pay to Thomas his illegal fee and takes possession of the checks. He considers that she owes him $600, and the bill under consideration gives him $601.27, the exact amount of the checks less $700.

Someone with more intelligence than this ignorant colored woman concocted the scheme to gain this fraudulent pension; and the circumstances point so suspiciously toward Thomas and Leatherbury, the claim of the latter upon the Government is infected with so much illegality, and the amount of his advances is arrived at so loosely that in my opinion he should not at this late day be relieved.

GROVER CLEVELAND.

To the Senate: EXECUTIVE MANSION, *August 7, 1888.*

I return without approval Senate bill No. 1870, entitled "An act granting the use of certain lands in Pierce County, Washington Territory, to the city of Tacoma, for the purpose of a public park."

It is proposed by this bill to permit the appropriation for a public park of a certain military reservation containing 635 acres, which was set apart for military and defensive purposes the 22d day of September, 1866.

The establishment of this reservation was strongly recommended by high military authority, and its preservation and maintenance have since that time been also urged by the same authority.

At this time, when the subject of national defense is much discussed, I can not account for the apparent willingness to grant, or permit to be used for other purposes, Government lands reserved for military uses.

I judge from an expression in the letter of the Chief of Engineers, made a part of the report of the committee of the House to which this bill was referred, that its original purpose was to absolutely transfer this reservation to the city of Tacoma. The Chief of Engineers suggested an amendment to the bill providing that the mere permission to use this land for a park should be granted, "and that this permission be given with the full understanding that the United States intends to occupy the lands or any part of them for military or other purposes whenever its proper officials see fit to order the same, and without any claim for compensation or damage on the part of said city of Tacoma.''

Instead of adopting the recommendation of the Chief of Engineers the provision of the bill limiting the extent of the use of this land declares—

That the United States reserves to itself the fee and the right forever to resume possession and occupy any portion of said lands for naval or military purposes whenever in the judgment of the President the exigency arises that should require the use and appropriation of the same for the public defense or for such other disposition as Congress may determine, without any claim for compensation to said city for improvements thereon or damages on account thereof.

The expediency of granting any right to the occupancy of this land is, in my opinion, very doubtful. If it is done, it should be in the form of a mere license, revocable at any time, for the purposes used by the officers to which its use and disposition are now subject.

It seems to me that if any use of this land is given to the city of Tacoma it should be with the proviso suggested by the Chief of Engineers, instead of the indefinite and restricted one incorporated in the bill.

GROVER CLEVELAND.

EXECUTIVE MANSION, *August 9, 1888.*

To the House of Representatives:

I return without approval House bill No. 8761, entitled ''An act granting a pension to Mrs. Anna Butterfield.''

It is proposed by this bill to pension the beneficiary therein named as the ''dependent mother of James A. B. Butterfield, late a sergeant in the Second Illinois Cavalry.''

The records show that the son of this beneficiary enlisted in the regiment mentioned in August, 1861, and was mustered out August 13, 1864. No claim is made in any quarter that he incurred the least disability during this service, and there is no dispute in regard to the date of enlistment or discharge, nor does there seem to be any definite claim that he again entered the military service.

The report of the committee states that his mother is advised that after his discharge her son still remained in the service of the Government and was killed by an explosion on board of the steamer *Sultana*, in April, 1865.

Her claim for pension is now pending in the Pension Bureau awaiting testimony, which seems to be entirely wanting, to support the allegation that at the time of his death the deceased was in the service of the Government in any capacity.

This evidence ought not to be difficult to obtain. Though the mother seems to have saved something, from which she draws a small income, her advanced age and the honorable service of her son would make the allowance of a pension in her case, upon any fair and plausible justification, very gratifying.

GROVER CLEVELAND.

EXECUTIVE MANSION, *August 9, 1888.*

To the House of Representatives:

I return without approval House bill No. 2140, entitled "An act granting a pension to Eliza Smith."

The husband of this beneficiary was a second lieutenant in an Indiana regiment, and was discharged from the service in April, 1864. It is proposed in the bill herewith returned to pension the beneficiary as the widow of a first lieutenant.

The deceased was pensioned for a gunshot wound in his left arm under the general law, and his pension was increased by a special act in 1883.

He died away from home at a hotel in Union City, Ind., on the 18th day of December, 1884, and it was determined at the time, and is still claimed, that his death was the result of an overdose of morphine self-administered.

It is represented that at times the wound of the deceased soldier was very painful and that he was in the habit of taking large doses of morphine to alleviate his suffering.

Two days before his death he was at the house of one Moore, in Union City; he complained of pain, and asked for a dose of morphine, but it does not appear that he obtained it.

On the same day he went to a hotel in the same town and remained there until his death. On the second evening after his arrival there he complained of asthma and pain in his arm, and retired about 9 o'clock p. m. In the afternoon of the next day the door of his room was forced open, and he was found prostrate and helpless, though able to talk. Medicine was administered, but he soon died.

His family physician testified that the deceased did not suffer from asthma; that when his wound was suppurating he had difficulty in breathing, and that at such times he was in the habit of taking morphine in large doses, and that at times he was intemperate, especially when suffering from his wound.

It seems to me it would establish a very bad precedent to allow a pension upon the facts developed in this case.

GROVER CLEVELAND.

EXECUTIVE MANSION, *August 9, 1888.*

To the House of Representatives:

I return without approval House bill No. 7510, entitled "An act granting a pension to Stephen A. Seavey."

This beneficiary served in a Maine regiment from November 11, 1861, to August 17, 1862, when he was discharged upon a surgeon's certificate of epilepsia and melancholia. The surgeon further stated in his certificate that the soldier had been unfit for duty for sixty days in consequence of epileptic fits, occurring daily, and requiring the constant attendance of two persons during the past thirty days.

In 1879 he applied for a pension, alleging that he incurred a sunstroke on July 20, 1862. This was within the sixty days during which he was unfit for duty and also within the thirty days during which he required the constant attendance of two persons.

He succeeded in securing a pension, and drew the same until December, 1885, when information was received at the Pension Bureau which caused an examination of the merits of the case.

This examination developed such facts as led the Pension Bureau to the conclusion that the condition of the soldier was then identical with that before enlistment and that his disability existed before he entered the service. His name was accordingly dropped from the rolls.

The object of the bill herewith returned is to restore the pensioner to the rolls.

An examination of the facts satisfies me that the act of the Pension Bureau in dropping this name from the pension rolls was entirely correct and should not be reversed.

GROVER CLEVELAND.

EXECUTIVE MANSION, *August 9, 1888.*

To the House of Representatives:

I return without approval House bill No. 6307, entitled "An act granting a pension to Sarah A. Corson."

Joshua Corson, the husband of the beneficiary named in this bill, enlisted in August, 1862, for nine months, was wounded by a ball which passed through the lower part of each buttock, and was discharged June 29, 1863. He was pensioned for his wound, and died December 12, 1885.

The cause of death is stated to have been femoral hernia by a physician who attended him shortly before his death. The official record of his death attributes it to a malignant tumor.

The widow filed a claim for pension in 1886, but furnished no evidence showing when or how the hernia originated. No disability of this description is shown by any service record, nor was it ever claimed by the soldier. It is stated in the report of the committee of the House of Representatives to whom this bill was referred that the hernia first made its appearance about four years prior to the soldier's death.

The claim of this beneficiary for pension was rejected by the Pension Bureau upon the ground that there was no possible connection between the soldier's wounds and the hernia from which he died.

I am forced to the conclusion that the case was properly disposed of, and base my disapproval of the bill herewith returned upon the same ground.

GROVER CLEVELAND.

EXECUTIVE MANSION, *August 9, 1888.*

To the House of Representatives:

I return without approval House bill No. 3521, entitled "An act granting a pension to Manuel Garcia."

From the records it appears that the beneficiary named in this bill enlisted as a substitute August 6, 1864, and was transferred to the Eighth New Jersey Volunteers; that he is reported absent sick, and never joined his regiment, and was discharged from a hospital July 2, 1865.

He filed a claim for pension March 4, 1880, alleging that in October, 1864, at Alexandria, Va., he became lame in both legs, and that subsequently his eyes became inflamed. His hospital record shows that he was treated for pneumonia.

The board of examining surgeons in 1883 found no such evidence of varicose veins, which seems to be the disability claimed, as would justify a rating, and there appears to be no proof of the existence of any disability between the date of discharge and the year 1867.

The application of this beneficiary is still pending in the Pension Bureau awaiting any further proof which may be submitted in its support.

GROVER CLEVELAND.

EXECUTIVE MANSION, *August 10, 1888.*

To the House of Representatives:

I return without approval House bill No. 149, entitled "An act granting a pension to Rachael Barnes."

The husband of this beneficiary served in the Regular Army of the United States from February 24, 1838, to February 24, 1841.

In 1880 he applied for a pension, alleging that he contracted disease of the eyes during the year 1840 while serving in Florida.

Pending the examination of his application, and on the 24th day of March, 1882, he committed suicide by hanging. His widow filed a claim for pension, alleging that he died of insanity, the result of disease of the head and eyes. Her claim was rejected on the ground that his insanity, forty-one years after discharge from the service, had no connection with his military service.

In July, 1886, a special act was passed granting a pension to the widow, which met with Executive disapproval.

At the time the soldier committed suicide he was 68 years old. Upon the facts I hardly think insanity is claimed. At least there does not appear to be the least evidence of it, unless it be the suicide itself. It is claimed, however, and with good reason, that he had become despondent on account of the delay in determining his application for a pension and because he supposed that important evidence to establish his claim which he expected would not be forthcoming. It is very likely that this despondency existed and that it so affected the mind of this old soldier that it led to his suicide. But the fact remains that he took his own life in a deliberate manner, and that the affection of his eyes, which was the disability claimed, was not in a proper sense even the remote cause of his death.

I confess that I have endeavored to relieve myself from again interposing objections to the granting of a pension to this poor and aged widow. But I can not forget that age and poverty do not themselves justify gifts of public money, and it seems to me that the according of pensions is a serious business which ought to be regulated by principle and reason, though these may well be tempered with much liberality.

I can find no principle or plausible pretext in this case which would not lead to granting a pension in any case of alleged disability arising from military service followed by suicide. It would be an unfair discrimination against many who, though in sad plight, have been refused relief in similar circumstances, and would establish an exceedingly troublesome and dangerous precedent.

GROVER CLEVELAND.

EXECUTIVE MANSION, *August 10, 1888.*

To the House of Representatives:

I return without approval House bill No. 8574, entitled "An act granting a pension to Sallie T. Ward, widow of the late W. T. Ward."

The husband of this beneficiary served about nine months in the Mexican War. He entered the service as a brigadier-general in 1861, and served through the War of the Rebellion with credit, and was wounded in the left arm on the 15th day of May, 1864.

For this wound he was pensioned according to his rank, and received such pension until his death, at the age of 70 years, which occurred October 12, 1878.

The cause of his death was brain disease, and it seems not to be seriously claimed that it had any relation to his wound.

His widow is now in receipt of the pension provided for those of her class by the Mexican pension law.

If this bill becomes a law, I am unable to see why, in fairness and justice, the widow of any officer of the grade of General Ward should not be allowed $50 a month, the amount proposed by this bill to be paid his widow, regardless of any other consideration except widowhood and the rank of the deceased husband.

The bill herewith returned, while fixing the monthly amount to be absolutely paid to the beneficiary, does not make the granting of the pension nor payment of the money subject to any of the provisions of the pension laws nor make any reference to the Mexican service pension she is now receiving. While it is the rule under general laws that two pensions shall not be pa d to the same person, inasmuch as the widow is entitled to the pension she is now receiving upon grounds different from those upon which the special bill was passed, and no intention is apparent in the special bill that the other pension should be superseded, it may result that under the peculiar wording of this bill she would be entitled to both pensions.

The beneficiary filed a claim for pension in the Pension Bureau in 1884, which is still pending, awaiting evidence connecting the death of the soldier with his wound.

GROVER CLEVELAND.

EXECUTIVE MANSION, *August 10, 1888.*

To the House of Representatives:

I herewith return without approval House bill No. 490, entitled "An act granting a pension to George W. Pitner."

It appears from the records that the beneficiary named in this bill entered the military service in June, 1863, and was discharged in March, 1866. He was treated while in the Army in the months of December, 1864, and January, 1865, for conjunctivitis.

He filed a claim for pension in 1886, alleging that he had a sunstroke in 1865, and that while at work in a basement in the year 1881 he fell into a well which was open near him and received serious injuries, resulting in the amputation of his right foot and also disability of his left foot. He attributes his fall to vertigo, consequent upon or related to the sunstroke he suffered in the Army.

The claim was rejected on the ground that the evidence taken failed to connect the disabilities for which a pension was claimed with army service.

Whatever may be said of the incurrence of sunstroke in the Army, though he fixes it as after the date of his only medical treatment during his service, and whatever may be said of the continuance of vertigo consequent upon the sunstroke for sixteen years, I find no proof that at the time he fell he was afflicted with vertigo, unless it be his own statement; and whatever disability naturally arose from sunstroke does not appear by him to have been deemed sufficient to induce him to apply for a pension previous to his fall.

In any event there seems to be no satisfactory evidence that anything which occurred in his army service was the cause of his fall and consequent injury.

GROVER CLEVELAND.

EXECUTIVE MANSION, *August 10, 1888.*

To the House of Representatives:

I return without approval House bill No. 9034, entitled "An act granting a pension to Lydia A. Heiny."

The husband of this beneficiary served in an Indiana regiment from
August, 1861, to March, 1864, when he reenlisted as a veteran volunteer and served as a private and teamster to July 20, 1865, when he was
discharged.

There is no record of any disability, and he never applied for a pension.

On the 12th day of December, 1880, in leaving a barber shop at the
place where he resided, he fell downstairs, and died the next day from
the injuries thus received.

His widow filed an application for a pension in the year 1885, alleging
that her husband contracted indigestion, bronchitis, nervous debility, and
throat disease in the Army, which were the cause of his death.

The claim was rejected upon the ground that the death of the soldier
was not due to an injury connected with his military service.

While there has been considerable evidence presented tending to show
that the deceased had a throat difficulty which might have resulted from
army exposure, the allegation or the presumption that it caused his fatal
fall, it seems to me, is entirely unwarranted.

GROVER CLEVELAND.

EXECUTIVE MANSION, *August 10, 1888.*

To the House of Representatives:

I return without approval House bill No. 9344, entitled "An act granting a pension to James C. White."

The records of the War Department show that this beneficiary enlisted in a Kentucky regiment September 29, 1861. On the muster roll
of April 30, 1862, he is reported as absent. On the roll of August 31,
1863, he is mentioned as having deserted July 19, 1862. His name is
not borne on subsequent muster rolls until it appears upon those of January and February, 1864, with the remark that he returned February,
1864, and that all pay and allowances were to be stopped from July 19,
1862, to February 5, 1864. It appears that he deserted again on the 18th
of December, 1864, and that his name was not borne upon any subsequent rolls.

Naturally enough, there does not appear to be any record of this soldier's honorable discharge.

It seems that this man during the time that he professed to be in the
service earned two records of desertion, the first extending over a period
of nearly a year and a half and the other terminating his military service.

He filed a claim for pension on the 4th day of August, 1883, alleging
that he contracted piles in December, 1861, and a hernia in April, 1862.

A medical examination in 1883 revealed the nonexistence of piles and the presence of hernia.

The fact of the incurrence of any disability at all in the service is not satisfactorily established, and the entire case in all its phases appears to be devoid of merit.

GROVER CLEVELAND.

EXECUTIVE MANSION, *August 10, 1888.*

To the House of Representatives:

I return without approval House bill No. 9183, entitled "An act granting a pension to William P. Riddle."

The records of the War Department show that the beneficiary named in this bill was enrolled October 4, 1861, in the Fifth Kentucky Regiment of Cavalry, and was mustered into the service on the 31st day of March, 1862.

From that time to April 30, 1862, he is reported absent sick. On the rolls for four months thereafter, ending August 31, 1862, he is reported as absent and deserted. His name is not borne on any subsequent rolls.

He did not file an application for pension until April, 1879, when the act granting arrears was in force. He then claimed that he contracted pneumonia February 15, 1862; that about a month after he was sent home, and was under medical treatment for two years; that he returned about May 1, 1864, and was discharged about May 15, 1864, but that his discharge papers were lost.

Though he has furnished some evidence in support of the claim that he was sick at about the time alleged and that he returned to the Army after an absence of two years, no record proof of any kind is furnished of an honorable discharge at any time.

He has been informed that the record of his desertion in the War Department will be investigated with a view to its correction if he will furnish direct proof that it is erroneous. No such proof has been supplied, and the case has not been finally acted upon in the Pension Bureau.

It does not seem to me that this case in its present condition should receive favorable consideration.

GROVER CLEVELAND.

EXECUTIVE MANSION, *August 10, 1888.*

To the House of Representatives:

I return without approval House bill No. 9126, entitled "An act granting a pension to Mrs. Caroline G. Scyfforth."

The husband of this beneficiary served as contract surgeon in the

United States Army from September 12, 1862, to August 17, 1865, and was stationed at Portsmouth Grove Hospital, in Rhode Island.

He never filed a claim for pension, and died July 21, 1874, of congestion of the liver. His widow filed an application for pension in 1882, alleging that her husband's death was caused by blood poisoning contracted while dressing the wound of a patient in January, 1863. There is proof that he suffered from blood poisoning.

The record of death states its cause as congestion of the liver, but the certificate was not signed. A young doctor named Adams, a friend and pupil of the deceased, seems to have been more than any other the attendant physician, but he appeared to think that one of three other doctors had actual charge of the case. These physicians, named, respectively, Sullivan, Dana, and Sargent, agreed that Adams had charge of the case and that they were consulting surgeons in the last illness.

Dr. Adams testified before a special examiner that from intimate association he knew that the deceased was subject to kidney disease and other symptoms of bad health from discharge to his death; that as he had lost a part of one hand from blood poisoning in the Army, he always supposed his subsequent troubles were referable to that cause; that he believed the cause of death was albuminuria, and that his liver was also affected. He further expresses the opinion that the death was the culmination of the disorders which affected him from the time of his discharge from the service.

Dr. Sullivan deposed that he knew the deceased well from about 1869, and never had any reason to think him the subject of blood poisoning or its results. He further says that he was called in consultation at the last illness of the deceased and diagnosed his trouble as liver disease, due to the patient's habits of intemperance.

Dr. Dana testified that he knew the deceased well from the time of his discharge; that he was called to consult in his case with young Dr. Adams a few days before the death occurred; that he took a general view of the case and considered that the trouble was due to habits of intemperance.

Dr. Sargent deposed that he knew the deceased well and knew that he had lost a part of his hand, as alleged, from septic poisoning in the Army, though he was not aware that the poisoning had left any other effect; that the deceased had several spells of alcoholism after the war; that he had heard him complain of his kidneys, but attributed his troubles to his excesses.

Other evidence suggested the same cause for sickness and death spoken of by these physicians, but there seems to be an almost entire absence of evidence connecting the death with service in the Army.

I am of the opinion that a case is not presented in any of its aspects justifying a pension.

GROVER CLEVELAND.

EXECUTIVE MANSION, *August 10, 1888.*

To the House of Representatives:

I return without approval House bill No. 6193, entitled "An act for the relief of Edson Saxberry."

The beneficiary named in this bill filed a declaration for a pension in 1879, alleging that in 1863 he bruised his leg, which became very sore, and when it began to heal his eyes became sore.

The evidence taken upon a careful examination of this application seems to establish, by the admission of the applicant and by other evidence, the correctness of the position taken by the Pension Bureau in rejecting the claim, that whatever disability was incurred existed before enlistment and was in no manner attributable to military service.

GROVER CLEVELAND.

EXECUTIVE MANSION, *August 10, 1888.*

To the House of Representatives:

I return without approval House bill No. 2233, entitled "An act granting a pension to Bernard Carlin."

By this bill it is proposed to pension the beneficiary therein named as of Company A, Fourteenth Regiment of Missouri Volunteer Infantry.

It seems that he served in the company and regiment named, but that he also served in Company A, Sixty-sixth Illinois Regiment, and it is claimed that while in the latter service exclusively he received the injuries for which a pension is claimed.

His application is still pending in the Pension Bureau, and the papers pertaining to the same are now in the hands of an examiner for special examination.

I think this should be completed before a special act is passed, and I understand this to be in accordance with a general rule adopted by Congress and its pension committees. This is certainly the correct course to be pursued in this case, in view of the failure to state in the special bill the regiment and company to which the soldier belonged at the time of the incurrence of disability. This can be corrected by the Pension Bureau if the claim is found meritorious.

GROVER CLEVELAND.

EXECUTIVE MANSION, *August 14, 1888.*

To the Senate:

I return herewith a joint resolution which originated in the Senate, and is numbered 17, providing for the printing of additional copies of the United States map of the edition of 1886, prepared by the Commissioner of Public Lands.

This resolution directs that 7,500 of these maps shall be printed at a rate not exceeding $1.35 each; that 2,000 of said maps shall be for the use of the Senate, 4,000 for the use of the House of Representatives, 500 for the Commissioner of the Land Office, and that 1,000 be mounted and sold at the price of $1.50 each. The sum of $10,125 is appropriated to pay the expense of the publication of said maps.

The propriety and expediency of this appropriation, to be applied so largely by the two branches of Congress, should be left to legislative discretion.

I believe, however, that through inadvertence the duplication of the edition of these maps issued in 1886 has been directed by this joint resolution instead of the edition of 1887.

The map of 1886 was published at a cost of $1.25 per copy.

The map of 1887 will very soon be issued at a cost of $1 per copy, and the publishers have offered to print an enlarged edition at the rate of 95 cents for each map. This map will be later, more correct, more valuable in every way, and cheaper than that issued the previous year.

Upon these facts I return the joint resolution without approval, in the belief that the Congress will prefer to correct the same by directing the publication of the latest, best, and cheapest map, and reducing the amount appropriated therefor.

GROVER CLEVELAND.

To the Senate: EXECUTIVE MANSION, *August 14, 1888.*

I return without approval Senate bill No. 2653, entitled "An act granting a pension to Mary Curtin."

The husband of this beneficiary was mustered into the military service October 8, 1862, was wounded in the right arm, and was discharged September 3, 1863.

He was pensioned for his wound to the time of his death, September 17, 1880.

The physician attending him in his last illness testified that the deceased was in the last stages of consumption when pneumonia intervened and caused his death.

I do not understand that this physician gives the least support to the theory that the wound for which this soldier was pensioned was in the slightest degree connected with his death, and there seems to be nothing in the case to justify the conclusion that such was the fact.

GROVER CLEVELAND.

To the Senate: EXECUTIVE MANSION, *August 14, 1888.*

I return without approval Senate bill No. 1076, entitled "An act granting a pension to the widow of John Leary, deceased."

This bill does not give the name of the intended beneficiary, but merely directs that the name of the widow of John Leary, late first sergeant in Battery F, Third Artillery, United States Army, be placed upon the pension roll, and that she be paid the sum of $20 per month.

John Leary first enlisted in the Regular Army July 26, 1854, and reenlisted in August, 1859. He was slightly wounded July 1, 1862, and appears to have been discharged March 25, 1863, on account of syphilitic iritis. In April, 1863, he entered the general service and acted as a clerk in the Adjutant-General's Office until April 1, 1864, when he was discharged.

Neither he nor his widow ever filed a claim in the Pension Bureau, but an application on behalf of his minor children was filed in 1882.

The soldier died on the 8th day of December, 1872, of pneumonia, and his widow remarried in 1876.

The application on behalf of the children was denied on the ground that the death of the soldier was not due to any cause arising from his military service. The youngest child will reach the age of 16 in September, 1888.

It is stated in the report of the Senate committee to whom this bill was referred that the second husband, to whom this widow was married in 1876, is now dead, and it is proposed to pension her as the widow of John Leary, her first husband, at the rate of $20 per month.

In the unusual cases when a widow has been pensioned on account of the death of her first husband, notwithstanding her remarriage, which forfeited her claim under the general law, it has been well established that she was again a widow by the death of her second husband, that beyond all controversy the death of the first husband was due to his military service, and such advanced age or disability has been shown on the part of the widow as prevented self-support.

In this case the name of the widow is not in the bill; there is hardly room for the pretense that her first husband's death was due to his military service, her age is given as over 40 years, and $20 a month is allowed her; being considerably more than is generally allowed in cases where a widow's right is clear, with no complications of second marriage, and her necessities great.

GROVER CLEVELAND.

To the Senate:

EXECUTIVE MANSION, *August 14, 1888.*

I return without approval Senate bill No. 1762, entitled "An act granting a pension to Benjamin A. Burtram."

The beneficiary named in this bill was mustered into the military service November 26, 1861; he was reported present until February 28, 1862, and was discharged for disability July 26, 1862.

The medical certificate of the disability of this soldier was made by the senior surgeon of a hospital in Louisville, Ky., and stated that the soldier had been disabled for sixty days; that his lungs were affected with tubercular deposits in both, and that there was some irregularity in the action of the heart; that he was of consumptive family, his mother, brother, and two sisters having died of that disease according to his and his father's account.

It is of course supposed that this certificate was based upon an examination of the patient, though both he and his father seem to have supplemented such an examination with statements establishing a condition and history which operated to bring about a discharge.

I do not find, however, either as the result of examinations or statements, any other trouble or disability alleged than those mentioned above.

But in 1879, seventeen years after the soldier's discharge, and during the period when arrearages of pensions were allowed on such applications, he filed a claim for pension, in which he alleged that about December 1, 1861, while unloading gun boxes, he incurred a rupture, and that in January, 1862, he was taken with violent pains in left arm and side, causing permanent disability.

It will be observed that the time of the incurrence of these disabilities is fixed as quite early in the very short military service of this soldier; and it certainly seems that, though short, his term of service was sufficiently long to develop such disabilities as he claims to have incurred to such an extent that they neither would have escaped in the succeeding July the examination of the surgeon nor the mention of the soldier.

A medical examination which followed the application for pension in 1879 disclosed a large scrotal hernia, but no discoverable trouble of left arm and side.

A special examination of the case was made and a large amount of testimony taken. Without giving it in any detail as it is reported to me, I fail to find in it reasonably satisfactory proof that the disabilities upon which he now bases his claim for a pension were incurred in the military service.

                                             GROVER CLEVELAND.

To the Senate: EXECUTIVE MANSION, *August 22, 1888.*

I return without approval Senate bill No. 3038, entitled "An act for the relief of P. E. Parker."

Mr. Parker was a surety with six other persons upon an official bond given by one Franklin Travis, a collector of internal revenue, which bond was dated on the 9th day of May, 1867. A few years after that the collector became a defaulter to the Government for something over $27,000. Suit was commenced against the sureties upon the bond, and the defense was presented in their behalf that by reason of the imposition of new duties and responsibilities upon the collector after the execution of the bond his sureties were released. Judgment, however, passed against them, and the property of the beneficiary named in this bill was sold upon said judgment for the sum of $2,366.95. But only $1,793.16

of such amount was paid into the United States Treasury, the remainder having been applied to the payment of fees and expenses.

After the application of this sum to the payment of the judgment a bill was passed by the Congress relieving all these sureties from liability upon the bond. It appears that the amount above stated was all the money collected thereupon. The grant of the relief of these sureties by the Congress apparently was the same interposed by them to the suit in which the judgment was recovered.

The present bill directs the Secretary of the Treasury to pay to the surety Parker the sum of $2,336.95, the entire amount for which his property was sold, though the Senate committee to which the bill was referred reported in favor of reducing this sum to $1,793.16, the amount actually received by the United States upon its indebtedness.

It seems to me that the action of Congress in relieving these sureties was generous in the extreme, and if money was to be refunded which was apparently legally recovered and collected it should not exceed the amount the Government actually received. The Government is in no default and should be put to no expense in refunding the small sum recovered on account of the defalcation of its officer whose good conduct this beneficiary guaranteed. I think it would better subserve public interests if no further relief should be granted than that already afforded.

There is another fact reported to me which deprives this surety of any equitable claim for further relief. It appears from an examination of this matter that the man who is now attempting to be reimbursed this money from the Government Treasury commenced a suit against his cosureties for this identical money on the ground of their liability with him, and that he actually collected from two of them in such suit the sum of $1,747.16.

If this is true, it is speaking mildly of the claim he now makes against the Government to say that it should not have been presented.

GROVER CLEVELAND.

EXECUTIVE MANSION, *August 22, 1888.*
To the Senate:

I return without approval Senate bill No. 2616, entitled "An act granting a pension to James E. Kabler."

This beneficiary enlisted August 10, 1862. He is reported as absent sick for November and December, 1862; present for January and February, 1863; on the rolls for March and April he is reported as deserted, and for May and June as under arrest. On the 17th of September, 1863, after having been in the service a little over a year, he was mustered out with his company with the remark "absent without leave and returned to duty with loss of fifty-two days' pay by order of General Boyle." The charge of desertion does not appear to have been removed.

He filed a claim for pension in 1870 on account of quinsy alleged to

have been contracted about December 7, 1862, with some evidence to sup
port the claim.   Three medical examinations fail to establish the exist
ence of this disease in a pensionable degree, and it is reported to me from
the Pension Bureau that in March, 1882, the family physician of th
beneficiary stated that though he had practiced in his family for eigh
or nine years he had no recollection of treating him for quinsy or an;
other disease.

It seems to me that neither the service nor the alleged disability of thi
beneficiary are of a meritorious character.

GROVER CLEVELAND.

To the Senate: EXECUTIVE MANSION, *August 22, 1888.*

I return without approval Senate bill No. 2370, entitled "An act grant
ing a pension to Sarah C. Anderson and children under 16 years of age.'

William H. Anderson, the husband and the father of the beneficia·
ries named in this bill, enlisted on the 27th day of August, 1862, and is
reported as sick or absent a large part of his short term of service.   He
was discharged April 23, 1863, to date November 5, 1862, on a surgeon's
certificate of disability for "tertiary syphilis, with ulcerated throat and
extensive nodes on the tibia of both legs."

He never filed an application for pension.   He was admitted to an
insane asylum in September, 1883, suffering with epilepsy, chronic diar·
rhea, and dementia, and died of pneumonia on the 26th day of February,
1884.

His symptoms and troubles after his discharge, so far as they are
stated, are entirely consistent with the surgeon's certificate of disability
given at the time of his discharge, and there seems to be an entire lack
of testimony connecting in any reasonable way his death with any incident of his military service.   GROVER CLEVELAND.

To the Senate: EXECUTIVE MANSION, *August 22, 1888.*

I return without approval Senate bill No. 2206, entitled "An act granting a pension to David H. Lutman."

The beneficiary named in this bill was pensioned in 1885 on account
of spinal irritation, the result of measles.

In 1886 he filed a claim for increase of pension, alleging rheumatism,
and the board of examining surgeons at Cumberland, Md., upon an examination, found no evidence of spinal irritation or rheumatism, and he was
dropped from the pension rolls on the ground that the disability for which
he was pensioned had ceased to exist.

He afterwards filed medical and lay testimony tending to show that
suffered from disease of the back, legs, and arms, and he was there-

upon, and on the 8th day of October, 1886, again examined by the board
of examining surgeons at Hagerstown, Md., who reported as follows:

> We have stripped him, and find a splendid specimen, square built from the ground
> up, muscles well developed, his appearance indicative of perfect health. No curva-
> ture of spine, disease or irritation of spinal cord; no atrophy of any muscles or evi-
> dence of weakness. No impairment of motion anywhere.

If there is any value to be placed upon the reports of these examining
boards, the refusal of the Pension Bureau to restore this beneficiary to
the rolls was fully justified; and this is not a proper case, in my opinion,
for interference with that determination.

GROVER CLEVELAND.

To the Senate: EXECUTIVE MANSION, *August 22, 1888.*

I return without approval Senate bill No. 645, entitled "An act granting a pension to Mrs. Margaret B. Todd."

This bill does not describe the beneficiary as related to any soldier of
the war, but from other data it is found that she is the widow of Frank
G. Todd, who served as a private in the One hundred and eighteenth
Volunteer Infantry from July, 1863, to May, 1864, when he was transferred to the Navy. It appears that he served in the Navy from May
13, 1864, until April 10, 1866. He died in January, 1878, from exhaustion, as stated by the physicians who attended him.

There is scarcely a particle of satisfactory evidence showing his condition from the time of his discharge to 1871, and there is almost an
entire lack of proof showing a connection between his death and any
incident of his service. The widow in her application to the Pension
Bureau for a pension states that she has children who were born in 1870,
1871, and 1878.

There seems to be no record of any disability during the husband's
service in the Army, and the only mention of disability while in the
Navy is an entry on the 30th day of May, 1864, showing that he was
admitted to treatment for "syphilis secondary."

The widow's claim is still pending in the Pension Bureau.

GROVER CLEVELAND.

To the Senate: EXECUTIVE MANSION, *August 22, 1888.*

I return without approval Senate bill No. 1542, entitled "An act granting a pension to John W. Reynolds."

The bill describes this beneficiary as being "late of the One hundred
and fifty-seventh Ohio Volunteer Infantry."

He filed a claim in 1872 that he was a deputy United States provost-
marshal for the Twelfth Ohio district from October, 1864, to March,
1865, and that in December, 1864, while ascending a stairway to arrest

two deserters who had been drafted, a barrel of cider was rolled down · upon him, by which he was severely injured.

The claim having been rejected on the ground that the claimant was not entitled to a pension as a civil employee of the Government, he afterwards, and in January, 1888, informed the Bureau that he was drafted in November, 1864, while serving as assistant deputy provost-marshal, and was sworn in and reserved for home duty, and was discharged from the One hundred and fifty-first Ohio Volunteers. The records of the War Department show that John W. Reynolds served in the One hundred and fifty-first Ohio Regiment from May 2, 1864, to August 27, 1864.

It is perfectly apparent that this beneficiary was injured while acting as a deputy assistant provost-marshal, arresting deserters for the pay and rewards allowed him, and that his injuries were not at all connected with actual military service.

GROVER CLEVELAND.

Executive Mansion, *August 22, 1888.*

To the House of Representatives:

I return without approval House bill No. 2088, entitled "An act for the relief of W. S. Carpenter."

This bill appropriates the sum of $126.26 to be paid to the beneficiary named therein for his salary as an employee in the Railway Mail Service from the 3d day of October until the 20th day of November, 1882.

Mr. Carpenter was employed as a railway postal clerk at a salary of $800 per annum. He abandoned his route about the 2d day of October, 1882, without any leave of absence or explanation at the time, leaving his work in charge of one Jones, another railway postal clerk. He appears to have been paid for all the work he did, unless it be for two or three days in October, for which he apparently makes no claim.

There is nothing in the Post-Office Department showing that the absence of Carpenter was claimed to be on account of sickness, though there are a number of communications relating to the case.

The regulations of the Department permit the performance of the duties of a postal clerk by an associate in case of sickness, but never without the written permission of the division superintendent after an arrangement between the parties in writing, signed by them and filed with the superintendent.

Among a number of communications from Railway Mail Service officials relating to the conduct of Carpenter, all tending in the same direction, there is a letter from the chief clerk of the Railway Mail Service at Peoria, Ill., under whose immediate supervision Mr. Carpenter performed service, written to the superintendent of the sixth division of said service at Chicago, and dated November 16, 1882, containing the following statement:

I desire to call your attention to the case of W. S. Carpenter. Gilman and Springd R. P. O., as follows: October 10 he was requested to appear at the post-office at

Springfield, Ill., for examination on Illinois scheme. I went to Springfield for the purpose of examining him, but he failed to put in an appearance. Upon my return home I found a letter from him stating that he did not expect to remain in the service, hence his failure to report for examination; and, furthermore, that he would send in his resignation to your office by the first of the following week. This he had not done the 12th instant. He has not been on duty but two days since October 1. He left the run in charge of Mr. Jones, of the same line, telling him he did not know when he would return, and for Jones to keep up the run. He has no leave of absence, either verbally or otherwise. What his motives are for conducting himself in this manner I can not imagine. I have written him on the subject, but can not hear from him. When in Springfield the 3d instant, I requested the postmaster there to not pay Carpenter for October until he received notice to do so. I then notified you of the facts in the matter. I would respectfully recommend that Carpenter be relieved from further duty and a successor be appointed. He is of no account at the best; he has no interest in the work, and should be removed. I would also recommend that he be paid for but the two days' run in the month of October.

Four days after the date of this letter Mr. Carpenter was notified that an order had been issued discontinuing his pay and services.

These facts stated present the case of an employee of the Government abandoning his duties without leave or notice, in direct violation of rules, and claiming compensation for work done in his absence by another employee whose entire services were due the Government.

To allow a claim so lacking in merit would endanger discipline and invite irregularity and loose methods in a very important branch of the public service.

GROVER CLEVELAND.

EXECUTIVE MANSION, *August 27, 1888.*

To the House of Representatives:

I return without approval House bill No. 2524, entitled "An act for the relief of Clement A. Lounsberry."

This bill appropriates the sum of $1,214.51 to reimburse him for clerk hire and fuel and lights in excess of allowances made to him by the Post-Office Department while he was postmaster at Bismarck, in the Territory of Dakota.

Seven hundred and fifty dollars of this sum is appropriated on account of clerk hire paid out from April 1, 1881, to June 30, 1882, and $464.51 for lights and fuel from July 1, 1883, to September 30, 1885.

As a general rule the allowances made by the Post-Office Department in these cases ought not to be interfered with. But sometimes a sudden rush of settlement in a locality, or some other cause, will so increase unexpectedly the need of clerks to distribute and handle the mails that the employment of more than have been provided for is absolutely necessary.

I am inclined to think the item for clerk hire in this bill should be so regarded. This was the only appropriation included in the bill presented in the Forty-eighth Congress in behalf of this postmaster upon which a favorable committee report was made and which was not unfavorably spoken of by the Department.

But it does not follow that the other item for fuel and lights should be allowed. I think it should not, on the grounds that the amount was fixed by the Department upon full examination, that there is no special reason shown why the postmaster should have exceeded the expenditures allowed, and that to give the least encouragement to postmasters that these allowances would be upon their application revised and increased by Congress would lead to demoralization in the service.

It appears that the allowance made to this officer for fuel and lights was increased October 1, 1883, and although the claim now made on this account embraces the period from July 1, 1883, to September, 1885, nothing was asked for fuel or lights in the bill presented to Congress for this beneficiary's relief in 1884.

It should not have been tacked upon the bill now presented.

GROVER CLEVELAND.

EXECUTIVE MANSION, *August 27, 1888.*

To the Senate:

I return without approval Senate bill No. 288, entitled "An act for the erection of a public building at Sioux City, Iowa."

On the 19th day of June, 1886, I was constrained to disapprove a bill embracing the same subject covered by the bill herewith returned. Further investigation on the second presentation of the matter fails to convince me that $150,000 should be expended at present for the erection of a public building at Sioux City.

From all the representations that are made in an effort to show the necessity for this building I gather that the only two purposes for which the Government should furnish quarters at this place are a term of the United States court not specially crowded with business and the post-office, which, though perhaps crowded, I am sure can get on very well for a time without a larger public building.

As far as the court is concerned, it was agreed when a term was located there in 1882 that it might be held in the county building, which from the description furnished me seems to be entirely adequate for the purpose and very well arranged. The term held in October, 1887, was in session for nine days.

I am decidedly of the opinion that if a public building is to be located at Sioux City it had better be delayed until a better judgment can be formed of its future necessity and proper size.

I see some of the parties interested have such confidence in the growth and coming needs of the place that in their opinion the work ought not to be entered upon with a less appropriation than $500,000.

GROVER CLEVELAND.

EXECUTIVE MANSION, *September 1, 1888.*

To the House of Representatives:

I return without approval House bill No. 9363, entitled "An act granting a pension to Edwin J. Godfrey."

The beneficiary named in this bill enlisted on the 27th day of May, 1861, in a New Hampshire regiment, and less than three months thereafter was discharged on a surgeon's certificate of his disability occasioned by "disease of heart existing prior to enlistment."

In 1881, twenty years after discharge, the beneficiary applied to the Pension Bureau for a pension, and alleged that his disease of the heart was the result of fatigue and overheating at Bull Run, Virginia, July 21, 1861.

If the heart disease of which the discharged soldier complained in 1861, and which the claimant of a pension in 1881 alleged still continued, could have been caused by fatigue and overheating in the only battle of his brief service, it seems to me that its manifestations and symptoms a month afterwards could not have been mistaken for such as belonged to a much longer continuance of the disease.

I am fully satisfied that the surgeon was not mistaken who made the certificate upon which the beneficiary was discharged, and that his military service is not properly chargeable with any disability he may have incurred.

GROVER CLEVELAND.

EXECUTIVE MANSION, *September 1, 1888.*

To the House of Representatives:

I return without approval House bill No. 5155, entitled "An act granting a pension to John S. Bryant."

The man for whom this pension is proposed never, so far as I can learn, did a single day's actual military service at the front, nor ever left in such service the State in which he was enlisted.

He enlisted December 7, 1863, in a Maine regiment; on the 16th day of the same month he is marked as a deserter, having failed to report after leave of absence; December 31, 1863, he is reported sick in hospital at Augusta, Me.; January 26, 1864, he is marked as having deserted from Camp Keyes, at Augusta, Me.

He was discharged January 14, 1865, for disability occasioned, as the surgeon's certificate declares, "by a fall from a wagon while at home on a furlough, December 22, 1863." The certificate continues as follows:

Never has done a day's duty. Is utterly worthless and unfit for the Veteran Reserve Corps.

After his discharge the second charge of desertion was removed, and the first charge does not seem to be serious.

But he was injured while home on a furlough, his regiment still being in camp within the State of his residence; and although there are cases in which it seems not improper that pensions should be granted for injuries sustained during furlough and before actual return to duty, this does not appear to me to be one of them.

GROVER CLEVELAND.

EXECUTIVE MANSION, *September 6, 1888*.

To the House of Representatives:

I herewith return without approval House bill No. 2507, entitled "An act granting a pension to Russel L. Doane, of Peck, Sanilac County, Mich."

It is proposed by this bill to pension the beneficiary therein named as the dependent father of the late Demster Doane, late Company D, Thirty-fifth New York Volunteers.

The only information I have concerning this case is furnished by the report of the committee of the House to whom the bill was referred. There is nothing alleged in the report except that Demster Doane, who was a second lieutenant in the company and regiment named, died at Peck, Mich., on the 22d day of September, 1881, and that the deceased up to the time of his death supported his father, the claimant, who is now over 81 years of age, incapable of manual labor, and destitute of the means of support.

There is no intimation that the death of the son sixteen years after the close of the war was caused or in any way related to his military service. I do not understand that it has ever been claimed that a parent should be pensioned for the death of a son who had been in the Army unless his death could be traced in some way to his army service.

While this case is probably one where the exercise of generosity would be pleasant and most timely to the recipient, I can not think that such a precedent should be established.

GROVER CLEVELAND.

EXECUTIVE MANSION, *September 7, 1888*.

To the House of Representatives:

I return without approval House bill No. 9372, entitled "An act granting a pension to John Dean."

The beneficiary named in this bill was mustered into the service of the United States February 25, 1863. He never went to the front, but while in camp at Staten Island, on the 21st day of April, 1863, was granted a pass for forty-eight hours, and on account of sickness did not again rejoin his company or regiment. The charge of desertion made against him has been removed. The Surgeon-General's report shows that he was treated at quarters on Staten Island in April, 1863, for syphilis, rheumatism, and debility.

He was admitted to Charity Hospital, Blackwells Island, New York Harbor, August 5, 1863, and discharged November 18, 1863. He was admitted to the Ladies' General Hospital in New York December 1, 1863, and was discharged from the service for disability April 7, 1864.

The discharge was granted, as stated by the surgeon of volunteers in charge of the hospital, "because of sloughing of both corneas from inflammation contracted while absent without leave, having received a forty-eight-hour pass from his regiment April 15, 1863, then stationed on Staten Island. He lost his sight in August, 1863, while absent without leave. Unfit for Invalid Corps. Admitted to this hospital December 1, 1863. Not a case for pension."

A claim for pension was filed by the beneficiary at the Pension Bureau in March, 1877, alleging that on or about April 1, 1863, he suffered from chronic rheumatism and sore eyes, occasioned by exposure and illness contracted in camp.

It will be observed that no affection of the eyes is mentioned in the record of his treatment in quarters.

The claimant was examined by the New York City board of surgeons in June, 1878, and no rheumatism was found to exist. He is now blind, and while his case is certainly a pitiable one I am forced to the belief that the conclusions reached in 1879 upon his application, that his disease was contracted while absent without leave and that his disability was due to syphilis, were correct.

GROVER CLEVELAND.

EXECUTIVE MANSION, *September 7, 1888.*

To the House of Representatives:

I return without approval House bill No. 217, entitled "An act granting a pension to C. T. Maphet."

This beneficiary enlisted August 1, 1863, and was discharged January 27, 1865, for disability.

The commander of the post certifies:

This soldier says that he was first affected with the present disease, conjunctivitis, in the spring of 1862, since which time his eyes have never been well, and for a great portion of the time since enlistment he has been unfit for duty.

The certificate of the surgeon is as follows:

Incapacitated by reason of long-standing conjunctivitis of both eyes, attended with partial opacity of the cornea. Disability existed prior to enlistment, consequently soldier is ineligible to the Veteran Reserve Corps.

The beneficiary filed no application for pension until April, 1883.

Notwithstanding some evidence of soundness prior to enlistment, it seems to be quite well established that the trouble with his eyes was not the result of his military service, but existed before enlistment.

GROVER CLEVELAND.

EXECUTIVE MANSION, *September 7. 1888.*

To the House of Representatives:

I return without approval House bill No. 5503, entitled "An act granting a pension to Charles Walster."

This case has been very exhaustively examined by the Pension Bureau upon the application for a pension filed there by the beneficiary named in this bill.   Upon a review of the evidence taken it appears to be well established that any disability of the beneficiary heretofore existing was not attributable to his military service.

In addition to this a board of pension surgeons, as late as July, 1886, determined, after a thorough medical investigation, that no pensionable disability existed.

It thus appears that even if this bill were approved there could be no rating, and the legislation would be of no advantage to the beneficiary named.   GROVER CLEVELAND.

EXECUTIVE MANSION, *September 7, 1888.*

To the House of Representatives:

I return without approval House bill No. 333, entitled "An act granting a pension to Catharine Bussey."

It does not appear that the husband of this beneficiary ever applied for a pension.   He was discharged from the Volunteer Army on the 9th day of December, 1864, after a service of more than three years.

He was found dead on a railroad track on the 11th day of June, 1870, apparently having been struck by a passing train.

It is claimed that the deceased suffered a sunstroke while in the Army, which so affected his mind that he wandered upon the railroad track and was killed in a fit of temporary insanity.

Though it would be gratifying to aid his widow, I do not think these facts are proven or can be assumed.

                        GROVER CLEVELAND.

EXECUTIVE MANSION, *September 7, 1888.*

To the House of Representatives:

I return without approval House bill No. 5525, entitled "An act granting a pension to Mrs. Jane Potts."

The husband of this beneficiary enlisted in 1861 and was mustered out of the service in April, 1865.

He was taken prisoner by the enemy and endured for a long time the hardship of prison life.

He never applied for a pension, though undoubtedly his health suffered to some extent as the result of his imprisonment.

The beneficiary married the soldier in 1871.

He conducted his business affairs, managed his farm, and accumulated property up to the year 1880, when by a decree of court he was adjudged insane, caused by sickness as far as was known, and that his disease was hereditary.

It also appears that his mother and sister had periods of insanity.

He committed suicide in 1882 by drowning.

The beneficiary, his widow, filed a claim for pension in 1885, claiming that the insanity which caused him to commit suicide resulted from the hardships of prison life.

. Upon this application the facts of the case have been thoroughly examined. Two witnesses indicate that domestic trouble was the cause of the soldier's suicide. Another says that his wife (the beneficiary) was a pretty rough woman—a hard talker—and that the soldier often consulted him about the matter, and said it was hard to live with her. This witness adds that he does not believe that the soldier would have committed suicide if she had not abused him till he could not longer endure it.

The special examiner, in summing up the proof, says in his report:

The general opinion in the community is to the effect that his wife drove him to commit suicide rather than to live with or to obtain a divorce from her. Her reputation is that of a virago.

This kind of evidence, while not perhaps determining the case, reconciles me to the conclusion, which seems inevitable from other facts developed, that the military service and prison experience of the deceased were in no manner connected with his death.

GROVER CLEVELAND.

EXECUTIVE MANSION, *September 7, 1888.*

To the House of Representatives:

I return without approval House bill No. 7717, entitled "An act granting a pension to Mrs. Catharine Reed."

The husband of this beneficiary served in the Army from July 25, 1862, to October 16, 1862, when he was discharged for disease of the lungs. He was pensioned for hernia and disease of the lungs.

On the 23d day of November, 1880, while working in a sawmill, a piece of board was thrown from a buzz saw and struck him in the groin, causing a wound from which he died two days afterwards.

It is impossible to connect this injury and the resulting death with the disability for which he was pensioned.

GROVER CLEVELAND.

EXECUTIVE MANSION, *September 7, 1888.*

To the House of Representatives:

I return without approval House bill No. 4855, entitled "An act granting a pension to Jacob Newhard."

The records show that this beneficiary was mustered into the service

August 20, 1862 as a lieutenant; that on the return for November, 1862, he is reported as absent without leave—left hospital at Louisville." He was treated for hemorrhoids in the hospital at Nashville from December 12 to December 23, 1862 when having served a few days more than four months, he tendered his resignation upon the ground of disability and procured the following surgeon's certificate, upon which his resignation was based:

Lieutenant Jacob Newhard having applied for a certificate upon which to ground a resignation, I do hereby certify that I have carefully examined this officer and find him suffering from hemorrhoids, * * * and in consequence thereof is, in my opinion, unfit for duty. I further declare my belief that he will not be fit for the duties of a soldier in any future time, having already been afflicted twelve years, as he asserts.

On the 14th day of February, 1880 nearly eighteen years after his resignation the beneficiary filed his claim for pension based upon hemorrhoids the result of diarrhea and fever.

He denied upon this application that he was unsound prior to enlistment, and filed evidence to support his denial. One of the witnesses, a surgeon, who testified to incurrence of disability in the service, on a special examination stated that he so testified, having satisfied himself of the fact by personal interviews with the beneficiary.

I do not think in the circumstances surrounding this case that the beneficiary should at this late day be permitted to impeach and set aside the medical certificate procured by himself and containing his own statements, upon which he secured exemption from further military service.

GROVER CLEVELAND.

EXECUTIVE MANSION, *September 13, 1888.*
To the House of Representatives:

I return without approval House bill No. 6371, entitled "An act granting a pension to Jesse M. Stilwell."

On the 6th day of May, 1885, twenty years after this beneficiary was discharged from the Army, he filed an application in the Pension Bureau for a pension, alleging that in December, 1863, one year and eight months before his discharge, a comrade assaulted him with a stick while he was sitting in front of his tent preparing for bed and injured his back. He alleged that the assault was unprovoked and unexpected.

The claim was rejected upon the facts stated, upon the ground that any injury incurred was not the result of military duty.

Unless the Government is to be held as an insurer against injuries suffered by anyone in the military service, no matter how incurred, and also as guarantor of the good and peaceable behavior toward each other of the soldiers at all times and under all circumstances, this is not a proper case for the allowance of a pension.

GROVER CLEVELAND.

EXECUTIVE MANSION, *September 24, 1888.*

To the House of Representatives:

I return without approval House bill No. 8310, entitled "An act to provide for the disposal of the Fort Wallace Military Reservation, in Kansas."

This bill provides that a portion of this reservation, which is situated in the State of Kansas, shall be set apart for town-site purposes, and may be entered by the corporate authorities of the adjoining city of Wallace.

The second section of the bill permits the Union Pacific Railroad Company to purchase within a limited time a certain part of the military reservation, which is particularly described, at the rate of $30 per acre.

I am informed that this privilege might, by reason of a faulty description of the lands, enable the railroad company to purchase at the price named property in which private parties have interests acquired under our laws.

It is evident that the description of the land which the railroad company is allowed the option of purchasing should be exact and certain for the interest of all concerned.

Section 4 of the bill grants a certain portion of the military reservation heretofore set apart by the military authorities as a cemetery to the city of Wallace for cemetery purposes.

There should, in my opinion, be a provision that no bodies heretofore interred in this ground should be disturbed, and that when the same is no longer used as a cemetery it should revert to the Government.

GROVER CLEVELAND.

EXECUTIVE MANSION, *September 24, 1888.*

To the House of Representatives:

I am unable to give my assent to a joint House resolution No. 14 and entitled "Joint resolution to authorize the Secretary of the Interior to certify lands to the State of Kansas for the benefit of agriculture and the mechanic arts," and I therefore return the same with a statement of my objections thereto.

By an act of Congress passed July 2, 1862, certain public lands were granted to such of the several States as should provide colleges for the benefit of agriculture and the mechanic arts.

Under the terms of this act the State of Kansas was entitled to 90,000 acres of land, subject, however, to the provisions of said statute, which declared that when lands which had been raised to double the minimum price, in consequence of railroad grants, should be selected by a State such lands should be computed at the maximum price and the number of acres proportionately diminished.

Of the lands selected by the State of Kansas, and which have been certified, 7,682.92 acres were within certain limits of a railroad grant, and had therefore been raised to the double minimum in price, so that the number of acres mentioned and thus situated really stood for double that number of acres in filling the grant to which the State of Kansas was entitled.

It is now claimed that after the selection of these lands the route of said railroad was abandoned and another one selected, and that in consequence thereof such lands included within its first location were reduced to the minimum price and restored to public market at that rate. It is supposed upon these allegations that justice and equity require that an additional grant should now be made to the State of Kansas from the public lands equal to the number of acres selected within the limits of the first railroad location.

But an examination discloses that the joint resolution is predicated upon an entire misunderstanding of the facts.

The lands heretofore mentioned as amounting to more than 7,000 acres, selected by the State of Kansas, and charged at double that amount because their price had been raised to the double minimum in consequence of their being within a railroad location, have all except 320 acres remained either in the new or old railroad location up to the present time, and if now vacant would be held by the Government at the double minimum price.

It seems clear to me that the State of Kansas has been granted all the public land to which it can lay any legal or equitable claim under the law of 1862

GROVER CLEVELAND.

To the Senate: EXECUTIVE MANSION, *October 10, 1888.*

I herewith return without approval Senate bill No. 2201, entitled "An act for the relief of Laura E. Maddox, widow and executrix, and Robert Morrison, executor, of Joseph H. Maddox, deceased."

An act of Congress approved July 2, 1864, provided among other things that the Secretary of the Treasury, with the approval of the President, might authorize agents "to purchase for the United States any products of States declared in insurrection, at such price as should be agreed on with the seller, not exceeding the market price thereof at the place of delivery."

Under the authority of said act the Secretary of the Treasury, with the approval of the President, prescribed rules and regulations to govern the transactions thus permitted, and appointed one H. A. Risley an agent to act for the United States in making such purchases.

On or about the 13th day of November, 1864, said Risley entered into a written contract with Joseph H. Maddox and two other parties, whereby the latter agreed to sell and deliver to Risley as such agent, at Norfolk or New York, 6,000 boxes of tobacco, 350 barrels of turpentine, and 700 barrels of rosin.   It was also agreed that all products transported under the contract should be consigned to said Risley as agent and shipped on a Government transport, or, if not so shipped, should be in the immediate charge of an agent of Risley's, whose compensation and expenses should be paid by the sellers.   Said products were to be sold in New York or Baltimore under Risley's direction, and one-fourth of the proceeds, after deducting certain expenses, costs, and charges, were to be retained for the United States and three-fourths paid to Maddox and his associates.

It was expressly provided in said contract as follows:

Nothing in this contract contained shall be construed as incurring any liability on behalf of the United States.

It appears that Maddox, very soon after the contract was made, acquired all the interest of his associates therein.

The President of the United States signed an order or permit for the transportation of the goods, in fulfillment of the contract, and for the passage of the parties selling such goods through the Federal military lines, the permit declaring, however, that such transportation and passage should be ''with strict compliance with the regulations of the Secretary of the Treasury, and for the fulfillment of said contract with the agent of the Government.''

Maddox and his associates were not at the time the contract was entered into the owners of any of the property they agreed to sell and deliver; but it is alleged that Maddox, as one of the parties to the contract and as assignee of his co-contractors, purchased 4,042 boxes of tobacco, worth at that time more than $735,000, for the purpose of fulfilling this contract.

The tobacco was purchased by him within the rebel lines in the State of Virginia.   A part of it, he charges, was forcibly taken by the military forces of the Government and converted to its use or destroyed while being transported to its destination, and the remainder of it, having been detained in storage at Richmond, Va., was afterwards appropriated to the use of the United States or was destroyed in the fires at Richmond upon the capture of the city by the United States forces in 1865.

An action predicated upon the contract with Risley was brought by Maddox in the Court of Claims to recover the value of this property, but it was held by the court that the contract was void.

On appeal to the Supreme Court of the United States the decision of the Court of Claims was affirmed, upon the ground, as had been previously decided by said court, that under the law, the Treasury regulations, and the Executive orders concerning the purchase of products of insurrectionary States a purchasing agent of the Government had no authority to negotiate with anyone in relation to the purchase of such products unless at the time of the negotiation the party either owned or controlled them; that neither the law nor the regulations for its execution protected a speculation wherein the products to be sold were to be procu by the contractor within the rebel lines after the contract was made; that private citizens were prohibited from trading at all in the insurrectionary districts, and that the object of the law and the regulations to carry it into effect was to encourage the insurgents themselves to bring their products to agents of the Government.

With this adverse decision all chance of recovery upon legal grounds or before the courts was dissipated. But recourse to Congress still remained. As appears from a memorandum furnished in support of this bill, the alleged equities of the case were presented to the Forty-second, the Forty-third, the Forty-fourth, the Forty-fifth, the Forty-sixth, the Forty-eighth, and the Forty-ninth Congresses. Two adverse and more than two favorable committee reports have been made upon the claim. No bill for the relief of the claimant has, however, passed Congress until the present session, when a favorable condition seems to have presented itself.

The bill herewith returned empowers and directs the accounting officers of the Treasury to settle and pay to the representatives of Maddox the amount found due him on account of the loss and damage he sustained by the seizure by our military forces of the tobacco purchased by him under the agreement referred to, excluding, however, the tobacco destroyed by fire in the city of Richmond, and provides that said claim shall be determined upon the evidence taken and now on file in the office of the clerk of the United States Court of Claims and the War Department and any other competent evidence.

I fail to appreciate the equities which entitle this claimant to further hearing.

Every intelligent man should be charged with the knowledge that as a general rule commercial intercourse with the enemy is entirely inconsistent with a state of war, and that the law of 1864 had for its object the encouragement of the insurgents themselves to bring their products to us, and not the authorization of persons to roam through the insurrectionary districts and purchase their products on speculation.

Even if the claimant did not understand these conditions, he certainly knew that his contract was based upon a statute; that the agent with whom he was contracting was a creature of statute, and that such statute and certain regulations of the Secretary of the Treasury made thereunder regulated the right and limited the action of all the parties to said contract. These things sufficiently appear from the very terms of the contract and the permit signed by the President. The privileges and liberties contained in this permit are expressly granted "with strict compliance with regulations of the Secretary of the Treasury."

If before or after entering into this contract the claimant had examined these regulations, he would have found that they provided that "commercial intercourse with localities beyond the lines of actual military occupation by the United States forces is absolutely prohibited."

He would have also found that such regulations expressly provided that the power of the agent of the Government to make contracts should be founded upon the statement that the contractor then owned or controlled the products for which he contracted. And yet the permit of the President, which so completely put the claimant upon inquiry as to what he might or might not do, seems now to be relied upon as the source of equities in his favor, and is pressed into his service under the guise of a sanction of his unlawful proceedings.

Besides the general knowledge the claimant should have possessed of the commercial disabilities consequent upon a state of war, and the information afforded him by his contract and permit, a proclamation of the President publicly issued September 24, 1864,* furnished abundant notice of the kind of trading which would be permitted.

The property for which compensation is asked constitutes a part only of that agreed to be furnished. None of it ever reached the possession of the agent of the Government, but, as I understand the case, was at the time of its seizure or destruction still in the territory of the enemy and in rebellious possession. If in the circumstances detailed it was treated by our military forces in like manner as other property in the same situation, there would seem to be no hardship in holding that the contractor assumed this risk as one arising from his unauthorized and, if successful, his profitable venture.

Not being satisfied that there are any especial equities which entitle this claim to more consideration than many others where equities might be claimed in behalf of those who long ago violated our nonintercourse laws, I am unwilling to sanction a precedent which if followed might substantially work a repeal of these laws, regarded necessary and expedient by those charged with legislation during the War of the Rebellion, and who had in full view all the necessities of that period.

GROVER CLEVELAND.

EXECUTIVE MANSION, *October 12, 1888.*
To the Senate:

I return without approval Senate bill No. 3276, entitled "An act granting restoration of pension to Sarah A. Woodbridge."

The first husband of this beneficiary, Anson L. Brewer, was an additional paymaster in the Army, and died February 2, 1866, from injuries received in an explosion of a steamer.

His widow, the beneficiary, was pensioned at the rate of $25 a month from the date of her husband's death until October 21, 1870, when she remarried, becoming the wife of Timothy Woodbridge.

Two children, who were minors at the time she was pensioned, became 16 years of age in April, 1870, and July, 1874, respectively.

---

* See Executive order of September 24, 1864, Vol. VI, pp. 240-241.

Upon the remarriage of the beneficiary her pension stopped under the law.

It is now proposed to restore her to the pension roll, notwithstanding the fact that her second husband is still alive.

Many cases have occurred in which pensions have been awarded by special acts to the widows of soldiers who, having remarried, were a second time made widows and rendered destitute by the death of their second husbands.   I have not objected to such charitable legislation.

But I think this is the first time that it has been proposed to grant a pension after such remarriage when the second husband still survives.

It seems to me that such a precedent ought not to be established.   If in pension legislation we attempt to determine the cases of this description in which the second husband can not or does not properly maintain the soldier's widow whom he has married, we shall open the door to much confusion and uncertainty, as well as unjust discrimination.

I am glad to learn from a statement contained in the committee's report that this beneficiary, though in a condition making the aid of a pension very desirable, has a small income derived from property inherited from her mother.

GROVER CLEVELAND.

To the Senate: Executive Mansion, *October 12, 1888.*

I herewith return without approval Senate bill No. 1044, entitled "An act authorizing the Secretary of the Treasury to state and settle the account of James M. Willbur with the United States and to pay said Willbur such sum of money as may be found due him thereon."

The claim mentioned in this bill grows out of alleged extra work done by the claimant in the construction of the post-office and court-house building in the city of New York.

The United States, in September, 1874, entered into a contract with Messrs. Bartlett, Robbins & Co. by which they agreed to furnish and put in place certain wrought and cast iron work and glass for the illuminated tiling required for the said building according to certain specifications and schedules which formed a part of said contract. The work was to be of a specified thickness and the contractors were to be paid for the same at certain rates per superficial foot.   The approximate estimate for the entire work was specified at $35,577.56.   Samples of the tiling to be put in were submitted to the Supervising Architect and accepted by him.

In August, 1874, the claimant entered into an agreement in writing with Bartlett, Robbins & Co. to do this work as subcontractor for them at certain prices for each superficial foot of said tiling put in place.

In neither contract was the weight of the tiling mentioned.   -

The work was, under the contract with Messrs. Bartlett, Robbins & Co., completed, and after such completion and the measurement of the work the said firm of Bartlett, Robbins & Co. were paid by the Government the sum of $35,217.57, in full satisfaction of their contract with the United States.

It appears that after the completion of the work the claimant gave notice to the Government that he had a claim against Bartlett, Robbins & Co., growing out of said work, for the sum of $8,744.44, and requested that payment be withheld from said firm until his claim against them was adjusted.

The fact that said claim had been made having been communicated by the Supervising Architect to Bartlett, Robbins & Co., on the 22d day of August, 1876, they responded to the Supervising Architect as follows:

DEAR SIR: We inclose copy of our account against Willbur and the Illuminated Tiling Company and a copy of Willbur's assignment to the Tile Company, which includes a copy of his agreement with us; and when the Department settles the measurement of the work the items in the contract will show just what the amount is, and, as we have repeatedly assured him, he will have all the measurements the Government gives us.

If anyone has cause of complaint in this case it is us. Four times the work came to a stand, or nearly so, and our Mr. B. was compelled to go to New York and stay until it was moving again, charging his expenses, by Willbur's request, and finally it had to be finished by others, etc. We know this does not interest you particularly, as you do not know him in the matter, but there has been so much willful misrepresentation we thought silence might be misconstrued.

It is charitable to think Willbur must be crazy.

Very respectfully, yours,   ·   BARTLETT, ROBBINS & CO.

In an opinion of the Solicitor of the Treasury concerning this claim, dated November 30, 1883, I find a statement that on the 20th day of October, 1876, a paper was filed by the attorneys of the claimant in which his claim for extra work and material in performing his contract was alleged to be $21,857.94. It is further stated that this claim was hastily drawn by one of Willbur's attorneys and without consultation with him.

On or about the 20th day of March, 1877, Mr. Willbur himself filed a statement of such extra work and material, in which he claimed for the same the sum of $42,685.20.

Another statement made by Willbur, in February, 1878, presents a claim on account of the same matters amounting to $47,159.62.

This claim, so variously stated, is based upon the allegation that tiling and frames of greater thickness than were required by the contract were put in the building. Although it is insisted by the claimant that these thicker tiles and frames were directed to be put in, or at least accepted by the person having charge of the construction of the building for the Government, I hardly think it will be seriously contended that the claimant has any legal claim against the United States.

But, with a view of discovering whether, upon equitable grounds, the claimant should be paid anything by the Government for glass and iron of greater thickness than its contract with Bartlett, Robbins & Co.

required, and which had been put in its building by their subcontractor, the Secretary of the Treasury in 1884 appointed a committee of three persons to examine and report upon this claim of Willbur's, "with a view of determining what portion, if any, it is proper for the Government to pay."

On the 24th day of January, 1885, this committee made a report by which they determined that there should be paid to the claimant on account of the matters alleged the sum of $1,214.90.

This report was based upon the measurements, examinations, and estimates of two experts, one selected by the claimant and the other by the committee. The report was transmitted to the House of Representatives by the Secretary of the Treasury and an appropriation asked to pay the amount awarded.

But Mr. Willbur was not satisfied, and on the 6th day of January, 1885, addressed a communication to the Secretary of the Treasury in which this passage occurs:

I shall insist on a remeasurement of the entire work, as this is vital to my claim. The excess which I furnished can only be ascertained by weight instead of by measuring the thickness of the plates and frames.

At the second session of the Forty-ninth Congress, and early in 1886, this claim was before the Senate Committee on Claims, and at the instance of the committee this work was again examined by experts, who came to the conclusion that the claimant was entitled to the sum of $45,615.67 for the extra work which he had performed and materials furnished.

It is only alleged that the glass tiling and frames actually put in the building were slightly thicker than those required by the contract, and this alleged increased thickness seems to be fairly represented in a general way by the claim that some of the glass and frames which were required to be 1 inch thick were actually put in 1 inch and a quarter thick.

Upon this statement it must be admitted that the sum above stated as the value of this extra thickness is somewhat startling. In the language of the report upon this bill by the Supervising Architect, "a claim of $47,159.02 for such slight excess on work the price of which was $35,217.57 is hardly entitled to consideration."

The claim, as well as the award of the experts last named, reach their astonishing proportions by the application of weights to the question in the following manner: A certain area is measured. A square foot of the tiling actually put in is weighed, and a square foot of the tiling required by the contract is also weighed. Both these weights are multiplied by the area. The lesser aggregate weight is deducted from the greater, and the difference is divided by the weight of a square foot of the lightest tiling, thus reducing it to square feet of such lightest tile. These square feet are multiplied by the price agreed to be paid by the contract for each superficial foot, and an item of extra work is determined. Thus additional weight in constructed and finished tiling is converted, as far as price and measurement are concerned, into finished tile, which more than doubles the quantity actually laid down.

This can not be right. And yet the bill herewith returned directs the Secretary of the Treasury to settle this claim for extra work upon the basis of the report of the experts who have adopted this mode of adjustment; or, if not satisfied with their report, he shall within thirty days from the passage of the act cause a reweighing of said material to be made by two sworn experts, one to be appointed by him and one by the claimant, and a third to be appointed by these two in case they can not agree. The bill further provides that he shall then pay to said Willbur the difference of excess in weight and superficial measurement as found by said experts between the illuminated tiling and frames furnished and that contracted for at the contract prices for such work and material.

There are features of this claim which suggest suspicion as to its merit. In any view of the matter, I regard the claimant as seeking equitable relief. He is not entitled to dictate the rule by which his claim is to be adjusted, and he should be quite satisfied if the officers of the Government charged with the settlement of such matters are permitted by the Congress to afford equitable relief according to such rules and methods as are best calculated to reach fair results.

GROVER CLEVELAND.

EXECUTIVE MANSION, *October 15, 1888.*

To the Senate:

I return without approval Senate bill No. 3306, entitled "An act granting a pension to Mary K. Richards."

The beneficiary named in this bill applied for a pension on the 14th day of November, 1878, and the same was rejected in April, 1879. Her claim has lately been reexamined, and since the passage of the bill herewith returned she has been allowed a pension by the Pension Bureau, it having been there determined that the former rejection was a manifest error.

With this action of the Pension Bureau I entirely concur.

I therefore venture, notwithstanding the persistent misrepresentations of my action in similar cases, to disapprove this bill, upon the ground that this deserving beneficiary will receive under the action of the Pension Bureau a much larger sum than she would if such action was superseded by the enactment of the proposed special statute in her behalf.

GROVER CLEVELAND.

EXECUTIVE MANSION, *October 15, 1888.*

To the Senate:

I herewith return without approval Senate bill No. 3208, entitled "An act granting a pension to William S. Bradshaw."

GROVER CLEVELAND.

EXECUTIVE MANSION, *October 29, 1888.*

To the House of Representatives:

I return without approval House bill No. 7657, entitled "An act granting a pension to Mary Woodworth, widow of Ebenezer F. Woodworth."

The husband of this beneficiary enlisted October 1, 1861. On the rolls of his company for May and June, 1862, he is reported as a deserter, and the report is the same on the muster-out roll of his regiment, dated October 19, 1864.

An effort was made on the application by the beneficiary for pension to the Pension Bureau to attribute the charge of desertion to the unfriendliness and injustice of the soldier's captain, and an unsuccessful effort was made to have the charge removed from the record by the Adjutant General.

The soldier, therefore, is still recorded as a deserter from camp near Farmington, Miss., since March 12, 1862.

The application of the widow to the Pension Bureau in 1867 states that her husband was missing at Hamburg, Tenn., May 7, 1862, and not having since been heard from is supposed to be dead.

The captain of the company testifies that the soldier was employed with the ambulance corps, and that for misconduct he (the captain) ordered him to his company and censured him; that very soon after that the soldier was absent at roll call and was marked as absent without leave; that in a day or two after that a member of a detail returned to camp from Hamburg Landing and reported that he had seen the soldier there and had been told by him that "he was off and would never go back." Thereupon he was dropped from the roll as a deserter.

Various theories are presented to account for the soldier's absence in other ways than by desertion, some of his comrades going so far as to express the opinion that he was murdered at the instigation of his captain. None of these theories, however, seem to be more than conjectures with various degrees of plausibility.

If the question of desertion could be solved favorably to the beneficiary, another difficulty immediately arises from the fact that there is absolutely no proof of death except the soldier's long absence without knowledge of his whereabouts; and if his death could be presumed the cause of it and whether connected at all with military service are matters regarding which we have no information whatever.

I am unable to see how a case in such a situation can be considered a proper subject for favorable pension legislation.

GROVER CLEVELAND.

EXECUTIVE MANSION, *October 16, 1888.*

To the House of Representatives:

I return without approval House bill No. 10661, entitled "An act granting a pension to Mrs. Sophia Vogelsang."

The husband of this beneficiary was severely wounded in the military service of the United States, and in consequence of said wound his left leg was amputated. This was in 1862. In January, 1863, another amputation was performed higher up above the knee. He appears at that time to have been living, or at least was treated, at Detroit, Mich. He was pensioned at the rate of $30 per month at the time of his death, which occurred at Louisville, Ky., where he appears to have then resided, on the 21st day of July, 1885.

The beneficiary filed a claim for pension in November, 1885, alleging that her husband died of gangrene.

There does not, however, seem to be a particle of evidence establishing that cause of death. On the contrary, the report received at the Pension

Bureau of his death attributes it to sunstroke, and this does not seem to be directly questioned.

The report of the House committee to whom this bill was referred proceeds upon the theory that death was caused from the use of opium to allay the pain of the wound. This theory is presented upon the alleged opinion of the surgeon living in Detroit, who made the second amputation in 1863. He says that the pain of the wound obliged the soldier to take morphine. But it does not appear that he observed the case for a long time preceding death. Instead of his giving an opinion that the disability and morphine produced death, he says, as it is reported to me, after describing the condition of the limb previous to its amputation in 1863 and immediately thereafter:

According to my opinion, said disability and the constant use of morphia in consequence of it may have been the cause of his death.

This and the statement of a druggist in Louisville that he sold him morphine to alleviate pain, and of two different persons with whom he boarded at that city in 1885 to the same effect, is all the evidence that I can discover tending in the least to hint that the death of the pensioner resulted from any cause but sunstroke, which really stands as the undisputed cause of death.

The allegation in the committee's report that the beneficiary's claim was rejected by the Pension Bureau on the ground that her husband's death proceeded from the use of morphine is erroneous. The cause of rejection is stated to be ''that the death cause (sunstroke) was not the result of the soldier's military service.''

We are not, therefore, left to the consideration of the question whether death from the use of morphine to allay pain can be charged to the disability incurred, for if death resulted from sunstroke it will hardly be claimed that it was in any way related to such disability.

GROVER CLEVELAND.

EXECUTIVE MANSION, *October 16, 1888.*

To the House of Representatives:

I return without approval House bill No. 6201, entitled ''An act granting a pension to John Robeson.''

The beneficiary named in this bill enlisted August 8, 1862, and was discharged for disability on the 21st day of November, 1862, after a service of a little more than three months.

In the certificate of disability upon which his discharge was granted the captain of the beneficiary's company states that ''he has been unfit for duty for sixty days; that the soldier represents that he has not done efficient service since enlistment by reason of phthisic, from which he has suffered since childhood, but has grown worse since entering the service.''

The surgeon of the regiment states in said certificate that "the soldier has asthma, with which he has been afflicted from his infancy."

Upon this certificate, based necessarily so far as his previous condition is concerned, this man procured his discharge after doing but very slight service.

He filed an application for pension in the Pension Bureau in October, 1879, basing his claim upon the allegation that he contracted asthma in September, 1862, about a month after he entered the service.

Two special examinations were had in his case, and his statement was taken in each.

On the first examination he said he could not account for the statements of his captain and surgeon, unless they arose from a remark he made that he had phthisic when he was small.

On the second he accounted for the statements of the captain and surgeon by saying that he felt very sick and feared that he could not live if he remained in the service; that he was suffering with jaundice as well as asthma; and having been told that he could not be discharged on account of jaundice, but could on account of asthma, he asked the captain to tell the surgeon that he had known him to have asthma before enlistment. He also says that he procured others to tell the same story.

On these examinations there was the usual negative testimony produced of certain parties who knew the claimant before enlistment and did not know that he was afflicted. This is balanced by the evidence of others, who testify that the claimant had asthma before enlistment.

Upon consideration of the character of the ailment, the testimony upon the two examinations, and the conduct of the beneficiary and his own admissions, I can not escape the conviction that whatever disability he had at the date of discharge he had when he enlisted, and that his claim was properly rejected by the Pension Bureau.

GROVER CLEVELAND.

EXECUTIVE MANSION, *October 16, 1888.*

To the House of Representatives:

I return without approval House bill No. 9106, entitled "An act granting a pension to Peter Liner."

The beneficiary named in this bill enlisted as a sergeant in the Regular Army in 1871, and he alleges that he served a previous term of enlistment, commencing in 1866.

While on a march from one post to another on the frontier, in September, 1874, the beneficiary was severely wounded by the bursting of a gun, necessitating the amputation of three of his fingers.

The reports of this occurrence develop the fact that the gun which burst in his hands was a shotgun, and that the accident happened while the beneficiary was hunting "for his own pleasure or benefit."

His wound was a severe one, and the injured man was probably a good and faithful soldier, but it seems quite clear to me that it would be extending the pension theory to an unwarrantable limit to hold the Government responsible for such an accident.

GROVER CLEVELAND.

EXECUTIVE MANSION, *October 16, 1888.*

To the House of Representatives:

I herewith return without approval House bill No. 10563, entitled "An act granting a pension to William S. Latham."

The beneficiary named in this bill enlisted in August, 1862. The rolls for March and April, 1863, report him a deserter, but it having been ascertained that sickness was the cause of his failure to return to his regiment at the end of a furlough granted to him, upon which failure the charge of desertion was based, he was restored to his company and the charge of desertion removed.

All this is stated in the report of the committee to which this bill was referred.

But it is not mentioned in said report that he was again furloughed on the 17th day of August, 1863, and, failing to return at the end of his furlough, one month thereafter, again became a deserter, but was not so reported until October 8, 1863.

He was arrested January 1, 1864, but there appears to be no record of his trial or his restoration.

He filed a claim for pension in the Pension Bureau in January, 1870, and he was informed twice during the year 1888 that no favorable action could be taken until the charge of desertion had been removed.

On application to the Adjutant-General that officer, on the 21st day of February, 1888, declined to remove said charge of desertion.

The claim is still pending before the Pension Bureau.

I do not suppose that the Congress is prepared to go so far in special pension legislation as to grant pensions to those against whom charges of desertion appear of record.

In the belief that the fact of the second desertion above mentioned was overlooked by the Congress, and because the application for pension in this case is still pending in the Pension Bureau, where complete justice can still be done, I am constrained to withhold my approval of this bill.

GROVER CLEVELAND.

EXECUTIVE MANSION, *October 17, 1888.*

To the House of Representatives:

I return without approval House bill No. 2472, entitled "An act granting a pension to Lydia A. Eaton."

The husband of this beneficiary was pensioned for chronic rheumatism, at the rate of $4 a month, up to the date of his death, August 4, 1884.

The beneficiary filed a claim for pension on the 2d day of September, 1884.

The cause of her husband's death was cystitis, which, being interpreted, is inflammation of the bladder.

The claim of the beneficiary was rejected on the ground that the fatal disease was not due to army service, and I fail to discover how any other conclusion can be reached. GROVER CLEVELAND.

EXECUTIVE MANSION, *October 17, 1888.*
To the House of Representatives:

I return without approval House bill No. 10342, entitled "An act granting a pension to John Dauper."

This beneficiary enlisted April 24, 1861, and was discharged August 28, 1861, four months after enlistment. .

He filed a claim for pension in September, 1879, alleging as cause of disability diarrhea and disease of the stomach, liver, kidneys, and bladder.

None of these ailments were established satisfactorily as originating in the soldier's brief service, and as constituting disabilities after discharge.

The claim was therefore rejected by the Pension Bureau, and this action appears to be entirely justified upon the facts presented.

GROVER CLEVELAND.

EXECUTIVE MANSION, *October 17, 1888.*
To the House of Representatives:

I return without approval House bill No. 11005, entitled "An act granting a pension to Ester Gaven."

This act provides that the beneficiary shall be placed upon the pension roll as the widow of Bernard Gaven, and the report of the committee to whom this bill was referred throughout speaks of her as bearing that relation to the soldier.

She filed a claim in the Pension Bureau for a pension on the 31st day of January, 1881, as the mother of Bernard Gaven.

This claim is still pending, and though evidence that the death of the soldier had any relation to his military service is entirely lacking and some other difficulties are apparent, the case may still be made out in the Pension Bureau. If it is, the beneficiary can be put upon the pension roll in her true character as mother of the soldier, instead of widow, as erroneously stated in the bill herewith returned.

Upon the merits as the case now stands, and because of the mistake in describing the relationship of the beneficiary, this bill, I think, should not become a law. GROVER CLEVELAND.

EXECUTIVE MANSION, *October 17, 1888.*

To the House of Representatives:

I return without approval House bill No. 10504, entitled "An act granting a pension to Mary Hooper."

The husband of this beneficiary was first lieutenant in the volunteer service from December 7, 1861, to February 28, 1862, a little over two months, when he resigned. His resignation was based upon a medical certificate in which it is stated that "this officer is unfit for duty on account of chronic pleuritis and pulmonary consumption, from which he has suffered for the past four months."

This certificate is dated February 14, 1862.

The soldier filed a claim in 1871 alleging typhoid fever resulting in paralysis, and that the fever was contracted in the latter part of February, 1862.

The soldier died January 17, 1884, of paralysis.

The beneficiary filed a claim for pension November 17, 1887, claiming that her husband died of disease contracted in the service.

The claims have been specially and thoroughly examined. The testimony does not establish any disease or disability in the service other than those stated in the certificate procured by him when he resigned, but it does tend to establish that about April 17, 1862, after his resignation, the soldier was sick with typhoid fever, and that afterwards he suffered from partial paralysis, which increased and finally caused his death.

I make no reference to the fact stated in the committee's report suggesting the idea that the courage of the deceased soldier had been questioned further than to correct the allegation of the report that either his or his widow's claim for pension has been rejected for cowardice. It appears from the record furnished to me that they were rejected on the ground that the evidence is insufficient to connect the death cause or disability with the soldier's military service.

I am unable to see what other conclusion could be reached in the face of the soldier's own statements, as contained in the medical certificate furnished him and elsewhere made, and upon consideration of the other facts in the case.

GROVER CLEVELAND.

EXECUTIVE MANSION, *October 17, 1888.*

To the House of Representatives:

I return without approval House bill No. 4820, entitled "An act granting a pension to Ellen Kelley."

The husband of this beneficiary was granted a furlough to go home and vote on the 31st day of October, 1864. On his way there he was severely injured by a railroad collision, and there does not seem to be a particle of doubt that the injuries thus sustained caused his death.

Upon these facts this does not seem to be a proper case for the granting of a pension.

GROVER CLEVELAND.

EXECUTIVE MANSION, *October 17, 1888.*

To the House of Representatives:

I return without approval House bill No. 11222, entitled "An act granting a pension to Elizabeth Heckler."

The husband of this beneficiary was pensioned for asthma, and there is no doubt of the propriety of such pension, nor is there doubt upon the evidence that this affection continued up to the time of his death.

But he died of acute inflammation of the bladder and chronic enlargement of prostate gland. There is no proof that these causes of death were in the least complicated with the difficulty for which the deceased was pensioned, or any other trouble which was the result of military service.

GROVER CLEVELAND

EXECUTIVE MANSION, *October 17, 1888.*

To the House of Representatives:

I return without approval House bill No. 4102, entitled "An act granting a pension to Mary A. Carr."

The husband of this beneficiary served in the Army from November 5, 1863, to June 15, 1865. He made a claim for pension for injury to his left ankle, caused by being thrown from a horse while in the service, and some time after his death a pension was allowed upon his claim, at the rate of $4 per month, commencing at the date of his discharge and ending at the date of his death.

He died on the 16th day of March, 1877, of apoplexy, and his widow filed a claim for pension on her own behalf in March, 1885, based upon the allegation that the injury for which her husband was pensioned was the cause of his death.

I can not upon the facts of this case arrive at a conclusion different from the Pension Bureau, where it was determined that the death of the soldier could not be accepted as having been caused by the injury to his ankle.

GROVER CLEVELAND.

EXECUTIVE MANSION, *October 17, 1888.*

To the House of Representatives:

I return without approval House bill No. 11332, entitled "An act granting a pension to Eliza S. Glass."

The husband of this beneficiary was in the military service from December 28, 1863, to April 27, 1864, a period of four months. He was discharged at the last-mentioned date for disability, the surgeon stating in the certificate his trouble to be "chronic hemorrhoids and rheumatism, both together producing lameness of back; unfit for Invalid Corps." The captain of the soldier's company in the same certificate states:

During the last two months said soldier has been unfit for duty fifty-four days in consequence of chronic rheumatism, owing to spinal affections and sprains received before entering the service, and made worse by drilling in double quick.

He filed a claim for pension December 24, 1879, more than fifteen years after discharge, in which he claimed that on the 15th day of January, 1864, he received an injury to his back by slipping and falling upon the ground.

After a thorough examination this claim was rejected on the ground that his disability existed prior to enlistment.

The beneficiary filed a claim for pension December 3, 1885, alleging the death of the soldier April 26, 1885. This claim was also rejected, on the ground that the death causes, "nervous prostration and spinal trouble," were not due to the service.

Both of these cases were appealed to the Secretary of the Interior, and in the decision of said appeals it is stated that upon an application for a discharge from the service the soldier first set up an injury to his back from a fall while on drill; that the regimental surgeon refused to entertain this proposition; that the next day the soldier returned, and upon the representations of himself and his captain that his trouble dated back of the alleged accident upon drill and was chronic the certificate for discharge was made out, and pursuant thereto his discharge was granted.

I am of the opinion that, considering the cause of death and all the facts and circumstances surrounding this case, the certificate of discharge which the soldier himself procured to be made out should stand as stating the true origin of his disability; and if the certificate was set aside and all the facts tending to support it were disregarded, the cause of death would still, in my opinion, appear to be disconnected with military service.

GROVER CLEVELAND.

PROCLAMATIONS.

By the President of the United States of America.

A PROCLAMATION.

Whereas the title to all that territory lying between the north and south forks of the Red River and the hundredth degree of longitude and jurisdiction over the same are vested in the United States, it being a part of the Indian Territory, as shown by surveys and investigation made on behalf of the United States, which territory the State of Texas also claims title to and jurisdiction over; and

Whereas said conflicting claim grows out of a controversy existing between the United States and the State of Texas as to the point where the hundredth degree of longitude crosses the Red River, as described in the treaty of February 22, 1819, between the United States and Spain, fixing the boundary line between the two countries; and

Whereas the commissioners appointed on the part of the United States under the act of January 31, 1885, authorizing the appointment of a commission by the President to run and mark the boundary lines between a portion of the Indian Territory and the State of Texas, in connection with a similar commission to be appointed by the State of Texas, have by their report determined that the South Fork is the true Red River designated in the treaty, the commissioners appointed on the part of said State refusing to concur in said report:

Now, therefore, I, Grover Cleveland, President of the United States, do hereby admonish and warn all persons, whether claiming to act as officers of the county of Greer, in the State of Texas, or otherwise, against selling or disposing of, or attempting to sell or dispose of, any of said lands or from exercising or attempting to exercise any authority over said lands.

And I also warn and admonish all persons against purchasing any part of said territory from any person or persons whomsoever.

In witness whereof I have hereunto set my hand and caused the seal of the United States to be affixed.

[SEAL.]   Done at the city of Washington, this 30th day of December, A. D. 1887, and of the Independence of the United States the one hundred and twelfth.

GROVER CLEVELAND.

By the President:

T. F. BAYARD,
Secretary of State.

BY THE PRESIDENT OF THE UNITED STATES OF AMERICA.

A PROCLAMATION.

Whereas satisfactory proof has been given to me by the Government of the Empire of Germany that no tonnage or light-house dues, or any equivalent tax or taxes whatever, are imposed upon American vessels entering the ports of the Empire of Germany, either by the Imperial Government or by the governments of the German maritime States, and that vessels belonging to the United States of America and their cargoes are not required in German ports to pay any fee or due of any kind or nature, or any import due higher or other than is payable by German vessels or their cargoes:

Now, therefore, I, Grover Cleveland, President of the United States of America, by virtue of the authority vested in me by section 11 of the act of Congress entitled "An act to abolish certain fees for official services to American vessels, and to amend the laws relating to shipping commissioners, seamen, and owners of vessels, and for other purposes," approved June 19, 1886, do hereby declare and proclaim that from and after the date of this my proclamation shall be suspended the collecti of the whole of the duty of 6 cents per ton, not to exceed 30 cents per ton per annum (which is imposed by said section of said act), upon vessels entered in the ports of the United States from any of the ports of the Empire of Germany.

Provided, That there shall be excluded from the benefits of the suspension hereby declared and proclaimed the vessels of any foreign country in whose ports the fees or dues of any kind or nature imposed on vessels of the United States, or the import or export duties on their cargoes, are in excess of the fees, dues, or duties imposed on the vessels of such foreign country or their cargoes, or of the fees, dues, or duties imposed on the vessels of Germany or the cargoes of such vessels.

And the suspension hereby declared and proclaimed shall continue so long as the reciprocal exemption of vessels belonging to citizens of the United States and their cargoes shall be continued in the said ports of the Empire of Germany, and no longer.

In witness whereof I have hereunto set my hand and caused the seal of the United States to be affixed.

[SEAL.]   Done at the city of Washington, this 26th day of January, A. D. 1888, and of the Independence of the United States the one hundred and twelfth.

GROVER CLEVELAND.

By the President:

T. F. BAYARD,
    Secretary of State.

BY THE PRESIDENT OF THE UNITED STATES OF AMERICA.

A PROCLAMATION.

Whereas satisfactory proof has been given to me that no light-house and light dues, tonnage dues, beacon and buoy dues, or other equivalent taxes of any kind are imposed upon vessels of the United States in the ports of the island of Guadeloupe, one of the French West India Islands:

Now, therefore, I, Grover Cleveland, President of the United States of America, by virtue of the authority vested in me by section 11 of the act of Congress entitled "An act to abolish certain fees for official services to American vessels, and to amend the laws relating to shipping commissioners, seamen, and owners of vessels, and for other purposes," approved June 19, 1886, do hereby declare and proclaim that from and after the date of this my proclamation shall be suspended the collection of the whole of the tonnage duty which is imposed by said section of said act upon vessels entered in the ports of the United States from any of the ports of the island of Guadeloupe.

Provided, That there shall be excluded from the benefits of the suspension hereby declared and proclaimed the vessels of any foreign country in whose ports the fees or dues of any kind or nature imposed on vessels of the United States, or the import or export duties on their cargoes, are in excess of the fees, dues, or duties imposed on the vessels of such foreign country or their cargoes, or of the fees, dues, or duties imposed on the vessels of the country in which are the ports mentioned in this proclamation or the cargoes of such vessels.

And the suspension hereby declared and proclaimed shall continue so long as the reciprocal exemption of vessels belonging to citizens of the United States and their cargoes shall be continued in the said ports of the island of Guadeloupe, and no longer.

In witness whereof I have hereunto set my hand and caused the seal of the United States to be affixed.

[SEAL.] Done at the city of Washington, this 16th day of April, A. D. 1888, and of the Independence of the United States the one hundred and twelfth.

GROVER CLEVELAND.

By the President:

T. F. BAYARD,
Secretary of State.

A PROCLAMATION

BY THE PRESIDENT OF THE UNITED STATES.

Constant thanksgiving and gratitude are due from the American people to Almighty God for His goodness and mercy, which have followed them since the day He made them a nation and vouchsafed to them a free government. With loving kindness He has constantly led us in the way of prosperity and greatness. He has not visited with swift punishment our shortcomings, but with gracious care He has warned us of our dependence upon His forbearance and has taught us that obedience to His holy law is the price of a continuance of His precious gifts.

In acknowledgment of all that God has done for us as a nation, and to the end that on an appointed day the united prayers and praise of a grateful country may reach the throne of grace, I, Grover Cleveland, President of the United States, do hereby designate and set apart Thursday, the 29th day of November instant, as a day of thanksgiving and prayer, to be kept and observed throughout the land.

On that day let all our people suspend their ordinary work and occupations, and in their accustomed places of worship, with prayer and songs of praise, render thanks to God for all His mercies, for the abundant harvests which have rewarded the toil of the husbandman during the year that has passed, and for the rich rewards that have followed the labors of our people in their shops and their marts of trade and traffic. Let us give thanks for peace and for social order and contentment within our borders, and for our advancement in all that adds to national greatness.

And mindful of the afflictive dispensation with which a portion of our land has been visited, let us, while we humble ourselves before the power of God, acknowledge His mercy in setting bounds to the deadly march of pestilence, and let our hearts be chastened by sympathy with our fellow-countrymen who have suffered and who mourn.

And as we return thanks for all the blessings which we have received from the hands of our Heavenly Father, let us not forget that He has enjoined upon us charity; and on this day of thanksgiving let us generously remember the poor and needy, so that our tribute of praise and gratitude may be acceptable in the sight of the Lord.

Done at the city of Washington on the 1st day of November, 1888, and in the year of the Independence of the United States the one hundred and thirteenth.

[SEAL.]

In witness whereof I have hereunto signed my name and caused the seal of the United States to be affixed.

GROVER CLEVELAND.

By the President:

T. F. BAYARD,
    Secretary of State.

EXECUTIVE ORDERS.

REVISED CIVIL-SERVICE RULES.

EXECUTIVE MANSION, *February 2, 1888.*

In the exercise of power vested in him by the Constitution and of authority given to him by the seventeen hundred and fifty-third section of the Revised Statutes and by an act to regulate and improve the civil service of the United States, approved January 16, 1883, the President hereby makes and promulgates the following rules and revokes the rules known as "Amended Civil-Service Rules" and "Special Rule No. 1," heretofore promulgated under the power and authority referred to herein: *Provided,* That this revocation shall not be construed as an exclusion from the classified civil service of any now classified customs district or classified post-office.

GENERAL RULES.

GENERAL RULE I.

Any officer in the executive civil service who shall use his official authority or influence for the purpose of interfering with an election or controlling the result thereof; or who shall dismiss, or cause to be dismissed, or use influence of any kind to procure the dismissal of any person from any place in the said service because such person has refused to be coerced in his political action, or has refused to contribute money for political purposes, or has refused to render political service; and any cer, clerk, or other employee in the executive civil service who shall willfully violate any of these rules, or any of the provisions of sections 11, 12, 13, and 14 of the act entitled "An act to regulate and improve the civil service of the United States," approved January 16, 1883, shall be dismissed from office

GENERAL RULE II.

There shall be three branches of the classified civil service, as follows:

1. The classified departmental service.
2. The classified customs service.
3. The classified postal service.

GENERAL RULE III.

1. No person shall be appointed or employed to enter the civil service, classified in accordance with section 163 of the Revised Statutes and under the "Act to regulate and improve the civil service of the United States," approved January 16, 1883, until he shall have passed an examination or shall have been shown to be specially exempted therefrom by said act or by an exception to this rule set forth in connection with the rules regulating admission to the branch of the service he seeks to enter.

2. No noncompetitive examination shall be held except under the following conditions:

(*a*) The failure of competent persons to be, after due notice, competitively examined, thus making it impracticable to supply to the appointing officer in due time the names of persons who have passed a competitive examination.

(*b*) That a person has been during one year or longer in a place excepted from examination, and the appointing or nominating officer desires the appointment of such person to a place not excepted.

(*c*) That a person has served two years continuously since July 16, 1883, in a place in the departmental service below or outside the classified service, and the appointing officer desires, with the approval of the President, upon the recommendation of the Commission, to promote such person into the classified service because of his faithfulness and efficiency in the position occupied by him, and because of his qualifications for the place to which the appointing officer desires his promotion.

(*d*) That an appointing or nominating officer desires the examination of a person to test his fitness for a classified place which might be filled under exceptions to examination declared in connection with the rules regulating admission to the classified service.

(*e*) That the Commission, with the approval of the President, has decided that such an examination should be held to test fitness for any particular place requiring technical, professional, or scientific knowledge, special skill, or peculiar ability, to test fitness for which place a competitive examination can not, in the opinion of the Commission, be properly provided.

(*f*) That a person who has been appointed from the copyist register wishes to take the clerk examination for promotion to a place the salary of which is not less than $1,000 per annum.

(*g*) To test the fitness of a person for a place to which his transfer has bee· requested.

(*h*) When the exigencies of the service require such examinations for prom provided by clause 6 of this rule.

3. All applications for examination must be made in forms and manner pr by the Commission.

4. No person serving in the Army or Navy shall be examined for a? the classified service until the written consent of the head of the D which he is enlisted shall have been communicated to the Commr·

No person who is an applicant for examination or who is an eli of the classified service shall at the same time be an applicant for examination in any other branch of said service.

5. The Commission may refuse to examine an applicant who would be physically unable to perform the duties of the place to which he desires appointment. The reason for any such action must be entered on the minutes of the Commission.

6. For the purpose of establishing in the classified civil service the principle of compulsory competitive examination for promotion, there shall be, so far as practicable and useful, compulsory competitive examinations of a suitable character to test fitness for promotion; but persons in the classified service who were honorably discharged from the military or naval service of the United States, and the widows and orphans of deceased soldiers and sailors, shall be exempt from such examinations.

The Commission may make regulations, applying them to any part of the classified service, under which regulations all examinations for promotion therein shall be conducted and all promotions be made; but until regulations in accordance herewith have been applied to any part of the classified service promotions therein shall be made in the manner provided by the rules applicable thereto. And in any part of the classified service in which promotions are made under examination as herein provided the Commission may in special cases, if the exigencies of the service require such action, provide noncompetitive examinations for promotion.

Persons who were in the classified civil service on July 16, 1883, and persons who have been since that date or may be hereafter put into that service by the inclusion of subordinate places, clerks, and officers, under the provisions of section 6 of the act to regulate and improve the civil service of the United States, approved January 16, 1883, shall be entitled to all rights of promotion possessed by persons of the same class or grade appointed after examination under the act referred to above.

7. No question in any examination shall be so framed as to elicit information concerning the political or religious opinions or affiliations of competitors, and no discrimination in examination, certification, or appointment shall be made by the Commission, the examiners, or the appointing or nominating officer in favor of or against any applicant, competitor, or eligible because of his political or religious opinions or affiliations. The Commission, the examiners, and the appointing or nominating officer shall discountenance all disclosures of such opinions or affiliations by or concerning any applicant, competitor, or eligible; and any appointing or nominating officer who shall make inquiries concerning or in any other way attempt to ascertain the political or religious opinions or affiliations of any eligible, or who shall discriminate in favor of or against any eligible because of the eligible's political or religious opinions or affiliations, shall be dismissed from office.

8. Every applicant must state under oath—

(*a*) His full name.

(*b*) That he is a citizen of the United States.

(*c*) Year and place of his birth.

(*d*) The State, Territory, or District of which he is a *bona fide* resident, and the length of time he has been a resident thereof.

(*e*) His post-office address.

(*f*) His business or employment during the three years immediately preceding the date of his application, and where he has resided each of those years.

(*g*) Condition of his health, and his physical capacity for the public service.

(*h*) His previous employment in the public service.

(*i*) Any right of preference in civil appointments he may claim under section 1754 of the Revised Statutes.

(*j*) The kind of school in which he received his education.

(*k*) That he does not habitually use intoxicating beverages to excess.

(*l*) That he has not within the one year next preceding the date of his application been dismissed from the public service for delinquency or misconduct.

(*m*) Such other facts as the Commission may require.

9. Every applicant for examination for the classified departmental service must support the statements of his application paper by certificates of persons acquainted with him, residents of the State, Territory, or District in which he claims *bona fide* residence; and the Commission shall prescribe the form and number of such certificates.

10. A false statement made by an applicant, or connivance by him with any person to make on his behalf a false statement in any certificate required by the Commission, and deception or fraud practiced by an applicant, or by any person on his behalf with his consent, to influence an examination, shall be good cause for refusal to examine such applicant or for refusing to mark his papers after examination.

11. All examinations shall be prepared and conducted under the supervision of the Commission; and examination papers shall be marked under rules made by the Commission, which shall take care that the marking examiners do not know the name of any competitor in an examination for admission whose papers are intrusted to them.

12. For the purpose of marking examination papers boards of examiners shall be appointed by the Commission, one to be known as the central board, which shall be composed of persons in the classified service, who shall be detailed for constant duty at the office of the Commission. Under supervision of the Commission the central board shall mark the papers of the copyist and of the clerk examinations, and such of the papers of the supplementary, special, and promotion examinations for the departmental service and of examinations for admission to or promotion in the other branches of the classified services as shall be submitted to it by the Commission.

13. No person shall be appointed to membership on any board of examiners until after the Commission shall have consulted with the head of the Department or of the office under whom such person is serving.

14. An examiner shall be allowed time during office hours to perform his duties as examiner, which duties shall be considered part of his official duties.

15. The Commission may change the membership of boards of examiners and—

(*a*) Prescribe the manner of organizing such boards.

(*b*) More particularly define their powers.

(*c*) Specifically determine their duties and the duties of the members thereof.

16. Each board shall keep such records and make such reports as the Commission may require, and such records shall be open to the inspection of any member of this Commission or other person acting under authority of the Commission, which may, for the purposes of investigation, take possession of such records.

GENERAL RULE IV.

1. The names of all competitors who shall successfully pass an examination shall be entered upon a register, and the competitors whose names have been thus registered shall be eligible to any office or place to test fitness for which the examination was held.

2. The Commission may refuse to certify—

(*a*) An eligible who is so defective in sight, speech, or hearing, or who is otherwise so defective physically as to be apparently unfit to perform the duties of the position to which he is seeking appointment.

(*b*) An eligible who has made a false statement in his application, or been guilty of fraud or deceit in any matter connected with his application or examination, or who has been guilty of a crime or of infamous or notoriously disgraceful conduct.

3. If an appointing or nominating officer to whom certification has been made shall object in writing to any eligible named in the certificate, stating that because of physical incapacity or for other good cause particularly specified such eligible is not capable of properly performing the duties of the vacant place, the Commission

may, upon investigation and ascertainment of the fact that the objection made is good and well founded, direct the certification of another eligible in place of the one to whom objection has been made.

GENERAL RULE V.

Executive officers shall in all proper ways facilitate civil-service examinations; and customs officers, postmasters, and custodians of public buildings at places where such examinations are to be held shall for the purposes of such examinations permit and arrange for the use of suitable rooms under their charge, and for heating, lighting, and furnishing the same.

GENERAL RULE VI.

No person dismissed for misconduct, and no probationer who has failed to receive absolute appointment or employment, shall be admitted to any examination within one year after having been thus discharged from the service.

GENERAL RULE VII.

1. Persons who have a *prima facie* claim of preference for appointments to civil offices under section 1754, Revised Statutes, shall be preferred in certifications made under the authority of the Commission to any appointing or nominating officer.

2. In making any reduction of force in any branch of the classified civil service those persons shall be retained who, being equally qualified, have been honorably discharged from the military or naval service of the United States, and also the widows and orphans of deceased soldiers and sailors.

GENERAL RULE VIII.

The Commission shall have authority to prescribe regulations under and in accordance with these general rules and the rules relating specially to each of the several branches of the classified service.

DEPARTMENTAL RULES.

DEPARTMENTAL RULE I.

1. The classified departmental service shall include the several officers, clerks, and other persons in any Department, commission, or bureau at Washington classified under section 163 of the Revised Statutes, or by direction of the President for the purposes of the examinations prescribed by the civil-service act of 1883, or for facilitating the inquiries as to fitness of candidates for admission to the departmental service in respect to age, health, character, knowledge, and ability, as provided for in section 1753 of the Revised Statutes.

2. The word "department," when used in the general or departmental rules, shall be construed to mean any such Department, commission, or bureau classified as above prescribed.

DEPARTMENTAL RULE II.

1. To test the fitness of applicants for admission to the classified departmental service there shall be examinations as follows:

Copyist examination.—For places of $900 per annum and under. This examination shall not include more than the following subjects:

(*a*) Orthography.
(*b*) Copying.
(*c*) Penmanship.
(*d*) Arithmetic—fundamental rules, fractions, and percentage.

Clerk examination.—For places of $1,000 per annum and upward. This examination shall not include more than the following subjects:

(*a*) Orthography.

(*b*) Copying.

(*c*) Penmanship.

(*d*) Arithmetic—fundamental rules, fractions, percentage, interest, and discount.

(*e*) Elements of bookkeeping and of accounts.

(*f*) Elements of the English language.

(*g*) Letter writing.

(*h*) Elements of the geography, history, and government of the United States.

Supplementary examinations.—For places which, in the opinion of the Commission, require, in addition to the knowledge required to pass the copyist or the clerk examination, certain technical, professional, or scientific knowledge, or knowledge of a language other than the English language, or peculiar or special skill.

Special examinations.—For places which, in the opinion of the Commission, require certain technical, professional, or scientific knowledge or skill. Each special examination shall embrace, in addition to the special subject upon which the applicant is to be tested, as many of the subjects of the clerk examination as the Commission may decide to be necessary to test fitness for the place to be filled.

Noncompetitive examinations.—For any place in the departmental service for which the Commission may from time to time (subject to the conditions prescribed by General Rule III, clause 2) determine that such examinations ought to be held.

2. An applicant may take the copyist or the clerk examination and any or all of the supplementary and special examinations provided for the departmental service, subject to such limitations as the Commission may by regulation prescribe; but no person whose name is on a departmental register of eligibles shall during the period of his eligibility be allowed reexamination unless he shall satisfy the Commission that at the time of his examination he was unable, because of illness or other good cause, to do himself justice in said examination; and the rating upon such reexamination shall cancel and be a substitute for the rating of such person upon the previous examination.

3. Exceptions from examination in the classified departmental service are hereby made as follows:

(*a*) One private secretary or one confidential clerk of the head of each classified Department and of each assistant secretary thereof, and also of each head of bureau appointed by the President by and with the advice and consent of the Senate.

(*b*) Direct custodians of money for whose fidelity another officer is under official bond; but this exception shall not include any officer below the grade of assistant cashier or assistant teller.

(*c*) Disbursing officers who give bonds.

(*d*) Persons employed exclusively in the secret service of the Government.

(*e*) Chief clerks.

(*f*) Chiefs of divisions.

4. No person appointed to a place under the exceptions to examination hereby made shall within one year after appointment be transferred from such place to a place not also excepted from examination, but after service of not less than one year in an examination-excepted place he may be transferred in the bureau in which he is serving to a place not excepted from examination: *Provided*, That before any such transfer may be made the Commission must certify that the person whom it is proposed to so transfer has passed an examination to test fitness for the place proposed to be filled by such transfer.

DEPARTMENTAL RULE III.

In compliance with the provisions of section 3 of the civil-service act the Commission shall provide examinations for the classified departmental service at least twice in each year in every State or Territory in which there are a sufficient number of applicants for such examinations; and the places and times of examinations shall when practicable, be so fixed that each applicant may know at the time of making his application when and where he may be examined; but applicants may be notified to appear at any place at which the Commission may order an examination.

DEPARTMENTAL RULE IV.

1. Any person not under 20 years of age may make application for admission to the classified departmental service, blank forms for which purpose shall be furnished by the Commission.

2. Every application for admission to the classified departmental service should be addressed as follows: "United States Civil Service Commission, Washington, D. C."

3. The date of reception and also of approval by the Commission of each application shall be noted on the application paper.

DEPARTMENTAL RULE V.

1. The papers of all examinations for admission to or promotion in the classified departmental service shall be marked as directed by the Commission.

2. The Commission shall have authority to appoint the following-named boards of examiners, which shall conduct examinations and mark examination papers as follows:

Central board.—As provided for by General Rule III, clause 12.

Special boards.—These boards shall mark such papers of special examinations for the classified departmental service as the Commission may direct, and shall be composed of persons in the public service.

Supplementary boards.—These boards shall mark the papers of such supplementary examinations for the classified departmental service as the Commission may direct, and shall be composed of persons in the public service.

Promotion boards.—One for each Department, of three members, and one auxiliary member for each bureau of the Department for which the board is to act. Unless the Commission shall otherwise direct, these boards shall mark the papers of promotion examinations.

Local boards.—These boards shall be organized at one or more places in each State and Territory where examinations for the classified departmental service are to be held, and shall conduct such examinations; and each shall be composed of persons in the public service residing in the State or Territory in which the board is to act.

Customs and postal boards.—These boards shall conduct such examinations for the classified departmental service as the Commission shall direct.

DEPARTMENTAL RULE VI.

1. The papers of the copyist and of the clerk examinations shall be marked by the central board; the papers of special and supplementary examinations shall be marked as directed by the Commission. Each competitor in any of the examinations mentioned or referred to above shall be graded on a scale of 100, according to the general average determined by the marks made by the examiners on his papers.

2. The papers of an examination having been marked, the Commission shall ascertain—

(*a*) The name of every competitor who has, under section 1754 of the Revised Statutes, claim of preference in civil appointments, and who has attained a general average of not less than 65 per cent; and all such competitors are hereby declared eligible to the class or place to test fitness for which the examination was held.

(*b*) The name of every other competitor who has attained a general average of not less than 70 per cent; and all such competitors are hereby declared eligible to the class or place to test fitness for which the examination was held.

3. The names of all preference-claiming competitors whose general average is not than 65 per cent, together with the names of all other competitors whose general

average is not less than 70 per cent, shall be entered upon the register of persons eligible to the class or place to test fitness for which the examination was held.

4. To facilitate the maintenance of the apportionment of appointments among the several States and Territories and the District of Columbia, required by section 2 of the act to regulate and improve the civil service of the United States, approved January 16, 1883, there shall be lists of eligibles for each State and Territory and for the District of Columbia, upon which shall be entered the names of the competitors from that State or Territory or the District of Columbia who have passed the copyist and the clerk examinations, the names of those who have passed the copyist examination and of those who have passed the clerk examination being listed separately; the names of male and of female eligibles in such examinations being also listed separately.

5. But the names of all competitors who have passed a supplementary or a special examination shall be entered, without regard to State residence, upon the register of persons eligible to the class or place to test fitness for which supplementary or special examination was held.

6. The grade of each competitor shall be expressed by the whole number nearest the general average attained by him, and the grade of each eligible shall be noted upon the register of eligibles in connection with his name. When two or more eligibles are of the same grade, preference in certification shall be determined by the order in which their application papers were filed.

7. Immediately after the general averages in an examination shall have been ascertained each competitor shall be notified that he has passed or has failed to pass.

8. If a competitor fail to pass, he may, with the consent of the Commission, be allowed reexamination at any time within six months from the date of failure without filing a new application; but a competitor failing to pass, desiring to take again the same examination, must, if not allowed reexamination within six months from the date of failure, make in due form a new application therefor.

9. No person who has passed an examination shall, while eligible on the register supplied by such examination, be reexamined, unless he shall furnish evidence satisfactory to the Commission that at the time of his examination he was, because of illness or other good cause, incapable of doing himself justice in said examination.

10. The term of eligibility to appointment under the copyist and the clerk examinations shall be one year from the day on which the name of the eligible is entered on the register. The term of eligibility under a supplementary or a special examination shall be determined by the Commission, but shall not be less than one year.

DEPARTMENTAL RULE VII.

1. Vacancies in the classified departmental service, unless among the places excepted from examination, if not filled by either promotion or transfer, shall be filled in the following manner:

(*a*) The appointing officer shall, in form and manner to be prescribed by the Commission, request the certification to him of the names of either males or females eligible to a certain place then vacant.

(*b*) If fitness for the place to be filled is tested by competitive examination, the Commission shall certify the names of three males or three females, these names to be those of the eligibles who, standing higher in grade than any other three eligibles of the same sex on the list of eligibles from which certification is to be made, have not been certified three times to the officer making the requisition: *Provided*, That if upon any register from which certification is to be made there are the names of eligibles who have, under section 1754 of the Revised Statutes, claim of preference in civil appointments, the names of such eligibles shall be certified before the names of other eligibles higher in grade. The Commission shall make regulations that will secure to each of such preference-claiming eligibles, in the order of his grade among other preference claimants, an opportunity to have his claim of preference considered and determined by the appointing officer.

2. Certifications hereunder sha 1 be made in such manner as to maintain as nearly as possible the apportionment of appointments among the several States and the Territories and the District of Columbia, as required by law.

3. If the three names certified are those of persons eligible on the copyist or the clerk register, the appointing officer shall select one, and one only, and shall notify the person whose name has been selected that he has been designated for appointment: *Provided,* That, for the purpose of maintaining the apportionment of appointments referred to in clause 2 of this rule, the Commission may authorize the appointing officer to select more than one of the three names certified.

When certification is made from a supplementary or a special register, and there are more vacancies than one to be filled, the appointing officer may select from the three names certified more than one.

4. The Commission may certify from the clerk register for appointment to a place the salary of which is less than $1,000 per annum any eligible on said register who has given written notice that he will accept such a place.

5. When a person designated for appointment shall have reported in person to the appointing officer, he shall be appointed for a probational period of six months, at the end of which period, if his conduct and capacity be satisfactory to the appointing officer, he shall receive absolute appointment; but if his conduct and capacity be not satisfactory to said officer he shall be notified that he will not receive absolute appointment, and this notification shall discharge him from the service. The appointing officer shall require the heads of bureaus or divisions under whom probationers are serving to keep a record and to make report of the punctuality, industry, habits, ability, and aptitude of each probationer.

6. All persons appointed to or promoted in the classified departmental service shall be assigned to the duties of the class or place to which they have been appointed or promoted, unless the interests of the service require their assignment to other duties; and when such assignment is made the fact shall be reported to the head of the Department.

DEPARTMENTAL RULE VIII.

1. Transfers will be made as follows:

(*a*) From one Department to another, upon requisition by the head of the Department to which the transfer is to be made.

(*b*) From a bureau of the Treasury Department in which business relating to the customs is transacted to a classified customs district, and from such a district to such a bureau of the Treasury Department, upon requisition by the Secretary of the Treasury.

(*c*) From the Post-Office Department to a classified post-office, and from such an office to the Post-Office Department, upon requisition by the Postmaster-General.

2. No person may be transferred as herein authorized until the Commission shall have certified to the officer making the transfer requisition that the person whom it is proposed to transfer has passed an examination to test fitness for the place to which he is to be transferred, and that such person has during at least six months preceding the date of the certificate been in the classified service of the Department, customs district, or post-office from which the transfer is to be made: *Provided,* That no person who has been appointed from the copyist register shall be transferred to a place the salary of which is more than $900 per annum until one year after appointment.

DEPARTMENTAL RULE IX.

1. A person appointed from the copyist register may, upon any test of fitness determined upon by the promoting officer, be promoted as follows:

(*a*) At any time after probational appointment, to any place the salary of which is not more than $900 per annum.

(*b*) At any time after one year from the date of probational appointment, upon certification by the Commission that he has passed the clerk examination or its equivalent, to any place the salary of which is $1,000 per annum or more.

(*c*) At any time after two years from the date of probational appointment, to any place the salary of which is $1,000 per annum or more.

2. A person appointed from the clerk register or from any supplementary or special register to a place the salary of which is $1,000 per annum or more may, upon any test of fitness determined upon by the promoting officer, be promoted at any time after absolute appointment.

3. A person appointed from the clerk register or from any supplementary or special register to a place the salary of which is $900 or less may, upon any test of fitness determined upon by the promoting officer, be promoted at any time after probational appointment to any place the salary of which is $1,000 per annum.

4. Other promotions may be made upon any tests of fitness determined upon by the promoting officer.

5. The provisions of clauses 1, 2, 3, and 4 of this rule shall become null and void in any part of the classified departmental service as soon as promotion regulations shall have been applied thereto under General Rule III, clause 6.

DEPARTMENTAL RULE X.

Upon requisition of the head of a Department the Commission shall certify for reinstatement in said Department, in a grade requiring no higher examination than the one in which he was formerly employed, any person who within one year next preceding the date of the requisition has, through no delinquency or misconduct, been separated from the classified service of that Department.

DEPARTMENTAL RULE XI.

Each appointing officer in the classified departmental service shall report to the Commission—

(*a*) Every probational and every absolute appointment made by him, and every appointment made by him under any exception to examination authorized by Departmental Rule II, clause 3.

(*b*) Every refusal by him to make an absolute appointment and every refusal or neglect to accept an appointment in the classified service under him.

(*c*) Every transfer within and into the classified service under him.

(*d*) Every assignment of a person to the performance of the duties of a class or place to which such person was not appointed.

(*e*) Every separation from the classified service under him, and whether the separation was caused by dismissal, resignation, or death. Places excepted from examination are within the classified service.

(*f*) Every restoration to the classified service under him of any person who may have been separated therefrom by dismissal or resignation.

CUSTOMS RULES.

CUSTOMS RULE I.

1. The classified customs service shall include the officers, clerks, and other persons in the several customs districts classified under the provisions of section 6 of the act to regulate and improve the civil service of the United States, approved January 16, 1883.

2. Whenever the officers, clerks, and other persons in any customs district number as many as fifty, any existing classification of the customs service made by the Secretary of the Treasury under section 6 of the act of January 16, 1883, shall apply thereto, and thereafter the Commission shall provide examinations to test the fitness

of persons to fill vacancies in said customs district and these rules shall be in force therein. Every revision of the classification of any customs office under section 6 of the act above mentioned, and every inclusion within the classified customs service of a customs district, shall be reported to the President.

CUSTOMS RULE II.

1. To test fitness for admission to the classified customs service, examinations shall be provided as follows:

*Clerk examination.**—This examination shall not include more than the following subjects:

(*a*) Orthography.
(*b*) Copying.
(*c*) Penmanship.
(*d*) Arithmetic—fundamental rules, fractions, percentage, interest, and discount.
(*e*) Elements of bookkeeping and of accounts.
(*f*) Elements of the English language.
(*g*) Letter writing.
(*h*) Elements of the geography, history, and government of the United States.

Law-clerk examination.—This examination shall not include more than the following subjects:

(*a*) Orthography.
(*b*) Copying.
(*c*) Penmanship.
(*d*) Arithmetic—fundamental rules, fractions, percentage, interest, and discount.
(*e*) Elements of the English language.
(*f*) Letter writing.
(*g*) Law questions.

Day-inspector examination.—This examination shall not include more than the following subjects:

(*a*) Orthography.
(*b*) Copying.
(*c*) Penmanship.
(*d*) Arithmetic—fundamental rules, fractions, and percentage.
(*e*) Elements of the English language.
(*f*) Geography of America and Europe.

Inspectress examination.—This examination shall not include more than the following subjects:

(*a*) Orthography.
(*b*) Copying.
(*c*) Penmanship.
(*d*) Arithmetic—fundamental rules.
(*e*) Geography of America and Europe.

Night-inspector, messenger, assistant weigher, and opener and packer examination.—This examination shall not include more than the following subjects:

(*a*) Orthography.
(*b*) Copying.
(*c*) Penmanship.
(*d*) Arithmetic—fundamental rules.

Gauger examination.—This examination shall not include more than the following subjects:

(*a*) Orthography.
(*b*) Copying.
(*c*) Penmanship.
(*d*) Arithmetic—practical questions.
(*e*) Theoretical questions.
(*f*) Practical tests.

* Storekeepers shall be classed as clerks, and vacancies in that class shall be filled by assignment.

Examiner examination.—This examination shall not include more than the following subjects:

(*a*) Orthography.
(*b*) Copying.
(*c*) Penmanship.
(*d*) Arithmetic—fundamental rules, fractions, percentage, and discount.
(*e*) Elements of the English language.
(*f*) Practical questions.
(*g*) Practical tests.

Sampler examination.—This examination shall not include more than the following subjects:

(*a*) Orthography.
(*b*) Copying.
(*c*) Penmanship.
(*d*) Arithmetic—fundamental rules.
(*e*) Practical questions.
(*f*) Practical tests.

Other competitive examinations.—Such other competitive examinations as the Commission may from time to time determine to be necessary in testing fitness for other places in the classified customs service.

Noncompetitive examinations.—Such examinations may, with the approval of the Commission, be held under conditions stated in General Rule III, clause 2.

2. Any person not under 21 years of age may be examined for any place in the customs service to test fitness for which an examination is prescribed, and any person not under 20 years of age may be examined for clerk or messenger.

3. A person desiring examination for admission to the classified customs service must make request, in his own handwriting, for a blank form of application, which request and also his application shall be addressed as directed by the Commission.

4. The date of reception and also of approval by the board of each of such applications shall be noted on the application paper.

5. Exceptions from examination in the classified customs service are hereby made as follows:

(*a*) Deputy collectors, who do not also act as inspectors, examiners, or clerks.
(*b*) Cashier of the collector.
(*c*) Assistant cashier of the collector.
(*d*) Auditor of the collector.
(*e*) Chief acting disbursing officer.
(*f*) Deputy naval officers.
(*g*) Deputy surveyors.
(*h*) One private secretary or one confidential clerk of each nominating officer.

6. No person appointed to a place under any exception to examination hereby made shall within one year after appointment be transferred from such place to another place not also excepted from examination, but a person who has served not less than one year in an examination-excepted place may be transferred in the customs office in which he is serving to a place not excepted from examination: *Provided,* That before any such transfer may be made the Commission must certify that the person whom it is proposed to so transfer has passed an examination to test fitness for the place proposed to be filled by such transfer.

CUSTOMS RULE III.

1. The papers of every examination shall be marked under direction of the Commission, and each competitor shall be graded on a scale of 100, according to the general average determined by the marks made by the examiners on his papers.

2. The Commission shall appoint in each classified customs district a board of examiners, which shall—

(*a*) Conduct all examinations held to test fitness for admission to or promotion in the classified service of the customs district in which the board is located.

(*b*) Mark the papers of such examinations, unless otherwise directed, as provided for by General Rule 111, clause 12.

(*c*) Conduct such examinations for the classified departmental service as the Commission may direct.

3. The papers of an examination having been marked, the board of examiners shall ascertain—

(*a*) The name of every competitor who has, under section 1754 of the Revised Statutes, claim of preference in civil appointments, and who has attained a general average of not less than 65 per cent; and all such competitors are hereby declared ·eligible to the class or place to test fitness for which the examination was held.

(*b*) The name of every other competitor who has attained a general average of not less than 70 per cent; and all such applicants are hereby declared eligible to the class or place to test fitness for which the examination was held.

4. The names of all preference-claiming competitors whose general average is not less than 65 per cent, together with the names of all other competitors whose general average is not less than 70 per cent, shall be entered upon the register of persons eligible to the class or place to test fitness for which the examination was held. The names of male and of female eligibles shall be listed separately.

5. The grade of each competitor shall be expressed by the whole number nearest the general average attained by him, and the grade of each eligible shall be noted upon the register of eligibles in connection with his name. When two or more eligibles are of the same grade, preference in certification shall be determined by the order in which their application papers were filed.

6. Immediately after the general averages in an examination shall have been ascertained each competitor shall be notified that he has passed or has failed to pass.

7. If a competitor fail to pass, he may, with the consent of the board, approved by the Commission, be allowed reexamination at any time within six months from the date of failure without filing a new application; but a competitor failing to pass, desiring to take again the same examination, must, if not allowed reexamination within six months from the date of failure, make in due form a new application therefor.

8. No person who has passed an examination shall while eligible on the register supplied by such examination be reexamined, unless he shall furnish evidence satisfactory to the Commission that at the time of his examination he was, because of illness or for other good cause, incapable of doing himself justice in said examination.

9. The term of eligibility to appointment in the classified customs service shall be one year from the day on which the name of the eligible is entered on the register.

CUSTOMS RULE IV.

1. Vacancies in the lowest class or grade of the classified service of a customs district shall be filled in the following manner:

(*a*) The nominating officer in any office in which a vacancy may exist shall, in form and manner to be prescribed by the Commission, request the board of examiners to certify to him the names of either males or females eligible to the vacant place.

(*b*) If fitness for the place to be filled is tested by competitive examination, the board of examiners shall certify the names of three males or three females, these names to be those of the eligibles who, standing higher in grade than any other three eligibles of the same sex on the register from which certification is to be made, have not been certified three times from said register: *Provided*, That if upon said register there are the names of eligibles who, under section 1754 of the Revised Statutes, have claim of preference in civil appointments, the names of such eligibles shall be certified before the names of other eligibles higher in grade. The Commission shall make regulations that will secure to each of such preference-claiming eligibles in the order of his grade among other preference claimants, an opportunity to have his claim of preference considered and determined by the appointing officer.

(*c*) Each name on a register of eligibles may be certified only three times: *Provided*, That when a name has been three times certified, if there are not three names on the register of higher grade, it may, upon the written request of a nominating officer to whom it has not been certified, be included in any certification made to said officer.

2. Of the three names certified the nominating officer must select one; and if at the time of making this selection there are more vacancies than one, he may select more than one name. Each person thus designated for appointment shall be notified, and upon reporting in person to the proper officer shall be appointed for a probational period of six months, at the end of which period, if his conduct and capacity be satisfactory to the nominating officer, he shall receive absolute appointment; but if his conduct and capacity be not satisfactory to said officer, he shall be notified that he will not receive absolute appointment, and this notification shall discharge him from the service.

3. Every nominating officer in the classified customs service shall require the officer under whom a probationer may be serving to carefully observe and report in writing the services rendered by and the character and qualifications of such probationer. These reports shall be preserved on file, and the Commission may prescribe the form and manner in which they shall be made.

4. All other vacancies, unless among the places excepted from examination, shall be filled by transfer or promotion.

CUSTOMS RULE V.

1. Until promotion regulations have been applied to a classified customs district, the following promotions may be made therein at any time after absolute appointment:

(*a*) A clerk, upon any test of fitness determined upon by the nominating officer, to any vacant place in the class next above the one in which he may be serving.

(*b*) A day inspector, upon any test of fitness determined upon by the nominating officer, to class 2 in the grade of clerk.

(*c*) A clerk, day inspector, opener and packer, or sampler, after passing the examiner examination, to the grade of examiner.

(*d*) A messenger, after passing the clerk examination, to the lowest class in the grade of clerk.

(*e*) A night inspector, after passing the day-inspector examination, to the grade of day inspector.

2. Other promotions may be made, in the discretion of the promoting officer, upon any test of fitness determined upon by him.

CUSTOMS RULE VI.

1. Transfers may be made as follows:

(*a*) From one office of a classified district to another office in the same district, subject to the provisions of Customs Rule V.

(*b*) From one classified district to another, upon requisition by the Secretary of the Treasury.

(*c*) From any bureau of the Treasury Department in which business relating to customs is transacted to any classified customs district, and from any such district to any such bureau, upon requisition by the Secretary of the Treasury.

2. No person may be transferred as herein authorized until the board of examiners, acting under (*a*) of clause 1, or until the Commission, acting under (*b*) or (*c*) of clause 1 of this rule, shall have certified to the officer making the transfer requisition that the person whom it is proposed to transfer has passed an examination to test fitness

for the place to which he is to be transferred, and that such person has been at least six months preceding the date of the certificate in the classified service of the Department or customs district from which the transfer is to be made.

CUSTOMS RULE VII.

Upon requisition of a nominating officer in any customs district the board of examiners thereof shall certify for reinstatement in any office under his jurisdiction, in a grade requiring no higher examination than the one in which he was formerly employed, any person who within one year next preceding the date of the requisition has, through no delinquency or misconduct, been separated from the classified service of said office.

CUSTOMS RULE VIII.

Each nominating officer of a classified customs district shall report to the board of examiners—

(*a*) Every probational and absolute appointment, and every appointment under any exception to examination authorized by Customs Rule II, clause 5, made within his jurisdiction.

(*b*) Every refusal by him to nominate a probationer for absolute appointment and every refusal or neglect to accept an appointment in the classified service under him.

(*c*) Every transfer into the classified service under him.

(*d*) Every separation from the classified service under him, and whether the separation was caused by dismissal, resignation, or death. Places excepted from examination are within the classified service.

(*e*) Every restoration to the classified service under him of any person who may have been separated therefrom by dismissal or resignation.

POSTAL RULES.

POSTAL RULE I.

1. The classified postal service shall include the officers, clerks, and other persons in the several post-offices classified under the provisions of section 6 of the act to regulate and improve the civil service of the United States, approved January 16, 1883.

2. Whenever the officers, clerks, and other persons in any post-office number as many as fifty, any existing classification of the postal service made by the Postmaster-General under section 6 of the act of January 16, 1883, shall apply thereto, and thereafter the Commission shall provide examinations to test the fitness of persons to fill vacancies in said post-office and these rules shall be in force therein. Every revision of the classification of any post-office under section 6 of the act above mentioned, and every inclusion of a post-office within the classified postal service, shall be reported to the President.

POSTAL RULE II.

1. To test fitness for admission to the classified postal service examinations shall be provided as follows:

Clerk examination.—This examination shall not include more than the following subjects:

(*a*) Orthography.

(*b*) Copying.

(*c*) Penmanship.

(*d*) Arithmetic—fundamental rules, fractions, and percentage.

(*e*) Elements of the English language.

(*f*) Letter writing.

(*g*) Elements of the geography, history, and government of the United States.

Carrier examination.—This examination shall not include more than the following subjects:

(*a*) Orthography.

(*b*) Copying.

(*c*) Penmanship.

(*d*) Arithmetic—fundamental rules.

(*e*) Elements of the geography of the United States.

(*f*) Knowledge of the locality of the post-office delivery.

(*g*) Physical tests.

Messenger examination.—This examination shall not include more than the following subjects:

(*a*) Orthography.

(*b*) Copying.

(*c*) Penmanship.

(*d*) Arithmetic—fundamental rules.

(*e*) Physical tests.

This examination shall also be used to test fitness for the position of piler, stamper, junior clerk, or other places the duties of which are chiefly manual.

Special examinations.—These examinations shall test fitness for positions requiring knowledge of a language other than the English language, or special or technical knowledge or skill. Each special examination shall include, in addition to the special subject upon which the applicant is to be tested, so many of the subjects of the clerk examination as the Commission may determine.

Noncompetitive examinations.—Such examinations may, with the approval of the Commission, be held under conditions stated in General Rule III, clause 2. -

2. No person shall be examined for the position of clerk if under 18 years of age; and no person shall be examined for the position of messenger, stamper, or junior clerk if under 16 or over 45 years of age; and no person shall be examined for the position of carrier if under 21 or over 40 years of age. No person shall be examined for any other position in the classified postal service if under 18 or over 45 years of age.

3. Any person desiring examination for admission to the classified postal service must make request, in his own handwriting, for a blank form of application, which request, and also his application, shall be addressed as directed by the Commission.

4. The date of reception and also of approval by the board of each of such applications shall be noted on the application paper.

5. Exceptions from examinations in the classified postal service are hereby made as follows:

(*a*) Assistant postmaster.

(*b*) One private secretary or one confidential clerk of the postmaster.

(*c*) Cashier.

(*d*) Assistant cashier.

(*e*) Superintendents designated by the Post-Office Department and reported as such to the Commission.

(*f*) Custodians of money, stamps, stamped envelopes, or postal cards, designated as such by the Post-Office Department and so reported to the Commission, for whose fidelity the postmaster is under official bond.

6. No person appointed to a place under any exception to examination hereby made shall within one year after appointment be transferred to another place not also excepted from examination; but a person who has served not less than one year in an examination-excepted place may be transferred in the post-office in which he is serving to a place not excepted from examination: *Provided*, That before any such transfer may be made the Commission must certify that the person whom it is proposed to so transfer has passed an examination to test fitness for the place proposed to be filled by such transfer.

POSTAL RULE III.

1. The papers of every examination shall be marked under the direction of the Commission, and each competitor shall be graded on a scale of 100, according to the general average determined by the marks made by the examiners on his papers.

2. The Commission shall appoint in each classified post-office a board of examiners, which shall—

(a) Conduct all examinations held to test fitness for entrance to or promotion in the classified service of the post-office in which the board is located.

(b) Mark the papers of such examinations, unless otherwise directed, as provided for by General Rule III, clause 12.

(c) Conduct such examinations for the classified departmental service as the Commission may direct.

3. The papers of an examination having been marked, the board of examiners shall ascertain—

(a) The name of every competitor who has, under section 1754 of the Revised Statutes, claim of preference in civil appointments, and who has attained a general average of not less than 65 per cent; and all such competitors are hereby declared eligible to the class or place to test fitness for which the examination was held.

(b) The name of every other competitor who has attained a general average of not less than 70 per cent; and all such applicants are hereby declared eligible to the class or place to test fitness for which the examination was held.

4. The names of all preference-claiming competitors whose general average is not less than 65 per cent, together with the names of all other competitors whose general average is not less than 70 per cent, shall be entered upon the register of persons eligible to the class or place to test fitness for which the examination was held. The names of male and of female eligibles shall be listed separately.

5. The grade of each competitor shall be expressed by the whole number nearest the general average attained by him, and the grade of each eligible shall be noted upon the register of eligibles in connection with his name. When two or more eligibles are of the same grade, preference in certification shall be determined by the order in which their application papers were filed.

6. Immediately after the general averages shall have been ascertained each competitor shall be notified that he has passed or has failed to pass.

7. If a competitor fail to pass, he may, with the consent of the board, approved by the Commission, be allowed reexamination at any time within six months from the date of failure without filing a new application; but a competitor failing to pass, desiring to take again the same examination, must, if not allowed reexamination within six months from the date of failure, make in due form a new application therefor.

8. No person who has passed an examination shall while eligible on the register supplied by such examination be reexamined, unless he shall furnish evidence satisfactory to the Commission that at the time of his examination he was, because of illness or for other good cause, incapable of doing himself justice in said examination.

9. The term of eligibility to appointment in the classified postal service shall be one year from the day on which the name of the eligible is entered on the register.

POSTAL RULE IV.

1. Vacancies in the classified service of a post-office, unless among the places excepted from examination, if not filled by either transfer or promotion, shall be filled in the following manner:

(a) The postmaster at a post-office in which a vacancy may exist shall, in form and manner to be prescribed by the Commission, request the board of examiners to certify to him the names of either males or females eligible to the vacant place.

(*b*) If fitness for the place to be filled is tested by competitive examination, the board of examiners shall certify the names of three males or three females, these names to be those of the eligibles who, standing higher in grade than any other three eligibles of the same sex on the register from which certification is to be made, have not been certified three times from said register: *Provided*, That if upon said register there are the names of eligibles who, under section 1754 of the Revised Statutes, have claim of preference in civil appointments, the names of such eligibles shall be certified before the names of other eligibles higher in grade. The Commission shall make regulations that will secure to each of such preference-claiming eligibles, in the order of his grade among other preference claimants, opportunity to have his claim of preference considered and determined by the appointing officer.

(*c*) Each name on any register of eligibles may be certified only three times.

2. Of the three names certified to him the postmaster must select one; and if at the time of making this selection there are more vacancies than one, he may select more than one name. Each person thus designated for appointment shall be notified, and upon reporting in person to the postmaster shall be appointed for a probational period of six months, at the end of which period, if his conduct and capacity be satisfactory to the postmaster, he shall receive absolute appointment; but if his conduct and capacity be not satisfactory to said officer, he shall be notified that he will not receive absolute appointment, and this notification shall discharge him from the service.

3. The postmaster of each classified post-office shall require the superintendent of each division of his office to carefully observe and report in writing the services rendered by and the character and qualifications of each probationer serving under him. These reports shall be preserved on file, and the Commission may prescribe the form and manner in which they shall be made.

POSTAL RULE V

Until promotion regulations shall have been applied to a classified post-office promotions therein may be made upon any test of fitness determined upon by the postmaster, if not disapproved by the Commission: *Provided*, That no employee shall be promoted to any grade he could not enter by appointment under the minimum age limitation applied thereto by Postal Rule II, clause 2.

POSTAL RULE VI.

1. Transfers may be made as follows:

(*a*) From one classified post-office to another, upon requisition of the Postmaster-General.

(*b*) From any classified post-office to the Post-Office Department, and from the Post-Office Department to any classified post-office, upon requisition of the Postmaster-General.

2. No person may be transferred as herein authorized until the Commission shall have certified to the officer making the transfer requisition that the person whom it is proposed to transfer has passed an examination to test fitness for the place to which he is to be transferred, and that such person has been at least six months next preceding the date of the certificate in the classified service of the Department or post-office from which the transfer is to be made.

POSTAL RULE VII.

Upon the requisition of a postmaster the board of examiners for his office shall certify for reinstatement, in a grade requiring no higher examination than the one in which he was formerly employed, any person who within one year next preceding the date of the requisition has through no delinquency or misconduct been separated from the classified service in said office.

POSTAL RULE VIII.

Each postmaster in the classified postal service shall report to the board of examiners—

(*a*) Every probational and every absolute appointment, and every appointment under any exception to examination authorized by Postal Rule II, clause 5, made in his office.

(*b*) Every refusal to make an absolute appointment in his office and every refusal or neglect to accept an appointment in the classified service under him.

(*c*) Every transfer into the classified service under him.

(*d*) Every separation from the classified service under him, and whether the separation was caused by dismissal, resignation, or death. Places excepted from examination are within the classified service.

(*e*) Every restoration to the classified service under him of any person who may have been separated therefrom by dismissal or resignation.

These rules shall take effect March 1, 1888.

GROVER CLEVELAND.

EXECUTIVE MANSION,
Washington, D. C., March 1, 1888.

In the exercise of authority vested in the President by the seventeen hundred and fifty-third section of the Revised Statutes to prescribe such regulations for the admission of persons into the civil service of the United States as may best promote the efficiency thereof and ascertain the fitness of each applicant in respect to age, health, character, knowledge, and ability for the branch of the service into which he seeks to enter, I hereby direct that the officers, clerks, and other employees of the United States Civil Service Commission, now authorized or that may hereafter be authorized by law, shall be arranged in the following classes, viz:

Class A, including all persons receiving compensation at the rate of less than $1,000 per annum.

Class B, including all persons receiving compensation at the rate of $1,000 or more, but less than $1,200 per annum.

Class 1, including all persons receiving compensation at the rate of $1,200 or more, but less than $1,400 per annum.

Class 2, including all persons receiving compensation at the rate of $1,400 or more, but less than $1,600 per annum.

Class 3, including all persons receiving compensation at the rate of $1,600 or more, but less than $1,800 per annum.

Class 4, including all persons receiving compensation at the rate of $1,800 or more, but less than $2,000 per annum.

Class 5, including all persons receiving compensation at the rate of $2,000 or more per annum.

No person who is appointed to an office by the President by and with the advice and consent of the Senate, or by the President alone, and no person who is to be employed merely as a laborer or workman or as a watchman, shall be considered as within this classification.

And it is ordered, That the United States Civil Service Commission thus classified, as provided by clause 2 of Departmental Rule I of the civil-service rules approved February 2, 1888, and in force on and after the date hereof, shall be considered a part of the classified departmental service, and the rules applicable thereto shall be in force therein.

GROVER CLEVELAND.

EXECUTIVE MANSION,
Washington, March 21, 1888.

To the United States Civil Service Commission.

GENTLEMEN: I desire to make a suggestion regarding subdivision (*c*), General Rule III, of the amended civil-service rules promulgated February 2, 1888. It provides for the promotion of an employee in a Department who is below or outside of the classified service to a place within said classified service in the same Department upon the request of the appointing officer, upon the recommendation of the Commission and the approval of the President, after a noncompetitive examination, in case such person has served continuously for two years in the place from which it is proposed to promote him, and "because of his faithfulness and efficiency in the position occupied by him," and "because of his qualifications for the place to which the appointing officer desires his promotion."

It has occurred to me that this provision must be executed with caution to avoid the application of it to cases not intended and the undue relaxation of the general purposes and restrictions of the civil-service law.

Noncompetitive examinations are the exceptions to the plan of the act, and the rules permitting the same should be strictly construed. The cases arising under the exception above recited should be very few, and when presented they should precisely meet all the requirements specified, and should be supported by facts which will develop the basis and reason of the application of the appointing officer and which will commend them to the judgment of the Commission and the President. The sole purpose of the provision is to benefit the public service, and it should never be permitted to operate as an evasion of the main feature of the law, which is competitive examinations.

As these cases will first be presented to the Commission for recommendation, I have to request that you will formulate a plan by which their merits can be tested. This will naturally involve a statement of all the facts deemed necessary for the determination of such applications, including the kind of work which has been done by the person proposed for promotion and the considerations upon which the allegations of the faithfulness, efficiency, and qualifications mentioned in the rule are predicated.

What has already been written naturally suggests another very important subject, to which I will invite your attention.

The desirability of the rule which I have commented upon would be nearly, if not entirely, removed, and other difficulties which now embarrass the execution of the civil-service law would be obviated, if there was a better and uniform classification of the employees in the different

Departments. The importance of this is entirely obvious. The present imperfect classifications, hastily made, apparently with but little care for uniformity, and promulgated after the last Presidential election and prior to the installation of the present Administration, should not have been permitted to continue to this time.

It appears that in the War Department the employees were divided on the 19th day of November, 1884, into eight classes and subclasses, embracing those earning annual salaries from $900 to $2,000.

The Navy Department was classified November 22, 1884, and its employees were divided into seven classes and subclasses, embracing those who received annual salaries from $720 to $1,800.

In the Interior Department the classification was made on the 6th day of December, 1884. It consists of eight classes and subclasses, and embraces employees receiving annual salaries from $720 to $2,000.

On the 2d day of January, 1885, a classification of the employees in the Treasury Department was made, consisting of six classes and subclasses, including those earning annual salaries from $900 to $1,800.

In the Post-Office Department the employees were classified on February 6, 1885, into nine classes and subclasses, embracing persons earning annual salaries from $720 to $2,000.

On the 12th of December, 1884, the Bureau of Agriculture was classified in a manner different from all the other Departments, and presenting features peculiar to itself.

It seems that the only classification in the Department of State and the Department of Justice is that provided for by section 163 of the Revised Statutes, which directs that the employees in the several Departments shall be divided into four classes. It appears that no more definite classification has been made in these Departments.

I wish the Commission would revise these classifications and submit to me a plan which will as far as possible make them uniform, and which will especially remedy the present condition which permits persons to enter a grade in the service in the one Department without any examination which in another Department can only be entered after passing such examination. This, I think, should be done by extending the limits of the classified service rather than by contracting them.

GROVER CLEVELAND.

EXECUTIVE MANSION, *March 23, 1888.*

To the People of the United States:

The painful duty devolves upon the President to announce the death, at an early hour this morning, at his residence in this city, of Morrison R. Waite, Chief Justice of the United States, which exalted office he had filled since March 4, 1874, with honor to himself and high usefulness to his country.

In testimony of respect to the memory of the honored dead it is ordered that the executive offices in Washington be closed on the day of the funeral and be draped in mourning for thirty days, and that the national flag be displayed at half-mast on the public buildings and on all national vessels on the day of the funeral.

By the President:

T. F. BAYARD, *Secretary.*

EXECUTIVE MANSION,
Washington, May 26, 1888.

Under the provisions of section 4 of the act approved March 3, 1883, it is hereby ordered that the several Executive Departments, the Department of Agriculture, and the Government Printing Office be closed on Wednesday, the 30th instant, to enable the employees to participate in the decoration of the graves of the soldiers who fell during the rebellion.

GROVER CLEVELAND.

UNITED STATES CIVIL SERVICE COMMISSION,
Washington, D. C., June 2, 1888.

The PRESIDENT.

SIR: In the force employed in the office of the collector of customs at the port of New York there are eight tellers who receive and count the money paid in at that office, amounting to $500,000 a day or upward, and who should be persons qualified to handle money with skill and to detect counterfeit coin and bills. One of these places is now vacant, and it is important that it should be filled at the earliest practicable date. The position is not one excepted from examination by Customs Rule II, clause 5; but the collector thinks that it would be imprudent and impracticable for him to be restricted in filling the vacancy to the three names that might be certified to him from the eligible register, and in this opinion the Commission concurs. But whether this class of positions and certain others in the customs service should be filled by noncompetitive examination or by special exception is a matter which the Commission has under consideration, but can not determine until after a visit to New York and perhaps other ports. In view, however, of the necessity for immediately filling the present vacancy—but without establishing a precedent—the Commission has the honor to recommend that a noncompetitive examination for the purpose be authorized under subdivision (*e*), clause 2 of General Rule III, Civil-Service Rules.

Your obedient servants,

JNO. H. OBERLY,
CHAS. LYMAN,
United States Civil Service Commissioners.

Approved, June 5. 1888.

GROVER CLEVELAND.

CLASSIFIED POSTAL SERVICE, SPECIAL RULE NO. 1.

JUNE 16, 1888.

In addition to the exceptions from examination in the classified postal service made by Postal Rule II, clause 5, the following exception to examination in that service is hereby made:

Printers, employed as such.

Provided, That before any person may be employed under this exception to examination the Post-Office Department shall inform the Commission of the authority given to employ printers at any post-office and of the number authorized to be employed at such office.

GROVER CLEVELAND.

Ordered, That noncompetitive examinations to test fitness for the following designated places in the classified departmental service be, and are hereby, authorized:

1. In all the Departments: Engineers, assistant engineers, pressmen, and compositors.

2. In the Department of the Treasury:

In the office of the Secretary: Storekeeper, inspector of electric lights, foreman of laborers, captain of watch, lieutenants of watch, and locksmith and electrician.

In the office of the Treasurer: Seventeen clerks employed as expert money tellers.

In the office of the Supervising Surgeon-General of Marine-Hospital Service: Hospital steward, employed as chemist.

3. In the Department of the Interior:

In the office of the Secretary: Stenographer (to be confidential clerk to Secretary), members of the boards of pension appeals, returns-office clerk, and six clerks to act as assistant disbursing clerks.

In the Bureau of Pensions: Superintendent of buildings and two qualified surgeons.

In the Patent Office: Librarian, principal examiners, machinists, and model attendants.

In the office of the Commissioner of Railroads: One bookkeeper.

In the Bureau of Education: Clerk of class 4, as librarian.

In the Geological Survey: In permanent force—Librarian. In temporary force—Assistant paleontologists, assistant geologists, topographers, and assistant photographers.

4. In the Department of Agriculture:

In the disbursing office: Four clerks.

5. In the Post-Office Department:

In the office of the Assistant Attorney-General: Stenographer (to be confidential clerk to the Assistant Attorney-General).

Approved, July 2, 1888.   GROVER CLEVELAND.

SPECIAL DEPARTMENTAL RULE NO. 1.

In addition to the exceptions from examination made by Departmental Rule III, clause 2, the following exceptions to examinations for the classified departmental service are hereby made, viz:

1. In the Department of State: Lithographer.

2. In the Department of the Treasury:

In the office of the Secretary: Government actuary.

In the office of the Comptroller of the Currency: Bond clerk.

In the office of the Supervising Architect: Supervising Architect, assistant supervising architect, confidential clerk to Supervising Architect, and photographer.

In the Bureau of the Mint: Assayer, examiner, computer of bullion, and adjuster of accounts.

In the Bureau of Navigation: Clerk of class 4, acting as deputy commissioner.

In the office of Construction of Standard Weights and Measures: Adjuster and mechanician.

In the Bureau of Engraving and Printing: Chief of the Bureau, assistant chief of Bureau, engravers, and plate printers.

In the Coast and Geodetic Survey: Superintendent, confidential clerk to Superintendent, the normal or field force, general office assistant, confidential clerk to general office assistant, engravers and contract engravers, electrotypist and photographer, electrotypist's helper. apprentice to electrotypist and photographer, copperplate printers, plate-printers' helpers, and mechanicians.

In the office of the Commissioner of Internal Revenue: Superintendent of stamp vault.

3. In the Department of the Interior:

In the office of the Secretary: Superintendent of documents, clerk of class 3 as custodian, clerk to sign land patents, and telephone operator.

In the office of the Assistant Attorney-General: Law clerks—One at $2,750 per annum, one at $2,500 per annum, one at $2,250 per annum, and thirteen at $2,000 per annum.

In the Patent Office: Financial clerk, examiner of interferences, and law clerk.

In the General Land Office: Two law clerks, two law examiners, clerk of class 4 acting as receiving clerk, and ten principal examiners of land claims and contests.

In the Bureau of Pensions: Assistant chief clerk, medical referee, assistant medical referee, and law clerk.

In the Bureau of Indian Affairs: Principal bookkeeper.

In the office of Commissioner of Railroads: Railroad engineer.

In the Bureau of Education: Collector and compiler of statistics and statistician.

In the Geological Survey: In permanent force--General assistant, executive officer, photographer, twelve geologists, two paleontologists, two chemists, chief geographer, three topographers, and three geographers. In temporary force—Six paleontologists, eight geologists, geographer, mechanician, and editor.

4. In the Department of War: Clerk for the General of the Army and clerk for the retired General of the Army.

In the office of the Chief Signal Officer: Lithographer.

5. In the Department of the Navy:

In the Hydrographic Office: Engravers, copperplate printers, printers' apprentices.

6. In the Department of Justice: Pardon clerk and two law clerks.

7. In the Department of Agriculture:

In the office of the Commissioner: Private secretary to the chief clerk, superintendent of grounds, and assistant chief of each of the following divisions: Of botany, of chemistry, of entomology, of forestry, and of statistics.

In the Bureau of Animal Industry: Chief of the Bureau, assistant chief, private secretary to chief, and chief clerk.

8. In the Post-Office Department: Assistant Attorney-General, law clerk, and agents and employees at postal-note, postage-stamp, postal-card, and envelope agencies.

9. In the Department of Labor: Statistical experts and temporary experts.

Approved, July 2, 1888.

GROVER CLEVELAND.

SPECIAL DEPARTMENTAL RULE NO. 2.

No substitute shall hereafter be employed in any Department; and the head of any Department in which substitutes are now employed may appoint any of such substitutes to take the place of his principal, or to any place of lower grade: *Provided,* That no substitute shall be appointed as herein authorized until he shall have passed an appropriate examination by the Civil Service Commission and his eligibility shall have been certified by said Commission to the head of the Department in which he is employed.

Approved, August 3, 1888.

GROVER CLEVELAND.

EXECUTIVE MANSION, *August 9, 1888.*
The Heads of Departments:

As a mark of respect to the memory of General Sheridan, the President directs that the several Executive Departments in the city of Washington be closed and all public business at the national capital suspended on Saturday, August 11 instant, the day of the funeral.

By direction of the President:

DANIEL S. LAMONT,
Private Secretary.

SPECIAL CUSTOMS RULE NO. 1.

In addition to exceptions from examination in the classified customs service made under Customs Rule II, clause 5, the following special exceptions are made:

In the Boston customs district, office of the naval officer: Assistant deputy naval officer.

Approved, August 10, 1888.

GROVER CLEVELAND.

WAR DEPARTMENT,
Washington City, August 14, 1888.

By direction of the President, Major-General John M. Schofield is assigned to the command of the Army of the United States.

WM. C. ENDICOTT,
Secretary of War.

UNITED STATES CIVIL SERVICE COMMISSION,
Washington, D. C., August 25, 1888.
The PRESIDENT.

SIR: The Commission respectfully submits for your consideration the following extract from the minutes of its proceedings of August 23, 1888:

"Navy Department, August 23. Harmony, Acting Secretary of the Navy, refers, with a request that the examination asked for therein be held at the earliest possible moment, a communication of the same date of G. S. Dyer, lieutenant, United States Navy, in charge of the Hydrographic Office, Navy Department, requesting that Francis A. Lewis, at New York City, and Joseph T. McMillan, of San Francisco, may be noncompetitively examined for the positions of assistants at the branch hydrographic offices at those places, respectively, under General Rule III, paragraph 2 (*e*), stating that the positions of assistants at those offices require men specially fitted by a technical nautical education, and therefore such as is only obtained in the Navy, and that the young men referred to are recent graduates of the Naval Academy and have been honorably discharged from the service.

"The positions named in this communication, and similar positions at other branch hydrographic offices, being regarded as in the classified departmental service in the Department of the Navy, and subject to examination, and in view of the qualifications required in such positions and of the fact that the service is to be rendered at points remote from the city of Washington, it is deemed impracticable to fill these places by competitive examination. It is therefore ordered that they be included among the places to be filled by noncompetitive examination under the provision of General Rule III, clause 2 (*e*), and that the President be asked to approve this order."

The Commission respectfully requests that you indorse this communication with your approval of the action above quoted and return it as the authority of the Commission for including the places mentioned among the noncompetitive examination places under General Rule III, clause 2 (*e*).

Very respectfully,

A. P. EDGERTON,
JOHN H. OBERLY,
CHAS. LYMAN,
United States Civil Service Commissioners.

Approved:

GROVER CLEVELAND.

UNITED STATES CIVIL SERVICE COMMISSION,
Washington, D. C., October 17, 1888.

The PRESIDENT.

SIR: This Commission has been informed by the Treasury Department that an additional teller has been authorized to be appointed at the custom-house in the city of New York, and that his immediate employment is desired.

This position is not one excepted from examination by Customs Rule II, clause 5, but the collector thinks, in view of its fiduciary character, that it ought to be filled by noncompetitive instead of by competitive examination, and in this view the Commission concurs. It is therefore respectfully recommended that a noncompetitive examination for the purpose be authorized under subdivision (*e*) of clause 2 of General Rule III, Revised Civil-Service Rules.

I have the honor to be, sir, your obedient servant,

CHAS. LYMAN,
Commissioner, in Charge.

Approved, October 17, 1888.

GROVER CLEVELAND.

UNITED STATES CIVIL SERVICE COMMISSION,
Washington, D. C., October 31, 1888.

The PRESIDENT.

SIR: Approval of the following order for noncompetitive examinations under the provisions of General Rule III, section 2, clause (*e*), of Revised Civil-Service Rules, is respectfully recommended:

Ordered, That noncompetitive examinations to test fitness for the following-designated places in the classified customs service are hereby authorized:

1. In the customs district of New York, collector's office: The tellers employed in the cashier's office; three stenographers employed under the immediate supervision of the collector.

2. In the customs district of San Francisco: Chinese interpreter.

I have the honor to be, sir, your obedient servant,

CHAS. LYMAN,
Commissioner, in Charge.

Approved, November 1, 1888.

GROVER CLEVELAND.

UNITED STATES CIVIL SERVICE COMMISSION,
Washington, D. C., October 31, 1888.

The PRESIDENT.

SIR: Approval of the following order for noncompetitive examinations under the provisions of General Rule III, section 2, clause (*e*), of Revised Civil-Service Rules, is respectfully recommended:

Ordered, That noncompetitive examinations to test fitness for the following-designated places in the classified departmental service are hereby authorized:

1. In the Department of the Interior, Geological Survey, permanent force: Assistant photographers.

2. In the Department of Labor: Special agents.

I have the honor to be, sir, your obedient servant,

CHAS. LYMAN,
Commissioner, in Charge.

Approved, November 1, 1888.   GROVER CLEVELAND

Clause (*e*) of section 2 of General Rule III is amended by adding thereto the following, and as thus amended is hereby promulgated:

But no person appointed to such a place upon noncompetitive examination shall within one year after appointment be transferred or appointed to any place not excepted from examination; but after having served in such noncompetitive place not less than one year he may be transferred or appointed in the bureau or office in which he is serving to a place not excepted from examination upon the certificate of the Commission or the proper board of examiners that he has passed an examination to test fitness for the place to which his transfer or appointment is proposed.

Approved, November 1, 1888.   GROVER CLEVELAND.

SPECIAL DEPARTMENTAL RULE NO. 1.

So much of Special Departmental Rule No. 1, approved July 2, 1888, as applies to the Department of Agriculture is hereby amended and promulgated as follows:

7. In the Department of Agriculture:

In the office of the Commissioner: Private secretary to the chief clerk, superintendent of grounds, and assistant chief of each of the following divisions: Of botany, of chemistry, of entomology, of forestry, and of statistics, and the director of experiment stations and the assistant director.

In the Bureau of Animal Industry: Chief of the Bureau, assistant chief, private secretary to the chief, and chief clerk.

Approved, November 1, 1888.   GROVER CLEVELAND.

SPECIAL CUSTOMS RULE NO. 1.

Special Customs Rule No. 1, specially excepting from examination certain places in the customs service, is hereby amended by including among those places the following:

At the port of New York, office of the collector: Bookbinder.

The foregoing amendment is hereby approved.

GROVER CLEVELAND.

Departmental Rule VII is hereby amended by inserting at the end of the first sentence of section 1 the following:

Provided, That no certification shall be made from the clerk or any supplementary register to any Department to which promotion regulations have been applied under General Rule III, section 6, to fill a vacancy above the grade of class 1.

So that as amended the first paragraph of section 1 will read:

1. Vacancies in the classified departmental service, unless among the places excepted from examination, if not filled by either promotion or transfer, shall be filled in the following manner: *Provided*, That no certification shall be made from the clerk or any supplementary register to any Department to which promotion regulations have been applied under General Rule III, section 6, to fill a vacancy above the grade of class 1.

Approved and promulgated.

EXECUTIVE MANSION, *November 1, 1888.*

The foregoing amendment is hereby approved.

GROVER CLEVELAND.

The following amendments to departmental rules are hereby made and promulgated:

To Departmental Rule IV: After the word "service," in section 1 of said rule, insert the following:

Provided, That any person may apply for the position of printer's assistant in the Bureau of Engraving and Printing who is not under 18 nor over 35 years of age.

And after the word "for," in the same section, strike out the words "which purpose" and insert in lieu thereof the words "such application," so that as amended section 1 will read:

1. Any person not under 20 years of age may make application for admission to the classified departmental service: *Provided*, That any person may apply for the position of printer's assistant in the Bureau of Engraving and Printing who is not under 18 nor over 35 years of age; and blank forms for such application shall be furnished by the Commission.

To Departmental Rule VI: After the word "examination," where it first occurs in section 5 of said rule, insert the words "or an examination for printer's assistant in the Bureau of Engraving and Printing." After the word "which" strike out the words "supplementary or special," where they last occur in said section, and insert in lieu thereof "the," so that as amended section 5 will read:

5. But the names of all competitors who have passed a supplementary or a special examination, or an examination for printer's assistant in the Bureau of Engraving

and Printing, shall be entered, without regard to State residence, upon the register of persons eligible to the class or place to test fitness for which the examination was held.

To Departmental Rule VII: After the word "or," in the second paragraph of section 3 of said rule, strike out the article "a," and after the word "register" in said paragraph insert the words "or the printer's-assistant register," so that as amended said second paragraph of section 3 will read:

When certification is made from a supplementary or special register, or the printer's-assistant register, and there are more vacancies than one to be filled, the appointing officer may select from the three names certified more than one.

EXECUTIVE MANSION,
Washington, November 5, 1888.

The foregoing amendments are hereby approved.

GROVER CLEVELAND.

UNITED STATES CIVIL SERVICE COMMISSION,
Washington, D. C., October 31, 1888.

The PRESIDENT.

SIR: The order heretofore approved by you authorizing noncompetitive examinations under General Rule III, section 2, clause (*e*), to test fitness for certain designated places in the classified departmental service, included among such places the following:

In the office of the Treasurer of the United States, seventeen clerks employed as expert money tellers.

The attempts thus far made to make appointments to these places under this order have fully satisfied the Commission and the Treasury Department of the impracticability of this method of procedure, not because of any difficulty of applying suitable tests to determine the expertness required, but because there are really no experts to be tested. The duties of these positions can not be learned elsewhere than in the positions themselves, and therefore the only experts are those now occupying them and the very few who have left them for one cause or another, but who are not seeking to return. Therefore, since experts are not available, and persons will have to be appointed who must learn the duties of the positions in the actual performance of those duties, there would seem to be no good reason why such persons should not be selected from the eligible registers of this Commission, which are at all times abundantly supplied with the names of persons who are both competent and worthy. And besides, so long as these tempting places are in the noncompetitive list, the Department will be subjected to solicitation and pressure concerning them which it would rather avoid.

In view of these considerations it is respectfully recommended that you approve the revocation of so much of the order above referred to as provides for the appointment upon noncompetitive examination of seventeen clerks in the office of the Treasurer of the United States employed as expert money tellers.

I have the honor to be, sir, your obedient servant,

CHAS. LYMAN,
Commissioner, in Charge,

Approved, November 13, 1888.

GROVER CLEVELAND.

FOURTH ANNUAL MESSAGE.

WASHINGTON, *December 3, 1888.*

To the Congress of the United States:

As you assemble for the discharge of the duties you have assumed as the representatives of a free and generous people, your meeting is marked by an interesting and impressive incident. With the expiration of the present session of the Congress the first century of our constitutional existence as a nation will be completed.

Our survival for one hundred years is not sufficient to assure us that we no longer have dangers to fear in the maintenance, with all its promised blessings, of a government founded upon the freedom of the people. The time rather admonishes us to soberly inquire whether in the past we have always closely kept in the course of safety, and whether we have before us a way plain and clear which leads to happiness and perpetuity.

When the experiment of our Government was undertaken, the chart adopted for our guidance was the Constitution. Departure from the lines there laid down is failure. It is only by a strict adherence to the direction they indicate and by restraint within the limitations they fix that we can furnish proof to the world of the fitness of the American people for self-government.

The equal and exact justice of which we boast as the underlying principle of our institutions should not be confined to the relations of our citizens to each other. The Government itself is under bond to the American people that in the exercise of its functions and powers it will deal with the body of our citizens in a manner scrupulously honest and fair and absolutely just. It has agreed that American citizenship shall be the only credential necessary to justify the claim of equality before the law, and that no condition in life shall give rise to discrimination in the treatment of the people by their Government.

The citizen of our Republic in its early days rigidly insisted upon full compliance with the letter of this bond, and saw stretching out before him a clear field for individual endeavor. His tribute to the support of his Government was measured by the cost of its economical maintenance, and he was secure in the enjoyment of the remaining recompense of his steady and contented toil. In those days the frugality of the people was stamped upon their Government, and was enforced by the free, thoughtful, and intelligent suffrage of the citizen. Combinations, monopolies, and aggregations of capital were either avoided or sternly regulated and restrained. The pomp and glitter of governments less free offered no temptation and presented no delusion to the plain people who, side by side, in friendly competition, wrought for the ennoblement and dignity of man, for the solution of the problem of free government, and for the achievement of the grand destiny awaiting the land which God had given them.

A century has passed. Our cities are the abiding places of wealth and luxury; our manufactories yield fortunes never dreamed of by the fathers of the Republic; our business men are madly striving in the race for riches, and immense aggregations of capital outrun the imagination in the magnitude of their undertakings.

We view with pride and satisfaction this bright picture of our country's growth and prosperity, while only a closer scrutiny develops a somber shading. Upon more careful inspection we find the wealth and luxury of our cities mingled with poverty and wretchedness and unremunerative toil. A crowded and constantly increasing urban population suggests the impoverishment of rural sections and discontent with agricultural pursuits. The farmer's son, not satisfied with his father's simple and laborious life, joins the eager chase for easily acquired wealth.

We discover that the fortunes realized by our manufacturers are no longer solely the reward of sturdy industry and enlightened foresight, but that they result from the discriminating favor of the Government and are largely built upon undue exactions from the masses of our people. The gulf between employers and the employed is constantly widening, and classes are rapidly forming, one comprising the very rich and powerful, while in another are found the toiling poor.

As we view the achievements of aggregated capital, we discover the existence of trusts, combinations, and monopolies, while the citizen is struggling far in the rear or is trampled to death beneath an iron heel. Corporations, which should be the carefully restrained creatures of the law and the servants of the people, are fast becoming the people's masters.

Still congratulating ourselves upon the wealth and prosperity of our country and complacently contemplating every incident of change inseparable from these conditions, it is our duty as patriotic citizens to inquire at the present stage of our progress how the bond of the Government made with the people has been kept and performed.

Instead of limiting the tribute drawn from our citizens to the necessities of its economical administration, the Government persists in exacting from the substance of the people millions which, unapplied and useless, lie dormant in its Treasury. This flagrant injustice and this breach of faith and obligation add to extortion the danger attending the diversion of the currency of the country from the legitimate channels of business.

Under the same laws by which these results are produced the Government permits many millions more to be added to the cost of the living of our people and to be taken from our consumers, which unreasonably swell the profits of a small but powerful minority.

The people must still be taxed for the support of the Government under the operation of tariff laws. But to the extent that the mass of our citizens are inordinately burdened beyond any useful public purpose and for the benefit of a favored few, the Government, under pretext of an exercise of its taxing power, enters gratuitously into partnership with these favorites, to their advantage and to the injury of a vast majority of our people.

This is not equality before the law.

The existing situation is injurious to the health of our entire body politic. It stifles in those for whose benefit it is permitted all patriotic love of country, and substitutes in its place selfish greed and grasping avarice. Devotion to American citizenship for its own sake and for what it should accomplish as a motive to our nation's advancement and the happiness of all our people is displaced by the assumption that the Government, instead of being the embodiment of equality, is but an instrumentality through which especial and individual advantages are to be gained.

The arrogance of this assumption is unconcealed. It appears in the sordid disregard of all but personal interests, in the refusal to abate for the benefit of others one iota of selfish advantage, and in combinations to perpetuate such advantages through efforts to control legislation and improperly influence the suffrages of the people.

The grievances of those not included within the circle of these beneficiaries, when fully realized, will surely arouse irritation and discontent. Our farmers, long suffering and patient, struggling in the race of life with the hardest and most unremitting toil, will not fail to see, in spite of misrepresentations and misleading fallacies, that they are obliged to accept such prices for their products as are fixed in foreign markets where they compete with the farmers of the world; that their lands are declining in value while their debts increase, and that without compensating favor they are forced by the action of the Government to pay for the benefit of others such enhanced prices for the things they need that the scanty returns of their labor fail to furnish their support or leave no margin for accumulation.

Our workingmen, enfranchised from all delusions and no longer frightened by the cry that their wages are endangered by a just revision of our tariff laws, will reasonably demand through such revision steadier employment, cheaper means of living in their homes, freedom for themselves and their children from the doom of perpetual servitude, and an open door to their advancement beyond the limits of a laboring class. Others of our citizens, whose comforts and expenditures are measured by moderate salaries and fixed incomes, will insist upon the fairness and justice of cheapening the cost of necessaries for themselves and their families.

When to the selfishness of the beneficiaries of unjust discrimination under our laws there shall be added the discontent of those who suffer from such discrimination, we will realize the fact that the beneficent purposes of our Government, dependent upon the patriotism and contentment of our people, are endangered.

Communism is a hateful thing and a menace to peace and organized government; but the communism of combined wealth and capital, the outgrowth of overweening cupidity and selfishness, which insidiously undermines the justice and integrity of free institutions, is not less dangerous than the communism of oppressed poverty and toil, which, exasperated by injustice and discontent, attacks with wild disorder the citadel of rule.

He mocks the people who proposes that the Government shall protect the rich and that they in turn will care for the laboring poor. Any intermediary between the people and their Government or the least delegation of the care and protection the Government owes to the humblest citizen in the land makes the boast of free institutions a glittering delusion and the pretended boon of American citizenship a shameless imposition.

A just and sensible revision of our tariff laws should be made for the relief of those of our countrymen who suffer under present conditions. Such a revision should receive the support of all who love that justice and equality due to American citizenship; of all who realize that in this justice and equality our Government finds its strength and its power to protect the citizen and his property; of all who believe that the contented competence and comfort of many accord better with the spirit of our institutions than colossal fortunes unfairly gathered in the hands of a few; of all who appreciate that the forbearance and fraternity among our people, which recognize the value of every American interest, are the surest guaranty of our national progress, and of all who desire to see the products of American skill and ingenuity in every market of the world, with a resulting restoration of American commerce.

The necessity of the reduction of our revenues is so apparent as to be generally conceded, but the means by which this end shall be accomplished and the sum of direct benefit which shall result to our citizens present a controversy of the utmost importance. There should be no scheme accepted as satisfactory by which the burdens of the people are only apparently removed. Extravagant appropriations of public money, with all their demoralizing consequences, should not be tolerated, either as a means of relieving the Treasury of its present surplus or as furnishing pretext for resisting a proper reduction in tariff rates. Existing evils and injustice should be honestly recognized, boldly met, and effectively remedied. There should be no cessation of the struggle until a plan is perfected, fair and conservative toward existing industries, but which will reduce the cost to consumers of the necessaries of life, while it provides for our manufacturers the advantage of freer raw materials and permits no injury to the interests of American labor.

The cause for which the battle is waged is comprised within lines clearly and distinctly defined. It should never be compromised. It is the people's cause.

It can not be denied that the selfish and private interests which are so persistently heard when efforts are made to deal in a just and comprehensive manner with our tariff·laws are related to, if they are not responsible for, the sentiment largely prevailing among the people that the General Government is the fountain of individual and private aid; that it may be expected to relieve with paternal care the distress of citizens and communities, and that from the fullness of its Treasury it should, upon the slightest possible pretext of promoting the general good, apply public funds to the benefit of localities and individuals. . Nor can it be denied that there is a growing assumption that, as against the Government and in favor of private claims and interests, the usual rules and limitations of business principles and just dealing should be waived.

These ideas have been unhappily much encouraged by legislative acquiescence. Relief from contracts made with the Government is too easily accorded in favor of the citizen; the failure to support claims against the Government by proof is often supplied by no better consideration than the wealth of the Government and the poverty of the claimant; gratuities in the form of pensions are granted upon no other real ground than the needy condition of the applicant, or for reasons less valid; and large sums are expended for public buildings and other improvements upon representations scarcely claimed to be related to public needs and necessities.

The extent to which the consideration of such matters subordinate and postpone action upon subjects of great public importance, but involving no special private or partisan interest, should arrest attention and lead to reformation.

A few of the numerous illustrations of this condition may be stated.

The crowded condition of the calendar of the Supreme Court, and the delay to suitors and denial of justice resulting therefrom, has been strongly urged upon the attention of the Congress, with a plan for the relief of the situation approved by those well able to judge of its merits. While this subject remains without effective consideration, many laws have been passed providing for the holding of terms of inferior courts at places to suit the convenience of localities, or to lay the foundation of an application for the erection of a new public building.

Repeated recommendations have been submitted for the amendment and change of the laws relating to our public lands so that their spoliation and diversion to other uses than as homes for honest settlers might be prevented. While a measure to meet this conceded necessity of reform remains awaiting the action of the Congress, many claims to the public lands and applications for their donation, in favor of States and individuals, have been allowed.

A plan in aid of Indian management, recommended by those well informed as containing valuable features in furtherance of the solution of the Indian problem, has thus far failed of legislative sanction, while grants of doubtful expediency to railroad corporations, permitting them to pass through Indian reservations, have greatly multiplied.

The propriety and necessity of the erection of one or more prisons for the confinement of United States convicts, and a post-office building in the national capital, are not disputed. But these needs yet remain unanswered, while scores of public buildings have been erected where their necessity for public purposes is not apparent.

A revision of our pension laws could easily be made which would rest upon just principles and provide for every worthy applicant. But while our general pension laws remain confused and imperfect, hundreds of private pension laws are annually passed, which are the sources of unjust discrimination and popular demoralization.

Appropriation bills for the support of the Government are defaced by items and provisions to meet private ends, and it is freely asserted by responsible and experienced parties that a bill appropriating money for public internal improvement would fail to meet with favor unless it contained items more for local and private advantage than for public benefit.

These statements can be much emphasized by an ascertainment of the proportion of Federal legislation which either bears upon its face its private character or which upon examination develops such a motive power.

And yet the people wait and expect from their chosen representatives such patriotic action as will advance the welfare of the entire country; and this expectation can only be answered by the performance of public duty with unselfish purpose. Our mission among the nations of the earth and our success in accomplishing the work God has given the American people to do require of those intrusted with the making and execution of our laws perfect devotion, above all other things, to the public good.

This devotion will lead us to strongly resist all impatience of constitutional limitations of Federal power and to persistently check the increasing tendency to extend the scope of Federal legislation into the domain of State and local jurisdiction upon the plea of subserving the public welfare. The preservation of the partitions between proper subjects of Federal and local care and regulation is of such importance under the Constitution, which is the law of our very existence, that no consideration of expediency or sentiment should tempt us to enter upon doubtful ground. We have undertaken to discover and proclaim the richest blessings of a free government, with the Constitution as our guide. Let us follow the way it points out; it will not mislead us. And surely no one who has taken upon himself the solemn obligation to support and preserve the Constitution can find justification or solace for disloyalty in the excuse that he wandered and disobeyed in search of a better way to reach the public welfare than the Constitution offers.

What has been said is deemed not inappropriate at a time when, from a century's height, we view the way already trod by the American people and attempt to discover their future path.

The seventh President of the United States—the soldier and statesman and at all times the firm and brave friend of the people—in vindication of his course as the protector of popular rights and the champion of true American citizenship, declared:

The ambition which leads me on is an anxious desire and a fixed determination to restore to the people unimpaired the sacred trust they have confided to my charge; to heal the wounds of the Constitution and to preserve it from further violation; to persuade my countrymen, so far as I may, that it is not in a splendid government supported by powerful monopolies and aristocratical establishments that they will find happiness or their liberties protection, but in a plain system, void of pomp, protecting all and granting favors to none, dispensing its blessings like the dews of heaven, unseen and unfelt save in the freshness and beauty they contribute to produce. It is such a government that the genius of our people requires—such an one only under which our States may remain for ages to come united, prosperous, and free.

In pursuance of a constitutional provision requiring the President from time to time to give to the Congress information of the state of the Union, I have the satisfaction to announce that the close of the year finds the United States in the enjoyment of domestic tranquillity and at peace with all the nations.

Since my last annual message our foreign relations have been strengthened and improved by performance of international good offices and by new and renewed treaties of amity, commerce, and reciprocal extradition of criminals.

Those international questions which still await settlement are all reasonably within the domain of amicable negotiation, and there is no existing subject of dispute between the United States and any foreign power that is not susceptible of satisfactory adjustment by frank diplomatic treatment.

The questions between Great Britain and the United States relating to the rights of American fishermen, under treaty and international comity, in the territorial waters of Canada and Newfoundland, I regret to say, are not yet satisfactorily adjusted.

These matters were fully treated in my message to the Senate of February 20, 1888,* together with which a convention, concluded under my authority with Her Majesty's Government on the 15th of February last, for the removal of all causes of misunderstanding, was submitted by me for the approval of the Senate.

This treaty having been rejected by the Senate, I transmitted a message to the Congress on the 23d of August last † reviewing the transactions and submitting for consideration certain recommendations for legislation concerning the important questions involved.

Afterwards, on the 12th of September,‡ in response to a resolution of the Senate, I again communicated fully all the information in my possession as to the action of the government of Canada affecting the commercial relations between the Dominion and the United States, including

* See pp. 603-607.   † See pp. 620-627.   ‡ See pp. 628-630.

the treatment of American fishing vessels in the ports and waters of British North America.

These communications have all been published, and therefore opened to the knowledge of both Houses of Congress, although two were addressed to the Senate alone.

Comment upon or repetition of their contents would be superfluous, and I am not aware that anything has since occurred which should be added to the facts therein stated.   Therefore I merely repeat, as applicable to the present time, the statement which will be found in my message to the Senate of September 12 last, that—

Since March 3, 1887, no case has been reported to the Department of State wherein complaint was made of unfriendly or unlawful treatment of American fishing vessels on the part of the Canadian authorities in which reparation was not promptly and satisfactorily obtained by the United States consul-general at Halifax.

Having essayed in the discharge of my duty to procure by negotiation the settlement of a long-standing cause of dispute and to remove a constant menace to the good relations of the two countries, and continuing to be of opinion that the treaty of February last, which failed to receive the approval of the Senate, did supply ''a satisfactory, practical, and final adjustment, upon a basis honorable and just to both parties, of the difficult and vexed question to which it related,'' and having subsequently and unavailingly recommended other legislation to Congress which I hoped would suffice to meet the exigency created by the rejection of the treaty, I now again invoke the earnest and immediate attention of the Congress to the condition of this important question as it now stands before them and the country, and for the settlement of which I am deeply solicitous.

Near the close of the month of October last occurrences of a deeply regrettable nature were brought to my knowledge, which made it my painful but imperative duty to obtain with as little delay as possible a new personal channel of diplomatic intercourse in this country with the Government of Great Britain.

The correspondence in relation to this incident will in due course be laid before you, and will disclose the unpardonable conduct of the official referred to in his interference by advice and counsel with the suffrages of American citizens in the very crisis of the Presidential election then near at hand, and also in his subsequent public declarations to justify his action, superadding impugnment of the Executive and Senate of the United States in connection with important questions now pending in controversy between the two Governments.

The offense thus committed was most grave, involving disastrous possibilities to the good relations of the United States and Great Britain, constituting a gross breach of diplomatic privilege and an invasion of the purely domestic affairs and essential sovereignty of the Government to which the envoy was accredited.

Having first fulfilled the just demands of international comity by affording full opportunity for Her Majesty's Government to act in relief of the situation, I considered prolongation of discussion to be unwarranted, and thereupon declined to further recognize the diplomatic character of the person whose continuance in such function would destroy that mutual confidence which is essential to the good understanding of the two Governments and was inconsistent with the welfare and self-respect of the Government of the United States.

The usual interchange of communication has since continued through Her Majesty's legation in this city.

My endeavors to establish by international cooperation measures for the prevention of the extermination of fur seals in Bering Sea have not been relaxed, and I have hopes of being enabled shortly to submit an effective and satisfactory conventional projet with the maritime powers for the approval of the Senate.

The coastal boundary between our Alaskan possessions and British Columbia, I regret to say, has not received the attention demanded by its importance, and which on several occasions heretofore I have had the honor to recommend to the Congress.

The admitted impracticability, if not impossibility, of making an accurate and precise survey and demarcation of the boundary line as it is recited in the treaty with Russia under which Alaska was ceded to the United States renders it absolutely requisite for the prevention of international jurisdictional complications that adequate appropriation for a reconnoissance and survey to obtain proper knowledge of the locality and the geographical features of the boundary should be authorized by Congress with as little delay as possible.

Knowledge to be only thus obtained is an essential prerequisite for negotiation for ascertaining a common boundary, or as preliminary to any other mode of settlement.

It is much to be desired that some agreement should be reached with Her Majesty's Government by which the damages to life and property on the Great Lakes may be alleviated by removing or humanely regulating the obstacles to reciprocal assistance to wrecked or stranded vessels.

The act of June 19, 1878, which offers to Canadian vessels free access to our inland waters in aid of wrecked or disabled vessels, has not yet become effective through concurrent action by Canada.

The due protection of our citizens of French origin or descent from claim of military service in the event of their returning to or visiting France has called forth correspondence which was laid before you at the last session.

In the absence of conventional agreement as to naturalization, which is greatly to be desired, this Government sees no occasion to recede from the sound position it has maintained not only with regard to France, but as to all countries with which the United States have not concluded special treaties.

Twice within the last year has the imperial household of Germany been visited by death; and I have hastened to express the sorrow of this people, and their appreciation of the lofty character of the late aged Emperor William, and their sympathy with the heroism under suffering of his son the late Emperor Frederick.

I renew my recommendation of two years ago for the passage of a bill for the refunding to certain German steamship lines of the interest upon tonnage dues illegally exacted.

On the 12th [2d] of April last* I laid before the House of Representatives full information respecting our interests in Samoa; and in the subsequent correspondence on the same subject, which will be laid before you in due course, the history of events in those islands will be found.

In a message accompanying my approval, on the 1st day of October last, of a bill for the exclusion of Chinese laborers, I laid before Congress full information and all correspondence touching the negotiation of the treaty with China concluded at this capital on the 12th day of March, 1888, and which, having been confirmed by the Senate with certain amendments, was rejected by the Chinese Government. This message contained a recommendation that a sum of money be appropriated as compensation to Chinese subjects who had suffered injuries at the hands of lawless men within our jurisdiction. Such appropriation having been duly made, the fund awaits reception by the Chinese Government.

It is sincerely hoped that by the cessation of the influx of this class of Chinese subjects, in accordance with the expressed wish of both Governments, a cause of unkind feeling has been permanently removed.

On the 9th of August, 1887, notification was given by the Japanese minister at this capital of the adjournment of the conference for the revision of the treaties of Japan with foreign powers, owing to the objection of his Government to the provision in the draft jurisdictional convention which required the submission of the criminal code of the Empire to the powers in advance of its becoming operative. This notification was, however, accompanied with an assurance of Japan's intention to continue the work of revision.

Notwithstanding this temporary interruption of negotiations, it is hoped that improvements may soon be secured in the jurisdictional system as respects foreigners in Japan, and relief afforded to that country from the present undue and oppressive foreign control in matters of commerce.

I earnestly recommend that relief be provided for the injuries accidentally caused to Japanese subjects in the island Ikisima by the target practice of one of our vessels.

A diplomatic mission from Korea has been received, and the formal intercourse between the two countries contemplated by the treaty of 1882 is now established.

*See p. 612.

Legislative provision is hereby recommended to organize and equip consular courts in Korea.

Persia has established diplomatic representation at this capital, and has evinced very great interest in the enterprise and achievements of our citizens. I am therefore hopeful that beneficial commercial relations between the two countries may be brought about.

I announce with sincere regret that Hayti has again become the theater of insurrection, disorder, and bloodshed. The titular government of President Saloman has been forcibly overthrown and he driven out of the country to France, where he has since died.

The tenure of power has been so unstable amid the war of factions that has ensued since the expulsion of President Saloman that no government constituted by the will of the Haytian people has been recognized as administering responsibly the affairs of that country. Our representative has been instructed to abstain from interference between the warring factions, and a vessel of our Navy has been sent to Haytian waters to sustain our minister and for the protection of the persons and property of American citizens.

Due precautions have been taken to enforce our neutrality laws and prevent our territory from becoming the base of military supplies for either of the warring factions.

Under color of a blockade, of which no reasonable notice had been given, and which does not appear to have been efficiently maintained, a seizure of vessels under the American flag has been reported, and in consequence measures to prevent and redress any molestation of our innocent merchantmen have been adopted.

Proclamation was duly made on the 9th day of November, 1887, of the conventional extensions of the treaty of June 3, 1875, with Hawaii, under which relations of such special and beneficent intercourse have been created.

In the vast field of Oriental commerce now unfolded from our Pacific borders no feature presents stronger recommendations for Congressional action than the establishment of communication by submarine telegraph with Honolulu.

The geographical position of the Hawaiian group in relation to our Pacific States creates a natural interdependency and mutuality of interest which our present treaties were intended to foster, and which make close communication a logical and commercial necessity.

The wisdom of concluding a treaty of commercial reciprocity with Mexico has been heretofore stated in my messages to Congress, and the lapse of time and growth of commerce with that close neighbor and sister Republic confirm the judgment so expressed.

The precise relocation of our boundary line is needful, and adequate appropriation is now recommended.

It is with sincere satisfaction that I am enabled to advert to the spirit of good neighborhood and friendly cooperation and conciliation that has marked the correspondence and action of the Mexican authorities i⁻

their share of the task of maintaining law and order about the line of our common boundary.

The long-pending boundary dispute between Costa Rica and Nicaragua was referred to my arbitration, and by an award made on the 22d of March last the question has been finally settled to the expressed satisfaction of both of the parties in interest.

The Empire of Brazil, in abolishing the last vestige of slavery among Christian nations, called forth the earnest congratulations of this Government in expression of the cordial sympathies of our people.

The claims of nearly all other countries against Chile growing out of her late war with Bolivia and Peru have been disposed of, either by arbitration or by a lump settlement. Similar claims of our citizens will continue to be urged upon the Chilean Government, and it is hoped will not be subject to further delays.

A comprehensive treaty of amity and commerce with Peru was proclaimed on November 7 last, and it is expected that under its operation mutual prosperity and good understanding will be promoted.

In pursuance of the policy of arbitration, a treaty to settle the claim of Santos, an American citizen, against Ecuador has been concluded under my authority, and will be duly submitted for the approval of the Senate.

Like disposition of the claim of Carlos Butterfield against Denmark and of Van Bokkelen against Hayti will probably be made, and I trust the principle of such settlements may be extended in practice under the approval of the Senate.

Through unforeseen causes, foreign to the will of both Governments, the ratification of the convention of December 5, 1885, with Venezuela, for the rehearing of claims of citizens of the United States under the treaty of 1866, failed of exchange within the term provided, and a supplementary convention, further extending the time for exchange of ratifications and explanatory of an ambiguous provision of the prior convention, now awaits the advice and consent of the Senate.

Although this matter, in the stage referred to, concerns only the concurrent treaty-making power of one branch of Congress, I advert to it in view of the interest repeatedly and conspicuously shown by you in your legislative capacity in favor of a speedy and equitable adjustment of the questions growing out of the discredited judgments of the previous mixed commission of Caracas. With every desire to do justice to the representations of Venezuela in this regard, the time seems to have come to end this matter, and I trust the prompt confirmation by both parties of the supplementary action referred to will avert the need of legislative or other action to prevent the longer withholding of such rights of actual claimants as may be shown to exist.

As authorized by the Congress, preliminary steps have been taken for the assemblage at this capital during the coming year of the representatives of South and Central American States, together with those of

Mexico, Hayti, and San Domingo, to discuss sundry important monetary and commercial topics.

Excepting in those cases where, from reasons of contiguity of territory and the existence of a common border line incapable of being guarded, reciprocal commercial treaties may be found expedient, it is believed that commercial policies inducing freer mutual exchange of products can be most advantageously arranged by independent but cooperative legislation.

In the mode last mentioned the control of our taxation for revenue will be always retained in our own hands unrestricted by conventional agreements with other governments.

In conformity also with Congressional authority, the maritime powers have been invited to confer in Washington in April next upon the practicability of devising uniform rules and measures for the greater security of life and property at sea. A disposition to accept on the part of a number of the powers has already been manifested, and if the cooperation of the nations chiefly interested shall be secured important results may be confidently anticipated.

The act of June 26, 1884, and the acts amendatory thereof, in relation to tonnage duties, have given rise to extended correspondence with foreign nations with whom we have existing treaties of navigation and commerce, and have caused wide and regrettable divergence of opinion in relation to the imposition of the duties referred to. These questions are important, and I shall make them the subject of a special and more detailed communication at the present session.

With the rapid increase of immigration to our shores and the facilities of modern travel, abuses of the generous privileges afforded by our naturalization laws call for their careful revision.

The easy and unguarded manner in which certificates of American citizenship can now be obtained has induced a class, unfortunately large, to avail themselves of the opportunity to become absolved from allegiance to their native land, and yet by a foreign residence to escape any just duty and contribution of service to the country of their proposed adoption. Thus, while evading the duties of citizenship to the United States, they may make prompt claim for its national protection and demand its intervention in their behalf. International complications of a serious nature arise, and the correspondence of the State Department discloses the great number and complexity of the questions which have been raised.

Our laws regulating the issue of passports should be carefully revised, and the institution of a central bureau of registration at the capital is again strongly recommended. By this means full particulars of each case of naturalization in the United States would be secured and properly indexed and recorded, and thus many cases of spurious citizenship would be detected and unjust responsibilities would be avoided.

The reorganization of the consular service is a matter of serious importance to our national interests. The number of existing principal

consular offices is believed to be greater than is at all necessary fc
conduct of the public business.   It need not be our policy to mai
more than a moderate number of principal offices, each supported
salary sufficient to enable the incumbent to live in comfort, and s
tributed as to secure the convenient supervision, through subord
agencies, of affairs over a considerable district.

I repeat the recommendations heretofore made by me that the a
priations for the maintenance of our diplomatic and consular s(
should be recast; that the so-called notarial or unofficial fees, whic'
representatives abroad are now permitted to treat as personal pe
sites, should be forbidden; that a system of consular inspection shou
instituted, and that a limited number of secretaries of legation at
should be authorized.

Preparations for the centennial celebration, on April 30, 1889, c
inauguration of George Washington as President of the United S'
at the city of New York, have been made by a voluntary organizat:
the citizens of that locality, and believing that an opportunity shot
afforded for the expression of the interest felt throughout the co'
in this event, I respectfully recommend fitting and cooperative acti(
Congress on behalf of the people of the United States.

The report of the Secretary of the Treasury exhibits in detail the
dition of our national finances and the operations of the several bra:
of the Government related to his Department.

The total ordinary revenues of the Government for the fiscal year (
June 30, 1888, amounted to $379,266,074.76, of which $219,091,1
was received from customs duties and $124,296,871.98 from inte
revenue taxes.

The total receipts from all sources exceeded those for the fiscal
ended June 30, 1887, by $7,862,797.10.

The ordinary expenditures of the Government for the fiscal year
ing June 30, 1888, were $259,653,958.67, leaving a surplus of $119,
116.09.

The decrease in these expenditures as compared with the fiscal
ended June 30, 1887, was $8,278,221.30, notwithstanding the paym
more than $5,000,000 for pensions in excess of what was paid fo
purpose in the latter-mentioned year.

The revenues of the Government for the year ending June 30,
ascertained for the quarter ended September 30, 1888, and estimat
the remainder of the time, amount to $377,000,000, and the actua
estimated ordinary expenditures for the same year are $273,00(
leaving an estimated surplus of $104,000,000.

The estimated receipts for the year ending June 30, 1890, are $
000,000, and the estimated ordinary expenditures for the same tin

necessary to be expended to meet the requirements of the sinking-fund act, amounting to more than $47,000,000 annually.

The cost of collecting the customs revenues for the last fiscal year was 2.44 per cent; for the year 1885 it was 3.77 per cent.

The excess of internal-revenue taxes collected during the last fiscal year over those collected for the year ended June 30, 1887, was $5,489,-174.26, and the cost of collecting this revenue decreased from 3.4 per cent in 1887 to less than 3.2 per cent for the last year. The tax collected on oleomargarine was $723,948.04 for the year ending June 30, 1887, and $864,139.88 for the following year.

The requirements of the sinking-fund act have been met for the year ended June 30, 1888, and for the current year also, by the purchase of bonds. After complying with this law as positively required, and bonds sufficient for that purpose had been bought at a premium, it was not deemed prudent to further expend the surplus in such purchases until the authority to do so should be more explicit. A resolution, however, having been passed by both Houses of Congress removing all doubt as to Executive authority, daily purchases of bonds were commenced on the 23d day of April, 1888, and have continued until the present time. By this plan bonds of the Government not yet due have been purchased up to and including the 30th day of November, 1888, amounting to $94,-700,400, the premium paid thereon amounting to $17,508,613.08.

The premium added to the principal of these bonds represents an investment yielding about 2 per cent interest for the time they still had to run, and the saving to the Government represented by the difference between the amount of interest at 2 per cent upon the sum paid for principal and premium and what it would have paid for interest at the rate specified in the bonds if they had run to their maturity is about $27,165,000.

At first sight this would seem to be a profitable and sensible transaction on the part of the Government, but, as suggested by the Secretary of the Treasury, the surplus thus expended for the purchase of bonds was money drawn from the people in excess of any actual need of the Government and was so expended rather than allow it to remain idle in the Treasury. If this surplus, under the operation of just and equitable laws, had been left in the hands of the people, it would have been worth in their business at least 6 per cent per annum. Deducting from the amount of interest upon the principal and premium of these bonds for the time they had to run at the rate of 6 per cent the saving of 2 per cent made for the people by the purchase of such bonds, the loss will appear to be $55,760,000.

This calculation would seem to demonstrate that if excessive and unnecessary taxation is continued and the Government is forced to pursue this policy of purchasing its own bonds at the premiums which it will be necessary to pay, the loss to the people will be hundreds of millions of dollars.

Since the purchase of bonds was undertaken as mentioned n that have been offered were at last accepted. It has been ma apparent that the Government was in danger of being subjected binations to raise their price, as appears by the instance cited by retary of the offering of bonds of the par value of only $326,000 that the aggregate of the sums demanded for their purchase a to more than $19,700,000.

Notwithstanding the large sums paid out in the purchase of the surplus in the Treasury on the 30th day of November, 18 $52,234,610.01, after deducting about $20,000,000 just drawn the payment of pensions.

At the close of the fiscal year ended June 30, 1887, there h coined under the compulsory silver-coinage act $266,988,280 i dollars, $55,504,310 of which were in the hands of the people.

On the 30th day of June, 1888, there had been coined $299,; and of this $55,829,303 was in circulation in coin, and $200, in silver certificates, for the redemption of which silver dollars amount were held by the Government.

On the 30th day of November, 1888, $312,570,990 had been $60,970,990 of the silver dollars were actually in circulation, an 418,346 in certificates.

The Secretary recommends the suspension of the further co silver, and in such recommendation I earnestly concur.

For further valuable information and timely recommendations] careful attention of the Congress to the Secretary's report.

The Secretary of War reports that the Army at the date of the l solidated returns consisted of 2,189 officers and 24,549 enlisted r

The actual expenditures of the War Department for the fis ended June 30, 1888, amounted to $41,165,107.07, of which sum 516.63 was expended for public works, including river and ha provements.

"The Board of Ordnance and Fortifications" provided for u act approved September 22 last was convened October 30, 1888, a and specifications for procuring forgings for 8, 10, and 12 inc under provisions of section 4, and also for procuring 12-inch bree ing mortars, cast iron, hooped with steel, under the provisions o 5 of the said act, were submitted to the Secretary of War for refe the board, by the Ordnance Department, on the same date.

These plans and specifications having been promptly approve board and the Secretary of War, the necessary authority to publis tisements inviting proposals in the newspapers throughout the was granted by the Secretary on November 12, and on Novembe

A board of ordnance officers was convened at the Watervliet Arsenal on October 4, 1888, to prepare the necessary plans and specifications for the establishment of an army gun factory at that point. The preliminary report of this board, with estimates for shop buildings and officers' quarters, was approved by the Board of Ordnance and Fortifications November 6 and 8. The specifications and form of advertisement and instructions to bidders have been prepared, and advertisements inviting proposals for the excavations for the shop building and for erecting the two sets of officers' quarters have been published. The detailed drawings and specifications for the gun-factory building are well in hand, and will be finished within three or four months, when bids will be invited for the erection of the building. The list of machines, etc., is made out, and it is expected that the plans for the large lathes, etc., will be completed within about four months, and after approval by the Board of Ordnance and Fortifications bids for furnishing the same will be invited. The machines and other fixtures will be completed as soon as the shop is in readiness to receive them, probably about July, 1890.

Under the provisions of the Army bill for the procurement of pneumatic dynamite guns, the necessary specifications are now being prepared, and advertisements for proposals will issue early in December. The guns will probably be of 15 inches caliber and fire a projectile that will carry a charge each of about 500 pounds of explosive gelatine with full-caliber projectiles. The guns will probably be delivered in from six to ten months from the date of the contract, so that all the guns of this class that can be procured under the provisions of the law will be purchased during the year 1889.

I earnestly request that the recommendations contained in the Secretary's report, all of which are, in my opinion, calculated to increase the usefulness and discipline of the Army, may receive the consideration of the Congress. Among these the proposal that there should be provided a plan for the examination of officers to test their fitness for promotion is of the utmost importance. This reform has been before recommended in the reports of the Secretary, and its expediency is so fully demonstrated by the argument he presents in its favor that its adoption should no longer be neglected.

The death of General Sheridan in August last was a national affliction. The Army then lost the grandest of its chiefs. The country lost a brave and experienced soldier, a wise and discreet counselor, and a modest and sensible man. Those who in any manner came within the range of his personal association will never fail to pay deserved and willing homage to his greatness and the glory of his career, but they will cherish with more tender sensibility the loving memory of his simple, generous, and considerate nature.

The Apache Indians, whose removal from their reservation in Arizona followed the capture of those of their number who engaged in a bloody and murderous raid during a part of the years 1885 and 1886, are now held as prisoners of war at Mount Vernon Barracks, in the State of Alabama. They numbered on the 31st day of October, the date of the last report, 83 men, 170 women, 70 boys, and 59 girls; in all, 382 persons. The commanding officer states that they are in good health and contented, and that they are kept employed as fully as is possible in the circumstances. The children, as they arrive at a suitable age, are sent to the Indian schools at Carlisle and Hampton.

Last summer some charitable and kind people asked permission to send two teachers to these Indians for the purpose of instructing the adults as well as such children as should be found there. Such permission was readily granted, accommodations were provided for the teachers, and some portions of the buildings at the barracks were made available for school purposes. The good work contemplated has been commenced, and the teachers engaged are paid by the ladies with whom the plan originated.

I am not at all in sympathy with those benevolent but injudicious people who are constantly insisting that these Indians should be returned to their reservation. Their removal was an absolute necessity if the lives and property of citizens upon the frontier are to be at all regarded by the Government. Their continued restraint at a distance from the scene of their repeated and cruel murders and outrages is still necessary. It is a mistaken philanthropy, every way injurious, which prompts the desire to see these savages returned to their old haunts. They are in their present location as the result of the best judgment of those having official responsibility in the matter, and who are by no means lacking in kind consideration for the Indians. A number of these prisoners have forfeited their lives to outraged law and humanity. Experience has proved that they are dangerous and can not be trusted. This is true not only of those who on the warpath have heretofore actually been guilty of atrocious murder, but of their kindred and friends, who, while they remained upon their reservation, furnished aid and comfort to those absent with bloody intent.

These prisoners should be treated kindly and kept in restraint far from the locality of their former reservation; they should be subjected to efforts calculated to lead to their improvement and the softening of their savage and cruel instincts, but their return to their old home should be persistently resisted.

The Secretary in his report gives a graphic history of these Indians, and recites with painful vividness their bloody deeds and the unhappy failure of the Government to manage them by peaceful means. It will be amazing if a perusal of this history will allow the survival of a desire for the return of these prisoners to their reservation upon sentimental or any other grounds.

The report of the Secretary of the Navy demonstrates very intelligent

management in that important Department, and discloses the most satisfactory progress in the work of reconstructing the Navy made during the
past year. Of the ships in course of construction five, viz, the *Charleston*, *Baltimore*, *Yorktown*, *Vesuvius*, and the *Petrel*, have in that time
been launched and are rapidly approaching completion; and in addition
to the above, the *Philadelphia*, the *San Francisco*, the *Newark*, the *Bennington*, the *Concord*, and the Herreshoff torpedo boat are all under contract for delivery to the Department during the next year. The progress
already made and being made gives good ground for the expectation that
these eleven vessels will be incorporated as part of the American Navy
within the next twelve months.

The report shows that notwithstanding the large expenditures for new
construction and the additional labor they involve the total ordinary or
current expenditures of the Department for the three years ending June
30, 1888, are less by more than 20 per cent than such expenditures for
the three years ending June 30, 1884.

The various steps which have been taken to improve the business
methods of the Department are reviewed by the Secretary. The purchasing of supplies has been consolidated and placed under a responsible
bureau head. This has resulted in the curtailment of open purchases,
which in the years 1884 and 1885 amounted to over 50 per cent of all
the purchases of the Department, to less than 11 per cent; so that at the
present time about 90 per cent of the total departmental purchases are
made by contract and after competition. As the expenditures on this
account exceed an average of $2,000,000 annually, it is evident that an
important improvement in the system has been inaugurated and substantial economies introduced.

The report of the Postmaster-General shows a marked increase of business in every branch of the postal service.

The number of post-offices on July 1, 1888, was 57,376, an increase of
6,124 in three years and of 2,219 for the last fiscal year. The latter-
mentioned increase is classified as follows:

New England States	5
Middle States	181
Southern States and Indian Territory (41)	1,406
The States and Territories of the Pacific Coast	190
The ten States and Territories of the West and Northwest	435
District of Columbia	2
Total	2,219

Free-delivery offices have increased from 189 in the fiscal year ended
June 30, 1887, to 358 in the year ended June 30, 1888.

In the Railway Mail Service there has been an increase in one year of
168 routes, and in the number of miles traveled per annum an increase
of 15,795,917.48. The estimated increase of railroad service for the year
was 6,000 miles, but the amount of new railroad service actually put on
was 12,764.50 miles.

The volume of business in the Money-Order Division, including transactions in postal notes, reached the sum of upward of $143,000,000 for the year.

During the past year parcel-post conventions have been concluded with Barbados, the Bahamas, British Honduras, and Mexico, and are now under negotiation with all the Central and South American States. The increase of correspondence with foreign countries during the past three years is gratifying, and is especially notable and exceptional with the Central and South American States and with Mexico. As the greater part of mail matter exchanged with these countries is commercial in its character, this increase is evidence of the improved business relations with them. The practical operation of the parcel-post conventions, so far as negotiated, has served to fulfill the most favorable predictions as to their benefits. In January last a general postal convention was negotiated with the Dominion of Canada, which went into operation on March 1, and which practically makes one postal territory of the United States and Canada. Under it merchandise parcels may now be transmitted through the mails at fourth-class rates of postage.

It is not possible here to touch even the leading heads of the great postal establishment to illustrate the enormous and rapid growth of its business and the needs for legislative readjustment of much of its machinery that it has outgrown. For these and valuable recommendations of the Postmaster-General attention is earnestly invited to his report.

A Department whose revenues have increased from $19,772,000 in 1870 to $52,700,000 in 1888, despite reductions of postage which have enormously reduced rates of revenue while greatly increasing its business, demands the careful consideration of the Congress as to all matters suggested by those familiar with its operations, and which are calculated to increase its efficiency and usefulness.

A bill proposed by the Postmaster-General was introduced at the last session of the Congress by which a uniform standard in the amount of gross receipts would fix the right of a community to a public building to be erected by the Government for post-office purposes. It was demonstrated that, aside from the public convenience and the promotion of harmony among citizens, invariably disturbed by change of leasings and of site, it was a measure of the highest economy and of sound business judgment. It was found that the Government was paying in rents at the rate of from 7 to 10 per cent per annum on what the cost of such public buildings would be. A very great advantage resulting from such a law would be the prevention of a large number of bills constantly introduced for the erection of public buildings at places, and involving expenditures not justified by public necessity. I trust that this measure will become a law at the present session of Congress.

Of the total number of postmasters 54,874 are of the fourth class. These, of course, receive no allowances whatever for expenses in the service, and their compensation is fixed by percentages on receipts at their respective offices. This rate of compensation may have been, and probably was, at some time just, but the standard has remained unchanged through the several reductions in the rates of postage. Such reductions have necessarily cut down the compensation of these officials, while it undoubtedly increased the business performed by them. Simple justice requires attention to this subject, to the end that fourth-class postmasters may receive at least an equivalent to that which the law itself, fixing the rate, intended for them.

Another class of postal employees whose condition seems to demand legislation is that of clerks in post-offices, and I call especial attention to the repeated recommendations of the Postmaster-General for their classification. Proper legislation of this character for the relief of carriers in the free-delivery service has been frequent. Provision is made for their promotion; for substitutes for them on vacation; for substitutes for holidays, and limiting their hours of labor. Seven million dollars has been appropriated for the current year to provide for them, though the total number of offices where they are employed is but 358 for the past fiscal year, with an estimated increase for the current year of but 40, while the total appropriation for all clerks in offices throughout the United States is $5,950,000.

The legislation affecting the relations of the Government with railroads is in need of revision. While for the most part the railroad companies throughout the country have cordially cooperated with the Post-Office Department in rendering excellent service, yet under the law as it stands, while the compensation to them for carrying the mail is limited and regulated, and although railroads are made post-roads by law, there is no authority reposed anywhere to compel the owner of a railroad to take and carry the United States mails. The only alternative provided by act of Congress in case of refusal is for the Postmaster-General to send mail forward by pony express. This is but an illustration of ill-fitting legislation, reasonable and proper at the time of its enactment, but long since outgrown and requiring readjustment.

It is gratifying to note from the carefully prepared statistics accompanying the Postmaster-General's report that notwithstanding the great expansion of the service the rate of expenditure has been lessened and efficiency has been improved in every branch; that fraud and crime have decreased; that losses from the mails have been reduced, and that the number of complaints of the service made to postmasters and to the Department are far less than ever before.

The transactions of the Department of Justice for the fiscal year ended June 30, 1888, are contained in the report of the Attorney-General, as well as a number of valuable recommendations, the most part of which are repetitions of those previously made, and ought to receive consideration.

It is stated in this report that though judgments in civil suits amounting to $552,021.08 were recovered in favor of the Government during the year, only the sum of $132,934 was collected thereon; and that though fines, penalties, and forfeitures were imposed amounting to $541,808.43, only $109,648.42 of that sum was paid on account thereof. These facts may furnish an illustration of the sentiment which extensively prevails that a debt due the Government should cause no inconvenience to the citizen.

It also appears from this report that though prior to March, 1885, there had been but 6 convictions in the Territories of Utah and Idaho under the laws of 1862 and 1882, punishing polygamy and unlawful cohabitation as crimes, there have been since that date nearly 600 convictions under these laws and the statutes of 1887; and the opinion is expressed that under such a firm and vigilant execution of these laws and the advance of ideas opposed to the forbidden practices polygamy within the United States is virtually at an end.

Suits instituted by the Government under the provisions of the act of March 3, 1887, for the termination of the corporations known as the Perpetual Emigrating Fund Company and the Church of Jesus Christ of Latter-day Saints have resulted in a decree favorable to the Government, declaring the charters of these corporations forfeited and escheating their property. Such property, amounting in value to more than $800,000, is in the hands of a receiver pending further proceedings, an appeal having been taken to the Supreme Court of the United States.

In the report of the Secretary of the Interior, which will be laid before you, the condition of the various branches of our domestic affairs connected with that Department and its operations during the past year are fully exhibited. But a brief reference to some of the subjects discussed in this able and interesting report can here be made; but I commend the entire report to the attention of the Congress, and trust that the sensible and valuable recommendations it contains will secure careful consideration.

I can not too strenuously insist upon the importance of proper measures to insure a right disposition of our public lands, not only as a matter of present justice, but in forecast of the consequences to future generations. The broad, rich acres of our agricultural plains have been long preserved by nature to become her untrammeled gift to a people civilized and free, upon which should rest in well-distributed ownership the numerous homes of enlightened, equal, and fraternal citizens. They came to national possession with the warning example in our eyes of the entail of iniquities in landed proprietorship which other countries have permitted and still suffer. We have no excuse for the violation of principles cogently taught by reason and example, nor for the allowance of pretexts which have sometimes exposed our lands to colossal greed. Laws which open a door to fraudulent acquisition, or administration which permits favor to rapacious seizure by a favored few of expanded areas that many should enjoy, are accessory to offenses against our national welfare and humanity not to be too severely condemned or punished.

It is gratifying to know that something has been done at last to redress the injuries to our people and check the perilous tendency of the reckless waste of the national domain. That over 80,000,000 acres have been arrested from illegal usurpation, improvident grants, and fraudulent entries and claims, to be taken for the homesteads of honest industry—although less than the greater areas thus unjustly lost—must afford a profound gratification to right-feeling citizens, as it is a recompense for the labors and struggles of the recovery. Our dear experience ought sufficiently to urge the speedy enactment of measures of legislation which will confine the future disposition of our remaining agricultural lands to the uses of actual husbandry and genuine homes.

Nor should our vast tracts of so-called desert lands be yielded up to the monopoly of corporations or grasping individuals, as appears to be much the tendency under the existing statute. These lands require but the supply of water to become fertile and productive. It is a problem of great moment how most wisely for the public good that factor shall be furnished. I can not but think it perilous to suffer either these lands or the sources of their irrigation to fall into the hands of monopolies, which by such means may exercise lordship over the areas dependent on their treatment for productiveness. Already steps have been taken to secure accurate and scientific information of the conditions, which is the prime basis of intelligent action. Until this shall be gained the course of wisdom appears clearly to lie in a suspension of further disposal, which only promises to create rights antagonistic to the common interest. No harm can follow this cautionary conduct. The land will remain, and the public good presents no demand for hasty dispossession of national ownership and control.

I commend also the recommendations that appropriate measures be taken to complete the adjustment of the various grants made to the States for internal improvements and of swamp and overflowed lands, as well as to adjudicate and finally determine the validity and extent of the numerous private land claims. All these are elements of great injustice and peril to the settlers upon the localities affected; and now that their existence can not be avoided, no duty is more pressing than to fix as soon as possible their bounds and terminate the threats of trouble which arise from uncertainty.

The condition of our Indian population continues to improve and the proofs multiply that the transforming change, so much to be desired, which shall substitute for barbarism enlightenment and civilizing education, is in favorable progress. Our relations with these people during the year have been disturbed by no serious disorders, but rather marked by a better realization of their true interests and increasing confidence and good will. These conditions testify to the value of the higher tone of consideration and humanity which has governed the later methods of dealing with them, and commend its continued observance.

Allotments in severalty have been made on some reservations until all those entitled to land thereon have had their shares assigned, and the work is still continued. In directing the execution of this duty I have not aimed so much at rapid dispatch as to secure just and fair arrangements which shall best conduce to the objects of the law by producing satisfaction with the results of the allotments made. No measure of general effect has ever been entered on from which more may be fairly hoped if it shall be discreetly administered. It proffers opportunity and inducement to that independence of spirit and life which the Indian peculiarly needs, while at the same time the inalienability of title affords security against the risks his inexperience of affairs or weakness of character may expose him to in dealing with others. Whenever begun upon any reservation it should be made complete, so that all are brought to the same condition, and as soon as possible community in lands should cease by opening such as remain unallotted to settlement. Contact with the ways of industrious and successful farmers will perhaps add a healthy emulation which will both instruct and stimulate.

But no agency for the amelioration of this people appears to me so promising as the extension, urged by the Secretary, of such complete facilities of education as shall at the earliest possible day embrace all teachable Indian youth, of both sexes, and retain them with a kindly and beneficent hold until their characters are formed and their faculties and dispositions trained to the sure pursuit of some form of useful industry. Capacity of the Indian no longer needs demonstration. It is established. It remains to make the most of it, and when that shall be done the curse will be lifted, the Indian race saved, and the sin of their oppression redeemed. The time of its accomplishment depends upon the spirit and justice with which it shall be prosecuted. It can not be too soon for the Indian nor for the interests and good name of the nation.

The average attendance of Indian pupils on the schools increased by over 900 during the year, and the total enrollment reached 15,212. The cost of maintenance was not materially raised. The number of teachable Indian youth is now estimated at 40,000, or nearly three times the enrollment of the schools. It is believed the obstacles in the way of instructing are all surmountable, and that the necessary expenditure would be a measure of economy.

The Sioux tribes on the great reservation of Dakota refused to assent to the act passed by the Congress at its last session for opening a portion of their lands to settlement, notwithstanding modification of the terms was suggested which met most of their objections. Their demand is for immediate payment of the full price of $1.25 per acre for the entire body of land the occupancy of which they are asked to relinquish.

The manner of submission insured their fair understanding of the law, and their action was undoubtedly as thoroughly intelligent as their capacity admitted. It is at least gratifying that no reproach of over-reaching can in any manner lie against the Government, however advisable the favorable completion of the negotiation may have been esteemed.

I concur in the suggestions of the Secretary regarding the Turtle Mountain Indians, the two reservations in California, and the Crees. They should, in my opinion, receive immediate attention.

The number of pensioners added to the rolls during the fiscal year ended June 30, 1888, is 60,252, and increase of pensions was granted in 45,716 cases. The names of 15,730 pensioners were dropped from the rolls during the year from various causes, and at the close of the year the number of persons of all classes receiving pensions was 452,557. Of these there were 806 survivors of the War of 1812, 10,787 widows of those who served in that war, 16,060 soldiers of the Mexican War, and 5,104 widows of said soldiers.

One hundred and two different rates of pensions are paid to these beneficiaries, ranging from $2 to $416.66 per month.

The amount paid for pensions during the fiscal year was $78,775,861.92, being an increase over the preceding year of $5,308,280.22. The expenses attending the maintenance and operation of the Pension Bureau during that period was $3,262,524.67, making the entire expenditures of the Bureau $82,038,386.57, being 21½ per cent of the gross income and nearly 31 per cent of the total expenditures of the Government during the year.

I am thoroughly convinced that our general pension laws should be revised and adjusted to meet as far as possible, in the light of our experience, all meritorious cases. The fact that 102 different rates of pensions are paid can not, in my opinion, be made consistent with justice to the pensioners or to the Government; and the numerous private pension bills that are passed, predicated upon the imperfection of general laws, while they increase in many cases existing inequality and injustice, lend additional force to the recommendation for a revision of the general laws on this subject.

The laxity of ideas prevailing among a large number of our people regarding pensions is becoming every day more marked. The principles upon which they should be granted are in danger of being altogether ignored, and already pensions are often claimed because the applicants are as much entitled as other successful applicants, rather than upon any disability reasonably attributable to military service. If the establishment of vicious precedents be continued, if the granting of pensions be not divorced from partisan and other unworthy and irrelevant considerations, and if the honorable name of veteran unfairly becomes by these means but another term for one who constantly clamors for the

aid of the Government, there is danger that injury will be done t
fame and patriotism of many whom our citizens all delight to h
and that a prejudice will be aroused unjust to meritorious applicat
pension.

The Department of Agriculture has continued, with a good me
of success, its efforts to develop the processes, enlarge the result
augment the profits of American husbandry. It has collected an
tributed practical information, introduced and tested new plants, ch
the spread of contagious diseases of farm animals, resisted the ad
of noxious insects and destructive fungous growths, and sought to
to agricultural labor the highest reward of effort and the fullest
nity from loss. Its records of the year show that the season of 188
been one of medium production. A generous supply of the domes
consumption has been secured, and a surplus for exportation, and
in certain products and bountiful in others, will prove a benediction
to buyer and grower.

Four years ago it was found that the great cattle industry of the
try was endangered, and those engaged in it were alarmed at the
extension of the European lung plague of pleuro-pneumonia. Se
outbreaks existed in Illinois, Missouri, and Kentucky, and in Texa
animals affected were held in quarantine. Five counties in New
and from one to four counties in each of the States of New Jersey, 1
sylvania, Delaware, and Maryland were almost equally affected.

With this great danger upon us and with the contagion alrea
the channels of commerce, with the enormous direct and indirect
already being caused by it, and when only prompt and energetic
could be successful, there were in none of these States any laws an
izing this Department to eradicate the malady or giving the State
cials power to cooperate with it for this purpose. The Department
lacked both the requisite appropriation and authority.

By securing State cooperation in connection with authority from
gress the work of eradication has been pressed successfully, and
dreaded disease has been extirpated from the Western States and
from the Eastern States, with the exception of a few restricted a
which are still under supervision. The danger has thus been rem
and trade and commerce have been freed from the vexatious State r
tions which were deemed necessary for a time.

During the past four years the process of diffusion, as applied t
manufacture of sugar from sorghum and sugar cane, has been introd
into this country and fully perfected by the experiments carried
the Department of Agriculture. This process is now universally co
ered to be the most economical one, and it is through it that the
glucose-sugar industry has been established upon a firm basis an
road to its future success opened. The adoption of this diffusion
ess is also extending in Louisiana and other sugar-producing po

the country, and will doubtless soon be the only method employed for the extraction of sugar from the cane.

An exhaustive study has also within the same period been undertaken of the subject of food adulteration and the best analytical methods for detecting it. A part of the results of this work has already been published by the Department, which, with the matter in course of preparation, will make the most complete treatise on that subject that has ever been published in any country.

The Department seeks a progressive development. It would combine the discoveries of science with the economics and amelioration of rural practice. A supervision of the endowed experimental-station system recently provided for is a proper function of the Department, and is now in operation. This supervision is very important, and should be wisely and vigilantly directed, to the end that the pecuniary aid of the Government in favor of intelligent agriculture should be so applied as to result in the general good and to the benefit of all our people, thus justifying the appropriations made from the public Treasury.

The adjustment of the relations between the Government and the railroad companies which have received land grants and the guaranty of the public credit in aid of the construction of their roads should receive early attention. The report of a majority of the commissioners appointed to examine the affairs and indebtedness of these roads, in which they favor an extension of the time for the payment of such indebtedness in at least one case where the corporation appears to be able to comply with well-guarded and exact terms of such extension, and the reenforcement of their opinion by gentlemen of undoubted business judgment and experience, appointed to protect the interests of the Government as directors of said corporation, may well lead to the belief that such an extension would be to the advantage of the Government.

The subject should be treated as a business proposition with a view to a final realization of its indebtedness by the Government, rather than as a question to be decided upon prejudice or by way of punishment for previous wrongdoing.

The report of the Commissioners of the District of Columbia, with its accompanying documents, gives in detail the operations of the several departments of the District government, and furnishes evidence that the financial affairs of the District are at present in such satisfactory condition as to justify the Commissioners in submitting to the Congress estimates for desirable and needed improvements.

The Commissioners recommend certain legislation which in their opinion is necessary to advance the interests of the District.

I invite your special attention to their request for such legislation as will enable the Commissioners without delay to collect, digest, and properly arrange the laws by which the District is governed, and which are now embraced in several collections, making them available only with great difficulty and labor. The suggestions they make touching desirable amendments to the laws relating to licenses granted for carrying on the retail traffic in spirituous liquors, to the observance of Sunday, to the proper assessment and collection of taxes, to the speedy punishment of minor offenders, and to the management and control of the reformatory and charitable institutions supported by Congressional appropriations are commended to careful consideration.

I again call attention to the present inconvenience and the danger to life and property attending the operation of steam railroads through and across the public streets and roads of the District. The propriety of such legislation as will properly guard the use of these railroads and better secure the convenience and safety of citizens is manifest.

The consciousness that I have presented but an imperfect statement of the condition of our country and its wants occasions no fear that anything omitted is not known and appreciated by the Congress, upon whom rests the responsibility of intelligent legislation in behalf of a great nation and a confiding people.

As public servants we shall do our duty well if we constantly guard the rectitude of our intentions, maintain unsullied our love of country, and with unselfish purpose strive for the public good.

GROVER CLEVELAND.

SPECIAL MESSAGES.

To the Congress: EXECUTIVE MANSION, *December 21, 1888.*

On the 2d of April last I transmitted to the House of Representatives, in response to its resolution of the 8th of the preceding March, a report of the Secretary of State, with accompanying correspondence, relative to affairs in Samoa.* On the same day I answered a resolution of the Senate of the 21st of the preceding December to the same effect, but adopted in executive session, and, in order to avoid duplication of the numerous documents involved, referred to the correspondence which accompanied my public response to the resolution of the House of Representatives, and which was duly printed and published by order of that body (House Executive Document No. 238, Fiftieth Congress, first session).

In my annual message of the 3d instant I announced my intention in due course to lay before Congress further correspondence on Samoan affairs. Accordingly, I now transmit a report of the Secretary of State, with accompanying correspondence, on that subject.

GROVER CLEVELAND.

*See p. 612.

To the Senate:

On or about the 25th day of September, 1888, I received a copy of a resolution adopted on that day by the Senate in executive session, requesting the transmission to that body by the President of all communications and correspondence (not heretofore sent to the Senate) under his control on the subject of the proposed convention with China, transmitted by him to the Senate by message dated 16th March, 1888,* and on the subject of the reported failure of the Government of China to finally agree to the same.

A few days after the copy of said resolution was received by me, and on the 1st day of October, 1888, I sent a communication to the Congress,† accompanying my approval of a bill prohibiting the return of Chinese laborers to the United States, in which I supposed all the information sought under the terms of the Senate resolution above recited was fully supplied.

I beg to refer in this connection to Senate Executive Document No. 273, first session of the Fiftieth Congress, and especially to page 3 thereof.

Believing the information contained in said document answered the purposes of said Senate resolution, no separate and explicit answer was made thereto.

But in my message of October 1, 1888, the tenor and purport of a cipher dispatch from our minister in China to the Secretary of State, dated September 21, 1888, was given instead of attempting to transmit a copy of the same.

For greater precision, however, and with the object of answering in more exact terms the resolution of the Senate, I transmit with this, in paraphrase of the cipher, a copy of the said dispatch. I also transmit copies of two notes which accompanied my message of October 1, 1888, one from Mr. Shu Cheon Pon, chargé d'affaires of the Chinese legation in this city, dated September 25, 1888, to the Secretary of State, and the other being the reply thereto by the Secretary of State, dated September 26, 1888, both of which will be found in Senate Executive Document No. 273.

The dispatch and notes above referred to comprise, in the language of the Senate resolution, "all communications and correspondence" the transmission of which is therein requested.

GROVER CLEVELAND.

EXECUTIVE MANSION, *January 3, 1889.*

To the Senate and House of Representatives:

I transmit herewith for the consideration of the Congress a report of the Secretary of State, with accompanying papers, recommending an

---

* See p. 610.   † See pp. 630–635.

appropriation for the relief of Japanese subjects injured and of the families of Japanese subjects killed on the island of Ikisima in consequence of target practice directed against the shore by the United States man-of-war *Omaha* in March, 1887.

GROVER CLEVELAND.

EXECUTIVE MANSION, *January 3, 1889.*

To the Senate:

I desire to supplement the message yesterday sent to your honorable body in response to a Senate executive resolution dated September 25, 1888, asking the transmission of certain communications and correspondence on the subject of the recent proposed convention with China and the reported failure of the Government of China to finally agree to the same, by adding to said response two telegrams I omitted therefrom, which were sent in cipher by the Secretary of State to our minister at Peking, and which may be considered by the Senate relevant to the subject of its inquiry.

One of said dispatches is as follows:

WASHINGTON, *September 4, 1888.*

DENBY,
   Minister, Peking:

Rejection of treaty is reported here. What information have you?

BAYARD.

Two replies to this dispatch were made by our minister to China, dated, respectively, September 5 and September 6, 1888. They were heretofore, and on September 7, 1888,* sent to the Senate, and are printed in Senate Executive Document No. 271.

The other of said dispatches is as follows:

WASHINGTON, *September 18, 1888.*

DENBY,
   Minister, Peking:

The bill has passed both Houses of Congress for total exclusion of Chinese and awaits President's approval. Public feeling on the Pacific Coast excited in favor of it, and situation is critical. Impress upon Government of China necessity for instant decision in the interest of treaty relations and amity.

BAYARD.

The answer of our minister at Peking to this dispatch, dated September 21, 1888, was yesterday sent to the Senate with the message to which this is a supplement.

The matters herein contained are now transmitted, to the end that they may, if deemed pertinent, be added to the response already made to the Senate resolution of inquiry, and with the intent that in any view of the subject the answer to said resolution may be full and complete.

GROVER CLEVELAND.

*See p. 627.

To the Senate:

I transmit, with a view to its ratification, an agreement signed by the plenipotentiaries of the United States and Denmark on the 6th ultimo, submitting to arbitration the claim of Carlos Butterfield & Co. against the Government of Denmark for indemnity for the seizure and detention of the steamer *Ben Franklin* and the bark *Catherine Augusta* by the authorities of the island of St. Thomas, of the Danish West India Islands, in the years 1854 and 1855; for the refusal of the ordinary right to land cargo for the purpose of making repairs; for the injuries resulting from a shot fired into one of the vessels, and for other wrongs. I also transmit a report from the Secretary of State inclosing the recent correspondence between the two Governments in regard to the claim.

GROVER CLEVELAND.

To the Senate and House of Representatives:

Whereas, by virtue of the provisions of the act of Congress approved June 22, 1860 (12 U. S. Statutes at Large, p. 73), entitled "An act to carry into effect provisions of the treaties between the United States, China, Japan, Siam, Persia, and other countries giving certain judicial powers to ministers and consuls or other functionaries of the United States in those countries, and for other purposes," Charles Denby, minister of the United States at Peking, has formally promulgated, under date of August 18, 1888, additional regulations governing the rendition of judgments by confession in the consular courts of the United States in China, the same having been previously assented to by all the consular officers of this Government in that Empire:

Now, therefore, in accordance with section 4119 of the Revised Statutes of the United States, being the sixth section of the act above mentioned, and which directs that all such regulations shall be transmitted to the Secretary of State, "to be laid before Congress for revision," I do herewith transmit to Congress a copy of Mr. Denby's dispatch No. 754, of November 5, 1888, containing the regulations so decreed.

GROVER CLEVELAND.

To the Senate and House of Representatives:

I transmit herewith, for the consideration of Congress and such legislation in respect of the matters therein presented as may seem necessary and proper, a report of the Secretary of State, with accompanying explanatory correspondence, in reference to the international questions arising from the imposition of differential rates of tonnage dues upon vessels entering ports of the United States from foreign countries under the provisions of the fourteenth section of the act of June 26, 1884, and the later amendatory provisions of the act of June 19, 1886, as set forth in said report.

GROVER CLEVELAND.

EXECUTIVE MANSION, *January 15, 1889.*

To the Congress:

On the 2d day of April, 1888, I transmitted to the House of Representatives, in response to a resolution passed by that body, a report from the Secretary of State, relating to the condition of affairs in the Samoan Islands, together with numerous letters, dispatches, and documents connected with the subject, which gave a history of all disorders in that locality up to that date.*

On the 21st day of December, 1888, this information was supplemented by the transmission to the Congress of such further correspondence and documents as extended this history to that time.†

I now submit a report from the Secretary of State, with later correspondence and dispatches, exhibiting the progress of the disturbances in Samoa up to the present date.

The information thus laid before the Congress is of much importance, since it has relation to the preservation of American interests and the protection of American citizens and their property in a distant locality and under an unstable and unsatisfactory government.

In the midst of the disturbances which have arisen at Samoa such powers have been exercised as seemed to be within Executive control under our Constitution and laws, and which appear to accord with our national policy and traditions, to restore tranquillity and secure the safety of our citizens.

Through negotiation and agreement with Great Britain and Germany, which, with our own Government, constitute the treaty powers interested in Samoan peace and quiet, the attempt has been made to define more clearly the part which these powers should assume in the Government of that country, while at the same time its autonomy has been insisted upon.

These negotiations were at one time interrupted by such action on the part of the German Government as appeared to be inconsistent with their further continuance.

Germany, however, still asserts, as from the first she has done, that she has no desire or intention to overturn the native Samoan Government or to ignore our treaty rights, and she still invites our Government to join her in restoring peace and quiet. But thus far her propositions on this subject seem to lead to such a preponderance of German power in Samoa as was never contemplated by us and is inconsistent with every prior

*See p. 612.   †See p. 800.

agreement or understanding, while her recent conduct as between native warring factions gives rise to the suspicion that she is not content with a neutral position.

Acting within the restraints which our Constitution and laws have placed upon Executive power, I have insisted that the autonomy and independence of Samoa should be scrupulously preserved according to the treaties made with Samoa by the powers named and their agreements and understanding with each other. I have protested against every act apparently tending in an opposite direction, and during the existence of internal disturbance one or more vessels of war have been kept in Samoan waters to protect American citizens and property.

These things will abundantly appear from the correspondence and papers which have been submitted to the Congress.

A recent collision between the forces from a German man-of-war stationed in Samoan waters and a body of natives rendered the situation so delicate and critical that the war ship *Trenton*, under the immediate command of Admiral Kimberly, was ordered to join the *Nipsic*, already at Samoa, for the better protection of the persons and property of our citizens and in furtherance of efforts to restore order and safety.

The attention of the Congress is especially called to the instructions given to Admiral Kimberly dated on the 11th instant and the letter of the Secretary of State to the German minister dated the 12th instant, which will be found among the papers herewith submitted.

By means of the papers and documents heretofore submitted and those which accompany this communication the precise situation of affairs in Samoa is laid before the Congress, and such Executive action as has been taken is fully exhibited.

The views of the Executive in respect of the just policy to be pursued with regard to this group of islands, which lie in the direct highway of a growing and important commerce between Australia and the United States, have found expression in the correspondence and documents which have thus been fully communicated to the Congress, and the subject in its present stage is submitted to the wider discretion conferred by the Constitution upon the legislative branch of the Government.

GROVER CLEVELAND.

EXECUTIVE MANSION, *January 15, 1889.*

To the Senate of the United States:

I transmit herewith, in response to the resolution of the Senate of the 4th instant, a report of the Secretary of State, with accompanying copies of correspondence, touching recent occurrences in the island of Hayti, both as relates to the state of the Government there and to the seizure and delivery up of the American vessel *Haytien Republic*.

GROVER CLEVELAND.

EXECUTIVE MANSION, *January 16, 1889.*

To the Senate and House of Representatives:

I have the honor to lay before you a report from the Secretary of State, with accompanying correspondence, in relation to the possible disturbances on the Isthmus of Panama in the event of the stoppage of work on the proposed interoceanic canal.   GROVER CLEVELAND.

EXECUTIVE MANSION, *January 21, 1889.*

To the Senate of the United States:

I transmit herewith, in response to a resolution of the Senate of the 5th instant, a report of the Secretary of State, touching correspondence with Venezuela in regard to the exchange of ratifications of the claims convention of December 5, 1885, between the United States and Venezuela and to the suspension by Venezuela of the monthly quotas of indebtedness under the convention between the two countries of April 25, 1866, together with copies of sundry correspondence between the Department of State and owners of Venezuelan certificates of award or their attorneys on the same subject, as requested in said resolution.

GROVER CLEVELAND.

EXECUTIVE MANSION, *January 30, 1889.*

To the Senate and the House of Representatives:

For the information of Congress I herewith transmit a report of the Secretary of State, with accompanying correspondence, relating to the execution of an agreement made between the representatives of certain foreign powers and the Korean Government in 1884 in respect to a foreign settlement at Chemulpo.   GROVER CLEVELAND.

To the Congress: EXECUTIVE MANSION, *January 30, 1889.*

I had the honor on the 15th instant to communicate to your honorable body certain correspondence and documents in relation to affairs in the Samoan Islands;* and having since that date received further dispatches from the vice-consul at Apia and the commander of the United States naval vessel *Nipsic* in those waters, I lose no time in laying them before you.

I also transmit herewith the full text of an instruction from Prince von Bismarck to the German minister at this capital, which was communicated to the Secretary of State on the afternoon of the 28th instant.

This appears to be an amplification of a prior telegraphic instruction on the same subject communicated through the same channel, and, being set forth in the note of the Secretary of State to Count von Arco-Valley,

*See pp. 804-805.

the German minister, of the 12th instant, was duly laid before Congress with my last message in relation to Samoan affairs.

It is also proper to inform you that on Monday, the 28th instant, the occasion of the communication of the note of the Prince Chancellor, the Secretary of State was given to understand by the German minister that a proposition from his Government to that of the United States for a conference on the Samoan subject was on its way by mail, having left Berlin on the 20th instant, so that its arrival here in due course of mail could be looked for in a very short time.

In reply to an inquiry from the Secretary of State whether the proposition referred to was for a renewal of the joint conference between the United States, Germany, and Great Britain which was suspended in July, 1887, or for a consideration of Samoan affairs *ab novo*, the German minister stated his inability to answer until the proposition which left Berlin on the 20th instant should have been received.

I shall hereafter communicate to the Congress all information received by me in relation to the Samoan status.

GROVER CLEVELAND.

EXECUTIVE MANSION,
Washington, February 1, 1889.

To the Senate and House of Representatives:

As supplementary to my previous messages on the subject, I have now the honor to transmit a report from the Secretary of State relating to affairs in Samoa.

GROVER CLEVELAND.

EXECUTIVE MANSION, *February 5, 1889.*

To the Congress:

I transmit herewith, for approval and ratification, a provisional agreement lately entered into between the Government of the United States and the Creek Nation of Indians, through their duly authorized representatives, and which has been approved by the National Council of said nation, by which agreement the title and interest of the said Creek Nation of Indians in and to all lands in the Indian Territory or elsewhere, except such as are held and occupied as the homes of said nation, are ceded to the United States.

The eighth section of the Indian appropriation bill approved March 3, 1885, authorized the President "to open negotiations with the Creeks, Seminoles, and Cherokees for the purpose of opening to settlement under the homestead laws the unassigned lands in the Indian Territory ceded by them respectively to the United States by the several treaties of August 11, 1866, March 21, 1866, and July 19, 1866." This section also contains an appropriation in furtherance of its purpose, and requires that the action of the President thereunder should be reported to Congress.

The "unassigned" lands thus referred to should be construed to be those which have not been transferred by the United States in pursuance of the treaties mentioned in the section quoted.

The treaty with the Creeks is dated June 14, 1866. It was confirmed by a Senate resolution passed July 19, 1866, and was proclaimed August 11, 1866 (14 U. S. Statutes at Large, p. 785).

The third article of the treaty makes a cession of lands in the following words:

In compliance with the desire of the United States to locate other Indians and freedmen thereon, the Creeks hereby cede and convey to the United States, to be sold to and used as homes for such other civilized Indians as the United States may choose to settle thereon, the west half of their entire domain, to be divided by a line running north and south; the eastern half of said Creek lands, being retained by them, shall, except as herein otherwise stipulated, be forever set apart as a home for said Creek Nation; and in consideration of said cession of the west half of their lands, estimated to contain 3,250,560 acres, the United States agree to pay the sum of 30 cents per acre, amounting to $975,168.

The provision that the lands conveyed were "*to be sold to* and used as homes for such other civilized Indians," etc., has been steadily regarded as a limitation upon the grant made to the United States. Such a construction is admitted to be the true one in many ways, especially by the continual reservation of the ceded lands from settlement by the whites, by the sale of a portion of the same to Indians, by the use of other portions as the home of Indians, and also by various provisions in proposed legislation in Congress. Thus the bill now pending for the organization of Oklahoma provides for the payment to the Creeks and Seminoles of the ordinary Government price of $1.25 per acre, less the amount heretofore paid.

The section of the law of 1885 first above quoted appears also to have been passed in contemplation not only of the existence of a claim on the part of the Creeks, but of the substantial foundation of that claim in equity, if not in law, and in acknowledgment of the duty of the Government to satisfactorily discharge the claim of the Indian people before putting the land to the free uses of settlement and territorial occupation by whites.

But it seems to have been considered that so far as the lands had been assigned they may fairly be taken to be such as under the treaty were "to be sold." As to these, they having been assigned or "sold" in accordance with said treaty, the claim of the Creeks thereto has been entirely discharged, and the title from the United States passed unburdened with any condition or limitation to the grantees. This seems to be an entirely clear proposition.

The unassigned lands must be those which are unsold, because not only is that the fair significance of the term, as used technically in conveyancing, but because the limiting condition in the Creek treaty was that the lands should be sold to, as well as used as homes for, other Indians.

The total quantity of lands in the western half of the Creek Nation, and
which were ceded in 1866, is.. 3,402,428.88 Acres.

The assigned lands as above defined are in three bodies: Acres.

  1. The Seminole country, by the treaty of 1866................ 200,000.00

  2. The Sac and Fox Reservation, sold and conveyed by article
    6 of the treaty of February 18, 1867 (15 U. S. Statutes at
    Large, p. 495), amounting to................ .... 479,668.05

  3. The Pawnee Reservation, granted by section 4 of the act of
    Congress of April 10, 1876 (19 U. S. Statutes at Large, p. 29),
    for which the Government received the price allowed the
    Creeks, 30 cents per acre................................... 53,005.94

Making a total of assigned or sold lands of..... .... 732,673.99

And leaving as the total unassigned lands 2,669,754.89

Of this total quantity of unassigned land which is subject to the negotiations provided for under the law of 1885 there should be a further
division made in considering the sum which ought fairly to be paid in
discharge of the Creek claim thereto.

I. In that part of these lands called the Oklahoma country no Indians
have been allowed to reside by any action of the Government, nor has
any execution been attempted of the limiting condition of the cession
of 1866.

The quantity of these lands carefully computed from the surveys is
1,392,704.70 acres.

II. The remainder of these unassigned lands has been appropriated
in some degree to Indian uses, although still within the control of the
Government.

Thus by three Executive orders the following Indian reservations have
been created:

  1. By President Grant, August 10, 1869, the reservation of the Cheyennes and
    Arapahoes, which embraces of this land.............................. . 619,450.59 Acres.

  2. By President Arthur, August 15, 1883, the reservation for the Iowas, con-
    taining.. 228,417.67

  3. By President Arthur, August 15, 1883, the Kickapoo Reservation, embra-
    cing.. 206,465.61

  4. A tract set apart for the Pottawatomies by the treaty of February 27, 1867
    (15 U. S. Statutes at Large, p. 531), followed by the act of May 23, 1872 (17
    U. S. Statutes at Large, p. 159), by which individual allotments were au-
    thorized upon the tract, though but very few Indians have selected and
    paid for such allotments according to the provisions of that law. The
    entire quantity of the Pottawatomie Reservation is..................... 222,716.32

    This shows the quantity of lands unassigned, but to some extent ap-
    propriated to Indian uses by the Government, amounting to....... 1,277,050.19

For the lands which are not only unassigned, but are unoccupied, and
which have been in no way appropriated, it appears clearly just and right
that a price of at least $1.25 should be allowed to the Creeks. They
held more than the ordinary Indian title, for they had a patent in fee
from the Government. The Osages of Kansas were allowed $1.25 per
acre upon giving up their reservation, and this land of the Creeks is
reported by those familiar with it to be equal to any land in the country. Without regard to the present enhanced value of this land, and if
reference be·only had to the conditions when the cession was made, no

less price ought to be paid for it than the ordinary Government price. Therefore in this provisional agreement which has been made with the Creeks the price of $1.25 has been settled upon for such land, with the deduction of the 30 cents per acre which has already been paid by the Government therefor.

As to the remainder of the unassigned lands, in view of the fact that some use has been made of them of the general character indicated by the treaty of 1866, and because some portion of them should be allotted to Indians under the general allotment act, and to cover the expenses of surveys and adjustments, a diminishment of 20 cents per acre has been acceded to. There is no difference in the character of the lands.

Thus, computing the unassigned and entirely unappropriated land, being the Oklahoma country, containing 1,392,704.70 acres, at 95 cents per acre, and the remainder which has been appropriated to the extent above stated, being 1,277,050.19 acres, at 75 cents per acre, the total price stipulated in the agreement has been reached—$2,280,857.10.

But as it was desirable that the Indian title should be beyond all question extinguished to all parts of the land ceded by the Creeks in 1866, with their full consent and understanding, the agreement of cession has been made to embrace a complete surrender of all claim to the western half of their domain, including the assigned as well as the unassigned lands, for the price named. So the agreement takes the form in the first article of such a cession, and in the second article is stipulated the price in gross of all the lands and interests ceded, with no detailed reference to the manner of its ascertainment.

The overtures which led to this agreement were made by representatives of the Creek Nation, who came here for that purpose. They were intelligent and evidently loyal to the interests of their people. The terms of the agreement were fully discussed and concessions were made by both parties. It was promptly confirmed by the National Council of the Creek Indians, and its complete consummation only waits the approval of the Congress of the United States.

I am convinced that such ratification will be of decided benefit to the Government, and that the agreement is entirely free from any suspicion of unfairness or injustice toward the Indians.

I desire to call especial attention to the fact that to become effective the agreement must be ratified by the Congress prior to the 1st day of July, 1889.

The draft of an act of ratification is herewith submitted.

                                        GROVER CLEVELAND.

EXECUTIVE MANSION, *February 8, 1889.*

To the Senate and House of Representatives:

I transmit herewith a further report of the Secretary of State, with accompanying correspondence, relating to Samoa, and the joint protocols

of the conferences held in this city in the summer of 1887, to the publication of which the Governments of Germany and Great Britain have consented.
                                                    GROVER CLEVELAND.

To the Senate: EXECUTIVE MANSION, *February 8, 1889.*

In response to the resolution of the Senate of the 23d ultimo, directing the Secretary of State to transmit to that body copies of all correspondence on the files of his Department relative to the case of the ship *Bridgewater*, I transmit herewith, being of the opinion that it is not incompatible with the public interest to do so, a report from the Secretary of State, accompanying which is the correspondence referred to.
                                                    GROVER CLEVELAND.

To the Senate: EXECUTIVE MANSION, *February 12, 1889.*

I herewith transmit, in reply to the resolution of the Senate of the 2d ultimo, a report from the Secretary of State, with the accompanying documents, in relation to the seal fisheries in Bering Sea.
                                                    GROVER CLEVELAND.

To the Congress: EXECUTIVE MANSION, *February 19, 1889.*

I herewith submit, for your consideration, a communication from the Secretary of the Interior, transmitting a proposition made on behalf of the Seminole Nation of Indians for the relinquishment to the Government of the United States of their right to certain lands in the Indian Territory.
                                                    GROVER CLEVELAND.

                                    EXECUTIVE MANSION, *February 19, 1889.*
To the Senate of the United States:

In compliance with a resolution of the Senate of the 18th instant, I return herewith the bill (S. 3640) entitled "An act to amend the laws relating to the selection and service of jurors in the supreme court of the District of Columbia."
                                                    GROVER CLEVELAND.

                                    EXECUTIVE MANSION, *February 20, 1889.*
To the Senate and House of Representatives:

I transmit herewith a report of the Secretary of State of this day's date, with accompanying correspondence, touching the case of Lord Sackville.*
                                                    GROVER CLEVELAND.

* The British minister at Washington, who was given his passports for writing an indiscreet letter on American politics.

EXECUTIVE MANSION,
Washington, February 22, 1889.

To the Senate:

I transmit herewith, with a view to its ratification, a convention signed on the 2d day of June, 1887, between the United States and the Netherlands, for the extradition of criminals; also a report from the Secretary of State, and accompanying papers, relating to the said convention.

GROVER CLEVELAND.

EXECUTIVE MANSION,
Washington, February 27, 1889.

To the Senate:

I herewith transmit, for the consideration of the Senate with a view to its ratification, a convention signed at Washington the 18th instant, between the United States and Mexico, to revive the provisions of the convention of July 29, 1882, to survey and relocate the existing boundary line between the two countries west of the Rio Grande, and to extend the time fixed in Article VIII of the said convention for the completion of the work in question.

Although the present convention fully explains the reasons for its negotiation, it may not be improper here to add that Article VII of the convention of July 29, 1882, stipulated that the said convention should continue in force until the completion of the work, "provided that such time does not exceed four years and four months from the date of the exchange of ratifications hereof."

The exchange of ratifications took place March 3, 1883, and the period within which the convention was in force ended July 3, 1887.

In order, therefore, to continue the provisions of the said convention of July 29, 1882, an additional article concluded at Washington December 5, 1885, further extended the time for the completion of the work for "eighteen months from the expiration of the term fixed in Article VIII of the said treaty of July 29, 1882," or until January 3, 1889.

As there was no further provision extending the said treaty of July 29, 1882, beyond that date, it expired by limitation. Hence the necessity for the convention of the 18th instant in its present form.

GROVER CLEVELAND.

EXECUTIVE MANSION,
Washington, February 27, 1889.

To the Senate:

I transmit herewith, in confidence, for the information of the Senate, a report from the Secretary of State, showing the progress of the correspondence in relation to the conference to be held at Berlin between the Governments of the United States, Germany, and Great Britain to settle the affairs of the Samoan Islands.

The nature of this information and the stage of the negotiations thus agreed upon and about to commence at Berlin make it proper that such report should be communicated to the Senate in the confidence of executive session.

As the conference has been proposed and accepted and the definitive bases of its proceedings agreed upon by all three Governments and on the lines with which the Senate has heretofore been made fully acquainted, nothing remains to be done but to select and appoint the commissioners to represent the United States, and the performance of this duty, in view of the few days that now remain of my term of office, can be most properly left to my successor.

In response to the inquiry of the German minister at this capital whether the names of the proposed representatives of the United States at the conference in Berlin could at once be given to him, he has been informed that the appointments in question would be made by my successor and not by me, and that in coming to this decision the expedition desired by Germany in the work of the conference would in my judgment be promoted.

GROVER CLEVELAND.

EXECUTIVE MANSION,
Washington, February 27, 1889.

To the Senate:

I transmit, with a view to its ratification, a convention for the extradition of criminals, signed by the plenipotentiaries of the United States and Russia on the 28th day of March, 1887; also a report from the Secretary of State and accompanying papers relating to the negotiations which terminated in the conclusion of the treaty in question.

GROVER CLEVELAND.

EXECUTIVE MANSION,
Washington, February 27, 1889.

To the Senate:

I herewith transmit a report of the Secretary of State and accompanying documents, relative to a naturalization treaty between the United States and Turkey signed the 11th day of August, 1874, as to the proclamation of which the advice of the Senate is desired. The advice and consent of the Senate were given to the ratification of the convention on the 22d of January, 1875, but with certain amendments which were not fully accepted by the Ottoman Porte. Because of such nonacceptance the treaty has never been proclaimed. Finally the Turkish Government, after the passage of fourteen years, has accepted the amendments as tendered. But in view of the long period that has elapsed since the Senate formerly considered the treaty I have deemed it wiser that before proclaiming it the Senate should have an opportunity to act upon the matter again, my own views being wholly favorable to the proclamation.

GROVER CLEVELAND.

EXECUTIVE MANSION,
Washington, February 27, 1889.

To the House of Representatives:

I transmit herewith, in response to the resolution of the House of Representatives of the 21st of December last, a report of the Secretary of State and accompanying documents, touching affairs in Madagascar.

GROVER CLEVELAND.

EXECUTIVE MANSION, *February 28, 1889.*

To the Senate of the United States:

I have the honor to transmit herewith a report of the Secretary of State, concerning the expenses of the representation of the United States at the Brussels Exhibition of 1888.

GROVER CLEVELAND.

[The same message was sent to the House of Representatives.]

EXECUTIVE MANSION, *February 28, 1889.*

To the Senate of the United States:

I have the honor to transmit herewith a report of the Secretary of State, respecting the representation of the United States at the Barcelona Exposition of 1888.

GROVER CLEVELAND.

[The same message was sent to the House of Representatives.]

EXECUTIVE MANSION, *March 2, 1889.*

To the Congress:

I herewith transmit the fifth report of the Civil Service Commission, covering the year which ended June 30, 1888.

The cause of civil-service reform, which in a great degree is intrusted to the Commission, I regard as so firmly established and its value so fully demonstrated that I should deem it more gratifying than useful if at this late day in the session of Congress I was permitted to enlarge upon its importance and present condition.

A perusal of the report herewith submitted will furnish information of the progress which has been made during the year to which it relates in the extension of the operations of this reform and in the improvement of its methods and rules.

It is cause for congratulation that watchfulness and care and fidelity to its purposes are all that are necessary to insure to the Government and our people all the benefits which its inauguration promised.

GROVER CLEVELAND.

EXECUTIVE MANSION,
Washington, March 2, 1889.

To the Senate of the United States:

I transmit herewith, for the consideration of the Senate with a view of giving its advice and consent to the ratification thereof, a convention signed in Washington on March 1, 1889, by duly authorized representatives of the United States and Mexico, providing for the institution of an international commission to determine questions between the United States and Mexico arising under the convention of November 12, 1884, by reason of changes in the river bed of the Rio Grande and the Colorado River when forming the boundary between the two countries.

A report of the Secretary of State, with the accompanying correspondence therein described, is also communicated for the information of the Senate.

GROVER CLEVELAND.

EXECUTIVE MANSION, *March 2, 1889.*

To the Senate and House of Representatives:

I herewith transmit a report of the Secretary of State and accompanying documents, relative to the undetermined boundary line between Alaska and British Columbia.

GROVER CLEVELAND.

EXECUTIVE MANSION, *March 2, 1889.*

To the House of Representatives:

I herewith transmit a report from the Secretary of State, in further response to the resolution of the House of Representatives of the 22d [21st] of December last, touching affairs in Madagascar.

GROVER CLEVELAND.

To the Senate:

EXECUTIVE MANSION, *March 2, 1889.*

I herewith transmit, for the information of Congress, a report from the Secretary of State, with its accompanying correspondence, in regard to the construction of certain dams or wing facings in the Rio Grande at Paso del Norte (Ciudad Juarez), opposite the city of El Paso, Tex.

GROVER CLEVELAND.

EXECUTIVE MANSION, *March 2, 1889.*

To the Senate of the United States:

I have the honor to transmit herewith a communication from the Secretary of State, covering the report of the commissioner of the United States to the Brussels Exhibition of 1888.

GROVER CLEVELAND.

VETO MESSAGES.

EXECUTIVE MANSION, *December 19, 1888.*

To the House of Representatives:

I return without approval House bill No. 5080, entitled "An act for the relief of C. B. Wilson."

This bill directs the Postmaster-General to credit to the beneficiary therein named, who is the postmaster at Buena Vista, in the State of Colorado, the sum of $225, being post-office funds forwarded by him to the deposit office at Denver, but which were lost in transmission.

A general law was passed on the 9th day of May, 1888, authorizing the Postmaster-General to make allowances and credits to postmasters in precisely such cases.

On the 8th day of September, 1888, under the sanction of that law, the credit directed by this bill was made.

It is plain, therefore, that the bill herewith returned ought not to become a law unless it is proposed to duplicate the credit therein mentioned.

GROVER CLEVELAND.

EXECUTIVE MANSION, *January 16, 1889.*

To the House of Representatives:

I return without approval House bill No. 8469, entitled "An act for the relief of Michael Pigott."

This bill appropriates the sum of $48 to the beneficiary therein named, formerly the postmaster at Quincy, Ill., which was paid by him for the use of a telephone for the year ending June 30, 1873.

There is evidently a mistake made in the statement of the period covered by the use of this telephone, for the official term of the beneficiary extended from May 16, 1881, to June 18, 1885.

Assuming, however, that it was intended to describe the period ending June 30, 1883, it appears that the use of a telephone during that time was wholly unauthorized by the Post-Office Department, and that the only authority given for any expenditure for that purpose covered the period of one year from the 1st day of January, 1884.

The following letter, dated July 16, 1884, was sent to the beneficiary from the salary and allowance division of the Post-Office Department:

In reply to your letter relative to amounts disallowed for use of telephone for your office, you are informed that the said expenditures were made without the authority of this office, and it is therefore deemed advisable not to approve the same.

Your authority for a telephone was for one year beginning January 1, 1884. At the expiration of the time named, if you desire to continue the telephone service, you should make application to the First Assistant Postmaster-General for a renewal of the same.

The multitude of claims of the same kind which the legislation proposed would breed and encourage, and the absolute necessity, in the interest of good administration, of limiting all public officers to authorized expenditures, constrain me to withhold my approval from this bill.

GROVER CLEVELAND.

EXECUTIVE MANSION, *January 16, 1889.*
To the House of Representatives:

I return without approval House bill No. 7, entitled "An act granting a pension to Thomas B. Walsh."

This beneficiary enlisted January 1, 1864, and was discharged August 1, 1865.

He is reported absent without leave in April, 1864, and further recorded as having deserted November 24, 1864. He was restored to duty in May, 1865, by the President's proclamation.

He filed an application for pension in December, 1881, alleging that he contracted rheumatism in May, 1865.

This statement of the claimant and nearly, if not all, the evidence in the case which tends to show the incurrence of the disability complained of appear to fix its appearance at a date very near the return of the beneficiary after his desertion.

In these circumstances the proof of disability, such as it is, is as consistent with its incurrence during desertion as it is with the theory that the beneficiary suffered therefrom as the result of honorable military service.

GROVER CLEVELAND.

EXECUTIVE MANSION, *January 16, 1889.*
To the House of Representatives:

I return without approval House bill No. 2236, entitled "An act granting a pension to Eli. J. Yamgheim."

The beneficiary named in this bill filed an application for pension in the Pension Bureau April 15, 1875, basing his claim upon an alleged wound of his left leg from a spent ball about October 15, 1861.

There is no record of his incurring any wound or injury during his service, and it does not appear that the company to which he belonged was in action nearer to the date he specifies than September 17, 1861, and his captain testifies that the beneficiary was not injured in the engagement of that day, which lasted only about fifteen minutes.

The proof taken in the case establishes that before enlistment the beneficiary had a sore on his leg which was quite troublesome, which suppurated, and after healing would break out again.

In the medical examinations made during the pendency of t.

the diseased leg was always found, but no mention is made of any oth
injury and no other injury seems to have been discoverable.

I can not avoid the conviction upon the facts presented that whatev
disability has existed since the discharge of the beneficiary arose fro
causes which were present before enlistment, and that the same is n
chargeable to his military service.   GROVER CLEVELAND.

EXECUTIVE MANSION, *January 16, 1889.*

To the House of Representatives:

I return without approval House bill No. 4887, entitled "An act gran
ing a pension to Charles E. Scott."

This beneficiary entered the volunteer service nearly at the close of tl
War of the Rebellion and served from the 8th day of March, 1865, to Ju
24, in the same year, a period of four months and sixteen days.

He filed a claim for pension in 1884, alleging that he incurred can
itch in July, 1865, which resulted in partial blindness.

Upon the proof presented, and after examination, the claim was r
jected upon the ground that it did not appear that the impairment of l
vision was the result of any incident of his army service.

I am entirely satisfied that this was a correct disposition of the cas
and that upon the same ground the bill herewith returned should not l
approved.   GROVER CLEVELAND.

To the Senate: EXECUTIVE MANSION, *January 17, 1889.*

I return without approval Senate bill No. 3646, entitled "An act f
the relief of William R. Wheaton and Charles H. Chamberlain, of Ca
fornia."

These parties were, respectively, for a number of years prior to 187
the register and receiver of the land office at San Francisco, in the Sta
of California.

Prior to July, 1877, they had collected and retained, apparently witho
question, certain fees allowed by law for reducing to writing the testimo
heard by them in establishing the rights of claimants to public lands.

On the 9th day of July, 1877, these officials were notified by the Actii
Commissioner of the General Land Office that monthly thereafter
dating from July 1, 1877, such fees should be reported with other fees
the General Land Office.

This notification furnished clear information that, whatever may ha
been the justification for their retention of these fees in the past, the pa
ties notified must thereafter account to the Government for the same.

On the 8th day of February, 1879, the beneficiaries were peremptori
required by the Commissioner of the General Land Office to deposit

the Treasury of the United States the sums which they had received for the services mentioned since July 1, 1877, and which, though reported, had not been paid over. Soon thereafter, and pursuant to this demand, the sum of $5,330.76, being the aggregate of such fees for the nineteen months between July 1, 1877, and February 1, 1879, was paid over to the Government.

On the 19th day of February, 1879, these officers were authorized to employ two clerks, each upon a salary of $100 per month.

The purpose of the bill now under consideration is to restore to the beneficiaries from the money paid over to the Government, as above stated, the sum of $3,800. This is proposed upon the theory that clerks were employed by the register and receiver to do the work for which the fees were received, and that these officials having paid them for their services they should be reimbursed from the fund.

It will be observed that whatever services were performed by clerks in the way of writing down testimony, and paid for by the beneficiaries, were performed and paid for after July, 1877, and after they had in effect received notice that such employment and payment would not be approved by the Government.

Upon this statement the claim covered by the bill can hardly be urged on legal grounds, whatever the Government may have allowed prior to such notice.

I am decidedly of the opinion that the relations, the duties, and the obligations of subordinates in public employment should be clearly defined and strictly limited. They should not be permitted to judge of the propriety or necessity of incurring expenses on behalf of the Government without authority, much less in disregard of orders. And yet there are cases when in an emergency money is paid for the benefit of the public service by an official which, though not strictly authorized, ought in equity to be reimbursed.

If there is any equity existing in favor of the beneficiaries named in the bill herewith returned, it is found in the fact that during the nineteen months from the 1st day of July, 1877, to the 1st day of February, 1879, they paid out certain moneys for which the Government, in the receipt of the fees which they paid over, received the benefit. Manifestly such equity in this case, if it can be claimed at all in view of the facts recited, is measured by the sum actually paid by these officials to the persons, if such there were, who did the work from which the fees arose which were paid over to the Government.

In other words, if certain clerks were paid by the beneficiaries from their private funds for doing this work, there should be a distinct statement of the sum so paid, and their claim should rest upon indemnity and reimbursement alone. But no such statement appears, so far as I can see from an examination of papers presented to me by the Interior Department and from the report of the Senate committee who reported this bill, except as it may be gathered from the rather indirect allegations contained in a paper prepared by counsel.

No vouchers have ever been received at the General Land Office for money paid for clerical services rendered during the period for which reimbursement is sought. The verified statement of the claimants annexed to the committee's report contains only the allegation that they paid for the necessary clerical services, and the affidavits of the clerks themselves furnish no clew to the amount they received. Such an omission, in my opinion, discredits the claim made, and the allowance of the sum of $100 per month for two clerks during the period of nineteen months covered by this claim, because that was the sum authorized to be paid thereafter for clerks' services, is, it seems to me, adopting a standard entirely inapplicable to the subject.

In any event these beneficiaries should be required to establish the sum necessary for such indemnification, and the amount appropriated for their relief should be limited to that sum.

GROVER CLEVELAND.

EXECUTIVE MANSION, *January 18, 1889.*

To the House of Representatives:

I return without approval House bill No. 9173, entitled "An act granting a pension to Mary J. Drake."

It is proposed by this bill to pension the beneficiary therein named as the widow of Newton E. Drake, who served as a soldier from August 1, 1863, to January 18, 1865.

The records do not show that he suffered from any disability during his term of service.

He filed an application for pension September 23, 1879, claiming that he contracted rheumatism about October, 1864.

He died June 7, 1881, and there does not appear to have been any evidence produced as to the cause of his death or establishing, except by the allegations of his own application, that he contracted any disease or disability in the service.

GROVER CLEVELAND.

EXECUTIVE MANSION, *January 18, 1889.*

To the House of Representatives:

I return without approval House bill No. 9791, entitled "An act for the relief of Charles W. Geddes."

This bill directs the Secretary of the Interior to include the name of the beneficiary mentioned, late assistant engineer in the United States Navy, among those who served in the Mexican War, and issue to him a land warrant for his services as assistant engineer on the United States steamer *General Taylor* during said war.

On an application made by this beneficiary for bounty land under general laws the Secretary of the Navy reported that the vessel to which he was attached was not considered as having been engaged in the war with Mexico, and thereupon his application was rejected. Upon appeal to the Secretary of the Interior he states the settled doctrine of such cases to be that "service must have been *in*, not simply *during*, a war to give title to bounty land."

The only claim made by the beneficiary is that the vessel upon which he was employed was engaged for a time in transporting seamen from New Orleans, where they were enlisted, to Pensacola, and that he was informed and believed that they were enlisted to serve on board vessels composing the Gulf Squadron, then cooperating with the land forces in the Mexican War.

It seems to me that it is establishing a bad precedent, tending to the breaking down of all distinctions between civil and military employment and service, to hold that a man engaged on a vessel transporting recruits to a rendezvous from which they may be sent to the scene of hostilities should be allowed the same advantages which are bestowed upon those actually engaged in or more directly related to the dangers and chances of military operations.

GROVER CLEVELAND.

EXECUTIVE MANSION, *January 18, 1889.*

To the House of Representatives:

I return without approval House bill No. 9252, entitled "An act granting a pension to Mrs. Catherine Barberick, of Watertown."

The beneficiary named in this bill is the mother of William Barberick, who enlisted February 19, 1862, and died of smallpox August 2, 1864, at his home while on veteran furlough.

It is not claimed that the soldier contracted the fatal disease while in the Army. On the contrary, the testimony taken upon his mother's application for pension to the Pension Bureau shows that he was taken sick after his arrival at his home on furlough, and that several of his family had died of the contagious disease to which he fell a victim before he was taken sick with it.

In these circumstances, unless there is to be a complete departure from the principle that pensions are to be granted for death or disability in some way related to the military service, this bill should not become a law.

GROVER CLEVELAND.

EXECUTIVE MANSION, *January 18, 1889.*

To the House of Representatives:

I return without approval House bill No. 7877, entitled "An act to place Mary Karstetter on the pension roll."

The beneficiary named in this bill is the widow of Jacob Karstette who enlisted in June, 1864, and was discharged in June, 1865, on accou of a wound in his left hand received in action. He died in August, 187 of gastritis, or inflammation of the stomach, and congestion of the live He was granted a pension for his gunshot wound and was in receipt such pension at the time of his death.

I was constrained to return without approval a bill identical with tl one herewith returned, and which was passed by the last Congress, an stated my objections to the same in a communication addressed to tl House of Representatives, dated July 6, 1886.*

It seemed to me at that time that the soldier's death could not be hel to be the result of his wound or any other cause chargeable to his mil tary service.

Upon reexamination I am still of the same opinion, which leads me 1 again return the bill under consideration without approval.

GROVER CLEVELAND.

EXECUTIVE MANSION, *January 18, 1889.*

To the House of Representatives:

I return without approval House bill No. 9296, entitled "An act gran ing a pension to Bridget Carroll."

This bill proposes to pension the beneficiary therein named as th dependent mother of Patrick Carroll, who was enrolled as a sergeant i the Regular Army in 1881, this being, as it is stated, his second term enlistment.

In September, 1886, being absent from his command at Fort Wai ren, Mass., he was drowned while sailing in a small boat with two con panions.

The beneficiary is aged and in need of assistance, but there is n pretense that the soldier's death was in the least degree related to hi military service.

I am sure no one could fail to be gratified by an opportunity to join i according aid to this dependent old mother of a faithful soldier, but can not believe that such a departure as is proposed should be mad from the just principles upon which pension legislation ought to b predicated.

GROVER CLEVELAND.

EXECUTIVE MANSION, *January 18, 1889.*

To the House of Representatives:

I return without approval House bill No. 9175, entitled "An act gran ing a pension to George Wallen."

* See pp. 469-470.

The beneficiary named in this bill filed an application for pension in June, 1873, alleging as his disability a fracture of his right arm.

In a subsequent affidavit filed in 1883 he alleged deafness, which appears to be the disability upon which the special act proposed for his relief is based.

The records establish that he enlisted July 27, 1861, that he deserted April 25, 1862, and returned February 20, 1863, after an absence of about ten months, and that he deserted again April 30, 1864, and returned prior to August 31, 1864. I am informed that his record shows two enlistments and desertion during each. He was discharged December 31, 1864.

An application to remove the charge of desertion against him was denied.

Without especially discussing the question of disability chargeable to military service, it seems to me that a soldier with such a record should not be pensioned. GROVER CLEVELAND.

To the Senate: EXECUTIVE MANSION, *January 31, 1889.*

I return without approval Senate bill No. 3264, entitled "An act granting a pension to Mrs. Ellen Hand."

The husband of the beneficiary named in this bill enlisted August 22, 1862, and was mustered out with his company July 10, 1865.

He filed a claim for pension in 1881, sixteen years after his discharge, alleging that he contracted rheumatism about December, 1862.

He died in February, 1883, the cause of death being, as then certified, typhoid fever.

His claim for pension on account of rheumatism seems to have been favorably determined after his death, for it was made payable to his widow and was allowed from the time of filing his petition to February 25, 1883, the day of his death.

The facts of the case as now presented appear to me to lead in the most satisfactory manner to the conclusion that the soldier's death was in no way related to any incident of his military service.

GROVER CLEVELAND.

EXECUTIVE MANSION, *February 12, 1889.*

To the House of Representatives:

I return without approval House bill No. 9163, entitled "An act granting a pension to Eli Garrett."

This beneficiary enlisted in the Confederate Army December 1, 1862. He was captured by the United States forces on the 26th of November, 1863, and enlisted in the Union Navy January 22, 1864.

He was discharged from the Navy for disability September 8, 1864, upon the certificate of a naval surgeon, which states that he had valvular cardiac disease (disease of the heart), and that there was no evidence that it originated in the line of duty.

His claim for pension was rejected in 1882 upon the ground that the act which permits pensions to Confederate soldiers who joined the Union Army did not extend to such soldiers who enlisted in the Navy.

I can see no reason why such a distinction should exist, and the recommendation of the Commissioner of Pensions, made in 1887, that this discrimination be removed should be adopted by the enactment of a law for that purpose.

In this case, however, I am unable to discover any evidence that the trouble with which this beneficiary appears to be afflicted is related to his naval service which should overcome the plain statement of the surgeon upon whose certificate he was discharged to the effect that there was no evidence that his disability originated in the line of naval duty.

GROVER CLEVELAND.

EXECUTIVE MANSION, *February 12, 1889.*

To the House of Representatives:

I return without approval House bill No. 11052, entitled "An act granting a pension to Clara M. Owen."

The husband of this beneficiary was pensioned for a gunshot wound in the left chest and lung, received in action on the 30th day of September, 1864.

He was drowned August 31, 1884.

It appears that he was found in a stream where he frequently bathed, in a depth of water variously given from 5 to 8 feet. He had undressed and apparently gone into the water as usual.

Medical opinions are produced tending to show that drowning was not the cause of death.

No *post mortem* examination was had, and it seems to me it must be conceded that a conclusion that death was in any degree the result of wounds received in military service rests upon the most unsatisfactory conjecture.

GROVER CLEVELAND.

EXECUTIVE MANSION, *February 12, 1889.*

To the House of Representatives:

I return without approval House bill No. 5752, entitled "An act for the relief of Julia Triggs."

This beneficiary filed an application for pension in 1882, claiming that her son, William Triggs, died in 1875 from the effects of poison taken during his military service in water which had been poisoned by the rebels and in food eaten in rebel houses, which had also been poisoned.

He was discharged from the Army with his company July 24, 1865, after a service of more than four years.

The cause of his death is reported to have been an abscess of the lung.

The case was specially examined, and the evidence elicited to support the claim of poisoning appears to have been anything but satisfactory.

The mother herself testified that her son was absent from Chicago, where she lived, and in the South from 1868 to 1869, and that he was in Indiana from 1869 to 1874.

The claim was rejected on the 12th day of February, 1887, on the ground that evidence could not be obtained upon special examination showing that the soldier's death was due to any disability contracted in the military service.

While I am unable to see how any other conclusion could have been reached upon the facts in this case, there is reason to believe that a favorable determination upon its merits would be of no avail, since, on the 17th day of April, 1888, a letter was filed in the Pension Office from a citizen of Chicago in which it is stated that the beneficiary named in this bill died on the 27th day of February, 1888, and an application is therein made on behalf of her daughter for reimbursement of money expended for her mother in her last illness and for her burial.

GROVER CLEVELAND.

To the Senate:

EXECUTIVE MANSION, *February 13, 1889.*

I return without approval Senate bill No. 2514, entitled "An act granting a pension to Michael Shong."

It appears that the beneficiary named in this bill, under the name of John M. Johns, enlisted in Company I, Fourteenth New York Volunteers, on the 17th day of May, 1861, and was discharged May 24, 1863.

In November, 1876, more than thirteen years after his discharge, under the same name of John M. Johns, he filed an application for pension, alleging a fever sore on his right leg contracted July 1, 1862, which resulted in the loss of the leg.

His claim was rejected in November, 1882, after a thorough special examination, on the ground that the disease of the leg resulting in amputation was contracted after the soldier's discharge from the service.

The leg was amputated in February, 1865.

While there is some evidence tending to show lameness in the service and following discharge, and while one witness swears to lameness and fever sores in the service, evidence was also produced showing that the soldier returned home from the Army in good physical condition and that the disease of his leg first manifested itself in the latter part of 1864.

It will be observed that he served in the Army nearly a year after it is alleged he contracted his disability, and that though his leg was amputated in February, 1865, he did not apply for a pension until 1876,

Moreover, the surgeon who amputated his leg testified that the soldier and his parents stated that he came out of the Army without a scratch; that on New Year's night in 1865 he became very warm at a dance; that he went outdoors and was taken with a chill and pain in his side, which subsequently settled in the leg and caused a gangrenous condition, and that upon amputating the leg the artery below the knee was found plugged by a blood clot, which caused the diseased condition of the leg and foot.

This testimony and the other facts established and the presumptions arising therefrom clearly indicate, in my opinion, that the claim made for a pension by this beneficiary is without merit.

GROVER CLEVELAND.

To the Senate: EXECUTIVE MANSION, *February 13, 1889.*

I return without approval Senate bill No. 3451, entitled "An act granting a pension to Frank D. Worcester."

The beneficiary named in this bill served in the Volunteer Army from February 4, 1863, to January 27, 1864, a period of less than one year, when he was discharged upon the certificate of a surgeon, alleging as his disability "manifest mental imbecility and incontinence of urine. Disease originated previous to enlistment."

In 1880, sixteen years after his discharge, a claim for pension was filed in his behalf by his father as his guardian, in which it was alleged that his mind, naturally not strong, became diseased in the Army by reason of excitement and exposure.

He was adjudged insane in 1872 and sent to an insane hospital, where he remained about six years, when he was discharged as a harmless incurable. His mental condition has remained about the same since that time.

Upon the declared inability to furnish testimony to rebut the record of mental disease prior to enlistment, the claim for pension was rejected in 1883.

In 1887 the case was reopened and a thorough examination was made as to soundness prior to enlistment and the origin and continuance of mental unsoundness.

Upon this examination evidence was taken showing that he was deficient intellectually when he joined the Army; that he was stationed where he was not much exposed, and that his duties were comparatively light, that he never was considered a boy of solid intelligence, and that he had epileptiform seizures prior to enlistment.

On the other hand, no disinterested and unbiased evidence was secured tending to rebut these conditions.

The claim was thereupon again rejected. This was a proper disposition of the case unless the Government is held liable for every disability which may afflict those who served in the Union Army.

GROVER CLEVELAND.

EXECUTIVE MANSION, *February 14, 1889.*

I return without approval Senate bill No. 2665, entitled "An act granting a pension to Charles J. Esty."

A bill in precisely the same words as the bill herewith returned was approved on the 8th day of July, 1886, and under its provisions the beneficiary is now upon the pension rolls.

It is supposed that the bill now under consideration was passed by the Congress in ignorance of the previous statute. A duplication of the act would manifestly be entirely useless.

GROVER CLEVELAND.

EXECUTIVE MANSION, *February 21, 1889.*

To the House of Representatives:

I herewith return without approval House bill No. 1368, entitled "An act to quiet title of settlers on the Des Moines River lands, in the State of Iowa, and for other purposes."

This bill is to all intents and purposes identical with Senate bill No. 150, passed in the first session of the Forty-ninth Congress, which failed to receive Executive approval. My objections to that bill are set forth in a message transmitted to the Senate on the 11th day of March, 1886.* They are all applicable to the bill herewith returned, and a careful reexamination of the matters embraced in this proposed legislation has further satisfied me of their validity and strength.

The trouble proposed to be cured by this bill grew out of the indefiniteness and consequent contradictory construction by the officers of the Government of a grant of land made in 1846 by Congress to the State of Iowa (then a Territory) for the purpose of aiding in the improvement of the Des Moines River. This grant was accepted on the 9th day of January, 1847, by the State of Iowa, as required by the act of Congress, and soon thereafter the question arose whether the lands granted were limited to those which adjoined the river in its course northwesterly from the southerly line of the State to a point called the Raccoon Fork, or whether such grant covered lands so adjoining the river through its entire course through the Territory, and both below and above the Raccoon Fork.

The Acting Commissioner of the General Land Office, on the 17th day of October, 1846, instructed the officers of the land office in Iowa that the grant extended only to the Raccoon Fork.

On the 23d day of February, 1848, the Commissioner of the General Land Office held that the grant extended along the entire course of the river.

Notwithstanding this opinion, the President, in June, 1848, proclaimed

See pp. 411-413.

the lands upon the river above the Raccoon Fork to be open for sale
and settlement under the land laws, and about 25,000 acres were sold
to and preempted by settlers under said proclamation.

In 1849, and before the organization of the Department of the Interior, the Secretary of the Treasury decided, upon a protest against opening said lands for sale and settlement, that the grant extended along the
entire course of the river.

Pursuant to this decision, and on the 1st day of June, 1849, the Commissioner of the General Land Office directed the reservation or the withholding from sale of all lands on the odd-numbered sections along the
Des Moines River above the Raccoon Fork.

This reservation from entry and sale under the general land laws seems
to have continued until a deed of the lands so reserved was made by the
State of Iowa and until the said deed was supplemented and confirmed
by the action of the Congress in 1861 and 1862.

In April, 1850, the Secretary of the Interior, that Department having
then been created, determined that the grant extended no farther than
the Raccoon Fork; but in view of the fact that Congress was in session
and might take steps in the matter, the Commissioner of the General
Land Office expressly continued the reservation.

In October, 1851, another Secretary of the Interior, while expressing
the opinion that the grant only extended to the Raccoon Fork, declared
that he would approve the selections made by the State of Iowa of lands
above that point, "leaving the question as to the construction of the statute entirely open to the action of the judiciary."

In this condition of affairs selections were made by Iowa of a large
quantity of land lying above the Raccoon Fork, which selections were
approved and the land certified to the State. In the meantime the State
had entered upon the improvement of the river and it appears had disposed of some of the land in furtherance of said improvement. But in
1854 the State of Iowa made a contract with the Des Moines Navigation and Railroad Company for the continuance of said work at a cost of
$1,300,000, the State agreeing in payment thereof to convey to the com-
pany all the land which had been or should thereafter be certified to the
State of Iowa under the grant of 1846.

In November, 1856, further certification of lands above the Raccoon
Fork under the grant to the State of Iowa was refused by the Interior
Department. This led to a dispute and settlement between the State of
Iowa and the Des Moines Navigation and Railroad Company, by which
the State conveyed by deed to said company—

All lands granted by an act of Congress approved August 8, 1846, to the then Territory of Iowa to aid in the improvement of the Des Moines River which have been
approved and certified to the State of Iowa by the General Government, saving and
excepting all lands sold and conveyed, or agreed to be sold and conveyed, by the
State, by its officers and agents, prior to the 23d day of December, 1853, under said
grant.

This exception was declared in the deed to cover the lands above the Raccoon Fork disposed of to settlers by the Government in 1848 under the proclamation of the President opening said lands to sale and settlement, which has been referred to; and it is conceded that neither these lands nor the rights of any settlers thereto are affected by the terms of the bill now under consideration.

The amount of land embraced in this deed located above the Raccoon Fork appears to be more than 271,000 acres.

It is alleged that the company in winding up its affairs distributed this land among the parties interested, and that said land, or a large part of it, has been sold to numerous parties now claiming the same under titles derived from said company.

In December, 1859, the Supreme Court of the United States decided that the grant to the Territory of Iowa under the law of 1846 conveyed no land above the Raccoon Fork, and that all selections and certifications of lands above that point were unauthorized and void, and passed no title or interest in said lands to the State of Iowa. In other words, it was determined that these lands were, in the language of the bill under consideration, "improperly certified to Iowa by the Department of the Interior under the act of August 8, 1846."

This adjudication would seem to conclusively determine that the title to these lands was, as the law then stood, and notwithstanding all that had taken place, still in the United States. And for the purpose of granting all claim or right of the Government to said lands for the benefit of the grantees of the State of Iowa, Congress, on the 2d day of March, 1861, passed a joint resolution providing that all the title still retained by the United States in the lands above the Raccoon Fork, in the State of Iowa, "which have been certified to said State improperly by the Department of the Interior as part of the grant by act of Congress approved August 8, 1846, and which is now held by *bona fide* purchasers under the State of Iowa, be, and the same is hereby, relinquished to the State of Iowa."

Afterwards, and on the 12th day of July, 1862, an act of Congress was passed extending the grant of 1846 so as to include lands lying above the Raccoon Fork.

The joint resolution and act of Congress here mentioned have been repeatedly held by the Supreme Court of the United States to supply a title to the lands mentioned in the deed from the State of Iowa to the Navigation and Railroad Company, which inured to the benefit of said company or its grantees.

No less than ten cases have been decided in that court more or less directly establishing this proposition, as well as the further proposition that no title to these lands could prior to said Congressional action be gained by settlers, for the reason that it had been withdrawn and reserved from entry and sale under the general land laws. It seems to be perfectly well settled also, if an adjudication was necessary upon that question, that all interest of the United States in these lands was entirely and completely granted by the resolution of 1861 and the act of 1862.

The act of 1862 provides for the setting apart of other lands in lieu of such as were covered by the act, but had been before its passage sold and disposed of by the United States, excepting such as had been released to the State of Iowa under the joint resolution of 1861.

It is claimed, I believe, that in a settlement of land grants thereafter had between the United States and the State of Iowa lands were allowed to the State in lieu or indemnity for some of the lands which it had conveyed to the Des Moines Navigation and Railroad Company. But if the title of the company is valid to lands along the river and above the Raccoon Fork, under the deed from Iowa and the joint resolution and act of Congress, it can not be in the least affected by the fact that the State afterwards, justly or unjustly, received other lands as indemnity.

The bill under consideration provides that all the lands "improperly certified to Iowa" under the grant of 1846, as referred to in the joint resolution of 1861, and for which indemnity lands were selected and received by the State, as provided in the act of 1862, "are, and are hereby, declared to be public lands of the United States."

The claims of persons and their heirs who, with intent in good faith to obtain title under the preemption and homestead laws of the United States, have entered and remained upon any tract of said land prior to 1880 are confirmed and made valid to them and their heirs, not exceeding 160 acres; and upon due proof and payment of the usual price or fees it is directed that such claims shall be carried to patent.

It is further provided that the claims of settlers and claimants which do not come in conflict with the claims of the parties above mentioned are confirmed and made valid. By the second section of the bill it is made the duty of the Attorney-General, as soon as practicable, and within three years after the passage of the act, to institute legal proceedings to assert and protect the title of the United States to said lands and to remove all clouds from its title thereto.

One result of this legislation, if consummated and if effectual, would be to restore to the United States, as a part of the public domain, lands which more than twenty-five years ago the Government expressly granted and surrendered, and which repeated decisions of the Supreme Court have adjudged to belong by virtue of this action of the Government to other parties.

Another result would be not only to validate claims to this land which our highest judicial tribunal have solemnly declared to be invalid, but to actually direct the issue of patents in confirmation of said claims.

Still another result would be to oblige the Government of the United States to enter the courts ostensibly to assert and protect its title to said land, while in point of fact it would be used to enforce private claims to the same and unsettle private ownership.

It is by no means certain that this proposed legislation, relating to a subject peculiarly within the judicial function, and which attempts to disturb rights and interests thoroughly intrenched in the solemn adjudications of our courts, would be upheld. In any event, it seems to me that it is an improper exercise of legislative power, an interference with the determinations of a coordinate branch of the Government, an arbitrary annulment of a public grant made more than twenty-five years ago, an attempted destruction of vested rights, and a threatened impairment of lawful contracts.

The advocates of this measure insist that a point in favor of the settlers upon these lands and important in the consideration of this bill is found in the following language of the constitution of the State of Iowa, which was adopted in 1857:

The general assembly shall not locate any of the public lands which have been or may be granted by Congress to this State, and the location of which may be given to the general assembly, upon lands actually settled, without the consent of the occupant.

The State under its constitution was perfectly competent to take the grants of 1861 and 1862. The clause of the constitution above quoted deals expressly with ''lands which have been or may be granted by Congress to the State,'' and thus of necessity recognizes its right to take such grants. This competency in the State as a grantee was all that was needed to create, under the joint resolution of 1861 and the act of 1862, a complete divestiture of the interests of the United States in these lands. It must be borne in mind, too, that prior to this time these lands. had been conveyed by the State of Iowa in furtherance of the purposes of the original Congressional grants, and that the joint resolution of 1861 and the act of 1862 were really made for the benefit of those who held under grants from the State. After these grants by the Government it had no concern with these lands. If in any stage of the proceedings the general assembly of Iowa was guilty of any neglect of duty or failed to act in accordance with the constitution of the State of Iowa, the remedy should be found in the courts of that State; and it is difficult to see how the situation in this aspect can be changed or improved by the bill under consideration.

I am not unmindful of the fact that there may be persons who have suffered or who are threatened with loss through a reliance upon the erroneous decisions of Government officials as to the extent of the original grant from the United States to the Territory of Iowa. I believe cases of this kind should be treated in accordance with the broadest sentiments of equity, and that where loss is apparent arising from a real or fairly supposed invitation of the Government to settle upon the lands mentioned in the bill under consideration such loss should be made good. But I do not believe that the condition of these settlers will be aided by encouraging them in such further litigation as the terms of this bill invite, nor do I believe that in attempting to right the wrongs of which they complain legislation should be sanctioned mischievous in principle, and in its practical operation doing injustice to others as innocent as they and as much entitled to consideration.

GROVER CLEVELAND.

EXECUTIVE MANSION, *February 23, 1889.*
To the House of Representatives:

I herewith return without approval House bill No. 220, entitled "An act granting a pension to John J. Lockrey."

It is stated that this beneficiary enlisted April 11, 1865, but it appears from the muster roll of his company for May and June, 1865, that he was a recruit assigned, but who had not joined. There is nothing appearing on the record which positively shows that he ever reached his regiment.

It is conceded that his real and nominal connection with the Army extended only from April 11, 1865, when he was mustered in, until August, 1865, when he was discharged for disability, consisting of a disease of the eye, called in the surgeon's certificate "iritis with conjunctivitis."

It seems that this claimant enlisted just at the close of the war, and was connected in a manner with the Army for four months. It is not probable that he ever saw any actual service, for none is stated in the papers before me; and it does appear that he spent a large part of his short term of enlistment in hospitals and under treatment for a trouble with his eye. As early as May 23, 1865, he was admitted to hospital with gonorrheal ophthalmia. His claim was rejected by the Pension Bureau on the ground that this was the cause of his disability, and the inferences from the proof presented make this extremely probable.

One of the witnesses who testified that the beneficiary caught cold in his eye in April, 1865, on the Mississippi River is shown to have been at that time with his regiment and company at Danville, Va.

The circumstances surrounding this case and the facts proved satisfy me that the determination of the Pension Bureau was correct, and there is certainly no sentiment in favor of the claimant which justifies the indulgence of violent presumptions for the purpose of overriding such determination.

GROVER CLEVELAND.

EXECUTIVE MANSION, *February 23, 1889.*
To the House of Representatives:

I return without approval House bill No. 5807, entitled "An act granting a pension to John McCool."

This beneficiary served in an Iowa regiment of volunteers from May 27, 1861, to July 12, 1865.

He filed a petition for pension, alleging an accidental wound in the right thumb while extracting a cartridge from a pistol in August, 1861.

There is no record of any such disability, though it appears that he was on a furlough about the date of his alleged injury. It appears that he served nearly four years after the time he fixed as the date of his injury.

No evidence was filed in support of the claim he filed, and he refused to appear for examination, though twice notified to do so.

His claim was rejected in May, 1888, no suggestion having been made of any other disability than the wound in the thumb, upon which his claim before the Bureau was based.

The report·of the committee in the House of Representatives recommending the passage of this bill contains no intimation that there exists any disability contracted in the military service, but distinctly declares the pension recommended a service pension, and states that the beneficiary is blind.

As long as the policy of granting pensions for disability traceable to the incidents of army service is adhered to, the allowance of pensions by special acts based upon service only gives rise to unjust and unfair discriminations among those equally entitled, and makes precedents which will eventually result in an entire departure from the principle upon which pensions are now awarded.   GROVER CLEVELAND.

EXECUTIVE MANSION, *February 23, 1889.*

To the House of Representatives:

I return without approval House bill No. 11803. entitled "An act granting a pension to Henry V. Bass."

This beneficiary enlisted September 9, 1862, and was mustered out August 15, 1865. The records show no disability during his service.

It is now alleged that the soldier was sitting on the ground near his tent while two comrades were wrestling near him, and that in the course of the scuffle one of the parties engaged in it was thrown or fell upon the beneficiary, injuring his right knee and ankle.

Upon these facts the claim was rejected by the Pension Bureau on the ground that the injury was not received in the line of duty.

I do not think that the Government should be held as an insurer against injuries of this kind, which are in no manner related to the performance of military service.   GROVER CLEVELAND.

EXECUTIVE MANSION, *February 23, 1889.*

To the House of Representatives:

I herewith return without approval House bill No. 11999, entitled "An act granting a pension to William Barnes."

The beneficiary named in this bill served in a Kentucky regiment from August 9, 1861, to December 6, 1864.

He made claim for pension in the Pension Bureau in September, 18:
alleging that in October, 1862, he was accidentally injured by a pis
shot in the thigh while in the line of duty.

It is conceded that he was wounded by the discharge of a pistol wh:
he was carrying while he was absent from his command with permiss
on a visit to his home, and that the discharge of the pistol was accident

The circumstances of the injury are neither given in the report of t
committee to whom the claim was referred by the House of Represe
atives nor in the report of the case furnished to me from the Pensi
Bureau, but on the conceded facts the granting of a pension in this c
can be predicated upon no other theory except the liability of the G
ernment for any injury by accident to a person in the military servi
whether in the line of duty or not.

I think the adoption of the principle that the Government is an
surer against accidents under any circumstances befalling those enlis
in its military service when visiting at home is an unwarrantable stre
of pension legislation.

GROVER CLEVELAND.

EXECUTIVE MANSION, *February 25, 1889.*

To the House of Representatives:

I herewith return without approval House bill No. 10448, entitled ".
act granting a pension to Squire Walter."

The son of the beneficiary named in this bill enlisted in a West V
ginia regiment on the 28th day of June, 1861.

On the 15th day of September, 1862, while bathing in the Poton
River near the Chain Bridge, with the knowledge and consent of
commanding officer, he was drowned.

It is perfectly clear that he lost his life while in the enjoyment
a privilege and when at his request military discipline was relaxed a
its restraints removed for his comfort and pleasure. His death resul
from his voluntary and perfectly proper personal indulgence, and can
be in the least attributed to military service.

The father does not appear to be so needy and dependent as is of
exhibited in cases of this class.

GROVER CLEVELAND.

To the Senate: EXECUTIVE MANSION, *February 25, 1889.*

I herewith return without approval Senate bill No. 3561, entitled ".
act granting a pension to Edwin W. Warner."

A claim for pension on behalf of the beneficiary named in this bill
filed in the Pension Bureau May 6, 1867. It has been examined and
examined and always rejected, until, on the 29th day of December, 18
as the result of a personal and thorough investigation by the Com

sioner, a pension was allowed and a certificate issued under which the claimant will be paid $18 a month hereafter and arrearages amounting to something near $2,000.

As the special act for the benefit of this claimant was passed by the Congress upon the supposition that nothing had been done for the beneficiary therein named, I deem it best, in his interest, and probably consistent with the intent of the Congress, that the bill herewith returned should not become a law. GROVER CLEVELAND.

EXECUTIVE MANSION, *February 26, 1889.*

To the House of Representatives:

I return without approval House bill No. 12047, entitled "An act granting an increase of pension to George Colwell."

The record shows that this beneficiary was enrolled in the military service August 10, 1862, and was mustered out June 1, 1865.

There is no record of any disability during his service.

He was pensioned at the rate of $2 a month for a dog bite just above the ankle.

In September, 1865, three months after his discharge, he strained the knee of the leg which had been bitten.

In 1887 he applied for an increase of pension, alleging increased disability. This increased disability appears plainly to be the result of the strain or injury to the knee, and in no way connected with the bite for which he was pensioned. GROVER CLEVELAND.

EXECUTIVE MANSION, *February 26, 1889.*

To the House of Representatives:

I herewith return without approval House bill No. 10791, entitled "An act granting a pension to Marinda Wakefield Reed."

This beneficiary filed an application for pension in November, 1876, alleging that her husband, William A. Reed, died in September of that year of consumption contracted in the line of military duty.

The records show that the soldier was in hospital in the year 1864 for chronic diarrhea and intermittent fever.

On the 5th day of November, 1864, he was injured in a railroad accident while on his way home to vote at the Presidential election of that year.

The beneficiary claimed in August, 1885, in support of her application for pension that those injuries resulted in consumption, from which the soldier died, and the favorable report of the House committee to which the bill herewith returned was referred seems to proceed upon the same theory.

Nothing appears which satisfactorily connects this injury, which w received in November, 1864, with death from consumption in 1876.

Another difficulty in the case is found in the fact that when the sold was injured he was clearly not engaged in any military duty nor was l injury in any degree attributable to military service.

GROVER CLEVELAND.

EXECUTIVE MANSION, *February 26, 1889.*

To the House of Representatives:

I return without approval House bill 11466, entitled "An act granti a pension to Mary A. Selbach."

This bill does not give the name of any soldier to whom the beneficia was related or in what capacity the pension provided for is to be paid her, but it appears from the report of the committee accompanying t bill that she is the widow of Gustavus Selbach, a volunteer in the Nin Regiment of Ohio Volunteers.

This soldier drew a pension from January, 1882, to January 16, 188 when he died. He claimed disability for disease of the ears and a resu ing deafness of his left ear. There appears to be no evidence in I record of any disability or medical treatment while in the service, and t medical examination upon his application for pension shows no rati for any disability other than that alleged by him and for which he w pensioned—disease of the ears and resulting deafness.

It is conceded that the soldier died January 16, 1886, of pneumonia.

The widow filed a claim for pension in May, 1887.

The testimony of physicians upon her claim covered seven years pri to his death, thus dating back to the year 1879, and they speak of t disease of the ear and of the kidneys, which, in their opinion, undermin his health, so that "he succumbed to an attack of pneumonia, which to person of ordinary good health would not have been considered serious

It can hardly be supposed that the trouble with his ears caused t soldier to fall a victim to pneumonia; and so far as the kidney disea tended in that direction, it is to be observed that it apparently did n make its appearance until fourteen years after the soldier's discharge.

GROVER CLEVELAND.

EXECUTIVE MANSION, *February 26, 1889.*

To the House of Representatives:

I return without approval House bill No. 11586, entitled "An act f the relief of Stephen Williams."

It appears from the records that the beneficiary for whom a pension provided in this bill served as a volunteer in an Illinois regiment fro October, 1862, to October, 1864, at which date he is reported as a desertu

He filed a claim for pension in 1881, in which he alleged that he was struck with a gunstock upon his head and injured in October, 1864.

The evidence shows that a drunken comrade struck the claimant with the stock of his gun because he would not buy whisky for him.

This, upon all the facts, does not appear to be a proper case for allowing a pension for an injury suffered in the line of military duty.

GROVER CLEVELAND.

To the Senate: EXECUTIVE MANSION, *March 2, 1889.*

I herewith return without approval Senate bill No. 139, entitled "An act to credit and pay to the several States and Territories and the District of Columbia all moneys collected under the direct tax levied by the act of Congress approved August 5, 1861."

The object of this bill is quite clearly indicated in its title. Its provisions have been much discussed in both branches of Congress and have received emphatic legislative sanction. I fully appreciate the interest which it has excited and have by no means failed to recognize the persuasive presentation made in its favor. I know, too, that the interposition of Executive disapproval in this case is likely to arouse irritation and cause complaint and earnest criticism. Since, however, my judgment will not permit me to assent to the legislation proposed, I can find no way of turning aside from what appears to be the plain course of official duty.

On the 5th day of August, 1861, a Federal statute was passed entitled "An act to provide increased revenue from imports, to pay interest on the public debt, and for other purposes."

This law was passed at a time when immense sums of money were needed by the Government for the prosecution of a war for the Union, and the purpose of the law was to increase in almost every possible way the Federal revenues. The first seven sections of the statute were devoted to advancing very largely the rates of duties on imports, and to supplement this the eighth section provided that a direct tax of $20,000,-000 should be annually laid and that certain amounts therein specified should be apportioned to the respective States. The remainder of the law, consisting of fifty sections, contained the most particular and detailed provisions for the collection of the tax through Federal machinery.

It was declared, among other things, that the tax should be assessed and laid on all lands and lots of ground, with their improvements and dwelling houses; that the annual amount of said taxes should be a lien upon all lands and real estate of the individuals assessed for the same, and that in default of payment the said taxes might be collected by distraint and sale of the goods, chattels, and effects of the delinquent persons.

This tax was laid in execution of the power conferred upon the General Government for that purpose by the Constitution. It was an exercise of the right of the Government to tax its citizens. It dealt with individuals, and the strong arm of Federal power was stretched out to exact from those who owed it support and allegiance their just share of the sum it had decreed should be raised by direct taxation for the general good. The lien created by this tax was upon the land and real estate of the "individuals" assessed for the same, and for its collection the distraint and sale of personal property of the "persons delinquent" were permitted.

But while the direct relationship and responsibility between the individuals taxed and the Federal Government were thus created by the exercise of the highest attribute of sovereignty, it was provided in the statute that any State or Territory and the District of Columbia might lawfully "assume, assess, collect, and pay into the Treasury of the United States" its quota of said tax in its own way and manner and by and through its own officers, assessors, and collectors; and it was further provided that such States or Territories as should give notice of their intention to thus assume and pay or to assess, collect, and pay into the Treasury of the United States such direct tax, should be entitled, in lieu of the compensation, pay, per diem, and percentage in said act prescribed and allowed to assessors, assistant assessors, and collectors of the United States, to a deduction of 15 per cent of the quota of direct tax apportioned to such States or Territories and levied and collected through their officers.

It was also provided by this law and another passed the next year that certain claims of the States and Territories against the United States might be applied in payment of such quotas. Whatever may be said as to the effect of these provisions of the law, it can hardly be claimed that by virtue thereof or any proceedings under them the apportioned quotas of this tax became debts against the several States and Territories, or that they were liable to the General Government therefor in every event, and as principal debtors bound by an enforceable obligation.

In the forty-sixth section of the law it is provided that in case any State, Territory, or the District of Columbia, after notice given of its intention to assume and pay or to levy, collect, and pay said direct tax apportioned to it, should fail to pay the amount of said direct tax, or any part thereof, it should be lawful for the Secretary of the Treasury to appoint United States officers as in the act provided, whose duty it should be to proceed forthwith to collect all or any part of said direct tax "the same as though said State, Territory, or District had not given notice nor assumed to levy, collect, and pay said taxes or any part thereof."

A majority of the States undertook the collection of their quotas and accounted for the amount thereof to the General Government by the payment of money or by setting off claims in their favor against the tax. Fifteen per cent of the amount of their respective quotas was retained as the allowance for collection and payment. In the Northern, or such as were then called the loyal States, nearly the entire quotas were collected and paid through State agencies. The money necessary for this purpose was generally collected from the citizens of the States with their other taxes, and in whatever manner their quotas may have been canceled, whether by the payment of money or setting off claims against the Government, it is safe to say, as a general proposition, that the people of these States have individually been obliged to pay the assessments made upon them on account of this direct tax and have intrusted it to their several States to be transmitted to the Federal Treasury.

In the Southern States, then in insurrection, whatever was actually realized in money upon this tax was collected directly by Federal officers without the interposition of State machinery, and a part of its quota has been credited to each of these States.

The entire amount applied upon this tax, including the 15 per cent for collection, was credited to the several States and Territories upon the books of the Treasury, whether collected through their instrumentalities or by Federal officers.

The sum credited to all the States was $17,359,685.51, which includes more than $2,000,000 on account of the 15 per cent allowed for collecting. Of the amount credited only about $2,300,000 is credited to the insurrectionary States. The amount uncollected of the twenty millions directed to be raised by this tax was $2,646,314.49, and nearly this entire sum remained due upon the quotas apportioned to these States.

In this condition of affairs the bill under consideration directs the Secretary of the Treasury " to credit to each State and Territory of the United States and the District of Columbia a sum equal to all collections, by set-off or otherwise, made from said States and Territories and the District of Columbia, or from any of the citizens or inhabitants thereof, or other persons, under the act of Congress approved August 5, 1861, and th amendatory acts thereto." An appropriation is also made of such ᵃ as may be necessary to reimburse each State, Territory, and the of Columbia for all money found due to it under the provisic bill, and it is provided that all money still due to the United Sta direct tax shall be remitted and relinquished.

The conceded effect of this bill is to take from the m the Treasury the sum of more than $17,000,000, or, if ᵗ allowed is not included, more than $15,000,000, and ₁ respective States and Territories the sums they or th more than twenty-five years ago upon a direct tax levicc ment of the United States for its defense and safety.

It is my belief that this appropriation of the public the constitutional power of the Congress. Under gated authority conferred by the Constitution upon ment the statement of the purposes for which m raised by taxation in any form declares also the 1 which it may be expended.

All must agree that the direct tax was lawfully and constitutionally laid and that it was rightfully and correctly collected. It can not be claimed, therefore, nor is it pretended, that any debt arose against the Government and in favor of any State or individual by the exaction of this tax. Surely, then, the appropriation directed by this bill can not be justified as a payment of a debt of the United States.

The disbursement of this money clearly has no relation to the common defense. On the contrary, it is the repayment of money raised and long ago expended by the Government to provide for the common defense.

The expenditure can not properly be advocated on the ground that the general welfare of the United States is thereby provided for or promoted. This "general welfare of the United States," as used in the Constitution, can only justify appropriations for national objects and for purposes which have to do with the prosperity, the growth, the honor, or the peace and dignity of the nation.

A sheer, bald gratuity bestowed either upon States or individuals, based upon no better reason than supports the gift proposed in this bill, has never been claimed to be a provision for the general welfare. More than fifty years ago a surplus of public money in the Treasury was distributed among the States; but the unconstitutionality of such distribution, considered as a gift of money, appears to have been conceded, for it was put into the State treasuries under the guise of a deposit or loan, subject to the demand of the Government.

If it was proposed to raise by assessment upon the people the sum necessary to refund the money collected upon this direct tax, I am sure many who are now silent would insist upon the limitations of the Constitution in opposition to such a scheme. A large surplus in the Treasury is the parent of many ills, and among them is found a tendency to an extremely liberal, if not loose, construction of the Constitution. It also attracts the gaze of States and individuals with a kind of fascination, and gives rise to plans and pretensions that an uncongested Treasury never could excite.

But if the constitutional question involved in the consideration of this bill should be determined in its favor, there are other objections remaining which prevent my assent to its provisions.

There should be a certainty and stability about the enforcement of taxation which should teach the citizen that the Government will only use the power to tax in cases where its necessity and justice are not doubtful, and which should also discourage the disturbing idea that the exercise of this power may be revoked by reimbursement of taxes once collected. Any other theory cheapens and in a measure discredits a process which more than any other is a manifestation of sovereign authority.

A government is not only kind, but performs its highest duty when it restores to the citizen taxes unlawfully collected or which have been erroneously or oppressively extorted by its agents or officers; but aside from these incidents, the people should not be familiarized with the spectacle of their Government repenting the collection of taxes and restoring them.

The direct tax levied in 1861 is not even suspected of invalidity. There never was a tax levied which was more needed, and its justice can not be questioned. Why, then, should it be returned?

The fact that the entire tax was not paid furnishes no reason that would not apply to nearly every case where taxes are laid. There are always delinquents, and while the more thorough and complete collection of taxes is a troublesome problem of government, the failure to solve the problem has never been held to call for the return of taxes actually collected.

The deficiency in the collection of this tax is found almost entirely in the insurrectionary States, while the quotas apportioned to the other States were, as a general rule, fully paid; and three-fourths or four-fifths of the money which it is proposed in this bill to return would be paid into the treasuries of the loyal States. But no valid reason for such payment is found in the fact that the Government at first could not, and afterwards, for reasons probably perfectly valid, did not, enforce collection in the other States.

There were many Federal taxes which were not paid by the people in the rebellious States; and if the nonpayment by them of this direct tax entitles the other States to a donation of the share of said taxes paid by their citizens, why should not the income tax and many other internal taxes paid entirely by the citizens of loyal States be also paid into the treasuries of these States? Considerations which recognize sectional divisions or the loyalty of the different States at the time this tax was laid should not enter into the discussion of the merits of this measure.

The loyal States should not be paid the large sums of money promised them by this bill because they were loyal and other States were not, nor should the States which rebelled against the Government be paid the smaller sum promised them because they were in rebellion and thus prevented the collection of their entire quotas, nor because this concession to them is necessary to justify the proposed larger gifts to the other States.

The people of the loyal States paid this direct tax as they bore other burdens in support of the Government, and I believe the taxpayers themselves are content. In the light of these considerations I am opposed to the payment of money from the Federal Treasury to enrich the treasuries of the States. Their funds should be furnished by their own citizens, and thus should be fostered the taxpayer's watchfulness of State expenditures and the taxpayer's jealous insistence upon the strict accountability of State officials. These elements of purity and strength in a State are not safely exchanged for the threatened demoralization and carelessness attending the custody and management of large gifts from the Federal Treasury.

The baneful effect of a surplus in the Treasury of the General Government is daily seen and felt. I do not think, however, that this surplus should be reduced or its contagion spread throughout the States by methods such as are provided in this bill.

There is still another objection to the bill, arising from what seems to me its unfairness and unjust discrimination.

In the case of proposed legislation of at least doubtful constitutionality, and based upon no legal right, the equities which recommend it should always be definite and clear.

The money appropriated by this bill is to be paid to the governors of the respective States and Territories in which it was collected, whether the same was derived through said States and Territories, or directly "from any of the citizens or inhabitants thereof or other persons;" and it is further provided that such sums as were collected in payment of this Federal tax through the instrumentality of the State or Territorial officials, and accounted for to the General Government by such States and Territories, are to be paid unconditionally to their governors, while the same collected in payment of said tax by the United States, or, in other words, by the Federal machinery created for that purpose, are to be held in trust by said States or Territories for the benefit of those paying the same.

I am unable to understand how this discrimination in favor of those who have made payment of this tax directly to the officers of the Federal Government, and against those who made such payments through State or Territorial agencies, can be defended upon fair and equitable principles. It was the General Government in every case which exacted this tax from its citizens and people in the different States and Territories, and to provide for reimbursement to a part of its citizens by the creation of a trust for their benefit, while the money exacted in payment of this tax from a far greater number is paid unconditionally into the State and Territorial treasuries, is an unjust and unfair proceeding, in which the Government should not be implicated.

It will hardly do to say that the States and Territories who are the recipients of these large gifts may be trusted to do justice to its citizens who originally paid the money. This can not be relied upon; nor should the Government lose sight of the equality of which it boasts, and, having entered upon the plan of reimbursement, abandon to other agencies the duty of just distribution, and thus incur the risk of becoming accessory to actual inequality and injustice.

If in defense of the plan proposed it is claimed that exact equality can not be reached in the premises, this may be readily conceded. The money raised by this direct tax was collected and expended twenty-seven years ago. Nearly a generation has passed away since that time. Even if distribution should be attempted by the States and Territories, as well as by the Government, the taxpayers in many cases are neither alive nor represented, and in many other cases if alive they can not be found. Fraudulent claims would often outrun honest applications and innumerable and bitter contests would arise between claimants.

Another difficulty in the way of doing perfect justice in the operation of this plan of reimbursement is found in the fact that the money to be appropriated therefor was contributed to the Federal Treasury for entirely different purposes by a generation many of whom were not born when the direct tax was levied and paid, who have no relation to said tax and can not share in its distribution. While they stand by and see the money they have been obliged to pay into the public Treasury professedly to meet present necessities expended to reimburse taxation long ago fairly, legally, and justly collected from others, they can not fail to see the unfairness of the transaction.

The existence of a surplus in the Treasury is no answer to these objections. It is still the people's money, and better use can be found for it than the distribution of it upon the plea of the reimbursement of ancient taxation. A more desirable plan to reduce and prevent the recurrence of a large surplus can easily be adopted—one that, instead of creating injustice and inequality, promotes justice and equality by leaving in the hands of the people and for their use the money not needed by the Government "to pay the debts and provide for the common defense and general welfare of the United States."

The difficulties in the way of making a just reimbursement of this direct tax, instead of excusing the imperfections of the bill under consideration, furnish reasons why the scheme it proposes should not be entered upon.

I am constrained, upon the considerations herein presented, to withhold my assent from the bill herewith returned, because I believe it to be without constitutional warrant, because I am of the opinion that there exists no adequate reasons either in right or equity for the return of the tax in said bill mentioned, and because I believe its execution would cause actual injustice and unfairness.
GROVER CLEVELAND.

PROCLAMATION.

By the President of the United States of America.

A PROCLAMATION.

Whereas public interests require that the Senate should be convened at 12 o'clock on the 4th day of March next to receive such communications as may be made by the Executive:

Now, therefore, I, Grover Cleveland, President of the United States

do hereby proclaim and declare that an extraordinary occasion requi·
the Senate of the United States to convene at the Capitol, in the city
Washington, on the 4th day of March next, at 12 o'clock noon, of whi
all persons who shall at that time be entitled to act as members of tl
body are hereby required to take notice.

Given under my hand and the seal of the United States, at Washir
ton, the 26th day of February, A. D. 1889, and of the Inc
[SEAL.] pendence of the United States of America the one hundr
and thirteenth.

GROVER CLEVELAND.

By the President:

T. F. BAYARD,
Secretary of State.

EXECUTIVE ORDERS.

EXECUTIVE MANSION,
Washington, December 5, 1888.

To the Civil Service Commission.

GENTLEMEN: The efficiency of the public service, in my opinion, re
ders it necessary to include in the classified service and subject to exa·
ination the employees in the railway mail service. The difficulties
the way of this movement can, I believe, be overcome by carefully p·
pared rules and regulations.

I have this day directed the Postmaster-General to so revise the clas
fication of his Department as to include these employees in one or mc
classes; and in furtherance of my purpose I have to request that, aft
conference with the Postmaster-General, you will prepare the necessa
modifications of the present rules and regulations to meet the propos
extension.

Yours, very truly,

GROVER CLEVELAND.

UNITED STATES CIVIL SERVICE COMMISSION,
Washington, D. C., December 5, 1888

The PRESIDENT.

SIR: The Commission recommends that Special Departmental Rule No. 1
amended by adding to the exceptions from examination therein declared the f
lowing:

"10. In all the Departments: Bookbinders."

Very respectfully,

A. P. EDGERTON,
CHAS. LYMAN,
United States Civil Service Commissioners

The above proposed amendment is hereby approved.

GROVER CLEVELAND.

Amendments to General Rules II, III, IV, Departmental Rules V, VIII, Customs Rule III, and Postal Rules II, VI, are hereby made and promulgated as follows:

GENERAL RULE II.

In line 1 strike out the word "three" and insert in place thereof the word "four." At the end of the rule insert the following: "4. The classified railway mail service." The rule as thus amended will read:

There shall be four branches of the classified civil service, as follows:
1. The classified departmental service.
2. The classified customs service.
3. The classified postal service.
4. The classified railway mail service.

GENERAL RULE III.

In section 9, line 2, after the word "service," insert the words "and the classified railway mail service." The section as thus amended will read:

9. Every applicant for examination for the classified departmental service and the classified railway mail service must support the statements of his application paper by certificates of persons acquainted with him, residents of the State, Territory, or district in which he claims *bona fide* residence; and the Commission shall prescribe the form and number of such certificates.

In section 10, line 1, after the word "or," insert the words "procured by his;" strike out all after the word "connivance" in line 1 to and including the word "and" in line 3, and in place of the words stricken out insert the words "or any;" strike out all after the word "consent" in line 4 to and including the word "examination" in line 5; strike out the words "for refusing" in line 6; change the period to a comma at the end of line 6 and insert after the comma the words "or to certify him for appointment, or for his removal after appointment." The section as thus amended will read:

10. A false statement made by an applicant, or procured by his connivance, or any deception or fraud practiced by an applicant, or by any person on his behalf with his consent, shall be good cause for refusal to examine such applicant, or to mark his papers after examination, or to certify him for appointment, or for his removal after appointment.

GENERAL RULE IV.

In section 2 strike out the letter "*a*," in brackets, in line 2; change the period to a semicolon at the end of line 4; in line 5 strike out the letter "*b*," in brackets, and strike out all after the word "has" to and

including the word "has" in line 7, and write the section as one pa
graph. The section as thus amended will read:

2. The Commission may refuse to certify an eligible who is so defective in sig
speech, or hearing, or who is otherwise so defective physically as to be apparen
unfit to perform the duties of the position to which he is seeking appointment,
an eligible who has been guilty of crime or of infamous or of notoriously disgrace
conduct.

DEPARTMENTAL RULE V.

In section 2, paragraph 6, after the word "service" in line 3, insert t
words "or the classified railway mail service;" in paragraph 7, line
strike out the word "and," and after the word "postal" in the same li
insert the words "and railway mail." The section as thus amended w
read:

Local boards.—These boards shall be organized at one or more places in each Sta
and Territory where examinations for the classified departmental service or the cl.
sified railway mail service are to be held, and shall conduct such examinations; a
each shall be composed of persons in the public service residing in the State or T
ritory in which the board is to act.

Customs, postal, and railway mail boards.—These boards shall conduct such exa·
inations for the classified departmental service as the Commission may direct.

DEPARTMENTAL RULE VIII.

In section 1, clause (*c*), line 1, after the word "post-office," insert "
to the classified railway mail service;" in line 2, after the word "from
strike out the words "such an office" and insert "a classified post-offi
or the classified railway mail service." The clause as thus amend
will read:

(*c*) From the Post-Office Department to a classified post-office or to the classifi
railway mail service, and from a classified post-office or the classified railway m.
service to the Post-Office Department, upon requisition by the Postmaster-General

In section 2, line 6, after the word "been," insert "in the classifi
railway mail service or." The section as thus amended will read:

2. No person may be transferred as herein authorized until the Commission sh.
have certified to the officer making the transfer requisition that the person whom
is proposed to transfer has passed an examination to test fitness for the place to whi
he is to be transferred, and that such person has during at least six months precedi
the date of the certificate been in the classified railway mail service or in the clas
fied service of the Department, customs district, or post-office from which the transf
is to be made: *Provided,* That no person who has been appointed from the copy
register shall be transferred to a place the salary of which is more than $900 ɪ
annum until one year after appointment.

CUSTOMS RULE III.

In section 2, clause (*c*), at the end of line 1, insert "and the classifi
railway mail service." The clause as thus amended will read:

(*c*) Conduct such examinations for the classified departmental service and t
classified railway mail service as the Commission may direct.

POSTAL RULE II.

In section 5, at the end of clause (*e*) of that section, strike out the period and insert a comma, and after the comma the following:

Provided, That superintendents of mails shall be selected from among the employees of the railway mail service.

The clause as thus amended will read:

Superintendents designated by the Post-Office Department, and reported as such to the Commission, *Provided*, That superintendents of mails shall be selected from among the employees of the railway mail service.

POSTAL RULE VI.

In section 1, clause (*a*), after the word "another" in line 1 of that clause, strike out the comma and insert a semicolon, and after the semicolon the following:

From any classified post-office to the classified railway mail service, and from the classified railway mail service to any classified post-office.

In clause (*b*), after the word "post-office" in line 1, insert "or from the classified railway mail service," and in line 2, after the word "post-office," insert "or to the classified railway mail service."

In section 2, line 6, after the word "certificate" insert "in the classified railway mail service or." The rule as thus amended will read:

1. Transfers may be made as follows:

(*a*) From one classified post-office to another, from any classified post-office to the classified railway mail service, and from the classified railway mail service to any classified post-office, upon requisition of the Postmaster-General.

(*b*) From any classified post-office or from the classified railway mail service to the Post-Office Department, and from the Post-Office Department to any classified post-office, or to the classified railway mail service, upon requisition of the Postmaster-General.

2. No person may be transferred as herein authorized until the Commission shall have certified to the officer making the transfer requisition that the person whom it is proposed to transfer has passed an examination to test fitness for the place to which he is to be transferred, and that such person has been at least six months next preceding the date of the certificate in the classified railway mail service or in the classified service of the Department or post-office from which the transfer is to be made.

Approved, January 4, 1889. **GROVER CLEVELAND.**

RAILWAY MAIL RULES.

RAILWAY MAIL RULE I.

The classified railway mail service shall include all the officers, clerks, and other persons in that service classified under the provisions of section 6 of the act to regulate and improve the civil service of the United States, approved January 16, 1883.

RAILWAY MAIL RULE II.

1. To test fitness for admission to the classified railway mail service the following examinations shall be provided:

Clerk examination.—This examination shall include not more than the following subjects:

(*a*) Orthography.

(*b*) Copying.

(*c*) Penmanship.

(*d*) Arithmetic—fundamental rules, fractions, and percentage.

(*e*) Letter writing.

(*f*) The geography of the United States, and especially of the State or railway m; division in which the applicant resides.

(*g*) The railway systems of the State or railway mail division in which the app cant resides.

(*h*) Reading addresses.

Other competitive examinations.—Such other competitive examinations as the Cor mission may from time to time deem necessary.

Noncompetitive examinations.—Such examinations may, with the approval of tl Commission, be held under conditions stated in General Rule III, clause 2.

2. No person shall be examined for the railway mail service if under 18 or ov 35 years of age, except that any person honorably discharged from the military naval service of the United States by reason of disability resulting from woun or sickness incurred in the line of duty, and whose claim of preference under sectic 1754 of the Revised Statutes has been allowed by the Commission, may be examine without regard to his age.

3. Any person desiring examination for admission to the classified railway ma service must, in his own handwriting, make request for a blank form of applicatio which request, and also his application, shall be addressed as follows: "United Stat Civil Service Commission, Washington, D. C."

4. The date of reception, and also of approval, by the Commission of each applic tion shall be noted on the application paper.

5. Exceptions from examination in the classified railway mail service are hereb made as follows:

(*a*) General superintendent.

(*b*) Assistant general superintendent.

6. No person appointed to a place under any exception to examination hereby mac shall within one year after appointment be transferred to another place not also e: cepted from examination; but after service of not less than one year in an examin; tion-excepted place he may be transferred to a place not excepted from examinatio upon the certificate of the Commission that he has passed an examination to te fitness for the place to which his transfer is proposed.

RAILWAY MAIL RULE III.

1. The papers of every examination shall be marked under the direction of tl Commission, and each competitor shall be graded on a scale of 100, according 1 the general average determined by the marks made by the examiners on his paper

2. The Commission shall appoint in each railway mail division as many boards examiners as it may deem necessary for the good of the service and the convenienc of applicants: *Provided*, That there shall be at least one such board in each Terr tory and not less than two in each State, except that the number may be limited 1 one each in the States of Rhode Island and Delaware.

3. These boards shall conduct such examinations for admission to and promotior in the classified railway mail service and such examinations for the other branches'; the classified service as the Commission may direct. They shall also mark such exa'; ination papers as the Commission may direct.

4. Unless otherwise directed by the Commission, the papers of examination fc admission to the classified railway mail service shall be marked by the central boar

5. The papers of an examination having been marked, the Commission shall asce tain—

(*a*) The name of every competitor who has, under section 1754 of the Revise statutes, claim of preference in civil appointments, and who has attained a gener average of not less than 65 per cent; and all such competitors are hereby declared eligible to the class or place to test fitness for which the examination was held.

(*b*) The name of every other competitor who has attained a general average of not less than 70 per cent; and all such applicants are hereby declared eligible to the class or place to test fitness for which the examination was held.

6. The names of all preference-claiming competitors whose general average is not less than 65 per cent, together with the names of all other competitors whose general average is not less than 70 per cent, shall be entered upon the register of persons eligible to the class or place to test fitness for which the examination was held.

7. The grade of each competitor shall be expressed by the whole number nearest the general average attained by him, and the grade of each eligible shall be noted upon the register of eligibles in connection with his name. When two or more eligibles are of the same grade, preference in certification shall be determined by the order in which their application papers were filed.

8. There shall be a register of eligibles for each State and Territory, and the names of all the eligibles of any State or Territory shall be entered upon the register for that State or Territory. The eligibles of the District of Columbia shall be entered, according to their election, upon the register of the State of Maryland or upon that of the State of Virginia.

9. Immediately after the general averages shall have been ascertained each competitor shall be notified that he has passed or has failed to pass.

10. If a competitor fail to pass, he may, with the consent of the Commission, be allowed a reexamination at any time within six months from the date of failure without filing a new application; but if such reexamination be not allowed within that time he shall not be again examined without making in due form a new application.

11. No eligible shall be allowed reexamination during the term of his eligibility unless he shall furnish evidence satisfactory to the Commission that at the time of his examination, because of illness or other good cause, he was incapable of doing himself justice in said examination.

12. The term of eligibility shall be such as the Commission may by regulation determine, but shall not be less than one year from the day on which the name of the eligible is entered upon the register: *Provided*, That for public and sufficient reasons the Commission shall have authority to extend the term of eligibility of the eligibles on the register of any State or Territory for such period, not exceeding one year, as it may deem necessary, without correspondingly extending the term of the eligibles on the registers of the other States and Territories as to which the same reasons do not exist.

RAILWAY MAIL RULE IV.

1. All vacancies in the classified railway mail service above class 1, unless among the places excepted from examination, shall be filled by promotion, upon such tests of fitness as the Postmaster-General, with the approval of the Commission, may prescribe: *Provided*, That a vacancy occurring in a State or railway mail division in any grade may be filled by the transfer of a clerk of the same grade from another State or division, under such regulations as the Postmaster-General, with the approval of the Commission, may prescribe, or by reappointment under the provisions of Railway Mail Rule VI.

2. All vacancies in class 1, unless filled by transfer or reappointment under Railway Mail Rule VI, shall be filled in the following manner:

(*a*) The general superintendent shall, in form and manner to be prescribed by the Commission, request the certification to him of eligibles from a State or Territory in which a vacancy then exists.

(*b*) The Commission shall certify from the register of the State or Territory in

which the vacancy exists the names of the three eligibles thereon having the high
averages who have not been three times certified: *Provided*, That if upon said
ister there are the names of eligibles having a claim of preference under section 1
Revised Statutes, the names of such eligibles shall be certified before the name
other elig'bles of higher grade: *Provided further*, That if there are not three e'
bles upon the register of the State or Territory in which the vacancy exists eligi
may be certified from the register of any adjoining State or Territory.

(*c*) The name of an eligible shall not be certified more than three times.

3. Of the three names certified to the general superintendent one shall be selec
and designated for appointment, and more than one may be if there be more t
one vacancy existing at the time.

4. Each person designated for appointment shall be notified, and upon report
to the proper officer shall be appointed for a probational period of six months, at
end of which period, if his conduct and capacity be satisfactory, he shall be al
lutely appointed; but if his conduct and capacity be not satisfactory he shall be
notified, and such notice shall be his discharge from the service.

5. The general superintendent, with the approval of the Postmaster-General, sl
prescribe regulations under which each probationer shall be observed and tested
a record kept of his conduct and capacity, and such record shall determine his
ness for the service and whether he shall be dropped during or at the end of p
bation or be absolutely appointed.

6. There may be certified and appointed in each State and Territory, in the m
ner provided for in this rule, such number of substitute clerks, not exceeding
ratio of one substitute to twenty regular clerks, in such State or Territory as the P
master-General may authorize, and any vacancies occurring in class 1 in any Stat
Territory in which substitutes have been appointed shall be filled by the appo
ment thereto of those substitutes in the order of their appointment as substitu
without further certification. The time during which any substitute is actua
employed in the service shall be counted as a part of his probation.

RAILWAY MAIL RULE V.

1. Transfers may be made as follows:

(*a*) From the classified railway mail service to any classified post-office, and fr
any classified post-office to the classified railway mail service, upon requisition of
Postmaster-General.

(*b*) From the classified railway mail service to the Post-Office Department,
from the Post-Office Department to the classified railway mail service, upon requ
tion of the Postmaster-General.

2. No person shall be transferred as herein authorized until the Commission sl
have certified to the Postmaster-General that the person whom it is proposed
transfer has passed an examination to test fitness for the place to which he is to
transferred, and that such person has been at least six months next preceding
date of the certificate in the classified railway mail service or in the classified se
ice of the post-office or Department from which the transfer is to be made: *Provia
That no employee shall be transferred to any grade which he could not enter
original appointment by reason of any age limitation prescribed by the civil-serv
rules.

RAILWAY MAIL RULE VI.

1. Upon requisition of the Postmaster-General the Commission shall certify
reinstatement in a grade or class no higher than that in which he was formerly
ployed any person who within one year next preceding the date of the requisit
has, through no delinquency or misconduct, been separated from the classified r
way mail service.

RAILWAY MAIL RULE VII.

1. The general superintendent of the railway mail service shall report to the Commission—

(*a*) Every probational (whether substitute or regular) and every absolute appointment in the railway mail service in each State or Territory; every appointment under any exception to examination authorized by Railway Mail Rule II, clause 5; every reappointment under Railway Mail Rule VI, and every appointment of a substitute to a regular place.

(*b*) Every refusal to make an absolute appointment and the reason therefor, and every refusal or neglect to accept an appointment in the classified railway mail service.

(*c*) Every transfer into the classified railway mail service.

(*d*) Every separation from the classified railway mail service and the cause of such separation.

(*e*) Every promotion or degradation in the classified railway mail service, if such promotion or degradation be from one class to another class.

(*f*) Once in every six months, namely, on the 30th of June and the 31st of December of each year, the whole number of employees in each railway mail division, arranged by States and classes, showing the number of substitutes and the number of regular employees in each class in each State or Territory.

> EXECUTIVE MANSION,
> *Washington, January 4, 1889.*

The above rules are hereby approved, to take effect March 15, 1889: *Provided*, That such rules shall become operative and take effect in any State or Territory as soon as an eligible register for such State or Territory shall be prepared, if it shall be prior to the date above fixed.

> GROVER CLEVELAND.

> UNITED STATES CIVIL SERVICE COMMISSION,
> *Washington, D. C., February 8, 1889.*

The PRESIDENT.

SIR: The Commission recommends that Special Departmental Rule No. 1 be amended by adding to the exceptions from examination therein declared the following:

"11. In the Department of Justice: Assistant attorneys.

"12. In the Department of Agriculture, Bureau of Experiment Stations: Private secretary to the Director."

Very respectfully,

> CHAS. LYMAN,
> *United States Civil Service Commissioner.*

Approved, February 11, 1889.

> GROVER CLEVELAND.

> UNITED STATES CIVIL SERVICE COMMISSION,
> *Washington, D. C., February 9, 1889.*

The PRESIDENT.

SIR: This Commission has the honor to recommend that the order of the President fixing the places to which appointments may be made upon noncompetitive examination under General Rule III, section 2, clause (*f*), may be amended by including among such places the following:

"In the Post-Office Department: Captain of the watch."

This recommendation is based upon the letter of the Postmaster-General dated December 19, 1888, in which he says:

"I would request that places in the Post-Office Department subject to noncompetitive examination be increased by including the position of captain of the watch, the duties of the position are of such a nature that the head of the Department should be permitted to recommend for examination such person as would possess such other qualifications in addition to the merely clerical ones as would commend him to the head of the Department to fill satisfactorily such position."

Very respectfully,

CHAS. LYMAN,
United States Civil Service Commissioner

Approved, February 11, 1889.

GROVER CLEVELAND.

UNITED STATES CIVIL SERVICE COMMISSION,
Washington, D. C., February 9, 1889.

The PRESIDENT.

SIR: This Commission has the honor to recommend that the order heretofore approved by you authorizing noncompetitive examination under General Rule I, section 2, clause (e), to test fitness for certain designated places in the classified departmental service, may be amended by the revocation of so much of the order above referred to as provides for the appointment upon noncompetitive examination of "inspector of electric lights" in the office of the Secretary in the Treasury Department.

Very respectfully,

CHAS. LYMAN,
United States Civil Service Commissioner.

Approved, February 11, 1889.

GROVER CLEVELAND.

EXECUTIVE MANSION, *February 26, 1889.*

Whereas by an act of Congress entitled "An act to enable the President to protect the interests of the United States in Panama," approved February 25, 1889, it was enacted as follows:

That there be, and is hereby, appropriated, out of any money in the Treasury not otherwise appropriated, the sum of $250,000 to enable the President to protect the interests of the United States and to provide for the security of persons and property of citizens of the United States at the Isthmus of Panama in such manner as he may deem expedient.

And whereas satisfactory information has been received by me that a number of citizens of the United States have been thrown out of employment and left destitute in the Republic of Colombia by the stoppage of work on the Panama Canal:

It is therefore ordered, That so much as is necessary of the fund appropriated by the said act be expended, under the direction and control of the Secretary of State, in furnishing transportation to the United States to any citizen or citizens of the United States who may be found destitute within the National Department of Panama, in the Republic of Colombia.

GROVER CLEVELAND.

GROVER CLEVELAN

Lightning Source UK Ltd.
Milton Keynes UK
UKHW020839110119
335238UK00009B/1033/P